Onshape 2025

A Power Guide for Beginners and Intermediate Users

CADArtifex

The premium provider of learning products and solutions

www.cadartifex.com

Onshape 2025: A Power Guide for Beginners and Intermediate Users

Author: Sandeep Dogra
Email: info@cadartifex.com

Published by
CADArtifex
www.cadartifex.com

ISBN: 978-9394074859

www.cadartifex.com

Dedication

First and foremost, I would like to thank my parents for being a great support throughout my career and while writing this book.

Heartfelt gratitude goes to my wife and my sisters for their patience and support in fulfilling this challenge.

I would also like to acknowledge the efforts of the employees at CADArtifex for their dedication in editing the contents of this textbook.

Contents at a Glance

Table of Contents

Preface

Onshape, developed by PTC Inc. (Parametric Technology Corporation), is a powerful 3D software suite for engineering and product design. As a leading technology provider, PTC offers advanced solid modeling tools that enable users to create, simulate, publish, and manage design data efficiently. With a strong focus on innovation, PTC helps businesses stay ahead of the competition by embracing the latest advancements, including IoT, 3D printing, digital twins, and augmented reality. By bridging the gap between the physical and digital worlds, PTC empowers companies to adapt quickly to industry changes and drive forward-thinking design solutions.

Onshape is a cloud-native CAD platform built entirely in the cloud, seamlessly integrating advanced solid modeling with next-generation product data management (PDM). By centralizing design data, it eliminates version control challenges, lost files, and inefficiencies, enabling agile and cost-effective workflows.

Onshape offers secure, real-time collaboration accessible from any web browser or mobile device. Users can create parametric solid models, convert 2D sketches into 3D components, assemble parts, and generate detailed engineering drawings for manufacturing and additive production. It also supports design validation, environmental impact analysis, CNC machining simulations from 2.5 to 5-axis operations, and more.

Onshape 2025: A Power Guide for Beginners and Intermediate Users is a comprehensive textbook designed for both instructor-led training and self-paced learning. It serves as an essential resource for students, professionals, hobbyists, engineers, and designers seeking to master Onshape for 3D mechanical design.

Tailored for new users and ideal for classroom instruction, this guide spans 10 chapters and 602 pages, thoroughly covering core Onshape environments, including Sketching, Part Studio, Assembly, and Drawing. With step-by-step instructions, it walks users through creating parametric 3D solid components, assemblies, and 2D drawings, making it a complete resource for mastering Onshape.

More than just a tool and command manual, this textbook emphasizes key design principles alongside software proficiency. Each chapter features in-depth tutorials with step-by-step guidance for efficiently creating mechanical designs and drawings. Additionally, every chapter concludes with hands-on test drives, allowing users to explore and experience Onshape's robust and intuitive technical capabilities.

Who Should Read This Book

This book is designed for a wide range of users, from beginners to advanced professionals, as well as Onshape instructors. With well-structured, easy-to-navigate chapters, it offers a clear understanding of various design methodologies, Onshape's tools, and fundamental design principles.

What Is Covered in This Textbook

Onshape 2025: A Power Guide for Beginners and Intermediate Users is designed to help you master Onshape through clear, step-by-step instructions and hands-on tutorials. This comprehensive textbook covers the following:

Chapter 1, "***Introduction to Onshape***," introduces Onshape, a cloud-native CAD platform, and guides you through accessing the software and creating a new design document. It explores Onshape's user interface components, which enhance navigation and streamline workflow. This chapter also covers sharing design documents via email or link for seamless collaboration, importing CAD and non-CAD files, and exporting designs in various formats. Additionally, it explains how Onshape automatically saves all design changes in the cloud, eliminating the need for manual saving.

Chapter 2, "***Creating and Editing Sketches with Onshape***," introduces the fundamentals of starting a new design by creating a design document and setting units. It covers sketching basics, including drawing lines, rectangles, circles, ellipses, arcs, polygons, splines, and slots, as well as adding control points and creating construction geometries.

This chapter also explores essential editing techniques such as trimming, extending, offsetting, and filleting sketch entities, along with advanced methods like mirroring, patterning, and transforming sketches. Additionally, it explains how to apply constraints and dimensions to ensure precision in designs.

Chapter 3, "***Creating Extrude & Revolve Base Features***," introduces the process of transforming 2D sketches into 3D models using extrude and revolve features in Onshape. It covers various methods for navigating a 3D model using the mouse, keyboard, and touchpad, along with view tools such as **Zoom to fit**, **Zoom to window**, and **Zoom to selection**.

This chapter also explores manipulating the view of a 3D model to standard planes, including trimetric, isometric, and perspective views, as well as creating custom-named views. Additionally, it discusses modifying the display style of a model, including shaded with or without edges, unshaded, translucent, and controlling the visibility of tangent edges.

Chapter 4, "***Creating Planes and Advanced Techniques***," discusses key techniques to enhance CAD modeling efficiency and precision. It begins with creating construction planes beyond the default Front, Top, and Right planes to support complex designs. The chapter then explores advanced Extrude and Revolve options for greater control over features.

Additionally, this chapter covers projecting edges onto the active sketching plane as sketch entities and using section views to inspect internal model details. It also explains how to display earlier model stages, reorder features to manage design flow, and refine models through feature editing and deletion. Finally, it discusses applying appearance and material properties to customize designs and calculating key mass properties.

*Chapter 5, "**Creating Sweep, Loft, and Thicken Features**,"* discusses three advanced modeling techniques: sweep, loft, and thicken. The sweep feature generates a 3D shape by sweeping a sketch profile along a defined path, making it ideal for designing components like pipes and rails. The loft feature enables smooth transitions between multiple similar or dissimilar sketch profiles, allowing for the creation of parts with varying cross-sections, such as turbine blades or ergonomic designs. Lastly, the thicken feature adds or removes thickness from an existing face of a model.

*Chapter 6, "**Creating Placed Features: Fillet, Chamfer, & More**,"* explores essential placed features that enhance the precision, strength, and realism of 3D models. It covers tools such as **Fillet**, **Face blend**, **Chamfer**, **Draft**, **Rib**, **Shell**, **Hole**, and **External thread** to refine designs. These techniques provide the skills needed to add greater functionality and detail to your 3D models.

*Chapter 7, "**Patterning and Mirroring**,"* explores techniques to enhance design efficiency through feature replication and symmetry. It covers linear, circular, and curve patterns to effectively duplicate features, faces, or parts. Additionally, it examines the mirroring of features, faces, or parts about a plane or planar face to create symmetrical designs. These tools streamline repetitive tasks, ensure accuracy, and optimize the design workflow.

*Chapter 8, "**Creating 3D Curves and Splitting Faces**,"* discusses techniques for generating complex curves and modifying models in Onshape. It covers creating helices using various methods, including selecting conical or cylindrical faces, axes, or circular edges. The chapter also explores projected curves by combining two sketches or projecting a sketch onto a face, as well as generating 3D fit splines through vertices and edges.

Additionally, this chapter examines bridging and intersection curves, composite curves for combining multiple curves or sketch entities, and methods for splitting parts and faces to enable detailed model modifications. These skills allow for the creation of intricate features such as internal and external threads, coils, 3D path features, and advanced geometry in your designs.

*Chapter 9, "**Working with Assemblies**,"* introduces the process of assembling components to build structured and functional designs. It begins with inserting and fixing the first component to establish a stable foundation before adding additional components. The chapter covers various mates, including **Fastened**, **Revolute**, **Slider**, **Planar**, **Cylindrical**, **Pin Slot**, **Ball**, **Parallel**, and **Tangent mates**, to define relationships and control movement between components.

Additionally, this chapter explores organizing assemblies by grouping components, enabling Snap Mode for easier alignment, and using Show Mate Mode to review and refine mates. It also discusses creating Linear and Circular Component Patterns and establishing advanced mechanical relations such as **Gear**, **Rack and Pinion**, **Screw**, and **Linear Relations** to simulate realistic motion. These tools and techniques enable you to design, refine, and manage complex assemblies with precision.

*Chapter 10, "**Working with Drawings**,"* discusses Onshape's Drawing Environment and the tools used to create and manage technical drawings. It covers accessing the drawing environment from both Part and Assembly workspaces and generating various view types, including base, projected, auxiliary, section, aligned section, broken-out section, detail, break, and crop views.

Additionally, this chapter explores view display and property controls, modifying drawing and sheet properties, and organizing multiple sheets within a drawing. It also examines editing hatch patterns in section views, repositioning views within a sheet or moving them to another sheet, and deleting views.

The chapter further introduces annotation tools such as centerlines, centermarks, virtual sharps, and different dimensioning techniques, including chamfer, ordinate, and hole/thread callouts. It also covers surface finish symbols, weld symbols, notes, and sheet format customization.

Finally, it discusses creating and customizing Bills of Materials (BOM), including adding balloons to improve clarity in assembly drawings. By mastering these tools, users can efficiently produce detailed, professional drawings for manufacturing and documentation in Onshape.

Some of the Icons/Terms used in this Textbook

Some of the icons and terms used in this textbook are as follows:

Note

Note: Notes highlight information requiring special attention.

Tip

Tip: Tips provide additional advice, which increases the efficiency of the users.

Drop-down Menu

A drop-down menu is a categorized list that groups related tools together, see Figure 1.

Dialog

A dialog is a pop-up window that offers task-specific options and input fields for user interaction, see Figure 2.

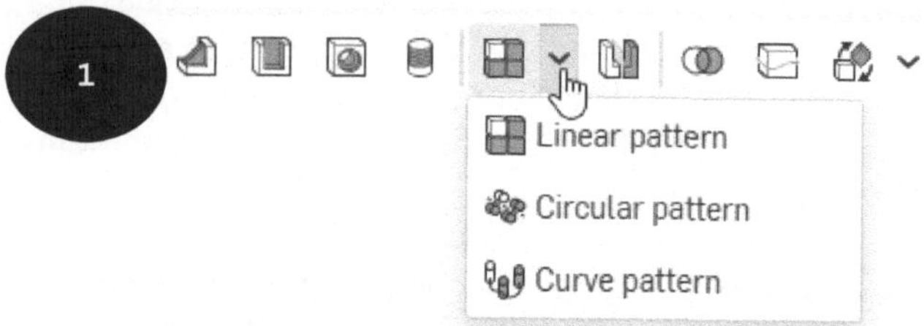

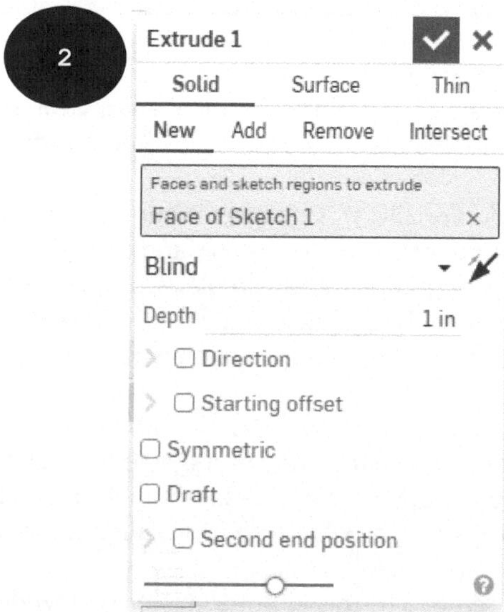

Rollout
A rollout is a section within a dialog that contains drop-down lists, fields, buttons, and/or check boxes for specifying various parameters, see Figure 3. It can be expanded or collapsed by clicking the arrow on its title bar.

Drop-down List
A drop-down list offers a set of selectable options related to a specific tool or function, see Figure 3.

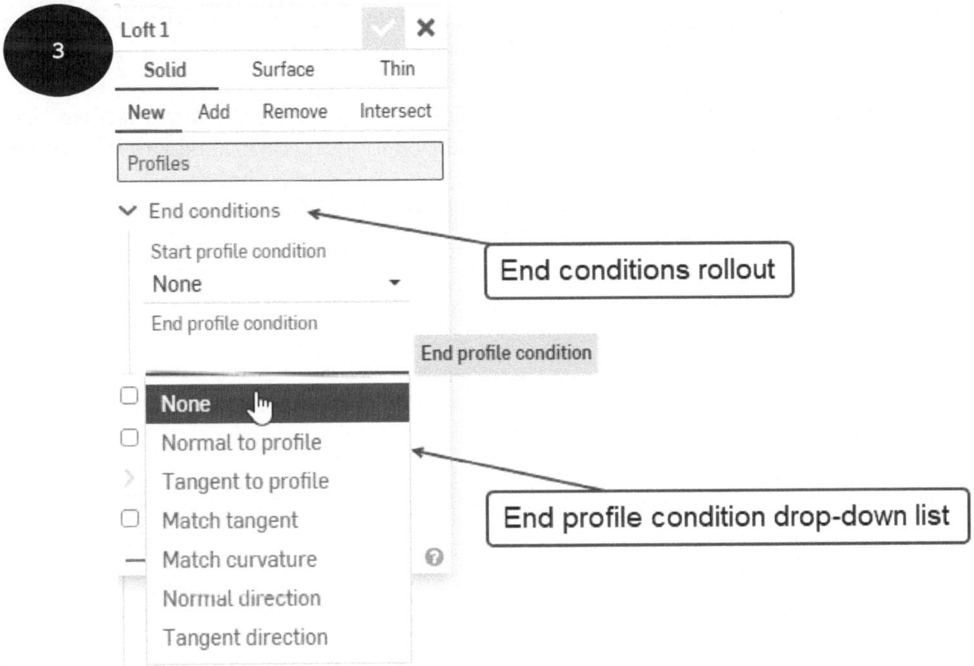

Field
A field enables you to input a new value or edit an existing one, see Figure 4.

Check Box
A check box lets you enable or disable a specific option, see Figure 4.

How to Download Online Resources

To access the free online teaching and learning resources for this textbook, visit the CADArtifex website at *cadartifex.com/login*. New users must first register at *cadartifex.com/register* to download the resources. You can also email us at *info@cadartifex.com* to request access.

How to Contact the Author

Your feedback and suggestions are highly appreciated. Feel free to email us at *info@cadartifex.com* or visit our website at *www.cadartifex.com* to share your thoughts about the textbook and access free learning resources.

Thank you for choosing **Onshape 2025: A Power Guide for Beginners and Intermediate Users**. We hope the knowledge and concepts presented in this textbook support you in achieving your professional objectives.

CHAPTER

1

Introduction to Onshape

In this chapter, the following topics will be discussed:

- Accessing Onshape: A Cloud-Native CAD Platform
- Getting Started with Onshape
- Starting a New Design Document
- Exploring Onshape's UI Components
- Sharing a Design Document
- Exporting a Design to Other CAD Formats
- Importing CAD or Non-CAD Files into Onshape
- Saving a Design Document

Welcome to Computer-Aided Design (CAD) with Onshape, a cloud-native product development platform by PTC Inc. As a leader in engineering technology, PTC provides a comprehensive suite of 3D software tools to design, simulate, publish, and manage product data efficiently. By integrating IoT, 3D printing, digital twins, and augmented reality, PTC helps companies stay ahead in an evolving industry.

Onshape is the only professional-grade CAD platform built entirely in the cloud, combining advanced solid modeling with next-generation product data management (PDM). By centralizing design data, it eliminates lost files, version control issues, and inefficiencies while supporting agile, cost-effective workflows.

Accessible from any web browser or mobile device, Onshape enables secure, real-time collaboration. Users can create parametric solid models, convert 2D sketches into 3D components, build assemblies, and generate detailed engineering drawings for manufacturing and additive production. It also supports design validation, environmental impact assessments, and CNC machining simulations for 2.5 to 5-axis operations.

Collaboration is at the core of Onshape, offering simultaneous editing, Follow Mode, and integrated commenting for streamlined feedback and teamwork. Flexible sharing options make it an ideal solution for multi-team product development.

With Onshape, design smarter, collaborate effortlessly, and bring innovative products to life, anytime, anywhere.

Accessing Onshape: A Cloud-Native CAD Platform

Onshape is a cloud-native CAD platform that runs entirely in a web browser, eliminating the need for downloads or installations. It is accessible from any internet-connected device, including Windows, Mac, Linux, and mobile devices (iOS and Android) via the Onshape App.

To get started, simply visit the Onshape website at ***www.onshape.com***, log in, and begin designing instantly.

Getting Started with Onshape

Go to the Onshape website at ***onshape.com*** from any web browser. Next, click the **SIGN IN** option at the top right corner to display the **Sign In** page, see Figure 1.1. On this page, enter your registered email ID and password, and then click on the **Sign In** button. After loading all the necessary files, the **Documents** page of Onshape appears as the startup user interface, see Figure 1.2.

1.1

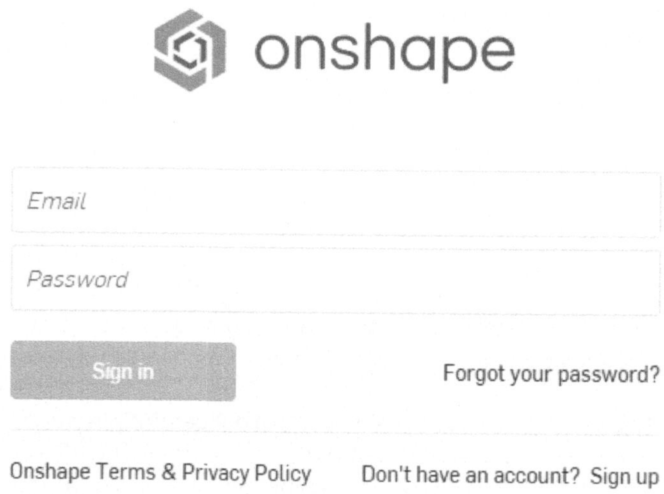

Note: If you're new to Onshape, click the **SIGN UP NOW** button in the top right corner of the browser to register for free, no credit card is required. You'll get instant access to start designing right away.

1.2

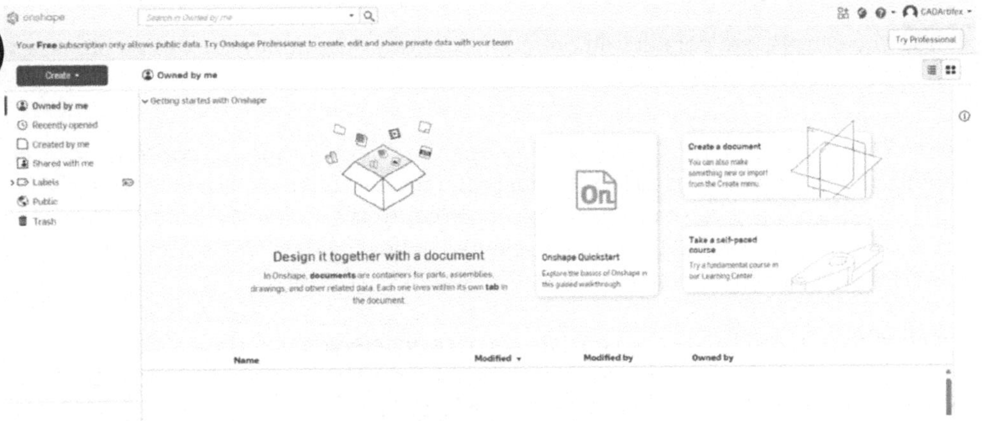

Note: Some of the options on the **Documents** page depend on your Onshape subscription type. With the **Free** subscription, files are stored as public data and available for anyone to use. To secure your files and get unlimited private storage, you need to upgrade your subscription from **Free** to **Standard**, **Professional**, or **Enterprise**. For more information, visit the Onshape website at: *onshape.com/en/pricing.*

If you are accessing Onshape for the first time after registration, a **Set your default units** pop-up window appears, see Figure 1.3. Here, you can define the default length, angle, and mechanical unit preferences for your Onshape documents.

1.3

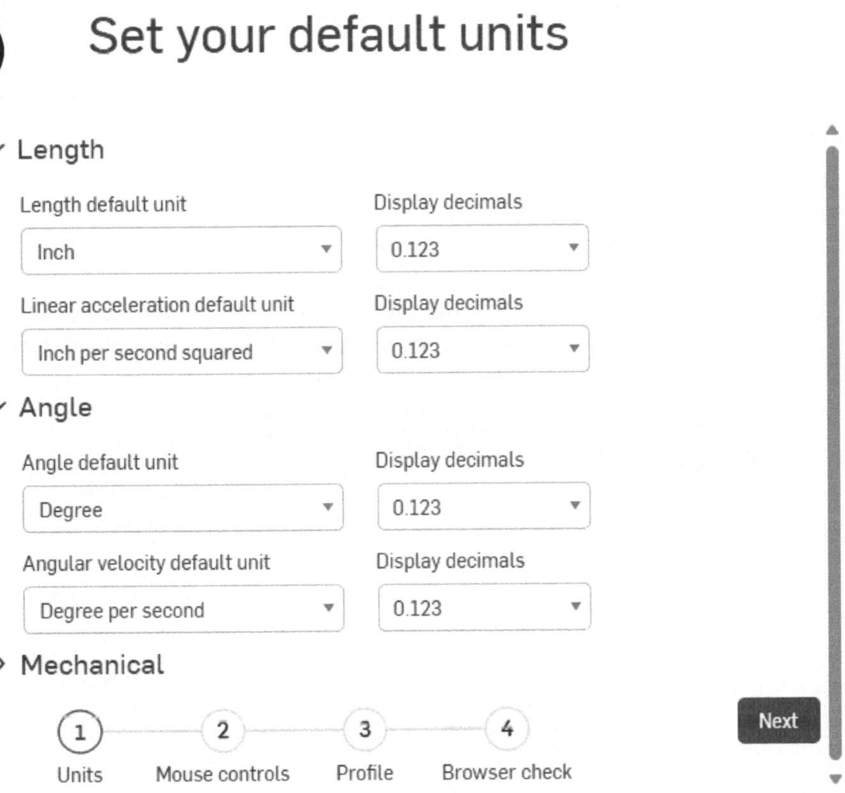

Tip: You can also set default unit preferences at any time during the design process, which will be covered in Chapter 2.

After setting the default units, click **Next** to open the **Set your mouse controls** page. Here, you can customize the mouse settings based on your preference. If you're familiar with other CAD software like SOLIDWORKS or Creo, you can adjust the mouse controls accordingly using the drop-down menu. By default, the **Onshape (default)** option is selected, following Onshape's standard navigation settings. You will learn more about Onshape navigation settings in Chapter 3.

Click **Next** to proceed to the **Set your profile** page, where you can set a nickname (displayed during collaboration) and upload a profile picture if desired. Press **Next** to continue and then **Done** to complete the setup and display the **Documents** page, see Figure 1.4.

1.4

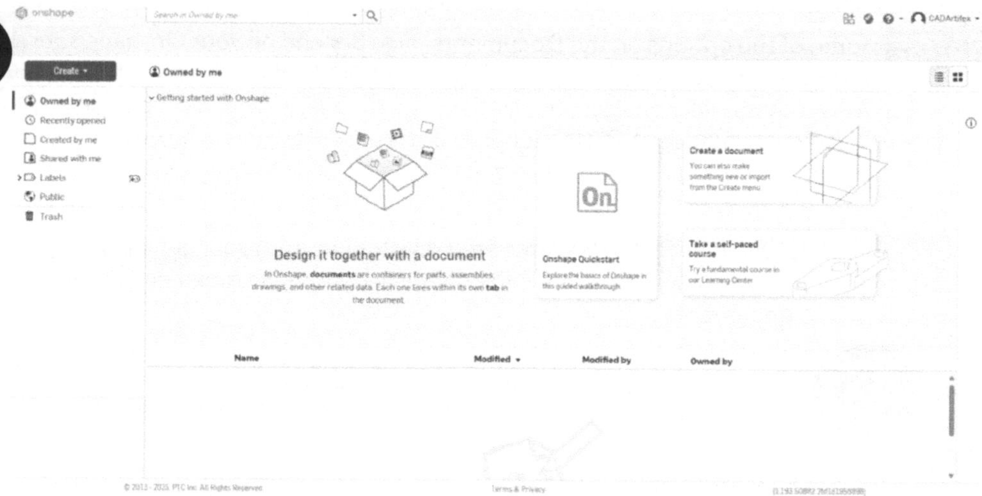

The **Documents** page is the first page you see when you sign in to your Onshape account. Here, you can create new design documents, view and open existing ones, organize them into folders, and access the Onshape QuickStart guide, among other features.

The left panel of the **Documents** page provides filter options such as **Owned by me, Recently opened, Created by me, Shared with me,** and **Public** to help you quickly locate relevant design documents, which are then displayed in the right panel, see Figure 1.5.

1.5

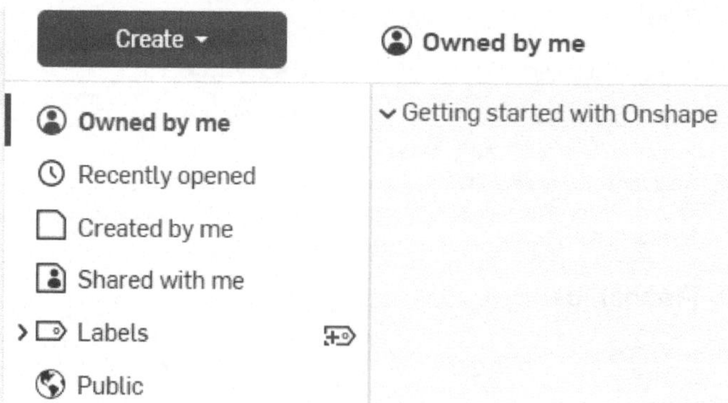

The **Create** button at the top left corner of the **Documents** page provides options to create a new design document, create a folder, or import files from your local computer, Dropbox, Google Drive, or Microsoft OneDrive, see Figure 1.6.

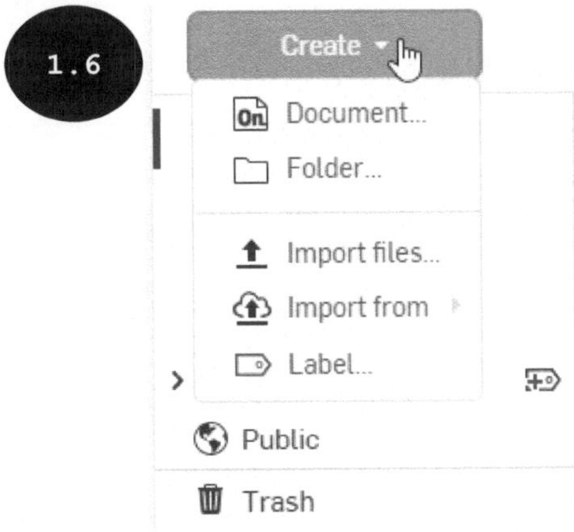

Starting a New Design Document

In the **Documents** page, click on the **Create** button at the top left corner and then click on the **Document** option in the menu that appears, refer to Figure 1.6. The **New document** window appears with a default name of the document "**Untitled document**", see Figure 1.7.

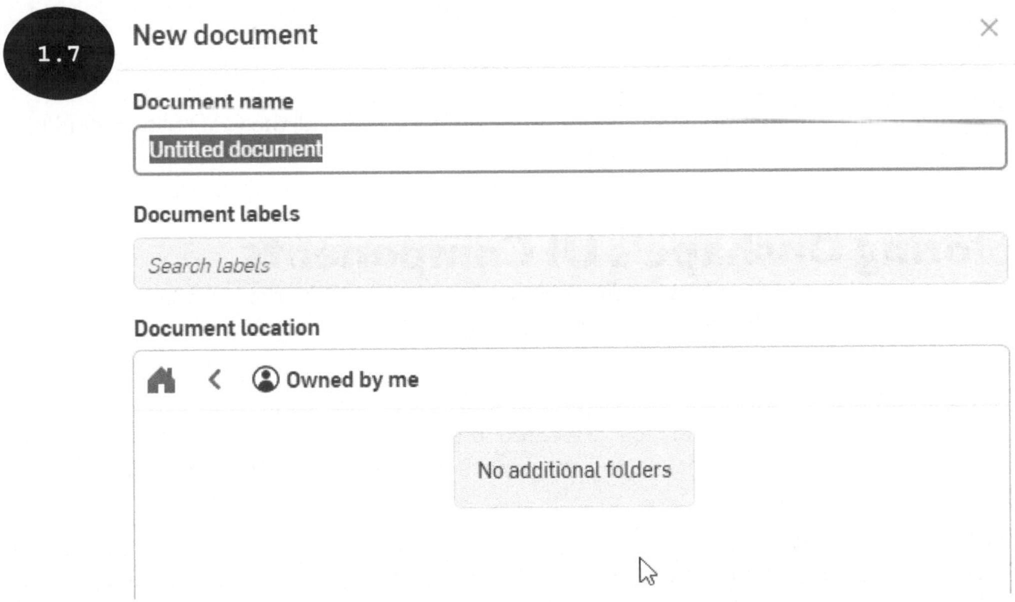

Tip: You can continue using the default document name, but it is recommended to assign a unique name for easier identification when searching or browsing. In Onshape, multiple documents can have the same name.

Enter a new name for the design document in the **New document** window, and then click on the **Create** button or the **Create Public Document** button, depending on your subscription type. A new document with the specified name is invoked and the **Part Studio 1** and **Assembly 1** tabs are added at the bottom, see Figure 1.8.

1.8

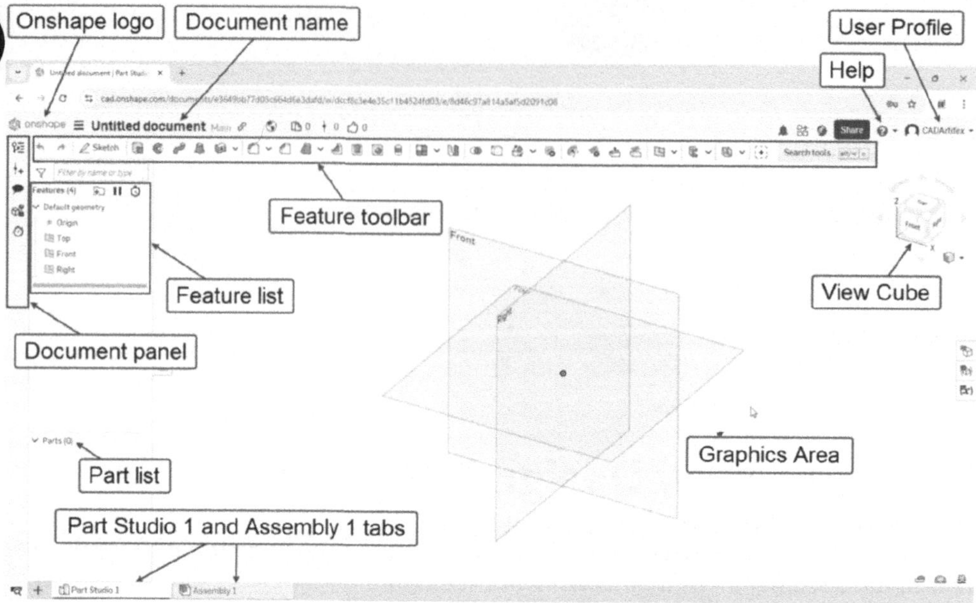

By default, the **Part Studio 1** tab is activated, allowing you to create a 3D solid part or a surface model using the tools in the **Feature** toolbar.

Note: In Onshape, a document refers to a project that contains all the CAD data, including parts, assemblies, drawings, and any other information related to the project.

Exploring Onshape's UI Components

The startup user interface of the Part Studio environment clearly shows that Onshape is user-friendly. Some key components of this interface are discussed next.

Onshape Logo

The Onshape logo (or your company logo), located in the top left corner of the browser, serves as a shortcut to return to the Documents page from any other page in the system by clicking it.

Document Name

The **Document Name** field, located next to the Onshape logo, displays the specified name of the design document. It also allows you to rename the document at any stage of the design process. To do this, simply click the **Document Name** field, enter a new name in the edit field that appears, and press ENTER to save the changes.

Feature Toolbar

The **Feature** toolbar provides various tools for creating 3D solid and surface models in the Part Studio environment. Figure 1.9 shows a partial view of the **Feature** toolbar, while Figure 1.10 shows a reference 3D solid model.

1.9

1.10

Note: The availability of the toolbar depends on the active environment. In the Assembly environment, the **Assembly** toolbar appears for tasks related to building assemblies, while in the Drawing environment, the Drawing toolbar is available for creating 2D technical drawings of parts or assemblies.

Feature List

The Feature list, located on the left side of the graphics area, records all features used in creating a model, see Figure 1.11. The first feature created appears at the top, with subsequent features listed sequentially below it. By default, the Feature list includes three default planes and an origin.

1.11

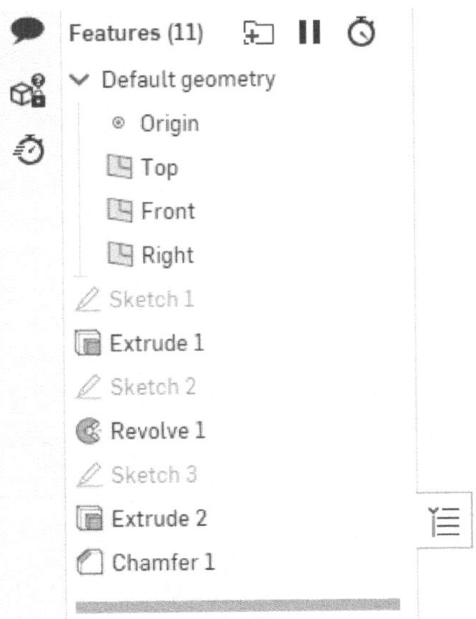

Tip: Features are sequential logical operations used to construct a design. Figure 1.12 displays the model, while Figure 1.13 illustrates the features used to create it in sequential order.

1.12

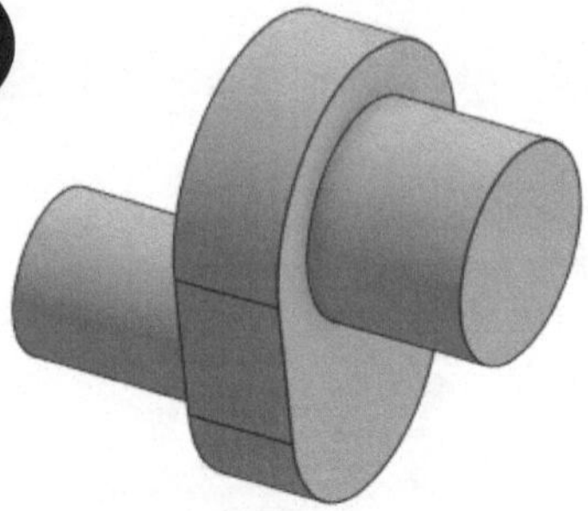

1.13

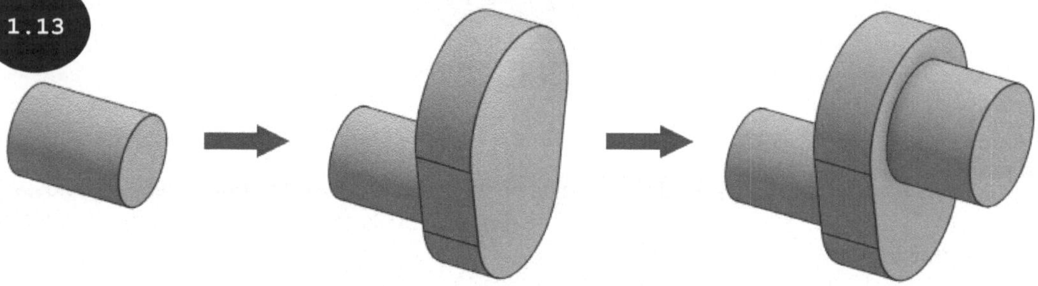

Part List

The Part list is located below the Feature list on the left side of the graphics area. It records all individual parts or bodies available in the current design file, see Figure 1.14.

1.14

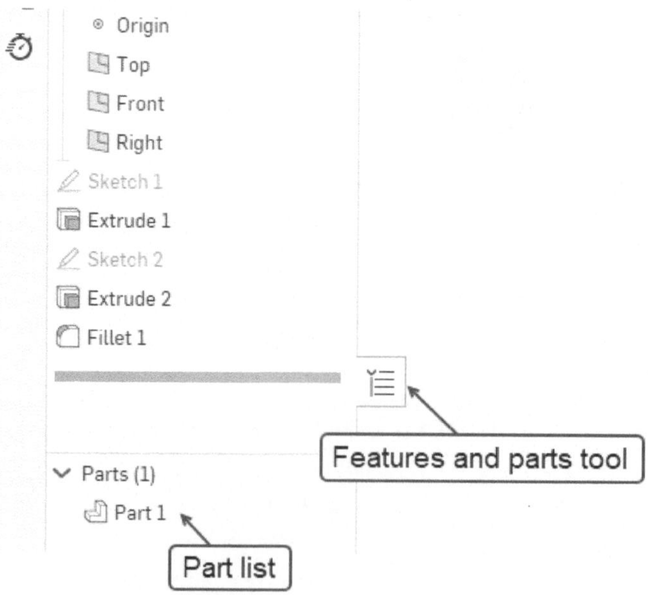

Tip: You can show or hide the Feature list and Part list using the **Features and parts** tool, refer to Figure 1.14.

Document Panel

The **Document panel** is vertically aligned in the top-left corner, below the Onshape logo, see Figure 1.15. It provides quick access to tools such as **Versions and history**, **Create version**, **Release drafts**, **Comments**, and **Performance** for every Onshape document.

1.15

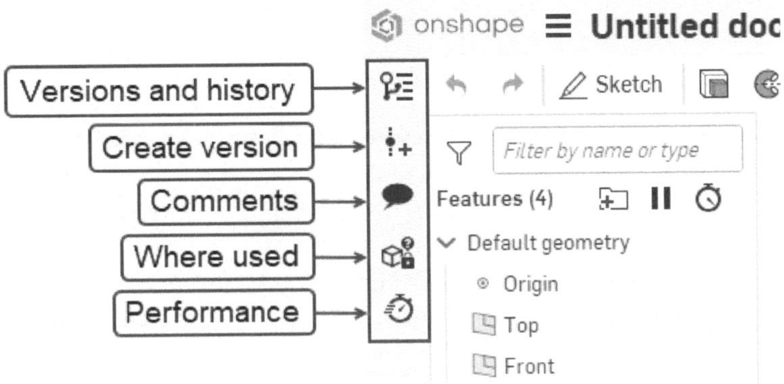

Versions and history

The **Versions and history** tool opens the **Document panel**, providing options to view changes and releases of the current design document, see Figure 1.16. It also enables you to create new workspaces, access previous stages of the design, compare history, create versions, and more. The availability of certain features depends on the current Onshape subscription type.

1.16

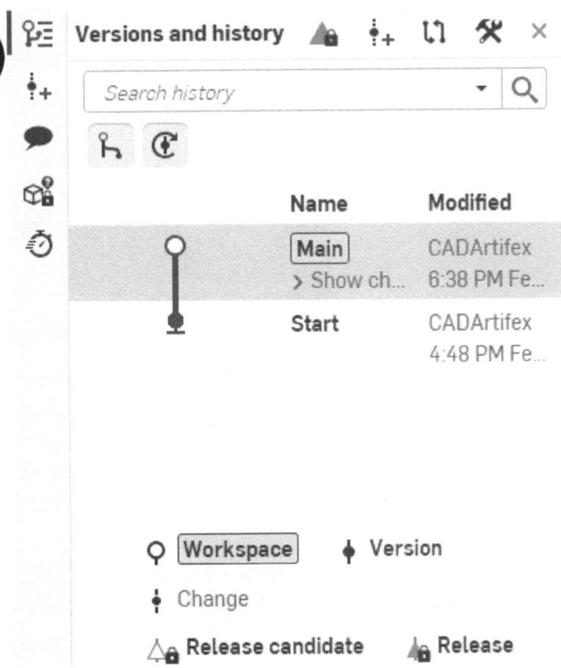

Create Version

The **Create version** tool opens the **Create version** dialog (see Figure 1.17), allowing you to create a new version of the design by capturing its current state.

1.17

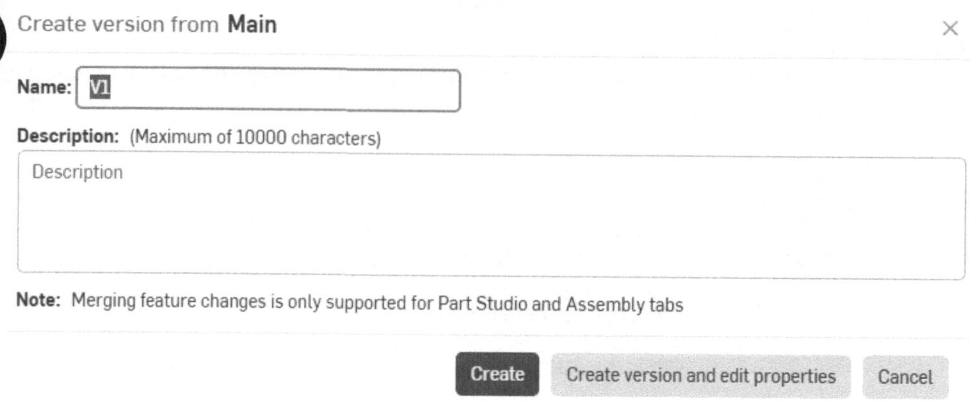

In the **Create version** dialog, you can enter a custom name for the version in the **Name** field or accept the default one. If needed, you can also add a description in the **Description** field, with a maximum limit of 10,000 characters. After defining the name and description, click the **Create** button to generate a new version of the design.

Comments

The **Comments** tool opens the **Document panel**, allowing you to add comments to the active document, see Figure 1.18.

1.18

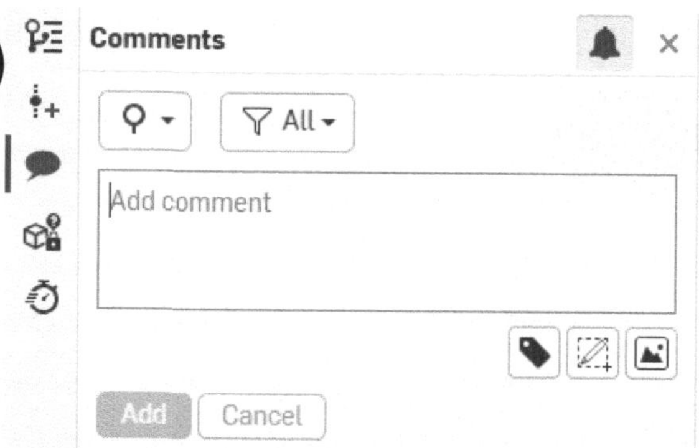

Where used

The **Where used** tool opens the **Document panel**, showing where the current design file (part or assembly) is used in other documents. This is particularly useful when making changes to the design, as it helps identify affected assemblies or drawings before making modifications. This feature is not available in the free Onshape subscription plan.

Performance

The **Performance** tool opens the **Document panel**, displaying statistics related to the model, graphics, and system details, see Figure 1.19. These insights help identify areas where the current design document can be optimized for better performance.

1.19

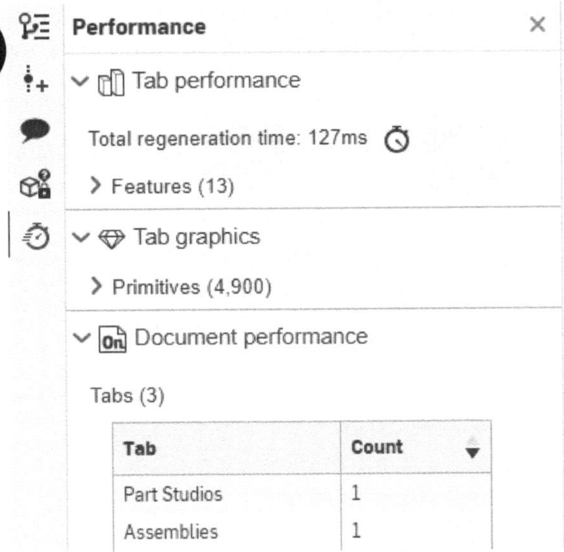

View Cube

1.20

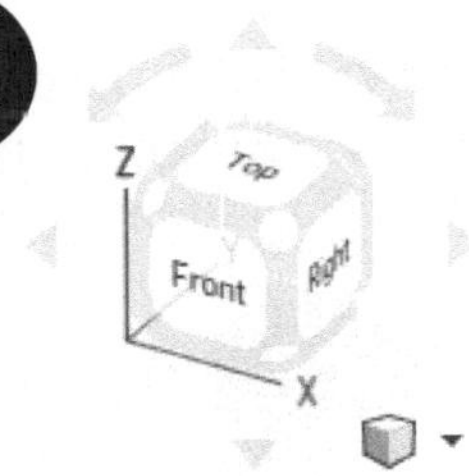

The View Cube is located in the upper right corner of the graphics area and is used for manipulating the view of the design, see Figure 1.20. You can orbit or switch between the standard views of the model using the View Cube. You will learn how to manipulate the view of a design using the View Cube in Chapter 3.

Onshape User Profile and Help Menus

The **Onshape User Profile** and **Help** menus are located in the upper-right corner of the interface. To access the **Onshape User Profile** menu, click on your account **User Profile**, see Figure 1.21. This menu displays general account information, including your name, nickname, bio, and company name, as well as options to set up account preferences such as default units and mouse controls. It also provides options to view support tickets, access the App Store, switch between Onshape's dark and light theme modes, and sign out of your account.

1.21

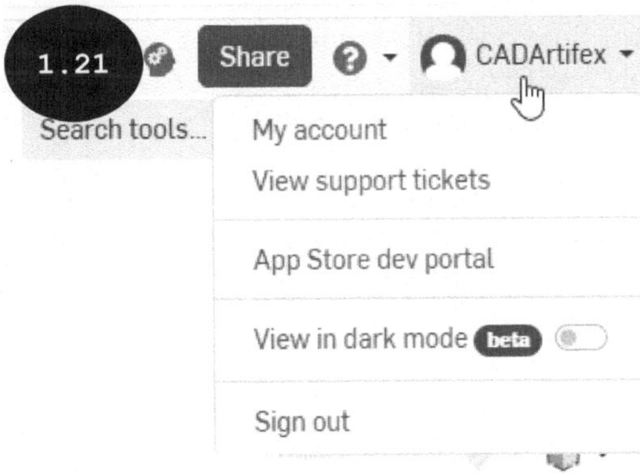

Similarly, to access the **Help** menu, click on the **Help** icon, see Figure 1.22. This menu provides access to help documents, keyboard shortcuts, What's New, community forums, Onshape license details, and more.

1.22

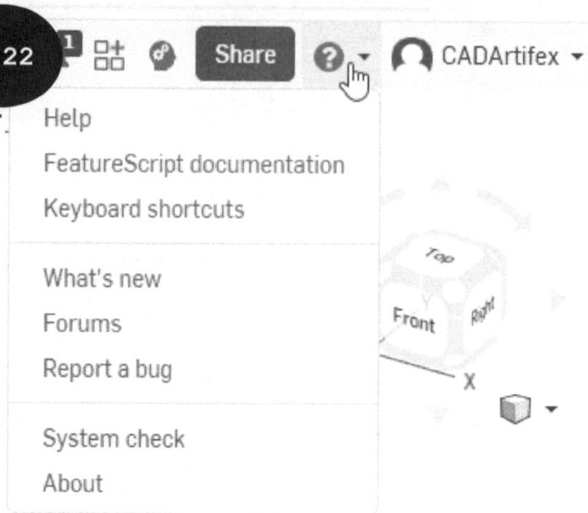

Part Studio 1 and Assembly 1 Tabs

As discussed earlier, when you start a new design document, the **Part Studio 1** and **Assembly 1** tabs appear at the bottom, representing different task-oriented environments, see Figure 1.23.

1.23

The **Part Studio 1** tab represents the Part Studio environment, providing tools to create a 3D solid part or a surface model, while the **Assembly 1** tab represents the Assembly environment, offering tools to create assemblies. You can switch between these environments by clicking their respective tabs.

In addition to the default **Part Studio 1** and **Assembly 1** tabs, you can add multiple new design tabs, such as **Part Studio**, **Assembly**, and **Drawing**, to organize all CAD data, including parts, assemblies, and drawings of a project, within a single design document.

To add a new design tab, click the **Insert new** tab (*plus sign*) at the lower-left corner of the screen, in front of the **Part Studio 1** tab, see Figure 1.24. A menu appears, displaying a list of available tab options. Select the desired tab, such as **Create Part Studio**, **Create Assembly**, or **Create Drawing**, to add it to the current design document.

1.24

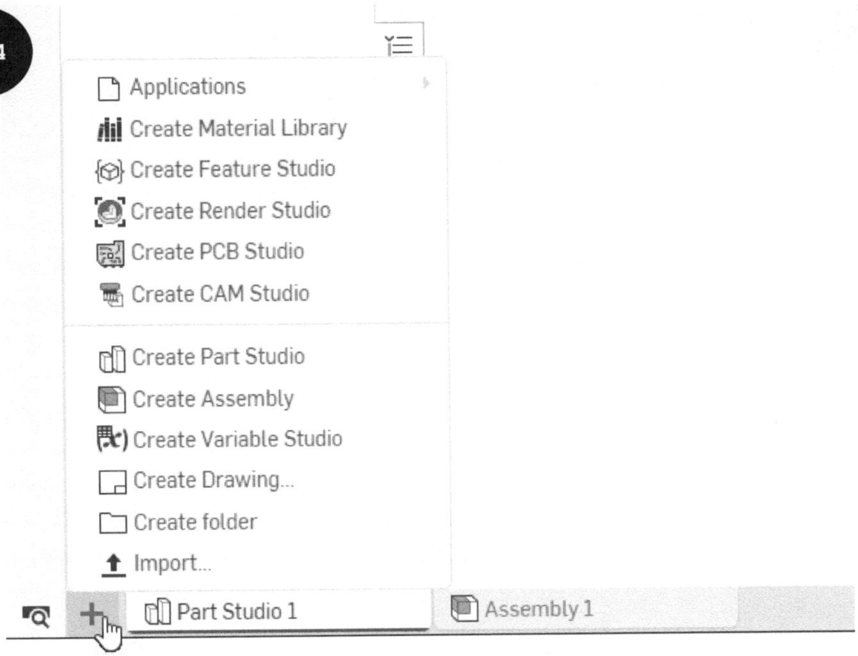

After adding a tab that represents a file (such as a part, assembly, or drawing), you can rename it as needed and begin working on the file. You will learn about creating parts in the Part Studio environment, assemblies in the Assembly environment, and 2D technical drawings in the Drawing environment of Onshape in later chapters.

Tip: You can switch between different environments by clicking on their respective tabs.

Sharing a Design Document

In Onshape, you easily collaborate with other designers by sharing your design via a link. To do this, click the **Share** tool in the top right corner, see Figure 1.25. The **Share** dialog appears, allowing you to manage sharing settings and invite collaborators, see Figure 1.26. This dialog provides various options to share your design with individuals via email and a unique link are discussed next.

1.25

1.26

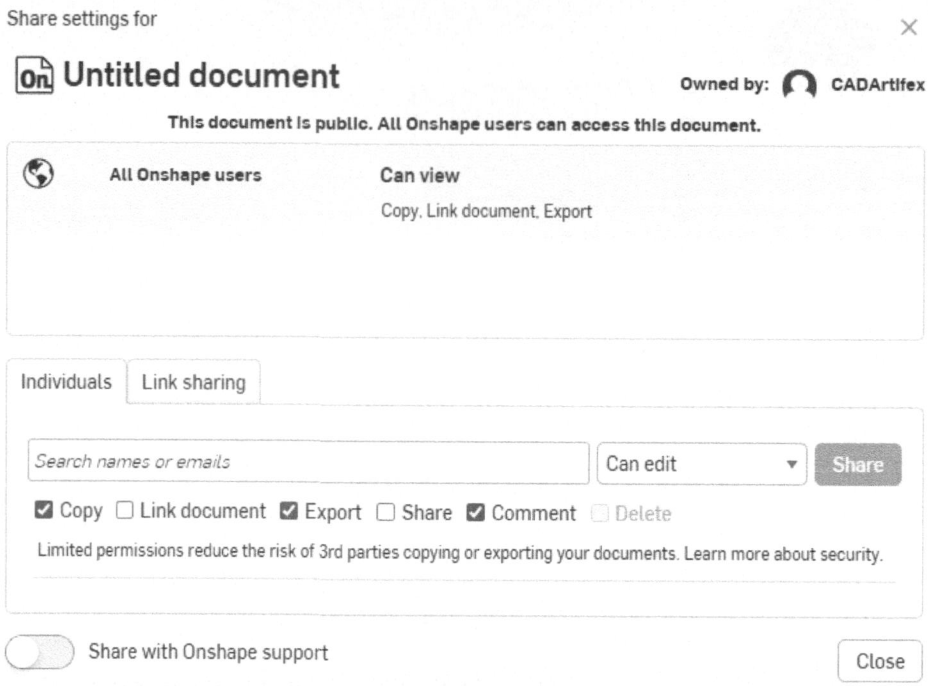

Sharing Your Design with Individual Users via Email

In the **Share** dialog, the **Individuals** tab is activated by default, allowing you to enter one or more email addresses in the **Search names or emails** field. After entering the email IDs, select the permission type as **Can edit** or **Can view** from the **Permission type** drop-down list next to the field, refer to Figure 1.26. The **Can edit** option grants full access, enabling users to edit, copy, link, export, share, and comment on the document. In contrast, the **Can view** option provides limited access, allowing users only to view, copy, link, export, and comment. You can also select the appropriate check boxes available below the **Search names or emails** field to customize sharing settings, as needed. Once the required email addresses are entered, click the **Share** button to send invitations and grant access to your design document.

Note: The options available in the **Share** dialog for sharing your design document depend on your current Onshape subscription type. Certain features, such as sharing with team or company members, may not be accessible with the free subscription.

Sharing Your Design via a Unique Link

To share your design document anyone using a unique link, click the **Link sharing** tab in the **Share** dialog and then click the **Turn on link sharing** button to generate a link. Once the link is generated, you can copy it using the **Copy to clipboard** button and share it via email or any other method to grant access to your design.

Tip: You can also share your design document with Onshape Support if you need assistance or have encountered a bug. To do this, activate the **Share with Onshape support** toggle button located at the bottom of the **Share** dialog.

Exporting a Design to Other CAD Formats

In Onshape, you can export your design to various CAD formats, including SOLIDWORKS, as well as neutral file formats such as PARASOLID, STEP, IGES, OBJ, and STL. To export a part, right-click on it either in the Part list or in the graphics area to open a shortcut menu, see Figure 1.27. This figure illustrates the shortcut menu that appears after right-clicking on a part in the Part list.

1.27

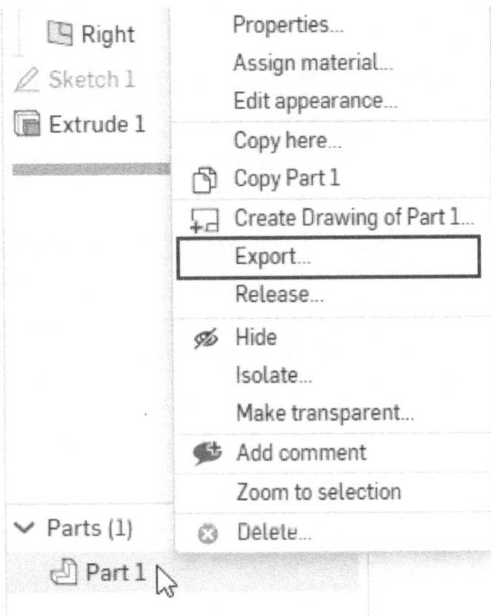

In this shortcut menu, select the **Export** option, refer to Figure 1.27. The **Export** dialog then appears, see Figure 1.28.

1.28

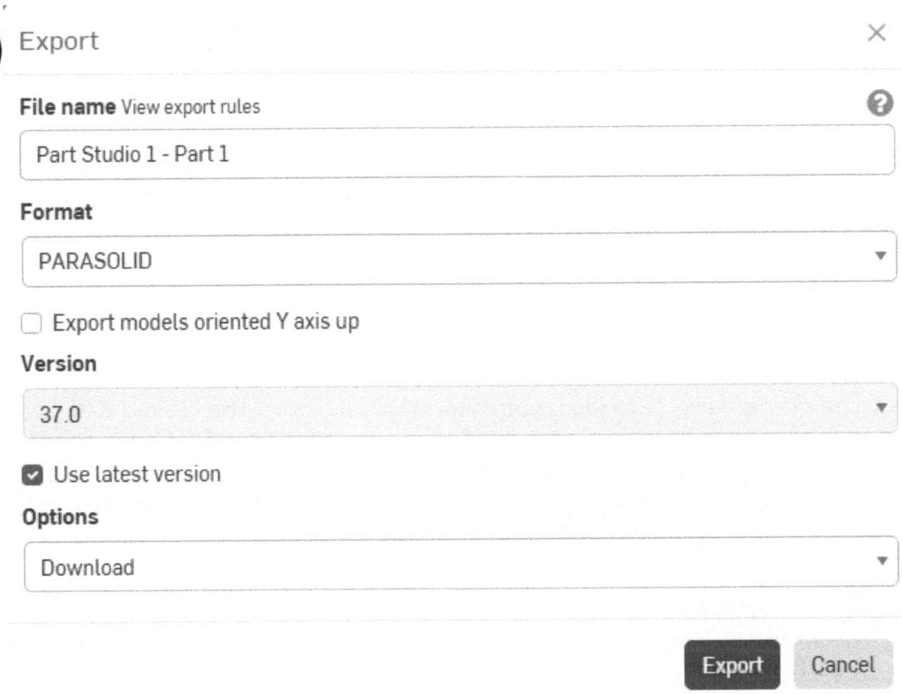

In the **Format** drop-down list of the **Export** dialog, select the desired format to export your design file. Additionally, in the **Options** drop-down list, choose the preferred download option: **Download**, **Download and store file in a new tab**, or **Store file in a new tab**.

After selecting the required format and related settings, click the Export button. The export process begins, and once completed, the file in the specified format is downloaded to your local computer.

Importing CAD or Non-CAD Files into Onshape

In Onshape, you can import various CAD or non-CAD files either into the current design document or as a new document. Both methods are discussed next.

Importing a File into the Current Document

To import a CAD or non-CAD file into the current design document, click the **Insert new** tab (*plus sign*) located next to the **Part Studio 1** tab in the lower left corner, see Figure 1.29. Then, select the **Import** option from the menu that appears. This opens the **Open** dialog, allowing you to choose the file to import.

1.29

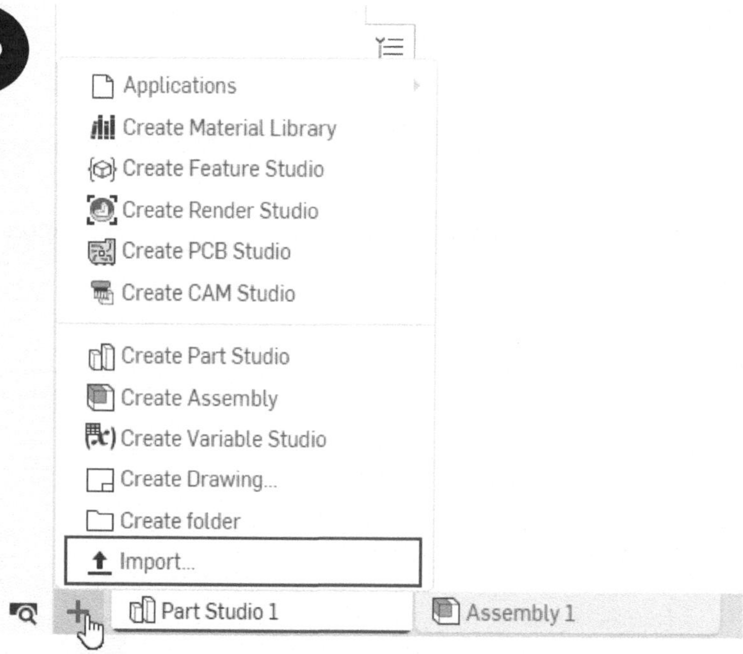

In the **Open** dialog, navigate to the required location and select the desired CAD or non-CAD file to import into the current design document. After selecting the file, click **Open**. The file import process begins, and the **Notifications** panel appears to display its progress. Once the import is complete, the selected file is added to the design document in a separate new tab at the bottom of the graphics area. You can click on this tab to access the imported file.

Note: If the imported file is not a supported Onshape file type, it may not be directly visible in the tab. Instead, the tab provides options to update and download the imported file.

Importing a File as a New Onshape Document

To import a CAD or non-CAD file as a new Onshape document, go to the **Documents** page, which is the first page that appears when you sign in to your Onshape account. If you are working within a document, you can access this page by clicking the Onshape logo at the top left corner.

In the **Documents** page, click **Create > Import** (see Figure 1.30). The **Open** dialog appears. In this dialog, select the desired file to import and click the **Open** button. The selected file is then imported as a new Onshape document.

1.30

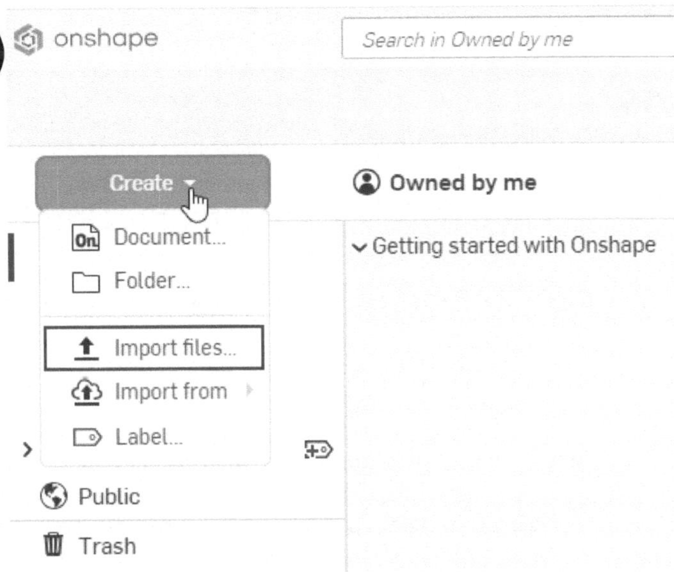

Saving a Design Document

In Onshape, there is no need to manually save a document, as it is automatically saved to the cloud. You can access a list of all saved documents anytime from the **Documents** page.

To do this, go to the **Documents** page and select a filter option such as **Owned by me**, **Recently opened**, **Created by me**, **Shared with me**, or **Public** (see Figure 1.31) to display a list of relevant design documents in the right panel of the **Documents** page. Next, double-click on the desired file to open it.

1.31

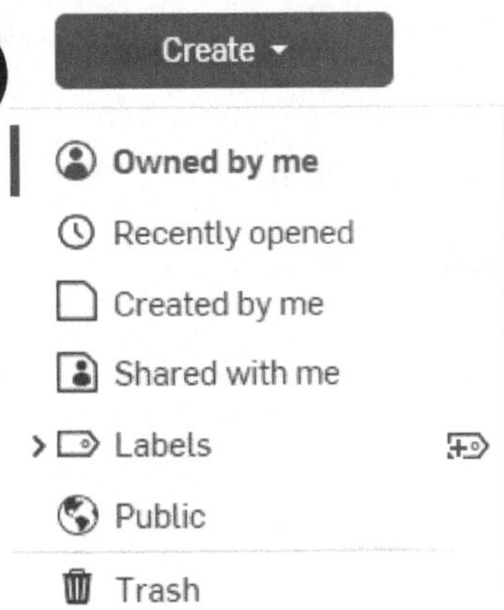

Summary

In this chapter, you have learned how to access Onshape, a cloud-native CAD platform, and get started with a new design document. You explored Onshape's user interface components, which help in efficient navigation and workflow.

You also discovered how to share design documents with others using email or a link, enabling seamless collaboration. Additionally, you learned how to export designs to different CAD formats and import both CAD and non-CAD files into Onshape. Finally, you understood that Onshape automatically saves all design changes in the cloud, eliminating the need for manual saving.

Questions

Complete and verify the following sentences:

- Onshape is a _________ platform that operates entirely within a web browser, removing the need for downloads or installations.
- The _________ page is the first screen displayed when you sign in to your Onshape account.
- The _________ serves as a shortcut to return to the **Documents** page from any other page with a single click.
- The _________ keeps track of all features used in constructing a model.
- The _________ tool is used to create a new version of the design by capturing its current state.
- Located in the upper right corner of the graphics area, the _________ is used to manipulate the view of the design.
- The _________ environment contains tools for creating 3D solid parts or surface models, whereas the _________ environment provides tools for assembling components.
- In Onshape, you can collaborate with other designers by sharing your design via _________ and a _________.
- In Onshape, you can export your design in multiple neutral file formats, including PARASOLID, STEP, IGES, OBJ, and STL. (True/False)
- Onshape does not allow you to import non-CAD files into a design document. (True/False)
- In Onshape, there is no need to manually save a document, as it is automatically saved to the cloud. (True/False)

CHAPTER

2

Creating and Editing Sketches with Onshape

In this chapter, the following topics will be discussed:

- Invoking a New Design Document
- Specifying Units
- Accessing the Sketch Toolbar
- Selecting a Sketching Plane
- Drawing a Line
- Switching Between Line and Tangent Arc Tools
- Drawing a Rectangle
- Drawing a Circle
- Drawing an Ellipse
- Drawing an Arc
- Drawing a Polygon
- Drawing a Spline
- Adding a Control Point to an Existing Spline
- Creating Construction Geometries
- Creating a Sketch Fillet
- Trimming Sketch Entities
- Extending Sketch Entities
- Splitting Sketch Entities
- Offsetting Sketch Entities
- Creating a Slot
- Mirroring Sketch Entities
- Patterning Sketch Entities
- Transforming Sketch Entities
- Applying Constraints
- Applying Dimensions
- Switching to the Part Studio environment

Onshape is a feature-based, parametric, solid modeling mechanical design, and automation software. To design a component in Onshape, you must create all its features individually, see Figures 2.1 and 2.2. The features are divided into two categories: sketch-based and placed. A feature created using a sketch is known as a sketch-based feature, whereas a feature created on an existing feature without a sketch is known as a placed feature. Among these, the sketch-based feature is typically the first feature of any real-world component to be designed. Therefore, it is important to focus first on drawing a sketch.

Figure 2.1 illustrates a component that includes an extrude feature and a chamfer. The extrude feature is created using a sketch, making it a sketch-based feature. Conversely, the chamfer is a placed feature, as it does not require a sketch for its creation. Figure 2.2 depicts the process for creating this model.

2.1

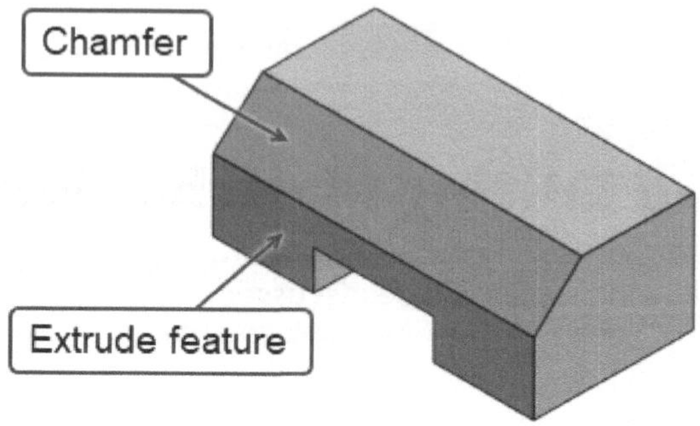

2.2

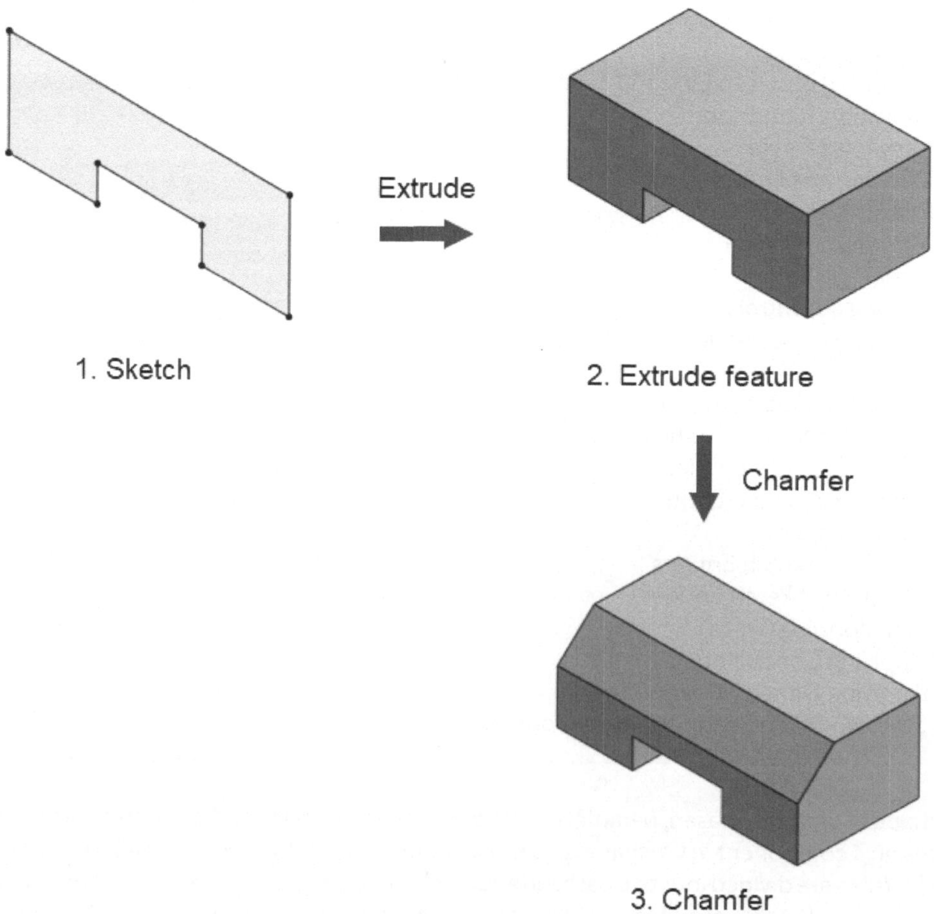

To start designing a component in Onshape, mastering sketch creation is crucial since the base or first feature of any component is typically sketch-based. In Onshape, you can create sketches by using the various sketching tools available in a design document.

Invoking a New Design Document

Go to the Onshape website at ***onshape.com*** from any web browser. Next, click the **SIGN IN** option at the top right corner to display the **Sign In** page, see Figure 2.3. On this page, enter your registered email ID and password, and then click on the **Sign In** button. After loading all the necessary files, the **Documents Page** of Onshape appears as the startup user interface, see Figure 2.4.

2.3

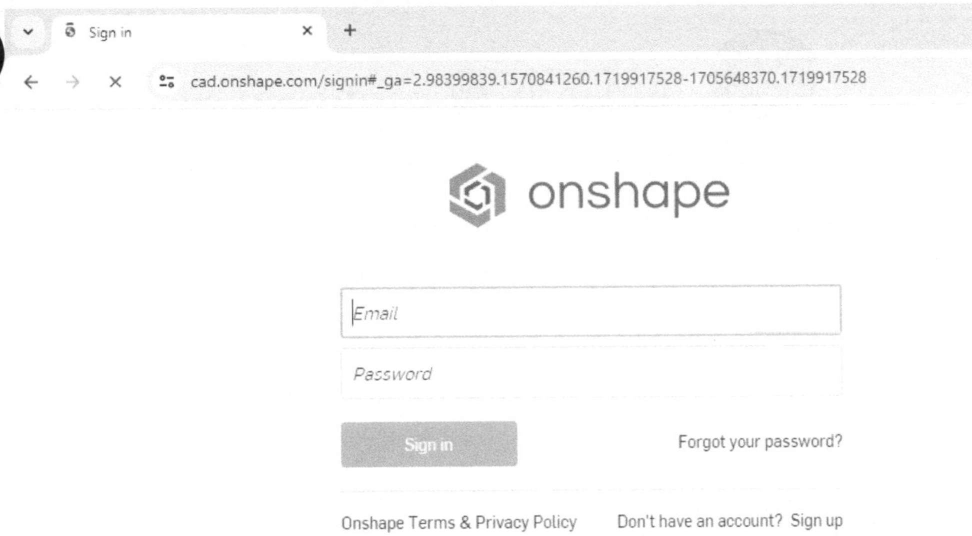

2.4

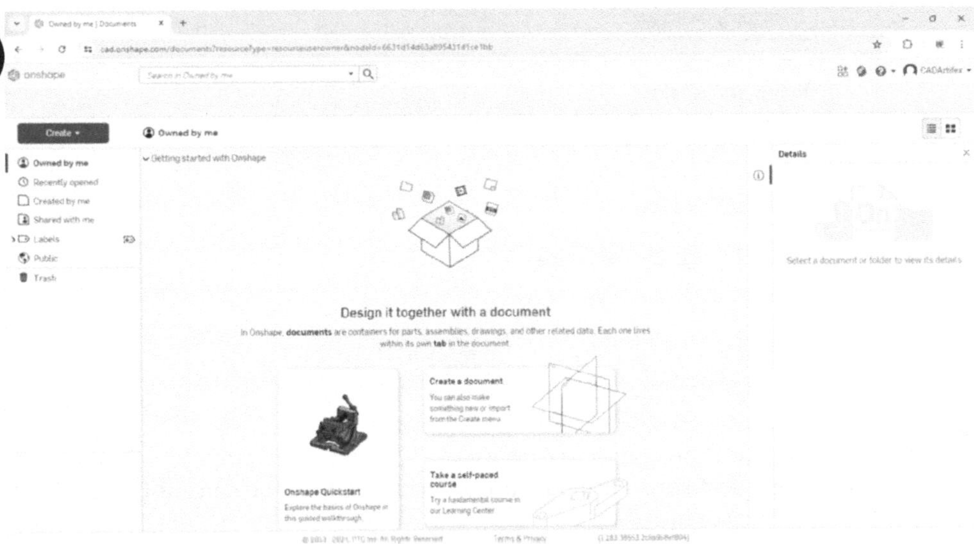

Note: Some of the options on the **Documents Page** depend on your Onshape subscription type. With the **Free** subscription, files are stored as public data and available for anyone to use. To secure your files and get unlimited private storage, you need to upgrade your subscription from **Free** to **Standard**, **Professional**, or **Enterprise**. For more information, visit the Onshape website at: *onshape.com/en/pricing.*

In the **Documents Page**, click on the **Create** button at the top left corner and then click on the **Document** option in the menu that appears, see Figure 2.5. The **New document** window appears with a default name of the document "**Untitled document**", see Figure 2.6.

2.5

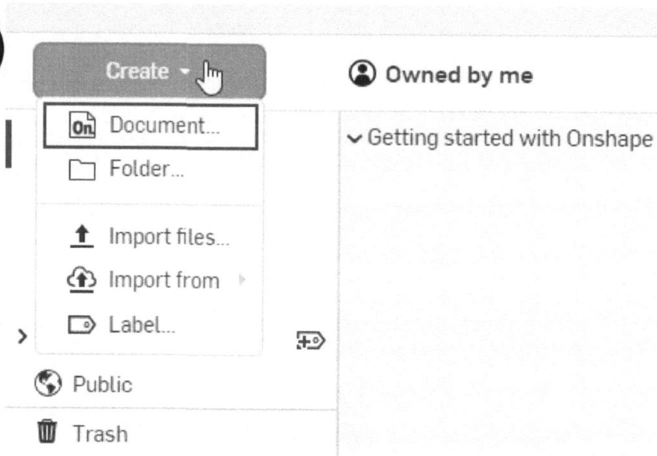

2.6

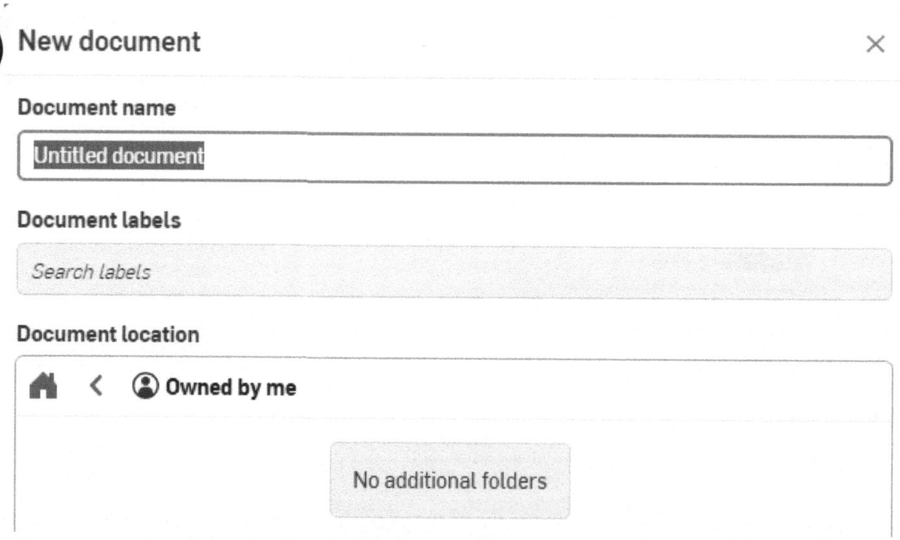

Tip: In Onshape, you can continue with the default specified name for a document. However, it is recommended to provide a new, unique name so that you can easily identify the document when searching or browsing.

Enter a new name for the design document in the **New document** window, and then click on the **Create** button or the **Create Public Document** button, depending on your subscription type. A new document with the specified name is invoked and the **Part Studio 1** and **Assembly 1** tabs are added at the bottom, see Figure 2.7. By default, the **Part Studio 1** tab is activated. As a result, you can create a 3D solid part and a surface model by using the tools available in the **Feature** toolbar. In Figure 2.7, the ***Suspension System*** is defined as the name of the document.

2.7

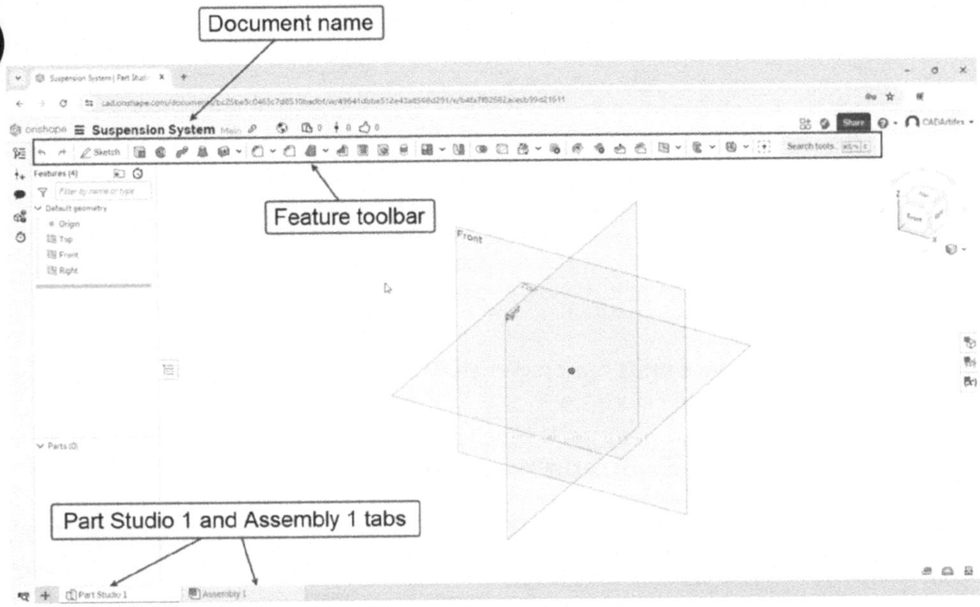

Note: In Onshape, a document refers to a project that contains all the CAD data, including parts, assemblies, drawings, and any other information related to the project.

In the Part Studio environment of Onshape, you can access the **Sketch** toolbar to create sketches. However, before you access the **Sketch** toolbar for creating sketches, it is essential to first set up units for the current document.

Specifying Units

Onshape defaults to inches and degrees for length and angle measurements for all documents. However, you can modify the default units of measurement at any point of your design for any particular document or workspace. The method for setting units is discussed below:

1. Invoke the **Document** menu by clicking on the ≡ icon (three horizontal lines) next to the Onshape logo at the top left corner, see Figure 2.8.

2.8

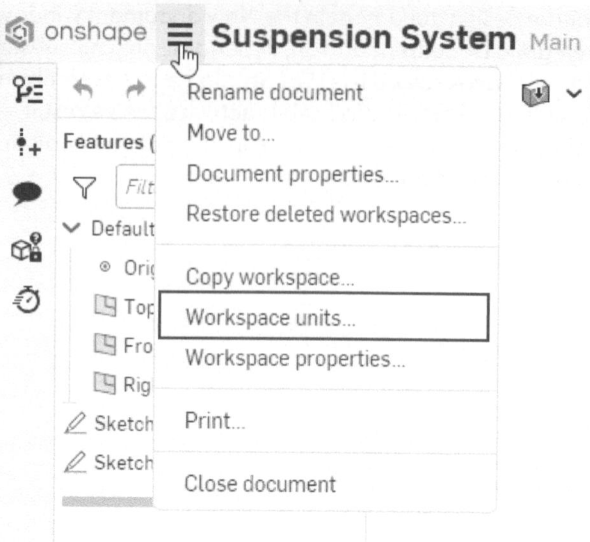

2. Click on the **Workspace units** option in the **Document** menu, refer to Figure 2.8. The **Workspace units** dialog appears, see Figure 2.9.

2.9

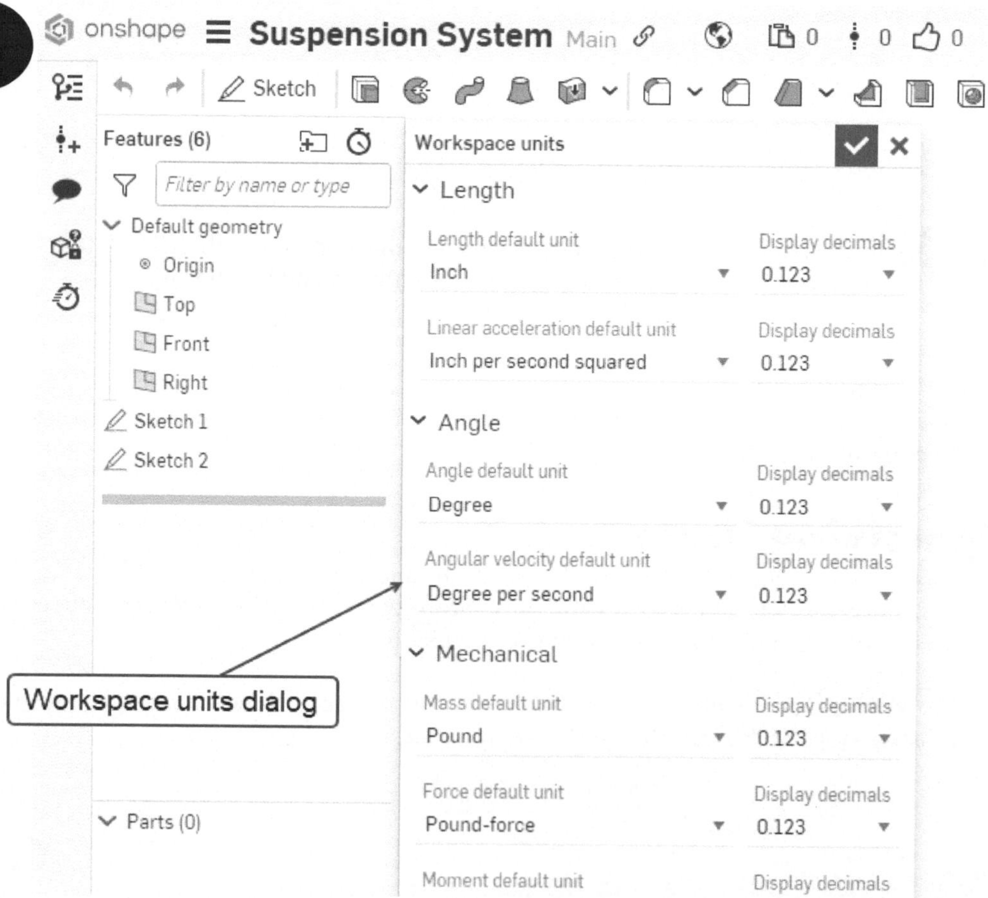

3. Select the required length and angle units of measurement, as well as their precision, from the respective drop-down lists in the **Workspace units** dialog.

4. After selecting the required units of measurement and precision for the current design document, click on the green checkmark ✓ to confirm the selection and exit the dialog.

Note: The units set in the **Workspace units** dialog apply as the default units for the current document only. To set the default unit for all new documents, click on your *name* or *Account user* icon in the upper right corner of the Onshape window (see Figure 2.10) and then select the **My account** option from the menu that appears. The **My account Profile** page appears, see Figure 2.11. In this page, click on the **Preferences** option to access the **My account Preferences** page. Next, scroll down to the **Units** section in the right panel of the **My account Preferences** page and then select the required default units of measurement. Next, click on the **Save changes** button at the bottom of the **Units** section.

After setting the default units for all new documents in the **My account Preferences** page, click on the **Return to document** option available at the top-right corner of the window (see Figure 2.12) to switch back to the currently active document.

2.10

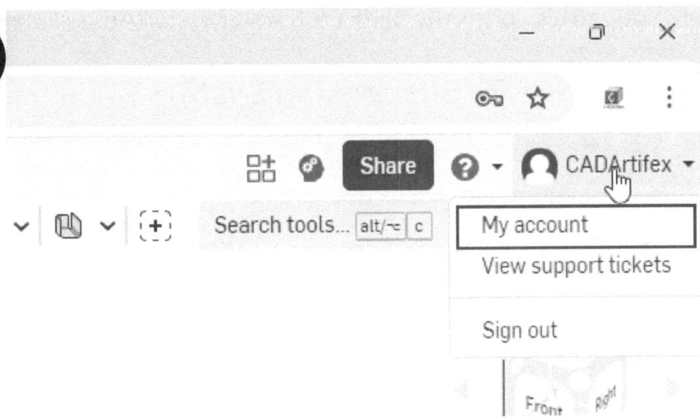

2.11

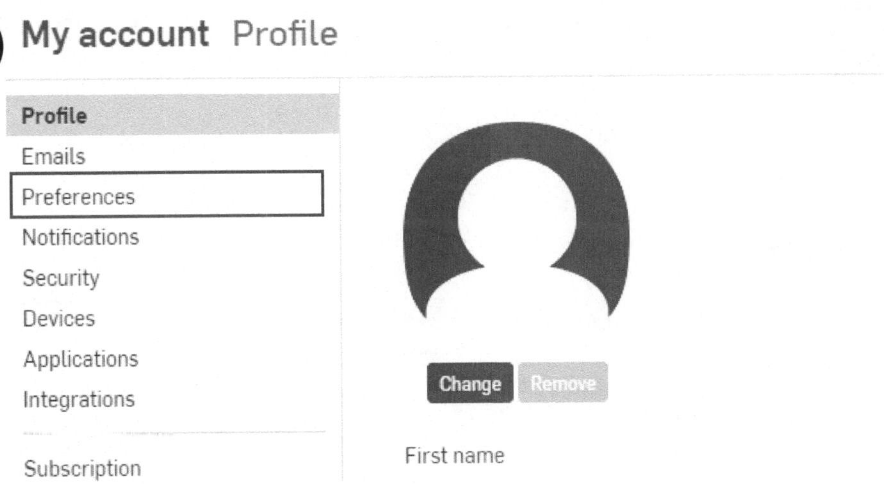

2.12

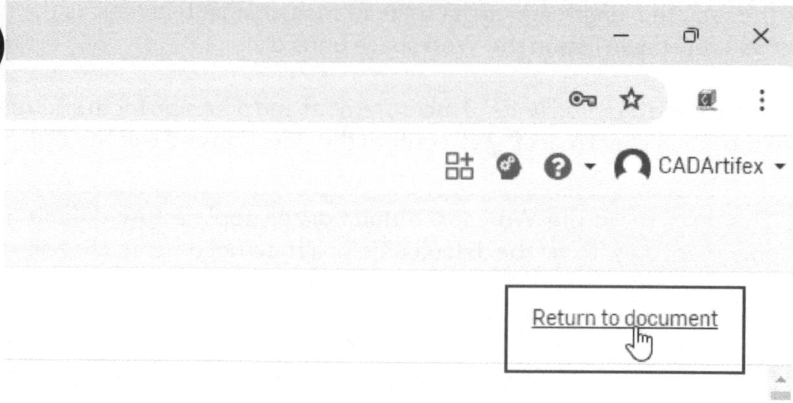

Accessing the Sketch Toolbar

After opening a document, you can access the **Sketch** toolbar in the Part Studio environment to create a sketch of the first feature of a part. The method to access the Sketch toolbar is discussed below:

1. Click on the **Sketch** tool in the **Feature** toolbar of the Part Studio environment, see Figure 2.13. The **Sketch** dialog appears (see Figure 2.14) and you are prompted to select a sketch plane. Alternatively, you can also press the SHIFT + S keys to invoke the **Sketch** dialog.

2.13

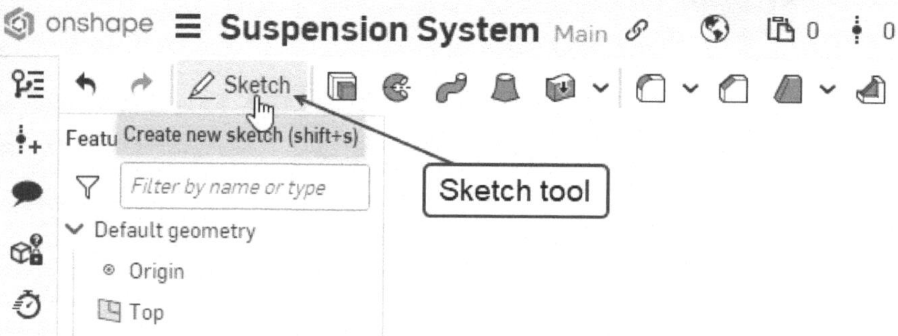

2.14

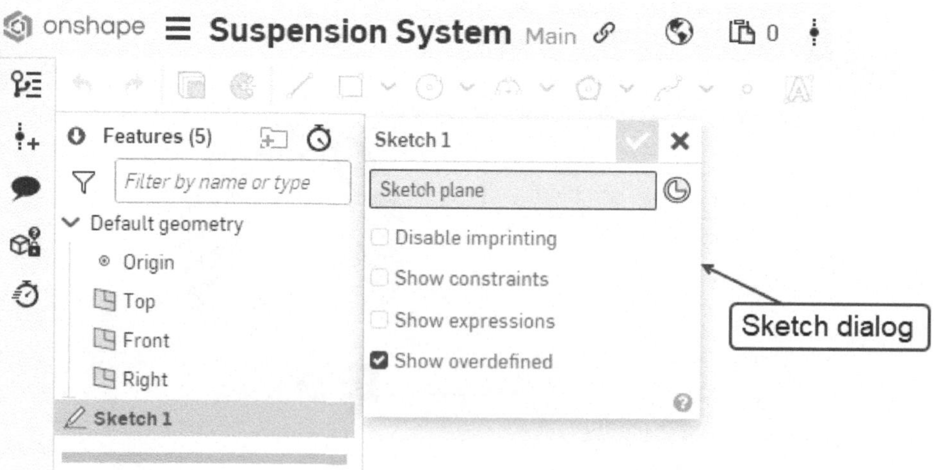

2. Select any of the three default planes in the graphics area (see Figure 2.15) or the **Feature list** (see Figure 2.16) as the sketching plane for creating a sketch. The selected plane becomes the sketching plane, and the **Sketch** toolbar appears, see Figure 2.17.

2.15

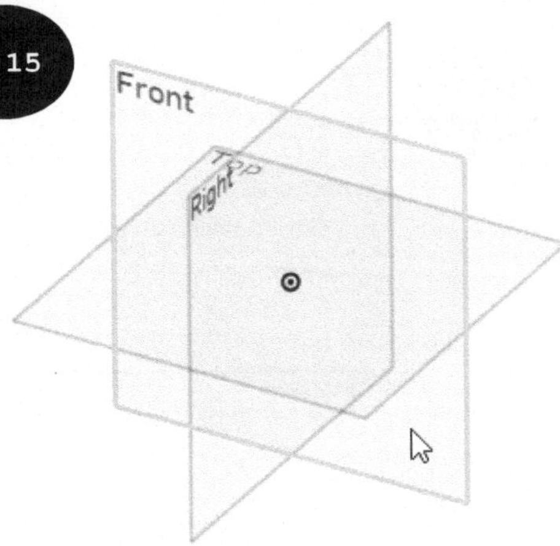

2.16

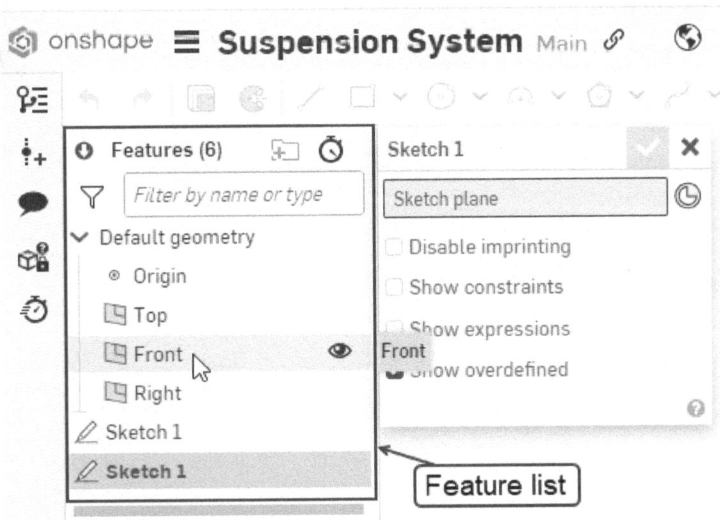

2.17

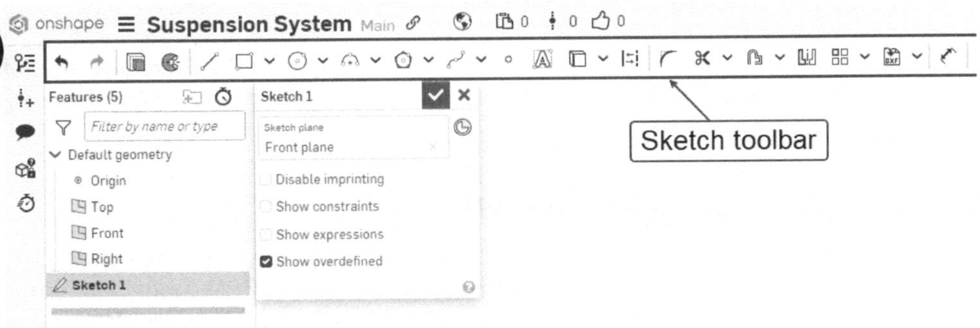

3. To orient the sketching plane normal to the viewing direction, right-click on an entity space in the graphics area and select the **View normal to sketch plane** option in the context menu that appears, see Figure 2.18. It makes it easier to create a sketch. Alternatively, press the **N** key to make the sketching plane normal to the viewing direction.

2.18

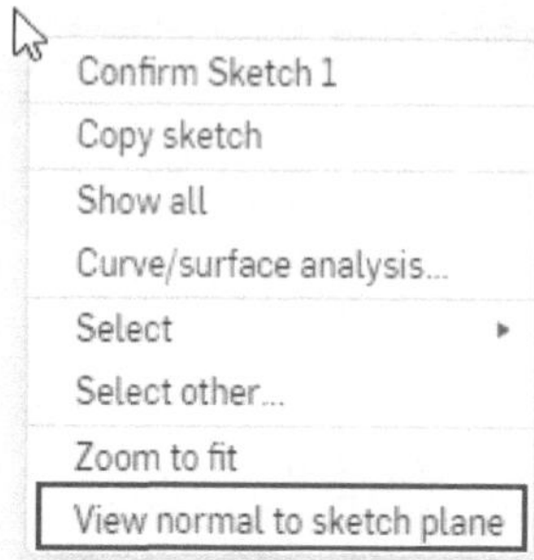

Note: A point located at the center of the graphics area represents the origin (0,0), see Figure 2.19. It is important to create sketches with reference to the origin to make them fully defined. You will learn more about making a sketch fully defined in later chapters.

2.19

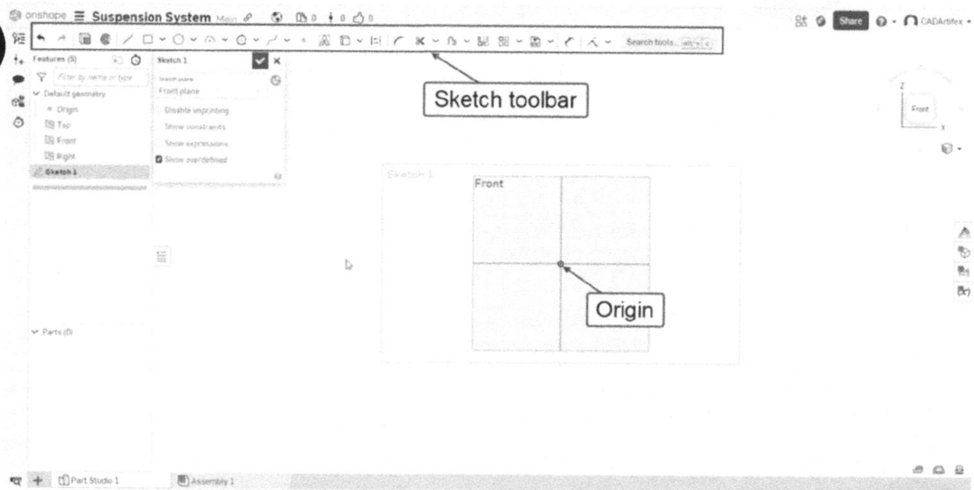

Now, you can start creating a sketch of a base feature by using the sketching tools of the **Sketch** toolbar. However, before we begin, let's first understand the importance of selecting the correct sketching plane for creating a sketch.

Selecting a Sketching Plane

As discussed earlier, to access the Sketch toolbar, you first need to select a sketching plane. Choosing the right sketching plane is crucial for defining the correct orientation of a model. For example, consider a model shown in Figure 2.20 with dimensions of 200 mm length, 100 mm width, and 40 mm height.

2.20

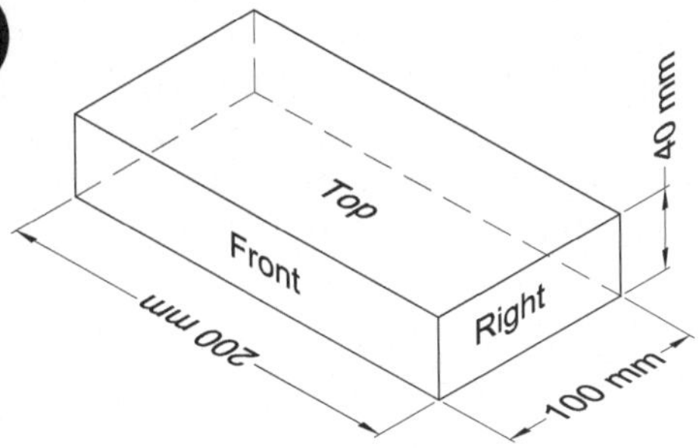

To create this model with the same orientation, you can select the Top plane as the sketching plane. Then, draw a rectangular sketch measuring 200 mm x 100 mm. After that, you can extrude the sketch to add material to a depth of 40 mm to create the model. You will learn more about creating 3D solid models in later chapters. However, if you select the Front plane as the sketching plane for creating this model, then you need to draw a rectangular sketch measuring 200 mm x 40 mm. Likewise, if you choose the right plane as the sketching plane, then you need to draw a rectangular sketch measuring 100 mm x 40 mm.

Drawing a Line

A line is defined as the shortest distance between two points. In Onshape, you can create a line or a continuous series of line segments by using the **Line** tool. The method for creating a line is discussed below:

1. Click on the **Line** tool in the **Sketch** toolbar, see Figure 2.21. The **Line** tool gets activated. Alternatively, you can press the **L** key to activate the **Line** tool.

2.21

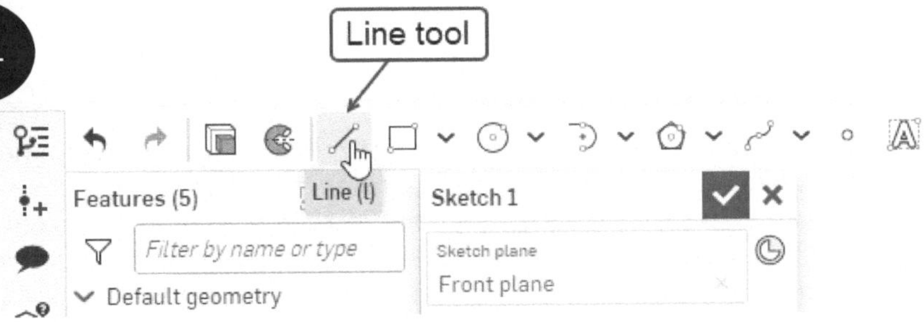

Tip: You can also invoke the **Sketch shortcut** toolbar by pressing the S key to access the sketching tools, see Figure 2.22.

2.22

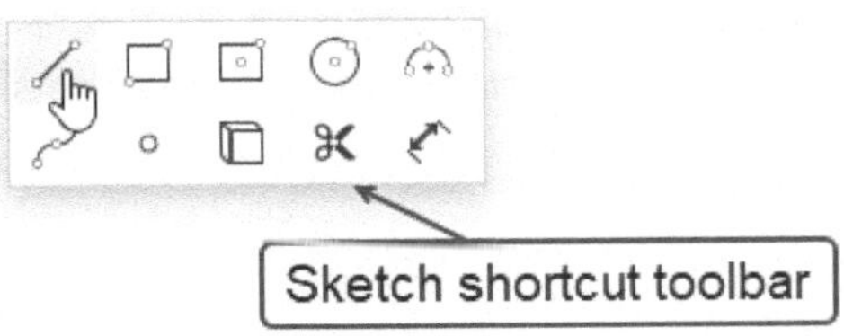

2. Click to specify a start point and an endpoint of a line one by one in the graphics area. A line is drawn between the specified points, see Figure 2.23. Notice that the current length of the line is displayed in a dimension field. Additionally, a rubber band line is displayed with one of its ends fixed to the last specified point and the other end attached to the cursor. This indicates that a series of continuous line segments can be drawn by clicking the left mouse button one after another in the graphics area, refer to Figure 2.24.

2.23

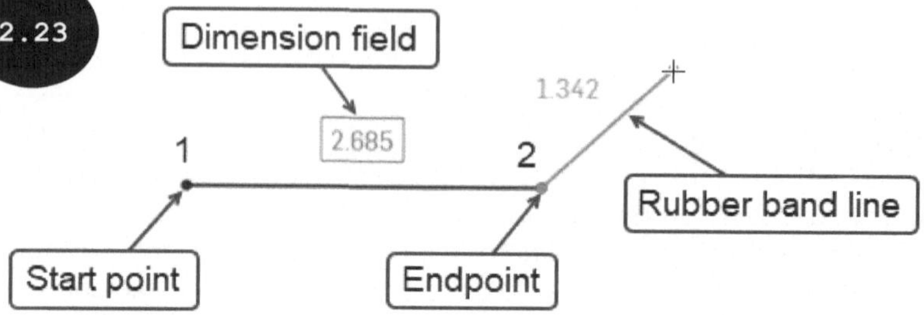

2.24

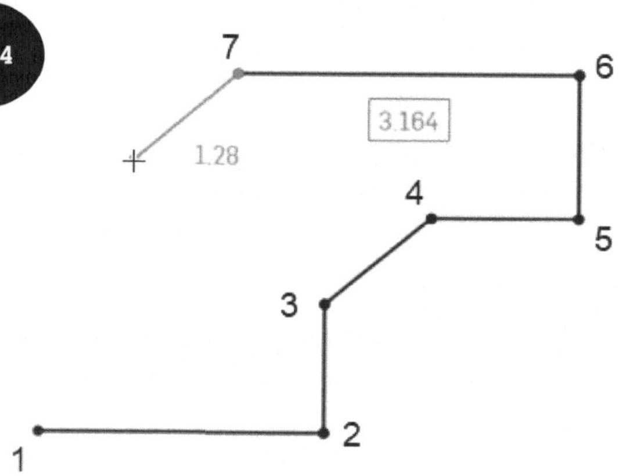

Note: In Onshape, while drawing a line segment, a symbol of the most appropriate constraint that can be applied appears near the line. For instance, when you move the cursor horizontally or vertically after specifying the start point of a line, a symbol of horizontal — or vertical I constraint appears near the line. It indicates that if you now click the left mouse button, the corresponding constraint will be applied to the line segment. You will learn more about constraints in later chapters.

Tip: You can also enter the length of the previously drawn line segment in the dimension field that appears (refer to Figure 2.23) and press ENTER. In doing so, a line of the specified length gets drawn and the respective dimension gets applied to the line. Also, the rubber band line remains visible and you can continue to draw other line segments.

3. Create a continuous series of line segments by specifying points arbitrarily one after another in the graphics area, if needed.

Tip: As Onshape is a parametric, 3D modeling software, you can first draw line segments by defining points arbitrarily in the drawing area and then apply dimensions using the **Dimension** tool. You will learn about dimensioning sketch in later chapters.

4. After drawing a single or a series of continuous line segments, right-click in the graphics area and then select the **Escape line** option in the context menu that appears to exit the **Line** tool, see Figure 2.25. Alternatively, press the ESC key to exit the **Line** tool.

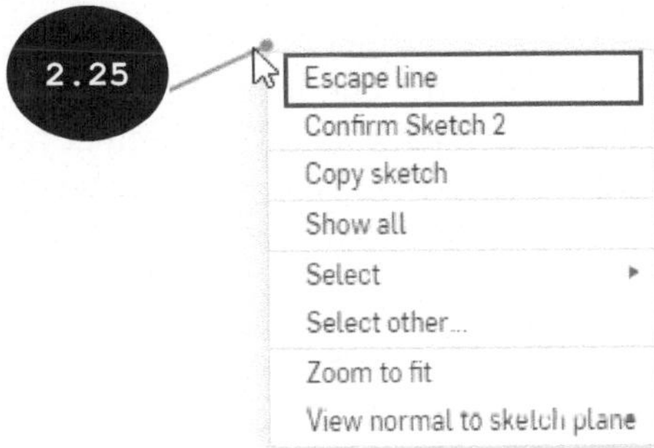

Note: Furthermore, to create a single line segment, click and hold the left mouse button after activating the **Line** tool and then drag the cursor to the endpoint. Next, release the left mouse button to end the creation of the line segment and exit the tool.

Switching Between Line and Tangent Arc Tools

In Onshape, you can switch between the **Line** and **Tangent Arc** tools and create a series of connected line and arc segments. The method to switch between the **Line** and **Tangent Arc** tools is discussed below:

1. Activate the **Line** tool and then create a line by specifying two points in the graphics area, see Figure 2.26.

Note: In this textbook, some of the figures are numbered for your reference only, see Figure 2.26. These numbers represent the sequence of points specified in the graphics area for creating an object by clicking the left mouse button.

2. After creating a line, press the SHIFT + A keys. The **Tangent arc** tool gets activated and the preview of a tangent arc appears in the graphics area, see Figure 2.27. Alternatively, move the cursor to the endpoint of the previously drawn line to switch to the **Tangent arc** tool.

3. Click the left mouse button to specify the endpoint of the tangent arc in the graphics area. A tangent arc is drawn, and the **Line** tool gets activated automatically. Also, the preview of a line appears in the graphics area, see Figure 2.28. You can continue creating a new line segment, or press the SHIFT + A keys to switch to the **Tangent arc** tool again.

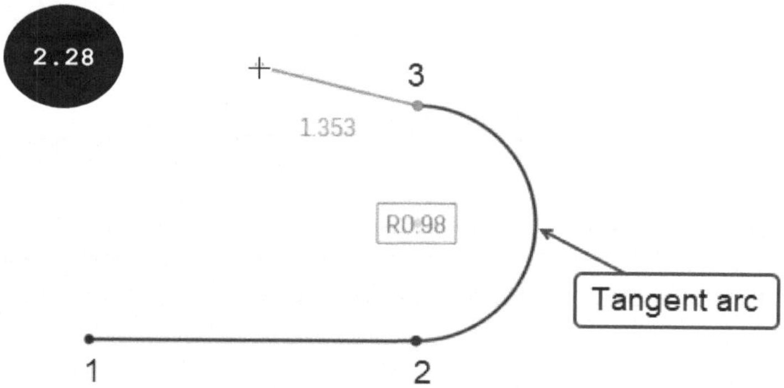

Tip: The direction of a tangent arc is defined by how you move the cursor in the graphics area from the last specified point.

Likewise, you can create a series of connected line and arc segments by switching between the tools, as required.

4. After creating a series of connected line and arc segments, press the ESC key to exit the tool.

Drawing a Rectangle

In Onshape, you can draw a rectangle by using the **Corner rectangle**, **Center point rectangle**, and **Aligned rectangle** tools. You can access these tools in the **Rectangle** drop-down menu of the **Sketch** toolbar, see Figure 2.29. The tools for drawing a rectangle are discussed next.

2.29

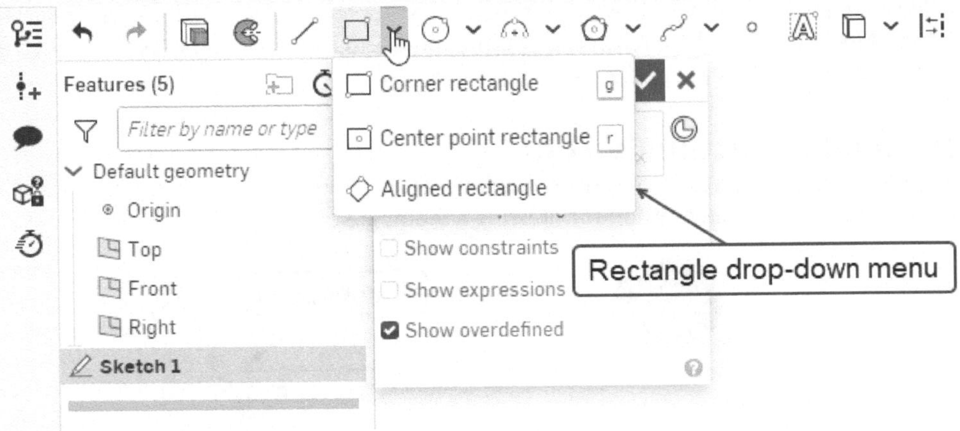

Corner rectangle Tool

The **Corner rectangle** tool is used for drawing a rectangle by specifying two diagonally opposite corners, see Figure 2.30. The method for drawing a rectangle by using this tool is discussed below:

2.30

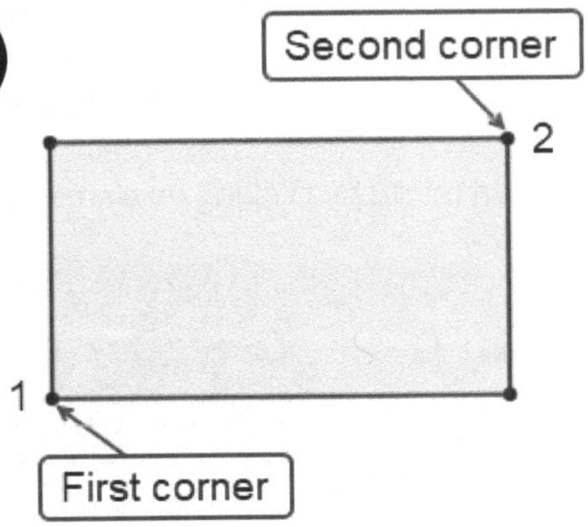

1. Click on the **Corner rectangle** tool in the **Sketch** toolbar, see Figure 2.31. Alternatively, press the **G** key to activate this tool.

2.31

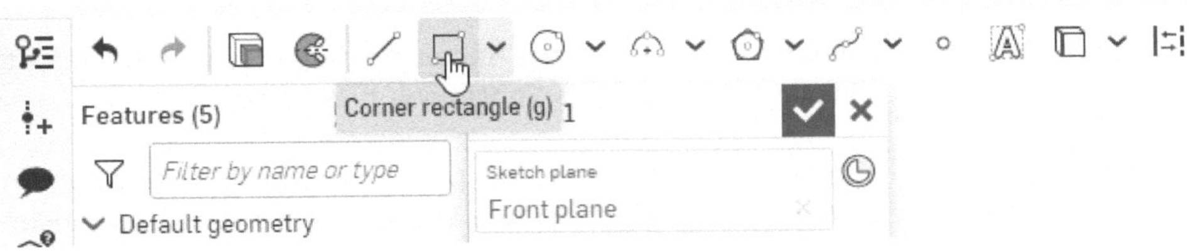

2. Click to specify two diagonally opposite corners of a rectangle one by one in the graphics area, refer to Figure 2.30. Note that the first corner defines the position of the rectangle, and the second corner defines its length and width.

Tip: To create a square with equal sides, press and hold the ALT key while drawing the rectangle.

3. After creating a rectangle, the **Corner rectangle** tool remains active. Press the ESC key to exit the tool. Alternatively, right-click in the graphics area and then select the **Escape rectangle** option in the context menu that appears to exit the tool.

Center point rectangle Tool

The **Center point rectangle** tool is used for drawing a rectangle by specifying its center and a corner point, see Figure 2.32. The method for drawing a rectangle by using this tool is discussed below:

2.32

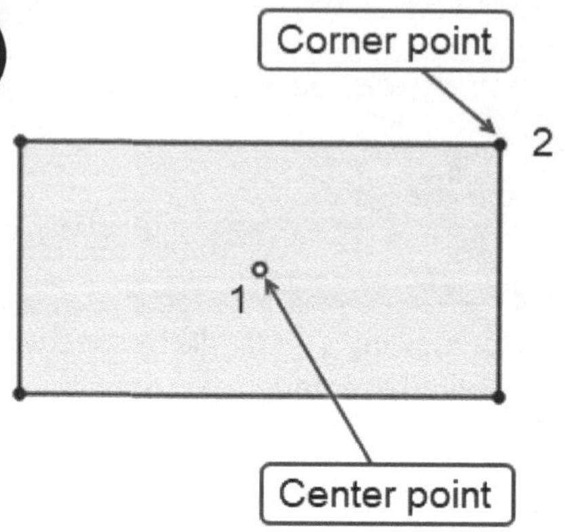

1. Invoke the **Rectangle** drop-down menu by clicking on a small arrow beside a rectangle tool in the **Sketch** toolbar, see Figure 2.33.

2.33

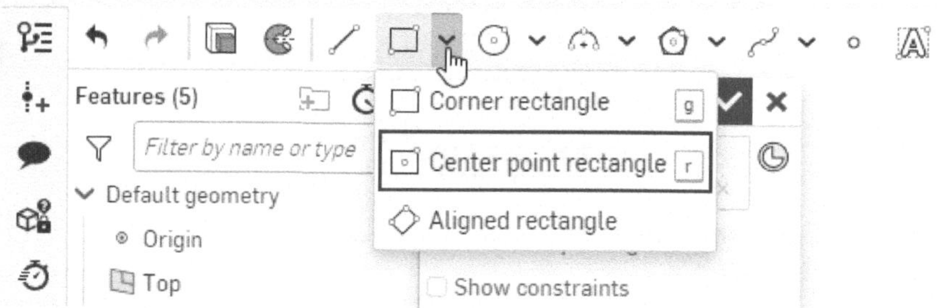

2. Click on the **Center point rectangle** tool in the **Rectangle** drop-down menu, refer to Figure 2.33. Alternatively, press the **R** key to activate the **Center point rectangle** tool.

3. Click to specify the center point and then a corner point of a rectangle one by one in the graphics area, refer to Figure 2.32. A rectangle gets drawn and the **Center point rectangle** tool remains active.

Tip: To create a square with equal sides, press and hold the ALT key while drawing the rectangle.

4. Press the ESC key to exit the tool. Alternatively, right-click in the graphics area and then select the **Escape center rectangle** option in the context menu that appears to exit the tool.

Aligned rectangle Tool

The **Aligned rectangle** tool is used for drawing an aligned rectangle by specifying three points, see Figure 2.34. The method for drawing an aligned rectangle is discussed below:

2.34

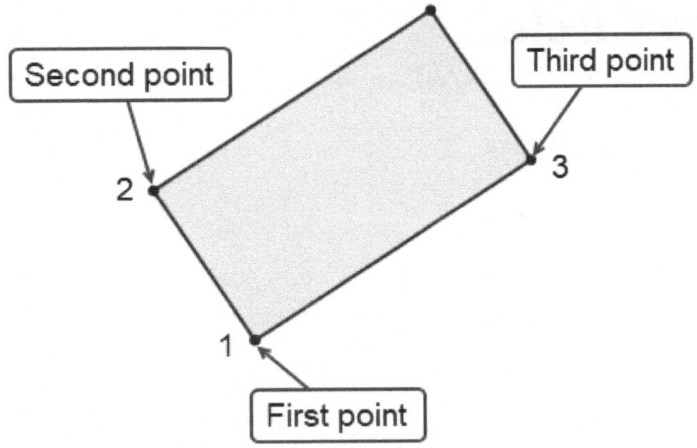

1. Invoke the **Rectangle** drop-down menu in the **Sketch** toolbar and then click on the **Aligned rectangle** tool, see Figure 2.35.

2.35

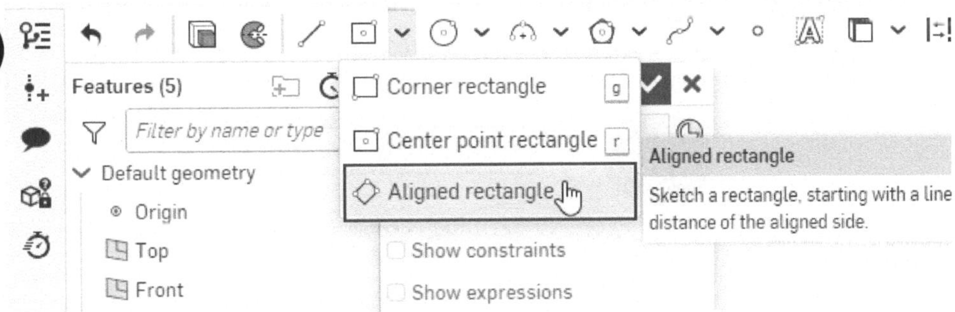

2. Click to specify three points of a rectangle one by one in the graphics area, see Figure 2.36. The first two points define the width and orientation of the rectangle, and the third point defines the length of the rectangle.

2.36

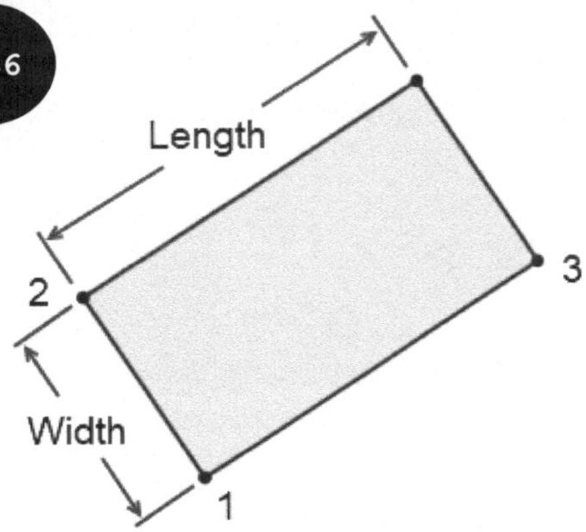

3. After creating the rectangle, the **Aligned rectangle** tool remains active. Press the ESC key to exit the tool. Alternatively, right-click in the graphics area and then select the **Escape aligned rectangle** option in the context menu that appears to exit the tool.

Drawing a Circle

In Onshape, you can draw a circle by using the **Center point circle** and **3 point circle** tools. You can access these tools in the **Circle** drop-down menu of the **Sketch** toolbar, see Figure 2.37. The tools for drawing a circle are discussed next.

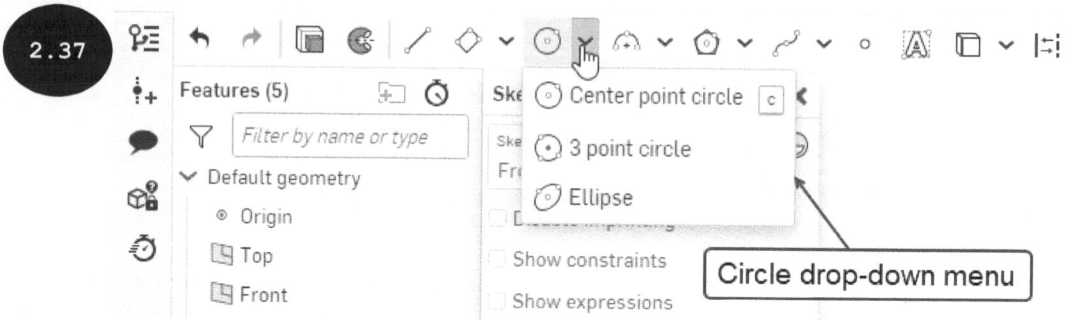

Center point circle Tool

The **Center point circle** tool is used for drawing a circle by specifying its center point and a point on its circumference, see Figure 2.38. The method for drawing a circle by using this tool is discussed below:

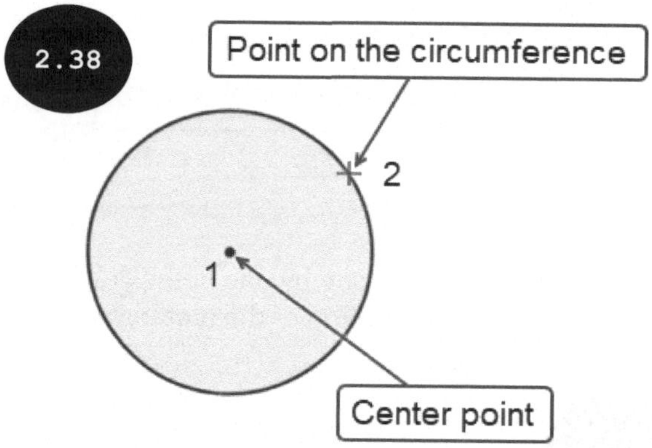

1. Click on the **Center point circle** tool in the **Sketch** toolbar, see Figure 2.39. Alternatively, press the C key to activate this tool.

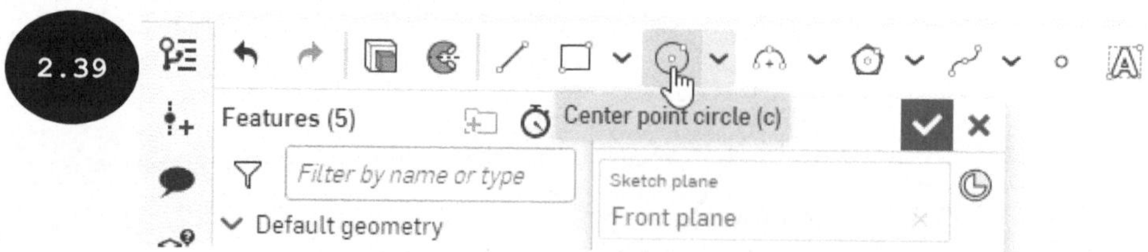

2. Click to specify the center point of a circle in the graphics area and then move the cursor to a distance. A preview of the circle appears with the display of its current diameter value, see Figure 2.40.

2.40

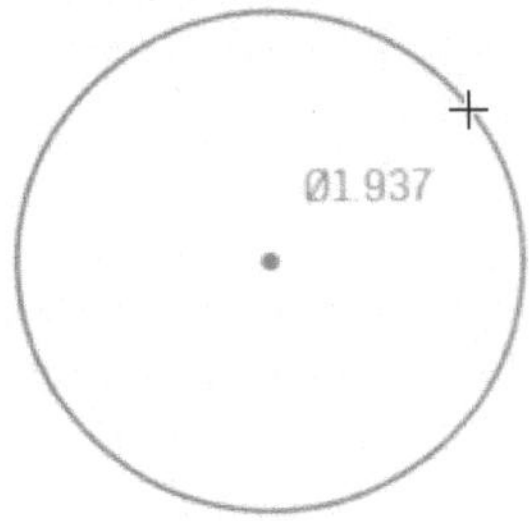

3. Click to specify a point on the circumference of the circle. A circle is drawn and the **Center point circle** tool remains active.

4. Right-click in the graphics area and then select the **Escape circle** option in the context menu that appears to exit the tool. Alternatively, press the ESC key.

3 point circle Tool

The **3 point circle** tool is used for drawing a circle by specifying three points on the circumference of the circle, see Figure 2.41. The method for drawing a circle by using this tool is discussed below:

2.41

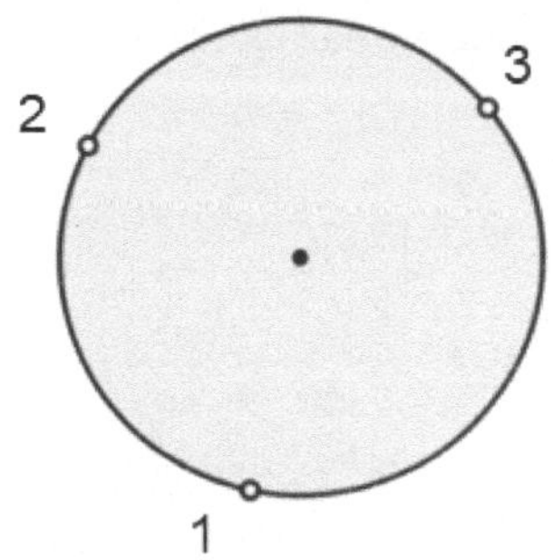

1. Invoke the **Circle** drop-down menu by clicking on a small arrow beside a circle tool in the **Sketch** toolbar, see Figure 2.42.

2.42

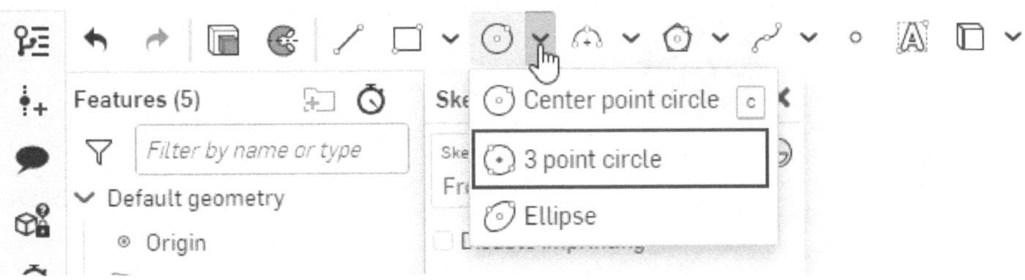

2. Click on the **3 point circle** tool in the **Circle** drop-down menu, refer to Figure 2.42. The **3 point circle** tool gets activated.

3. Click to specify three points on the circle's circumference one by one in the graphics area. A circle gets drawn and the **3 point circle** tool remains active.

4. Right-click in the graphics area and then select the **Escape 3 point circle** option in the context menu that appears to exit the tool. Alternatively, press the ESC key.

Drawing an Ellipse

An ellipse is drawn by defining its major axis and minor axis, see Figure 2.43. You can draw an ellipse by using the **Ellipse** tool. The method for drawing an ellipse is discussed below:

2.43

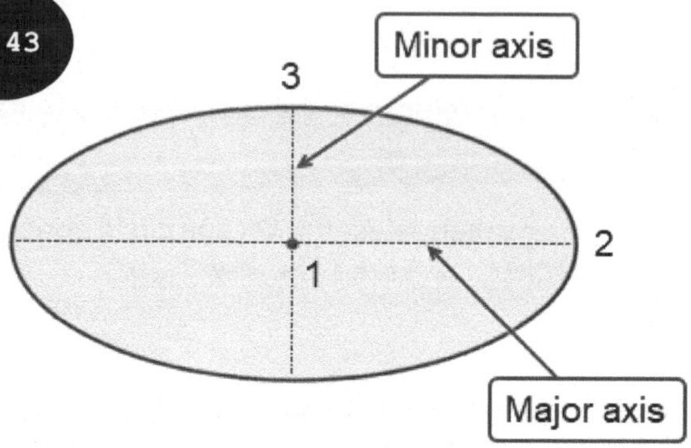

1. Click on a small arrow beside a circle tool in the **Sketch** toolbar and then click on the **Ellipse** tool in the drop-down menu that appears, see Figure 2.44.

2.44

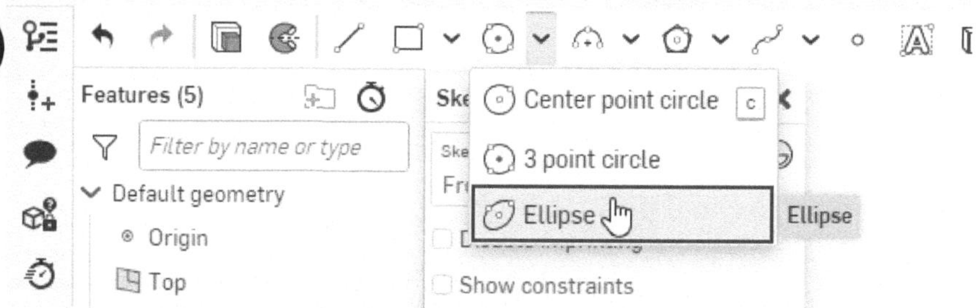

2. Click to specify the center point of the ellipse in the graphics area and then move the cursor to a distance. The preview of an ellipse appears, see Figure 2.45.

2.45

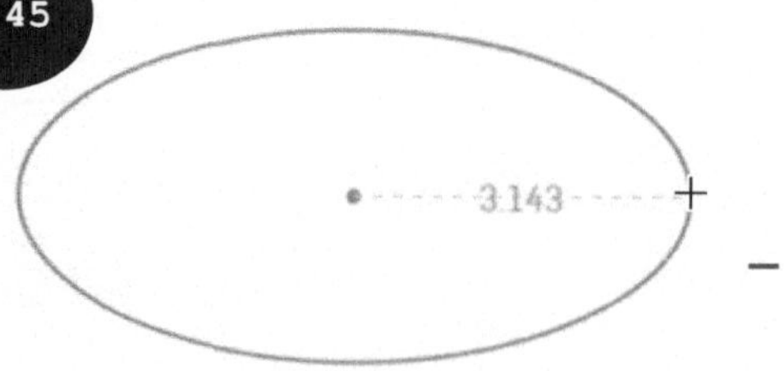

3. Click to define the major and minor axes of the ellipse one by one in the graphics area. An ellipse gets drawn (see Figure 2.46) and the **Ellipse** tool remains active.

2.46

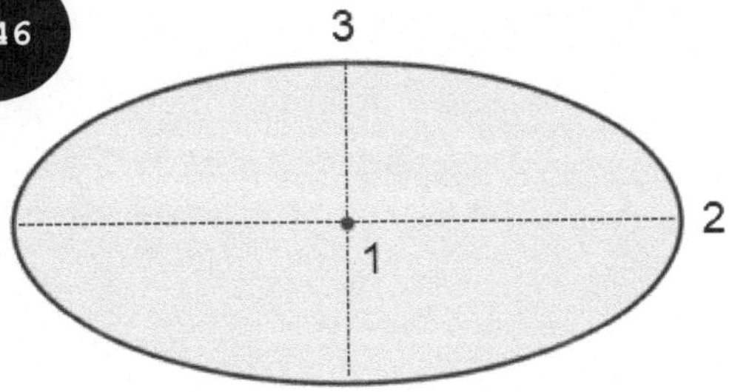

4. Press the ESC key to exit the tool. Alternatively, right-click in the graphics area and then select the **Escape ellipse** option in the context menu that appears.

Drawing an Arc

In Onshape, you can draw various types of arcs using the tools in the **Arc** drop-down menu of the **Sketch** toolbar, see Figure 2.47. These include a 3-point arc, tangent arc, center point arc, elliptical arc, and conic arc. The tools for creating these arcs are discussed below:

2.47

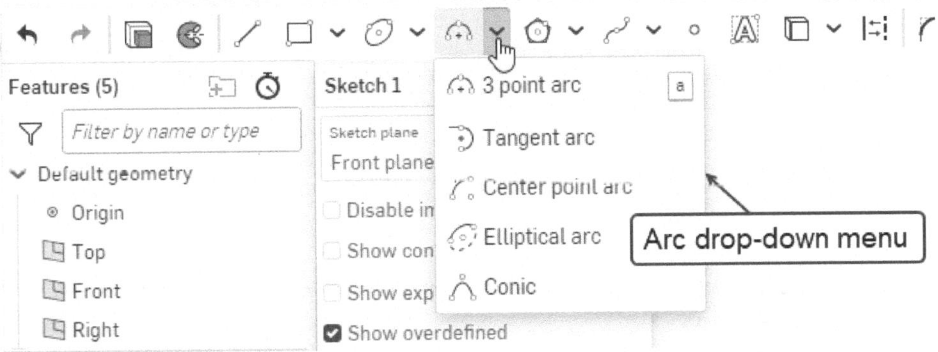

3 point arc Tool

The **3 point arc** tool is used for drawing an arc by specifying three points on its arc length, see Figure 2.48. To do so, click on the **3 point arc** tool in the **Sketch** toolbar and then specify three points in the graphics area one by one. The first point defines the start point of the arc, the second point defines the endpoint of the arc, and the third point defines the arc radius. After creating the arc, press ESC to exit the tool.

2.48

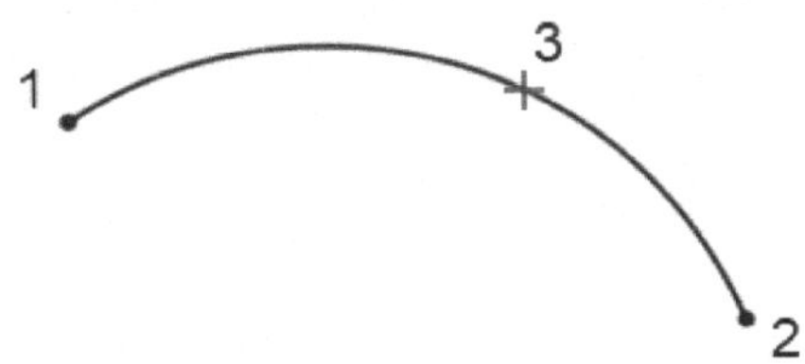

Tangent arc Tool

The **Tangent arc** tool is used for drawing an arc tangent to an existing line, arc, or spline entity, refer to Figure 2.49. In this figure, a tangent arc is created to an existing line entity. The method for creating an arc tangent to an existing entity is discussed below:

2.49

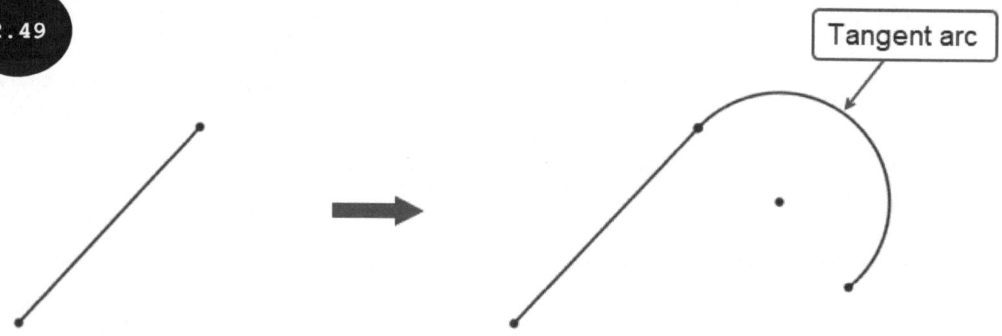

1. Invoke the **Arc** drop-down menu by clicking on a small arrow beside an arc tool in the **Sketch** toolbar, see Figure 2.50.

2.50

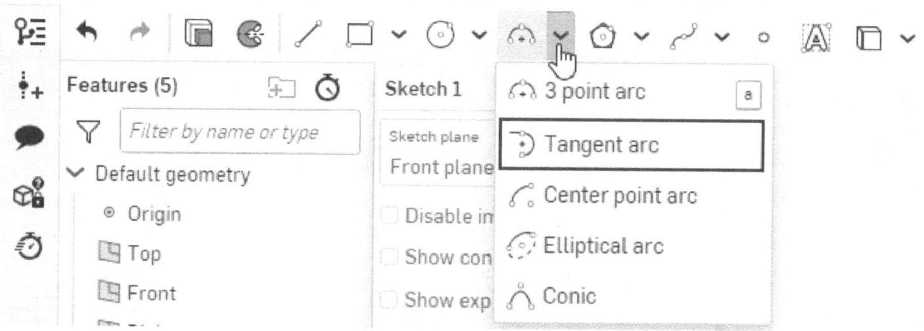

2. Click on the **Tangent arc** tool in the **Arc** drop-down menu, refer to Figure 2.50. The **Tangent arc** tool gets activated.

3. Select an endpoint of an existing entity (line, arc, or spline) in the graphics area. A preview of an arc tangent to the selected entity appears in the graphics area such that its endpoint is attached to the cursor, see Figure 2.51.

2.51

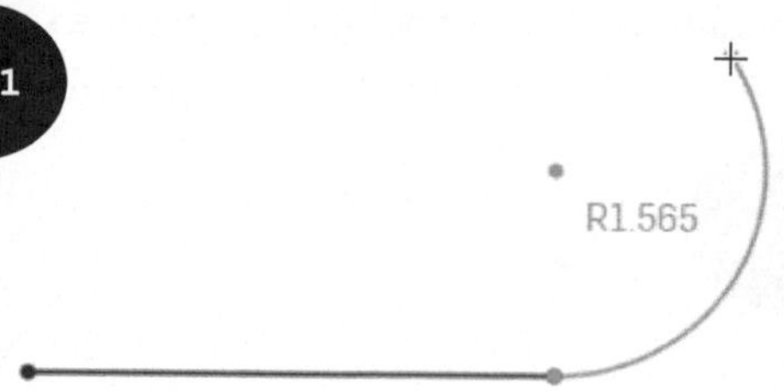

Tip: You can also select an entity to initiate a tangent arc from its closest endpoint of the selection.

4. Move the cursor in the required direction and then click to specify the endpoint of the tangent arc in the graphics area. An arc tangent to the selected entity gets created and the **Tangent arc** tool remains active.

5. Press the ESC key to exit the tool. Alternatively, right-click in the graphics area and then select the **Escape tangent arc** option in the context menu that appears.

Center point arc Tool

The **Center point arc** tool is used for drawing an arc by specifying its center point, start point, and endpoint one by one in the graphics area, refer to Figure 2.52. The method for creating an arc by using this tool is discussed below:

2.52

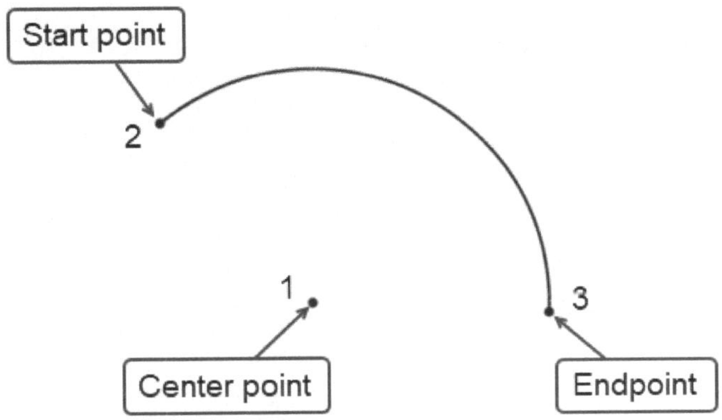

1. Invoke the **Arc** drop-down menu in the **Sketch** toolbar and then click on the **Center point arc** tool, see Figure 2.53.

2.53

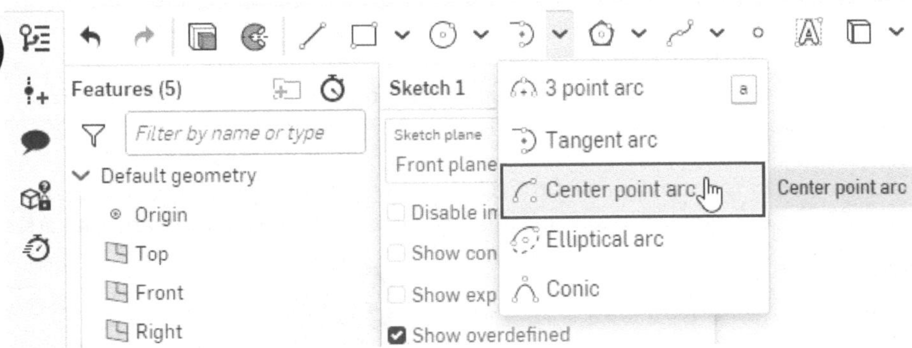

2. Click to specify a center point of an arc in the graphics area, refer to Figure 2.52. The preview of a construction circle appears.

3. Click to define the start point of the arc and then move the cursor clockwise or anti-clockwise. The preview of an arc appears in the drawing area.

4. Click to define the endpoint of the arc in the graphics area. An arc is drawn by specifying its center point, start point, and endpoint, refer to Figure 2.52.

Elliptical arc Tool

The **Elliptical arc** tool is used for drawing an elliptical arc in the graphics area, refer to Figure 2.54. The method for drawing an elliptical arc by using this tool is discussed below:

2.54

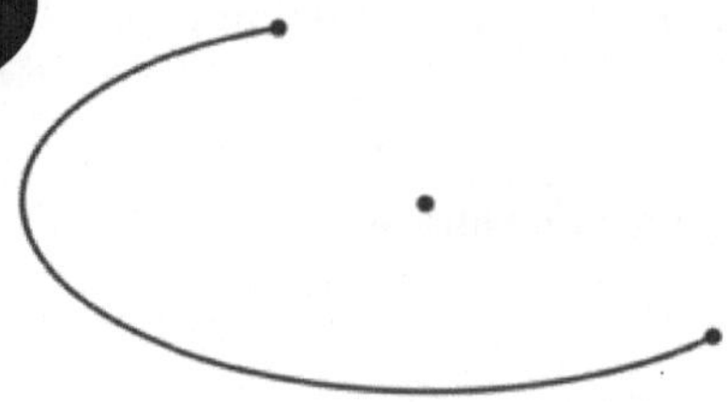

1. Invoke the **Arc** drop-down menu in the **Sketch** toolbar and then click on the **Elliptical arc** tool, see Figure 2.55.

2.55

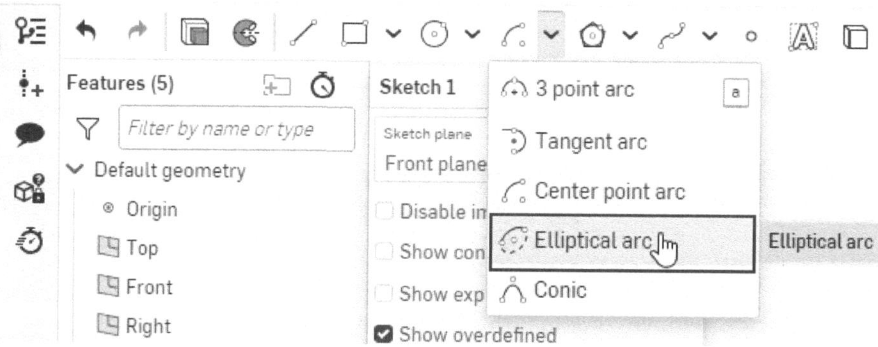

2. Click to specify the center point of the elliptical arc in the graphics area and then move the cursor to a distance. A preview of a construction ellipse appears.
3. Click to define the major axis of the elliptical arc in the graphics area and then move the cursor to a distance, see Figure 2.56.
4. Click to specify the start point of the elliptical arc in the graphics area and then move the cursor clockwise or anti-clockwise to a distance. The preview of an elliptical arc appears, see Figure 2.57.

2.56

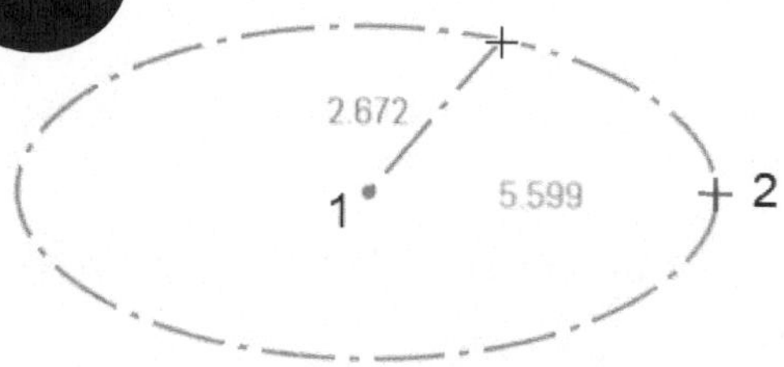

2.57

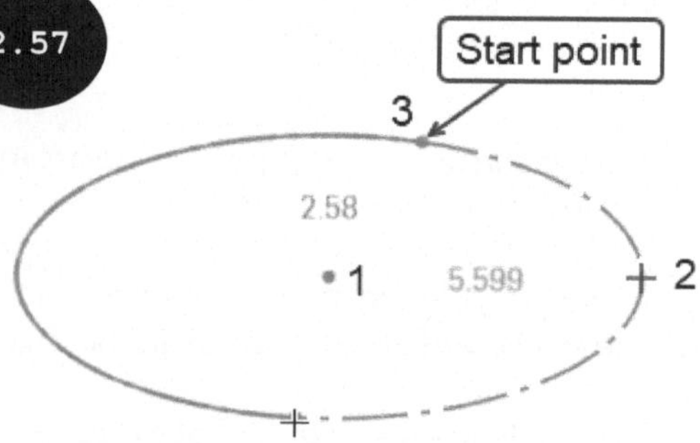

5. Click to specify the endpoint of the elliptical arc. An elliptical arc is created, see Figure 2.58. Next, press the ESC key to exit the **Elliptical arc** tool.

2.58

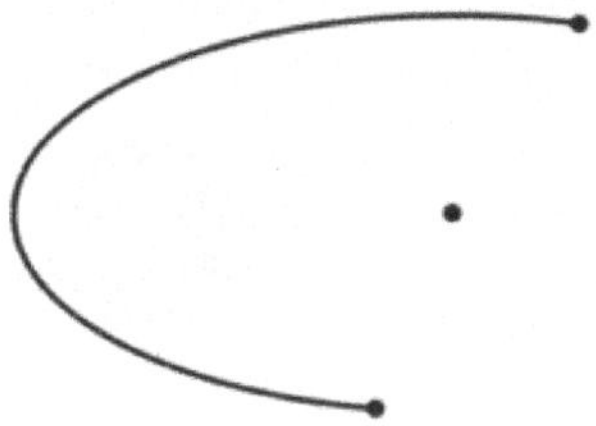

Conic Tool

The **Conic** tool is used to draw conic arcs, including elliptical, parabolic, and hyperbolic arcs, by specifying the start point, endpoint, top vertex, and Rho value, refer to Figure 2.59. The method for drawing a conic arc by using this tool is discussed below:

2.59

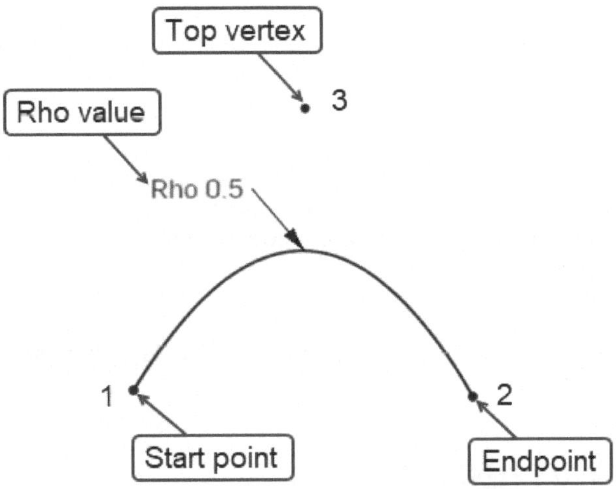

1. Invoke the **Arc** drop-down menu in the **Sketch** toolbar and then click on the **Conic** tool, see Figure 2.60.

2.60

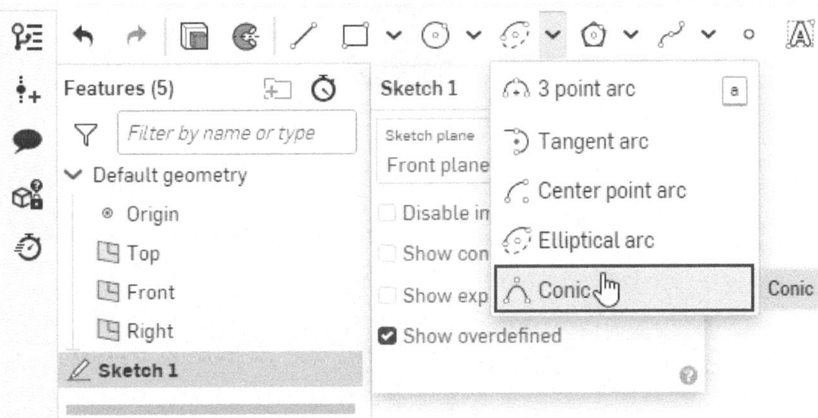

2. Click to specify a start point, followed by an endpoint, in the graphics area. A preview of the conic arc appears, with its top vertex attached to the cursor, see Figure 2.61.

3. Click to specify the top vertex of the arc at a desired location in the graphics area. The default Rho value of the arc appears in a dimension field, see Figure 2.62.

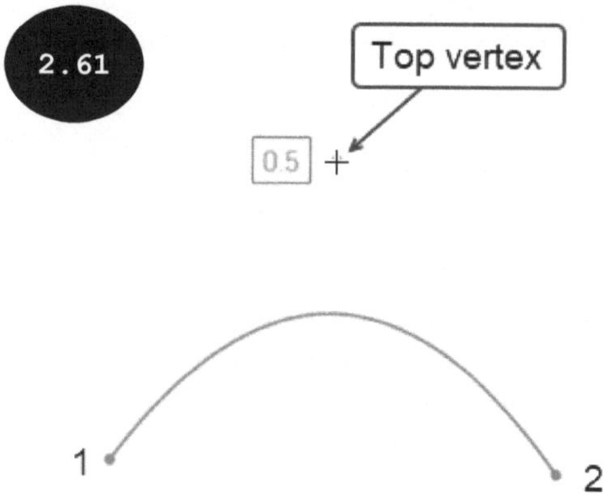

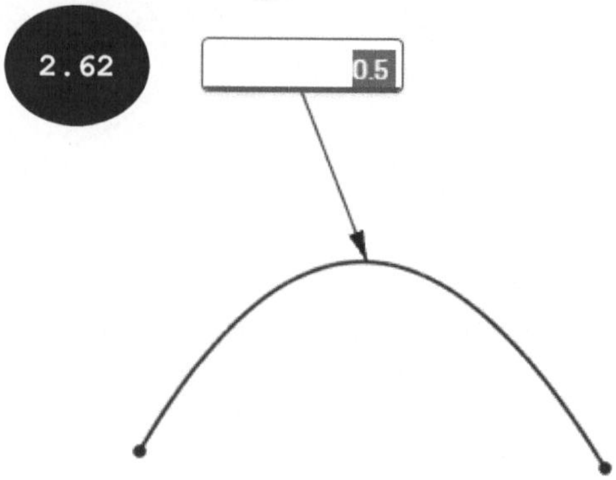

4. Enter the required Rho value (greater than 0 and less than 1) in the dimension field.

Note: The Rho value of a conic arc defines the type of curve. If the Rho value is less than 0.5 then the conic arc will be an elliptical curve. If the Rho value is equal to 0.5 then the conic arc will be a parabolic curve. If the Rho value is greater than 0.5 then the conic arc will be a hyperbolic curve.

5. After entering the required Rho value, press the ENTER key. The respective conic arc gets drawn. Next, press the ESC key to exit the tool.

Drawing a Polygon

A polygon is a multi-sided geometry with all sides of equal length and angles, see Figure 2.63. In Onshape, you can draw a polygon using the **Inscribed polygon** and **Circumscribed polygon** tools, see Figure 2.64. The tools for drawing a polygon are discussed next.

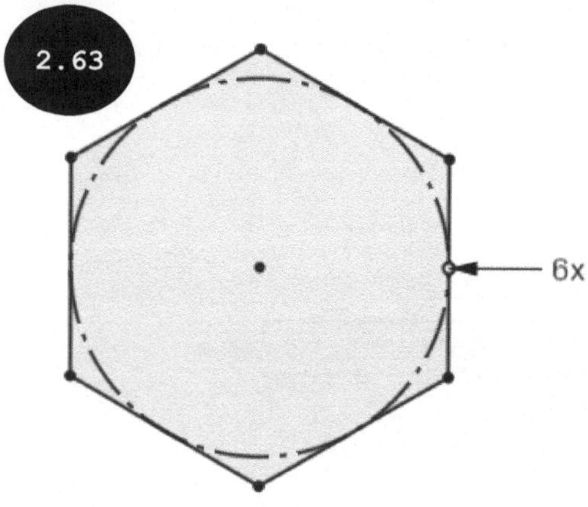

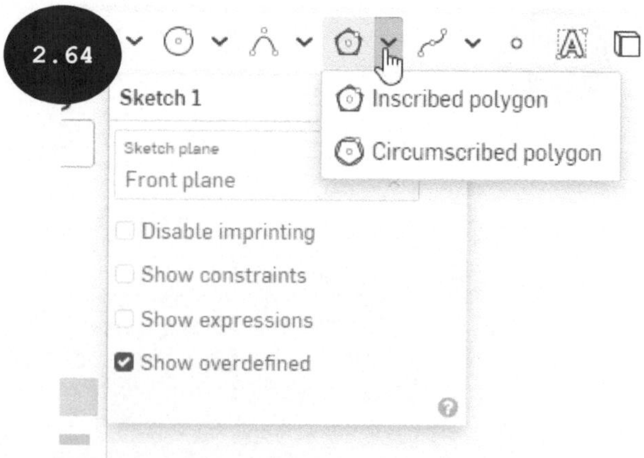

Inscribed polygon Tool

The **Inscribed polygon** tool is used for drawing a polygon using a construction circle inside the polygon, see Figure 2.65. This ensures that the midpoints of all polygon sides touch the construction circle. The method for creating a polygon by using this tool is discussed below:

2.65

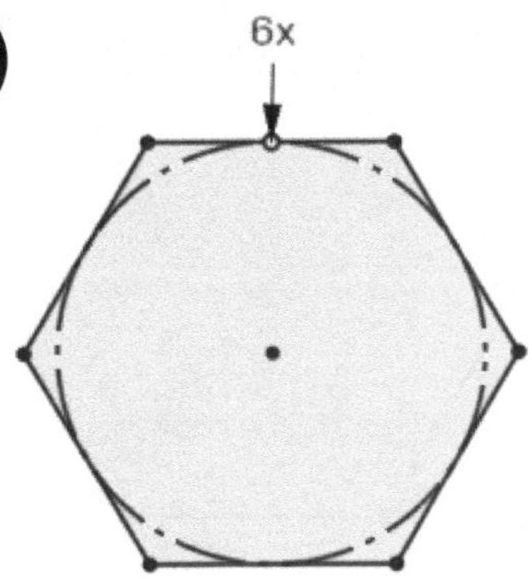

1. Click on the **Inscribed polygon** tool in the **Sketch** toolbar, see Figure 2.66.

2.66

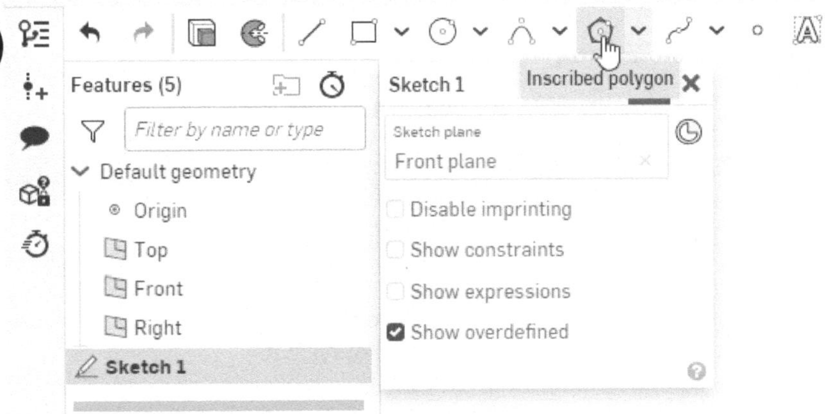

2. Click to specify the center point of a polygon in the graphics area. The preview of a polygon appears with a construction circle positioned inside it.

3. Click to define the diameter of the construction circle in the graphics area. An inscribed polygon is created and you are prompted to specify the number of sides for the polygon, ranging from 3 to 50.

4. Move the cursor towards or away from the polygon to adjust the number of polygon sides as needed, within the range of 3 to 50.

5. Click when the desired number of polygon sides is displayed in the spinner. A polygon of specified sides is created. Next, press the ESC key to exit the tool.

Circumscribed polygon Tool

The **Circumscribed polygon** tool is used for drawing a polygon using a construction circle outside the polygon, see Figure 2.67. This ensures that all vertices of the polygon touch the construction circle. The method for creating a polygon by using this tool is discussed below:

2.67

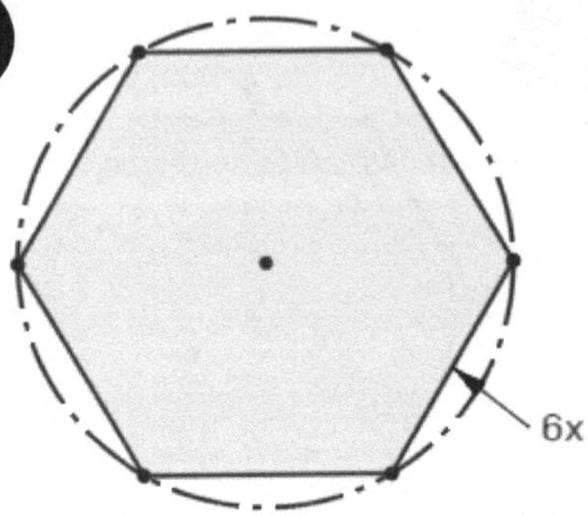

1. Click on a small arrow beside a polygon tool in the **Sketch** toolbar and then click on the **Circumscribed polygon** tool in the drop-down menu that appears, see Figure 2.68.

2.68

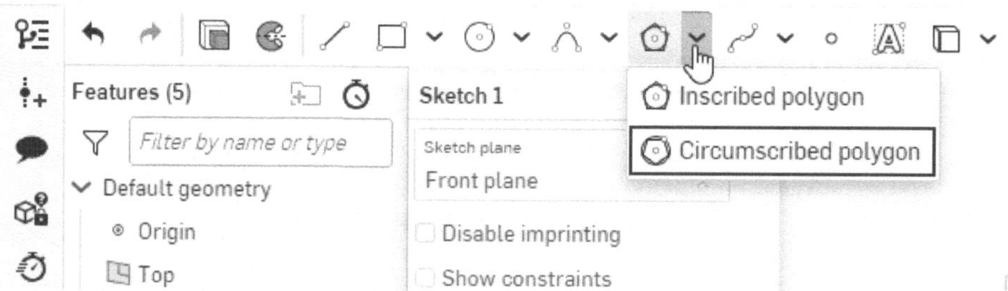

2. Click to specify the center point of a polygon in the graphics area. The preview of a polygon appears with a construction circle positioned outside it.

3. Click to define the diameter of the construction circle in the graphics area. A circumscribed polygon is created and you are prompted to specify the number of sides for the polygon, ranging from 3 to 50.

4. Move the cursor towards or away from the polygon to adjust the number of polygon sides as needed, within the range of 3 to 50.

5. Click when the desired number of polygon sides is displayed in the spinner. A polygon of specified sides is created. Next, press the ESC key to exit the tool.

Drawing a Spline

A spline is a multiple-point curve with a high degree of smoothness. In Onshape, you can draw a spline by specifying two or more control points in the graphics area using the **Spline** and **Bezier** tools. Both of these tools for drawing a spline are discussed next.

Spline Tool

The **Spline** tool is used to create a spline by defining two or more control points along its length, see Figure 2.69. In this figure, a spline is created by using five control points. The method for drawing a spline by using the **Spline** tool is discussed below:

2.69

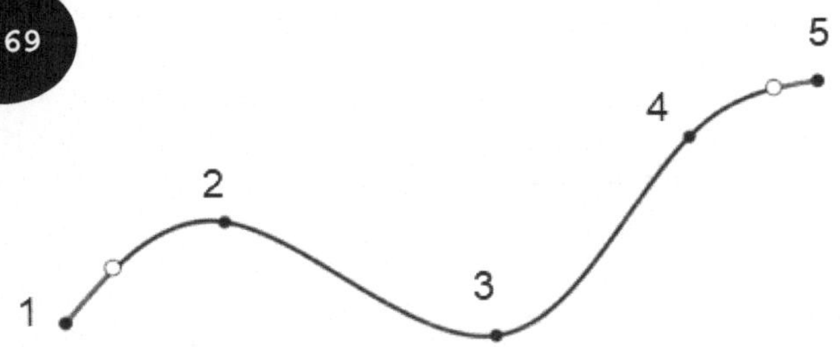

1. Click on the **Spline** tool in the **Sketch** toolbar, see Figure 2.70.

2.70

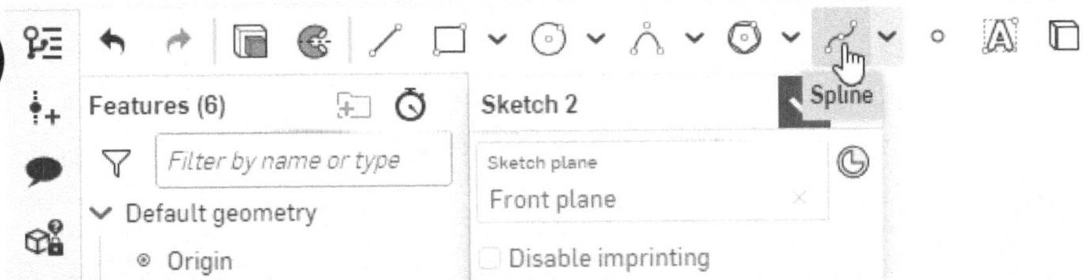

2. Click to specify two or more control points one by one in the graphics area as needed. A preview of the spline curve appears such that it passes through the specified control points, see Figure 2.71.

2.71

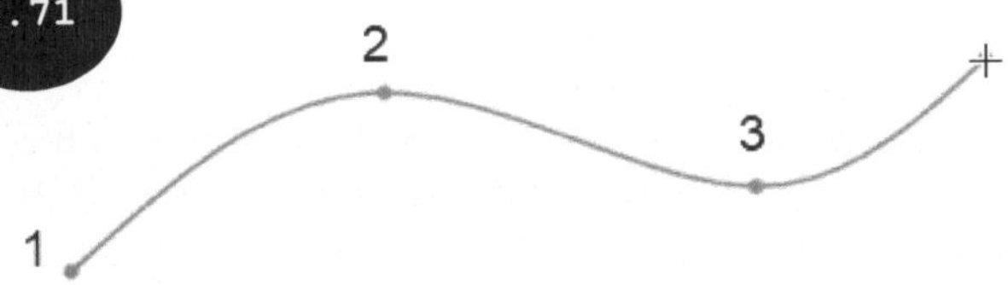

3. After specifying the required number of control points for drawing a spline, press the ESC key. A spline of specified control points is created and the **Spline** tool remains active.

4. Press the ESC key again to exit the **Spline** tool. Alternatively, right-click in the graphics area and then select the **Escape spline** option in the context menu that appears to exit the tool.

Note: Once a spline is created, you can edit it by dragging its control points to new locations within the graphics area, as desired.

Bezier Tool

The **Bezier** tool is used to create a bezier spline by defining two or more control points along the control polygon that influence the shape of the spline, see Figure 2.72. In this figure, a bezier spline is created by specifying five control points. The method for drawing a bezier spline by using the **Bezier** tool is discussed below:

2.72

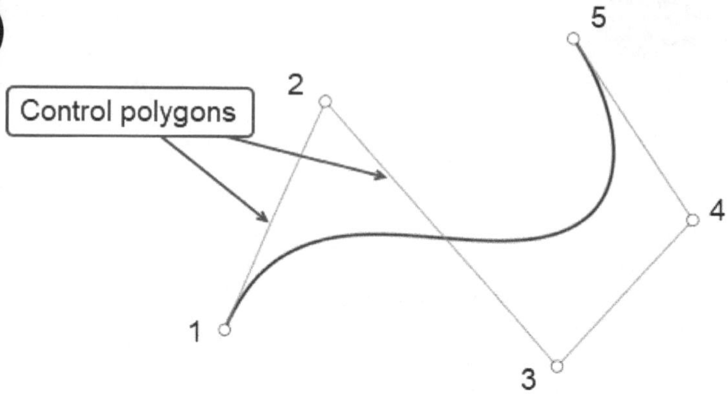

1. Click on a small arrow beside a spline tool in the **Sketch** toolbar and then click on the **Bezier** tool in the drop-down menu that appears, see Figure 2.73.

2.73

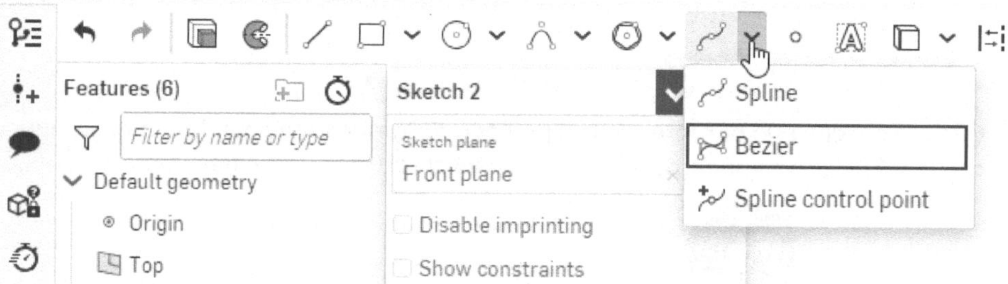

2. Click to specify two or more control points one by one in the graphics area along the control polygon as needed. A preview of a bezier spline appears such that it passes near the specified control points, which are connected by control polygons, see Figure 2.74.

2.74

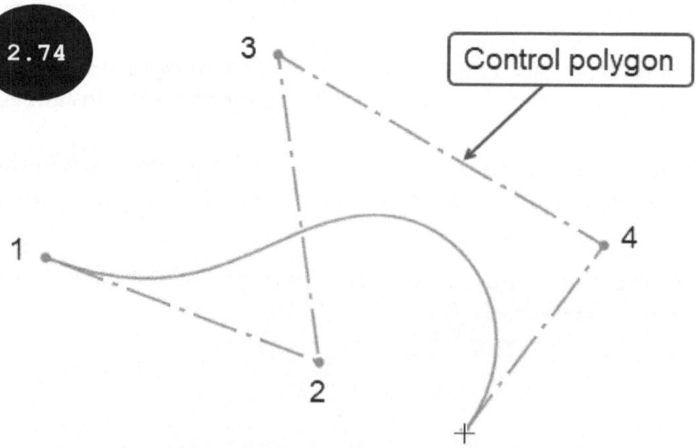

3. After specifying the required number of control points, press the ESC key. A bezier spline is created and the **Bezier** tool remains active.

4. Press the ESC key again to exit the **Bezier** tool. Alternatively, right-click in the graphics area and then select the **Escape bezier** option in the context menu that appears to exit the tool.

Note: Once a bezier spline is created, you can edit it by dragging its control points and control polygons to new locations within the graphics area, as desired.

Adding a Control Point to an Existing Spline

In Onshape, you can add additional control points along the length of a spline or the control polygon of a bezier spline to further manipulate the shape. You can add a control point by using the **Spline control point** tool. The method for adding a control point is discussed below:

1. Click on a small arrow beside a spline tool in the **Sketch** toolbar and then click on the **Spline control point** tool in the drop-down menu that appears, see Figure 2.75.

2.75

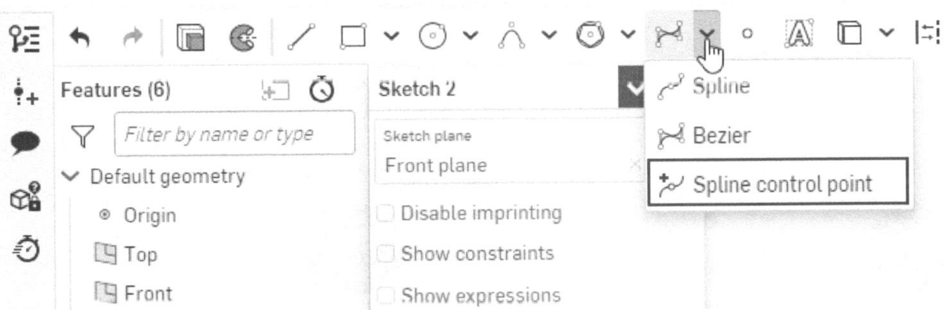

2. Move the cursor to the desired location along a spline, then click to add a control point exactly where you need it, see Figure 2.76. You can add multiple control points one by one along the length of the spline.

2.76

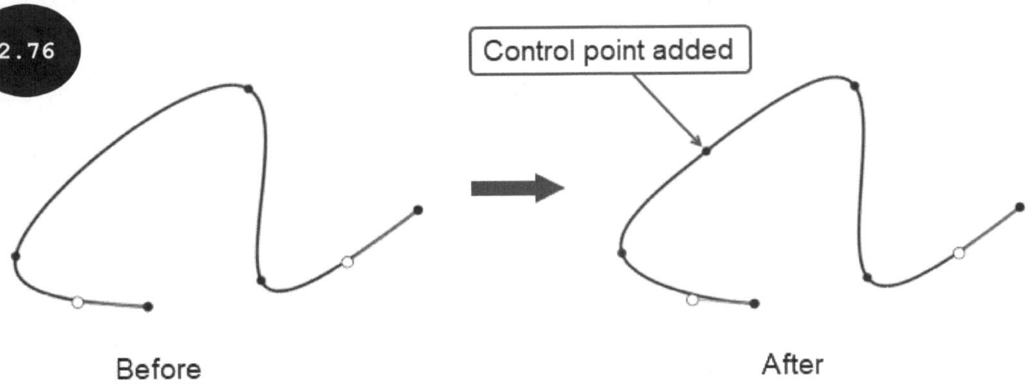

3. Similarly, you can add control points along a control polygon of a bezier spline

4. After adding the control points, right-click in the graphics area and then select the **Escape spline control point** option in the context menu that appears.

Creating Construction Geometries

In Onshape, you can create new construction geometries or convert existing sketch entities into construction geometries by using the **Construction** tool. The method for creating construction geometries is discussed below:

1. Click to activate the **Construction** tool in the **Sketch** toolbar (see Figure 2.77) or press the **Q** key. The construction mode gets activated.

2.77

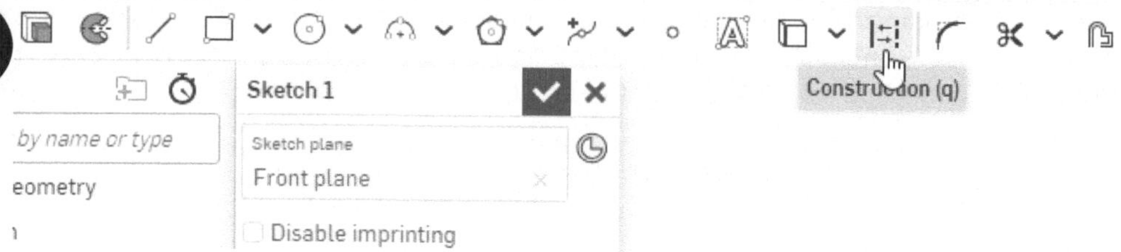

Now, you can create a construction geometry.

2. Create a construction geometry such as a line or a circle by using the respective sketching tool, as required. Figure 2.78 shows a construction line created using the **Line** tool, while Figure 2.79 shows a construction circle created using the **Center point circle** tool.

2.78

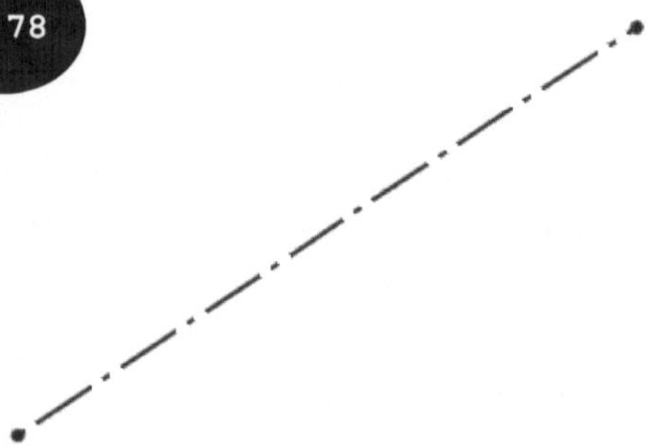

2.79

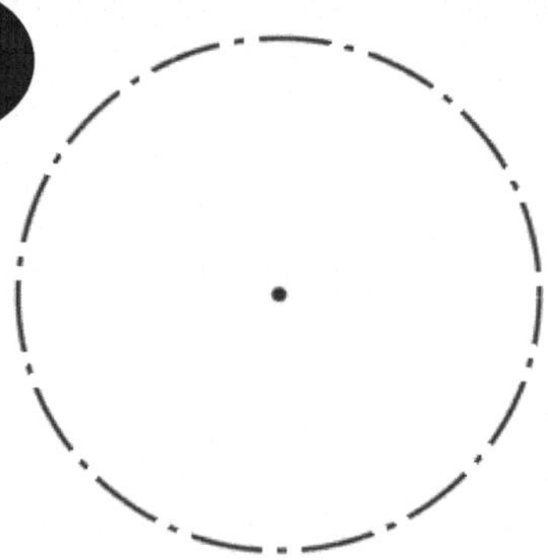

Tip: After creating a construction geometry, when you exit the tool, the **Construction** tool gets deactivated automatically. You need to activate it again to create another construction geometry.

Note: You can also convert an existing sketch entity into a construction geometry. To do so, select a sketch entity in the graphics area and then click to activate the **Construction** tool in the **Sketch** toolbar.

Creating a Sketch Fillet

A fillet is created at the intersection of two sketch entities, such as lines, by removing the sharp corner with a tangent arc of a constant radius, see Figure 2.80. The method for creating a sketch fillet is discussed below:

2.80

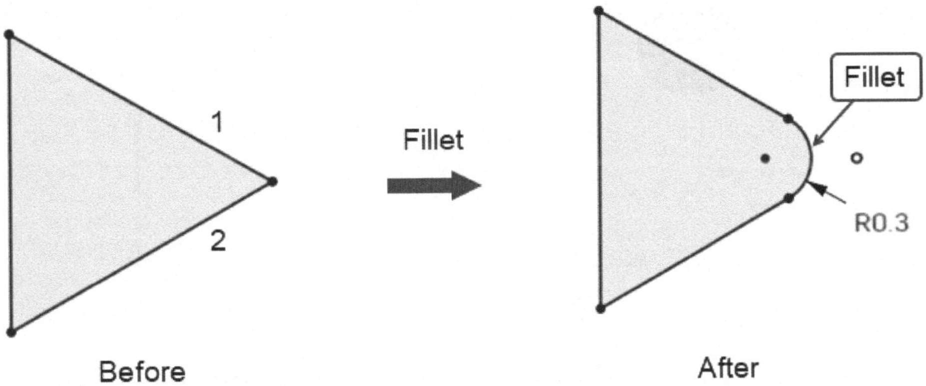

1. Click on the **Sketch fillet** tool in the **Sketch** toolbar, see Figure 2.81. Alternatively, press the **SHIFT + F** keys to activate this tool.

2.81

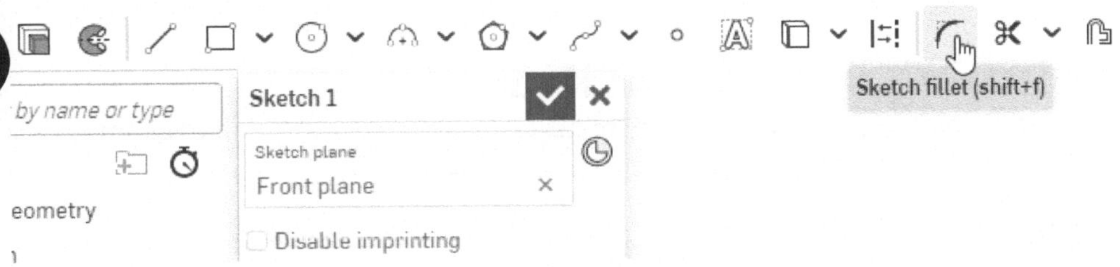

2. Select two connected line entities one by one in the graphics area, see Figure 2.82. A fillet preview appears at the intersection of the selected entities, displaying an arrow and the current radius dimension, see Figure 2.83. You can drag the arrow to dynamically adjust the radius of the fillet in the graphics area.

2.82

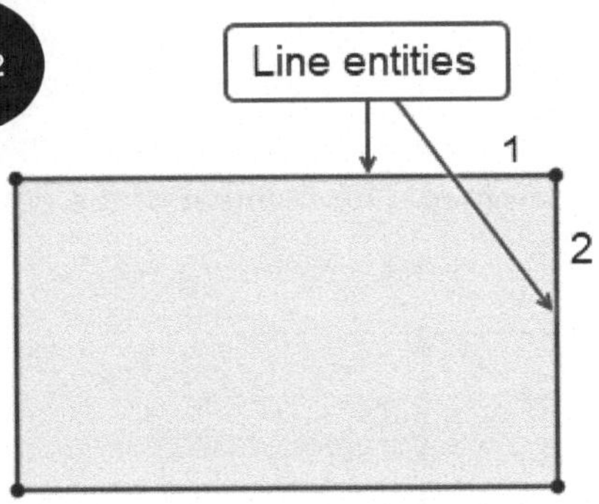

2.83

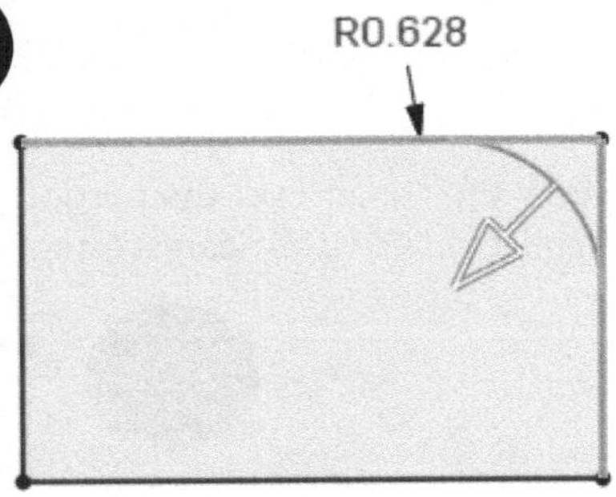

Tip: Instead of selecting two connected line entities, you can alternatively select a corner (vertex) formed at the intersection of two lines to create a fillet.

3. Click anywhere in the graphics area to create the fillet. The current radius value of the fillet then appears in the dimension field.

4. Enter the required radius value in the dimension field and then press ENTER. A fillet of a specified radius is created, see Figure 2.84. Also, the **Sketch fillet** tool remains active.

2.84

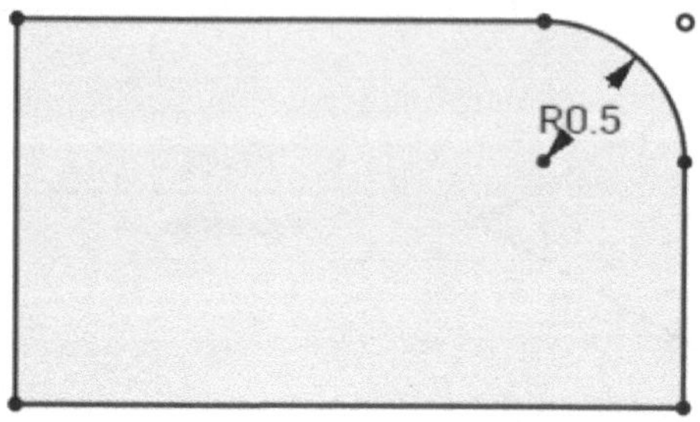

5. Similarly, you can create multiple fillets between two intersecting sketch entities one by one.

6. After creating the fillets, right-click in the graphics area and then select the **Escape fillet** option in the context menu that appears to exit the tool.

Trimming Sketch Entities

In Onshape, you can trim a sketch entity to its nearest intersection point or geometry using the **Trim** tool. The method for trimming sketch entities is discussed below:

1. Click on the **Trim** tool in the **Sketch** toolbar, see Figure 2.85. Alternatively, press the M key to activate this tool.

2.85

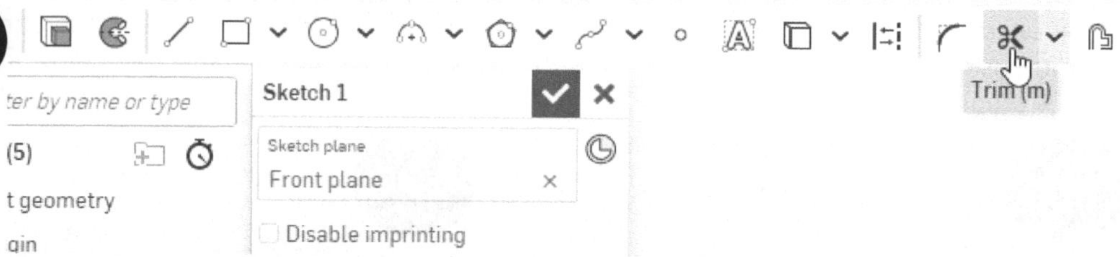

2. Move the cursor over the portion of the entity to be trimmed. The segment of the entity gets highlighted up to its nearest intersection, see Figure 2.86.

2.86

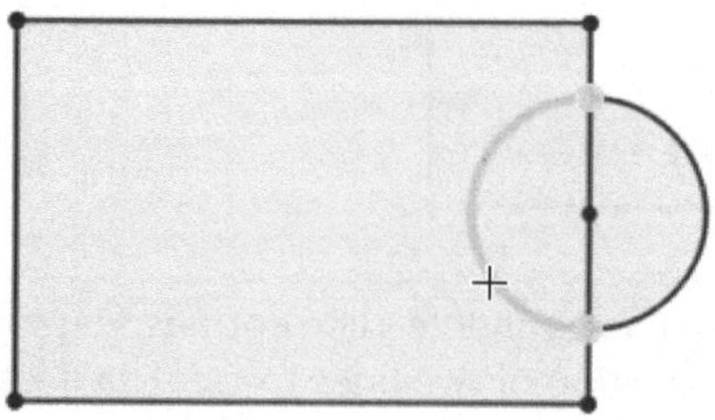

3. Click on the portion of the sketch entity to be trimmed. The selected segment of the entity gets trimmed up to its nearest intersection with the other entity, see Figure 2.87. Also, the **Trim** tool remains activated, and you can continue trimming other sketch entities by clicking the left mouse button.

2.87

Tip: If the selected entity does not intersect with any other entities or boundaries, it will be entirely deleted.

Note: You can also drag the cursor by pressing and holding the left mouse button to trim multiple entities. As you drag the cursor, a light-colored tracing line will appear, and any entities intersected by this tracing line will be trimmed at their nearest intersection, see Figure 2.88. After trimming entities, release the CTRL key. The **Trim** tool remains active.

2.88

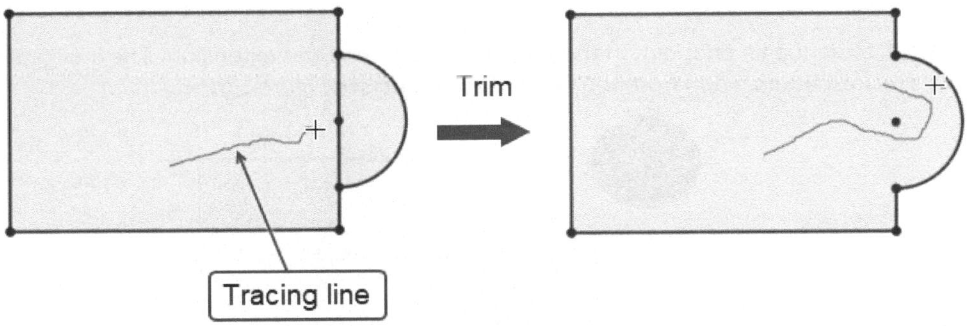

4. Right-click in the graphics area and then select the **Escape trim** option in the context menu that appears to exit the tool.

Extending Sketch Entities

In Onshape, you can extend a sketch entity up to an intersection point or geometry using the **Extend** tool. The method for extending a sketch entity is discussed below:

1. Click on a small arrow beside the **Trim** tool in the **Sketch** toolbar and then click on the **Extend** tool in the drop-down menu that appears, see Figure 2.89. Alternatively, press the X key to activate this tool.

2.89

2. Click to select an entity (line or arc) to be extended, see Figure 2.90. Then, move the cursor in the desired direction. As you move the cursor, a preview of the extended entity appears, following the cursor's movement, see Figure 2.91.

2.90

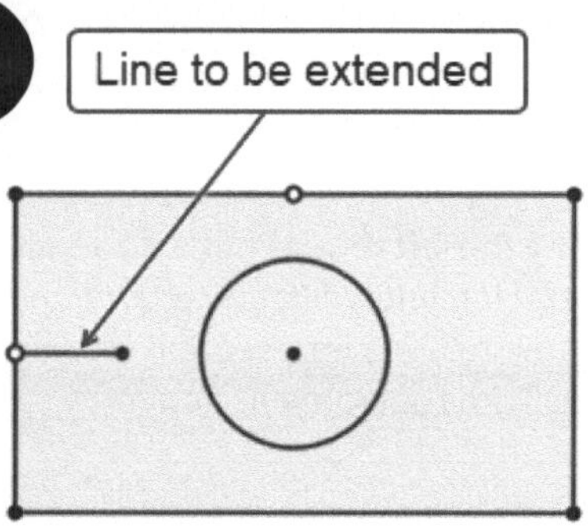

2.91

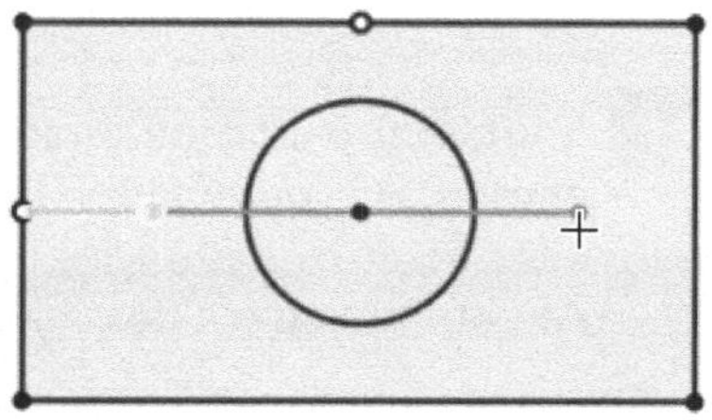

3. Click to define an endpoint in the graphics area to end the extension. The line gets extended to its nearest intersection from the defined endpoint, see Figure 2.92.

2.92

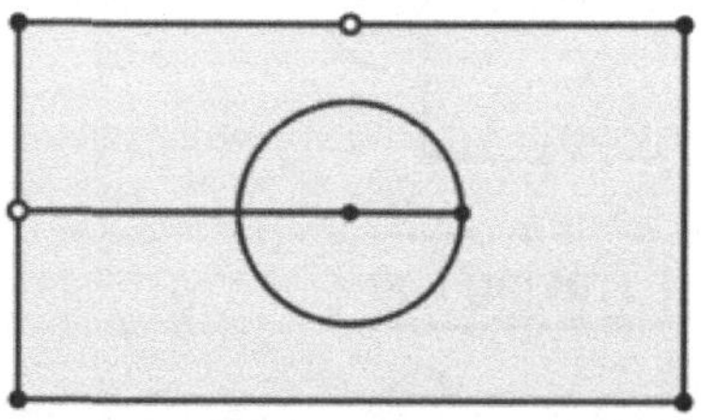

Note: If the entity being extended does not intersect with any other entities, it will be extended to the defined endpoint in the graphics area.

4. Similarly, you can extend other sketch entities (lines or arcs), as desired.

5. Right-click in the graphics area and then select the **Escape extend** option in the context menu that appears to exit the tool.

Splitting Sketch Entities

You can split an open or closed sketch entity into two or more segments using the **Split** tool. The method for splitting a sketch entity is discussed below:

1. Click on a small arrow beside the **Trim** or **Extend** tool in the **Sketch** toolbar and then click on the **Split** tool in the drop-down menu that appears, see Figure 2.93.

2.93

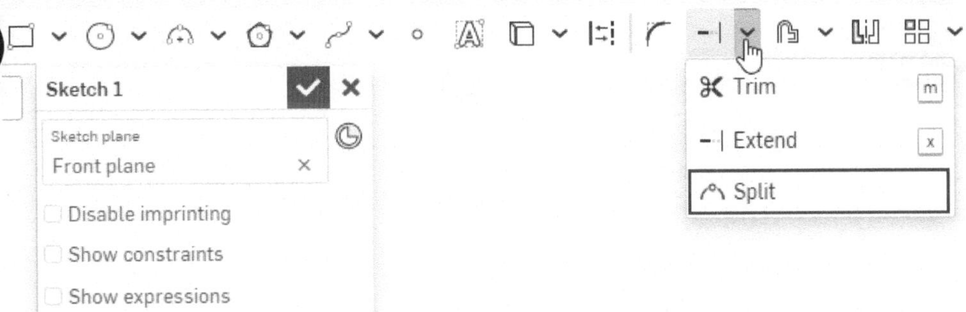

2. Click to define a split point on a sketch entity. The selected entity gets divided into two segments at the specified split point, see Figure 2.94.

2.94

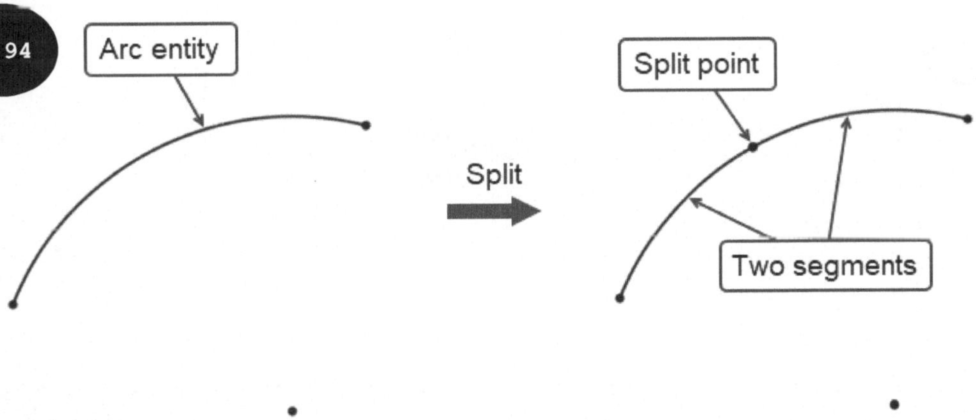

Note: If the selected entity is a closed curve, such as a circle, you need to define two split points to divide it into two segments.

3. Similarly, you can continue defining split points to divide the entity into multiple segments.

4. After splitting an entity into one or more segments, right-click in the graphics area and then select the **Escape split** option in the context menu that appears to exit the tool.

Offsetting Sketch Entities

You can offset a sketch entity or a loop (closed or open) at a specified offset distance using the **Offset** tool. The method for offsetting an entity or a loop at a specified distance is discussed below:

1. Click on the **Offset** tool in the **Sketch** toolbar, see Figure 2.95. Alternatively, press the O key to activate this tool.

2.95

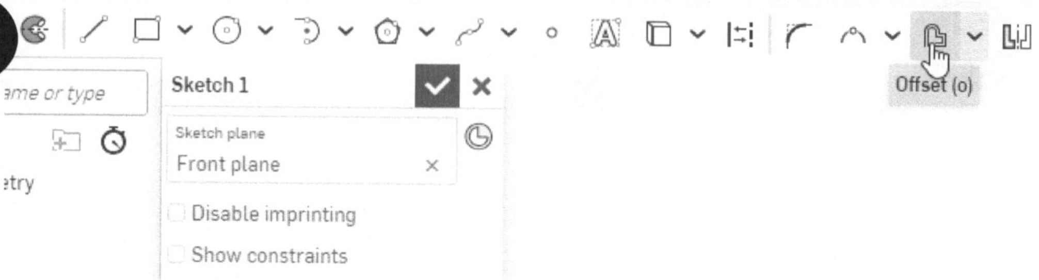

2. Select one or more sketch entities in the graphics area. A preview of the offset entities appears at an offset distance, along with an arrow indicating the direction of the offset, see Figure 2.96. You can drag the arrow to dynamically adjust the offset distance in the graphics area.

2.96

Tip: To select multiple sketch entities, you can click each one individually with the left mouse button or draw a selection window around them by dragging the cursor, see Figure 2.97.

2.97

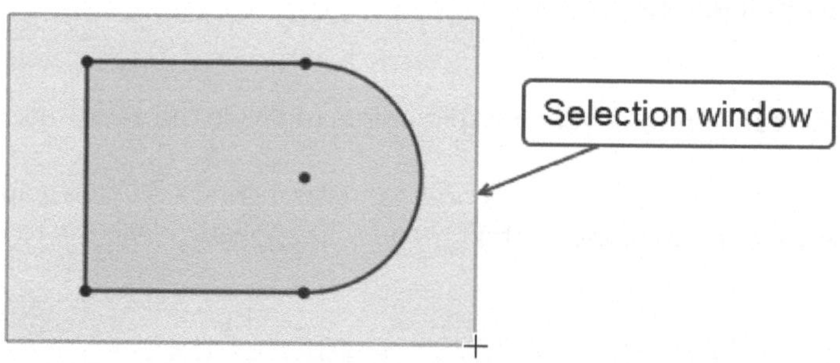

Note: You can offset a single chain of connected sketch entities at a time.

3. Click on the arrow to reverse the offset direction to the other side of the parent sketch entity or entities, if needed.

4. Click anywhere in the graphics area to offset the selected entities. The current offset distance appears in the dimension field, see Figure 2.98.

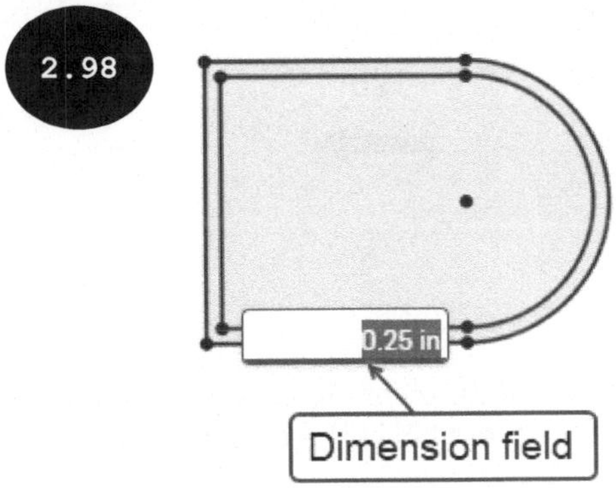

5. Enter the desired offset distance in the dimension field and press ENTER. The offset entities get created at the specified distance from the parent entities.

Note: A negative offset distance value reverses the offset's direction to the other side of the parent entities.

6. Right-click in the graphics area and then select the **Escape offset** option in the context menu that appears to exit the tool.

Creating a Slot

In Onshape, you can create a slot around a selected line, arc, or spline entity using the **Slot** tool. The method for creating a slot is discussed below:

1. Click on a small arrow beside the **Offset** tool in the **Sketch** toolbar and then click on the **Slot** tool in the drop-down menu that appears, see Figure 2.99.

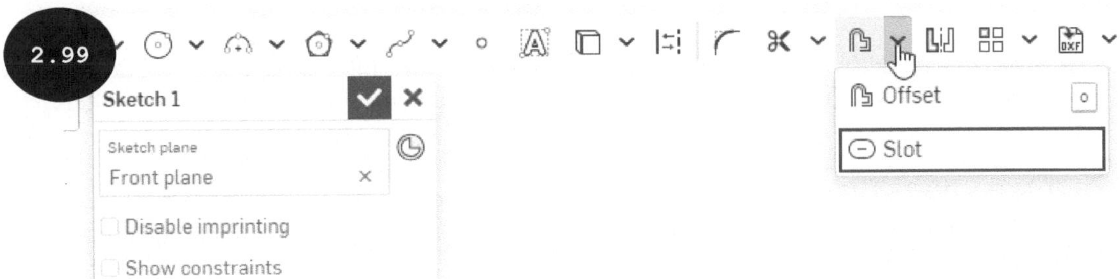

2. Select a line, arc, or spline in the graphics area. A slot preview appears around the selected entity, see Figure 2.100. In this figure, an arc is selected to create a slot.

2.100

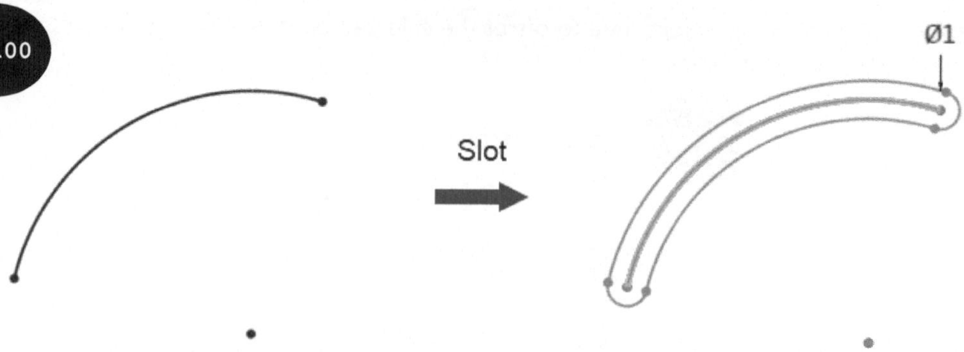

3. Double-click the slot dimension in the graphics area and enter the desired slot arc diameter in the dimension field that appears. Next, press ENTER. The slot gets updated in the graphics area.

4. Click anywhere in the graphics area. A slot of a specified dimension gets created around the selected entity. Next, right-click in the graphics area and then select the **Escape slot** option in the context menu that appears to exit the tool.

Mirroring Sketch Entities

You can create a mirrored copy of one or more sketch entities about a mirror line by using the **Mirror** tool. The method for mirroring sketch entities is discussed below:

1. Click on the **Mirror** tool in the **Sketch** toolbar, see Figure 2.101. You are prompted to select a mirror line.

2.101

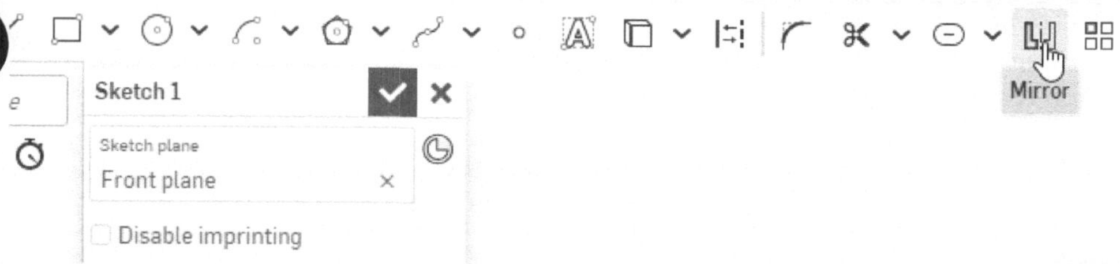

2. Select a mirror line (which could be a line, centerline, plane, or linear edge) in the graphics area, see Figure 2.102. After the mirror line is selected, you are prompted to select sketch entities to be mirrored.

3. Select the sketch entities to be mirrored by either clicking on them with the left mouse button or by drawing a selection window around the entities. A mirrored copy of the selected entities appears, see Figure 2.103.

Tip: You can also select the entities to be mirrored before activating the **Mirror** tool.

2.102

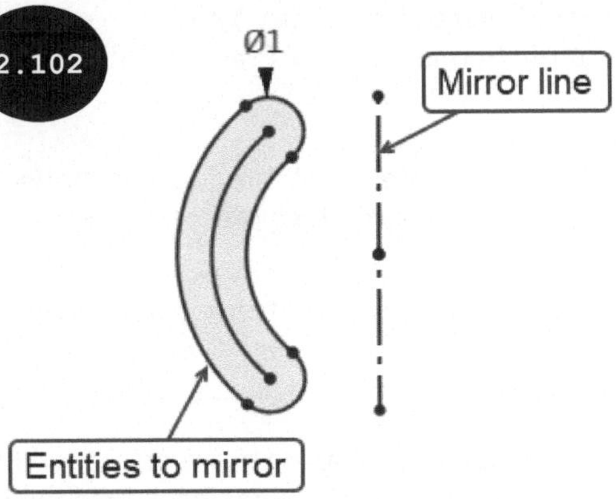

2.103

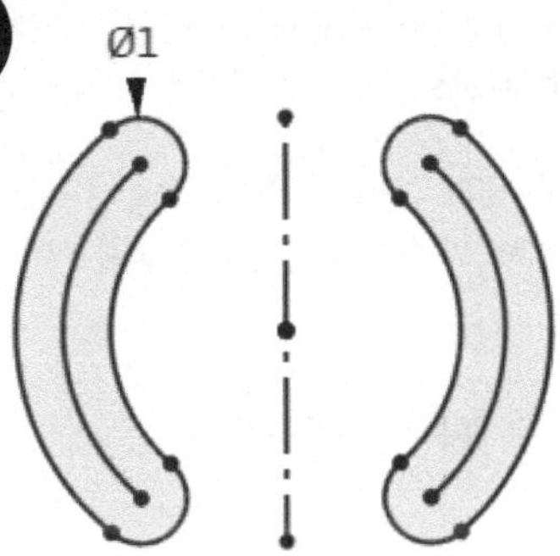

4. Press the ESC key to exit the **Mirror** tool.

Patterning Sketch Entities

In Onshape, you can create multiple instances of sketch entities using the **Linear pattern** and **Circular pattern** tools. Both these tools are discussed next.

Creating a Linear Sketch Pattern

A linear sketch pattern creates multiple instances of sketch entities along one or two linear directions. The method for creating a linear sketch pattern using the **Linear pattern** tool is discussed next.

1. Click on the **Linear pattern** tool in the **Sketch** toolbar, see Figure 2.104.

2.104

2. Select one or more sketch entities by either clicking on them with the left mouse button or by drawing a selection window around them. A preview of the linear pattern appears with default parameters (Spacing 1, No. of instances in Direction 1, and No. of instances in Direction 2), see Figure 2.105.

2.105

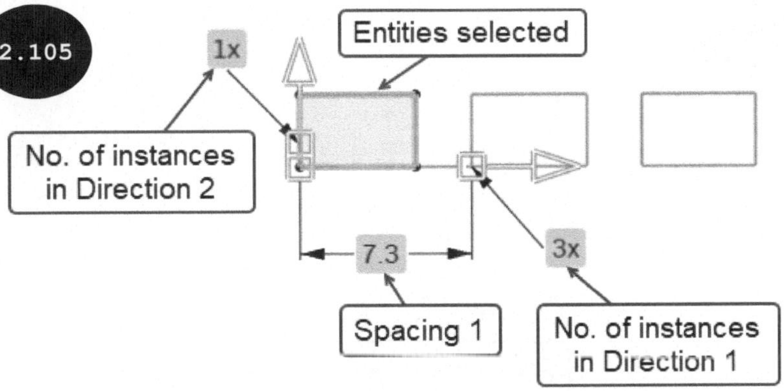

3. Double-click on the **No. of instances in Direction 1** field (refer to Figure 2.105) and then enter the desired number of instances for Direction 1 in the edit field that appears. Press ENTER to apply the changes.

4. Double-click on the **Spacing 1** field (refer to Figure 2.105), then enter the desired spacing between consecutive instances along Direction 1 in the edit field that appears. Next, press ENTER.

Tip: You can also drag the arrows to adjust the spacing between the pattern instances in the respective directions.

5. Similarly, you can specify the number of pattern instances and the spacing between them along Direction 2 by double-clicking on the respective fields. Note that the **Spacing 2** field, which defines the spacing between instances along Direction 2, will only appear after you have set 2 or more instances along Direction 2. Figure 2.106 shows the preview of a linear sketch pattern with 6 number of instances along Direction 1 and 3 instances along Direction 2.

2.106

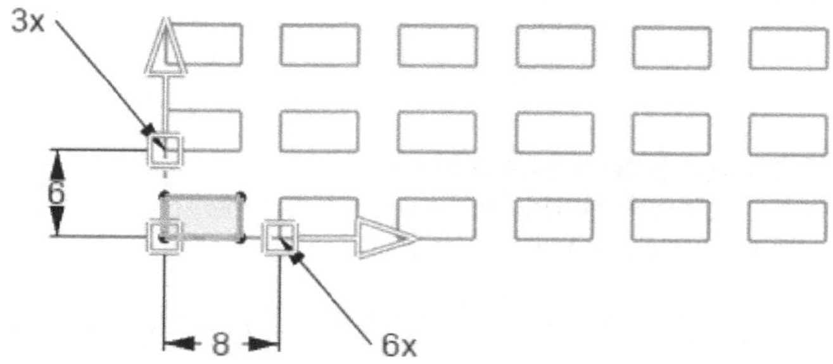

Note: The number of pattern instances includes the parent instance. For example, if you specify 6 instances along Direction 1, 6 instances will be created, including the parent instance.

Tip: You can also drag the arrow manipulator base to create a pattern at an angle, if needed, see Figure 2.107.

2.107

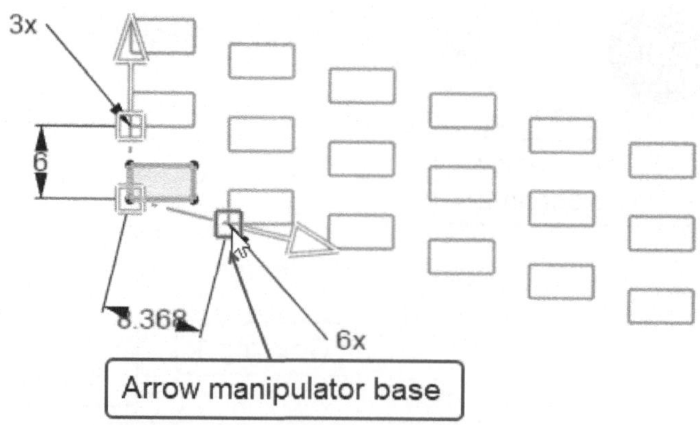

6. After specifying all the desired parameters, click anywhere in the graphics area. A linear sketch pattern with the specified parameters is created.

Creating a Circular Sketch Pattern

A circular sketch pattern generates multiple instances of sketch entities around a central point or axis. The method for creating a circular sketch pattern using the **Circular pattern** tool is discussed next.

1. Click on a small arrow beside the **Linear pattern** tool in the **Sketch** toolbar and then click on the **Circular pattern** tool in the drop-down menu that appears, see Figure 2.108.

2.108

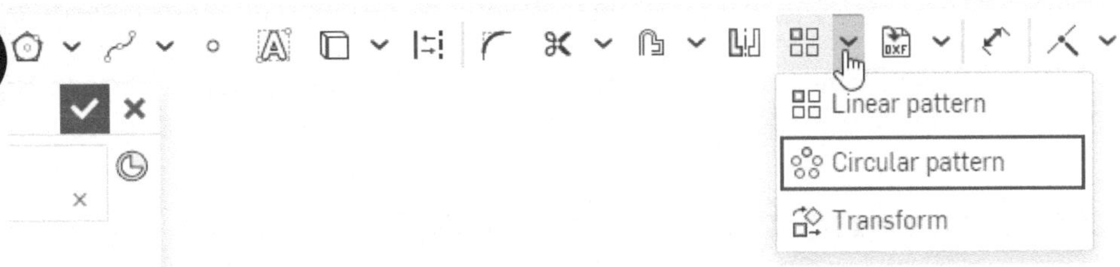

2. Select one or more sketch entities by either clicking on them with the left mouse button or by drawing a selection window around them. A preview of a circular pattern appears with default parameters around the origin, see Figure 2.109.

2.109

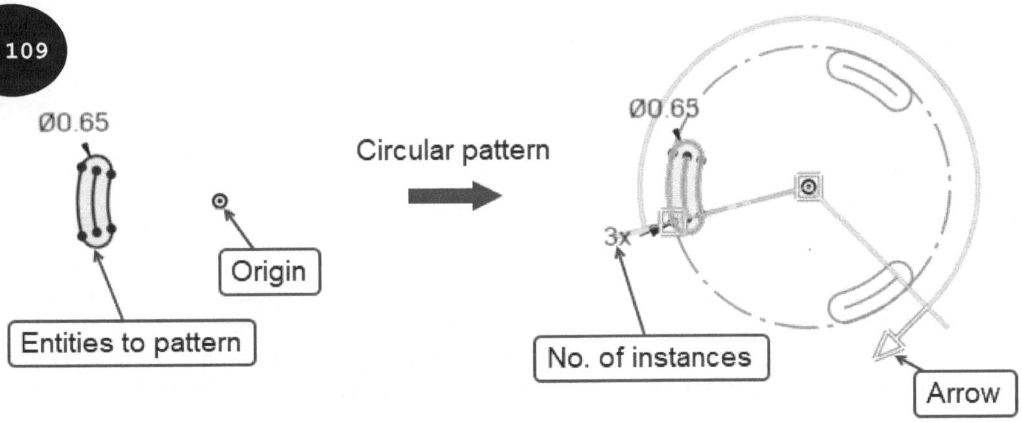

3. Double-click on the **No. of instances** field (refer to Figure 2.109) and then enter the desired number of instances in the edit field that appears. Press ENTER to apply the changes. Figure 2.110 shows the preview of a circular sketch pattern with 5 number of instances defined.

2.110

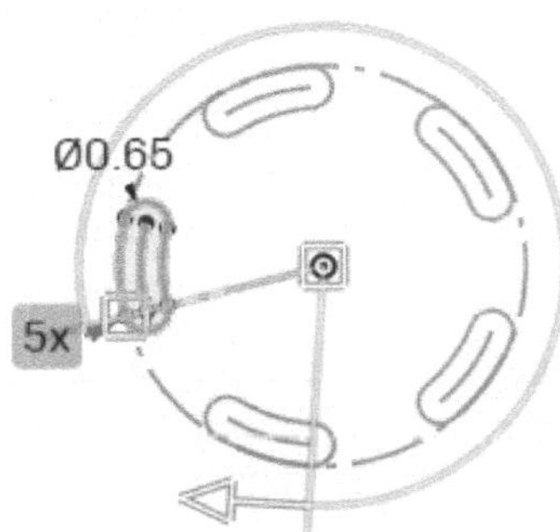

Note: The number of pattern instances includes the parent instance. For example, if you specify 5 instances, a total of 5 instances will be created, including the parent instance.

4. Drag the arrow near the last pattern instance to adjust the total angle value. All pattern instances are evenly distributed within this angle. You can further edit the total angle by double-clicking on the angle dimension that appears after dragging or clicking on the arrow.

5. By default, the origin is set as the center of the circular pattern. However, you can drag the center point icon to a new location to redefine the center of the circular pattern, if needed.

6. After specifying all the desired parameters, click anywhere in the graphics area. A circular sketch pattern with the specified parameters is created.

Transforming Sketch Entities

You can transform one or more sketch entities by moving, rotating, and scaling them in the graphics area using the **Transform** tool. The method for transforming entities is discussed below.

1. Invoke the **Pattern** drop-down menu and then click on the **Transform** tool, see Figure 2.111.

2.111

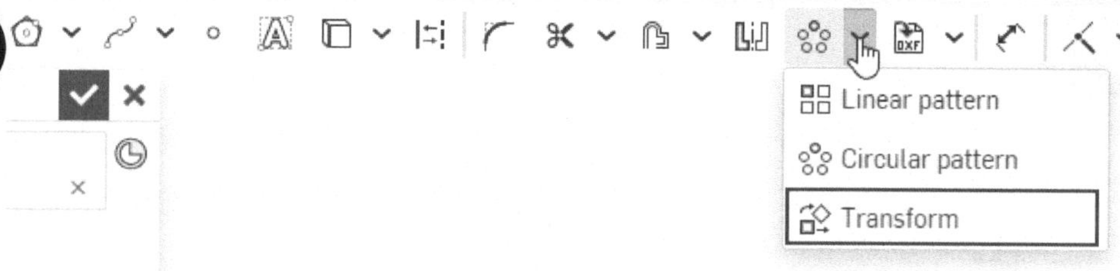

2. Select one or more sketch entities in the graphics area. The manipulator handles appear on the selected entities. Figure 2.112 shows different manipulator handles. You can use these handles to translate, rotate, scale, and move the sketch entities in the graphics area. Additionally, the Base Point handle allows you to set a new base point for transforming the entities relative to it.

2.112

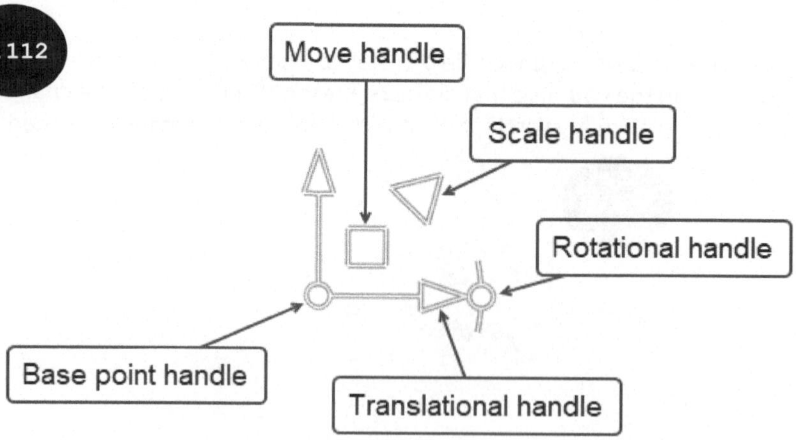

Note: When using manipulate handles to translate, rotate, or scale selected sketch entities, an edit field appears in the graphics area. You can enter the specific values for translation, rotation, or scaling in this field to precisely adjust the entities.

3. After transforming the selected sketch entities relative to the base point, click anywhere in the graphics area to confirm the transformation and exit the tool.

Applying Constraints

Constraints are used to limit or restrict the degrees of freedom of sketch entities. You can apply constraints to individual sketch entities, between multiple entities, or between a sketch point and the origin. Some constraints, such as horizontal, vertical, and coincident, may be applied automatically while sketching. For example, when drawing a line, if you move the cursor horizontally to the left or right, a horizontal constraint icon will appear near the cursor, see Figure 2.113. This indicates that if you specify the endpoint of the line at that moment, the horizontal constraint will be applied, locking the line's movement horizontally. Similarly, if you move the cursor vertically upward or downward, a vertical constraint icon will appear, see Figure 2.114. This indicates that if you specify the endpoint of the line, the vertical constraint will be applied, locking the line's movement vertically.

2.113

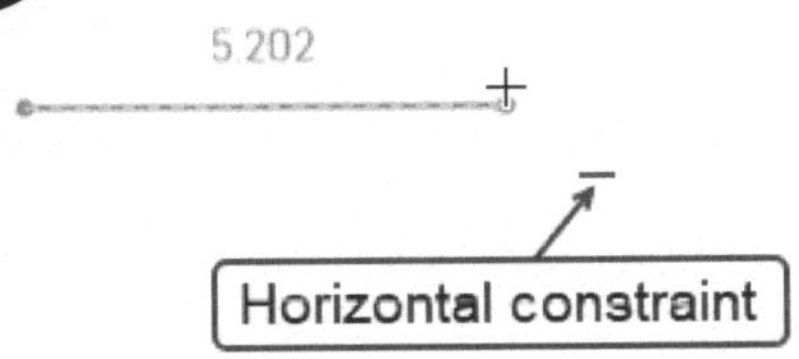

2.114

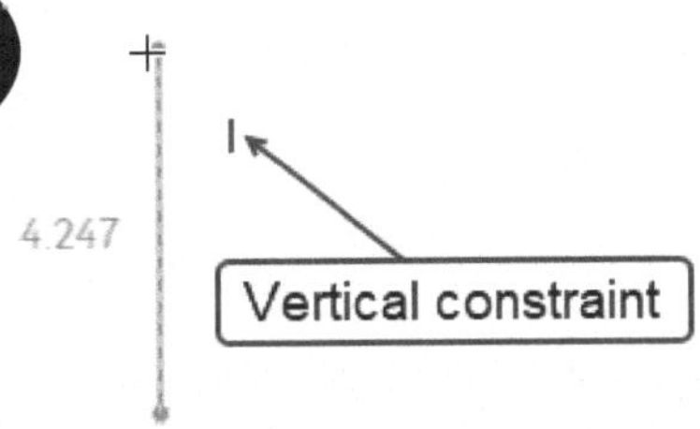

In Onshape, you can apply different types of constraints using the tools available in the **Constraints** drop-down menu, see Figure 2.115. These constraints are discussed next.

2.115

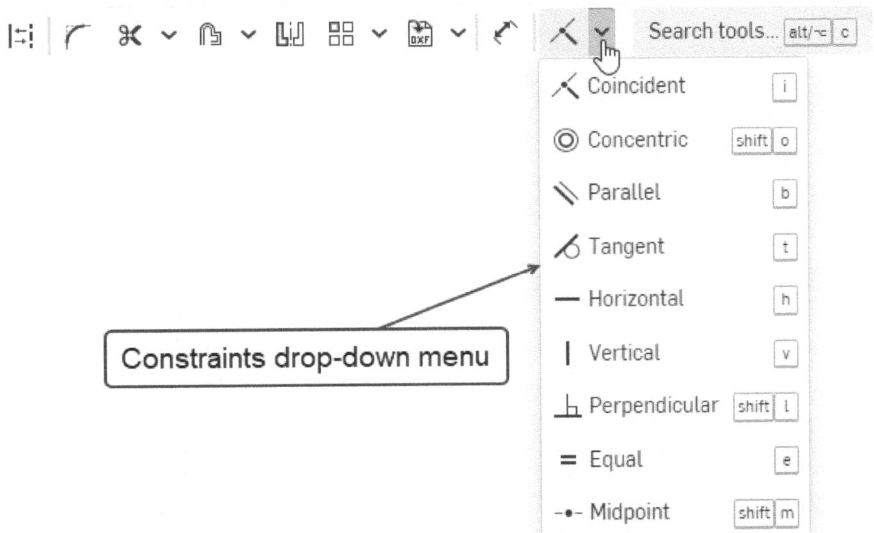

A coincident constraint is used to make two or more sketch entities or points, aligned or coincident with each other, see Figures 2.116 and 2.117. It can also be applied to make a sketch entity coincident with a plane.

2.116

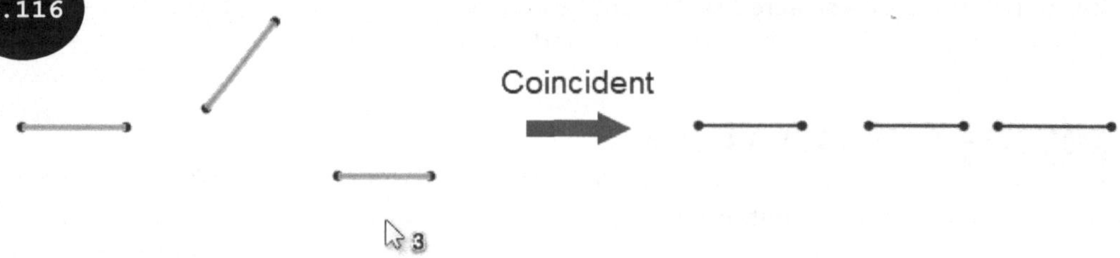

2.117

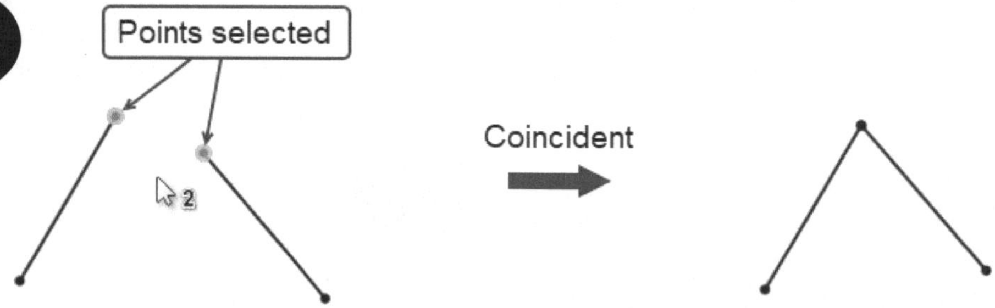

To apply a coincident constraint, select two or more sketch entities or points in the graphics area and then click on the **Coincident** tool in the **Constraints** drop-down menu (see Figure 2.118) or press the **I** key. The selected sketch entities get aligned or coincident with each other.

2.118

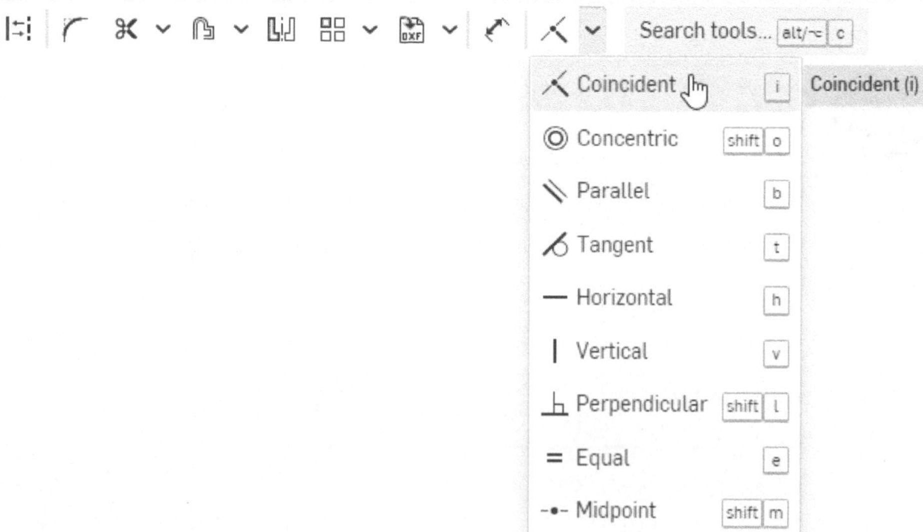

Concentric Constraint

A concentric constraint is used to make two or more arcs or circles, or a combination of them, concentric with each other by sharing the same center point, see Figure 2.119.

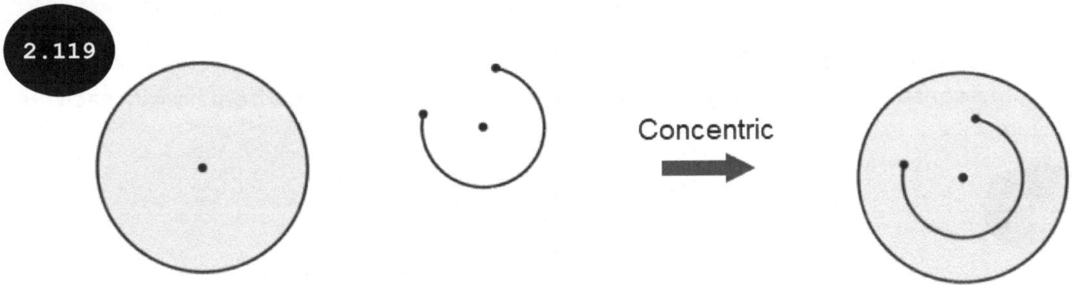

To apply a concentric constraint, select two or more arcs, circles, or a combination of them in the graphics area. Next, click on the **Concentric** tool in the **Constraints** drop-down menu or press SHIFT + O. The selected sketch entities become concentric, sharing the same center point.

Parallel Constraint

A parallel constraint is used to make two or more lines parallel to each other, see Figure 2.120.

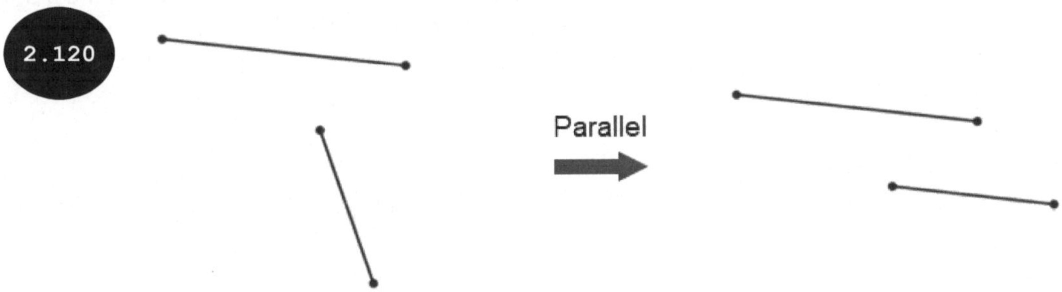

To apply a parallel constraint, select two or more lines in the graphics area and click on the **Parallel** tool in the **Constraints** drop-down menu or press the B key. The selected lines become parallel to each other.

Tangent Constraint

A tangent constraint is used to make two sketch entities such as a circle and a line tangent to each other, see Figure 2.121.

You can also make two circles, two arcs, two ellipses, two splines, and a combination of these entities tangent to each other. Besides, you can also make a sketch entity tangent to a plane. To do so, select two or more sketch entities in the graphics area and click on the **Tangent** tool in the **Constraints** drop-down menu or press the T key. The selected entities become tangent to each other.

Horizontal Constraint

A horizontal constraint is used to align one or more lines or sketch points horizontally with each other, see Figure 2.122.

2.122

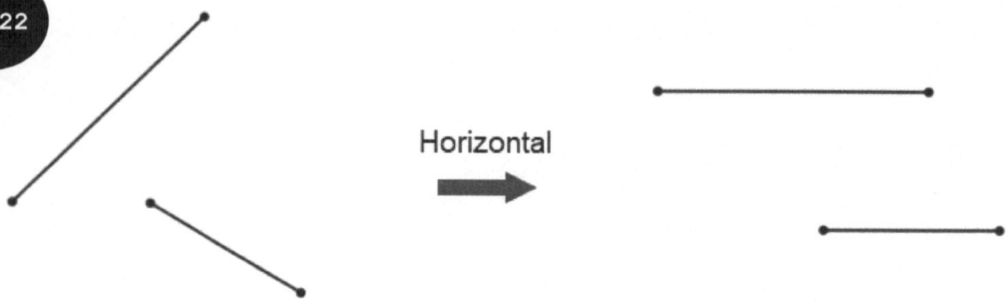

To apply a horizontal constraint, select one or more lines or sketch points in the graphics area, then click the **Horizontal** tool in the **Constraints** drop-down menu or press the **H** key. The selected entities get aligned horizontally to each other. You can also select an entity to be aligned horizontally after invoking the **Horizontal** tool.

Vertical Constraint

A vertical constraint is used to align one or more lines or sketch points vertically with each other, see Figure 2.123.

2.123

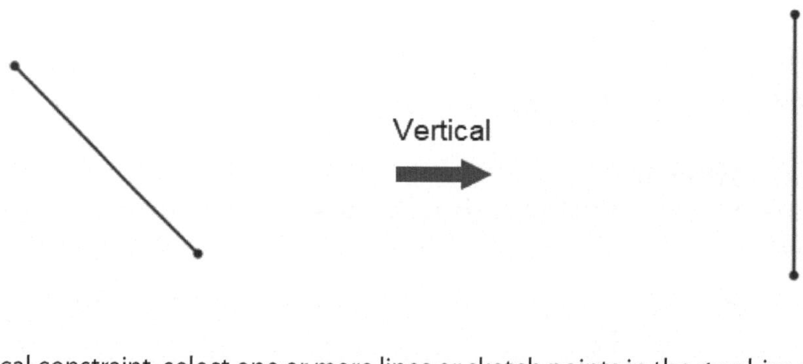

To apply a vertical constraint, select one or more lines or sketch points in the graphics area, then click the **Vertical** tool in the **Constraints** drop-down menu or press the V key. The selected entities get aligned vertically to each other. You can also select a line to be aligned vertically after invoking the **Vertical** tool.

Perpendicular Constraint

A perpendicular constraint is used to make two or more lines perpendicular to each other, see Figure 2.124.

2.124

To apply a perpendicular constraint, select two or more lines and then click on the **Perpendicular** tool in the **Constraints** drop-down menu or press **SHIFT + L**.

Equal Constraint

An equal constraint is used to make two or more sketch entities, such as lines, arcs, or circles, equal in size, ensuring that the selected lines have the same length and the selected arcs or circles have equal radii. In Figure 2.125, an equal constraint is applied between two lines.

2.125

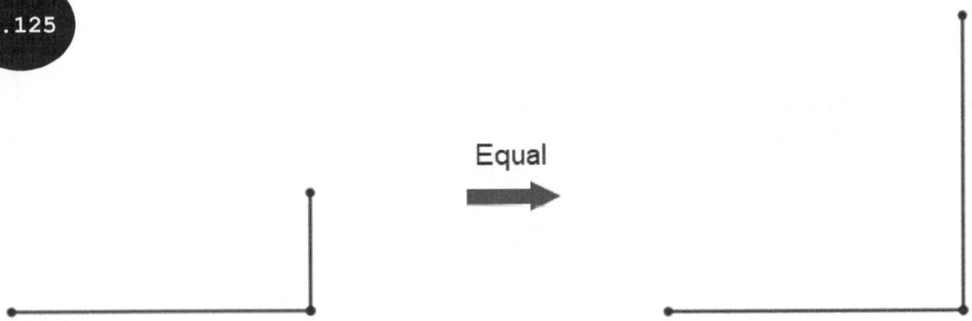

To apply an equal constraint, select two or more sketch entities and then click on the **Equal** tool in the **Constraints** drop-down menu or press the **E** key. You can also select entities after invoking the tool.

Midpoint Constraint

A midpoint constraint is used to constrain a sketch point at the midpoint of a line or an arc. In Figure 2.126, an endpoint of one line is constrained to the midpoint of another line.

2.126

To apply a midpoint constraint, select a sketch point and a line or an arc in the graphics area and then click on the **Midpoint** tool in the **Constraints** drop-down menu or press **SHIFT + M**. You can also select entities after invoking the **Midpoint** tool.

Normal Constraint

A normal constraint is used to make a line and a curve, such as a circle or an arc, perpendicular to each other, see Figure 2.127. In this figure, the line is constrained to be normal to the circle, passing through the circle's center point. Additionally, you can use a normal constraint to make a curve (like an arc or a circle) perpendicular to a plane.

2.127

To apply a normal constraint, select a line or a curve in the graphics area and then click on the **Normal** tool in the **Constraints** drop-down menu or press **SHIFT + K**. You can select entities before or after invoking the **Normal** tool.

Pierce Constraint

A pierce constraint aligns a sketch entity, such as a point or curve, with an entity from a different sketch on another plane, ensuring they coincide exactly at the intersection of the two planes, see Figures 2.128 and 2.129. Figure 2.128 shows a spline created on the currently active sketching plane alongside an existing sketch (an ellipse) created on a different plane. Figure 2.129 displays the resulting sketch after applying a pierce constraint between the endpoint of the spline and the ellipse from the other sketch.

2.128

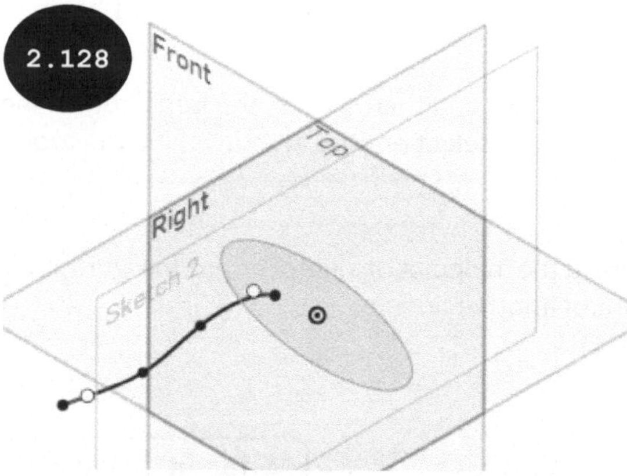

2.129

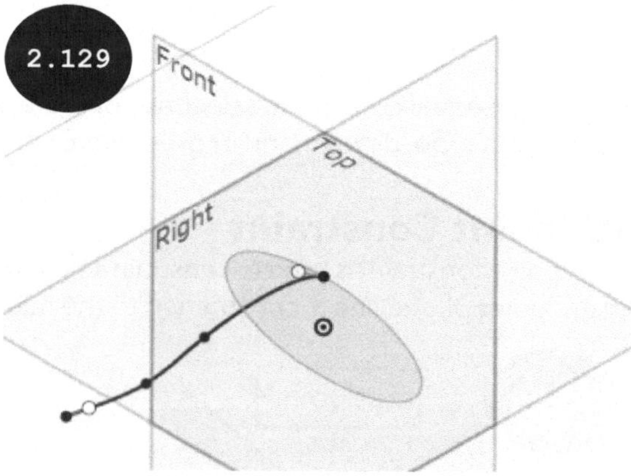

To apply a pierce constraint, first select a sketch entity, such as a point or curve, from the currently active sketching plane. Then, select an entity from another sketch created on a different sketching plane. Next, invoke the **Constraints** drop-down menu and click on the **Pierce** tool. Alternatively, you can activate the **Pierce** tool by pressing SHIFT + G.

Symmetric Constraint

A symmetric constraint is used to make two sketch entities of the same geometry type, such as two circles, two lines, or two points, symmetric relative to a line, centerline, or plane, see Figure 2.130. In this figure, a symmetric constraint is applied between two circles relative to a line.

2.130

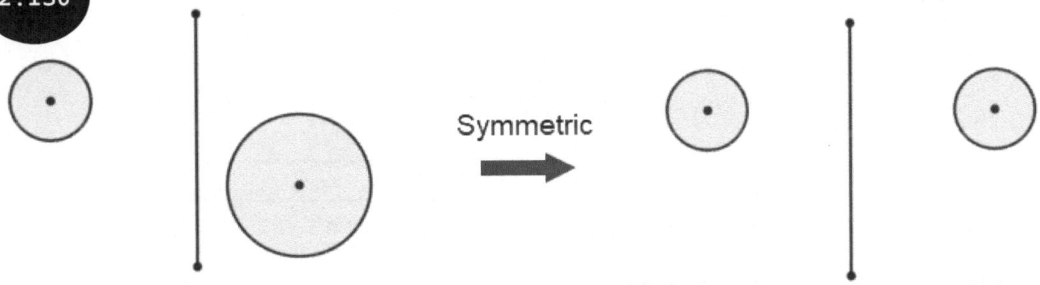

To apply a symmetric constraint, first select two sketch entities, such as two circles, arcs, lines, or points, in the graphics area. Then, invoke the **Constraints** drop-down menu and click on the **Symmetric** tool. Finally, select a line or centerline to make the selected entities symmetric about it.

Fix Constraint

A fix constraint is used to ground or lock the current position and size of a sketch entity on the sketching plane. However, for a fixed line or arc entity, the endpoints can still move without altering the position of the entity itself.

To apply a fix constraint, select one or more sketch entities in the graphics area and then click on the **Fix** tool in the **Constraints** drop-down menu or press SHIFT + J.

Curvature Constraint

A curvature constraint is used to establish a curvature-continuous transition between a spline and another sketch entity, such as a line, arc, spline, or conic curve, see Figure 2.131. In this figure, a curvature constraint is applied between two splines.

2.131

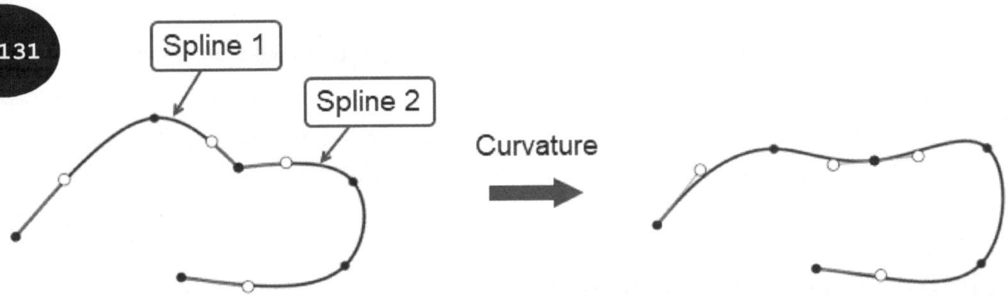

To apply a curvature constraint, select two splines or a spline and another sketch entity, such as a line, arc, or conic curve, in the graphics area. Then, click on the **Curvature** tool in the **Constraints** drop-down menu or press SHIFT + U.

Note: In Onshape, you can enable the display of constraint symbols in the graphics area by selecting the **Show constraints** check box in the **Sketch** dialog box, see Figure 2.132.

2.132

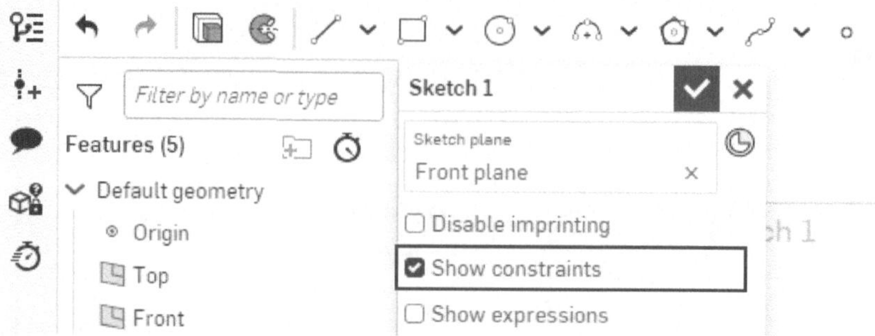

Applying Dimensions

After creating a sketch, you can apply the necessary dimensions to the sketch entities. You can apply a dimension to a sketch entity or between two sketch entities using the **Dimension** tool, see Figure 2.133. This tool allows you to apply various types of dimensions, including horizontal, vertical, aligned, angular, diameter, radius, or arc length depending upon the type of selected entity or entities. For example, selecting a circle will apply a diameter dimension, while choosing two parallel lines will result in a linear dimension, see Figure 2.134. The methods to apply various types of dimensions are discussed next.

2.133

2.134

a. Diameter dimension

b. Linear dimension

Tip: In Onshape, a parametric software, the parameters of sketch entities such as length and angle are driven by dimension values. Changing a dimension value will automatically adjust the corresponding sketch entity.

Applying a linear Dimension

You can apply an aligned, horizontal, or vertical linear dimension to a sketch entity (line) or between two sketch entities, such as lines or points. The method for applying a linear dimension is discussed below:

1. Click the **Dimension** tool in the **Sketch** toolbar (refer to Figure 2.133) or press the **D** key. The **Dimension** tool gets activated.

2. Select a line, two parallel lines, or two points in the graphics area. A linear dimension appears attached to the cursor, based on the type of entities selected. For example, selecting an inclined line will show an aligned dimension, whereas choosing two sketch points will result in either a horizontal or vertical dimension, respectively, see Figure 2.135.

2.135

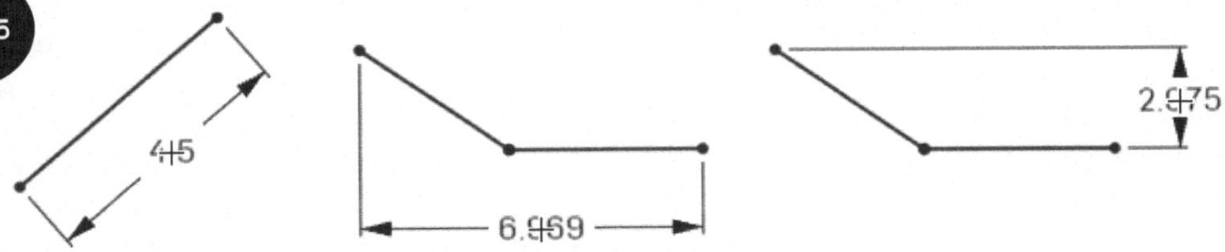

a. Aligned dimension b. Horizontal dimension c. Vertical dimension

3. Move the cursor to the desired location, then click to place the dimension in the graphics area. A dimension field appears, displaying the current dimension value of the selected entity or between the selected entities, see Figure 2.136.

4. Enter the required value in the dimension field and then press ENTER to accept the dimension value. The dimension is applied to the selected entity or between the selected entities, see Figure 2.137. In this figure, a horizontal dimension is applied between two points.

2.136

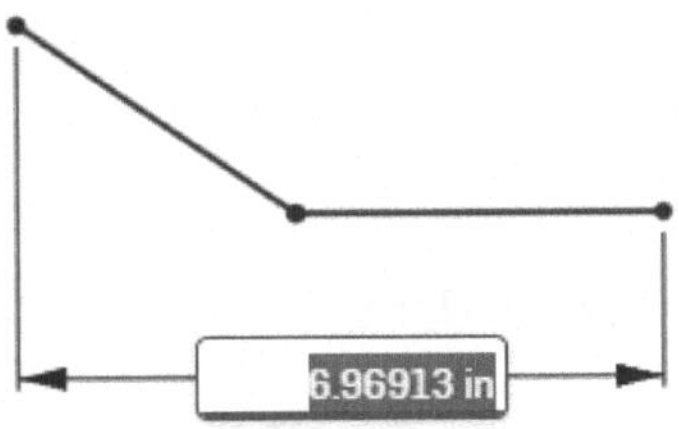

2.137

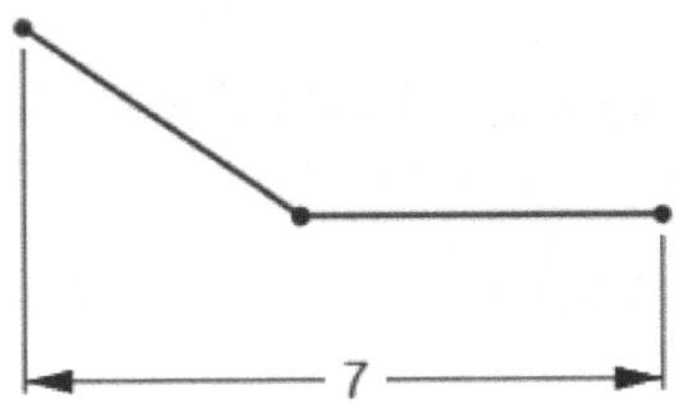

Applying Angular Dimensions

Similar to applying a linear dimension, you can apply an angular dimension between two line entities using the **Dimension** tool, see Figure 2.138. You can specify the desired location for the angular dimension between the selected entities to apply it accordingly.

2.138

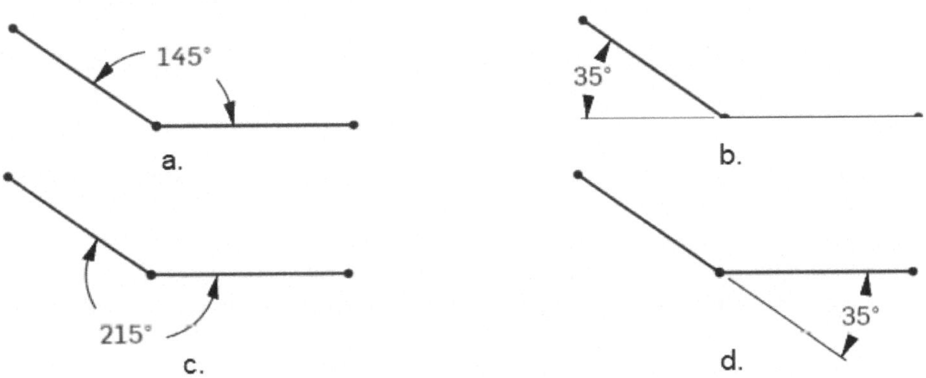

Tip: For linear and angular dimensions, you can also enter a negative value to flip the direction of the sketch entity or entities.

Applying a Diameter and a Radius Dimension

You can apply a diameter dimension to a circle and a radius dimension to an arc using the **Dimension** tool. To do so, activate the **Dimension** tool and then select a circle or an arc in the graphics area. A diameter dimension or a radius dimension appears attached to the cursor, respectively. Next, click to place the dimension in the graphics area and then enter the required dimension value in the field that appears. Next, press ENTER to apply the dimension. Figure 2.139 shows a diameter dimension applied to a circle and a radius dimension is applied to an arc. You can press the ESC key to exit the tool.

2.139

a. Diameter dimension b. Radius dimension

Applying an Arc Length Dimension

The method for applying an arc length dimension is discussed below:

1. Click on the **Dimension** tool of the **Sketch** toolbar or press the **D** key.

2. Select the endpoints of an arc one by one, then hover the cursor over the arc. The arc length dimension appears attached to the cursor, see Figure 2.140.

2.140

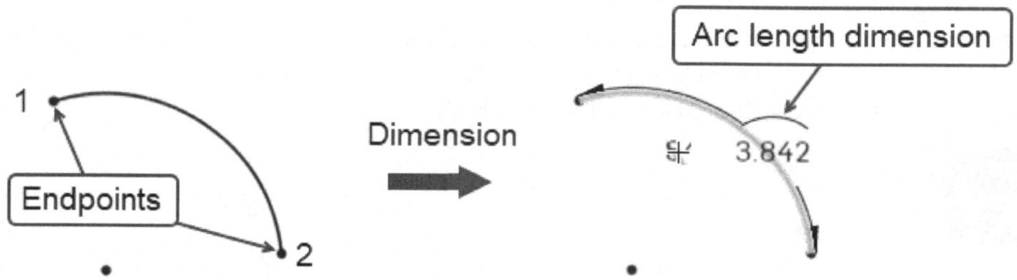

3. Click when the arc length dimension appears, then click again to place the dimension in the desired location in the graphics area. A dimension field appears.

4. Enter the required arc length value in the dimension field and press ENTER to apply the arc length dimension to the arc entity, see Figure 2.141. You can press the ESC key to exit the tool.

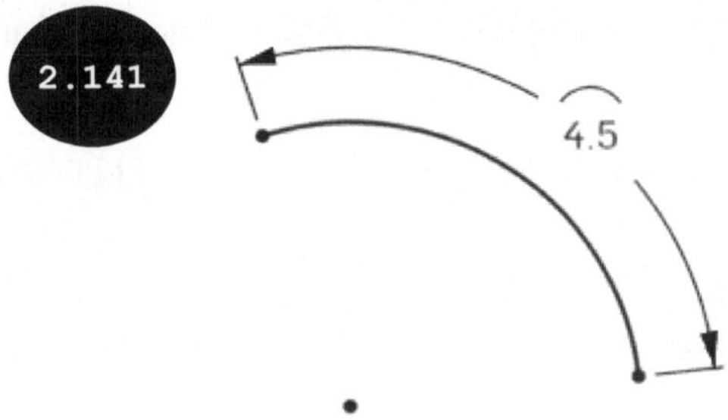

Applying a Centerline Dimension

A centerline dimension also referred to as a linear diameter dimension, is applied to sketch entities that define the diameter of a revolve feature. The method for applying a centerline dimension is discussed below:

1. Activate the **Dimension** tool by pressing the **D** key.

2. Select a linear sketch entity and a construction line in the graphics area. A linear dimension between the selected entities appears attached to the cursor, see Figure 2.142.

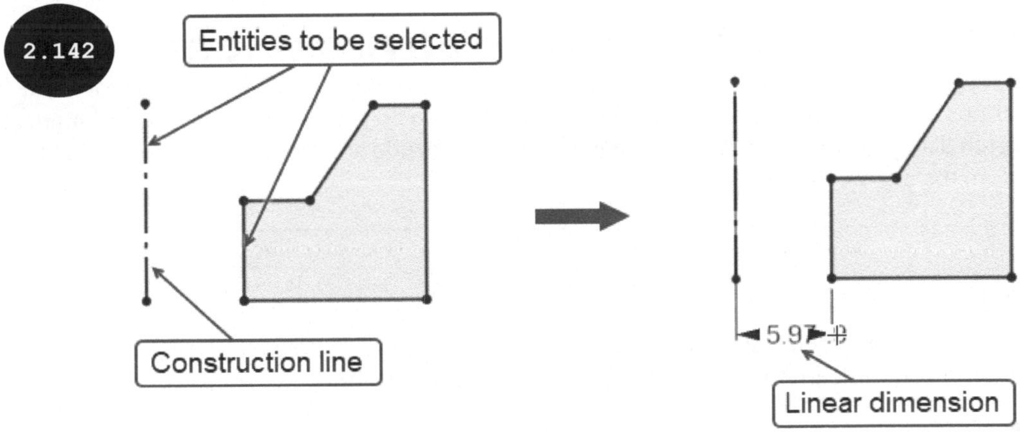

3. Move the cursor to the other side of the construction line to toggle the dimension to a centerline dimension, see Figure 2.143.

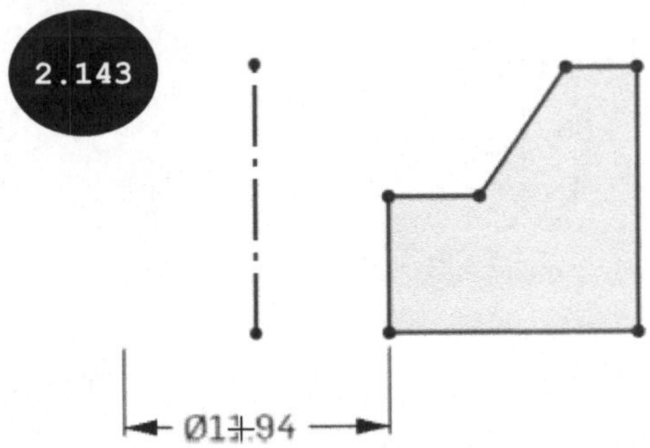

4. Click to place the dimension in the graphics area. A dimension field appears with the display of the current dimension value.

5. Enter the required value in the dimension field and then press ENTER. A centerline dimension is applied, see Figure 2.144.

2.144

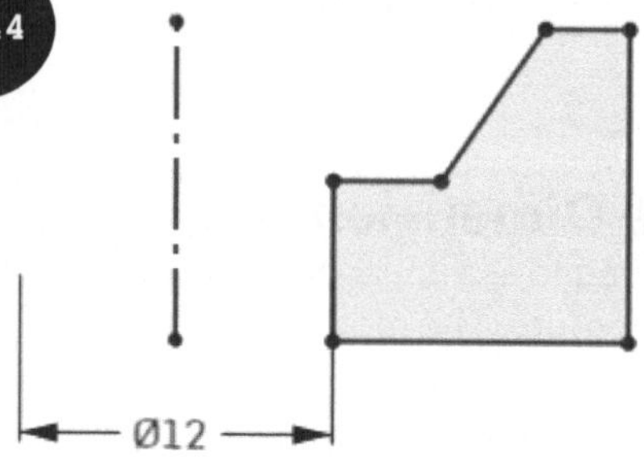

6. Similarly, you can apply multiple centerline dimensions to sketch entities relative to a construction line. Next, press the ESC key to exit the **Dimension** tool.

Switching to the Part Studio environment

After creating a sketch, you can confirm its creation and switch to the Part Studio environment to access various feature modeling tools in the **Feature** toolbar. To do this, click the green checkmark ✓ in the **Sketch** dialog. Note that feature modeling tools like **Extrude** and **Revolve** can also be accessed directly from the **Sketch** toolbar.

Tutorial 1

Draw the sketch of the model shown in Figure 2.145. The 3D model shown in the figure is for your reference only. You will learn to create 3D models in later chapters. All dimensions are in mm.

2.145

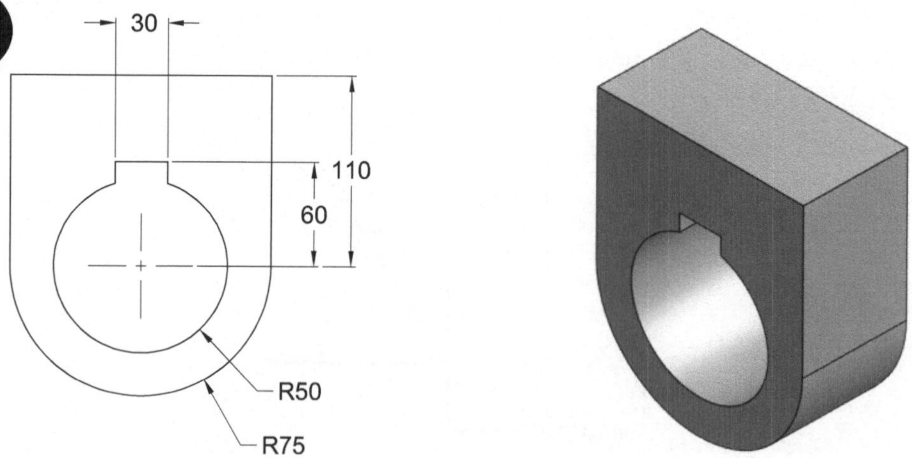

Section 1: Launching Onshape and Starting a New Design Document

1. Visit the Onshape website at ***onshape.com*** using any web browser, and then click the **SIGN IN** option in the top right corner to access the **Sign In** page, see Figure 2.146.

2.146

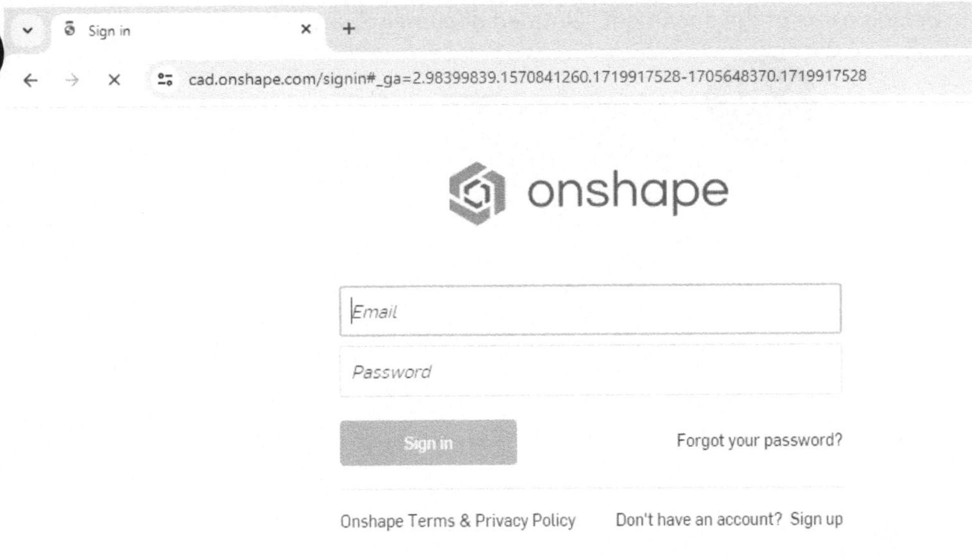

2. On the **Sign In** page, enter your registered email ID and password, then click the **Sign in** button. After the necessary files have loaded, the startup user interface of Onshape appears, see Figure 2.147.

2.147

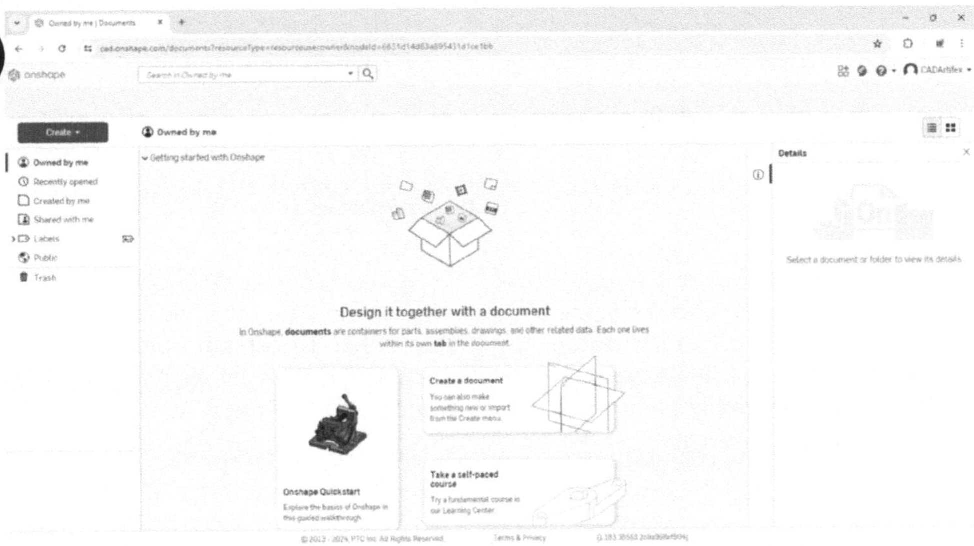

Now, you can start a new design document.

3. Click on the **Create** button at the top left corner of the page and then click on the **Document** option in the menu that appears, see Figure 2.148. The **New document** window appears with the default name of the document "**Untitled document**", see Figure 2.149.

2.148

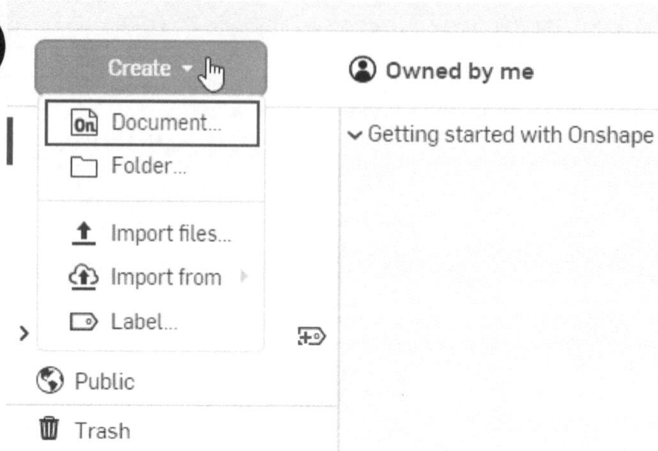

2.149

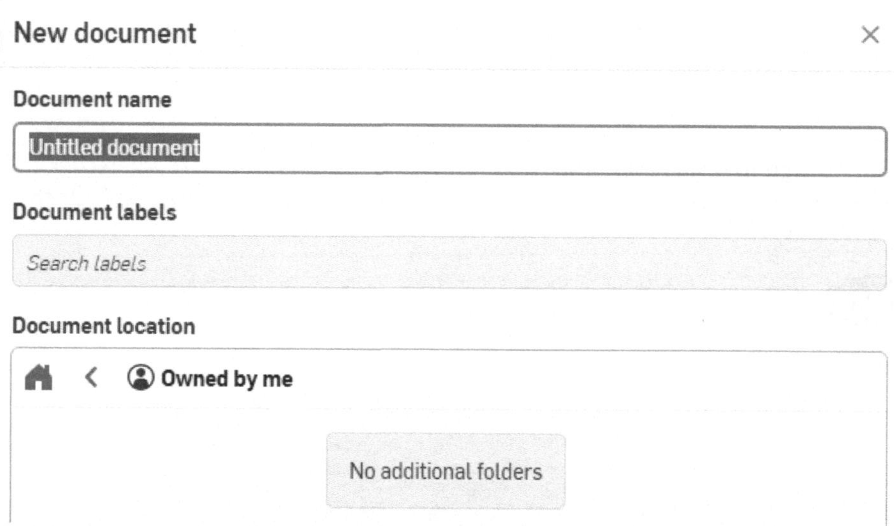

4. Enter **C02 Tutorial 01** as the name of the design document in the **New document** window, and then click on the **Create** button or the **Create Public Document** button, depending on your subscription type. A new document with the specified name is invoked, see Figure 2.150. The **Part Studio 1** and **Assembly 1** tabs are displayed at the bottom of the document. By default, the **Part Studio 1** tab is activated.

2.150

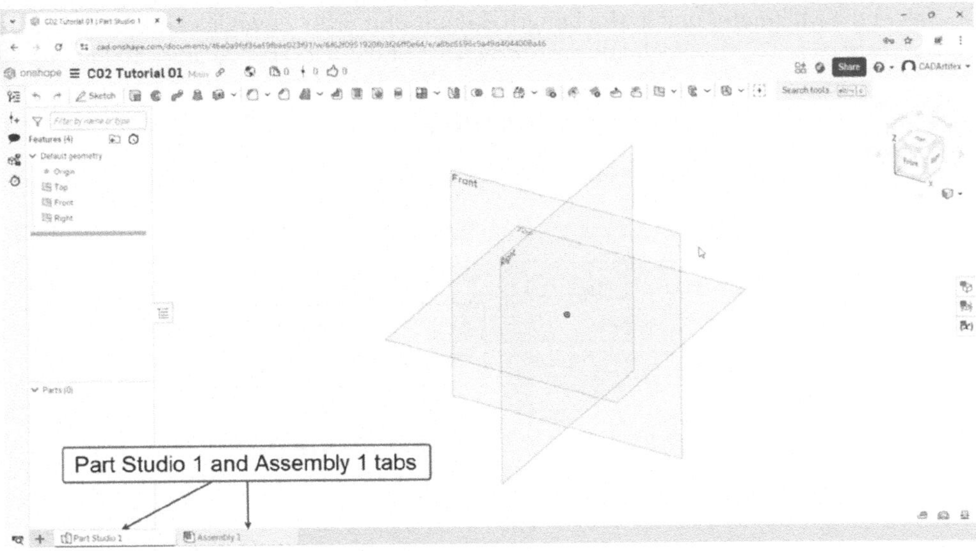

Section 2: Settings Units

Now, you can set millimeters (mm) as the default unit for the length in the current design document.

1. Invoke the **Document** menu by clicking on the ≡ icon (three horizontal lines) next to the Onshape logo at the top left corner, see Figure 2.151.

2.151

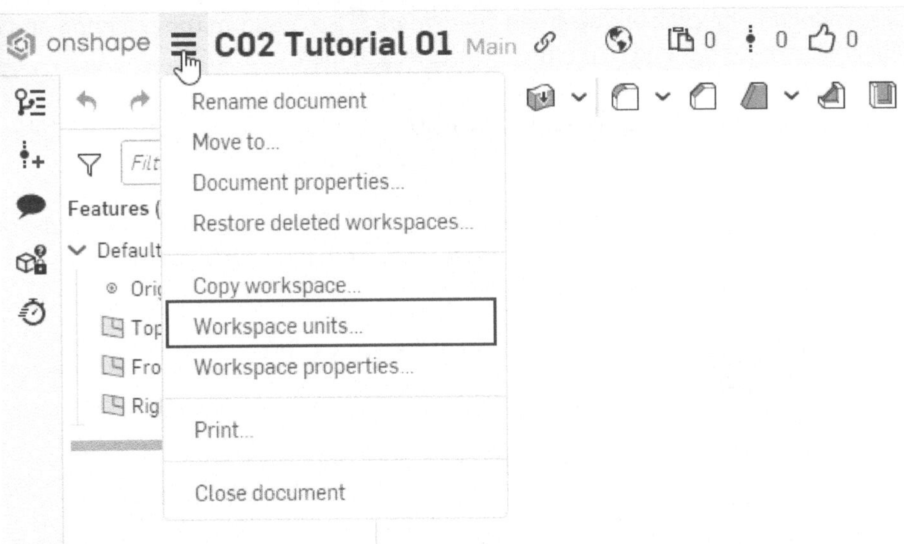

2. Click on the **Workspace units** option in the **Document** menu, refer to Figure 2.151. The **Workspace units** dialog appears, see Figure 2.152.

3. Select the **Millimeter** unit in the **Length default unit** drop-down list and set its precision to **0.1** in the respective **Display decimals** drop-down list of the **Workspace units** dialog, see Figure 2.152.

2.152

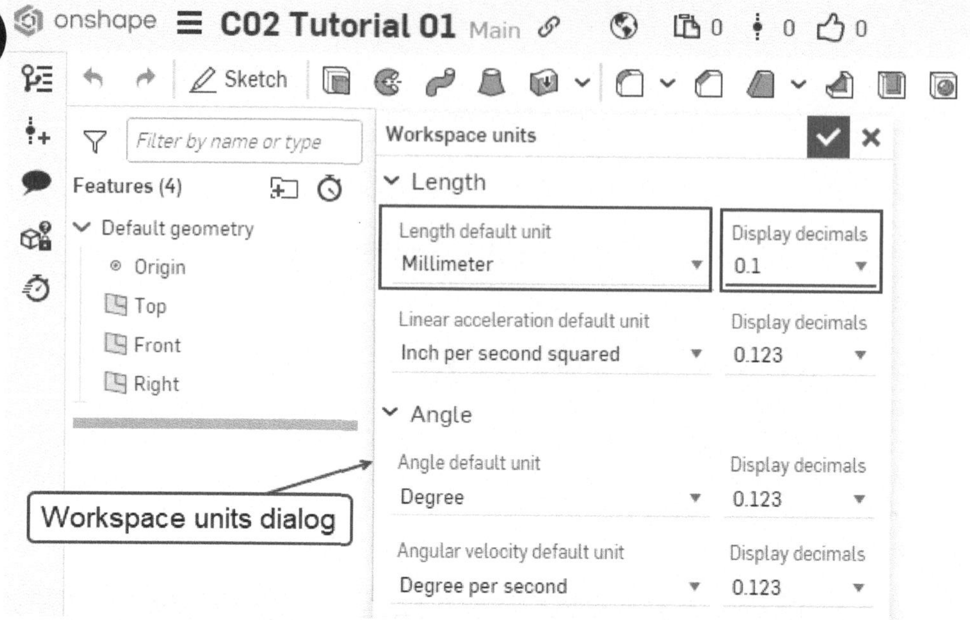

4. After selecting the required unit of length measurement and the decimal precision for the current design document, click on the green checkmark ✓ to confirm the selection and exit the dialog. The millimeter is defined as the unit for the length measurement.

Section 3: Accessing the Sketch Toolbar

Now, you can access the **Sketch** toolbar to create a sketch.

1. Click on the **Sketch** tool in the **Feature** toolbar, see Figure 2.153. The **Sketch** dialog appears (see Figure 2.154) and you are prompted to select a sketch plane. Alternatively, you can also press the SHIFT + S keys to invoke the **Sketch** dialog.

2.153

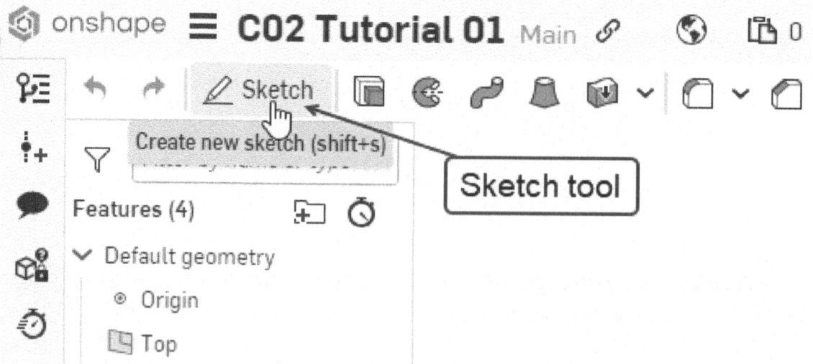

2.154

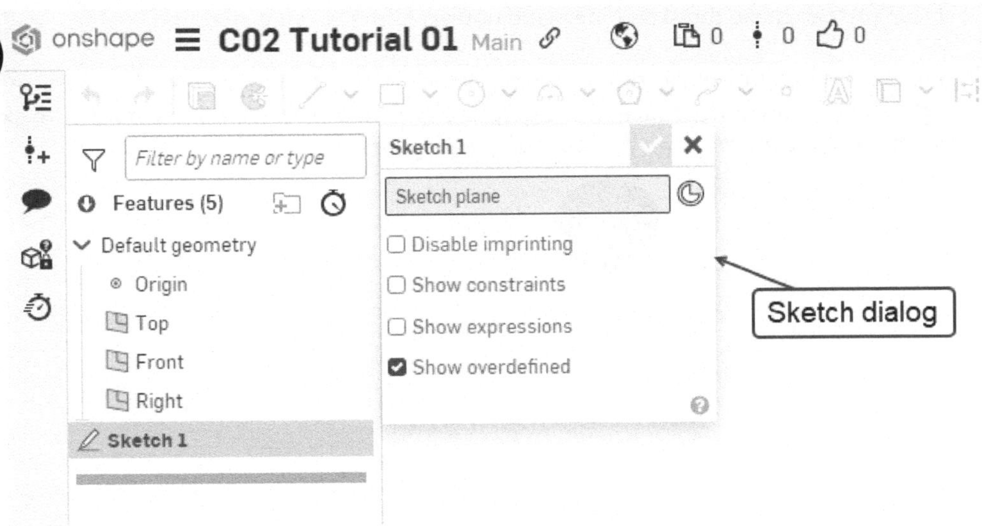

2. Select the Front plane as the sketching plane in the graphics area, see Figure 2.155. The selected plane becomes the sketching plane, and the **Sketch** toolbar appears with the display of various sketching tools, see Figure 2.156.

2.155

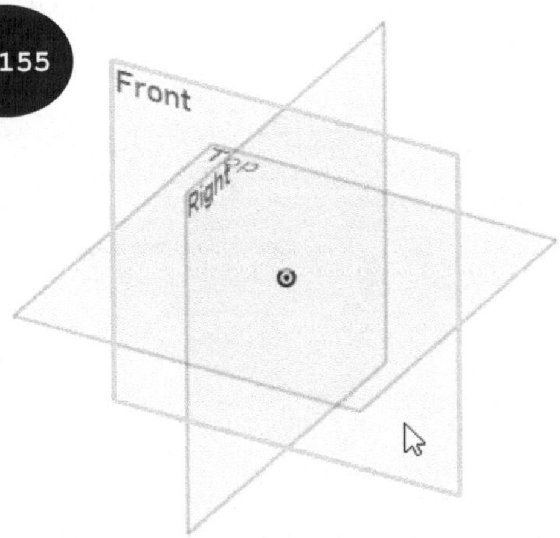

2.156

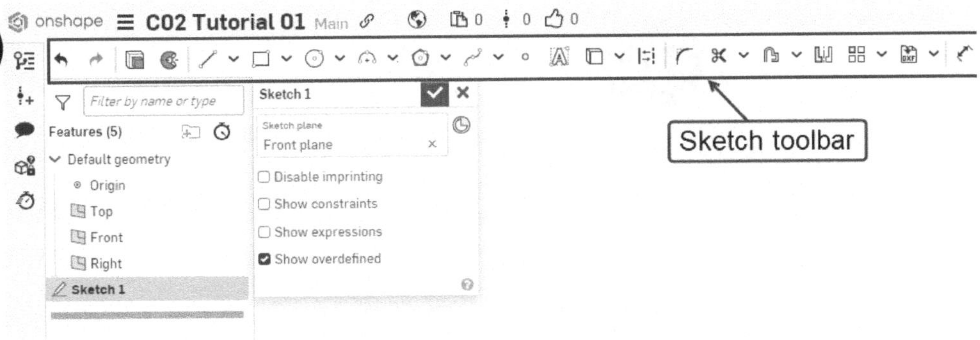

Now, you can make the sketching plane normal to the viewing direction.

3. Press the **N** key to make the sketching plane normal to the viewing direction. Alternatively, right-click on an entity space in the graphics area and select the **View normal to sketch plane** option in the context menu that appears, see Figure 2.157.

2.157

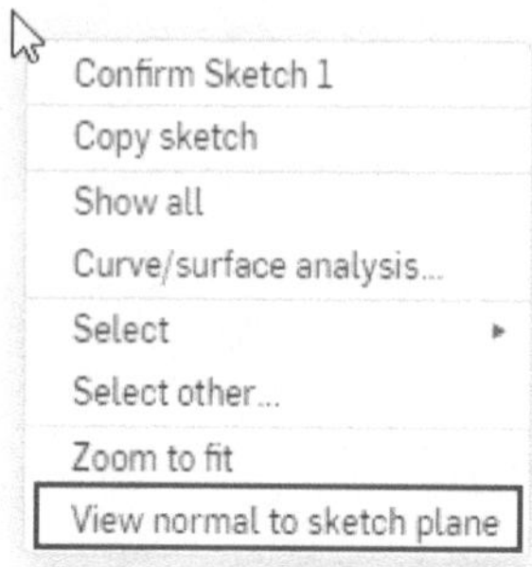

Section 4: Creating the Sketch

Now, you can start creating the sketch using the sketching tools available in the **Sketch** toolbar.

1. Click on the **Center point circle** tool in the **Sketch** toolbar, see Figure 2.158. Alternatively, press the C key to activate the **Center point circle** tool.

2.158

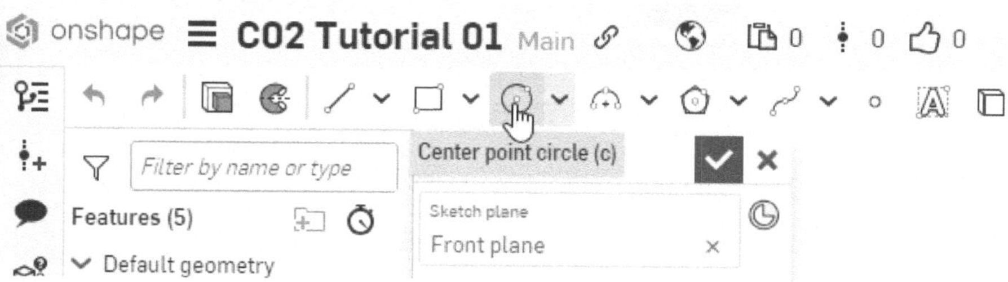

2. Move the cursor to the origin and then click to specify the center point of the circle when the cursor snaps to the origin.

3. Move the cursor to the right and click anywhere in the graphics area to set an arbitrary circle diameter. A circle is drawn, refer to Figure 2.159. Also, the **Center point circle** tool remains active.

2.159

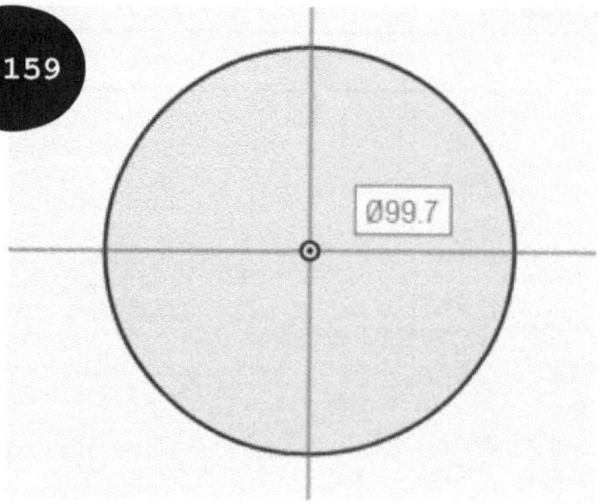

4. Right-click in the graphics area and then select the **Escape circle** option in the context menu that appears to exit the tool. Alternatively, press the ESC key.

   Now, you need to create an arc.

5. Invoke the **Arc** drop-down menu in the **Sketch** toolbar and then click on the **Center point arc** tool, see Figure 2.160.

2.160

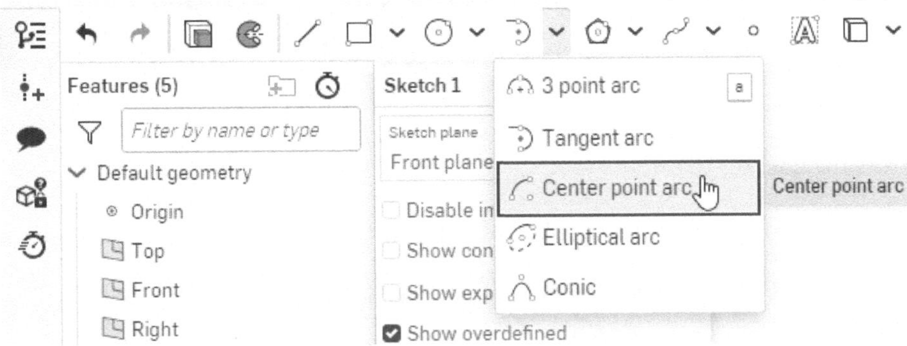

6. Move the cursor to the origin and then click to specify the center point of an arc when the cursor snaps to the origin.

7. Move the cursor horizontally to the right along the X-axis and click to specify the start point of the arc at a location outside the previously created circle, see Figure 2.161. Ensure that the start point is horizontally aligned with the origin.

2.161

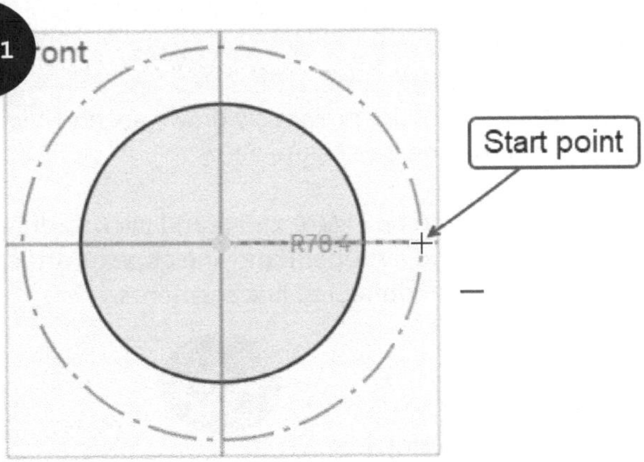

8. After specifying the start point of the arc, move the cursor clockwise. A preview of the arc appears in the graphics area.

9. Click to define the endpoint of the arc when the cursor aligns horizontally with the origin along the X-axis, on the opposite side of the start point, see Figure 2.162. The arc is drawn and the **Center point circle** tool remains active.

2.162

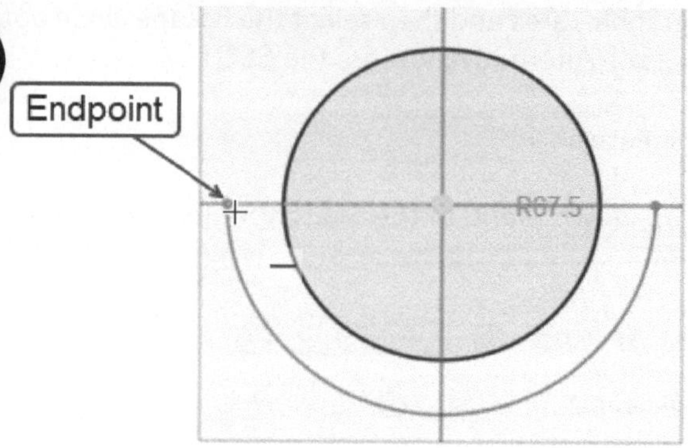

10. Press the ESC key to exit the tool.

    Now, you can create the line entities of the sketch.

11. Click on the **Line** tool in the **Sketch** toolbar (see Figure 2.163) or press the **L** key. The **Line** tool gets activated.

2.163

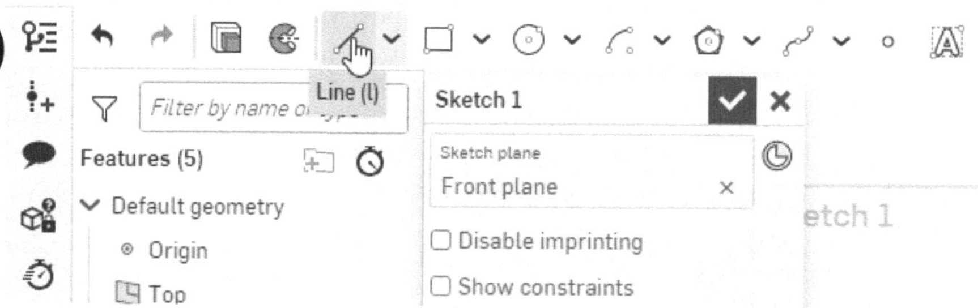

12. Move the cursor to the start point of the previously drawn arc and click when the cursor snaps to it to specify the start point of the line, see Figure 2.164.

13. Move the cursor vertically upward (see Figure 2.165) and click to draw a vertical line of arbitrary length. A vertical line is created, and a rubber band line appears attached to the cursor, allowing you to continue drawing a series of connected line segments.

2.164

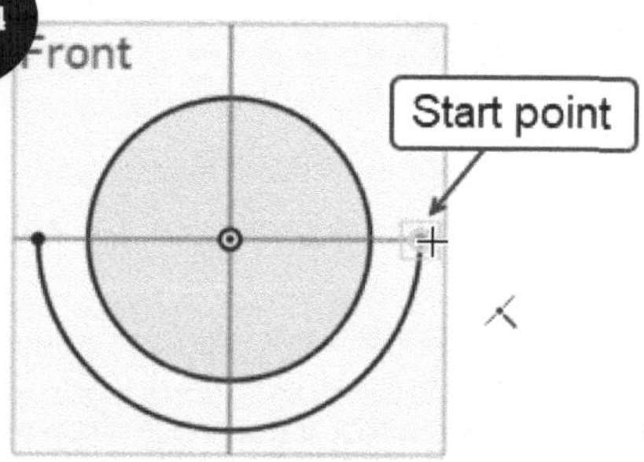

2.165

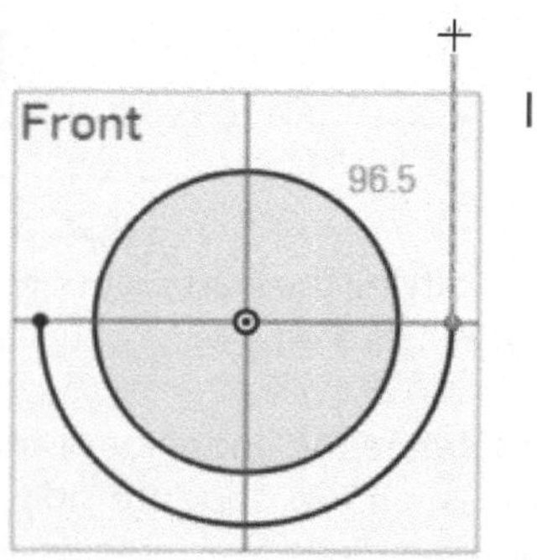

14. Move the cursor to the endpoint of the arc, then move it horizontally to the left from the previously specified point until a light-colored dotted reference line appears originating from the endpoint of the arc, see Figure 2.166.

2.166

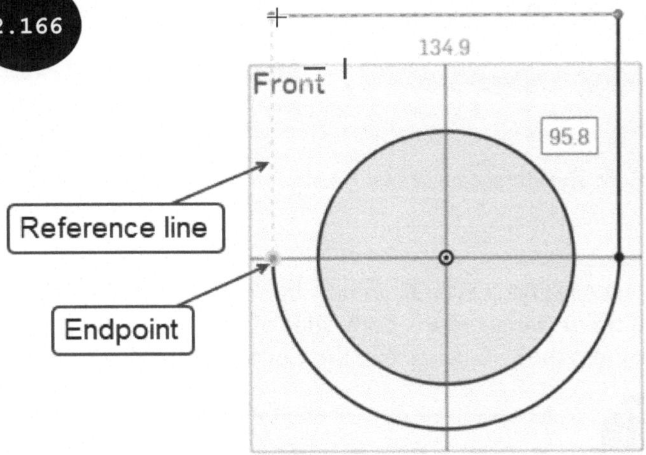

15. Click to specify the endpoint of the line when the cursor snaps to the reference line, refer to Figure 2.166. A horizontal line between the specified points is created.

16. Move the cursor vertically downward and click when the cursor snaps to the endpoint of the arc, see Figure 2.167.

17. Press the ESC key to exit the Line tool. The sketch appears similar to the one shown in Figure 2.168.

2.167

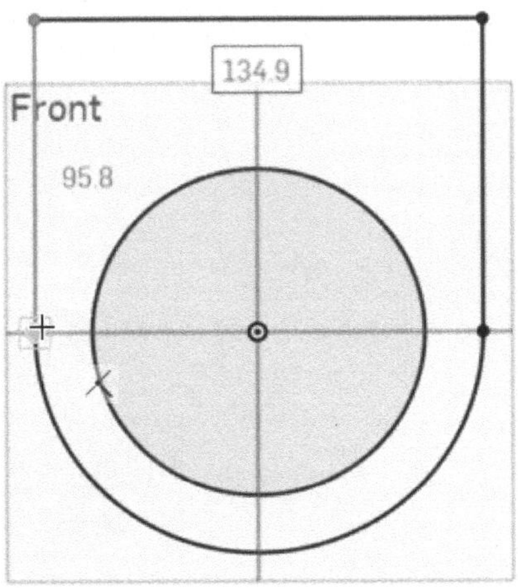

2.168

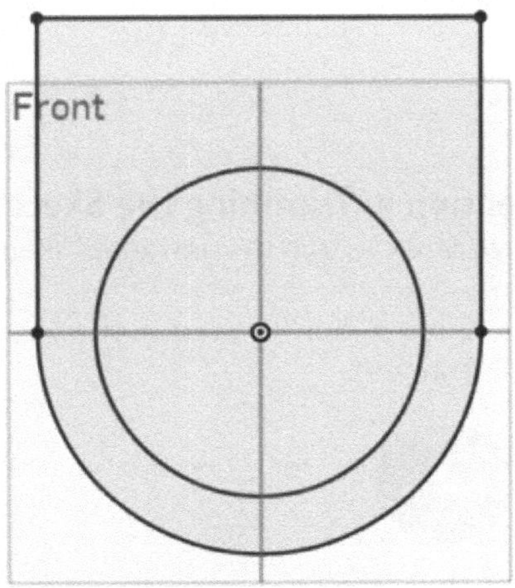

Now, you can create the remaining entities of the sketch.

18. Click on the **Corner rectangle** tool in the **Sketch** toolbar (see Figure 2.169) or press the **G** key.

2.169

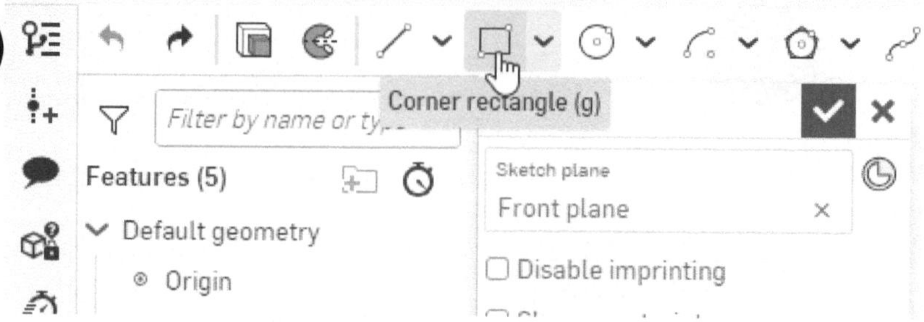

19. Create a rectangle by specifying two diagonally opposite corners, similar to the one shown in Figure 2.170. Ensure the rectangle spans both sides of the Y-axis and is partially inside the inner circle of the sketch. Press the ESC key to exit the **Corner rectangle** tool.

2.170

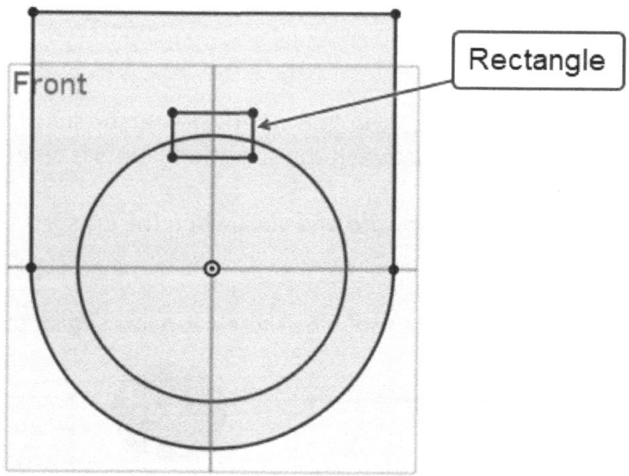

Section 5: Trimming the Sketch Entities

Now, you can trim the unwanted sketch entities.

1. Click on the **Trim** tool in the **Sketch** toolbar (see Figure 2.171) or press the **M** key to activate the **Trim** tool.

2.171

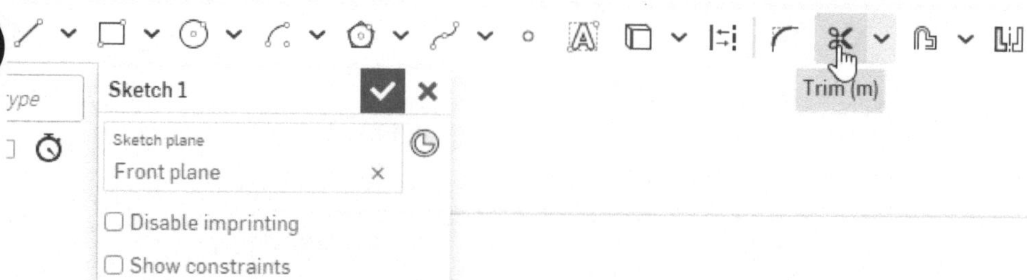

2. Click on the entities of the rectangle that lie inside the circle one at a time. Each selected entity gets trimmed to its nearest intersection, see Figure 2.172. The **Trim** tool remains active.

3. Similarly, trim the portion of the circle that lies between the two vertical lines of the previously drawn rectangle. Figure 2.173 shows the sketch after trimming all unwanted entities. Next, press the ESC key to exit the **Trim** tool.

2.172

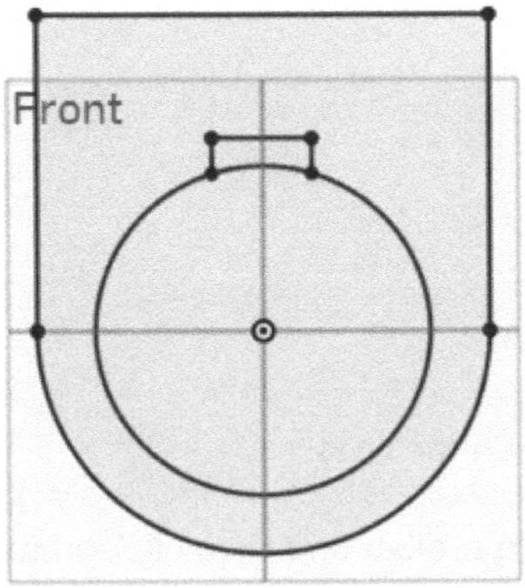

2.173

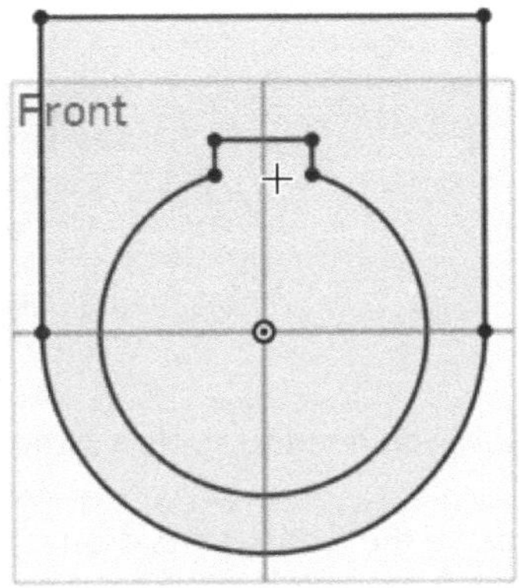

Section 6: Applying Constraints

Now, you can apply the required constraints to the sketch entities.

1. Invoke the **Constraints** drop-down menu in the **Sketch** toolbar and then click on the **Equal** tool, see Figure 2.174. Alternatively, press the **E** key to activate the **Equal** tool.

2.174

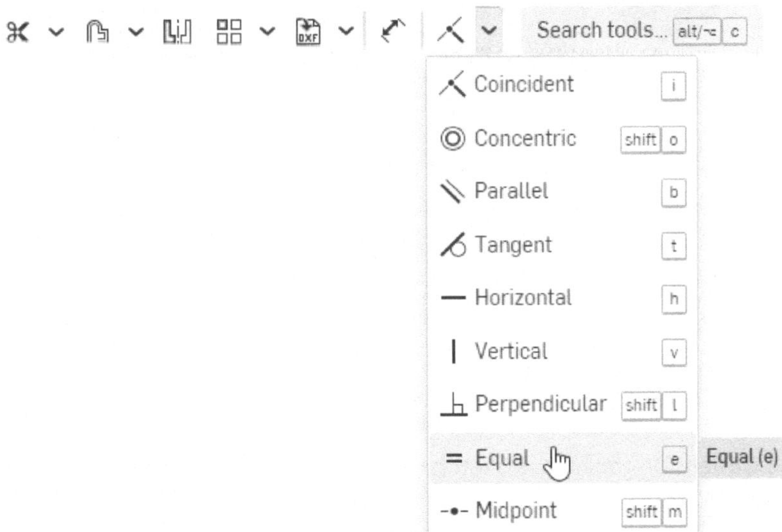

2. Select the two inner vertical lines of the sketch, see Figure 2.175. The lines become equal in length, and an equal constraint is applied between them. Press the ESC key to exit the tool.

2.175

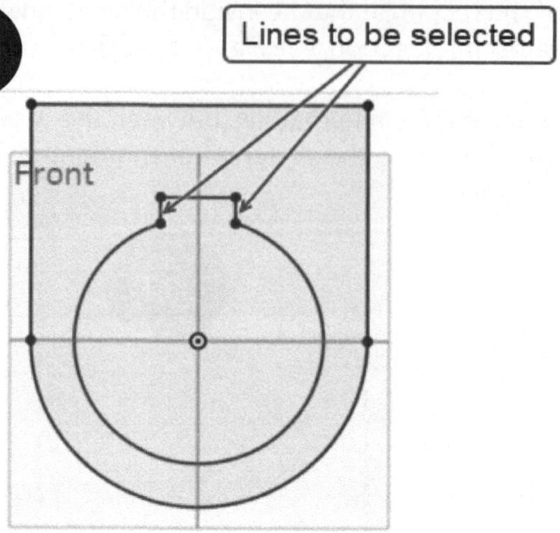

Now, you need to apply a symmetric constraint between the lines.

3. Invoke the **Constraints** drop-down menu in the **Sketch** toolbar and then click on the **Symmetric** tool or press SHIFT + Q.

4. Select the two inner vertical lines of the sketch shown in Figure 2.175 and then select the vertical plane (Right), see Figure 2.176. Both the lines become symmetric to each other relative to the selected vertical plane and a symmetric constraint is applied. Press the ESC key to exit the tool.

2.176

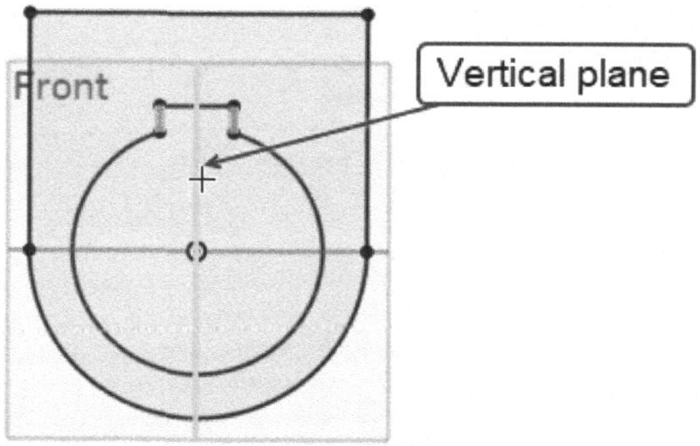

Section 7: Applying Dimensions

Now, you can apply the required dimensions to the sketch entities.

1. Click on the **Dimension** tool in the **Sketch** toolbar or press the D key to activate the **Dimension** tool, see Figure 2.177.

2.177

2. Select the outer arc of the sketch. A radius dimension appears attached to the cursor, see Figure 2.178.

3. Click in the graphics area to define the placement for the radius dimension. A dimension field appears, displaying the current radius of the selected arc.

4. Enter **75** mm in the dimension field and press ENTER. The radius of the arc gets modified accordingly, and the radius dimension is applied, see Figure 2.179. The **Dimension** tool remains active.

2.178

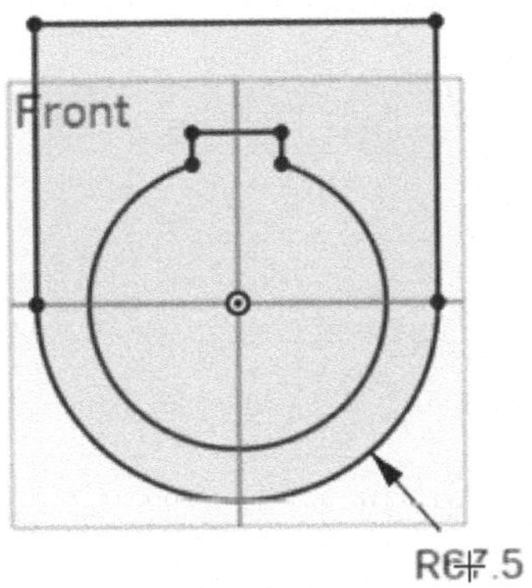

2.179

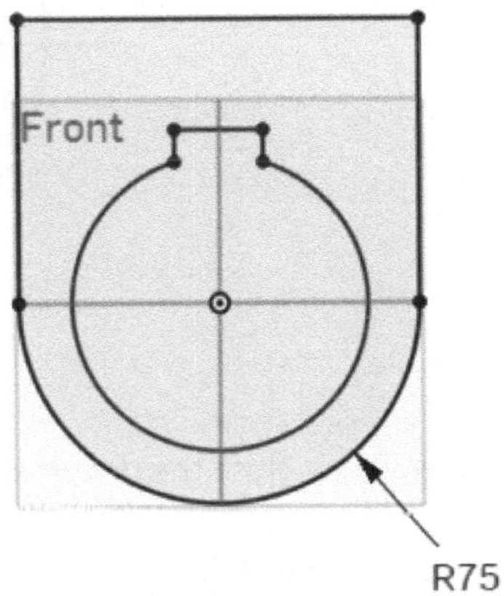

5. Select the rightmost vertical line of the sketch. A vertical dimension appears attached to the cursor, see Figure 2.180. Next, click to define its placement point in the graphics area. A dimension field appears, displaying the current length of the selected line.

6. Enter **110** mm in the dimension field and press ENTER. The length of the line gets modified accordingly, and the dimension is applied, see Figure 2.181. The **Dimension** tool remains active.

2.180

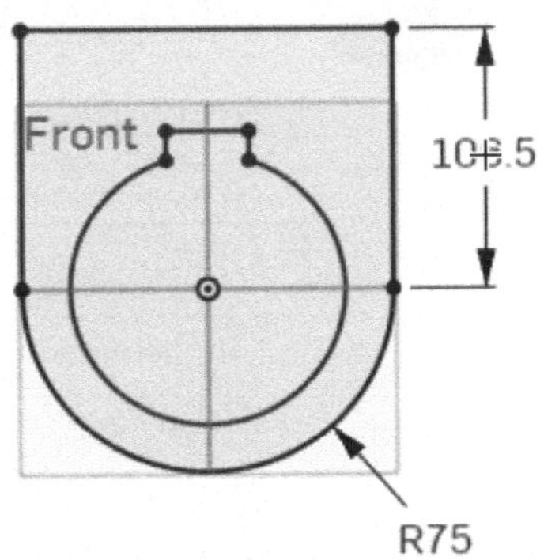

2.181

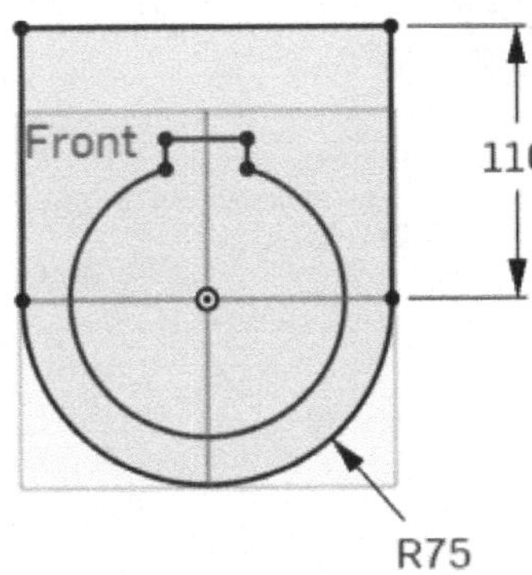

7. Similarly, apply the remaining dimensions to the sketch. Figure 2.182 shows the final sketch after applying all the dimensions.

2.182

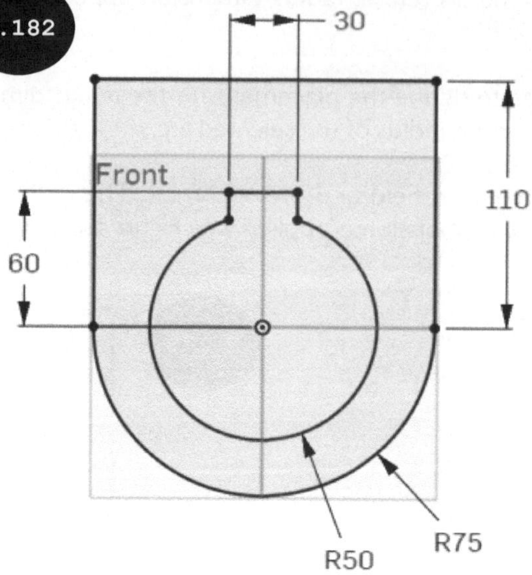

Now, you can close the document.

8. Invoke the **Document** menu by clicking on the ≡ icon (three horizontal lines) next to the Onshape logo at the top left corner and click on the **Close document** option, see Figure 2.183. The current document gets closed and the **Documents Page** appears.

Tip: In Onshape, the documents save automatically in cloud. You can access a list of all the saved documents anytime by clicking on the **Created by me** option in the left menu of the **Documents Page**, see Figure 2.184.

2.183

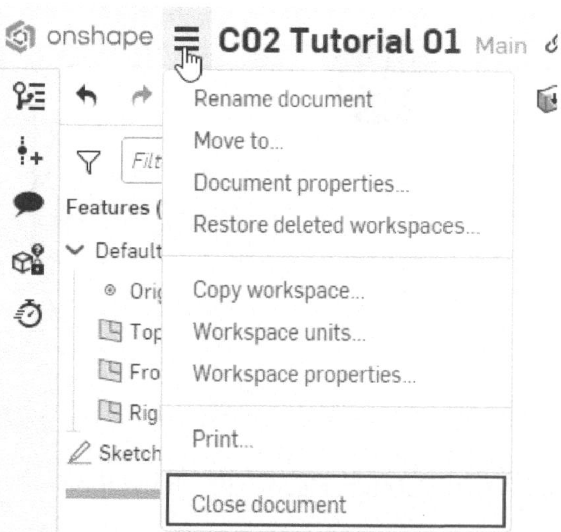

2.184

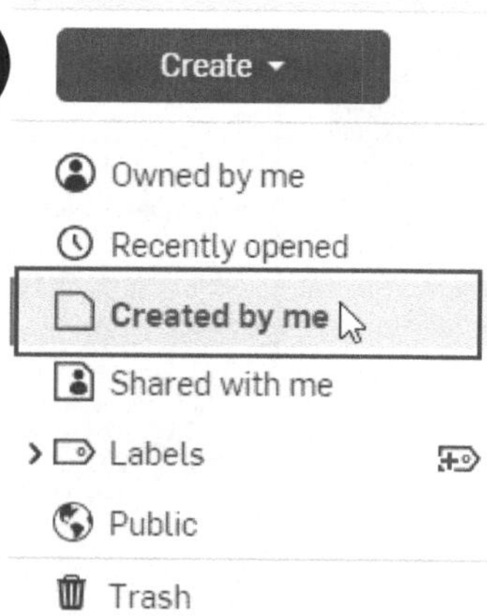

Tutorial 2

Draw the sketch of the model shown in Figure 2.185. The 3D model shown in the figure is for your reference only. You will learn to create models in later chapters. All dimensions are in inches.

2.185

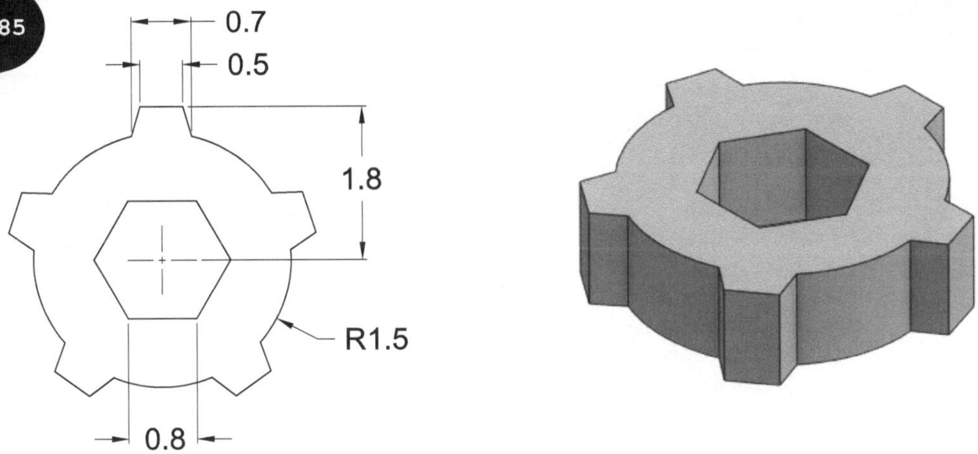

Section 1: Starting a New Design Document

1. Launch Onshape (***onshape.com***) and log in to your account if you're not already logged in.

2. Click on the **Create** button at the top left corner of the **Documents Page** and then click on the **Document** option in the menu that appears, see Figure 2.186. The **New document** window appears with the default name of the document "**Untitled document**".

2.186

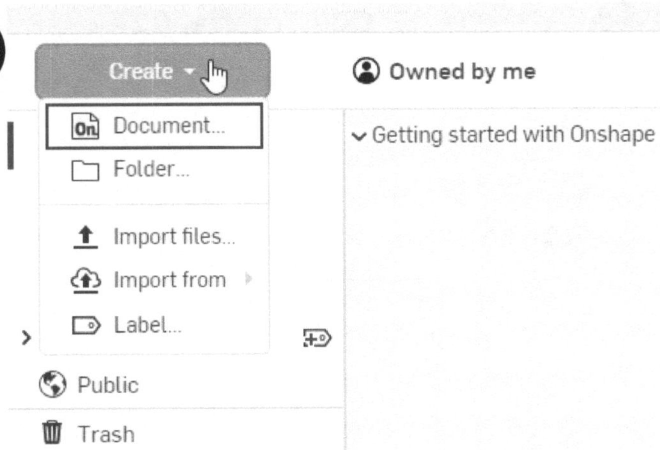

Note: The **Documents Page** automatically appears each time you launch Onshape. You can also access it at any time by clicking the Onshape logo in the top left corner of the screen.

3. Enter **C02 Tutorial 02** as the name of the design document in the **New document** window (see Figure 2.187), and then click on the **Create** button or the **Create Public Document** button, depending on your subscription type. A new document with the specified name is invoked.

2.187

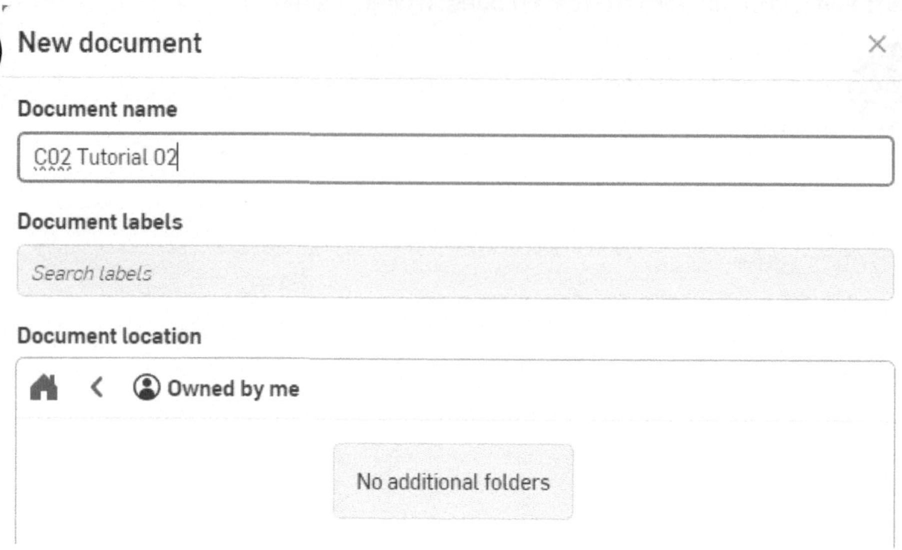

Section 2: Settings Units

Now, you can set inches (in) as the default unit for the length in the current design document.

1. Invoke the **Document** menu by clicking on the ≡ icon (three horizontal lines) next to the Onshape logo at the top left corner, see Figure 2.188.

2.188

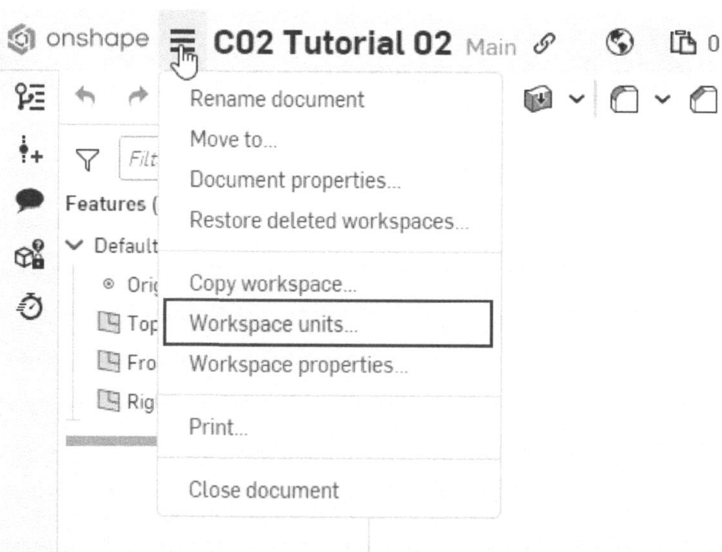

2. Click on the **Workspace units** option in the **Document** menu, refer to Figure 2.188. The **Workspace units** dialog appears.

3. Ensure that the **Inch** unit is selected in the **Length default unit** drop-down list and set its precision to **0.12** in the respective **Display decimals** drop-down list of the **Workspace units** dialog, see Figure 2.189.

2.189

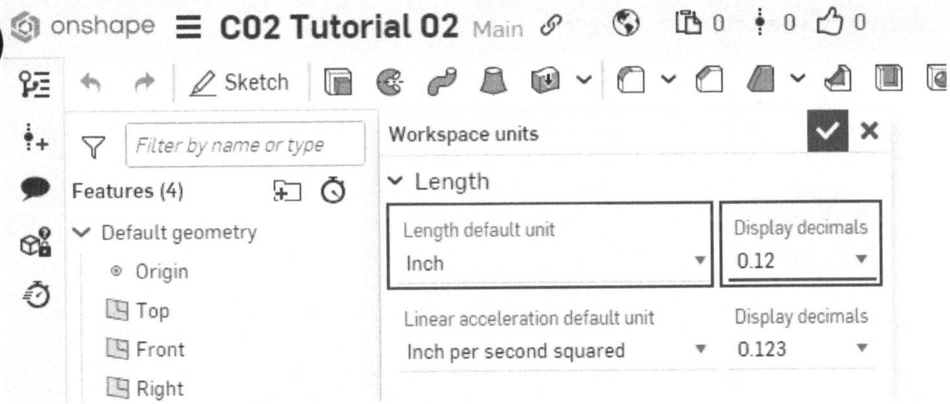

4. Click on the green checkmark ✓ to confirm the selection and exit the dialog. The inches unit is defined as the unit for the length measurement.

Section 3: Accessing the Sketch Toolbar

1. Click on the **Sketch** tool in the **Feature** toolbar, see Figure 2.190. The **Sketch** dialog appears and you are prompted to select a sketch plane.

2.190

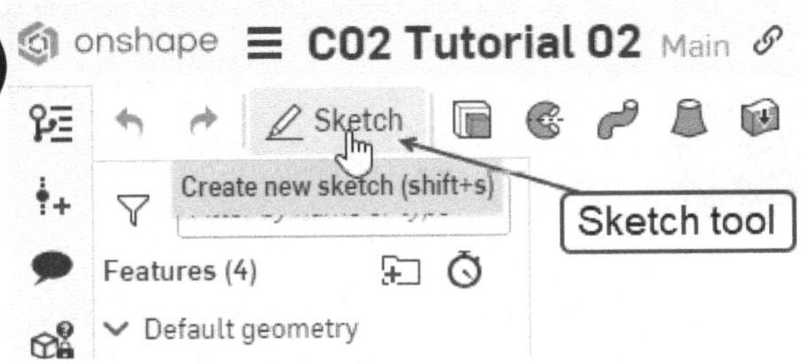

2. Select the Top plane as the sketching plane in the graphics area, see Figure 2.191. The selected plane becomes the sketching plane, and the **Sketch** toolbar appears with the display of various sketching tools.

2.191

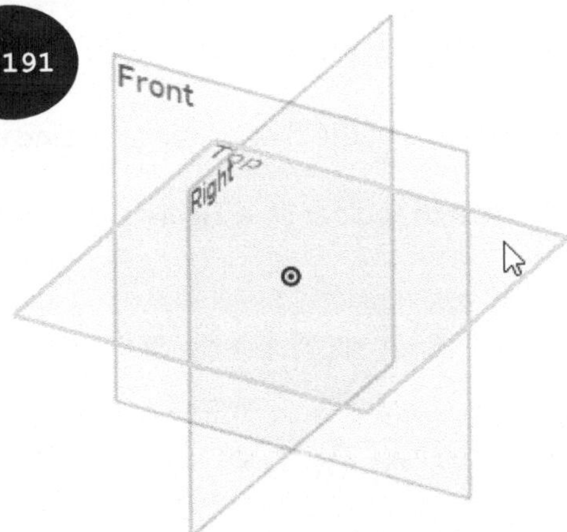

Now, you can make the sketching plane normal to the viewing direction.

3. Press the **N** key to make the sketching plane normal to the viewing direction.

Section 4: Creating the Sketch

Now, you can start creating the sketch using the sketching tools available in the **Sketch** toolbar.

1. Click on the **Center point circle** tool in the **Sketch** toolbar, see Figure 2.192. Alternatively, press the C key to activate the **Center point circle** tool.

2.192

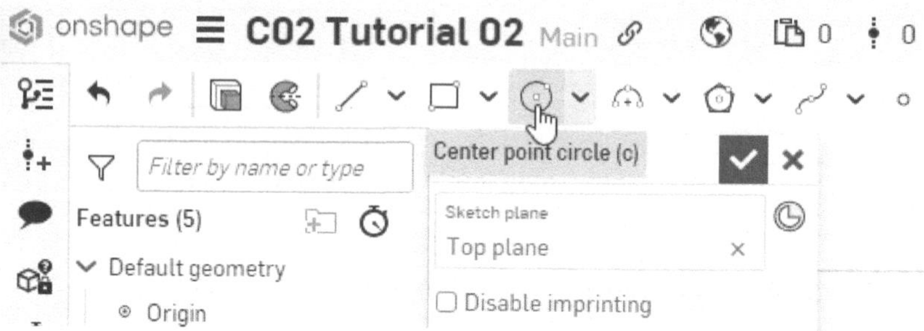

2. Move the cursor to the origin and then click to specify the center point of the circle when the cursor snaps to the origin.

3. Move the cursor to the right and click anywhere in the graphics area to set an arbitrary circle diameter. A circle is drawn, refer to Figure 2.193. Next, press the ESC key to exit the **Center point circle** tool.

2.193

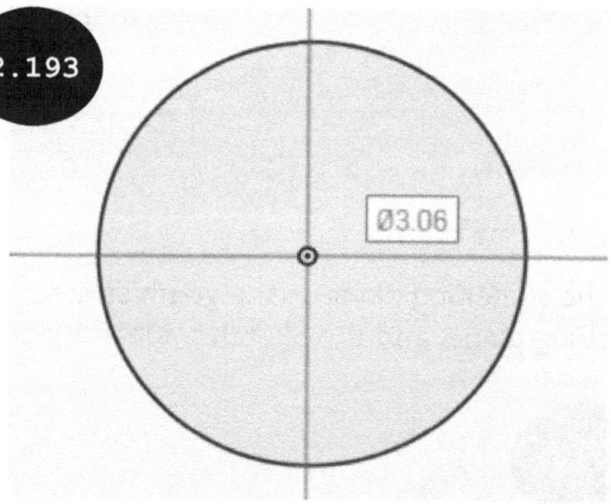

Now, you need to create line entities of the sketch using the **Line** tool.

4. Click on the **Line** tool in the **Sketch** toolbar (see Figure 2.194) or press the **L** key to activate the **Line** tool.

2.194

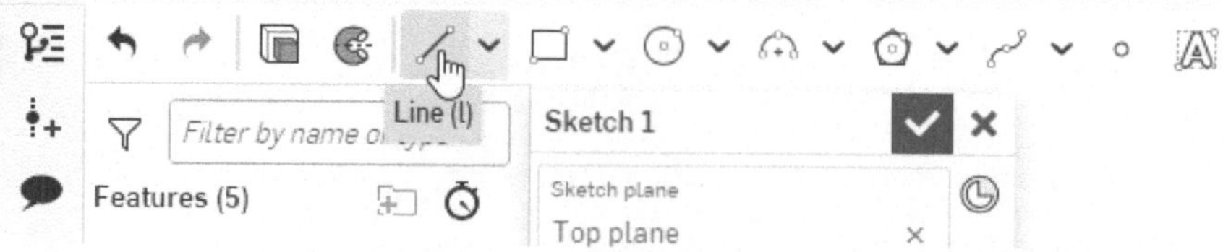

5. Create three connected lines, including two inclined lines and one horizontal line, by defining points in the graphics area similar to the lines shown in Figure 2.195. Ensure that both inclined lines partially intersect the circle. After creating the lines, press the ESC key to exit the **Line** tool.

2.195

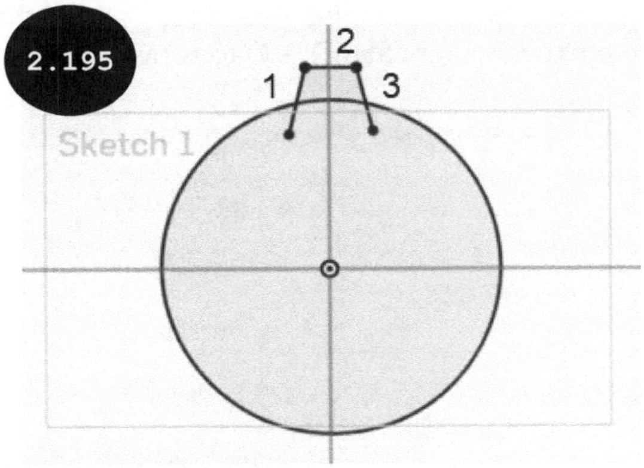

Section 5: Trimming the Sketch Entities

Now, you can trim the excess portion of line entities.

1. Click on the **Trim** tool in the **Sketch** toolbar (see Figure 2.196) or press the **M** key to activate the **Trim** tool.

2.196

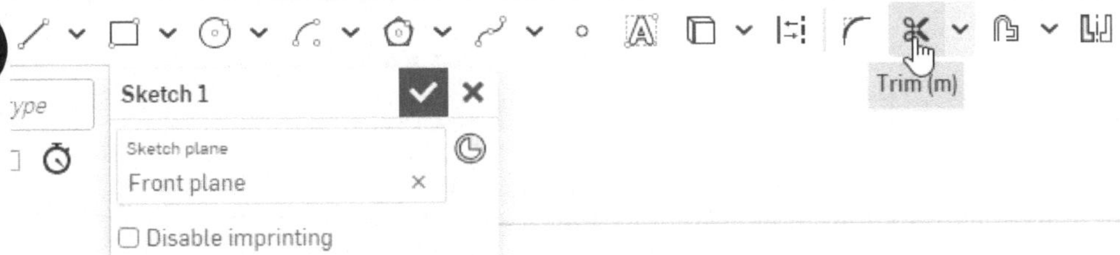

2. Click on the portion of the inclined lines that lie inside the circle one at a time. Each selected line gets trimmed to its nearest intersection, see Figure 2.197. The **Trim** tool remains active.

3. Similarly, trim the portion of the circle that lies between the two inclined lines. Figure 2.198 shows the sketch after trimming all entities. Next, press the ESC key to exit the **Trim** tool.

2.197

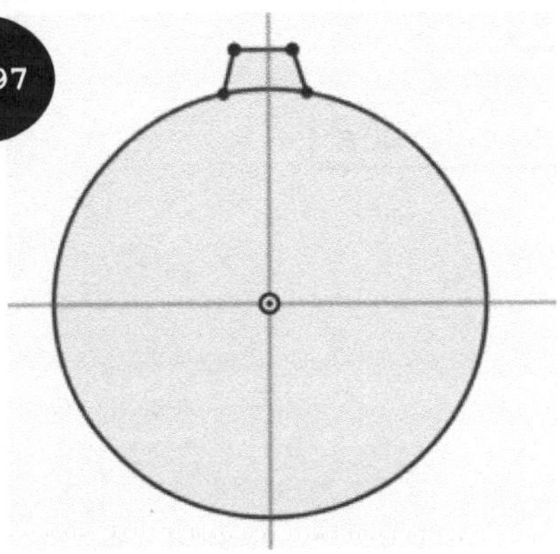

2.198

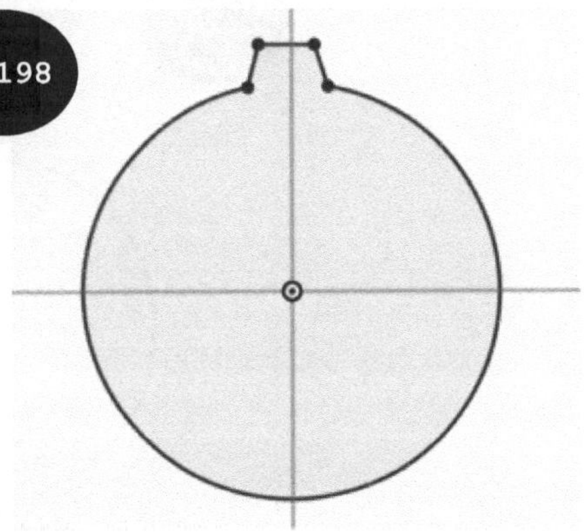

Section 6: Applying Constraints

Now, you can apply the required constraints to the sketch entities.

1. Invoke the **Constraints** drop-down menu in the **Sketch** toolbar and then click on the **Symmetric** tool, see Figure 2.199. Alternatively, press **SHIFT + Q** to activate this tool.

2.199

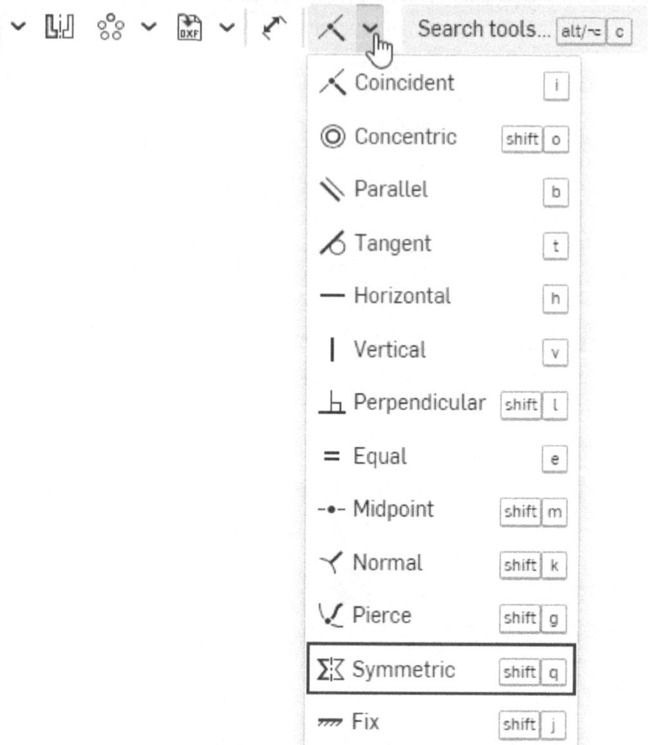

2. Select the two inclined lines in the sketch one by one, and then choose the vertical plane that passes between them, see Figure 2.200. The lines become symmetrical relative to the selected vertical plane, and the **Symmetric** constraint is applied. Next, press the ESC key to exit the tool.

2.200

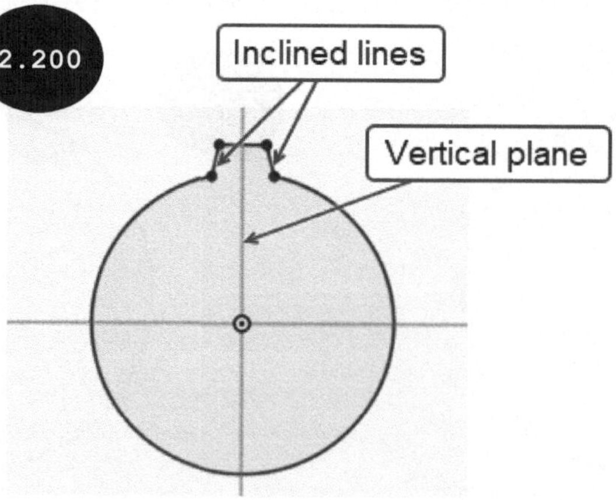

Section 7: Creating the Circular Pattern

1. Click on a small arrow beside the **Linear pattern** tool in the **Sketch** toolbar and then click on the **Circular pattern** tool in the drop-down menu that appears, see Figure 2.201.

2.201

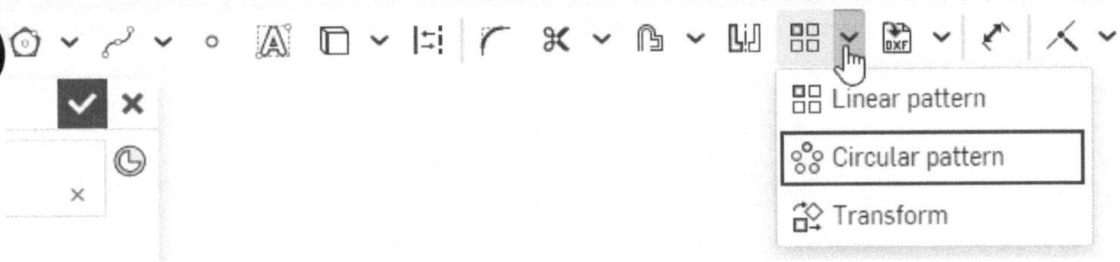

2. Select three line entities of the sketch by either clicking on them with the left mouse button or by drawing a selection window around them. A preview of a circular pattern appears around the origin, see Figure 2.202.

3. Double-click on the **3x** (No. of instances) in the graphics area and then enter **5** as the desired number of instances to be created in the edit field that appears. Next, press ENTER to apply the changes. Figure 2.203 shows the preview of a circular sketch pattern with 5 number of instances.

2.202

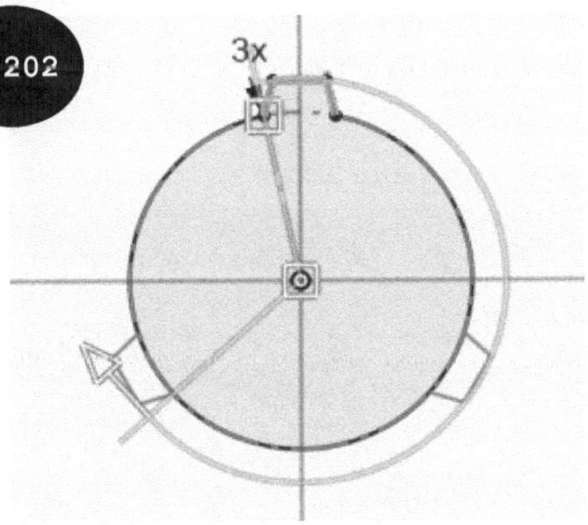

2.203

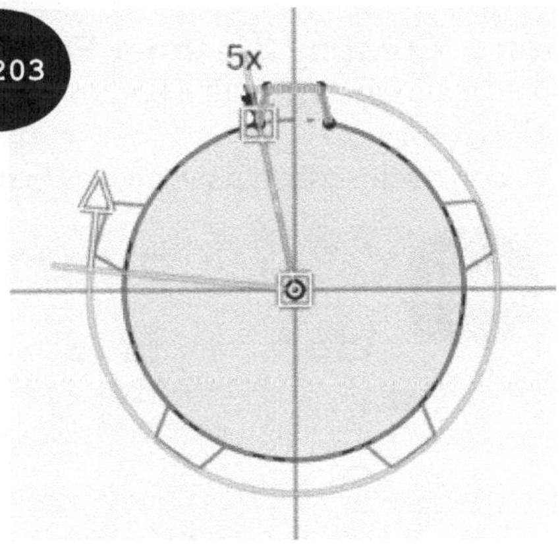

4. Click anywhere in the graphics area. A circular sketch pattern with the specified instances is created, see Figure 2.204.

2.204

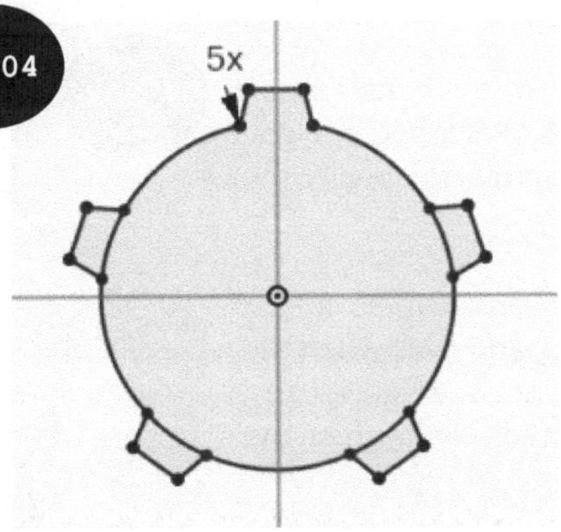

Section 8: Trimming the Circle

Now, you can trim the portions of the circle that lie between two inclined line entities.

1. Press the **M** key to activate the **Trim** tool and then click on the portions of the circle that lie between two inclined lines one at a time. Figure 2.205 shows the sketch after trimming the circle. Next, press the ESC key to exit the tool.

2.205

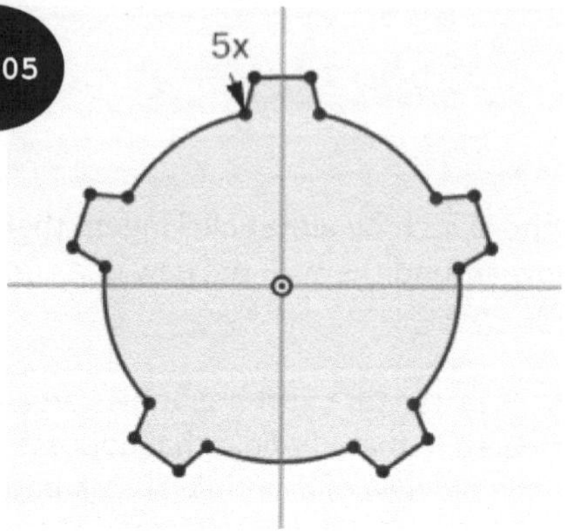

Section 9: Creating the Inner Polygon

Now, you can create a six-sided polygon within the sketch.

1. Click on the **Inscribed polygon** tool in the **Sketch** toolbar, see Figure 2.206.

2.206

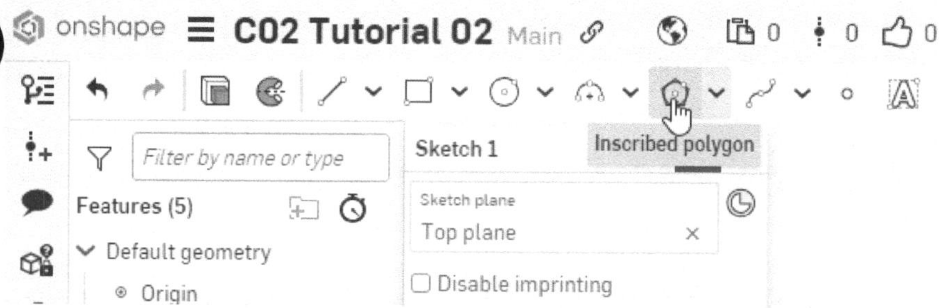

2. Click to specify the center point of a polygon at the origin. The preview of a polygon appears with a construction circle positioned inside it.

3. Click to define the diameter of the construction circle in the graphics area. An inscribed polygon is created and you are prompted to specify the number of sides for the polygon.

4. Slowly move the cursor up or down to adjust the number of polygon sides, and click when the number **6** appears in the spinner, see Figure 2.207. A six-sided polygon is created. Next, press the ESC key to exit the tool

2.207

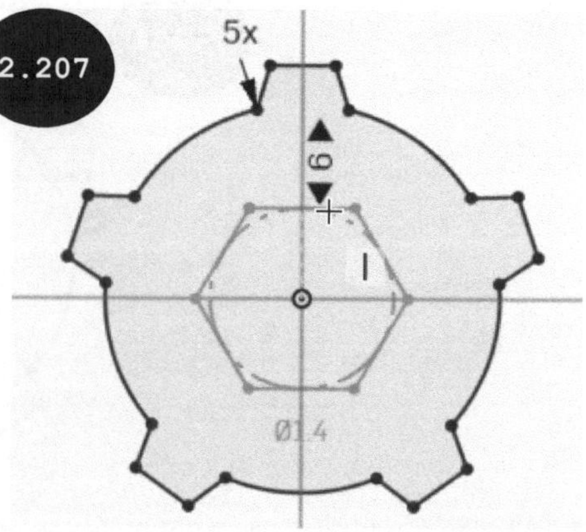

Section 10: Applying Dimensions

1. Click on the **Dimension** tool in the **Sketch** toolbar or press the D key to activate the **Dimension** tool, see Figure 2.208.

2.208

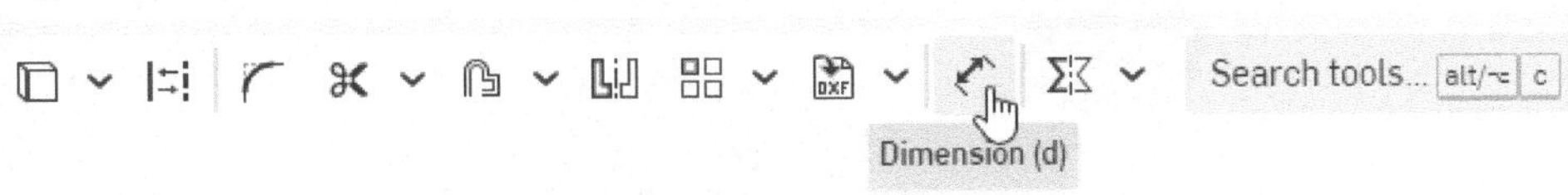

2. Select the outer arc of the sketch. A radius dimension appears attached to the cursor, see Figure 2.209.

3. Click in the graphics area to define the placement for the radius dimension. A dimension field appears, displaying the current radius of the selected arc.

4. Enter **1.5** inches in the dimension field and press ENTER. The radius of the arc gets modified accordingly, and the radius dimension is applied, see Figure 2.210. The tool remains active.

2.209

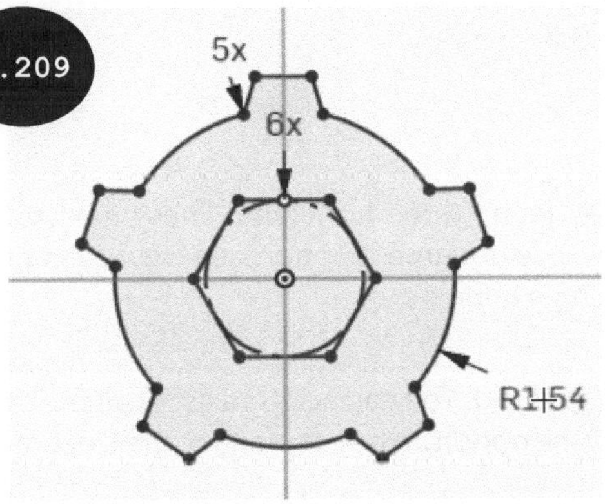

2.210

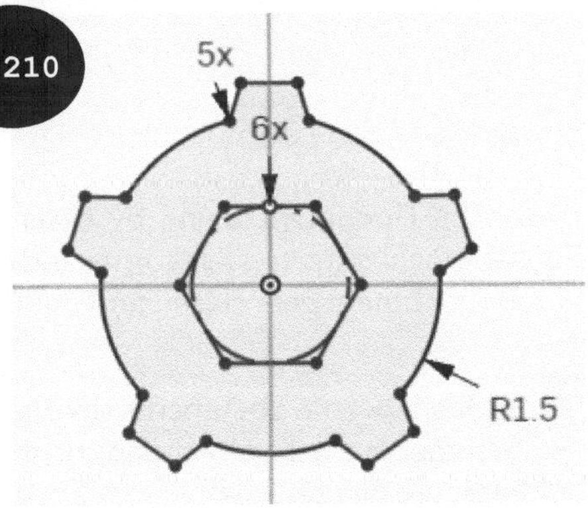

5. Select the origin and then the upper horizontal line of the sketch. A vertical dimension appears attached to the cursor, see Figure 2.211. Next, click to define its placement point in the graphics area. A dimension field appears, displaying the current distance between the selected entities.

6. Enter **1.8** inches in the dimension field and press ENTER. The distance between the origin and the upper horizontal line gets modified accordingly, and the dimension is applied, see Figure 2.212. The **Dimension** tool remains active.

2.211

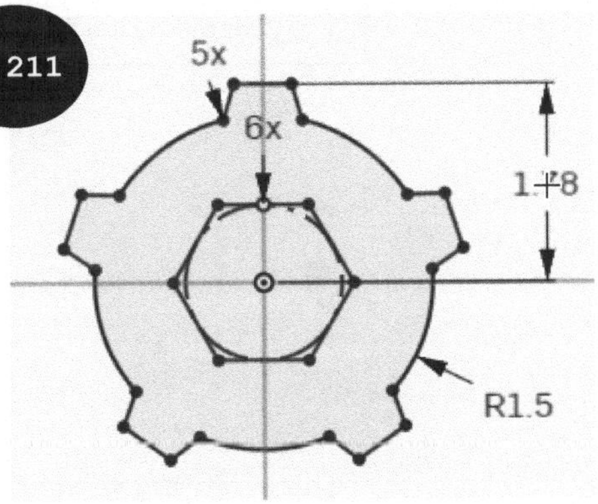

2.212

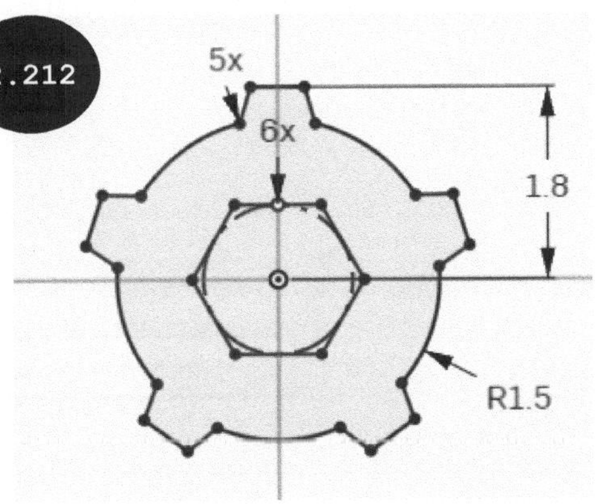

7. Similarly, apply the remaining dimensions to the sketch. Figure 2.213 shows the final sketch after applying all the dimensions.

2.213

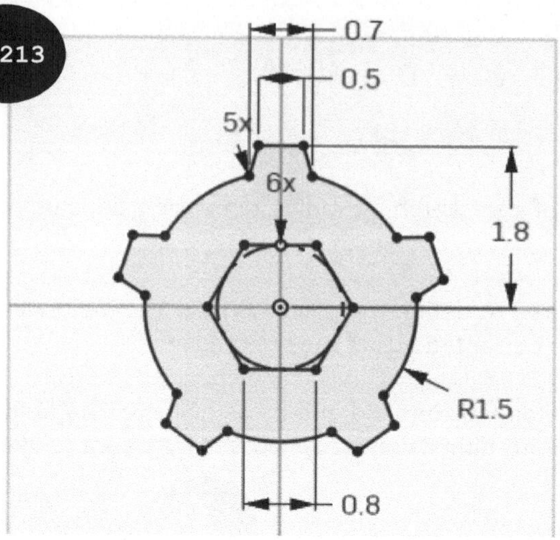

Now, you can close the document.

8. Invoke the **Document** menu by clicking on the ≡ icon (three horizontal lines) next to the Onshape logo at the top left corner and click on the **Close document** option, see Figure 2.214. The current document gets closed and the **Documents Page** appears.

Tip: In Onshape, the documents save automatically in cloud. You can access a list of all the saved documents anytime by clicking on the **Created by me** option in the left menu of the **Documents Page**, see Figure 2.215.

2.214

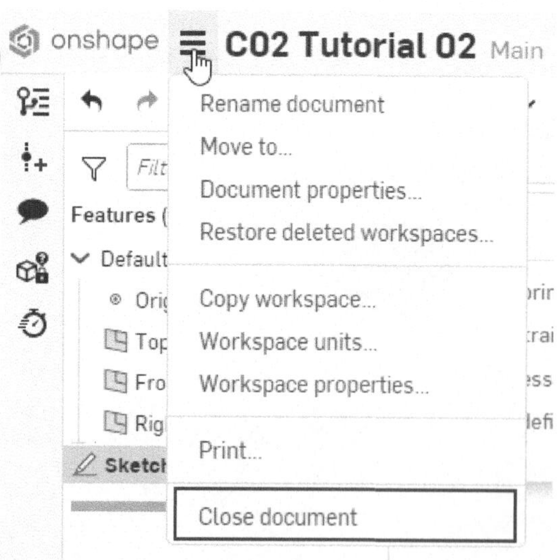

2.215

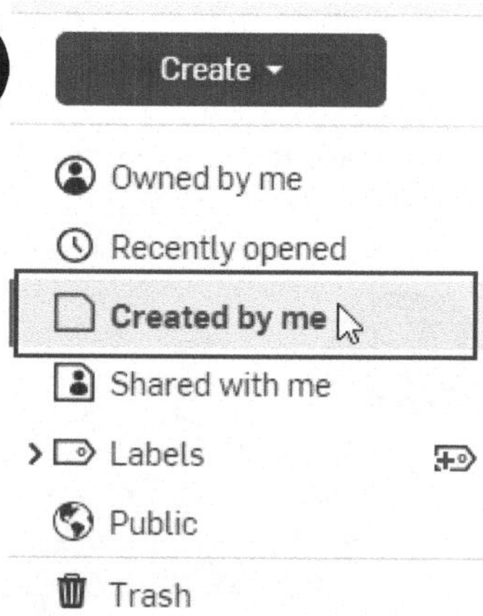

Hands-on Test Drive 1

Draw a sketch of the model shown in Figure 2.216. The 3D model shown in the figure is for your reference only. All dimensions are in inches.

2.216

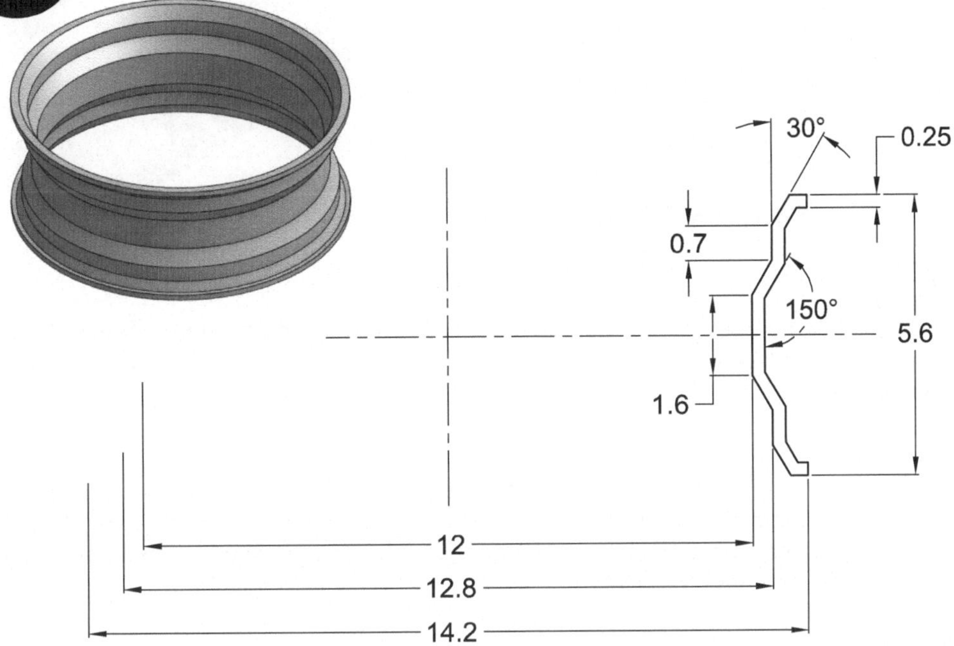

Hands-on Test Drive 2

Draw a sketch of the model shown in Figure 2.217. The 3D model shown in the figure is for your reference only. All dimensions are in inches.

2.217

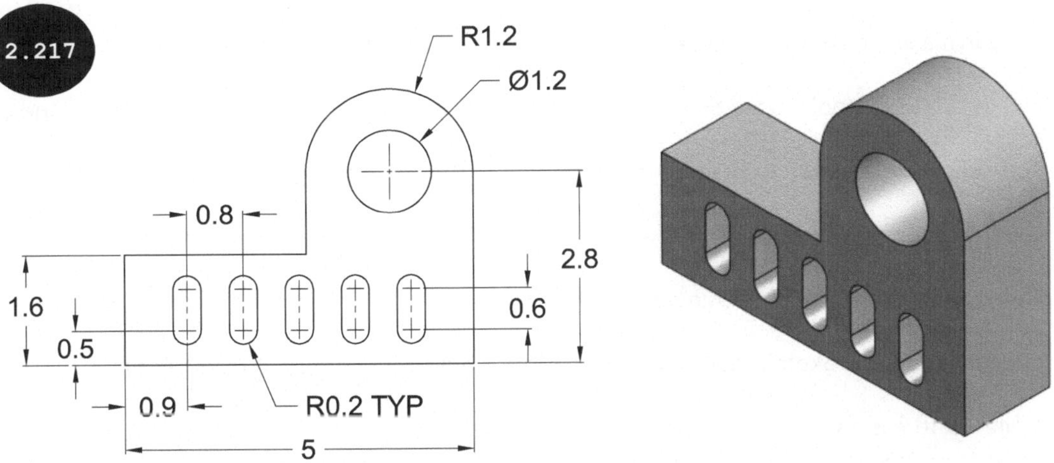

Hands-on Test Drive 3

Draw a sketch of the model shown in Figure 2.218. All dimensions are in mm.

2.218

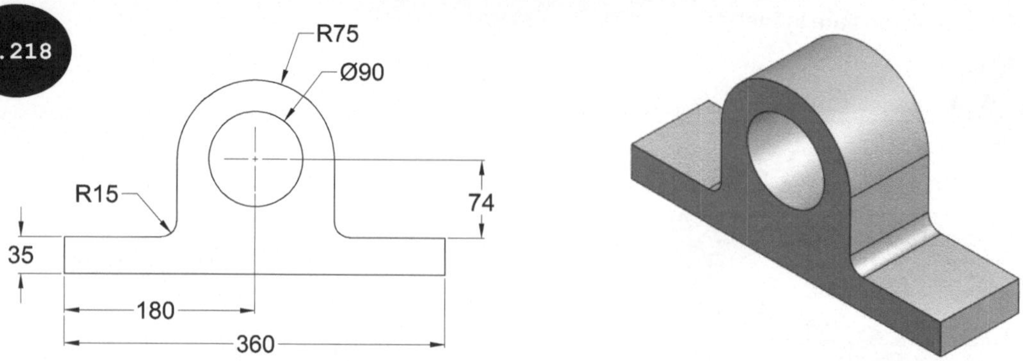

Summary

In this chapter, you learned how to start a new design in Onshape by creating a design document and setting units. You explored sketching basics, including drawing lines, rectangles, circles, ellipses, arcs, polygons, splines, and slots. You also practiced adding control points and creating construction geometries.

It also covered essential editing techniques like trimming, extending, offsetting, and filleting sketch entities and advanced methods such as mirroring, patterning, and transforming sketches. Finally, you learned to apply constraints and dimensions to ensure precision in your designs. These skills will help you create and modify sketches effectively in Onshape.

Questions

Complete and verify the following sentences:

- Features are divided into two main categories: _________ and _________.
- The _________ feature of a real-world component is typically sketch-based.
- You can make the sketching plane normal to the viewing direction by pressing the ________ key.
- The _________ tool is used to draw a rectangle by specifying two diagonally opposite corners.
- If the Rho value of a conic curve is less than 0.5 then the conic curve is an _______.
- The _______ tool is used to create a spline by defining control points along its length.
- The _______ tool is used to transform sketch entities by moving, rotating, and scaling them.
- You can access the **Sketch** toolbar within the Part Studio environment. (True/False)
- A fillet feature is a sketch-based feature. (True/False)

CHAPTER

3

Creating Extrude & Revolve Base Features

This chapter discusses the following topics:

- Creating an Extrude Feature
- Creating a Revolve Feature
- Navigating a 3D Model
- Manipulating View of a 3D Model
- Changing the Display Style of a Model

Once a sketch has been created, you can convert it into a 3D solid feature in the Part Studio environment of Onshape, see Figure 3.1.

3.1

In the Part Studio environment, you can transform a sketch into a 3D solid feature using the modeling tools available in the **Feature** toolbar, see Figure 3.2. To build a complete 3D solid model, each feature must be created sequentially using these tools, refer to Figure 3.3. The first feature created in a model is referred to as the base or parent feature.

3.2

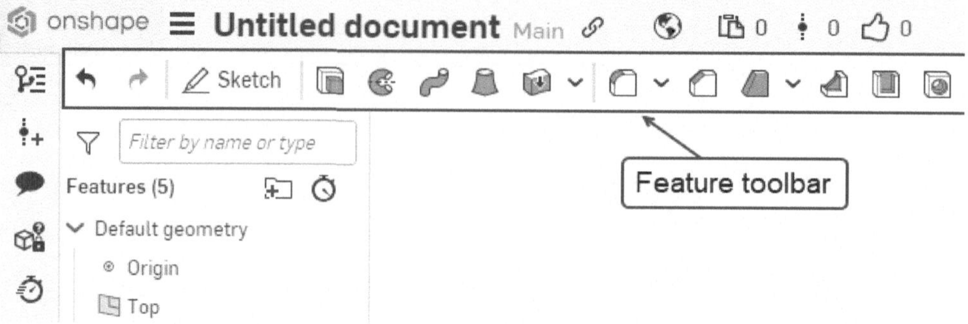

3.3

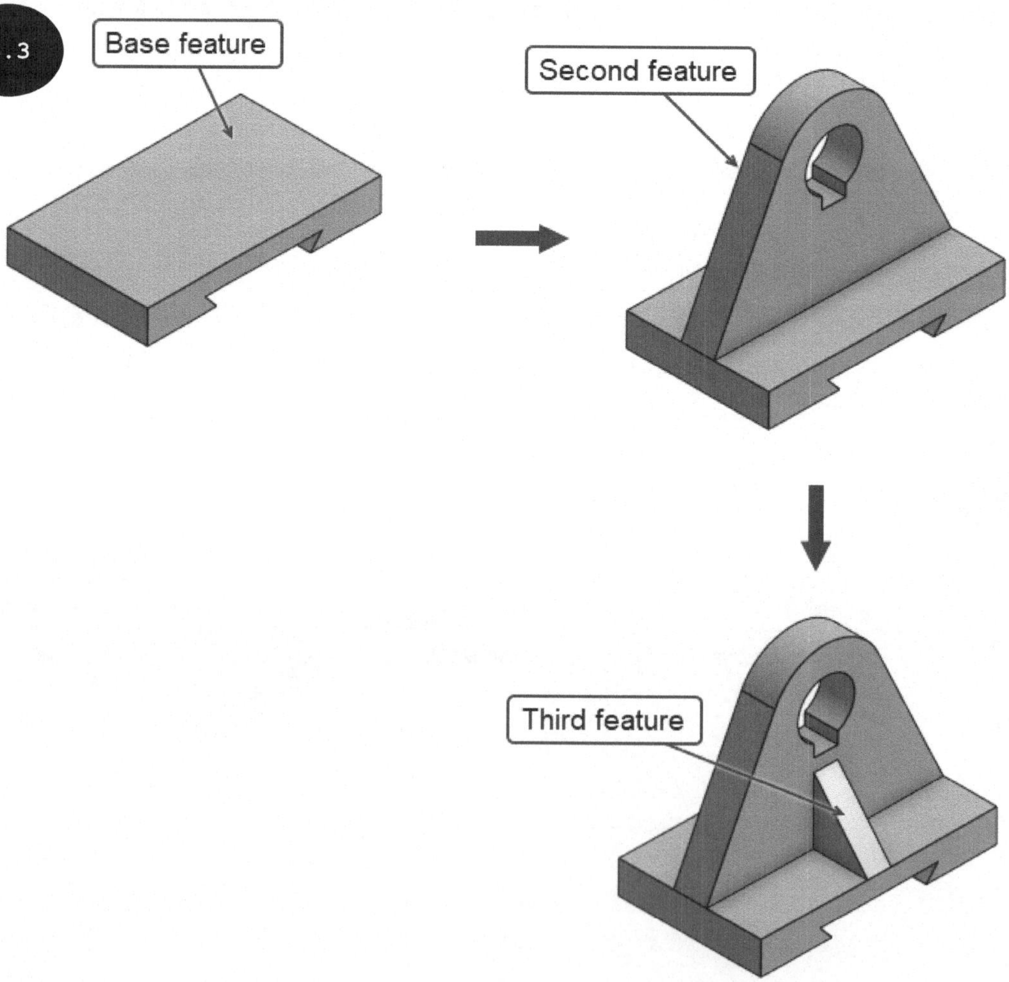

In Onshape, the base feature of a model can be created using various feature modeling tools like **Extrude, Revolve, Sweep**, and **Loft**. This chapter focuses on creating a base feature using the **Extrude** and **Revolve** tools, while the remaining tools will be covered in later chapters.

Creating an Extrude Feature

An extrude feature is created by adding or removing material perpendicular to the sketching plane. The sketch for the extrude feature defines its geometry, refer to Figure 3.4. Base extrude features are typically created by adding material. Figure 3.4 shows different extrude features created from their corresponding sketches. In Onshape, you can create an extrude feature using the **Extrude** tool. The method to create an extrude feature is discussed below:

3.4

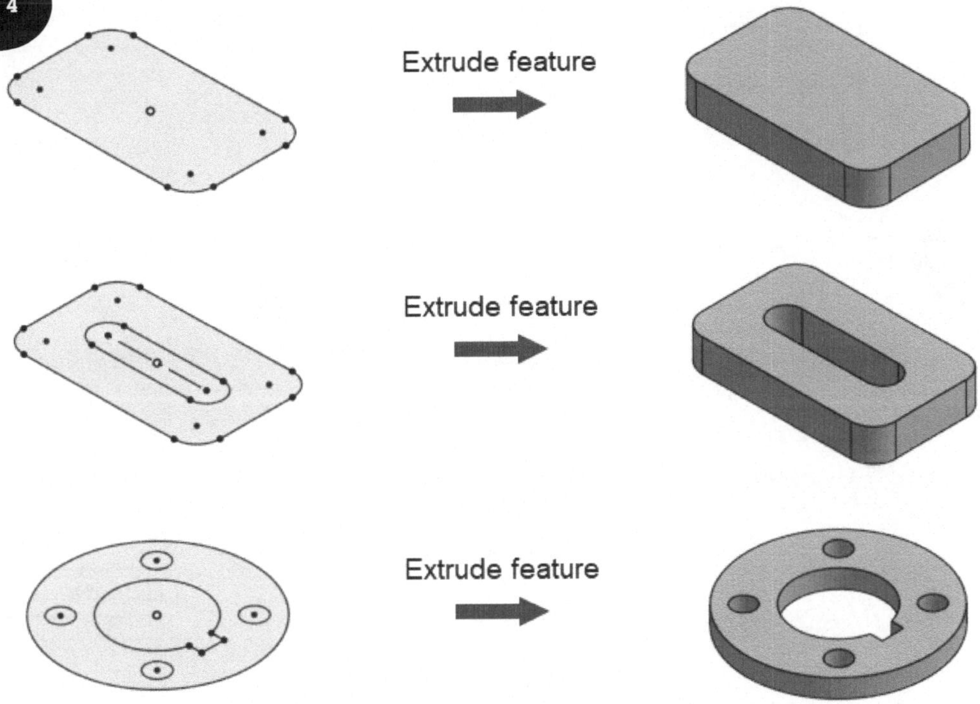

Note: It is evident from the above figure that the sketch for an extrude feature must be closed, containing one or more enclosed regions.

1. After creating a sketch using various sketching tools, click on the **Extrude** tool in the **Sketch** toolbar (see Figure 3.5) or press SHIFT + E. The **Extrude** dialog appears (see Figure 3.6), and the sketch is automatically selected. Consequently, a preview of an extruded feature with the default extrusion depth appears in the graphics area, see Figure 3.7. In this figure, a circular sketch created on the Top Plane is shown with the resulting extruded feature. Note that if the extrude feature preview does not appear, you will need to manually select the sketch region.

2. Press SHIFT + 7 to change the view orientation of the feature to isometric.

3.5

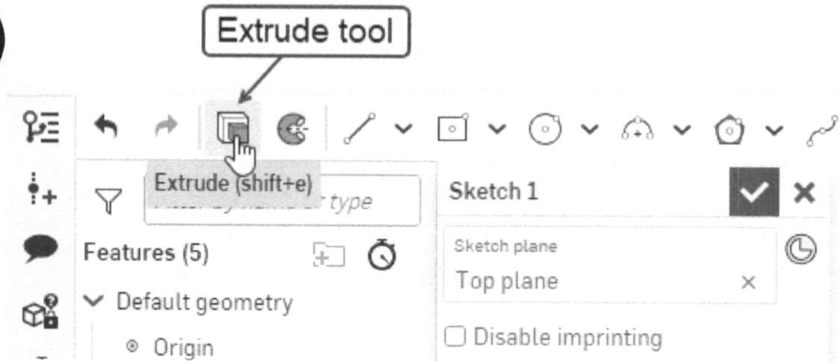

3.6

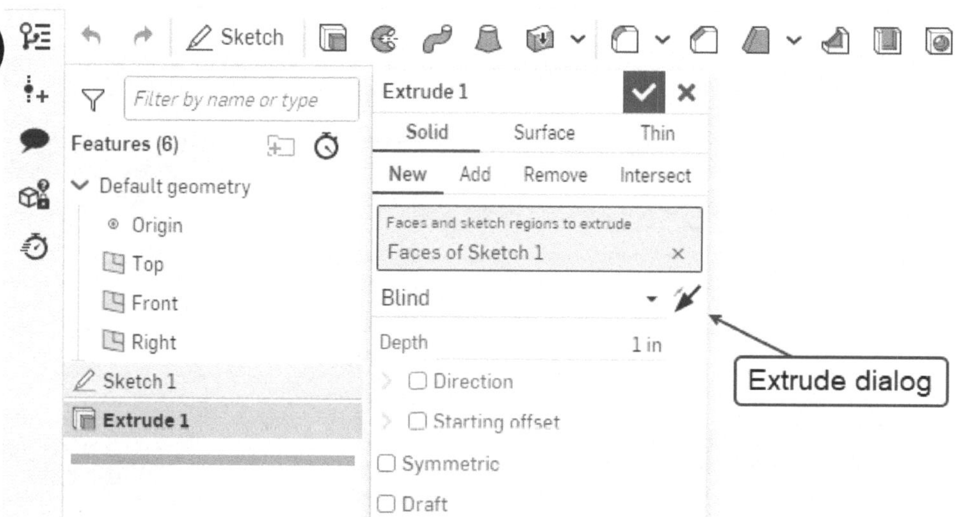

3.7

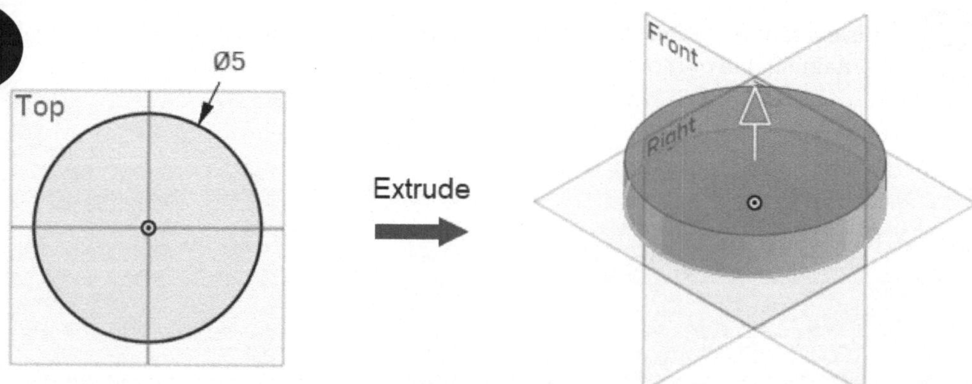

Note: After creating a sketch, if you have switched to the Part Studio environment by clicking the green checkmark in the **Sketch** dialog, you can then access the **Extrude** tool in the **Feature** toolbar to extrude the sketch.

The options in the **Extrude** dialog are used for specifying the required parameters to create an extrude feature and the same are discussed below:

Creation Type: By default, the **Solid** option is activated in the **Creation Type** area of the **Extrude** dialog, see Figure 3.8. Consequently, the preview of a solid extrude feature is shown by adding material to the sketch.

3.8

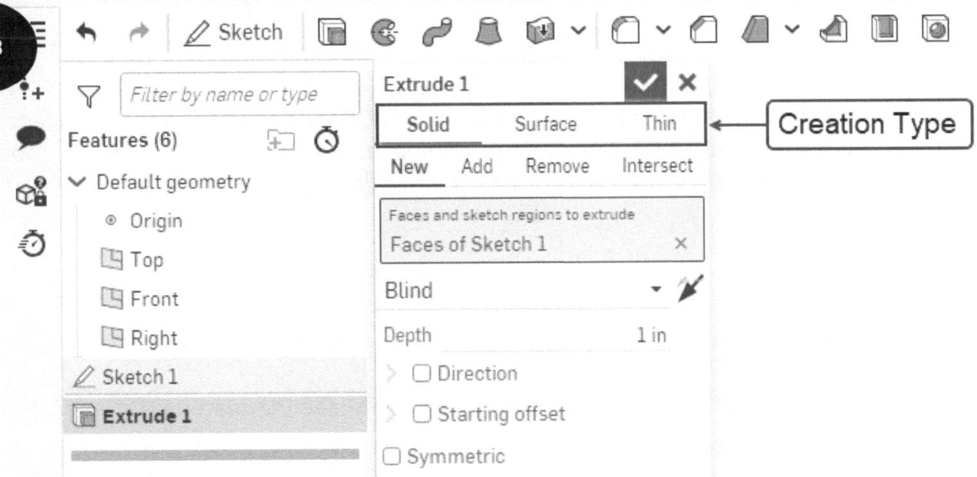

By activating the **Surface** or **Thin** option in the **Creation Type** area, you can create a surface feature or a thin solid feature, respectively. A surface feature has no thickness and does not have mass properties, whereas a thin solid feature has a uniform wall thickness. Figure 3.9 displays the preview of a surface feature, while Figure 3.10 shows a thin solid feature with a uniform thickness. The methods for creating both surface and thin features are the same as those used for creating a solid feature.

3.9

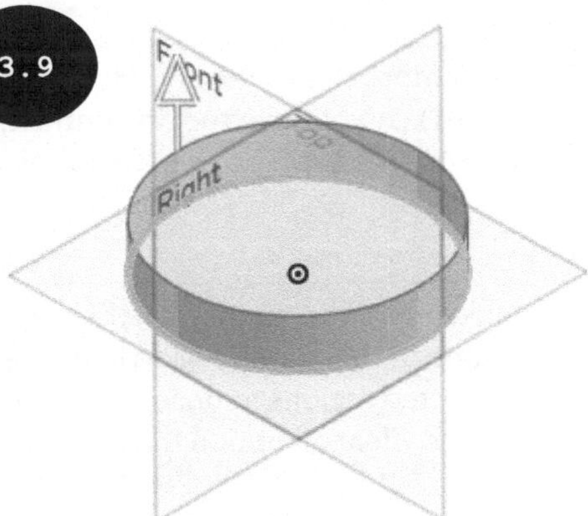

3.10

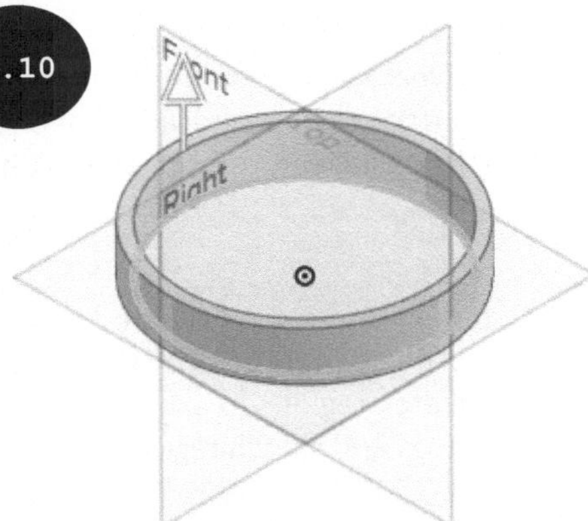

Operation Type: The Operation Type area includes four options: **New**, **Add**, **Cut**, and **Intersect**, refer to Figure 3.11.

3.11

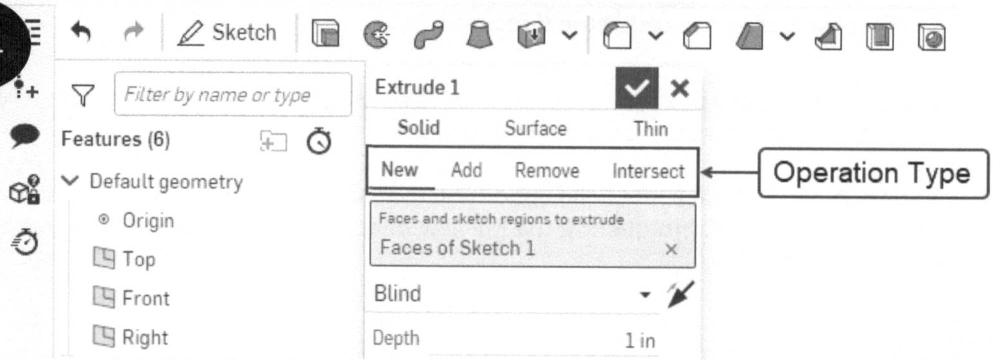

New: When creating the first or base feature of a model, the **New** option is automatically selected. This option creates a base extrude feature by adding material and forms a new part (body). After the base feature of a part is created, you can use the **Add**, **Remove**, and **Intersect** options to build its additional features.

Add: Extrudes the sketch by adding material, merging it with existing features.

Remove: Extrudes the sketch by subtracting material, creating a cut feature.

Intersect: Creates a feature by retaining only the intersecting material between the existing feature and the new one.

You will learn creating features using the **Add**, **Remove**, and **Intersect** options in later chapters.

Faces and sketch regions to extrude: The **Faces and Sketch Regions to Extrude** field in the **Extrude** dialog is used to select one or more sketch regions for extrusion. By default, this field is activated, so if the sketch contains a valid closed region, it will be automatically selected when the **Extrude** dialog is invoked. You can also manually select one or more sketch regions for extrusion by clicking on them individually.

Note: To create a solid feature, the sketch must contain one or more closed regions. However, for a surface feature, individual open sketch entities (curves) can be selected. In contrast, for a thin solid feature, both open sketch entities and closed regions can be used for extrusion.

Tip: To remove an existing selected region, click on the sketch region to be removed in the graphics area. Alternatively, click on the cross mark next to the name of the sketch region in the **Faces and sketch regions to extrude** field. To remove all the selected regions at once, right-click in the **Faces and sketch regions to extrude** field and select the **Clear all** option that appears.

End Type: The options in the **End Type** drop-down list allow you to specify the end condition or termination method for the extruded feature. The available options are discussed below:

Blind: The **Blind** option is selected by default and is used to extrude the sketch to a specified depth, which you can set in the **Depth** field of the **Extrude** dialog, see Figures 3.12 and 3.13.

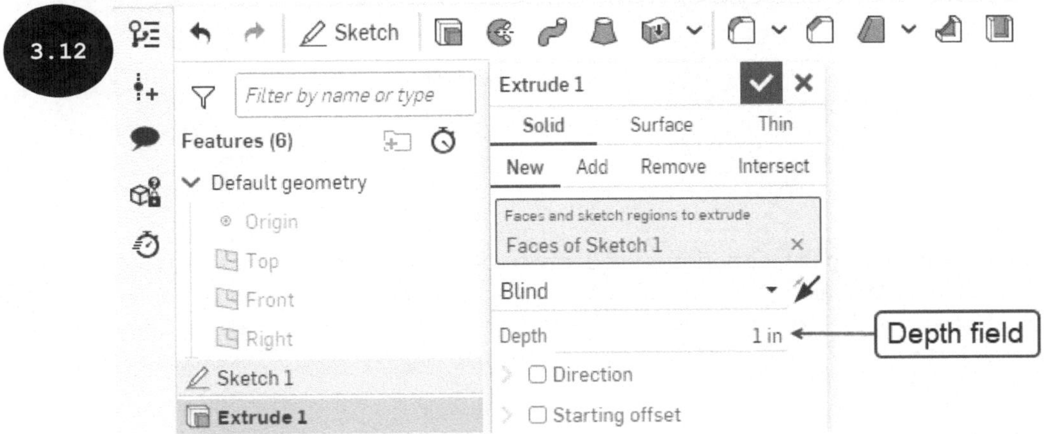

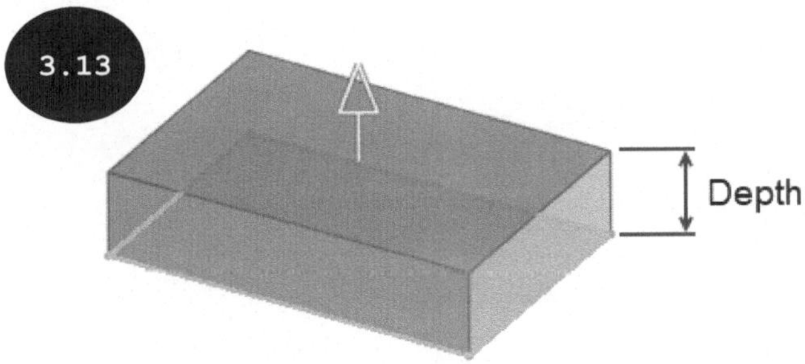

The remaining options in the **End Type** drop-down list: **Up to Next**, **Up to face**, **Up to part**, **Up to vertex**, and **Through all** are particularly useful when creating subsequent features in a part (model). These options may not work when creating a base feature of a part. In later chapters, you will learn how to use these options to build a multi-feature part. For now, each option is discussed below.

Up to next: The **Up to next** option is used to extrude the sketch up to its next or nearest intersecting face of an existing feature along the direction of extrusion. Figure 3.14 shows a sketch (circle) and the preview of a resultant extrude feature up to its next intersection. If needed, you can reverse the direction of extrusion to other sides of the sketching plane by clicking on the **Opposite direction** button available next to the **End Type** drop-down list.

3.14

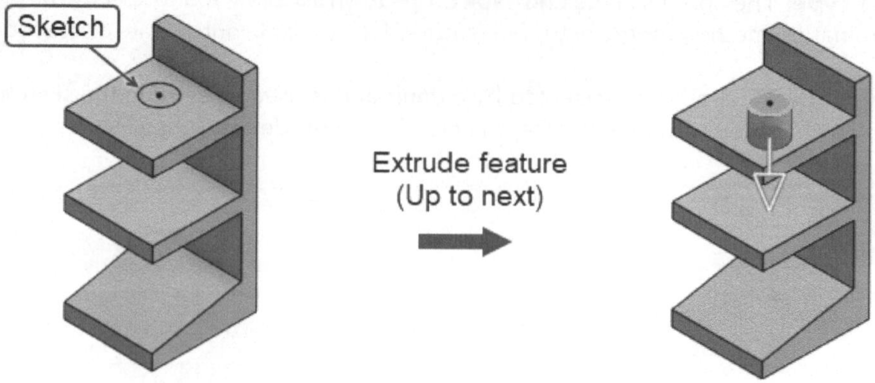

Up to face: The **Up to face** option is used to extrude the sketch up to a selected face of an existing feature or a plane along the direction of extrusion. When you select this option, the **Up to face** field appears in the **Extrude** dialog (see Figure 3.15) and is activated, by default. Consequently, you can select a face of an existing feature or a plane up to which you would like to extrude the sketch, see Figure 3.16.

3.15

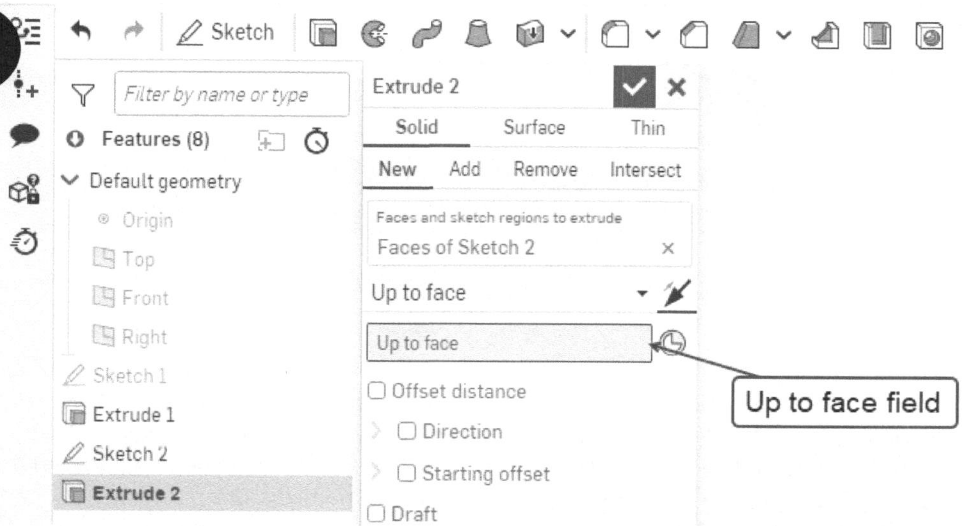

3.16

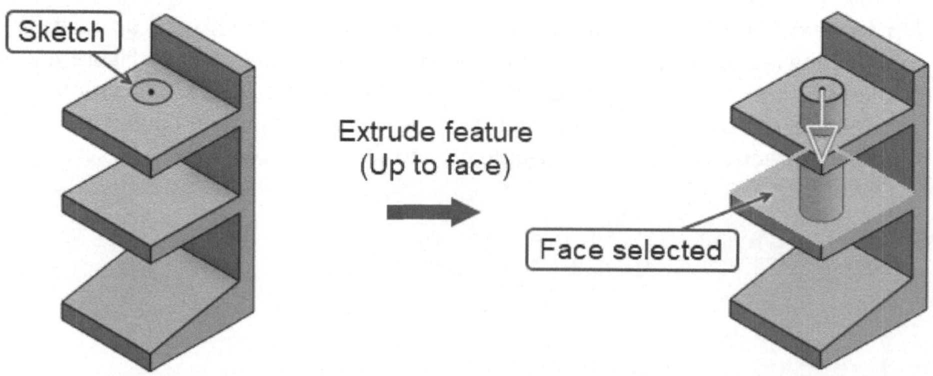

Up to part: The **Up to part** option is used to extrude the sketch up to a selected part or a surface. When you select this option, the **Up to surface or part** field appears in the **Extrude** dialog. Consequently, you can select an existing available part or a surface up to which you would like to extrude the sketch.

Tip: In Onshape, you can create a multi-body design by using the **New** option of the **Extrude** dialog, which has been discussed earlier.

Up to vertex: The **Up to vertex** option is used to extrude the sketch up to a selected vertex (point) or mate connector. When you select this option, the **Up to vertex or mate connector** field appears in the **Extrude** dialog. Consequently, you can select a vertex (point) or define a mate connector up to which you would like to extrude the sketch, see Figure 3.17. In this figure, the preview an extrude feature appears up to a selected vertex.

3.17

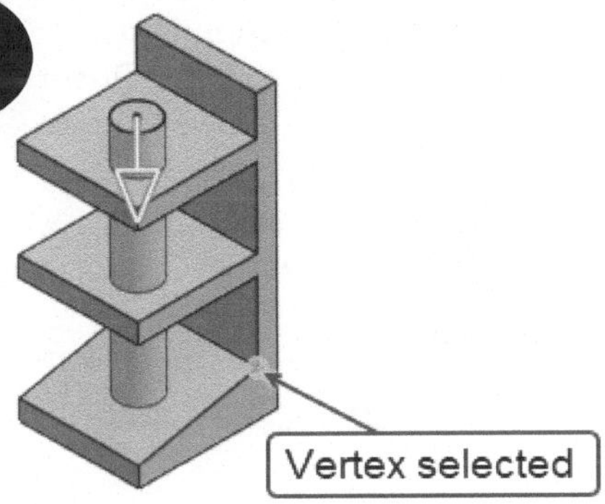

To define a mate connector, click the **Select mate connector** button next to the **Up to vertex or mate connector** field or press CTRL + M. Then, move your cursor over a face or edge of the model. The face or edge highlights, revealing all of its snap points, see Figure 3.18. Also, the mate connector appears attached to the cursor tip on the highlighted face or edge, as illustrated. Now, position the mate connector on the desired snap point of the highlighted face or edge by clicking the left mouse button to extrude the sketch up to the defined mate connector, see Figure 3.19.

3.18

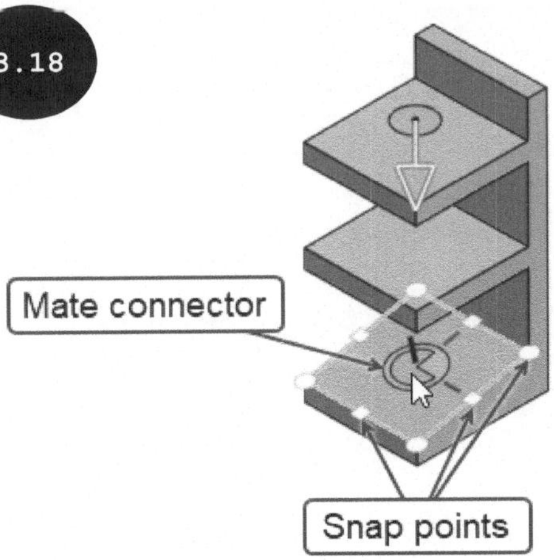

3.19

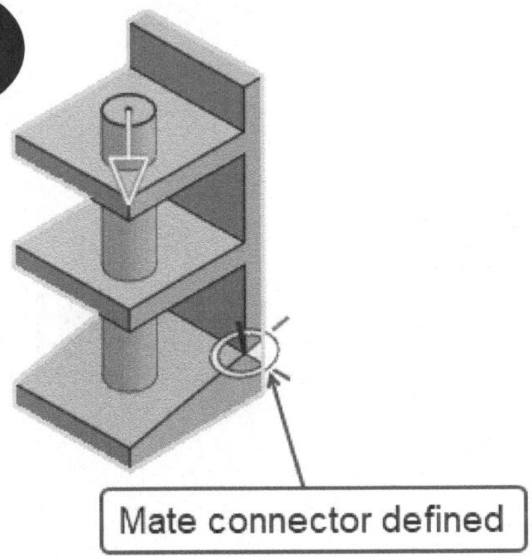

Note: Sometimes, when you move the cursor toward a snap point on a highlighted face or edge to define the position of the mate connector, snap points on other faces or edges might get highlighted. To avoid this, you can lock the face or edge from which you want to select the snap point by pressing the SHIFT key when the snap points appear.

Through all: The **Through all** option is used to extrude the sketch through all the length of the model in the extrusion direction. If needed, you can reverse the direction of extrusion to other sides of the sketching plane by clicking on the **Opposite direction** button available next to the **End Type** drop-down list.

Offset distance: The **Offset distance** check box is used to terminate an extrusion at a specified offset distance from the selected geometry, such as a face, part, or vertex. This check box is available when the **Up to next**, **Up to face**, **Up to part**, or **Up to vertex** option is selected in the **End Type** drop-down list to define the extrusion's end condition, see Figure 3.20. In this figure, the **Up to face** option is selected in the **End Type** drop-down list. When the **Offset distance** checkbox is selected, the **Offset distance** field appears, allowing you to enter the desired offset value. Figure 3.21 shows a preview of an extruded feature at an offset distance from a selected face of the model.

3.20

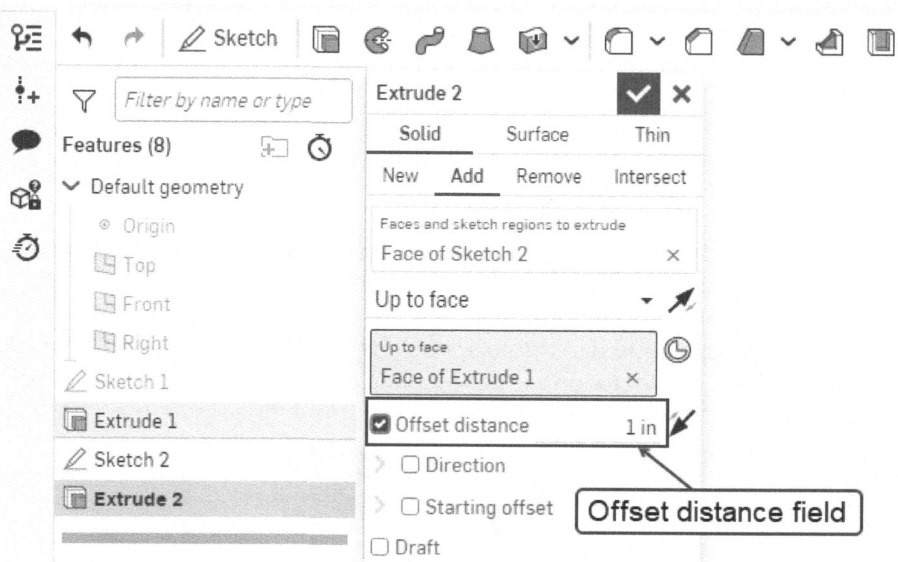

3.21

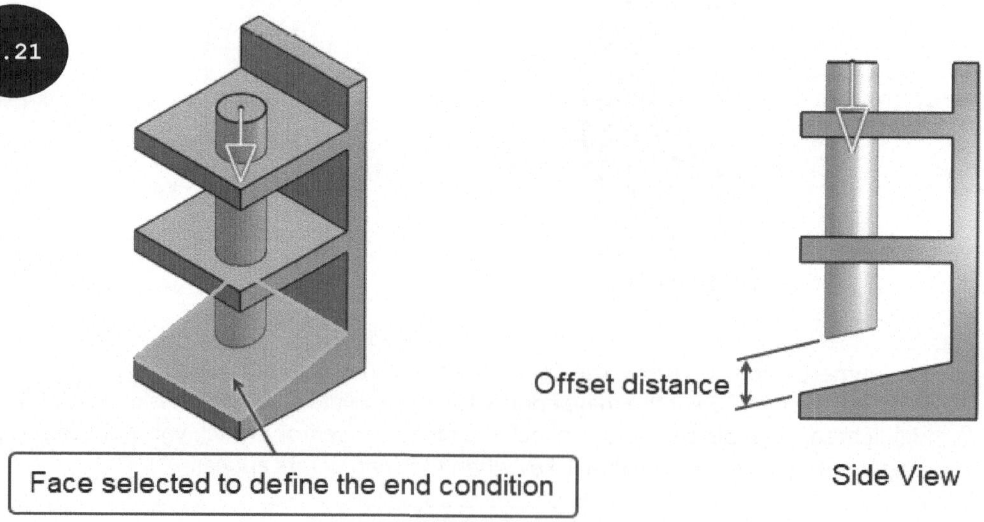

Starting offset: The **Starting offset** check box allows you to begin an extrusion at a specified offset distance from the sketching plane. When this check box is selected, the **Starting Offset Bound** drop-down list appears, with the default option set to **Blind**, see Figure 3.22. This enables you to enter the desired offset value in the **Depth** field that appears below. Figure 3.23 shows a front-view preview of an extruded feature with an offset distance defining its starting position. To reverse the offset direction to the opposite side of the sketching plane, you can click the **Opposite Direction** button located next to the **Depth** field.

3.22

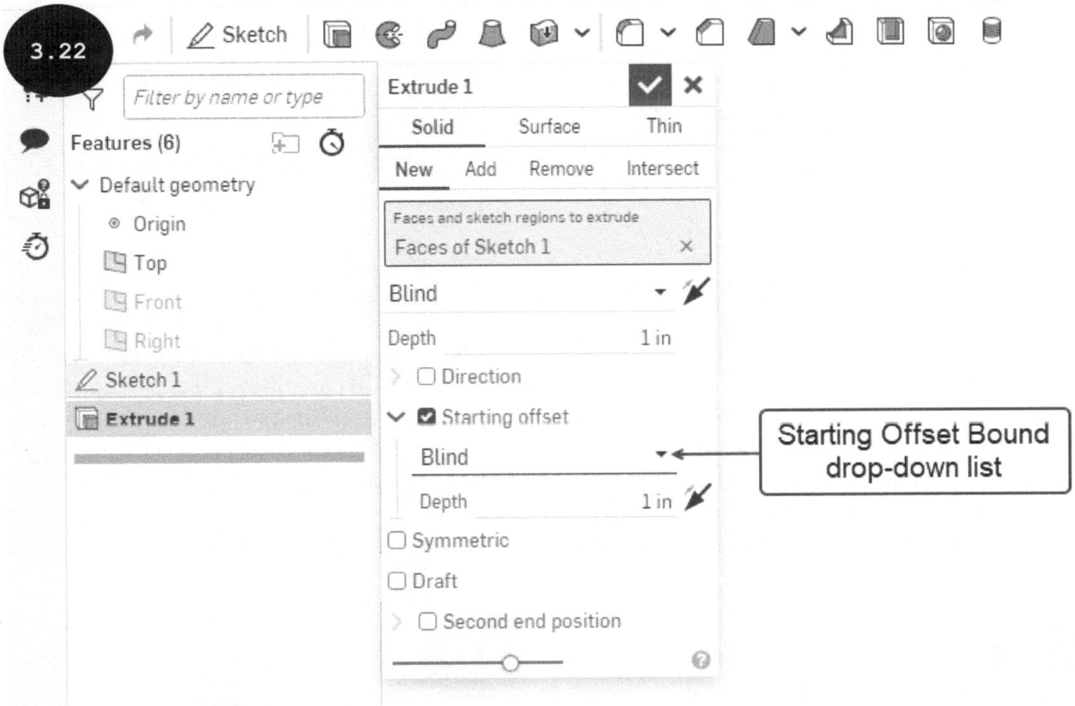

3.23

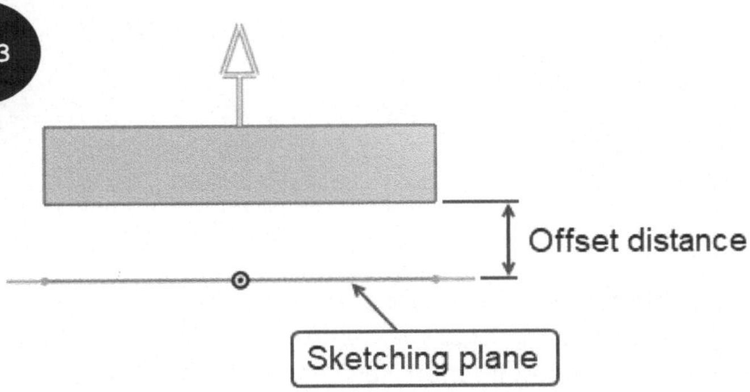

The **Entity** option in the **Starting Offset Bound** drop-down list allows you to begin an extrusion from a selected entity, such as a face, edge, vertex, or plane. Once the **Entity** option is selected, the **Entity** field appears, enabling you to select the desired entity to start the extrusion. This option is particularly useful when creating subsequent features in a part (model). It may not be useful when creating the base feature.

Symmetric: The **Symmetric** check box allows you to extrude a sketch symmetrically on both sides of the sketching plane. When selected, the depth specified in the **Depth** field is divided equally between both sides, resulting in a symmetrically extruded feature, see Figure 3.24. For example, if you enter a depth of 2 inches in the **Depth** field, the extrusion will add 1 inch of material to each side of the sketching plane.

3.24

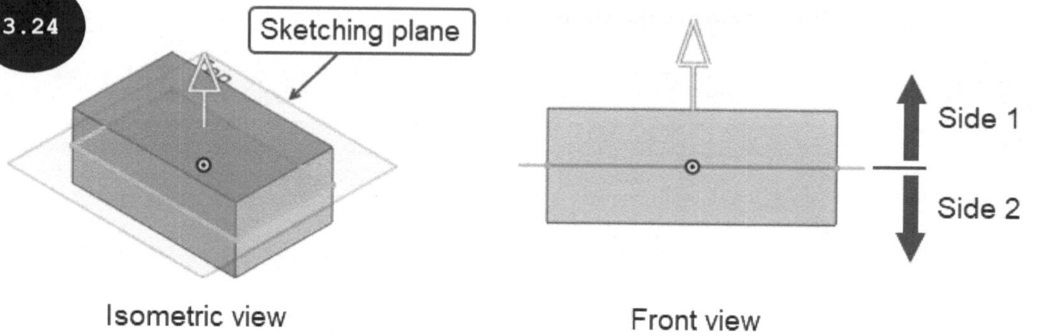

Draft: The **Draft** check box is used to apply a draft or taper to an extruded feature. When selected, the **Draft Angle** field appears with a default value. You can enter the desired draft angle in this field and press ENTER to apply the change. The preview of the extruded feature, including the draft angle along the extrusion direction, appears in the graphics area, see Figure 3.25. To reverse the draft angle direction from outward to inward or vice versa, click the **Opposite Direction** button next to the **Draft Angle** field. Figure 3.25 shows the preview of an extruded feature with an outward draft angle direction, while Figure 3.26 shows the preview with an inward draft angle direction.

3.25

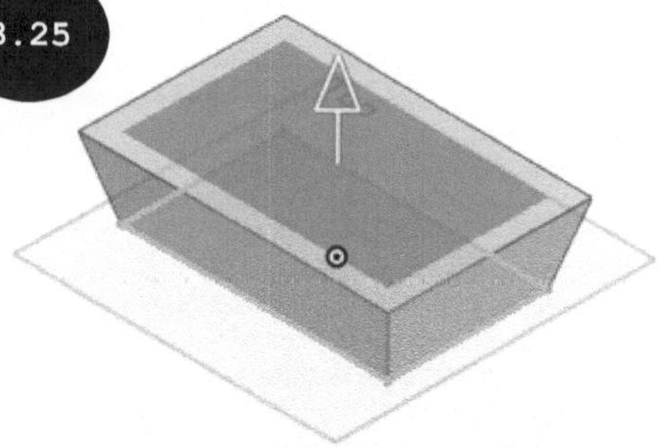

3.26

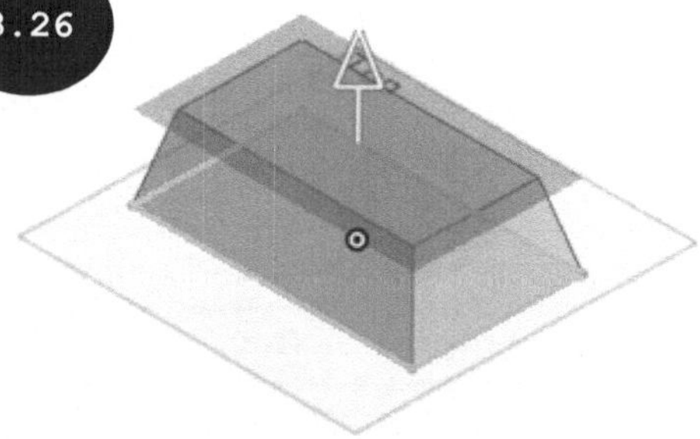

Direction: The **Direction** check box is used to define the extrusion direction along a linear sketch entity, a linear edge, or an axis. By default, the extrusion direction is normal to the sketching plane. To specify a different extrusion direction, select the **Direction** checkbox to display the **Extrude Direction** field, then select a linear sketch entity, linear edge, or axis in the graphics area to set the desired direction of extrusion. Figure 3.27 shows a sketch to be extruded with a linear sketch line created on a different plane to define the direction of extrusion. Figure 3.28 displays a preview of the resulting extruded feature.

3.27

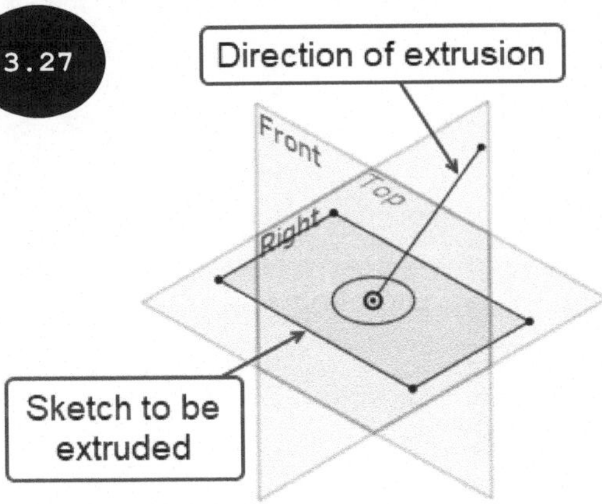

3.28

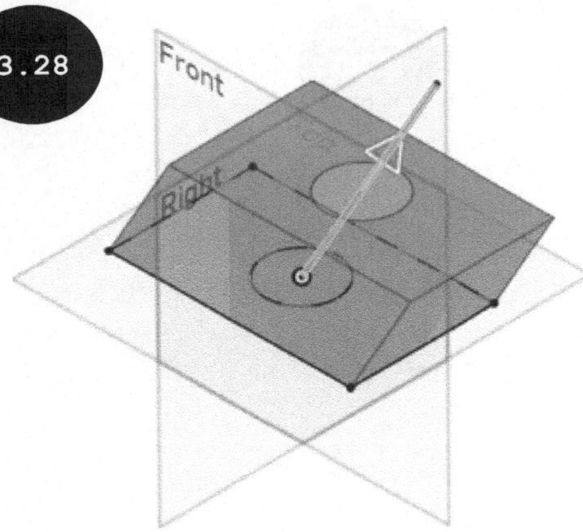

Second end position: The **Second end position** check box allows you to define the end condition or termination of the extrusion in the opposite direction of the sketching plane. By default, this option is unchecked, meaning extrusion occurs only in one direction of the sketching plane. To apply an extrusion with a different depth in the second direction, select the **Second end position** check box, then choose the appropriate option from the **End Type** drop-down list that appears, see Figure 3.29. The options in this list for defining the extrusion depth in the second direction are the same as those previously discussed. Figure 3.30 shows a preview of an extruded feature with different depths and draft angles on both sides of the sketching plane.

3.29

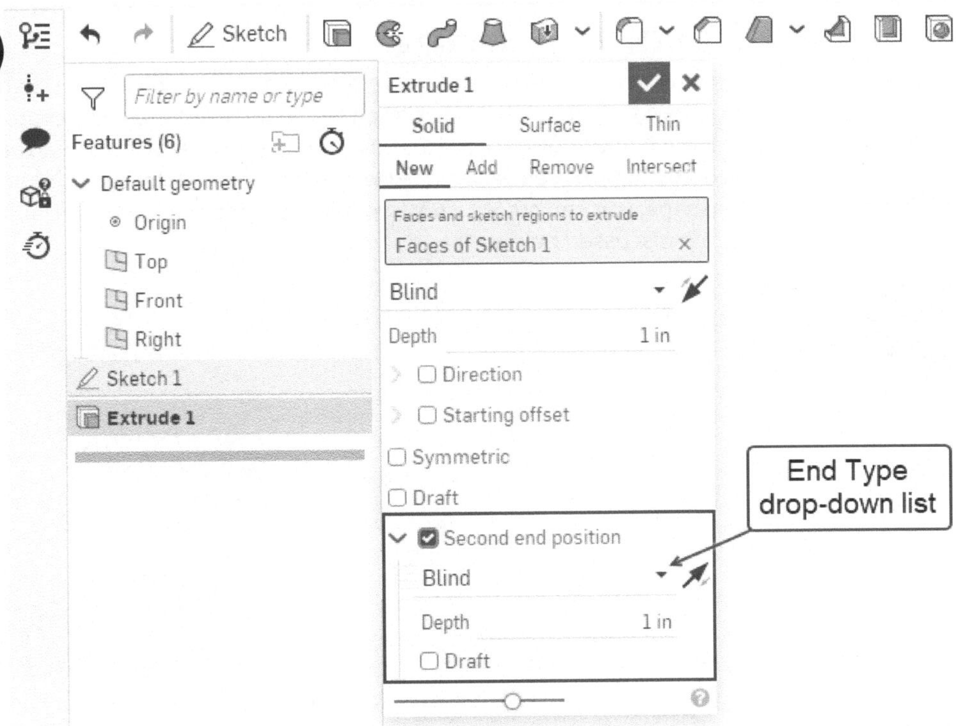

3.30

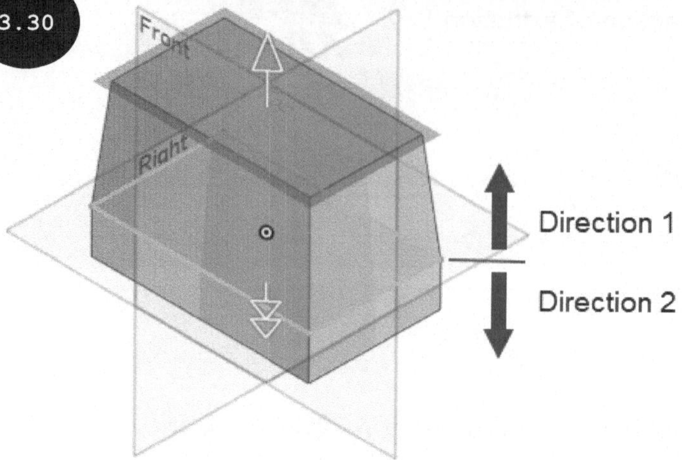

3. Specify the required parameters for creating the extrude feature in the **Extrude** dialog, as discussed above.

4. After specifying all the necessary parameters, click the green checkmark ✓ in the **Extrude** dialog box to confirm the creation of the extrude feature and close the dialog.

Creating a Revolve Feature

A revolve feature is created by adding or removing material through the revolving of a sketch around a central axis, as shown in Figure 3.31. In this figure, the sketch region revolved 270 degrees around the axis to create the revolve feature. It is important to note that the sketch being revolved should be positioned on either side of the axis of revolution (central axis). Also, the base revolve feature is typically created by adding material. In Onshape, you can create a revolve feature using the **Revolve** tool. The method to create a revolve feature is discussed below:

3.31

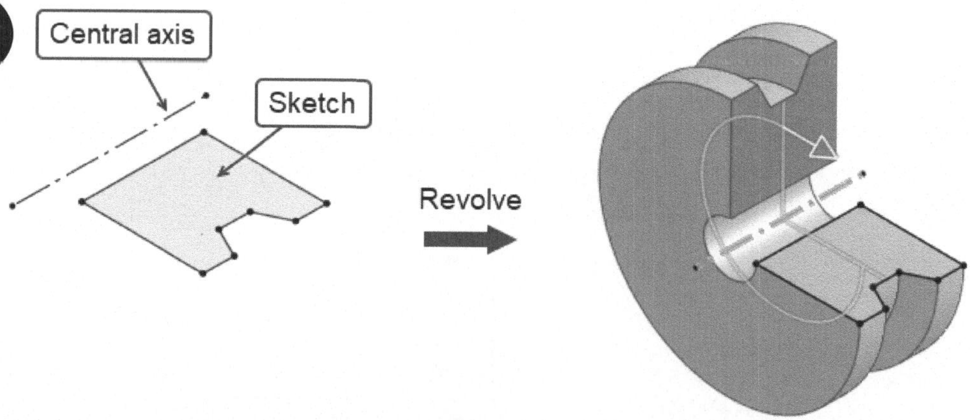

Note: The sketch a revolve feature must be a closed sketch, containing one or more enclosed regions.

1. After creating a sketch with a central axis, click on the **Revolve** tool in the **Sketch** toolbar, see Figure 3.32. The **Revolve** dialog appears, see Figure 3.33. Also, all closed regions in the sketch are automatically selected, see Figure 3.34. This sketch contains only one closed region.

3.32

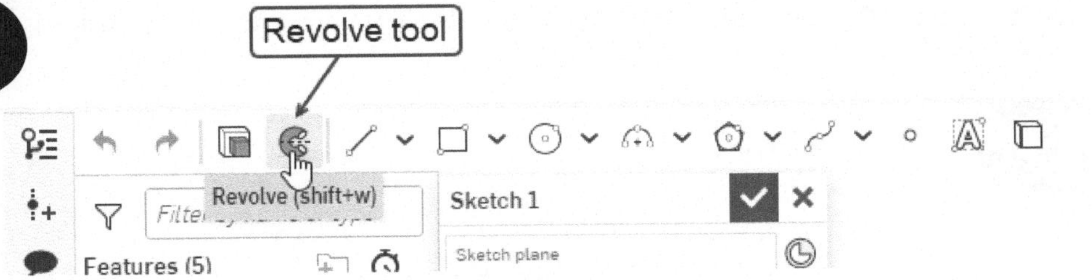

3.33

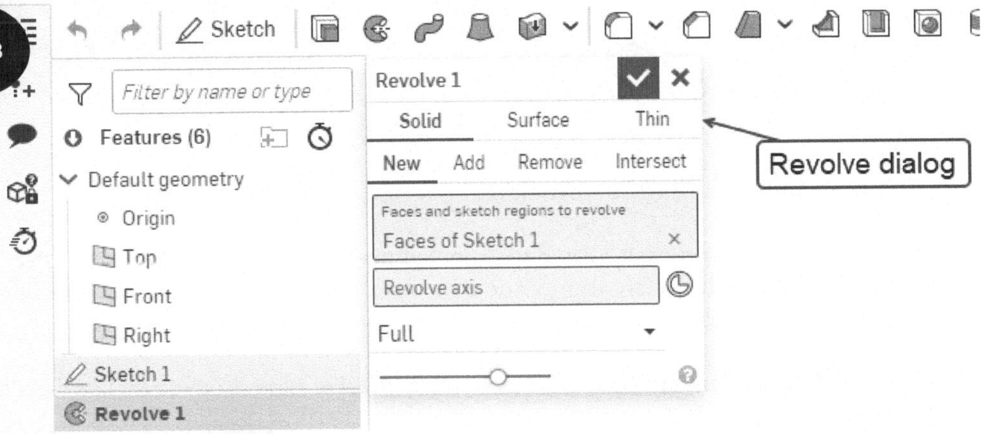

3.34

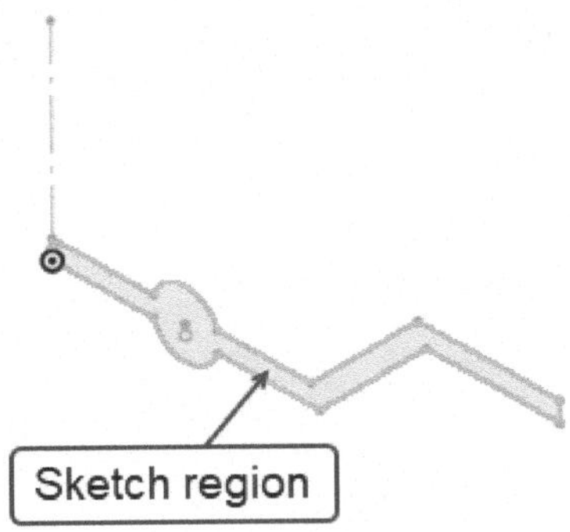

Tip: You can clear a selected sketch region or include a new one by clicking the left mouse button on the desired region to remove it from the selection or add it.

Note: After creating a sketch, if you have switched to the Part Studio environment by clicking the green checkmark ✓ in the **Sketch** dialog, you can then access the **Revolve** tool in the **Feature** toolbar. You may then need to manually select the sketch regions to be revolved by clicking on them with the left mouse button.

Now, you need to select an axis of revolution.

2. Click on the **Revolve axis** field in the **Revolve** dialog and then select a line, construction line, or a linear edge as the axis of revolution. A preview of a revolve feature appears by revolving the sketch around the selected axis, see Figure 3.35. In this figure, a construction line is selected as the axis of revolution.

3.35

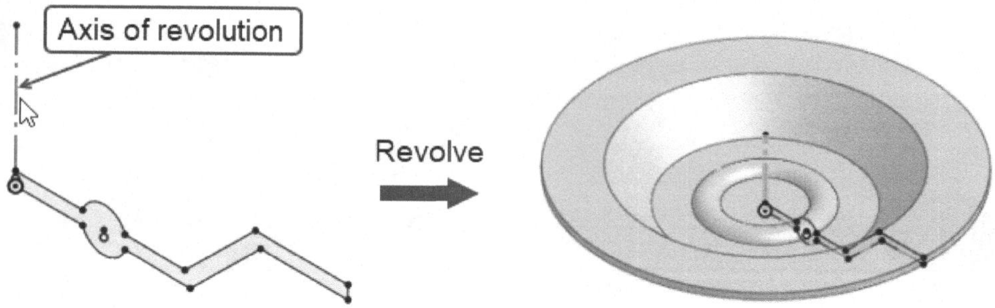

Now, you can define the angle of revolution.

3. Select the desired option (**Full**, **One direction**, **Symmetric**, or **Two directions**) from the **Revolve type** drop-down list to specify the method for revolving the sketch around the selected axis. These options are discussed below:

Full: By default, the **Full** option is selected in the **Revolve type** drop-down list. This causes the sketch to revolve a full 360 degrees around the selected axis of revolution, refer to Figure 3.35.

One Direction: The **One direction** option is used to revolve the sketch by a specified angle on one side of the sketching plane around the axis. When this option is selected, the **Revolve angle** field appears below, see Figure 3.36. In this field, you can enter the desired angle for revolving the sketch around the axis on one side of the sketching plane. If needed, you can reverse the rotational direction to the other side of the sketching plane by clicking the **Opposite direction** button next to the **Revolve Type** drop-down list.

3.36

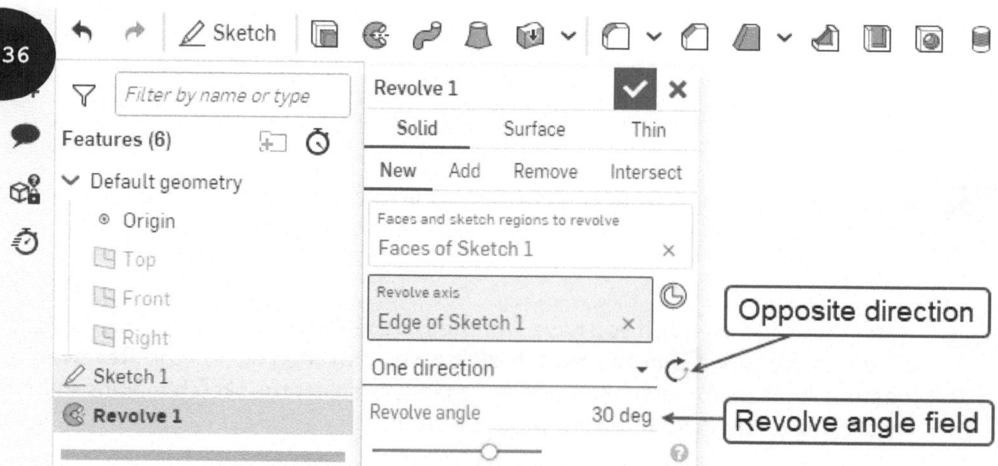

Figure 3.37 shows the preview of a revolve feautre with 270 degrees angle of revoution on one side of the sketching plane.

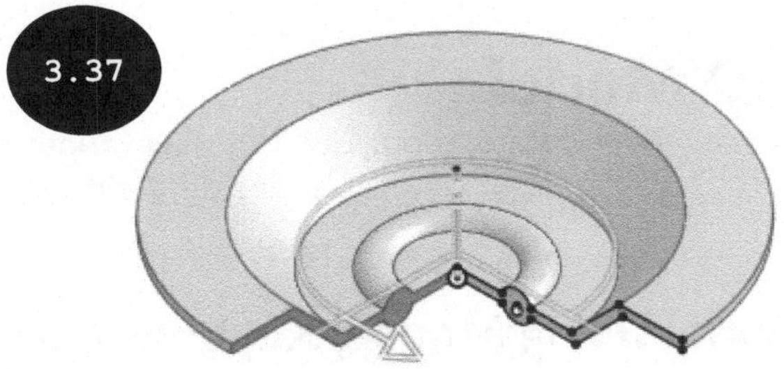

Symmetric: The **Symmetric** option is used to revolve the sketch symmetrically on both sides of the sketching plane, see Figure 3.38. When this option is selected, the angle value specified in the **Revolve Angle** field is divided equally between both sides, resulting in a symmetrically revolved feature.

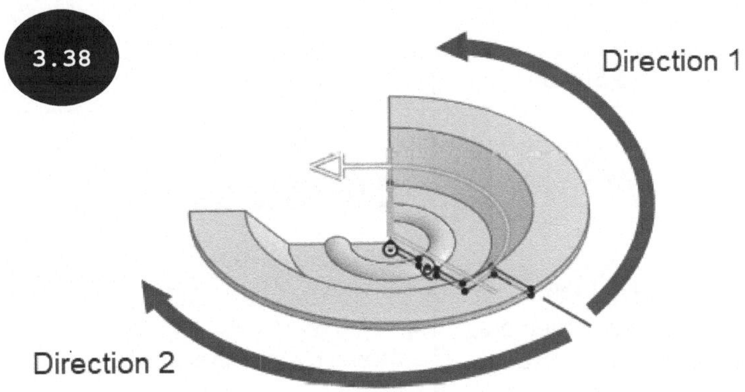

Two directions: The **Two directions** option is used to revolve the sketch on both sides of the sketching plane with different angles of revolution. When this option is selected, the **Revolve angle** and **Second revolve angle** fields appear below. In these fields, you can enter the different angles for revolving the sketch on each side of the sketching plane, as required. Figure 3.39 shows a preview of a revolve feature with a 90-degree angle of revolution on one side (Direction 1) and a -30-degree angle on the other side (Direction 2) of the sketching plane.

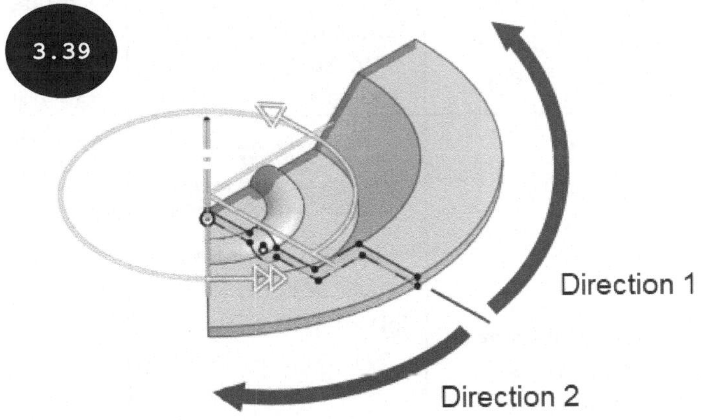

4. After specifying the necessary parameters, click the green checkmark ✓ in the **Revolve** dialog box to confirm the creation of the revolve feature and close the dialog.

Navigating a 3D Model

In Onshape, you can navigate a model (rotate, zoom, or pan) using various methods such as mouse buttons, keyboard keys, touchpad gestures, or view tools. The different methods for navigating a 3D model are discussed next.

Navigating a 3D Model Using Mouse, Keyboard, and Touchpad

The methods for rotating, zooming, and panning a 3D model using mouse buttons, keyboard keys, and touchpad gestures are detailed below:

Rotating a 3D Model

The table below outlines various methods for rotating a 3D model using mouse buttons, keyboard keys, and touchpad gestures.

<table>
<tr><th></th><th>Mouse Buttons</th><th>keyboard</th><th>Touchpad</th></tr>
<tr><td rowspan="3">3D Rotate</td><td>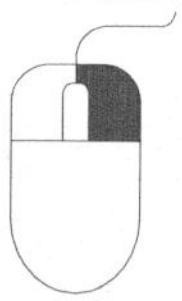
Press and hold the right mouse button, then drag the cursor to rotate the model freely.</td><td>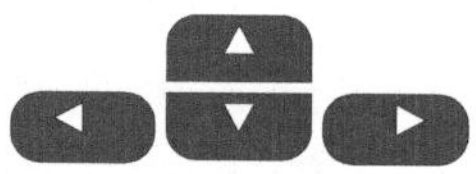
Press the keyboard's up, down, left, or right arrow keys to rotate the model by 15 degrees.</td><td rowspan="3">
Press and hold the right mouse button, then drag a finger on the touchpad to rotate the model freely.

For Apple Mac OS, tap two fingers on the touchpad and drag to rotate the model.

For iOS & Android OS, tap a single finger on the touchpad and drag to rotate the model.</td></tr>
<tr><td>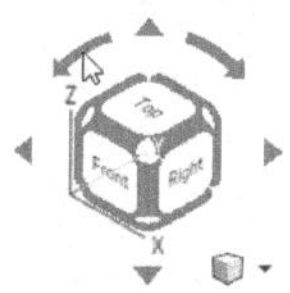
Click the View Cube arrows with the left mouse button to rotate the model in 15-degree increments.</td><td>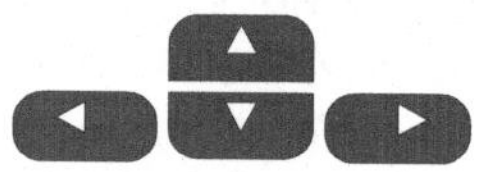
Hold the SHIFT key and press the keyboard's up, down, left, or right arrow keys to rotate the model in 5-degree increments.</td></tr>
<tr><td>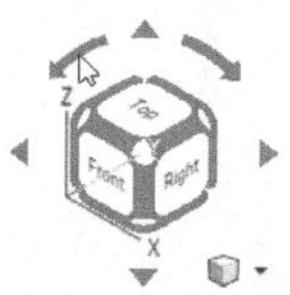
Hold the SHIFT key and click the View Cube arrows to rotate the model in 5-degree increments.</td><td>
Press and hold the keyboard's up, down, left, or right arrow keys to rotate the model continuously.</td></tr>
</table>

Zooming In/Out on a 3D Model

The table below outlines different methods for zooming in or out of a 3D model using mouse buttons, keyboard keys, and touchpad gestures.

	Mouse Buttons	keyboard	Touchpad
Zoom In / Out	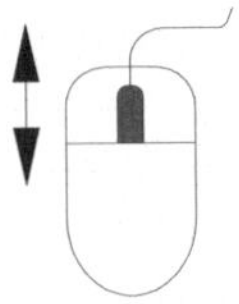 Scroll the middle mouse button (wheel) down to zoom out and up to zoom in on the model.	 Press the Z key to zoom out, and press SHIFT + Z to zoom in on the model.	 Tap two fingers on the touchpad and drag up to zoom out, and drag down to zoom in on the model.

Panning/Moving a 3D Model

The table below outlines different methods for panning or moving a 3D model using mouse buttons, keyboard keys, and touchpad gestures.

	Mouse Buttons	keyboard	Touchpad
Pan	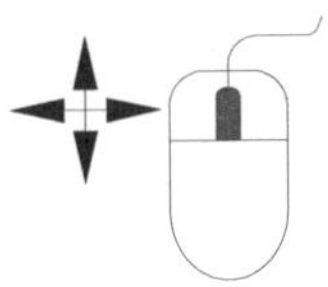 Press and hold the middle mouse button, then drag the cursor to move or pan the model. 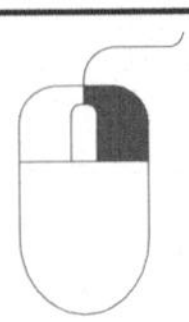 Press and hold the CTRL key, then drag the right mouse button to pan the model.	 Hold the CTRL and SHIFT keys, then press the keyboard's up, down, left, or right arrow keys to pan the model.	 Hold the CTRL key and the right mouse button, then drag a finger on the touchpad to pan the model. For Apple Mac OS, hold the CTRL key, then tap with two fingers on the touchpad and drag to pan the model. For iOS & Android OS, tap two fingers on the touchpad and drag to pan the model.

Navigating a 3D Model Using View Tools

The different view tools for navigating a 3D model are discussed below:

Zoom to fit

The **Zoom to fit** tool adjusts the view of the model so that all objects or bodies in the current document fit entirely within the graphics area. To access this tool, right-click in the graphics area and select the **Zoom to fit** tool from the shortcut menu (see Figure 3.40) or pres the F key. Alternatively, click on the small cube located at the top right corner, just below the View Cube, and choose the **Zoom to fit** tool from the menu that appears, see Figure 3.41. You can also double-click the middle mouse button to fit the view entirely within the graphics area.

3.40

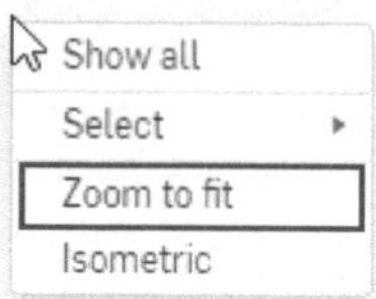

3.41

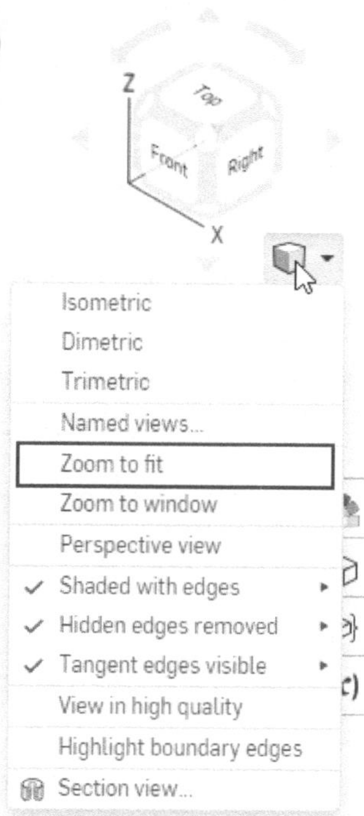

Zoom to window

The **Zoom to window** tool is used to zoom in on a specific portion or area of a model within the graphics area. To access this tool, click on the small cube located at the top right corner, just below the View Cube, and select the **Zoom to window** tool from the menu that appears, refer to Figure 3.41. Next, define a rectangular window by dragging the cursor around the portion or area of the model to be zoomed. The area inside the defined window gets enlarged. You can also access this tool by pressing the W key.

Zoom to selection

The **Zoom to selection** tool is used to zoom in on one or more selected geometries within the graphics area. To do so, select a geometry, such as a face, edge, or vertex, and then right-click to open the shortcut menu. From there, choose the **Zoom to selection** option. The selected geometry is zoomed in and displayed prominently in the graphics area.

Manipulating View of a 3D Model

Manipulating the view orientation of a 3D model is important for reviewing it from various perspectives and angles. In Onshape, you can adjust the view of a 3D model to standard orientations, including front, back, top, right, left, bottom, and trimetric, using the View Cube and other tools. Various methods for manipulating the views of a model are discussed next.

Standard Plane View

To change the view of a model to one of the standard plane views (Front, Back, Top, Right, Left, Bottom), click on the corresponding side face of the View Cube.

Note: The View Cube, located at the upper right corner of the graphics area (see Figure 3.42), is a tool for adjusting the view of a 3D model in Onshape. It allows you to toggle between standard plane views (Front, Back, Top, Right, Left, Bottom) and trimetric views.

3.42

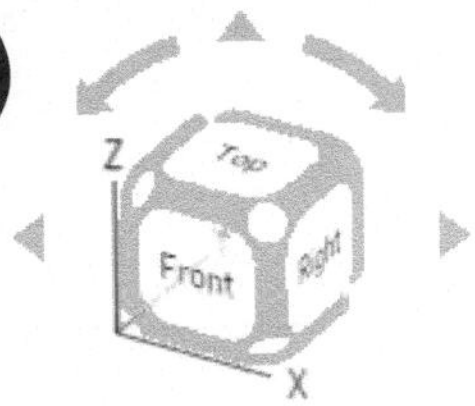

Trimetric View

To change the view of a model to a trimetric view, click on the corresponding corner of the View Cube, see Figure 3.43. Alternatively, click on the small cube located at the top right corner, just below the View Cube, and choose the **Trimetric** tool from the menu that appears, see Figure 3.44.

3.43

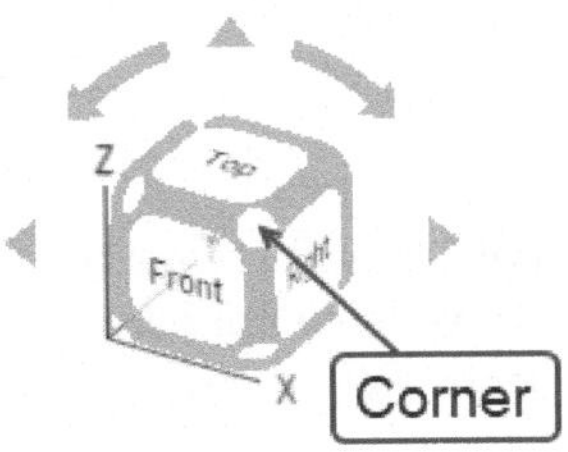

3.44

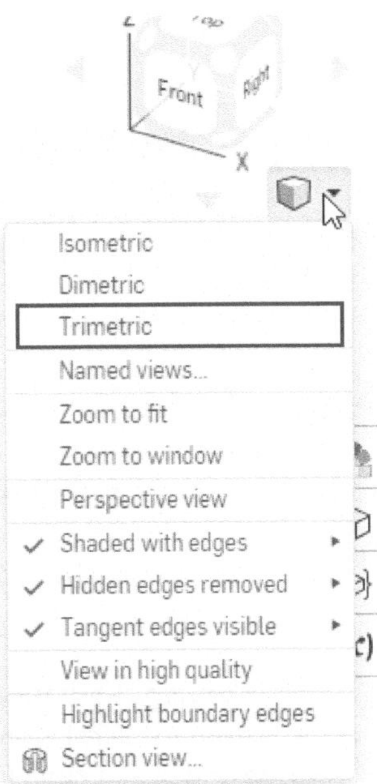

Isometric View

To change the view of a model to the isometric, press the SHIFT + 7 keys. Alternatively, right-click in the graphics area and then click on the **Isometric** option in the shortcut menu that appears, see Figure 3.45.

3.45

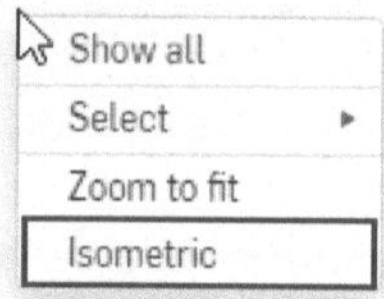

You can also click on the small cube and choose the **Isometric** tool from the menu that appears, see Figure 3.46.

3.46

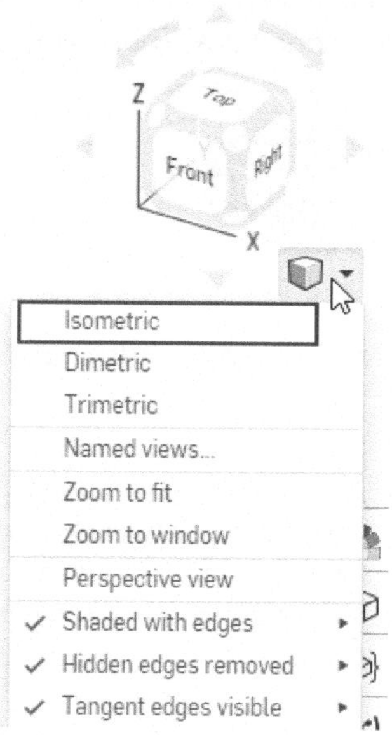

Perspective View

To change the view of a model to the perspective view, click on the small cube and select the **Perspective** tool from the menu that appears, refer to Figure 3.46. The perspective view appears as it is viewed normally from the human eyes. Note that the display of the perspective view can vary based on the model's size and the distance between the model and the viewer.

Named View

In Onshape, you can create custom or user-defined named views of a model for future use. The method to create a named view is discussed below:

1. Set the view of the model as desired in the graphics area using different navigating operations including zoom, rotate, and pan.

2. After setting the desired view of the model, press the SHIFT + V keys. The **Named views** dialog box appears, see Figure 3.47. Alternatively, click on the small cube located just below the View Cube and select the **Named views** tool from the menu to display the **Named views** dialog.

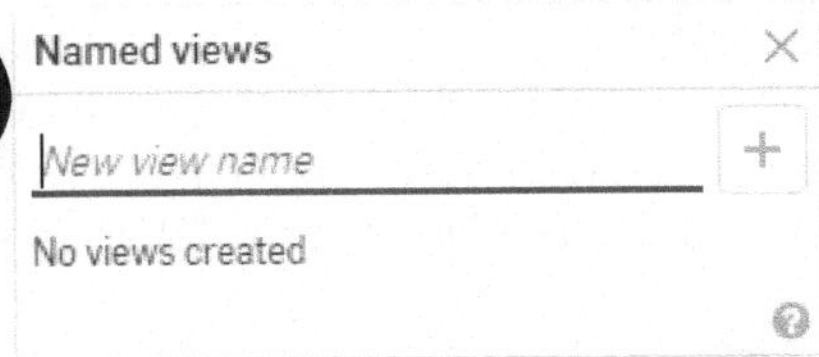

3. Enter a name for the view in the **New view name** field of the dialog, then click on the **+** icon next to the field, see Figure 3.48. The named view of the model is created and saved to the list at the bottom of the **Named views** dialog, see Figure 3.49.

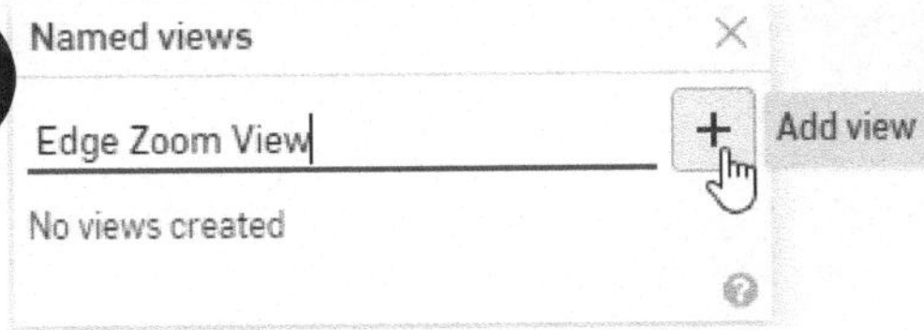

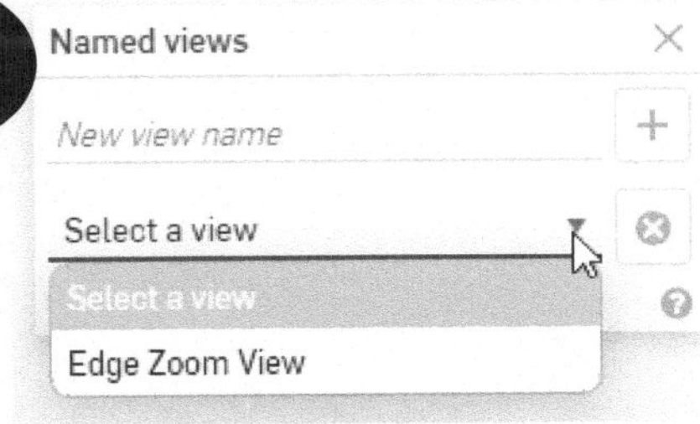

4. Similarly, you can create multiple custom views of the model and save them for later use.

5. After creating the desired named views, exit the dialog box by clicking the cross mark × in the top right corner.

Tip: You can display the model in any of the saved named views at any time. To do this, open the **Named views** dialog box by pressing the SHIFT + V keys and then select the desired named view from the drop-down list, refer to Figure 3.49.

Changing the Display Style of a Model

In Onshape, you can modify the display style of a model to various options, such as shaded with or without edges, unshaded, translucent, or hidden edges removed. The display style tools can be accessed through the **Camera and render options** menu, which appears when you click the small cube, see Figure 3.50. The different display style tools are discussed next.

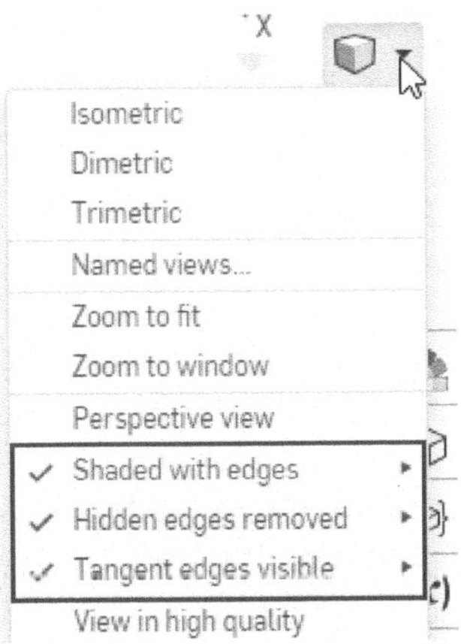

Shaded with edges Tool

The **Shaded with edges** tool displays the model in shaded mode with the outer visible edges highlighted in black, see Figure 3.51. This tool is enabled by default in the **Camera and render options** menu (refer to Figure 3.50), meaning the model is displayed in the "shaded with edges" style in the graphics area by default.

3.51

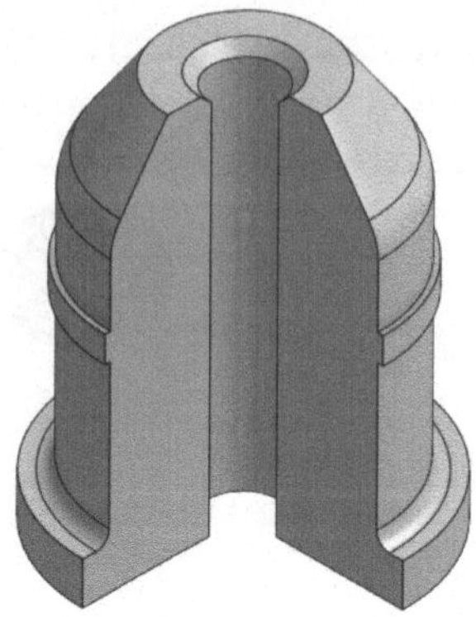

It is evident from the above figure that hidden edges are not displayed by default in the "shaded with edges" style. However, you can manage the visibility of hidden edges as needed. To do this, open the **Camera and render options** menu and hover over **Hidden Edges Removed** to access a cascading menu, see Figure 3.52. In this menu, you can toggle the visibility of hidden edges by selecting either **Hidden Edges Visible** or **Hidden Edges Removed**, according to your preference. Figure 3.53 shows the model in the "shaded with edges" style with the visibility of hidden edges turned on.

3.52

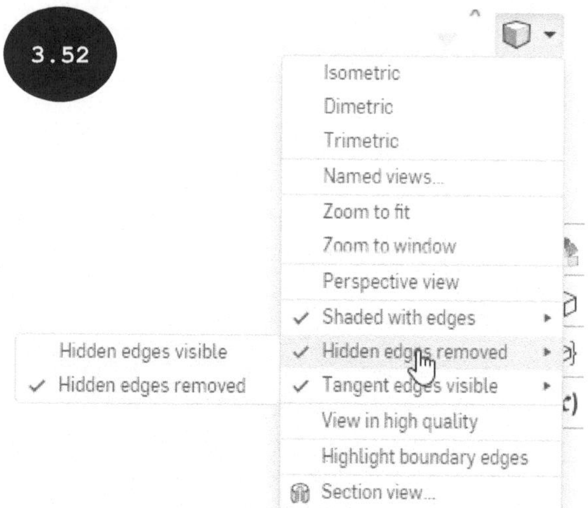

3.53

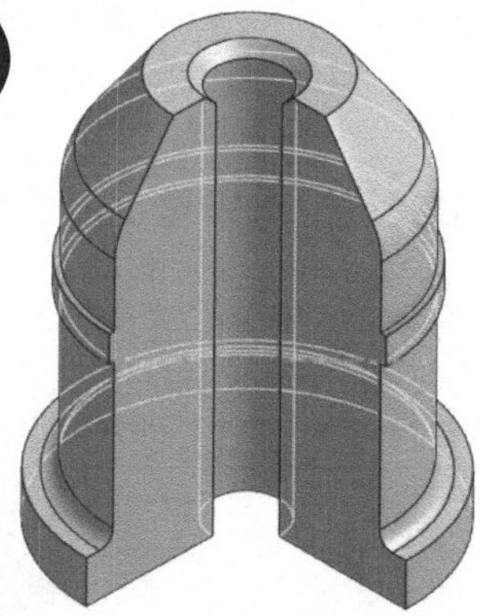

Shaded without edges Tool

The **Shaded without edges** tool displays the model in shaded mode with the outer visible edges turned off, see Figure 3.54. To switch to this style, invoke the **Camera and render options** menu by clicking the small cube. Then, hover over the active display style tool, see Figure 3.55. A cascading menu appears. In this menu, select the **Shaded without edges** tool.

3.54

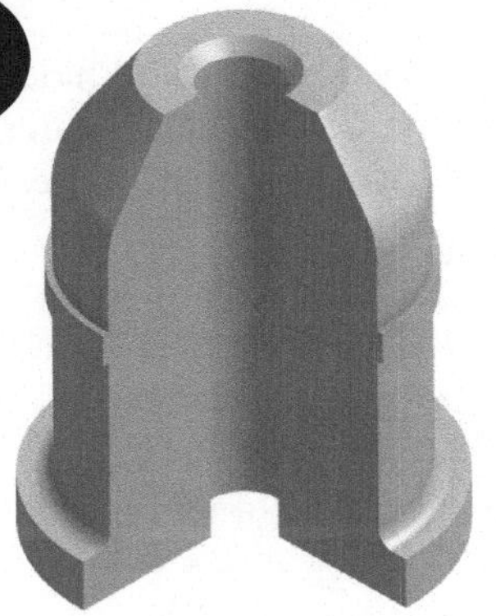

3.55

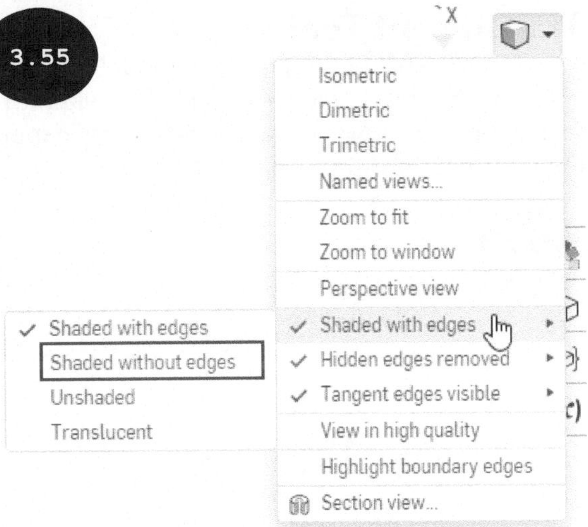

Unshaded Tool

The **Unshaded** tool displays the model in unshaded mode with the outer visible edges highlighted in black, see Figure 3.56. To switch to this style, invoke the **Camera and render options** menu by clicking the small cube. Then, hover over the active display style tool, refer to Figure 3.55. A cascading menu appears. In this menu, select the **Unshaded** tool.

It is evident from Figure 3.56 that hidden edges are not displayed by default in the "unshaded" style. However, you can manage the visibility of hidden edges as needed. To do this, open the **Camera and render options** menu and hover over **Hidden Edges Removed** to access a cascading menu, see Figure 3.57. In this menu, select either **Hidden Edges Visible** or **Hidden Edges Removed** to toggle the visibility of hidden edges according to your preference.

3.56

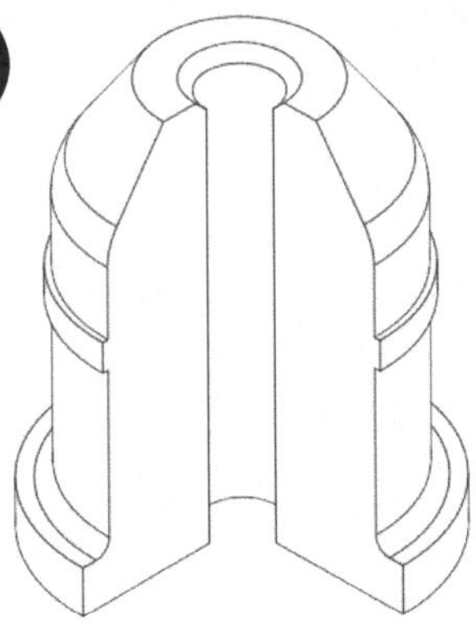

3.57

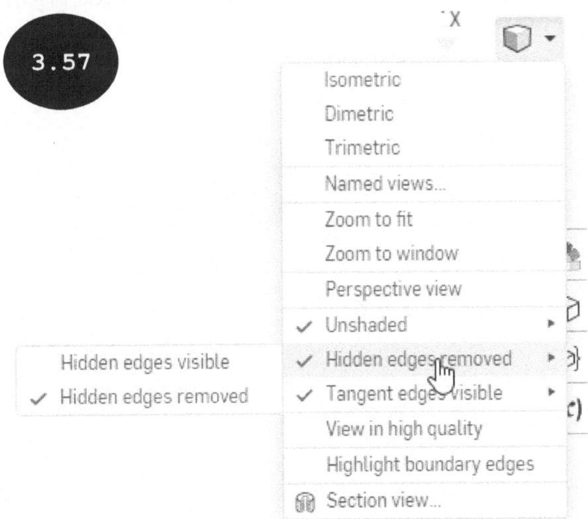

Translucent Tool

The **Translucent** tool displays the model in translucent mode, with both visible and hidden edges highlighted in black, see Figure 3.58. To switch to this style, invoke the **Camera and render options** menu, then hover over the active display style tool, see Figure 3.59. A cascading menu appears. In this menu, select the **Translucent** tool.

3.58

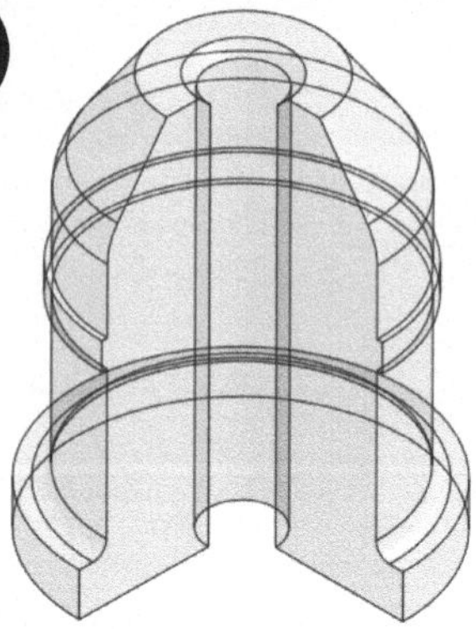

3.59

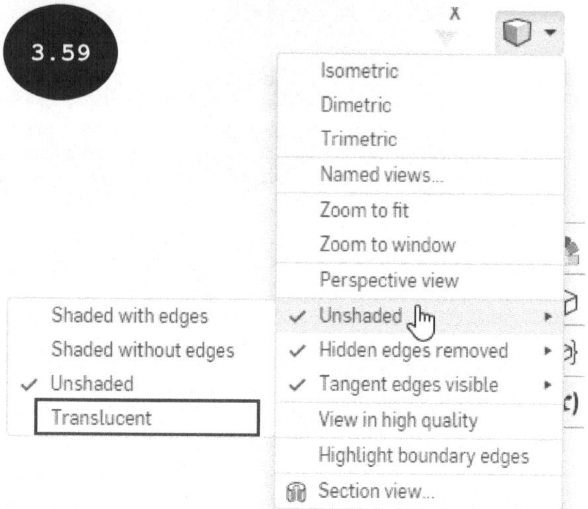

Tangent Edges Visibility

In Onshape, you can control the visibility of tangent edges (visible, phantom, or removed) for the shaded with edges, unshaded, and translucent display styles. By default, tangent edges are visible in all these styles. To modify their visibility, invoke the **Camera and render options** menu and hover over **Tangent edges visible** to reveal a cascading menu, see Figure 3.60. In this menu, choose **Tangent edges visible, Tangent edges phantom**, or **Tangent edges removed** to set the visibility of tangent edges according to your preference. Figure 3.61 shows the "shaded with edges" style with tangent edges set to visible, phantom, and removed.

3.60

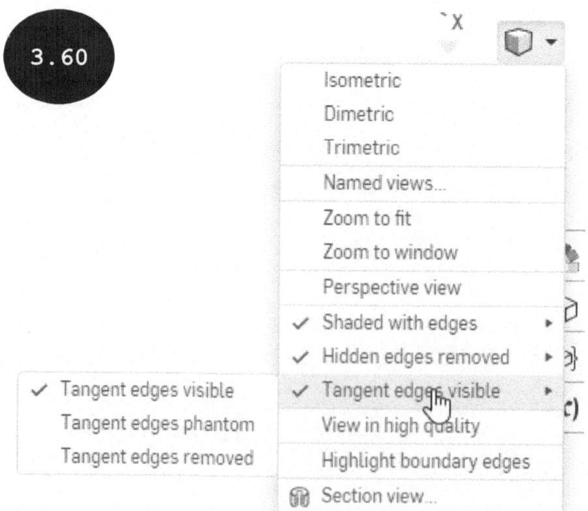

3.61

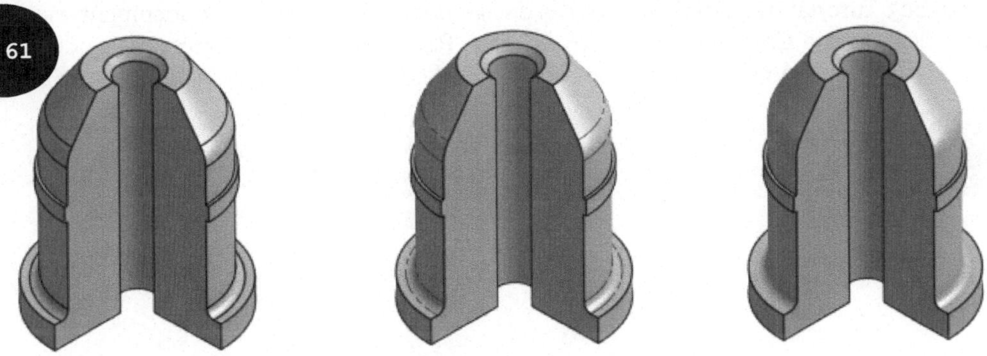

a. Tangent edges visible b. Tangent edges phantom c. Tangent edges removed

Tutorial 1

Create a sketch of the model shown in Figure 3.62 and then extrude it to a depth of 18 mm symmetrically about the sketching plane. All dimensions are in mm.

3.62

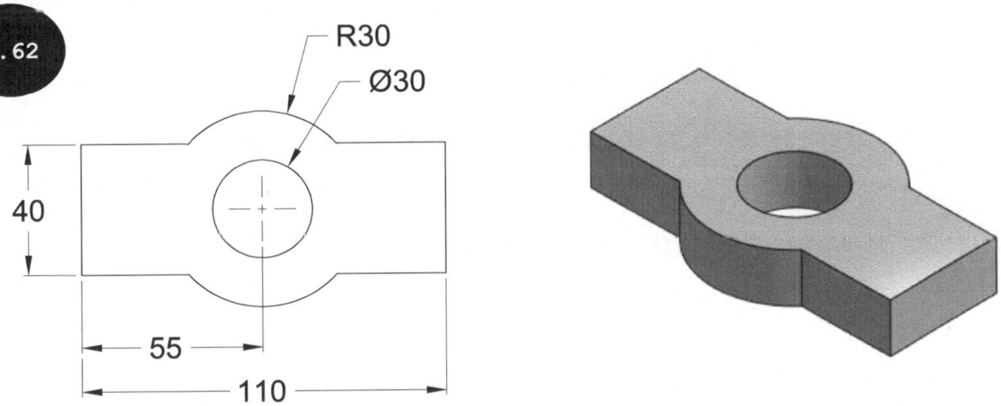

Section 1: Launching Onshape and Starting a New Design Document

1. Launch Onshape (*onshape.com*) and log in to your account if you're not already logged in.

2. Click on the **Create** button at the top left corner of the **Documents Page** and then click on the **Document** option in the menu that appears, see Figure 3.63. The **New document** window appears with the default name of the document as "**Untitled document**".

3.63

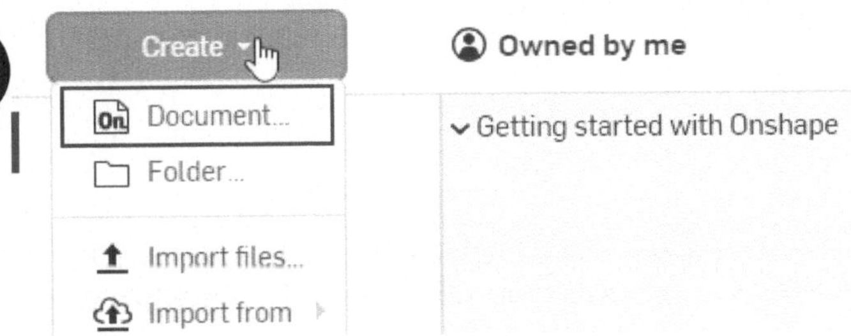

3. Enter **C03 Tutorial 01** as the name of the design document in the **New document** window, and then click on the **Create** button or the **Create Public Document** button, depending on your subscription type. A new document with the specified name is invoked, see Figure 3.64.

3.64

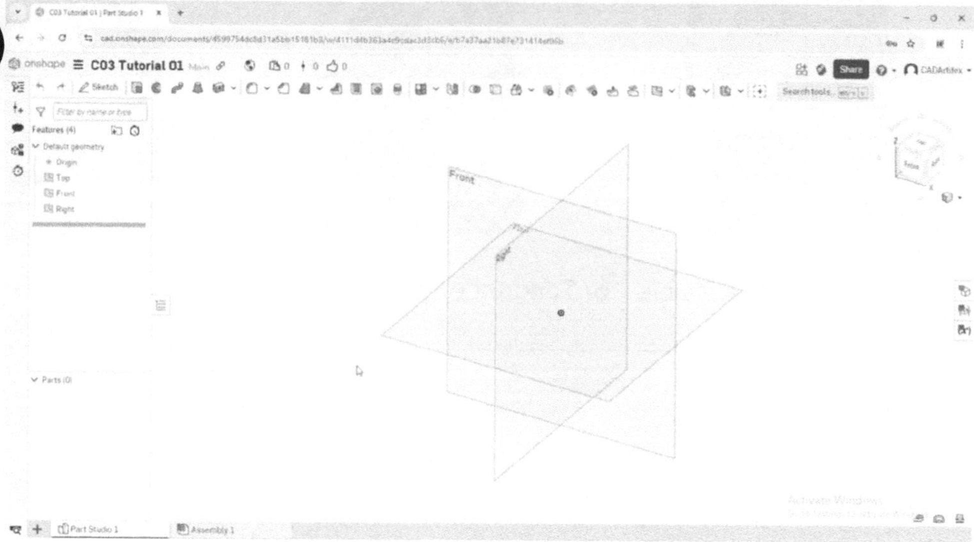

Section 2: Settings Units

Now, you can set millimeters (mm) as the unit for the length measuement in the current document.

1. Invoke the **Document** menu by clicking on the ≡ icon (three horizontal lines) next to the Onshape logo at the top left corner, see Figure 3.65.

3.65

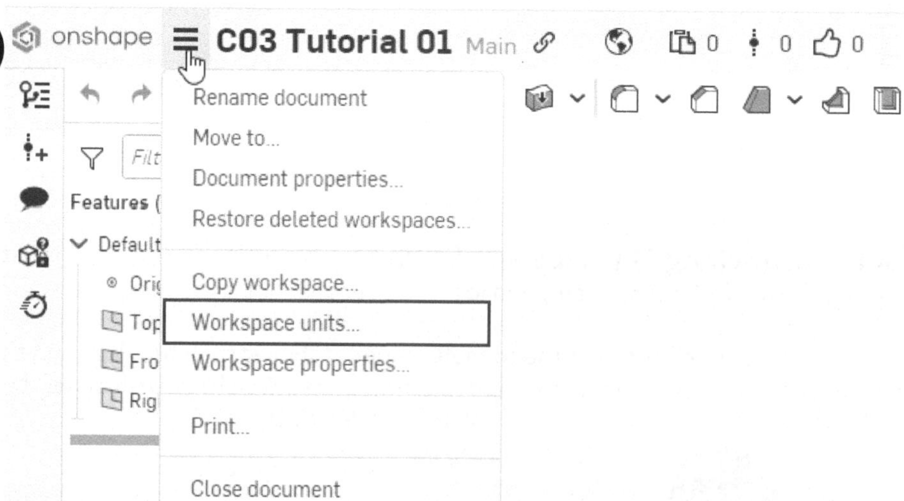

2. Click on the **Workspace units** option in the **Document** menu, refer to Figure 3.65. The **Workspace units** dialog appears, see Figure 3.66.

3. Select the **Millimeter** unit in the **Length default unit** drop-down list and set its precision to **0.1** in the respective **Display decimals** drop-down list of the **Workspace units** dialog, see Figure 3.66.

3.66

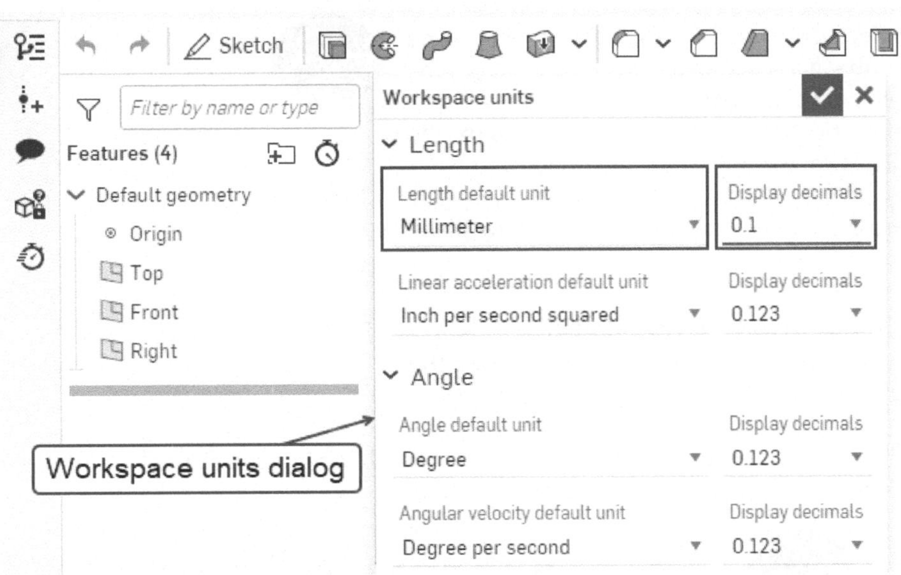

4. After selecting the required unit of length measurement and the decimal precision for the current design document, click on the green checkmark ✓ to confirm the selection and exit the dialog. The millimeter is defined as the unit for the length measurement.

Section 3: Accessing the Sketch Toolbar

Now, you can access the **Sketch** toolbar to create the sketch of the feature.

1. Click on the **Sketch** tool in the **Feature** toolbar, see Figure 3.67. The **Sketch** dialog appears (see Figure 3.68) and you are prompted to select a sketch plane.

3.67

3.68

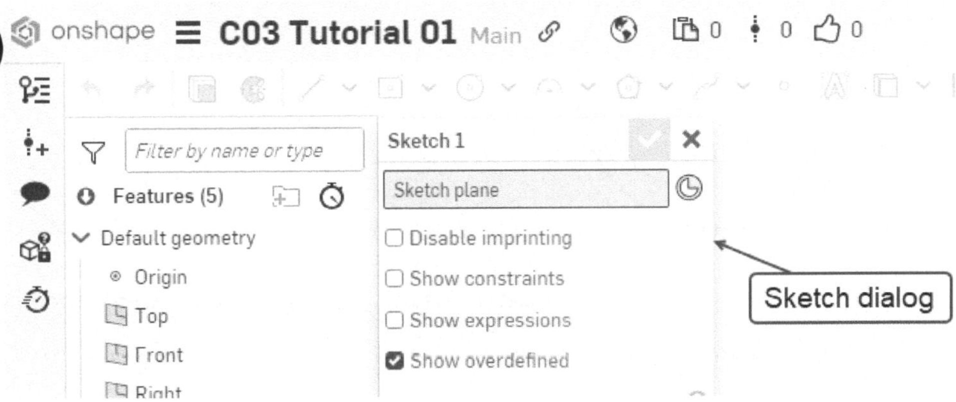

2. Select the Top plane as the sketching plane in the graphics area, see Figure 3.69. The selected plane becomes the sketching plane, and the **Sketch** toolbar appears with the display of various sketching tools.

3. Press the N key to make the sketching plane normal to the viewing direction.

3.69

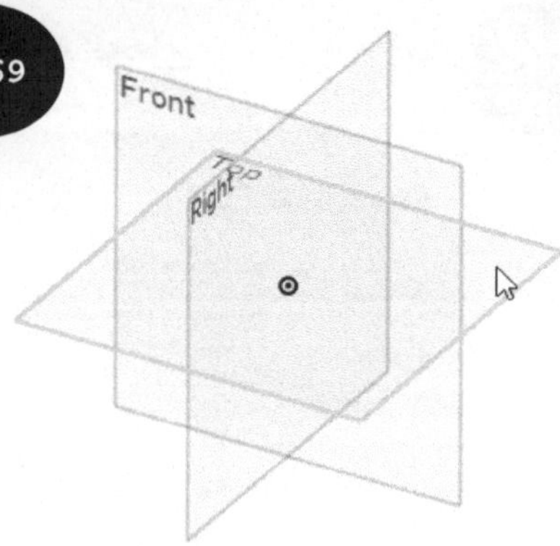

Section 4: Creating the Sketch

Now, you can start creating the sketch using the sketching tools available in the **Sketch** toolbar.

1. Click on the **Center point circle** tool in the **Sketch** toolbar, see Figure 3.70. Alternatively, press the C key to activate the **Center point circle** tool.

3.70

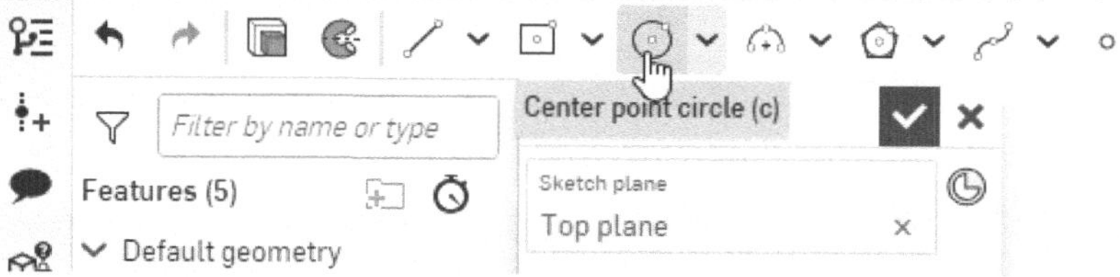

2. Move the cursor to the origin and then click to specify the center point of the circle when the cursor snaps to the origin.

3. Move the cursor to the right and click anywhere in the graphics area to set an arbitrary circle diameter. A circle is drawn, refer to Figure 3.71. Also, the **Center point circle** tool remains active.

4. Similarly, create another circle with a larger diameter, ensuring the center point is located at the origin, see Figure 3.72.

3.71

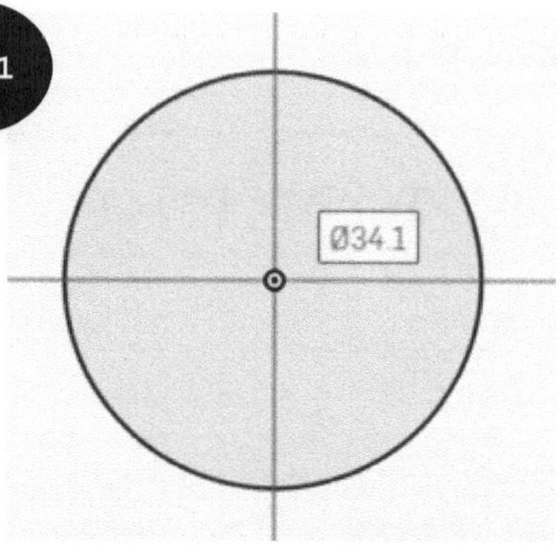

3.72

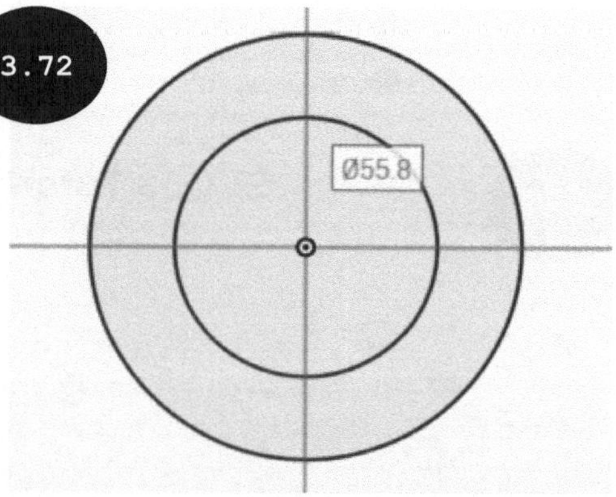

5. After creating the two concentric circles, press the ESC key to exit the **Center point circle** tool.

Now, you need to create a rectangle with its center at the origin.

6. Invoke the **Rectangle** drop-down menu in the **Sketch** toolbar and then click on the **Center point rectangle** tool, see Figure 3.73.

3.73

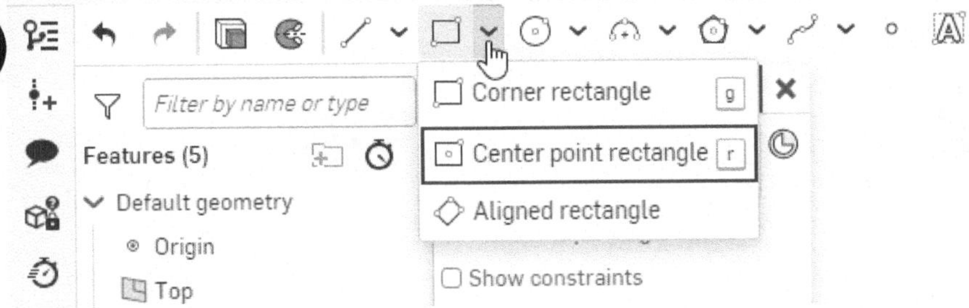

7. Move the cursor to the origin and then click to specify the center of a rectangle when the cursor snaps to the origin.

8. Move the cursor diagonally to the right and click to define a corner of the rectangle, see Figure 3.74. Ensure the rectangle's top and bottom horizontal lines are positioned between the circles similar to the one shown in Figure 3.74. In this figure, the smallest circle in the sketch is fully enclosed by the rectangle being drawn. Figure 3.75 shows the sketch after drawing the rectangle.

3.74

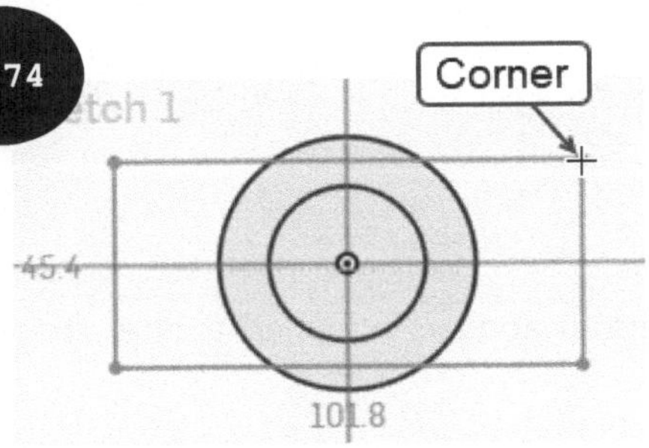

3.75

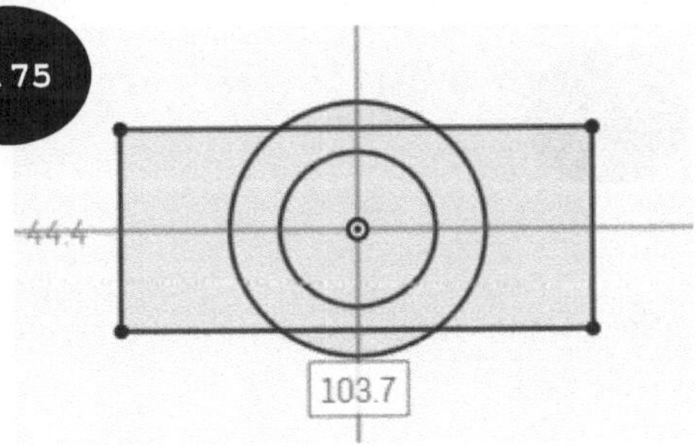

9. Press the ESC key to exit tool.

Now, you can trim the unwanted sketch entities.

10. Click on the **Trim** tool in the **Sketch** toolbar (see Figure 3.76) or press the **M** key to activate the **Trim** tool.

3.76

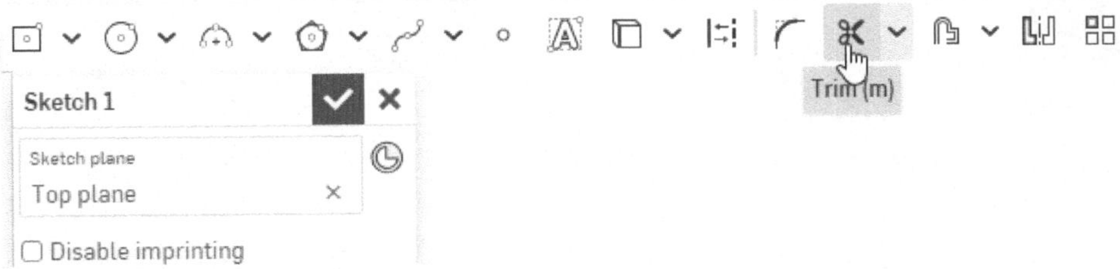

11. Click on the entities of the rectangle that lie inside the outer circle one at a time. Each selected entity gets trimmed to its nearest intersection, see Figure 3.77. The **Trim** tool remains active.

12. Similarly, trim the portion of the outer circle that lies between the rectangle segments. Figure 3.78 shows the sketch after trimming all unwanted entities. Next, press the ESC key to exit the **Trim** tool.

3.77

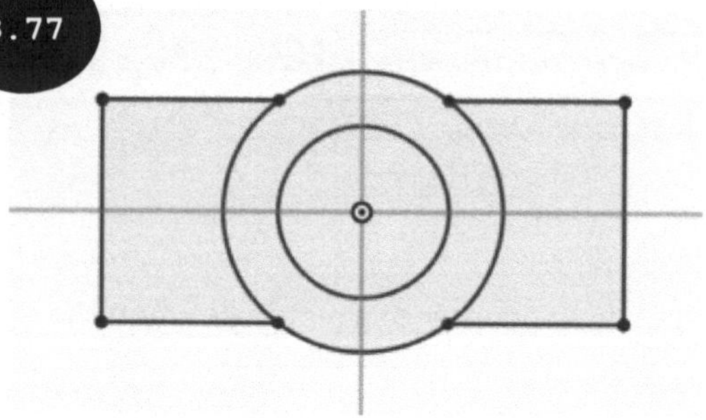

3.78

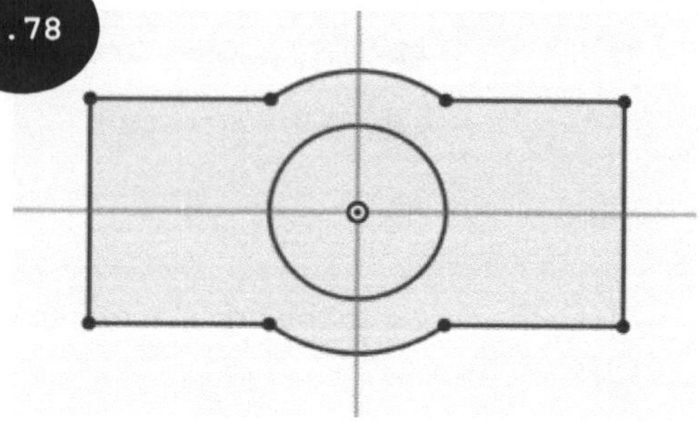

Now, you can apply required constraints and dimensions to the sketch.

13. Click on the **Dimension** tool in the **Sketch** toolbar (see Figure 3.79) or press the D key to activate the **Dimension** tool.

3.79

14. Select the outer arc of the sketch. A radius dimension appears attached to the cursor, see Figure 3.80.

15. Click in the graphics area to define the placement for the radius dimension. A dimension field appears, displaying the current radius of the selected arc.

16. Enter **30** mm in the dimension field and press ENTER. The radius of the arc gets modified accordingly, and the radius dimension is applied, see Figure 3.81. The **Dimension** tool remains active.

3.80

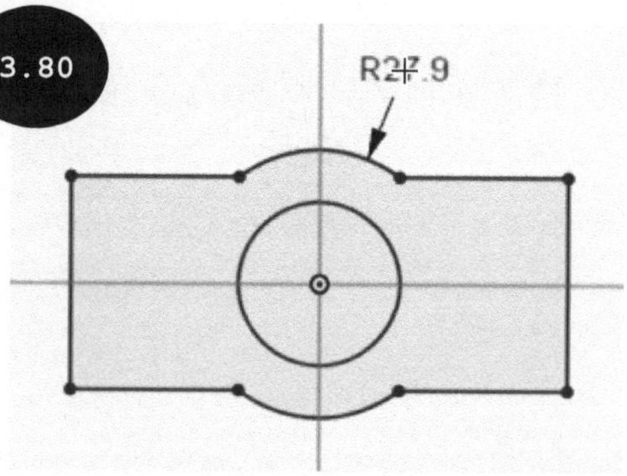

3.81

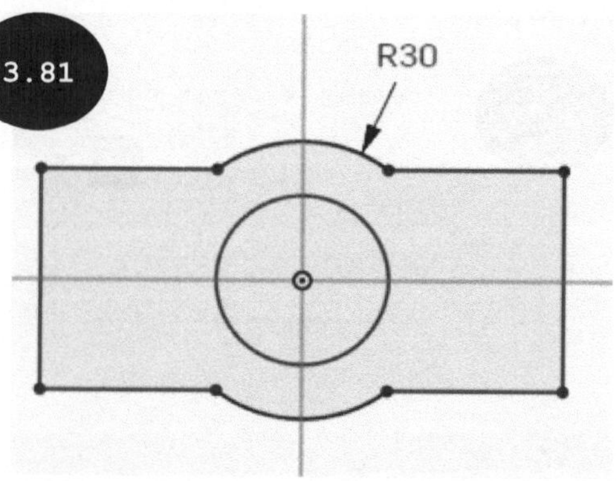

17. Similarly, apply the remaining dimensions to the sketch entities. Figure 3.82 shows the final sketch after applying all the required dimensions.

3.82

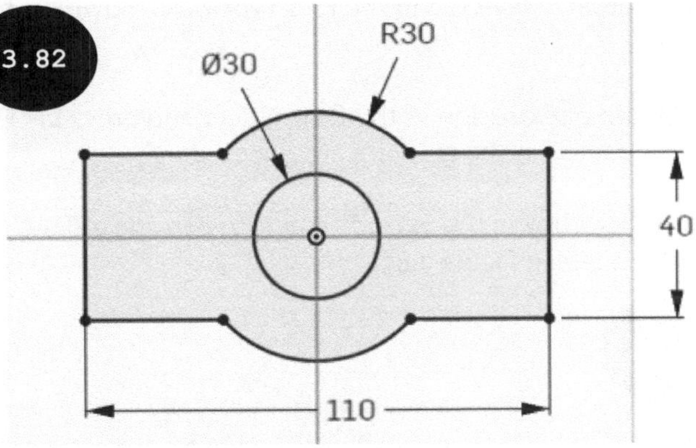

Section 5: Creating an Extrude Feature

Now, you need to create an extrude feature by extruding the sketch to a depth of 18 mm symmetrically on both sides of the sketching plane.

1. Click on the **Extrude** tool in the **Sketch** toolbar (see Figure 3.83) or press SHIFT + E. The **Extrude** dialog appears (see Figure 3.84), and the sketch is automatically selected. Consequently, a preview of an extruded feature with the default extrusion depth appears in the graphics area.

3.83

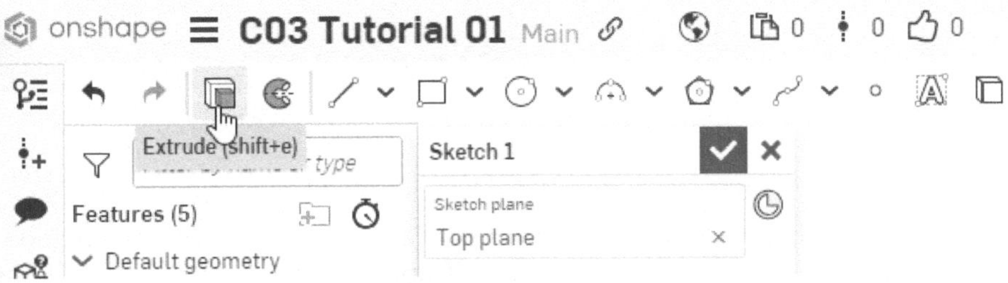

3.84

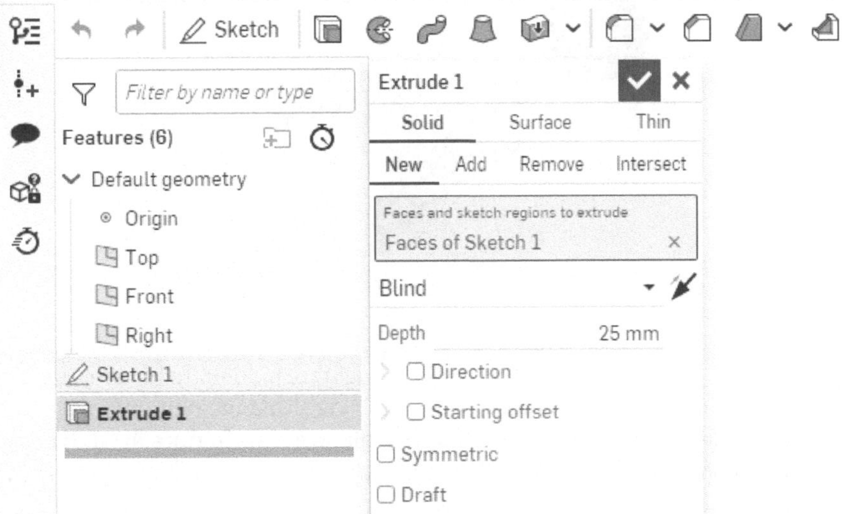

2. Press the SHIFT + 7 keys to change the view of the model to isometric.

3. Ensure that the **Blind** option is selected in the **End Type** drop-down list for extruding the sketch to a specific depth.

4. Enter **18** mm as the depth of extrusion in the **Depth** field and press ENTER. The preview of the extruded feature gets updated in the graphics area, accordingly.

5. Select the **Symmetric** check box in the **Extrude** dialog to extrude a sketch symmetrically on both sides of the sketching plane, see Figure 3.85.

3.85

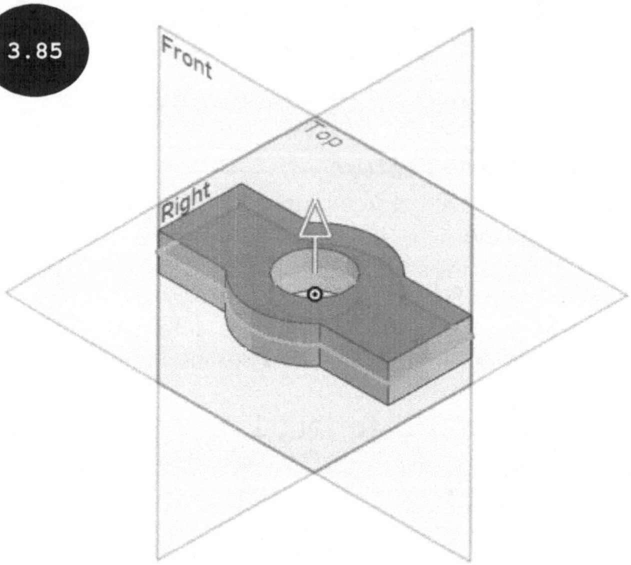

6. Click the green checkmark in the **Extrude** dialog box to confirm the creation of the extrude feature and close the dialog. The extruded feature of specified depth is created, see Figure 3.86.

3.86

Note: In Figure 3.86, the reference planes and origin are hidden. To hide reference planes, right-click on a plane in the graphics area and select **Hide all planes** in the shortcut menu, see Figure 3.87. Alternatively, hover over the reference plane in the **Feature list** and click the **Hide** icon, as see Figure 3.88. You can use the same approach to hide the Origin.

3.87

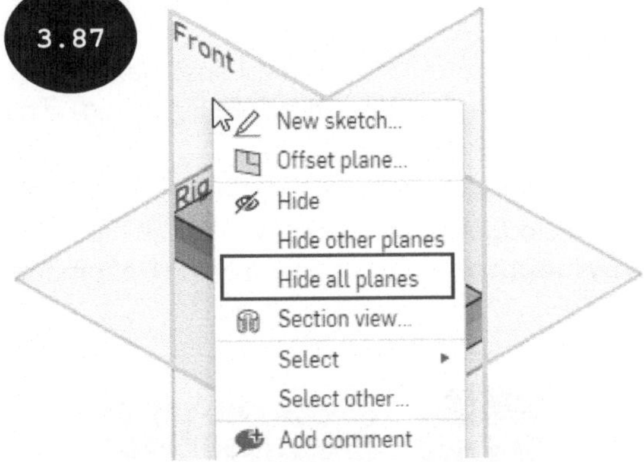

3.88

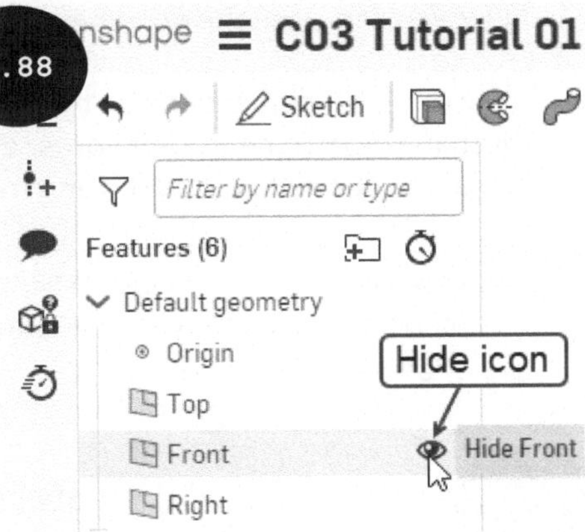

Section 6: Creating a Version

After creating a model, you can create a version in the document to capture the current state of the design for future reference or comparison.

1. Click on the **Create version** tool in the **Document panel**, which is aligned vertically with the Onshape logo, see Figure 3.89. The **Create version from Main** window appears with default version name **V1** in its **Name** field, see Figure 3.90.

3.89

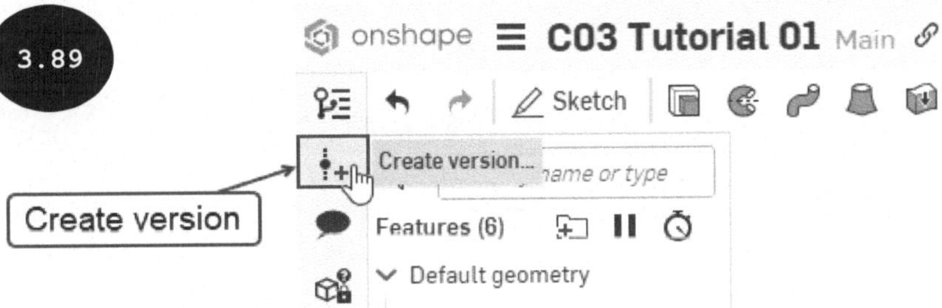

3.90

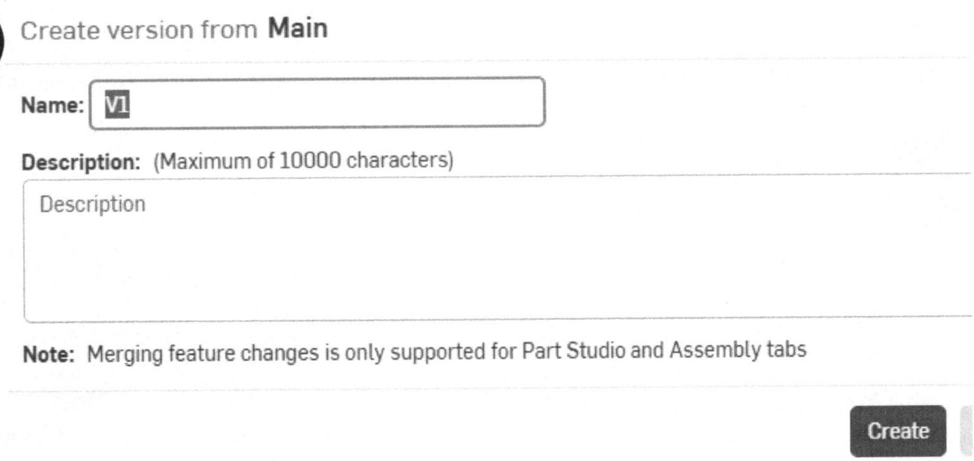

2. Accept the default specified name "V1" and click the **Create** button. A new version, "V1," is created in the document, capturing the model's current state.

Now, you can close the document.

3. Invoke the **Document** menu by clicking on the ≡ icon (three horizontal lines) next to the Onshape logo at the top left corner and click on the **Close document** option, see Figure 3.91. The current document gets closed and the **Documents Page** appears.

Tip: In Onshape, the documents save automatically in cloud. You can access a list of all the saved documents anytime by clicking on the **Created by me** option in the left menu of the **Documents Page**, see Figure 3.92.

3.91

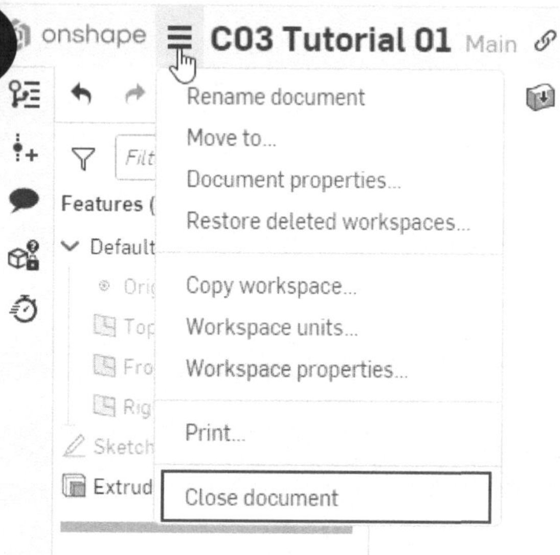

3.92

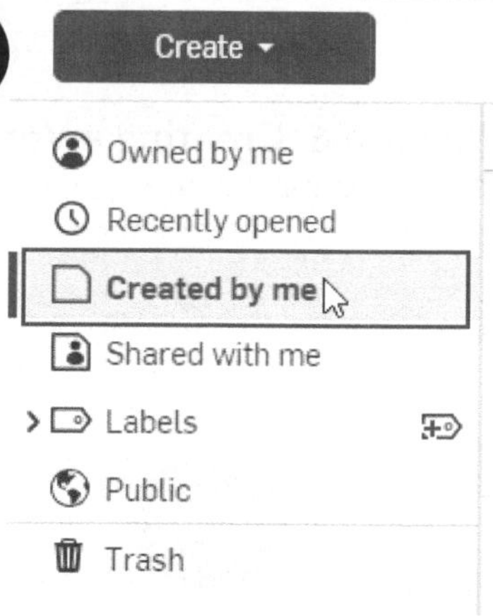

Tutorial 2

Create a sketch of the model shown in Figure 3.93 and then revolve it around the vertical axis at an angle of 270 degrees. All dimensions are in inches (in).

3.93

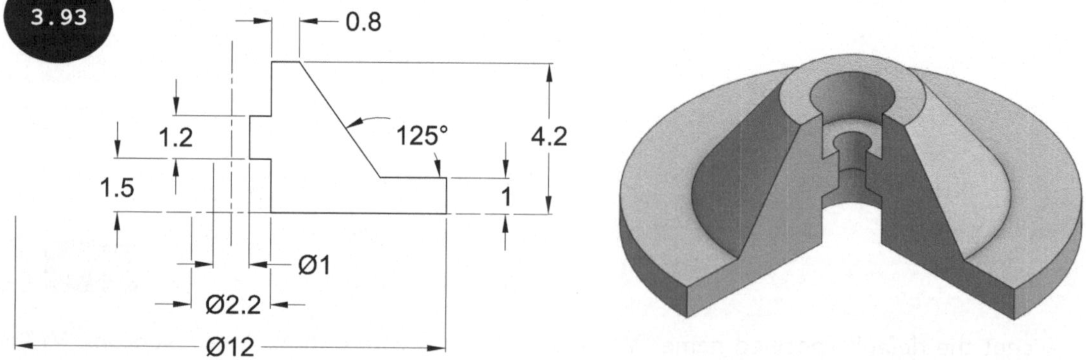

Section 1: Starting a New Design Document

1. Launch Onshape (*onshape.com*) and log in to your account if you're not already logged in.

2. Click on the **Create** button at the top left corner of the **Documents Page** and then click on the **Document** option in the menu that appears, see Figure 3.94. The **New document** window appears with the default name of the document "**Untitled document**".

3.94

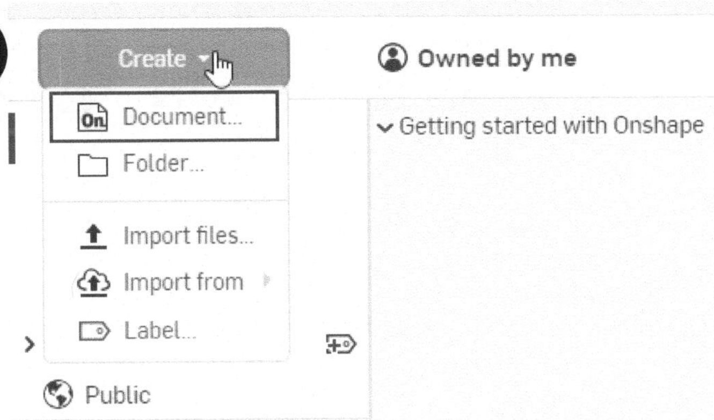

Note: The **Documents Page** automatically appears each time you launch Onshape. You can also access it at any time by clicking the Onshape logo in the top left corner of the screen.

3. Enter **C03 Tutorial 02** as the name of the design document in the **New document** window, and then click on the **Create** button or the **Create Public Document** button, depending on your subscription type. A new document with the specified name is invoked.

Section 2: Settings Units

Now, you can set inches (in) as the default unit for the length measurement in the current document.

1. Invoke the **Document** menu by clicking on the ≡ icon (three horizontal lines) next to the Onshape logo at the top left corner, see Figure 3.95.

3.95

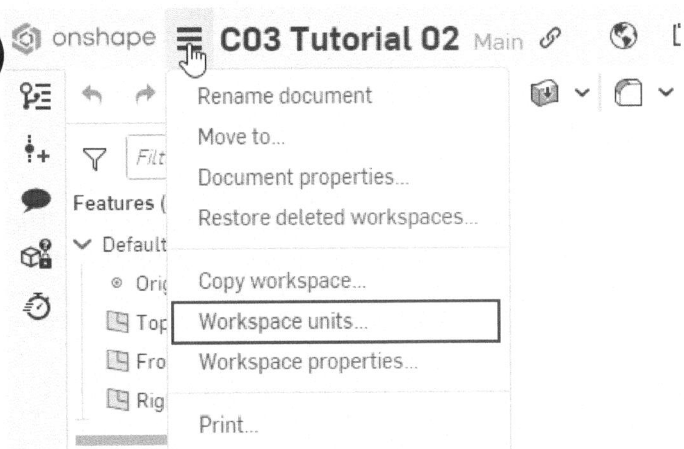

2. Click on the **Workspace units** option in the **Document** menu, refer to Figure 3.95. The **Workspace units** dialog appears.

3. Ensure that the **Inch** unit is selected in the **Length default unit** drop-down list and set its precision to **0.1** in the respective **Display decimals** drop-down list of the **Workspace units** dialog, see Figure 3.96.

3.96

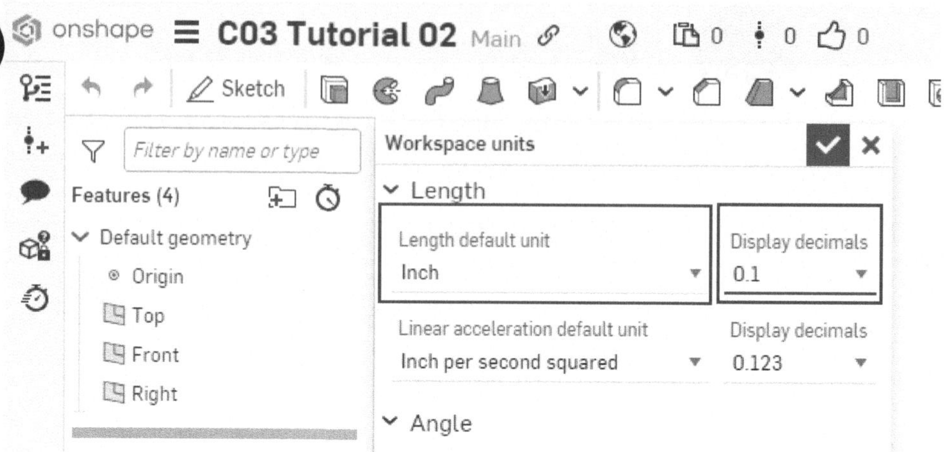

4. Click on the green checkmark ✓ to confirm the selection and exit the dialog. The inches unit is defined as the unit for the length measurement.

Section 3: Accessing the Sketch Toolbar

1. Click on the **Sketch** tool in the **Feature** toolbar, see Figure 3.97. The **Sketch** dialog appears and you are prompted to select a sketch plane.

3.97

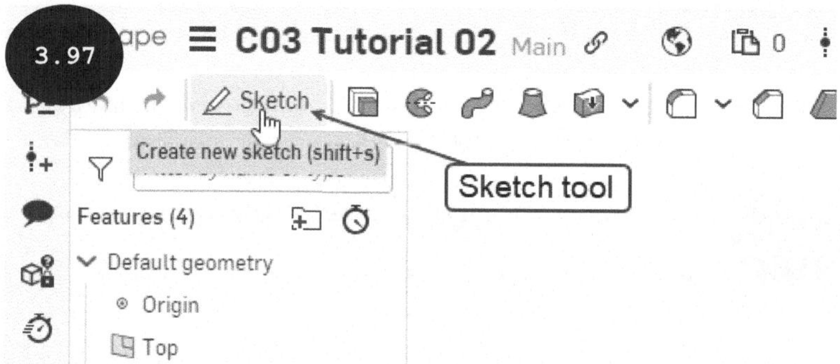

2. Select the Front plane as the sketching plane in the graphics area. The selected plane becomes the sketching plane, and the **Sketch** toolbar appears with the display of various sketching tools.

3. Press the N key to make the sketching plane normal to the viewing direction.

Section 4: Creating the Sketch

Now, you can start creating the sketch using the sketching tools available in the **Sketch** toolbar.

1. Click on the **Line** tool in the **Sketch** toolbar (see Figure 3.98) or press the **L** key to activate the **Line** tool.

3.98

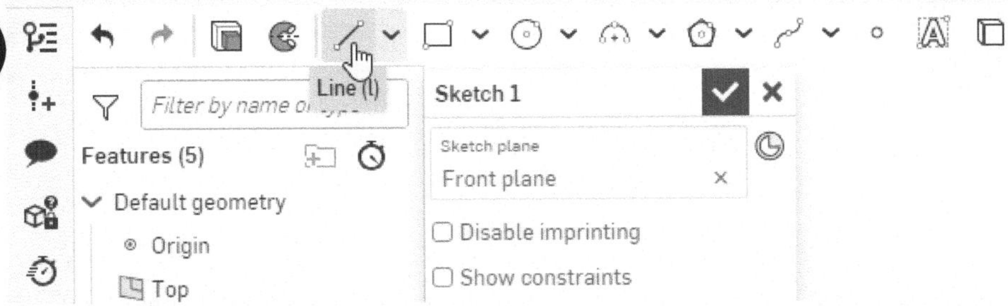

2. Move the cursor over the horizontal axis, at a small distance from the origin and then click to specify the start point of the line, refer to Figure 3.99.

3. Move the cursor vertically upward and then click anywhere to specify the endpoint of the vertical line, refer to Figure 3.99. A vertical line is created and the **Line** tool remains activated.

3.99

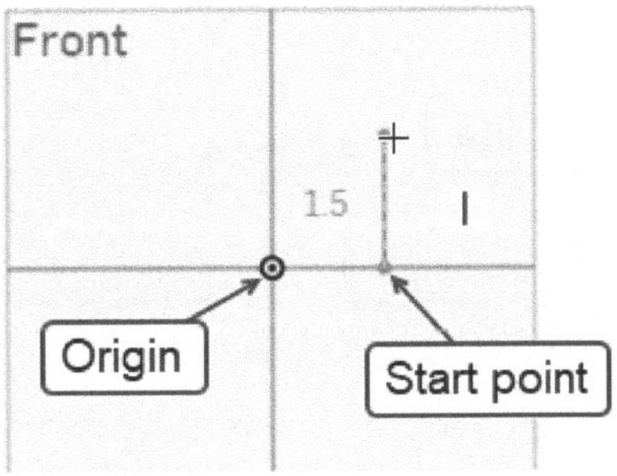

4. Continue creating a chain of line segments of the sketch by specifying points arbitrarily in the graphics area like the one shown in Figure 3.100. Ensure that the sketch forms a closed loop by making sure the endpoint of the last line segment coincident with the start point of the first line segment. Notice the **Line** tool remains active.

3.100

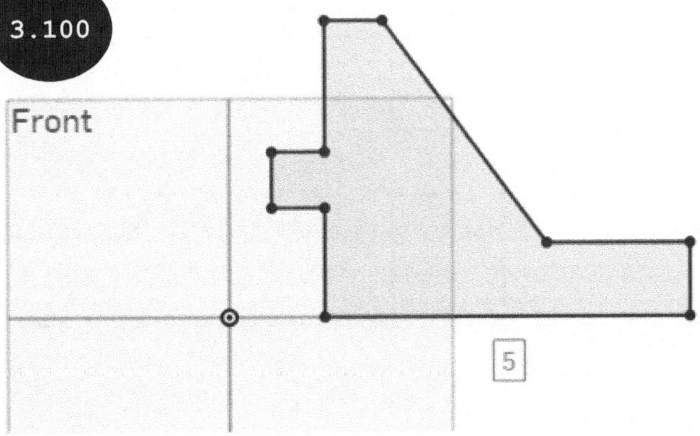

Now, you need to create a vertical construction line. It will be used as the axis of revolution for creating the revolve feature.

5. Click the **Construction** tool in the **Sketch** toolbar to activate construction mode, which allows you to create construction entities, see Figure 3.101.

3.101

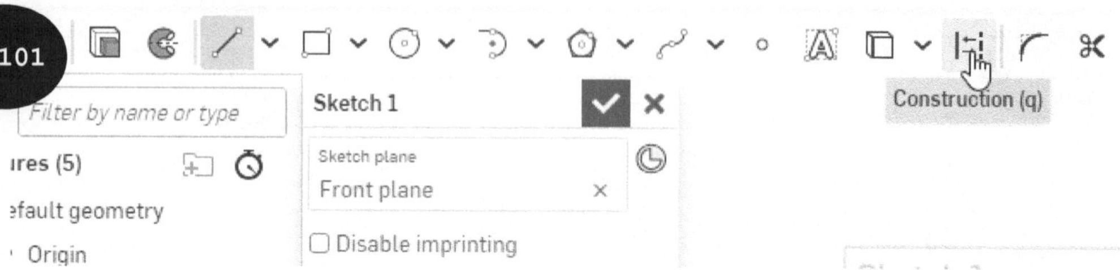

6. Create a vertical construction line of any length starting from the origin, see Figure 3.102. Next, press the ESC key to exit the **Line** tool.

3.102

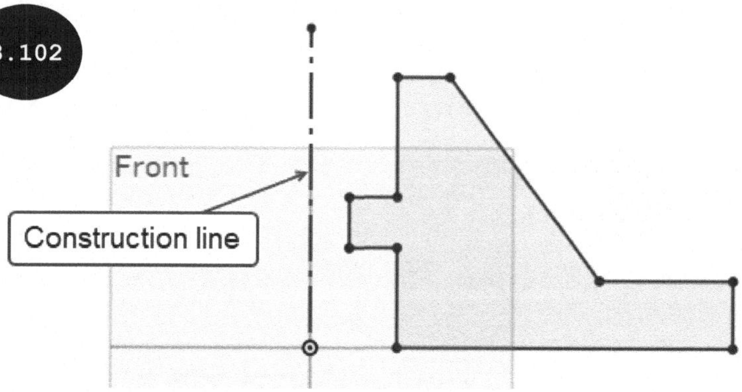

Now, you need to apply the required constraints and dimensions to make the sketch fully defined.

7. Ensure that the endpoints of the vertical lines shown in Figure 3.103 are vertically aligned by applying a vertical constraint between them.

3.103

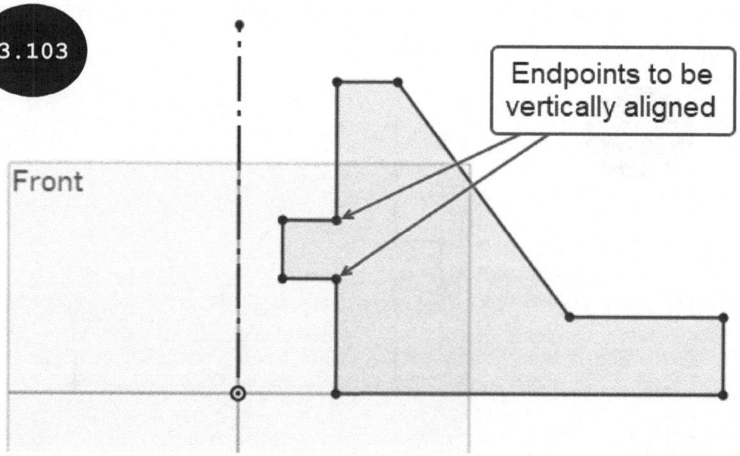

8. Activate the **Dimension** tool and apply the required dimensions to the sketch. Figure 3.104 shows the sketch with all necessary dimensions applied.

3.104

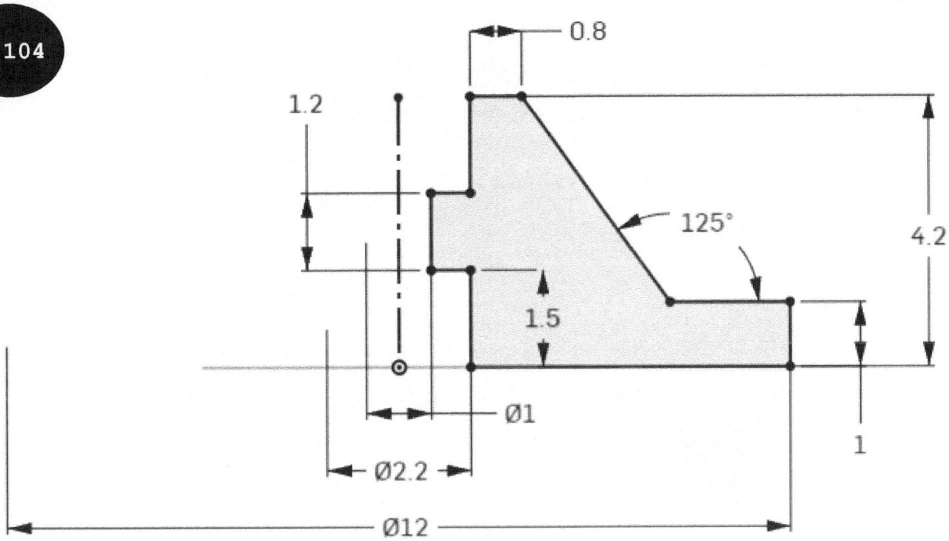

Tip: In Figure 3.104, the bottom dimensions (1, 2.2, and 12) are linear diameter dimensions, applied to the corresponding sketch entities concerning the vertical construction line.

Section 5: Creating a Revolve Feature

Now, you need to create a revolve feature by revolving the sketch around the vertical construction line.

1. Click on the **Revolve** tool in the **Sketch** toolbar (see Figure 3.105) or press SHIFT + R. The **Revolve** dialog appears (see Figure 3.106), and the sketch is automatically selected.

3.105

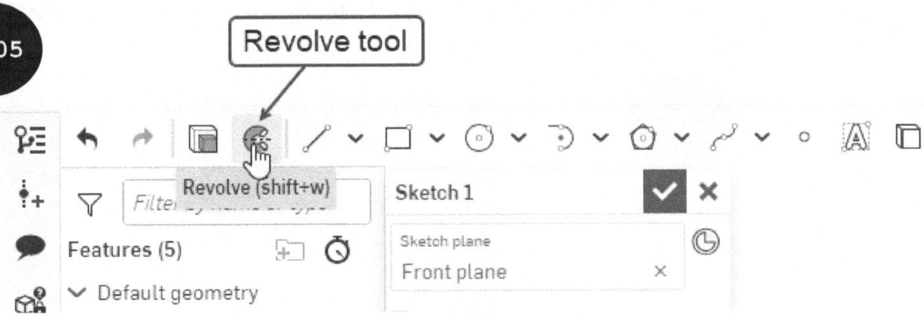

3.106

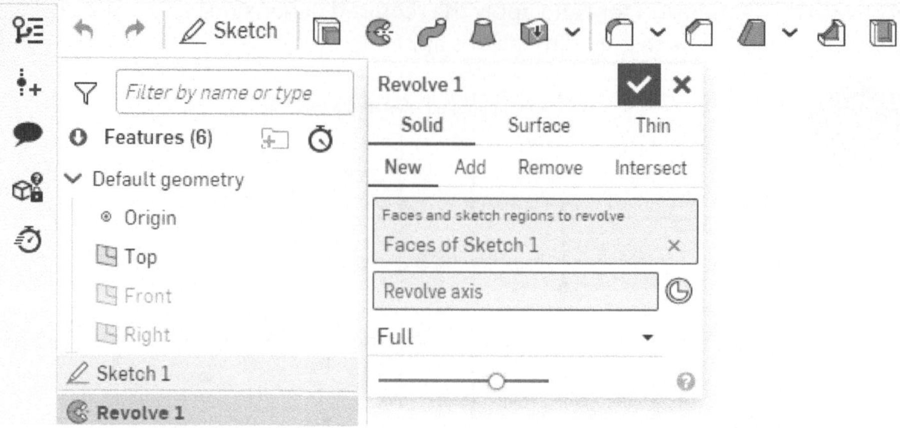

2. Press the SHIFT + 7 keys to change the view orientation to isometric, see Figure 3.107.

3.107

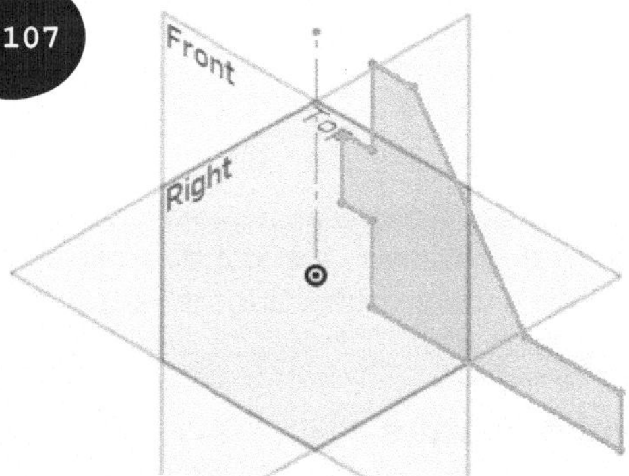

Now, you need to define an axis of revolution.

3. Click the **Revolve axis** field in the **Revolve** dialog, then select the vertical construction line in the graphics area. A preview of the revolve feature appears by revolving the sketch around the selected construction line, see Figure 3.108.

3.108

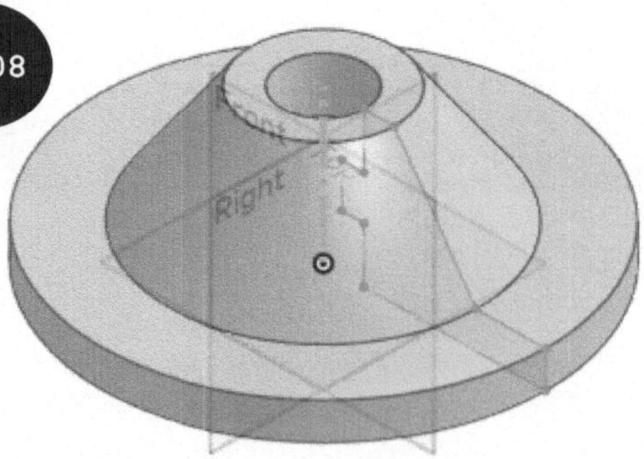

Tip: By default, the sketch revolves 360 degrees around the axis to create a revolve feature, as the **Full** option is selected in the **Revolve type** drop-down list in the **Revolve** dialog.

4. Select the **One Direction** option in the **Revolve type** drop-down list to revolve the sketch at a specific angle around one side of the sketching plane, see Figure 3.109.

5. Enter **270** degrees as the angle of revolution in the **Revolve angle** field of the dialog box. The preview of the revolve feature appears similar to the one shown in Figure 3.110.

3.109

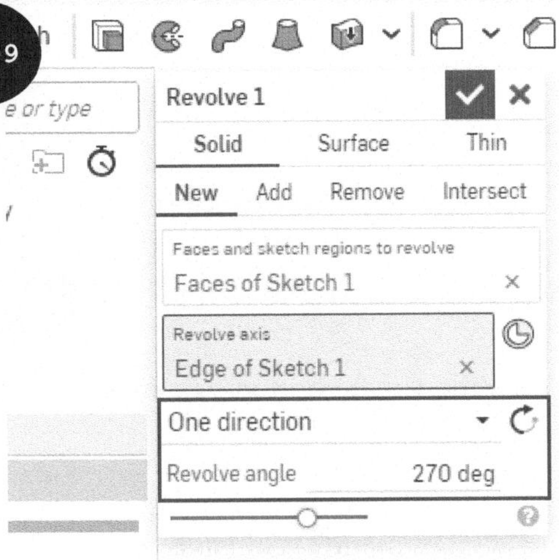

3.110

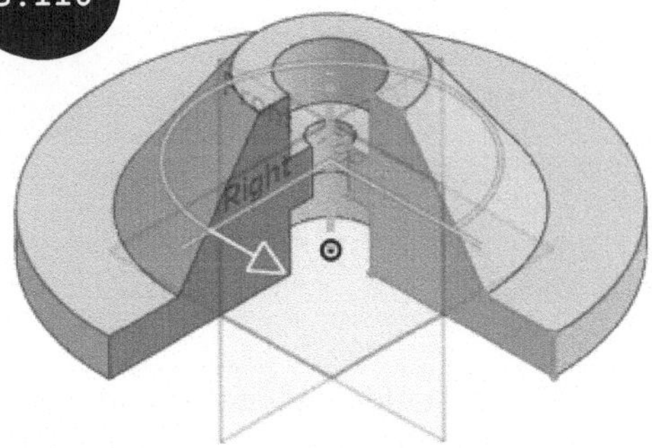

6. Click the green checkmark in the **Revolve** dialog to confirm the creation of the revolve feature and close the dialog. The revolved feature of specified angle of revolution is created, see Figure 3.111.

3.111

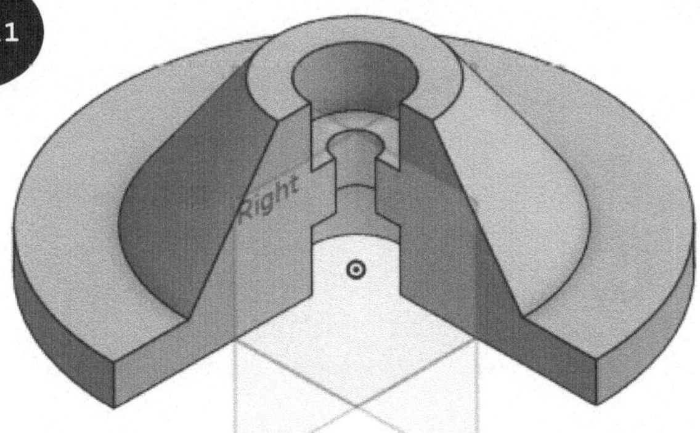

Section 6: Creating a Version

After creating a model, you can create a version in the document to capture the current state of the design for future reference or comparison.

1. Click on the **Create version** tool in the **Document panel**, which is aligned vertically with the Onshape logo, see Figure 3.112. The **Create version from Main** window appears with default version name **V1** in its **Name** field, see Figure 3.113.

3.112

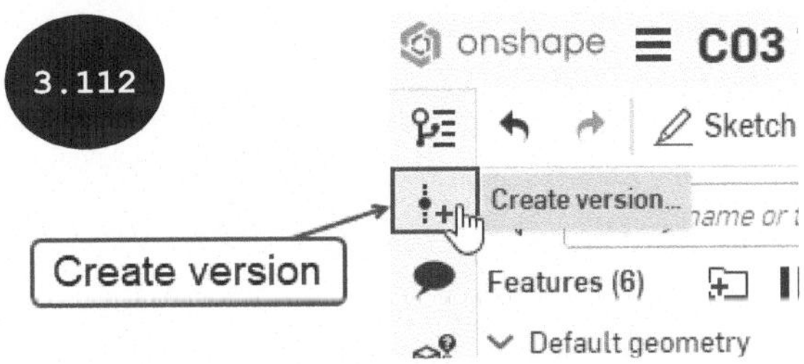

3.113

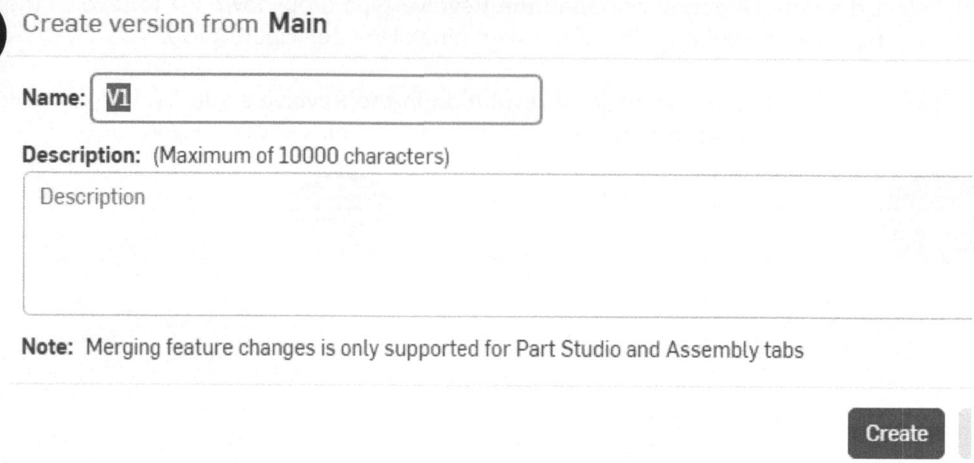

2. Accept the default specified name "V1" and click the **Create** button. A new version, "V1," is created in the document, capturing the model's current state.

   Now, you can close the document.

3. Invoke the **Document** menu by clicking on the ≡ icon (three horizontal lines) next to the Onshape logo at the top left corner and click on the **Close document** option, see Figure 3.114. The current document gets closed.

3.114

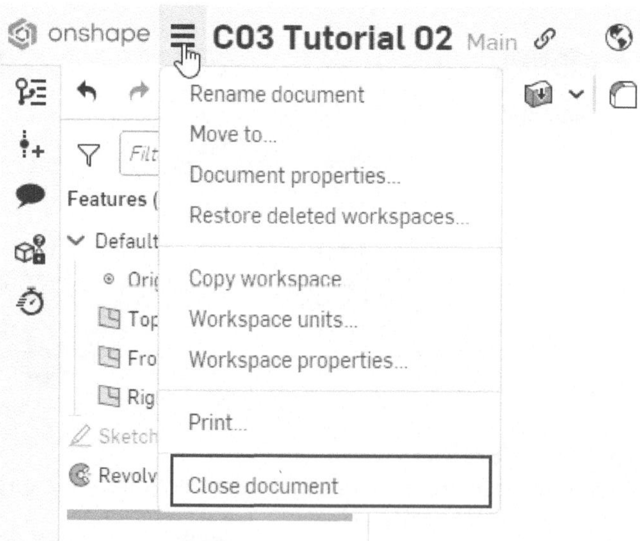

Hands-on Test Drive 1

Create a sketch of the model shown in Figure 3.115 and then revolve it around the vertical axis at an angle of 360 degrees. All dimensions are in inches (in).

3.115

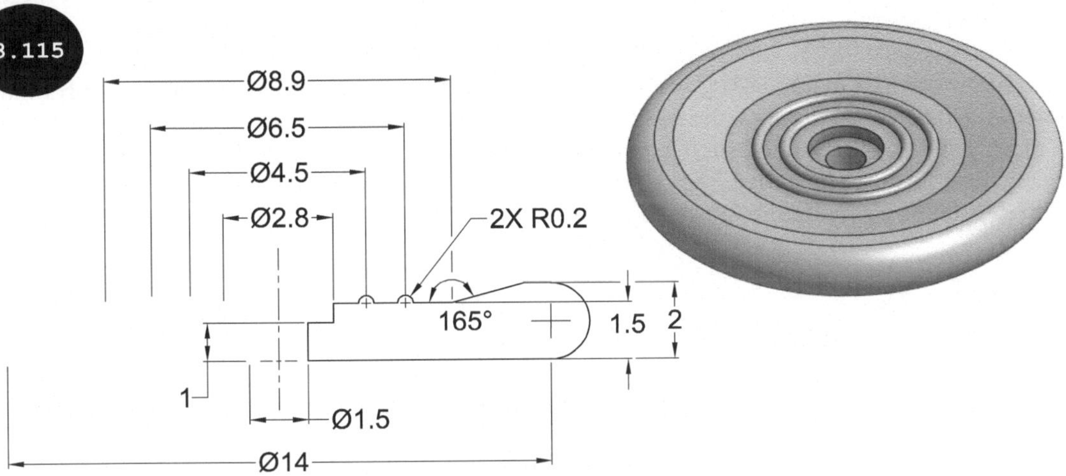

Hands-on Test Drive 2

Create a sketch of the model shown in Figure 3.116 and then extrude it to a depth of 125 mm symmetrically about the sketching plane. All dimensions are in mm.

3.116

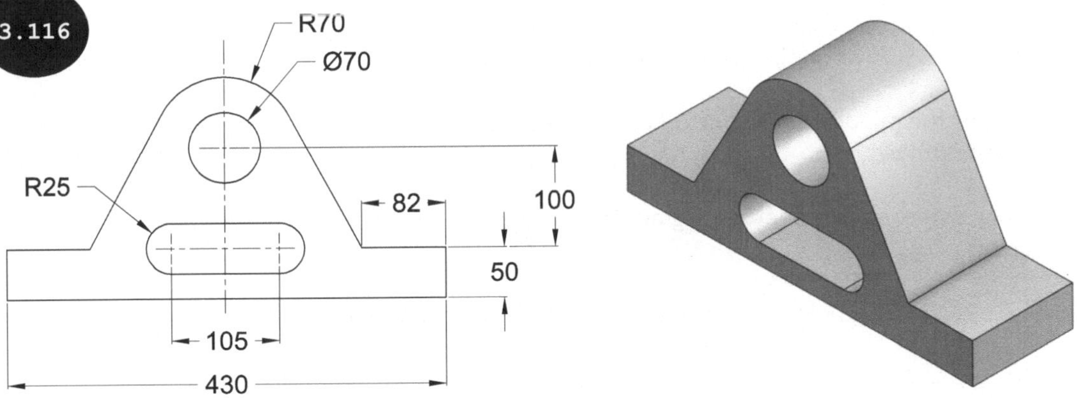

Summary

In this chapter, you learned how to create extrude and revolve features in Onshape, essential for transforming 2D sketches into 3D models. You also explored various methods for navigating a 3D model using the mouse, keyboard, and touchpad, along with view tools like Zoom to Fit, Zoom to Window, and Zoom to Selection.

The chapter covered manipulating the view of a 3D model to standard planes, including trimetric, isometric, and perspective views, and creating custom named views. Additionally, it discussed changing the display style of the model, such as shaded with or without edges, unshaded, translucent, and toggling the visibility of tangent edges. These skills are fundamental for efficiently creating, navigating, and manipulating 3D models in Onshape.

Questions

Complete and verify the following sentences:

- An _________ is created by adding or removing material perpendicular to the sketching plane.
- The _________ option creates a base extrude feature by adding material and forms a new part.
- The _________ option is used to extrude the sketch up to a selected face of an existing feature.
- A _________ feature is created by adding or removing material through the revolving of a sketch around an axis.
- To freely rotate the model in the graphics area, hold down the _________ mouse button and move the cursor.
- Clicking the arrows on the View Cube rotates the model in _________ -degree increments.
- Scrolling the middle mouse button down will _________, while scrolling it up will _________ the model view.
- To pan or move the model in the graphics area, hold the _________ mouse button and drag the cursor.
- The _________ tool is used to adjust the model to fit completely within the graphics area.
- The _________ tool is used to create custom, user-defined views of a model.
- The _______ checkbox allows extrusion on both sides of the sketch plane, with varying extrusion lengths for each side.
- In Onshape, you can customize the direction of an extrusion beyond the default normal to the sketching plane. (True/False)
- Base extrude features are typically created by adding material. (True/False)

CHAPTER

4

Creating Planes and Advanced Techniques

In this chapter, **the following topics will be discussed:**

- Creating Construction Planes
- Exploring Additional Extrude / Revolve Options
- Projecting Edges onto a Sketching Plane
- Displaying Section View of a Model
- Displaying an Earlier Stage of a Model
- Reordering Features of a Model
- Editing Features and Sketches
- Deleting a Feature of a Model
- Assigning Appearance
- Assigning Material
- Computing Mass Properties

In Onshape, there are three default construction planes: Front, Top, and Right. These planes can be used to create features like extrudes and revolves, as covered in previous chapters. However, for more complex real-world models that require multiple features, these three planes may not suffice. Onshape provides the capability to create additional construction planes as needed. You can create various types of construction planes using the Plane tool to support the creation of complex real-world models.

Figure 4.1 displays a model created by sequentially creating its features. This model includes four features: the first is an extrude feature created on the right plane, the second is a construction plane established at an angle, the third is another extrude feature made on the previously created construction plane, and the fourth is a cut feature created to the top planar face of the third feature.

4.1

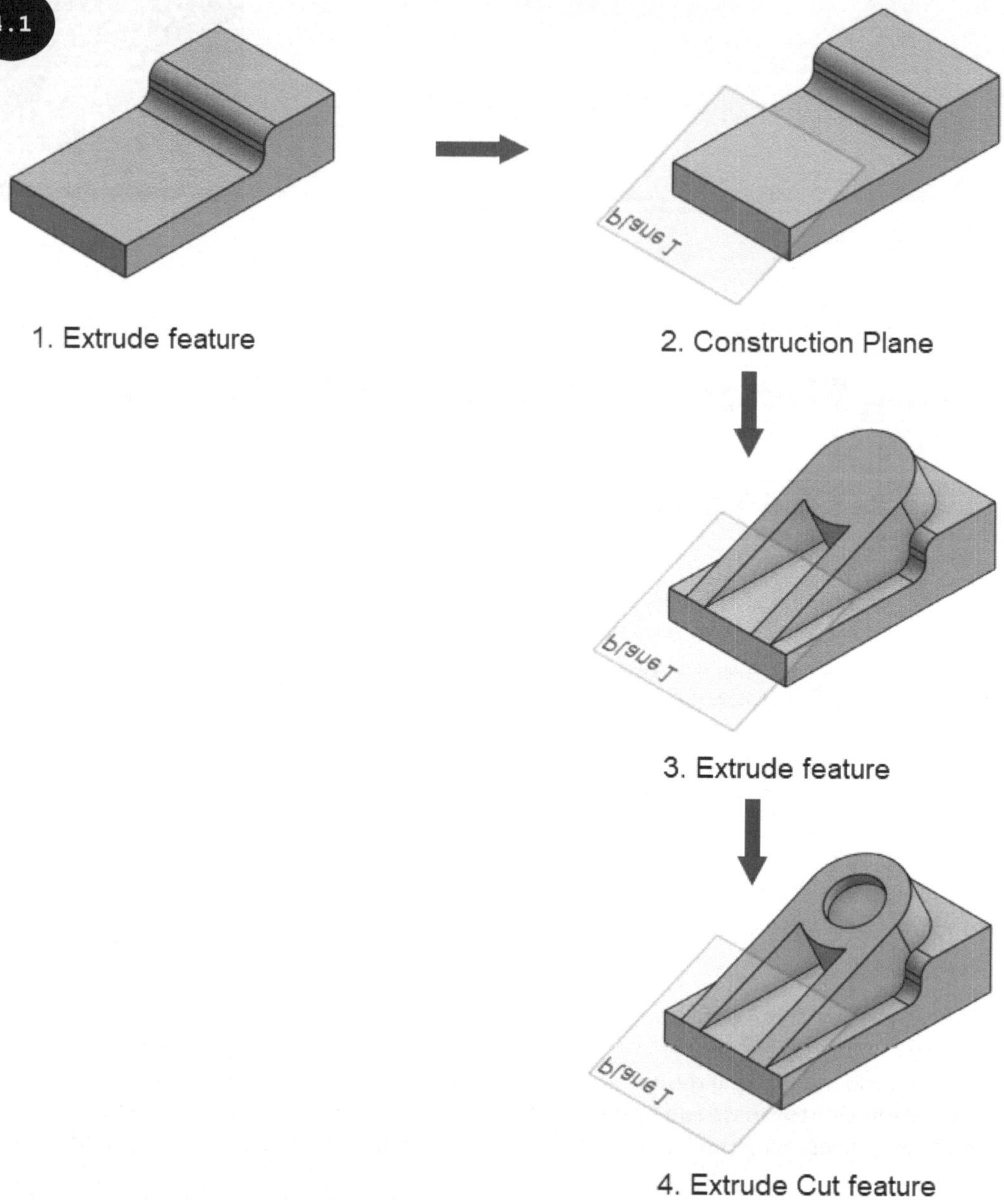

Note: It is evident from the above figure that additional construction planes may be necessary to create certain features of a 3D model. In this figure, for instance, the second extrude feature is created on a construction plane established at an angle.

Creating Construction Planes

In Onshape, you can create construction planes using the **Plane** tool through various methods, including:

- Creating a plane at an offset distance.
- Creating a plane parallel to a face or plane through a point.
- Creating a plane at an angle to a planar face or a plane.
- Creating a plane normal to a line or linear edge.
- Creating a plane through three points or vertices.
- Creating a plane in the middle of two planar faces.
- Creating a plane normal to a curve or curved edge.
- Creating a plane tangent to a cylindrical face.

All these methods of creating construction planes are discussed next.

Creating a Plane at an Offset Distance

The method for creating a plane at an offset distance from an existing plane or planar face is discussed below:

1. Click on the **Plane** tool in the **Feature** toolbar, see Figure 4.2. The **Plane** dialog appears, see Figure 4.3.

4.2

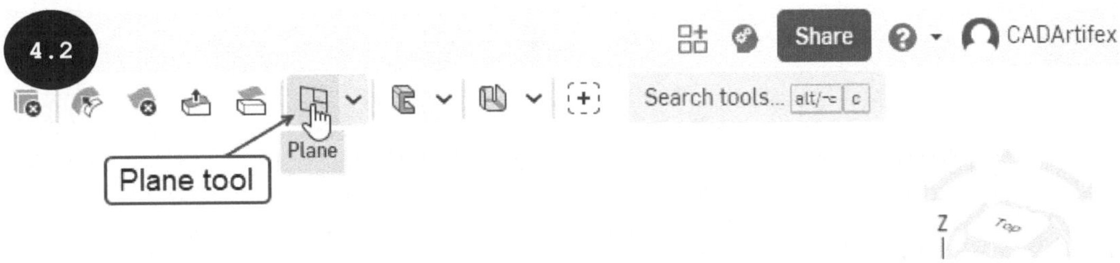

2. Ensure that the **Offset** option is selected in the **Plane type** drop-down list of the **Plane** dialog, see Figure 4.3. This will allow you to create a plane at a specified offset distance from an existing plane or planar face.

4.3

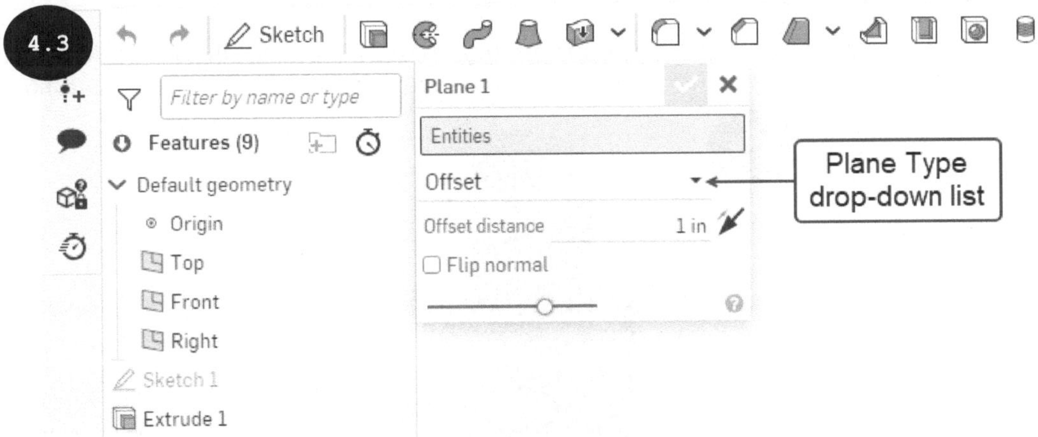

3. Select a planar face or a plane as a reference entity in the graphics area. A preview of a construction plane appears at a default offset distance from the selected face, see Figure 4.4. Also, the name of the selected face appears in the **Entities** field of the **Plane** dialog. In this case, the top planar face of the model is selected as the reference entity.

4.4

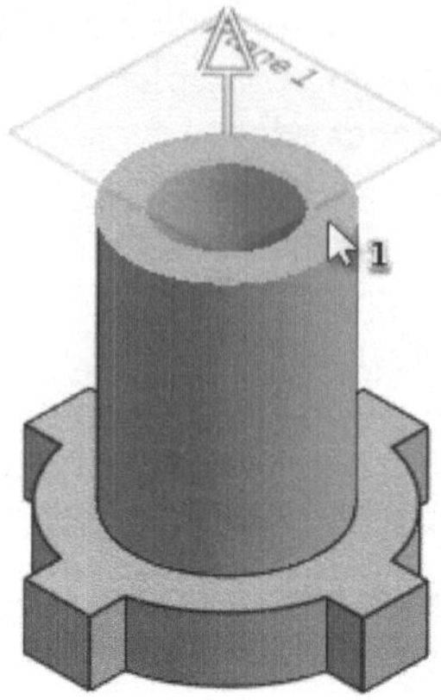

4. Enter the required offset distance in the **Offset distance** field (see Figure 4.5) and press **ENTER** to apply the change. Alternatively, you can drag the arrow that appears in the graphics area to dynamically adjust the offset distance visually.

4.5

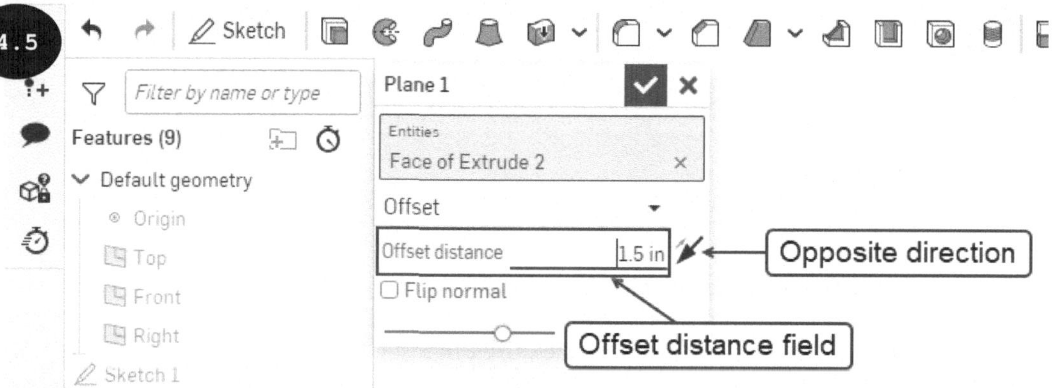

5. If needed, click on the **Opposite direction** button next to the **Offset distance** field to reverse the direction of the construction plane to the other side of the selected face, see Figure 4.6.

4.6

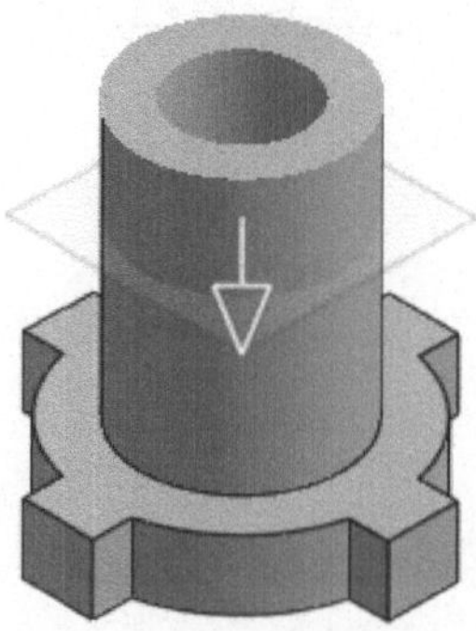

6. If needed, select the **Flip normal** check box to reverse the plane's normal direction; this step is optional. You can identify the current normal direction by viewing the plane's name (e.g., Plane1) in the graphics area.

7. Click the green checkmark ✅ in the **Plane** dialog to confirm the creation of the construction plane at the specified offset distance from the selected face and close the dialog.

Creating a Plane Parallel to a Face or Plane Through a Point

The method for creating a plane parallel to a planar face or existing plane and passing through a specified point is discussed below:

1. Click on the **Plane** tool in the **Feature** toolbar, see Figure 4.7. The **Plane** dialog appears, see Figure 4.8.

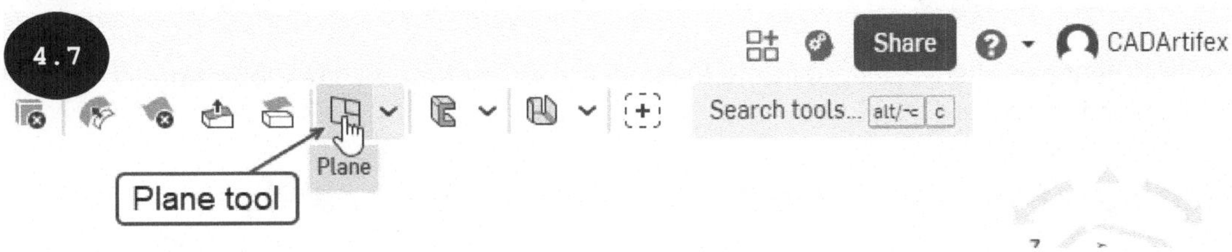

2. Invoke the **Plane type** drop-down list in the **Plane** dialog and then select the **Plane point** option, see Figure 4.8. This option allows you to create a plane that is parallel to a planar face or an existing plane while passing through a specific point or vertex.

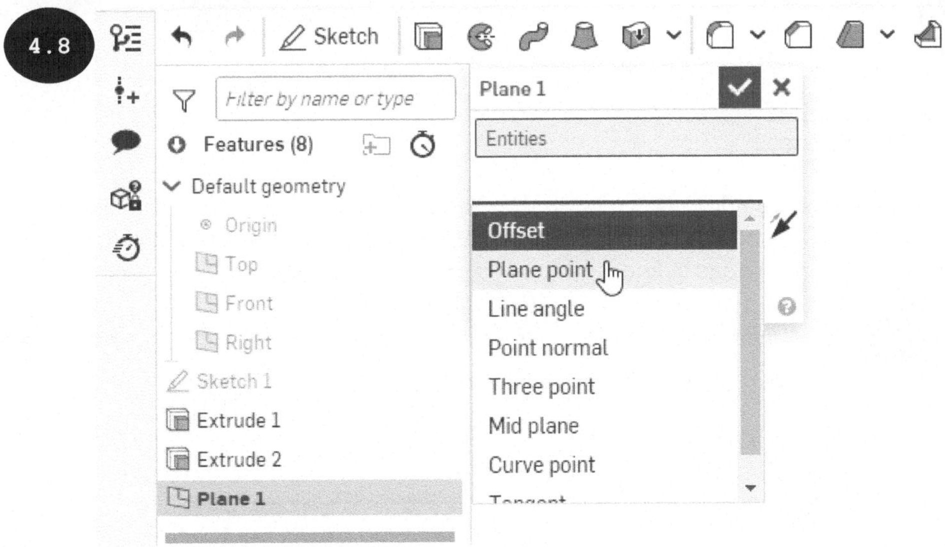

3. Select a planar face or a plane as the first reference entity in the graphics area, see Figure 4.9.

4. Select a point or a vertex as the second reference entity in the graphics area, see Figure 4.9. A preview of the reference plane appears, parallel to the selected face and passes through the chosen point or vertex, see Figure 4.10.

4.9

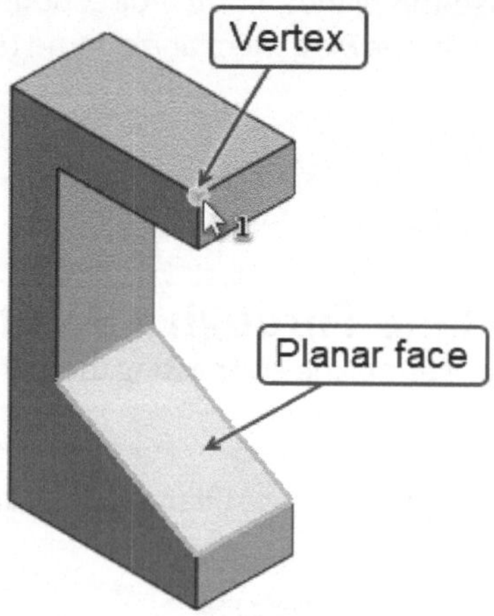

4.10

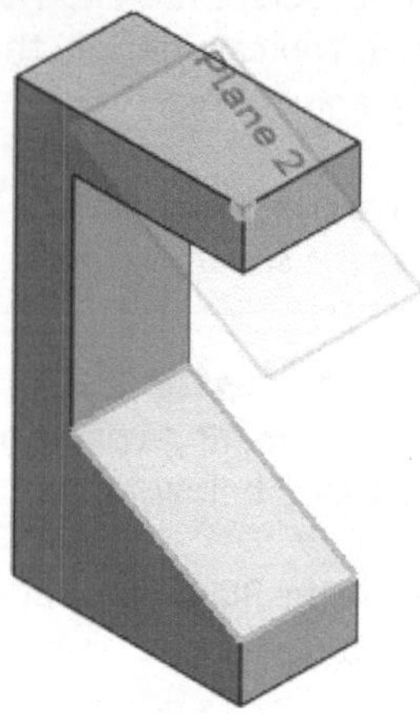

5. Click the green checkmark in the **Plane** dialog to confirm the creation of the construction plane and close the dialog.

Creating a Plane at an Angle to a Planar Face or a Plane

The method for creating a plane at an angle to a planar face or existing plane that passes through a linear edge or line is discussed below:

1. Click on the **Plane** tool in the **Feature** toolbar, see Figure 4.11. The **Plane** dialog appears.

4.11

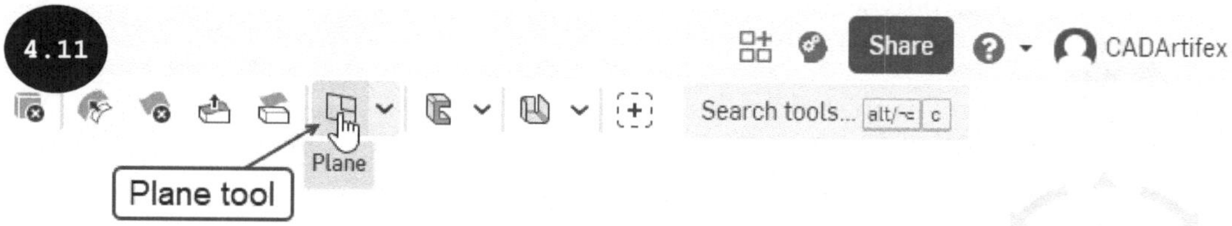

2. Invoke the **Plane type** drop-down list in the **Plane** dialog and then select the **Line angle** option, see Figure 4.12. This option enables you to create a plane at an angle to a planar face or existing plane around a linear edge or line.

4.12

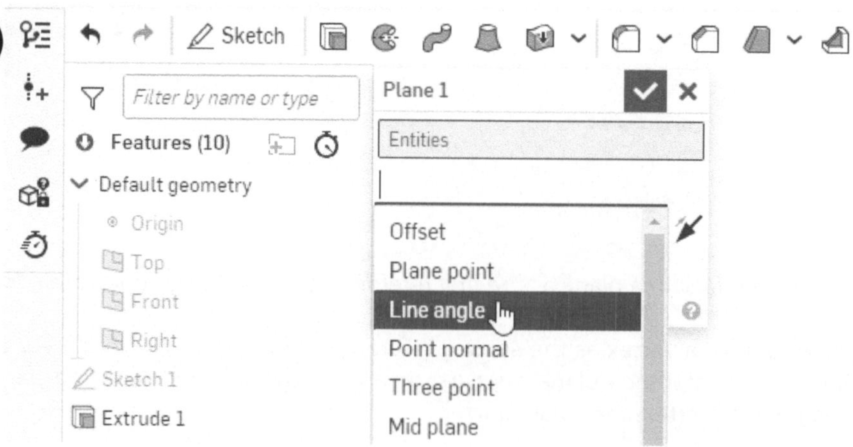

3. Select a planar face or a plane as the first reference entity in the graphics area, see Figure 4.13.

4. Select a linear edge or a line as the second reference entity in the graphics area, see Figure 4.14. A preview of the reference plane appears at a default angle (0-degree) to the selected face around the chosen edge or line, see Figure 4.15. Also, the **Angle** field displayed in the **Plane** dialog.

4.13

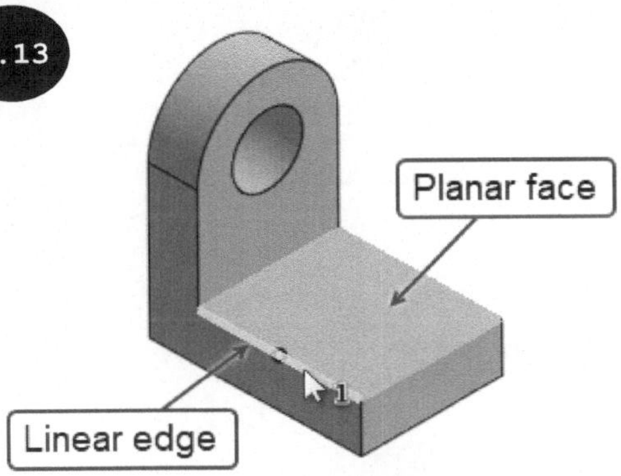

4.14

4.15

5. If needed, you can reverse the angle direction to the opposite side of the selected face by clicking on the **Opposite direction** button next to the **Angle** field.

6. Click the green checkmark in the **Plane** dialog to confirm the creation of the construction plane and close the dialog.

Creating a Plane Normal to a Line or Linear Edge

The method for creating a plane that is normal to a line or a linear edge and passing through a specified point is discussed below:

1. Click on the **Plane** tool in the **Feature** toolbar, see Figure 4.16. The **Plane** dialog appears.

4.16

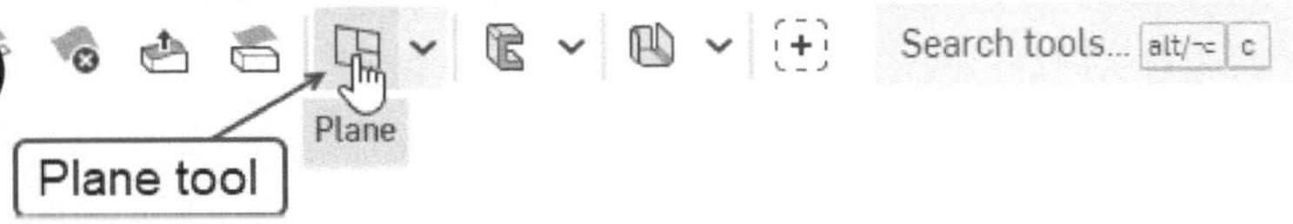

2. Invoke the **Plane type** drop-down list in the **Plane** dialog and then select the **Point normal** option, see Figure 4.17. This option enables you to create a plane that is normal to a line or a linear edge while passing through a specific point or vertex.

4.17

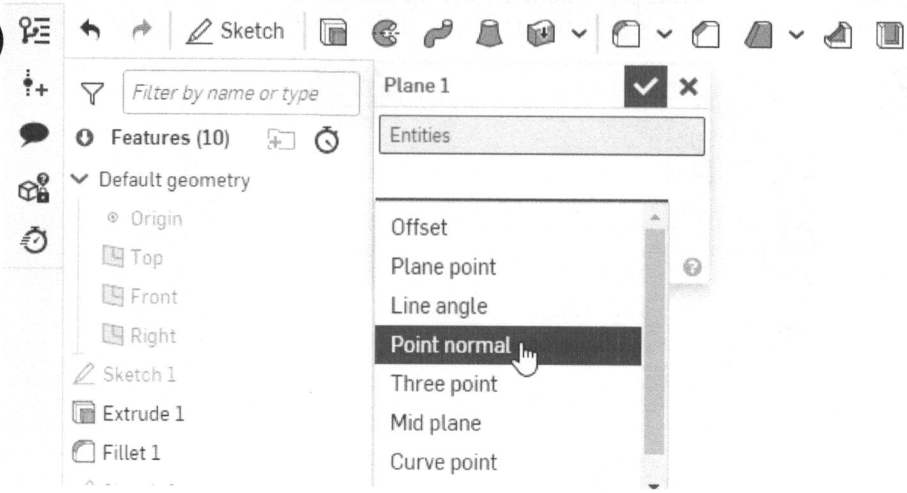

3. Select a line or linear edge as the first reference entity in the graphics area, see Figure 4.18.

4. Select a point or vertex as the second reference entity in the graphics area, see Figure 4.18. A preview of the reference plane appears normal to the selected linear edge and passes through the chosen vertex or point, see Figure 4.19.

4.18

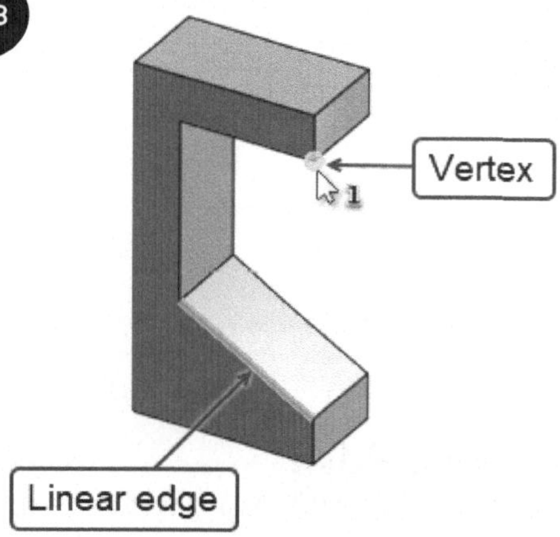

4.19

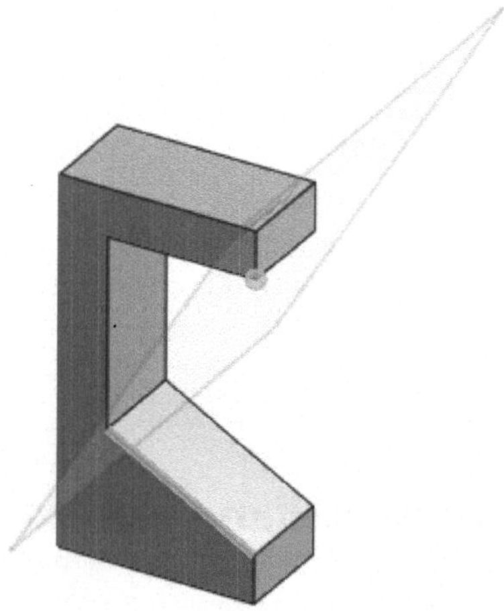

5. Click the green checkmark in the **Plane** dialog to confirm the creation of the construction plane and close the dialog.

Creating a Plane Through Three Points or Vertices

The method for creating a plane that passes through three points or vertices is discussed below:

1. Click on the **Plane** tool in the **Feature** toolbar, see Figure 4.20. The **Plane** dialog appears.

4.20

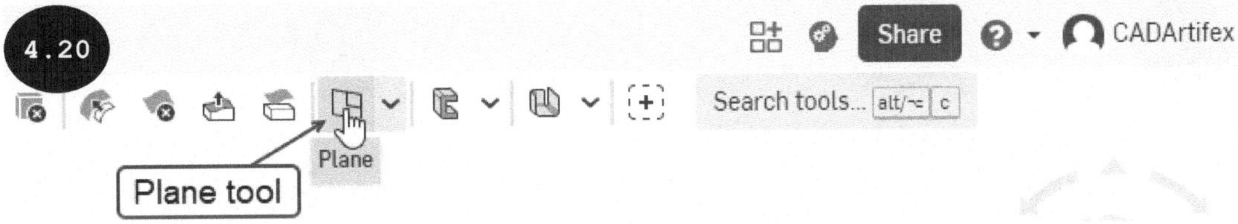

2. Invoke the **Plane type** drop-down list in the **Plane** dialog and then select the **Three point** option, see Figure 4.21. This option enables you to create a plane that passes through three points or vertices.

4.21

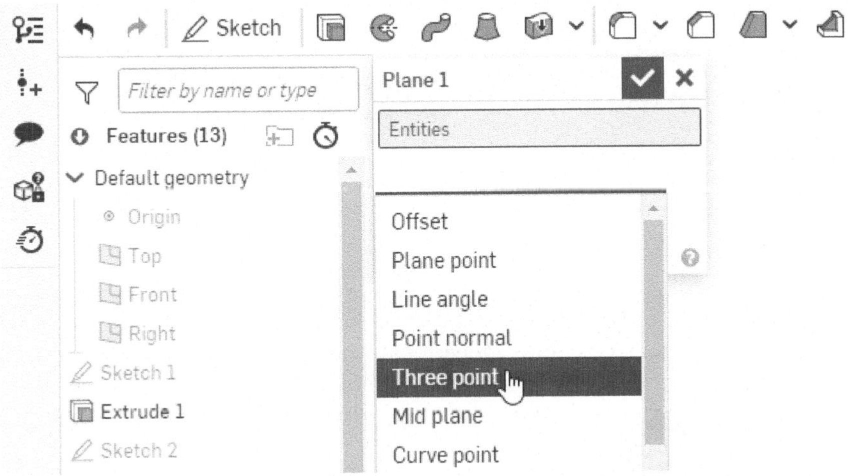

3. Select three points or vertices individually as the reference entities in the graphics area. A preview of the reference plane appears, passing through the selected points or vertices, see Figure 4.22.

4.22

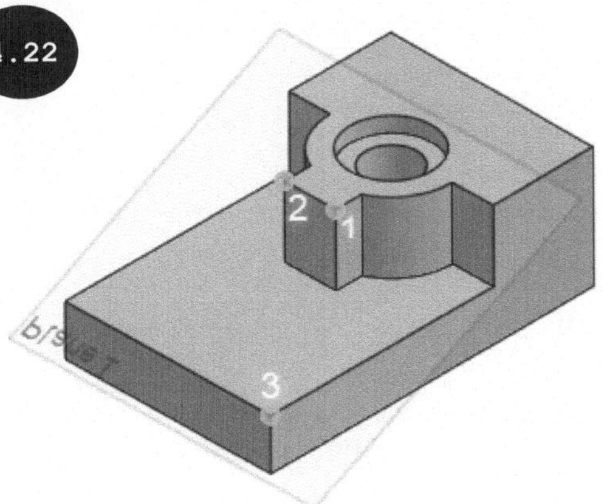

4. Click the green checkmark ✓ in the **Plane** dialog to confirm the creation of the construction plane and close the dialog.

Creating a Plane in the Middle of Two Planar Faces

The method for creating a plane in the middle of two planar faces or planes is discussed below:

1. Click on the **Plane** tool in the **Feature** toolbar, see Figure 4.23. The **Plane** dialog appears.

4.23

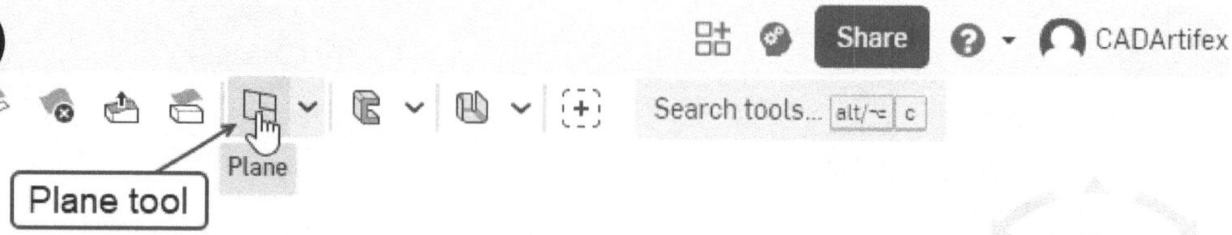

2. Select the **Mid plane** option in the **Plane type** drop-down list of the **Plane** dialog, see Figure 4.24. This option enables you to create a plane in the middle of two planar faces.

4.24

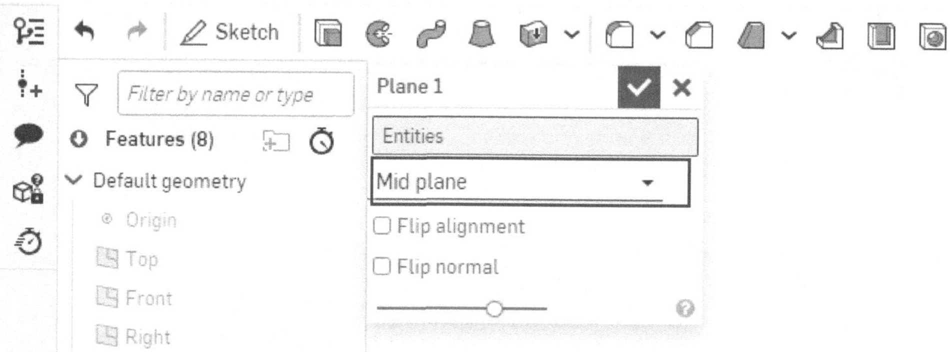

3. Select two planar faces or planes individually as the reference entities in the graphics area. A preview of the reference plane appears in the middle of the selected faces, see Figure 4.25.

4.25

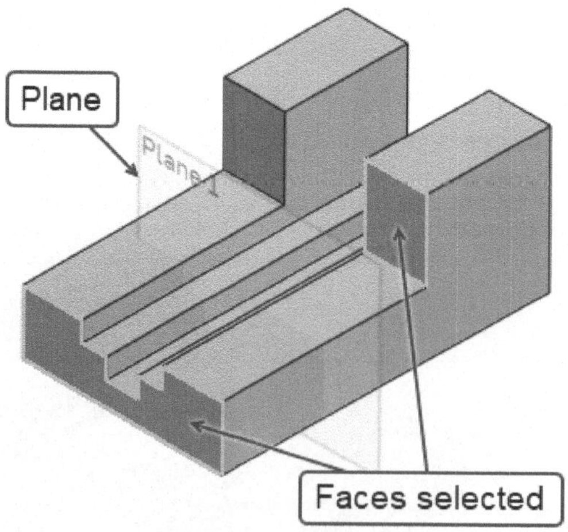

4. Click the green checkmark in the **Plane** dialog to confirm the creation of the construction plane and close the dialog.

Creating a Plane Normal to a Curve or Curved Edge

The method for creating a plane that is normal to a curve or curved edge and passes through a specified point is discussed below:

1. Click on the **Plane** tool in the **Feature** toolbar, see Figure 4.26. The **Plane** dialog appears.

4.26

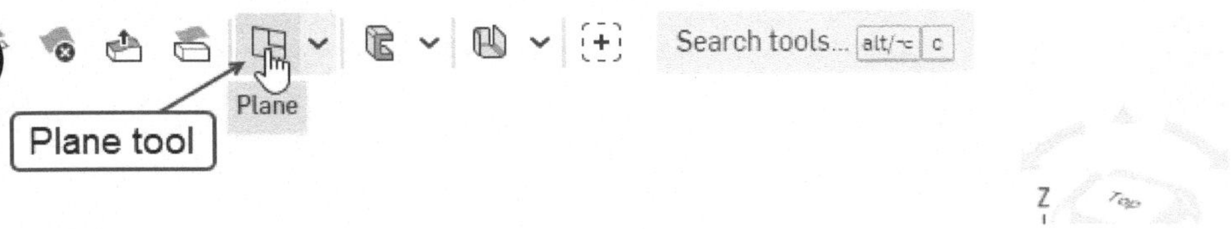

2. Select the **Curve point** option in the **Plane type** drop-down list of the **Plane** dialog, see Figure 4.27.

4.27

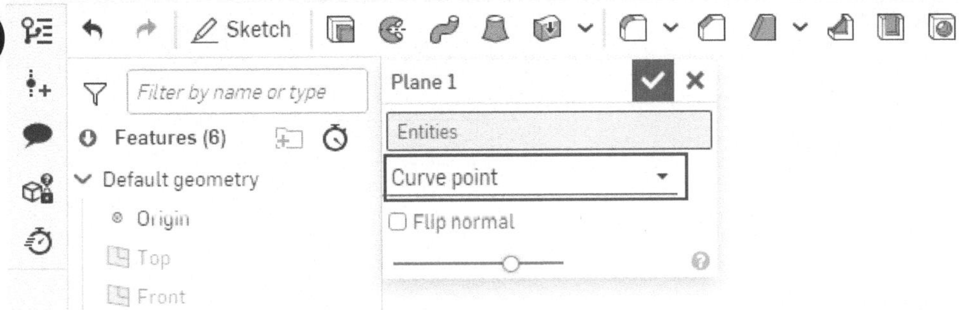

3. Select a curve or edge as the first reference entity in the graphics area, see Figure 4.28.

4. Select a point or vertex as the second reference entity, see Figure 4.28. A preview of the reference plane appears normal to the selected curve and passes through the chosen point, see Figure 4.29.

4.28

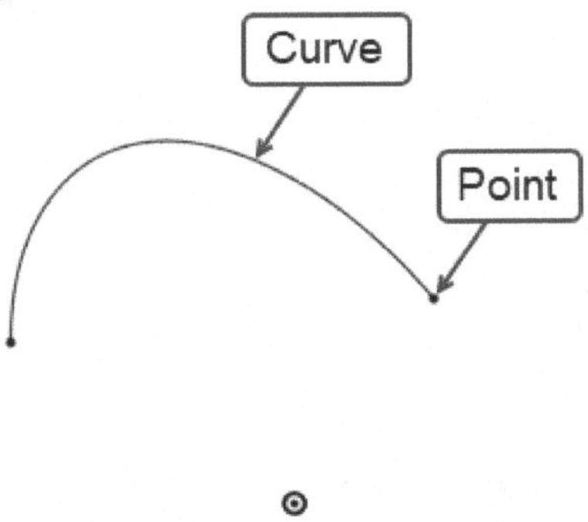

4.29

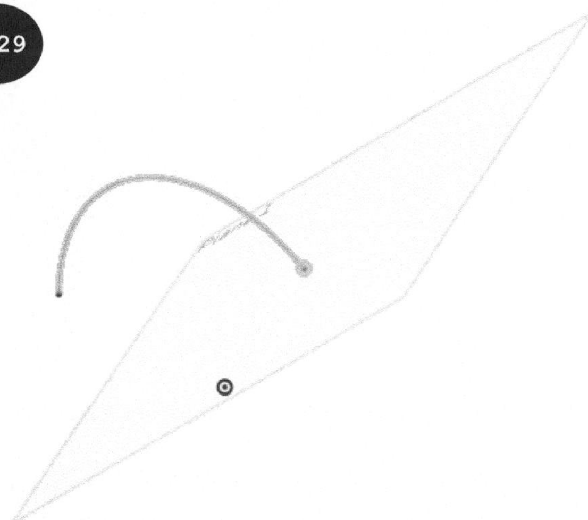

5. Click the green checkmark in the **Plane** dialog to confirm the creation of the construction plane and close the dialog.

Creating a Plane Tangent to a Cylindrical Face

The method for creating a plane that is tangent to a cylindrical face and either passes through a specific point or is parallel to a planar face is discussed below:

1. Click on the **Plane** tool in the **Feature** toolbar, see Figure 4.30. The **Plane** dialog appears.

4.30

2. Select the **Tangent** option in the **Plane type** drop-down list of the **Plane** dialog, see Figure 4.31.

4.31

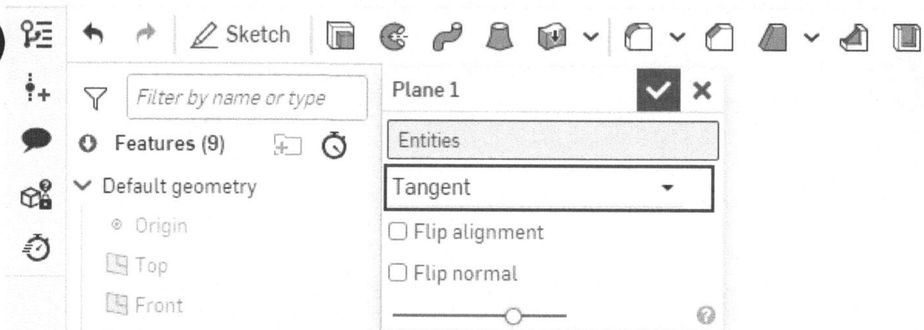

3. Select a cylindrical face of the model as the first reference entity, see Figure 4.32. A preview of a reference plane appears tangent to the selected face.

4.32

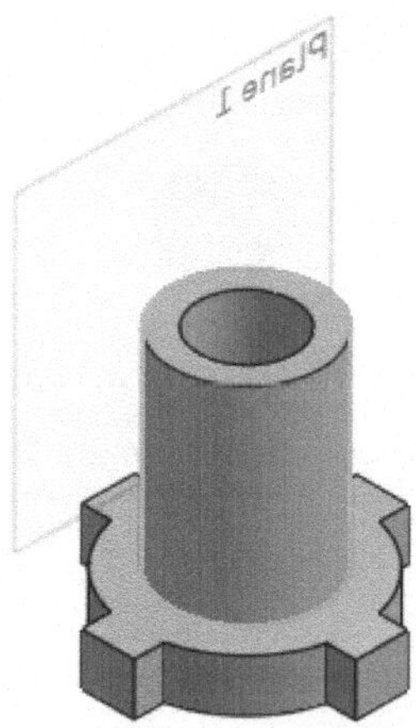

Now, if needed, you can select either a point or a planar face as the second reference entity.

4. Select either a point (vertex) or a planar face as the second reference entity in the graphics area. A preview of the reference plane appears based on the selection, see Figures 3.33 and 3.34. In Figure 3.33, a vertex is selected as the second reference entity, resulting in a plane that is tangent to the cylindrical face and passes through the selected vertex. However, Figure 3.34 shows a planar face selected as the second reference entity, resulting in a plane that is tangent to the cylindrical face and parallel to the chosen planar face.

4.33

4.34

5. If needed, you can reverse the alignment of the resulting reference plane to the opposite side relative to the selected entities by selecting the **Flip alignment** check box in the **Plane** dialog.

6. Click the green checkmark ✅ in the **Plane** dialog to confirm the creation of the construction plane and close the dialog.

Exploring Additional Extrude / Revolve Options

In earlier chapters, you learned how to create base features using the **Extrude** and **Revolve** tools. This chapter will explore additional options for these tools, such as **Add**, **Remove**, and **Intersect**. The additional options for both of these tools are discussed next.

Exploring Additional Options of the Extrude Tool

In Onshape, after creating the base feature of a model, you can proceed to create the second feature and then continue adding additional features sequentially. To create the sketch for the second feature, you can select any reference plane or a planar face of an existing feature as the sketching plane. For example, in Figure 4.35, the sketch is created on the right planar face of the model.

4.35

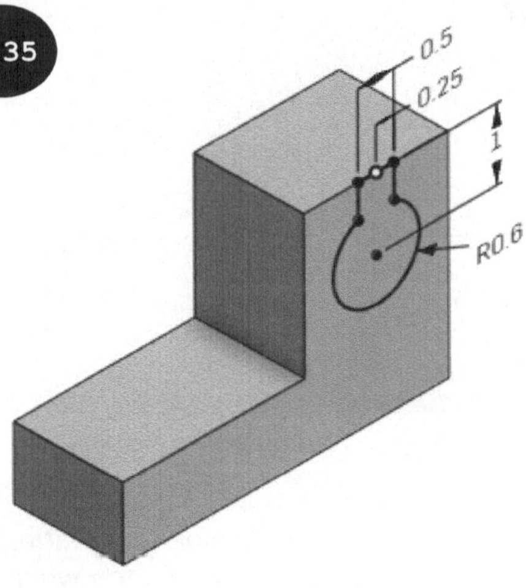

After creating a sketch for an extrude feature, click on the **Extrude** tool in the **Sketch** toolbar. The **Extrude** dialog box appears, see Figure 4.36. Most of the options in this dialog have been covered previously when creating the base extrude feature, and the remaining options are discussed below:

4.36

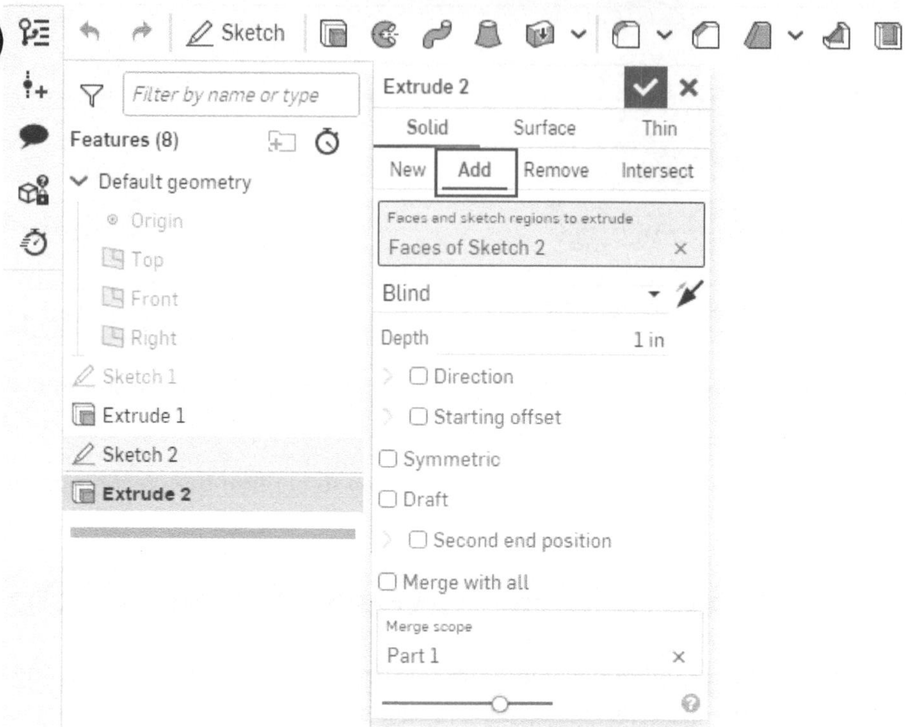

Add

When creating the second or additional extrude features of a model, the **Add** option is automatically selected in the **Operation type** area of the dialog, refer to Figure 3.36. This option extrudes the sketch by adding material and merging the resulting feature with the existing features of the model, see Figure 4.37.

4.37

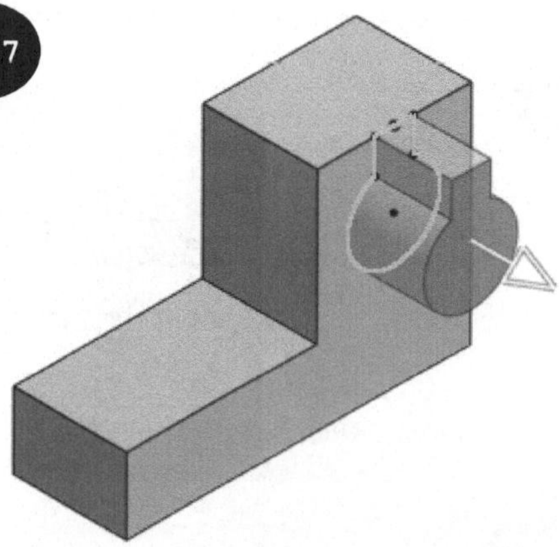

Note that the additional options that appear in the dialog for creating an extrude feature by adding material are the same as those discussed in the previous chapter when creating the base feature.

Remove

On activating the **Remove** option in the **Operation type** area of the dialog, you can create a cut feature by removing material from the model, refer to Figure 4.38. To ensure material is removed from the model, make sure the direction of extrusion is set toward the model, see Figure 4.39. You can reverse the extrusion direction toward the model by clicking the **Opposite Direction** button next to the **End type** drop-down list in the dialog.

4.38

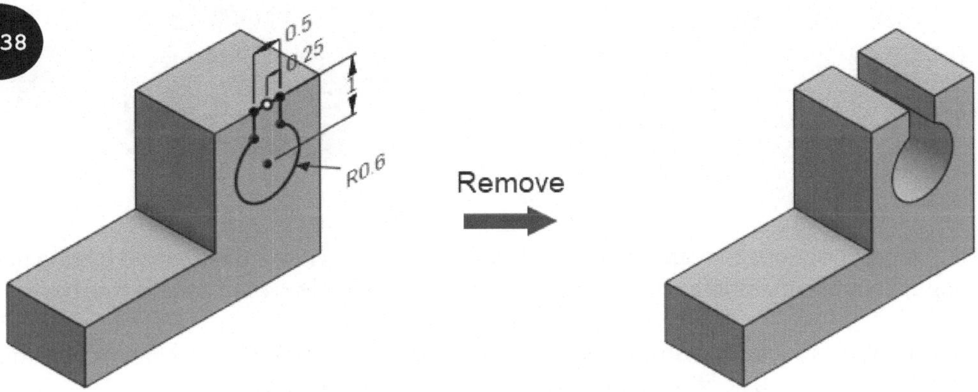

4.39

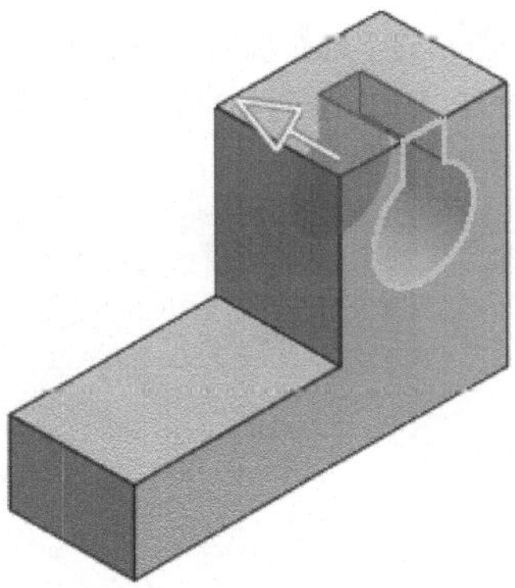

Note that the other options that appear in the dialog for creating an extrude cut feature by removing material are the same as those discussed in the previous chapter when creating the base feature.

Intersect

The **Intersect** option is used for creating a feature by keeping only the overlapping or common material between the existing feature and the new feature being created, refer to Figure 4.40. On activating this option, the preview of the overlapping or common material between the features is highlighted in the graphics area.

4.40

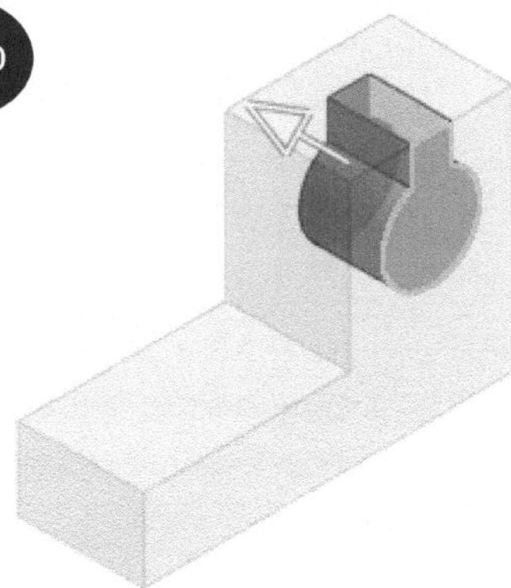

Figure 4.41 shows a sketch, which is created on the top planar face of the model and Figure 4.42 shows the resultant intersect feature.

4.41

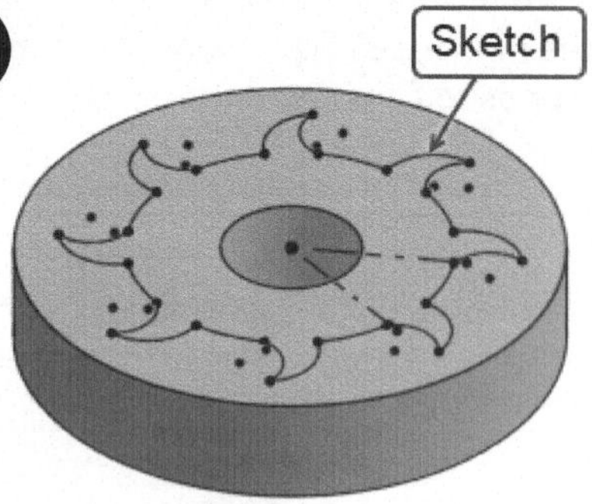

4.42

Note that the other options that appear in the dialog for creating an extrude feature by retaining the overlapping or common material are the same as those discussed earlier when creating the base feature.

After specifying all the required parameters for creating an extrude feature, click the green checkmark in the **Extrude** dialog box to confirm the creation of the feature and close the dialog.

Exploring Additional Options of the Revolve Tool

In Onshape, when creating a revolve feature by revolving a sketch around an axis using the **Revolve** tool, the **Revolve** dialog appears, see Figure 4.43.

4.43

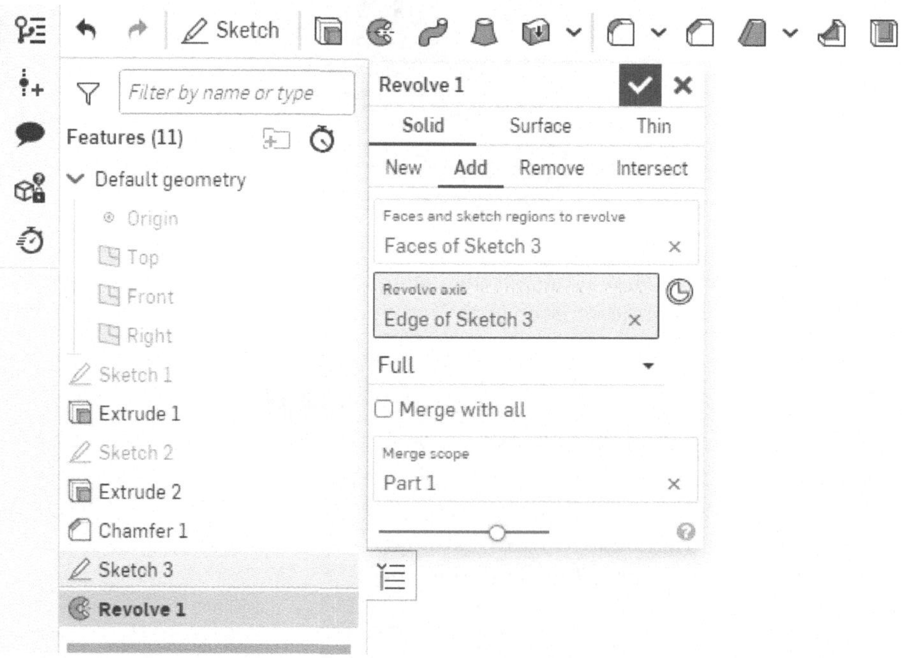

The options in the **Revolve** dialog are used to create a revolve feature by revolving a sketch around an axis. Most of these options, including **New** in the **Operation type** area, were discussed in the previous chapter when creating the base revolve feature. The remaining options: **Add**, **Remove**, and **Intersect** are used to add, remove, or retain the intersecting material, respectively in a similar manner as explained earlier when extruding a sketch.

Figure 4.44 shows a sketch with an axis of revolution (construction line) for creating a revolve feature. Figure 4.45 shows the resultant revolve feature created by adding material, removing material, and intersecting material using the respective **Add**, **Remove**, and **Intersect** operation types.

4.44

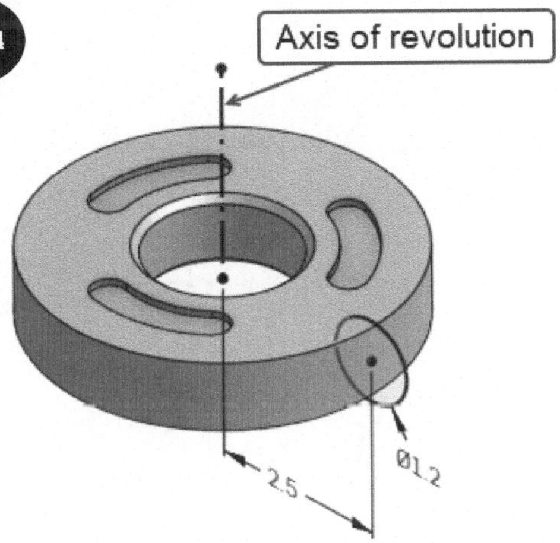

4.45

Tutorial 1

Create a model shown in Figure 4.46 by creating each feature individually. All dimensions are in mm.

4.46

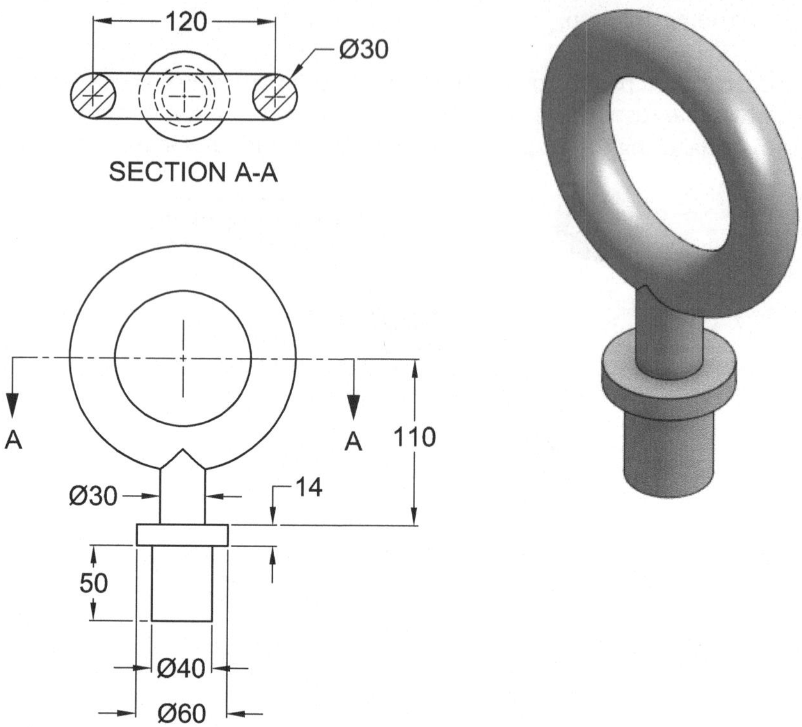

Section 1: Starting a New Design Document

1. Launch Onshape (***onshape.com***) and log in to your account if you're not already logged in.

2. If you are within a document, click on the **Onshape** logo located in the top left corner of the browser to display the **Documents Page**, see Figure 4.47.

4.47

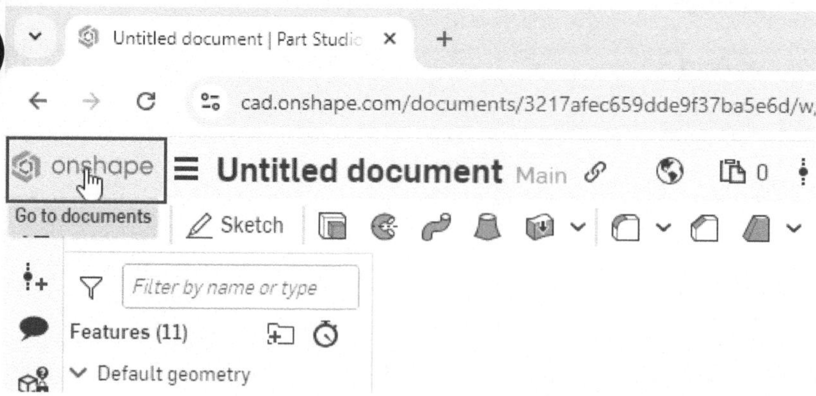

3. Click on the **Create** button at the top left corner of the **Documents Page** and then click on the **Document** option in the menu that appears, see Figure 4.48. The **New document** window appears with the default name of the document as "**Untitled document**".

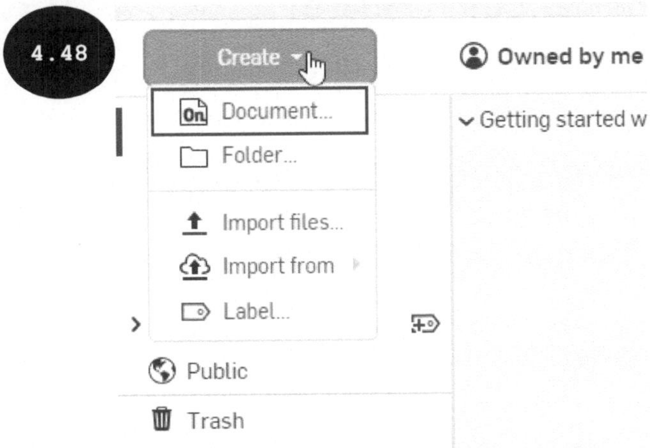

4. Enter **C04 Tutorial 01** as the name of the design document in the **New document** window, and then click on the **Create** button or the **Create Public Document** button, depending on your subscription type. A new document with the specified name is opened.

Section 2: Settings Units

Now, you can set millimeters (mm) as the unit for the length measurement in the current document.

1. Invoke the **Document** menu by clicking on the ☰ icon (three horizontal lines) next to the **Onshape** logo at the top left corner, see Figure 4.49.

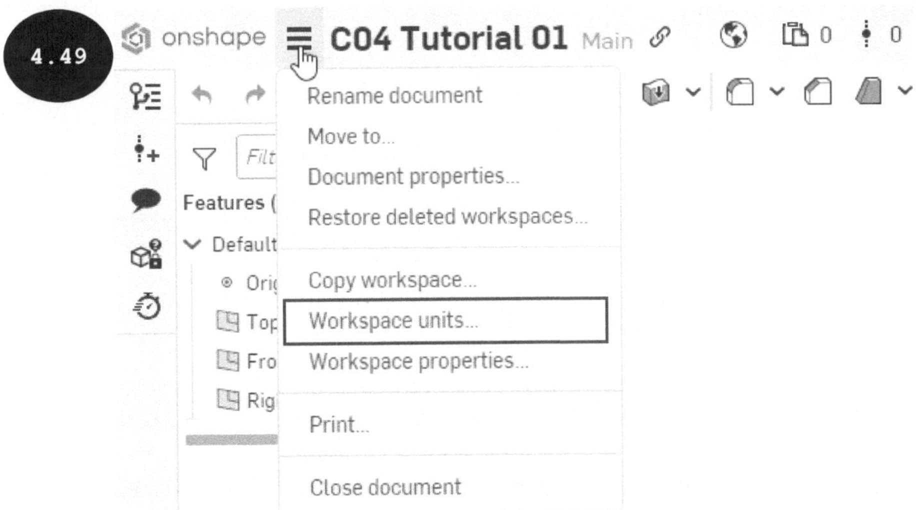

2. Click on the **Workspace units** option in the **Document** menu, refer to Figure 4.49. The **Workspace units** dialog appears, see Figure 4.50.

3. Select the **Millimeter** unit in the **Length default unit** drop-down list and set its precision to **0.1** in the respective **Display decimals** drop-down list of the **Workspace units** dialog, see Figure 4.50.

4.50

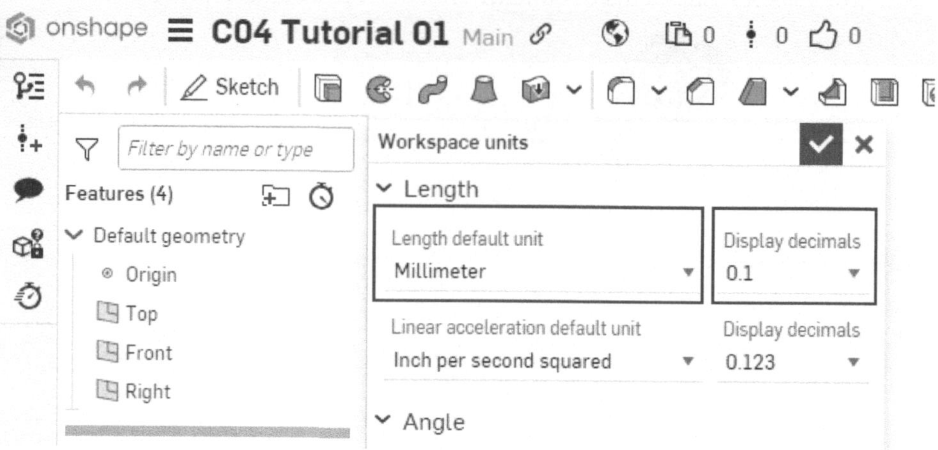

4. After selecting the required unit of length measurement and the decimal precision for the current design document, click on the green checkmark ✓ to confirm the selection and exit the dialog. The millimeter is defined as the unit for the length measurement.

Section 3: Accessing the Sketch Toolbar

Now, you can access the **Sketch** toolbar to create the sketch of the base feature, which is a revolve feature.

1. Click on the **Sketch** tool in the **Feature** toolbar, see Figure 4.51. The **Sketch** dialog appears and you are prompted to select a sketch plane.

4.51

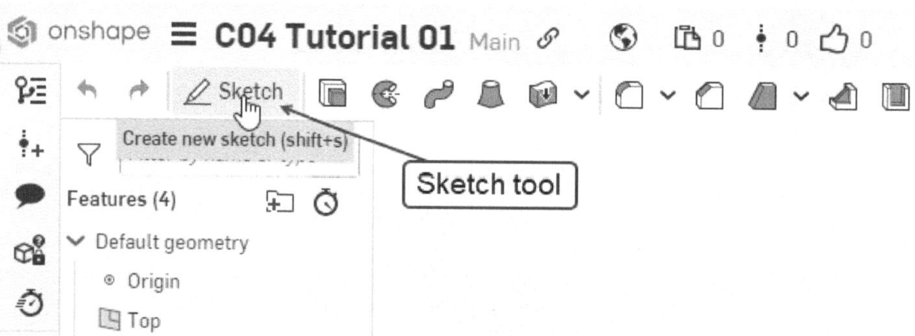

2. Select the Top plane as the sketching plane in the graphics area. The selected plane becomes the sketching plane, and the **Sketch** toolbar appears with the display of various sketching tools.

3. Press the **N** key to make the sketching plane normal to the viewing direction.

Section 4: Creating the Base Feature - Revolve

Now, you can create the base feature of the model, which is a revolve feature.

1. Create a circle of diameter 30 mm and a vertical construction line originating from the origin as the sketch of the revolve feature, see Figure 4.52. In this figure, a linear diameter dimension (centerline dimension) is applied to the center of the circle relative to the construction line.

4.52

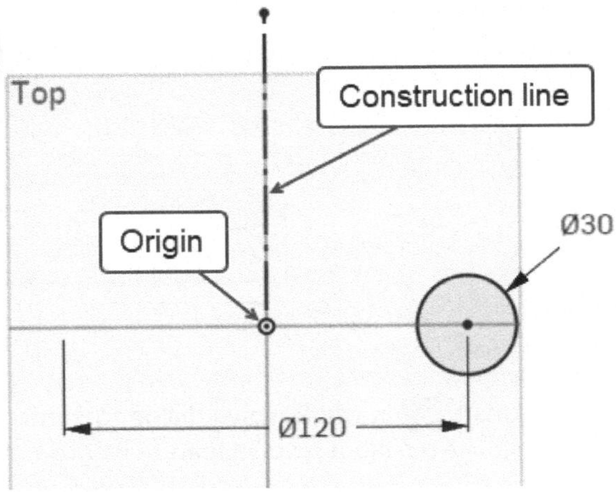

2. Click on the **Revolve** tool in the **Sketch** toolbar, see Figure 4.53. The **Revolve** dialog appears and the sketch profile is automatically selected.

4.53

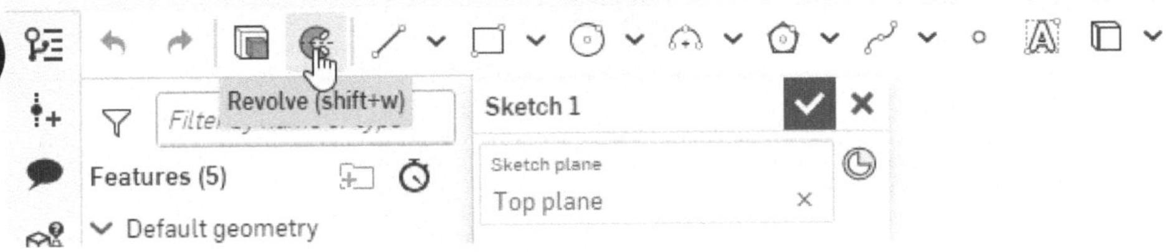

3. Press the SHIFT + 7 keys to change the view orientation to isometric.

4. Click on the **Revolve axis** field in the **Revolve** dialog and then select the construction line of the sketch as the axis of revolution. A preview of a revolve feature appears in the graphics area, see Figure 4.54.

4.54

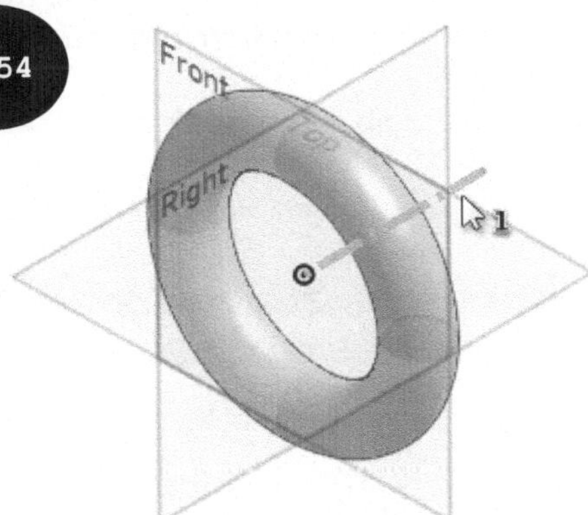

5. Ensure that the **Full** option is selected in the **Revolve type** drop-down list of the dialog to create a revolve feature by revolving the sketch 360 degrees around the axis, see Figure 4.55.

4.55

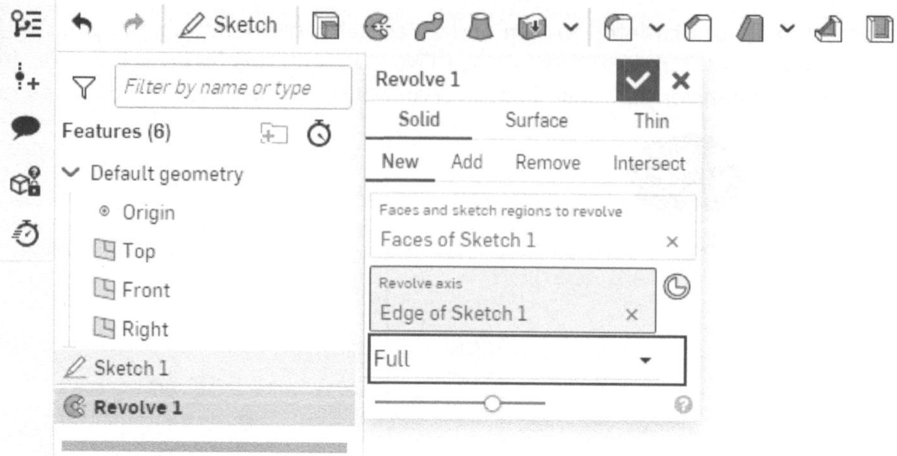

6. Click on the green checkmark in the **Revolve** dialog to confirm the creation of the revolve feature and exit the dialog. The resultant revolve feature is shown in Figure 4.56.

4.56

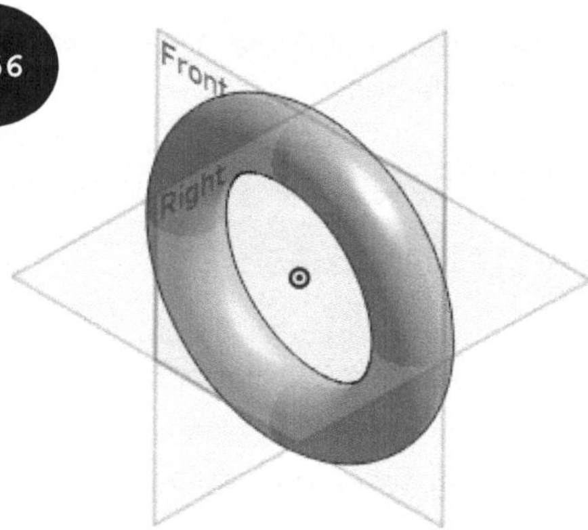

Section 5: Creating the Second Feature - Extrude

Now, you can create the second feature of the model, which is an extrude feature. To begin, you first need to create a construction plane offset by 110 mm from the Top plane.

1. Click on the **Plane** tool in the **Feature** toolbar, see Figure 4.57. The **Plane** dialog appears.

4.57

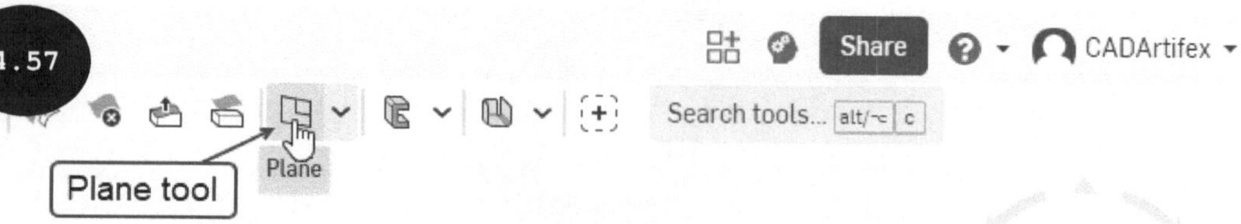

2. Select the **Offset** option in the **Plane type** drop-down list of the **Plane** dialog, see Figure 4.58.

4.58

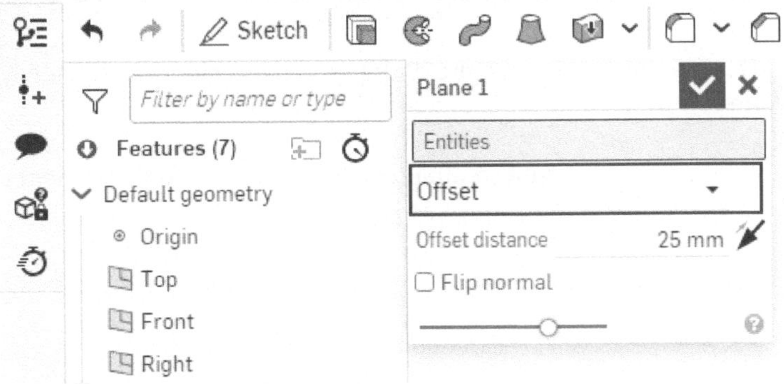

3. Select the Top plane as the reference entity in the graphics area. A preview of a construction plane appears at an offset distance from the selected plane (Top), see Figure 4.59.

4.59

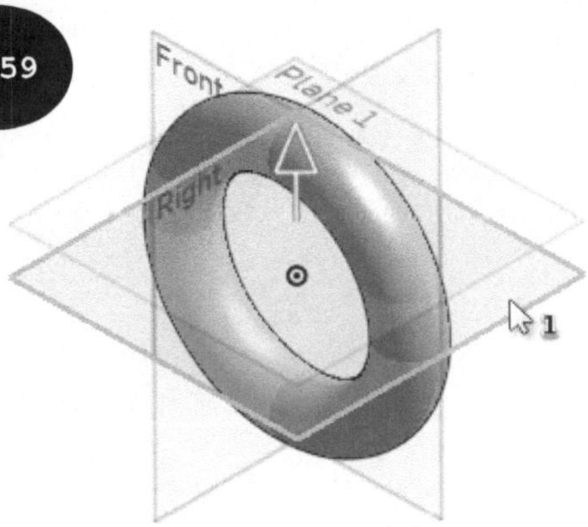

4. Enter **110** mm in the **Offset distance** field of the **Plane** dialog and press ENTER. The preview of the construction plane updates in the graphics area accordingly.

5. Click the **Opposite direction** button next to the **Offset distance** field in the dialog to reverse the direction of the construction plane downwards, as shown in Figure 4.60.

4.60

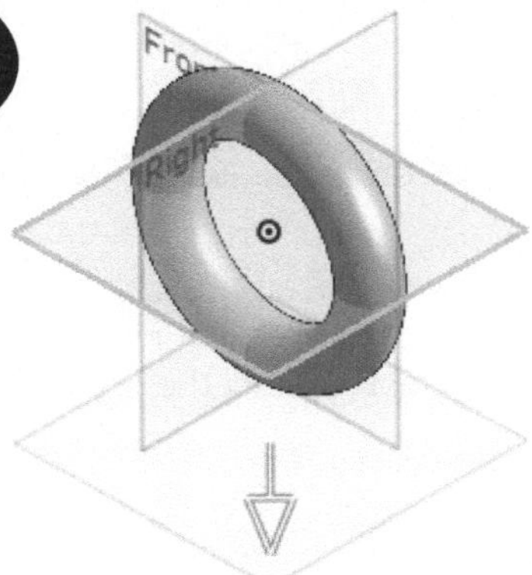

6. Click on the green checkmark ✓ to confirm the creation of the construction plane and exit the dialog.

   Now, you need to create the second feature of the model by selecting the newly created plane as the sketching plane.

7. Click on the **Sketch** tool in the **Feature** toolbar (see Figure 4.61) and then select the newly created construction plane as the sketching plane, see Figure 4.62.

4.61

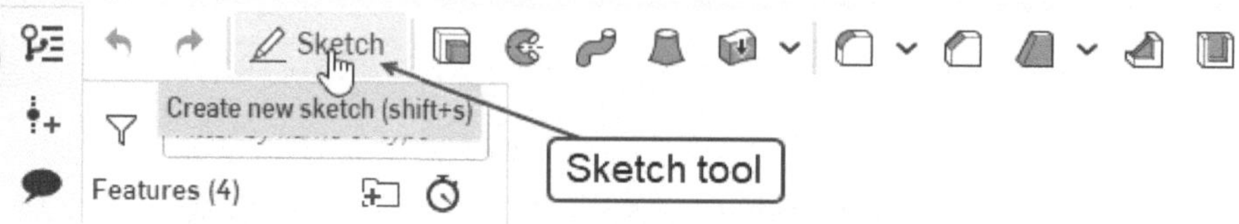

4.62

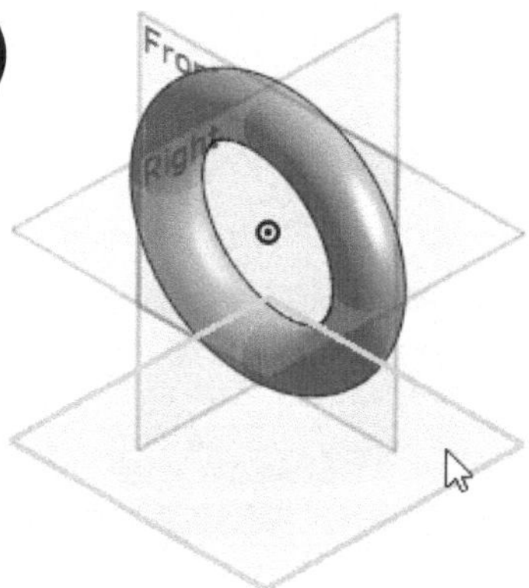

8. Press the **N** key to make the sketching plane normal to the viewing direction.

9. Create a circle of diameter 30 mm and apply the diameter dimension, see Figure 4.63. Note that the center of the circle is at the origin.

4.63

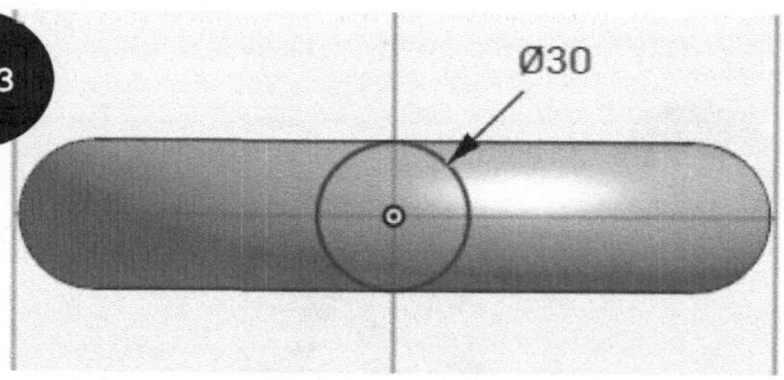

10. Click on the **Extrude** tool in the **Sketch** toolbar, see Figure 4.64. The **Extrude** dialog appears and the sketch profile is automatically selected. Also, the preview of an extrude feature appears.

4.64

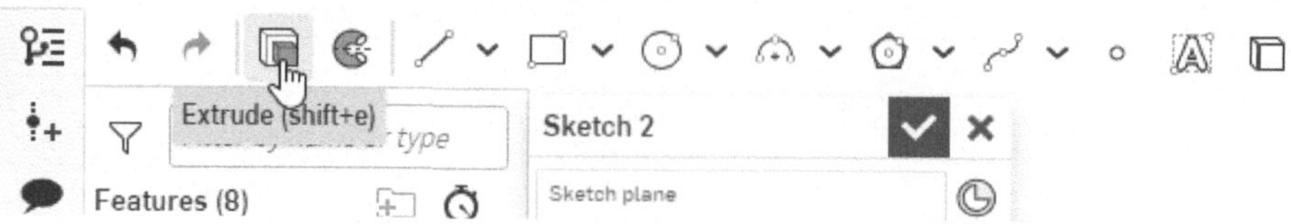

11. Press the SHIFT + 7 keys to change the view orientation to isometric, see Figure 4.65.

4.65

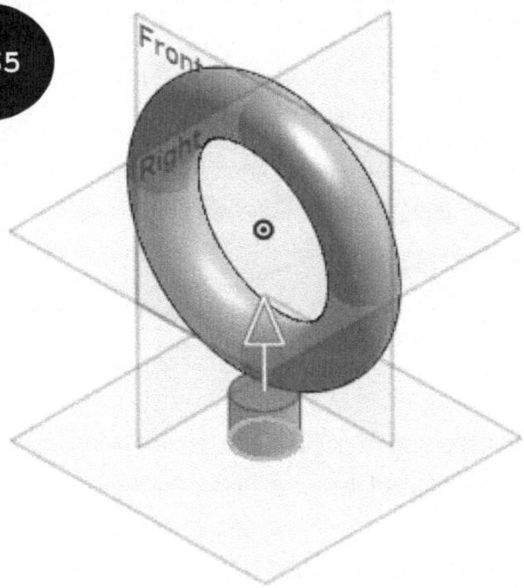

12. Ensure that the direction of extrusion is towards the base feature as shown in Figure 4.65.

13. Select the **Up to next** option in the **End type** drop-down list of the dialog, see Figure 4.66. The preview of the extrude feature appears up to its next intersection, see Figure 4.67.

4.66

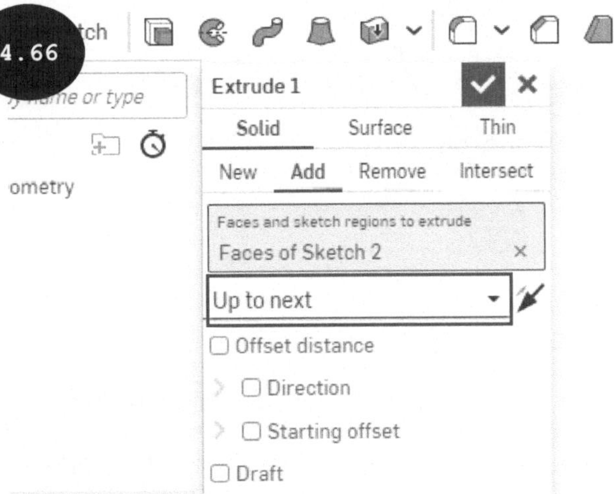

4.67

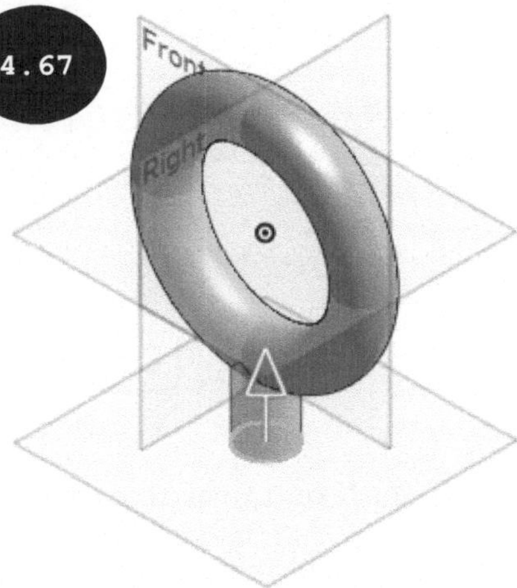

Note: The **Add** option is activated in the **Operation type** area of the **Extrude** dialog, by default. Consequently, the feature will be created by adding material and merging with the existing feature, forming a single body or part.

14. Click on the green checkmark ✓ in the **Extrude** dialog to confirm the creation of the feature and exit the dialog.

Section 6: Creating the Third Feature - Extrude

Now, you can create the third feature of the model, which is also an extrude feature.

1. Click on the **Sketch** tool in the **Feature** toolbar, see Figure 4.68. The **Sketch** dialog appears and you are prompted to select a sketching plane.

4.68

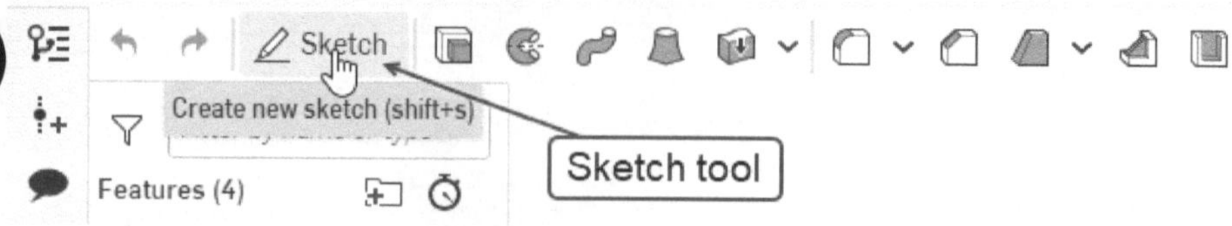

2. Rotate the model by holding the right mouse button and dragging the cursor until the bottom planar face of the model becomes visible, see Figure 4.69.

3. Select the bottom planar face of the model as the sketching plane, see Figure 4.69. The **Sketch** toolbar appears with various sketching tools.

4.69

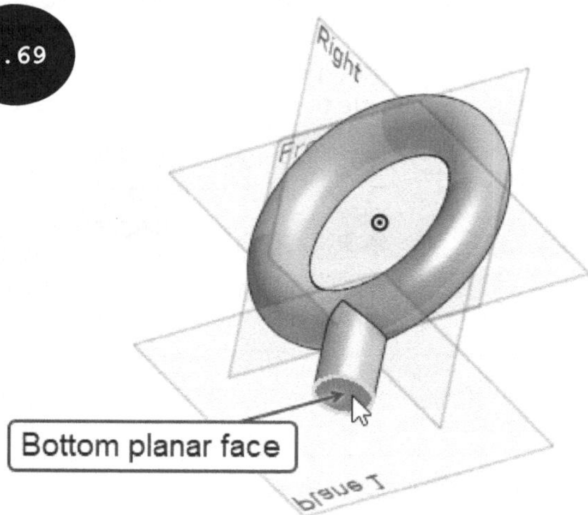

4. Press the **N** key to make the sketching plane (bottom planar face) normal to the viewing direction.

5. Create a circle of diameter 60 mm as the sketch of the feature, see Figure 4.70. The center of the circle is at the origin.

4.70

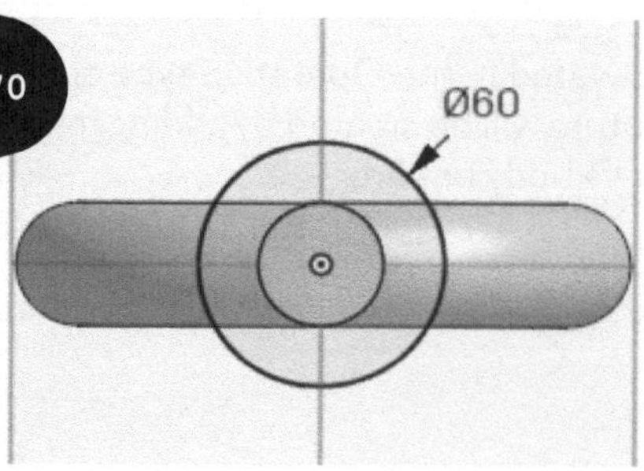

6. Click on the **Extrude** tool in the **Sketch** toolbar, see Figure 4.71. The **Extrude** dialog appears and the sketch profile is automatically selected. Also, the preview of an extrude feature appears in the graphics area.

4.71

7. Press the SHIFT + 7 keys to change the view orientation to isometric, see Figure 4.72.

4.72

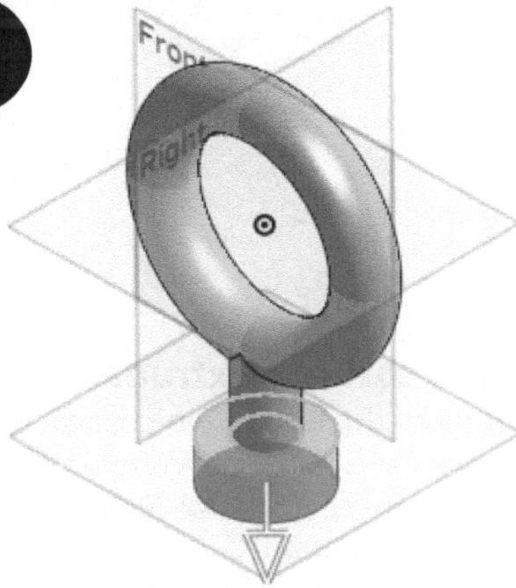

8. Ensure that the direction of extrusion is downwards as shown in Figure 4.72.

9. Enter **12** mm as the depth of extrusion in the **Depth** field of the **Extrude** dialog (see Figure 4.73) and press ENTER. The preview of the extrude feature gets updated, accordingly.

4.73

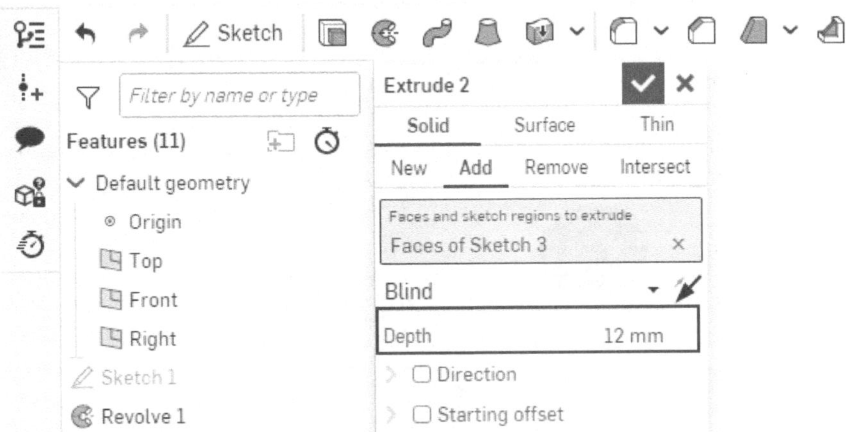

Note: The **Add** option is activated in the **Operation type** area of the **Extrude** dialog, by default. Consequently, the feature will be created by adding material and merging with the existing features, forming a single body or part.

10. Click on the green checkmark ✓ in the **Extrude** dialog to confirm the creation of the feature and exit the dialog. The resultant extrude feature is shown in Figure 4.74.

4.74

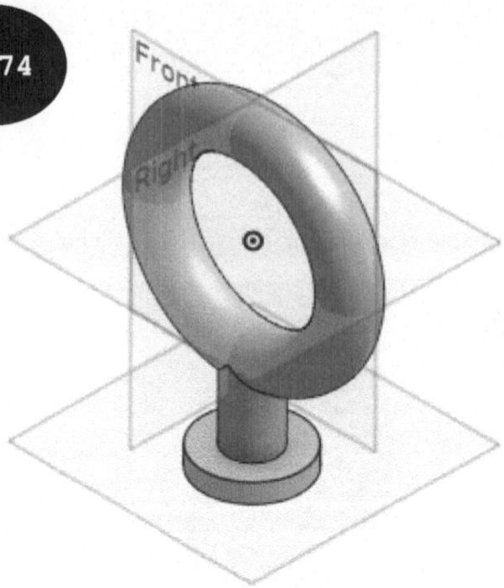

Section 7: Creating the Fourth Feature - Extrude

Now, you can create the fourth feature of the model, which is an extrude feature.

1. Click on the **Sketch** tool in the **Feature** toolbar, see Figure 4.75. The **Extrude** dialog appears and you are prompted to select a sketching plane.

4.75

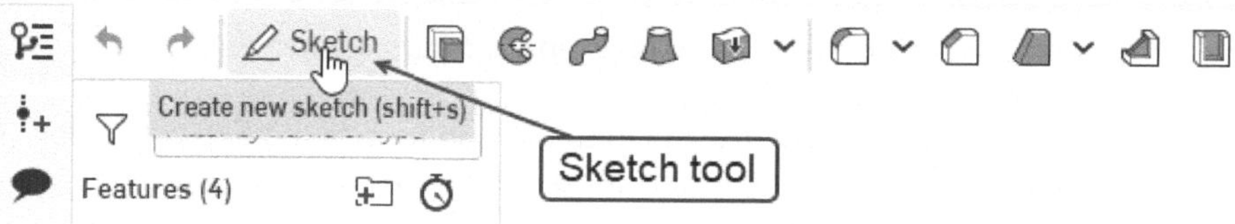

2. Rotate the model by holding the right mouse button and dragging the cursor until the bottom planar face of the model becomes visible, refer to Figure 4.76.

3. Select the bottom planar face of the model as the sketching plane, see Figure 4.76. The **Sketch** toolbar appears with various sketching tools.

4.76

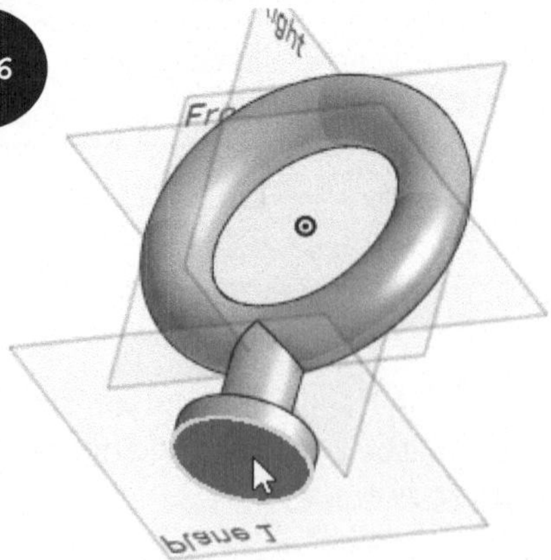

4. Press the N key to make the sketching plane (bottom planar face) normal to the viewing direction.

5. Create a circle of diameter 40 mm as the sketch of the feature, see Figure 4.77. The center of the circle is at the origin.

4.77

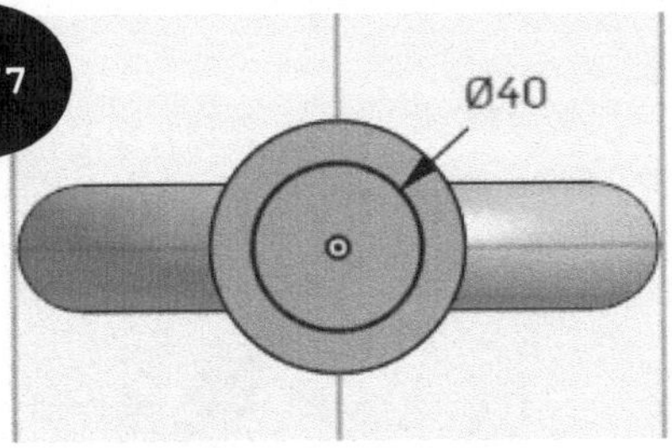

6. Click on the **Extrude** tool in the **Sketch** toolbar, see Figure 4.78. The **Extrude** dialog appears and the sketch profile is automatically selected. Also, the preview of an extrude feature appears in the graphics area.

4.78

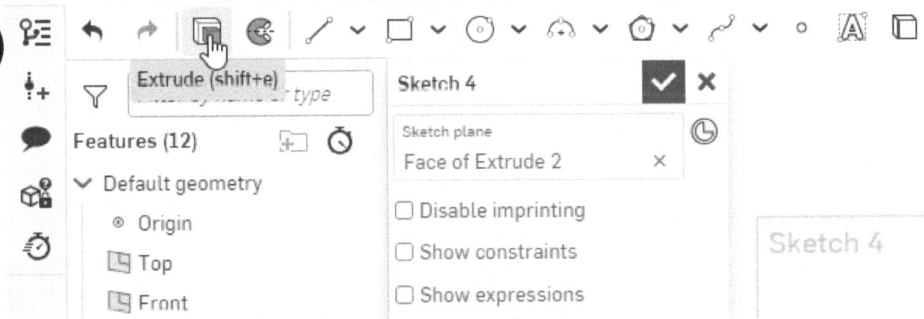

7. Press the SHIFT + 7 keys to change the view orientation to isometric, see Figure 4.79.

4.79

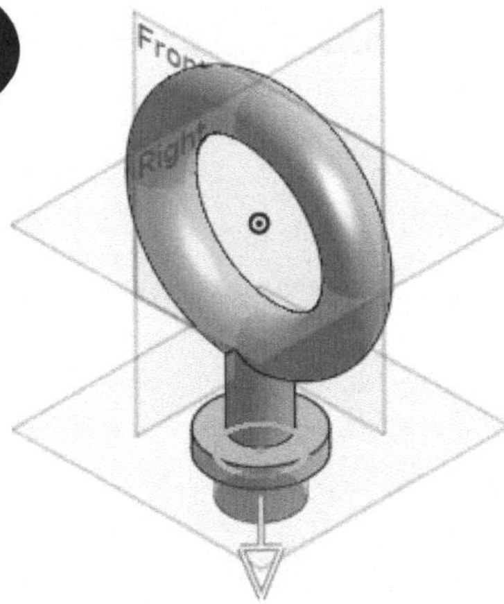

8. Ensure that the direction of extrusion is downwards as shown in Figure 4.79.

9. Ensure that the **Add** option is activated in the **Operation type** area of the **Extrude** dialog to create the extrude feature by adding material and merging with the existing features of the model.

10. Enter **50** mm as the depth of extrusion in the **Depth** field of the **Extrude** dialog and press ENTER. The preview of the extrude feature gets updated, accordingly.

11. Click on the green checkmark ✓ in the **Extrude** dialog to confirm the creation of the feature and exit the dialog. Figure 4.80 shows the final model after creating all its features, sequentially.

4.80

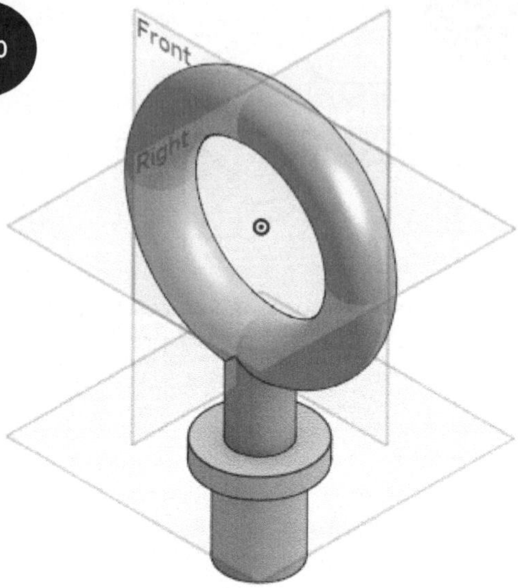

Now, you can close the document.

12. Invoke the **Document** menu by clicking on the ≡ icon (three horizontal lines) next to the Onshape logo at the top left corner and click on the **Close document** option, see Figure 4.81. The current document gets closed.

4.81

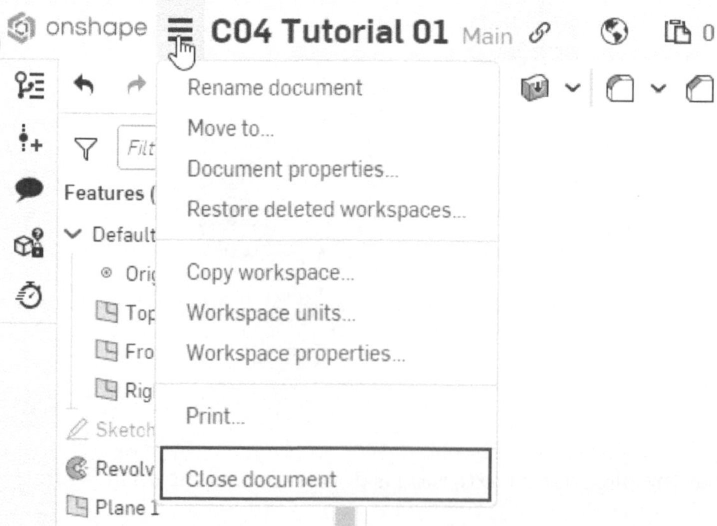

Projecting Edges onto the Sketching Plane

In Onshape, while sketching, you can project the edges or faces of existing features of the model onto the active sketching plane using the **Use (Project/Convert)** tool. Figure 4.82 shows a model where the edges of existing features have been projected onto the active sketching plane as sketch entities. The method for projecting edges or faces onto the sketching plane is discussed below:

4.82

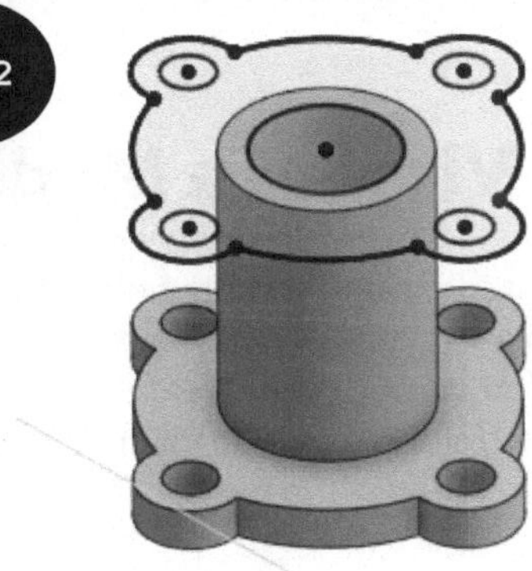

1. Invoke the Sketch mode by selecting a plane or a planar face as the sketching plane using the **Sketch** tool.

2. Click on the **Use (Project/Convert)** tool in the **Sketch** toolbar, see Figure 4.83.

4.83

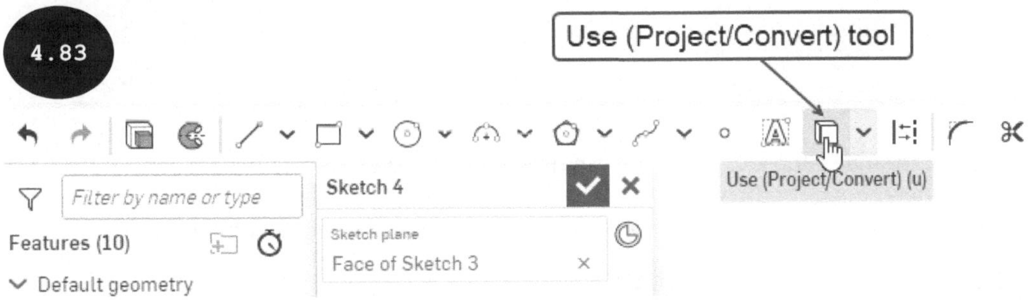

Now, you can project the edges or faces of the existing features onto the active sketching plane.

3. Select the edges or faces of the existing features to be projected onto the sketching plane, see Figure 4.84. In this figure, the outer edges of the model are projected onto the sketching plane. Note that when a face is selected, all the edges in its outer loop will be projected, simultaneously.

4.84

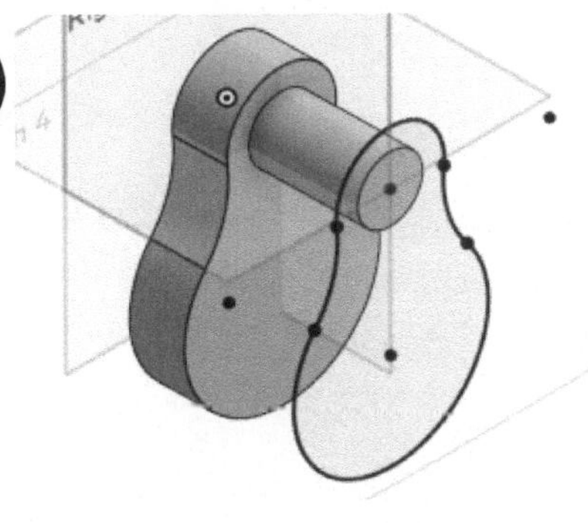

Tip: You can also project the existing sketch entities or curves as sketch entities onto the active sketching plane.

4. After projecting the edges of the existing features, press the ESC key to exit the tool. To confirm the creation of the sketch and exit the Sketch mode, click on the green checkmark in the **Sketch** dialog.

Displaying Section View of a Model

In Onshape, you can create a section view of a model in the graphics area using the **Section view** tool, see Figure 4.85. A section view is created by temporarily hiding the material in front of the chosen section plane. You can select either a plane or a planar face as the section plane. It is important to note that creating a section view does not alter or modify the model's geometry; it is solely for visualizing the internal features or geometries of the model. The method for creating a section view is discussed below:

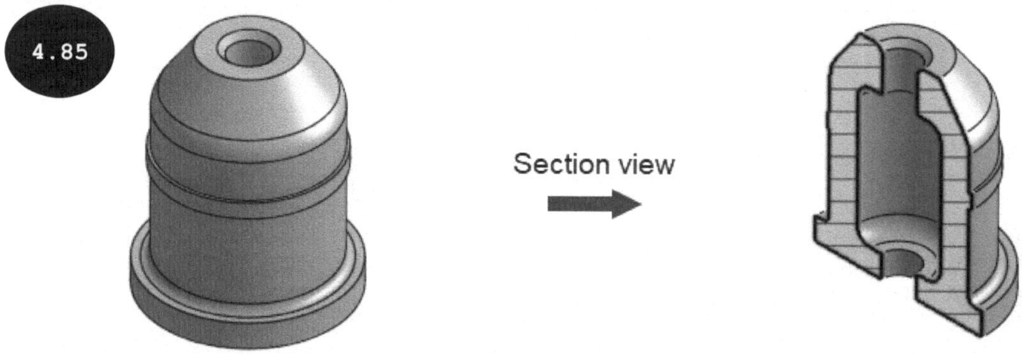

1. Click on the small cube located at the top right corner, just below the View Cube, and choose the **Section view** tool from the menu that appears, see Figure 4.86. The **Section view** dialog appears (see Figure 4.87) and you are prompted to select one or more section planes.

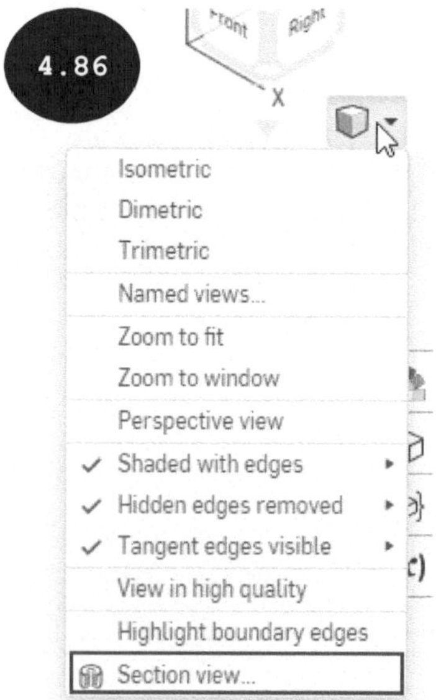

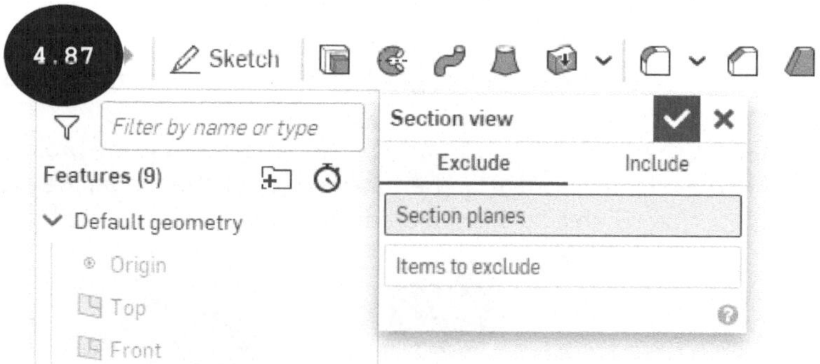

2. Select a plane or a planar face in the graphics area to set as the section plane. A preview of the section view appears, temporarily hiding the material in front of the section plane, see Figure 4.88. Additionally, one translational and two rotational handles appear in the preview.

3. If needed, you can drag the translational and rotational handles to dynamically adjust the section view of the model in the graphics area.

4. Similarly, you can define multiple section planes in the graphics area, see Figure 4.89. In this figure, a quarter-section view of the model is created by selecting two section planes.

4.88

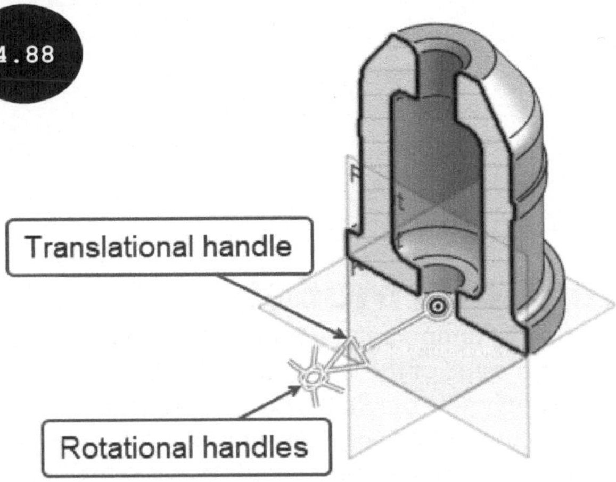

4.89

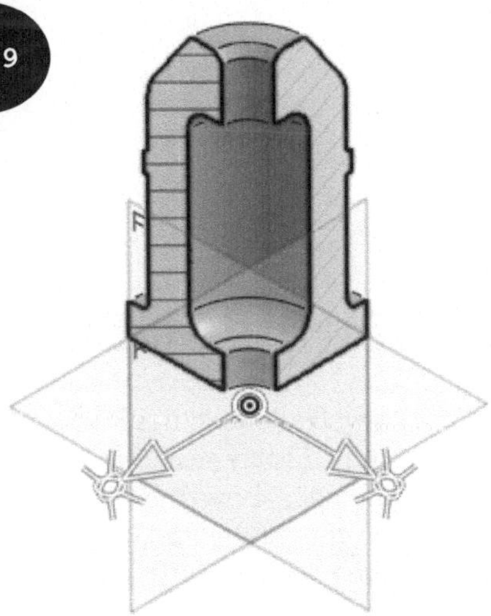

Note: When working with a multi-body part, you can choose to include or exclude parts from the section view. Excluded parts will remain un-sectioned, while included parts will be sectioned or cut in the view. To exclude parts, activate the **Items to exclude** field in the **Exclude** tab of the **Section View** dialog box. Then, select the parts you want to exclude. Similarly, to include parts, switch to the **Include** tab and select one or more parts to be sectioned in the view.

5. Once the desired section view of the model is created, click on the green checkmark ✓ in the **Section view** dialog to confirm.

   After creating the section view, you can return to the full or original view of the model again.

6. Click on the small cube located at the top right corner and choose the **Turn off section view** tool from the menu that appears, see Figure 4.90. The display of section view gets turned off and the entire or original view of the model appears in the graphics area.

4.90

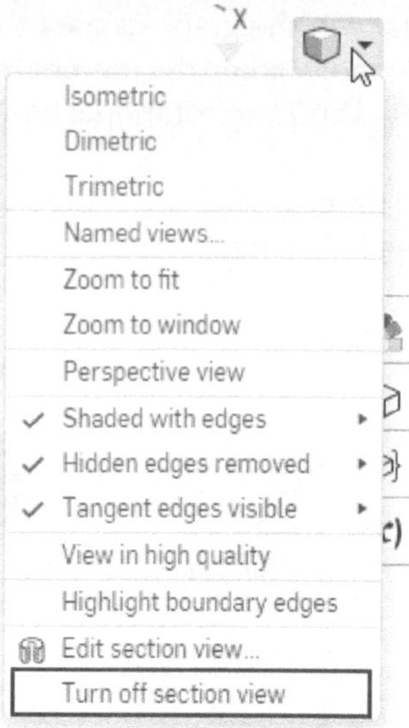

Displaying an Earlier Stage of a Model

In Onshape, you can display an earlier stage of a model by temporarily hiding its later features using the **Rollback bar**. By default, the **Rollback bar** displays at the end of the last feature in the Feature list, see Figure 4.91. To display an earlier stage of the model, simply drag the **Rollback bar** upward in the Feature list, positioning it above the specific features you want to exclude or hide, refer to Figure 4.92. When you do this, the model updates in the graphics area, displaying only the features above the **Rollback bar**, while the ones below it are hidden and appear faded in the Feature list.

4.91

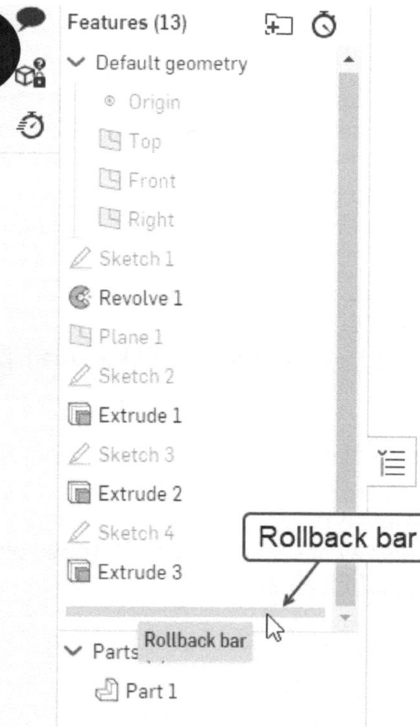

4.92

In the rolled-back stage, you can create new features or modify existing ones, as needed. To return to the full model view, simply drag the **Rollback bar** to the end of the Feature list, after the last feature. Alternatively, you can right-click on the **Rollback bar** and select the **Roll to end** option (see Figure 4.93), which will automatically move the bar to the end of the Feature list.

4.93

Reordering Features of a Model

By default, features in a model are organized sequentially in the order they are created in the Feature list. If needed, you can change the order of a feature by dragging it to a new position, either above or below another feature. However, ensure that you do not drag a child feature above its parent feature to avoid errors. This means a dependent feature should not be moved above the feature it relies on.

Editing Features and Sketches

Onshape allows you to edit individual features and their sketches at any stage of the design process. The methods for editing a feature and a sketch are discussed next.

Editing a Feature

The method for editing a feature of a model is discussed below:

1. Right-click on the feature to be edited in the Feature list and select the **Edit** option from the shortcut menu, see Figure 4.94. A dialog box appears based on the selected feature. For example, if you are editing an extrude feature, the **Extrude** dialog box will open, whereas for a revolve feature, the **Revolve** dialog box will appear, allowing you to modify its parameters accordingly.

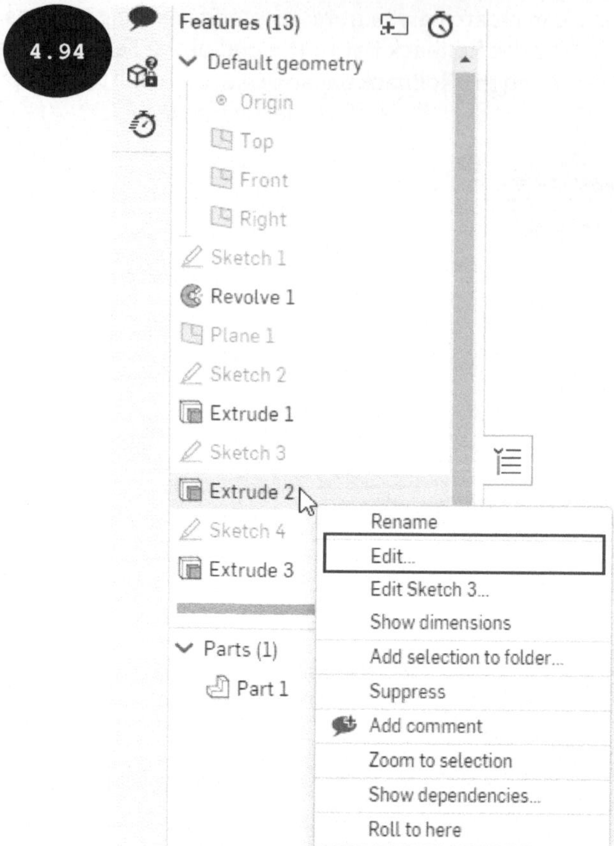

2. Edit the parameters of the feature as needed in the corresponding dialog box that appears.

3. After editing the feature parameters, click on the green checkmark ✓ in the dialog to confirm the changes made in the feature and exit the dialog.

Editing a Sketch

The method for editing a sketch is discussed below:

1. Right-click on the sketch to be edited in the Feature list and select the **Edit** option from the shortcut menu. The **Sketch** dialog appears along with the **Sketch** toolbar, allowing you to modify the sketch using the available sketching tools. Alternatively, right-click on the feature associated with the sketch you want to modify and then click on the **Edit Sketch** option in the shortcut menu that appears.

2. Edit the sketch using the sketching tools, as needed.

3. After editing the sketch, click on the green checkmark ✓ in the dialog to confirm the changes made and exit the dialog.

Deleting a Feature of a Model

To delete an existing feature from a model, right-click on the feature in the Feature list and choose the **Delete** option from the shortcut menu. The selected feature is then removed from the model and is no longer part of it. Alternatively, select the feature and press the DELETE key.

Note: If the detected feature has some dependent features, then they will also be removed or deleted from the model. However, their names remain appear in the Feature list in red. When you hover the cursor over any of the deleted feature names, the corresponding error message appears.

Assigning Appearance

In Onshape, you can edit the default appearance of a part, its features, and its faces by assigning a new appearance as needed. The methods for assigning an appearance to a part, feature, or face are discussed next.

Assigning Appearance to a Part

The method for assigning an appearance to a part is discussed below:

1. Right-click on the name of the part (*Part1*) in the Part list located below the Feature list on the left side of the graphics area, and select the **Edit Appearance** option from the shortcut menu that appears, see Figure 4.95. The **Appearance** dialog appears with the **Palette** tab activated by default, see Figure 4.96.

4.95

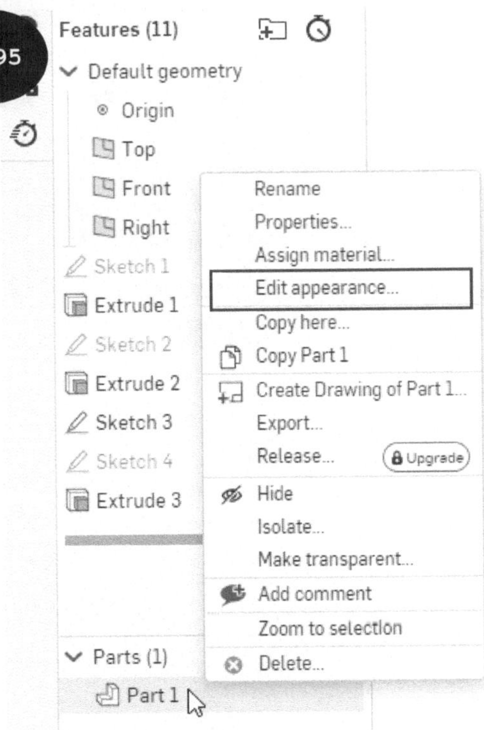

4.96

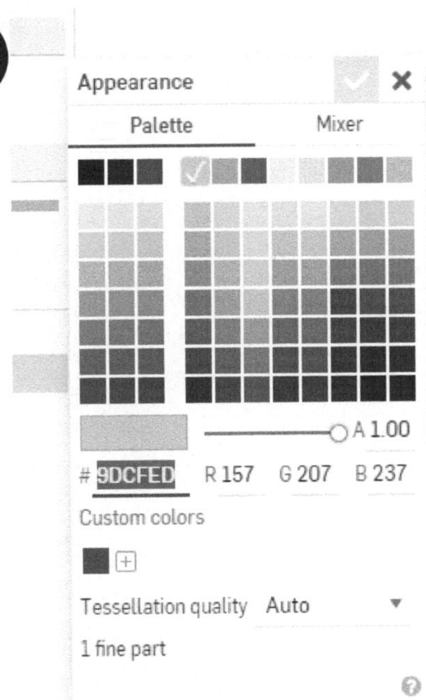

Alternatively, right-click on a face of the part in the graphics area and select the **Edit Appearance for Part1** option from the shortcut menu that appears. The **Appearance** dialog appears, allowing you to change the part's appearance.

2. Select the required color swatch in the **Palette** tab of the **Appearance** dialog. You can also enter the color code or RGB in the respective fields of the dialog.

3. If needed, you can activate the **Mixer** tab in the **Appearance** dialog to further adjust the color as desired.

4. After assigning the required appearance to the part, click on the green checkmark in the dialog to confirm the changes and exit the dialog.

Assigning Appearance to a Feature

The method for assigning an appearance to a feature is discussed below:

1. Right-click on the name of the feature in the Feature list and select the **Add appearance to feature** option from the shortcut menu that appears, see Figure 4.97. The selected feature gets highlighted in the graphics area and the **Face appearance** dialog appears with the **Palette** tab activated by default, see Figure 4.98.

4.97

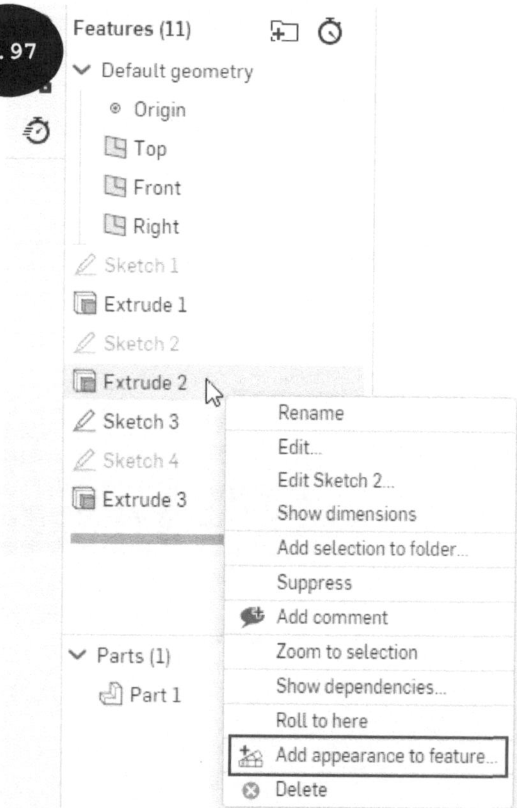

4.98

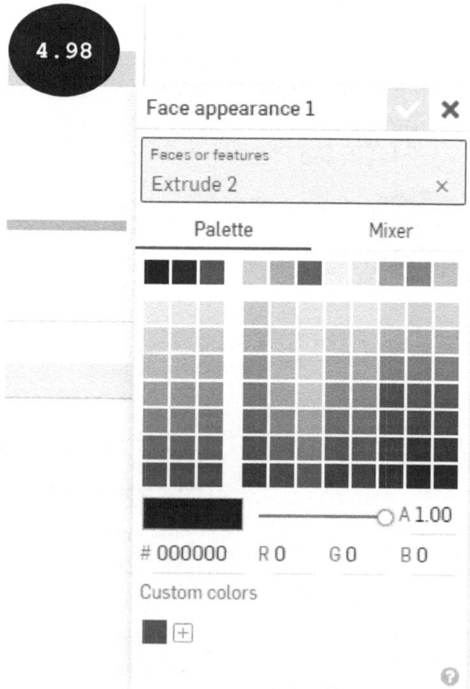

2. Select the required color swatch in the **Palette** tab of the **Appearance** dialog. You can also enter the color code or RGB in the respective fields of the dialog.

3. After assigning the required appearance to the selected feature, click on the green checkmark ✓ in the dialog to confirm the changes and exit the dialog.

Assigning Appearance to Faces

The method for assigning an appearance to one or more faces of a model is discussed below:

1. Right-click on a face of the model in the graphics area and select the **Add appearance to face** option from the shortcut menu that appears, see Figure 4.99. The **Face appearance** dialog appears with the **Palette** tab activated by default.

4.99

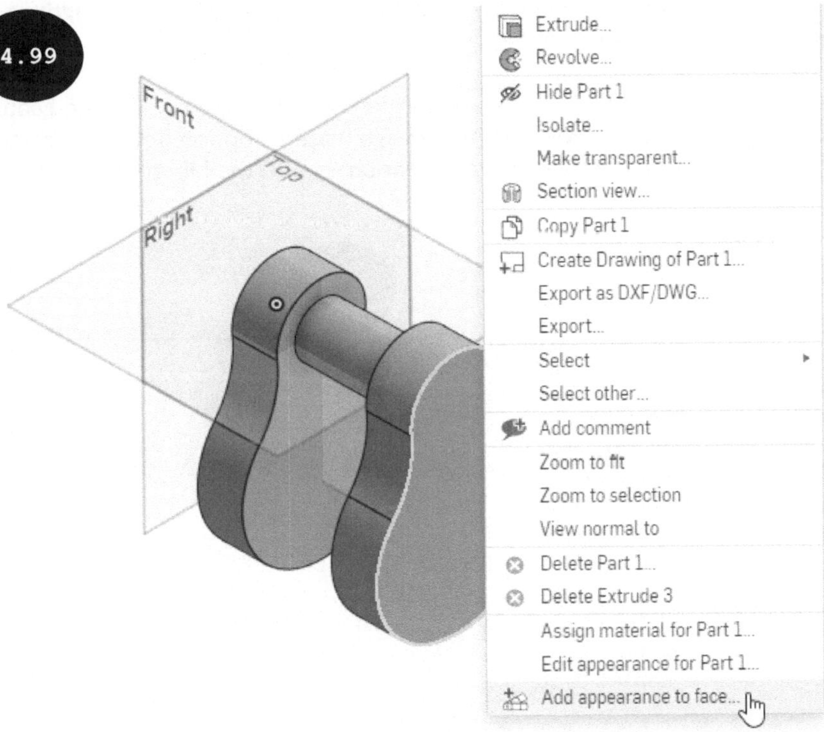

2. Select the required color swatch in the **Appearance** dialog. The chosen appearance is assigned to the selected face of the model. You can also enter the color code or RGB in the respective fields of the dialog.

3. If needed, select additional faces of the model to apply the same appearance to them.

4. After assigning the required appearance, click on the green checkmark ✓ in the dialog to confirm the changes and exit the dialog.

Note: In Onshape, you can also assign appearance to a sketch just like you do for parts, features, and faces. To do this, right-click on the sketch in the Feature list and select the **Edit sketch appearance** option from the shortcut menu. The **Appearance** dialog appears, allowing you to assign an appearance to the selected sketch.

Assigning Material

In Onshape, you can apply the required standard material, such as stainless steel, carbon steel, iron, aluminum, or ABS, to a model. Assigning a material is essential for calculating mass and performing analysis. Onshape's material library contains nearly all standard materials, allowing you to directly apply the needed material to your model. Additionally, you can apply a custom material to a model by defining its properties such as density, Poisson's ratio, young's modulus, and tensile strength as required. The methods for applying a material is discussed below:

1. Right-click on the name of the part (*Part1*) in the Part list located below the Feature list on the left side of the graphics area, and select the **Assign material** option from the shortcut menu that appears, see Figure 4.100. The **Material** dialog appears with the **Library** tab activated by default, see Figure 4.101.

4.100

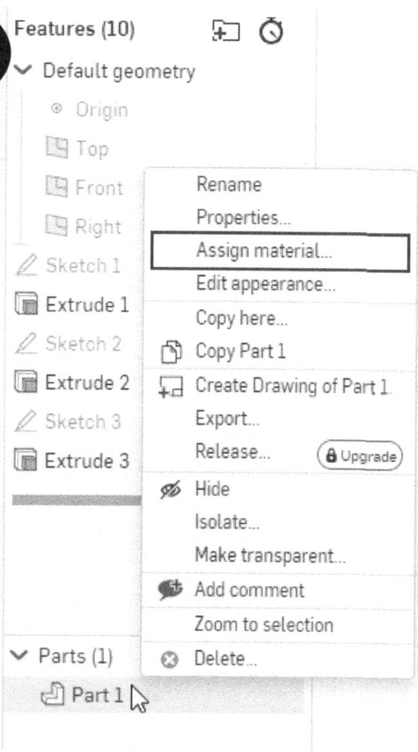

4.101

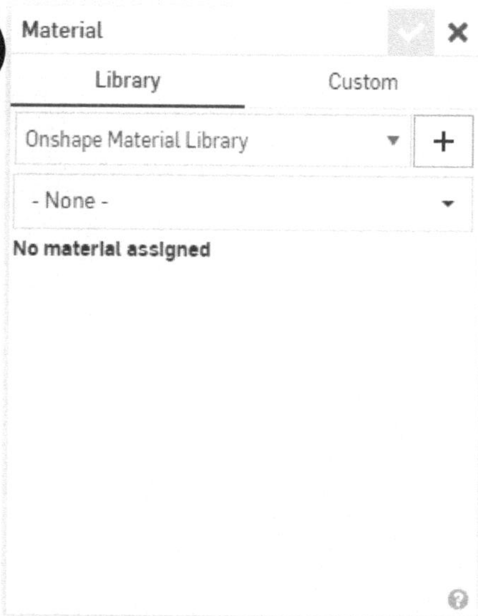

2. Ensure that the **Onshape Material Library** is selected in the **Library** drop-down list of the dialog, refer to Figure 9.101.

3. Invoke the **Material** drop-down list by clicking on the down arrow, see Figure 4.102. A list of all the materials available in the Onshape Material Library appears, see Figure 4.103.

4.102

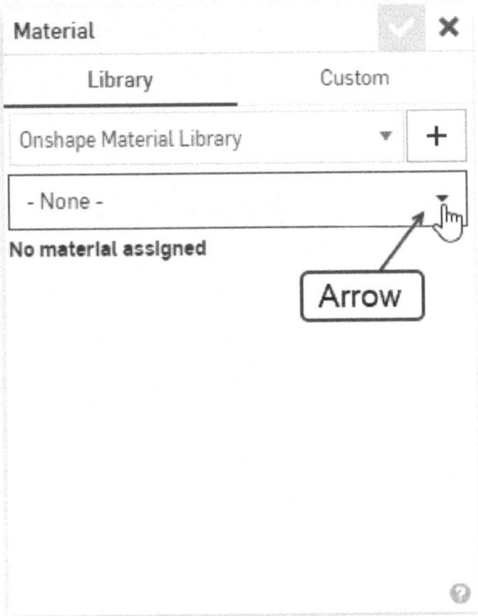

4.103

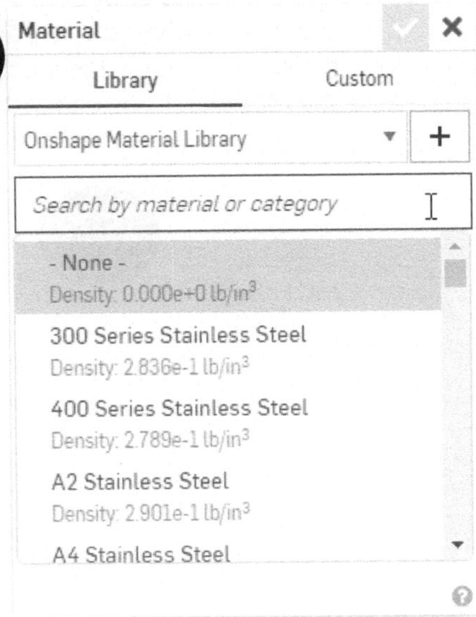

4. Scroll through the material list and select the required material to apply. Alternatively, you can search for the material by typing its name in the **Search by material or category** field in the dialog, then select it to apply. The material properties of the selected material are displayed in the dialog, see Figure 4.104.

4.104

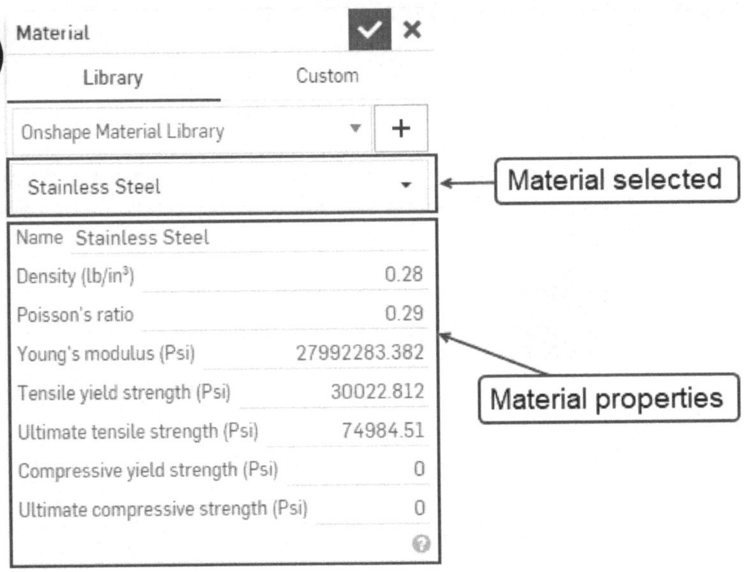

Note: You cannot edit the properties of a standard material. However, if needed, you can create a custom material by defining its properties such as density, Poisson's ratio, young's modulus, and tensile strength. To do this, click on the **Custom** tab in the **Material** dialog and enter the custom material properties in the respective fields, including its name. Figure 4.105 shows the **Material** dialog box with the **Custom** tab activated.

4.105

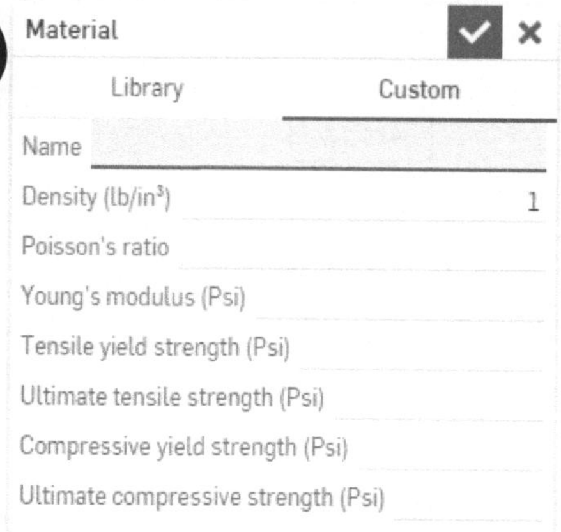

5. After select a material, click on the green checkmark in the dialog to confirm the application of the material and exit the dialog.

Computing Mass Properties

After assigning material to a model, you can calculate its mass properties, including mass, volume, surface area, center of mass, and mass moments of inertia, using the **Display mass and section properties** tool. The method for computing the mass properties of a part is discussed below:

1. Click on the **Display mass and section properties** tool, located at the lower right corner of the graphics area, see Figure 4.106. The **Mass and section properties** dialog appears with the **Part** tab activated by default, see Figure 4.107.

4.106

4.107

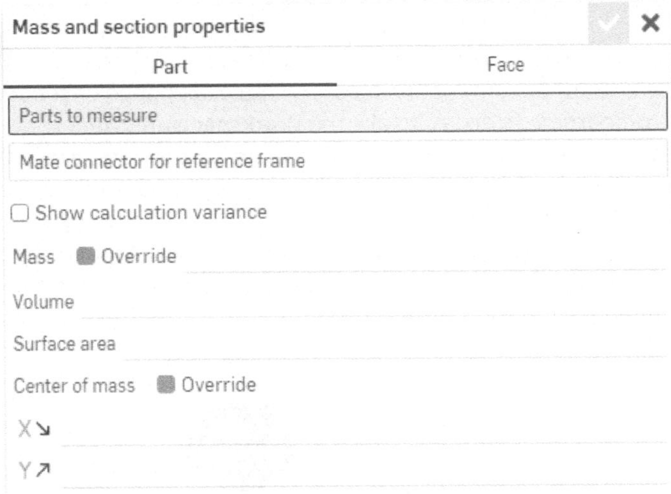

2. Select the part from the graphics area or the Part list. The mass properties of the selected part are computed and displayed in the dialog, see Figure 4.108. Notice that the selected part is highlighted in the graphics area and the center of mass is marked with the ⯐ symbol on the model.

4.108

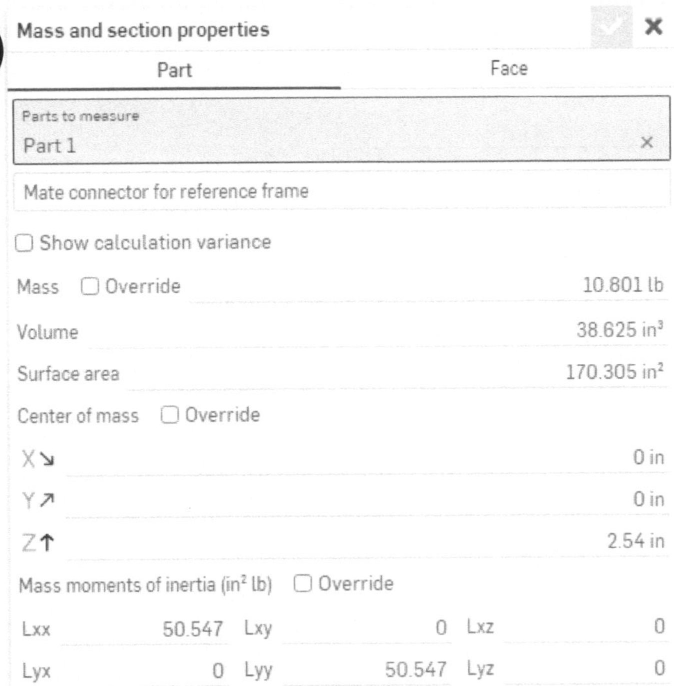

Tip: If you are working with a multi-body part document, you can select multiple parts to calculate their combined mass properties. If any selected part does not have a material assigned, an error message stating, "**One or more parts do not have a material defined,**" will pop-up. You must first assign material to the part before computing its mass properties.

Note: By default, the mass properties of a model are calculated using the default units specified for the current document. If necessary, you can change or set custom units for calculating these properties. To do so, invoke the **Workspace units** dialog by clicking the ≡ icon (three horizontal lines) next to the Onshape logo in the top-left corner, then select the **Workspace units** option, see Figure 4.109. In the **Workspace units** dialog, under the **Mechanical** section, choose the preferred units for properties like mass and moment from the corresponding drop-down lists, see Figure 4.110. Once done, click the green checkmark ✓ to confirm and exit the dialog. The mass properties of the part will now be calculated using the newly selected units.

4.109

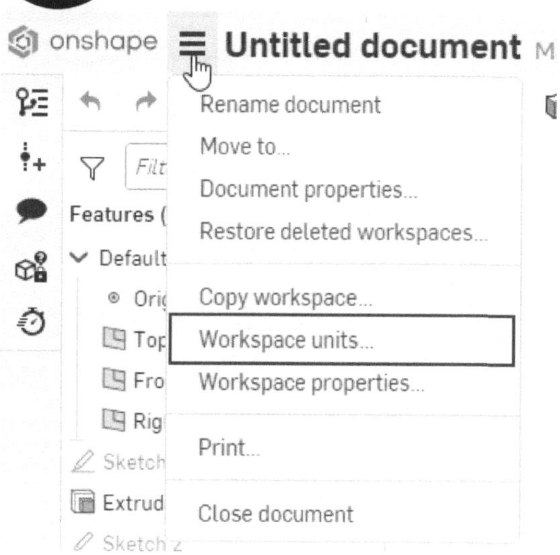

4.110

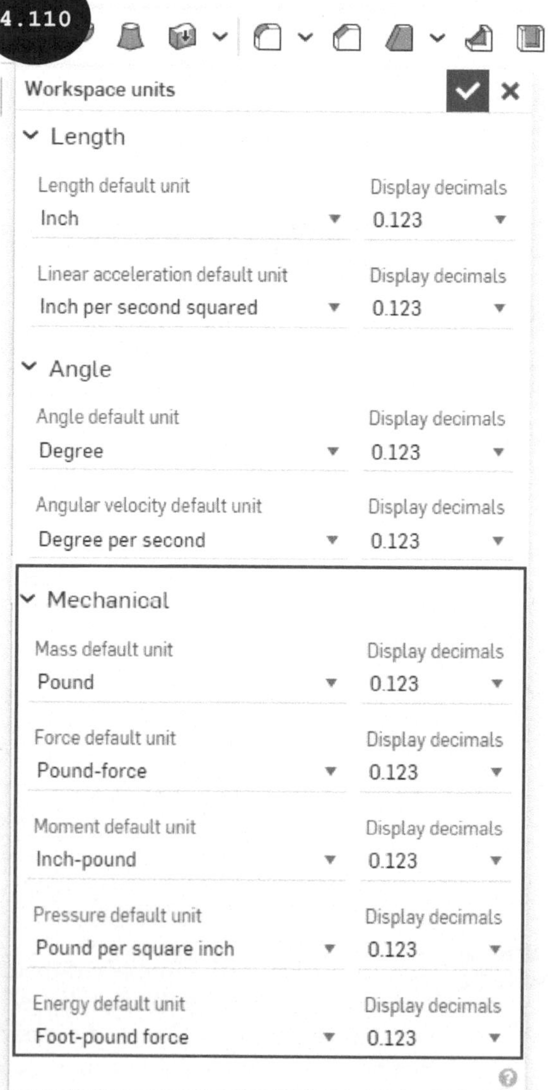

Override: In Onshape, you can override the calculated mass properties of a model if needed. To change the calculated mass, select the **Override** check box next to the **Mass** field and enter the desired mass value in the **Mass** field that is enabled. Similarly, to override the center of mass and mass moments of inertia, simply select the corresponding **Override** check box in the dialog. Note that the overridden properties specified for a model do not reflect the model's actual properties.

Face Tab: On activating the **Face** tab in the **Mass and section properties** dialog, you can select one or more coplanar faces of a model to calculate their properties such as surface area, perimeter, area moment of inertia, and polar moment of inertia, see Figure 4.111. In this figure, a planar face is selected, and its properties are displayed.

4.111

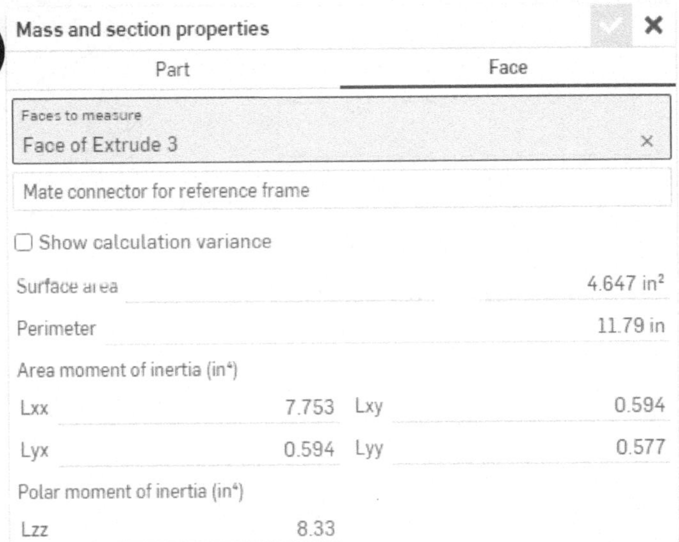

3. After reviewing the mass properties of a model, click the green checkmark or cross mark to exit the dialog.

Tutorial 2

Create a model shown in Figure 4.112. Different drawing views with dimensions are given in Figure 4.113. All dimensions are in inches.

4.112

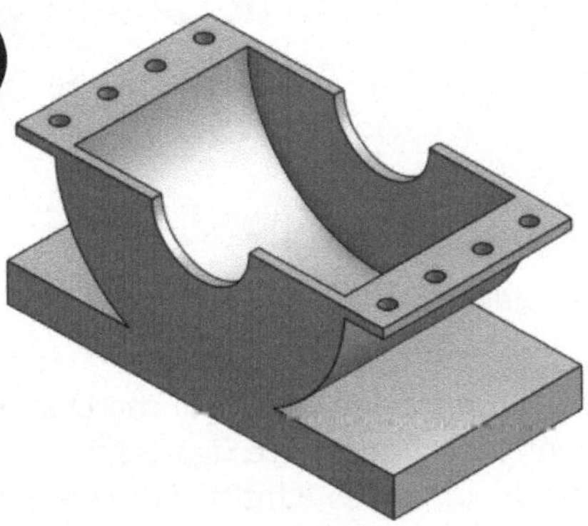

4.113

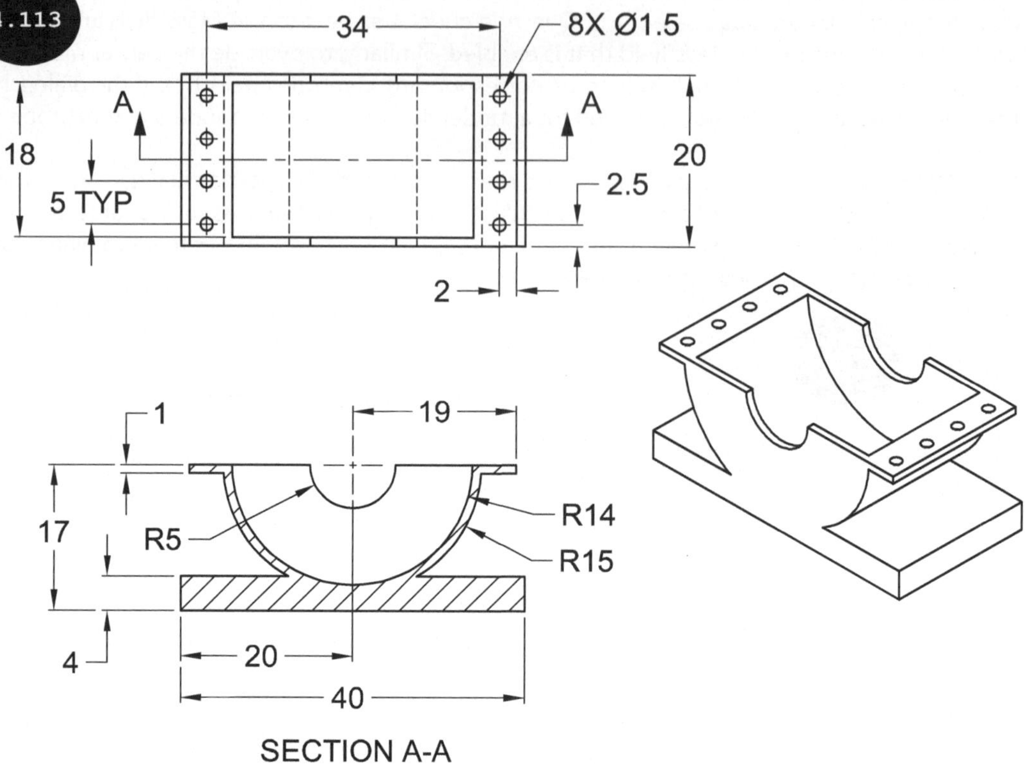

Section 1: Starting a New Design Document

1. Launch Onshape (***onshape.com***) and log in to your account if you're not already logged in.

2. If you are within a document, click on the **Onshape** logo located in the top left corner of the browser to display the **Documents Page**, see Figure 4.114.

4.114

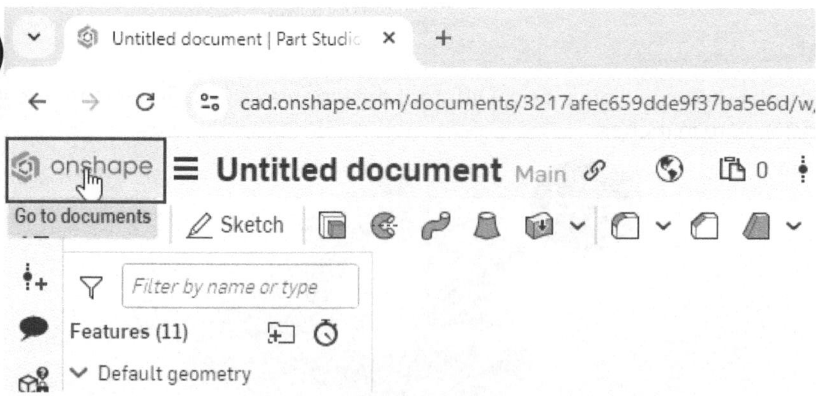

3. Click on the **Create** button at the top left corner of the **Documents Page** and then click on the **Document** option in the menu that appears, see Figure 4.115. The **New document** window appears with the default name of the document as "**Untitled document**".

4.115

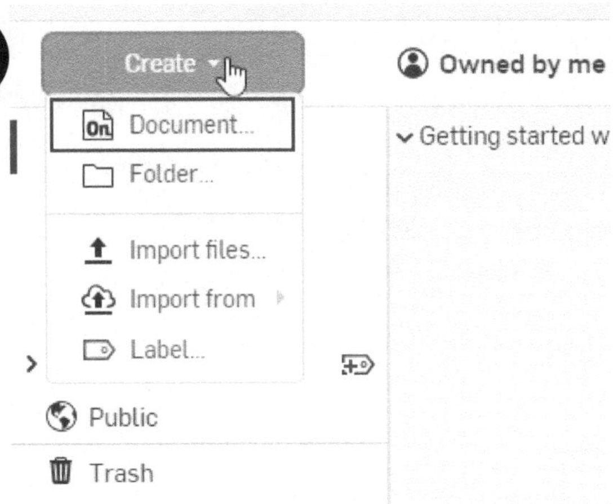

4. Enter **C04 Tutorial 02** as the name of the design document in the **New document** window, and then click on the **Create** button or the **Create Public Document** button, depending on your subscription type. A new document with the specified name is opened.

Section 2: Settings Units

Now, you can set inches (in) as the unit for the length measurement in the current document.

1. Invoke the **Document** menu by clicking on the ☰ icon (three horizontal lines) next to the **Onshape** logo at the top left corner, see Figure 4.116.

4.116

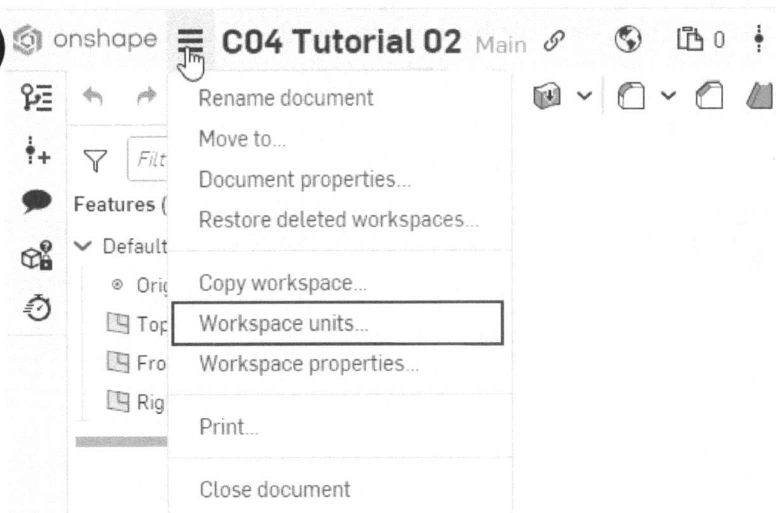

2. Click on the **Workspace units** option in the **Document** menu, refer to Figure 4.116. The **Workspace units** dialog appears, see Figure 4.117.

4.117

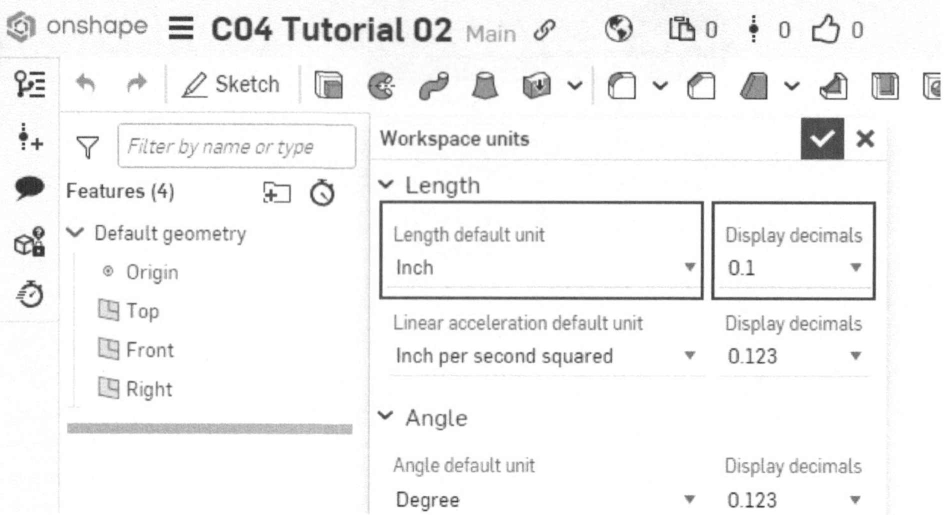

3. Select the **Inch** unit in the **Length default unit** drop-down list and set its precision to **0.1** in the respective **Display decimals** drop-down list of the **Workspace units** dialog, refer to Figure 4.117.

4. After selecting the required unit of length measurement and the decimal precision for the current design document, click on the green checkmark ✓ to confirm the selection and exit the dialog. The inch is defined as the unit for the length measurement.

Section 3: Accessing the Sketch Toolbar

Now, you can access the **Sketch** toolbar to create the sketch of the base feature, which is an extrude feature.

1. Click on the **Sketch** tool in the **Feature** toolbar, see Figure 4.118. The **Sketch** dialog appears and you are prompted to select a sketch plane.

4.118

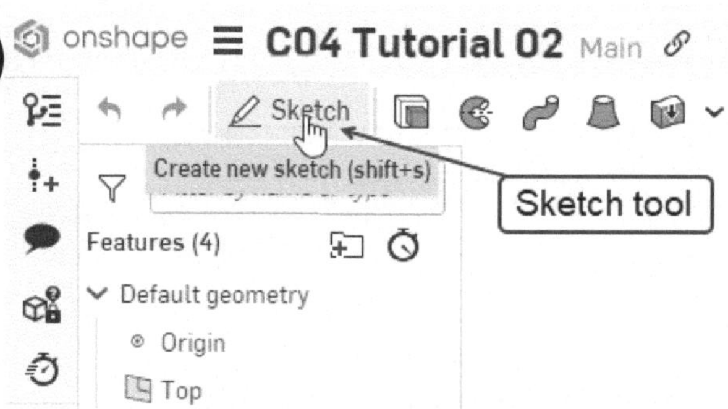

2. Select the Front plane as the sketching plane in the graphics area. The selected plane becomes the sketching plane, and the **Sketch** toolbar appears with the display of various sketching tools.

3. Press the N key to make the sketching plane normal to the viewing direction.

Section 4: Creating the Base Feature - Extrude

Now, you can create the base feature of the model, which is an extrude feature.

1. Create the sketch of the base feature using the sketching tools and apply the required dimensions, see Figure 4.119.

4.119

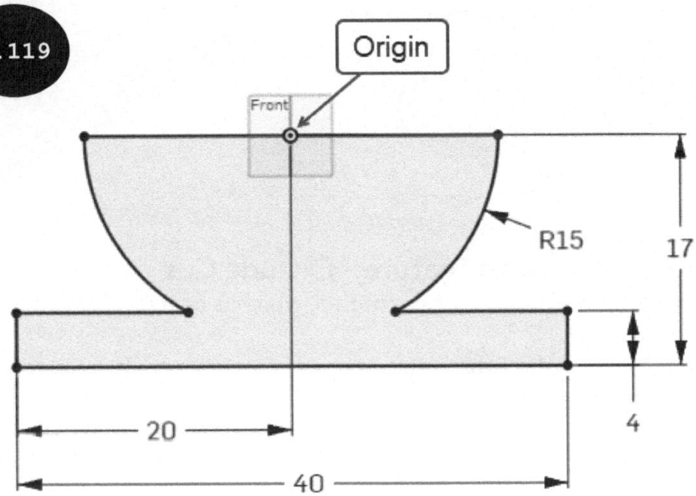

2. Click on the **Extrude** tool in the **Sketch** toolbar (see Figure 4.120) or press SHIFT + E. The **Extrude** dialog appears, and the sketch is automatically selected. Consequently, a preview of an extruded feature with the default extrusion depth appears in the graphics area.

4.120

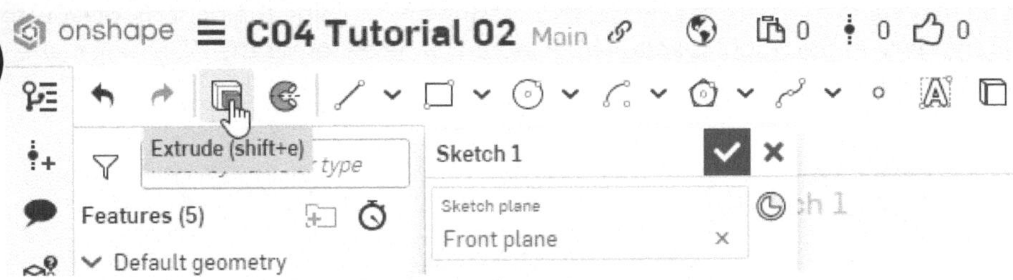

3. Press the SHIFT + 7 keys to change the view of the model to isometric.

4. Ensure that the **Blind** option is selected in the **End Type** drop-down list for extruding the sketch to a specific depth.

5. Enter **20** inches as the depth of extrusion in the **Depth** field and press ENTER. The preview of the extruded feature gets updated in the graphics area, accordingly.

6. Select the **Symmetric** check box in the **Extrude** dialog to extrude a sketch symmetrically on both sides of the sketching plane, see Figure 4.121.

7. Click the green checkmark ✓ in the **Extrude** dialog box to confirm the creation of the extrude feature and close the dialog. The extruded feature of specified depth is created, see Figure 4.122.

4.121

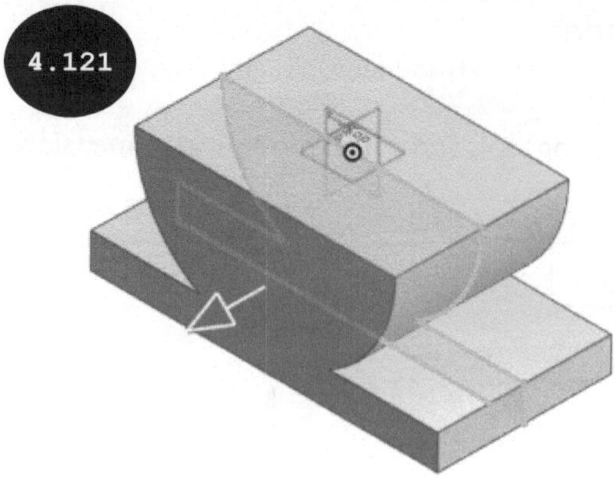

4.122

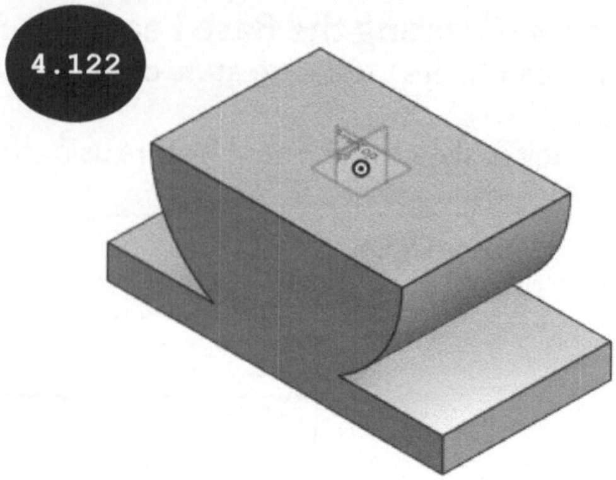

Section 5: Creating the Second Feature - Extrude Cut

Now, you can create the second feature of the model, which is an extruded cut feature.

1. Click on the **Sketch** tool in the **Feature** toolbar, see Figure 4.123. The **Sketch** dialog appears and you are prompted to select a sketch plane.

4.123

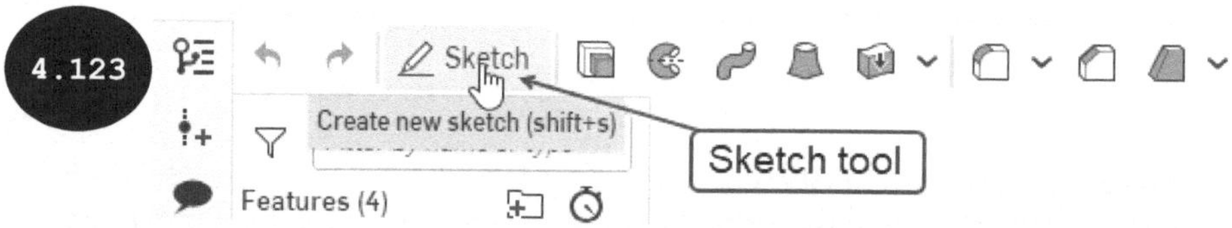

2. Select the Front plane as the sketching plane in the graphics area, see Figure 4.124. Note that you may need to rotate the model by pressing and holding the right mouse button to select the Front plane in the graphics area. The selected plane becomes the sketching plane, and the **Sketch** toolbar appears.

4.124

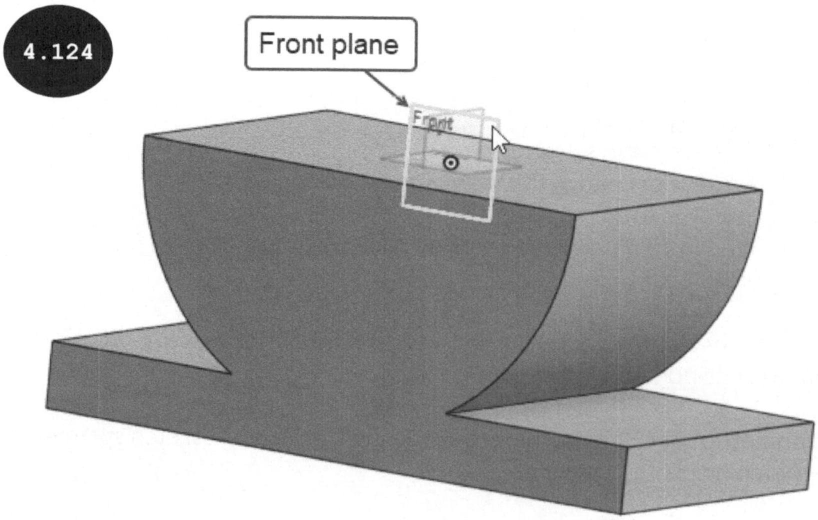

3. Press the **N** key to make the sketching plane normal to the viewing direction.

4. Create a circle of diameter 28 inches as the sketch of the feature, see Figure 4.125. The center point of the circle is at the origin.

4.125

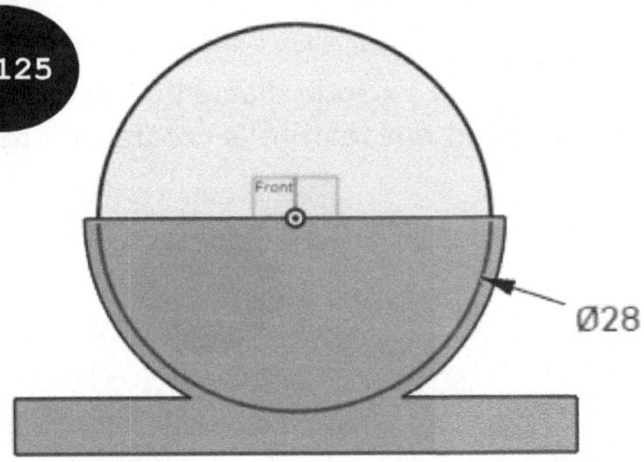

5. Click on the **Extrude** tool in the **Sketch** toolbar (see Figure 4.126) or press SHIFT + E. The **Extrude** dialog appears with the **Add** option is automatically selected in the **Operation type** area. Also, a preview of an extruded feature by adding material to the sketch.

4.126

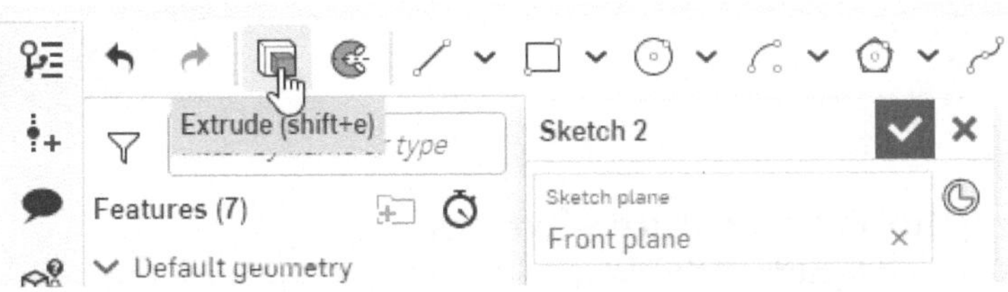

6. Press the SHIFT + 7 keys to change the view of the model to isometric.

7. Select the **Remove** option in the **Operation type** area to create an extruded feature by removing the material from the model, see Figure 4.127.

4.127

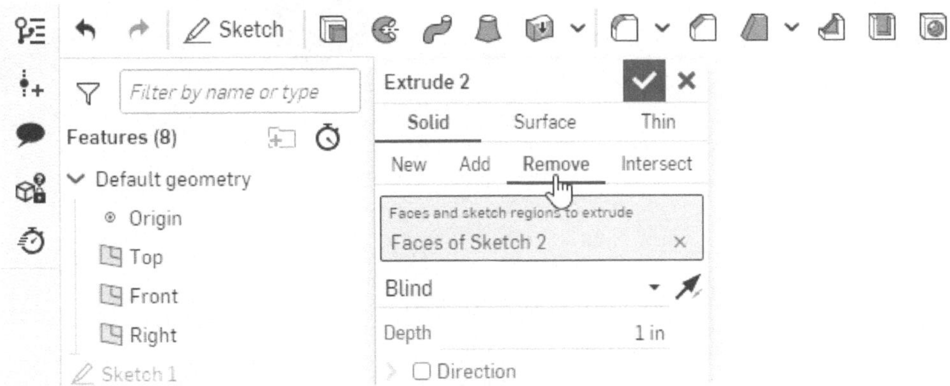

8. Ensure that the **Blind** option is selected in the **End Type** drop-down list for extruding the sketch to a specific depth.

9. Enter **18** inches as the depth of extrusion in the **Depth** field and press ENTER. The preview of the extruded feature gets updated in the graphics area, accordingly.

10. Select the **Symmetric** check box in the **Extrude** dialog to extrude a sketch symmetrically on both sides of the sketching plane, see Figure 4.128.

11. Click the green checkmark ✓ in the **Extrude** dialog box to confirm the creation of the feature and close the dialog. The extruded cut feature is created by removing the material from the model, see Figure 4.129.

4.128

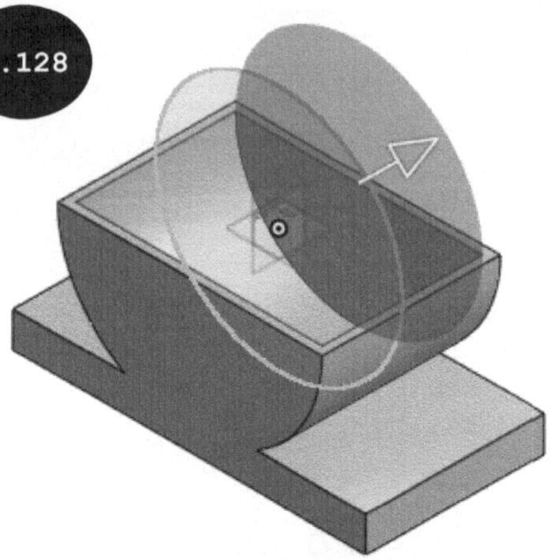

4.129

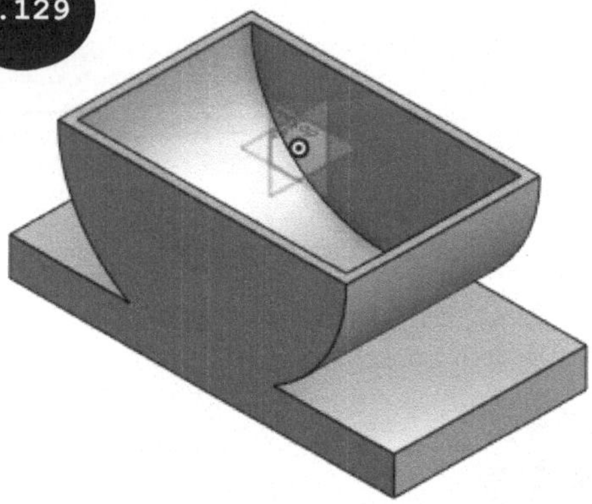

Section 6: Creating the Third Feature - Extrude

Now, you can create the third feature of the model, which is an extruded feature.

1. Click on the **Sketch** tool in the **Feature** toolbar (see Figure 4.130) and then select the front planar face of the model as the sketching plane, see Figure 4.131.

4.130

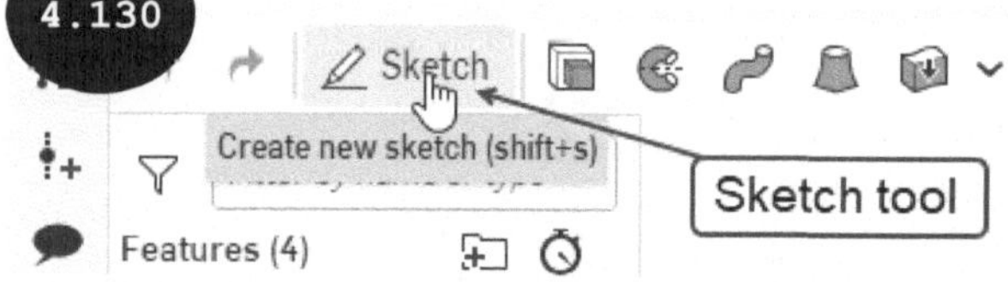

4.131

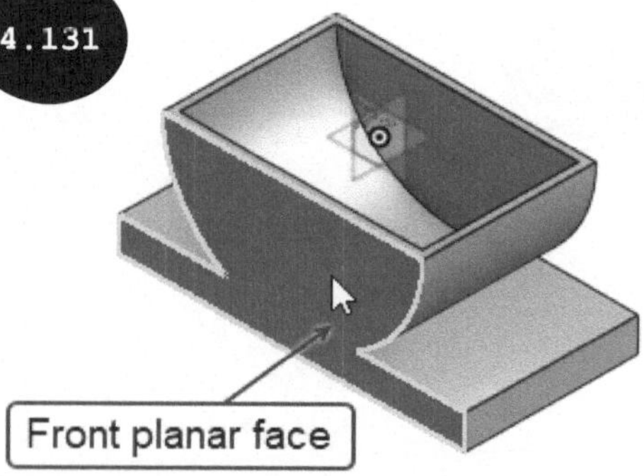

2. Press the **N** key to make the sketching plane normal to the viewing direction.

3. Click on the **Use (Project/Convert)** tool in the Sketch toolbar (see Figure 4.132) and then select the right curved edge of the model, see Figure 4.133. The selected edge of the model gets projected as sketch entity onto the current sketching plane. Next, press the ESC key to exit the tool.

4.132

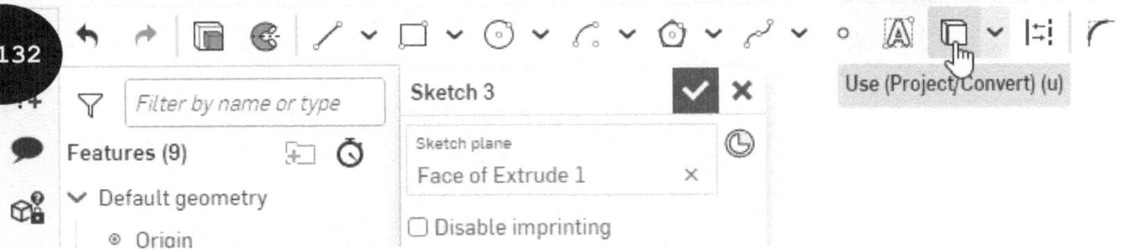

4.133

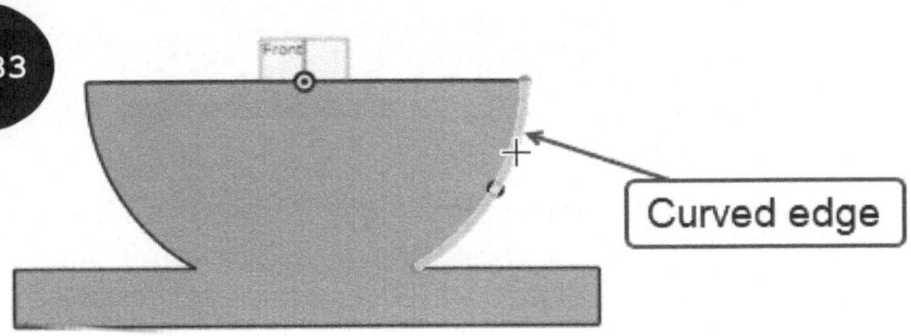

4. Create the other line entities of the sketch using the **Line** tool, refer to Figure 4.134.

5. Trim the bottom portion of the projected sketch entity, see Figure 4.134. The entity gets trimmed up to its next intersection.

4.134

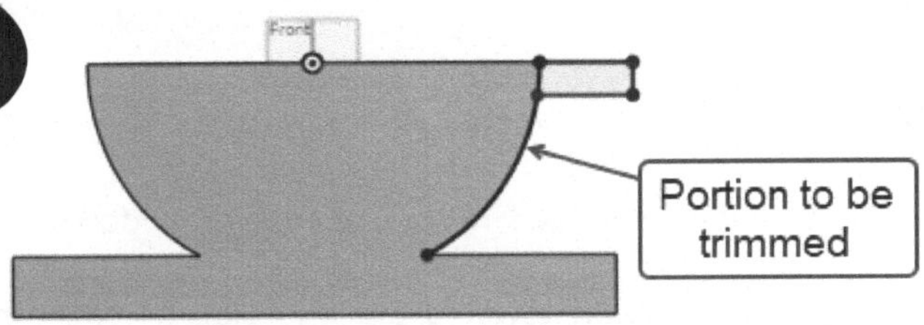

6. Apply the required dimensions to the sketch, see Figure 4.135.

4.135

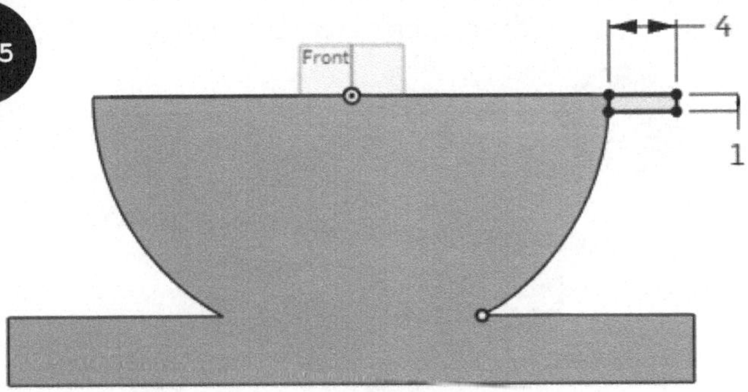

7. Mirror the sketch including the projected curve about the Right plane (vertical) using the **Mirror** tool, see Figure 4.136.

4.136

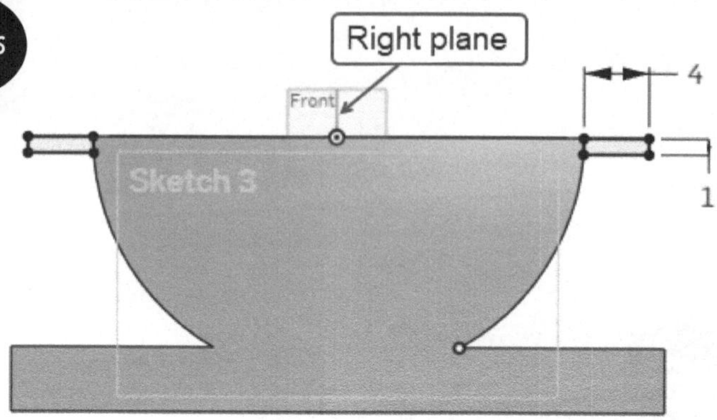

8. Click on the **Extrude** tool in the **Sketch** toolbar, see Figure 4.137. The **Extrude** dialog appears with the **New** option is selected in the **Operation type** area, by default. Also, a preview of an extruded feature appears.

4.137

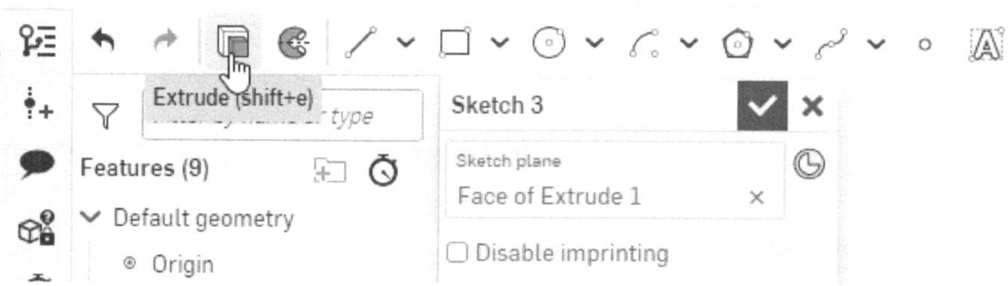

9. Press the SHIFT + 7 keys to change the view of the model to isometric.

10. Ensure that the **Blind** option is selected in the **End Type** drop-down list.

11. Reverse the direction of extrusion towards the rear side by click on the **Opposite direction** button next to the **Depth** field of the dialog, refer to Figure 4.138.

12. Enter **20** inches as the depth of extrusion in the **Depth** field and press ENTER. The preview of the extruded feature gets updated in the graphics area, accordingly, see Figure 4.138.

4.138

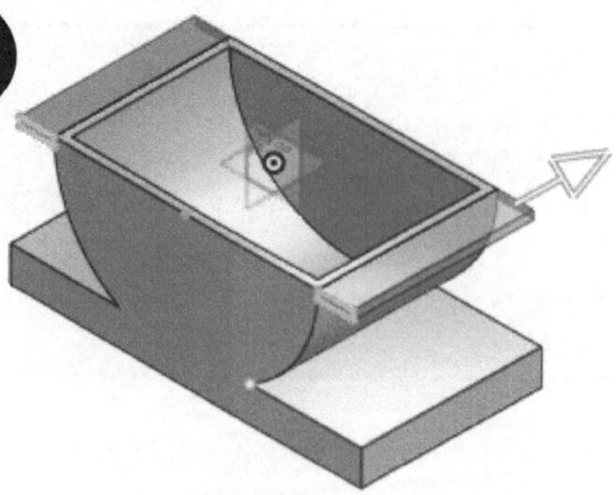

13. Select the **Add** option in the **Operation type** area to create an extruded feature by merging it with the existing features of the model, see Figure 4.139.

4.139

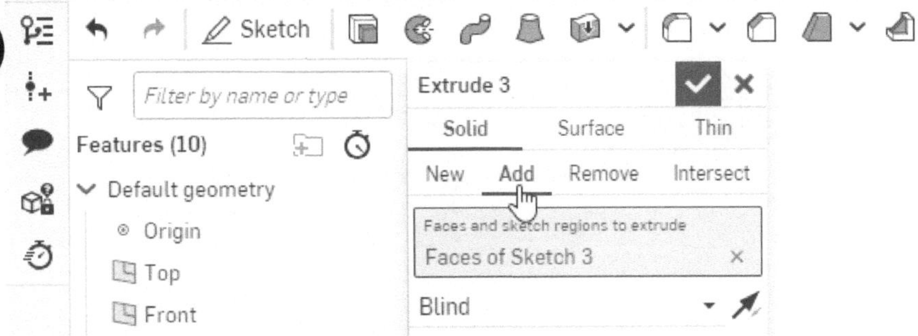

14. Click the green checkmark ✓ in the **Extrude** dialog box to confirm the creation of the feature and close the dialog. The extruded feature of specified depth is created, see Figure 4.140.

4.140

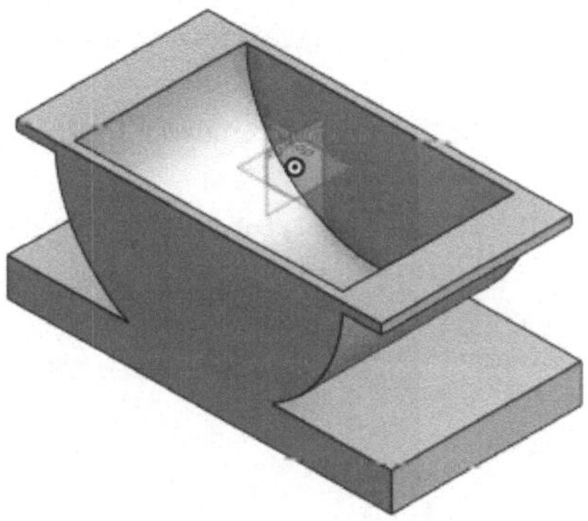

Section 7: Creating the Fourth Feature - Extrude Cut

Now, you can create the fourth feature of the model, which is an extruded cut feature.

1. Click on the **Sketch** tool in the **Feature** toolbar (see Figure 4.141) and then select the front planar face of the model as the sketching plane in the graphics area, see Figure 4.142.

4.141

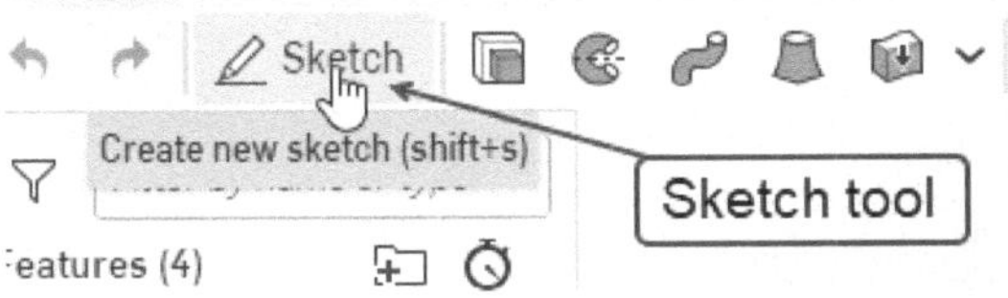

4.142

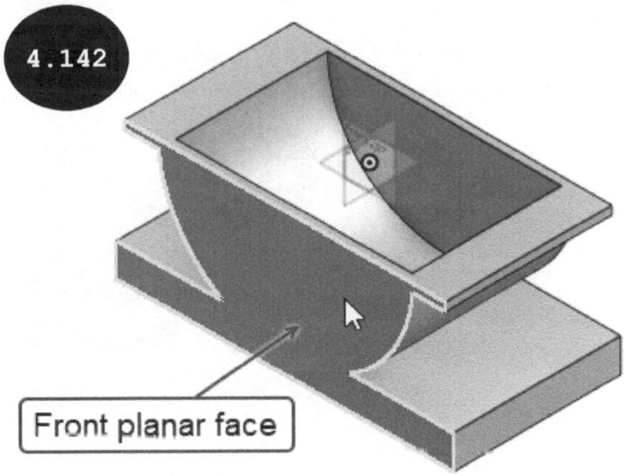

2. Press the **N** key to make the sketching plane normal to the viewing direction.

3. Create a circle of diameter 10 inches as the sketch of the feature, see Figure 4.143. The center point of the circle is at the origin.

4.143

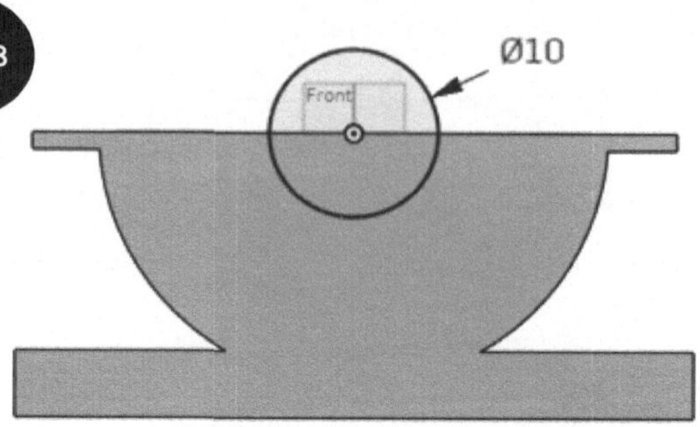

4. Press the SHIFT + E keys to activate the **Extrude** tool. The **Extrude** dialog appears and the preview of an extruded feature appears by adding material to the sketch.

5. Press the SHIFT + 7 keys to change the view of the model to isometric.

6. Select the **Remove** option in the **Operation type** area to create an extruded feature by removing the material from the model, see Figure 4.144.

4.144

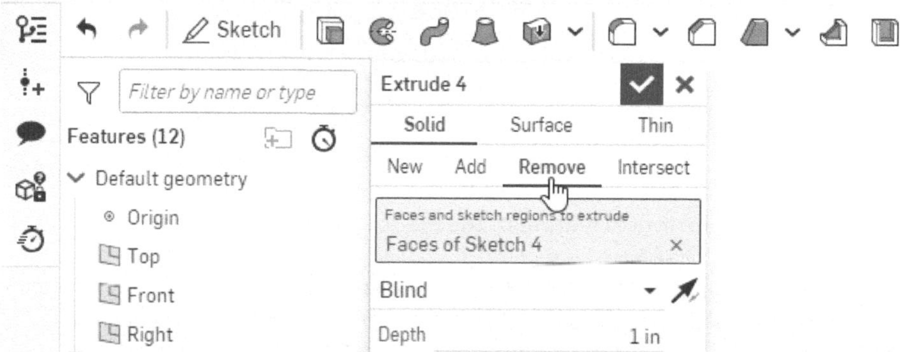

7. Ensure that the direction of extrusion is towards the rear side of the model, see Figure 4.145. If needed, you can reverse the direction of extrusion by click on the **Opposite direction** button.

4.145

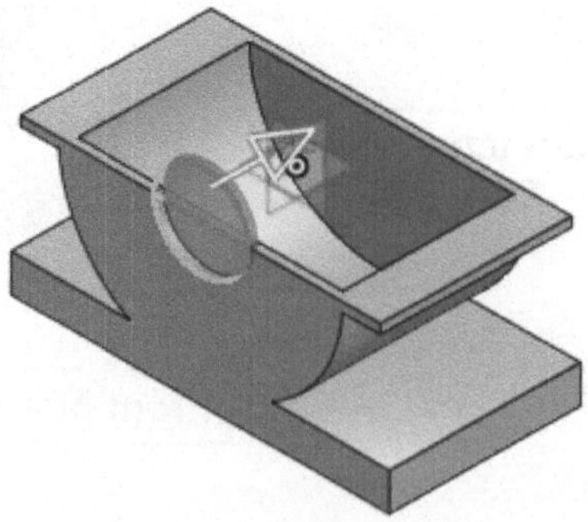

8. Select the **Through all** option in the **End Type** drop-down list for extruding the sketch through the entire length of the model, see Figure 4.146.

4.146

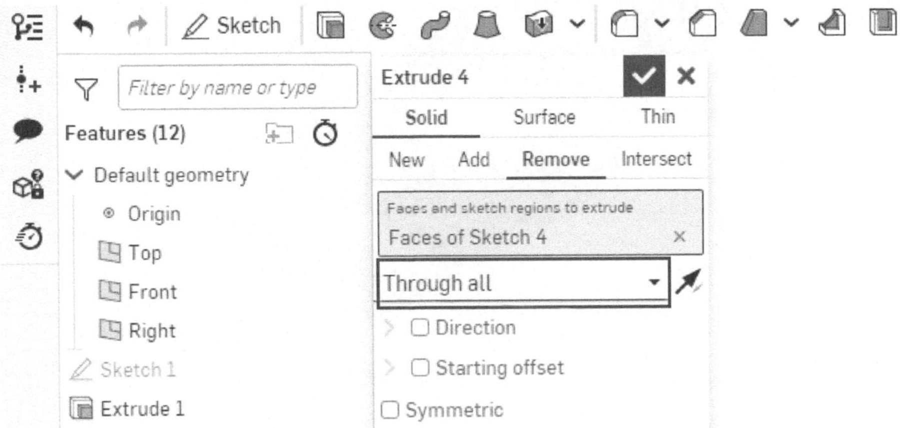

9. Click the green checkmark in the **Extrude** dialog box to confirm the creation of the feature and close the dialog. The extruded cut feature is created by removing the material through the entire length of the model, see Figure 4.147.

4.147

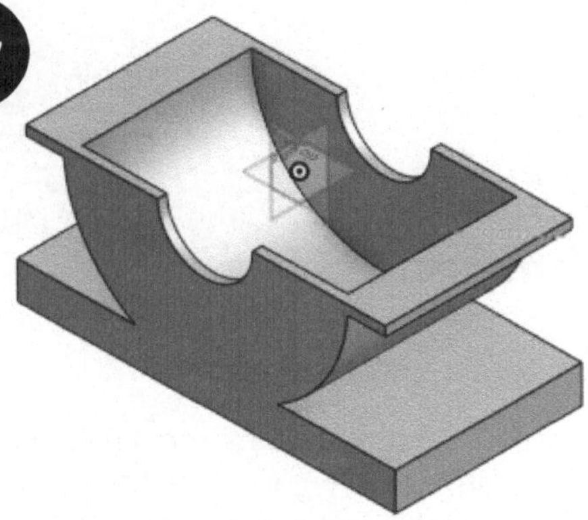

Section 8: Creating the Fifth Feature - Extrude Cut

Now, you can create the fifth feature of the model, which is also an extruded cut feature.

1. Click on the **Sketch** tool in the **Feature** toolbar, see Figure 4.148. The **Sketch** dialog appears and you are prompted to select a sketch plane.

4.148

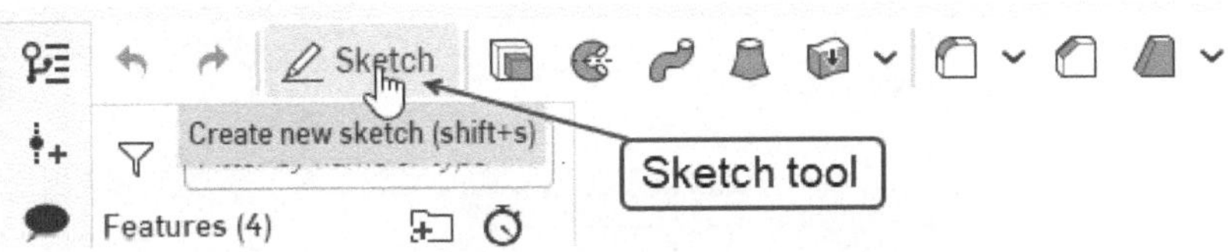

2. Select the top planar face of the model as the sketching plane in the graphics area, see Figure 4.149.

4.149

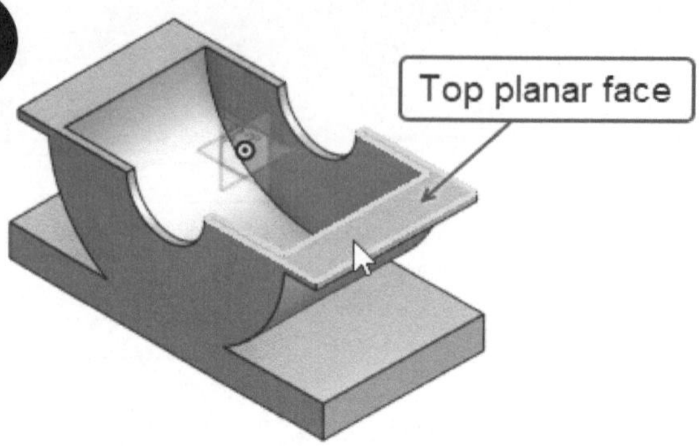

3. Press the **N** key to make the sketching plane normal to the viewing direction.

4. Create a circle of diameter 1.5 inches and apply the required dimensions, see Figure 4.150.

4.150

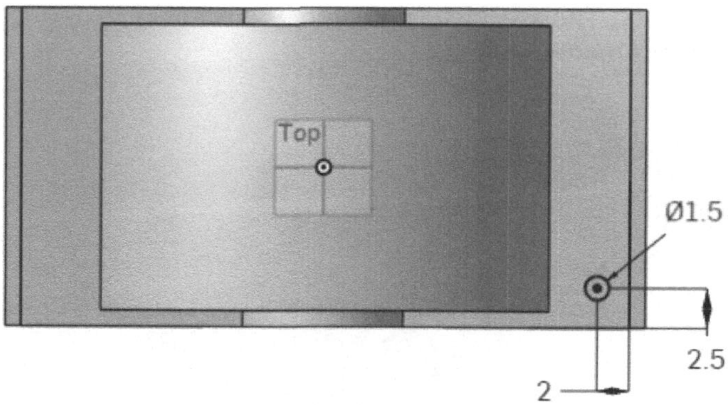

5. Create a linear pattern of the circle to create its remaining instances using the **Linear pattern** tool, see Figure 4.151. As illustrated in Figure 4.151, the pattern consists of 4 instances (4x) in Direction 1 with a spacing of 5 inches and 2 instances (2x) in Direction 2 with a spacing of 34 inches.

4.151

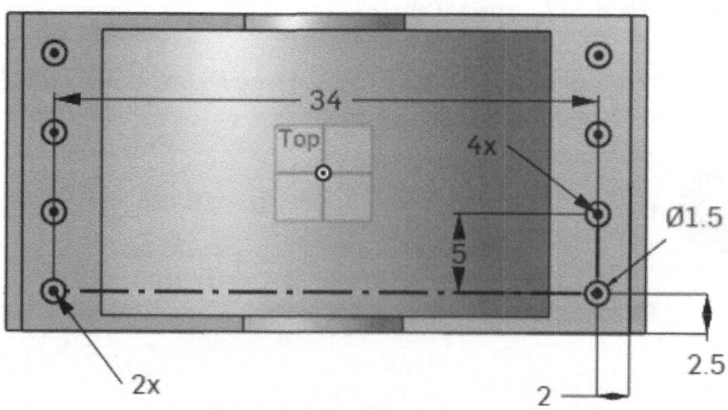

6. Click on the **Extrude** tool in the **Sketch** toolbar, see Figure 4.152. The **Extrude** dialog appears. Also, the preview of an extruded feature appears by adding material to the sketch profiles in the graphics area.

4.152

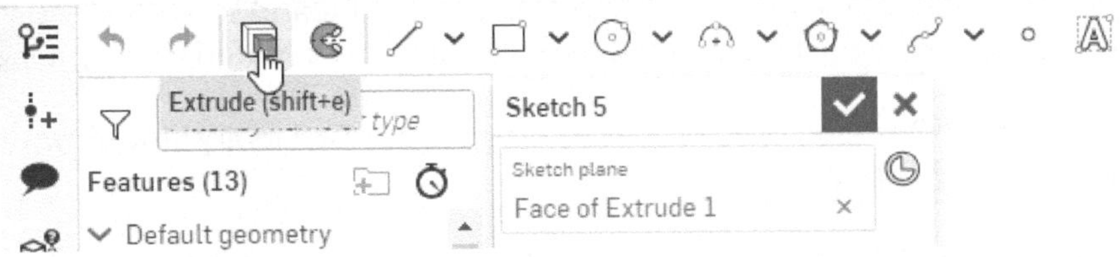

7. Press the SHIFT + 7 keys to change the view of the model to isometric.

8. Select the **Remove** option in the **Operation type** area to create an extruded feature by removing the material from the model, see Figure 4.153.

9. Select the **Up to next** option in the **End Type** drop-down list for extruding the sketch up to the next intersection, see Figure 4.153.

4.153

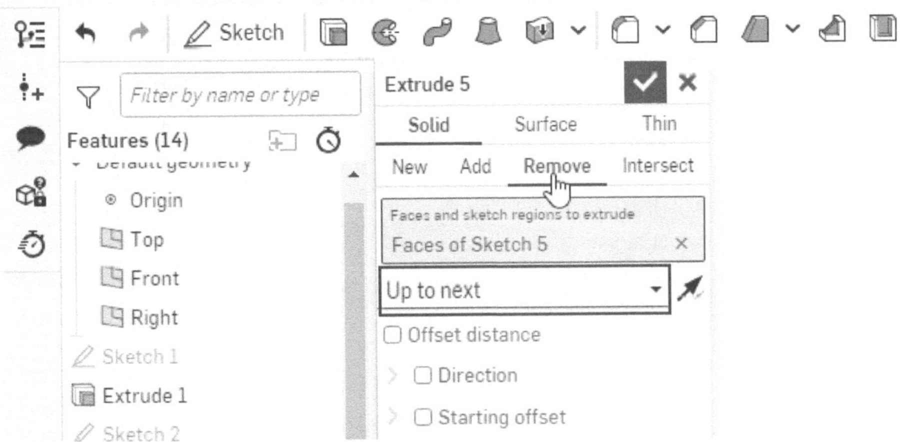

10. Click the green checkmark  in the **Extrude** dialog box to confirm the creation of the feature and close the dialog. The extruded cut feature is created by removing the material. Figure 4.154 shows the final model after creating all its features.

4.154

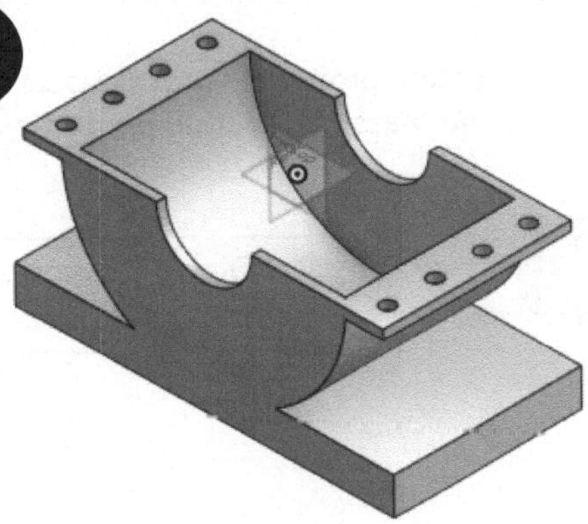

Section 9: Assigning the Material

Now, you need to assign the Carbon Steel material to the model.

1. Right-click on the name of the part (*Part1*) in the Part list and select the **Assign material** option from the shortcut menu that appears, see Figure 4.155. The **Material** dialog appears.

2. Ensure that the **Onshape Material Library** is selected in the **Library** drop-down list of the **Material** dialog, refer to Figure 4.156.

3. Invoke the **Material** drop-down list and select the Carbon Steel material, see Figure 4.156. The material properties of the selected material are displayed in the dialog.

4.155

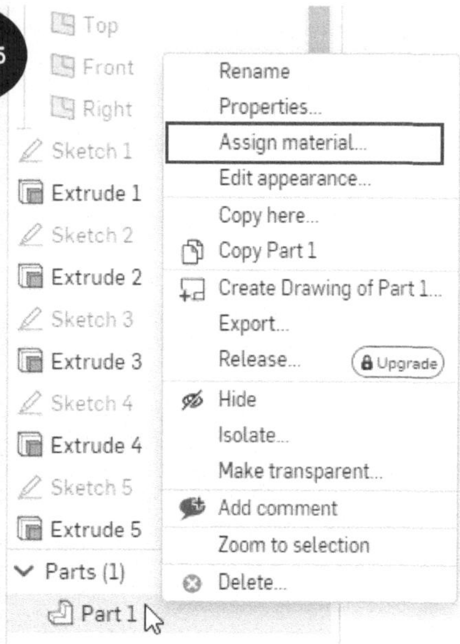

4.156

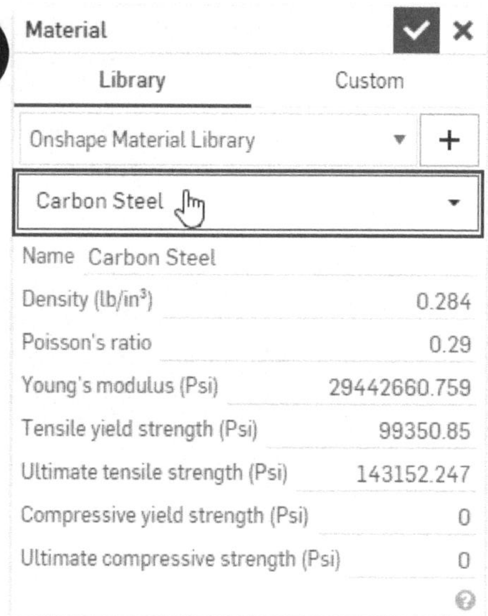

4. After select a material, click on the green checkmark in the dialog to confirm the application of the material and exit the dialog.

Section 10: Calculating Mass Properties

Now, you can calculate the mass properties of the model such as mass, area, and volume.

1. Click on the **Display mass and section properties** tool, located at the lower right corner of the graphics area, see Figure 4.157. The **Mass and section properties** dialog appears with the **Part** tab activated by default.

4.157

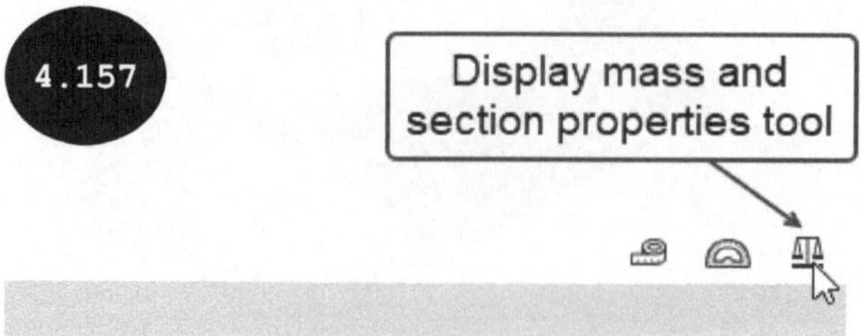

2. Select the part from the graphics area or the Part list. The mass properties of the selected part are computed and displayed in the dialog, see Figure 4.158. Notice that the selected part is highlighted in the graphics area and the center of mass is marked with the ⯐ symbol on the model.

4.158

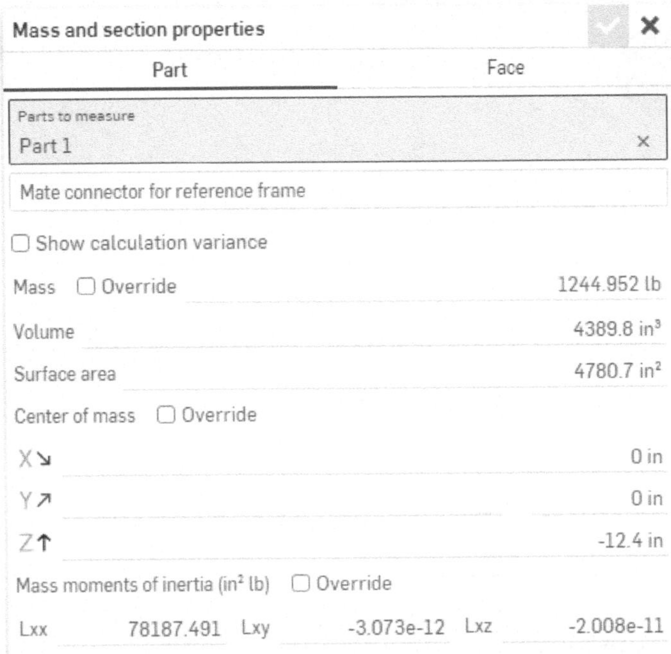

3. After reviewing the mass properties of a model, click the exit the dialog.

Section 11: Creating a Version and Closing the Document

Now, you can create a version in the document to capture the current state of the design, and then close the document.

1. Click on the **Create version** tool in the **Document panel**, which is aligned vertically with the Onshape logo, see Figure 4.159. The **Create version from Main** window appears with default version name **V1** in its **Name** field.

4.159

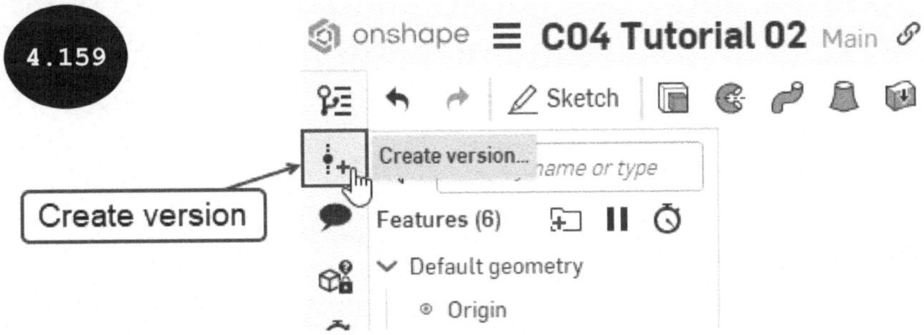

2. Accept the default specified name "V1" and click the **Create** button. A new version, "V1," is created in the document, capturing the model's current state.

Now, you can close the document.

3. Invoke the **Document** menu by clicking on the ≡ icon next to the Onshape logo and click on the **Close document** option, see Figure 4.160. The current document gets closed.

4.160

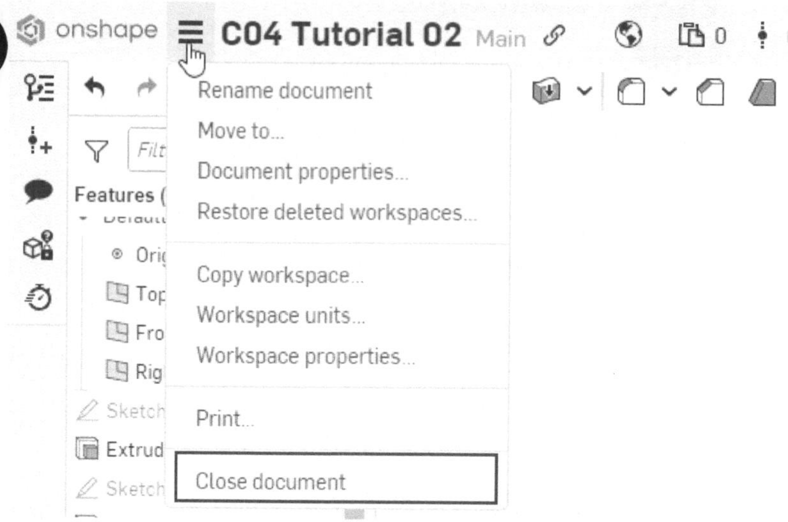

Hands-on Test Drive 1

Create a model shown in Figure 4.161. After creating the model, apply the Copper material to the model and calculate its mass properties. All dimensions are in inches.

4.161

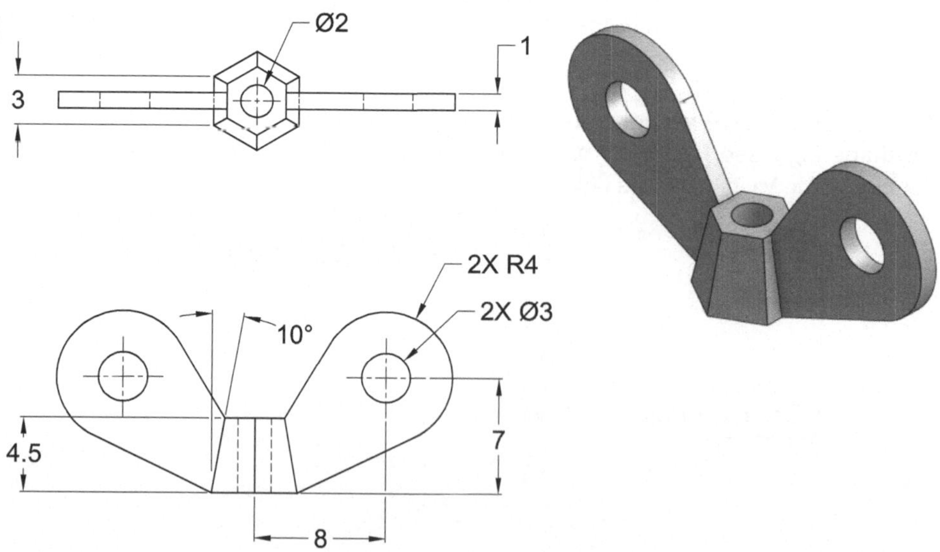

Hint: *To create this model, start by extruding a six-sided polygon to a depth of 4.5 inches with a 10-degree inward draft angle, and then proceed with creating the other features of the model.*

Hands-on Test Drive 2

Create a model shown in Figure 4.162. After creating the model, apply the Copper material to the model and calculate its mass properties. All dimensions are in mm.

4.162

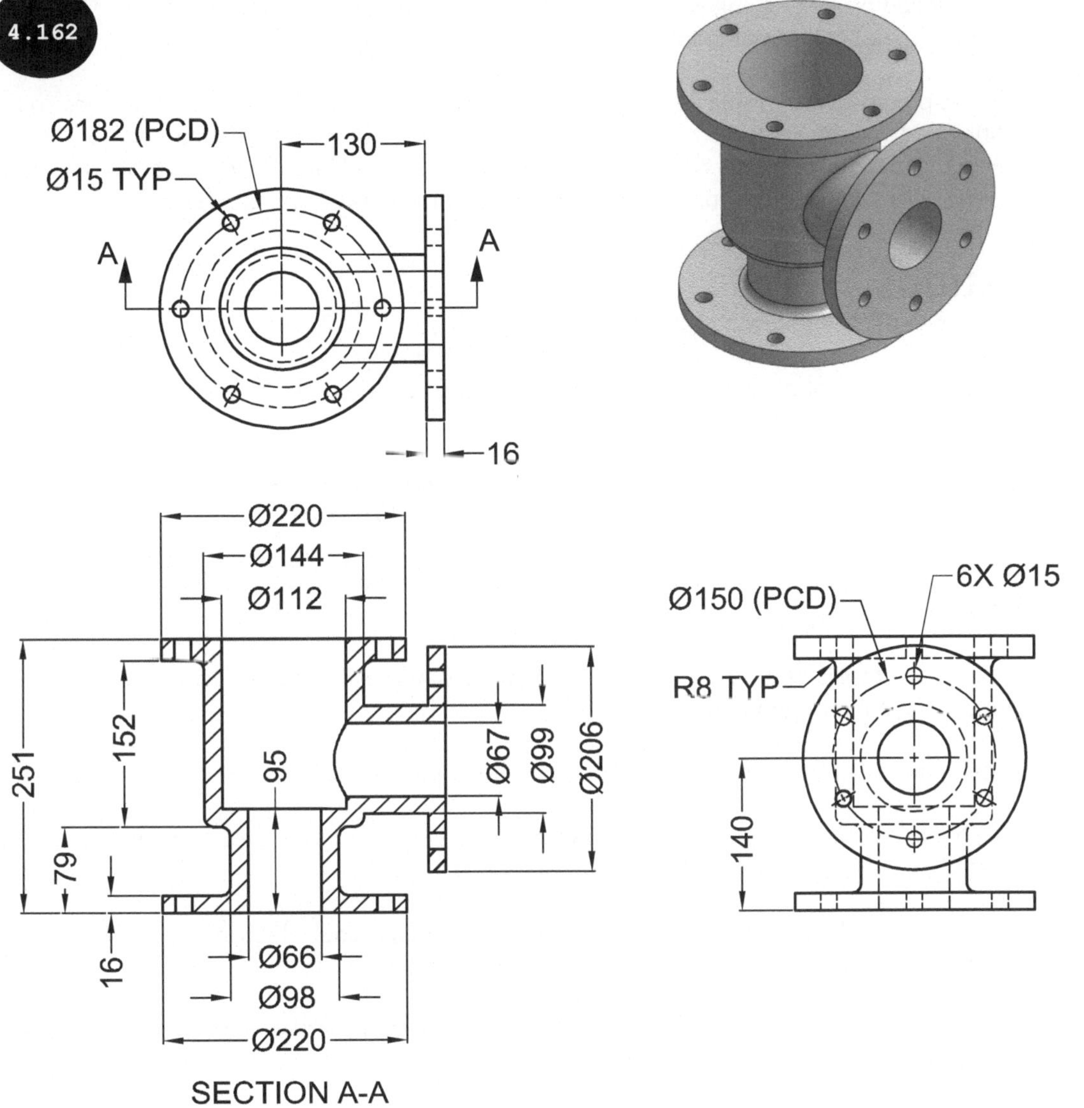

Summary

In this chapter, you learned key techniques to enhance your CAD modeling. You started with creating construction planes, as the default three planes (Front, Top, and Right) may not suffice for complex designs. Next, you explored advanced options in Extrude/Revolve to gain greater control over features. You also practiced projecting edges onto the active sketching plane as sketch entities and creating section views to inspect internal model details.

You further explored how to display earlier model stages and reorder features to manage design flow, while editing and deleting features helped refine your model. Additionally, you learned how to apply appearance and material properties to customize your design and calculate key mass properties. These fundamental skills significantly improve your CAD modeling precision and efficiency.

Questions

Complete and verify the following sentences:

- The _________ option in the **Plane** dialog is used to create a plane at an angle relative to a planar face around a linear edge or line.
- The _________ option in the **Extrude** dialog is used to extrude the sketch by adding material and merging the new feature with the existing features of the model.
- The _________ option is used to create an extruded cut feature by removing material from the model.
- The _______ tool is used to create a section view of a model in the graphics area for visualizing its internal features or geometries.
- To display an earlier stage of a model by temporarily hiding later features, you can use the_______.
- In Onshape, you can edit the default appearance of a _______, its _______, and its _______ by assigning a new appearance.
- The _______ tool is used to calculate mass properties of a model which includes mass, volume, surface area, center of mass, and mass moments of inertia.
- You can apply a custom material to a model by defining its properties such as density, Poisson's ratio, young's modulus, and tensile strength. (True/False)
- Assigning a material to a model is essential for calculating its mass properties. (True/False)
- When creating a section view of a multi-body part, you can choose to include or exclude parts from the section view. (True/False)

CHAPTER

5

Creating Sweep, Loft, and Thicken Features

In this chapter, the following topics will be discussed:

- Creating a Sweep Feature
- Creating a Loft feature
- Creating a Thicken feature

In the previous chapters, you learned about the fundamental modeling tools used to create features such as extrude and revolve, either by adding or removing material. You also covered the essential workflow for building models; starting with the base feature and then adding subsequent features step by step. Additionally, techniques such as navigating models, adjusting view orientation, changing display styles, assigning materials, and calculating mass properties, along with many more essential tools and methods, were discussed.

In this chapter, you will explore some of the advanced modeling tools: **Sweep**, **Loft**, and **Thicken**.

Creating a Sweep Feature

A sweep feature is created by adding or removing material by sweeping a profile along a path. Figure 5.1 shows a profile and a path along with the resulting sweep feature created by sweeping the profile along the path. In this figure, the sweep feature is created by adding material.

5.1

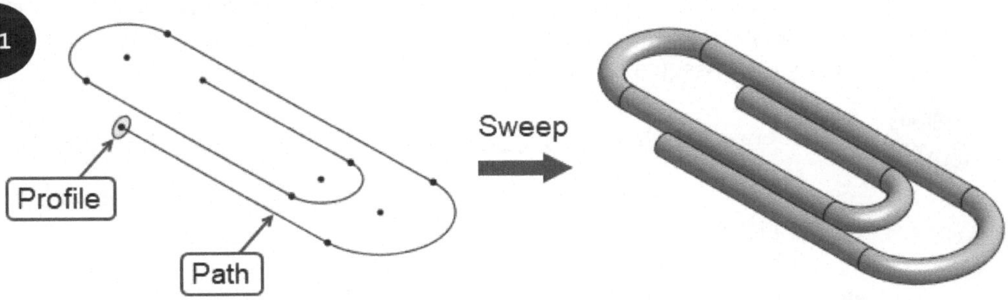

It is clear from the above figure that creating a sweep feature involves developing both a profile and a path as separate sketches. The profile represents the cross-sectional shape of the feature, while the path determines the route the profile will follow. To begin, you must create the profile by identifying the cross-section of the desired feature. Similarly, the path should be established based on the intended direction for the profile to move along. After both the profile and path are created, you can use the **Sweep** tool to create the sweep feature. In Onshape, you can create solid, surface, and thin sweep features. When creating a sweep feature, keep the following points in mind:

1. The profile must be a closed sketch; you can also select the face of a model as the profile. For surface and thin sweep features, both open and closed sketch profiles can be selected.
2. The path can be either an open or closed sketch made up of end-to-end connected sketched entities or curves. Alternatively, you can select a set of model edges as the path.
3. The starting point of the path should intersect with the plane of the profile for better results.
4. The profile, path, and resulting sweep feature must not have any self-intersections.

The method for creating a solid sweep feature is discussed below:

1. Create a path and a profile of the sweep feature as separate sketches, refer to Figure 5.2. In this example, the path is created on the Right plane, while the profile is created on the Top plane.

5.2

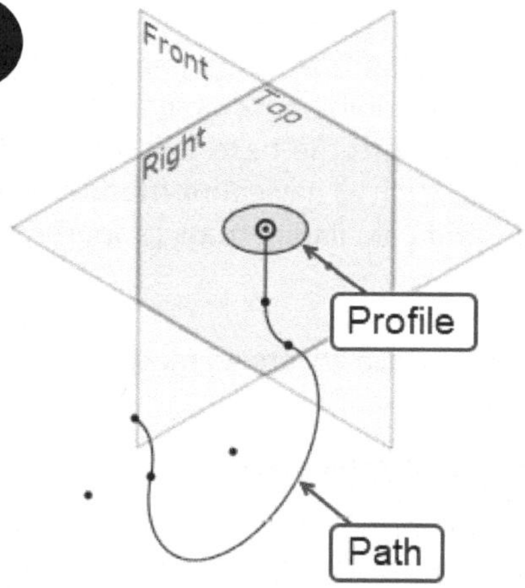

2. After creating the path and the profile, click on the **Sweep** tool in the **Feature** toolbar, see Figure 5.3. The **Sweep** dialog appears, with the **Solid** option automatically activated in the **Creation Type** section, see Figure 5.4. Consequently, you can create a solid sweep feature.

5.3

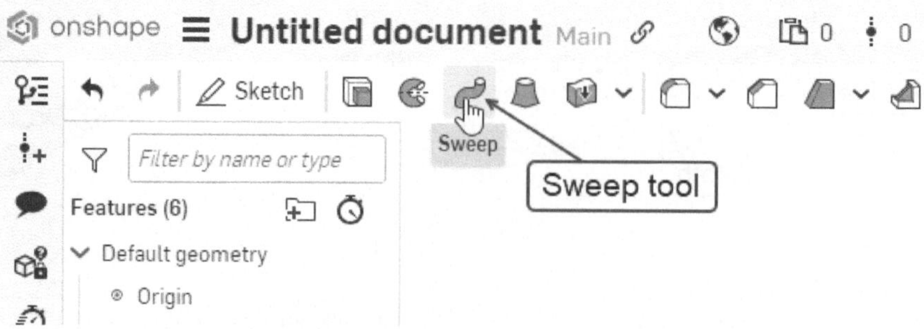

5.4

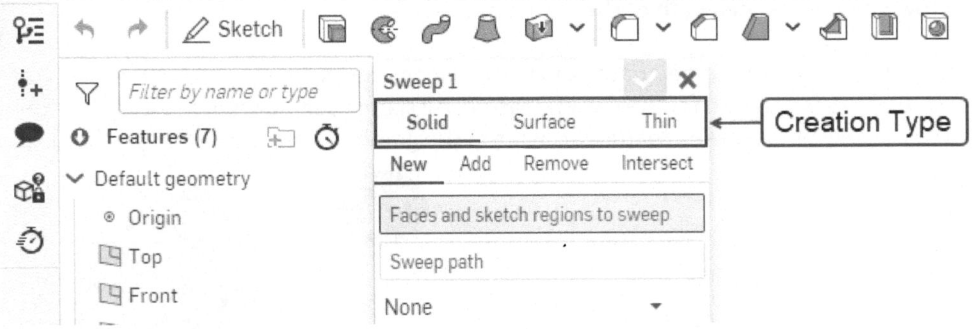

Creating Type: By default, the **Solid** option is activated in the **Creation Type** area of the **Sweep** dialog, see Figure 5.4. This enables you to create a solid sweep feature by adding material, allowing the closed profile to follow the designated path.

By activating the **Surface** or **Thin** option in the **Creation Type** area, you can create either a surface feature or a thin solid feature. A surface feature has no thickness and does not have mass properties, whereas a thin solid feature has a uniform wall thickness. The methods for creating both surface and thin features are the same as those used for creating a solid feature, which is covered in this section.

Faces and sketch regions to sweep: The **Faces and sketch regions to sweep** field allows you to select a face or a sketch region as the profile for the sweep feature. Note that when creating a solid sweep feature, you must choose a closed sketch region or profile. However, for surface or thin sweep features, you can select either a closed or an open sketch profile.

Sweep path: The **Sweep path** field allows you to select a path for the sweep feature. You can select either a closed or an open sketch as the path for sweep features.

3. Ensure that the **Solid** option is activated in the **Creation Type** area of the **Sweep** dialog for creating a solid sweep feature.

4. Select a closed sketch region as the profile of the solid sweep feature in the graphics area, see Figure 5.5. The name of the selected profile appears in the **Faces and sketch regions to sweep** field of the dialog. You can select one or more closed regions of a sketch as the profile. Alternatively, you can also select a face of a model as the profile of the sweep feature, see Figure 5.6.

5.5

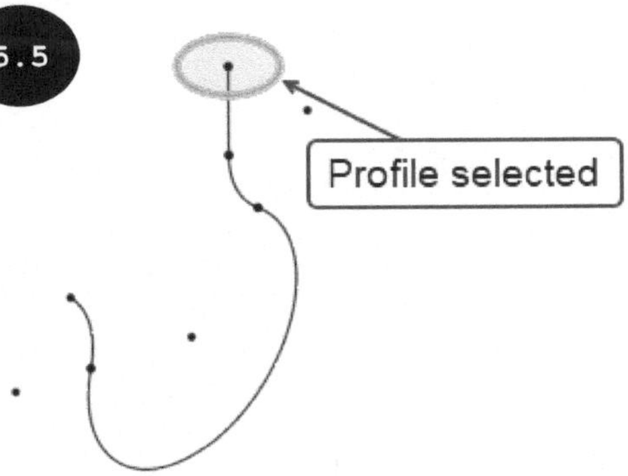

5.6

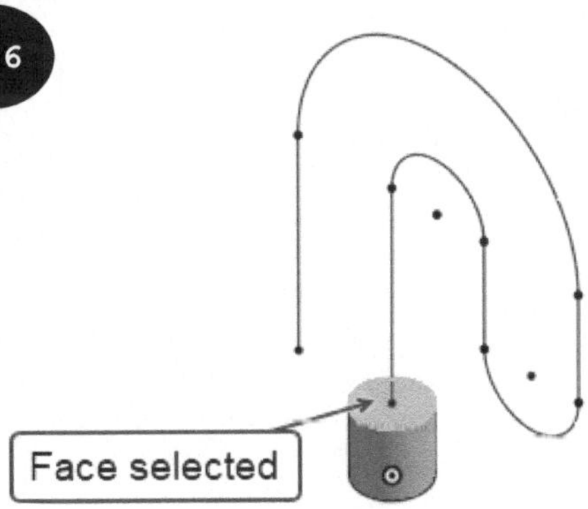

Now, you can select a path of the sweep feature.

5. Click to activate the **Sweep path** field in the dialog, then select an open or closed sketch from the Feature list as the path for the sweep feature. All sketch segments are selected automatically, and the preview of the sweep feature appears in the graphics area, see Figures 5.7 and 5.8.

5.7

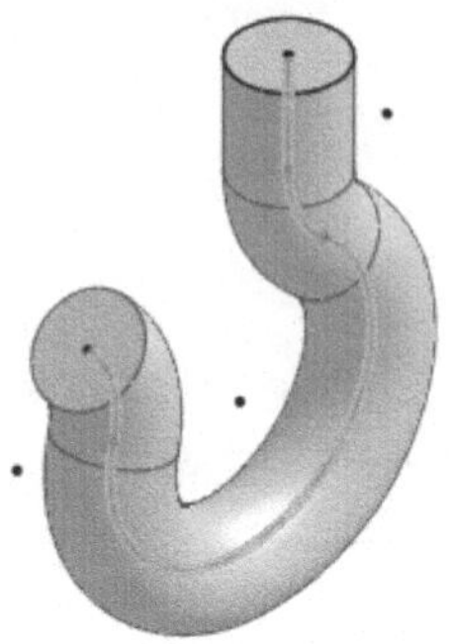

5.8

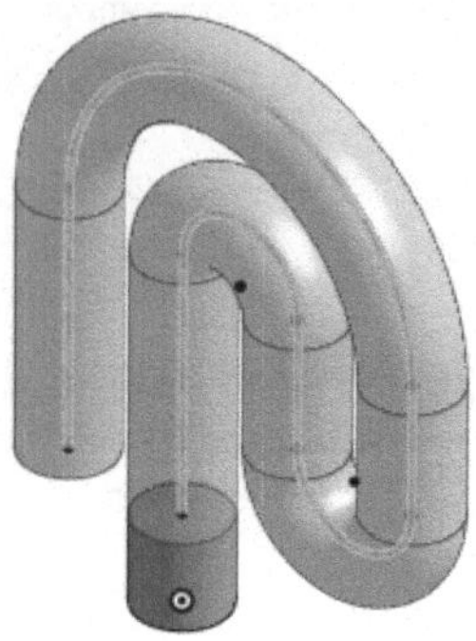

Note: When you select a sketch from the Feature list, all its segments are automatically selected as the path of the feature. However, in the graphics area, you can only select individual segments of the sketch as the path for the feature, refer to Figure 5.9. Moreover, you can also select individual edges of the model to define the path of the feature.

5.9

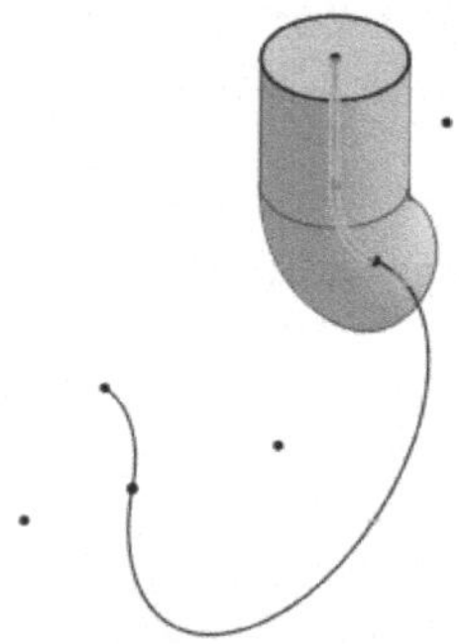

6. Ensure that the required option: **New**, **Add**, **Remove**, or **Intersect** is selected in the **Operation Type** area of the dialog, see Figure 5.10. The options are discussed below:

5.10

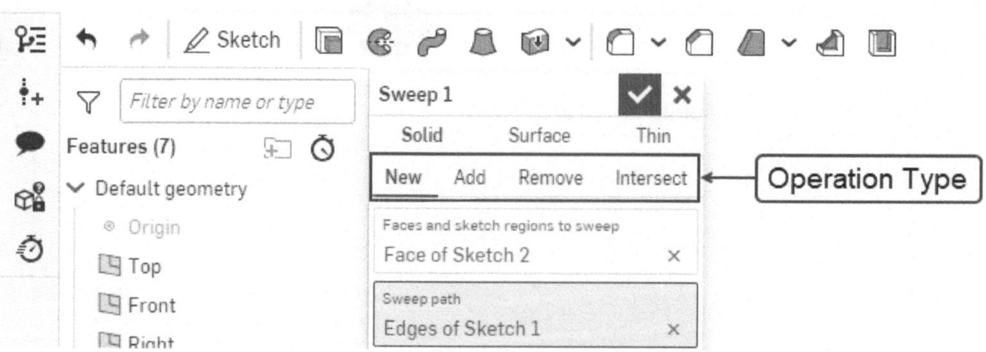

New: The **New** option creates a sweep feature by adding material and forming a new part (body). This option is selected automatically, when creating the first or base feature of a model.

Add: The **Add** option creates a sweep feature by adding material and merging it with existing features of the model, refer to Figure 5.11.

5.11

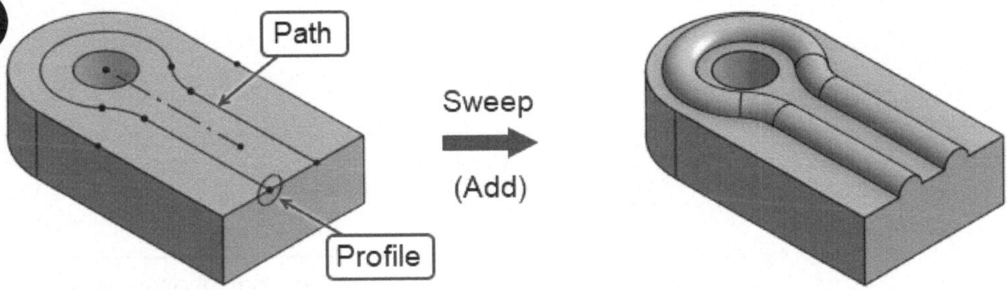

Remove: The **Remove** option creates a sweep feature by subtracting or removing material from the model, creating a cut feature, refer to Figure 5.12.

5.12

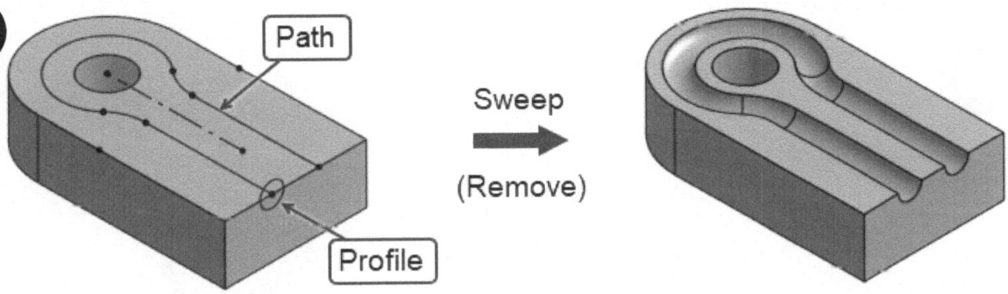

Intersect: The **Intersect** option creates a sweep feature by keeping the intersecting material between the existing feature and the new one, refer to Figure 5.13.

5.13

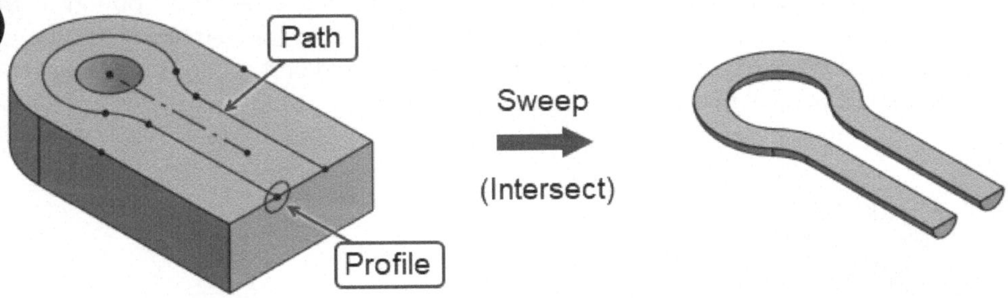

7. If needed, you can define the orientation of the profile along the path by selecting the required option in the **Profile control** drop-down list, see Figure 5.14. The options are discussed below:

5.14

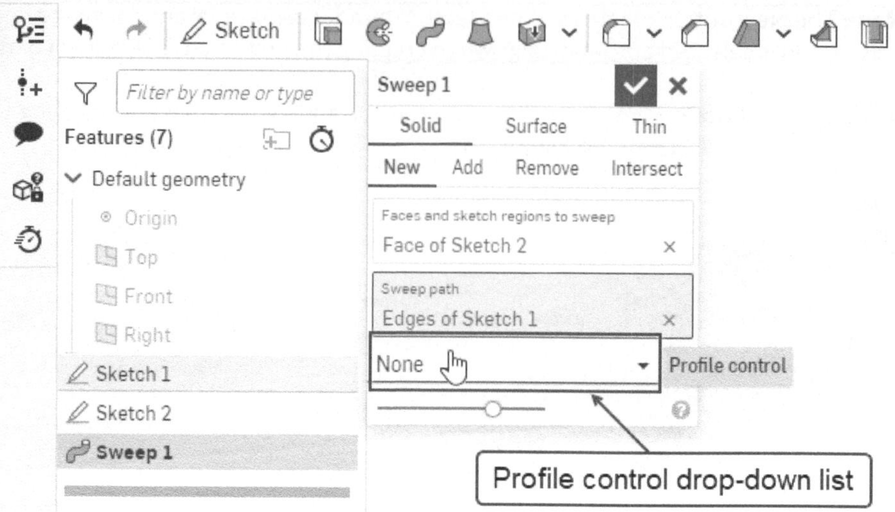

None: By default, the **None** option is selected in the **Profile control** drop-down list. Consequently, no profile control is applied, and the profile follows the path while maintaining the angle of orientation relative to the path from start to end, see Figure 5.15.

5.15

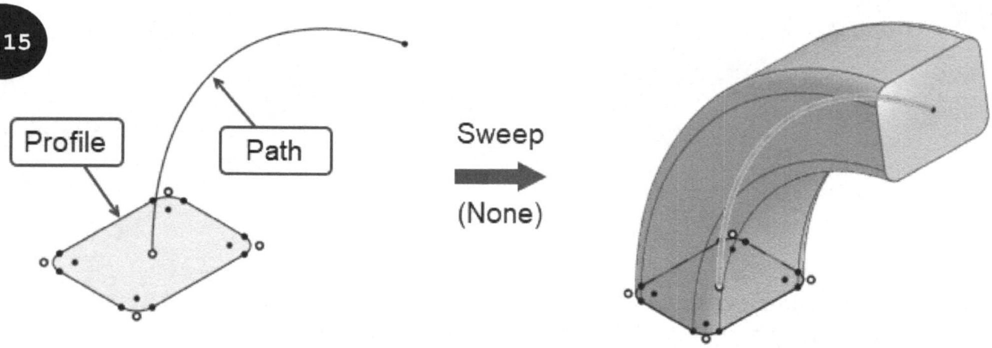

Keep profile orientation: By selecting the **Keep profile orientation** option in the **Profile control** drop-down list, the profile follows the specified path while remaining parallel, preventing any twisting along the path. This ensures that the start and end sections of the resulting sweep feature remain parallel to each other, see Figure 5.16.

5.16

Lock profile faces: The **Lock profile faces** option creates a sweep feature where the profile follows a specified path while maintaining its orientation based on a selected face. When this option is selected, the **Lock face** field appears in the dialog, allowing you to choose a face (the locked face) that will control the orientation of the profile during the sweep operation. Figures 5.17 and 5.18 show previews of sweep features with a locked face selected, illustrating how the profile follows the path while maintaining its orientation concerning the locked face. This option is particularly useful for ensuring that the profile maintains a specific alignment or angle relative to the selected face, which can be critical in complex geometries.

5.17

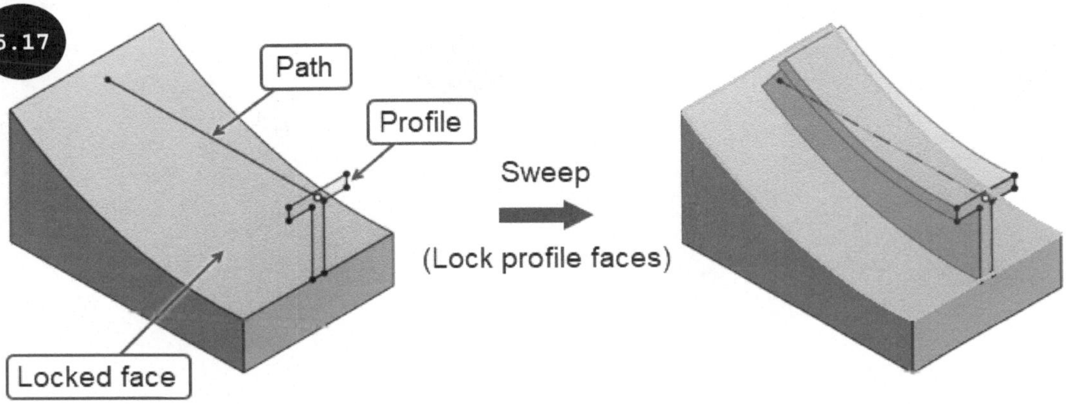

5.18

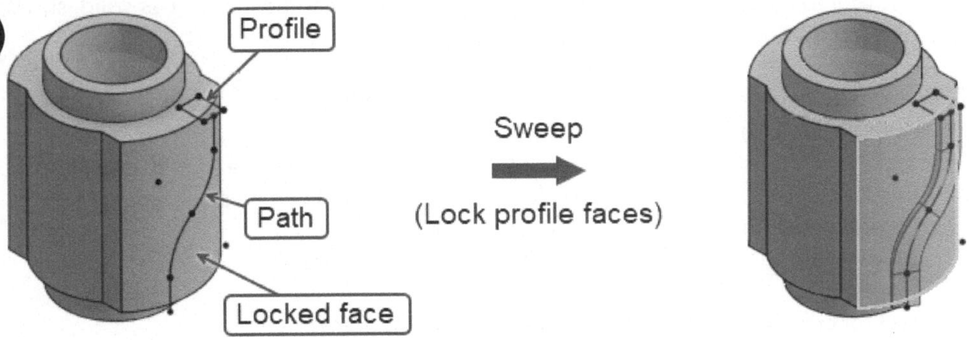

Lock profile direction: The **Lock profile direction** option creates a sweep feature where the profile follows the specified path while maintaining a normal relation to a specified direction (e.g., an axis or plane), see Figure 5.19. In this figure, the Right plane is selected to define the direction. This feature is particularly useful for preserving a consistent shape and orientation throughout the sweep, helping to avoid rotational distortion in the resultant feature.

5.19

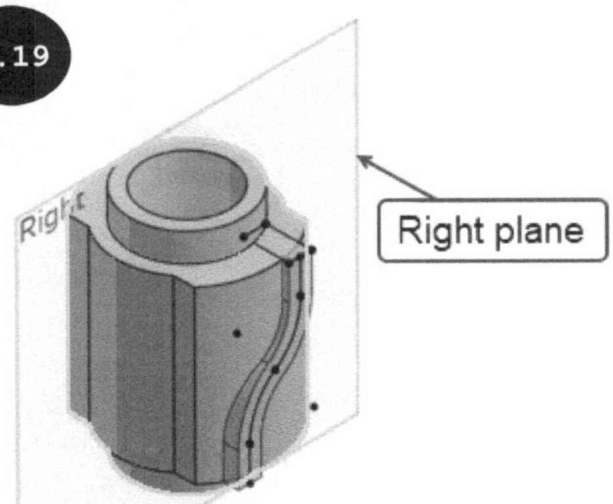

8. After select the profile and path, click the green checkmark ✓ to confirm the creation of the sweep feature and exit the dialog.

Creating a Loft feature

A loft feature is created by lofting two or more sketch profiles (sections), allowing the cross-sectional shape to smoothly transition from one profile to another. Figure 5.20 shows three dissimilar sketch profiles (sections) created on different planes with an offset distance between them and Figure 5.21 shows the resultant loft feature.

5.20

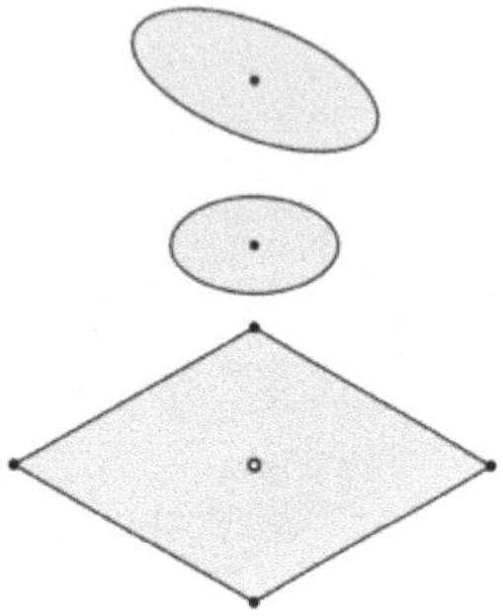

5.21

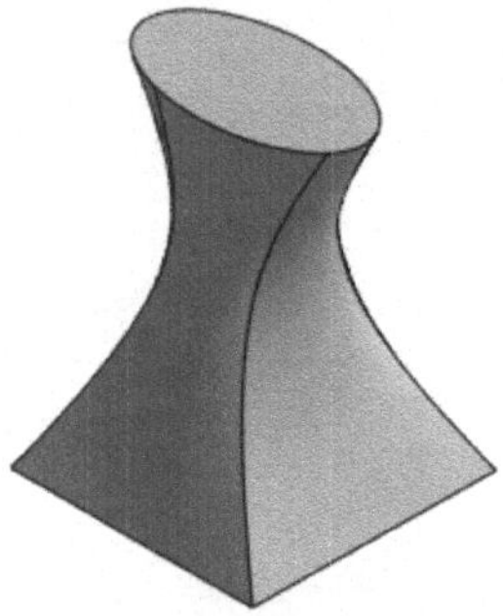

It is evident from the above figures that to create a loft feature, the first step is to create all the necessary sketch profiles that define its cross-sectional shape. Once the sketch profiles are created, you can use the Loft tool to create the loft feature. In Onshape, lofts can be created as solid, surface, or thin features. When creating a loft feature, keep the following points in mind:

1. Ensure that two or more profiles (whether similar or different) are available in the graphics area before using the **Loft** tool.
2. Profiles must be closed sketch regions; you can also select faces of a model as profiles. For surface and thin loft features, both open and closed sketch profiles can be selected.
3. Each profile must be created in a separate sketch.
4. The profiles and the resulting loft must not intersect themselves.

The method for creating a loft sweep feature is discussed below:

1. Create each of the required sketch profiles that define the cross-sectional shape of the feature as separate sketches, refer to Figure 5.22. In the figure, the construction planes have been turned off to enhance image clarity.

5.22

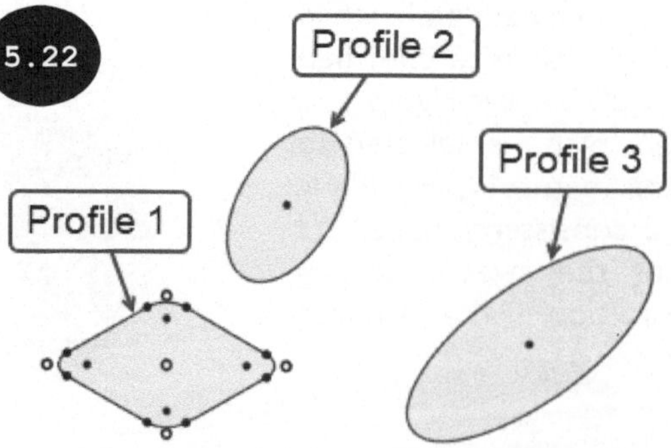

2. After creating the sketch profiles, click on the **Loft** tool in the **Feature** toolbar, see Figure 5.23. The **Loft** dialog appears, with the **Solid** option automatically activated in the **Creation Type** section, see Figure 5.24. Consequently, you can create a solid loft feature.

5.23

5.24
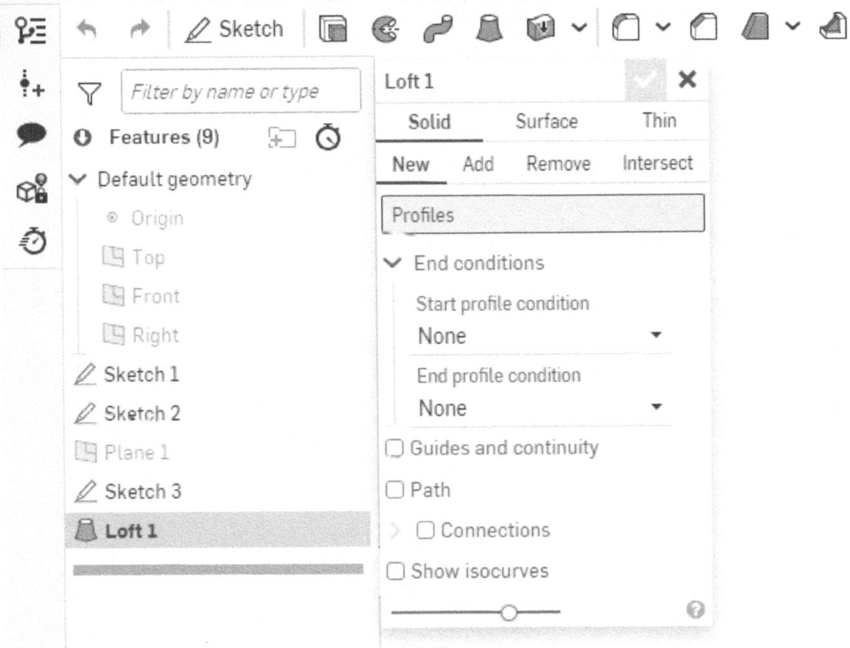

Creating Type: By default, the **Solid** option is activated in the **Creation Type** area of the **Loft** dialog, refer to Figure 5.24. This enables you to create a solid loft feature by adding material.

By activating the **Surface** or **Thin** option in the **Creation Type** area, you can create a surface feature or a thin solid feature, respectively. A surface feature has no thickness and does not have mass properties, whereas a thin solid feature has a uniform wall thickness. The methods for creating both surface and thin features are the same as those used for creating a solid feature, which is covered in this section.

Profiles: The **Profiles** field allows you to select two or more sketch profiles to create a loft feature. When creating a solid loft feature, it is essential to choose closed sketch regions or profiles. However, for surface or thin loft features, you can use either closed or open sketch profiles.

3. Select two or more closed sketch profiles in the graphics area sequentially. As you select them, the loft feature preview appears, see Figure 5.25. Also, the names of the selected profiles appear in the **Profiles** field of the **Loft** dialog.

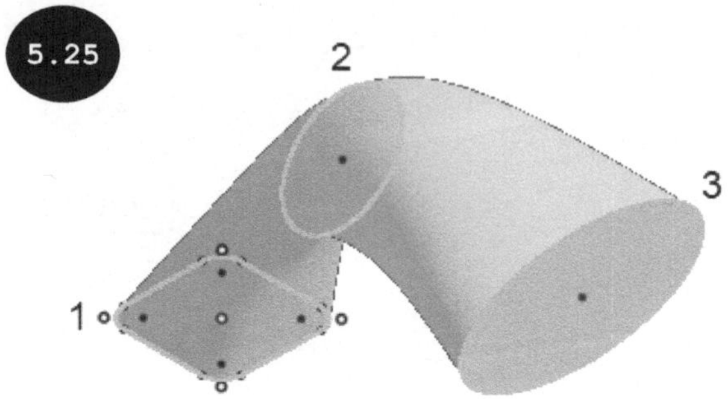

The remaining options in the Loft dialog are discussed below:

Start profile condition: The **Start profile condition** drop-down list is located in the **End conditions** rollout, see Figure 5.26. The options in this list are used to specify the constraint (end condition) for the first or starting profile of the loft feature. The options are discussed below:

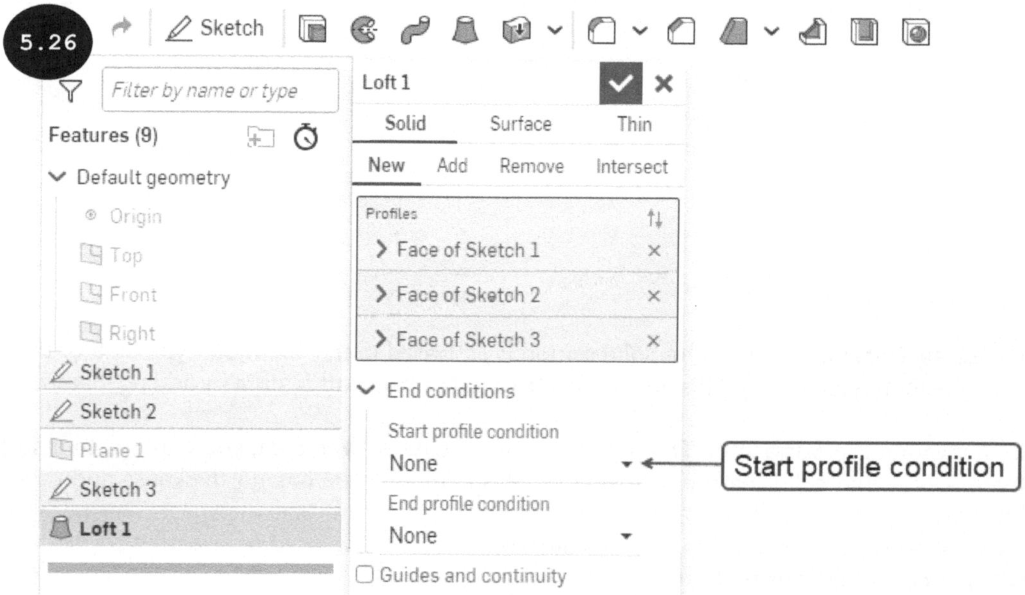

None: By default, the **None** option is selected in the **Start profile condition** drop-down list. Consequently, no constraint is applied to the start profile of the loft feature, allowing it to transition linearly to the second or subsequent profiles, see Figure 5.27.

5.27

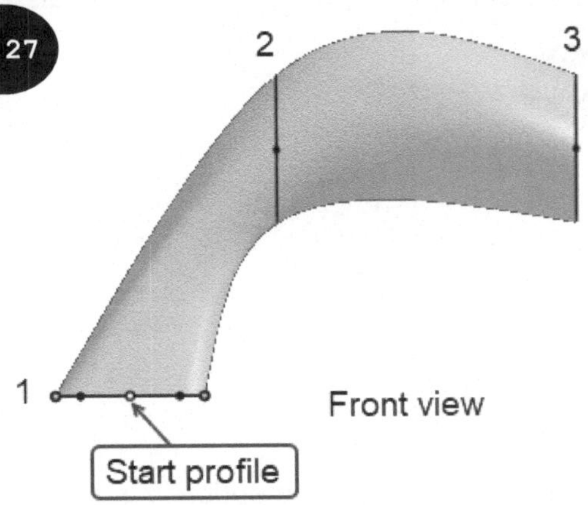

Normal to profile: By selecting the **Normal to profile** option in the **Start profile condition** drop-down list, a tangency constraint is applied normal to the start profile of the loft feature, see Figure 5.28. Also, the **Start magnitude** field becomes available below the drop-down list, allowing you to specify the magnitude or length of the start tangency. Figure 5.28 shows a preview of a loft feature with the start tangency magnitude set to 1, while Figure 5.29 shows a preview of the loft feature with the start tangency magnitude set to 2.

5.28

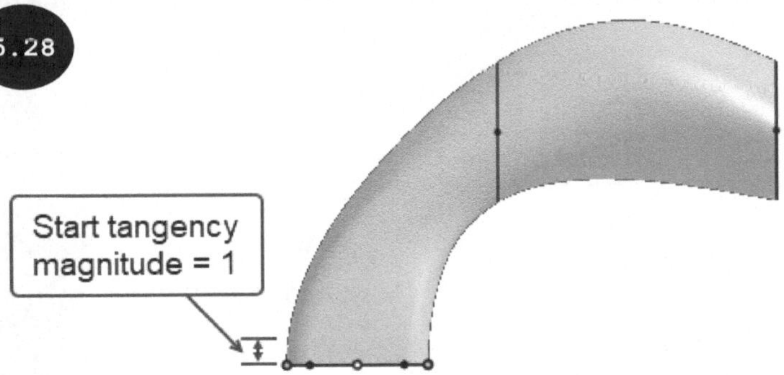

5.29

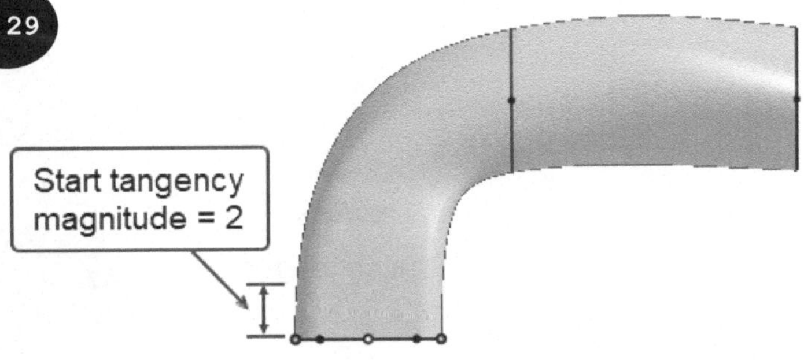

Tangent to profile: By selecting the **Tangent to profile** option in the **Start profile condition** drop-down list, a tangency constraint is applied tangent to the plane of the start profile, see Figure 5.30. Also, the **Start magnitude** field becomes available below the drop-down list, allowing you to specify the magnitude or length of the start tangency, as discussed earlier.

5.30

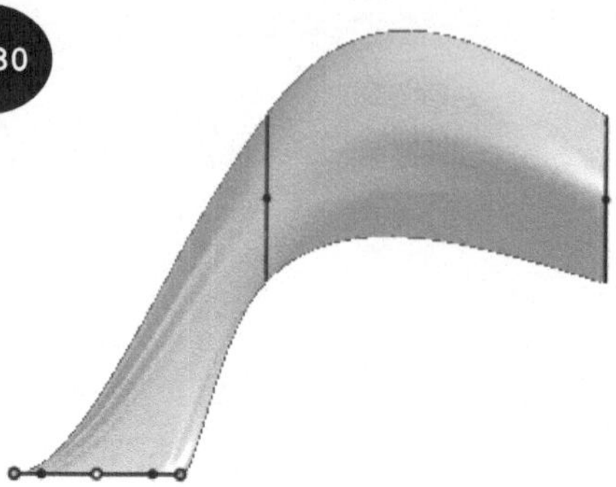

Match tangent: By selecting the **Match tangent** option in the **Start profile condition** drop-down list, the start profile of the loft feature maintains tangency with its adjacent face on the model, see Figure 5.31. Note that if the start profile has adjacent faces, they will be automatically selected in the **Adjacent faces** field when this option is chosen. For instance, in Figure 5.31, the start profile (top planar face) has one adjacent face, which is automatically selected. In contrast, Figure 5.32 shows a start profile with four adjacent faces. If needed, you can also manually select adjacent faces by choosing them from the graphics area. Moreover, if needed, you can define tangency magnitude in the **Start magnitude** field that appears, as discussed earlier. This **Match tangent** option is particularly useful when the start profile has an adjacent face to maintain tangency.

5.31

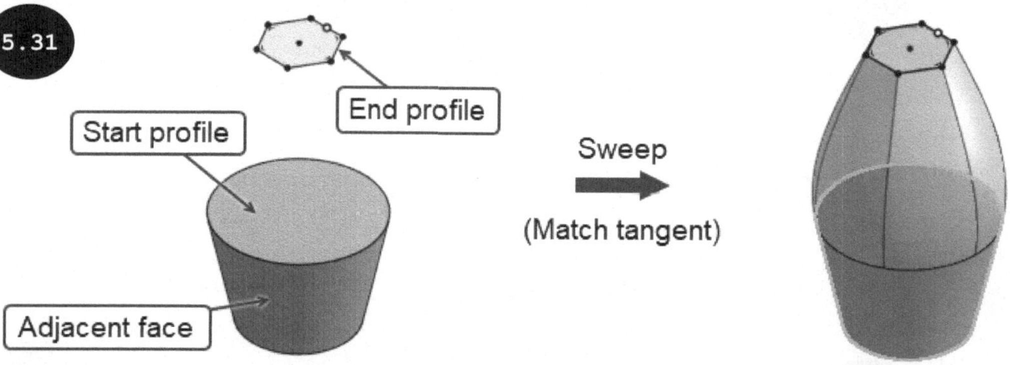

5.32

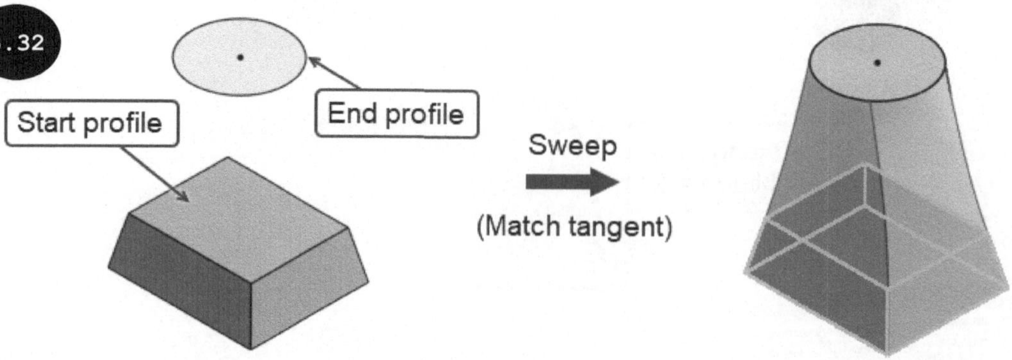

Match curvature: By selecting the **Match curvature** option in the **Start profile condition** drop-down list, the start profile of the loft feature maintains curvature continuity with its adjacent face on the model, see Figure 5.33. If needed, you can define curvature magnitude in the **Start magnitude** field that appears, as discussed earlier. This option is particularly useful when the start profile has an adjacent face to maintain curvature continuity.

5.33

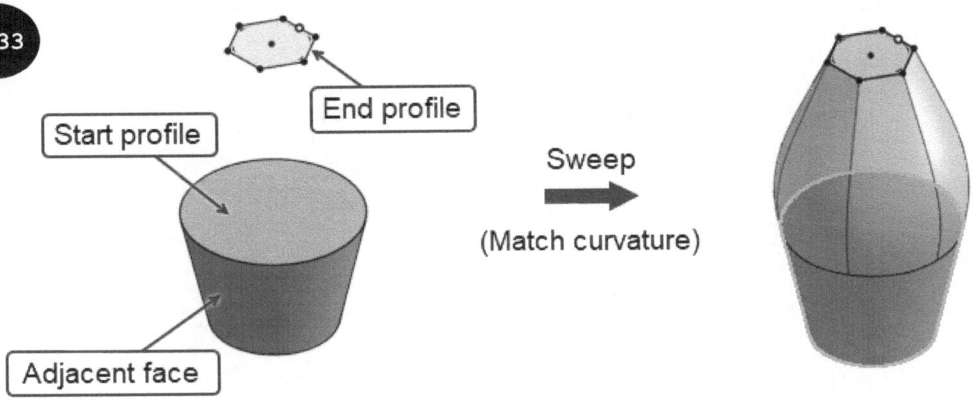

End profile condition: The options in the **End profile condition** drop-down list are the same as those discussed for the start profile, with the only difference being that these options apply constraints to the last or end profile of the loft feature. Figure 5.34 shows a preview of a loft feature where a tangency constraint is applied normal to the end profile (3). Similarly, Figure 5.35 shows a loft feature with a tangency constraint applied tangent to the plane of the end profile.

5.34

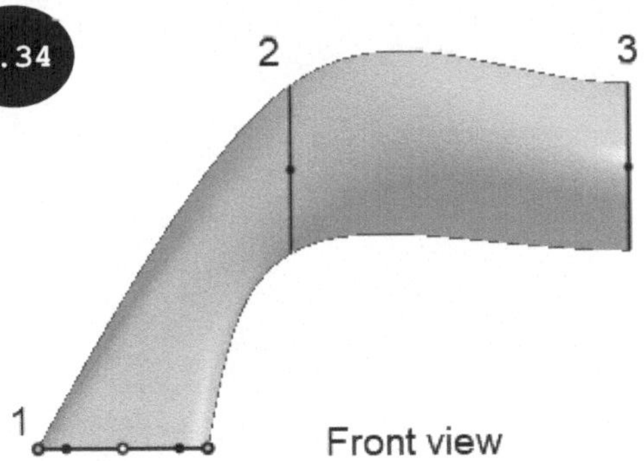

5.35

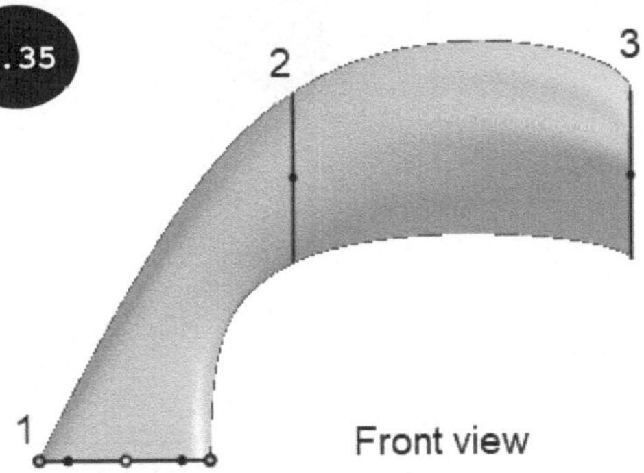

Guides and continuity: When the **Guides and continuity** check box is selected, the **Guides** field appears in the **Loft** dialog, see Figure 5.36. This allows you to select one or more guide curves to control or guide the cross-sectional shape of the loft feature, refer to Figures 5.37 and 5.38.

Note: The endpoints of the guide curves must have pierce constraints with the profiles of the loft feature to achieve optimal results.

5.36

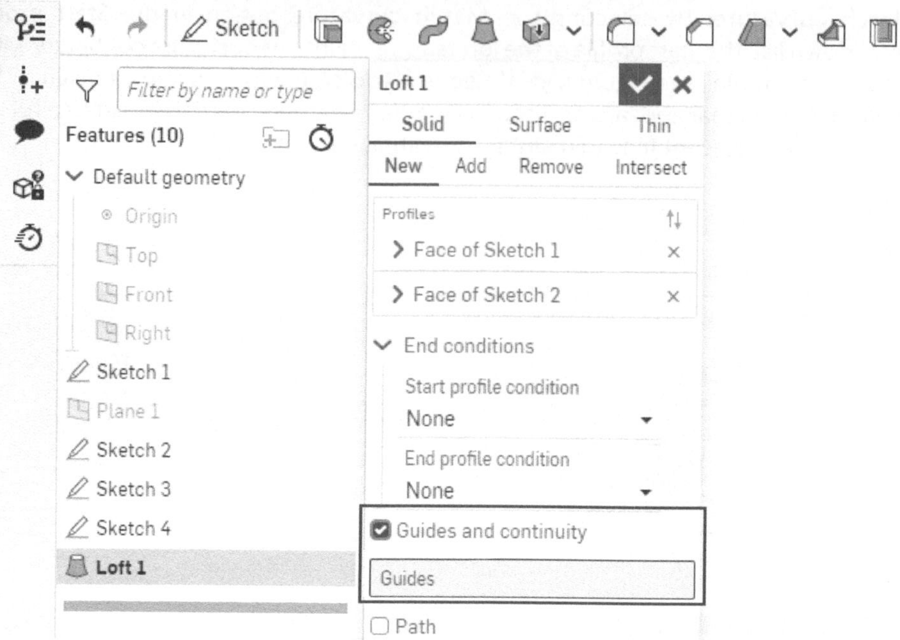

Figure 5.37 shows two profiles with one guide curve, while Figure 5.38 displays a preview of the loft feature before and after selecting the guide curve. As mentioned earlier, the endpoints of the guide curves must have pierce constraints with the profiles of the loft feature.

5.37

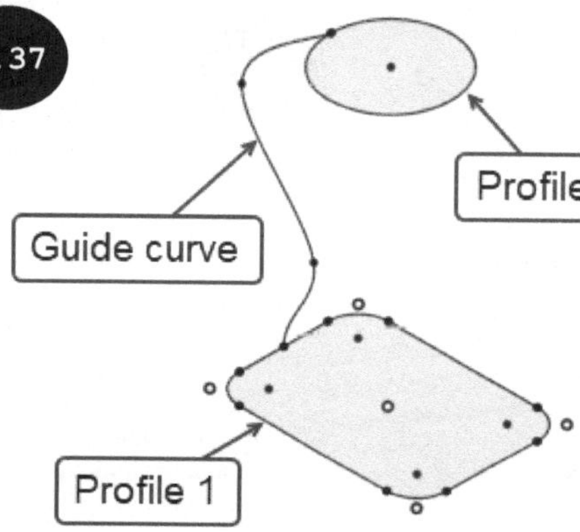

5.38

Path: When the **Path** check box is selected, the **Edges, curves and sketches** field appears in the **Loft** dialog, see Figure 5.39. This allows you to select a centerline guide (path), which helps maintain the neutral axis of the loft feature, see Figures 5.40 and 5.41. The centerline guide can be defined using edges, curves, or sketch segments. In Figure 5.40, a sketch consisting of an arc and line segments is created as the centerline guide. It is important to ensure that the endpoints of the centerline guide are coincident with the profiles of the loft feature.

5.39

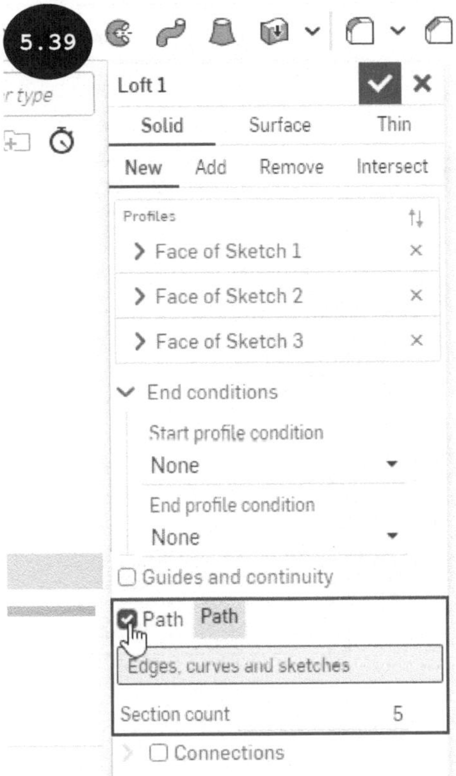

5.40

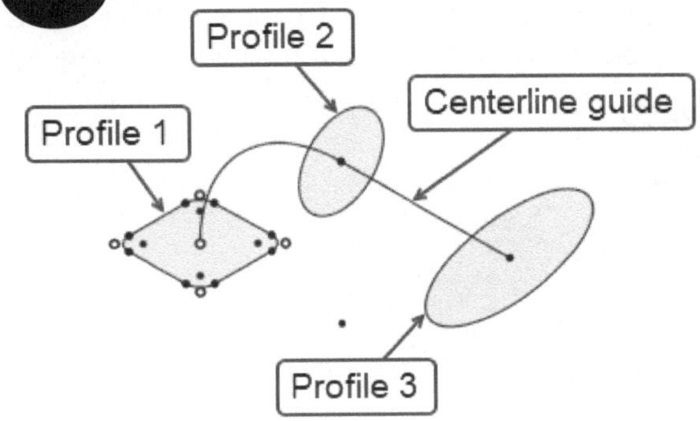

Figure 5.40 shows three profiles with a centerline guide (path), while Figure 5.41 displays a preview of the loft feature both before and after the centerline guide is selected.

5.41

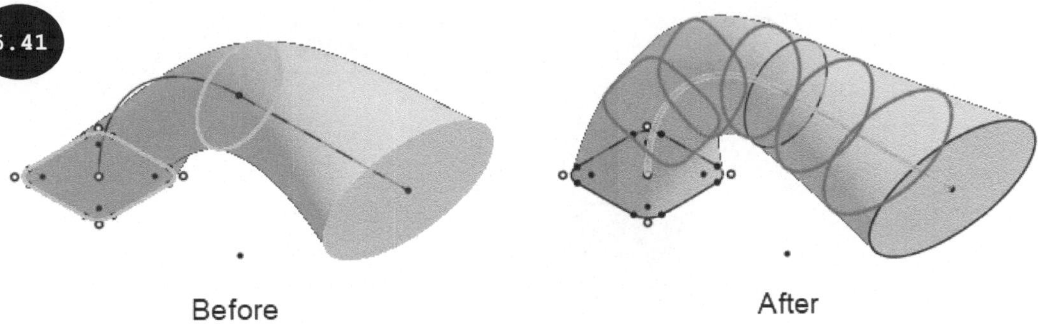

You can also define the number of intermediate sections along the centerline guide in the **Section count** field of the **Loft** dialog. Increasing the number of sections enables the profiles to follow the centerline guide more closely.

Connections: The **Connections** check box allows you to manually define connections to gain more control over the twist of the resulting loft feature. By default, connections between profiles are automatically set based on their geometry. To manually define these connections, select the **Connections** check box, which displays the **Match connections** field in the dialog. Also, the default automatic applied connections between the profiles are displayed in magenta in the graphics area, see Figure 5.42.

After selecting the **Connections** check box, click to define a set of connection points or vertices to link the profiles, see Figure 5.43. This figure shows the loft feature preview where manually defined connection points result in twisting.

5.42

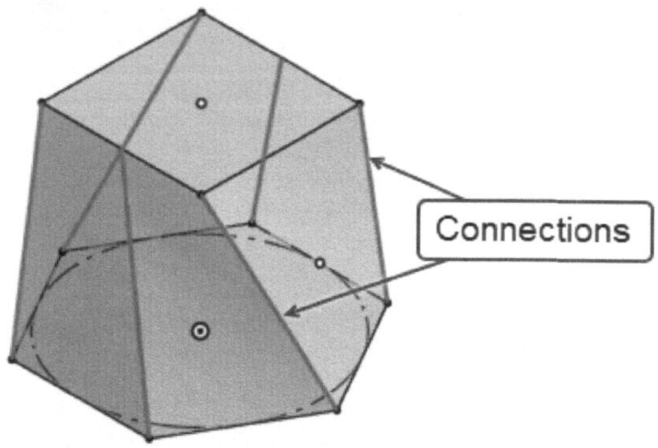

5.43

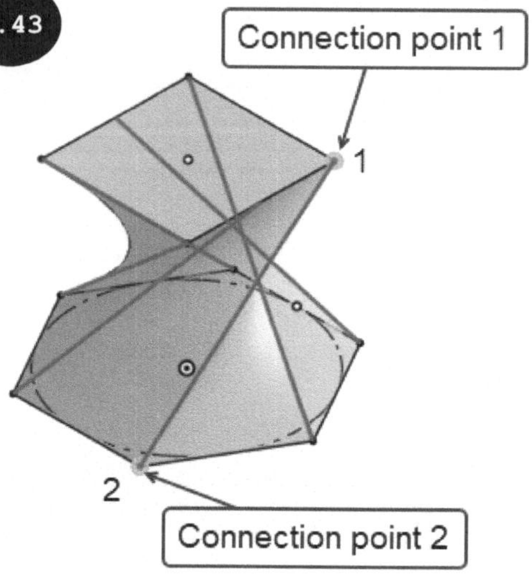

Note: If a control point is defined on a curved or circular profile, such as a circle, the **Connection handle** will appear on the profile, see Figure 5.44. You can drag this handle to the desired position on the profile to adjust or control the twist in the loft feature.

5.44

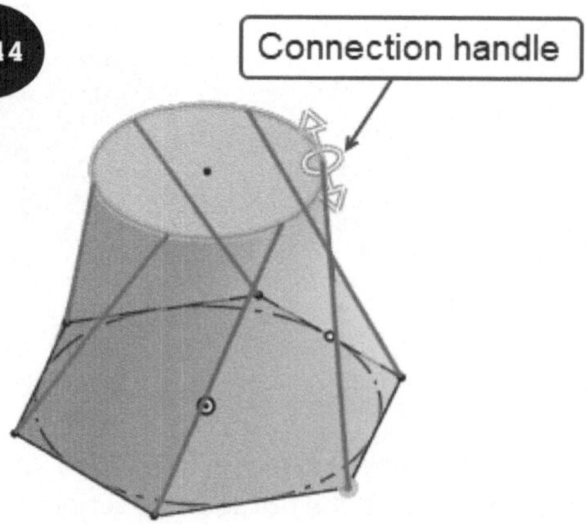

Tip: If needed, you can define multiple connections, with each connection requiring a set of two selections (connection points or vertices). To define a new connection between the profiles, activate the **Match connections** field in the dialog, then select the desired connection points or vertices to link the profiles.

Show isocurves: On selecting the **Show isocurves** check box, a mesh overlay is displayed on the faces of the loft feature preview, see Figure 5.45. In this mesh, you can adjust the number of isocurves per loft face by entering the desired value in the **Count** field that appears below the **Show isocurves** check box.

5.45

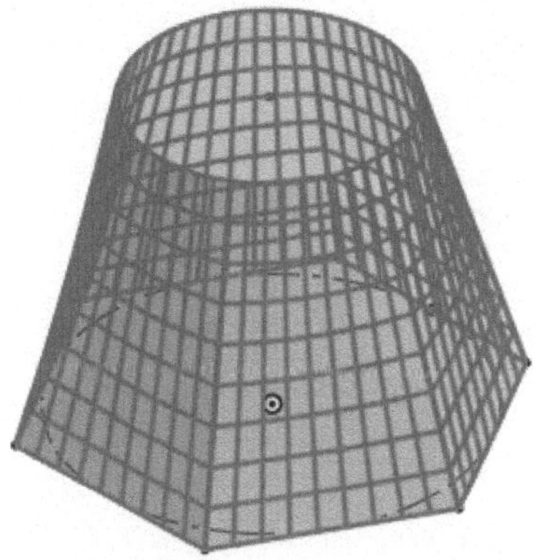

4. After selecting the profiles and the other parameters, ensure that the required option: **New**, **Add**, **Remove**, or **Intersect** is selected in the **Operation Type** area of the dialog for creating a loft feature, see Figure 5.46.

5.46

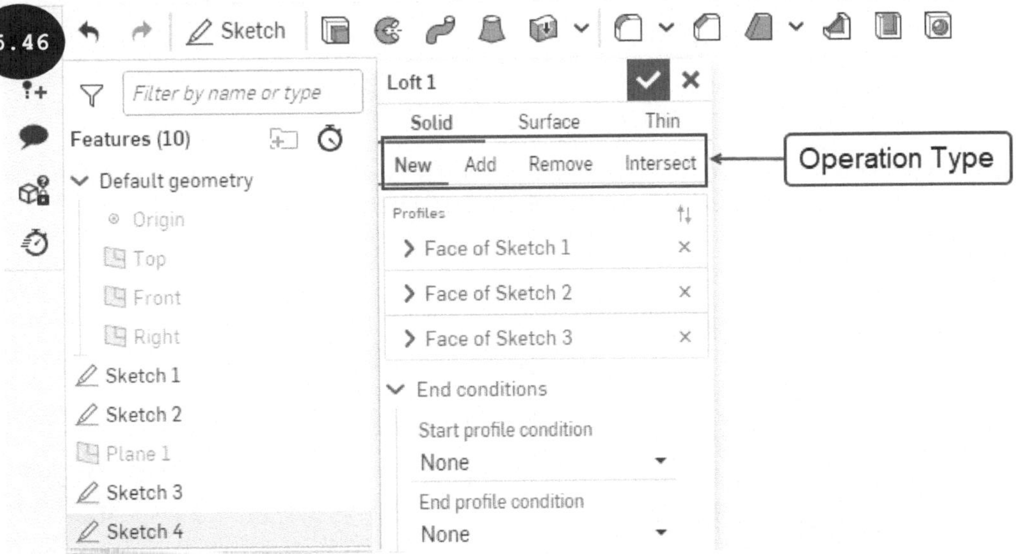

New: The **New** option creates a loft feature by adding material and forming a new part (body). This option is selected automatically, when creating the first or base feature of a model.

Add: The **Add** option creates a loft feature by adding material and merging it with existing features of the model, refer to Figure 5.47.

5.47

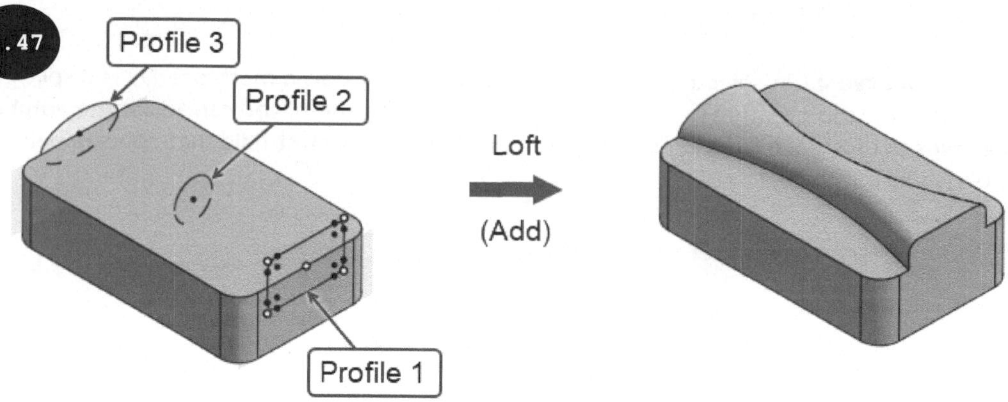

Remove: The **Remove** option creates a loft feature by subtracting or removing material from the model, creating a cut feature, refer to Figure 5.48.

5.48

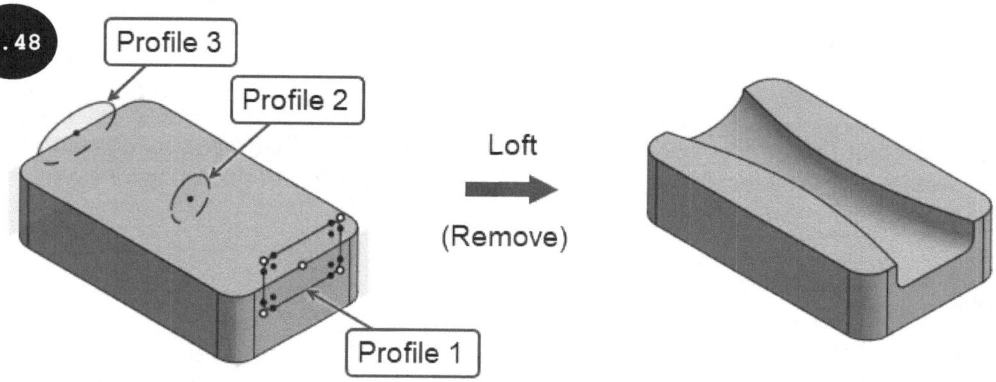

Intersect: The **Intersect** option creates a sweep feature by keeping the intersecting material between the existing feature and the new one, refer to Figure 5.49.

5.49

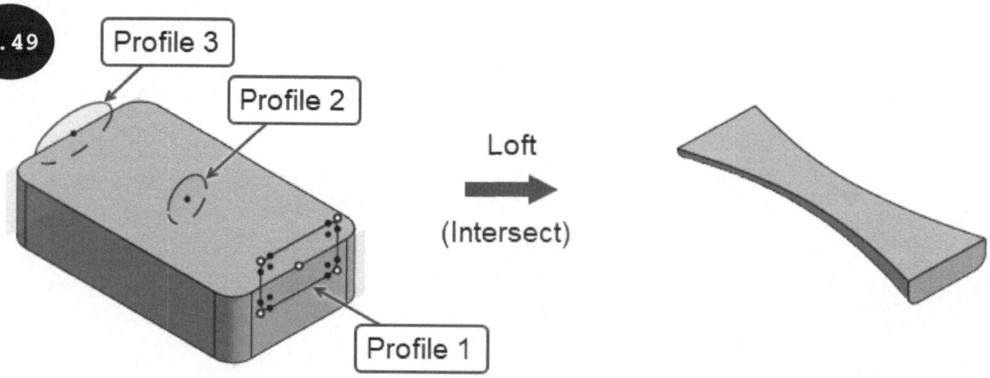

Note: If a sketch contains two or more closed regions that need to be selected as a single profile, it is recommended to select the sketch from the Feature list.

5. After select the profiles and the other parameters, click the green checkmark ✓ to confirm the creation of the loft feature and exit the dialog.

Creating a Thicken feature

A thicken feature modifies a model by either adding or removing material to a specified depth or thickness from an existing face. It can also be created by retaining the material at the intersection of the existing and new features. The method for creating a thicken feature is discussed below:

1. Click on the **Thicken** tool in the **Feature** toolbar, see Figure 5.50. The **Thicken** dialog appears, with the **Faces and surfaces to thicken** field activated, see Figure 5.51.

5.50
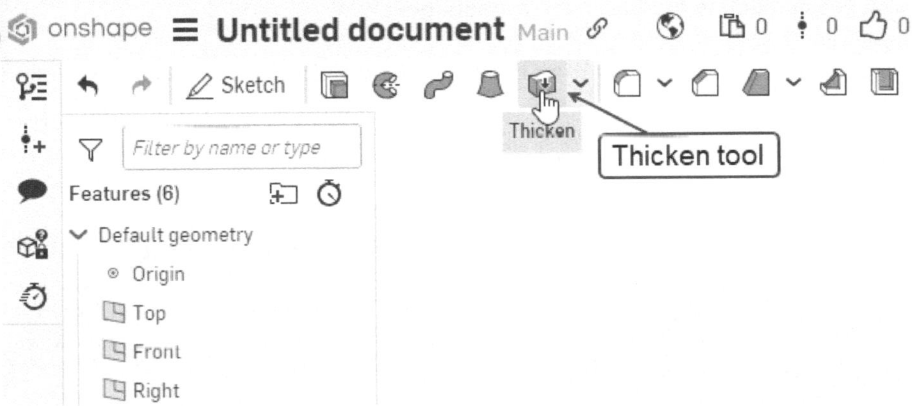

5.51
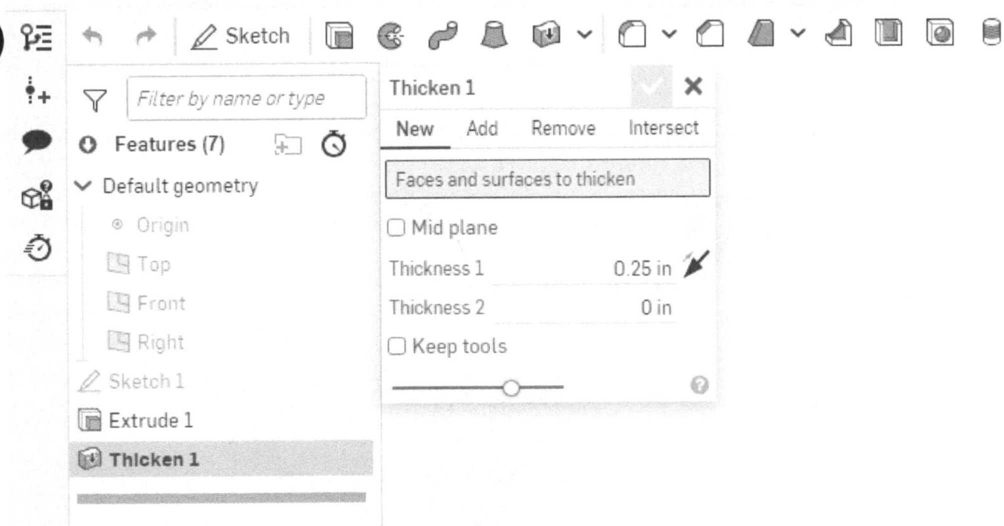

2. Select one or more faces of the model in the graphics area to thicken. A preview appears, showing the specified thickness extending from the selected face(s) of the model, see Figure 5.52.

5.52

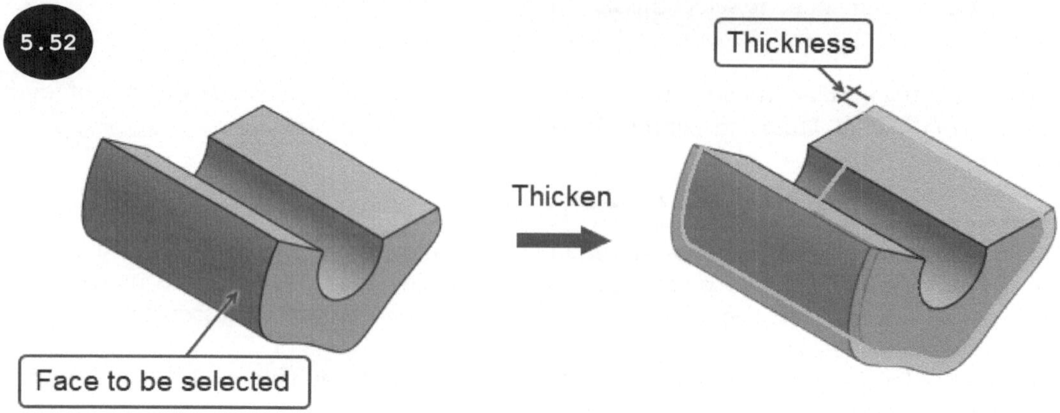

Now, you can define the thickness, as required.

3. Enter the desired thickness in the **Thickness 1** field to add material in one direction (Direction 1) of the selected face, refer to Figure 5.53. In this figure, a thickness is added to a surface in one direction.

5.53

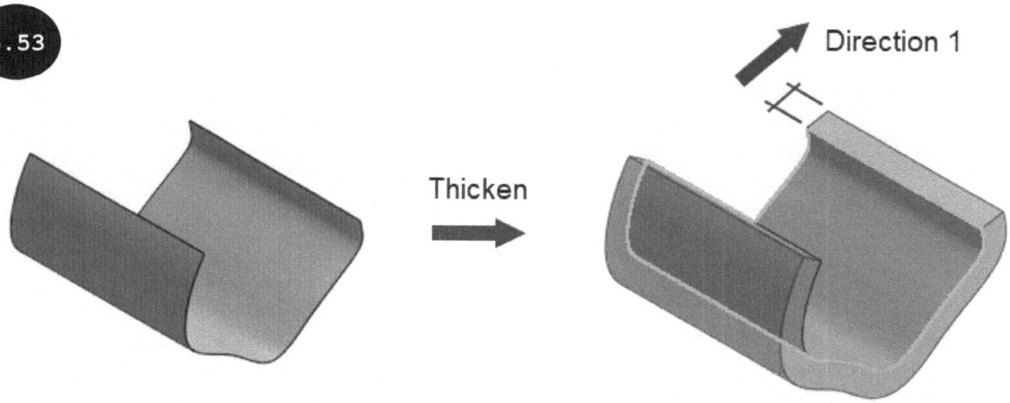

4. If needed, you can also add thickness in the second direction (Direction 2) of the selected face using the **Thickness 2** field, refer to Figure 5.54.

5.54

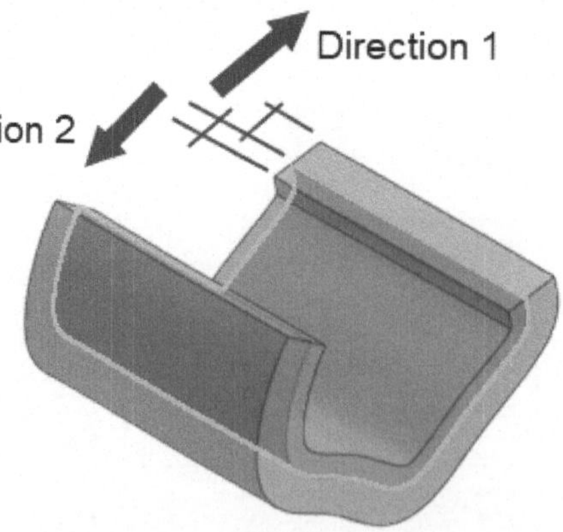

Mid plane: On selecting the **Mid plane** check box, the thickness specified in the **Thickness** field is added symmetrically to both sides of the selected face.

5. Ensure that the required option: **New, Add, Remove,** or **Intersect** is selected in the **Operation Type** area of the dialog for creating a thicken feature, see Figure 5.55. These options function as described earlier. Figure 5.56 shows the preview of a thicken feature when the **Add, Remove,** or **Intersect** option is selected.

5.55

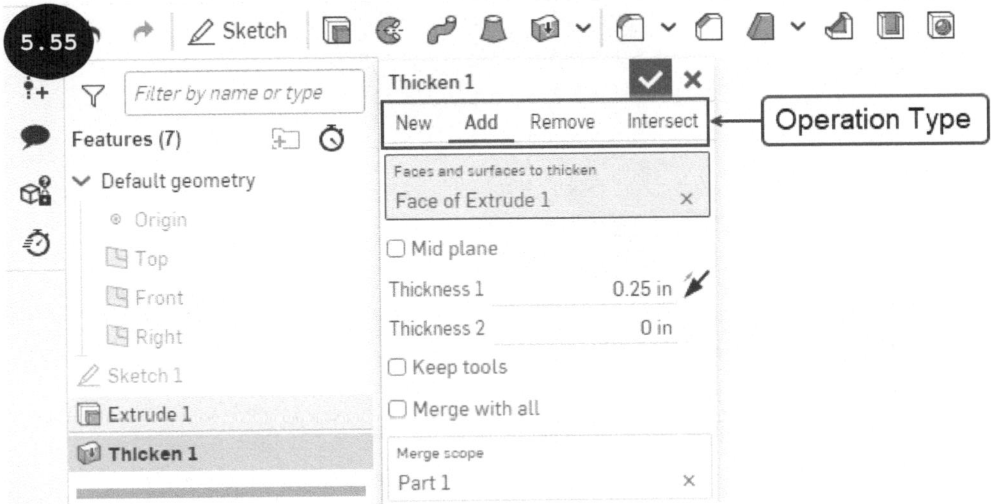

5.56

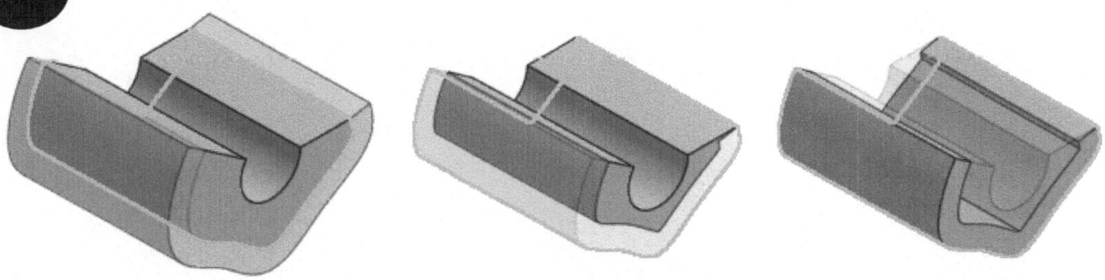

a. Add b. Remove c. Intersect

6. After specifying the desired parameters, click the green checkmark ✓ to confirm the creation of the thicken feature and exit the dialog.

Tutorial 1

Create a model, as shown in Figure 5.57. The different views and dimensions are given in the same figure. All dimensions are in mm.

5.57

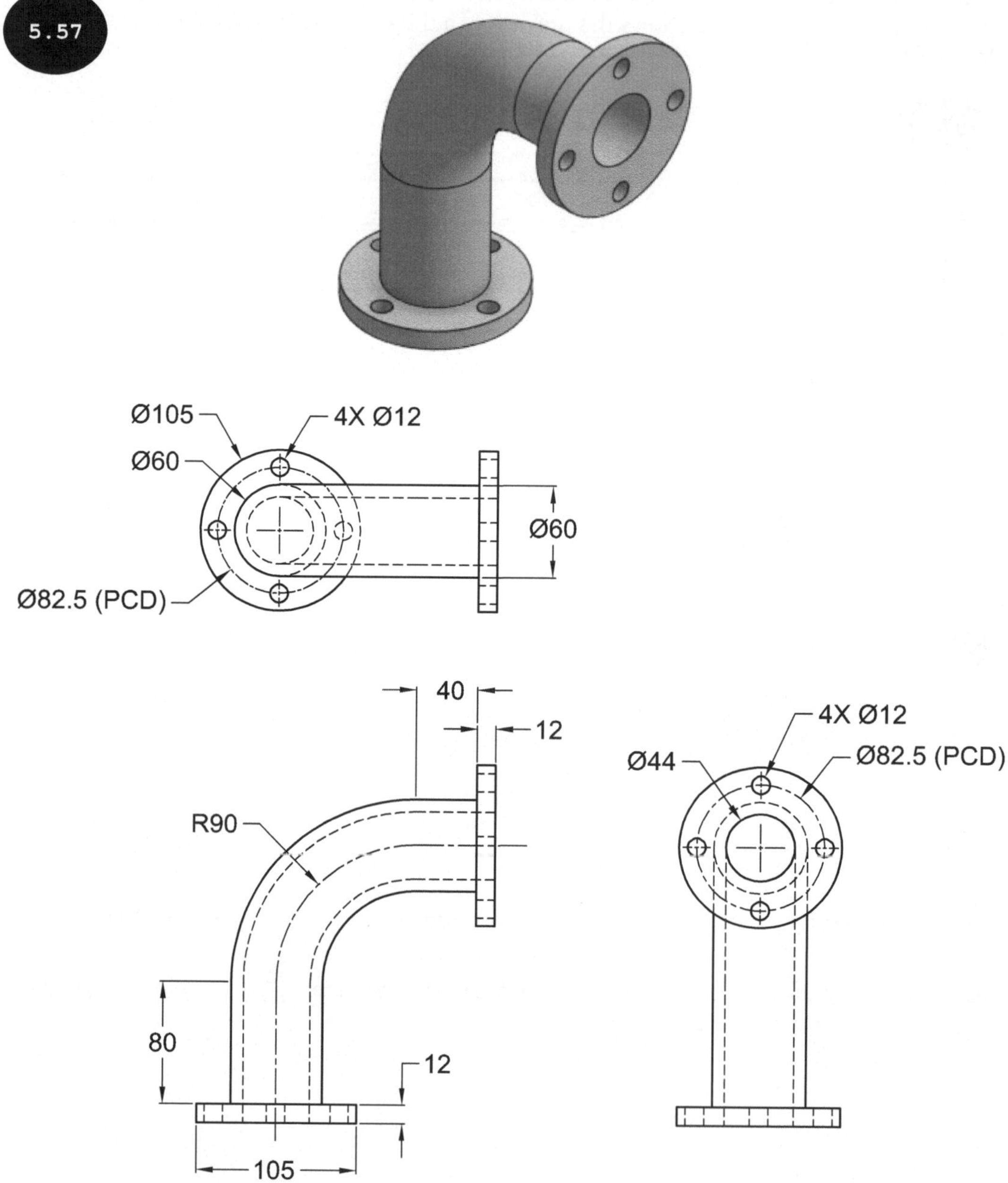

Section 1: Starting a New Design Document

1. Launch Onshape (***onshape.com***) and log in to your account if you're not already logged in.

Note: If you are within a document, click on the **Onshape** logo located in the top left corner of the browser to display the **Documents Page**, see Figure 5.58.

5.58

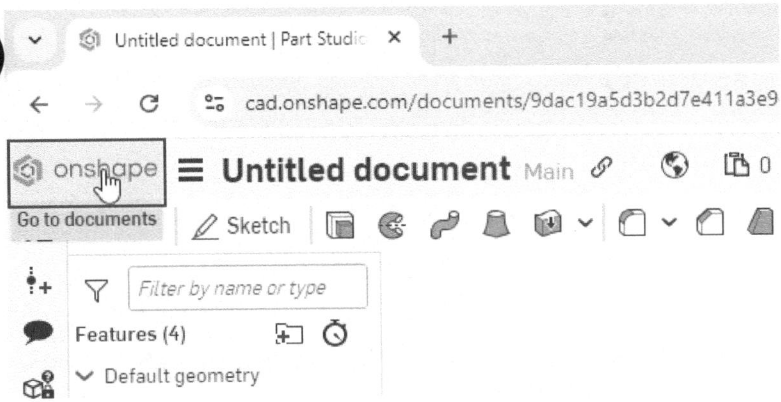

2. Click on the **Create** button at the top left corner of the **Documents Page** and then click on the **Document** option in the menu that appears, see Figure 5.59. The **New document** window appears with the default name of the document as "**Untitled document**".

5.59

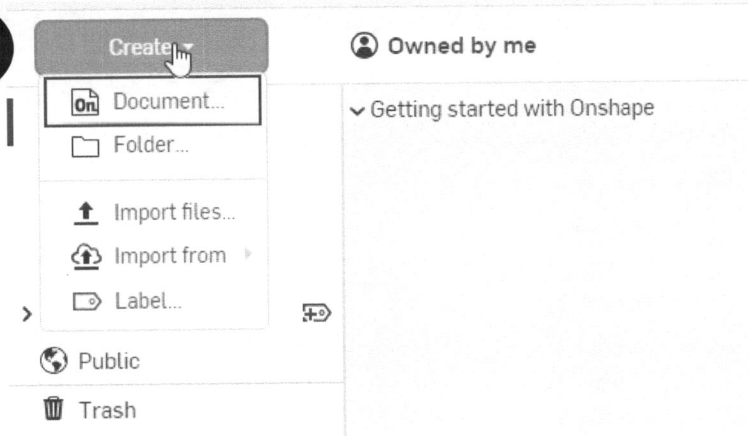

3. Enter **C05 Tutorial 01** as the name of the design document in the **New document** window, and then click on the **Create** button or the **Create Public Document** button, depending on your subscription type. A new document with the specified name is opened.

Section 2: Settings Units

Now, you can set millimeters (mm) as the unit for the length measurement in the current document.

1. Invoke the **Document** menu by clicking on the ≡ icon (three horizontal lines) next to the **Onshape** logo at the top left corner, see Figure 5.60.

5.60

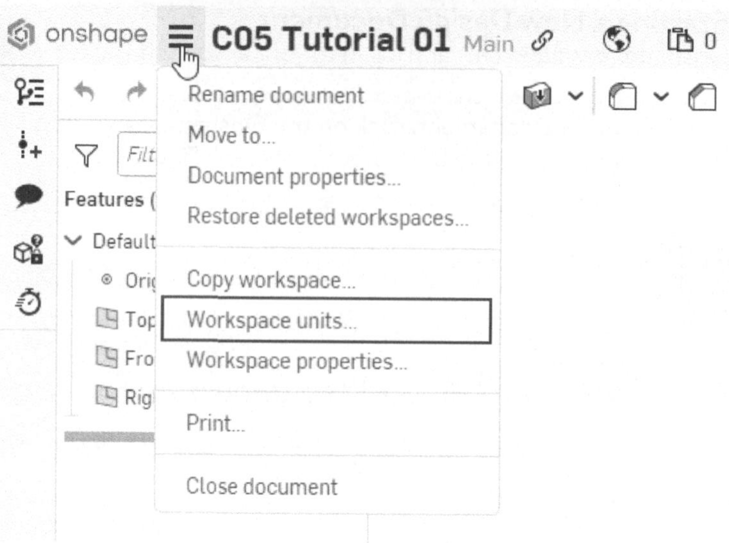

2. Click on the **Workspace units** option in the **Document** menu, refer to Figure 5.60. The **Workspace units** dialog appears, see Figure 5.61.

3. Select the **Millimeter** unit in the **Length default unit** drop-down list and set its precision to **0.1** in the respective **Display decimals** drop-down list of the **Workspace units** dialog, see Figure 5.61.

5.61

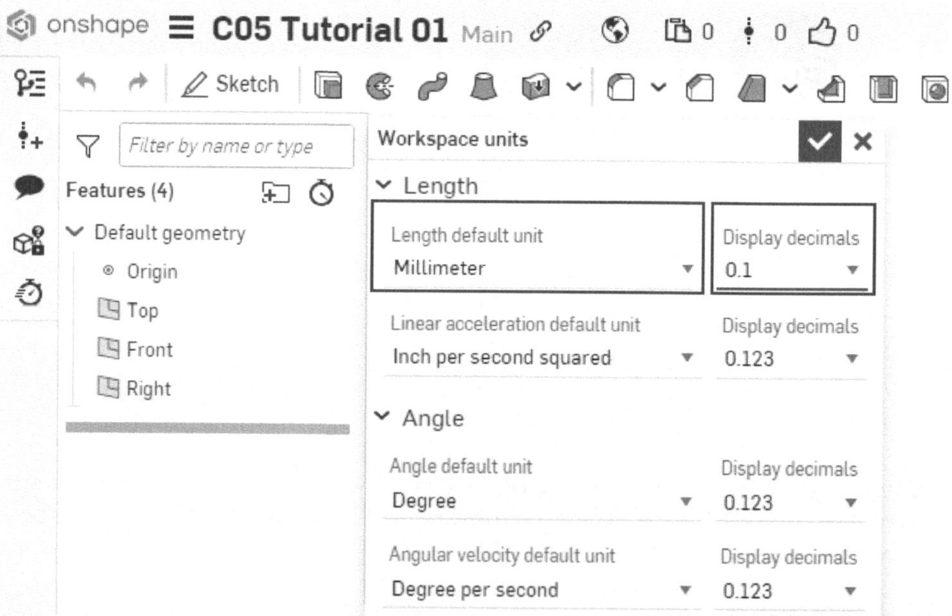

4. After selecting the required unit of length measurement and the decimal precision for the current design document, click on the green checkmark ✓ to confirm the selection and exit the dialog. The millimeter is defined as the unit for the length measurement.

Section 3: Creating the Base Feature - Sweep

To create a sweep feature, you must first create the path and profile as individual sketches.

1. Click on the **Sketch** tool in the **Feature** toolbar, see Figure 5.62. The **Sketch** dialog appears and you are prompted to select a sketching plane.

5.62

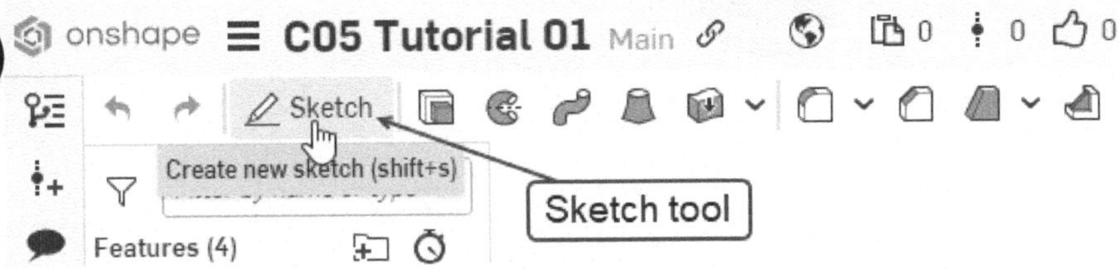

2. Select the Front plane as the sketching plane in the graphics area. The selected plane becomes the sketching plane, and the **Sketch** toolbar appears with the display of various sketching tools.

3. Press the **N** key to make the sketching plane normal to the viewing direction.

   Now, you can create the path of the sweep feature.

4. Create the sketch of the path and apply the required dimensions and constraints, see Figure 5.63.

5.63

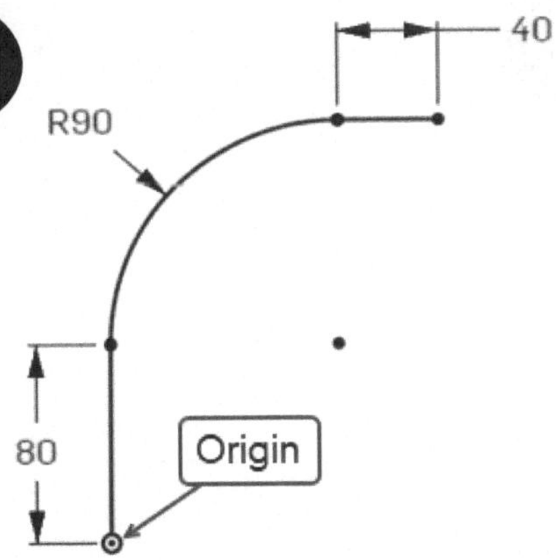

5. Click the green checkmark in the **Sketch** dialog to confirm the creation of the path and exit the dialog. Next, press the SHIFT + 7 keys to change the view orientation to isometric.

   Now, you need to create the profile of the sweep feature.

6. Click on the **Sketch** tool in the **Feature** toolbar (see Figure 5.64) and then select the Top plane as the sketching plane.

5.64

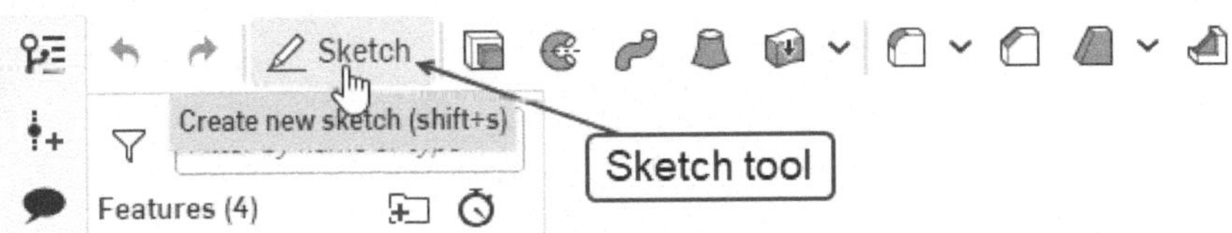

7. Press the **N** key to make the sketching plane normal to the viewing direction.

8. Create a circle of diameter 60 mm as the profile of the sweep feature, see Figure 5.65. The center of the circle is at the origin.

5.65

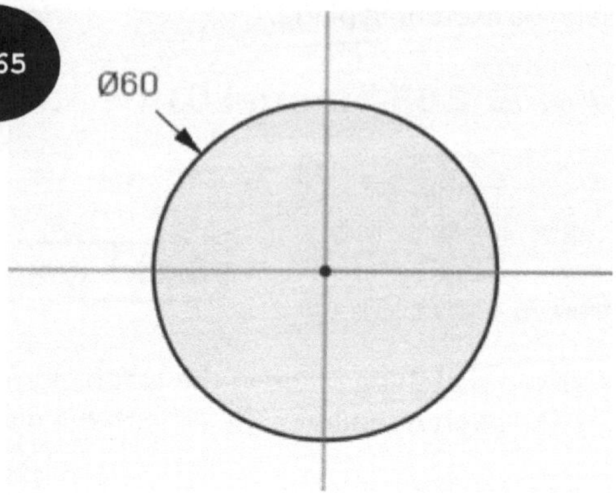

9. Click the green checkmark in the **Sketch** dialog to confirm the creation of the profile and exit the dialog.

10. Press the SHIFT + 7 keys to change the view orientation to isometric, see Figure 5.66.

5.66

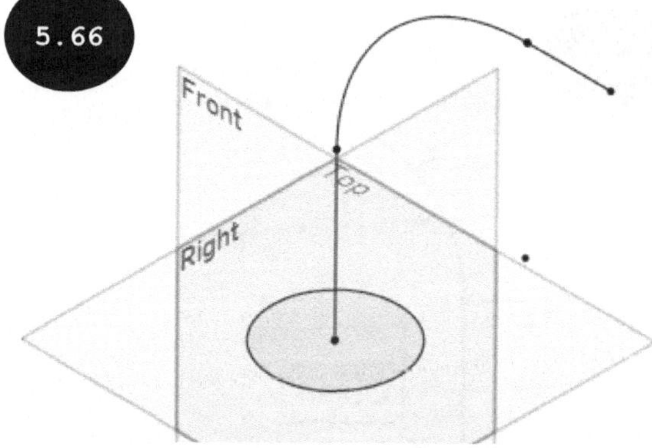

Now, you can create the sweep feature.

11. Click on the **Sweep** tool in the **Feature** toolbar, see Figure 5.67. The **Sweep** dialog appears with the **Solid** option activated automatically to create a solid sweep feature.

5.67

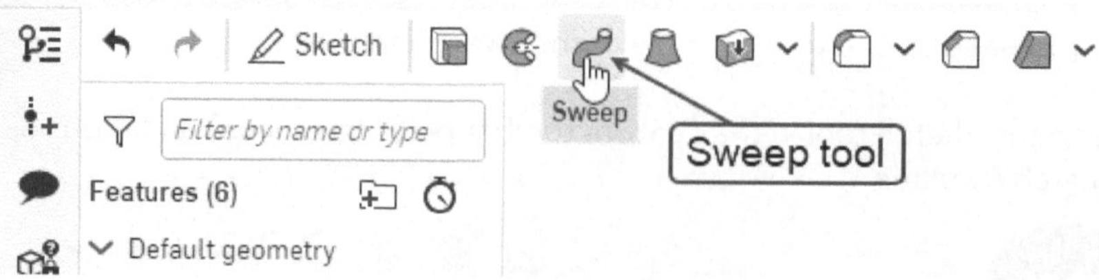

12. Click to activate the **Thin** option in the **Creation Type** area of the **Sweep** dialog to create a thin sweep feature, see Figure 5.68.

5.68

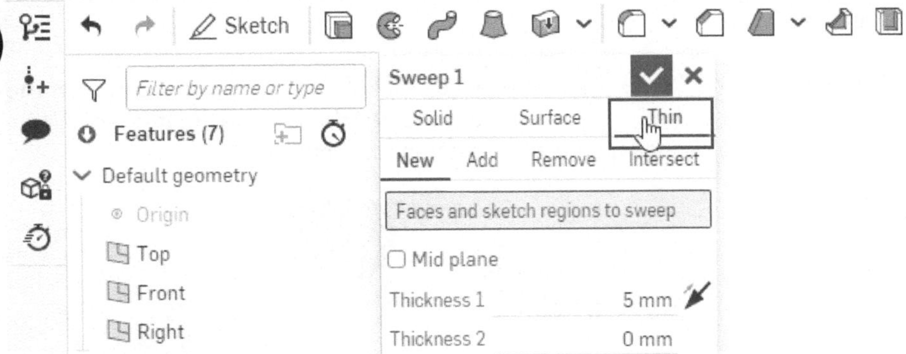

13. Select the profile (circle) of the sweep feature in the graphics area, see Figure 5.69. The profile is selected, and its name appears in the **Faces and sketch regions to sweep** field of the dialog box.

5.69

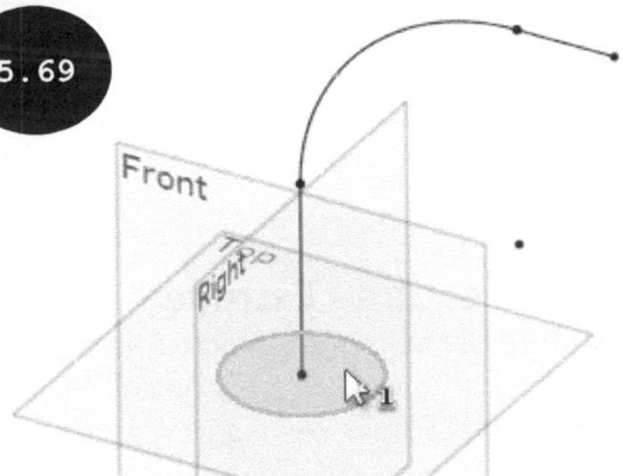

14. Click on the **Sweep path** field in the **Sweep** dialog and then select the path (**Sketch 1**) of the feature in the Feature list, see Figure 5.70. A preview of the thin sweep feature appears with the default specified thickness, showing the profile following the path, see Figure 5.71.

5.70

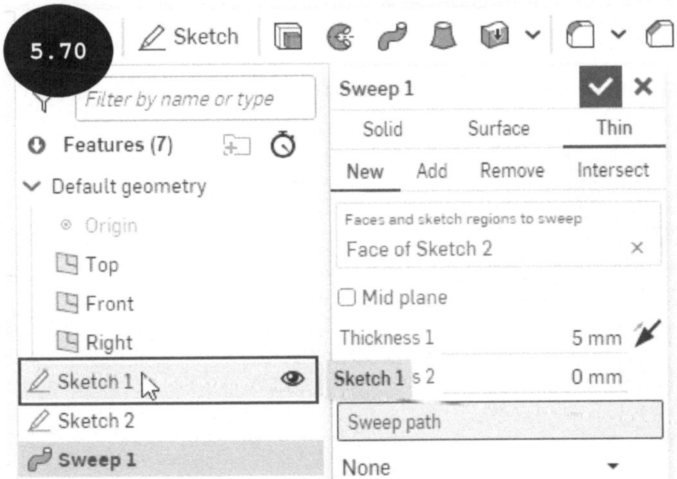

5.71

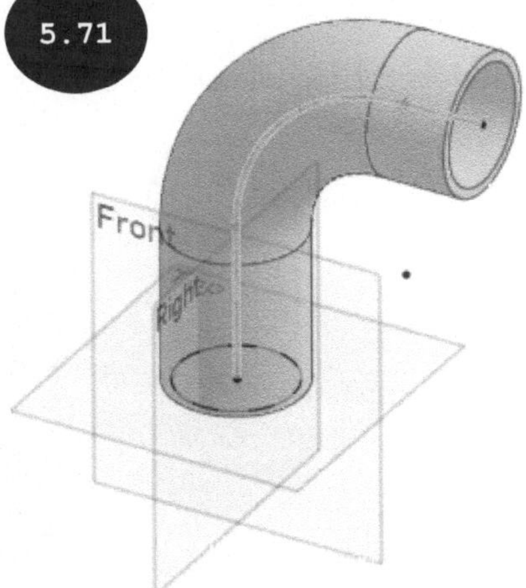

15. Enter **8** mm as the thickness of the sweep feature in the **Thickness 1** field of the **Sweep** dialog.

16. Click on the **Flip wall** button next to the **Thickness 1** field to reverse the thickness direction inward, see Figure 5.72.

17. Click the green checkmark in the **Sweep** dialog to confirm the creation of the sweep feature and exit the dialog. The sweep feature of specified thickness is created, see Figure 5.73. Press the SHIFT + 7 keys to change the view orientation to isometric.

5.72

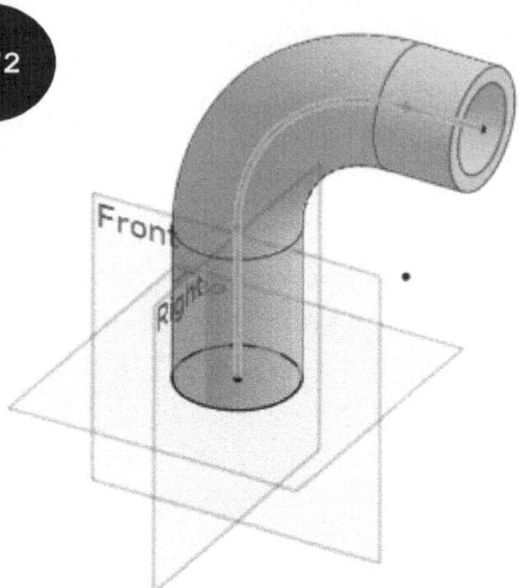

5.73

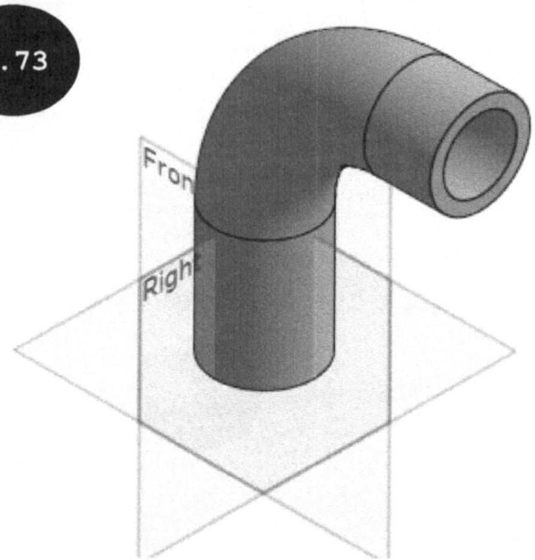

Section 4: Creating the Second Feature - Extrude

Now, you can create the second feature of the model, which is an extruded feature.

1. Click on the **Sketch** tool in the **Feature** toolbar, see Figure 5.74. The **Sketch** dialog appears and you are prompted to select a sketching plane.

5.74

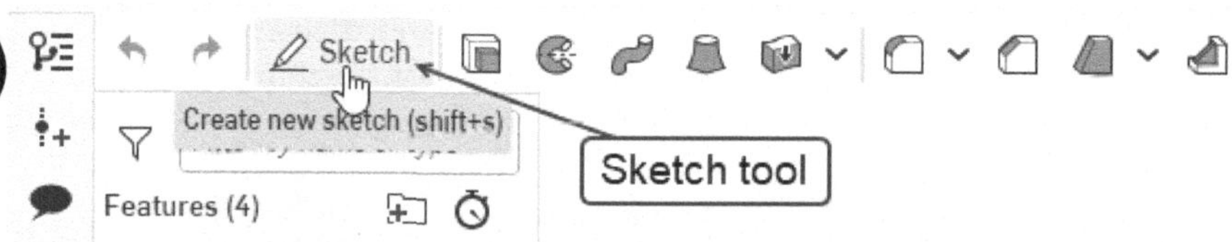

2. Select the top planar face of the sweep feature as the sketching plane, see Figure 5.75.

4.75

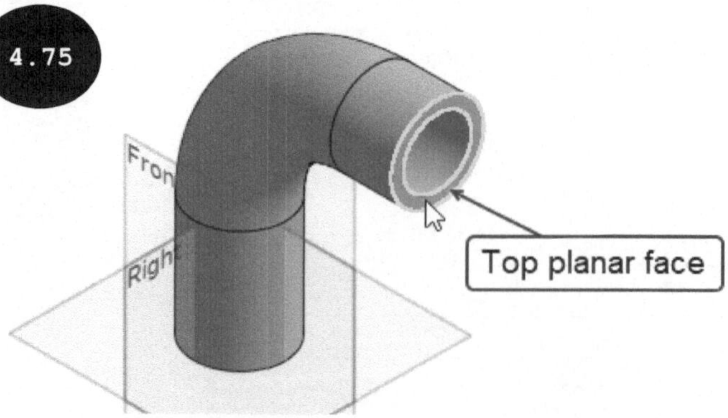

3. Press the **N** key to make the sketching plane (top planar face) normal to the viewing direction.

4. Create two concentric circles as the sketch of the feature using the sketching tools, see Figure 5.76. The center point of the circles is coincident with the center of the model's circular edge.

4.76

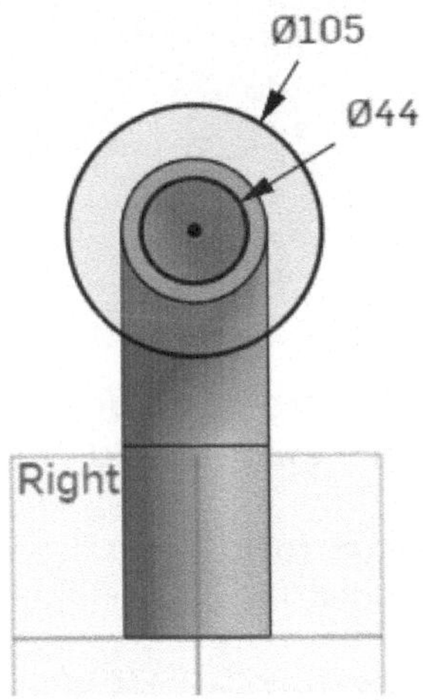

5. Click on the **Extrude** tool in the **Sketch** toolbar, see Figure 5.77. The **Extrude** dialog appears and the sketch profile is automatically selected. Also, the preview of an extrude feature appears in the graphics area.

5.77

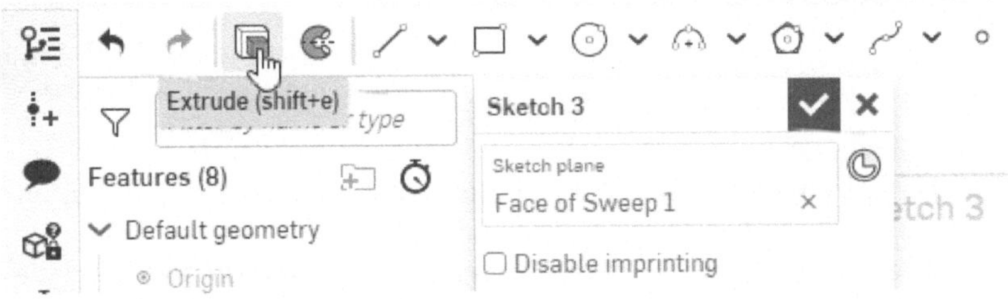

6. Press the SHIFT + 7 keys to change the view orientation to isometric, see Figure 5.78.

5.78

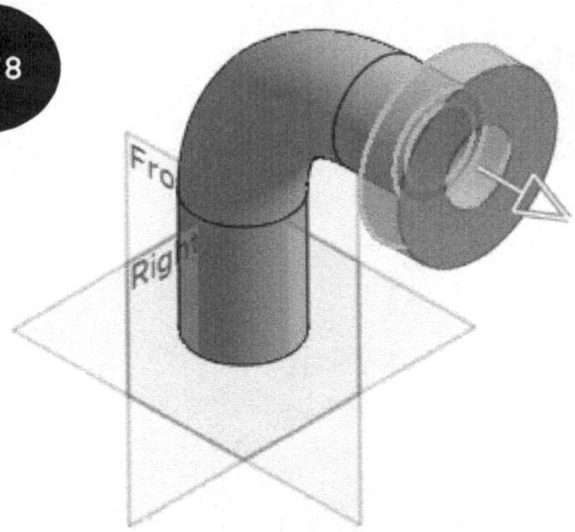

7. Enter **12** mm as the depth of extrusion in the **Depth** field of the **Extrude** dialog.

8. Click the green checkmark ✓ in the **Extrude** dialog to confirm the creation of the extrude feature and exit the dialog. The extrude feature of specified depth is created, see Figure 5.79.

5.79

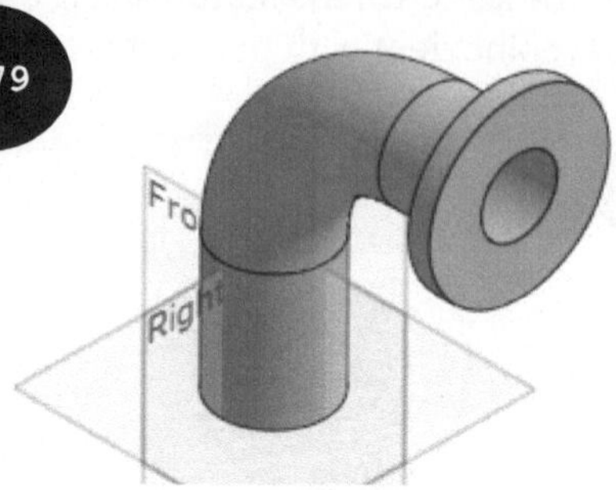

Section 5: Creating the Third Feature - Extrude Cut

Now, you can create the third feature of the model, which is an extruded cut feature.

1. Click on the **Sketch** tool in the **Feature** toolbar (see Figure 5.80) and then select the front planar face of the previously created extruded feature, see Figure 5.81.

5.80

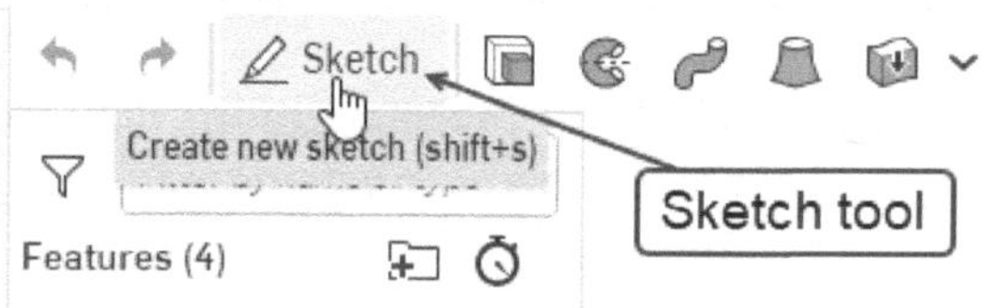

5.81

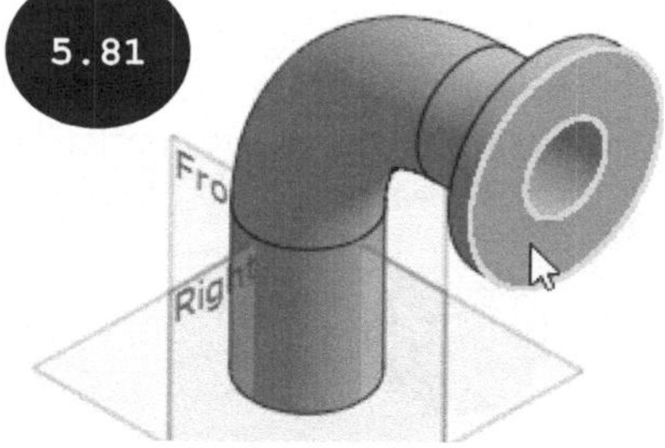

2. Press the **N** key to make the sketching plane normal to the viewing direction.

3. Create four circles of equal diameter (10 mm), positioned on a pitch circle diameter (PCD) of 82.5 mm as the sketch of the feature, see Figure 5.82. In this figure, the equal constraint is applied among all the circles of equal diameter. Ensure that the center point of the construction circle representing the PCD coincides with the center of the model's circular edge.

5.82

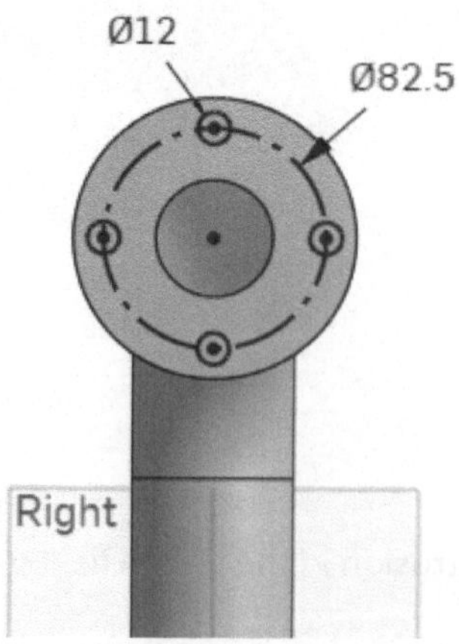

4. Click on the **Extrude** tool in the **Sketch** toolbar, see Figure 5.83. The **Extrude** dialog appears, all closed profiles of the sketch are automatically selected, and a preview of the extruded feature is displayed in the graphics area, see Figure 5.84.

5.83

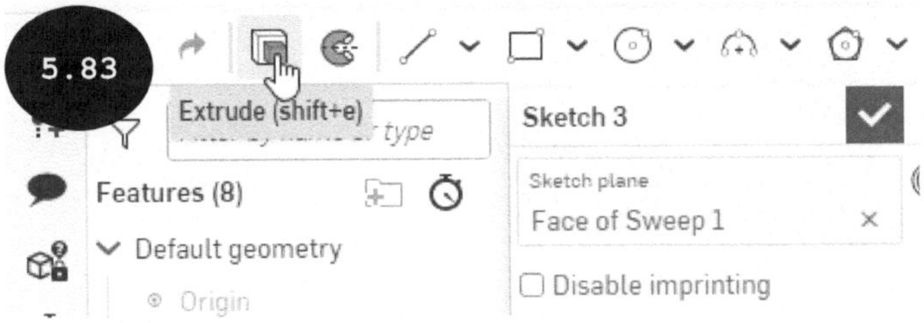

5.84

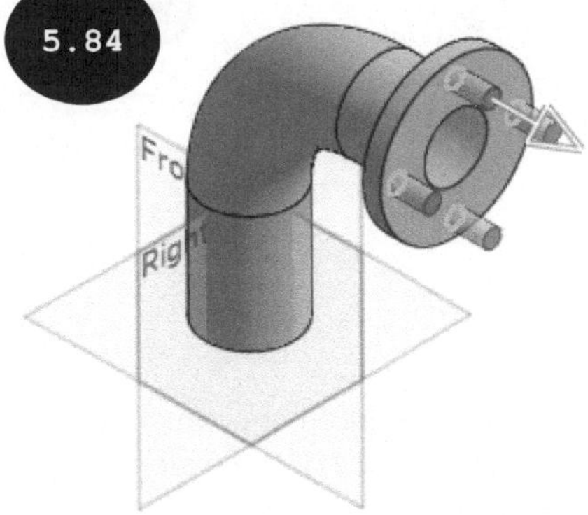

5. Click to activate the **Remove** option in the **Operation Type** area of the dialog (refer to Figure 5.85) to create the cut feature by removing the material.

6. Select the **Up to next** option in the **End type** drop-down list of the **Extrude** dialog to extrude the sketch up to its next intersection, see Figure 5.85.

5.85

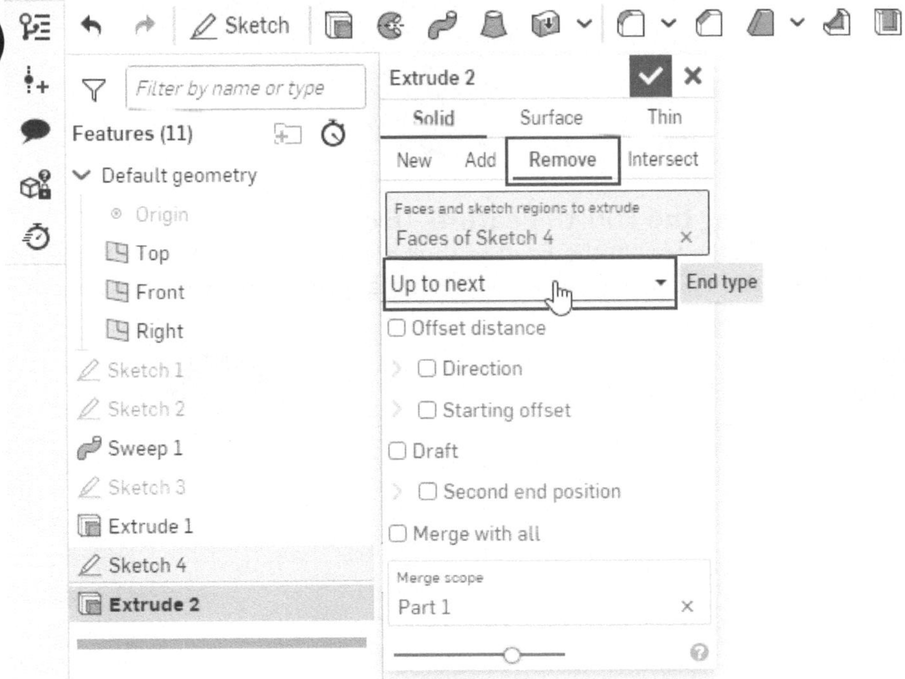

7. Ensure that the direction of extrusion is reversed toward the rear side of the model, refer to Figure 5.86.

5.86

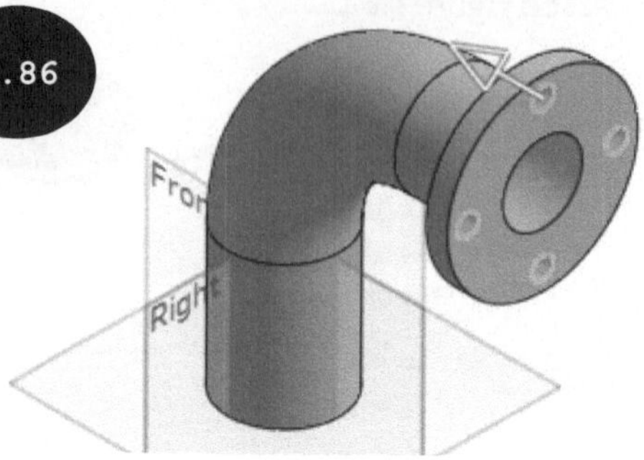

8. Click the green checkmark ✅ in the **Extrude** dialog to confirm the creation of the extrude cut feature and exit the dialog. The extrude cut feature is created by removing the material from the model, see Figure 5.87.

5.87

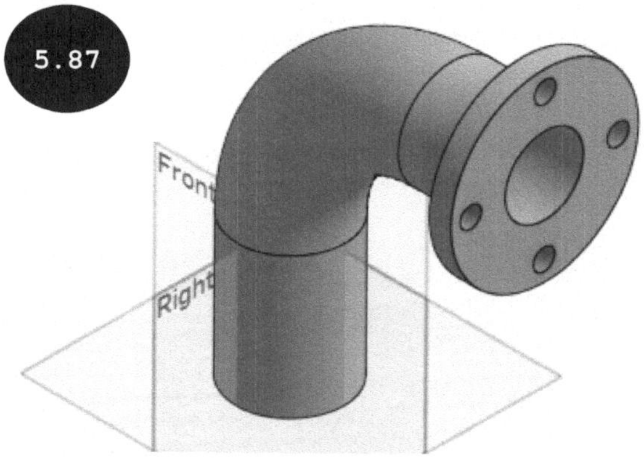

Section 6: Creating the Fourth Feature - Extrude

1. Click on the **Sketch** tool in the **Feature** toolbar (see Figure 5.88) and then select the bottom planar face of the model, see Figure 5.89. Note that you may need to rotate the model to select its bottom planar face.

5.88

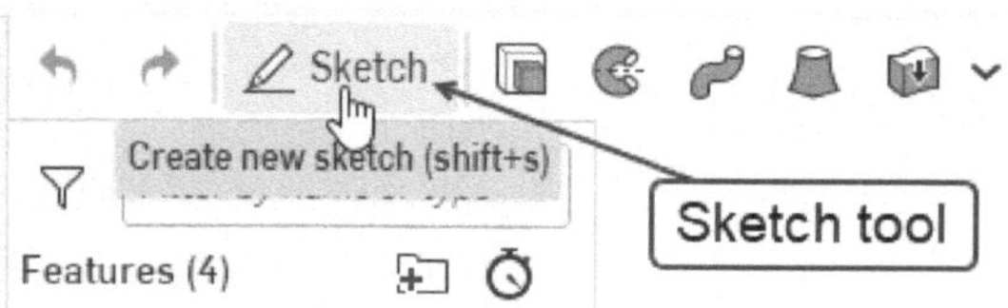

5.89

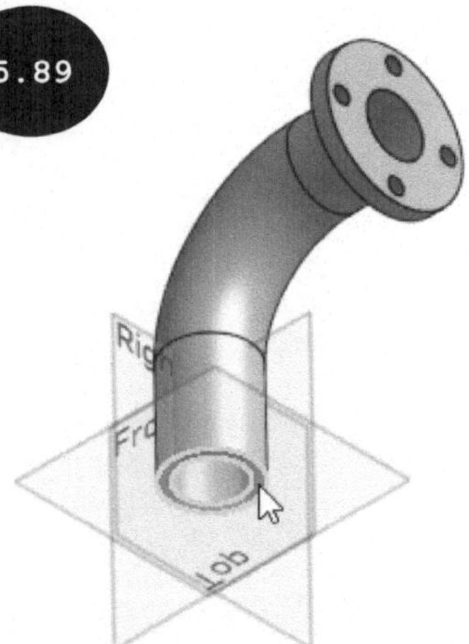

2. Press the **N** key to make the sketching plane (bottom planar face) normal to the viewing direction.

3. Create the sketch of the feature using the sketching tools, as shown in Figure 5.90. This figure consists of two concentric circles sharing a center point at the origin, along with four smaller circles of 12 mm diameter, positioned on a pitch circle diameter (PCD) of 82.5 mm.

5.90

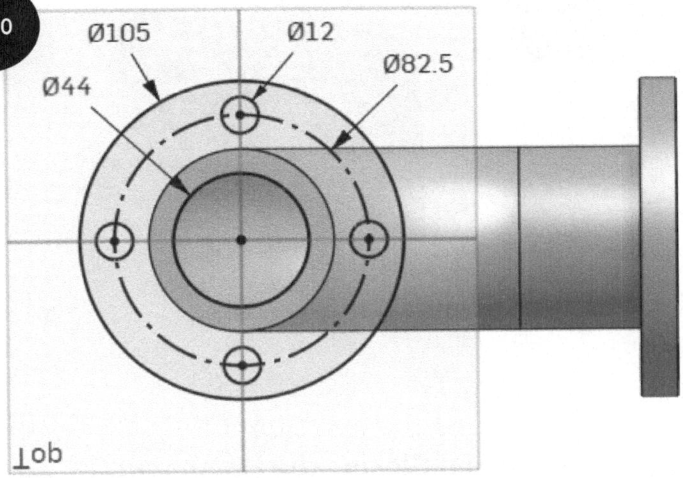

4. After creating the sketch, click on the **Extrude** tool in the **Sketch** toolbar, see Figure 5.91. The **Extrude** dialog appears and the sketch profile is automatically selected. Also, the preview of an extruded feature appears in the graphics area.

5.91

5. Press the SHIFT + 7 keys to change the view orientation to isometric, see Figure 5.92. Ensure that the direction of extrusion is downwards.

5.92

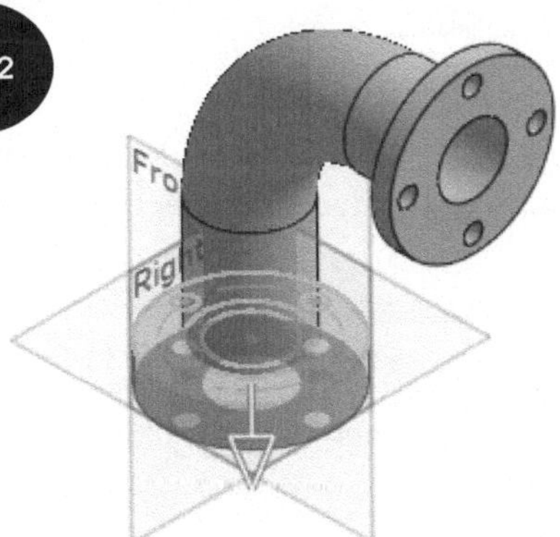

6. Enter **12** mm as the depth of extrusion in the **Depth** field of the **Extrude** dialog.

7. Click the green checkmark ✅ in the **Extrude** dialog to confirm the creation of the extrude feature and exit the dialog. The extrude feature of specified depth is created. Figure 5.93 shows the final model after creating all its features.

5.93

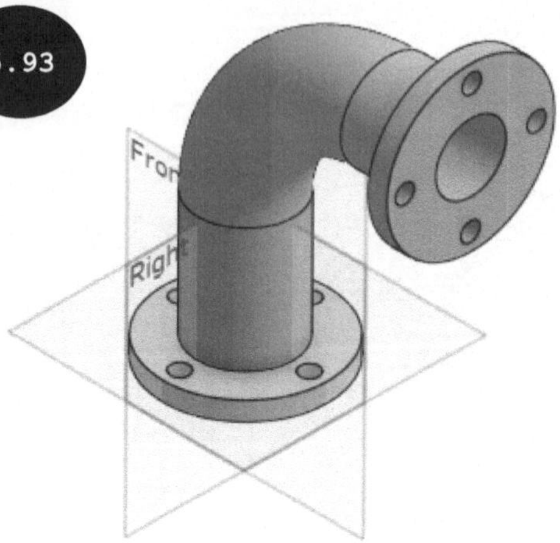

Section 7: Creating a Version and Closing the Document

Now, you can create a version in the document to capture the current state of the design, and then close the document.

1. Click on the **Create version** tool in the **Document panel**, which is aligned vertically with the Onshape logo, see Figure 5.94. The **Create version from Main** window appears with default version name **V1** in its **Name** field.

5.94

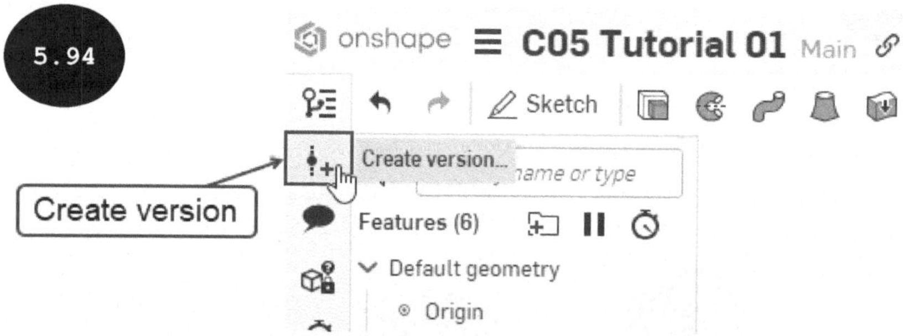

2. Accept the default specified name "V1" and click the **Create** button. A new version, "V1," is created in the document, capturing the model's current state.

   Now, you can close the document.

3. Invoke the **Document** menu by clicking on the ≡ icon next to the Onshape logo and click on the **Close document** option. The current document gets closed.

Tutorial 2

Create a model, as shown in Figure 5.95. The different views and dimensions are given in the same figure. All dimensions are in inches.

5.95

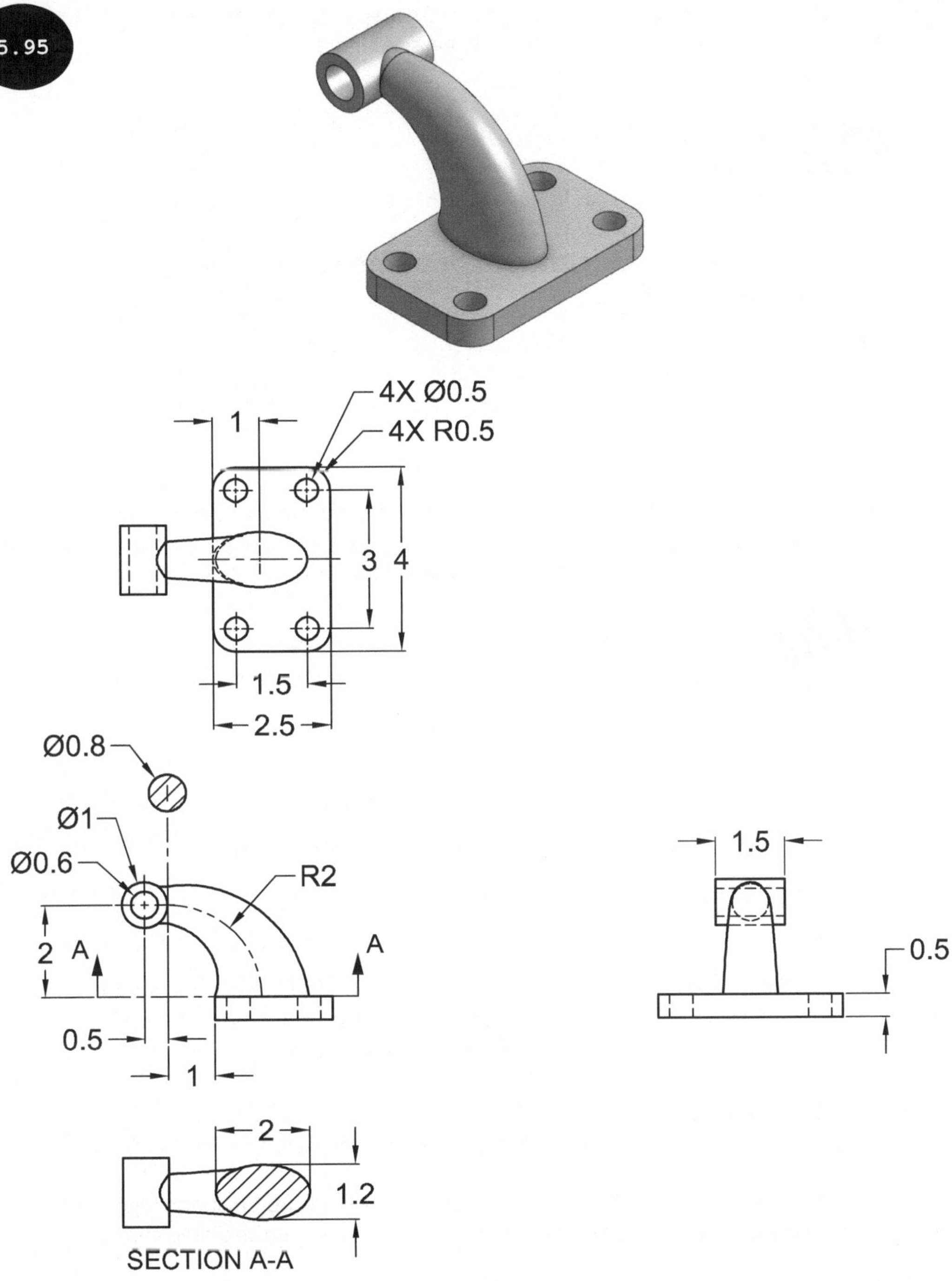

Section 1: Starting a New Design Document

1. Launch Onshape (*onshape.com*) and log in to your account if you're not already logged in. The **Documents Page** appears.

Note: If you are within a document, click on the **Onshape** logo located in the top left corner of the browser to display the **Documents Page**, see Figure 5.96.

5.96

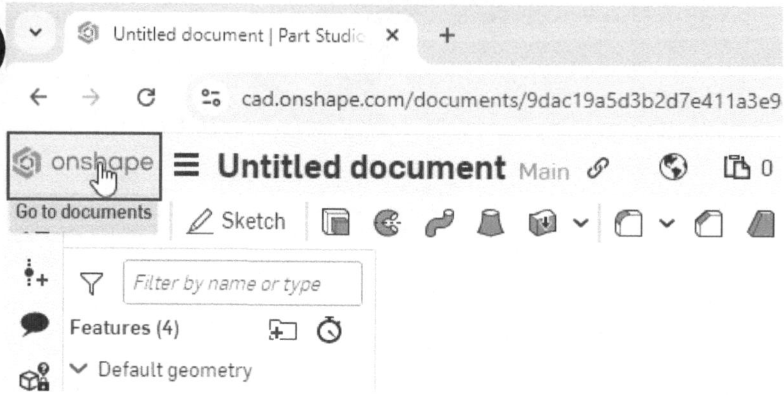

2. Click on the **Create** button at the top left corner of the **Documents Page** and then click on the **Document** option in the menu that appears, see Figure 5.97. The **New document** window appears with the default name of the document as "**Untitled document**".

5.97

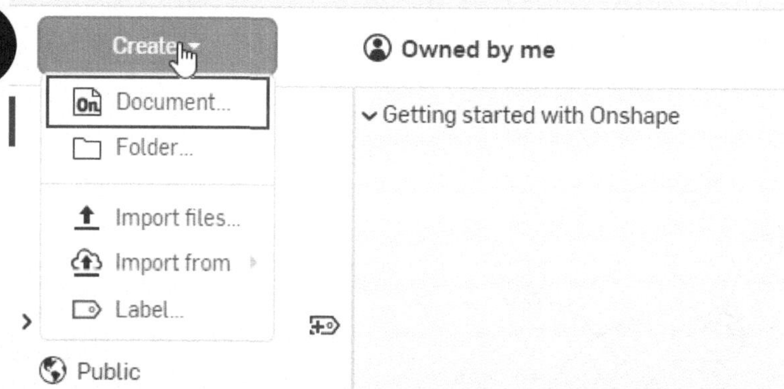

3. Enter **C05 Tutorial 02** as the name of the design document in the **New document** window, and then click on the **Create** button or the **Create Public Document** button, depending on your subscription type. A new document with the specified name is opened.

Section 2: Settings Units

Now, you can set inches (in) as the unit for the length measurement in the current document.

1. Invoke the **Document** menu by clicking on the ☰ icon next to the **Onshape** logo and then click on the **Workspace units** option, see Figure 5.98. The **Workspace units** dialog appears.

5.98

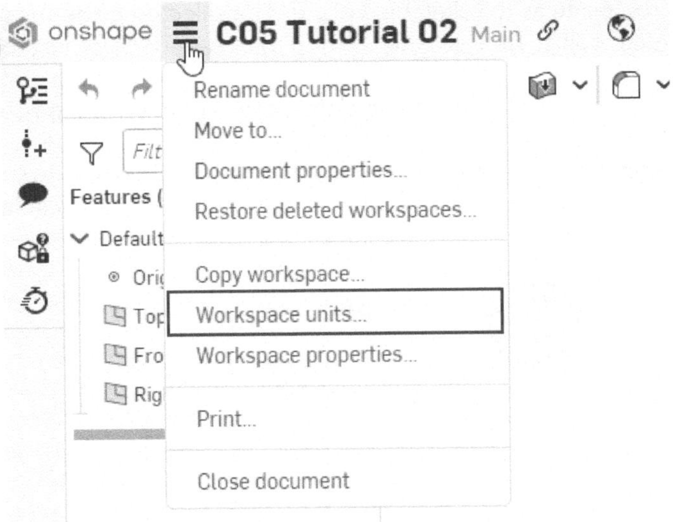

2. Ensure that the **Inch** unit is selected in the **Length default unit** drop-down list of the **Workspace units** dialog, see Figure 5.99.

5.99

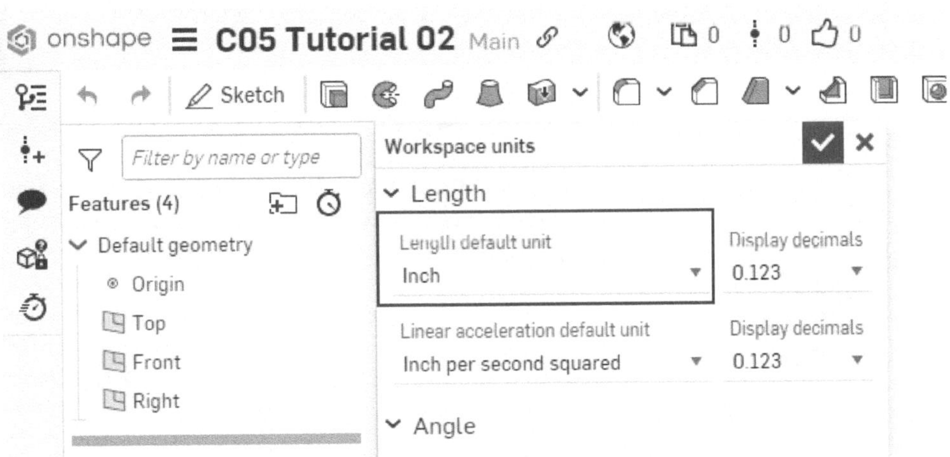

3. Click on the green checkmark to confirm the selection and exit the dialog.

Section 3: Creating the Base Feature - Extrude

Now, you can create the base feature of the model, which is an extruded feature.

1. Click on the **Sketch** tool in the **Feature** toolbar, see Figure 5.100. The **Sketch** dialog appears and you are prompted to select a sketching plane.

5.100

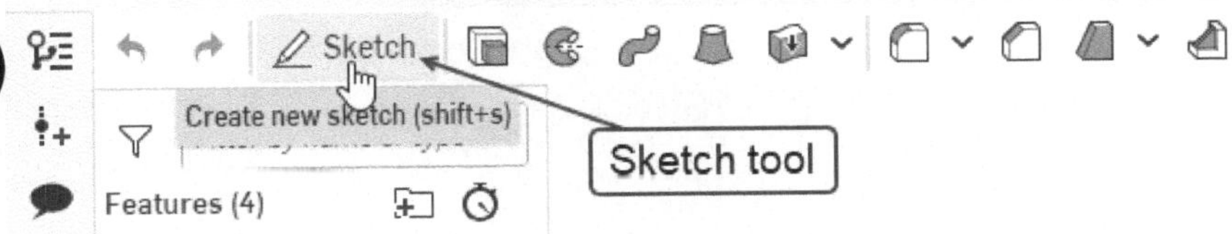

2. Select the Top plane as the sketching plane. The selected plane becomes the sketching plane, and the **Sketch** toolbar appears with the display of various sketching tools.

3. Press the **N** key to make the sketching plane normal to the viewing direction.

4. Create the sketch of the feature using the sketching tools, see Figure 5.101. The sketch consists of a rectangle with fillets of 0.5 inches radius at each corner and four circles, each with a diameter of 12 inches. Ensure the center of the rectangle is at the origin.

5.101

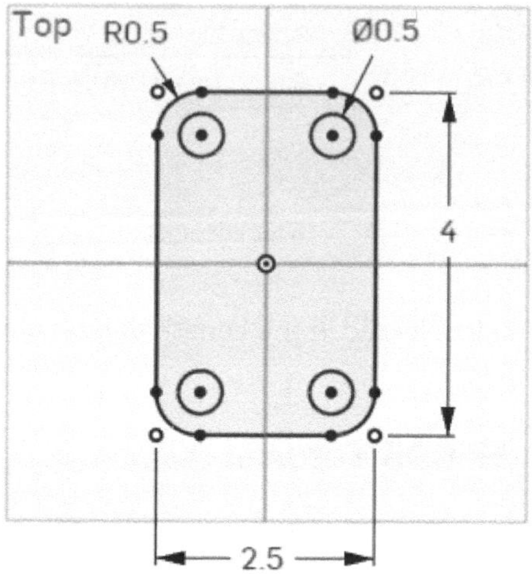

5. After creating the sketch, click on the **Extrude** tool in the **Sketch** toolbar, see Figure 5.102. The **Extrude** dialog appears and the sketch profile is automatically selected. Also, the preview of an extruded feature appears in the graphics area.

5.102

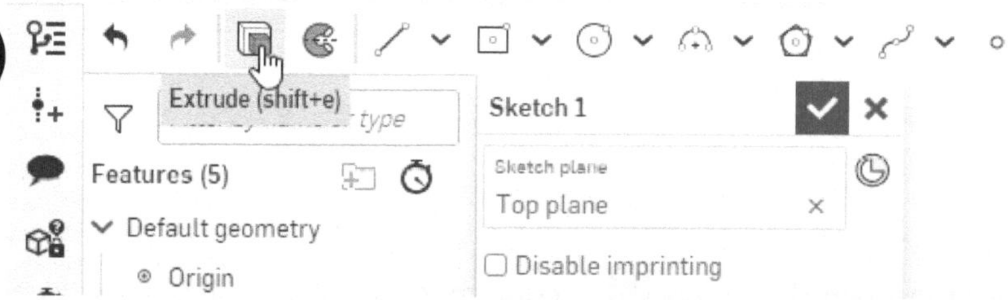

6. Press the SHIFT + 7 keys to change the view orientation to isometric, see Figure 5.103. Ensure that the extrusion is directed upwards.

5.103

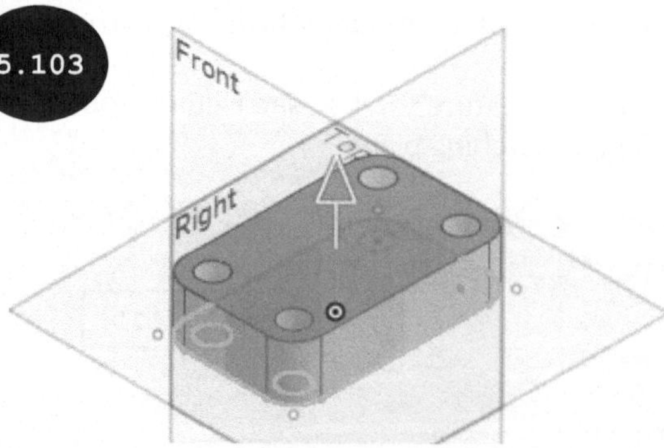

7. Enter **0.5** inches as the depth of extrusion in the **Depth** field of the **Extrude** dialog and then press ENTER.

8. Click the green checkmark ✓ in the **Extrude** dialog to confirm the creation of the extrude feature and exit the dialog. The extrude feature of specified depth is created, see Figure 5.104.

5.104

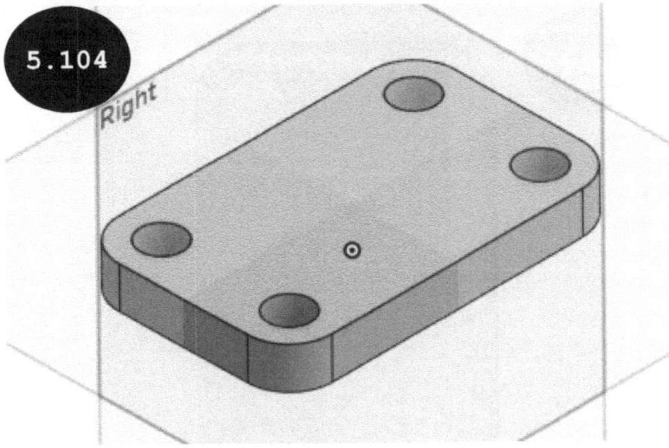

Section 4: Creating the Second Feature - Loft

To create a Loft feature, you must first create the necessary profiles as individual sketches.

1. Click on the **Sketch** tool in the **Feature** toolbar, see Figure 5.105. The **Sketch** dialog appears and you are prompted to select a sketching plane.

5.105

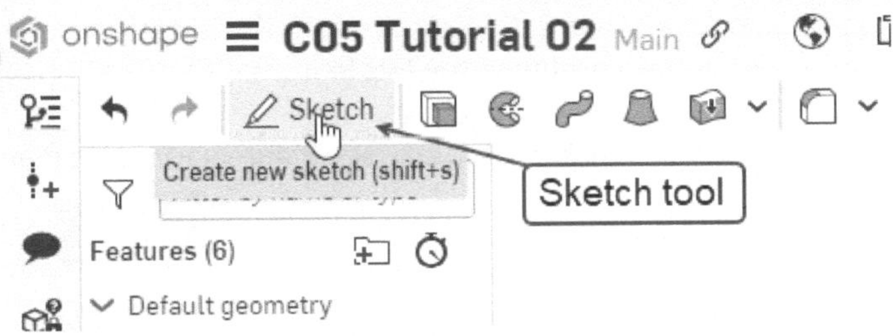

2. Select the top planar face of the base feature as the sketching plane in the graphics area, see Figure 5.106. The **Sketch** toolbar appears.

5.106

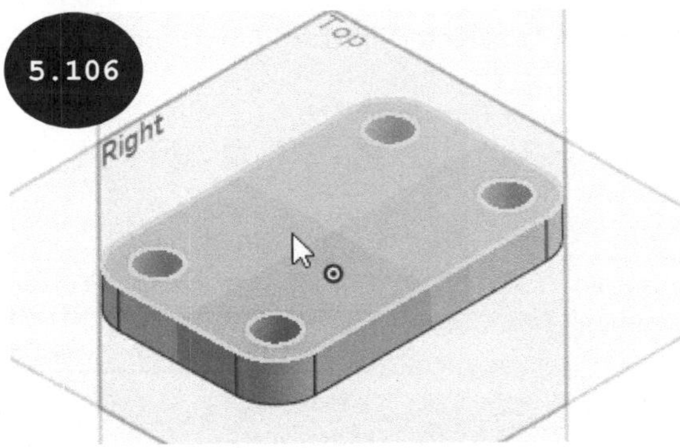

3. Press the **N** key to make the sketching plane normal to the viewing direction.

Now, you can create the first profile of the loft feature.

4. Create an ellipse as the first profile and apply the required dimensions, see Figure 5.107. Ensure that the center of the ellipse is horizontally aligned with the origin by applying a horizontal constraint.

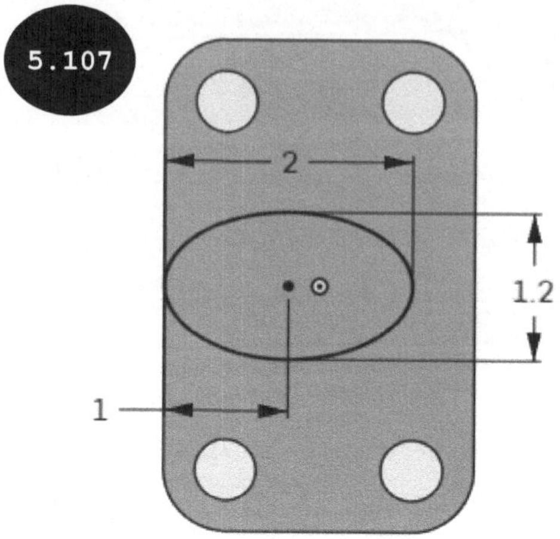

5. Click the green checkmark in the **Sketch** dialog to confirm the creation of the profile and exit the dialog. Next, press the SHIFT + 7 keys to change the view orientation to isometric.

   Now, you need to create a construction plane at an offset distance of 2.25 inches from the Right plane for creating the second profile of the loft feature.

6. Click on the **Plane** tool in the **Feature** toolbar, see Figure 5.108. The **Plane** dialog appears.

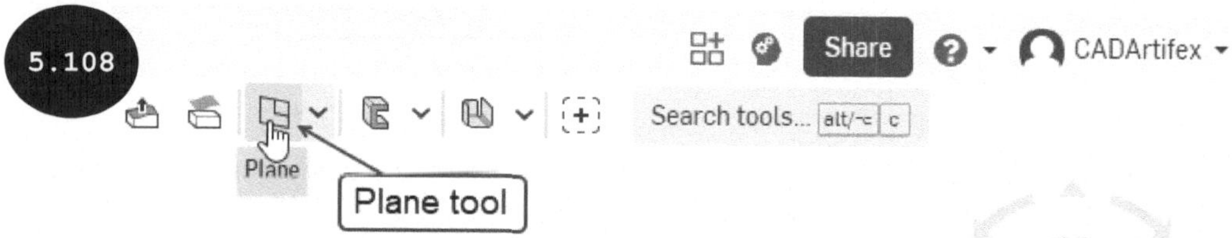

7. Ensure that the **Offset** option is selected in the **Plane type** drop-down list of the dialog, see Figure 5.109.

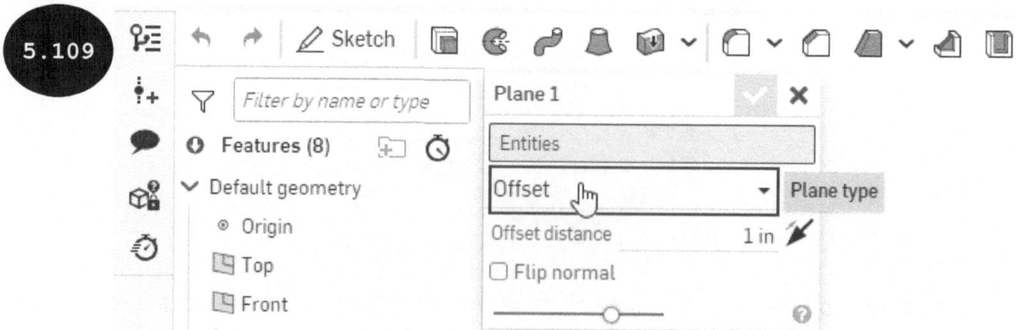

8. Select the Right plane as the reference entity in the graphics area. A preview of the construction plane appears at a default offset distance.

9. Enter **2.25** inches as the offset distance in the **Offset distance** field and press ENTER.

10. Click on the **Opposite direction** button located next to the **Offset distance** field to reverse the creation of the construction plane towards the rear side of the Right plane, see Figure 5.110.

5.110

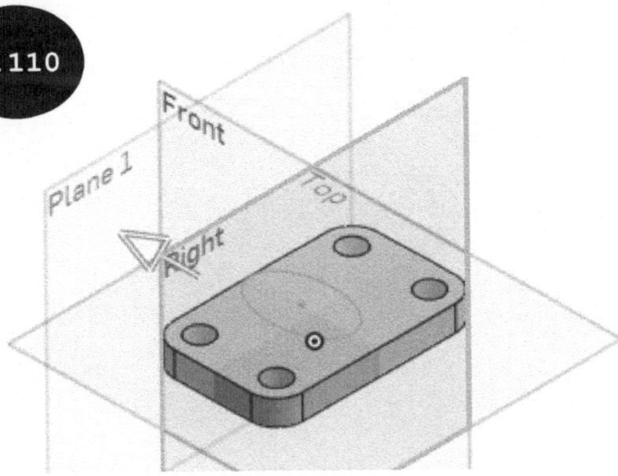

11. Click the green checkmark in the **Plane** dialog to confirm the creation of the construction plane and exit the dialog.

    Now, you can create the second profile of the loft feature.

12. Click on the **Sketch** tool in the **Feature** toolbar (see Figure 5.111) and then select the newly created construction plane (**Plane 1**) as the sketching plane.

5.111

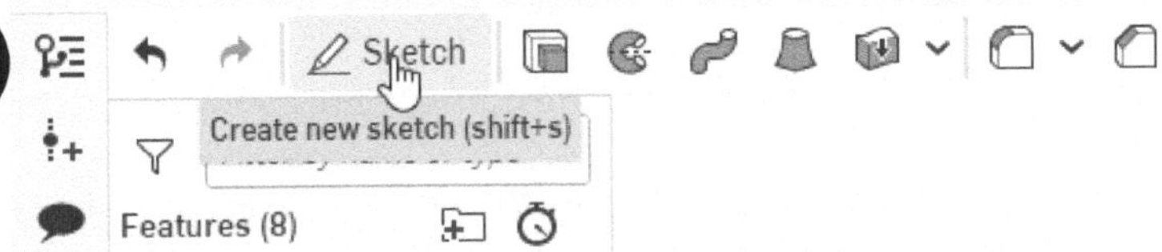

13. Press the **N** key to make the sketching plane normal to the viewing direction.

14. Select a circle of diameter 0.8 inches as the profile of the loft feature, see Figure 5.112.

5.112

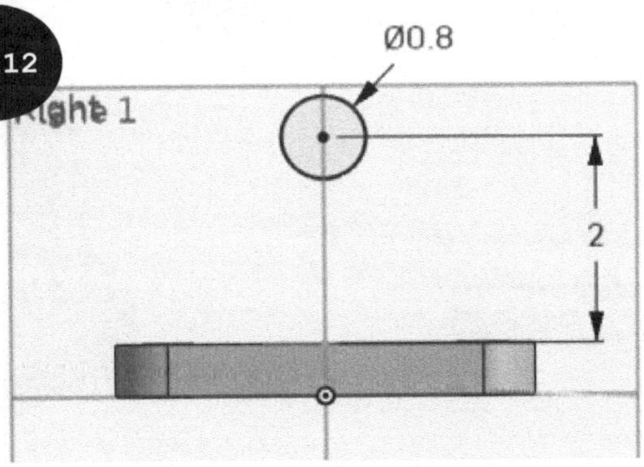

15. Click the green checkmark ✅ in the **Sketch** dialog to confirm the creation of the profile and exit the dialog. Next, press the SHIFT + 7 keys to change the view orientation to isometric, see Figure 5.113.

5.113

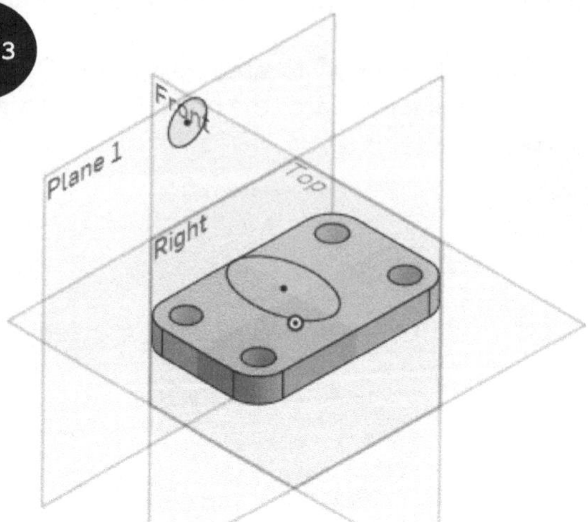

Now, you need to create a centerline guide (path) to maintain the neutral axis of the loft feature.

16. Click on the **Sketch** tool in the **Feature** toolbar (see Figure 5.114) and then select the Front plane as the sketching plane in the graphics area.

5.114

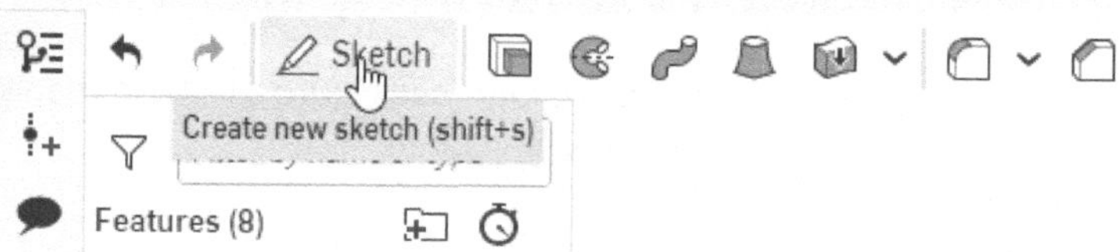

17. Press the **N** key to make the sketching plane normal to the viewing direction.

18. Create an arc with a radius of 2 inches in the graphics area, see Figure 5.115. Note that both endpoints of the arc are coincident with the center points of the respective profiles, refer to Figure 5.116.

5.115

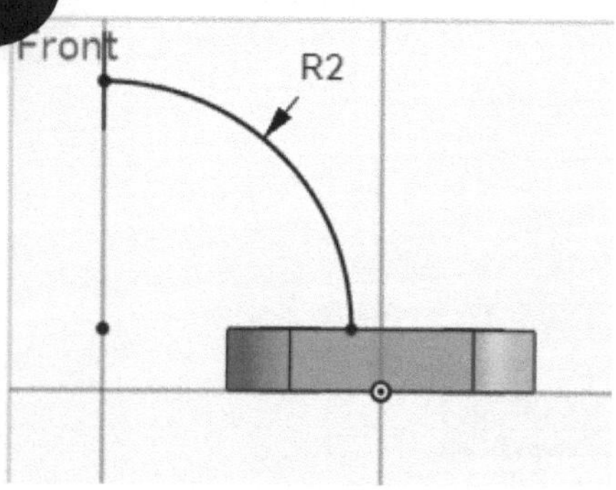

5.116

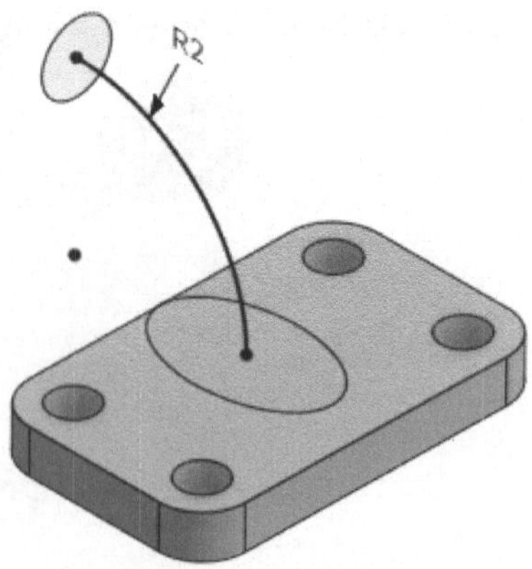

19. Click the green checkmark in the **Sketch** dialog to confirm the creation of the sketch and exit the dialog. Next, press the SHIFT + 7 keys to change the view orientation to isometric.

    Now, you can create the loft feature.

20. Click on the **Loft** tool in the **Feature** toolbar, see Figure 5.117. The **Loft** dialog appears.

5.117

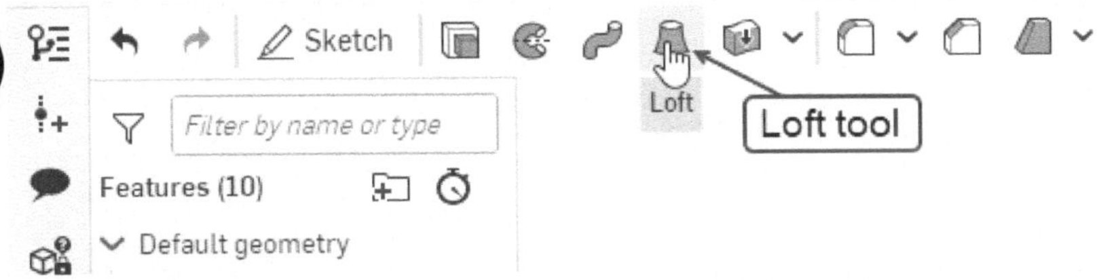

21. Ensure that the **Solid** option is activated in the **Creation Type** area of the **Loft** dialog to create a solid loft feature, refer to Figure 5.118.

5.118

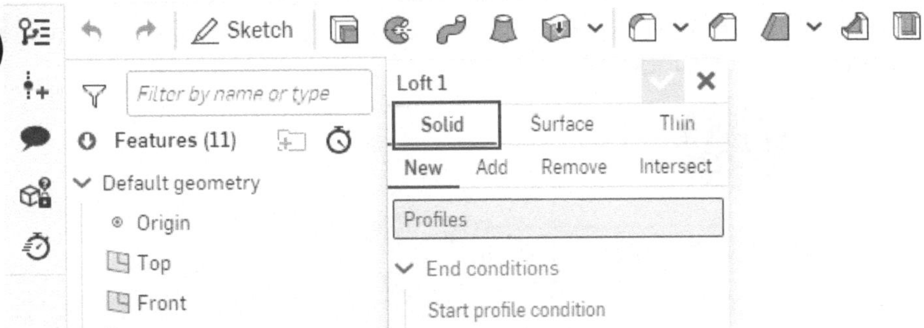

22. Select both profiles (the ellipse and the circle) in the graphics area, one at a time. The preview of the loft feature appears. You may notice that the preview of the loft feature displays a self-intersection or twist during the transition between the two profiles, see Figure 5.119.

5.119

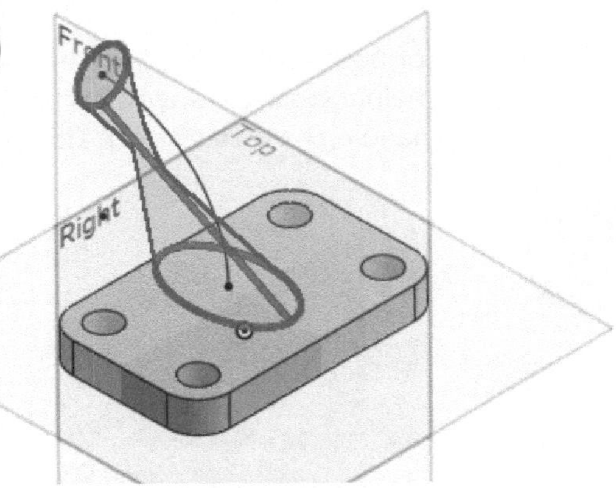

23. Click on the **Connections** check box to define the connection between both profiles, helping to avoid self-intersections or twists. The **Match connection** field appears below the check box.

24. Click on the circle profile in the graphics area. The Connection handle appears on the circle, see Figure 5.120.

5.120

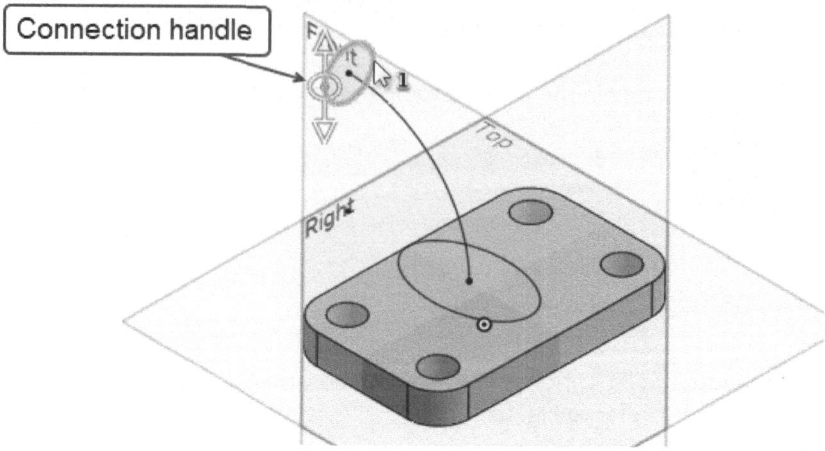

25. Similarly, click on the ellipse profile in the graphics area. The Connection handle appears on the ellipse as well, see Figure 5.121.

5.121

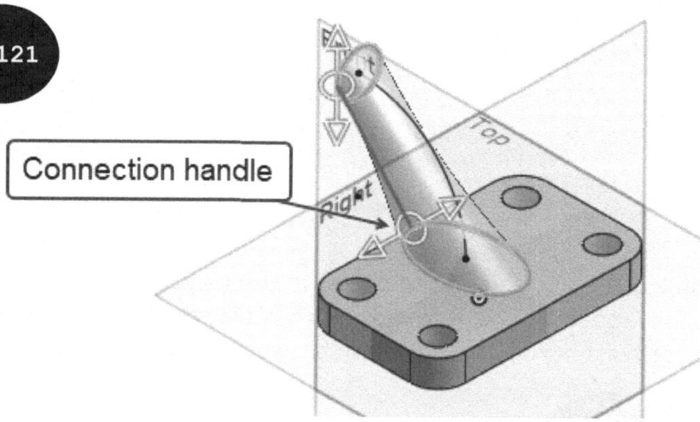

26. Adjust the Connection handles of both profiles by dragging them as needed so that they align with each other in one direction, helping to avoid any twists between them, see Figure 5.122. Note that as you drag the Connection handle, the preview of the loft feature updates accordingly in the graphics area.

5.122

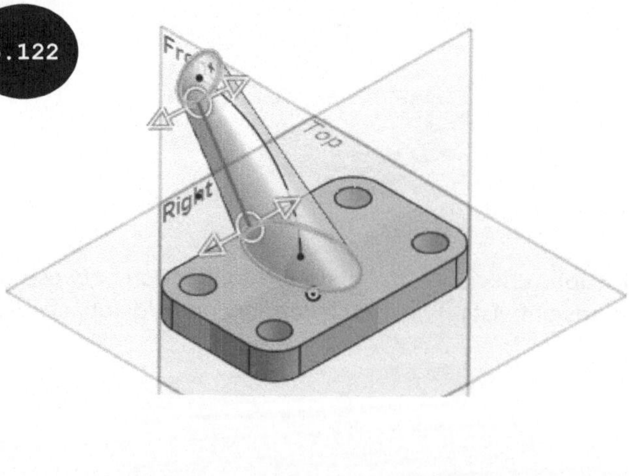

Now, you can select the centerline guide (path) of the loft feature.

27. Select the **Path** check box in the **Loft** dialog and then select the arc in the graphics area as the centerline guide of the feature, see Figure 5.123. The preview of the loft feature updates in the graphics area, maintaining the neutral axis of the loft feature.

5.123

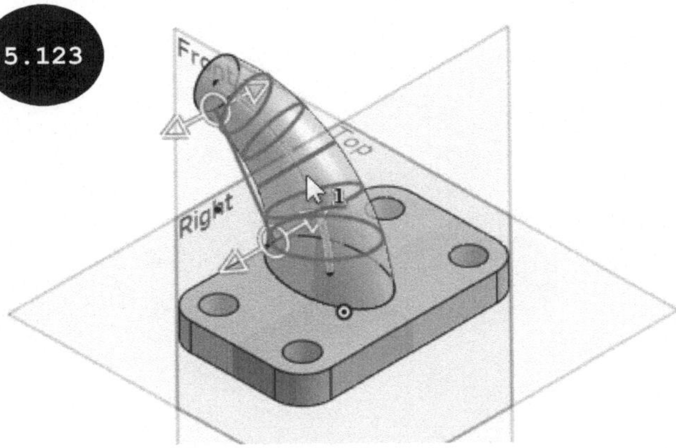

28. Click the green checkmark in the **Loft** dialog to confirm the creation of the feature and exit the dialog. Figure 5.124 shows the model after the loft feature.

5.124

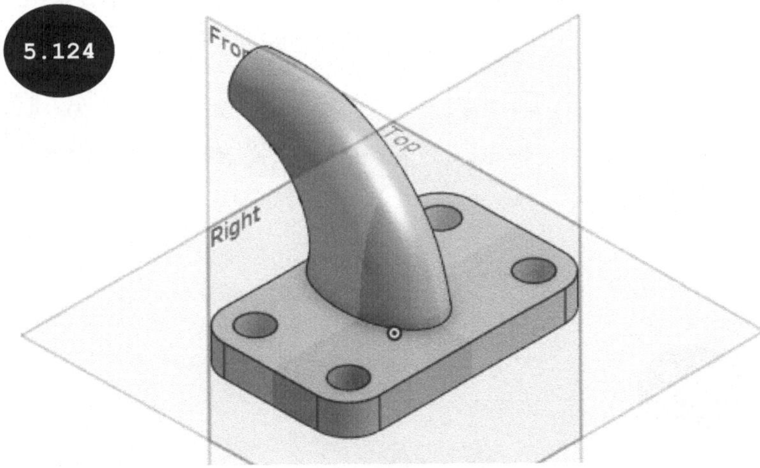

Section 5: Creating the Third Feature - Extrude

Now, you can create the third feature of the model, which is an extruded feature.

1. Click on the **Sketch** tool in the **Feature** toolbar, see Figure 5.125. The **Sketch** dialog appears and you are prompted to select a sketching plane.

5.125

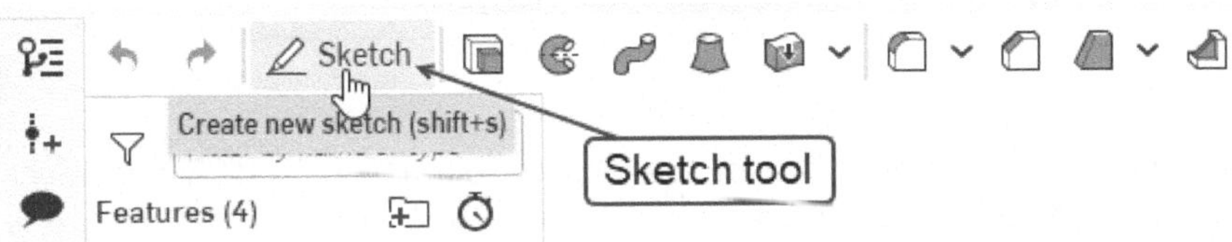

2. Rotate the model to bring the end planar face of the previously created loft feature into view, see Figure 5.126. Once the face is visible, select it to set as the sketching plane.

5.126

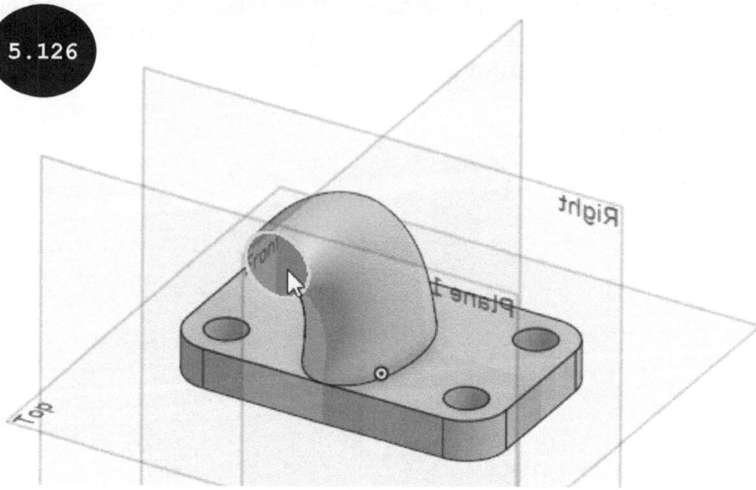

3. Press the **N** key to make the sketching plane normal to the viewing direction.

4. Activate the **Use (Project/Convert)** tool in the **Sketch** toolbar (see Figure 5.127) and select the circular edge of the model, see Figure 5.128. The circular edge projects as a sketch entity onto the current sketching plane.

5.127

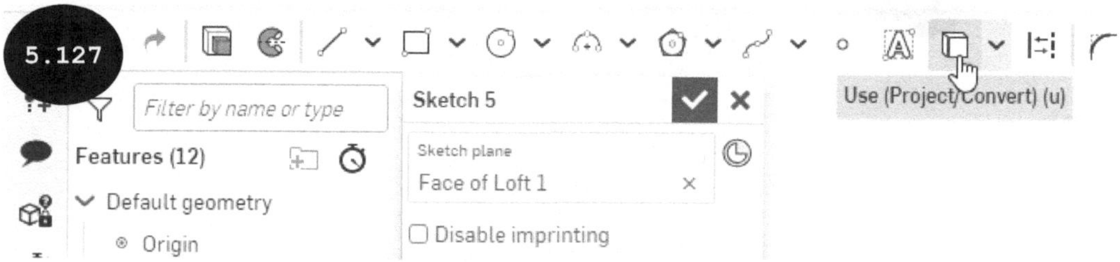

5.128

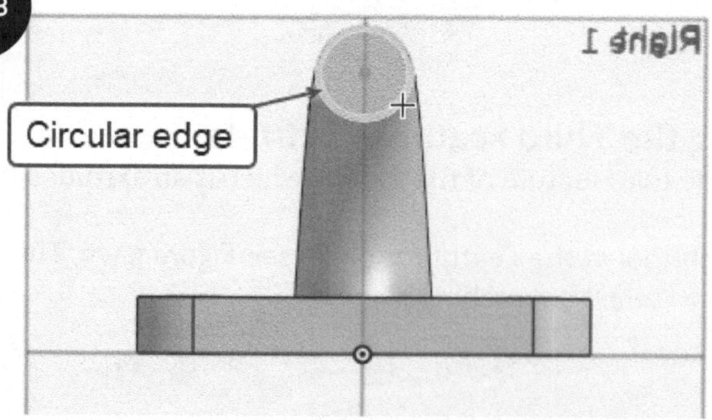

5. Press the SHIFT + E keys to activate the **Extrude** tool. The **Extrude** dialog appears and the sketch profile is automatically selected. Also, the preview of an extruded feature is displayed in the graphics area.

6. Press the SHIFT + 7 keys to change the view orientation to isometric, see Figure 5.129. Ensure that the extrusion direction is towards the rear side of the model.

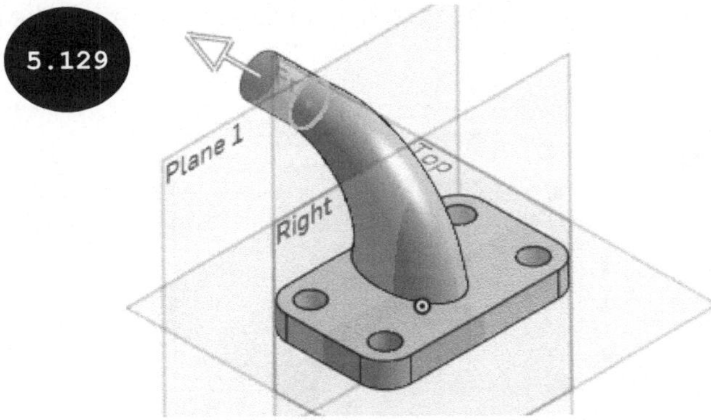

7. Enter **0.5** inches as the extrusion depth in the **Depth** field of the dialog and then press ENTER.

8. Click the green checkmark ✓ in the **Extrude** dialog to confirm the creation of the extrude feature and exit the dialog. The extrude feature of specified depth is created, see Figure 5.130.

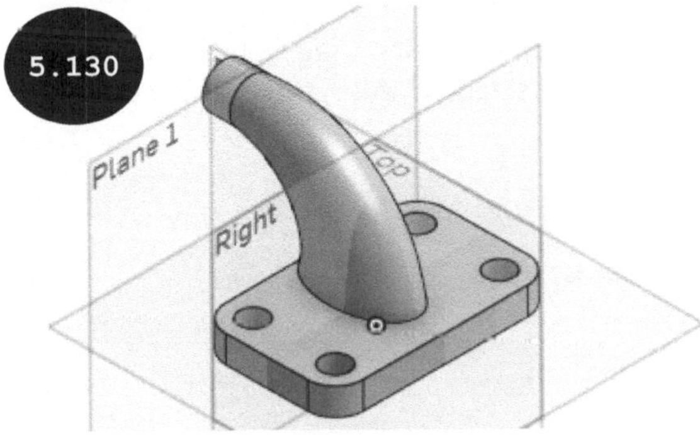

Section 6: Creating the Fourth Feature - Extrude

Now, you can create the fourth feature of the model, which is also an extruded feature.

1. Click on the **Sketch** tool in the **Feature** toolbar and select the Front plane as the sketching plane, see Figure 5.131.

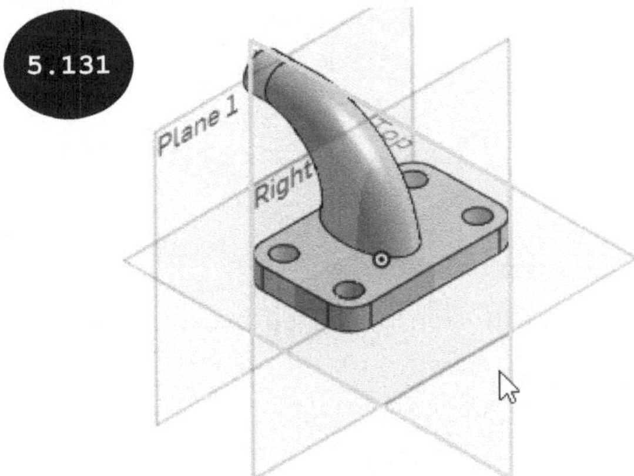

2. Press the **N** key to make the sketching plane normal to the viewing direction.

3. Create a circle of diameter 1 inch as the sketch of the feature and apply the necessary dimensions, see Figure 5.132.

5.132

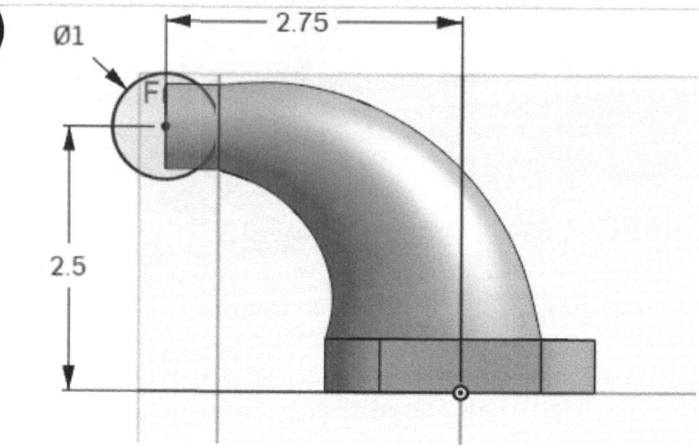

4. Click on the **Extrude** tool in the **Sketch** toolbar, see Figure 5.133. The **Extrude** dialog appears and the sketch profile is automatically selected. Also, the preview of an extruded feature appears in the graphics area.

5.133

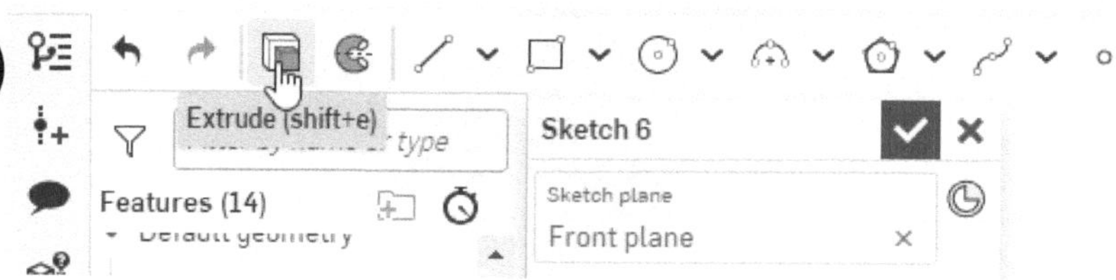

5. Press the SHIFT + 7 keys to change the view orientation to isometric, see Figure 5.134.

5.134

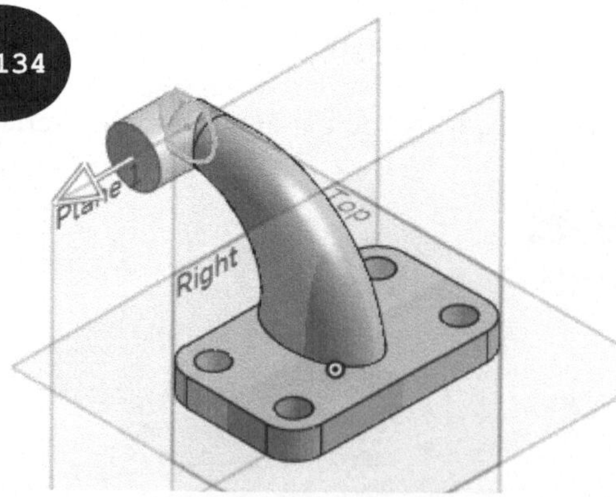

6. Enter **1.5** inches as the depth of extrusion in the **Depth** field of the **Extrude** dialog and then press ENTER.

7. Select the **Symmetric** check box in the **Extrude** dialog to extrude the sketch symmetrically on both sides of the sketching plane, see Figure 5.135.

8. Click the green checkmark in the **Extrude** dialog to confirm the creation of the extrude feature and exit the dialog. The extrude feature of specified depth is created, see Figure 5.136. In this figure, the display of construction planes is turned off for clarity.

5.135

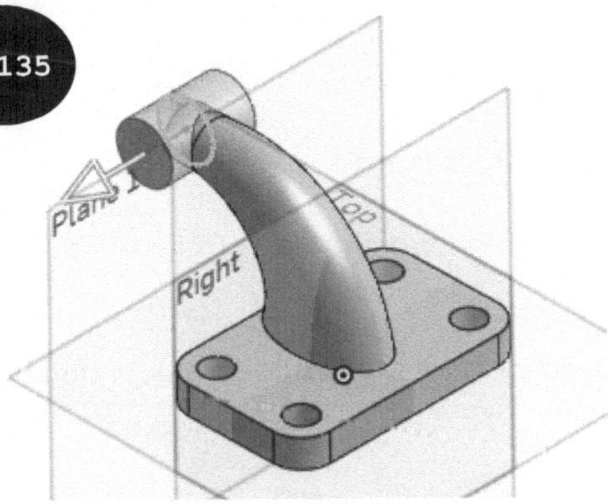

5.136

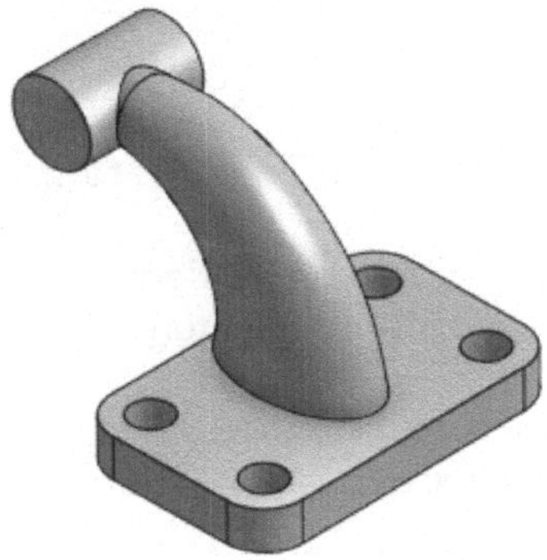

Section 7: Creating the Fifth Feature - Extrude Cut

1. Click on the **Sketch** tool in the **Feature** toolbar (see Figure 5.137) and then select the front planar face of the previously created extruded feature, see Figure 5.138.

5.137

5.138

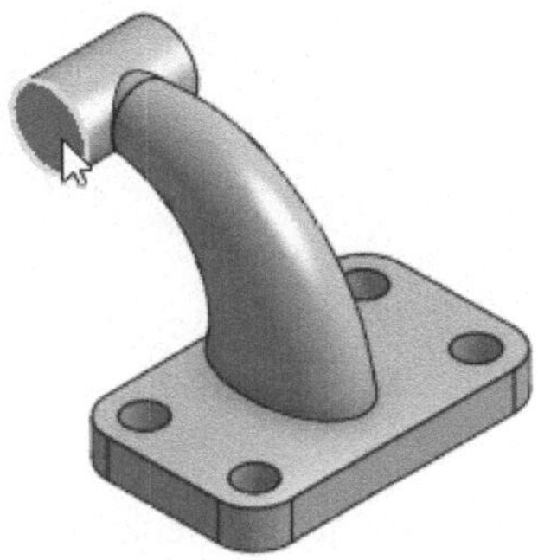

2. Press the **N** key to make the sketching plane normal to the viewing direction.

3. Create a circle of diameter 0.6 inches as the sketch of the cut feature, see Figure 5.139. The center point of the circle is concentric with the circular edge of the model.

5.139

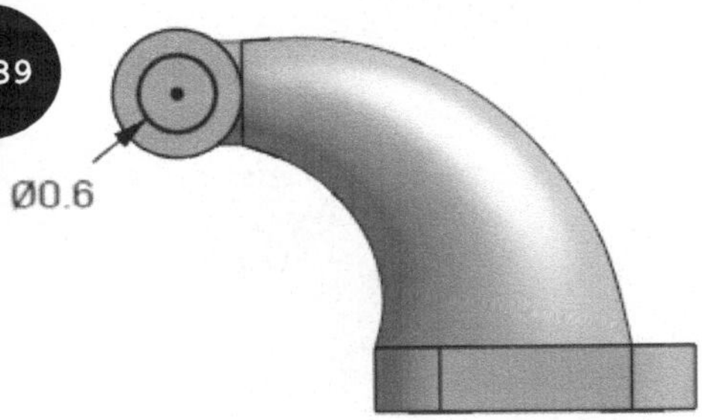

4. Click on the **Extrude** tool in the **Sketch** toolbar, see Figure 5.140. The **Extrude** dialog appears and the preview of an extruded feature appears in the graphics area.

5.140

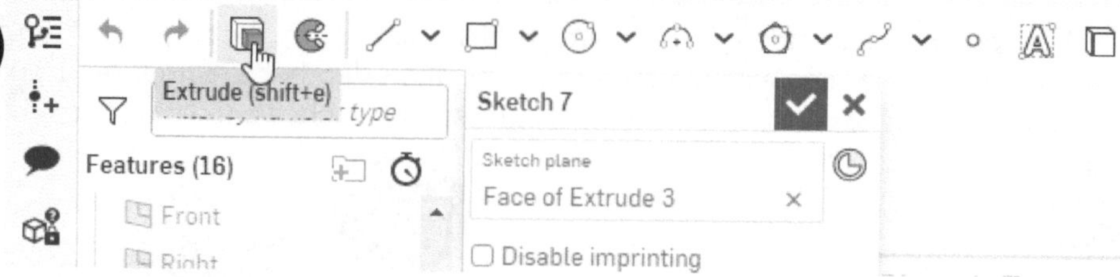

5. Press the SHIFT + 7 keys to change the view orientation to isometric.

6. Click to activate the **Remove** option in the **Operation Type** area of the dialog (refer to Figure 5.141) to create the cut feature by removing the material.

7. Select the **Through all** option in the **End type** drop-down list of the **Extrude** dialog to remove the material through the entire geometry of the model, see Figure 5.141.

5.141

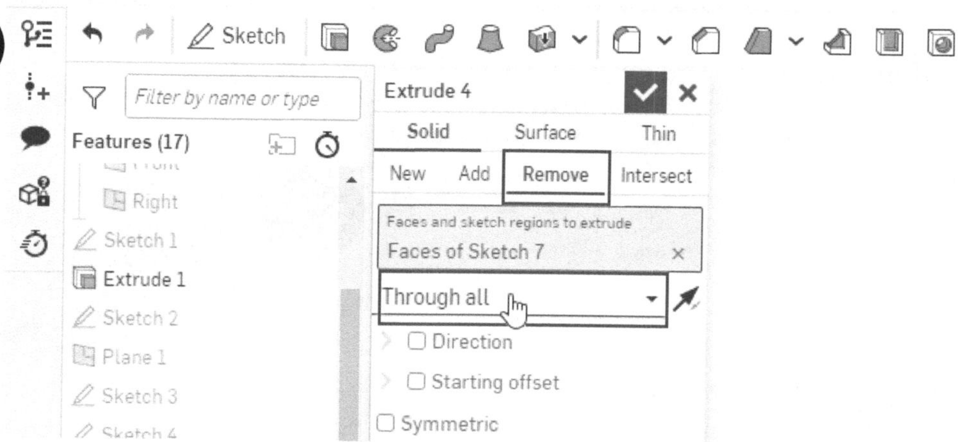

8. Click the green checkmark ✅ in the **Extrude** dialog to confirm the creation of the extrude cut feature and exit the dialog. The extrude cut feature is created by removing the material from the model. Figure 5.142 shows the final model after creating all its features.

5.142

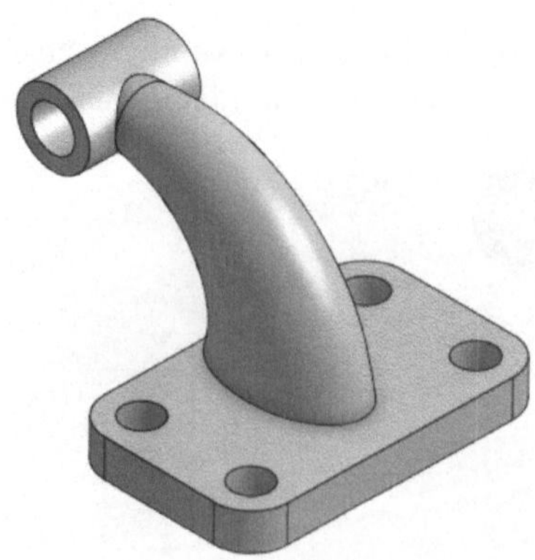

Section 8: Creating a Version and Closing the Document

Now, you can create a version in the document to capture the current state of the design, and then close the document.

1. Click on the **Create version** tool in the **Document panel**, which is aligned vertically with the Onshape logo, see Figure 5.143. The **Create version from Main** window appears with default version name **V1** in its **Name** field.

5.143

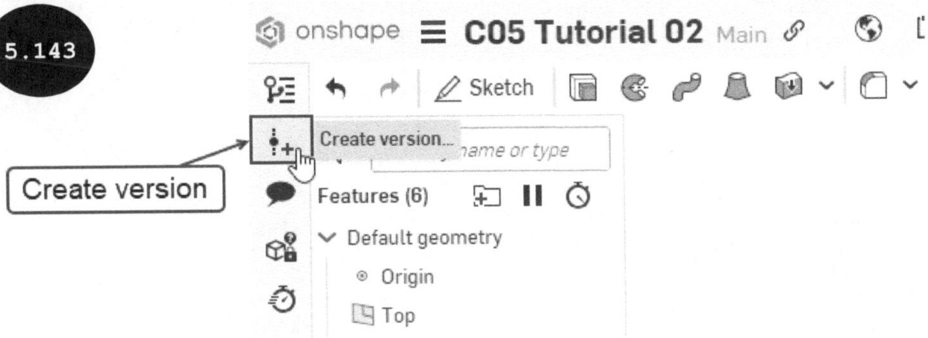

2. Accept the default specified name "V1" and click the **Create** button. A new version, "V1," is created in the document, capturing the model's current state.

   Now, you can close the document.

3. Invoke the **Document** menu by clicking on the ≡ icon (three horizontal lines) next to the Onshape logo at the top left corner and click on the **Close document** option, see Figure 5.144. The current document gets closed.

5.144

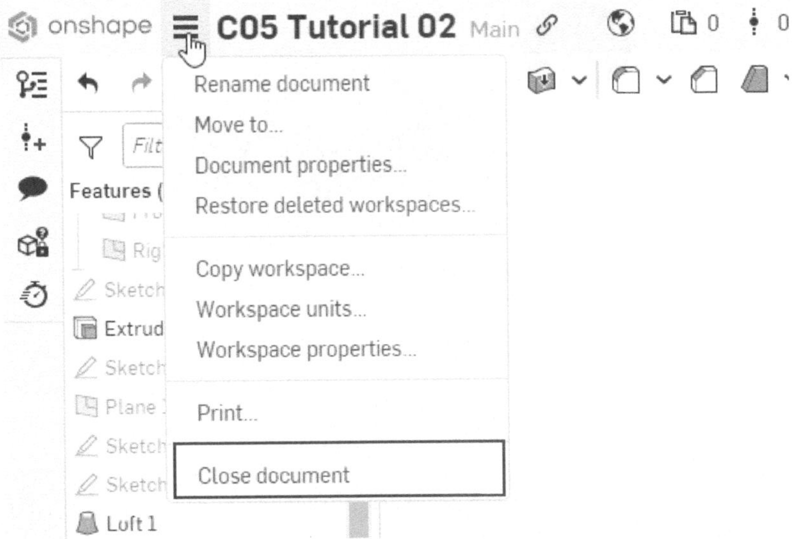

Hands-on Test Drive 1

Create a model, as shown in Figure 5.145. All dimensions are in mm.

5.145

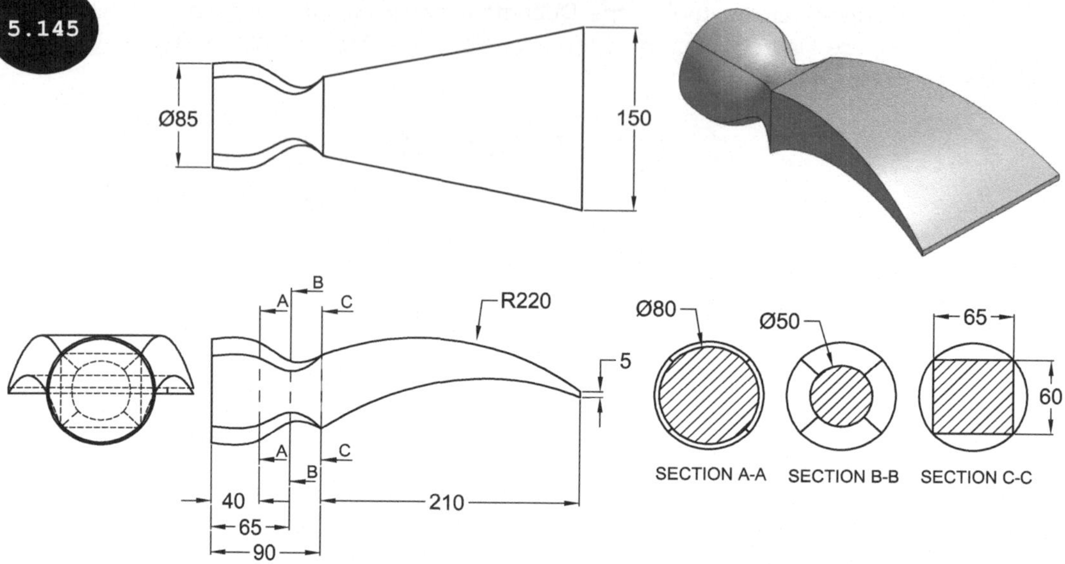

Hands-on Test Drive 2

Create a model, as shown in Figure 5.146. The different views and dimensions for crating this model are given in Figure 5.147. All dimensions are in inches.

5.146

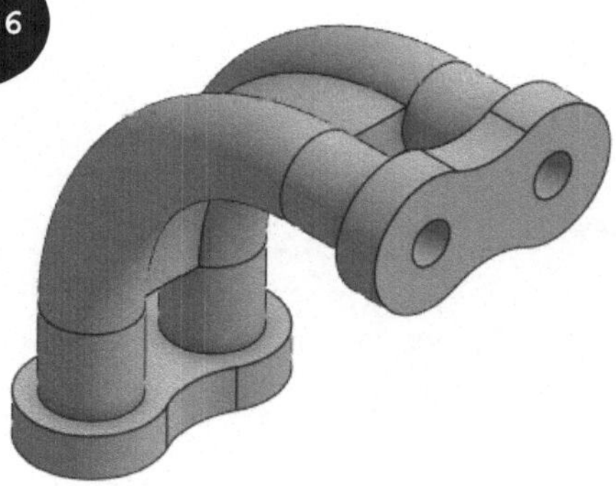

5.147

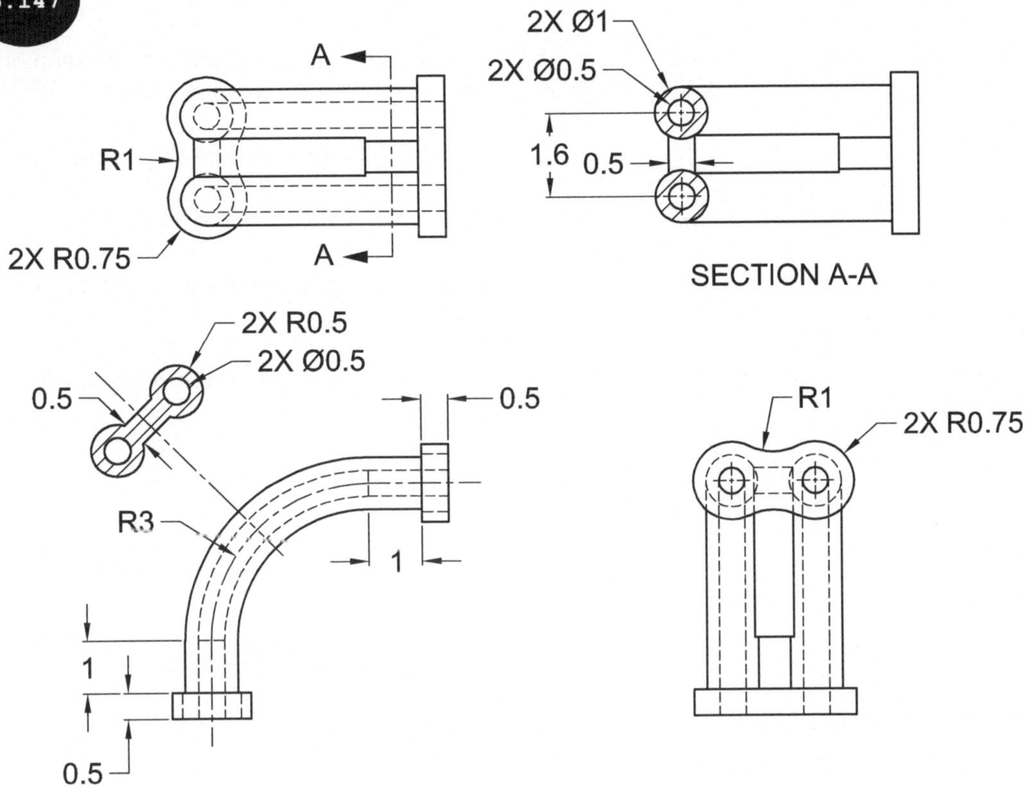

Summary

In this chapter, you explored three advanced modeling features: sweep, loft, and thicken. The sweep feature is created by sweeping a sketch profile along a path, ideal for designing parts like pipes and rails. The loft feature enables smooth transitions between multiple similar or dissimilar sketch profiles, making it perfect for creating parts with varying cross-sections, such as turbine blades or ergonomic shapes. Lastly, the thicken feature adds or removes thickness from an existing face of a model. Together, these tools enhance your ability to create complex and precise models in Onshape.

Questions

Complete and verify the following sentences:

- The _________ tool is used for creating a sweep feature.
- The profile for a solid sweep feature must be a _________ sketch, but for surface and thin sweep features, both _________ and _________ sketch profiles can be selected.

- The _________ option creates a sweep feature by _________ material and merging it with existing features.
- On selecting the _________ option in the **Profile control** drop-down list of the **Sweep** dialog, the profile follows the path while remaining parallel, preventing any twisting along the path.
- A _________ feature allows for a smooth transition between two or more sketch profiles.
- To create a Loft feature, you need at least _________ profiles to generate the transition.
- The _________ tool is used to add or remove material to a specified thickness from an existing face of a model.
- While create a loft feature, you can select a _________ to maintain the neutral axis of the feature.
- The _________ check box in the **Loft** dialog allows you to select guide curves to control the cross-sectional shape of the loft feature.
- The _________ option creates a sweep feature by keeping the intersecting material between the existing feature and the new one.
- A surface feature created with the **Sweep** tool has mass properties. (True/False)
- The **Keep profile orientation** option prevents twisting of the profile along the sweep path. (True/False)
- You need at least one profile to create a loft feature. (True/False)
- The thicken feature can only add material to a model, not remove it. (True/False)
- The profile for the thin sweep feature can only be a closed sketch. (True/False)

CHAPTER

6

Creating Placed Features: Fillet, Chamfer, & More

In this chapter, the following topics will be discussed:

- Creating Fillets
- Creating Face Blends
- Creating Chamfers
- Adding a Draft Angle
- Creating a Rib Feature
- Creating a Shell Feature
- Creating Holes
- Creating an External Thread

In this chapter, you will explore essential placed features that add precision, strength, and refinement to your 3D models. This chapter covers the **Fillet**, **Face blend**, **Chamfer**, **Draft**, **Rib**, **Shell**, **Hole**, and **External thread** tools, each critical for adding detail and functionality to your designs. You will learn how to smoothly round edges, add angled faces, create supporting ribs, apply external threads, and more to your parts. By the end of this chapter, you will be equipped with a comprehensive set of techniques to bring your designs to a new level of precision and realism.

Creating Fillets

A fillet is a rounded face with a constant or variable radius, used to remove the sharp edges of a model. Figure 6.1 shows a model before and after creating a constant radius fillet on two of its edges. In Onshape, you can create constraint and variable radius edge fillets, as well as full round fillets, using the **Fillet** tool. The methods for creating each type of fillet are discussed next.

6.1

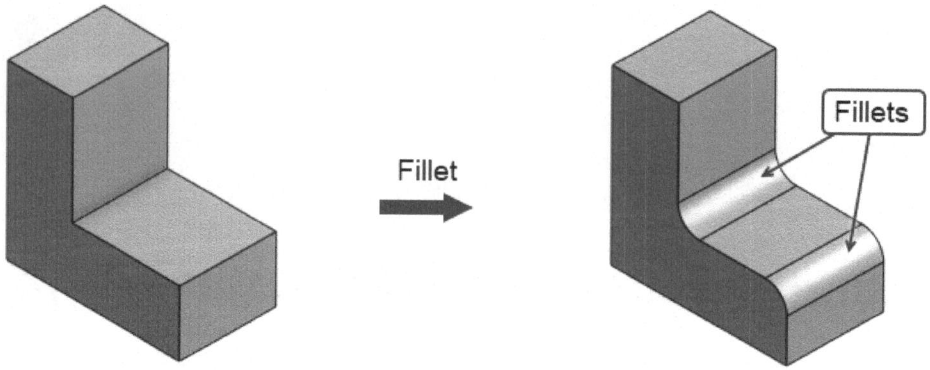

Creating a Constraint Radius Edge Fillet

Edge fillets are created on the edges of a model. In Onshape, you can create constraint and variable radius edge fillets. The method for creating a constraint radius edge fillet is discussed below:

1. Click on the **Fillet** tool in the **Feature** toolbar (see Figure 6.2) or press Shift + F. The **Fillet** dialog appears with the **Edge** tab activated by default, see Figure 6.3.

6.2

6.3

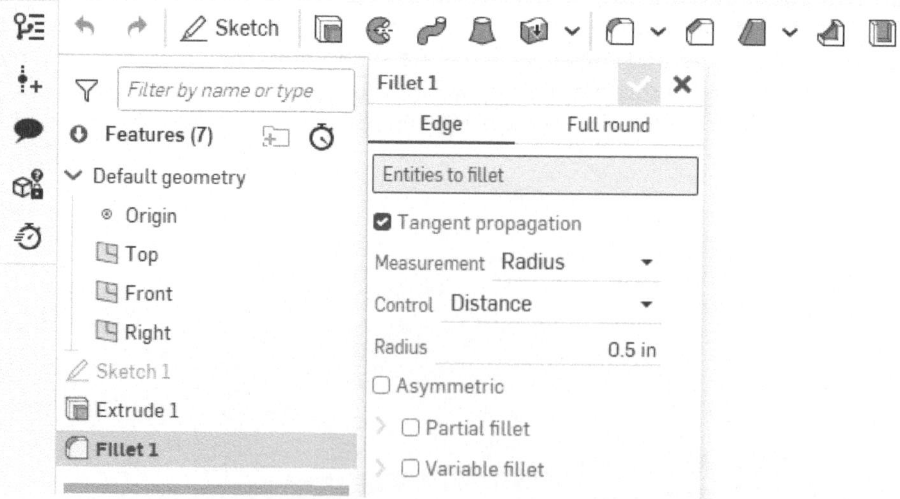

Note: The **Edge** tab is activated by default in the **Fillet** dialog, resulting in the display of options for creating fillets on the edges of a model.

Entities to fillet: The **Entities to fillet** field is activated by default, allowing you to select entities to be filleted. You can choose one or more edges or faces as the entities to be filleted. Note that when you select a face, all its edges will automatically be selected as entities to be filleted.

2. Select one or more edges or faces of the model as the entities to fillet. A preview of the fillet appears on the selected edge(s) or face(s) with a default radius value, see Figures 6.4 and 6.5. Figure 6.4 shows an edge selected for filleting, while Figure 6.5 displays a face selected for the same purpose. Note that when you select a face, the preview of the fillet appears on all the edges of the selected face.

6.4

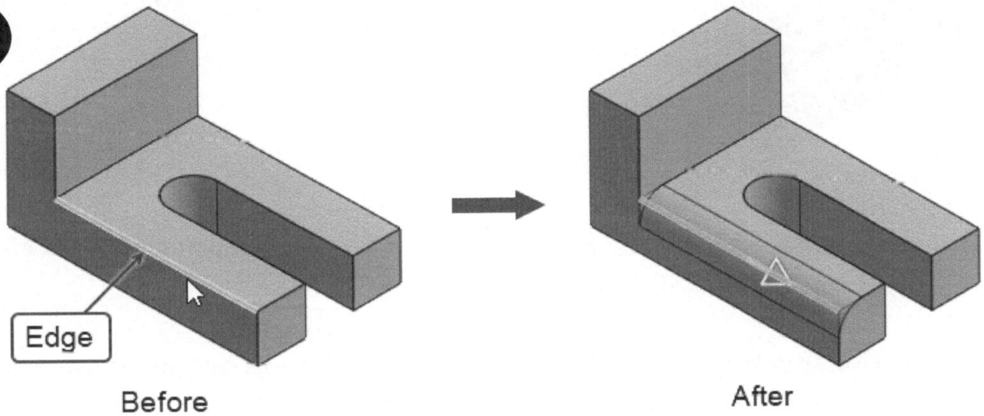

6.5

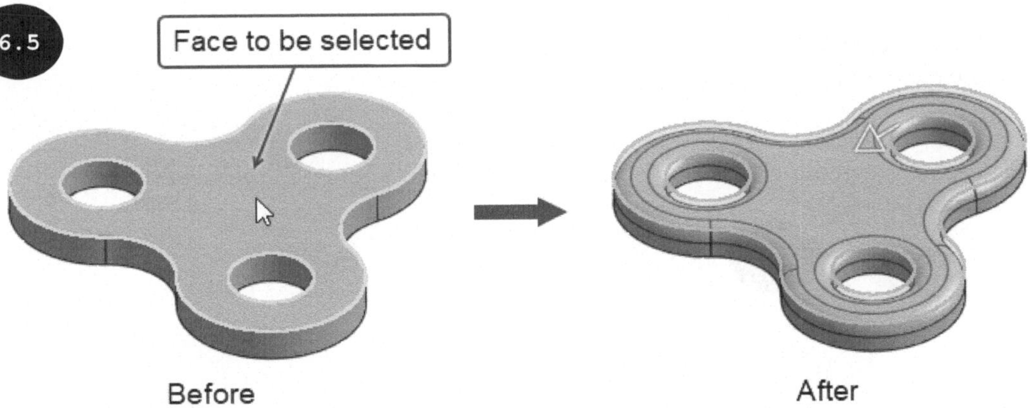

Tangent propagation: The **Tangent propagation** check box is selected by default. Consequently, all edges tangent to the selected edge are automatically filleted. Figure 6.6 shows the edge to be filleted, while Figure 6.7 displays the preview of the fillet with the **Tangent propagation** check box selected. In contrast, Figure 6.8 shows the preview when this check box is cleared.

6.6

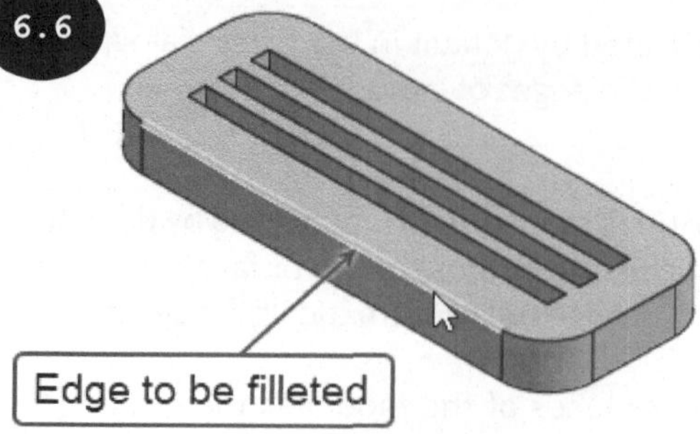

6.7

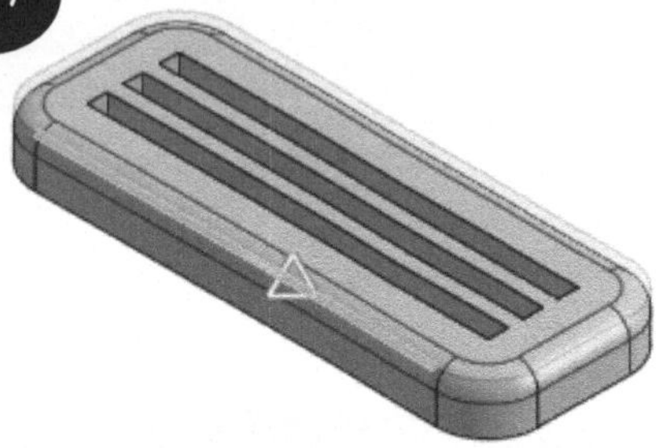

Tangent propagation check box selected

6.8

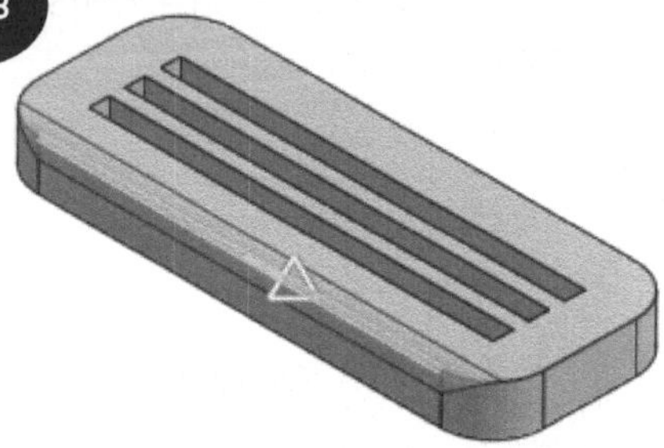

Tangent propagation check box cleared

Tip: To select an individual edge of a model without including all its tangentially connected edges, it is advisable to clear the **Tangent propagation** check box.

Measurement: The options in the **Measurement** drop-down list define the measurement type for the radius of the fillet. The options are discussed below:

Radius: The **Radius** option allows you to specify the radial measurement of the fillet, see Figure 6.9. When this option is selected, the **Radius** field appears in the **Fillet** dialog for defining the fillet's radius.

6.9

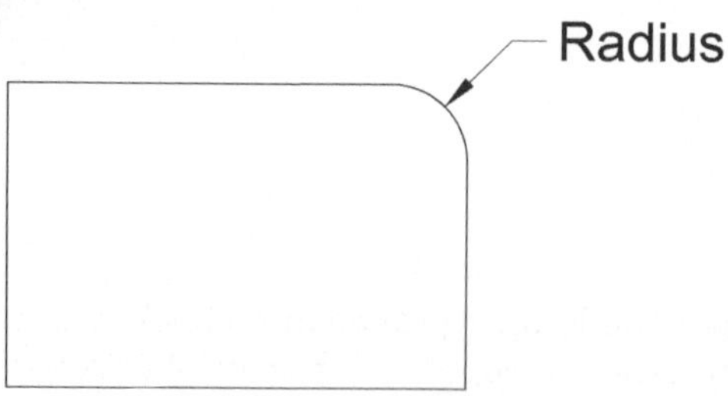

Width: The **Width** option allows you to specify the width of the fillet, see Figure 6.10. The width of the fillet refers to the distance between its two ends. When this option is selected, the **Width** field appears in the **Fillet** dialog for defining the fillet's width.

6.10

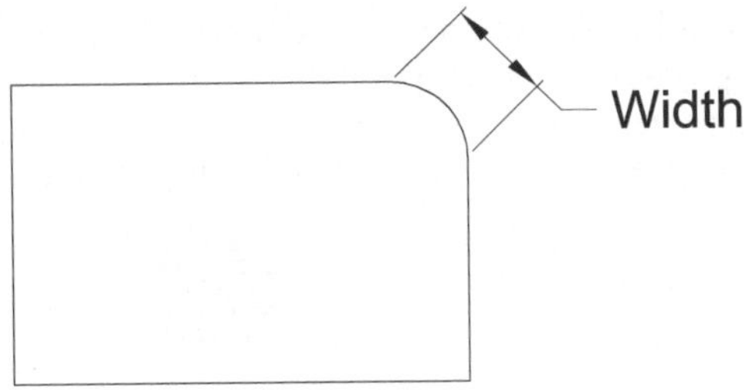

Control: The options in the **Control** drop-down list control the cross-sectional shape of the fillet. The options are discussed below:

Distance: The **Distance** option creates a fillet with a circular cross-section, defined by the specified radius value. You can enter the radius in the **Radius** field of the dialog to set the size of the fillet's circular edge (cross-section).

Conic: The **Conic** option creates a fillet with a conical cross-section, defined by the specified radius and Rho values. You can enter the radius in the **Radius** field and Rho value in the Rho field of the dialog.

The Rho value defines the type of conical curve or cross-section (elliptical, parabolic, or hyperbolic) for the fillet. You can set the Rho value within the range of 0 to 1. When the Rho value is:

- **Less than 0.5:** The fillet will have an elliptical curve, see Figure 6.11 (a).
- **Equal to 0.5:** The fillet will have a parabolic curve, see Figure 6.11 (b).
- **Greater than 0.5:** The fillet will have a hyperbolic curve, see Figure 6.11 (c).

6.11

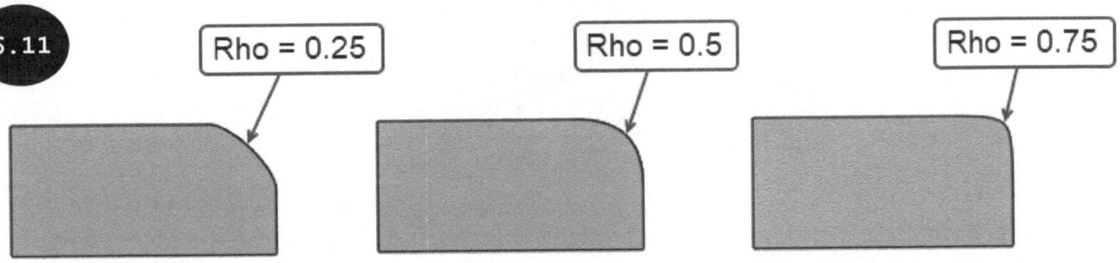

a. Elliptical curve b. Parabolic curve c. Hyperbolic curve

Curvature: The **Curvature** option creates a fillet with a specified radius value, ensuring curvature continuity with the surrounding edges. In addition to defining the radius value, you can specify a magnitude value between 0 and 0.999 in the **Magnitude** field to control the tweak of the tangency.

Radius: The **Radius** field is used to define the radius value of the fillet. You can also drag the arrow that appears on the fillet edge in the preview to adjust the radius dynamically.

Asymmetric: The **Asymmetric** check box allows you to create a fillet with a different radius on each side of the selected edge. When you select this check box, the **Second radius** field appears below it in the dialog, where you can specify a radius value different from the one in the **Radius** field to set the radius for the other side. Figure 6.12 shows a fillet with a symmetric radius on both sides of the edge, while Figure 6.13 shows a fillet with different radii on each side of the edge.

6.12

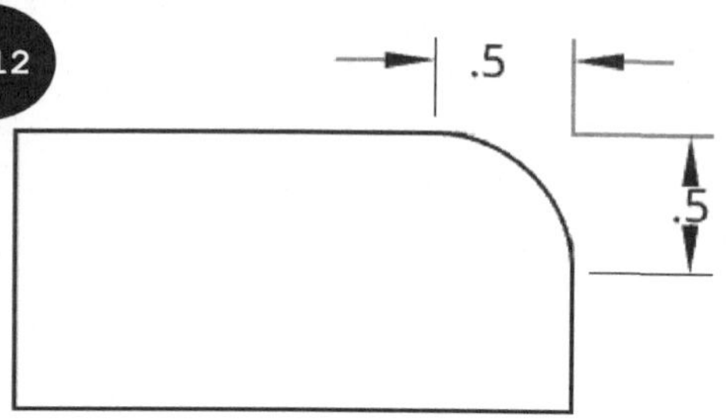

6.13

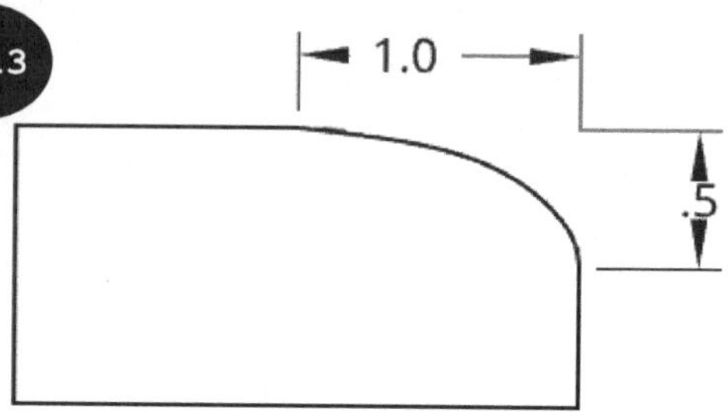

Note that if needed, you can flip the sides with different radii by selecting the **Flip asymmetric** button that appears next to the **Second radius** field in the dialog.

Partial fillet: The **Partial fillet** check box allows you to set the starting position of the fillet along the selected edge. By default, the fillet extends over the entire length of the edge. However, by using this check box, you can create a fillet of a specific length by defining its starting position, see Figure 6.14. To do this, select the **Partial fillet** check box and choose the required option (**Position**, **Entity**, or **Offset**) from the **End type** drop-down list that appears to define the fillet's starting position. The options are discussed below:

6.14

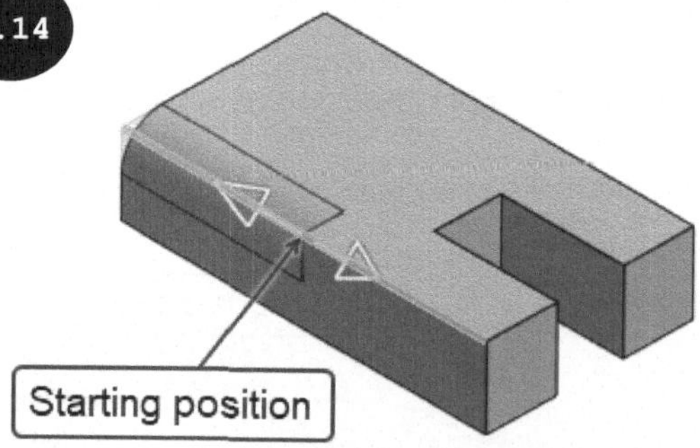

Position: By selecting the **Position** option, you can specify the starting point of the fillet from an end vertex of the selected edge as a percentage value ranging from 0 to 1 in the **Start position** field that appears below the drop-down list. This percentage is based on the total length of the selected edge. For instance, a value of 0.5 indicates that the fillet will begin at the midpoint of the selected edge. If needed, you can reverse the direction of the fillet along the selected edge by clicking the **Opposite direction** button next to the **Start position** field. This adjustment changes the fillet's extension to the opposite side of the specified starting point.

6.15

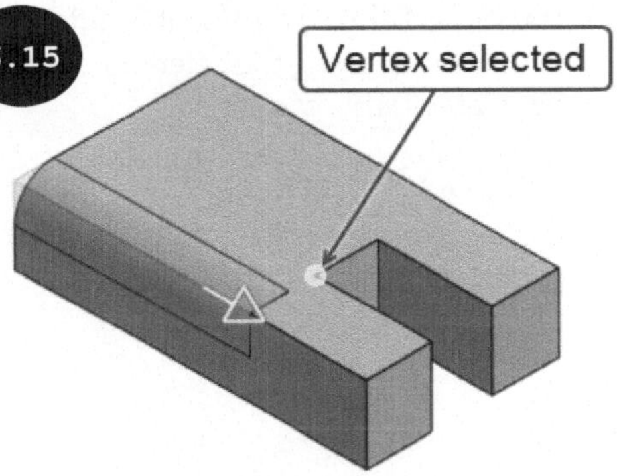

Entity: By selecting the **Entity** option, the **Select an entity or mate connector** field appears below the drop-down list, allowing you to define the starting position of the fillet by selecting an entity (face, vertex, plane, or mate connector), see Figure 6.15. In this example, a vertex is chosen to establish the fillet's starting position along the selected edge.

Offset: By selecting the **Offset** option, the **Start offset** field appears, allowing you to specify an offset distance to set the starting position of the fillet from an end vertex, see Figure 6.16. If needed, you can reverse the direction of the fillet along the selected edge by clicking the **Opposite direction** button next to the **Start position** field, see Figure 6.17. This adjustment changes the fillet's extension to the opposite side of the specified starting point.

6.16

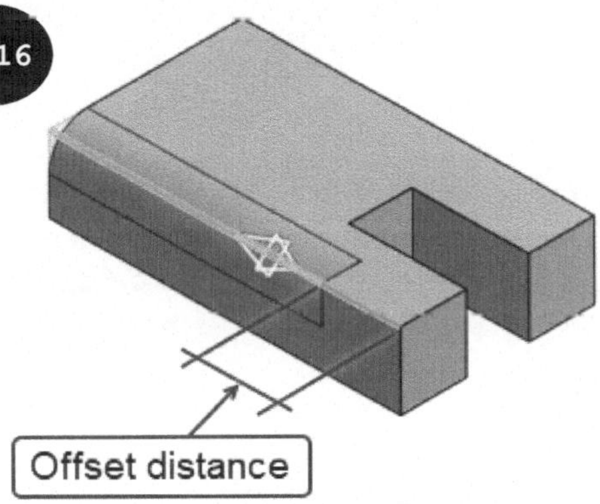

6.17

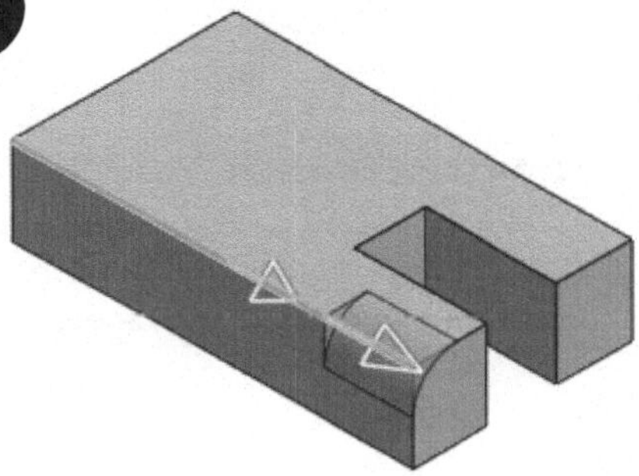

Second bound: The **Second bound** option allows you to set the ending position of the fillet from the second end vertex of the selected edge, see Figure 6.18. This check box is available only when either the **Position** or **Offset** option is selected in the **End type** drop-down list discussed above. The options that appear after selecting this check box are the same as those discussed previously, with the key difference being that these options define the ending position of the fillet relative to the second end vertex.

6.18

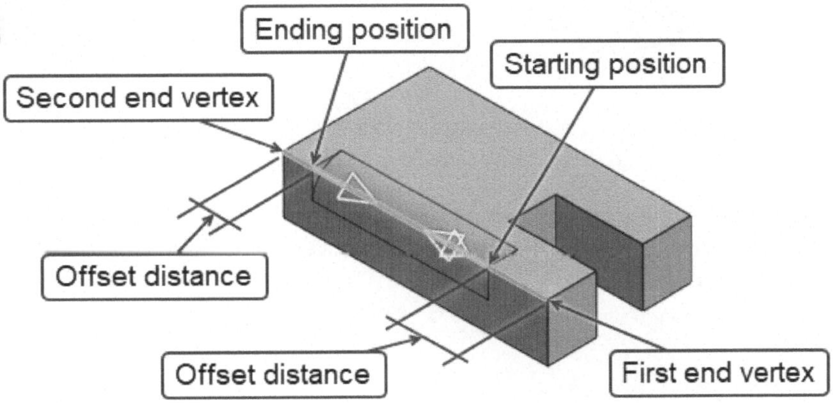

Variable fillet: The **Variable fillet** check box is used to create a variable radius fillet that has variable radii along the selected edge of the model. You will learn about creating a variable radius fillet later in this chapter.

Allow edge overflow: When the **Allow edge overflow** check box is selected, fillets can adjust the surrounding edges of the model, resulting in a smooth, continuous fillet surface. Figure 6.19 shows the fillet with the **Allow edge overflow** check box selected, while Figure 6.20 shows the fillet with the check box cleared.

6.19

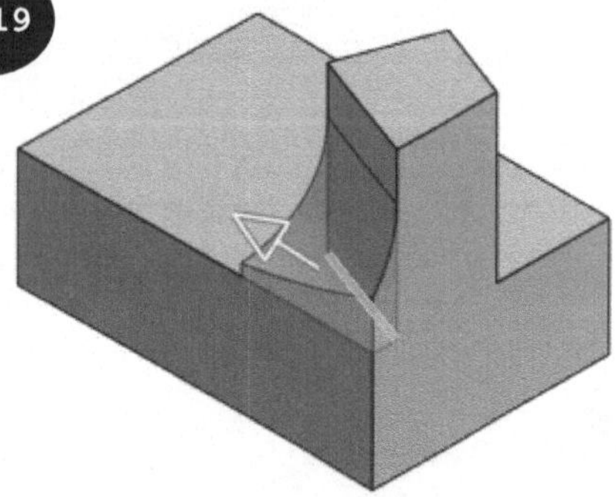

6.20

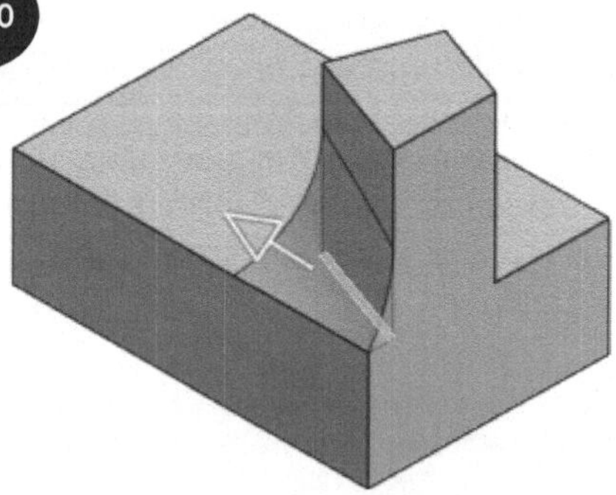

Smooth fillet corners: When the **Smooth fillet corners** check box is selected, smooth rounded corners are created at the intersection of filleted edges. Figure 6.21 shows the preview of the fillets with smooth rounded corners when the check box is selected, while Figure 6.22 displays the preview of the fillets with sharp corners when this check box is cleared.

6.21

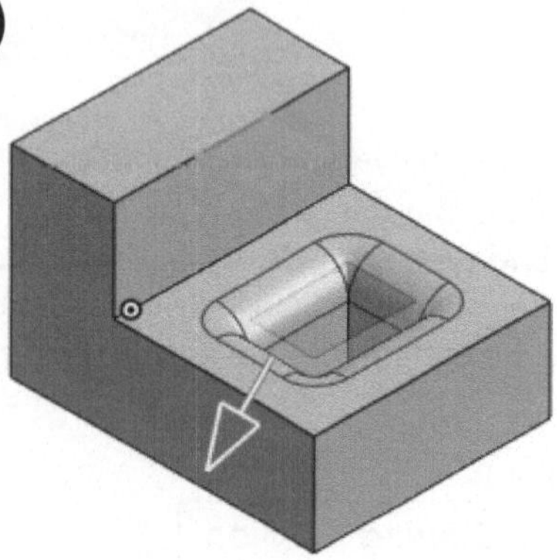

6.22

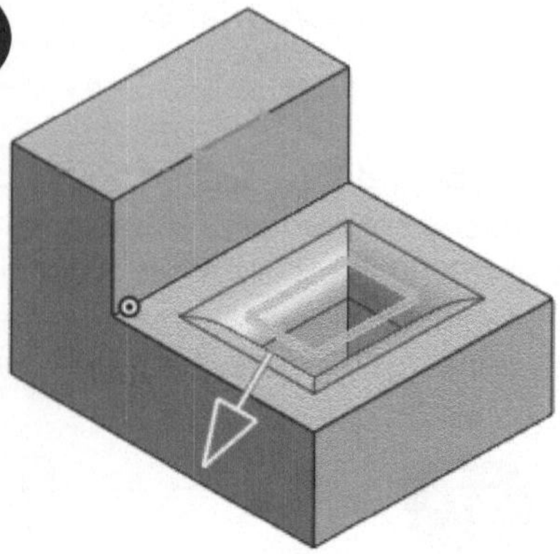

Note that after selecting the **Smooth fillet corners** check box, you can also exclude some of the corners or vertices from being smoothed by selecting them in the graphics area. The names of the selected corners appear in the **Corners to exclude** field enabled below the **Smooth fillet corners** check box. Figure 6.23 shows the preview of the fillets with two intersecting corners selected or excluded from being smooth.

6.23

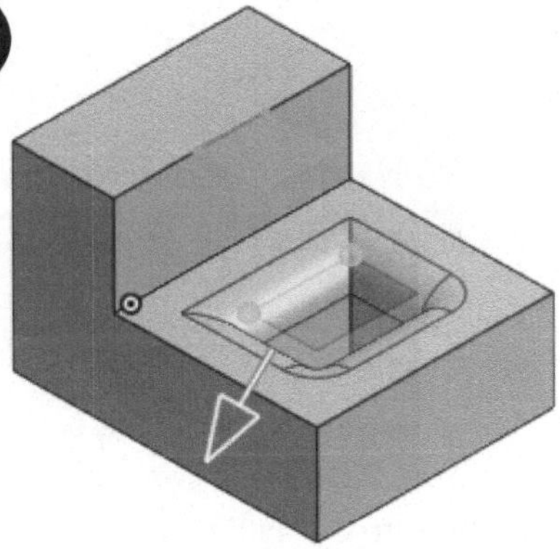

3. After specifying the required parameters, click the green checkmark ✅ to confirm the creation of the fillet and exit the dialog. The fillet of specified radius created on the selected edges of the model.

Creating a Variable Radius Edge Fillet

A variable radius fillet has variable radii along an edge, see Figure 6.24. The method for creating a variable radius edge fillet is discussed below:

6.24

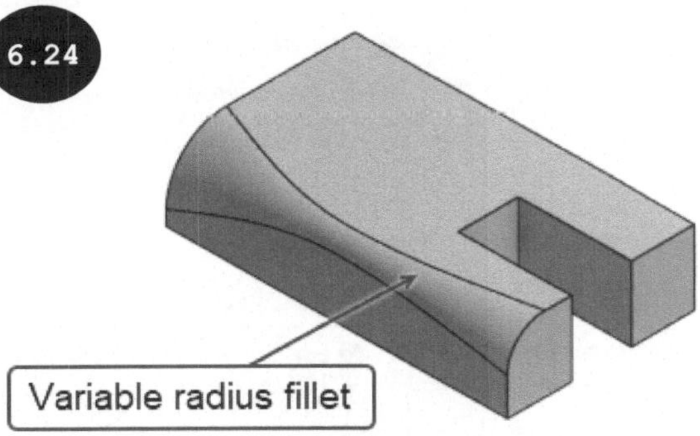

1. Click on the **Fillet** tool in the **Feature** toolbar (see Figure 6.25) or press Shift + F. The **Fillet** dialog appears with the **Edge** tab activated by default.

6.25

2. Select an edge of the model as the entity to fillet. A preview of the constraint radius fillet appears on the selected edge using the default specified radius in the **Radius** field, see Figure 6.26. You can select multiple edges or faces as entities to fillet. Note that selecting a face creates fillets on all its edges.

6.26

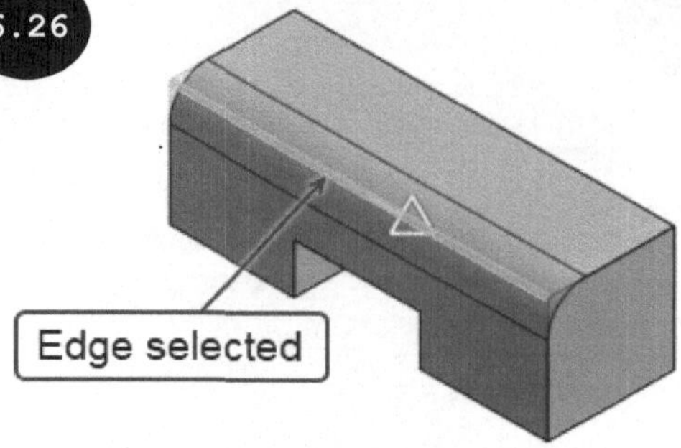

3. Select the **Variable fillet** check box in the Fillet dialog to create a variable radius fillet, see Figure 6.27. The **Vertices** field and the **Add point on edge** button appear. Additionally, both end vertices of the selected edge are highlighted with black dots in the graphics area, see Figure 6.28.

6.27

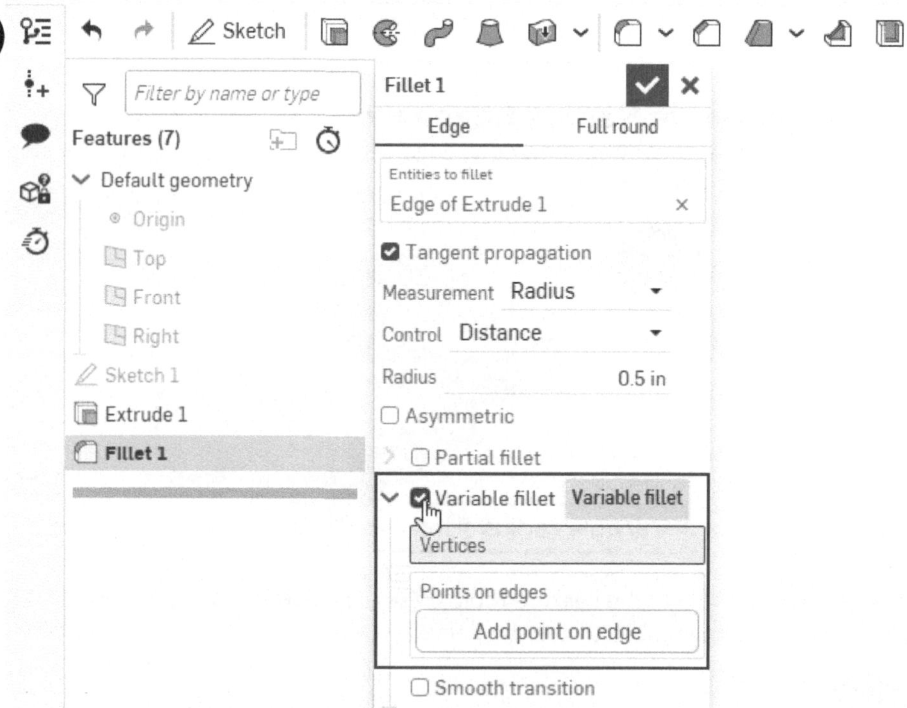

6.28

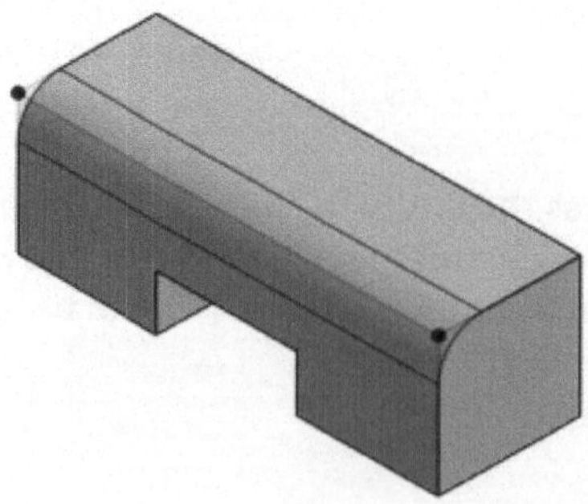

Now, you can define variable radii for both highlighted end vertices. Additionally, you can add points along the edge to specify different radius values at each point.

4. Click to select the end vertices (black dots) of the selected edge to assign different radius values to them. The names of the selected vertices appear in the **Vertices** field, along with the radius value specified in the **Radius** field of the dialog.

Tip: By default, the radius value specified in the **Radius** field of the dialog is applied to the entire selected edge.

5. Edit or specify the required radius values for the selected end vertices in the **Vertices** field of the dialog, see Figure 6.29. In this figure, a radius value of 0.2 is defined for one vertex, while 0.6 is defined for the second vertex. Figure 6.30 displays the preview of the resultant fillet in the graphics area.

6.29

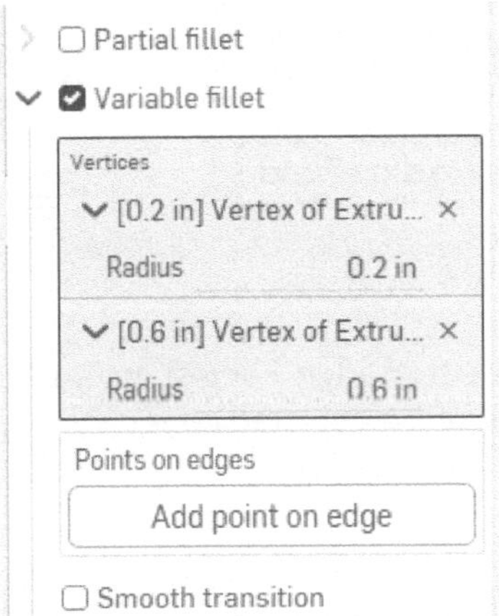

6.30

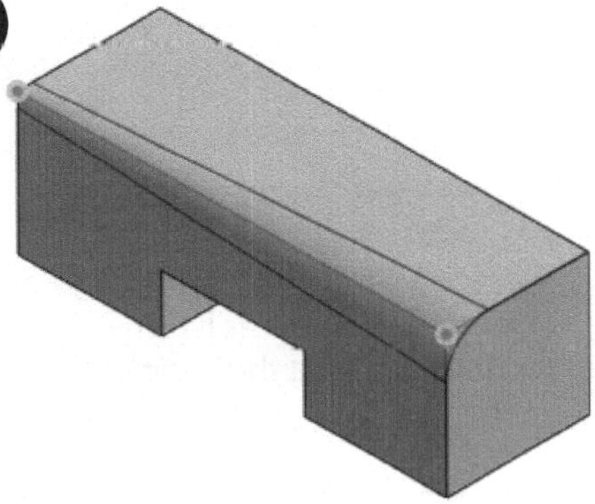

In addition to defining variable radii at both ends of the selected edge, you can add multiple points along the edge and specify a different radius for each point.

6. Click the **Add point on edge** button in the **Fillet** dialog, then click anywhere on the selected edge. A new point is added along the selected edge, along with the display of an arrow handle, see Figure 6.31.

6.31

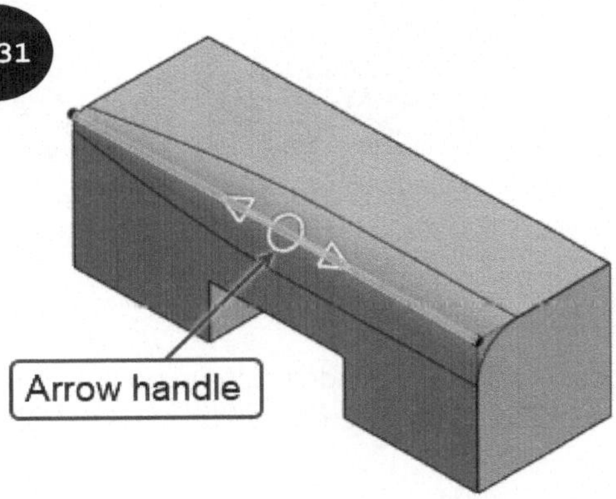

7. Move the arrow handle to adjust the position of the newly added point along the edge, if needed. You can also define the precise position of the specified point by entering a percentage value ranging from 0 to 1 in the **Location** field that appears in the dialog, see Figure 6.32.

6.32

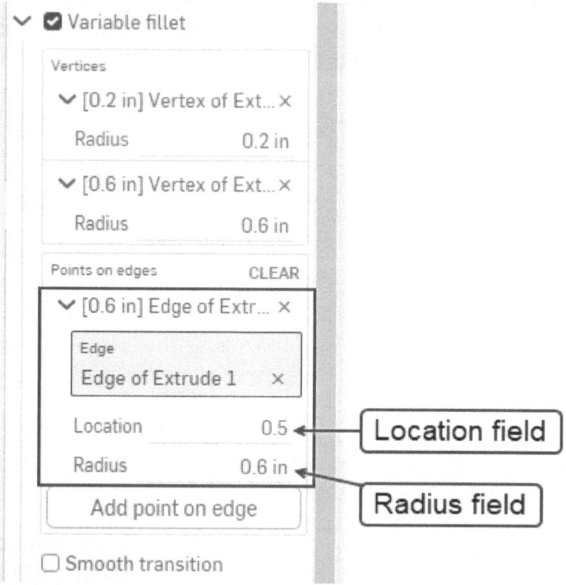

Tip: The percentage is based on the total length of the selected edge. For instance, a value of 0.5 indicates that the point will be added at the midpoint of the selected edge.

Now, you can define a different radius value for the newly added point.

8. Enter the required radius value for the newly added point in the **Radius** field of the dialog and press ENTER. The preview of the fillet updates accordingly in the graphics area, refer to Figure 6.33.

6.33

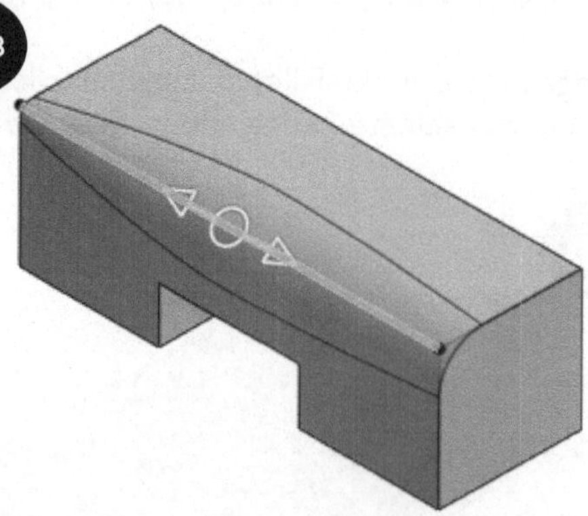

9. Similarly, by repeating steps 6 to 8, you can add multiple points along the selected edge using the **Add point on edge** button and assign a different radius to each point.

10. After specifying the desired variable radii at different points or vertices along the selected edge, click the green checkmark ✓ to confirm the fillet creation and exit the dialog. The fillet with the specified variable radii is created on the selected edge of the model, refer to Figure 6.34.

6.34

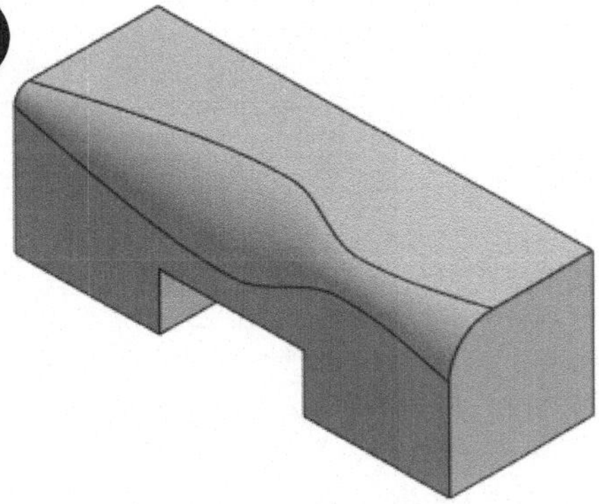

Creating a Full Round Fillet

A full round fillet creates a smooth, tangent transition across three adjacent faces of a model, see Figure 6.35. The method for creating a full round fillet is discussed below:

6.35

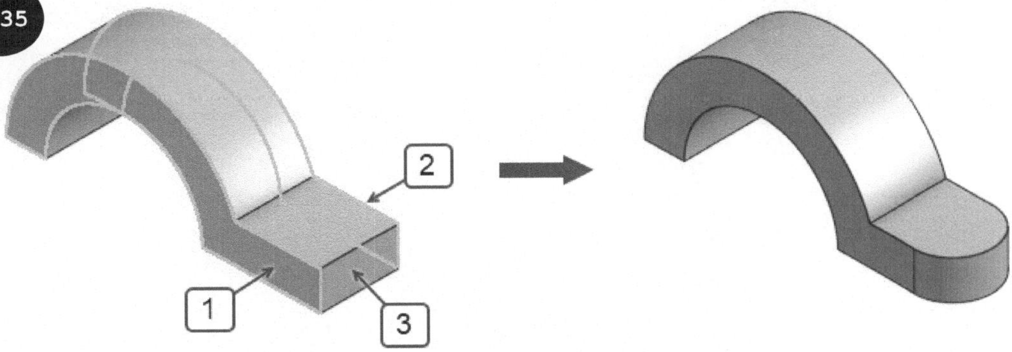

1. Click on the **Fillet** tool in the **Feature** toolbar (see Figure 6.36) or press Shift + F. The **Fillet** dialog appears with the **Edge** tab activated by default.

6.36

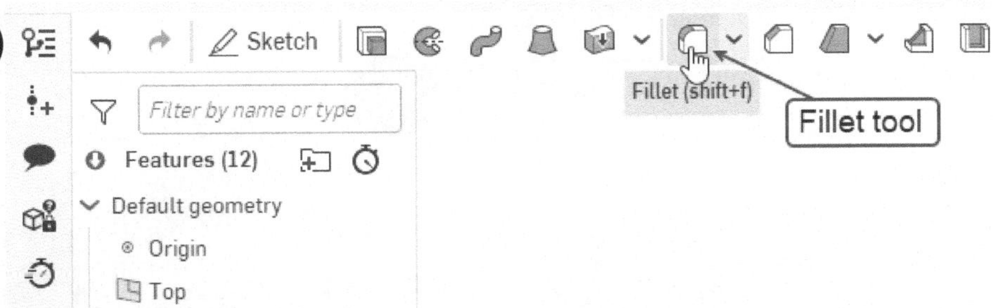

2. Click to activate the **Full round** tab in the **Fillet** dialog. The options to create a full round fillet appears, see Figure 6.37.

6.37

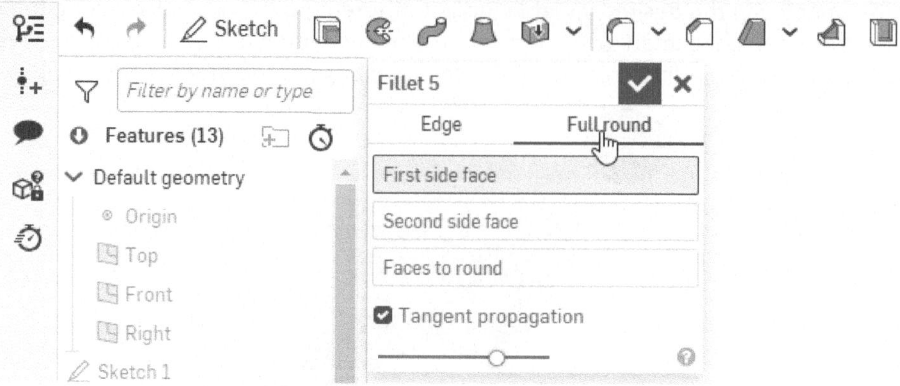

Now, you can create a full round fillet by selecting two side faces and one central face to round.

3. Select the first side face of the model, see Figure 6.38. After you select the first side face, the **Second side face** field activates automatically.

4. Select the second side face of the model, see Figure 6.38. You may need to rotate the model to select the second side face of the model. After you select the second side face, the **Faces to round** field activates automatically.

6.38

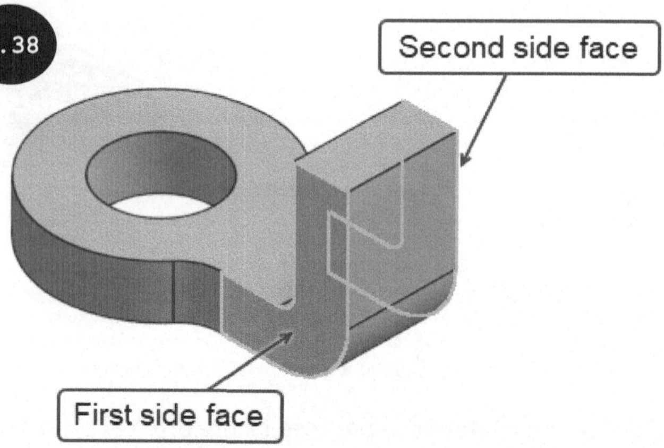

5. Select the central face of the model to round, see Figure 6.39. A preview of the full round fillet appears in the graphics area, see Figure 6.40.

6.39

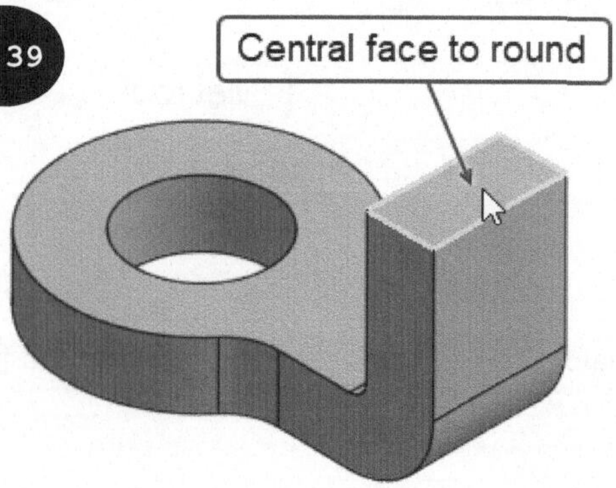

6.40

6. Click the green checkmark ✓ to confirm the fillet creation and exit the dialog. The full round fillet is created, see Figure 6.41.

6.41

Creating Face Blends

A face blend creates smooth blends or rounds between connected or disconnected faces of a model, see Figure 6.42. It provides more control than a fillet, allowing you to specify parameters like blend cross-section type, measurement type, symmetry, control type, and trim options. You can create a face blend using the **Face blend** tool. The method for creating a face blend is discussed below:

6.42

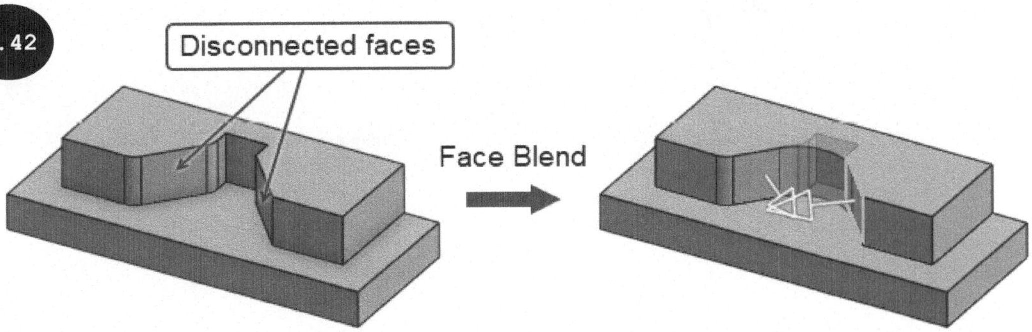

1. Click on a small arrow beside the **Fillet** tool in the **Feature** toolbar and then click on the **Face blend** tool in the drop-down menu that appears, see Figure 6.43. The **Face blend** dialog appears, see Figure 6.44.

6.43

6.44

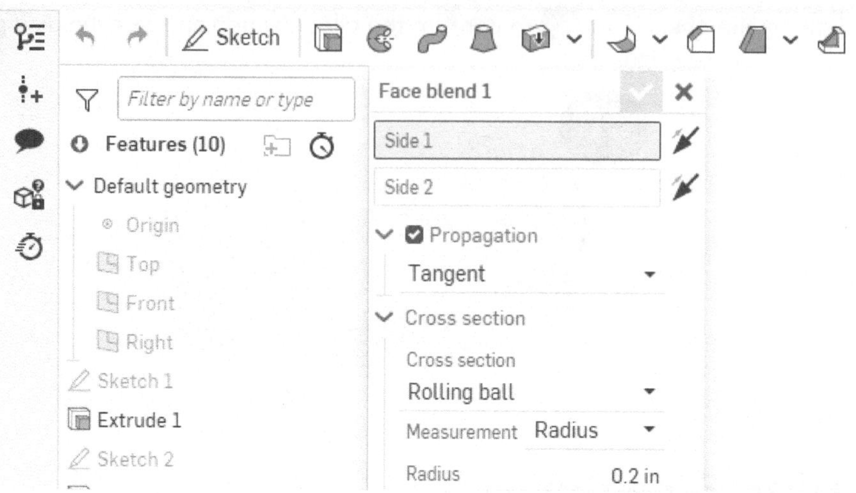

Now, you can select connected or disconnected faces to create a face blend between them.

2. Select the first side face of the model, see Figure 6.45. The name of the select face appears in the **Side 1** field of the dialog.

6.45

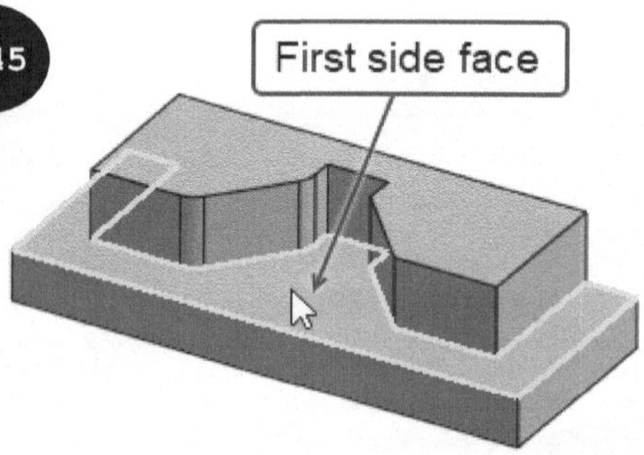

3. Click to activate the **Side 2** field in the dialog and select the second side face, see Figure 6.46. A preview of the face blend appears between the selected faces with default radius, see Figure 6.47.

6.46

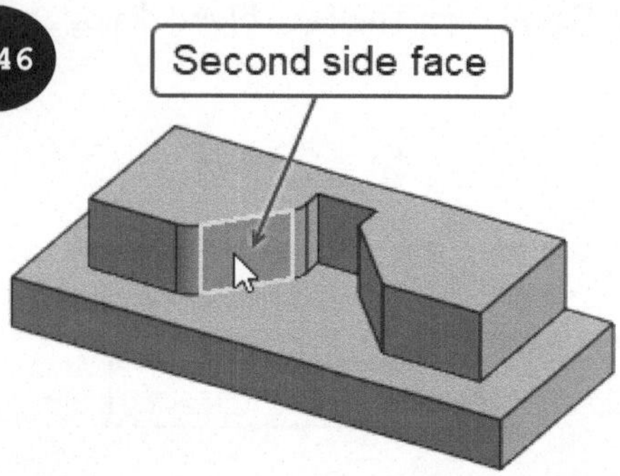

6.47

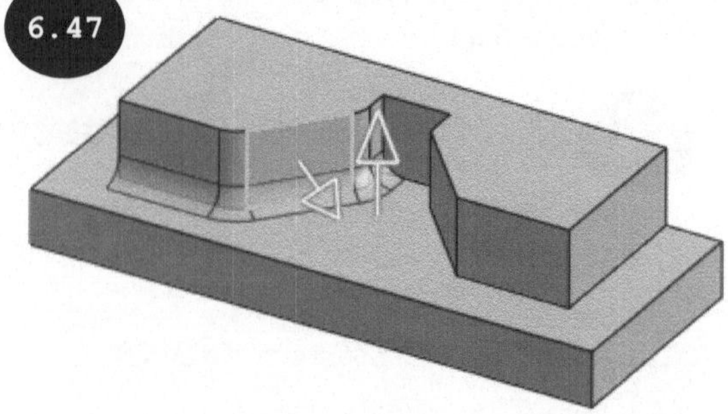

Note: If the preview of the face blend does not appear between the selected faces of the model, you may need to adjust the blend radius in the **Radius** field of the dialog.

4. Enter the required blend radius in the **Radius** field of the dialog and press ENTER. The preview of the face blend updates accordingly in the graphics area. The other options to control the face blend are discussed next.

   Propagation: By default, the **Propagation** check box is selected, allowing you to choose an option from the **Propagation** drop-down list to extend the blend to the connected faces. The options are discussed below:

   Tangent: By selecting the **Tangent** option, the blend extends to faces that are tangentially connected to the selected set, see Figure 6.48.

6.48

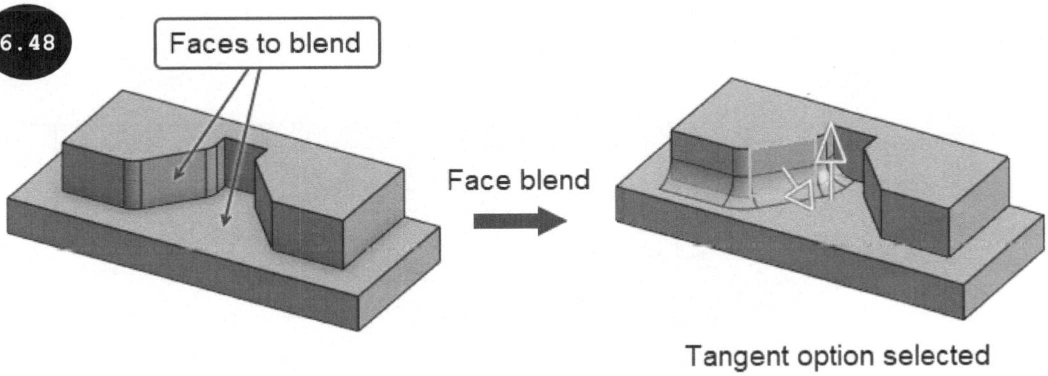

   Adjacent: By selecting the **Adjacent** option, the blend extends to all faces adjacent to the selected set, particularly the first side face, see Figure 6.49.

6.49

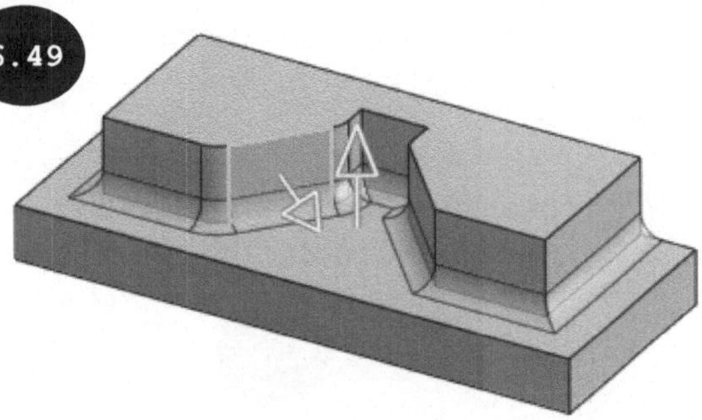

   Custom: By selecting the **Custom** option, the blend extends to all adjacent faces that have an angle less than the value specified in the **Maximum angle** field that appears below the drop-down list.

Tip: If the **Propagation** check box is cleared, the blend will be created only between the selected set of faces.

Cross section: The options in the **Cross section** drop-down list allow you to select the desired cross-section type for the blend. The options are discussed below:

Rolling ball: By default, the **Rolling ball** option is selected in the **Cross section** drop-down list, allowing you to create a curved blend (fillet) of a specified radius between the selected faces.

Swept profile: By selecting the **Swept profile** option, the **Spine** field appears below the drop-down list, allowing you to select an edge or a sketch as the spine, see Figure 6.50. This creates a blend between the selected set that remains perpendicular to the chosen spine.

6.50

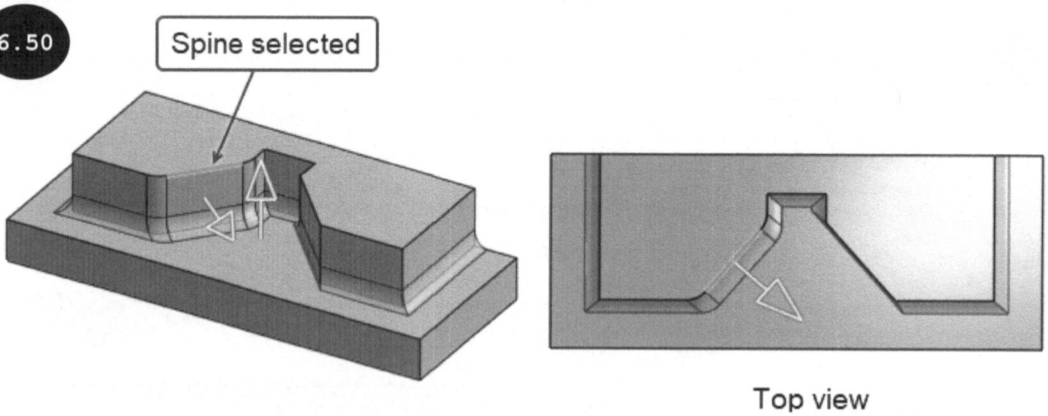

Measurement: The options in the **Measurement** drop-down list are used to select the desired measurement type for the cross-section of the blend (curve). The options are discussed below:

Radius: By default, the **Radius** option is selected in the **Measurement** drop-down list, allowing you to specify the required radius of the blend (curve) in the **Radius** field (see Figure 6.51), which appears below the drop-down list.

Width: By selecting the **Width** option, the **Width** field appears below the drop-down list, allowing you to specify the distance between the two ends of the blend (curve), see Figure 6.52.

6.51

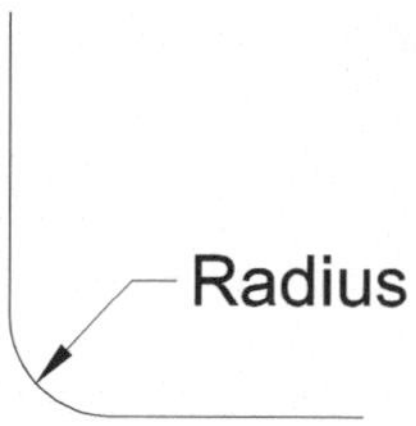

6.52

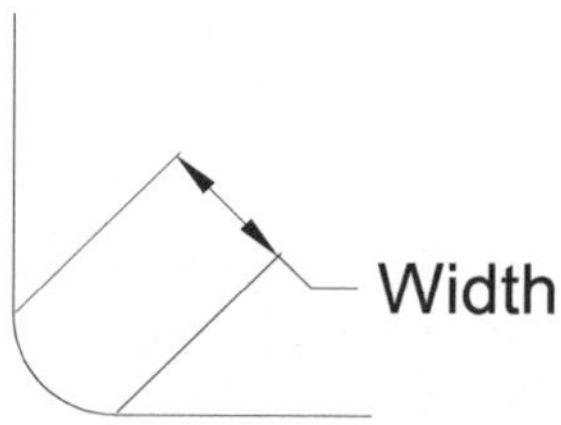

Asymmetric: The **Asymmetric** check box allows you to create a blend with a different radius or width at each end, depending on whether the **Radius** or **Width** option is selected in the **Measurement** drop-down list.

Note: If the Radius option is selected, you can specify a second radius for the blend in the Second Radius field. If the Width option is selected, you can define a ratio between the widths at each end in the Ratio field that appears.

Control: The **Control** drop-down list allows you to define the cross-sectional shape of the blend as circular, conical, curvature continuity, or chamfer by selecting the respective option.

Note: The conical cross-section of the blend depends upon the rho value while, curvature continuity with the surrounding edges of the blend depends upon the magnitude value, as discussed earlier while creating a fillet.

Trim type: The **Trim type** drop-down list provides options to define how the trim applies to the blend in relation to the selected faces. These options are discussed below:

Wall: By selecting the **Wall** option, the blend is created along the entire wall edges of the selected **Side 1** and **Side 2** faces, see Figure 6.53.

6.53

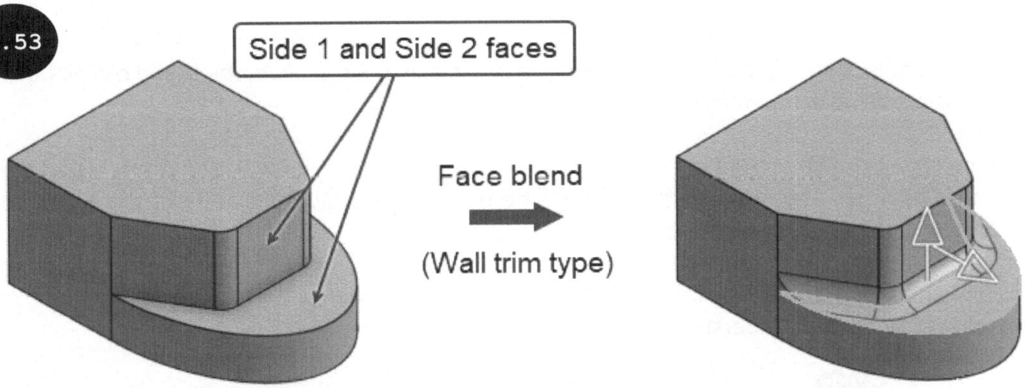

Short: By selecting the **Short** option, the blend is created as the shortest possible connection along the wall edges of the selected **Side 1** and **Side 2** faces, refer to Figure 6.54.

6.54

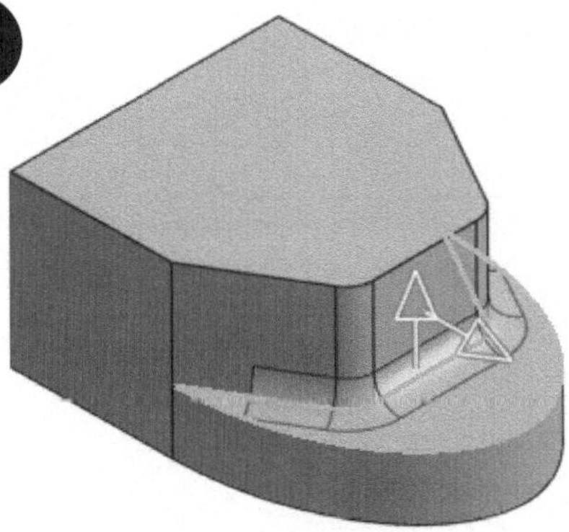

Long: By selecting the **Long** option, the blend is created as the longest possible connection along the wall edges of the selected **Side 1** and **Side 2** faces, refer to Figure 6.55. In this example, the **Detached** check box is selected to illustrate the longest possible connection between the faces.

No trim: By selecting the **No Trim** option, the blend is not trimmed and extends beyond the **Side 1** and **Side 2** faces, refer to Figure 6.56. In this example, the **Detached** check box is selected to illustrate the extension of the blend beyond the faces.

6.55

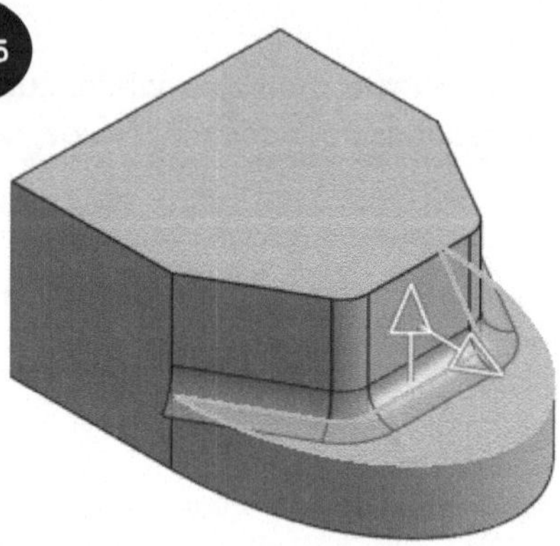

6.56

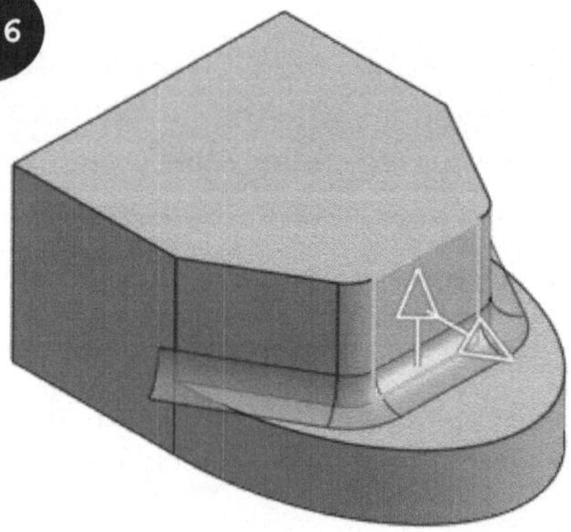

Detached: By default, the **Detached** check box is cleared. As a result, the blend merges with the existing model, and together they act as a single part or body.

On selecting the **Detached** check box, the blend does not merge with the model (part) and is created as a new, separate surface body. The resulting new surface body of the blend is also added to the Part List, located at the bottom of the Feature List on the left side of the graphics area. Figure 6.57 shows the Part List displaying a separate blend surface body, while Figure 6.58 shows the resulting new surface body of the blend after hiding the existing model or part for reference and better understanding.

6.57

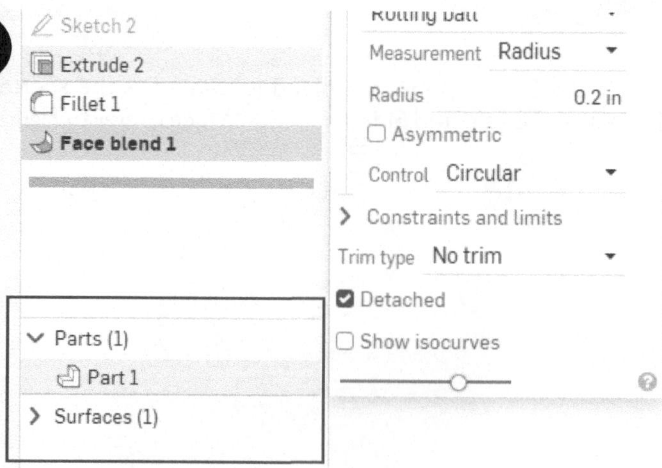

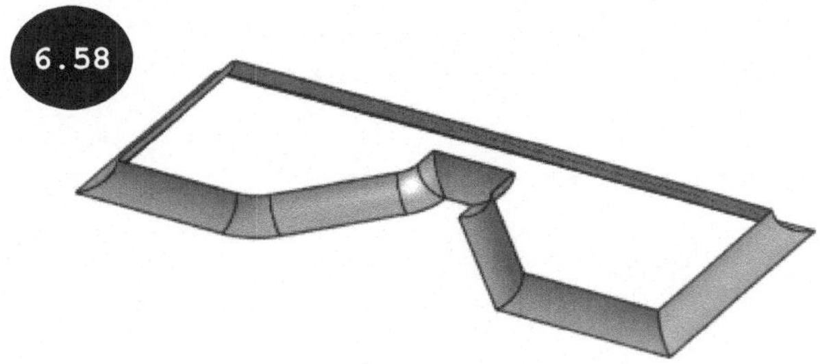

Tip: You can show or hide a part or body while designing by clicking the **Show** or **Hide** icon that appears next to the part name in the **Part List** when you hover the cursor over it.

Show isocurves: On selecting the **Show isocurves** check box, a mesh overlay is displayed on the blend preview, refer to Figure 5.59. In this mesh, you can adjust the number of isocurves per blend face by entering the desired value in the **Count** field that appears below the check box.

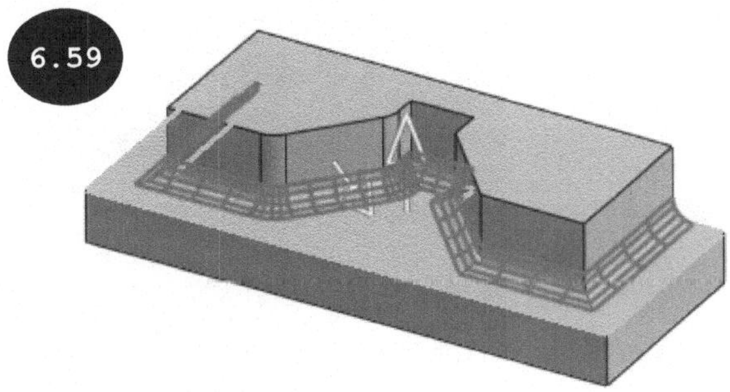

5. After specifying the required parameters, click the green checkmark to confirm the creation of the face blend and exit the dialog.

Creating Chamfers

A chamfer is a beveled face that is not perpendicular to its adjacent faces. It is used to remove the sharp edges of a model by adding angled surfaces or bevels. Figure 6.60 shows a model before and after creating a chamfer on its edge. The method for creating a chamfer is discussed below:

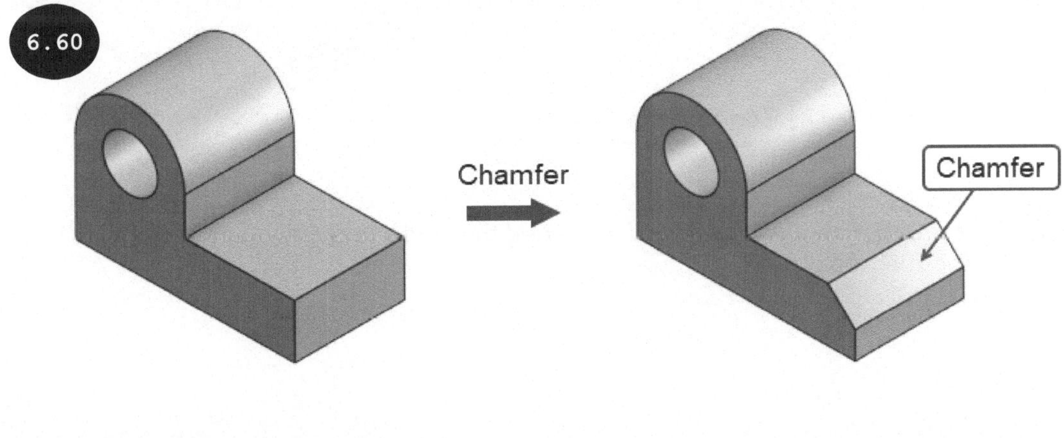

1. Click on the **Chamfer** tool in the **Feature** toolbar, see Figure 6.61. The **Chamfer** dialog appears with the **Edge** tab activated by default, see Figure 6.62.

6.61

6.62

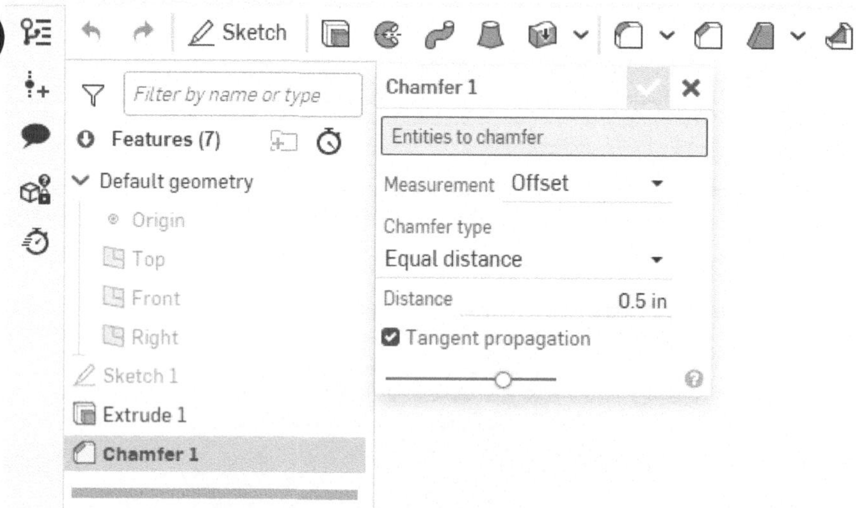

2. Select one or more edges or faces of the model as entities for chamfering. A preview of the chamfer appears on the selected edges or faces using default parameters, see Figure 6.63. In this figure, an edge is selected for chamfering. Note that when you select a face, a preview of the chamfer appears on all its edges.

6.63

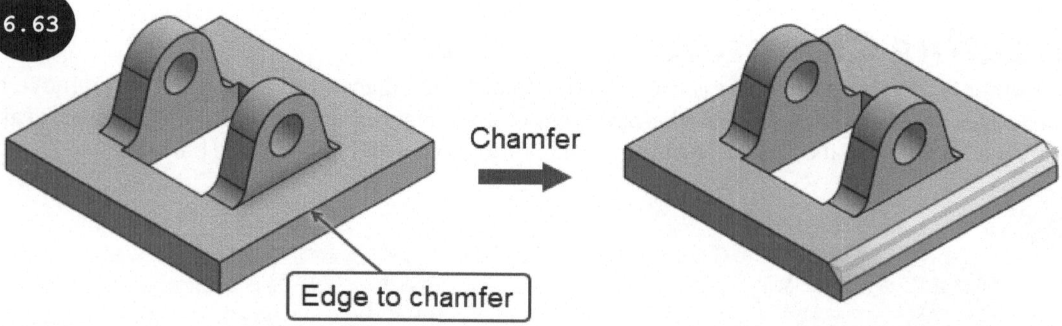

Tip: You can also draw a selection window around the model to quickly capture all edges within the specified area.

The options in the Chamfer dialog are discussed below:

Tangent propagation: By default, the **Tangent propagation** check box is selected, which causes all edges tangent to the selected edge to be automatically chamfered. Figure 6.64 shows the edge and the resulting chamfer preview with **Tangent propagation** enabled. In contrast, Figure 6.65 shows the preview when this check box is cleared.

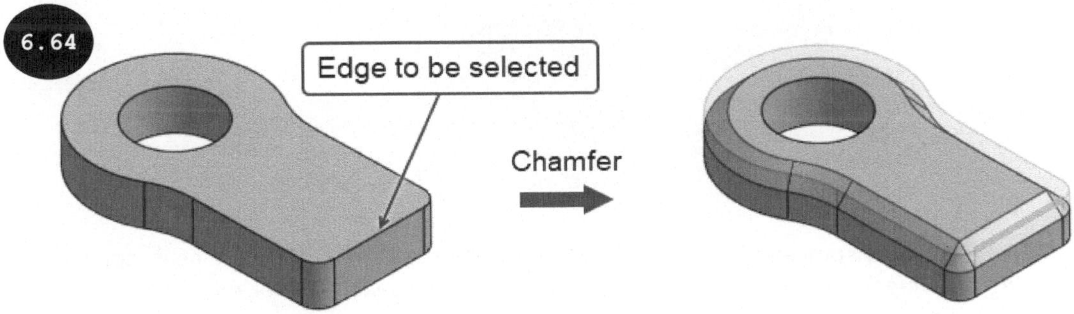

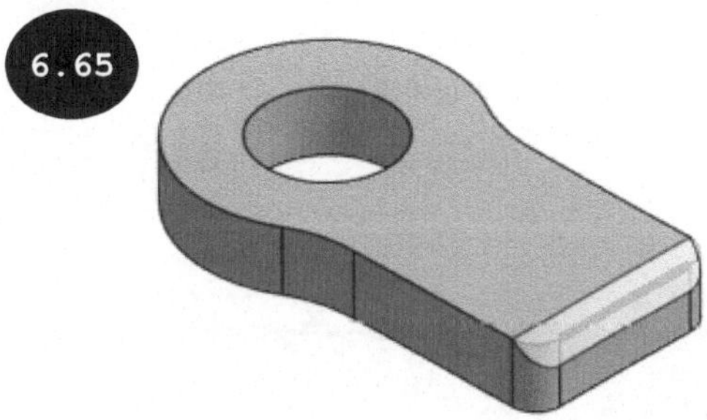

Tangent propagation check box cleared

Chamfer type: The options in the **Chamfer type** drop-down list are used to select the type of chamfer to be created. The options are discussed next.

Equal distance: The **Equal distance** option creates a chamfer that extends an equal distance on both sides of the chamfered edge, see Figure 6.66.

When this option is selected, the **Distance** field appears in the dialog, allowing you to specify a distance that will be applied equally on both sides of the chamfered edge.

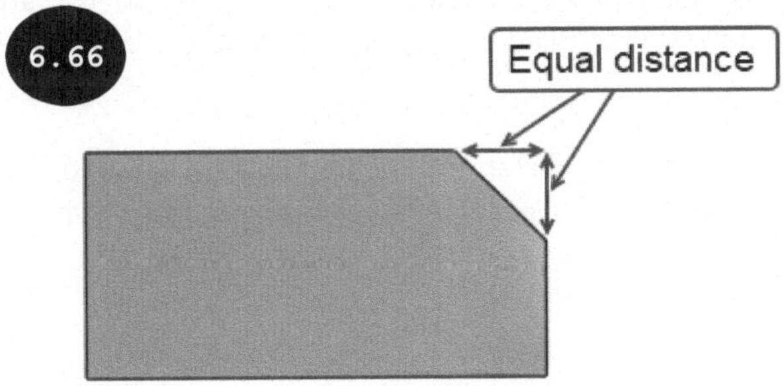

Two distances: The **Two distance** option creates a chamfer that extends with different distances on both sides of the chamfered edge, see Figure 6.67.

6.67

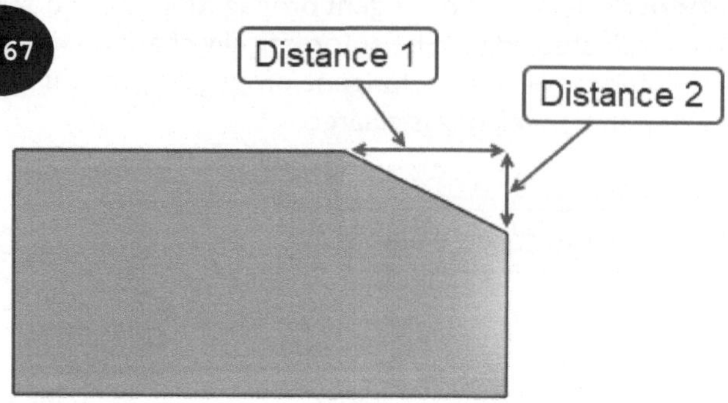

When the **Two Distances** option is selected, the **Distance 1** and **Distance 2** fields appear in the dialog, allowing you to specify different distance values for each side of the chamfered edge. If needed, you can also reverse the sides of the chamfer by clicking the **Opposite direction** button next to the **Distance 1** field in the dialog.

Distance and angle: The **Distance and angle** option creates a chamfer that extends with a specified distance in one direction and a specified angle in the other direction, see Figure 6.68.

6.68

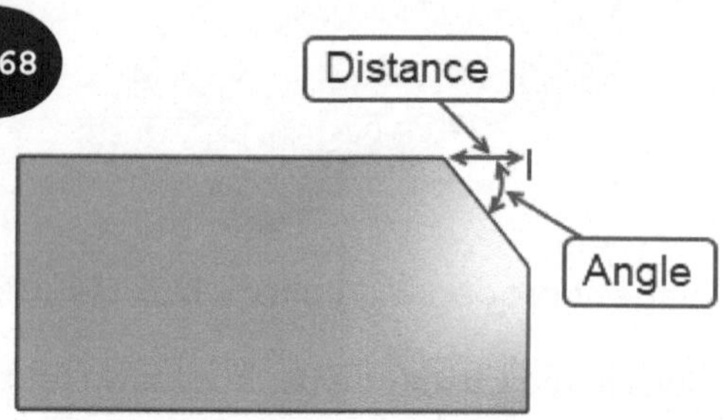

When the **Distance and angle** option is selected, the **Distance** and **Angle** fields appear in the dialog, allowing you to specify a distance value for one side and an angle value for the other side. If needed, you can reverse the sides of the chamfer by clicking the **Opposite direction** button next to the **Distance** field in the dialog.

Measurement: The options in the **Measurement** drop-down list are used to define the measurement type for non-planar adjacent faces of a chamfered edge. The options are discussed next.

Offset: The **Offset** option sets the distance specified in the **Distance** field from the start of the chamfered edge, see Figure 6.69. This option is especially useful when the chamfered edge has non-planar adjacent faces.

6.69

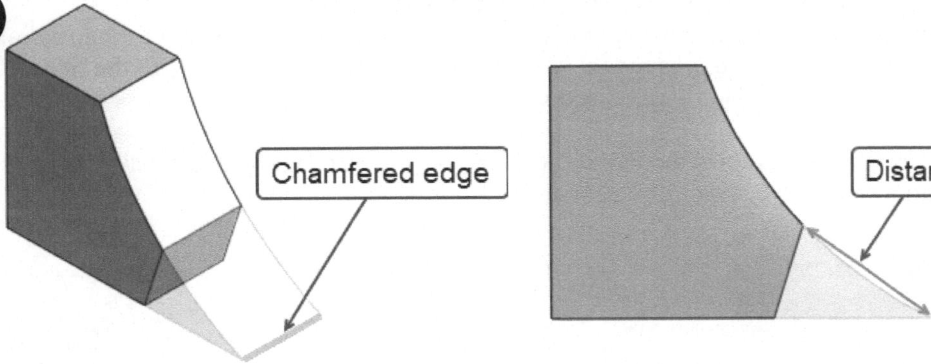

Tangent: The **Tangent** option sets the distance specified in the **Distance** field from the point where the tangents of the two adjacent faces of the chamfer intersect, see Figure 6.70. You can visualize the result of the option when the chamfered edge has non-adjacent faces.

6.70

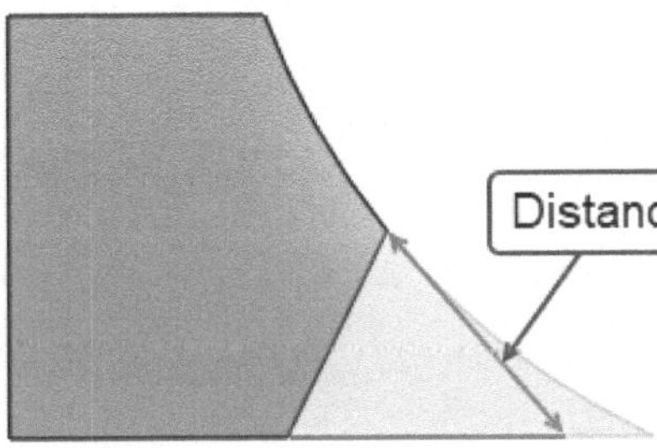

3. Select the required option (**Equal distance, Two distances**, or **Distance and angle**) in the **Chamfer type** drop-down list for creating a chamfer, as discussed above.

4. Enter either an equal distance, two distance values, or a distance and an angle value in the respective fields that appear, depending on the option selected in the **Chamfer type** drop-down list of the dialog.

5. After specifying the required parameters, click the green checkmark ✓ to confirm the creation of the chamfer and exit the dialog. The chamfer with the specified parameters is created to the selected edge or edges of the model.

Adding a Draft Angle

Adding a draft angle is the process of tapering one or more faces of a model (part) to ensure it can easily separate from its cast during manufacturing. In Onshape, the **Draft** tool allows you to add a draft angle to selected faces of a model using either a neutral plane or a parting line. The methods for adding different types of draft angle are discussed next.

Adding a Draft Angle Using a Neutral Plane

A neutral plane is defined as a plane or face that remains fixed and unchanged when a draft angle is applied to the selected faces of a model. The method for adding a draft angle to the selected faces of a model using a neutral plane is discussed below:

1. Click on the **Draft** tool in the **Feature** toolbar, see Figure 6.71. The **Draft** dialog appears with the **Neutral plane** tab activated, by default, see Figure 6.72.

6.71

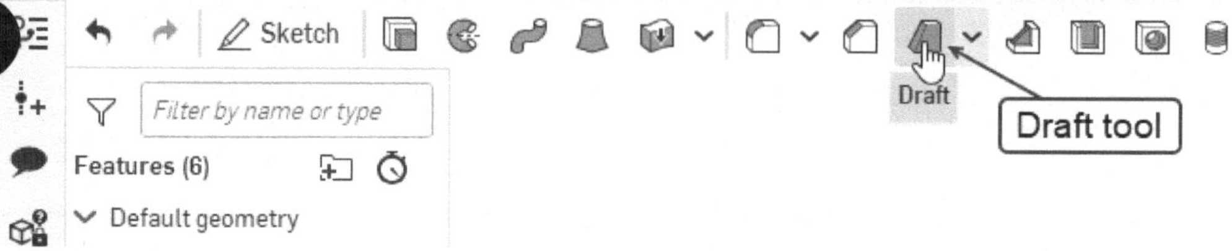

6.72

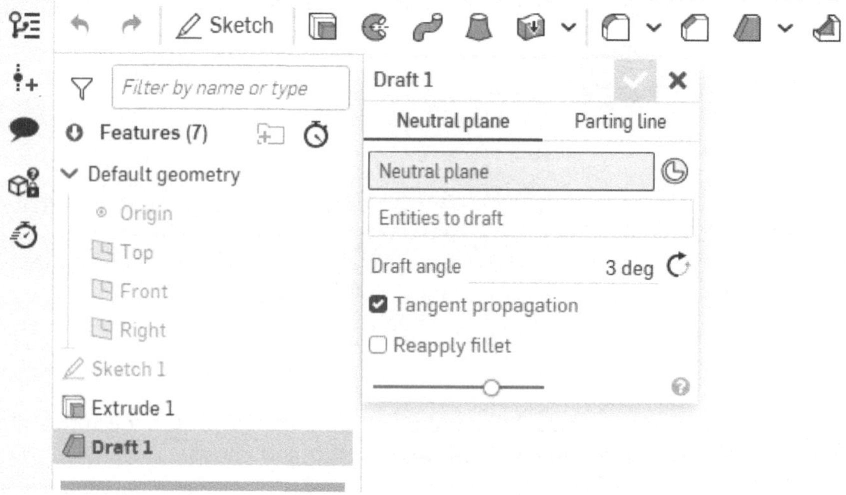

Neutral plane: The neutral plane, also known as the fixed plane, remains dimensionally stable or fixed when a draft angle is applied to the selected faces of a model.

2. Select a plane or a planar face as the neutral plane, refer to Figure 6.73. In this figure, the top planar face of the model is selected as the neutral plane. Once the neutral plane is selected, the **Entities to draft** field automatically activates.

6.73

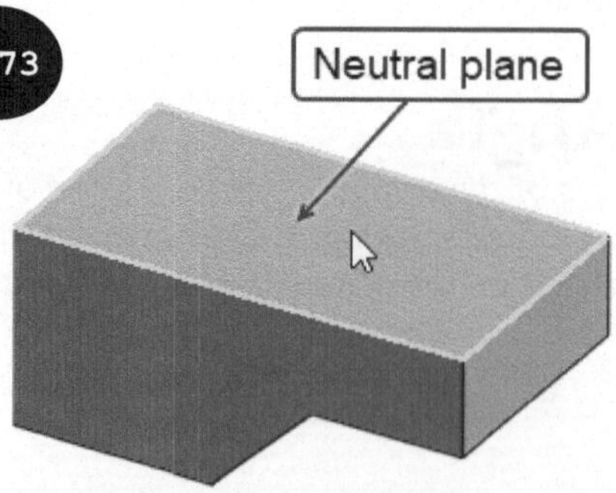

Now, you need to select faces for adding a draft angle.

3. Select one or more faces of the model to be drafted, see Figure 6.74. In this example, the front planar face of the model is selected as the draft face, and the default draft angle is applied to it.

6.74

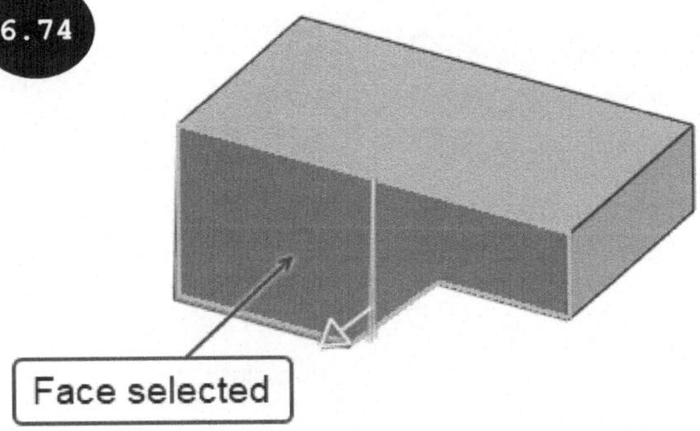

4. Enter the desired draft angle in the **Draft angle** field of the dialog box and press ENTER. The preview of the draft angle applied to the selected face(s) updates in the graphics area.

Tip: You can also drag the arrow that appears in the graphics area to dynamically adjust the draft angle.

5. Click the **Opposite direction** button next to the **Draft angle** field to reverse the draft angle direction from outward to inward, or vice versa, if needed.

Note: By default, the **Tangent Propagation** check box is selected, automatically drafting all faces tangent to the selected face. If needed, you can clear this check box to exclude tangent faces from the draft.

6. After specifying the required parameters, click the green checkmark to confirm the addition of the draft angle to the selected face(s) and exit the dialog.

Adding a Draft Angle Using a Parting Line

A parting line is defined as a fixed boundary line used to apply a draft angle on one or both sides of the line, with either similar or different draft angles on each side. The method for adding a draft angle using a parting line is discussed below:

1. Click on the **Draft** tool in the **Feature** toolbar, see Figure 6.75. The **Draft** dialog appears.

6.75

2. Click to activate the **Parting line** tab in the **Draft** dialog, see Figure 6.76.

6.76

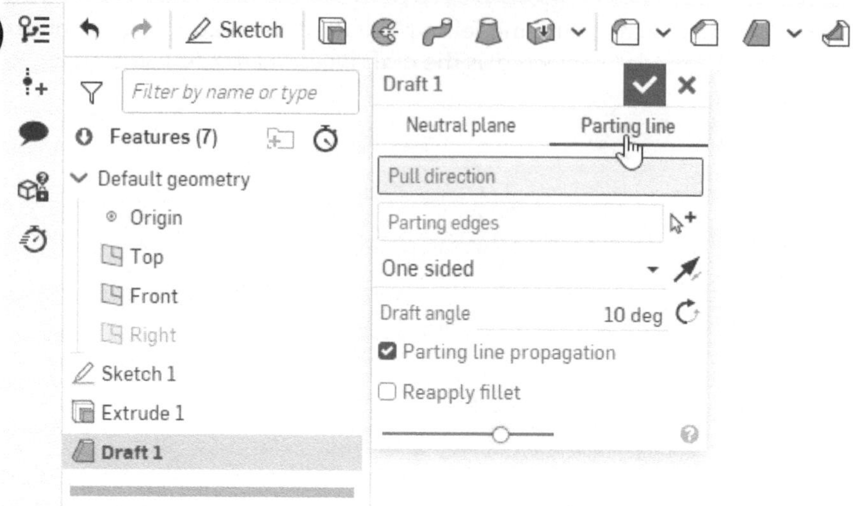

Now, you need to first define the pulling direction for adding a draft angle.

3. Select an edge, plane, or planar face to define the pulling direction for adding the draft, see Figure 6.77. In this figure, the top planar face of the model is selected, setting the pulling direction normal to the chosen face. Once the pulling direction is defined, the **Parting edges** field automatically activates

6.77

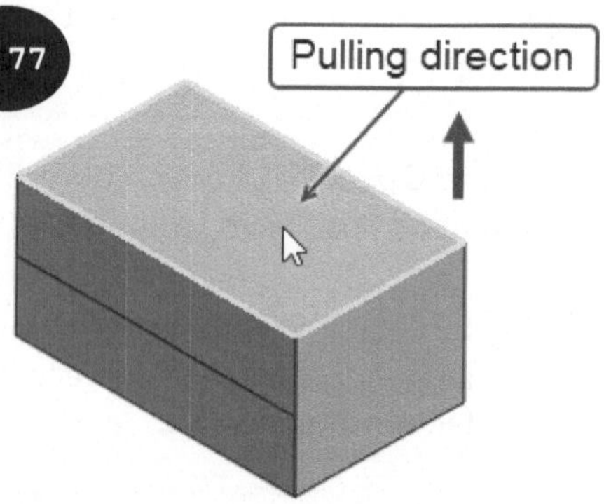

Now, you need to select a parting line.

4. Select an edge of the model as the parting line, see Figure 6.78. A preview of the draft is applied on either side of the parting line (see Figure 6.79), since the **One sided** option is selected in the **Sides** drop-down list of the dialog, by default.

6.78

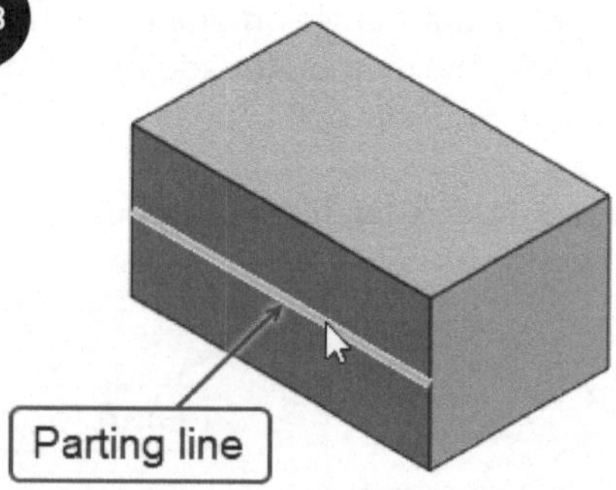

6.79

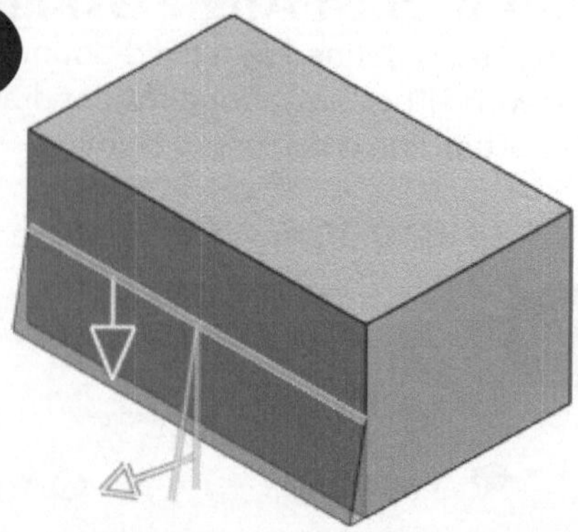

Note: In the figures above, the parting line (edge) is created by splitting the face of the model. You will learn how to split one or more faces of a model in later chapters.

One sided: By default, the **One sided** option is selected in the **Sides** drop-down list of the **Draft** dialog, allowing you to add a draft of a specified angle on one side of the selected parting line, refer to Figure 6.79. You can define the required draft angle in the **Draft angle** field of the dialog.

If needed, you can reverse the draft to the other side of the parting line by clicking the **Switch face** button available next to the **Sides** drop-down list.

Symmetric: The **Symmetric** option applies the specified draft angle symmetrically to both sides of the parting line, see Figure 6.80.

6.80

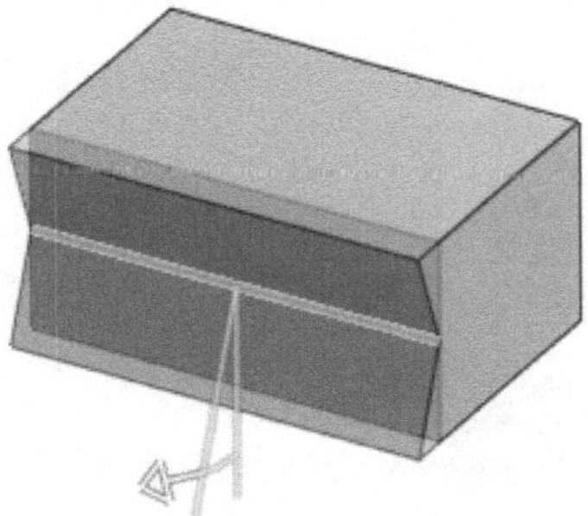

Two sided: The **Two sided** option allows you to apply different draft angles to both sides of the parting line, see Figure 6.81. When you select this option, the **Draft angle** and **Second draft angle** fields appear in the dialog, where you can specify different draft angles for each side of the parting line. If needed, you can also reverse the draft direction of each side from inward to outward, or vice versa, by clicking the **Opposite direction** button next to these fields.

6.81

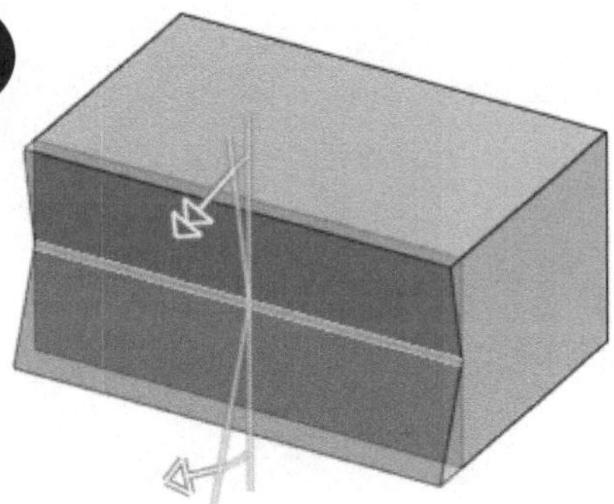

5. Select the required option (**One sided**, **Symmetric**, or **Two sided**) in the **Sides** drop-down list of the dialog, as discussed above.

6. Specify the draft angle in the **Draft angle** field of the dialog, depending on the option selected in the **Sides** drop-down list. You can also drag the arrow handle that appears in the graphics area to dynamically adjust the draft angle.

7. After specifying the required parameters, click the green checkmark ✓ to confirm the addition of the draft with respect to the parting line and exit the dialog.

Creating a Rib Feature

Rib features act as supporting elements and are typically used to increase the strength of a model. You can create a rib feature from an open or closed sketch entity by adding thickness in a specified direction, see Figure 6.82. This figure shows an open sketch created on the Front plane and a preview of the resulting rib feature parallel to the sketching plane. In Onshape, you can use the **Rib** tool to create a rib feature that is either normal or parallel to the sketching plane. The method for creating a rib feature normal or parallel to the sketching plane is discussed below:

6.82

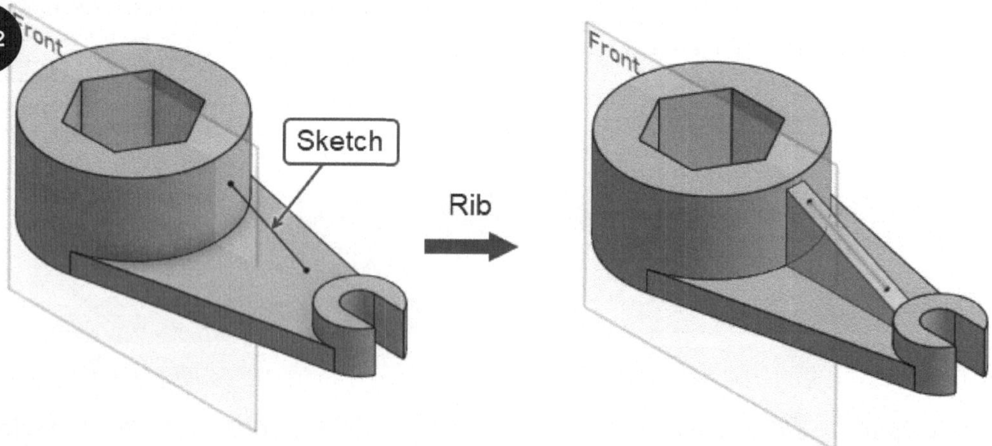

1. Click on the **Rib** tool in the **Feature** toolbar, see Figure 6.83. The **Rib** dialog appears, see Figure 6.84.

6.83

6.84

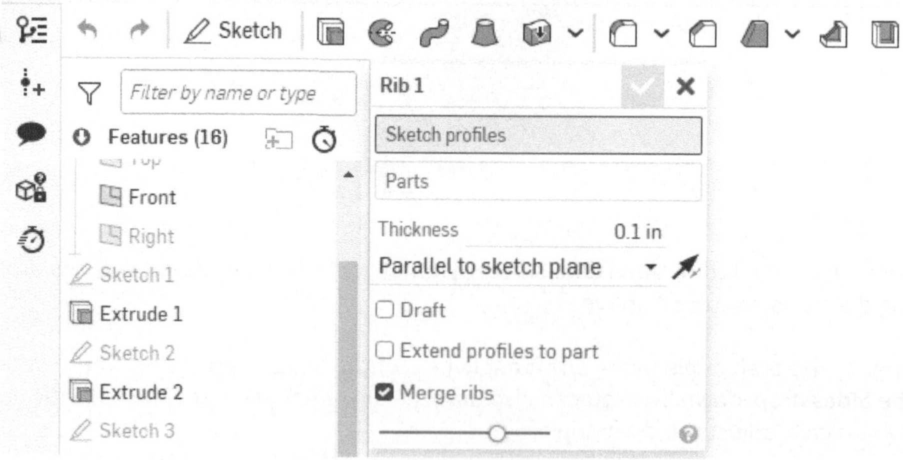

2. Select an open or closed sketch entity as the profile to create a rib feature, refer to Figure 6.85. In this figure, an open sketch entity is selected for creating the rib feature. Note that the projection of both ends of the open sketch entity should lie on the geometry of the model.

Note: You can also select multiple sketch entities as the profiles to create a rib feature of a specified thickness. In Figure 6.86, multiple sketch entities of a sketch are selected.

6.85

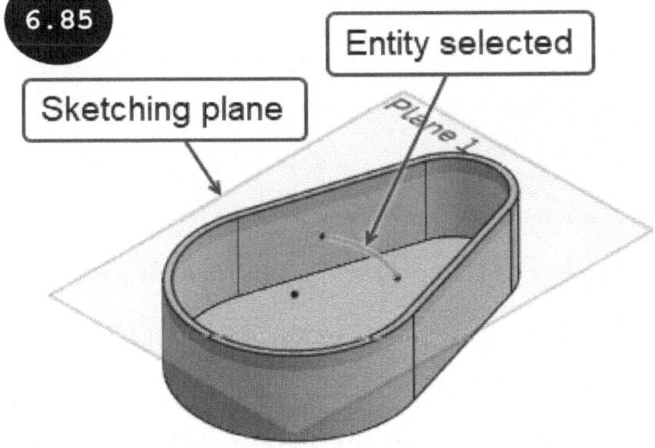

6.86

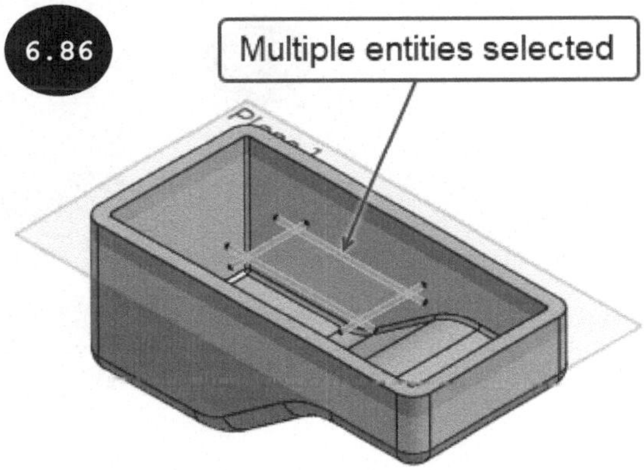

3. After selecting one or more sketch entities, enter the required thickness value for the rib feature in the **Thickness** field of the dialog and press ENTER.

4. Select the required option (**Parallel to sketch plane** or **Normal to sketch plane**) in the **Rib extrusion direction** drop-down list of the dialog. The preview of the rib feature appears either parallel to the sketching plane or normal to the sketching plane depending upon the option selected, see Figures 6.87 and 6.88.

6.87

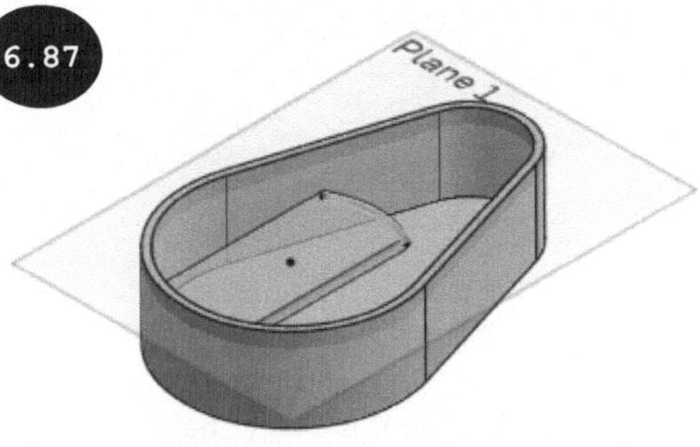

Parallel to sketch plane

6.88

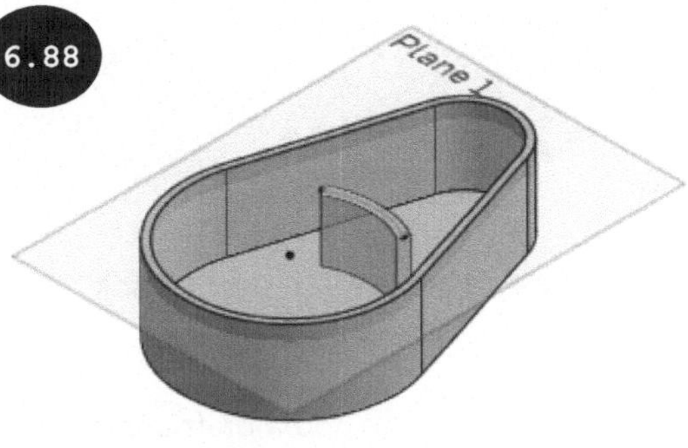

Normal to sketch plane

Note: If the preview of the rib feature does not appear, you may need to reverse its extension direction toward the model geometry by clicking the **Opposite direction** button.

Additionally, ensure that the extension of the selected sketch entity ends, which is being used to create the rib feature, lies completely on the model's geometry.

Tip: In the figures above, the sketch is placed on a construction plane offset downward from the model's top planar face. This downward offset ensures that the extensions of the sketch entity ends lie on the model's geometry.

5. Select the **Extend profiles to part** check box to extend the open ends of the sketch entity or entities up to the intersection with the model geometry, see Figure 6.89.

6.89

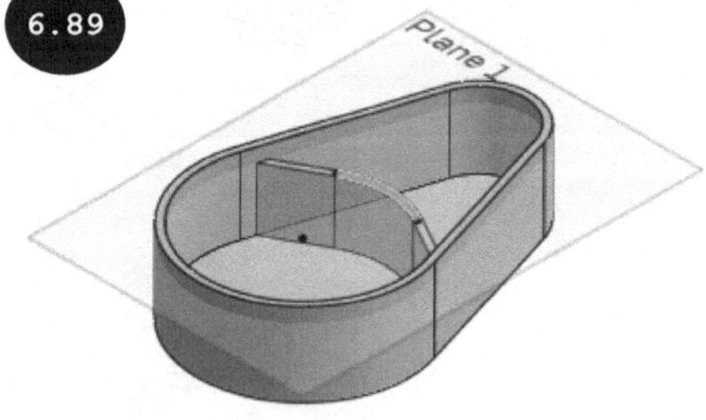

Figures 6.90 and 6.91 show another example of a rib feature, with the **Extend profiles to part** check box cleared in Figure 6.90 and selected in Figure 6.91. In this example, multiple sketch entities are used as the profiles for creating the rib feature. Additionally, the projection type is defined as normal to the sketching plane.

6.90

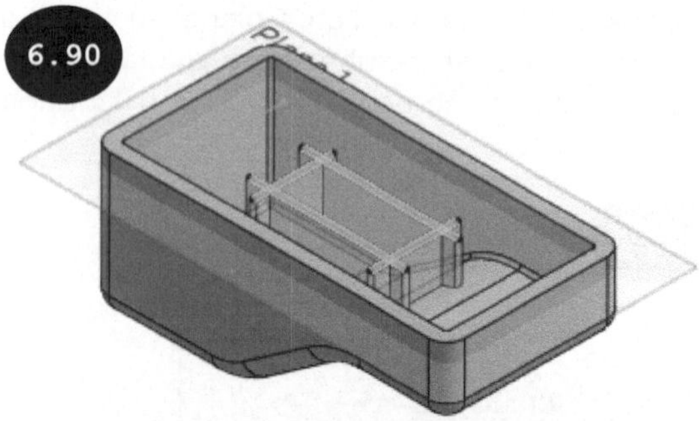

Extend profiles to part check box is cleared

6.91

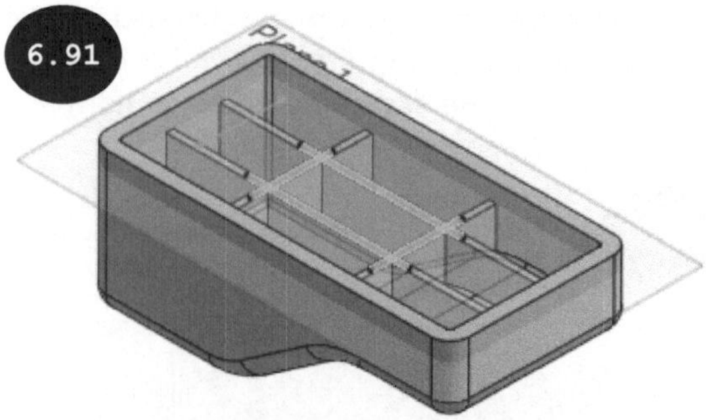

Extend profiles to part check box is selected

6. If needed, you can add a draft angle to the rib feature by selecting the **Draft** check box in the dialog. Once selected, you can enter the desired draft angle in the **Draft angle** field that appears next to this check box.

7. Ensure that the **Merge ribs** check box is selected in the dialog box to merge the resulting rib feature with the model. If this check box is cleared, the rib feature will be created as a separate body or part.

8. After specifying the required parameters, click the green checkmark ✓ to confirm the creation of the rib feature and exit the dialog.

Creating a Shell Feature

A shell feature creates a thin-walled structure with uniform thickness by removing one or more faces from a model, as shown in Figure 6.92. In this example, the top planar face is removed to create the shell. Additionally, this feature enables you to convert a solid model into a hollow one with consistent wall thickness. The method for creating a shell feature is discussed below:

6.92

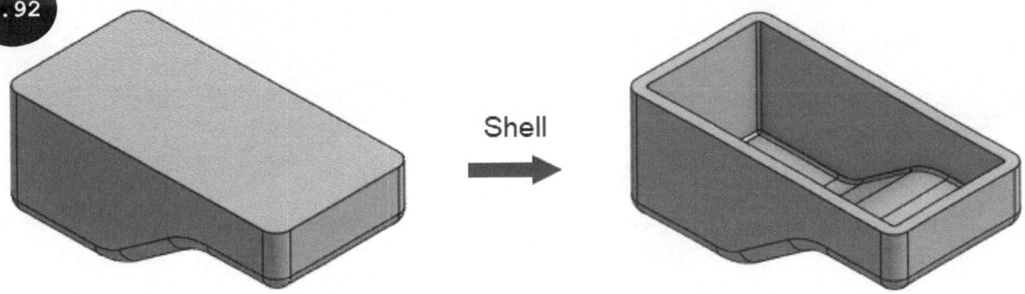

1. Click on the **Shell** tool in the **Feature** toolbar, see Figure 6.93. The **Shell** dialog appears, see Figure 6.94.

6.93

6.94

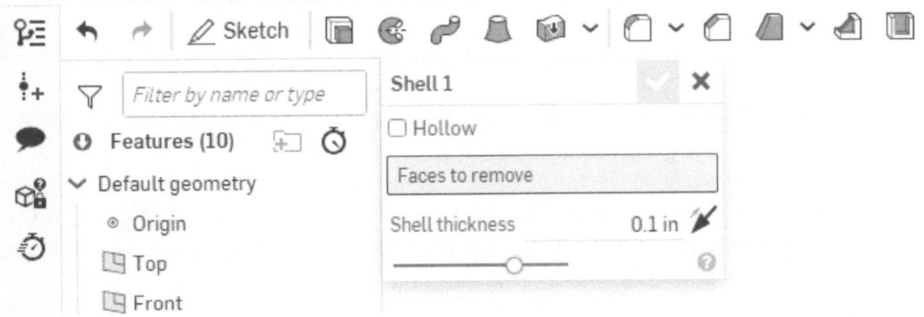

Hollow: By default, the **Hollow** check box is cleared, allowing you to select one or more faces of a model to remove and create a thin-walled structure with a specified thickness. To create a hollow model, select this **Hollow** check box, then select the part or model to hollow it out from the inside with a specified thickness. The thickness can be defined in the **Shell thickness** field of the dialog.

2. Ensure the **Hollow** check box is cleared to create a shell feature by removing one or more faces. To create a hollow model, remember to select this check box, as explained above.

3. Select one or more faces of the model to remove, see Figure 6.95. After selecting the face(s), a preview of the shell feature with the specified thickness appears in the graphics area, see Figure 6.96.

6.95

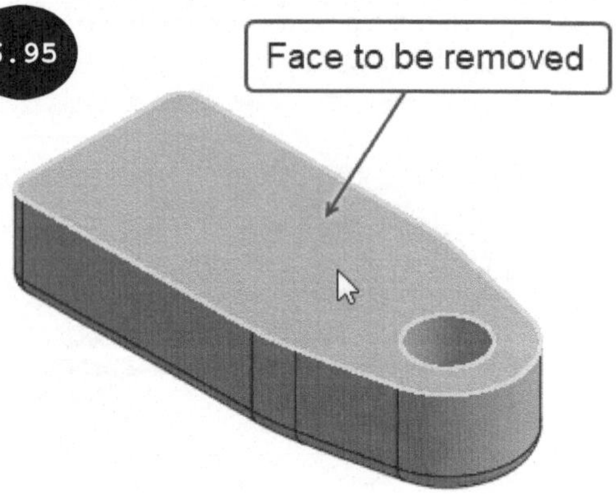

6.96

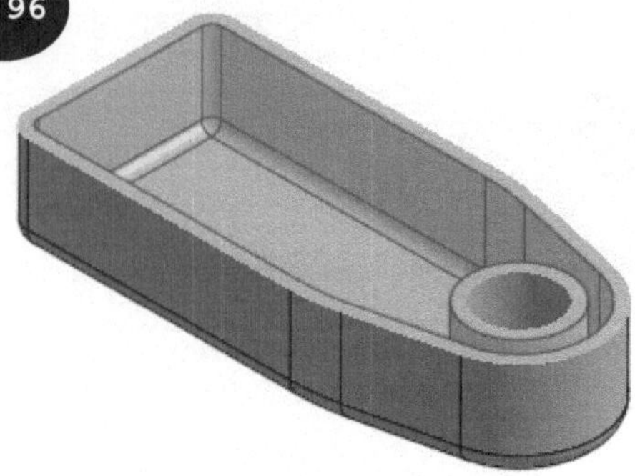

Figure 6.97 shows an example where multiple faces of the model are selected for removal.

6.97

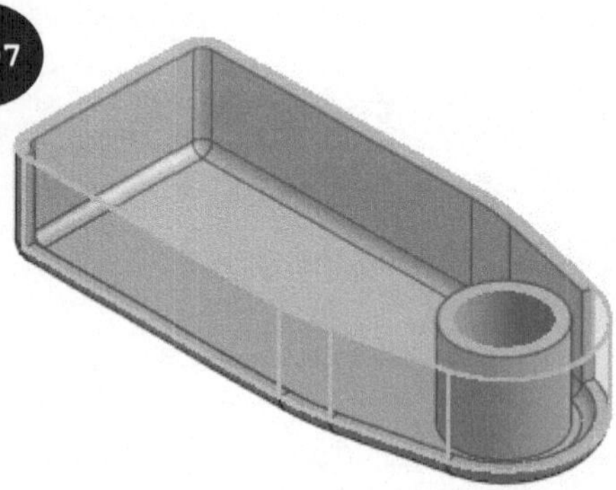

4. Enter the required thickness in the **Shell thickness** field of the dialog and press ENTER. The preview updates in the graphics area accordingly.

5. After specifying the required parameters, click the green checkmark ✓ to confirm the creation of the shell feature and exit the dialog. Figure 6.98 shows the shell model after removing the top planar face, while Figure 6.99 shows the model with multiple faces removed.

6.98

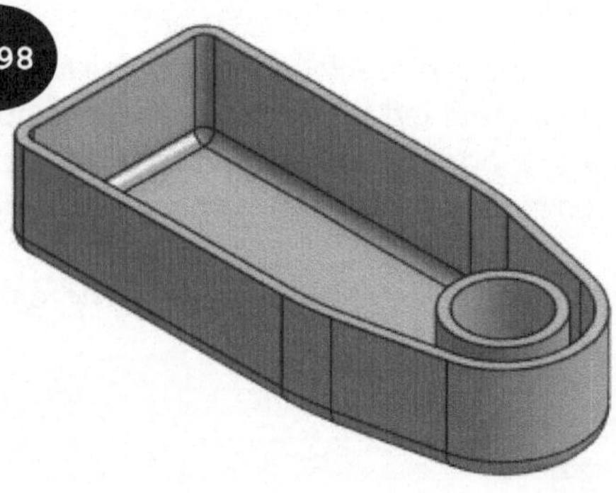

6.99

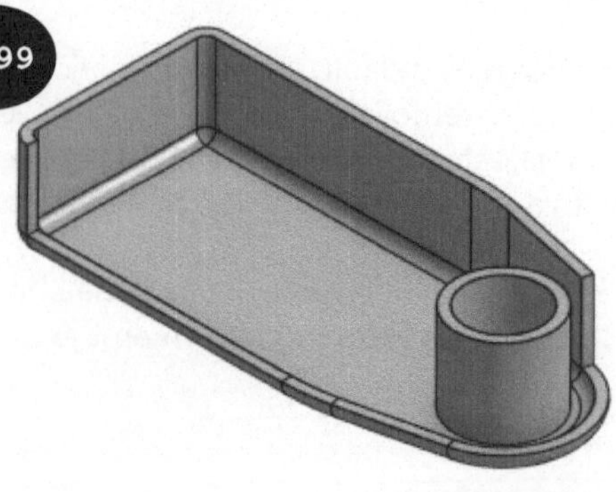

Creating Holes

In Onshape, you can create standard or customized holes, including simple, counterbore, and countersink types. The placement of these holes can be defined using either sketch points or mate connectors. Figure 6.100 illustrates a counterbore hole positioned using a sketch point. The method for creating different types of holes is discussed below:

6.100

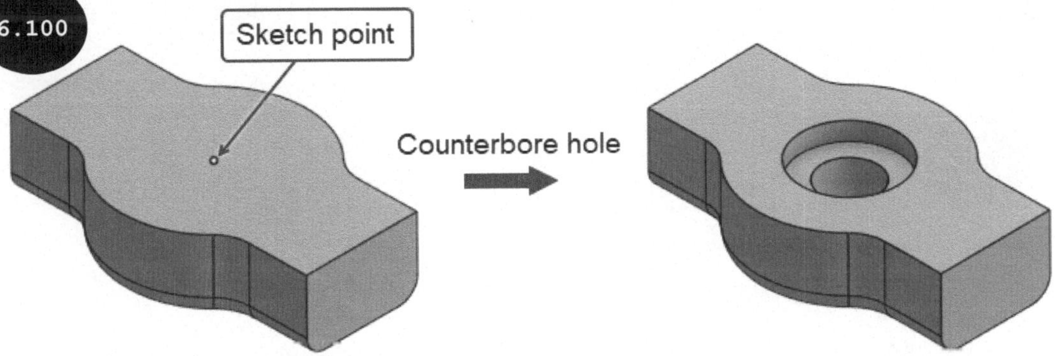

1. Create one or more sketch points on the face of the model to define the positions of the holes.

Note: To define the position of a hole using a sketch point, first create the sketch point on the face of the model. To do this, access the **Sketch** toolbar by selecting a planar face as the sketching plane. Then, activate the **Point** tool in the **Sketch** toolbar, see Figure 6.101. Next, click on the planar face to create a sketch point. You can create multiple sketch points by clicking the left mouse button one by one, refer to Figure 6.102. In this figure, four sketch points are created at the center of their respective semi-circular edges. After creating one or more sketch points, you can apply dimensions to define their position. Once done, switch back to the Part Studio environment by clicking the green checkmark ✓ in the **Sketch** dialog.

6.101

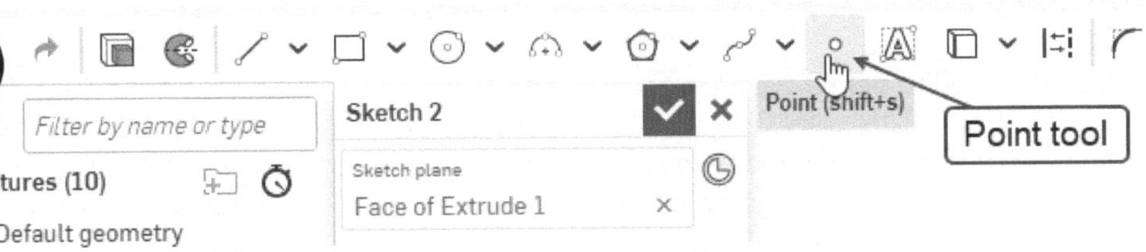

6.102

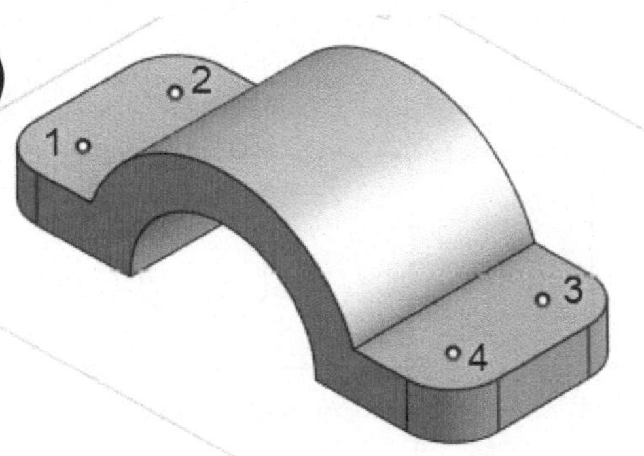

2. After creating sketch points to define the positions of the holes, click on the **Hole** tool in the **Feature** toolbar, see Figure 6.103. The **Hole** dialog appears with **Inch** and **Metric** tabs at the top, see Figure 6.104.

6.103

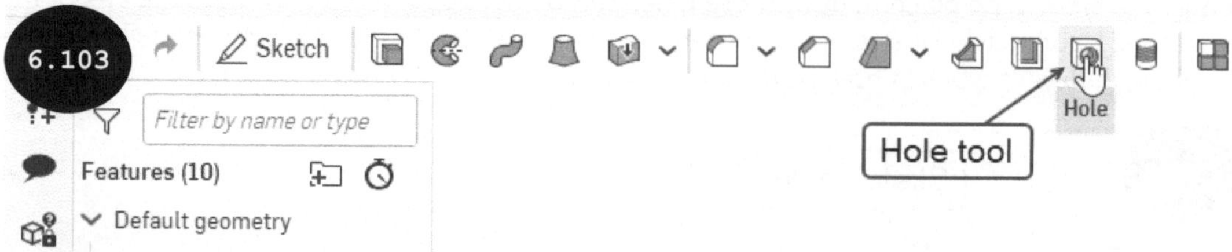

6.104

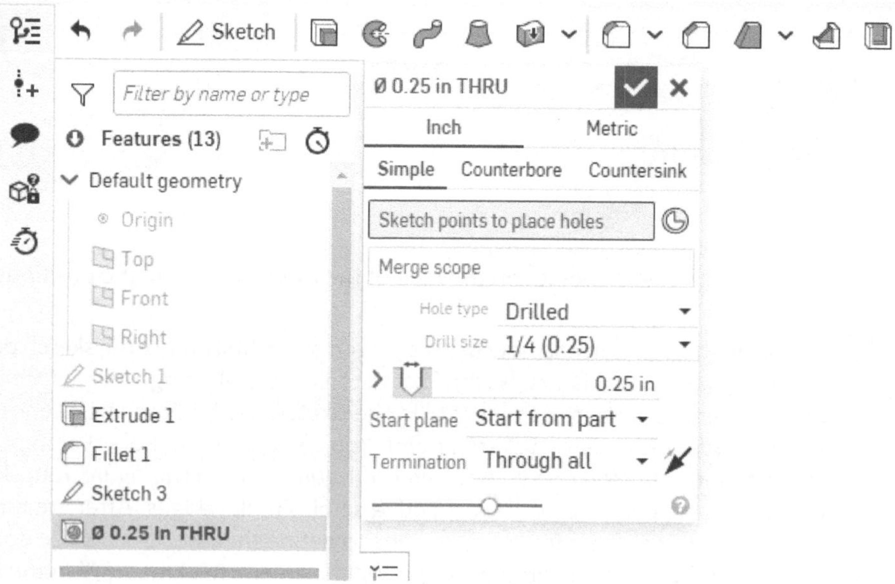

3. Activate the appropriate tab, **Inch** or **Metric**, to define the hole parameters in the desired unit system. By default, the Inch tab is selected, enabling you to define hole parameters in inches.

Now, you need to define the type of hole to be created.

4. Click to activate the required hole type: **Simple**, **Counterbore**, or **Countersink** in the **Hole** dialog. Figure 6.105 illustrates an example of a simple hole, a counterbore hole, and a countersink hole, shown from the front view with hidden edges visible.

6.105

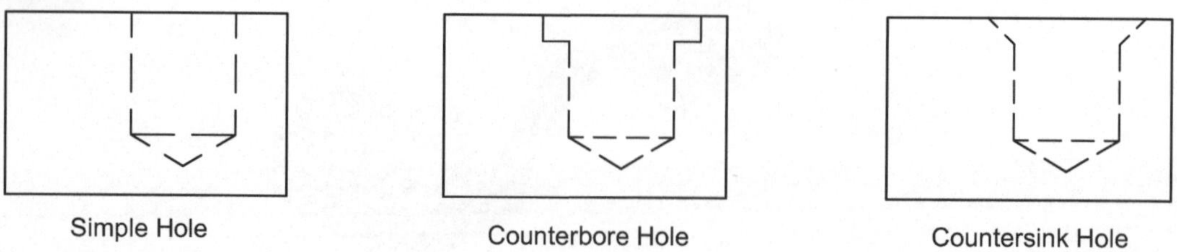

After selecting the type of hole to be created, you need to define the position of the hole using either a sketch point or a mate connector.

5. Select the sketch point in the graphics area, see Figure 6.106. A preview of the hole appears, centered at the selected sketch point, with default parameters, see Figure 6.107. You can select one or more sketch points one by one. Note that the type of hole depends on whether the **Simple**, **Counterbore**, or **Countersink** tab is selected in the **Hole** dialog. Figure 6.107 displays the preview of a simple hole.

6.106

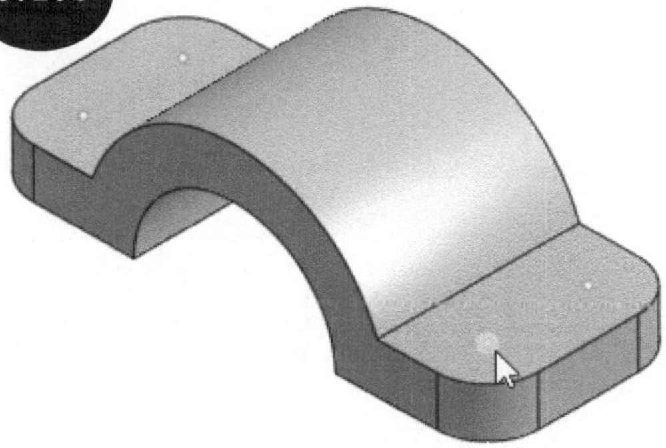

6.107

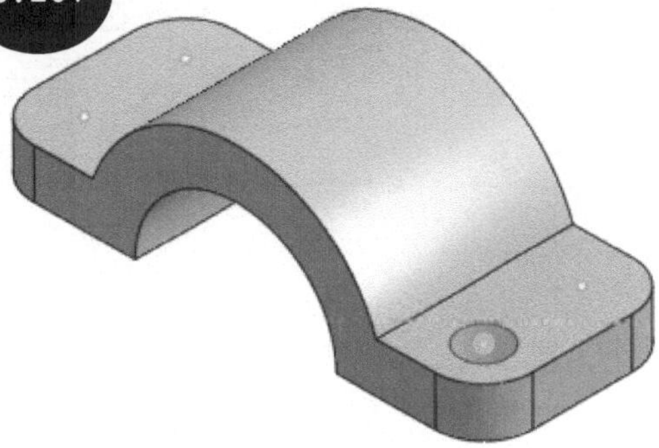

Note: To define the position of a hole using a mate connector, click the **Select mate connectors** button next to the **Sketch points to place holes** field. Then, move the cursor over a face or edge of the model. The face or edge highlights, revealing all of its snap points, see Figure 6.108. Also, the mate connector appears attaches to the cursor tip on the highlighted face or edge. Position the mate connector at the desired snap point by clicking the left mouse button. The hole position is defined at the specified mate connector, refer to Figure 6.109. This figure shows the preview of a countersink hole.

6.108

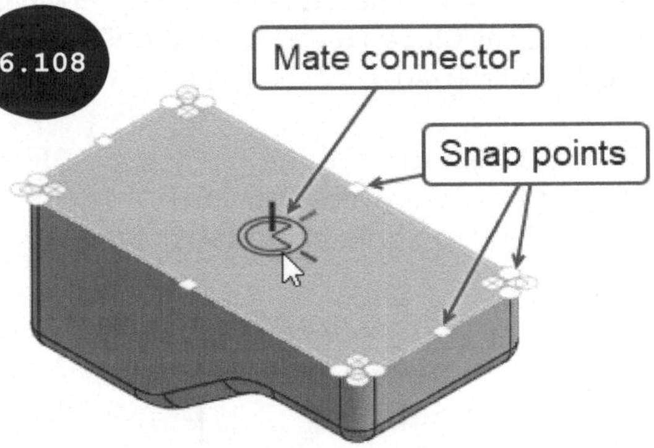

6.109

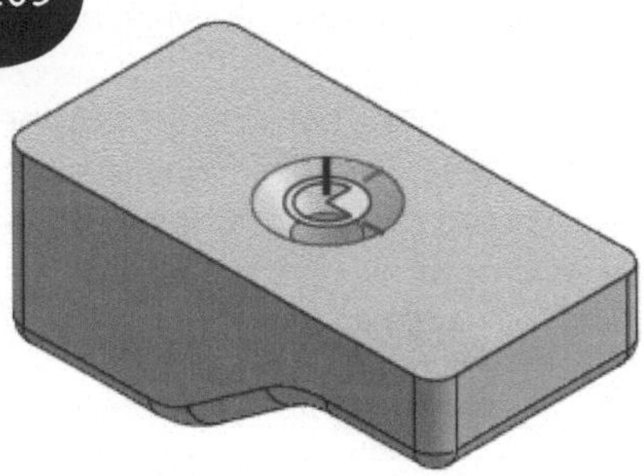

Tip: You can also select the endpoints of sketch entities, such as the endpoints of a line, the center point of a circle, and other similar points, to define the position of the hole.

After defining the position of the hole, you need to define its parameters. The available options in the dialog for defining hole parameters depend on the selected hole type.

Hole type: The **Hole type** drop-down list lets you select the type of hole to create, such as a drilled hole, clearance hole, or tapped hole, by choosing the appropriate option, see Figure 6.110. For a simple hole, an additional option, **PEM®**, is available for creating holes designed for PennEngineering® fasteners. The associated parameters for each hole type are discussed below:

6.110

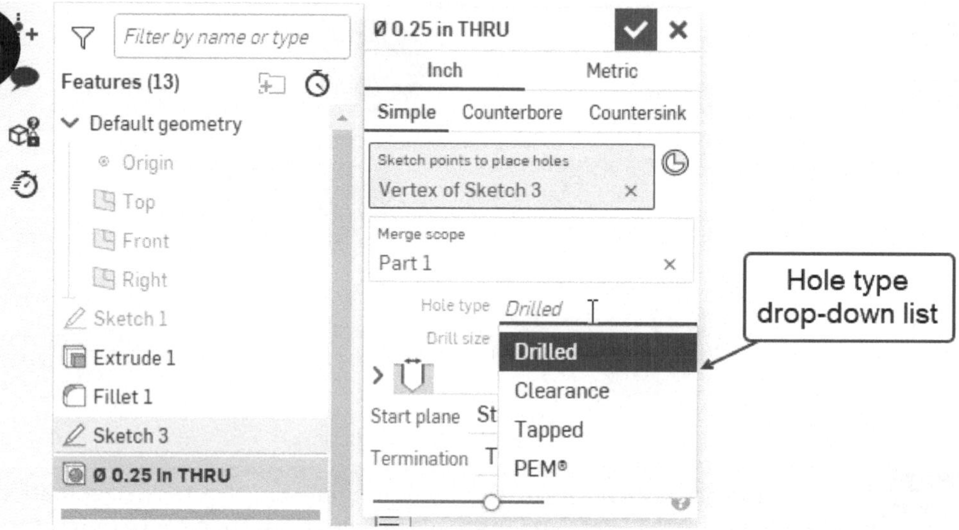

Drilled: This option creates a drilled hole. When the **Drilled** option is selected, the **Drill size** drop-down list becomes available in the **Hole** dialog. It enables you to select the appropriate standard drill size to create the hole, ensuring precision and compliance with design specifications.

Clearance: This option creates a clearance hole. When the **Clearance** option is selected, the **Size** and **Fastener fit** drop-down lists become available in the **Hole** dialog. The **Size** drop-down list allows you to select the appropriate clearance size for the hole. The **Fastener fit** drop-down list lets you choose the type of fastener fit, with options such as **Close**, **Free**, **Close (ASME)**, **Normal (ASME)**, and **Loose (ASME)**, based on the desired fit and tolerance for the fastener.

Tapped: This option creates a tapped hole with threads. When selected, the **Tap type**, **Size**, **Pitch**, and **Fastener fit** drop-down lists become available in the **Hole** dialog, see Figure 6.111. Additionally, the **Thread class** check box becomes available, allowing you to toggle the visibility of the **Thread class** drop-down list.

6.111

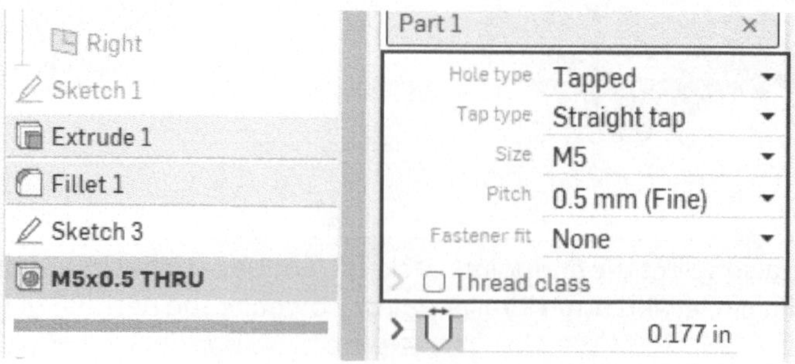

These drop-down lists let you define the tap type (**Straight tap** or **Tapered pipe tap**), tapped hole size, thread pitch or threads per inch, and the fastener fit type for the tapped hole. Note that the **Fastener fit** drop-down list is available only when **Straight tap** is selected as the tap type.

To define a thread class for the threads of the tapped hole, select the **Thread class** check box, then choose the desired thread class from the drop-down list that appears below the check box in the dialog.

PEM®: This option creates a hole specifically designed for PennEngineering® fasteners. This option is available only when creating a simple hole. When selected, the **Hole** dialog displays additional drop-down lists for specifying parameters such as fastener, fastener type, size, and fastener fit. These selections enable you to configure the hole to meet PennEngineering® fastener requirements.

Diameter: By default, the hole diameter is automatically determined based on the standard hole size and other specified parameters, see Figure 6.112. In this example, the diameter is set to 0.257 inches, derived from the standard hole size of 1/4 inch and the selected fastener fit type, which is Close. However, if required, you can customize the hole diameter directly in the **Diameter** field to meet your specific requirements.

6.112

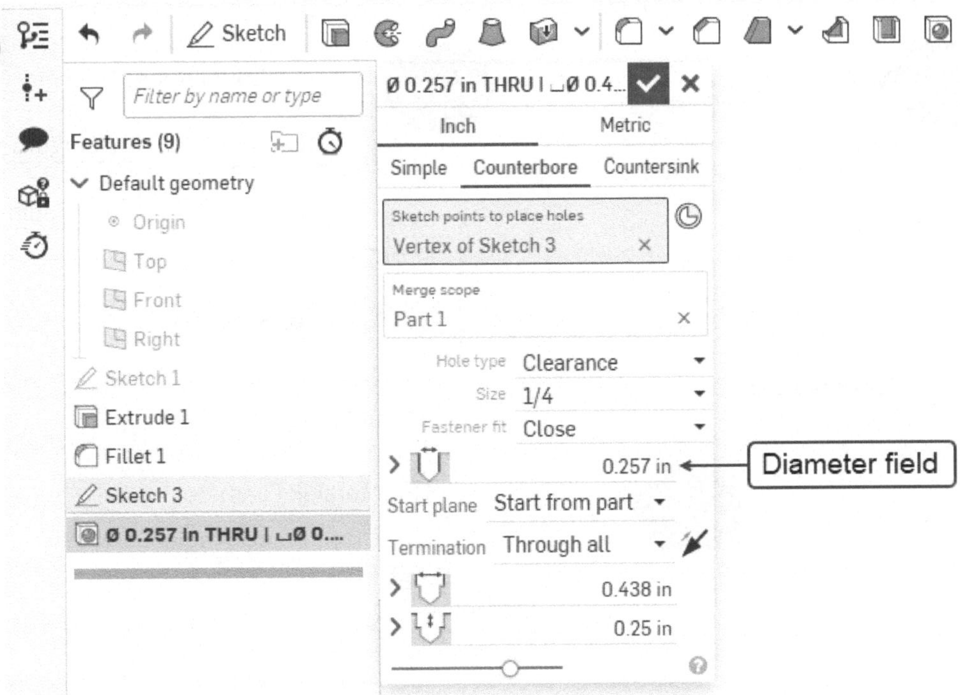

Note: If needed, you can control or define the precision and tolerance for the hole diameter. To do this, expand the **Diameter** rollout in the **Hole** dialog, see Figure 6.113. Then, specify the desired precision, tolerance type, and corresponding tolerance values for the hole diameter using the available drop-down lists.

6.113

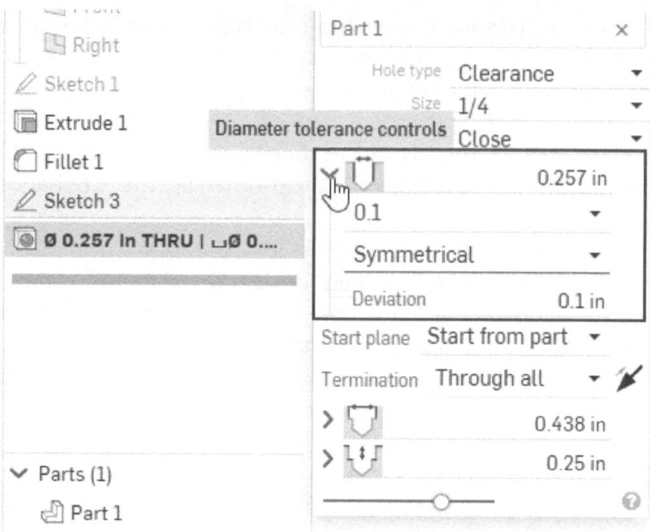

Similarly, you can control or adjust the other parameters of the hole in the corresponding fields, which appear based on the selected hole type. Figures 6.114 to 6.116 illustrate the specific parameters for simple, counterbore, and countersink holes.

6.114

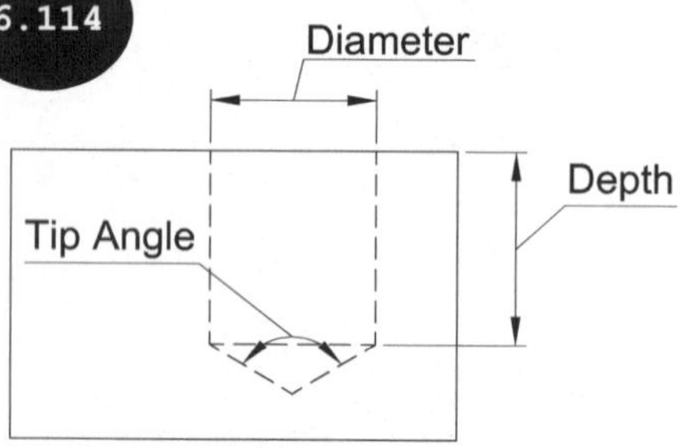

Simple Hole

6.115

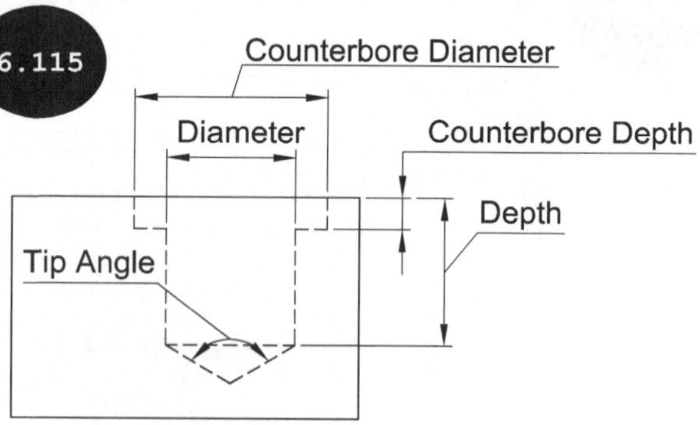

Counterbore Hole

6.116

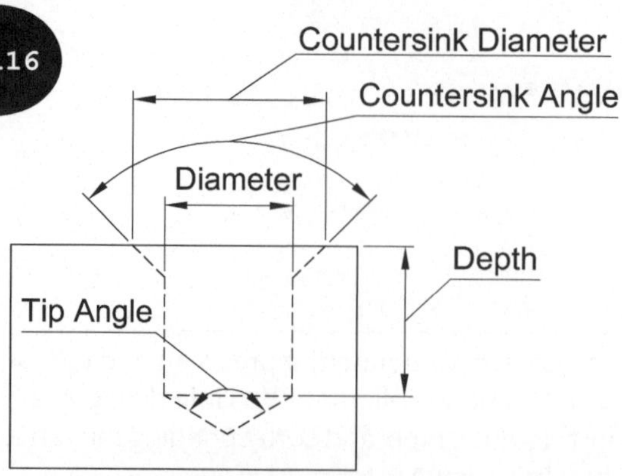

Countersink Hole

Start plane: The options in the **Start plane** drop-down list allow you to define the hole's starting condition. By default, the **Start from part** option is selected, meaning the hole begins from the closest intersection face of the part, regardless of the sketching plane. Figure 6.117 illustrates this concept, where the endpoints of the line define the hole's position. Although the line is created on the topmost planar face of the model, each hole starts from its respective part face.

6.117

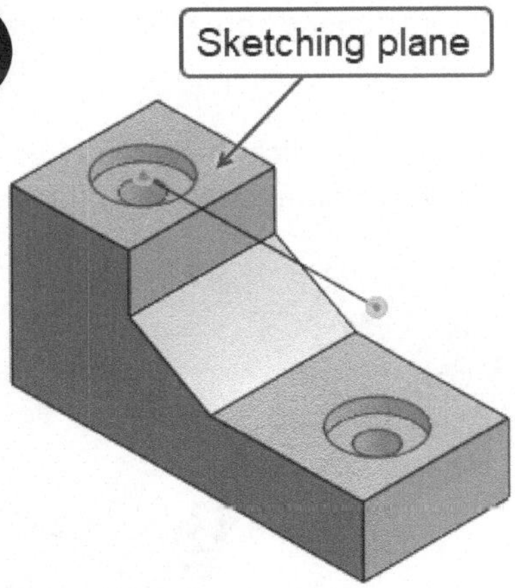

When you select the **Start from sketch plane** option, the hole creation begins from the sketching plane, as shown in Figure 6.118. In the figure, the counterbore section of the second hole is not visible due to the offset distance between the sketching plane and the part face.

6.118

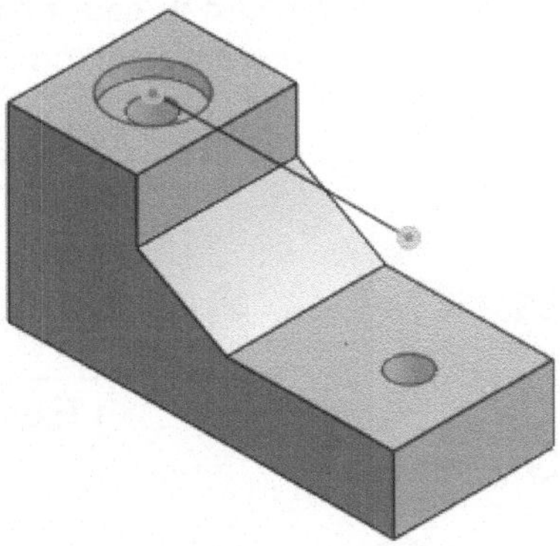

When you select the **Start from selected plane** option, the **Hole start plane or mate connector** field appears, allowing you to choose a plane or a planar face of the model to define the starting condition for the hole.

Termination: The options in the **Termination** drop-down list allow you to define the hole's end or termination condition. These options are the same as those discussed earlier when creating extruded and other features in the model.

6. Select the desired hole type, such as a drilled hole, clearance hole, or tapped hole, from the **Hole type** drop-down list, and specify the corresponding parameters, as discussed above.

7. Specify the start and end condition of the hole, as discussed above.

8. Edit the standard hole parameters, such as diameter, counterbore diameter, and depth, if needed. The availability of these parameters depends on whether a simple, counterbore, or countersink hole is being created.

9. After specifying the required parameters, click the green checkmark ✓ to confirm the creation of the hole feature and exit the dialog. Figure 6.119 shows four countersink holes created.

6.119

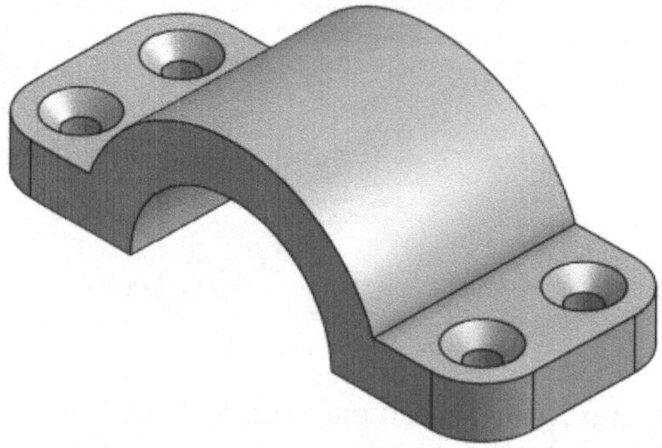

Creating an External Thread

In Onshape, you can create ANSI and ISO standard threads on the cylindrical faces of a model using the **External thread** tool. The method for creating external threads is discussed below:

1. Click on the **External thread** tool in the **Feature** toolbar, see Figure 6.120. The **External thread** dialog appears, see Figure 6.121.

6.120

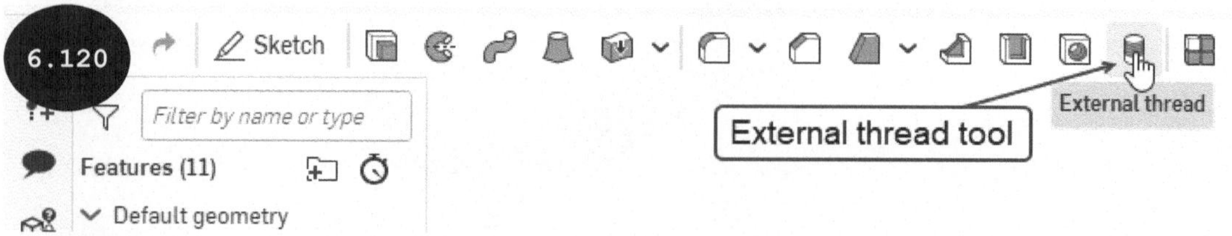

6.121

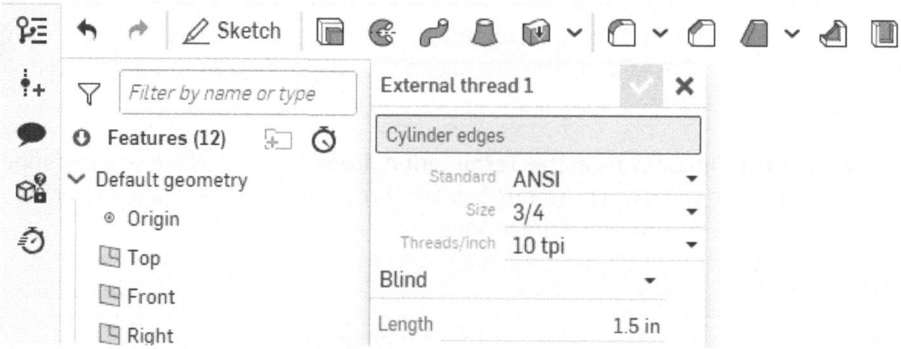

2. Select the circular edge of a cylindrical feature on the model, see Figure 6.122. A shaded preview of the thread appears on the cylindrical feature, starting from the selected circular edge.

6.122

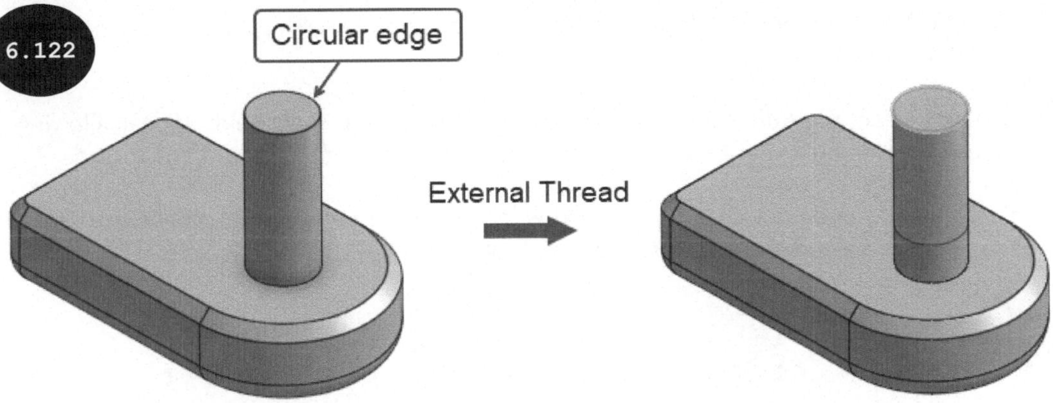

You can also select multiple circular edges one by one to create threads of similar parameters, see Figure 6.123.

6.123

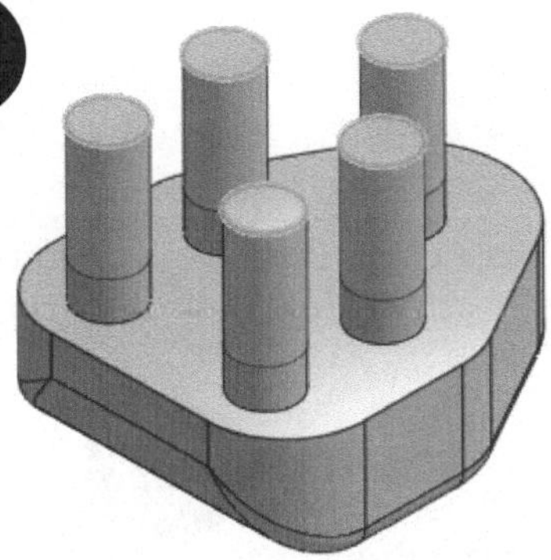

3. In the **Standard** drop-down list, select the appropriate thread standard: **ANSI** or **ISO**, depending on your design specifications and requirements for creating the thread.

4. Select the appropriate size for the thread in the **Size** drop-down list, if needed. By default, the thread size is automatically computed based on the cylinder diameter and the selected standard (ANSI or ISO). However, you can manually adjust the size if needed for your specific requirements.

5. Select the number of threads per inch in the **Threads/inch** drop-down list if you are using the ANSI standard. For the ISO standard, you will need to define the pitch of the thread in the respective drop-down list. This will determine the spacing between the threads for your design.

6. Select the **Blind** or **Up to next** option in the **End type** drop-down list to define the end condition or termination of the thread. Both these options are discussed below:

   Blind: By default, the **Blind** option is selected in the **End type** drop-down list. This allows you to specify the length of the thread in the **Length** field of the dialog. The thread will terminate at the specified depth from the selected circular edge.

Up to next: When you select the **Up to next** option, the thread extends up to the next intersecting face automatically.

7. Select the **Add chamfer** check box if you want to add a chamfer with specified parameters at the start of the thread, see Figure 6.124.

   When you select the **Add chamfer** check box, the **Length** and **Angle** fields appear, allowing you to specify the length and angle values for the chamfer created at the start of the thread.

8. Select the **Add undercut** check box if you want to add an undercut or groove with specified parameters at the end of the thread depth, see Figure 6.125.

6.124

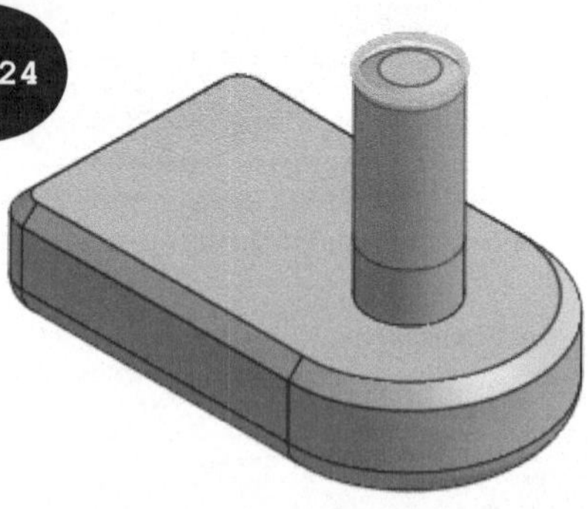

6.125

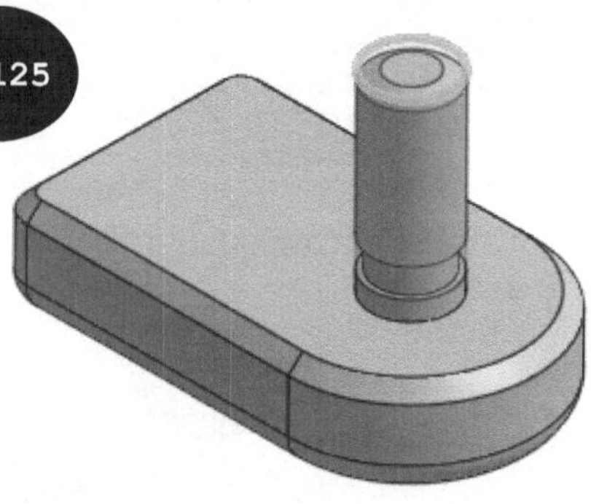

When you select the **Add undercut** check box, the **Diameter** and **Length** fields appear, allowing you to specify the diameter and length values for the undercut or groove created at the end of the thread.

Split face: By default, the **Split face** check box is selected. This splits the face of the cylindrical feature at the end of the thread, refer to Figure 6.126. Note that this check box is not available when the **Add undercut** check box is selected.

6.126

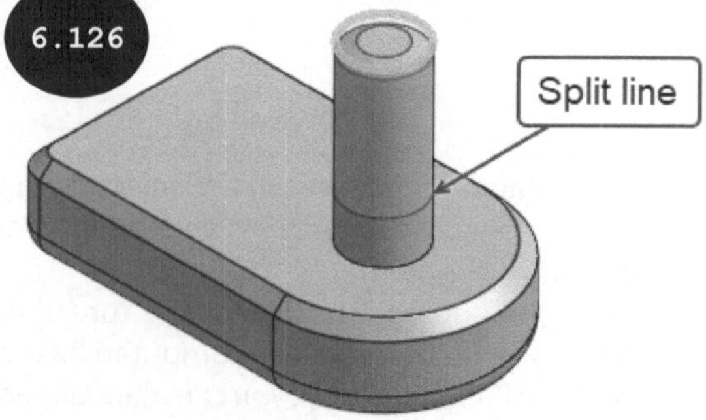

9. After specifying the required parameters, click the green checkmark ✓ to confirm the creation of the external thread and exit the dialog.

Note: In Onshape, the external thread is created without removing the material from the model. It helps in reducing the complexity of the model and improves the overall performance of the system. These threads can be viewed in drawings as dashed lines, providing a clear representation without affecting the geometry of the part.

Tutorial 1

Create a model, as shown in Figure 6.127. The different views and dimensions are given in the same figure. All dimensions are in mm.

6.127

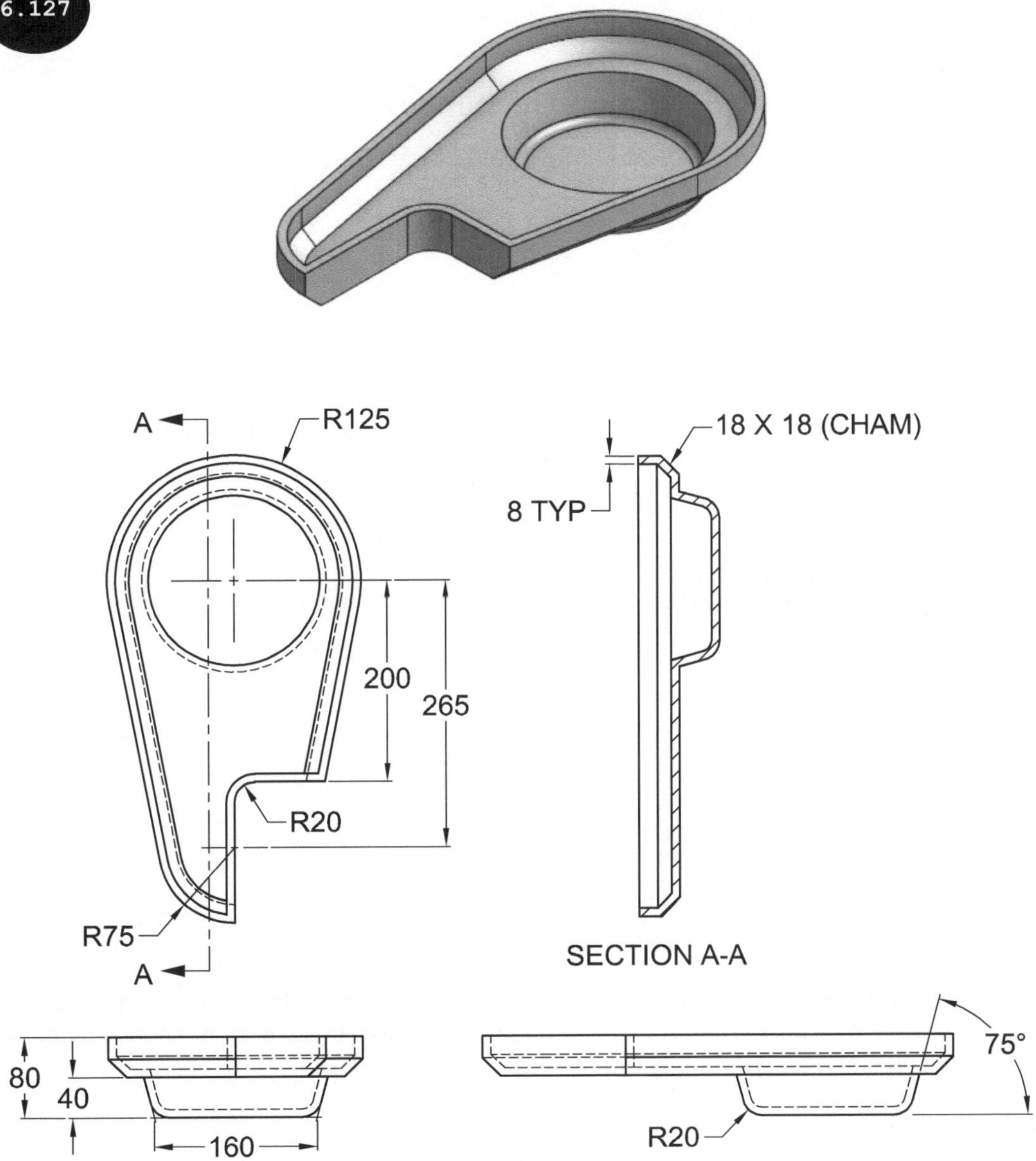

Section 1: Starting a New Design Document

1. Launch Onshape (*onshape.com*) and log in to your account if you're not already logged in.

Note: If you are within a document, click on the **Onshape** logo located in the top left corner of the browser to display the **Documents Page**, see Figure 6.128.

6.128

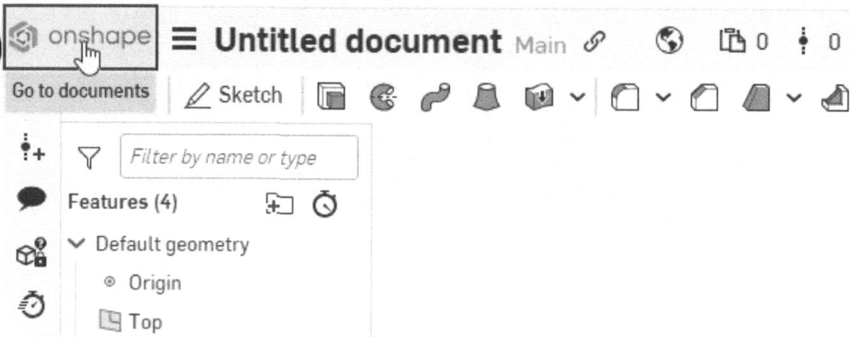

2. Click on the **Create** button at the top left corner of the **Documents Page** and then click on the **Document** option in the menu that appears, see Figure 6.129. The **New document** window appears with the default name of the document as "**Untitled document**".

6.129

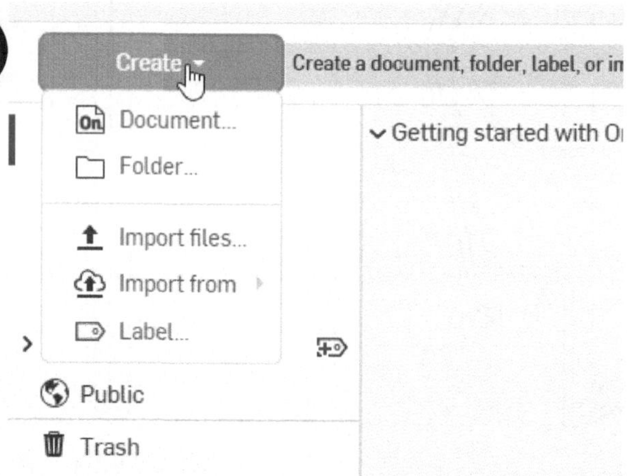

3. Enter **C06 Tutorial 01** as the name of the design document in the **New document** window, and then click on the **Create** button or the **Create Public Document** button, depending on your subscription type. A new document with the specified name is opened.

Section 2: Settings Units

Now, you can set millimeters (mm) as the unit for the length measurement in the current document.

1. Invoke the **Document** menu by clicking on the ≡ icon (three horizontal lines) next to the **Onshape** logo at the top left corner, see Figure 6.130.

6.130

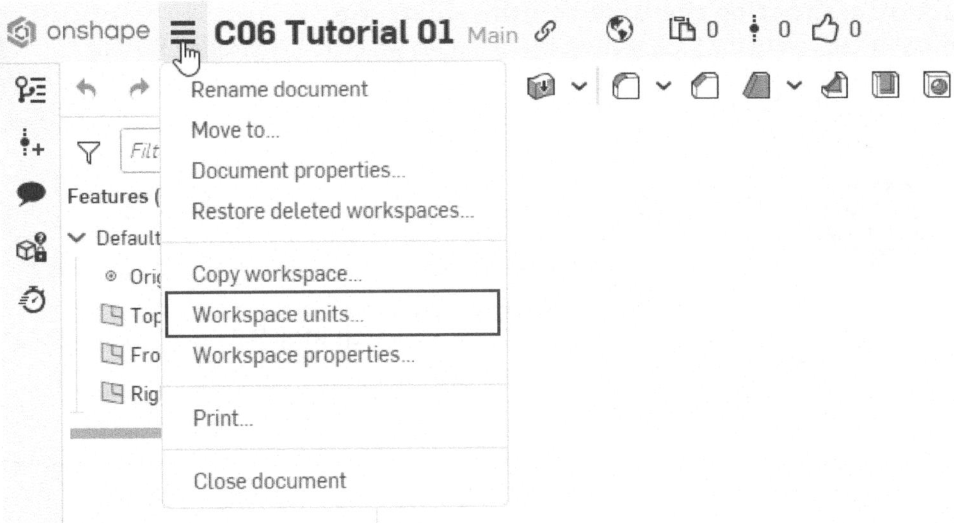

2. Click on the **Workspace units** option in the **Document** menu, refer to Figure 6.130. The **Workspace units** dialog appears, see Figure 6.131.

3. Select the **Millimeter** unit in the **Length default unit** drop-down list and set its precision to **0.1** in the respective **Display decimals** drop-down list of the **Workspace units** dialog, see Figure 6.131.

6.131

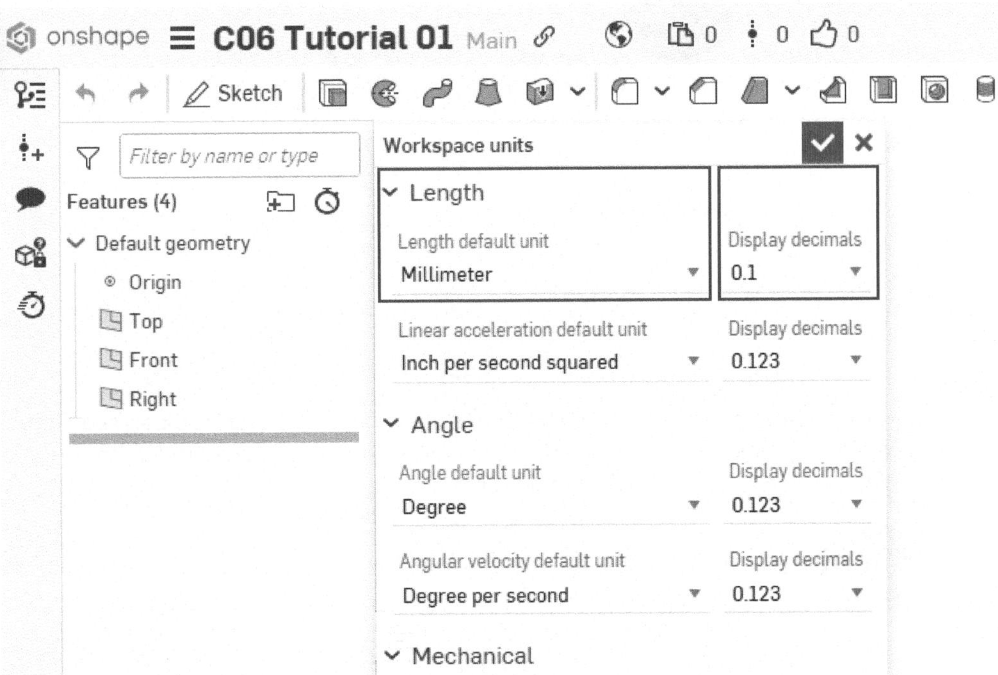

4. After selecting the required unit of length measurement and the decimal precision for the current design document, click on the green checkmark ✓ to confirm the selection and exit the dialog. The millimeter is defined as the unit for the length measurement.

Section 3: Creating the Base Feature - Extrude

Now, you can create the base feature of the model, which is an extruded feature.

1. Click on the **Sketch** tool in the **Feature** toolbar, see Figure 6.132. The **Sketch** dialog appears and you are prompted to select a sketching plane.

6.132

2. Select the Top plane as the sketching plane. The selected plane becomes the sketching plane, and the **Sketch** toolbar appears with the display of various sketching tools.

3. Press the N key to make the sketching plane normal to the viewing direction.

4. Create a circle of diameter 160 mm as the sketch of the base feature, see Figure 6.133. The center point of the circle is at the origin.

6.133

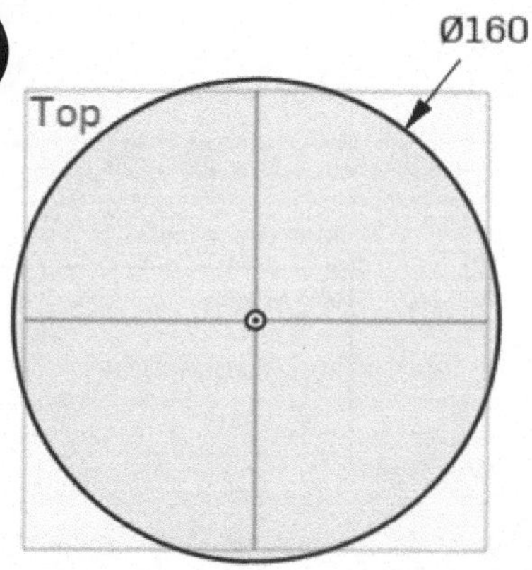

5. After creating the sketch, click on the **Extrude** tool in the **Sketch** toolbar, see Figure 6.134. The **Extrude** dialog appears and the sketch profile is automatically selected. Also, the preview of an extruded feature appears in the graphics area.

6.134

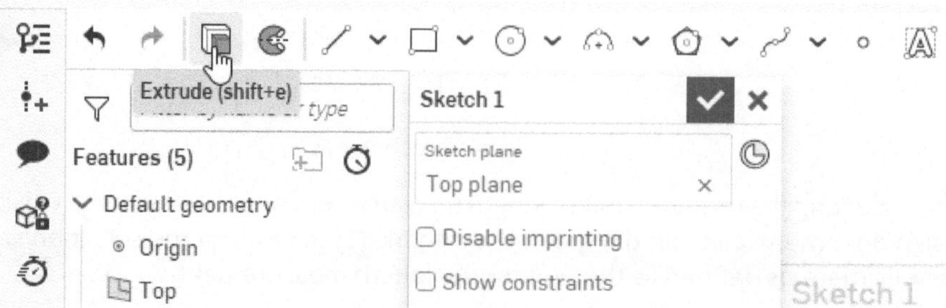

6. Press the SHIFT + 7 keys to change the view orientation to isometric, see Figure 6.135. Ensure that the extrusion is directed upwards.

7. Enter **40** mm as the depth of extrusion in the **Depth** field of the **Extrude** dialog and then press ENTER.

   Now, you can add the draft angle to the extrude feature.

8. Select the **Draft** check box in the **Extrude** dialog, enter **15** degrees in the **Draft angle** field that appears, and press ENTER to apply the changes. Ensure the draft angle is applied outwards, as shown in Figure 6.136.

6.135

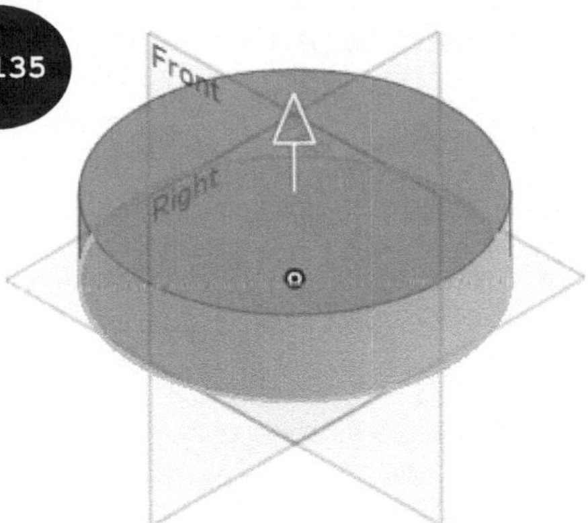

6.136

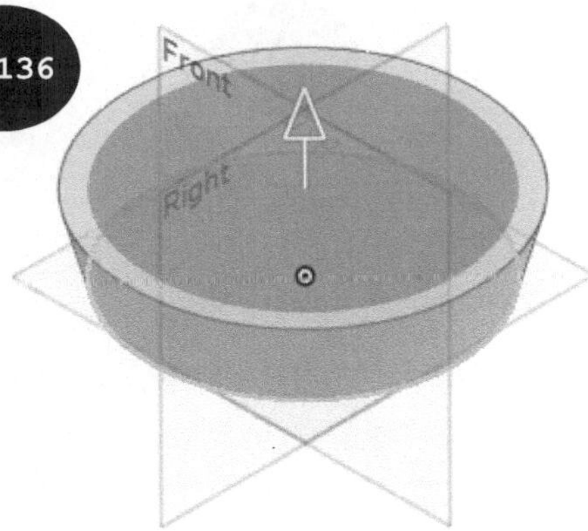

9. Click the green checkmark ✓ in the **Extrude** dialog to confirm the creation of the extrude feature and exit the dialog. The extrude feature of specified depth and draft angle is created, see Figure 6.137.

6.137

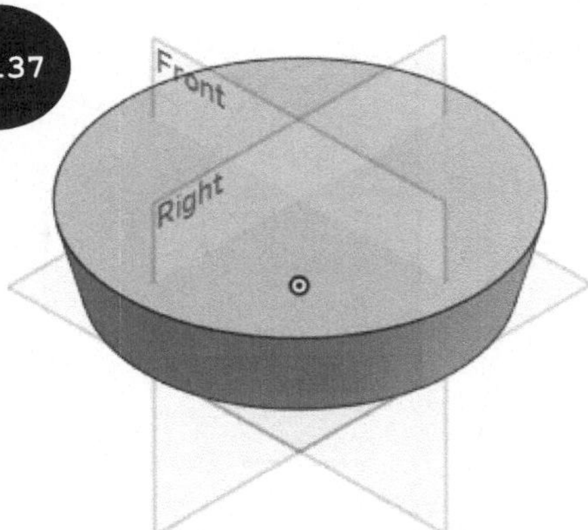

Section 4: Creating the Second Feature - Extrude

Now, you can create the second feature of the model, which is also an extruded feature.

1. Click on the **Sketch** tool in the **Feature** toolbar, see Figure 6.138. The **Sketch** dialog appears and you are prompted to select a sketching plane.

6.138

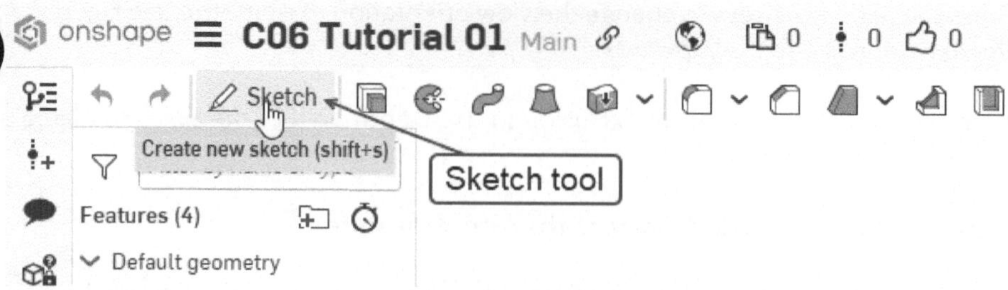

2. Select the top planar face of the base feature as the sketching plane, see Figure 6.139. The selected plane becomes the sketching plane, and the **Sketch** toolbar appears.

6.139

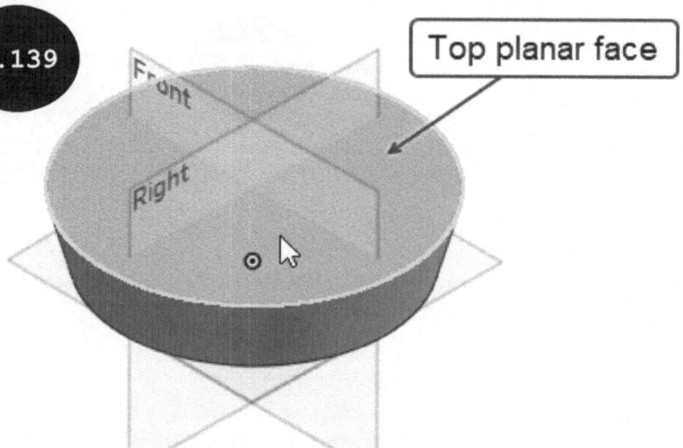

3. Press the **N** key to make the sketching plane normal to the viewing direction.

4. Create the sketch of the feature using the sketching tools, see Figure 6.140.

6.140

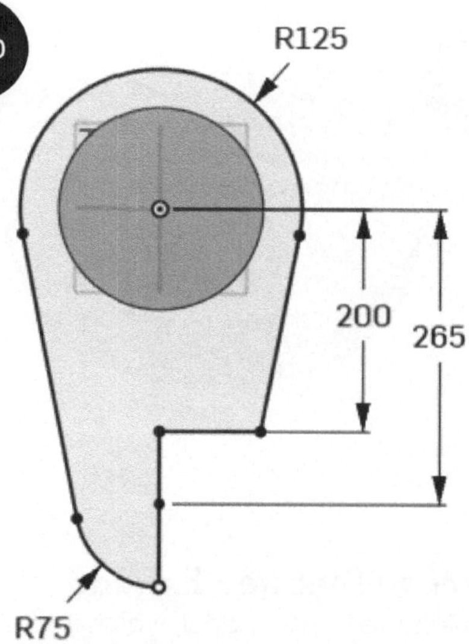

5. After creating the sketch, click on the **Extrude** tool, see Figure 6.141. The **Extrude** dialog appears and the sketch profile is automatically selected. Also, the preview of an extruded feature appears in the graphics area.

6.141

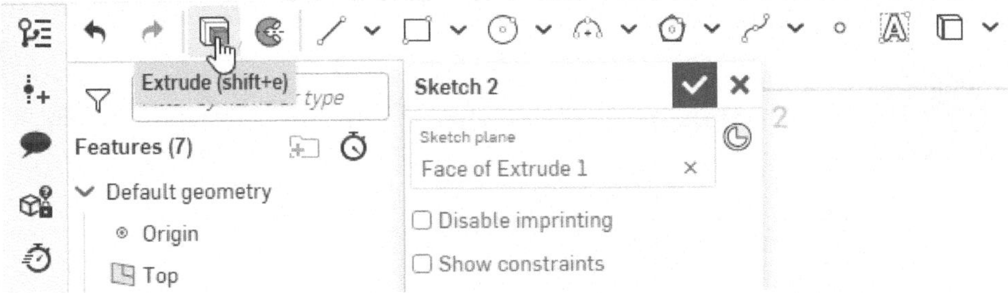

6. Press the SHIFT + 7 keys to change the view orientation to isometric, see Figure 6.142. Ensure that the extrusion is directed upwards.

6.142

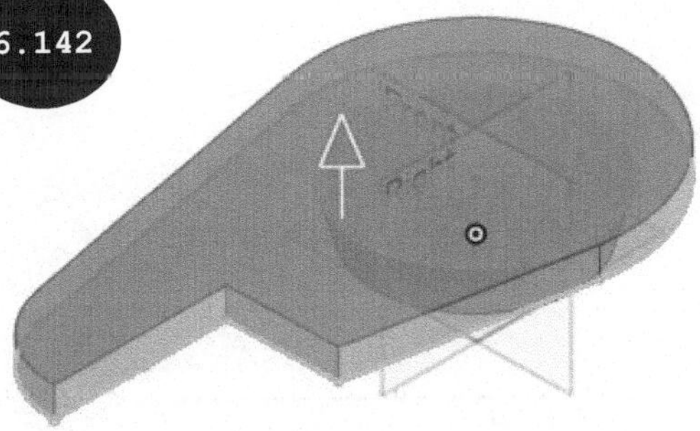

7. Enter **40** mm as the depth of extrusion in the **Depth** field of the **Extrude** dialog and then press ENTER.

8. Click the green checkmark ✓ in the **Extrude** dialog to confirm the creation of the extrude feature and exit the dialog. The extrude feature of specified depth is created, see Figure 6.143.

6.143

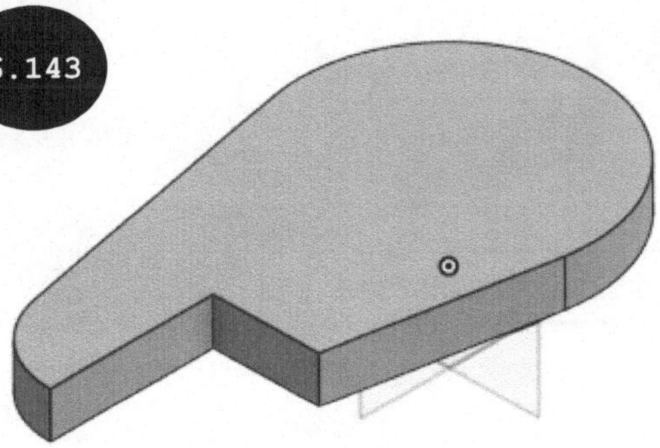

Section 5: Creating the Fillet

Now, you can create the fillet with a radius of 20 mm on the edges of the model.

1. Click on the **Fillet** tool in the **Feature** toolbar, see Figure 6.144. The **Fillet** dialog appears with the **Edge** tab activated, by default.

6.144

2. Rotate the model by pressing and holding the right mouse button until the bottom circular edge becomes visible, as shown in Figure 6.145.

6.145

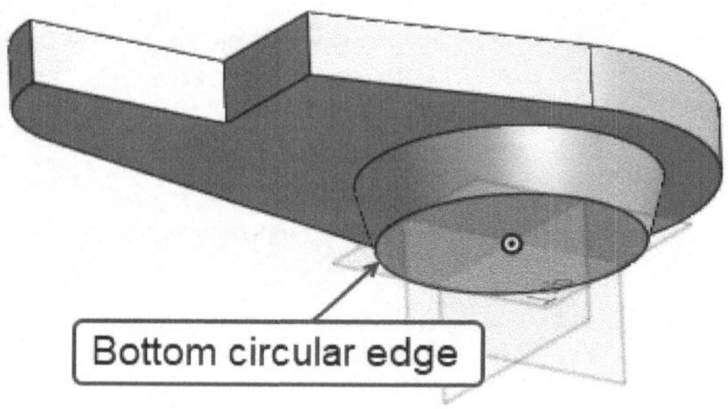

3. Select the bottom circular edge of the model. A preview of the fillet appears with the default radius on the selected edge, refer to Figure 6.146.

4. Select the second edge of the model to apply the fillet of a similar radius, see Figure 6.146.

6.146

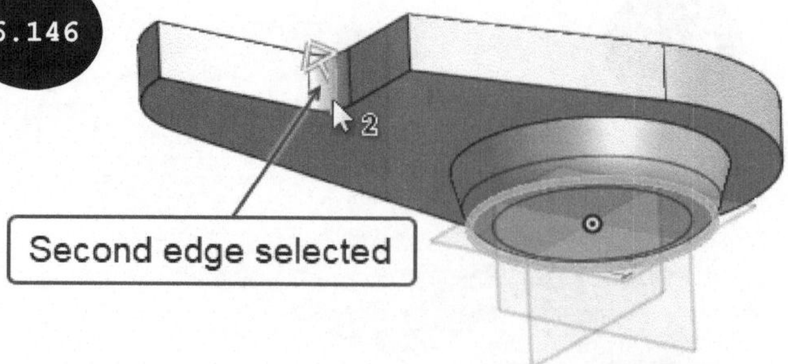

5. Ensure that the **Radius** option is selected in the **Measurement** drop-down list and the **Distance** option is selected in the **Control** drop-down list of the dialog.

6. Enter **20** mm as the radius of the fillet in the Radius field of the dialog and press ENTER. The preview of the fillet updates accordingly on the selected edges of the model.

7. Click the green checkmark ✓ in the **Fillet** dialog to confirm the creation of the fillet and exit the dialog. The fillet of specified radius is created on the selected edges of the model, see Figure 6.147.

8. Press the SHIFT + 7 keys to change the view orientation to isometric, see Figure 6.148.

6.147

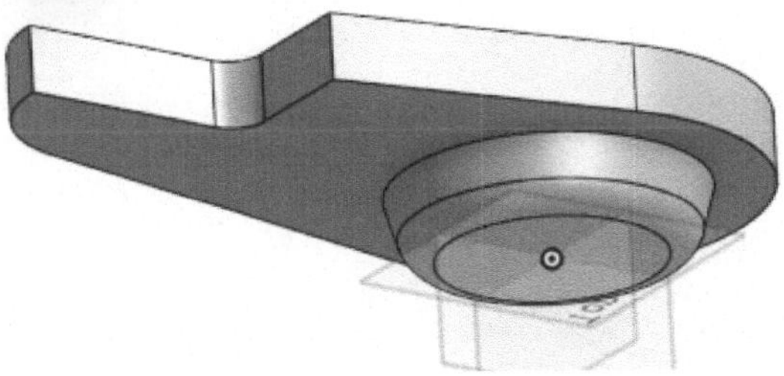

6.148

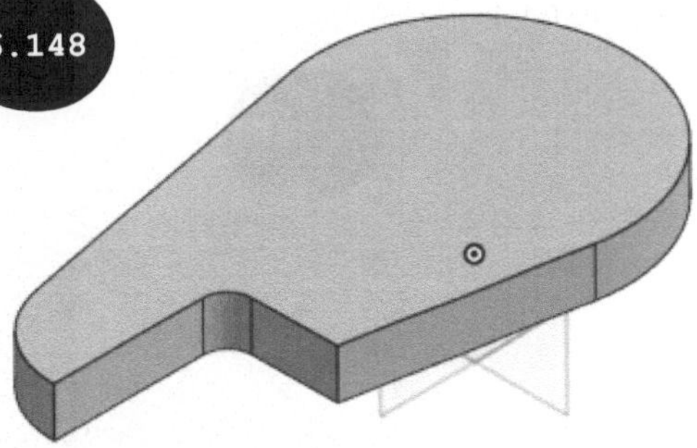

Section 6: Creating the Chamfer

Now, you can create the chamfer on the edges of the model.

1. Click on the **Chamfer** tool in the **Feature** toolbar, see Figure 6.149. The **Chamfer** dialog appears.

6.149

2. Select a bottom edge of the model to chamfer, see Figure 6.150. A preview of the chamfer appears on all tangentially connected edges of the selected one, as the **Tangent propagation** check box is selected by default, see Figure 6.151.

6.150

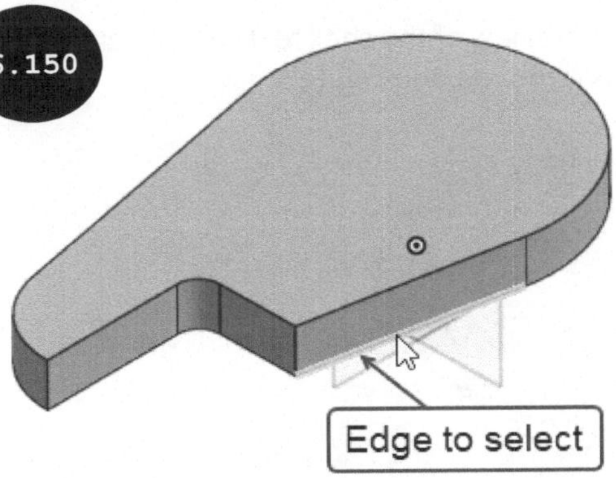

6.151

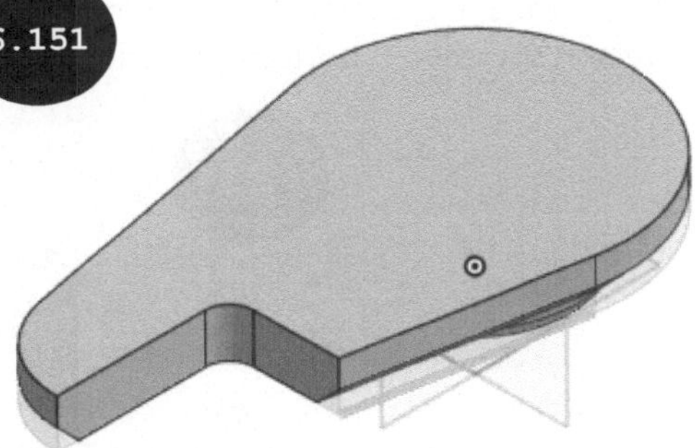

3. Ensure the **Equal distance** option is selected in the **Chamfer type** drop-down list to create a chamfer with equal distances on both sides of the chamfered edges.

4. Enter **18** mm in the **Distance** field of the dialog and press ENTER. The preview of the chamfer updates accordingly in the graphics area.

5. Click the green checkmark in the **Chamfer** dialog to confirm the creation of the chamfer and exit the dialog. The chamfer of specified distance is created on the edges of the model, see Figure 6.152.

6.152

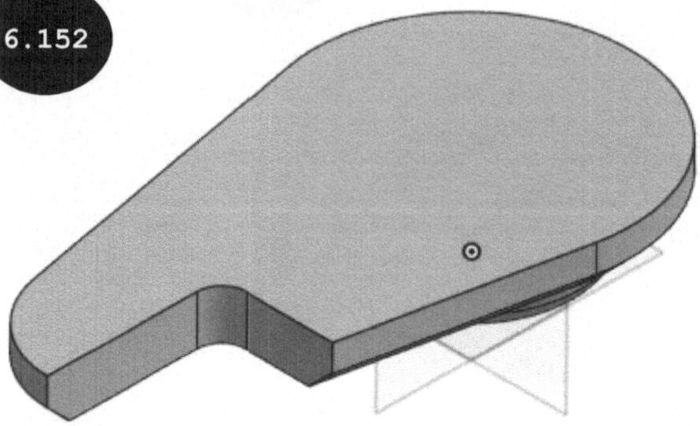

Section 7: Creating the Shell

Now, you can create the shell feature by removing the top planar face of the model.

1. Click on the **Shell** tool in the **Feature** toolbar, see Figure 6.153. The **Shell** dialog appears.

6.153

2. Ensure that the **Hollow** check box is cleared in the dialog to create a shell feature by removing the top planar face of the model.

3. Select the top planar face of the model to remove. A preview of the shell feature appears with the default specified thickness after the selected face is removed, see Figure 6.154.

6.154

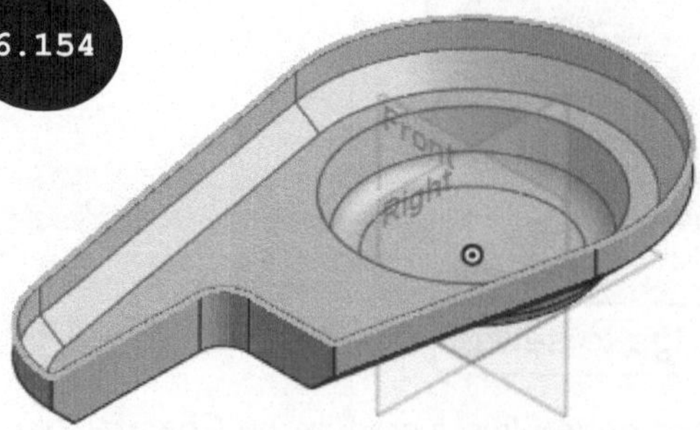

4. Enter **8** mm as the wall thickness of the feature in the **Shell thickness** field of the dialog and press ENTER. The preview of the shell feature updates accordingly in the graphics area.

5. Click the green checkmark ✓ in the **Shell** dialog to confirm the creation of the feature and exit the dialog. The shell feature of specified thickness is created by removing the top planar face of the model. Figure 6.155 shows the final model after creating all its features.

6.155

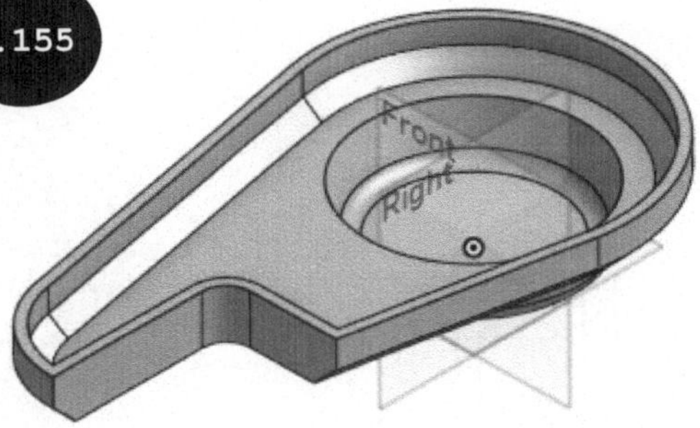

Tip: In Onshape, the document automatically saves to the specified location in the cloud. You can access a list of all the saved documents anytime by clicking on the **Created by me** option in the left menu of the **Documents Page**.

6. Create a version in the document to capture the current state of the design using the **Create version** tool in the **Document panel**.

   Now, you can close the document.

7. Invoke the **Document** menu by clicking on the ☰ icon (three horizontal lines) next to the Onshape logo at the top left corner and click on the **Close document** option, see Figure 6.156. The current document gets closed.

6.156

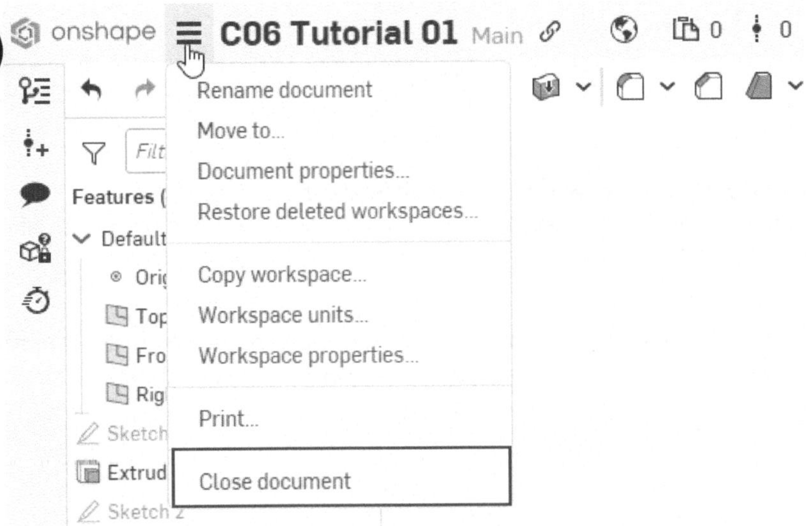

Tutorial 2

Create a model, as shown in Figure 6.157. The different views and dimensions are given in the same figure. All dimensions are in inches.

6.157

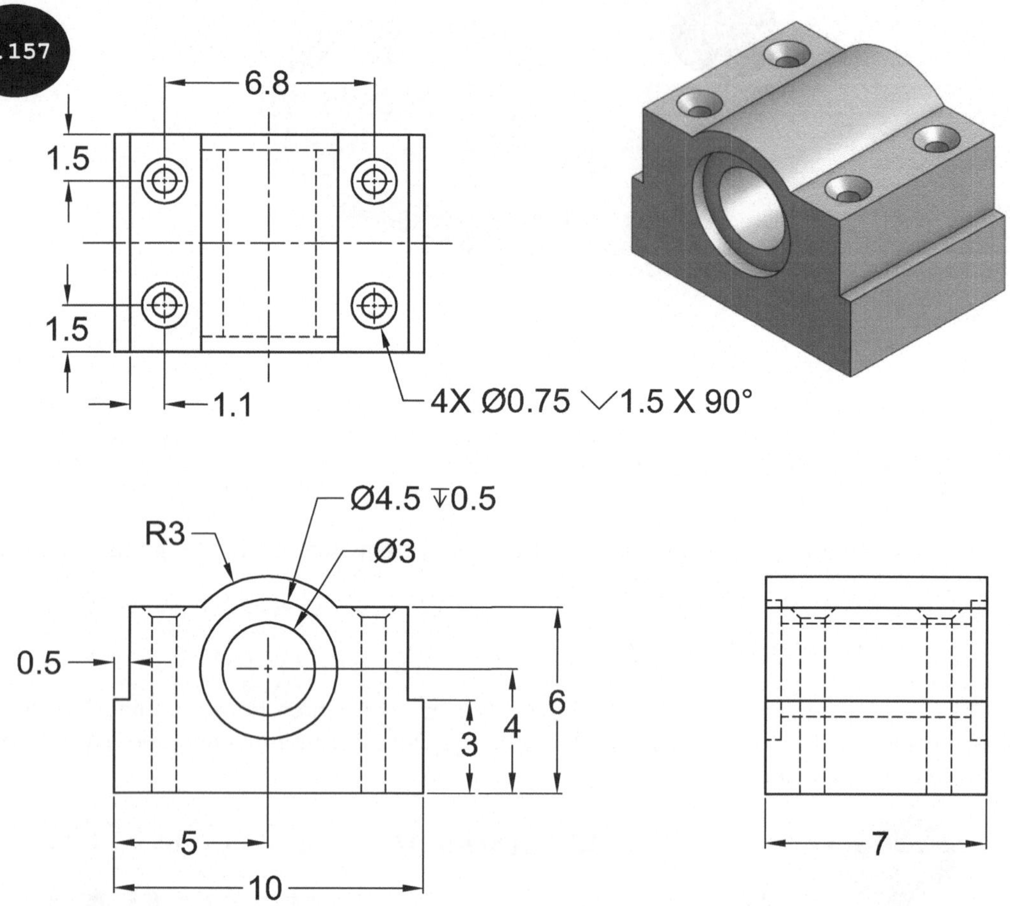

Section 1: Starting a New Design Document

1. Launch Onshape (***onshape.com***) and log in to your account if you're not already logged in. The **Documents Page** appears.

Note: If you are within a document, click on the **Onshape** logo located in the top left corner of the browser to display the **Documents Page**, see Figure 6.158.

6.158

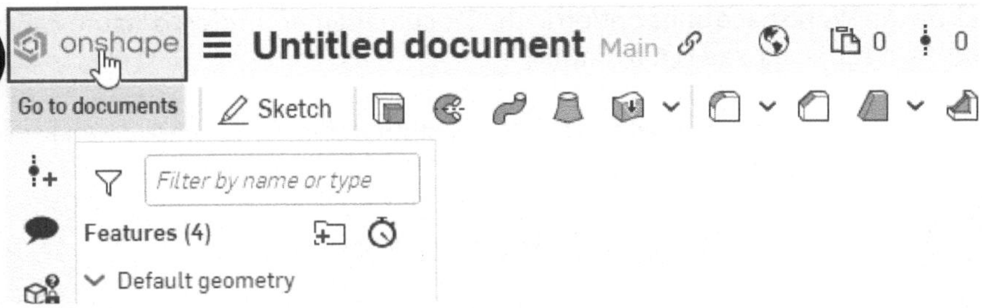

2. Click on the **Create** button at the top left corner of the **Documents Page** and then click on the **Document** option in the menu that appears, see Figure 6.159. The **New document** window appears with the default name of the document as "**Untitled document**".

6.159

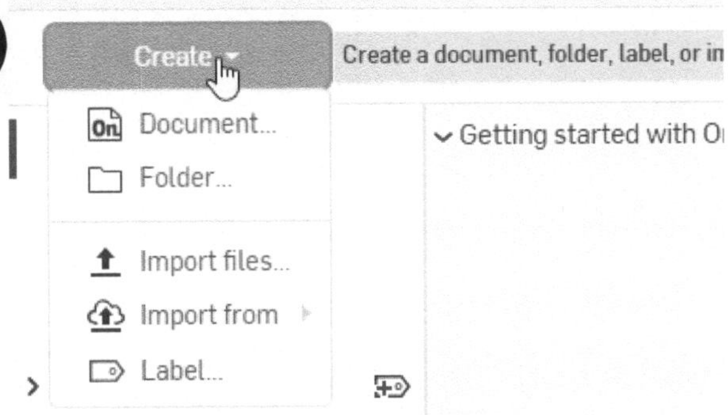

3. Enter **C06 Tutorial 02** as the name of the design document in the **New document** window, and then click on the **Create** button or the **Create Public Document** button, depending on your subscription type. A new document with the specified name is opened.

Section 2: Settings Units

Now, you can set inches (in) as the unit for the length measurement in the current document.

1. Invoke the **Document** menu by clicking on the ≡ icon (three horizontal lines) next to the **Onshape** logo at the top left corner, see Figure 6.160.

6.160

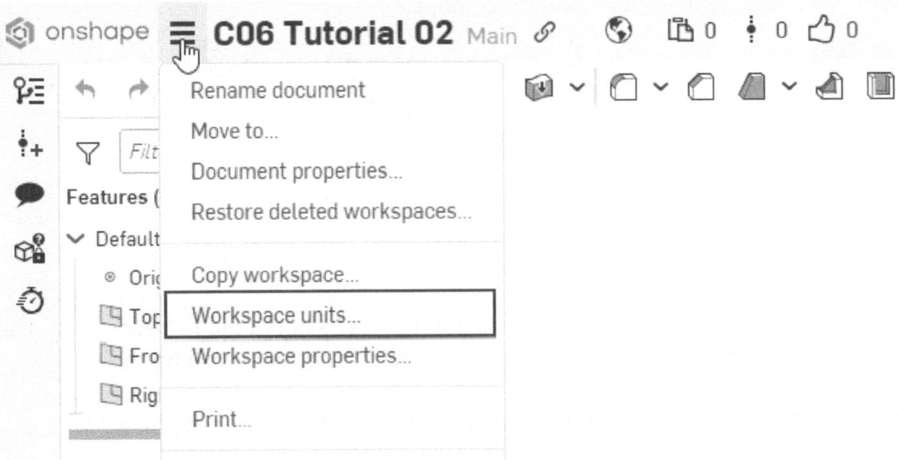

2. Click on the **Workspace units** option in the **Document** menu, refer to Figure 6.160. The **Workspace units** dialog appears, see Figure 6.161.

3. Ensure that the **Inch** unit is selected in the **Length default unit** drop-down list of the **Workspace units** dialog, see Figure 6.161.

6.161

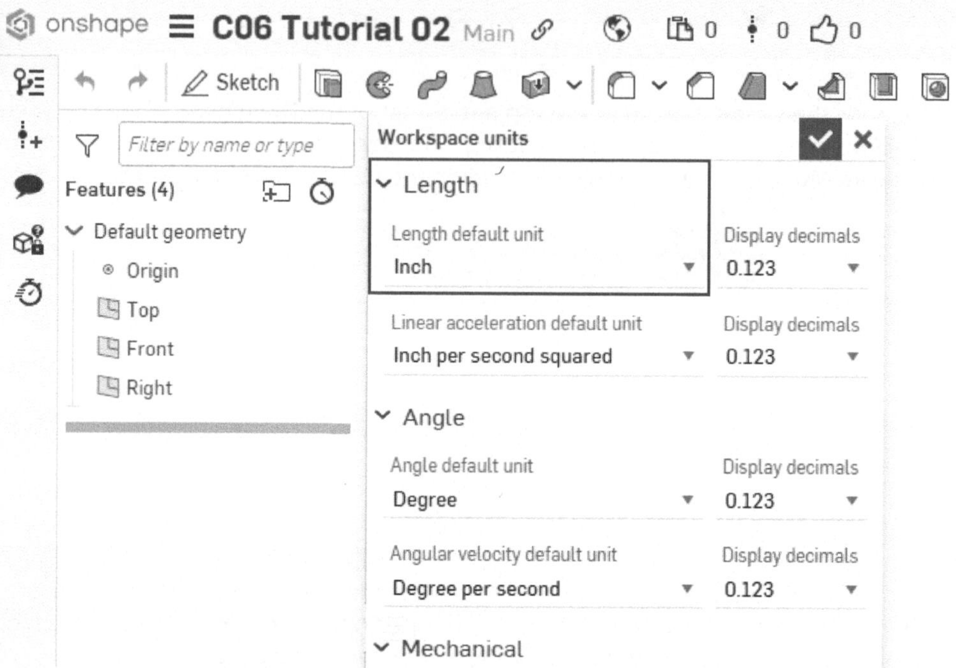

4. Click on the green checkmark to confirm the selection and exit the dialog.

Section 3: Creating the Base Feature - Extrude

Now, you can create the base feature of the model, which is an extruded feature.

1. Click on the **Sketch** tool in the **Feature** toolbar, see Figure 6.162. The **Sketch** dialog appears and you are prompted to select a sketching plane.

6.162

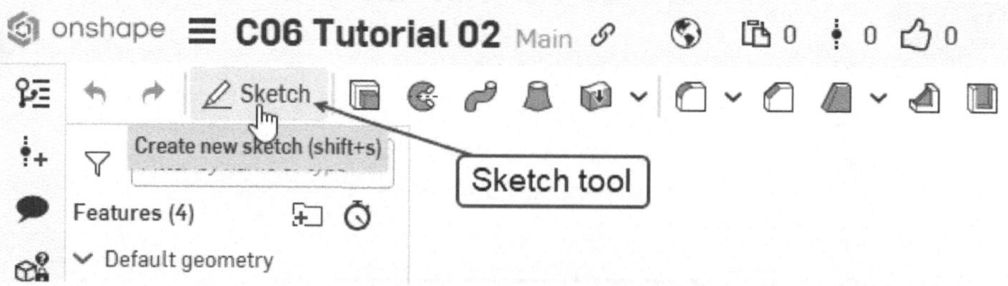

2. Select the Front plane as the sketching plane. The selected plane becomes the sketching plane, and the **Sketch** toolbar appears with the display of various sketching tools.

3. Press the N key to make the sketching plane normal to the viewing direction.

4. Create the sketch of the feature using the sketching tools, see Figure 6.163. Note that an equal constraint is applied between lines of equal length to fully define the sketch.

6.163

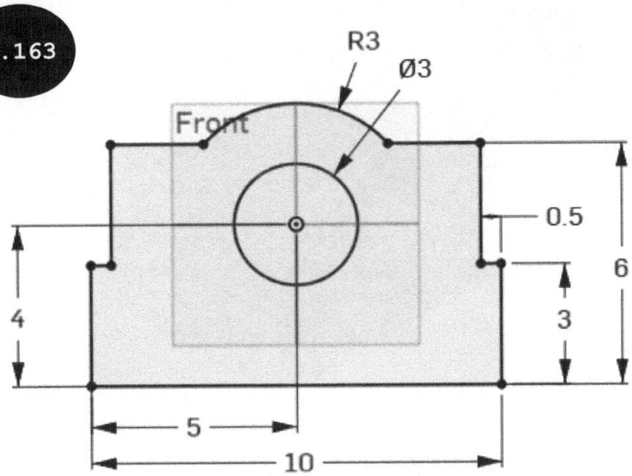

5. After creating the sketch, click on the **Extrude** tool in the **Sketch** toolbar, see Figure 6.164. The **Extrude** dialog appears and the sketch profile is automatically selected. Also, the preview of an extruded feature appears in the graphics area.

6.164

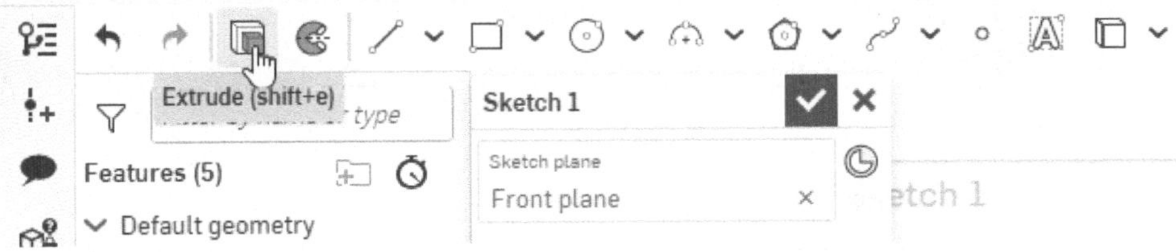

6. Press the SHIFT + 7 keys to change the view orientation to isometric.

7. Enter **7** inches as the depth of extrusion in the **Depth** field of the **Extrude** dialog and then press ENTER. The preview of the extrude feature updates accordingly in the graphics area.

8. Select the **Symmetric** check box in the dialog to extrude the sketch symmetrically on both sides of the sketching plane, see Figure 6.165.

6.165

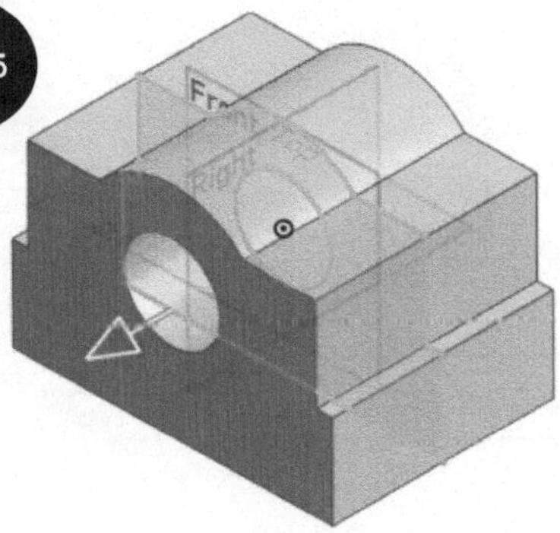

9. Click the green checkmark ✅ in the **Extrude** dialog to confirm the creation of the extrude feature and exit the dialog. The extrude feature of specified depth is created, see Figure 6.166.

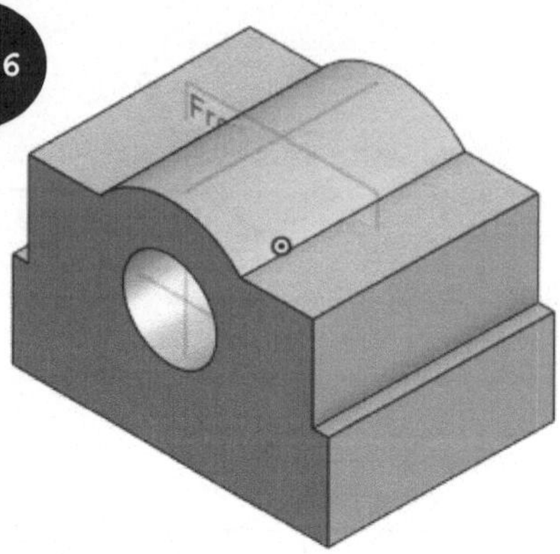

6.166

Section 4: Creating the Second Feature - Extrude Cut

Now, you can create the second feature of the model, which is an extruded cut feature.

1. Click on the **Sketch** tool in the **Feature** toolbar, see Figure 6.167. The **Sketch** dialog appears and you are prompted to select a sketching plane.

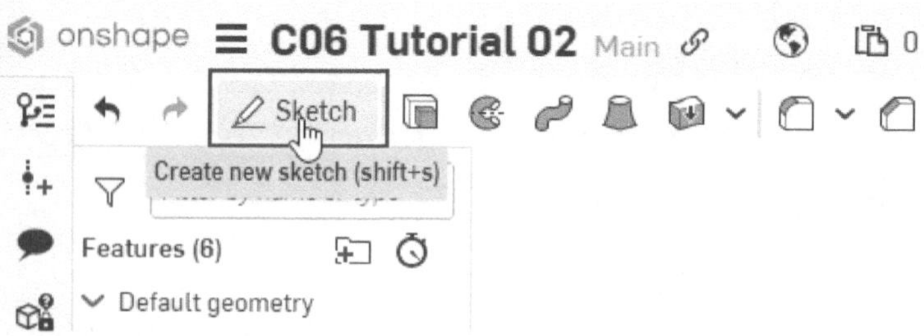

6.167

2. Select the front planar face of the model as the sketching plane, see Figure 6.168. The selected plane becomes the sketching plane, and the **Sketch** toolbar appears with the display of various sketching tools.

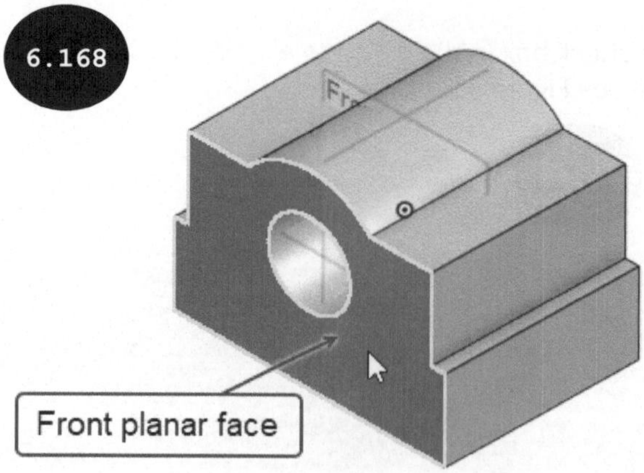

6.168

3. Press the **N** key to make the sketching plane normal to the viewing direction.

4. Create a circle of diameter 4.5 inches as the sketch of the feature, see Figure 6.169.

6.169

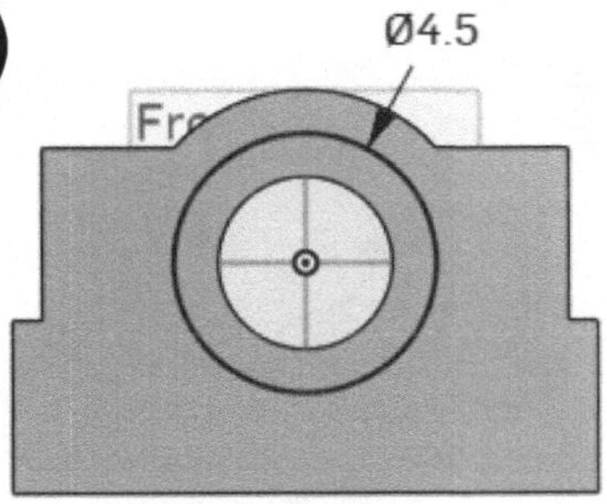

5. After creating the sketch, press the SHIFT + E keys to activate the **Extrude** tool. The **Extrude** dialog appears, and a preview of the extruded feature is displayed in the graphics area.

6. Press the SHIFT + 7 keys to change the view orientation to isometric.

7. Enter **0.5** inches in the **Depth** field of the **Extrude** dialog and then press ENTER.

8. Click on the **Remove** tab in the **Extrude** dialog to create an extruded cut feature by removing the material from the model, see Figure 6.170. The preview of the feature updates accordingly in the graphics area, see Figure 6.171.

6.170

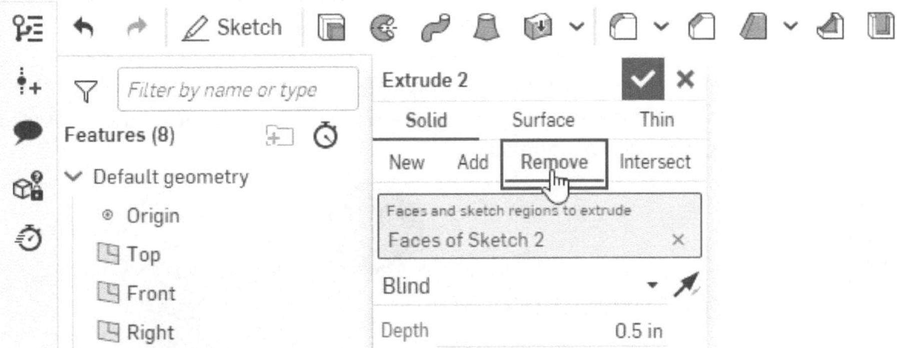

6.171

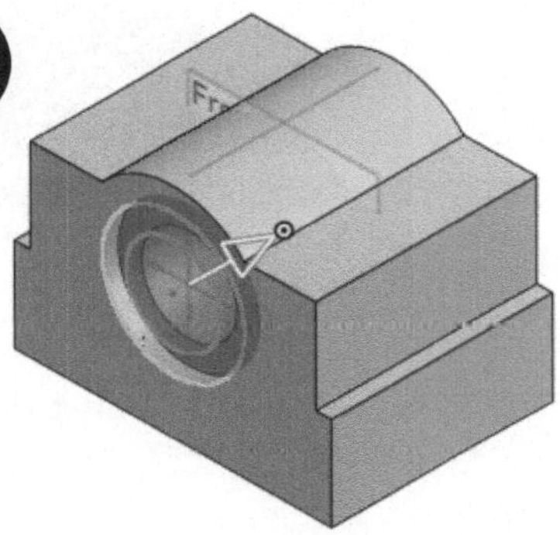

9. Ensure the extrusion direction is set toward the rear side of the model, refer to Figure 6.171.

10. Click the green checkmark ✓ in the **Extrude** dialog to confirm the creation of the extruded cut feature and exit the dialog. The extruded cut feature is created, see Figure 6.172.

6.172

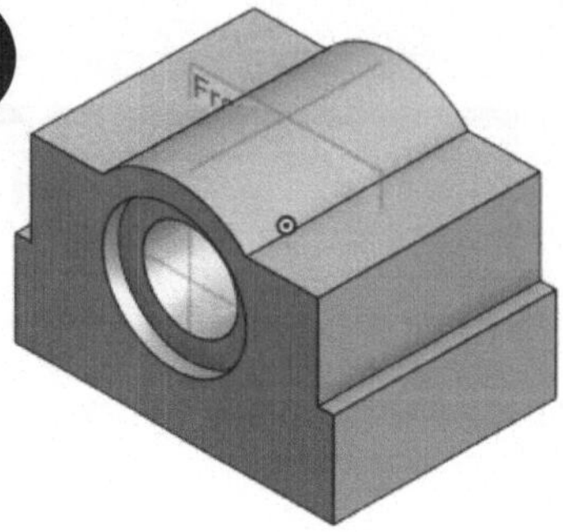

Section 5: Creating the Third Feature - Extrude Cut

Now, you can create the third feature of the model, an extruded cut feature on the rear side.

Note: You can mirror the previously created cut feature about the Front plane to create this extruded cut feature. However, since the topic of mirroring features is covered in later chapters, this section guides you to create it as a separate extruded cut feature in a similar way as explained earlier.

1. Click on the **Sketch** tool in the **Feature** toolbar, see Figure 6.173. The **Sketch** dialog appears and you are prompted to select a sketching plane.

2. Rotate the model by pressing and holding the right mouse button, then select the rear planar face of the model as the sketching plane, see Figure 6.174. The selected plane becomes the sketching plane, and the **Sketch** toolbar appears.

6.173

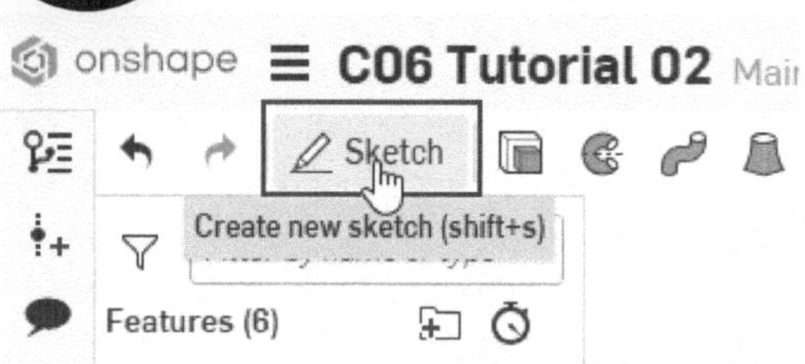

6.174

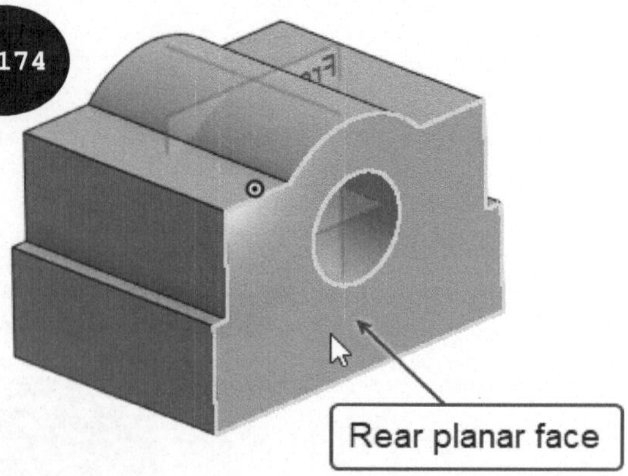

3. Press the N key to make the sketching plane normal to the viewing direction.

4. Create a circle of diameter 4.5 inches as the sketch of the feature, see Figure 6.175.

5. Press the SHIFT + E keys. The **Extrude** dialog invokes, and a preview of the extruded feature appears in the graphics area.

6. Rotate the model by pressing and holding the right mouse button to make the rear side visible, see Figure 6.176.

6.175

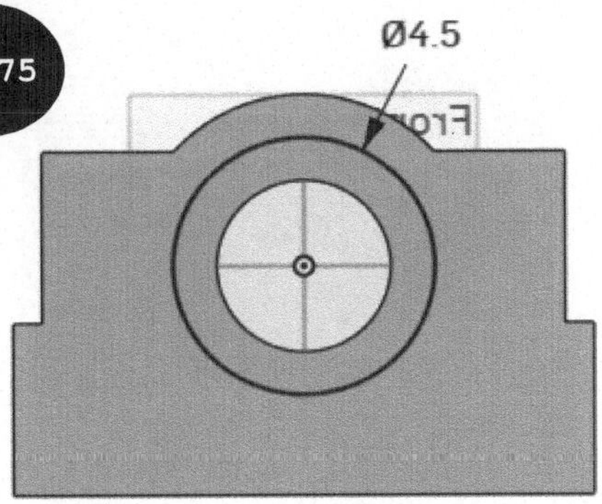

6.176

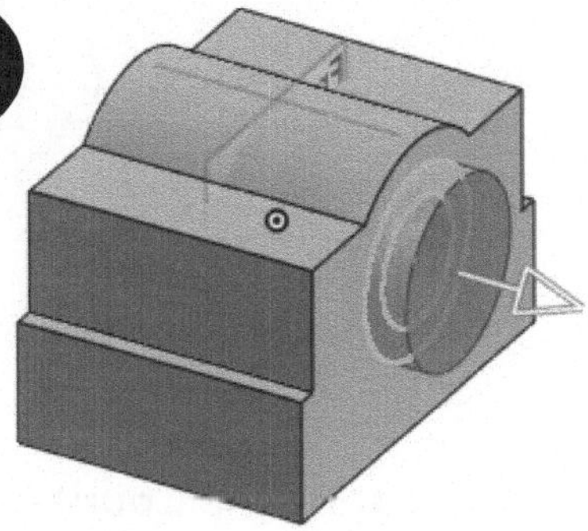

7. Enter **0.5** inches in the **Depth** field of the **Extrude** dialog and then press ENTER.

8. Click to activate the **Remove** tab in the **Extrude** dialog to create an extruded cut feature by removing the material from the model, see Figure 6.177. The preview of the feature updates accordingly in the graphics area, see Figure 6.178.

6.177

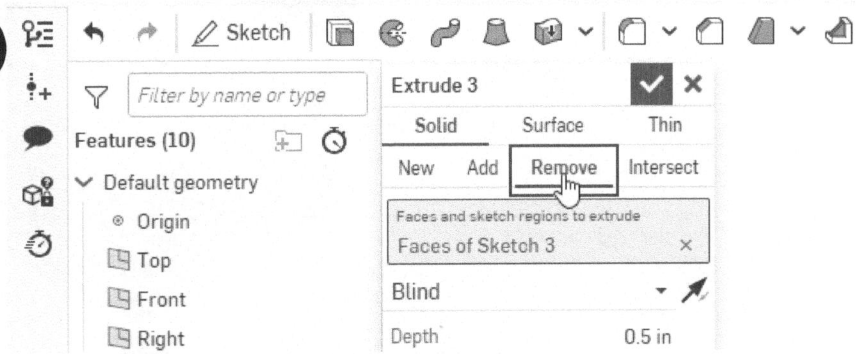

6.178

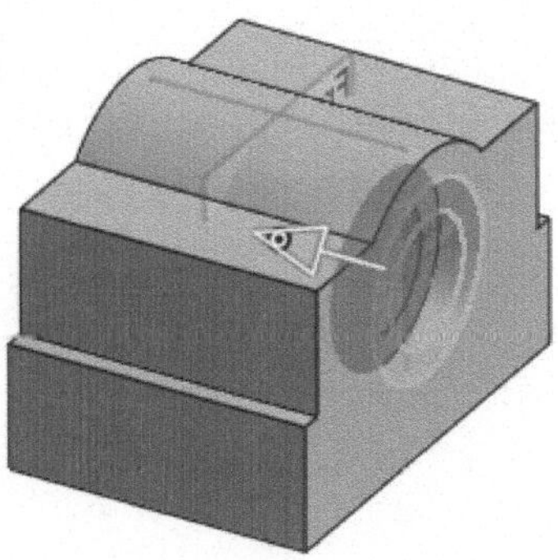

9. Click the green checkmark in the **Extrude** dialog to confirm the creation of the extruded cut feature and exit the dialog. The extruded cut feature is created, see Figure 6.179.

10. Press SHIFT + 7 to change the view orientation of the model to isometric, see Figure 6.180.

6.179

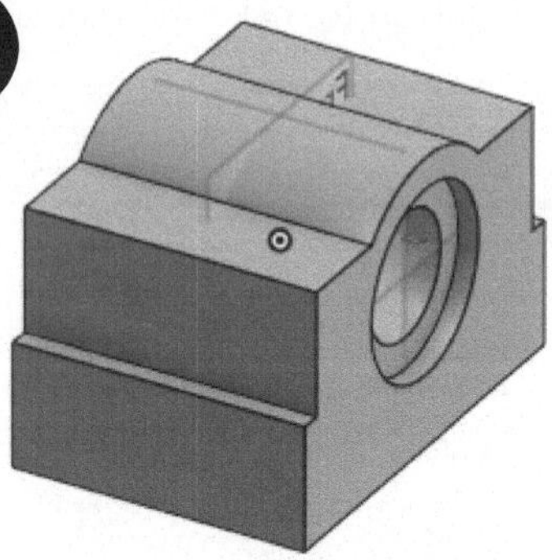

6.180

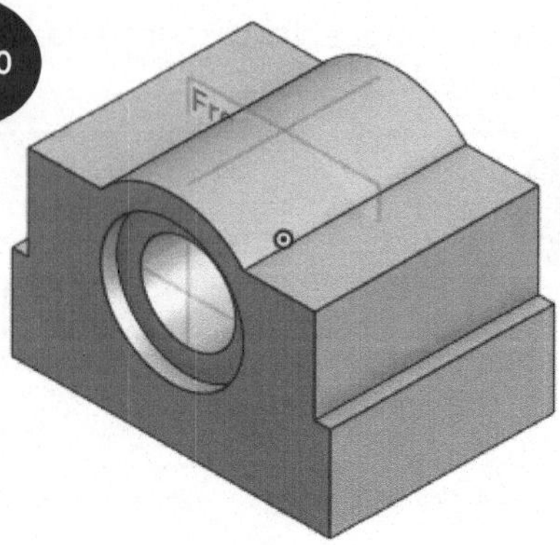

Section 6: Creating the Countersink Holes

Now, you can create the countersink holes as the fourth feature of the model.

1. Click on the **Sketch** tool in the **Feature** toolbar (see Figure 6.181) and select the top planar face of the model as the sketching plane, see Figure 6.182. The **Sketch** dialog appears and you are prompted to select a sketching plane.

6.181

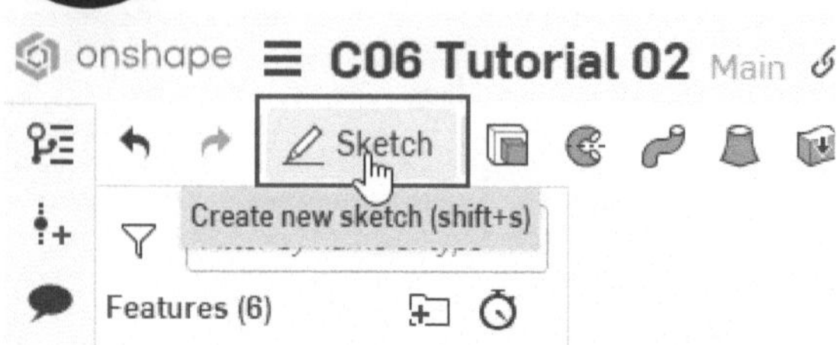

6.182

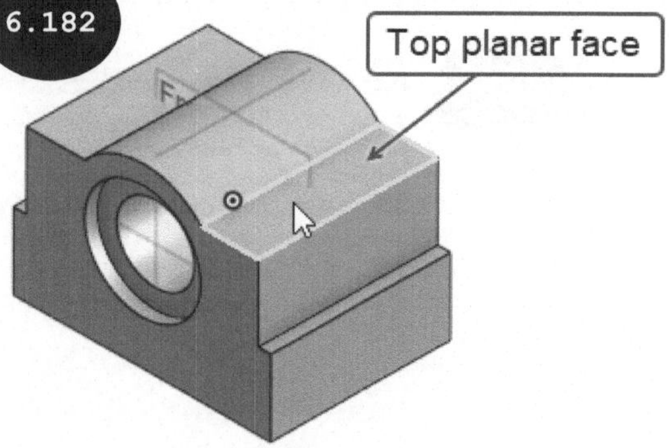

2. Press the **N** key to make the sketching plane normal to the viewing direction.

3. Click on the **Point** tool in the Sketch toolbar (see Figure 6.183) or press SHIFT + S. Next, create four sketch points on the top planar face by clicking the left mouse button, refer to Figure 6.184.

6.183

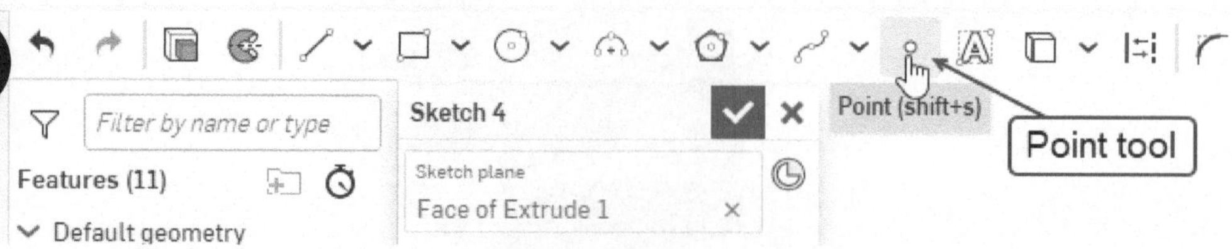

4. Apply the required dimensions and constraints to the sketch points, see Figure 6.184. Note that the sketch points are numbered in the figure for reference only. Points 1 and 3, as well as points 2 and 4, are horizontally aligned, while points 1 and 2, and points 3 and 4, are vertically aligned.

6.184

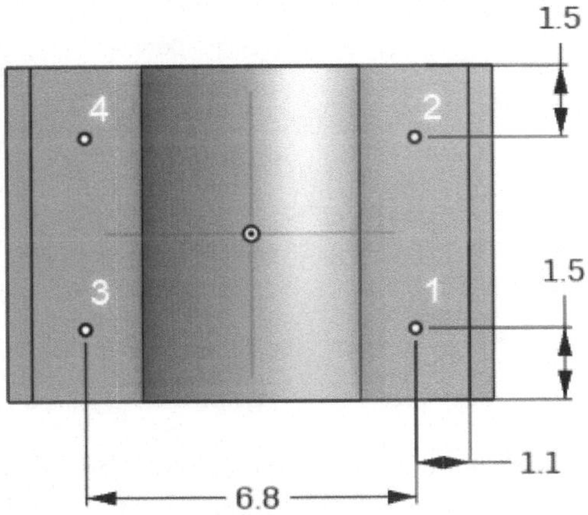

5. Click the green checkmark in the **Sketch** dialog to confirm the creation of the sketch points and exit the dialog. The four sketch points are created. Next, press the SHIFT + 7 keys to change the view orientation to isometric, see Figure 6.185.

6.185

Now, you can create the countersink holes.

6. Click on the **Hole** tool in the **Feature** toolbar, see Figure 6.186. The **Hole** dialog appears.

6.186

7. Ensure the **Inch** tab is activated to define the hole parameters in the inches, refer to Figure 6.187.

8. Click on the **Countersink** tab in the **Hole** dialog to select it as the type of hole to be created, see Figure 6.187.

6.187

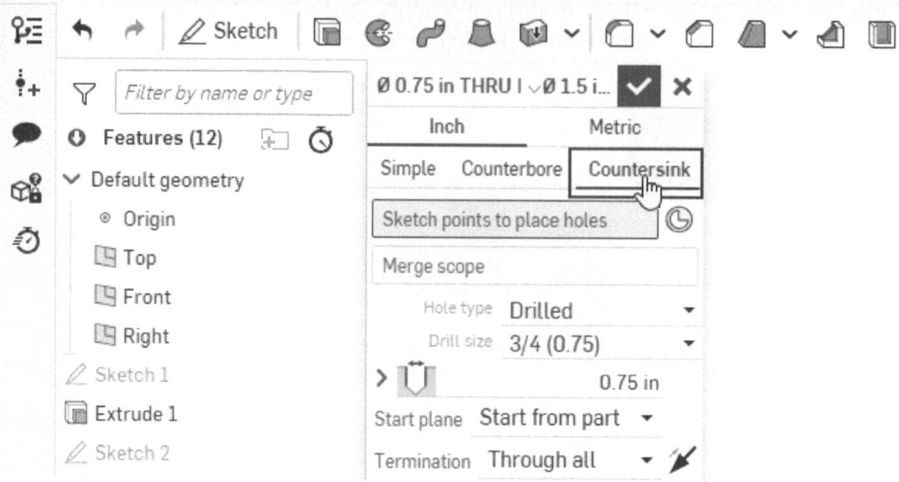

9. Click to select the four sketch points in the graphics area, one by one. A preview of the countersink holes appears, centered on the selected sketch points with default parameters, see Figure 6.188.

6.188

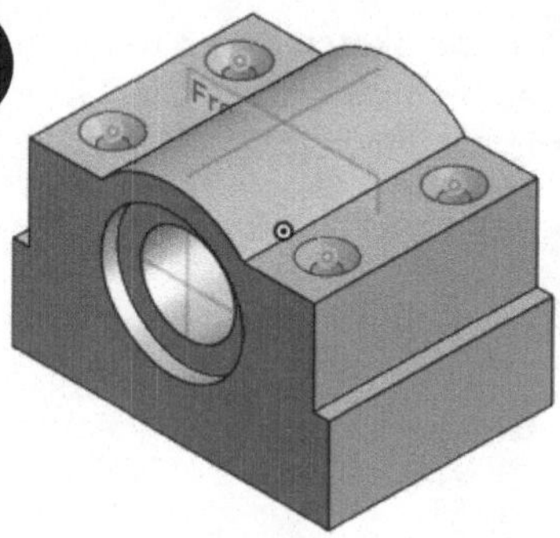

Tip: The default parameters are based on the settings of the last created countersink hole. Therefore, the preview of the countersink hole may vary in your case.

10. Ensure the **Drilled** option is selected in the **Hole type** drop-down list, see Figure 6.189.
11. Select **3/4 (0.75)** as the size of the drill hole in the **Drill size** drop-down list, see Figure 6.189.
12. Ensure the diameter of the hole is set to **0.75** inches in the **Diameter** field, see Figure 6.189.
13. Ensure the **Start from part** option is selected in the **Start plane** drop-down list to define the start condition of the hole, refer to Figure 6.189.
14. Select the **Through all** option in the **Termination** drop-down list to create the hole through the entire length of the model, refer to Figure 6.189.

6.189

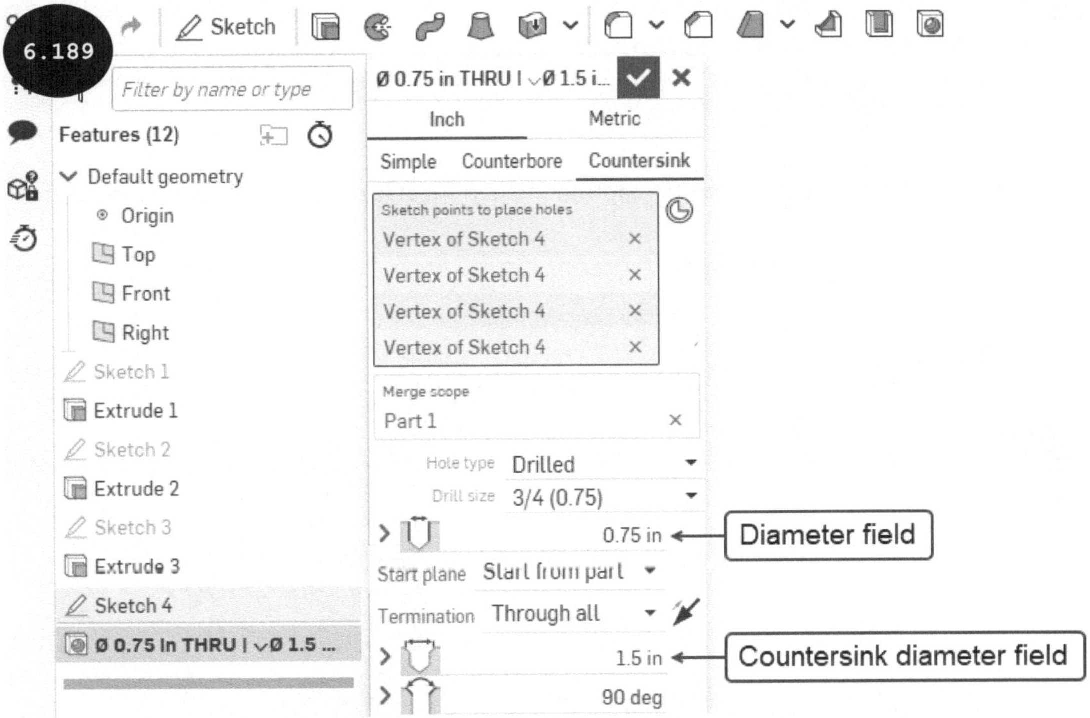

15. Set the countersink diameter to **1.5** inches in the **Countersink diameter** field. Figure 6.190 illustrates the parameters of a countersink hole when the depth is set to **Through All**.

16. Ensure that the countersink angle is set to **90** degrees in the **Countersink angle** field of the dialog.

17. After specifying all the required parameters, click the green checkmark ✔ in the **Hole** dialog to confirm the creation of the countersink holes and exit the dialog. The four countersink holes with the same parameters are created at the defined positions. Figure 6.191 shows the final model.

6.190

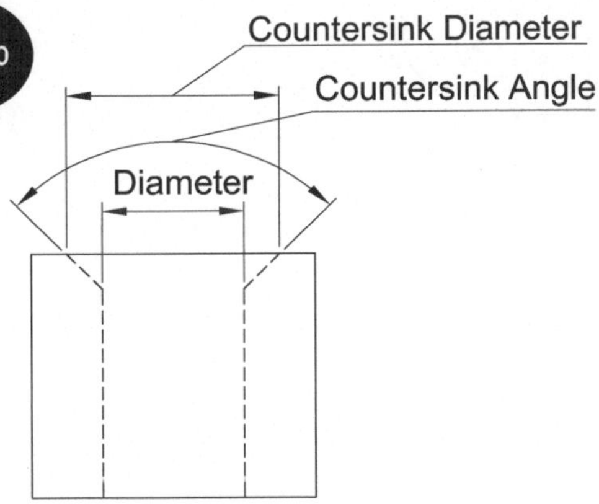

6.191

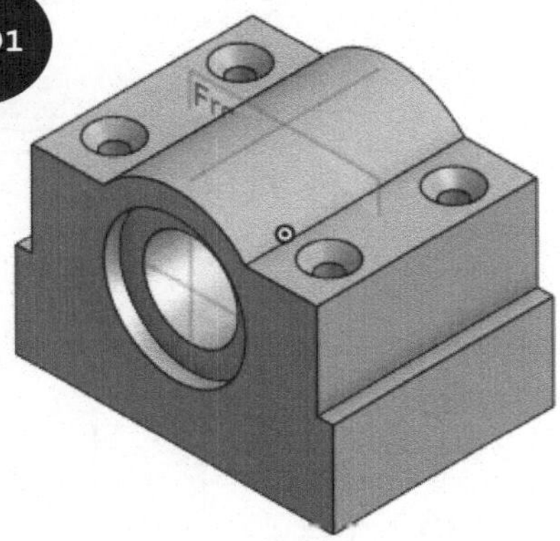

Tip: In Onshape, the document automatically saves to the specified location in the cloud. You can access a list of all the saved documents anytime by clicking on the **Created by me** option in the left menu of the **Documents Page**.

18. Create a version in the document to capture the current state of the design, and then close the document.

Hands-on Test Drive 1

Create the model shown in Figure 6.192. All dimensions are in mm.

6.192

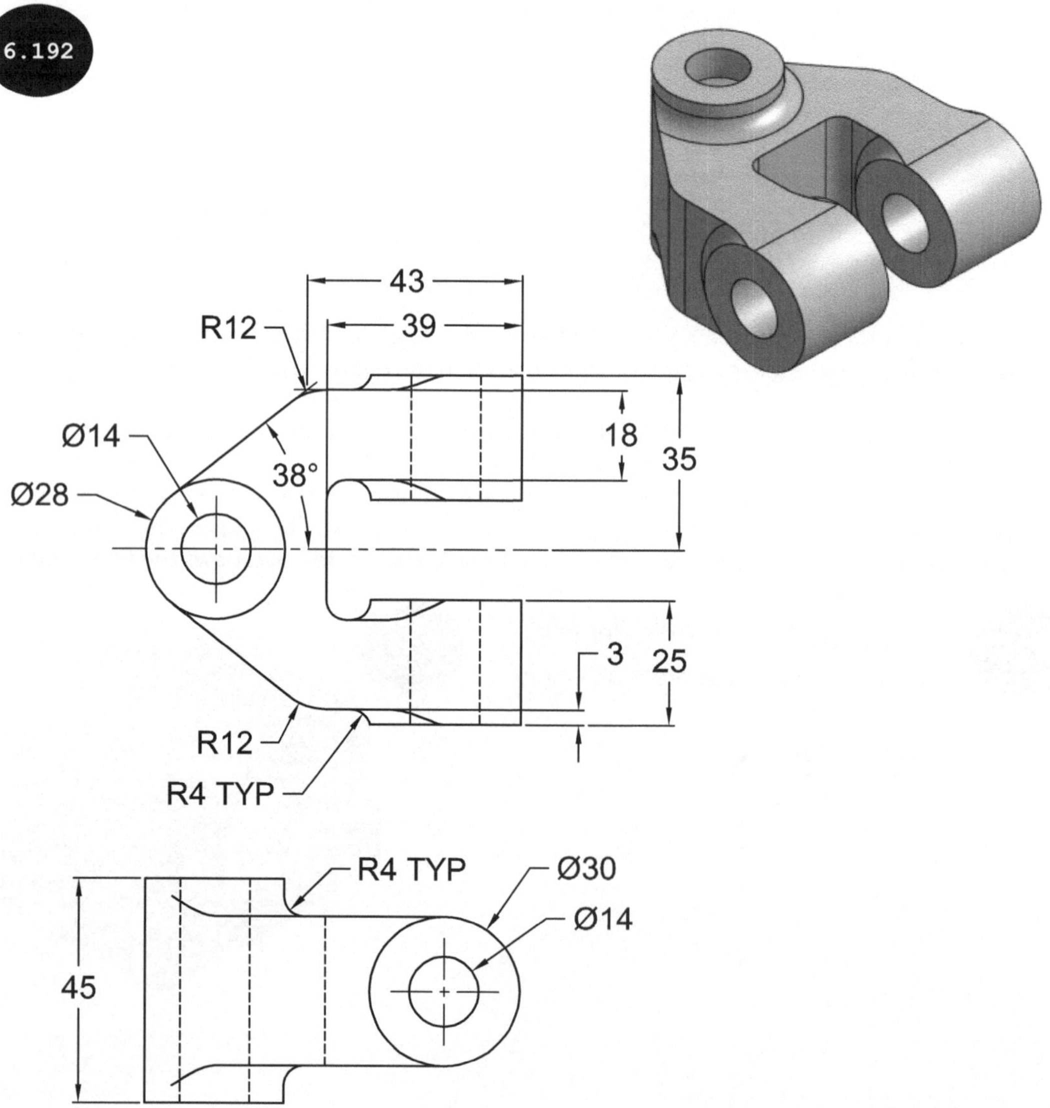

Hands-on Test Drive 2

Create the model shown in Figure 6.193. All dimensions are in inches.

6.193

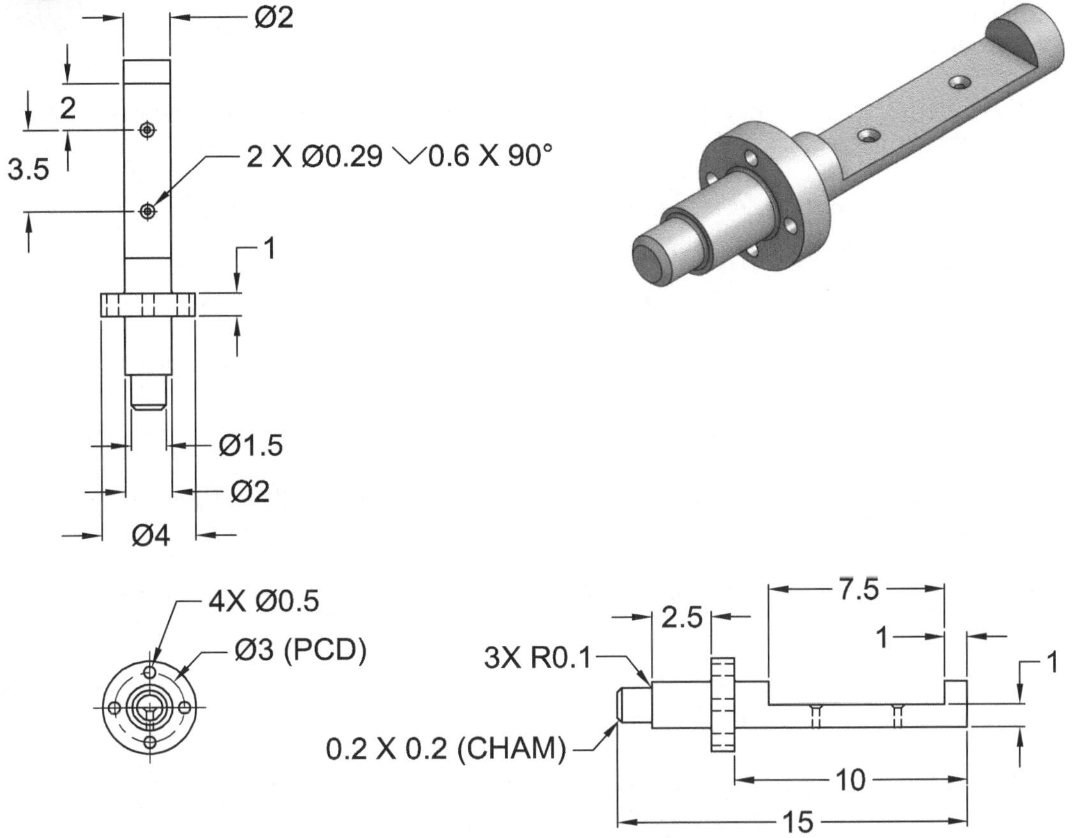

Summary

In this chapter, you explored essential placed features to enhance the precision, strength, and realism of your 3D models. You learned how to use tools such as **Fillet**, **Face Blend**, **Chamfer**, **Draft**, **Rib**, **Shell**, **Hole**, and **External thread** to refine your designs. These techniques equip you with the skills to add greater functionality and detail to your 3D models.

Questions

Complete and verify the following sentences:

- A _________ is a rounded face with a constant or variable radius, used to remove the sharp edges of a model.
- In Onshape, the **Fillet** tool allows you to create a _________ radius fillet, a _________ radius fillet, and a _________ round fillet.
- When the _________ check box is selected, all edges tangent to the selected edge are automatically filleted.
- The _________ option creates a fillet with a conical cross-section, defined by the specified radius and Rho values.
- If the Rho value is less than 0.5, the fillet will have an _________ curved shape.
- A _________ is a beveled face that is not perpendicular to its adjacent faces.
- The _________ tool allows you to add a draft angle to selected faces of a model.
- A _________ plane remains fixed and unchanged when a draft angle is applied to the selected faces of a model.
- A _________ feature acts as supporting element and is typically used to increase the strength of a model.
- A _________ feature creates a thin-walled structure with uniform thickness by removing one or more faces from a model.
- Selecting the _________ check box in the **Shell** dialog hollows out the selected part from the inside by applying a specified thickness.
- In Onshape, the Hole tool enables you to create _________, _________, and _________ holes.
- You can control the precision and tolerance for a hole's diameter while creating it. (True/False)
- In Onshape, you can create ANSI standard threads on the cylindrical faces of a model, but ISO standard threads are not supported. (True/False)
- If the Rho value is equal to 0.5, the fillet will have a parabolic curved shape. (True/False)
- Multiple faces of a model can be removed to create a shell feature. (True/False)

CHAPTER

7

Patterning and Mirroring

In this chapter, the following topics will be discussed:

- Creating a Linear Pattern
- Creating a Circular Pattern
- Creating a Curve pattern
- Mirroring Features, Faces, or Parts

Patterning and mirroring are essential tools that boost design efficiency by simplifying repetitive tasks and saving considerable time. For instance, consider designing a plate with 600 identical holes (refer to Figure 7.1). Instead of manually modeling each hole, you can create one and use the pattern tool to replicate it efficiently. Similarly, when working with symmetrical geometries, designing one side and mirroring it to create the other ensures consistency and save time.

7.1

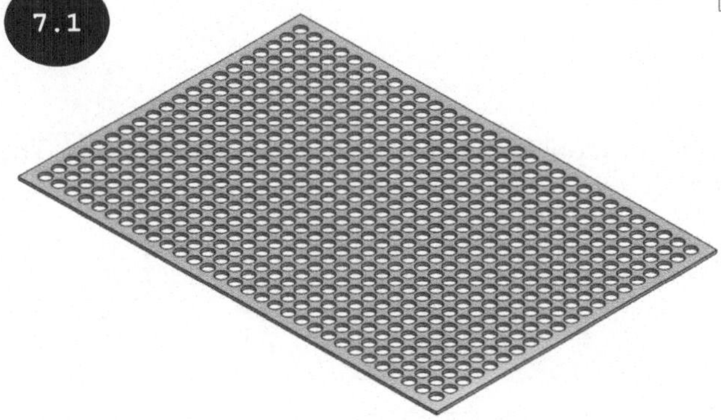

Onshape provides powerful tools for patterning, including **Linear pattern**, **Circular pattern**, and **Curve pattern**, along with robust mirroring capabilities. These features enable you to replicate faces, features, and parts with ease, ensuring accuracy and saving time. This chapter explores both patterning and mirroring tools in detail, guiding you through their application to optimize design workflow and boost productivity.

Creating a Linear Pattern

In Onshape, you can create a linear pattern by creating multiple instances of parts, features, or faces along one or two linear directions using the **Linear pattern** tool, see Figures 7.2 through 7.4. Figure 7.2 illustrates the feature to be patterned and the two linear directions (Direction 1 and Direction 2). Figure 7.3 shows the resulting linear pattern created by pattering the feature along Direction 1, while Figure 7.4 demonstrates the pattern created by pattering the feature along both Direction 1 and Direction 2. The method for creating a linear pattern is discussed below:

7.2

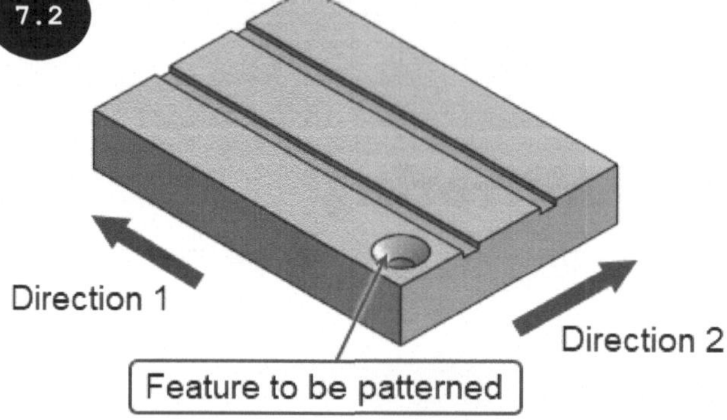

7.3

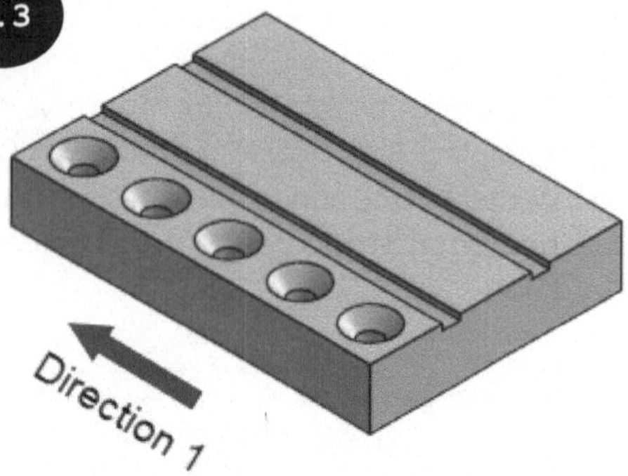

7.4

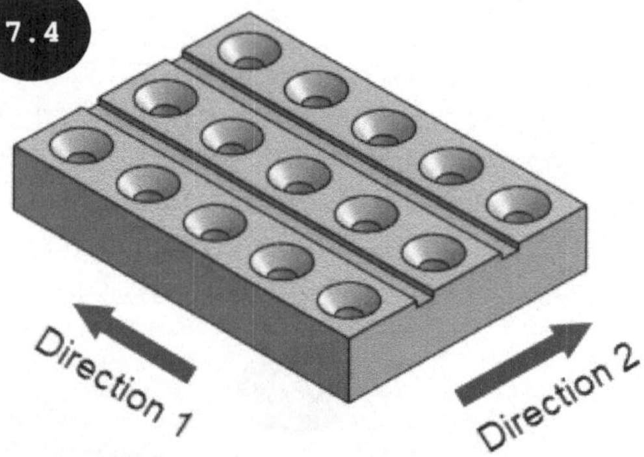

1. Click on the **Linear pattern** tool in the **Feature** toolbar, see Figure 7.5. The **Linear pattern** dialog appears, see Figure 7.6.

7.5

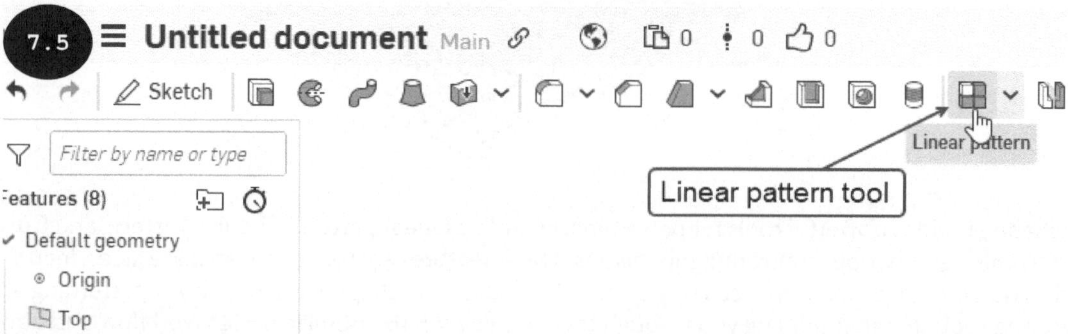

7.6

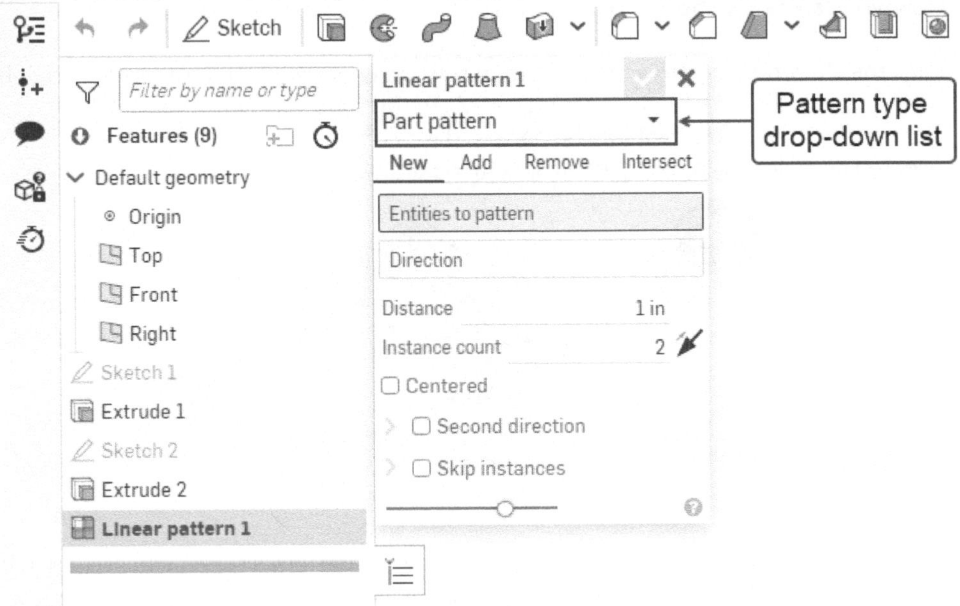

Pattern type: The **Pattern type** drop-down list lets you choose to pattern parts, features, or faces by selecting the corresponding option. By default, the **Part pattern** option is selected (see Figure 7.6), allowing you to pattern the entire part. Selecting the **Feature pattern** option enables you to pattern one or more features along one or two linear directions. Similarly, choosing the **Face pattern** option lets you pattern faces along specified directions. However, ensure that the selected faces form a closed volume for the pattern to be created successfully.

2. Select the **Feature pattern** option in the **Pattern type** drop-down list to create a pattern of one or more features. However, you can choose the desired option (**Part pattern**, **Feature pattern**, or **Face pattern**) in this drop-down list, as discussed above.

3. Select one or more features of a model to pattern, either from the graphics area or the **Feature list**, see Figure 7.7. The selected features highlight in the graphics area, and their names appear in the **Features to pattern** field of the dialog. In Figure 7.7, an extruded cut feature is selected as the feature to pattern.

7.7

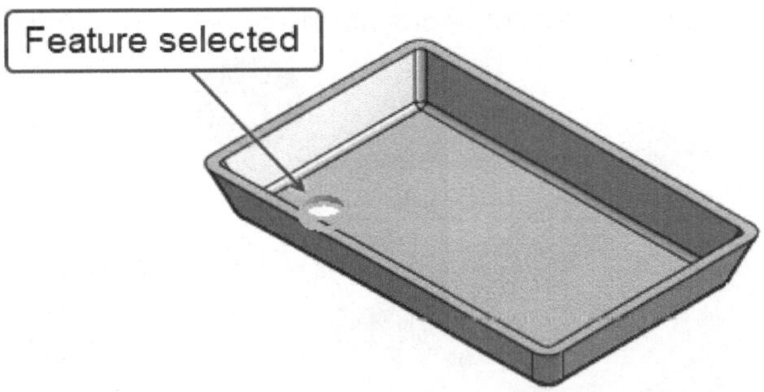

Now, you can define the first pattern direction along with other related parameters.

4. Click the **Direction** field to activate it, then select a linear edge or a planar face to define the first pattern direction (Direction 1), see Figure 7.8. In this figure, a linear edge is selected to define the pattern direction. After defining the pattern direction, a preview of the pattern appears along the selected direction, using the default specified parameters.

7.8

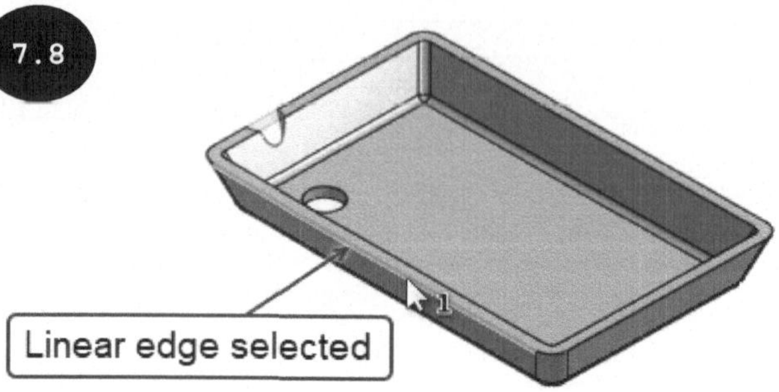

Tip: If you select a planar face or a plane to define the pattern direction, the pattern direction will be set normal to the selected face or plane.

5. Enter the required spacing between two consecutive instances in the **Distance** field and press ENTER.

6. Enter the required number of pattern instances in the **Instance count** field of the dialog box and press ENTER. The pattern preview updates accordingly in the graphics area along the specified pattern direction, see Figure 7.9.

Note: The total number of pattern instances specified in the **Instance count** field includes the parent or original instance. For example, if 7 is entered in this field, 7 pattern instances will be created along the specified pattern direction, with the parent instance counted as one of them.

7. Reverse the pattern direction by clicking the **Opposite direction** button located next to the **Instance count** field, if needed, see Figure 7.10. In this figure, a total of 7 pattern instances are defined, which includes the parent or original instance in the count.

7.9

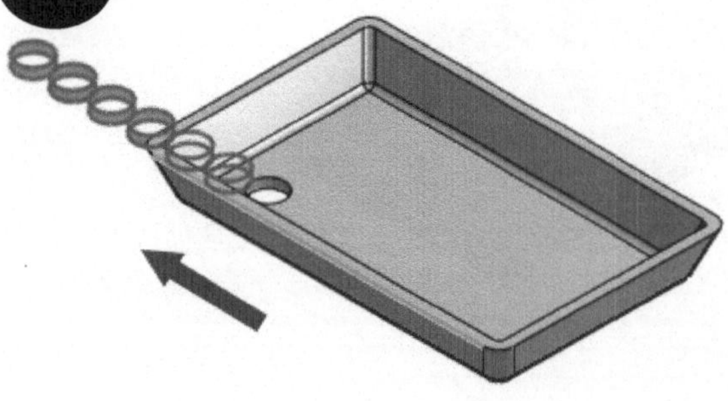

7.10

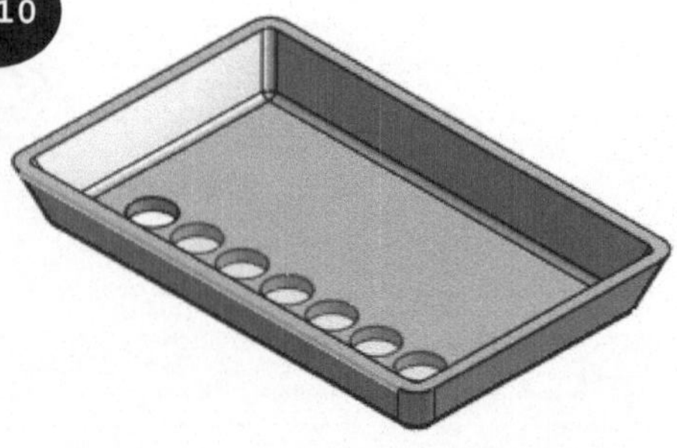

Centered: By selecting the **Centered** check box, the instances are patterned symmetrically on both sides of the parent feature along the specified pattern direction, refer to Figure 7.11. This option makes the parent feature the center of the pattern.

7.11

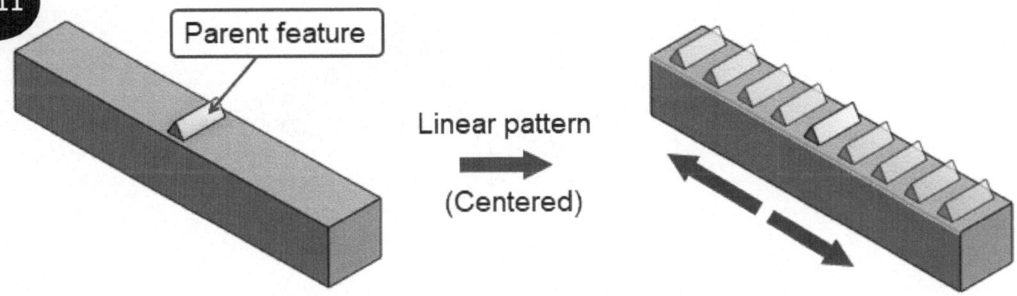

Second direction: By selecting the **Second direction** check box, you can pattern the selected features, faces, or part along the second direction (Direction 2), in addition to the first pattern direction.

8. Select the **Second direction** check box in the **Linear pattern** dialog to pattern the selected feature along the second direction (Direction 2), if needed. The **Direction** field appears below the check box to define the second direction, along with the **Distance** field, **Instance count** field, and **Centered** check box for specifying the respective parameters, see Figure 7.12.

7.12

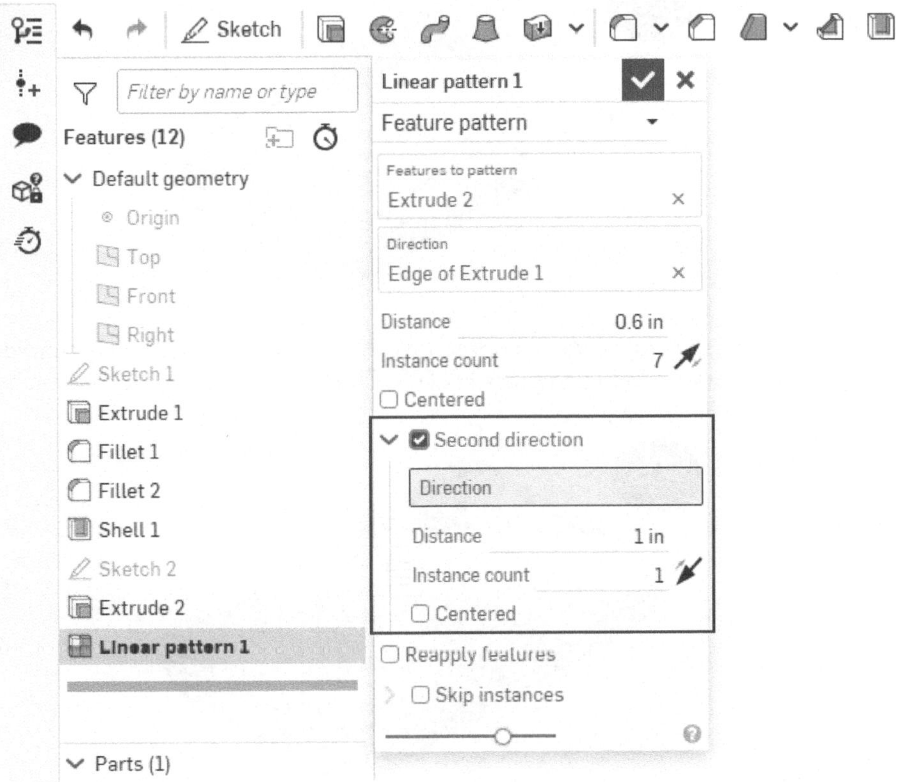

9. Select a linear edge or a planar face to define the second pattern direction (Direction 2), see Figure 7.13. In this figure, a linear edge is selected to define the second pattern direction.

7.13

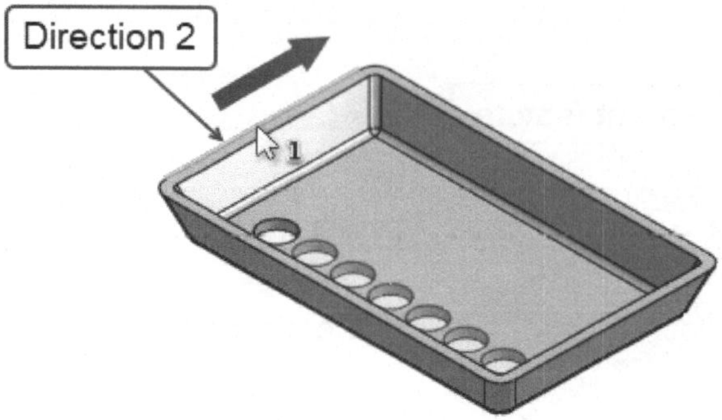

Now, you can specify the total number of instances and the spacing among them along the second pattern direction.

10. Enter the required number of pattern instances for the second pattern direction in the corresponding **Instance count** field and press ENTER. The pattern preview updates accordingly in the graphics area, see Figure 7.14. In this figure, a total of 3 pattern instances are specified along the second pattern direction, including the parent feature.

7.14

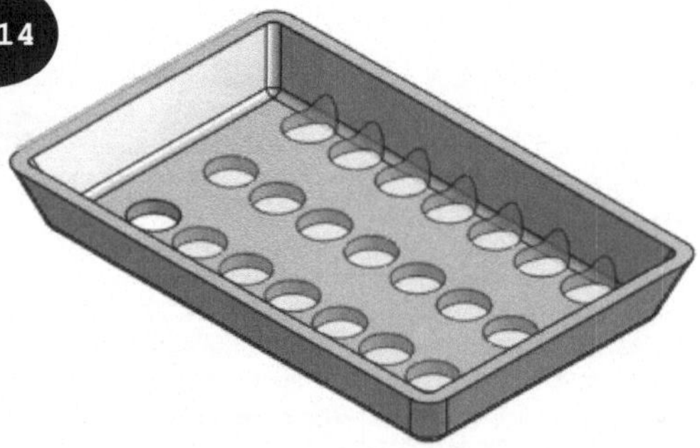

11. Enter the required spacing between consecutive instances for the second pattern direction in the corresponding **Distance** field and press ENTER. The pattern preview updates accordingly in the graphics area, see Figure 7.15.

7.15

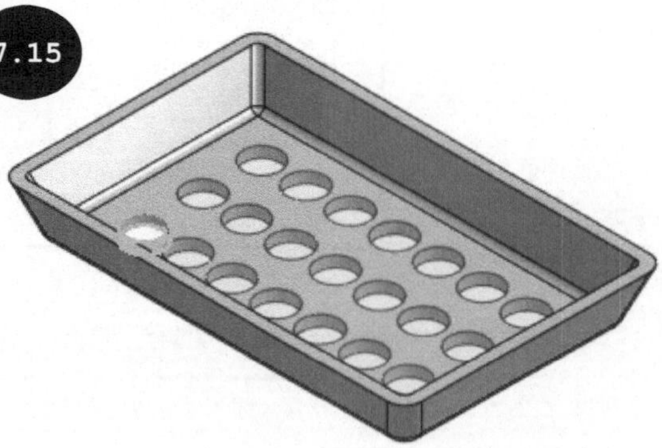

Centered: The **Centered** check box that appears after selecting the **Second direction** check allows you to pattern the instances symmetrically on both sides of the parent feature along the second pattern direction, refer to Figure 7.16.

7.16

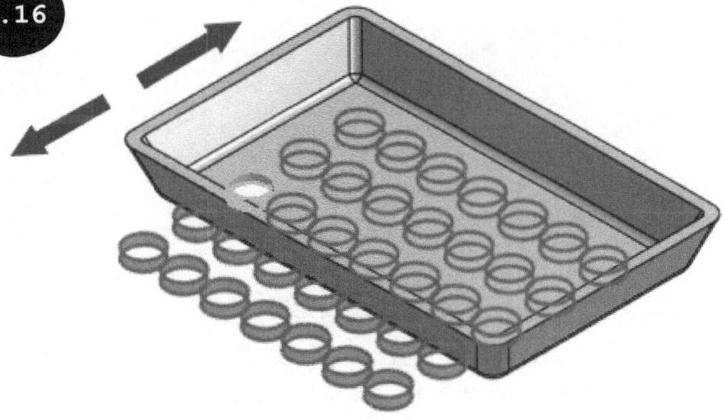

Reapply features: Selecting the **Reapply features** check box regenerates the feature for each instance, ensuring that only the instances that can be created based on the model geometry are generated, thereby avoiding geometrical errors. For example, in Figure 7.17, five instances are defined along the second pattern direction. However, the last two instances cannot be created because they extend beyond the model geometry, leading to an error in the pattern. By selecting this check box, the system automatically excludes these invalid instances and adjusts the pattern, see Figure 7.18. This resolves the issue effectively and maintains the integrity of the pattern. Note that this check box is available only when patterning a feature

7.17

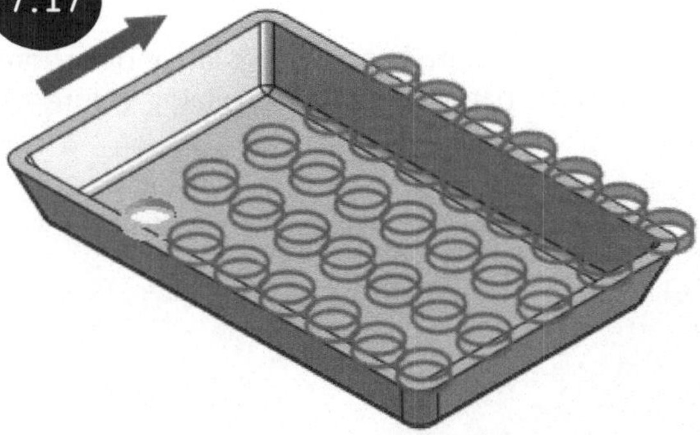

7.18

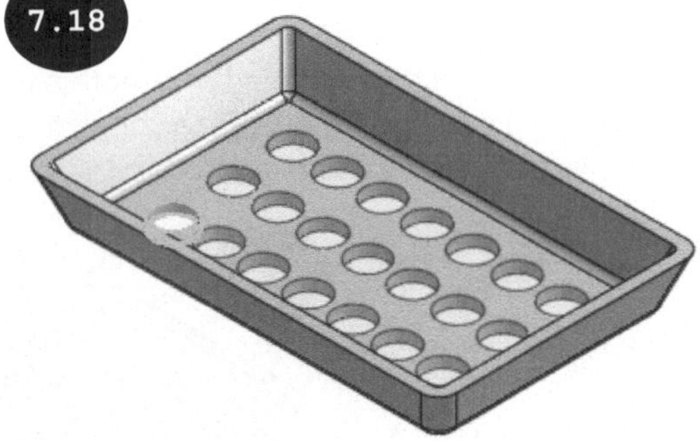

Skip instances: The **Skip instances** check box allows you to exclude specific instances from a pattern. To do this, select the **Skip instances** check box in the dialog. White dots appear at the center of each pattern instance in the graphics area, see Figure 9.19. Hover over the white dot of the instance you want to skip and click the left mouse button. The selected instance disappears or is skipped, but its white dot remains visible in its position, as illustrated in Figure 9.20. To skip multiple instances, click on their respective dots one at a time. The skipped instances are listed in the **Instances to skip** field located below the **Skip instances** check box in the dialog.

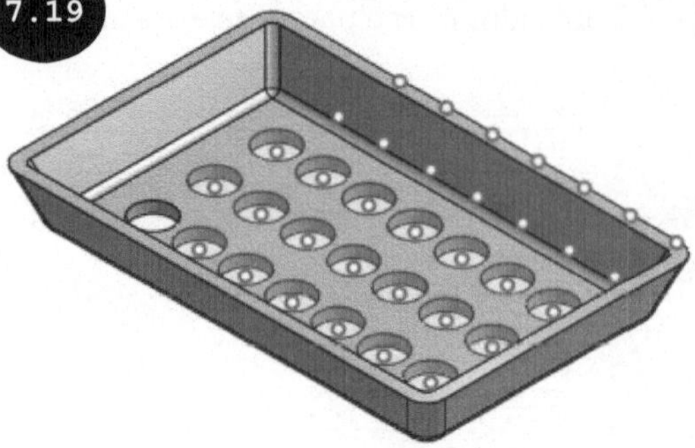
7.19

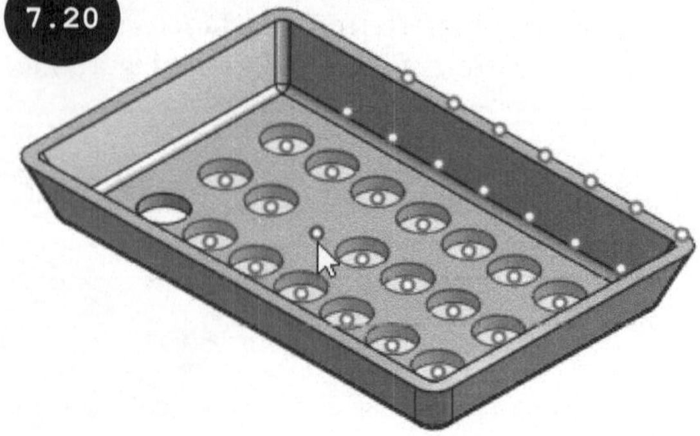
7.20

To recall skipped instances, click their white dots again in the graphics area or click on the cross-mark × next to their name in the **Instances to skip** field. To restore all skipped instances at once, right-click in the **Instances to skip** field and select the **Clear all** option, see Figure 7.21.

7.21

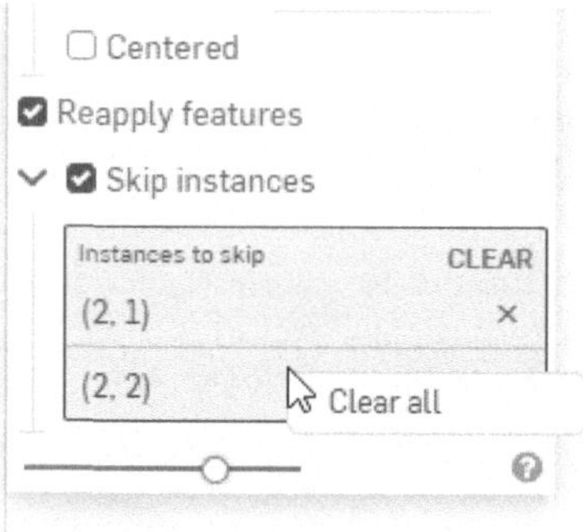

12. After specifying the required parameters for creating linear pattern in one or two linear directions, click the green checkmark ✓ to confirm the creation of the pattern and exit the dialog. Figure 7.22 shows the linear pattern created.

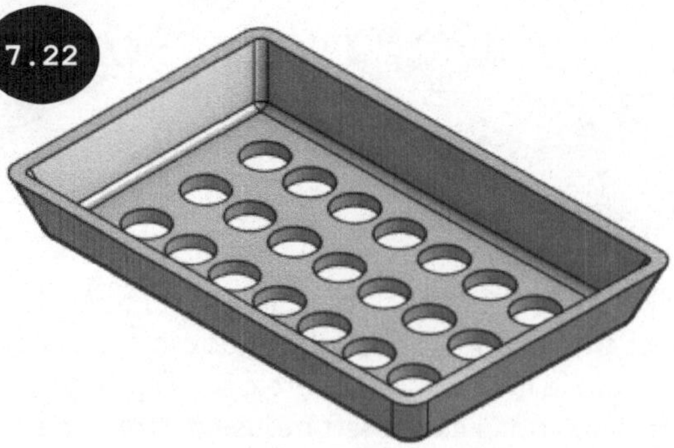
7.22

Creating a Circular Pattern

A circular pattern is created by creating multiple instances of parts, features, or faces circularly around an axis using the **Circular pattern** tool, see Figure 7.23. This figure illustrates the feature to be patterned and the resulting circular pattern, formed by replicating the feature around the centered vertical axis of the model. The method for creating a circular pattern is discussed below:

7.23

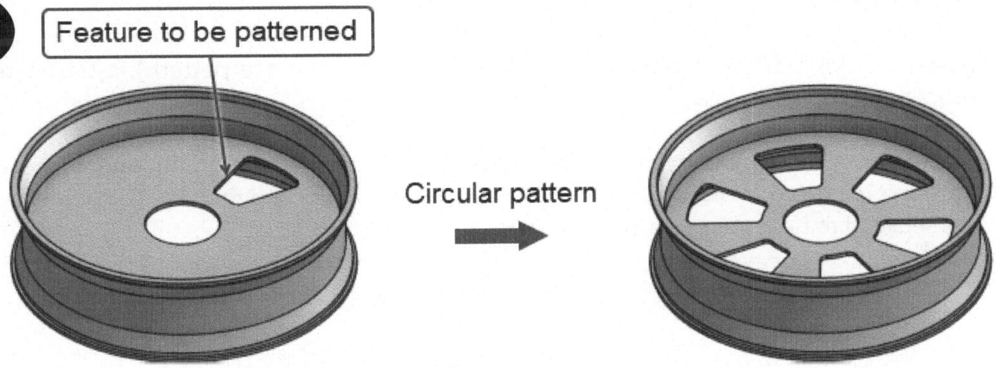

1. Click on a small arrow beside the **Linear pattern** tool in the **Feature** toolbar and then click on the **Circular pattern** tool in the **Pattern** drop-down menu that appears, see Figure 7.24. The **Circular pattern** dialog appears, see Figure 7.25.

7.24

7.25

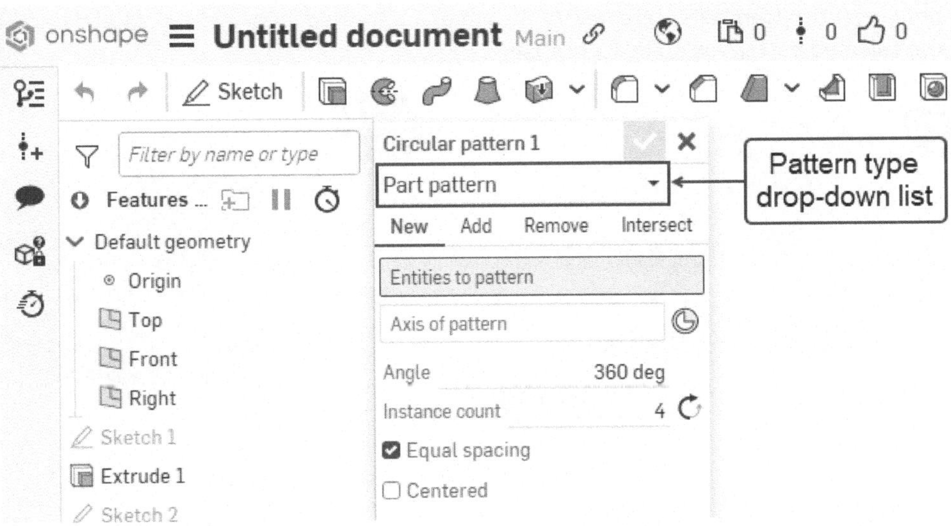

Pattern type: The **Pattern type** drop-down list allows you to choose whether to pattern parts, features, or faces by selecting the corresponding option. By default, the **Part pattern** option is selected (see Figure 7.25), enabling you to pattern an entire part around an axis of revolution. Selecting the **Feature pattern** option allows you to replicate one or more features around the axis of revolution. Likewise, the **Face pattern** option lets you pattern faces around the axis; however, it is essential to ensure that the selected faces form a closed volume for the pattern to be created successfully.

2. Select the desired option (**Part pattern**, **Feature pattern**, or **Face pattern**) in the **Pattern type** drop-down list, as discussed above.

3. Select one or more parts, features, or faces to be patterned, based on the option chosen in the **Pattern type** drop-down list, see Figure 7.26. In this example, two features (rib and extrude cut) are selected to be patterned around an axis.

7.26

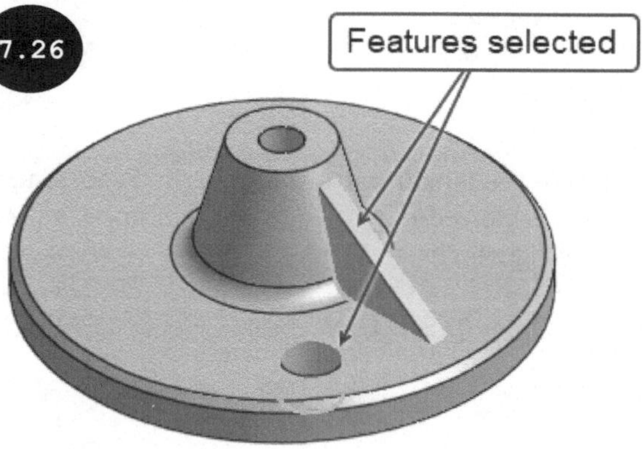

Now, you can define a pattern axis.

4. Click the **Axis of pattern** field in the dialog to activate it, then select a circular face, a circular edge, a linear edge, or a linear sketch entity to define the pattern axis, see Figure 7.27. This figure illustrates the outer circular edge of the model being selected to define the pattern axis. After defining the pattern axis, a preview of the circular pattern appears with default parameters around the selected pattern axis, see Figure 7.28.

7.27

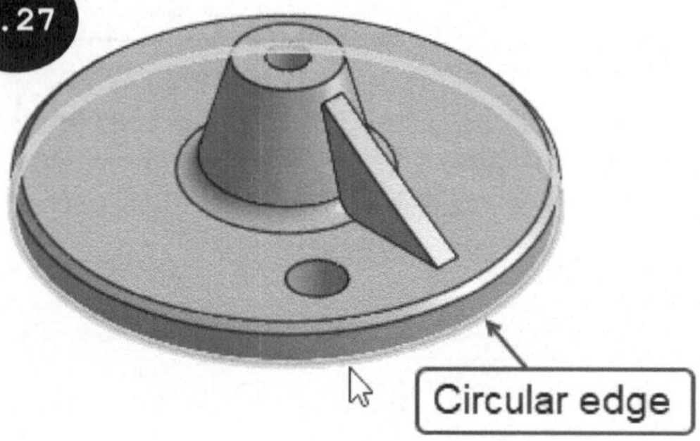

7.28

Note: When selecting a circular face or a circular edge as the pattern axis, the corresponding center axis is automatically determined and used as the axis for the circular pattern.

Angle: The **Angle** field defines the angle value between pattern instances. When the **Equal spacing** check box is selected, the angle value in the **Angle** field represents the total angle of the pattern, with all instances evenly spaced within this specified angle. Conversely, if the **Equal spacing** check box is cleared, the angle value in the **Angle** field defines the spacing between two consecutive pattern instances.

5. Ensure that the **Equal spacing** check box is selected in the dialog to define the total angle value for the pattern instances. If you want to define the angle value between two consecutive pattern instances, clear this check box.

6. Enter the desired total angle value in the **Angle** field of the dialog. All pattern instances are evenly distributed within this specified total angle. By default, the field is set to **360** degrees.

7. Enter the desired number of pattern instances in the **Instance count** field of the dialog, see Figure 7.29. This figure illustrates the preview of a circular pattern with 5 instances evenly distributed within a total angle of 360 degrees. Note that the number of instances specified in the **Instance count** field includes the parent feature.

7.29

Centered: The **Centered** check box allows you to pattern the instances symmetrically on both sides of the parent feature around the pattern axis, refer to Figure 7.30.

7.30

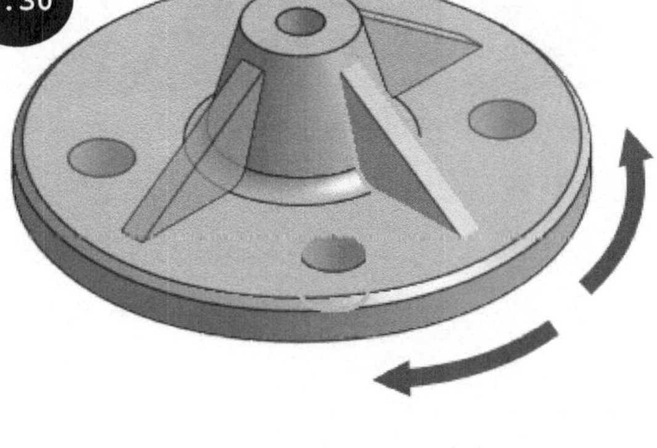

Reapply features: Selecting the **Reapply features** check box regenerates the feature for each instance, ensuring that only the instances that can be created based on the model geometry are generated, thereby avoiding geometrical errors. This check box is available only when patterning a feature.

Skip instances: The **Skip instances** check box allows you to exclude specific instances from a pattern. To do this, select the **Skip instances** check box in the dialog. White dots appear at the center of each pattern instance in the graphics area, see Figure 9.31. Hover over the white dot of the instance you want to skip and click the left mouse button. The selected instance disappears or is skipped, but its white dot remains visible in its position, as illustrated in Figure 9.32. To skip multiple instances, click on their respective dots one at a time. The skipped instances are listed in the **Instances to skip** field located below the **Skip instances** check box in the dialog.

7.31

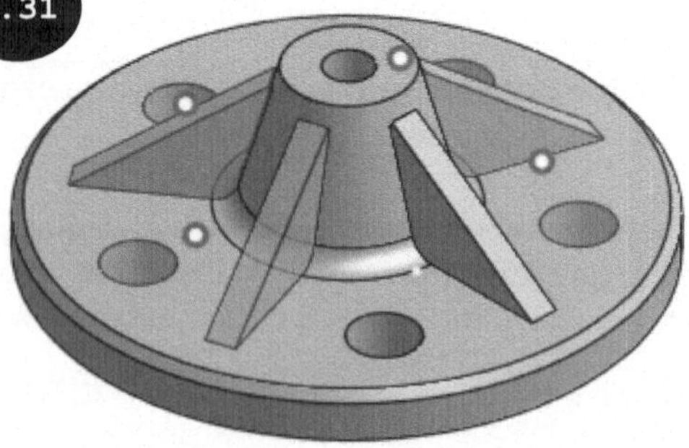

7.32

To recall skipped instances, click their white dots again in the graphics area or click on the cross-mark × next to their name in the **Instances to skip** field.

8. After specifying the required parameters for creating circular pattern, click the green checkmark ✓ to confirm the creation of the pattern and exit the dialog. Figure 7.33 shows the circular pattern created.

7.33

Creating a Curve pattern

A curve pattern is created by creating multiple instances of parts, features, or faces along a path (curve) using the **Curve pattern** tool, see Figure 7.34. This figure illustrates the feature to be patterned and the path, with the resulting curve pattern formed by replicating the feature along the path. The method for creating a curve pattern is discussed below:

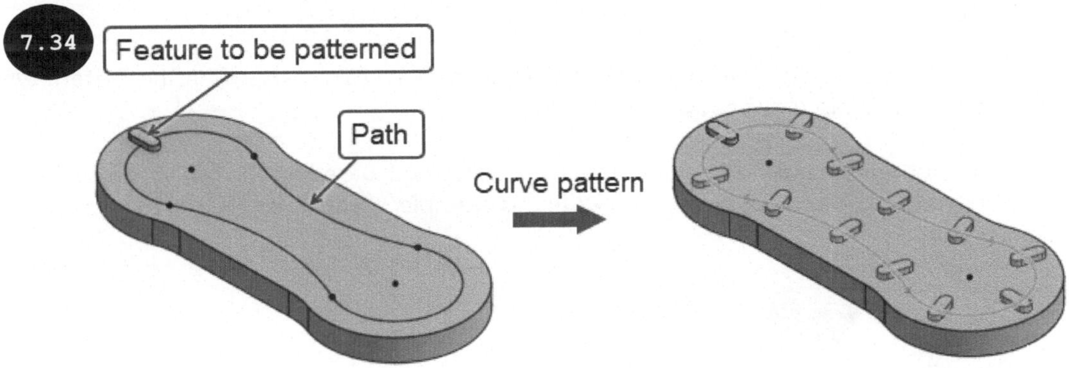

1. Invoke the **Pattern** drop-down menu by clicking on a small arrow beside the active pattern tool and then click on the **Curve pattern** tool, see Figure 7.35. The **Curve pattern** dialog appears, see Figure 7.36.

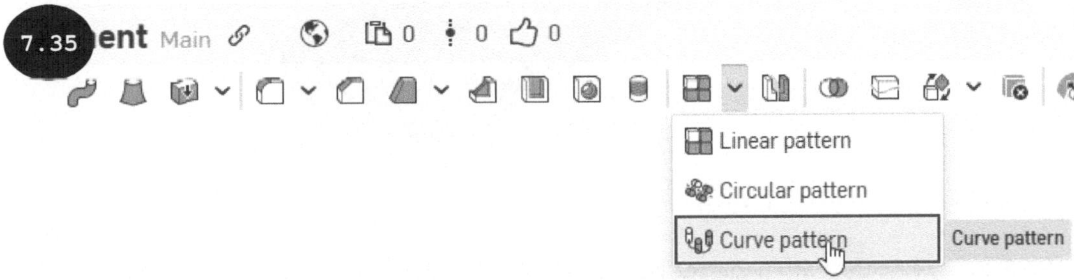

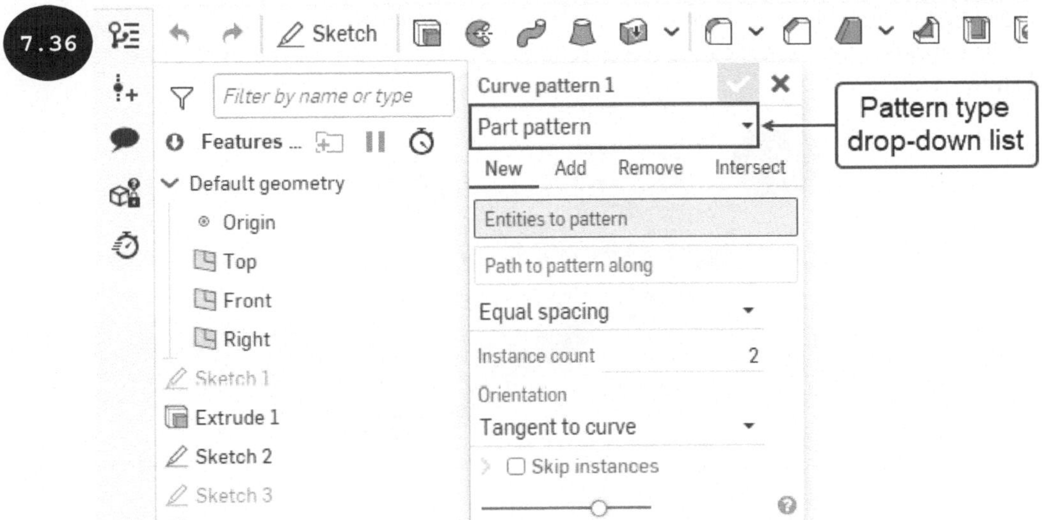

Pattern type: The **Pattern type** drop-down list allows you to choose whether to pattern parts, features, or faces by selecting the corresponding option. By default, the **Part pattern** option is selected (see Figure 7.36), enabling you to pattern an entire part along a selected path (curve). Selecting the **Feature pattern** option allows you to replicate one or more features along the specified path. Likewise, the **Face pattern** option lets you pattern faces along the path; however, it is essential to ensure that the selected faces form a closed volume for the pattern to be created successfully.

2. Select the desired option (**Part pattern**, **Feature pattern**, or **Face pattern**) in the **Pattern type** drop-down list, as discussed above.

3. Select one or more parts, features, or faces to be patterned, based on the option chosen in the **Pattern type** drop-down list, see Figure 7.37. In this example, a feature is selected to be patterned along a path.

7.37

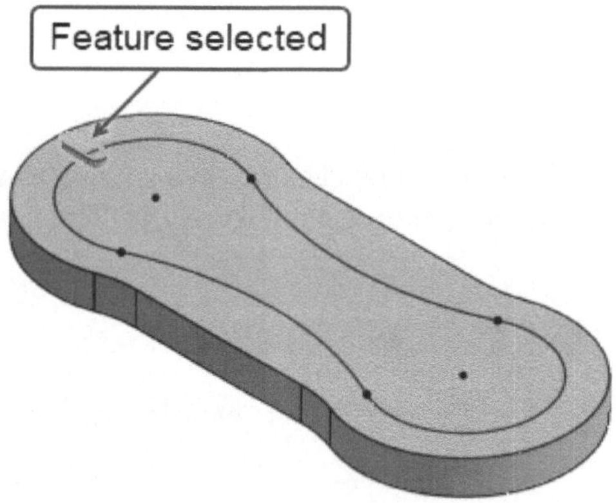

Now, select a path to replicate the chosen features, faces, or parts along it.

4. Click to activate the **Path to pattern along** field in the dialog, then select an open or closed sketch from the **Feature list** as the path to drive the pattern instances. Alternatively, you can select individual model edges to define the pattern's path. Once the path is defined, a preview of the curve pattern appears, replicating the specified number of instances along the selected path, see Figure 7.38.

7.38

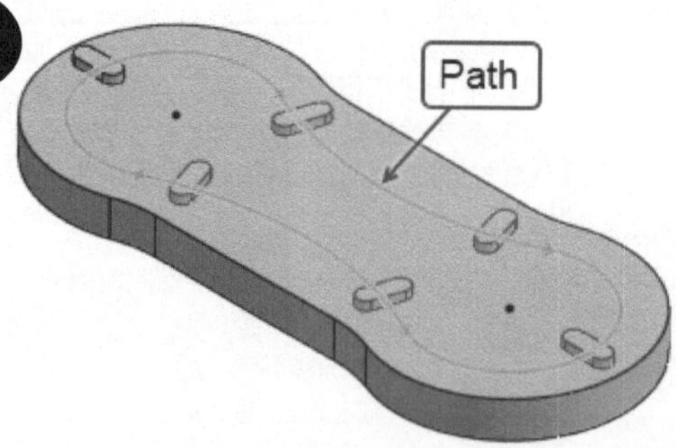

Note: If the sketch contains multiple segments, it is recommended to select it from the **Feature list** to automatically include all segments as the path. In the graphics area, only individual sketch segments can be selected as the path.

Tip: Ensure that the path and the parent feature are coincident or touch each other for the best results. This ensures proper alignment and helps the pattern instances be created accurately along the selected path.

5. Enter the desired number of pattern instances to be created in the **Instance count** field of the dialog and press ENTER. The preview of the curve pattern updates, accordingly, refer to Figure 7.39. This figure illustrates the preview of the curve pattern with 12 instances evenly distributed along the selected path. Note that the number of instances specified in the **Instance count** field includes the parent feature.

7.39

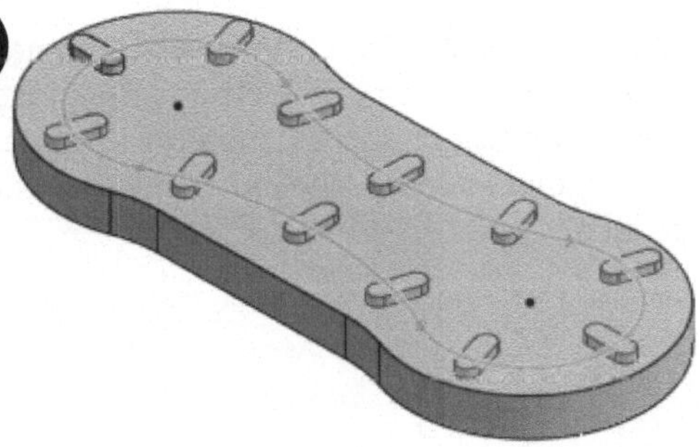

Spacing type: By default, the **Equal spacing** option is selected in the **Spacing type** drop-down list. This ensures that the specified number of pattern instances are evenly distributed along the entire length of the selected path, refer to Figure 7.39. If you select the **Distance** option, the **Distance** field becomes active in the dialog (see Figure 7.40), enabling you to specify the distance between two consecutive pattern instances.

7.40

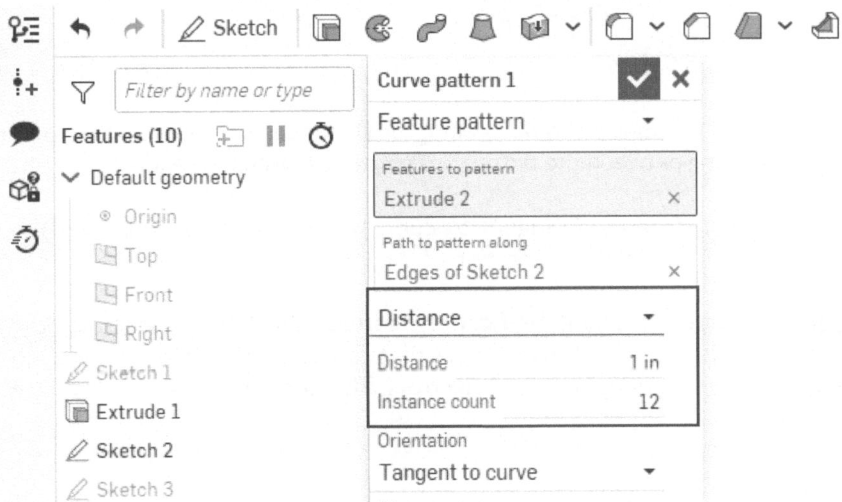

Orientation: By default, the **Tangent to curve** option is selected in the **Orientation** drop-down list, aligning all the pattern instances tangentially to the selected path (curve), see Figure 7.41. If you select the **Locked** option, the orientation of the pattern instances is fixed to match the orientation of the parent instance, see Figure 7.42.

7.41

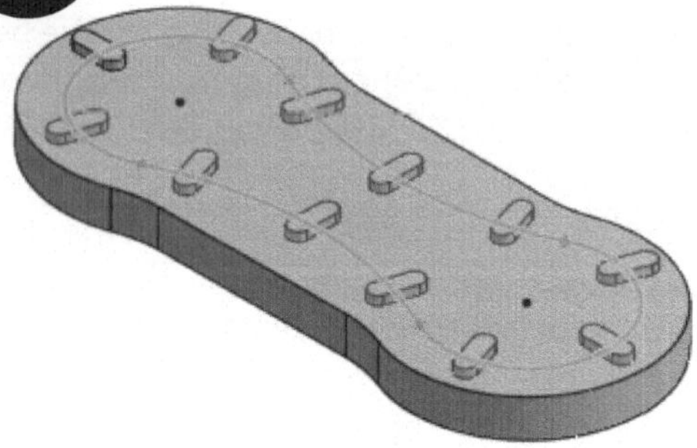

7.42

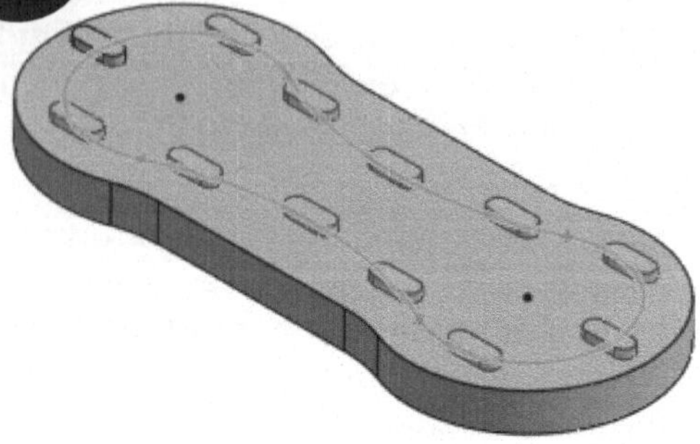

When you select the **Normal to face** option, the **Faces to be normal to** field becomes available, allowing you to choose one or more faces to align the pattern instances normal to them along the selected path (curve), see Figure 7.43. In this example, all the side faces of the model are selected. Consequently, the pattern instances follow the path while maintaining a normal relationship with their corresponding side face.

7.43

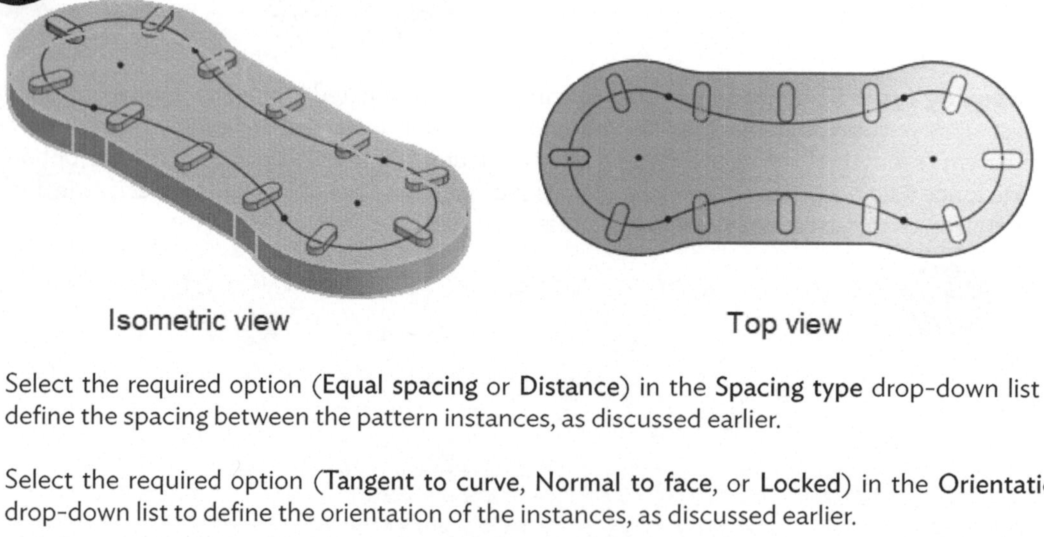

Isometric view

Top view

6. Select the required option (**Equal spacing** or **Distance**) in the **Spacing type** drop-down list to define the spacing between the pattern instances, as discussed earlier.

7. Select the required option (**Tangent to curve, Normal to face**, or **Locked**) in the **Orientation** drop-down list to define the orientation of the instances, as discussed earlier.

   Reapply features: Selecting the **Reapply features** check box regenerates the feature for each instance, ensuring that only the instances that can be created based on the model geometry are generated, thus preventing geometrical errors. This check box is available only when patterning a feature.

Skip instances: The **Skip instances** check box allows you to exclude specific instances from a pattern. To do this, select the **Skip instances** check box in the dialog. White dots appear at the center of each pattern instance in the graphics area, see Figure 7.44. Hover over the white dot of the instance you want to skip and click the left mouse button. The selected instance disappears or is skipped, but its white dot remains visible in its position, as illustrated in Figure 7.45. To skip multiple instances, click on their respective dots one at a time. The skipped instances are listed in the **Instances to skip** field located below the **Skip instances** check box in the dialog.

7.44

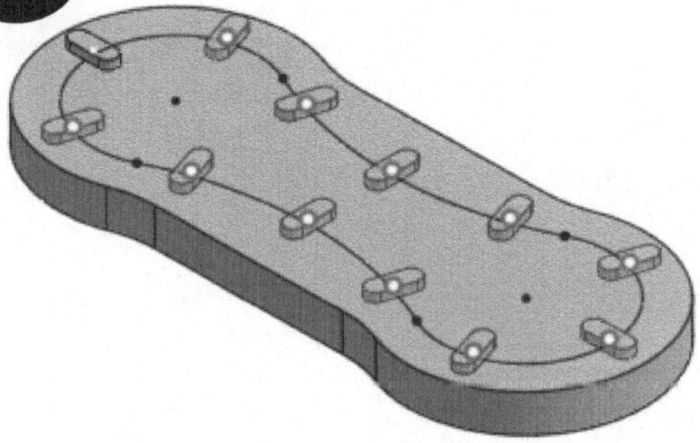

7.45

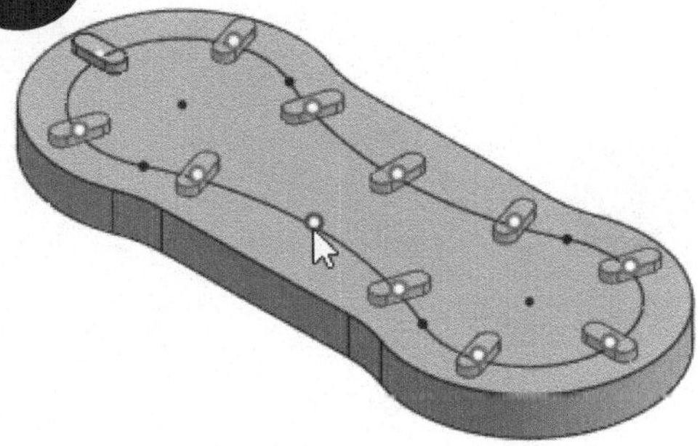

To recall skipped instances, click their white dots again in the graphics area or click on the cross-mark × next to their name in the **Instances to skip** field.

8. After specifying the required parameters, click the green checkmark ✓ to confirm the creation of the curve pattern and exit the dialog.

Mirroring Features, Faces, or Parts

In Onshape, you can mirror features, faces, or parts about a mirroring plane using the **Mirror** tool. You can select a plane or a planar face as the mirroring plane. Figure 7.46 illustrates a feature to be mirrored, the mirroring plane, and the resulting mirror feature created. The method for mirroring features, faces, or parts is discussed below:

7.46

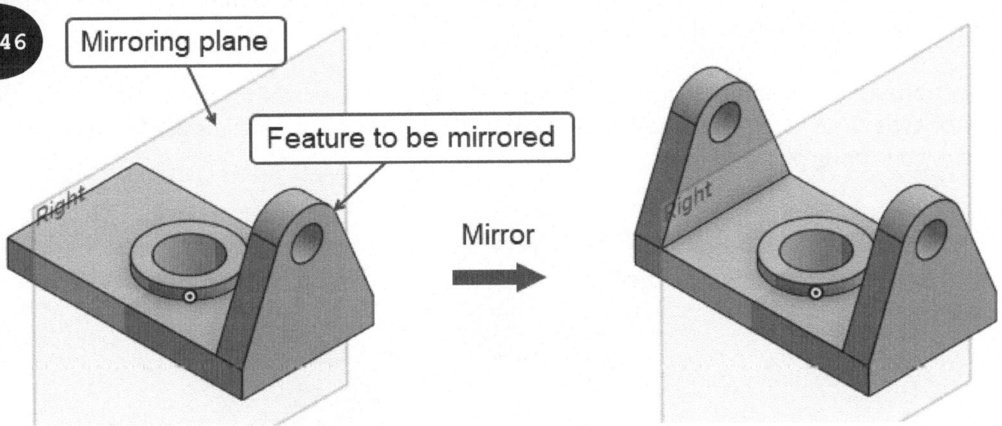

1. Click on the **Mirror** tool in the **Feature** toolbar, see Figure 7.47. The **Mirror** dialog appears, see Figure 7.48.

7.47

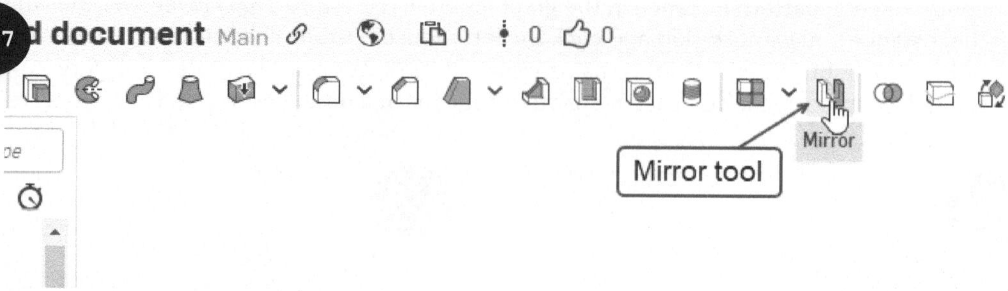

7.48

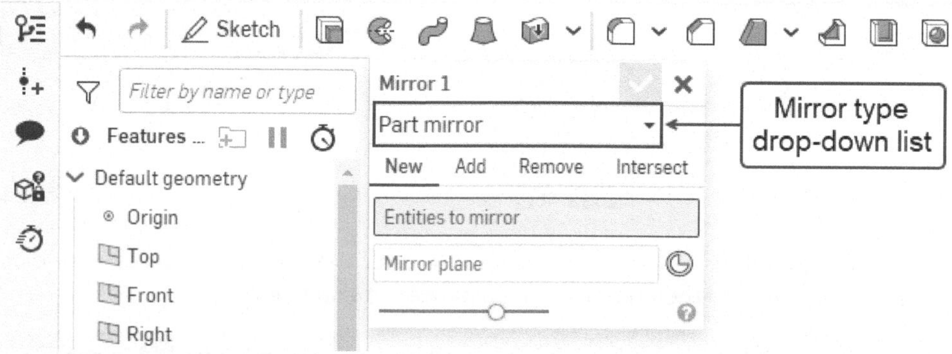

Mirror type: The **Mirror type** drop-down list allows you to choose whether to mirror parts, features, or faces by selecting the corresponding option. By default, the **Part mirror** option is selected (see Figure 7.48), enabling you to mirror an entire part about a mirroring plane. Selecting the **Feature mirror** option allows you to mirror one or more features about a mirroring plane. Likewise, the **Face mirror** option lets you mirror faces about a mirroring plane; however, it is essential to ensure that the selected faces form a closed volume for the mirror to be created successfully.

2. Select the desired option (**Part mirror**, **Feature mirror**, or **Face mirror**) in the **Mirror type** drop-down list, as discussed above.

3. Select one or more parts, features, or faces to be mirrored, based on the option chosen in the **Mirror type** drop-down list, see Figure 7.49. In this example, a part is selected to be mirrored about a mirroring plane.

7.49

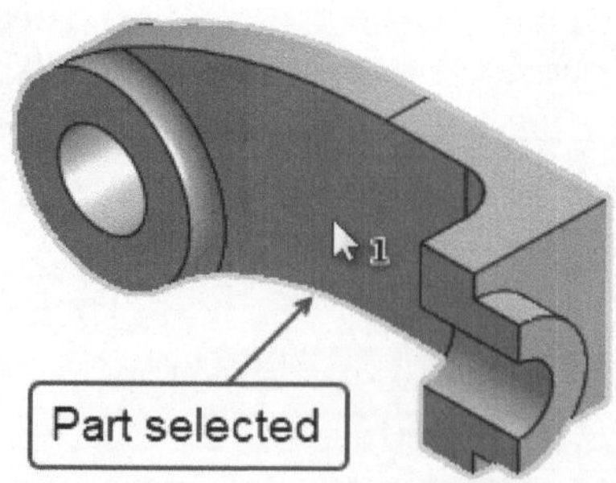

4. Click on the **Mirror plane** field in the dialog to activate it, then select a plane or a planar face of the model as the mirroring plane, see Figure 7.50. In this example, the cursor is placed over a planar face of the model to indicate its selection as the mirroring plane. As soon as you select the mirroring plane, a preview of the mirror feature appears in the graphics area, see Figure 7.51.

7.50

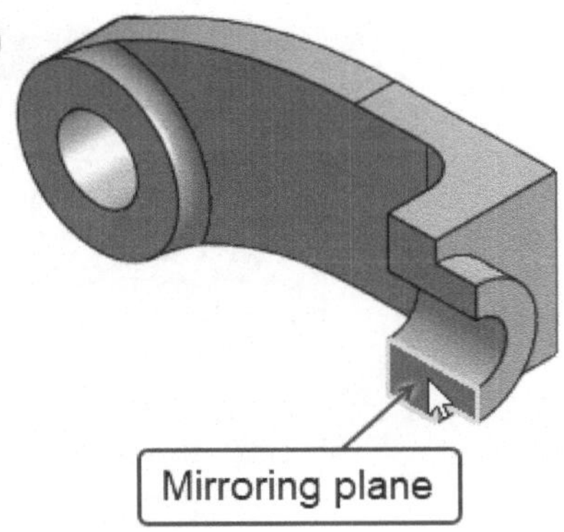

7.51

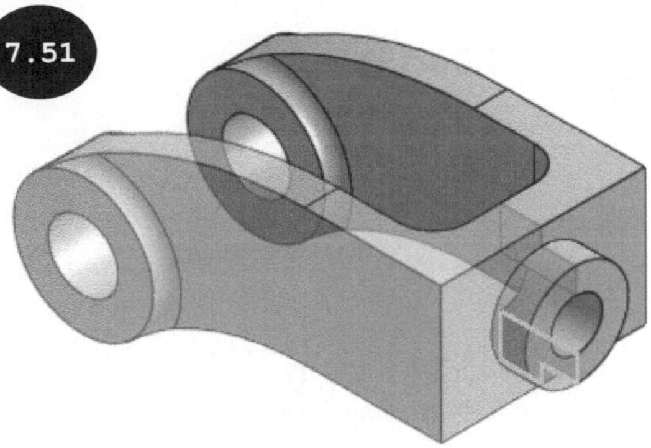

5. Ensure that the required option (**New**, **Add**, **Remove**, or **Intersect**) is selected in the **Operation type** area of the dialog, see Figure 7.52. This area is available only when mirroring a part.

7.52

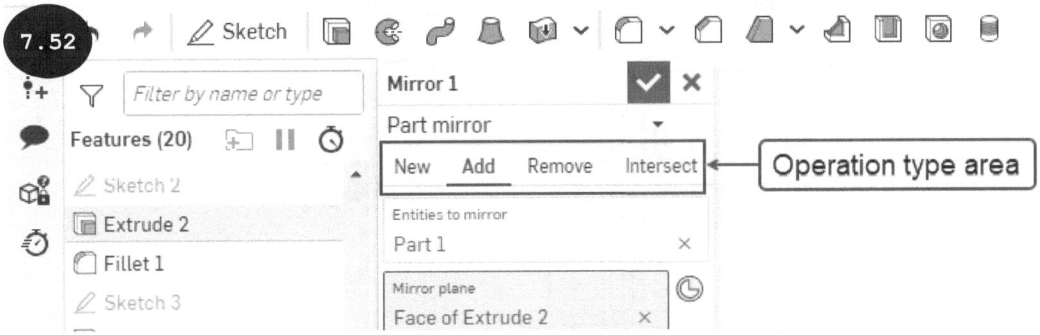

6. Select the **Reapply features** check box in the **Mirror** dialog, if needed. Note that this check box is available only when mirroring a feature.

7. After specifying the required parameters, click the green checkmark ✓ to confirm the creation of the mirror and exit the dialog. Figure 7.53 illustrates the model created by mirroring one half about a mirroring plane to form the other half.

7.53

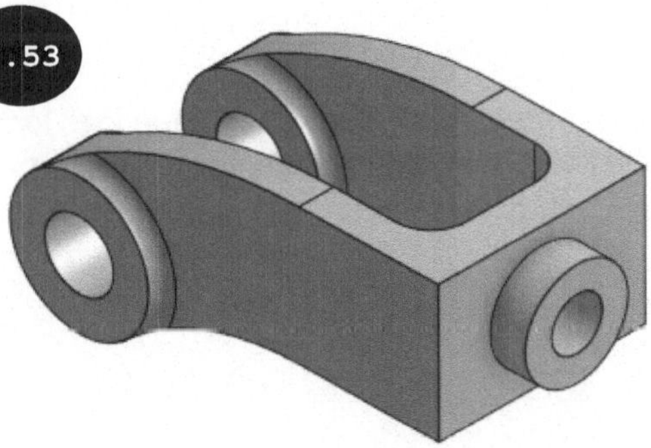

Tutorial 1

Create a model, as shown in Figure 7.54. The different views and dimensions are given in the same figure. All dimensions are in inches.

7.54

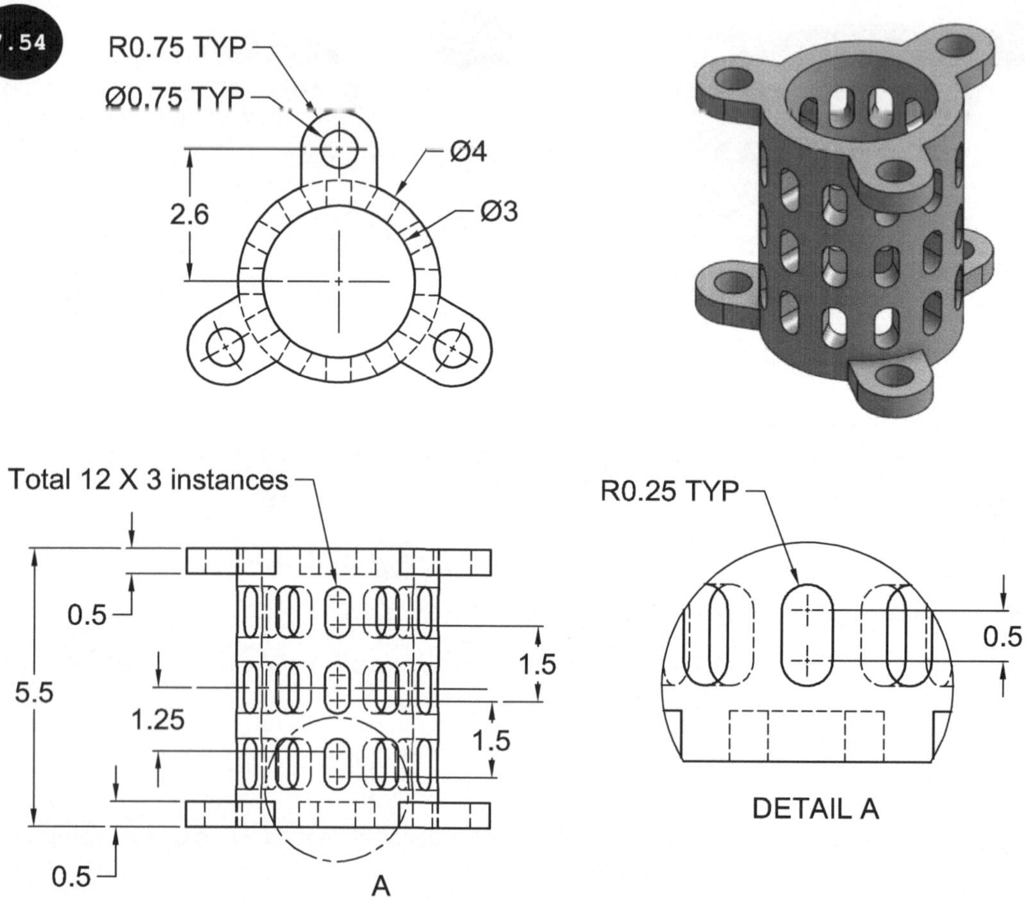

Section 1: Starting a New Design Document

1. Launch Onshape (***onshape.com***) and log in to your account if you're not already logged in. The **Documents Page** appears.

Note: If you are within a document, click on the **Onshape** logo located in the top left corner of the browser to display the **Documents Page**, see Figure 7.55.

7.55

2. Click on the **Create** button at the top left corner of the **Documents Page** and then click on the **Document** option in the menu that appears, see Figure 7.56. The **New document** window appears with the default name of the document as "**Untitled document**".

7.56

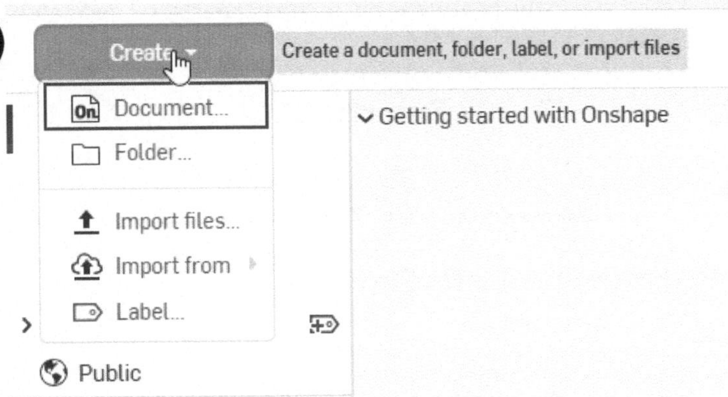

3. Enter **C07 Tutorial 01** as the name of the design document in the **New document** window, and then click on the **Create** button or the **Create Public Document** button, depending on your subscription type. A new document with the specified name is opened.

Section 2: Settings Units

Before creating the model, ensure that the document's units are properly defined.

1. Invoke the **Document** menu by clicking on the ≡ icon (three horizontal lines) next to the **Onshape** logo at the top left corner, see Figure 7.57.

7.57

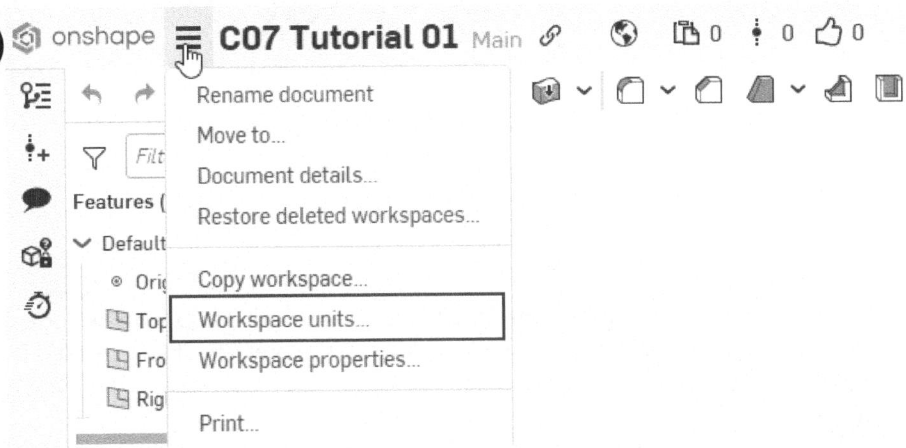

2. Click on the **Workspace units** option in the **Document** menu, refer to Figure 7.57. The **Workspace units** dialog appears.

3. In this dialog, ensure that the **Inch** unit is selected for length measurement in the **Length default unit** drop-down list. Next, click on the green checkmark ✓ to confirm the selection and exit the dialog.

Section 3: Creating the Base Feature - Extrude

Now, you can create the base feature of the model, which is an extruded feature.

1. Click on the **Sketch** tool in the **Feature** toolbar, see Figure 7.58. The **Sketch** dialog appears and you are prompted to select a sketching plane.

7.58

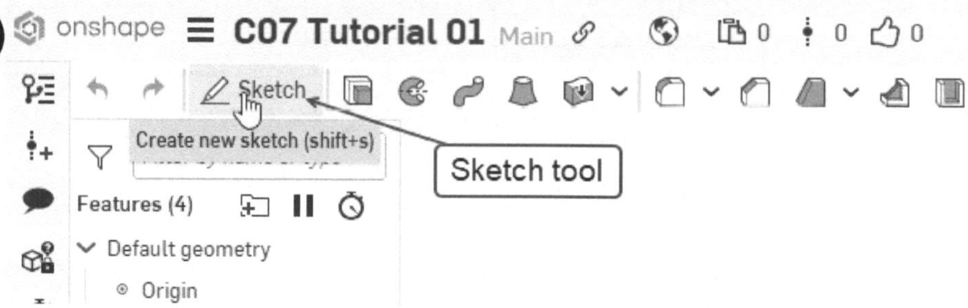

2. Select the Top plane as the sketching plane. The selected plane becomes the sketching plane, and the **Sketch** toolbar appears with the display of various sketching tools.

3. Press the N key to make the sketching plane normal to the viewing direction.

4. Sketch two concentric circles with their center points at the origin and apply dimensions, see Figure 5.59.

7.59

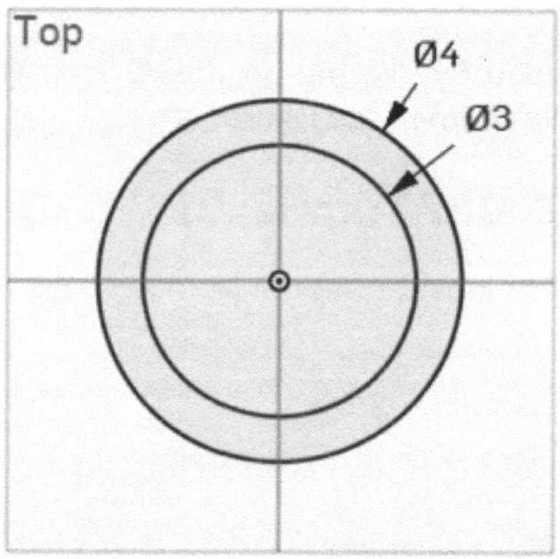

5. After creating the sketch, click on the **Extrude** tool, see Figure 7.60. The **Extrude** dialog appears and the sketch profile is automatically selected. Also, the preview of an extruded feature appears in the graphics area.

7.60

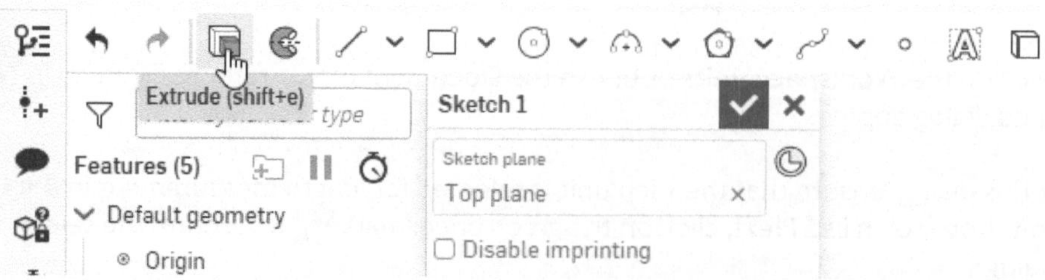

6. Press the SHIFT + 7 keys to change the view orientation to isometric.
7. Enter **5.5** inches as the extrusion depth in the **Depth** field of the **Extrude** dialog and press ENTER. The preview of the extrude feature updates accordingly in the graphics area.
8. Select the **Symmetric** check box in the dialog to extrude the sketch symmetrically on both sides of the sketching plane, see Figure 7.61.
9. Click the green checkmark in the **Extrude** dialog to confirm the creation of the extrude feature and exit the dialog. The extrude feature of specified depth is created, see Figure 7.62.

7.61

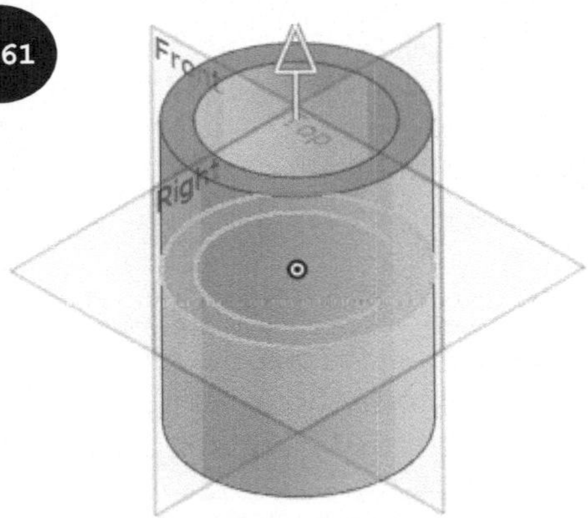

7.62

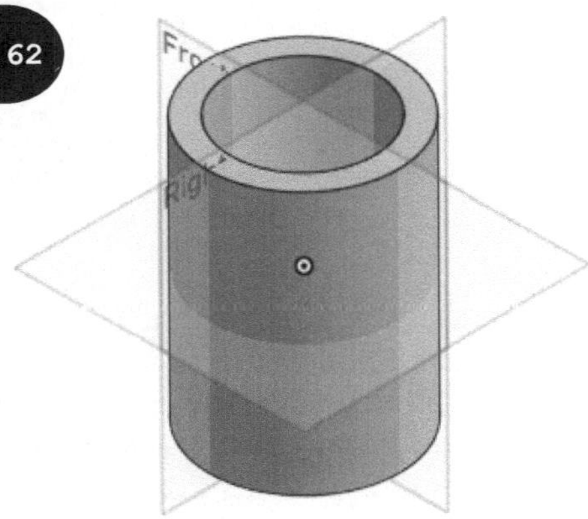

Section 4: Creating the Second Feature - Extrude

Now, you can create the second feature of the model, which is also an extruded feature.

1. Click the **Sketch** tool in the **Feature** toolbar (see Figure 7.63) and select the top planar face of the model as the sketching plane, see Figure 7.64.

7.63

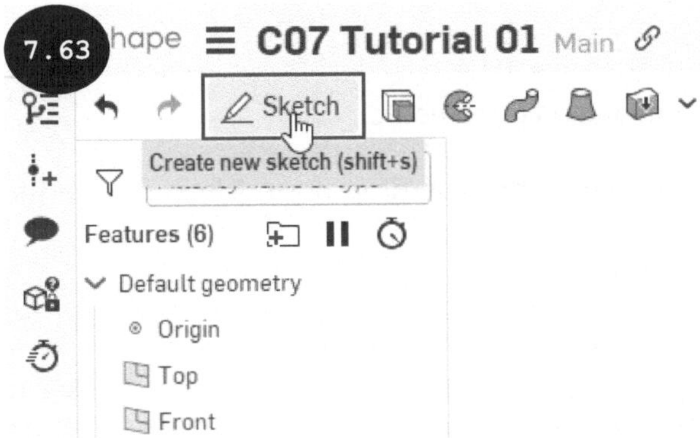

7.64

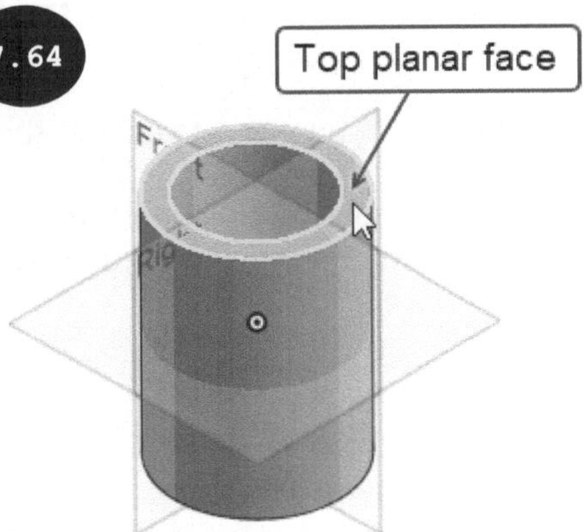

2. Press the N key to make the sketching plane normal to the viewing direction.

3. Create the sketch of the feature using the sketching tools, see Figure 7.65.

7.65

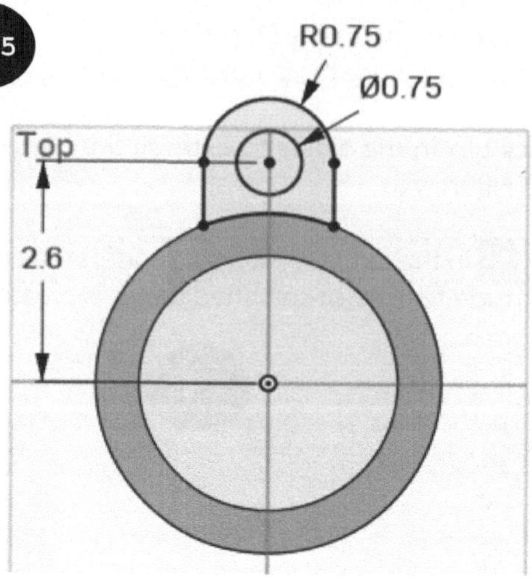

Tip: In Figure 7.65, the outer circular edge of the base feature is projected onto the current sketching plane as a sketch entity using the **Use (Project/Convert)** tool. After creating all the sketch entities, the unwanted portions are trimmed.

4. After creating the sketch, click on the **Extrude** tool, see Figure 7.66. The **Extrude** dialog appears, and a preview of the extruded feature is displayed in the graphics area.

7.66

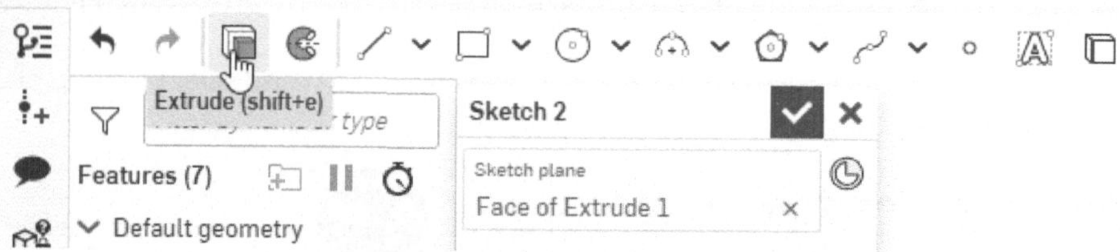

5. Press the SHIFT + 7 keys to change the view orientation to isometric.

6. Click the **Opposite direction** button next to the **End type** drop-down list to reverse the extrusion direction downward, see Figure 7.67.

7.67

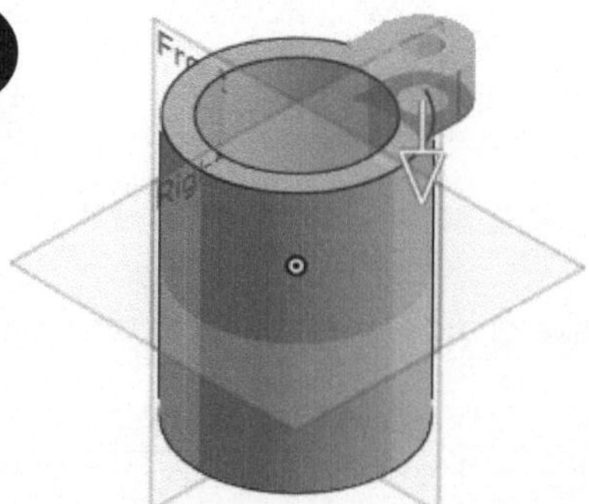

7. Enter **0.5** inches in the **Depth** field of the **Extrude** dialog and press ENTER. The preview of the extrude feature updates accordingly in the graphics area.

8. Click on the **Add** tab in the **Extrude** dialog to create the extrude feature and merge it with the existing feature in the model, see Figure 7.68.

7.68

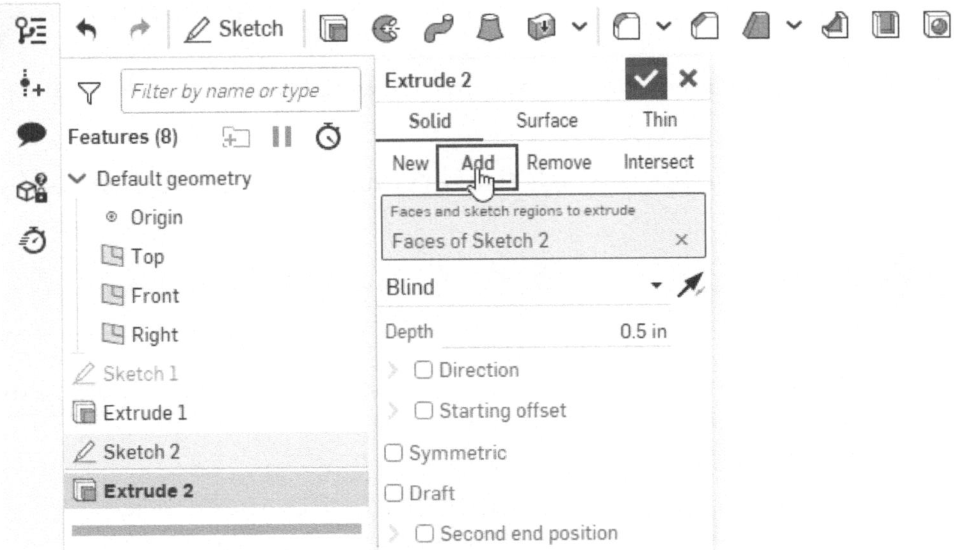

9. Click the green checkmark in the **Extrude** dialog to confirm the creation of the extrude feature and exit the dialog. The extrude feature with the specified depth is created, see Figure 7.69.

7.69

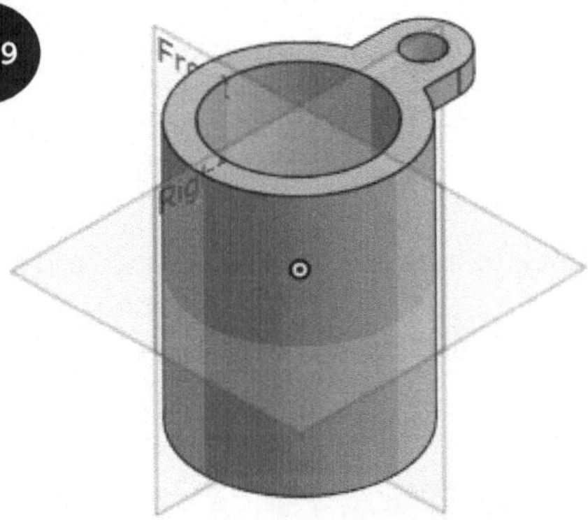

Section 5: Creating the Circular Pattern

Now, you can create the circular pattern of the previously created extrude feature to generate its remaining instances.

1. Click on a small arrow beside the **Linear pattern** tool in the **Feature** toolbar and then click on the **Circular pattern** tool in the **Pattern** drop-down menu that appears, see Figure 7.70. The **Circular pattern** dialog appears.

7.70

2. Select the **Feature pattern** option in the **Pattern type** drop-down list to select features to pattern, refer to Figure 7.71.

3. Select the previously created extrude feature (**Extrude 2**) in the **Feature list** (see Figure 7.71) or the graphics area.

7.71

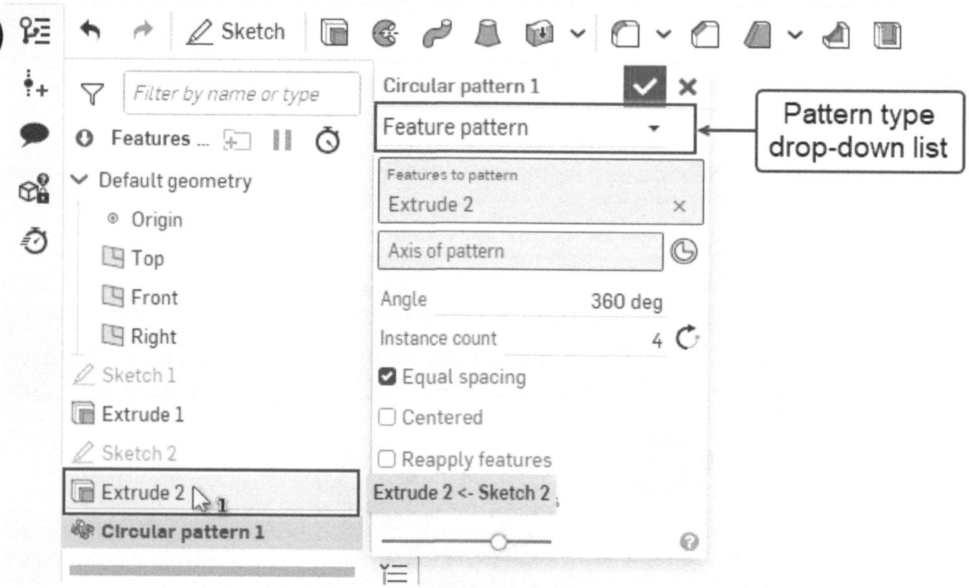

4. After selecting the feature, click to activate the **Axis of pattern** field in the dialog, then select the outer cylindrical face of the model, see Figure 7.72. The center axis of the selected face is defined as the axis of the circular pattern, and a preview of the circular pattern appears with the default parameters.

7.72

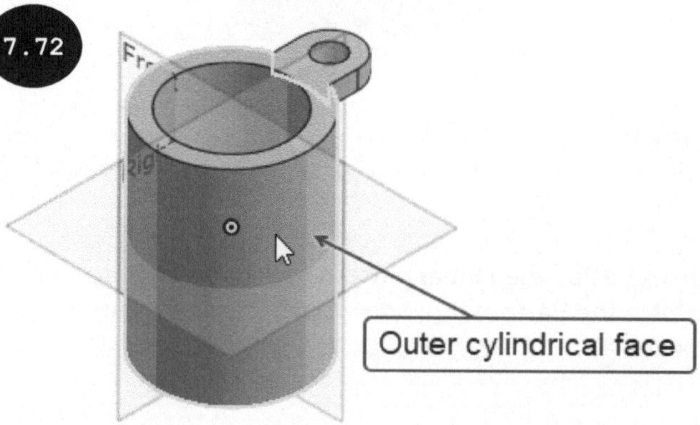

5. Ensure that **360** degrees is specified in the **Angle** field and the **Equal spacing** check box is selected in the dialog.

6. Enter **3** as the number of pattern instances to be created in the **Instance count** field of the dialog, then press ENTER. The preview of the circular pattern updates accordingly in the graphics area, see Figure 7.73.

7.73

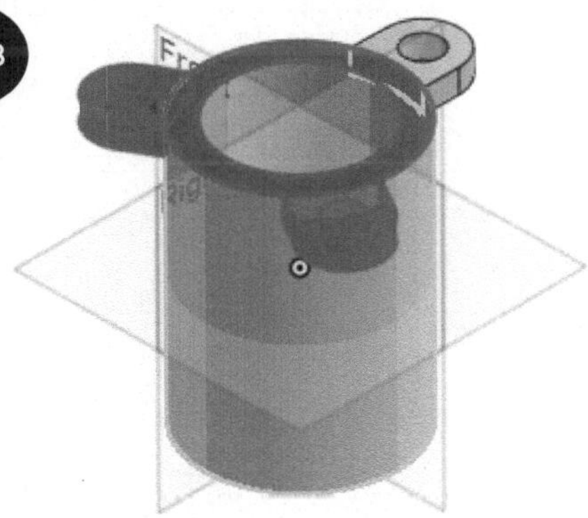

7. Select the **Reapply features** check box in the dialog to reapply pattern instances on the model geometry.

8. Click the green checkmark in the **Circular pattern** dialog to confirm the creation of the pattern and exit the dialog. The circular pattern with the specified total number of instances is created, see Figure 7.74.

7.74

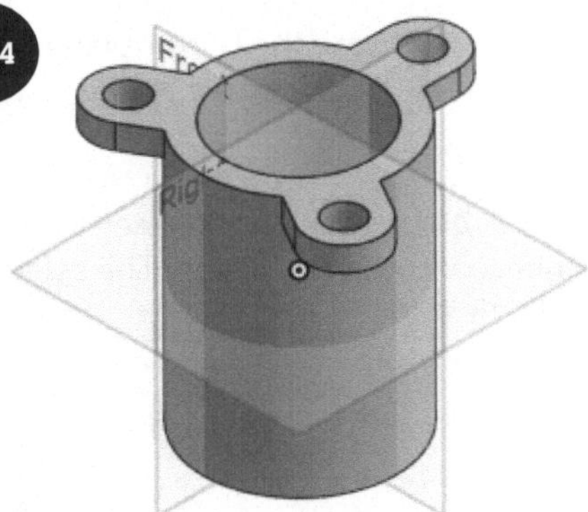

Section 6: Mirroring Features

Now, you can create the mirror the previously created circular pattern and its parent feature.

1. Click on the **Mirror** tool in the **Feature** toolbar, see Figure 7.75. The **Mirror** dialog appears.

7.75

2. Select the **Feature mirror** option in the **Mirror type** drop-down list to select features to mirror, refer to Figure 7.76.

3. Select the previously created circular pattern and extrude features (**Circular pattern 1** and **Extrude 2**) in the **Feature list**, see Figure 7.76.

7.76

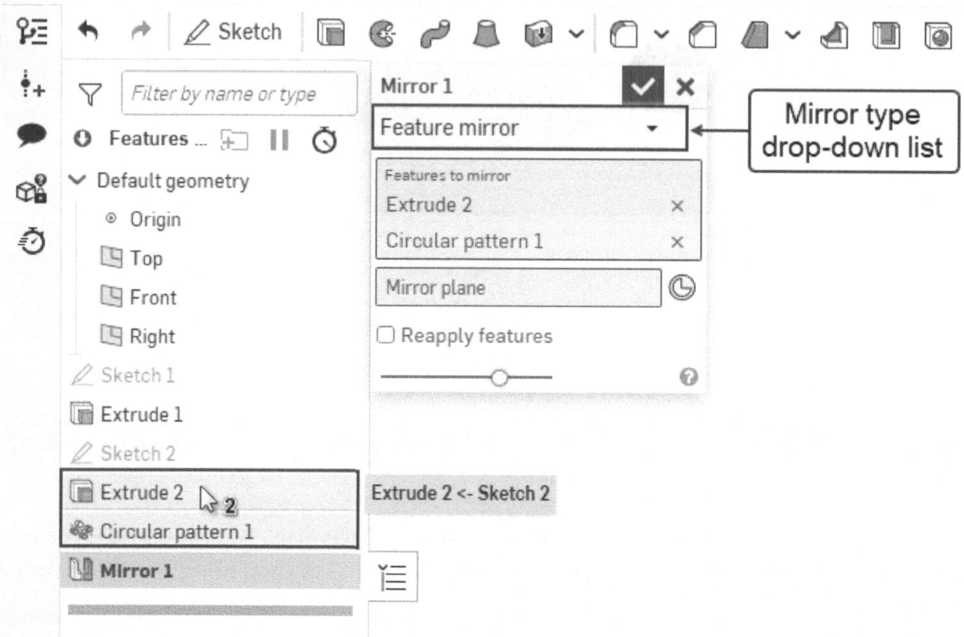

4. After selecting the features, click to activate the **Mirror plane** field in the dialog, then select the Top plane as the mirroring plane in the graphics area. A preview of the mirror appears about the mirroring plane, see Figure 7.77.

5. Select the **Reapply features** check box, then click the green checkmark ✓ in the **Mirror** dialog to confirm the creation of the mirror and exit the dialog. The selected features are mirrored about the mirroring plane, see Figure 7.78.

7.77

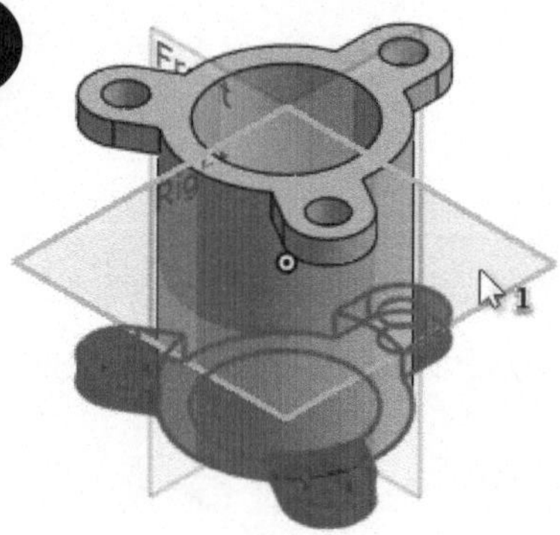

7.78

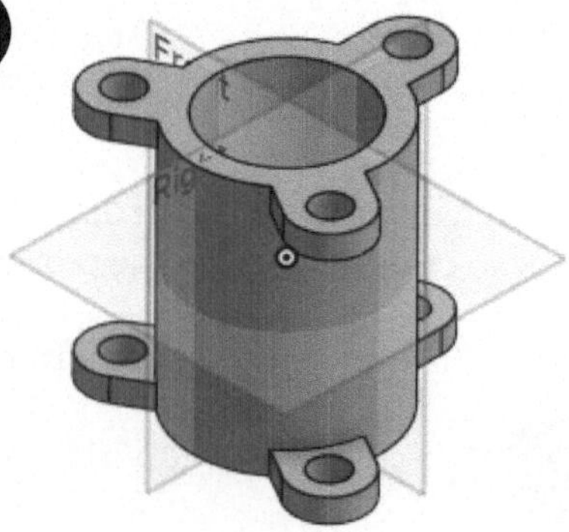

Section 7: Creating the Extrude Cut Feature

Now, you can create an extruded cut feature by removing material from the model.

1. Click the **Sketch** tool in the **Feature** toolbar (see Figure 7.79) and select the Front plane as the sketching plane, see Figure 7.80.

7.79

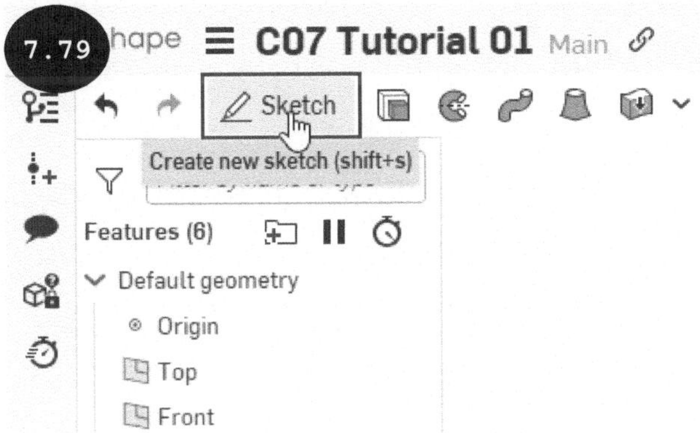

7.80

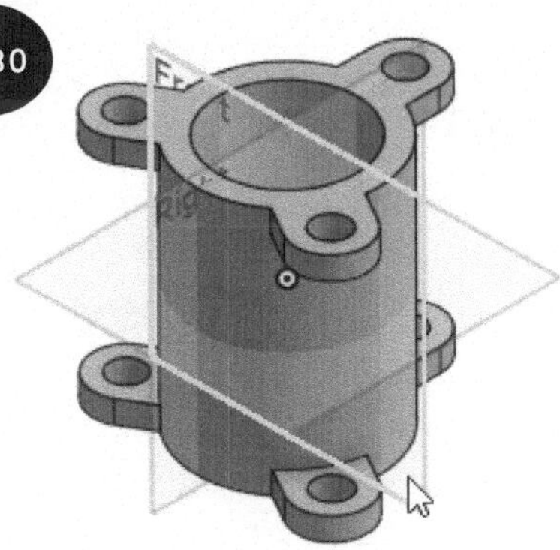

2. Press the **N** key to make the sketching plane normal to the viewing direction.

3. Create the sketch (slot) of the feature using the sketching tools, see Figure 7.81.

7.81

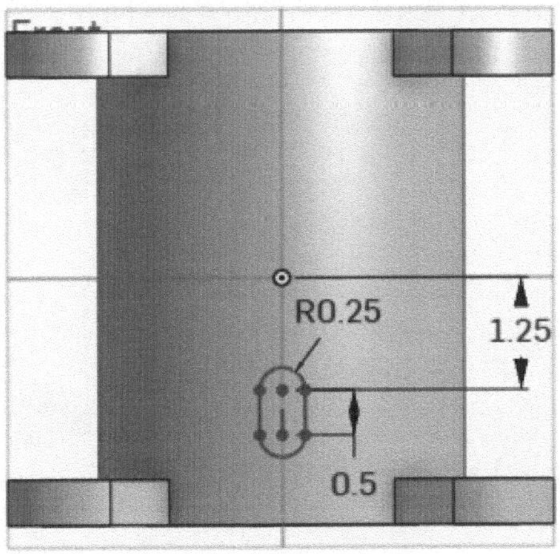

4. After creating the sketch, click on the **Extrude** tool, see Figure 7.82. The **Extrude** dialog appears, and a preview of the extruded feature is displayed in the graphics area.

7.82

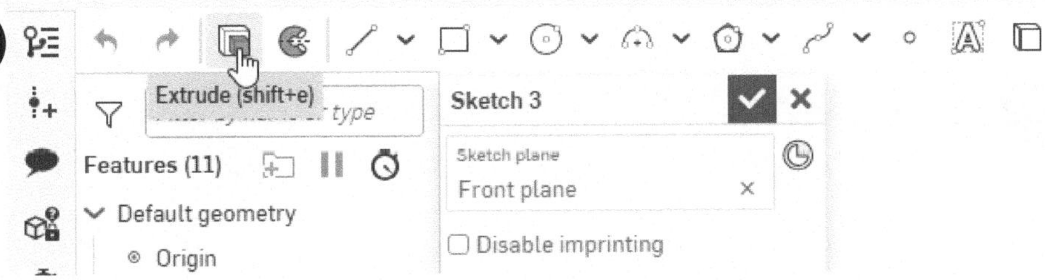

5. Press the SHIFT + 7 keys to change the view orientation to isometric.

6. Select the **Through all** option in the **End type** drop-down list, see Figure 7.83.

7. Click on the **Remove** tab in the **Extrude** dialog to create the extrude cut feature by removing material, see Figure 7.83.

7.83

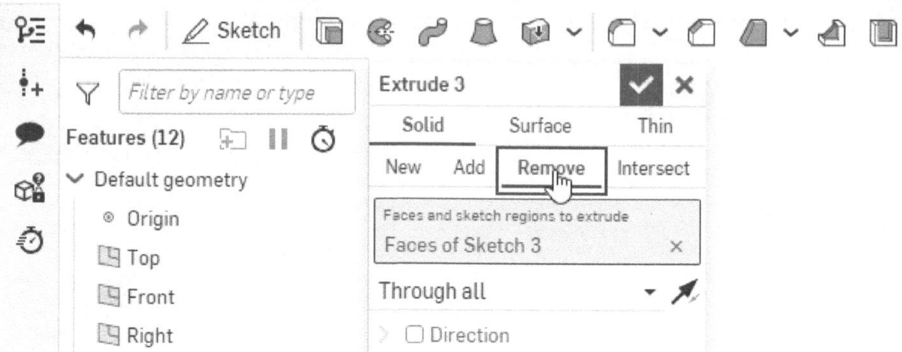

8. Click the **Opposite direction** button next to the **End type** drop-down list to reverse the extrusion direction toward the front, if needed, see Figure 7.84.

9. Click the green checkmark in the **Extrude** dialog to confirm the creation of the feature and exit the dialog. The extrude cut feature is created, see Figure 7.85.

7.84

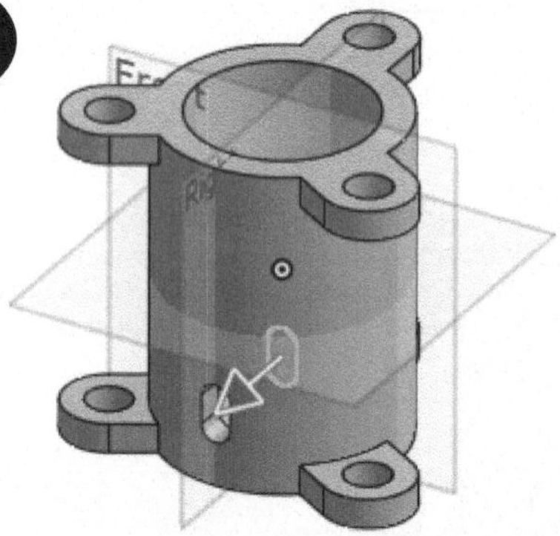

7.85

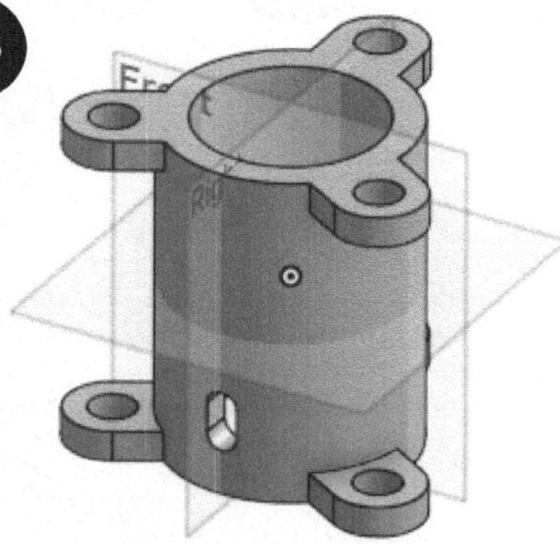

Section 8: Creating the Linear Pattern

Now, you can create the linear pattern of the previously created cut feature.

1. Invoke the **Pattern** drop-down menu, then click on the **Linear pattern** tool, see Figure 7.86. The **Linear pattern** dialog appears.

7.86

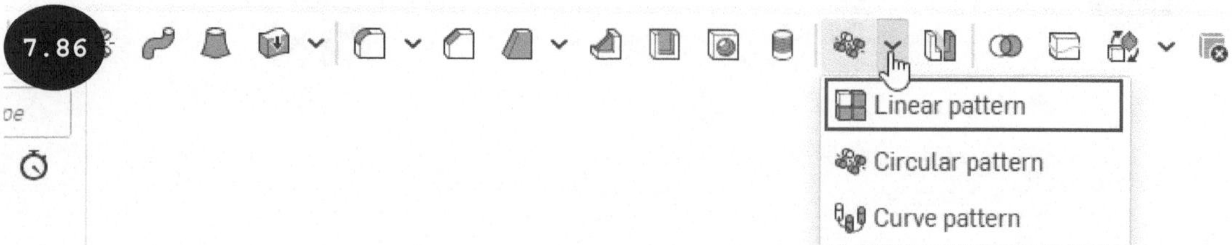

2. Select the **Feature pattern** option in the **Pattern type** drop-down list to select features to pattern, refer to Figure 7.87.

3. Select the previously created extrude feature (**Extrude 3**) in the **Feature list** (see Figure 7.87) or the graphics area.

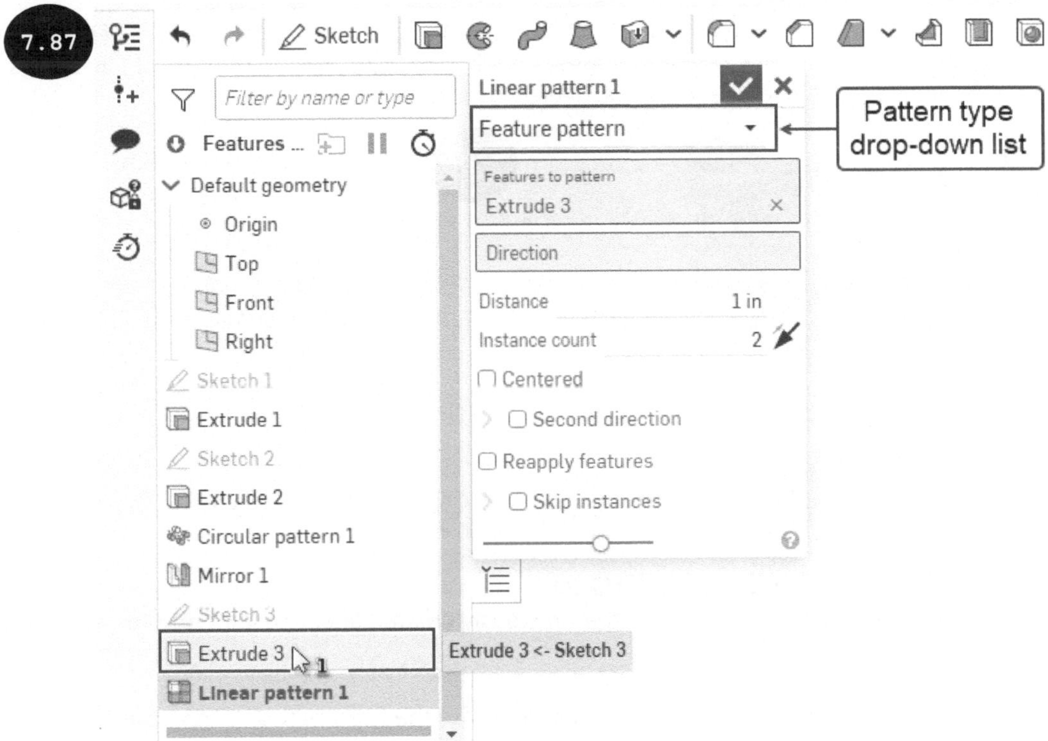

4. After selecting the feature, click to activate the **Direction** field in the dialog, then select the Top plane in the graphics area to define the first pattern direction normal to it. A preview of the linear pattern appears with the default parameters in the direction normal to the Top plane, see Figure 7.88.

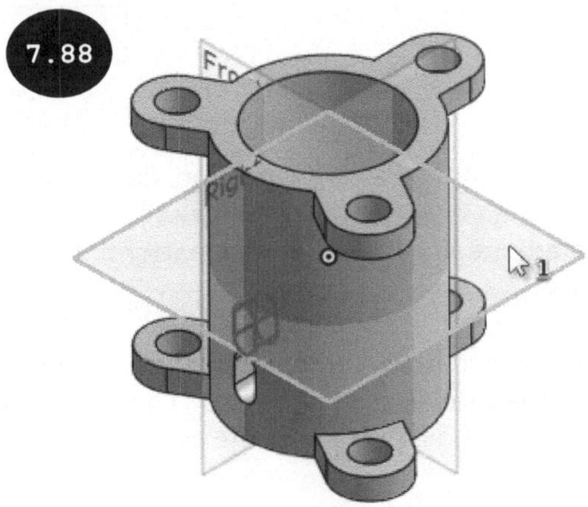

5. Enter **1.5** inches as the distance between two instances in the **Distance** field of the dialog.

6. Enter **3** as the total number of instances to be created in the **Instance count** field of the dialog, then press ENTER. The preview of the linear pattern updates accordingly in the graphics area, see Figure 7.89.

7. Click the green checkmark in the **Linear pattern** dialog to confirm the creation of the pattern and exit the dialog. The linear pattern with the specified number of instances is created along the defined direction, see Figure 7.90.

7.89

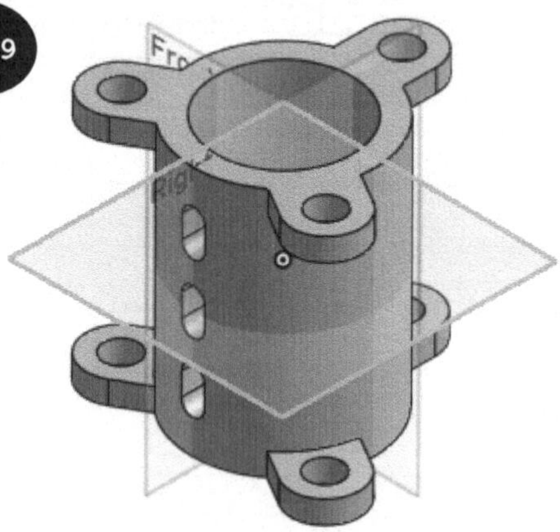

7.90

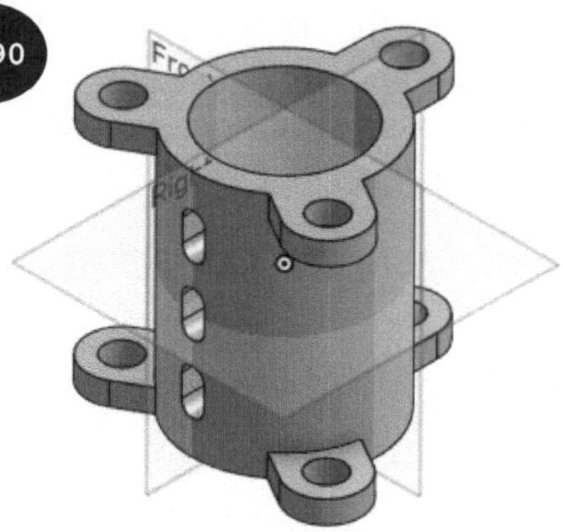

Section 9: Creating the Circular Pattern

Now, you can create a circular pattern of the previously created linear pattern and the extrude cut feature.

1. Click on a small arrow beside the **Linear pattern** tool in the **Feature** toolbar and then click on the **Circular pattern** tool in the **Pattern** drop-down menu that appears, see Figure 7.91. The **Circular pattern** dialog appears.

7.91

2. Select the **Feature pattern** option in the **Pattern type** drop-down list to select features to pattern.

3. Select the previously created linear pattern (**Linear pattern 1**) and the extrude cut feature (**Extrude 3**) in the **Feature list**.

4. After selecting the features, click to activate the **Axis of pattern** field in the dialog, then select the outer cylindrical face of the model, see Figure 7.92. The center axis of the selected face is defined as the axis of revolution, and a preview of the circular pattern appears with the default parameters.

7.92

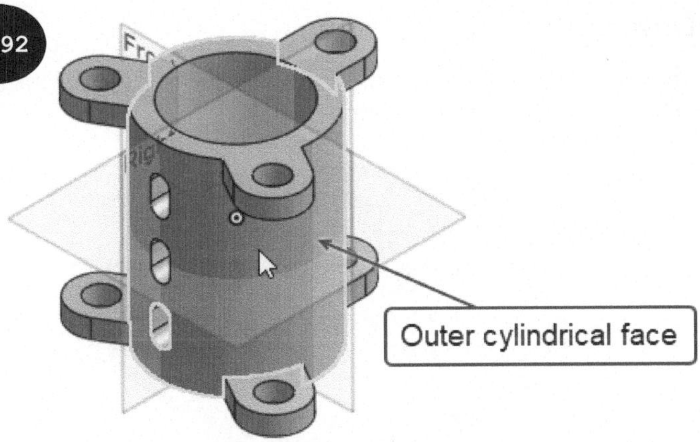

5. Ensure that **360** degrees is specified in the **Angle** field and the **Equal spacing** check box is selected in the dialog.

6. Enter **12** as the number of pattern instances to be created in the **Instance count** field of the dialog, then press ENTER. The preview of the circular pattern updates accordingly in the graphics area, see Figure 7.93.

7. Click the green checkmark ✔ in the **Circular pattern** dialog to confirm the creation of the pattern and exit the dialog. The circular pattern with the specified total number of instances is created. Figure 7.94 shows the final model after creating all its features.

7.93

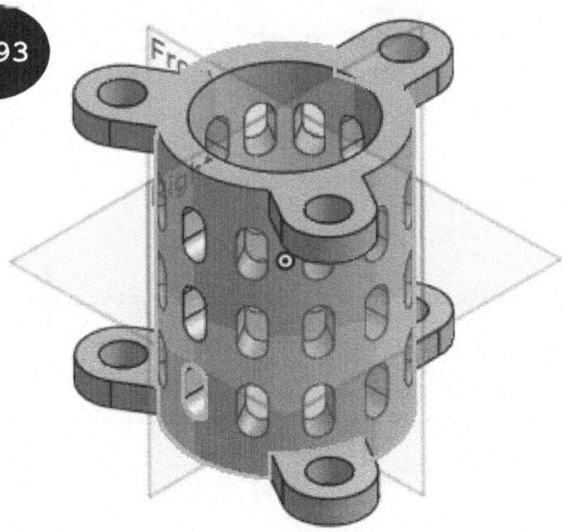

7.94

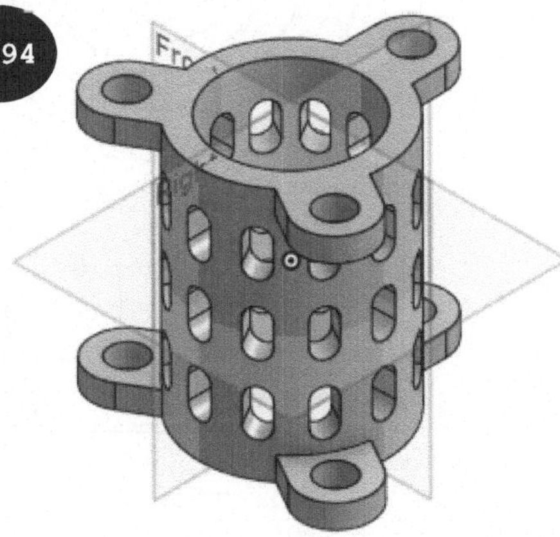

Tip: In Onshape, the document automatically saves to the specified location in the cloud. You can access a list of all the saved documents anytime by clicking on the **Created by me** option in the left menu of the **Documents Page**.

8. Create a version in the document to capture the current state of the design using the **Create version** tool in the **Document panel**.

Hands-on Test Drive 1

Create a model, as shown in Figure 7.95. The different views and dimensions are given in the same figure for your reference. All dimensions are in inches.

7.95

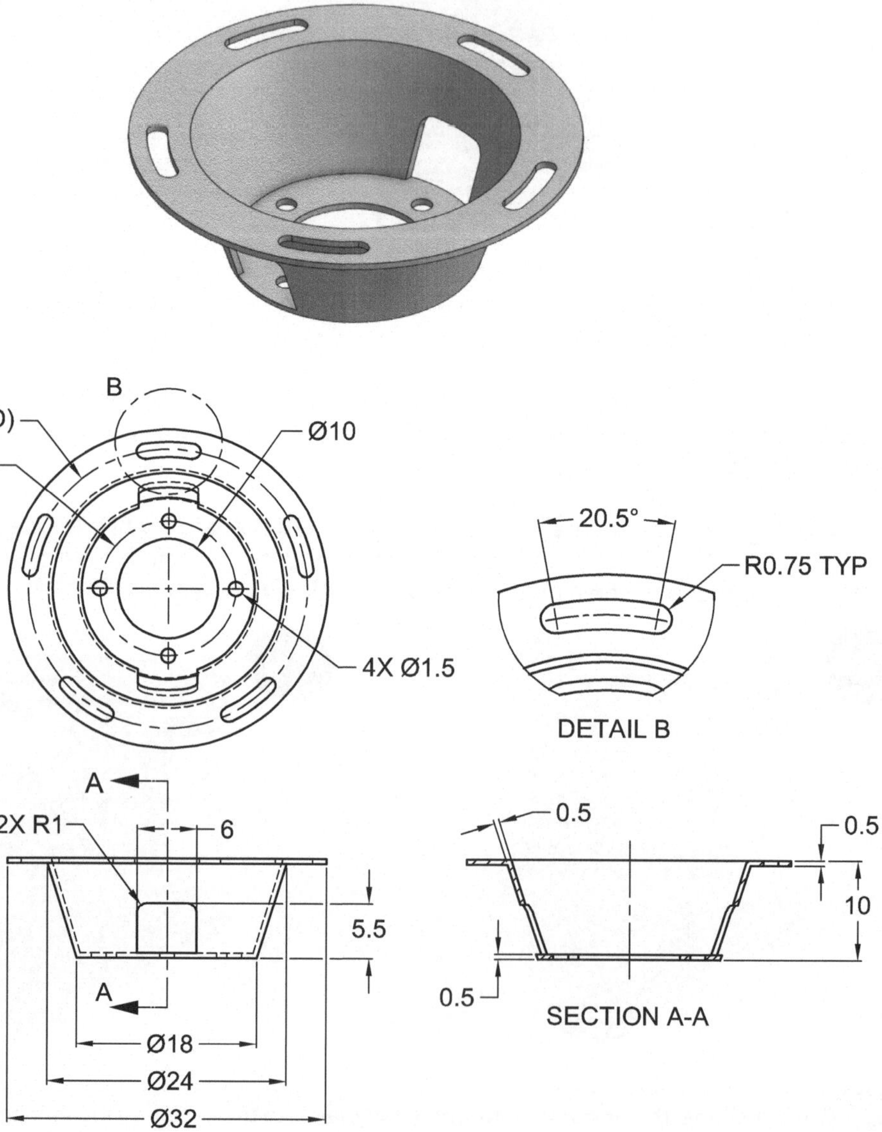

Hands-on Test Drive 2

Create a model, as shown in Figure 7.96. The different views and dimensions are given in the same figure for your reference. All dimensions are in mm.

7.96

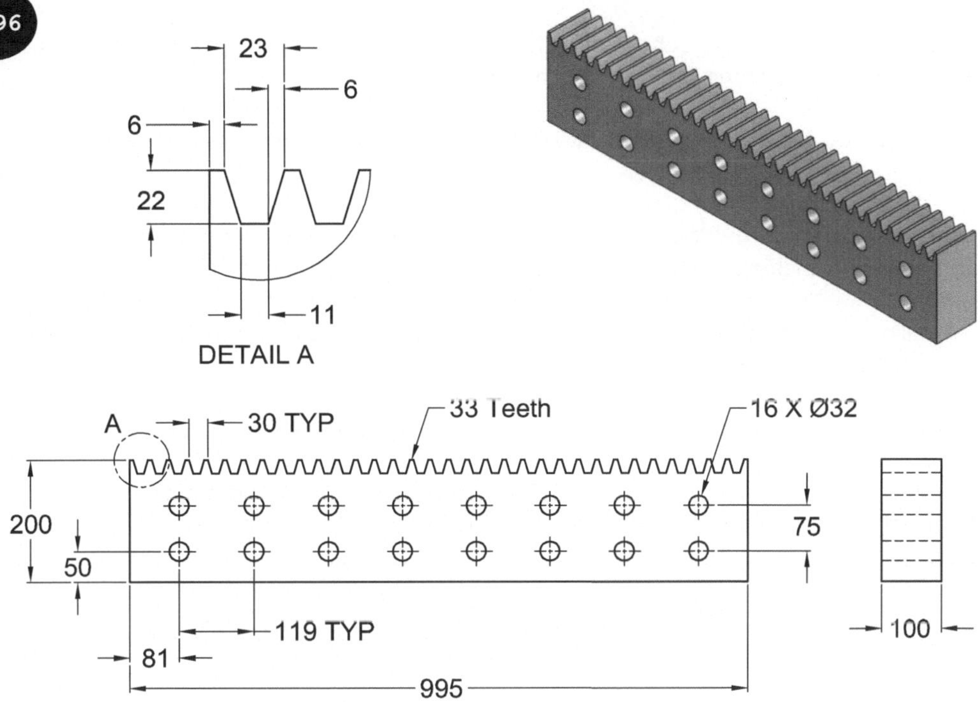

Summary

In this chapter, you have learned how to enhance design efficiency using linear, circular, and curve patterns to replicate features, faces, or parts effectively. Additionally, you explored the mirroring of features, faces, or parts about a plane or a planar face to create symmetrical designs. These tools simplify repetitive tasks, ensure accuracy, and optimize your design workflow.

Questions

Complete and verify the following sentences:

- The _________ tool is used to create multiple instances of parts, features, or faces circularly around an axis.
- The _________ tool is used to create multiple instances of parts, features, or faces along a path.
- A _________ pattern creates multiple instances of parts, features, or faces along one or two linear directions.

- Selecting the _________ option while creating a curve pattern ensures that all pattern instances retain the same orientation as the parent feature.
- In Onshape, you can exclude specific instances from a pattern by selecting the _________ check box.
- By selecting the _________ check box, the instances are patterned symmetrically on both sides of the parent feature along the specified pattern direction.
- In Onshape, you can mirror features, faces, or parts about a mirroring plane using the _________ tool.
- If the sketch contains multiple segments, it is recommended to select it from the _________ list to automatically include all segments as the path.
- The total number of pattern instances specified in the Instance count field includes the parent or original instance. (True/False)
- In Onshape, you cannot recall or include the skipped instances of the pattern. (True/False)
- If you select a planar face or a plane to define the pattern direction, the pattern direction will be set normal to the selected face or plane. (True/False)

CHAPTER
8

Creating 3D Curves and Splitting Faces

In this chapter, the following topics will be discussed:

- Creating a Helix
- Creating a Projected Curve
- Creating a 3D Fit Spline
- Creating a Bridging Curve
- Creating an Intersection Curve
- Creating a Composite Curve
- Splitting a Part and the Face of a Model

Onshape provides powerful tools for creating and refining curves in 3D designs. This chapter covers the creation of various curve types, including helix, projected, bridge, intersection, offset, and composite curves. You will also explore methods for trimming and editing curves, along with techniques for splitting model faces, which will enhance your design flexibility and control over geometry.

Creating a Helix

In Onshape, the **Helix** tool allows you to create a helix with specific parameters using a conical or cylindrical face, an axis, or a circular edge or circle, see Figures 8.1 through 8.3. Figure 8.1 illustrates a helix created using a cylindrical face.

8.1

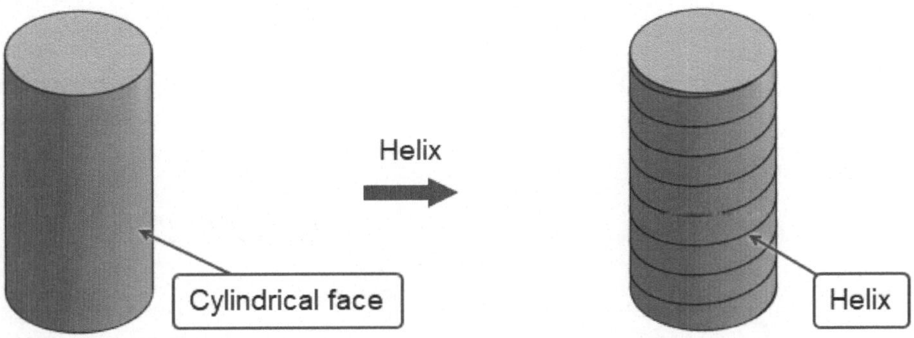

Figure 8.2 illustrates a helix created using an axis. You can define the axis of the helix by selecting a line, a construction line, or a linear edge.

8.2

Figure 8.3 depicts a helix created using a circle, where the diameter of the circle defines the diameter of the helix. The different methods for creating a helix using the **Helix** tool are discussed next.

8.3

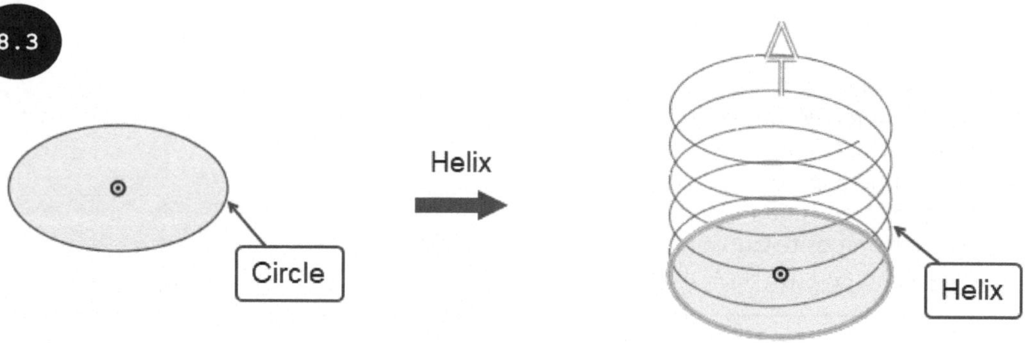

Creating a Helix Using a Conical or Cylindrical Face

The method for creating a helix using a conical or cylindrical face is discussed below:

1. Click on the down arrow next to the **Plane** tool in the **Feature** toolbar to display a drop-down menu, see Figure 8.4.

8.4

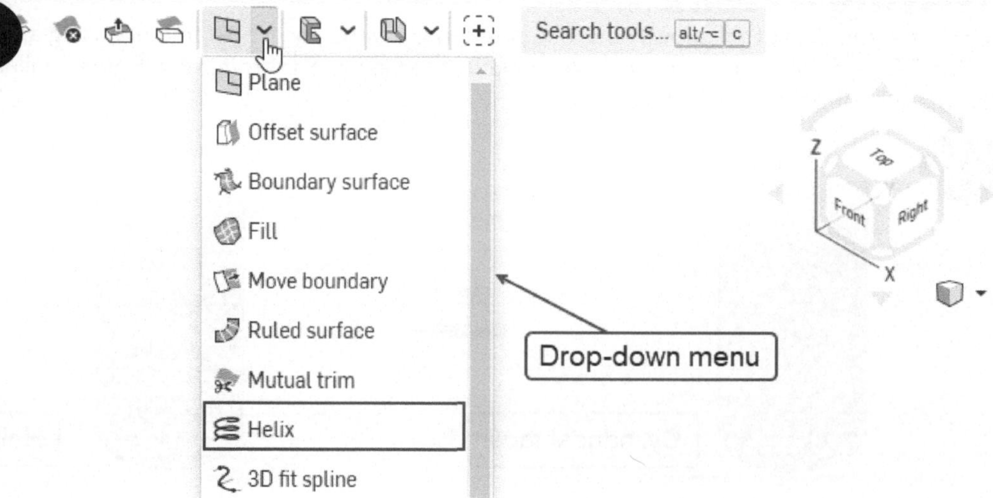

2. Click on the **Helix** tool in the drop-down menu, refer to Figure 8.4. The **Helix** dialog appears, see Figure 8.5.

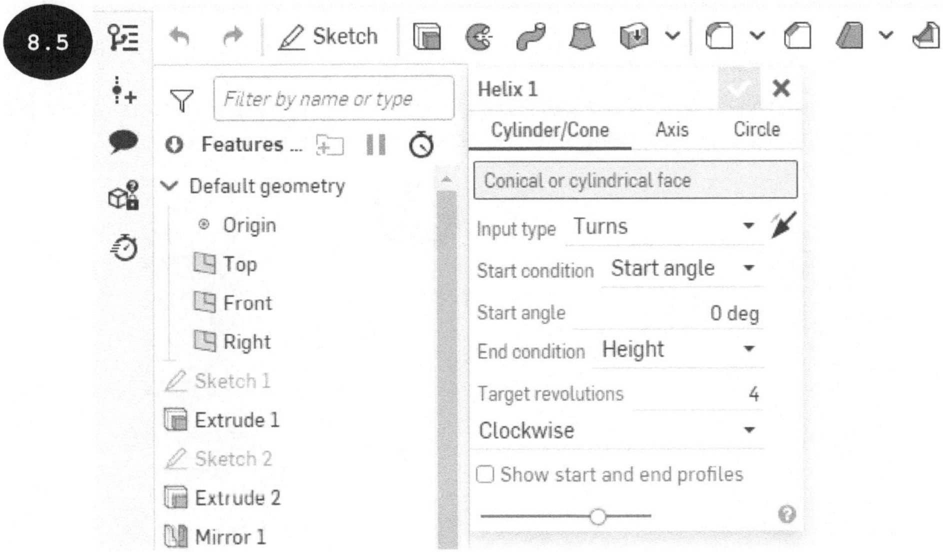

3. Ensure that the **Cylinder/Cone** tab is activated in the **Helix** dialog, see Figure 8.5. This allows you to create a helix on the conical or cylindrical face of the model.

4. Select a conical or cylindrical face of the model, see Figure 8.6. A preview of the helix appears along the entire length of the selected face with default parameters, see Figure 8.7.

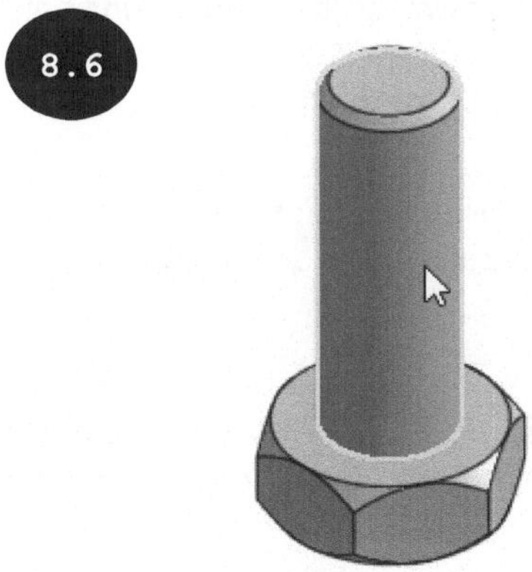

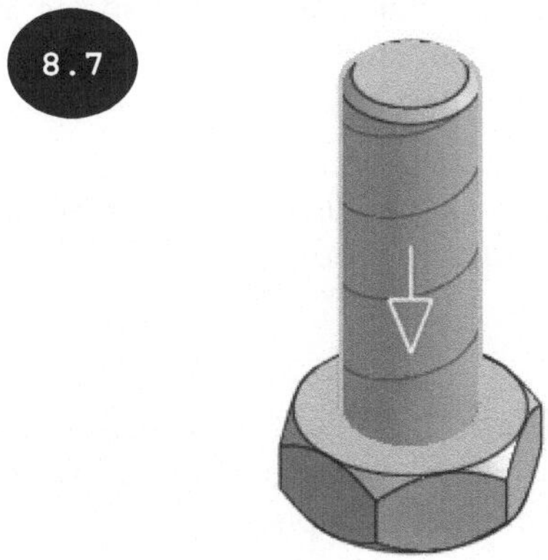

Input type: The **Input type** drop-down list allows you to choose an option (**Turns**, **Pitch**, or **Turns and pitch**) based on the parameters you want to define for creating the helix. The options are discussed below:

Turns: This option allows you to create a helix by specifying the required number of revolutions or turns along the full height of the helix in the **Target revolutions** field of the dialog.

Tip: By default, the height of the helix is define along the entire length of the selected geometry.

Pitch: This option allows you to create a helix by specifying a constant pitch value along the full height of the helix in the **Target pitch** field of the dialog, see Figure 8.8.

Turns and pitch: This option allows you to create a helix by specifying the required number of revolutions and the pitch value in the **Target revolutions** and **Target pitch** fields of the dialog, respectively. Here, the height of the helix is determined by these parameters rather than being directly defined along the entire length of the selected geometry, see Figure 8.9.

8.8

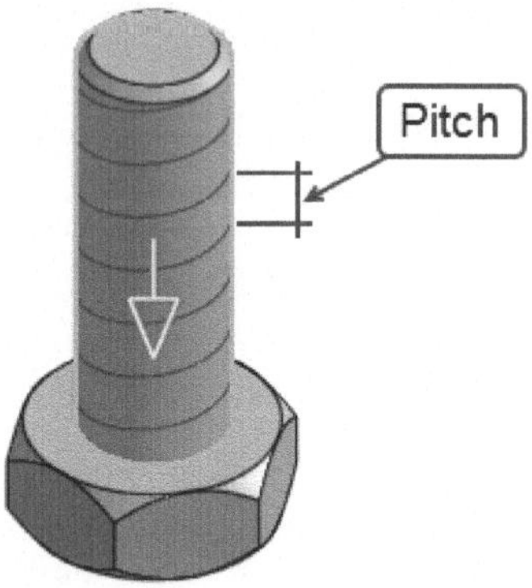

8.9

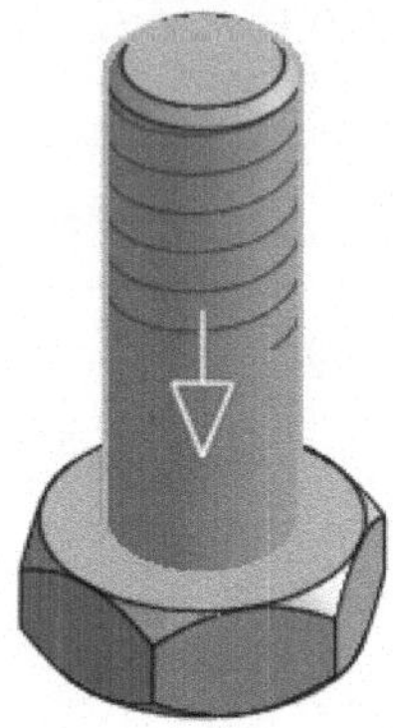

Start condition: By default, the **Start angle** option is selected in this drop-down list, allowing you to specify the starting angle for the helix in the **Start angle** field. The default start angle value is set to 0; however, you can enter the desired starting angle as needed.

On selecting the **Start point** option in the **Start condition** drop-down list, the **Start point** field becomes available. This field allows you to select a vertex or a point on the starting circular edge of the selected geometry (cylindrical face) to define the starting point of the helix.

Tip: If needed, you can flip the helix's direction by clicking the **Opposite direction** button next to the **Input type** drop-down list. This alters the start and end circular edges defined for creating the helix.

End condition: By default, the **Height** option is selected in this drop-down list. This creates a helix along the entire length of the selected geometry (cylindrical face) based on the defined number of revolutions or pitch.

On selecting the **End point** option in the **End condition** drop-down list, the **End point** field becomes available. This field allows you to select a vertex or a point coplanar with the ending circular edge of the selected geometry (cylindrical face) to define the end point of the helix and compute the number of revolutions or pitch accordingly. It overrides the value set in the **Target revolutions** or **Target pitch** field.

Note: The **End condition** drop-down list is available only when the **Turns** or **Pitch** option is selected in the **Input type** drop-down list of the dialog.

Handedness: By default, the **Clockwise** option is selected in the drop-down list, setting the direction of turns or revolutions to clockwise.

On selecting the **Counterclockwise** option, the direction of turns or revolutions switches to counterclockwise.

Show start and end profiles: Selecting the **Show start and end profiles** check box highlights the start and end profiles of the helix in the graphics area.

5. Select the desired option (**Turns**, **Pitch**, or **Turns and pitch**) in the **Input type** drop-down list. Then, define the helix parameters in the corresponding fields within the dialog, as discussed above.

6. After defining all the required parameters, click the green checkmark ✓ to confirm the creation of the helix along the selected conical or cylindrical face and exit the dialog. Figure 8.10 illustrates a helix created along the entire length of the cylindrical face.

8.10

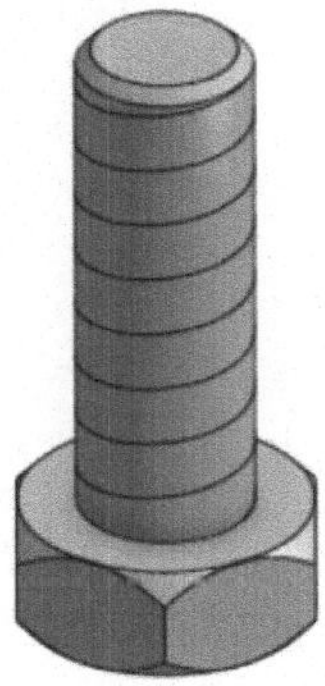

Tip: After creating a helix, you can use it as a path for creating sweep features, such as springs or threads on a cylindrical face, by either adding or removing material.

Creating a Helix Using an Axis

The method for creating a helix using an axis is discussed below:

1. Invoke the **Helix** dialog by clicking the down arrow next to the **Plane** tool in the **Feature** toolbar and selecting the **Helix** tool from the drop-down menu, see Figure 8.11.

8.11

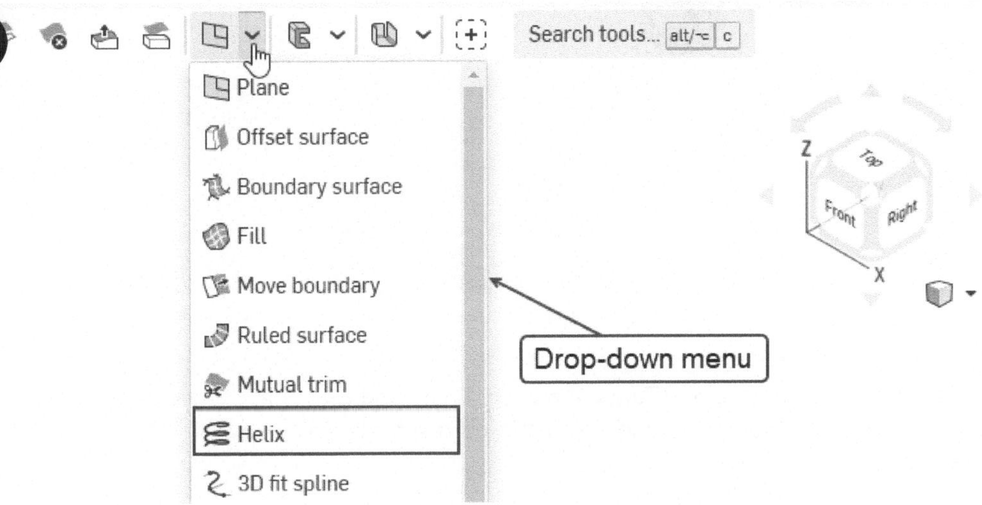

2. Click the **Axis** tab in the **Helix** dialog to access options for creating a helix by defining an axis, see Figure 8.12.

8.12

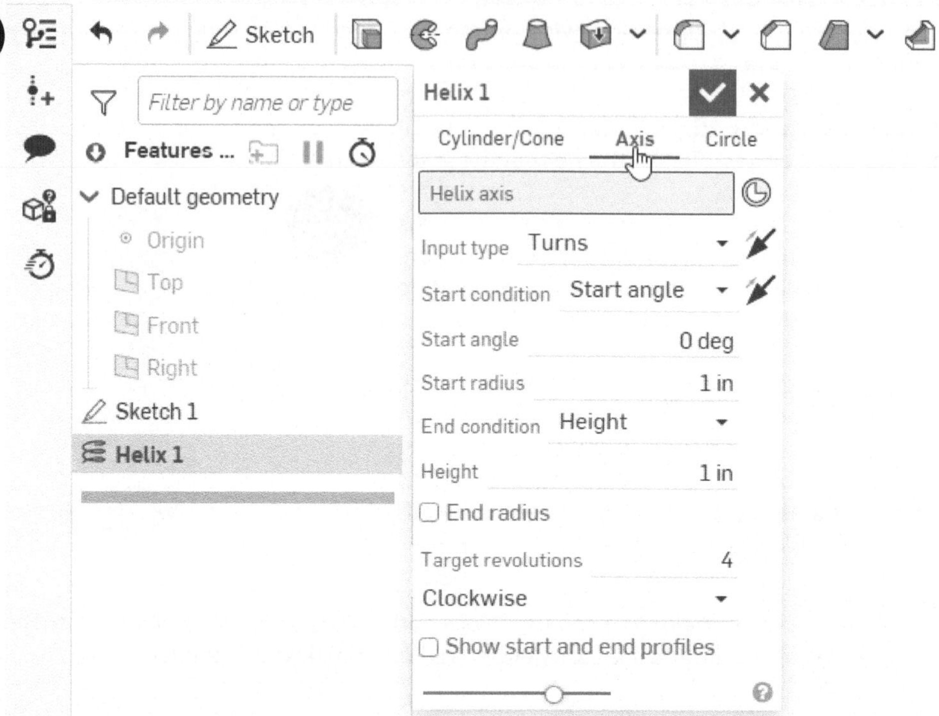

3. Select a line, construction line, or linear edge to define the axis of the helix. A preview of the helix with default parameters appears in the graphics area, see Figure 8.13. In this example, a construction line is selected to define the axis of the helix. You can also use the mate connector to define the axis of the helix.

8.13

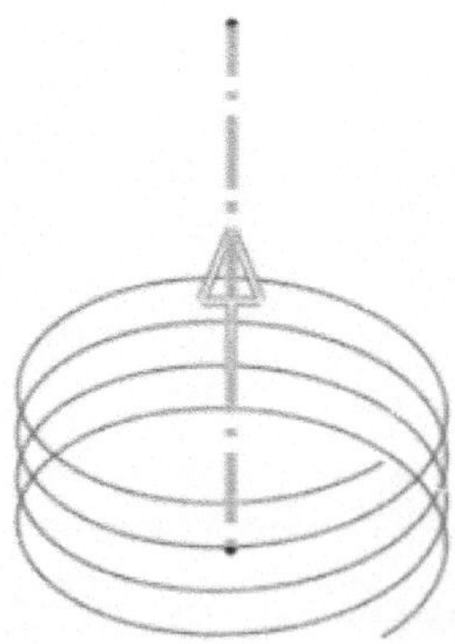

4. Select the desired option (**Turns**, **Pitch**, or **Turns and pitch**) in the **Input type** drop-down list. Then, define the helix parameters in the corresponding fields within the dialog, as discussed earlier.

Most of the options in the **Helix** dialog are the same as those discussed previously, except for **Start radius** and **End radius**, which are explained next.

Start radius: The **Start radius** field is used to define the start radius of the helix, refer to Figure 8.14.

End radius: By selecting the **End radius** check box, the **End radius** field becomes available in the dialog, allowing you to define the end radius of the helix. By default, the end radius is set to the same value as the start radius, creating a straight helix with a uniform radius throughout the entire length, see Figure 8.14. However, you can enter a different end radius to add tapering to the resulting helix, see Figure 8.15.

8.14

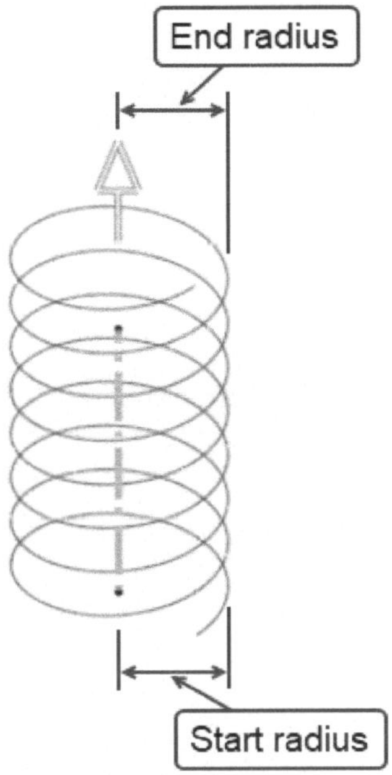

8.15

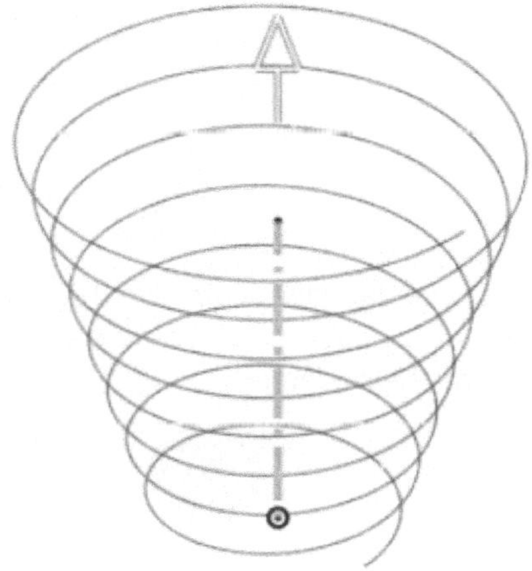

Tip: If needed, you can flip the helix's direction by clicking the **Opposite direction** button next to the **Input type** drop-down list. This alters the start and end position of the helix.

5. After defining all the required parameters, click the green checkmark to confirm the creation of the helix around the selected axis and exit the dialog.

Creating a Helix Using a Circular Edge or Circle

The method for creating a helix using a circular edge or a circle that defines its diameter is discussed below:

1. Invoke the **Helix** dialog by clicking the down arrow next to the **Plane** tool in the **Feature** toolbar and selecting the **Helix** tool from the drop-down menu.

2. Click the **Circle** tab in the **Helix** dialog to access options for creating a helix by selecting a circular edge or circle, see Figure 8.16.

8.16

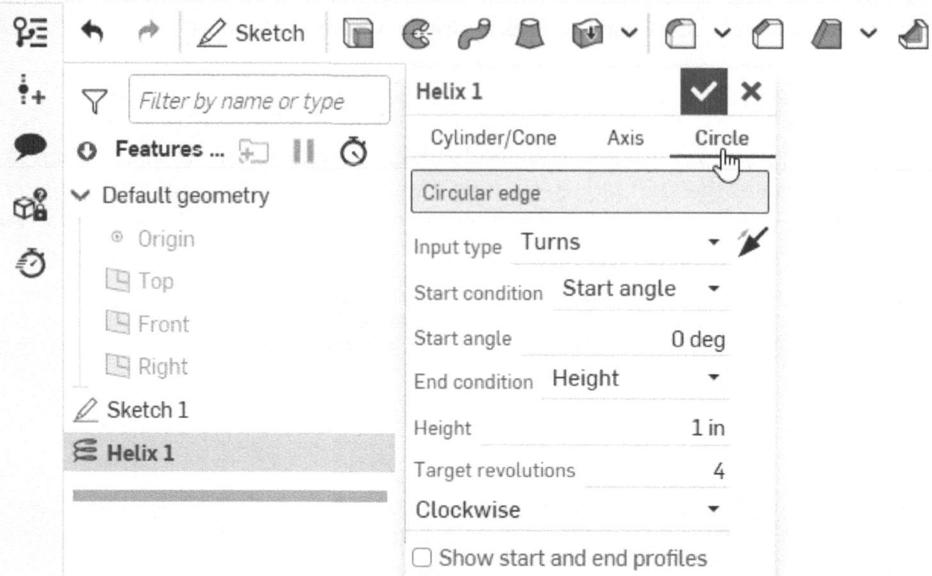

3. Select a circular edge or circle in the graphics area that defines the diameter of the helix. A preview of the helix appears with default parameters, see Figure 8.17. In this example, a circle is selected to define the helix diameter.

8.17

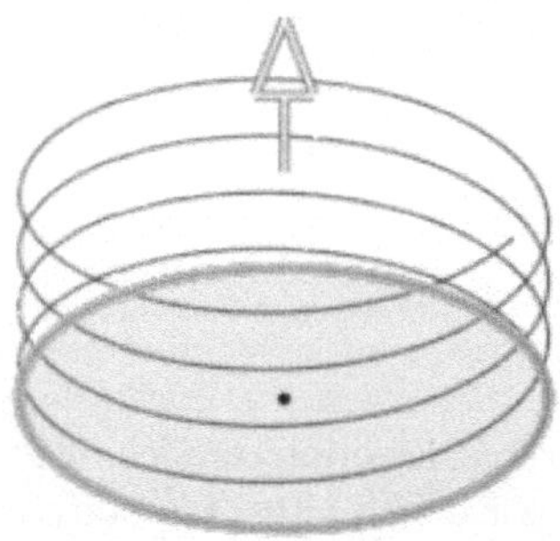

4. Select the desired option (**Turns**, **Pitch**, or **Turns and pitch**) in the **Input type** drop-down list. Then, define the helix parameters in the corresponding fields within the dialog. The options in the **Helix** dialog are the same as those discussed previously.

5. After defining all the required parameters, click the green checkmark ✓ to confirm the creation of the helix and exit the dialog.

Creating a Projected Curve

In Onshape, you can create a projected curve by projecting one sketch onto another or by projecting a sketch onto a model's face using the **Projected curve** tool. The methods for creating these types of projected curves are discussed next.

Creating a Projected Curve by Projecting Two Sketches

The method for creating a projected curve by projecting one sketch onto another is discussed below:

1. Ensure that the two sketches to be projected onto each other for creating a projected curve are already created in the graphics area, refer to Figure 8.18.

8.18

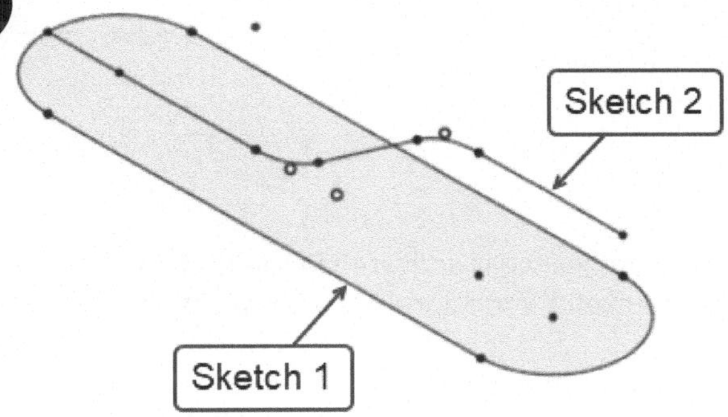

Note: In Figure 8.18, Sketch 1 is created on the Top plane, while Sketch 2 is created on the Front plane as individual sketches.

2. Click on the down arrow next to the **Plane** tool in the **Feature** toolbar to display a drop-down menu, see Figure 8.19.

8.19

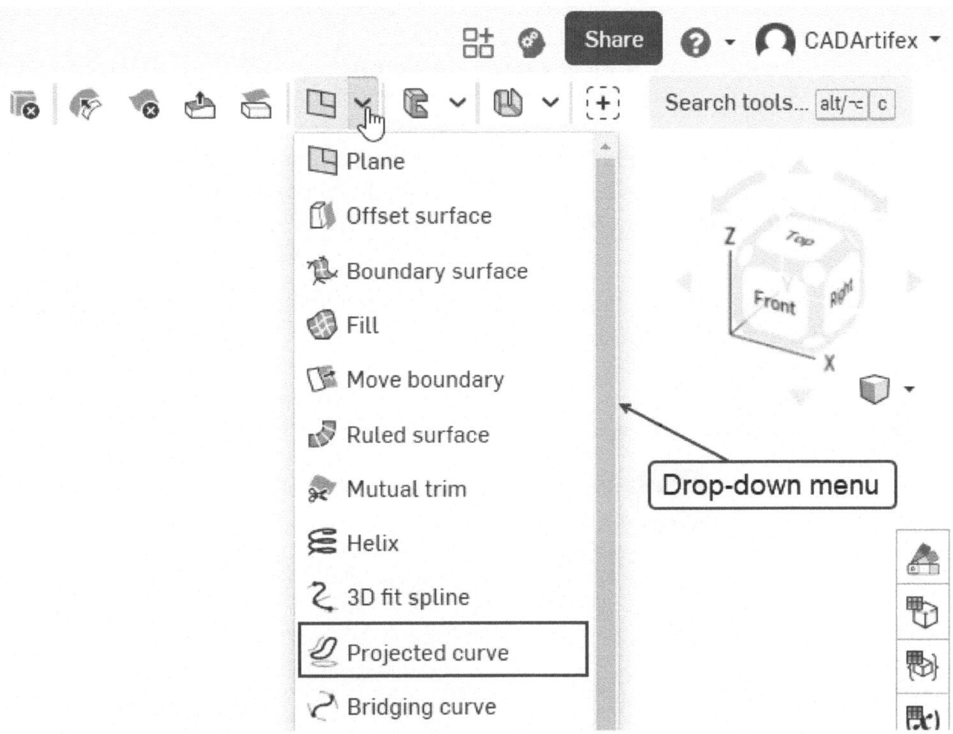

3. Click on the **Projected curve** tool in the drop-down menu, refer to Figure 8.19. The **Projected curve** dialog appears, see Figure 8.20.

8.20

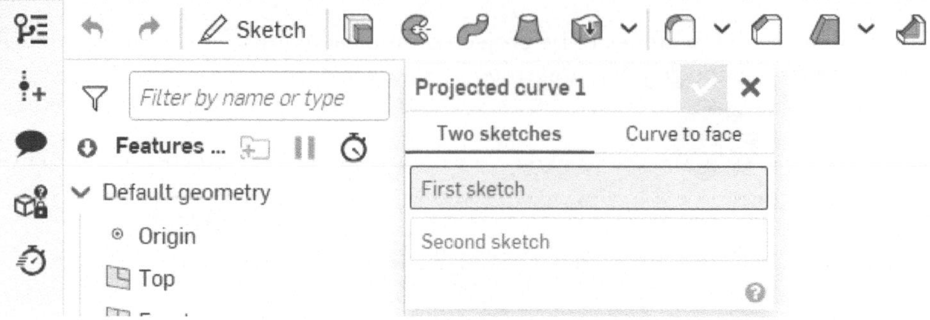

4. Ensure that the **Two sketches** tab is activated in the **Projected curve** dialog to create a projected curve by projecting one sketch onto another, refer to Figure 8.20.

5. Select the first sketch from the Feature list. The sketch highlights in the graphics area (refer to Figure 8.21), and its name appears in the **First sketch** field in the dialog.

8.21

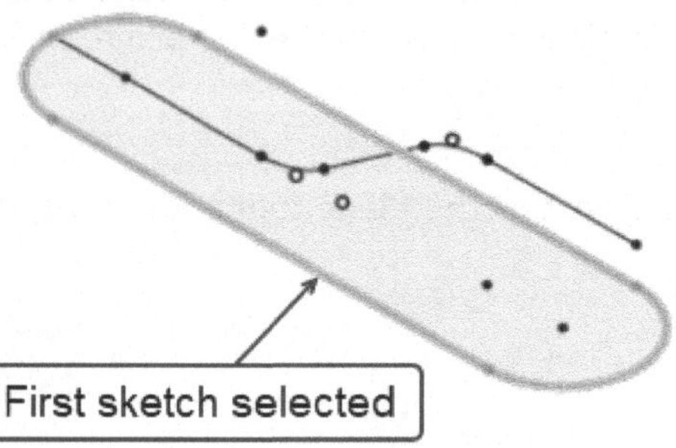

Tip: If the sketch contains multiple segments, it is recommended to select it from the Feature list to include all its segments at once. However, if you prefer to select the sketch directly from the graphics area, you must select each segment individually.

6. After selecting the first sketch, click the **Second sketch** field in the dialog to activate it for selecting the second sketch to project.

7. Select the second sketch from the Feature list. A preview of the projected curve appears in the graphics area, see Figure 8.22.

8.22

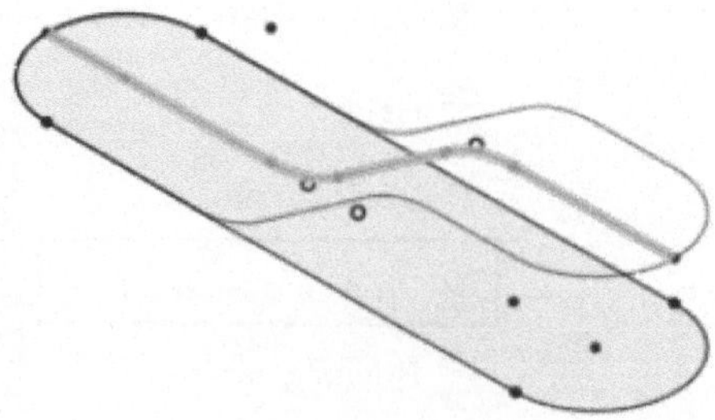

8. After selecting two individual sketches, click the green checkmark ✓ to confirm the creation of a projected curve and exit the dialog. Figure 8.23 shows a projected curve created by selecting two sketches.

8.23

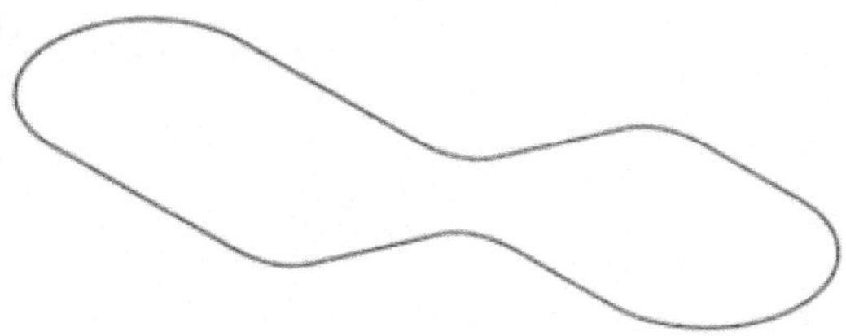

Creating a Projected Curve by Projecting a Sketch onto a Face

The method for creating a projected curve by projecting a sketch onto a model face is discussed below:

1. Invoke the **Projected curve** dialog by clicking the down arrow next to the **Plane** tool in the **Feature** toolbar and selecting the **Projected curve** tool from the drop-down menu, see Figure 8.24.

8.24

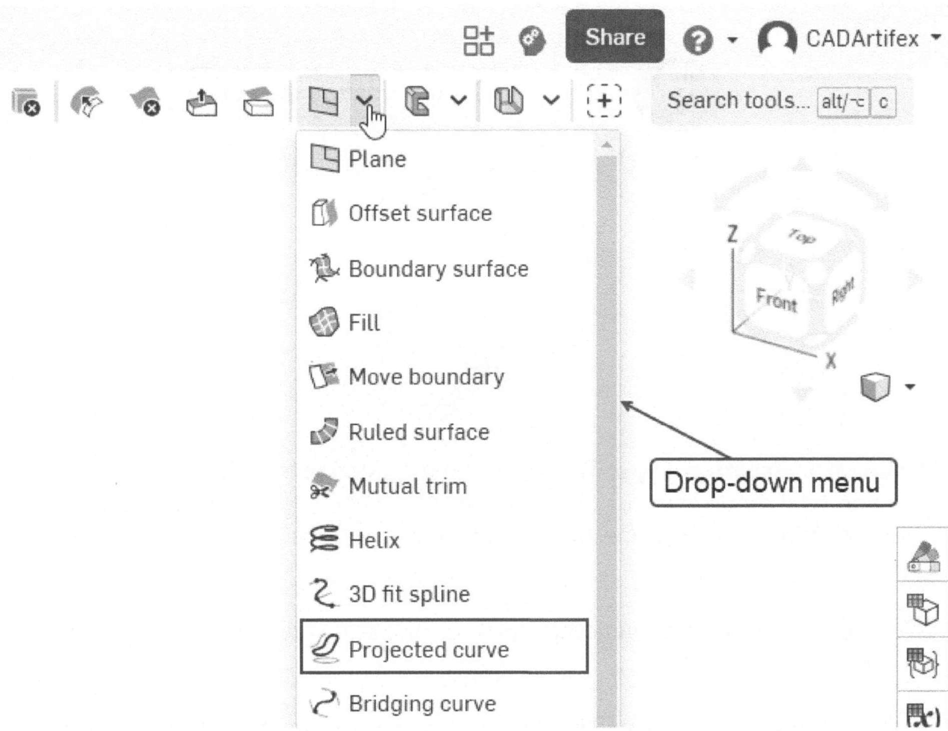

2. Click on the **Curve to face** tab in the dialog to access options for projecting a sketch or curve onto a face of a model, see Figure 8.25.

8.25

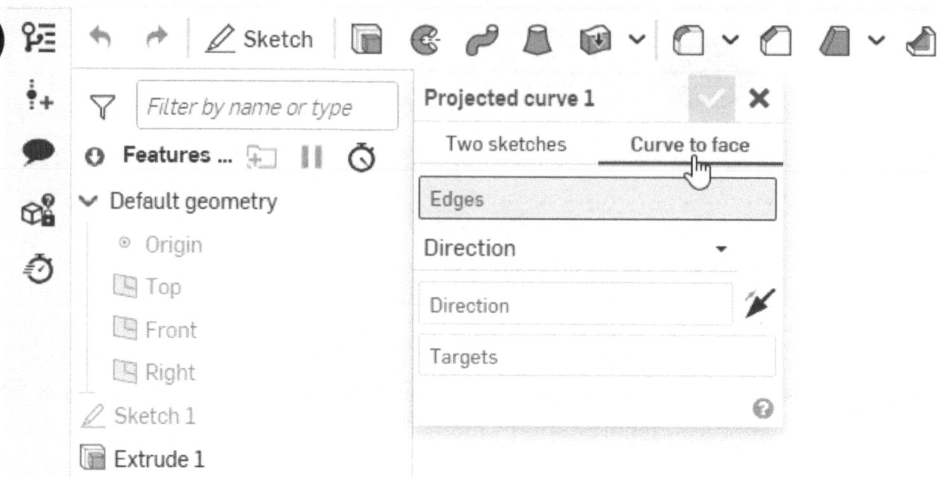

3. Select one or more sketch entities or edges to project onto a face. The selected sketch entities or edges highlight in the graphics area (see Figure 8.26), and their names appear in the **Edges** field of the dialog.

8.26

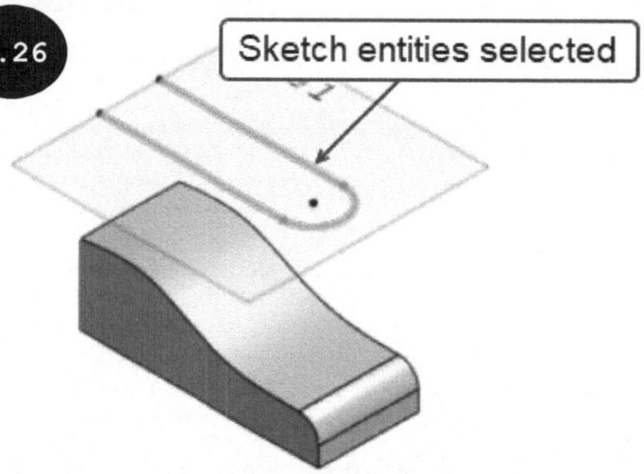

Projection direction type: By default, the **Direction** option is selected in the **Projection direction type** drop-down list of the dialog. As a result, the **Direction** field is enabled, allowing you to select a linear edge, line, or plane to define the direction for projecting the selected sketch entities.

Selecting the **Normal to target** option projects the selected sketch entities in the direction that is normal to the target face.

4. Select the required options (**Direction** or **Normal to target**) in the **Projection direction type** drop-down list of the dialog, as discussed above.

5. Click the **Direction** field and select a linear edge, line, planar face, or plane to define the projection direction, see Figure 8.27. Note that this field is enabled only when the **Direction** option is selected in the previous step.

8.27

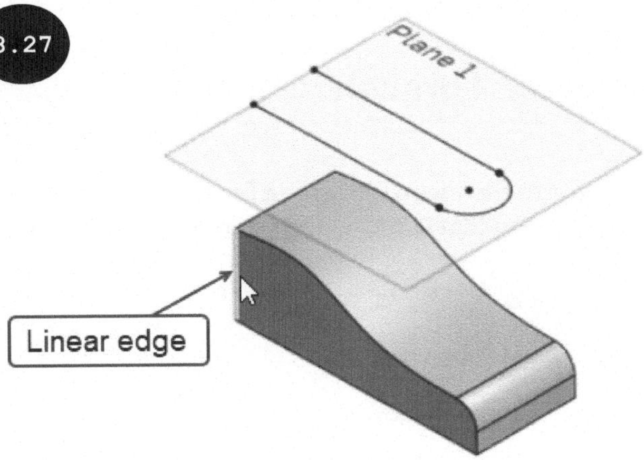

Now, you need to select one or more target faces to project the selected sketch entities or edges.

6. Select one or more target faces of a model in the graphics area. A preview of the projected curve appears on the selected face(s) of the model based on the defined direction, see Figure 8.28.

7. Ensure that the direction of projection is toward the target face. If needed, you can reverse the direction of projection by clicking on the **Opposite direction** button available next to the **Direction** field of the dialog.

8. Click the green checkmark to confirm the creation of a projected curve and exit the dialog. Figure 8.29 shows a projected curve created by projecting a sketch onto a face of a model.

8.28

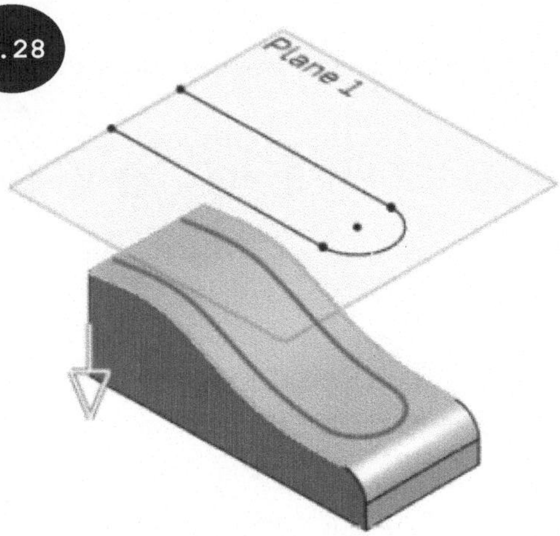

8.29

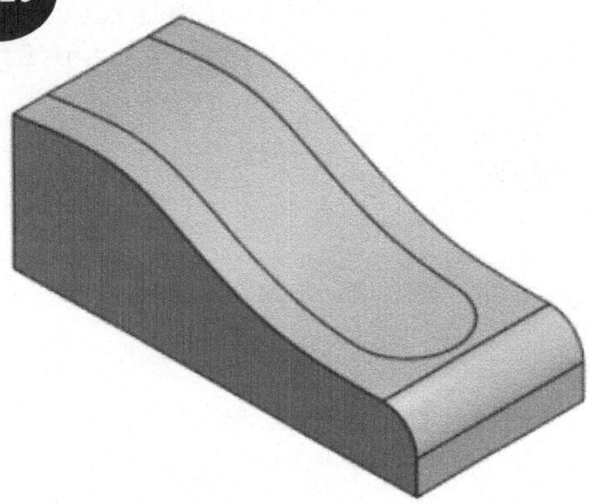

Creating a 3D Fit Spline

You can create a 3D fit spline through a series of vertices or edges using the **3D fit spline** tool. Note that the edges must be tangentially connected to create a 3D fit spline using them. The methods for creating different types of 3D fit splines are outlined below.

Creating a 3D Fit Spline Through Vertices

The method for creating a 3D fit spline through a series of vertices or points is discussed below:

1. Click the down arrow next to the **Plane** tool in the **Feature** toolbar, then select the **3D fit spline** tool from the drop-down menu that appears, see Figure 8.30. The **3D fit spline** dialog appears.

8.30

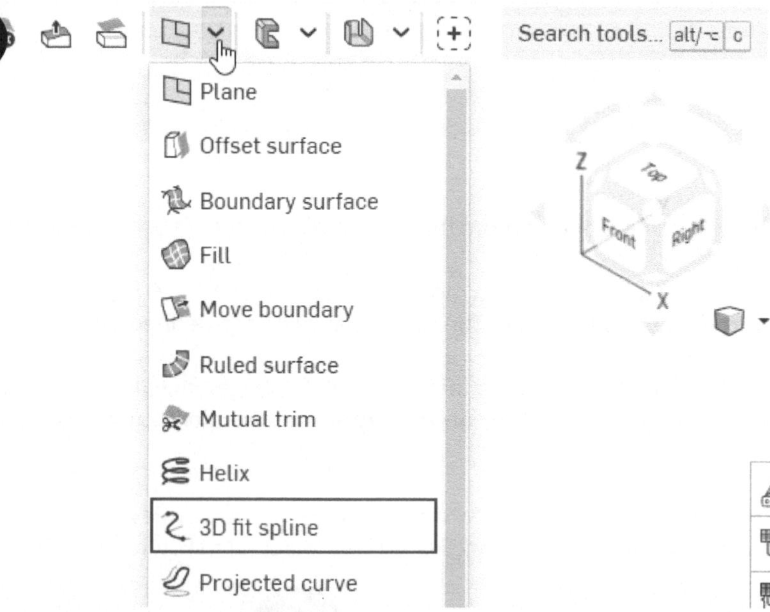

2. Ensure that the **Vertices** tab is activated in the **3D fit spline** dialog to create a spline through a series of vertices or points, see Figure 8.31.

8.31

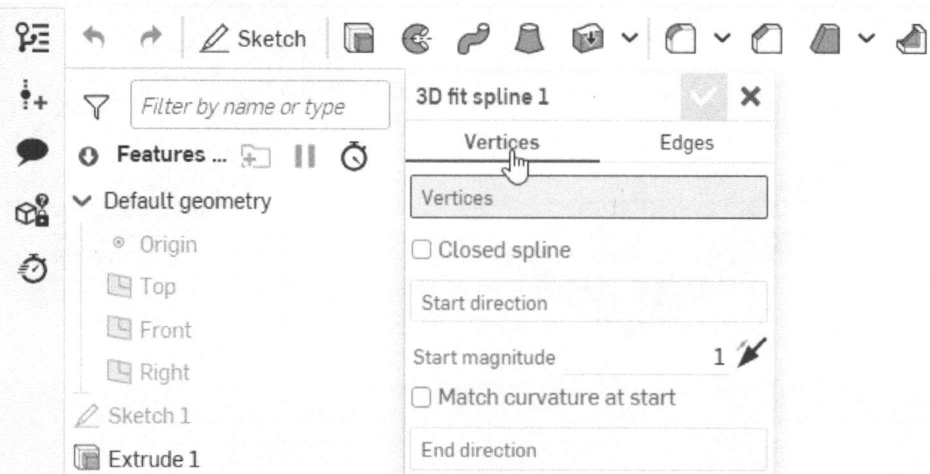

3. Select a series of vertices or points sequentially in the graphics area, see Figure 8.32. Note that as you select vertices or points, a preview of the spline appears passing through the selected points. In this example, five points are selected, and the preview of the spline is displayed accordingly.

8.32

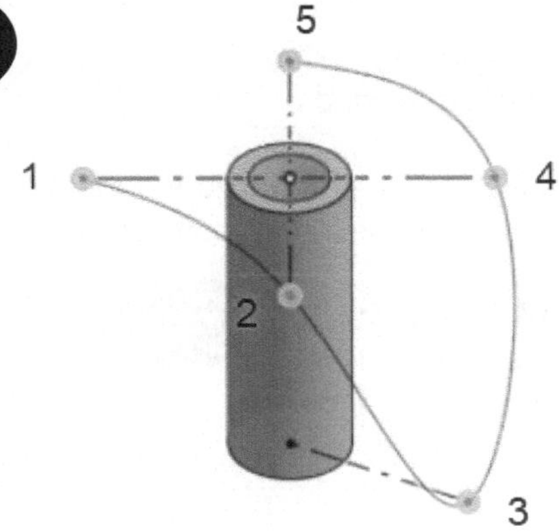

Closed spline: Selecting the **Closed spline** check box creates a closed 3D fit spline, where the start and end vertices or points connect to each other, see Figure 8.33.

8.33

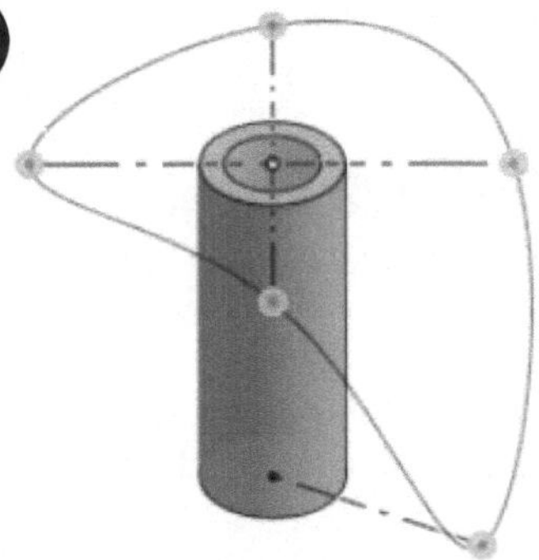

Start direction: The **Start direction** field allows you to select an entity to define the start direction of the spline. You can choose from various entities, such as a linear edge, line, plane, planar face, or cylindrical face, to set the start direction, see Figure 8.34. In this example, the start direction is define downward by selecting a cylindrical face. Note that this field is enabled only when the **Closed spline** check box is cleared.

8.34

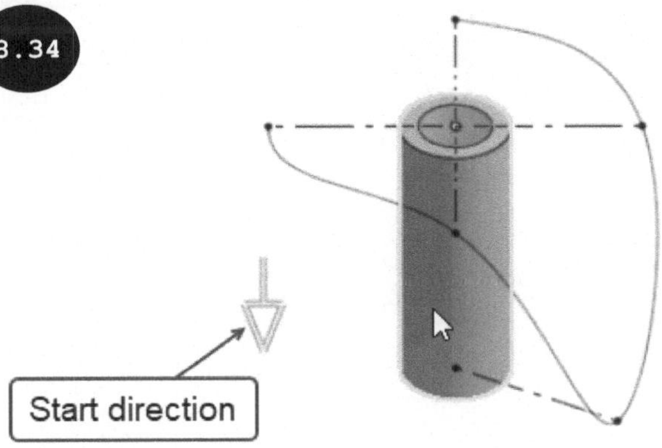

Tip: When a plane or planar face is selected, the start direction is defined as normal to the selection. However, if a cylindrical face is selected, the start direction is defined along its axis.

Start magnitude: After defining the start direction, you can specify the start magnitude along the defined direction of the spline, if needed.

Match curvature at start: Selecting the **Match curvature at start** check box matches the start curvature of the spline with the entity selected to define the start direction.

End Direction and End Magnitude: Similar to defining the start direction and start magnitude, you can define the end direction and end magnitude for the spline in their respective fields within the dialog.

4. After defining the required parameters, click the green checkmark ✓ to confirm the creation of the 3D fit spline and exit the dialog. Figure 8.35 shows a 3D fit spline created by selecting five different points.

8.35

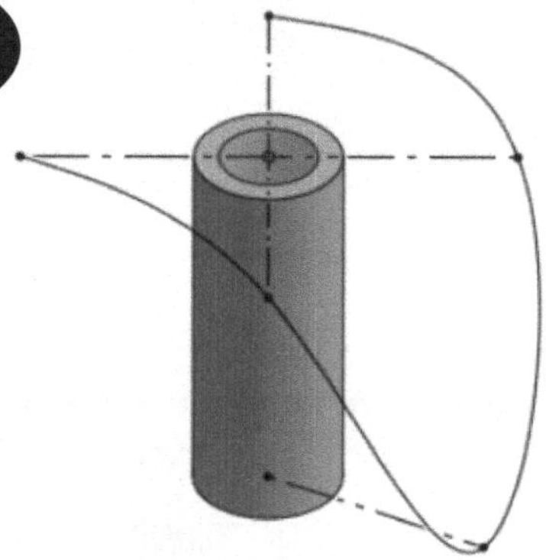

Creating a 3D Fit Spline Through Edges

The method for creating a 3D fit spline through a series of tangentially connected edges is discussed below:

1. Invoke the **3D fit spline** dialog by clicking the down arrow next to the **Plane** tool in the **Feature** toolbar and selecting the **3D fit spline** tool from the drop-down menu.

2. Click on the **Edges** tab in the dialog to access options for creating a 3D fit spline through a series of tangentially connected edges, see Figure 8.36.

8.36

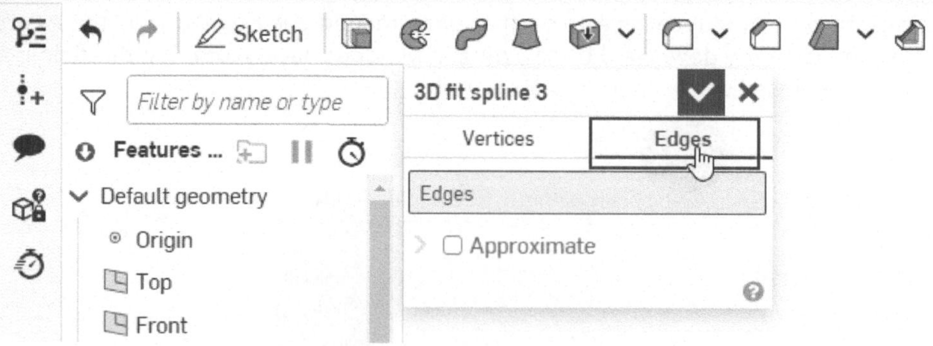

3. Select the tangentially connected edges of the model sequentially in the graphics area. The selected edges are highlighted (see Figure 8.37), and their names appear in the **Edges** field of the dialog. In Figure 8.37, a total of five edges are selected and labeled for your reference.

4. After selecting the edges, click the green checkmark ✓ to confirm the creation of the 3D fit spline and exit the dialog. The 3D fit spline is created along the selected edges of the model.

8.37

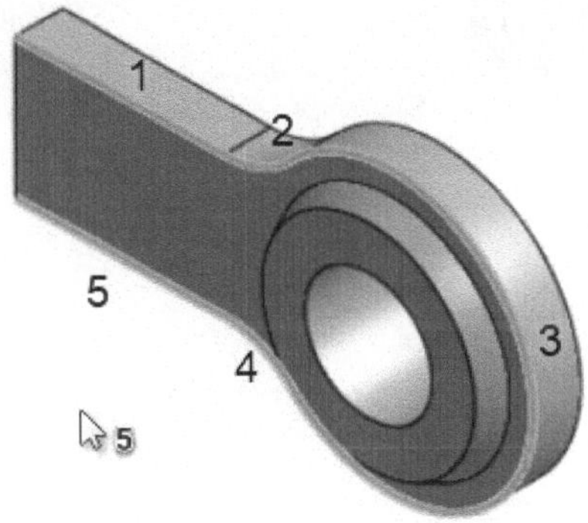

Creating a Bridging Curve

You can create a bridging curve between any two points, vertices, or edges. The method for creating a bridging curve is discussed below:

1. Click the down arrow next to the **Plane** tool in the **Feature** toolbar and select the **Bridging curve** tool from the drop-down menu that appears, see Figure 8.38. The **Bridging curve** dialog appears, see Figure 8.39.

8.38

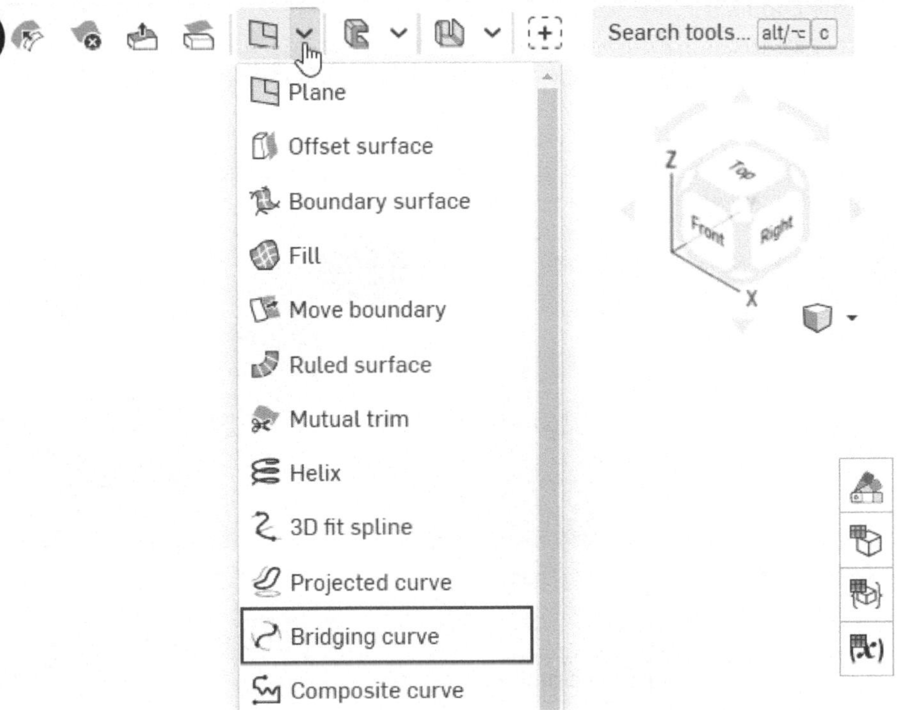

8.39

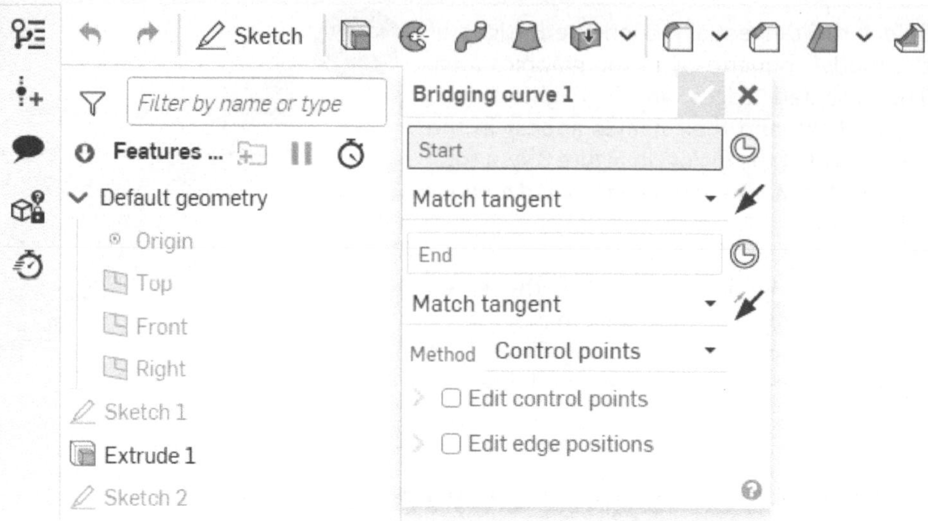

2. Select a point, vertex, or edge to define the start position of the bridging curve, refer to Figures 8.40 and 8.41. The selected entity is highlighted in the graphics area, and its name appears in the **Start** field of the dialog.

   Now, you need to define the end position of the bridging curve.

3. Click the **End** field in the dialog, then select a point, vertex, or edge in the graphics area, refer to Figures 8.40 and 8.41. A preview of the bridging curve appears, connecting the selected points or vertices. If two edges are selected, the curve connects the endpoints of the selected edges, by default.

   Figure 8.40 shows a preview of the bridging curve after selecting two points, while Figure 8.41 shows a preview after selecting two edges of a model.

8.40

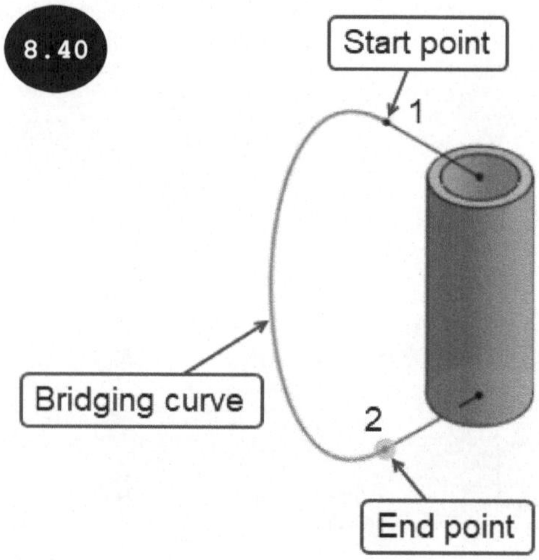

8.41

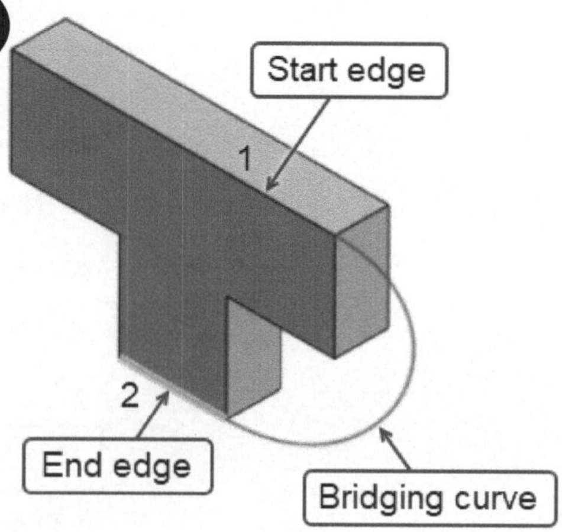

Match Drop-down lists: The options in the **Start Match** and **End Match** drop-down lists are used to define the type of continuity between the bridging curve and the selected start and end entities, such as points or vertices. The options are discussed next.

Match tangent: By default, the **Match tangent** option is enabled in both the **Start Match** and **End Match** drop-down lists. This ensures that the bridging curve maintains tangency with the selected start and end entities, refer to Figures 8.40 and 8.41.

Match position: Selecting the **Match position** option in the **Start Match** drop-down list aligns the start position of the bridging curve with the selected start point, without preserving tangency or curvature. Similarly, choosing the **Match position** option in the **End Match** drop-down list aligns the end position of the bridging curve with the selected end point. Figure 8.42 illustrates the preview of a bridging curve when the **Match position** option is selected for both the **Start Match** and **End Match** drop-down lists.

8.42

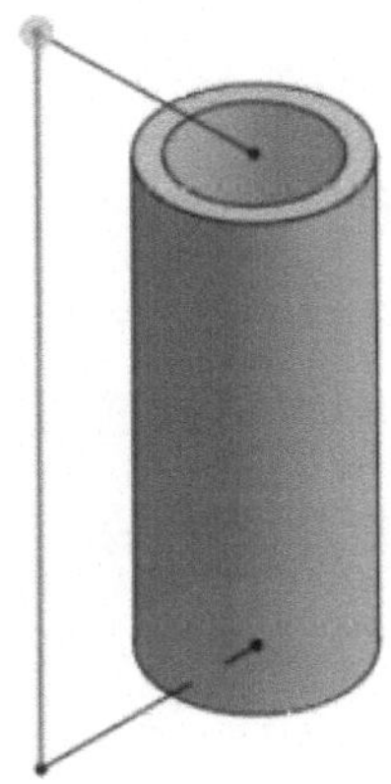

Match curvature: Selecting the **Match curvature** option ensures that the bridging curve maintains curvature continuity with the selected start and end entities.

Match flow (G3): Selecting the **Match flow (G3)** option ensures that the bridging curve maintains flow (G3) continuity with the selected start and end entities.

Edit control points: Selecting the **Edit control points** check box allows you to adjust the magnitude of the start and end points of the bridging curve. When this check box is selected, additional options appear to control the magnitude of the start and end control points, based on the options chosen in the **Match** drop-down lists. This check box is not available if the **Match position** option is selected in both the **Match** drop-down lists of the dialog.

Edit edge positions: Selecting the **Edit edge positions** check box allows you to adjust the start and end positions of the bridging curve along the selected edges of the model. This option is available only when two edges are selected for creating the bridging curve. When the **Edit control points** check box is selected, the **Start edge position** and **End edge position** fields become available in the dialog box. These fields let you define the start and end positions of the bridging curve along the selected edges as percentage values ranging from 0 to 1. For example, a value of 0.5 specifies the position at the midpoint of the edge. Additionally, you can dynamically adjust these positions by dragging the handles that appear along the edges.

4. After defining the required parameters, click the green checkmark ✓ to confirm the creation of the bridging curve and exit the dialog.

Creating an Intersection Curve

You can create an intersection curve at the intersection of two or more geometries. The method for creating an intersection curve is discussed below:

1. Click the down arrow next to the **Plane** tool in the **Feature** toolbar and select the **Intersection curve** tool from the drop-down menu that appears, see Figure 8.43. The **Intersection curve** dialog appears, see Figure 8.44.

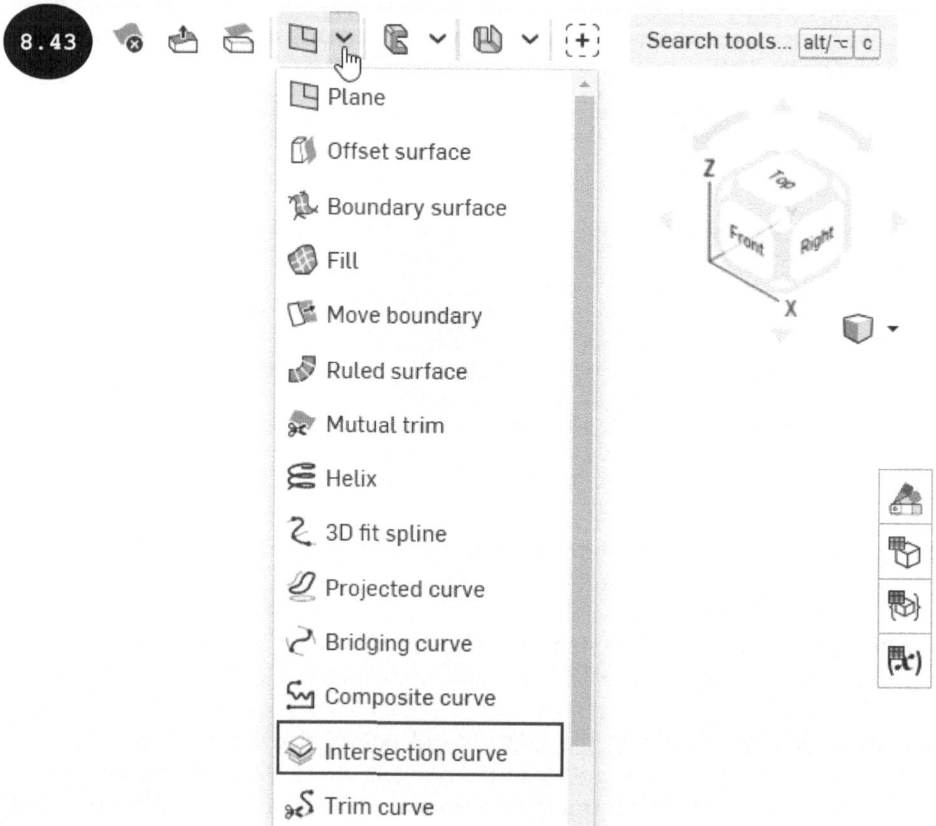

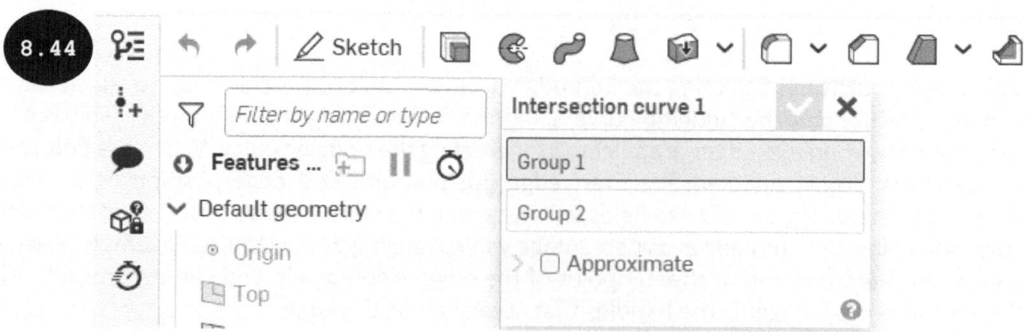

Now, you can select two groups of entities to create an intersection curve at the point where they intersect.

2. Select one or more entities, such as faces, surfaces, parts, or planes, as the first group of entities, see Figure 8.45. In this example, a face of a model is chosen as the first group of entities.

8.45

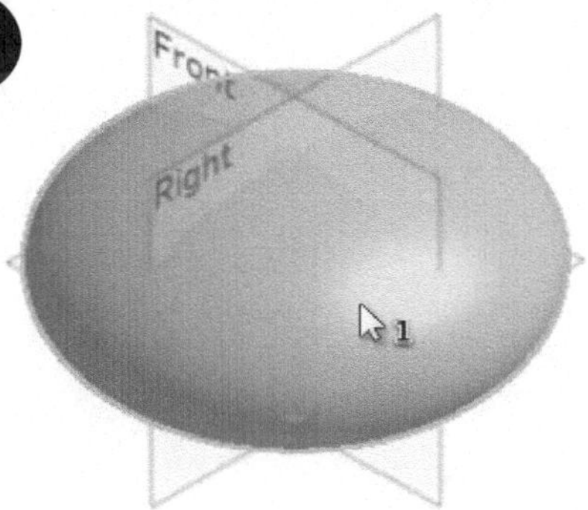

Now, you can select the second group of entities.

3. Click on the Group 2 field in the dialog to activate it, then select one or more entities, such as faces, surfaces, parts, or planes, as the second group of entities. A preview of the intersection curve appears at the intersection of the two selected groups, see Figure 8.46. In this example, two planes (Front and Right) are selected as the second group of entities.

8.46

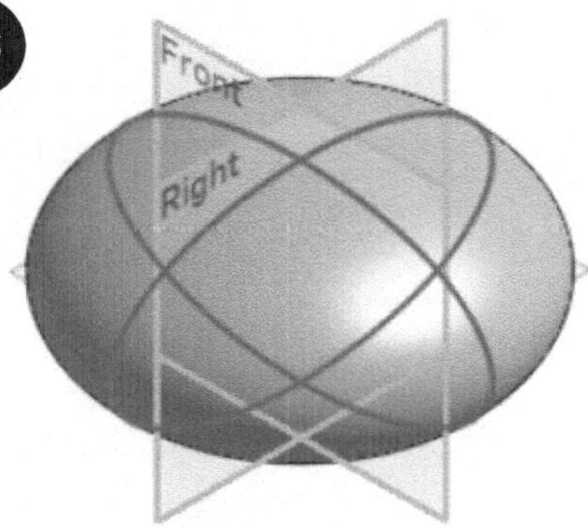

4. After selecting the first and second groups of entities, click the green checkmark ✓ to confirm the creation of the intersection curve and exit the dialog. Figure 8.47 shows the resultant intersection curves. For a better understanding, refer to Figure 8.48 for the resultant intersection curves. In this example, the model display is turned off to show only the intersection curves.

8.47

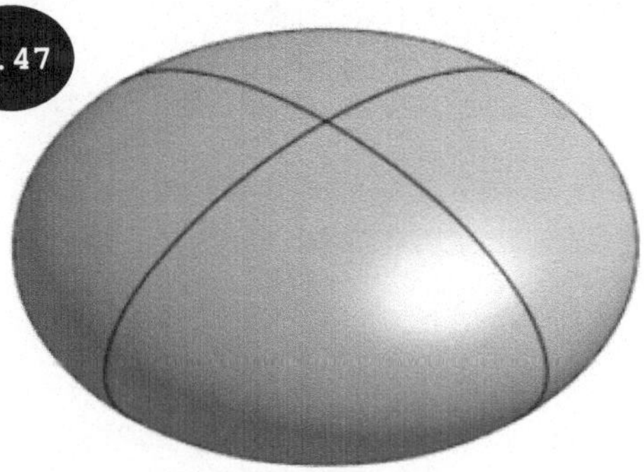

8.48

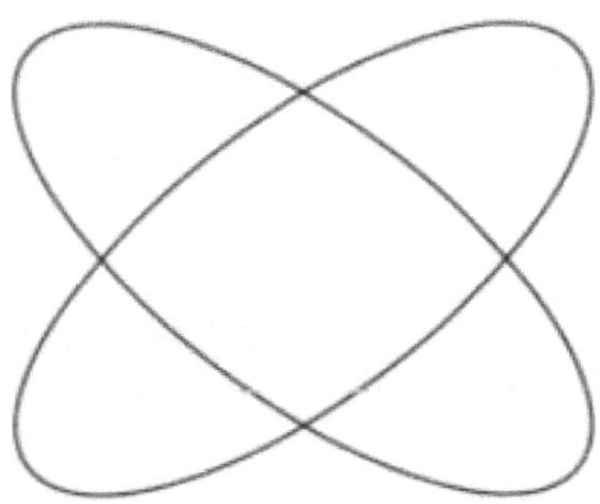

Creating a Composite Curve

A composite curve is formed by connecting two or more individual curves or sketch entities into a unified curve using the **Composite curve** tool.. The method for creating a composite curve is discussed below:

1. Click the down arrow next to the **Plane** tool in the **Feature** toolbar and select the **Composite curve** tool from the drop-down menu that appears, see Figure 8.49. The **Composite curve** dialog appears, see Figure 8.50.

8.49

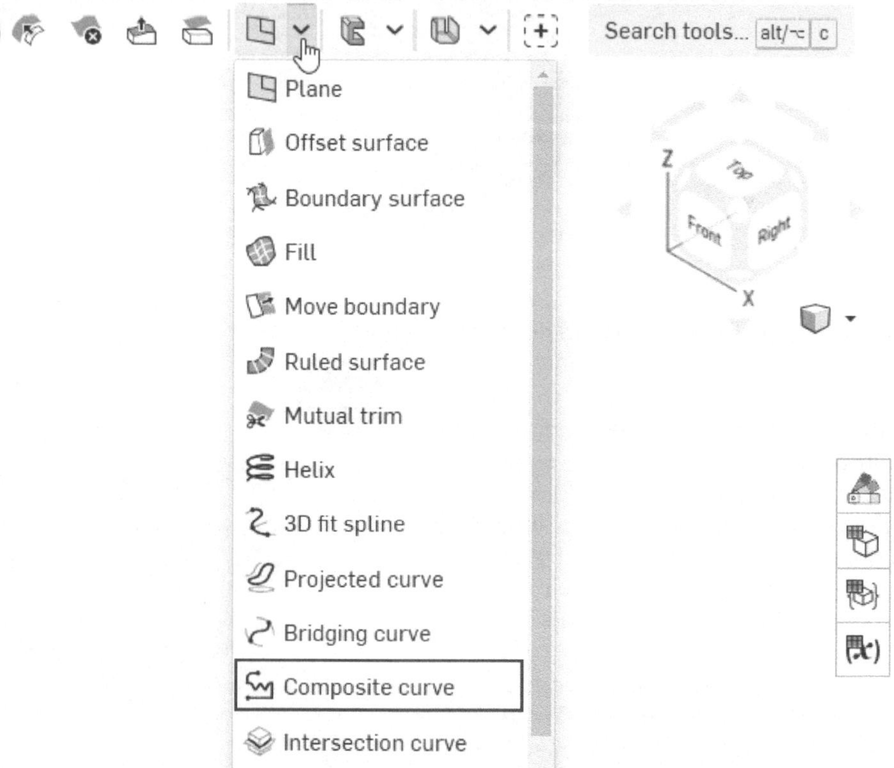

8.50

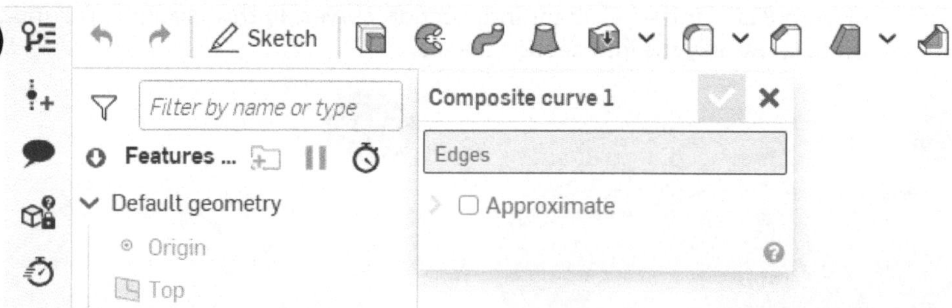

2. Select one or more curves, edges, sketch entities, or a combination of these entities individually in the graphics area, see Figure 8.51. In this example, two helices and a sketch containing multiple entities are selected.

8.51

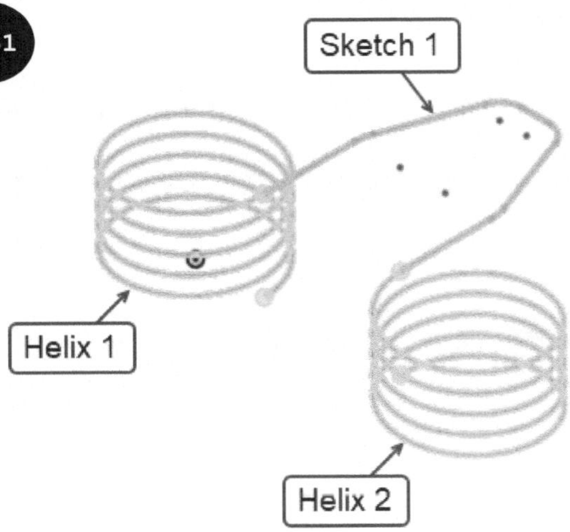

Note: A sketch with multiple entities can be selected either from the Feature list or directly in the graphics area. However, when selecting in the graphics area, you need to select each entity of the sketch individually.

3. After selecting all the entities for creating a composite curve, click the green checkmark ✓ to confirm the creation of the composite curve and exit the dialog. Figure 8.52 shows the resultant composite curve.

8.52

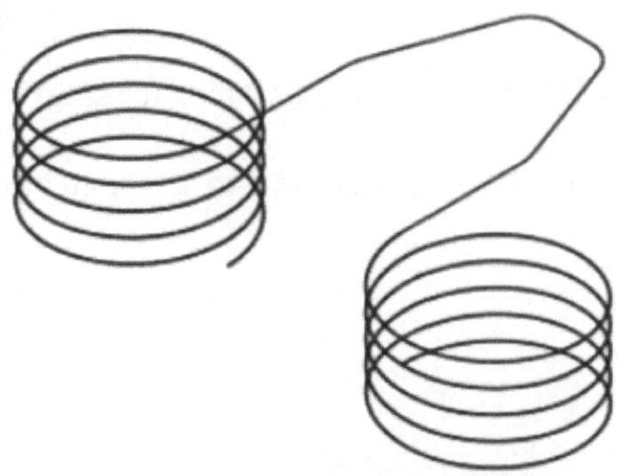

Note: The method for editing a curve is the same as for editing a feature. To edit a curve, right-click on it in the Feature list and select the **Edit** option from the shortcut menu. The respective dialog appears, allowing you to make the necessary changes. Once done, click the green checkmark ✓ to accept the modification and exit the dialog.

Splitting a Part and the Face of a Model

In Onshape, you can divide a part into multiple separate parts, as well as a face of a model into multiple individual faces, using the **Split** tool. The methods for splitting both parts and faces are discussed next.

Splitting a Part

The method for splitting a part into multiple separate parts is discussed below:

1. Click on the **Split** tool in the **Feature** toolbar, see Figure 8.53. The **Split** dialog appears, see Figure 8.54.

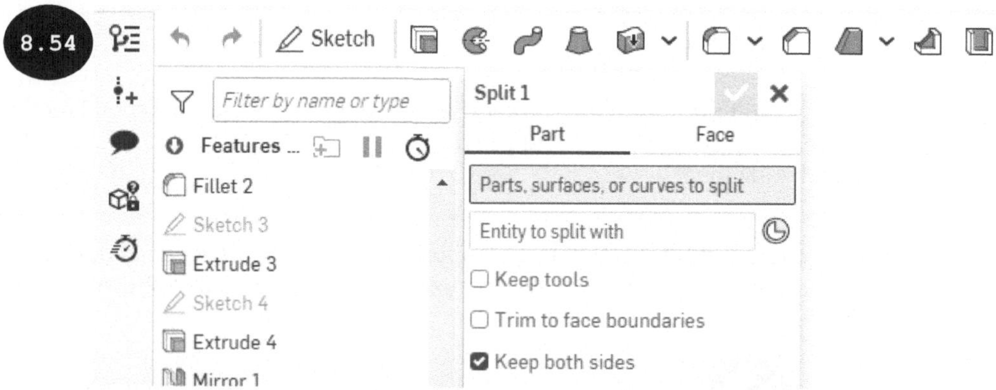

2. Ensure that the **Part** tab is activated in the **Split** dialog for splitting a part.

3. Select one or more parts in the graphics area to be split into multiple individual parts, see Figure 8.55.

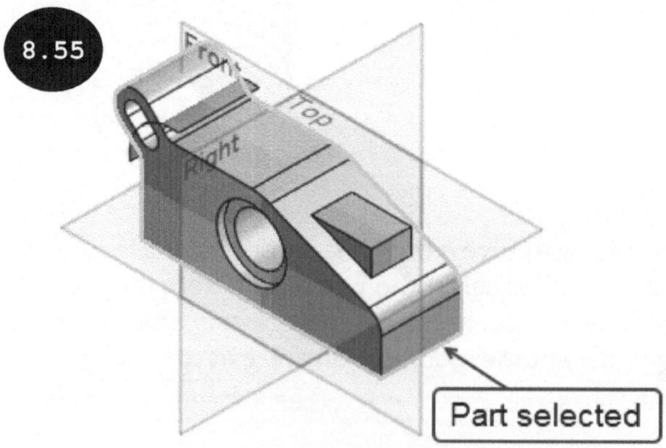

Now, select an entity to use as the tool for splitting the selected part(s).

4. Click on the **Entity to split with** field in the dialog to activate it, then select a plane, face, surface, or mate connector as the tool to split the selected part(s). The selected part is then divided into two or more parts based on the chosen tool, refer to Figures 8.56 and 8.57. In Figure 8.56, the Front plane is selected as the split tool, dividing the part into two individual parts along the Front plane. In Figure 8.57, a surface is selected as the split tool, dividing the part into three individual parts.

8.56

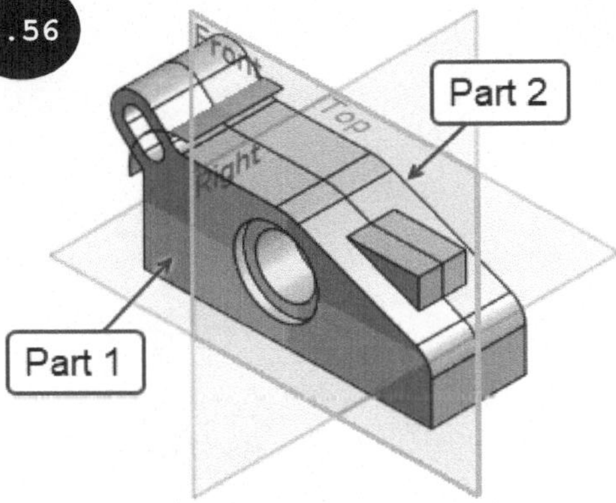

8.57

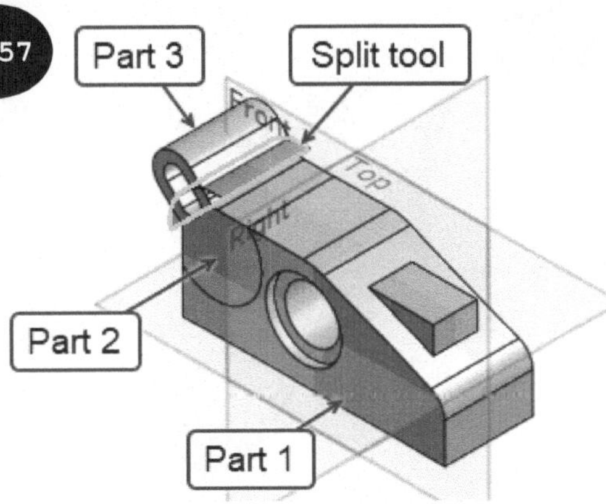

Keep tools: Selecting the **Keep tools** check box retains the display of the selected split tool in the resultant model. If you clear this check box, the selected tool will be hidden in the resultant split model. This option works better when a face or surface is selected as the split tool. However, planes and mate connectors will remain displayed in the resultant model even if this check box is cleared.

Trim to face boundaries: Selecting the **Trim to face boundaries** check box limits the split operation to the bounding edges of the selected split tool, refer to Figure 8.58. In this example, the model is split into two individual parts relative to the selected split tool.

Clearing the check box allows the bounding edges of the split tool to extend to their full length to perform the split operation, see Figure 8.59. In this case, the model is split into four individual parts relative to the split tool.

8.58

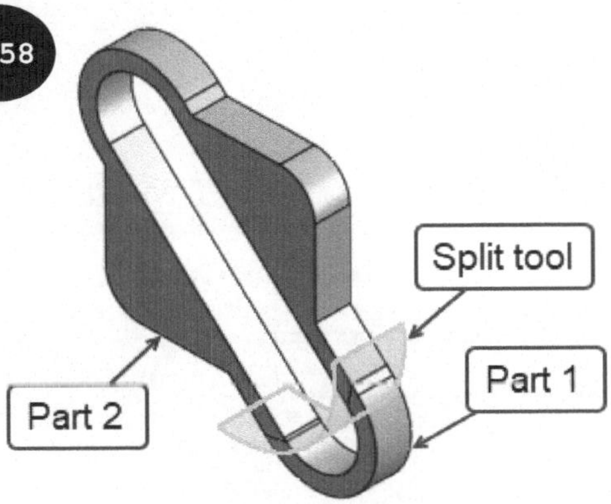

8.59

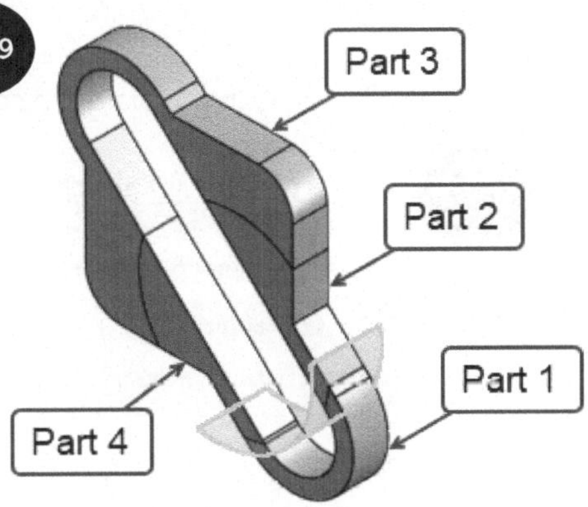

Keep both sides: By default, the **Keep both sides** check box is selected, retaining both sides (split parts) of the model relative to the selected split tool, see Figure 8.60.

When you clear this check box, only one side (split part) of the model will be retained, see Figure 8.61. The side displayed as transparent in the preview will be removed. You can toggle the side of the part to be kept by clicking the **Opposite direction** button, which becomes available when the check box is cleared.

8.60

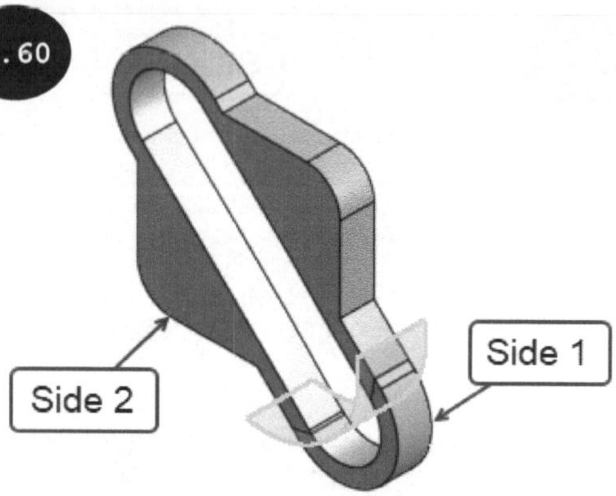

8.61

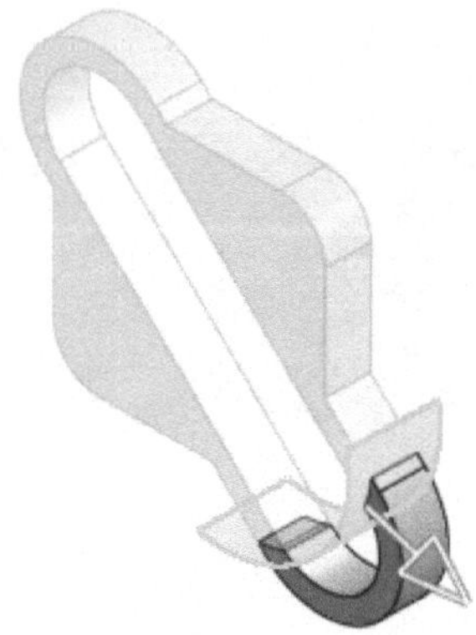

5. After selecting the part to be split and the split tool, click the green checkmark to confirm the split operation and exit the dialog. The selected part splits into two or more parts relative to the selected split tool.

Splitting the Face of a Model

The method for splitting the face of a model is discussed below:

1. Click on the **Split** tool in the **Feature** toolbar, see Figure 8.62. The **Split** dialog appears.

8.62

2. Click on the **Face** tab in the dialog to split one or more faces of a model, see Figure 8.63.

8.63

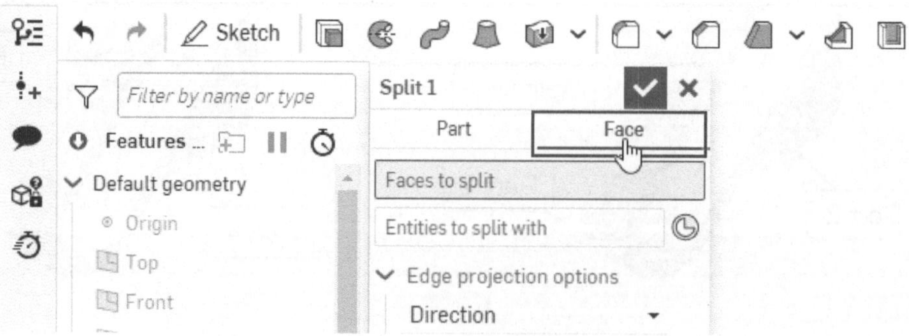

3. Select one or more faces of a model to be split, see Figure 8.64. In the figure, a face is selected.

8.64

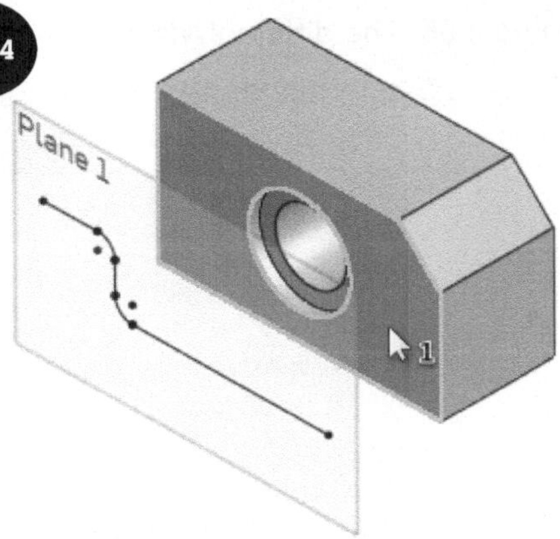

Now, select an entity to use as the tool for splitting the selected face(s).

4. Click on the **Entity to split with** field in the dialog, then select one or more entities as the tool to split the selected face(s), see Figure 8.65. In this example, a sketch is selected as the split tool. You can choose sketch entities, planes, faces, surfaces, or curves as the split tool. Once you select the split tool, the selected face of the model splits into two or more faces relative to the selected split tool, see Figure 8.65.

8.65

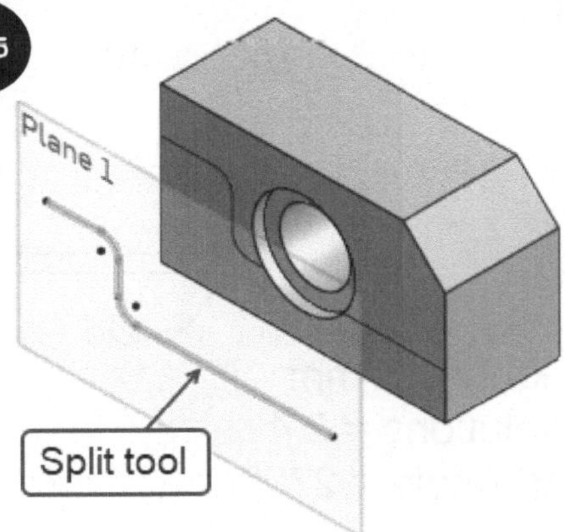

Tip: You can select the entire sketch or all its entities at once by selecting it from the Feature list.

5. Click the green checkmark to confirm the split operation and exit the dialog. The selected face(s) splits into two or more faces relative to the selected split tool.

Tutorial 1

Create a model, as shown in Figure 8.66. The different views and dimensions are given in the same figure. All dimensions are in inches.

8.66

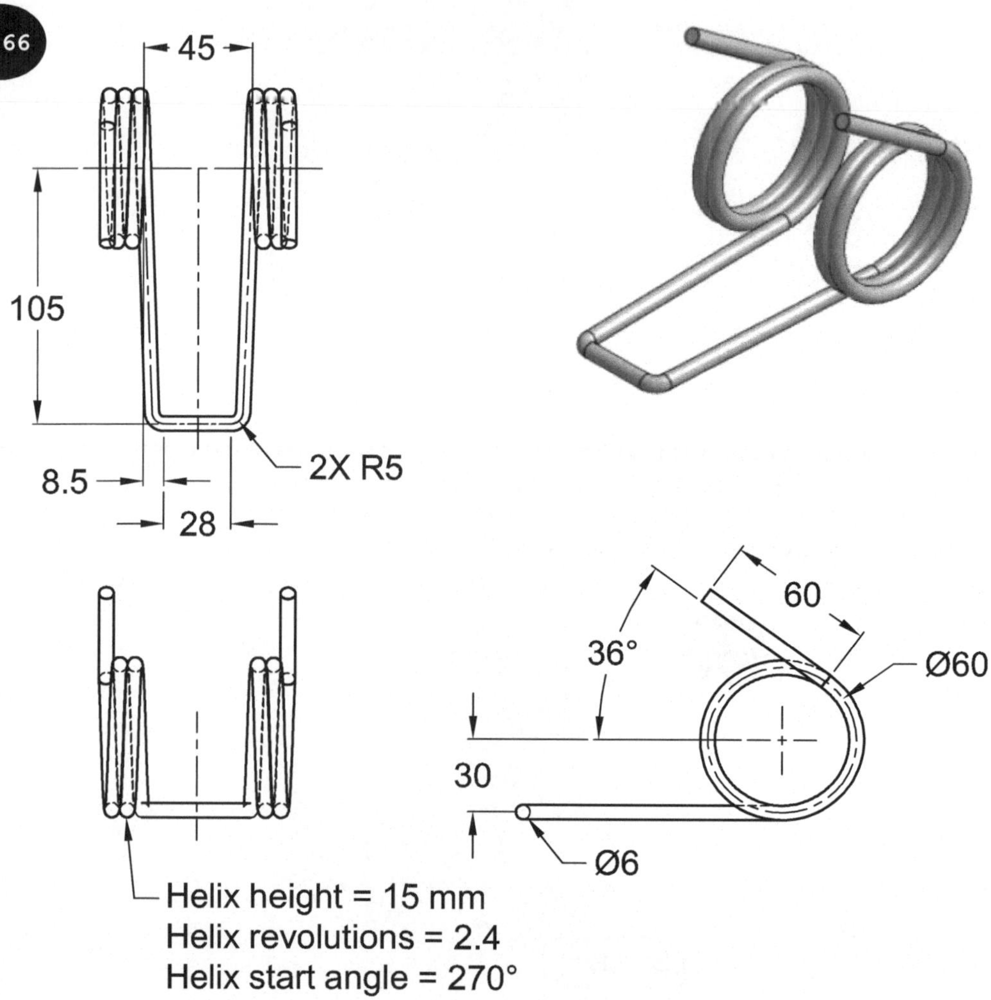

Section 1: Starting a New Design Document

1. Launch Onshape (***onshape.com***) and log in to your account if you're not already logged in. The **Documents Page** appears.

Note: If you are within a document, click on the **Onshape** logo located in the top left corner of the browser to display the **Documents Page**, see Figure 8.67.

8.67

2. Click on the **Create** button at the top left corner of the **Documents Page** and then click on the **Document** option in the menu that appears, see Figure 8.68. The **New document** window appears with the default name of the document as "**Untitled document**".

8.68

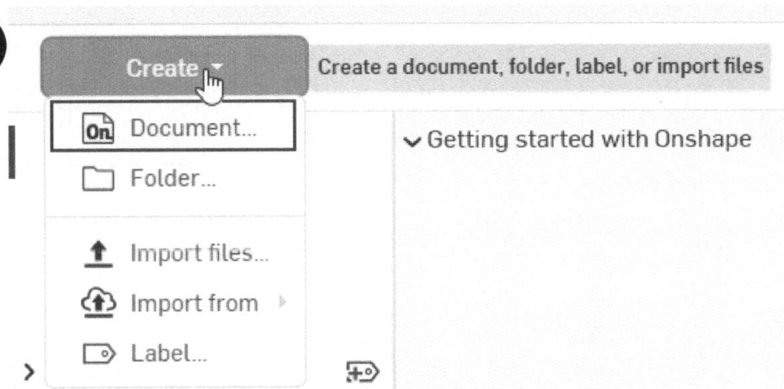

3. Enter **C08 Tutorial 01** as the name of the design document in the **New document** window, and then click on the **Create** button or the **Create Public Document** button, depending on your subscription type. A new document with the specified name is opened.

Section 2: Settings Units

Before creating the model, ensure that the document's units are properly defined.

1. Invoke the **Document** menu by clicking on the ≡ icon (three horizontal lines) next to the **Onshape** logo at the top left corner, see Figure 8.69.

8.69

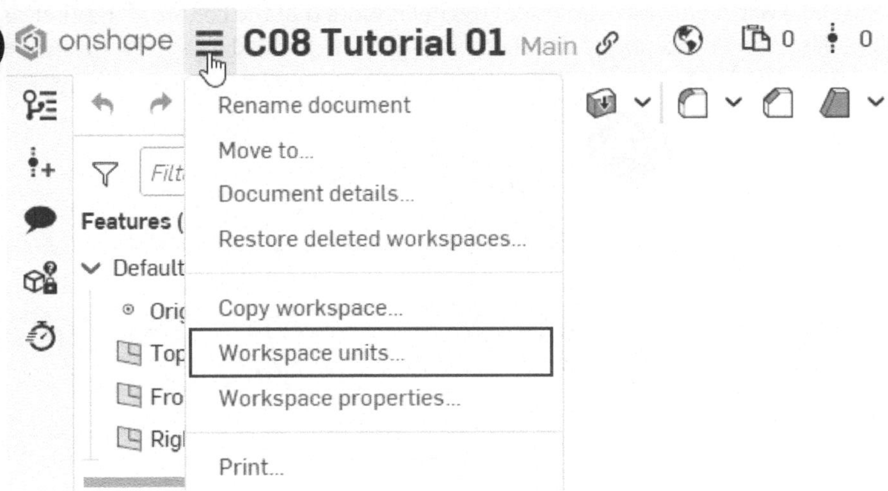

2. Click on the **Workspace units** option in the **Document** menu, refer to Figure 8.69. The **Workspace units** dialog appears.

3. Select the **Millimeter** unit in the **Length default unit** drop-down list and set its precision to **0.1** in the respective **Display decimals** drop-down list of the **Workspace units** dialog, see Figure 8.70.

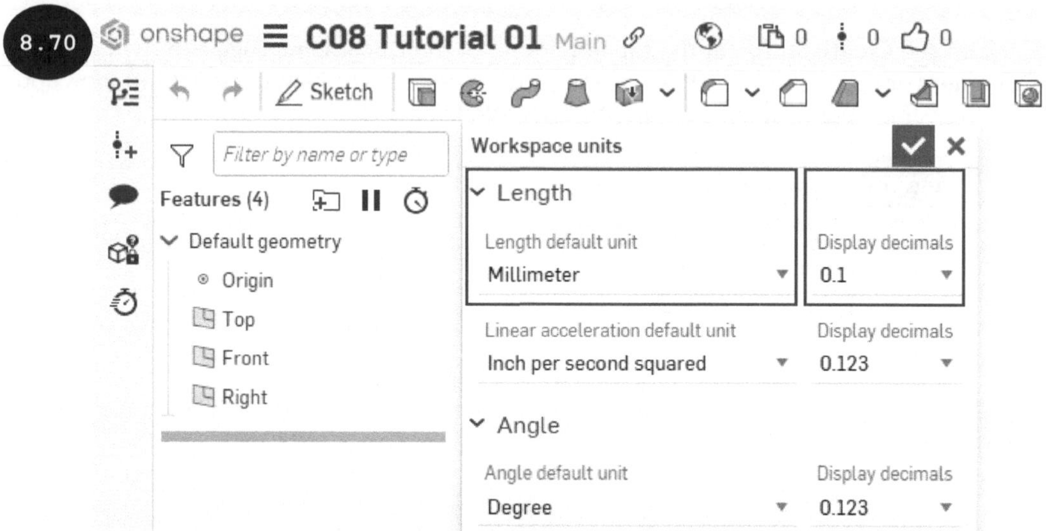

4. After selecting the required unit of length measurement and the decimal precision for the current design document, click on the green checkmark ✓ to confirm the selection and exit the dialog. The millimeter is defined as the unit for the length measurement.

Section 3: Creating the First Curve - Helix

Now, you can create a helix curve.

1. Access the **Sketch** toolbar by selecting the Right plane as the sketching plane. Then, create a circle with a diameter of 60 mm using the **Center point circle** tool, see Figure 8.71. The diameter of the circle will define the diameter of the helix. Note that the center of the circle is located at the origin. Also, the orientation of the sketching plane is changed to normal to the viewing direction by pressing the N key.

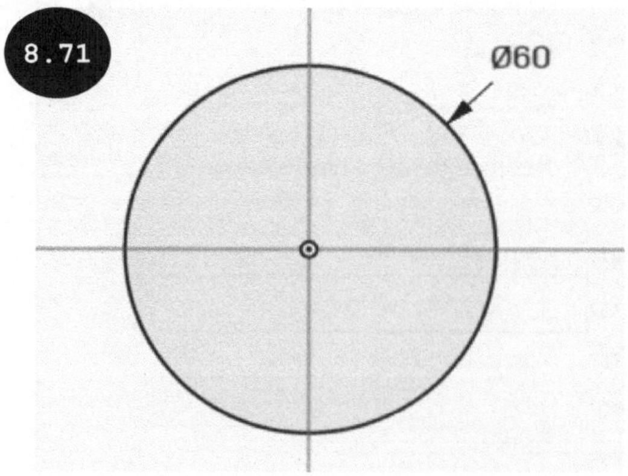

2. After creating the circle, green checkmark ✓ in the Sketch dialog to confirm the creation of the circle and switch back to the Part Studio environment.

3. Press the SHIFT + 7 keys to change the view orientation to isometric.

   Now, you can create a helix using the previously created circle.

4. Click on the down arrow next to the **Plane** tool in the **Feature** toolbar to display a drop-down menu, see Figure 8.72.

8.72

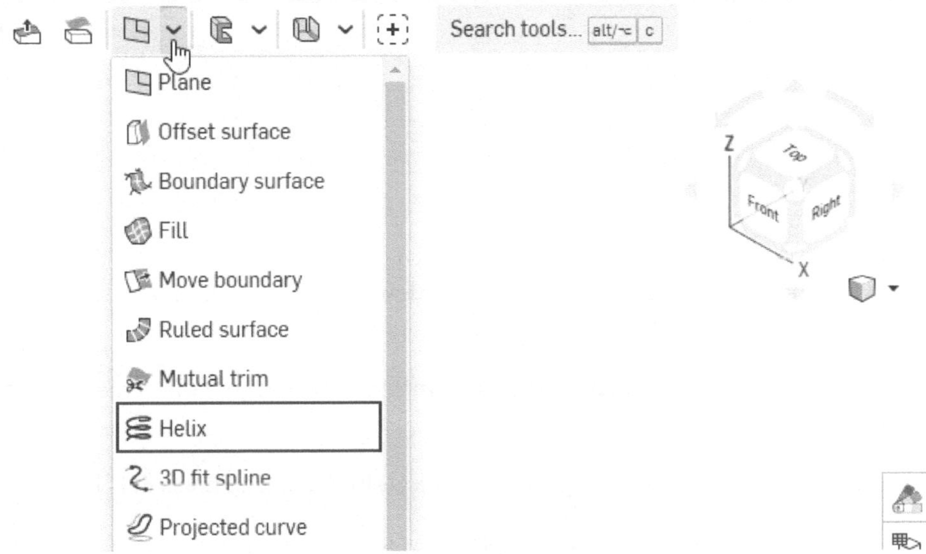

5. Click on the **Helix** tool in the drop-down menu, refer to Figure 8.72. The **Helix** dialog appears.

6. Click the **Circle** tab in the **Helix** dialog to access options for creating a helix using a circular edge or circle, see Figure 8.73.

8.73

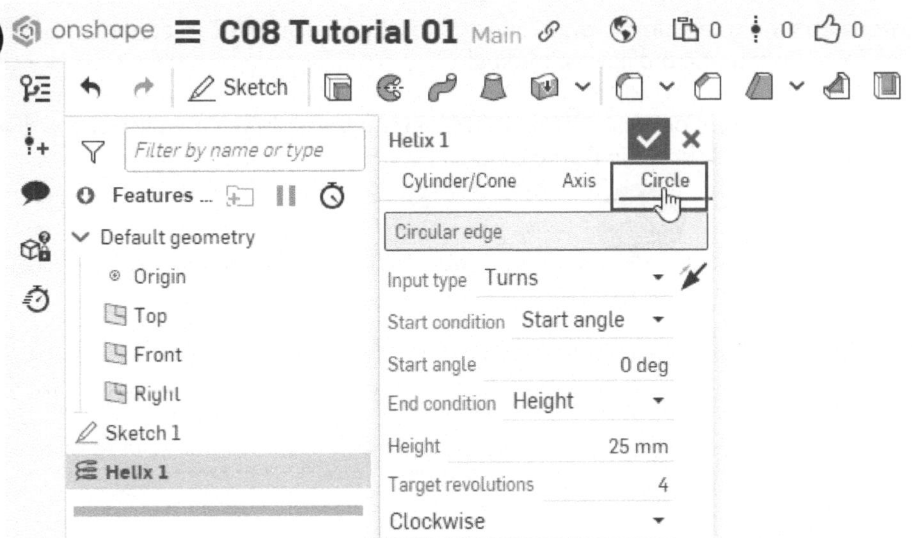

7. Select the circle in the graphics area. A preview of the helix appears with default parameters, see Figure 8.74.

8.74

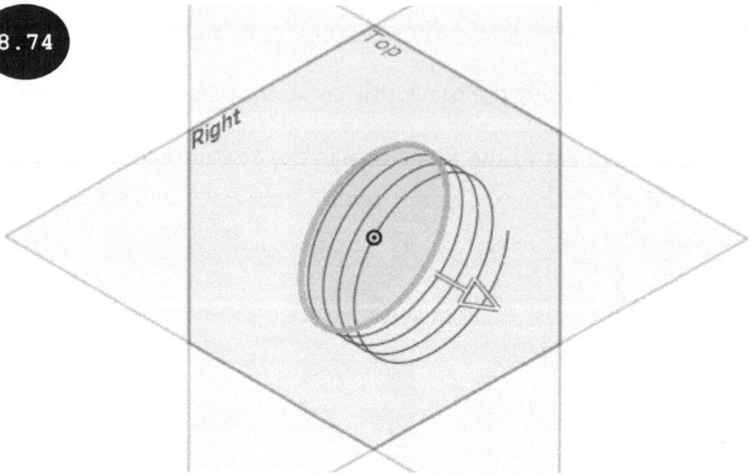

8. Select the **Turns** option in the **Input type** drop-down list to create a helix by specifying the number of revolutions or turns.

9. Click on the **Opposite direction** button to reverse the helix direction to the opposite side of the sketching plane.

10. Enter **270** degrees in the **Start angle** field of the **Helix** dialog and press ENTER.

11. Ensure that the **Height** option is selected in the **Height** drop-down list to define the height of the helix.

12. Enter **15** mm as the total height of the helix in the **Height** field of the dialog and press ENTER. The helix preview is updated accordingly in the graphics area.

13. Enter **2.4** as the total number of revolutions for the helix in the **Target revolutions** field and press ENTER to update the preview accordingly.

14. Select the **Counterclockwise** option in the **Handedness** drop-down list of the dialog. The helix preview appears as shown in Figure 8.75.

8.75

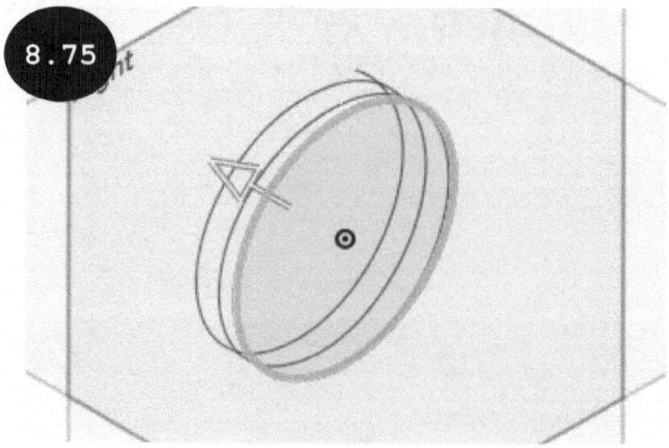

15. After defining all the required parameters, click the green checkmark ✓ to confirm the creation of the helix and exit the dialog. Figure 8.76 shows the created helix. In this figure, the display of construction planes and the origin is turned off for clarity.

8.76

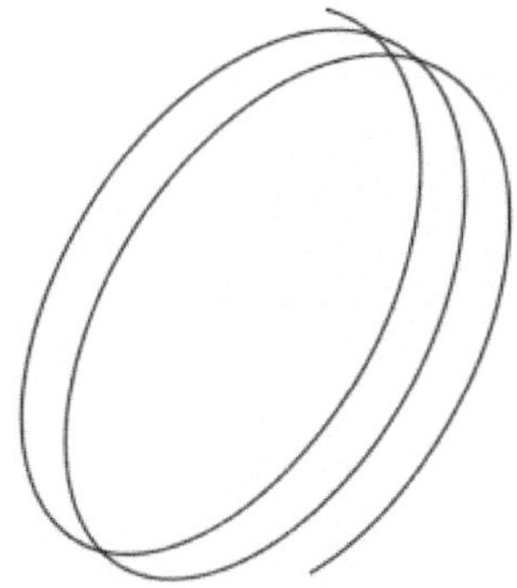

Section 4: Creating the Second Curve - Helix

After creating the first helix, you can create the second helix of similar parameters at an offset distance of 45 mm from the Right plane.

1. Click on the **Plane** tool in the **Feature** toolbar (see Figure 8.77) to open the **Plane** dialog.

8.77

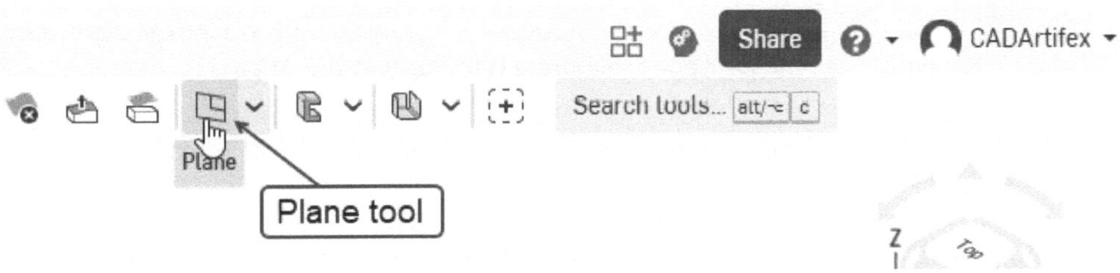

2. Ensure that the **Offset** option is selected in the **Plane type** drop-down list of the dialog (see Figure 8.78) to create a plane at the specified offset distance.

8.78

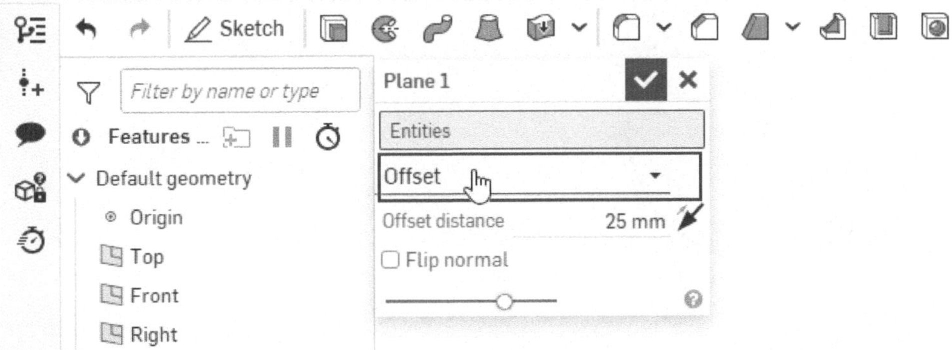

3. Select the Right plane as the reference entity in the graphics area. A preview of the construction plane appears at a default offset distance.

4. Enter **45** mm in the **Offset distance** field and press ENTER. The construction plane preview is updated accordingly in the graphics area, see Figure 8.79.

8.79

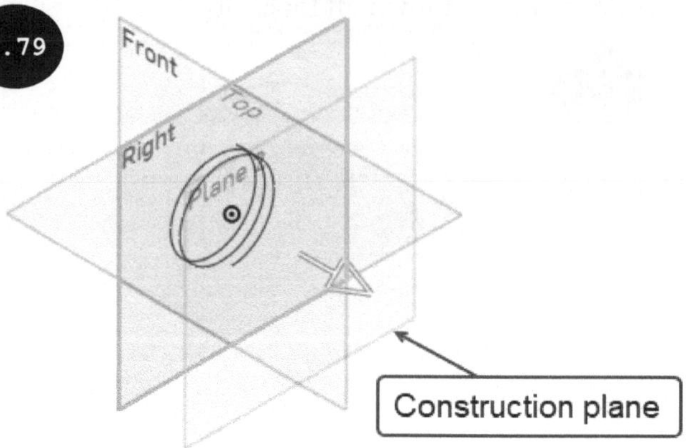

5. Click the green checkmark in the **Plane** dialog to confirm the creation of the construction plane and exit the dialog.

   Now, you can create the second helix.

6. Access the **Sketch** toolbar by selecting the newly created construction plane as the sketching plane. Then, create a circle with a diameter of 60 mm using the **Center point circle** tool, see Figure 8.80. Note that the center of the circle is located at the origin.

7. After creating the circle, green checkmark in the Sketch dialog to confirm the creation of the circle and switch back to the Part Studio environment.

8. Press the SHIFT + 7 keys to change the view orientation to isometric, see Figure 8.81.

8.80

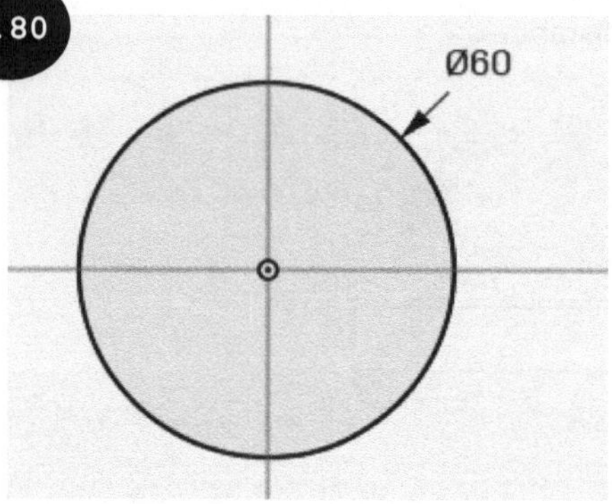

8.81

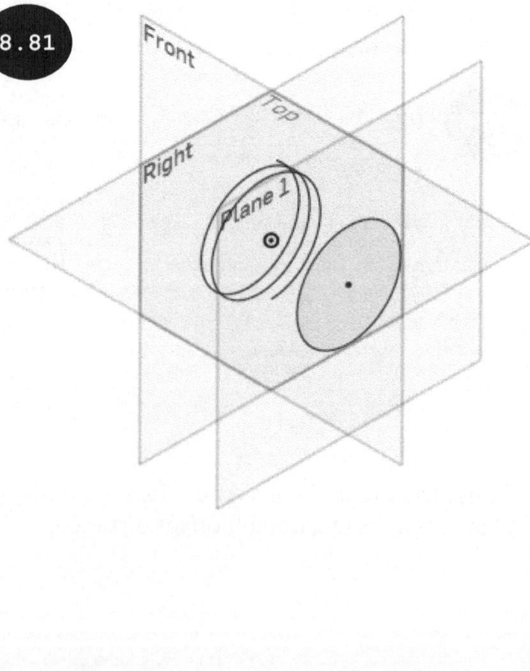

Now, you can create the helix using the previously created circle.

9. Click on the down arrow next to the **Plane** tool in the **Feature** toolbar and then select the **Helix** tool in the drop-down menu that appears, see Figure 8.82. The **Helix** dialog appears.

8.82

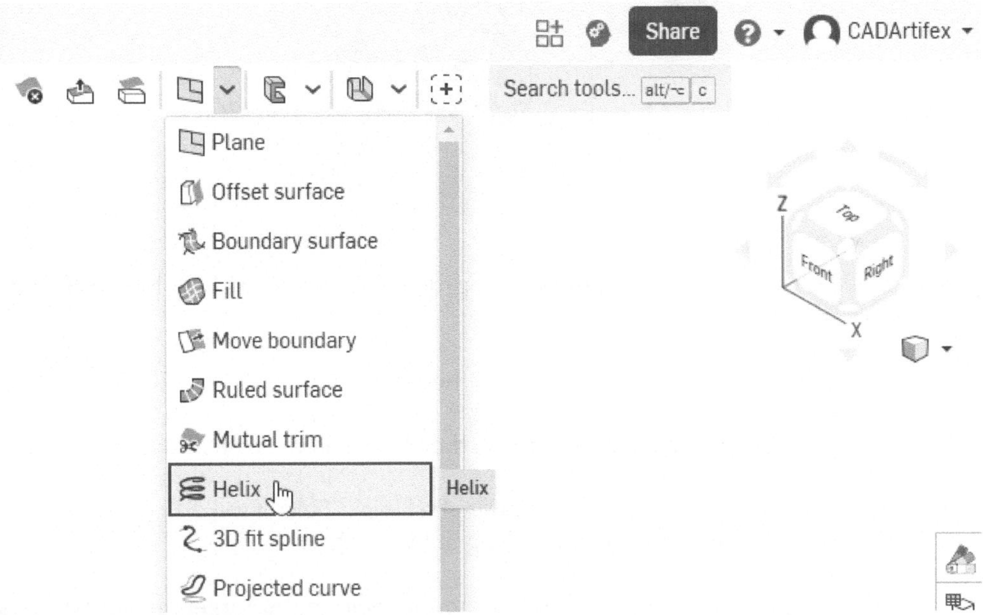

10. Click the **Circle** tab in the **Helix** dialog to access options for creating a helix using a circular edge or circle, see Figure 8.83.

8.83

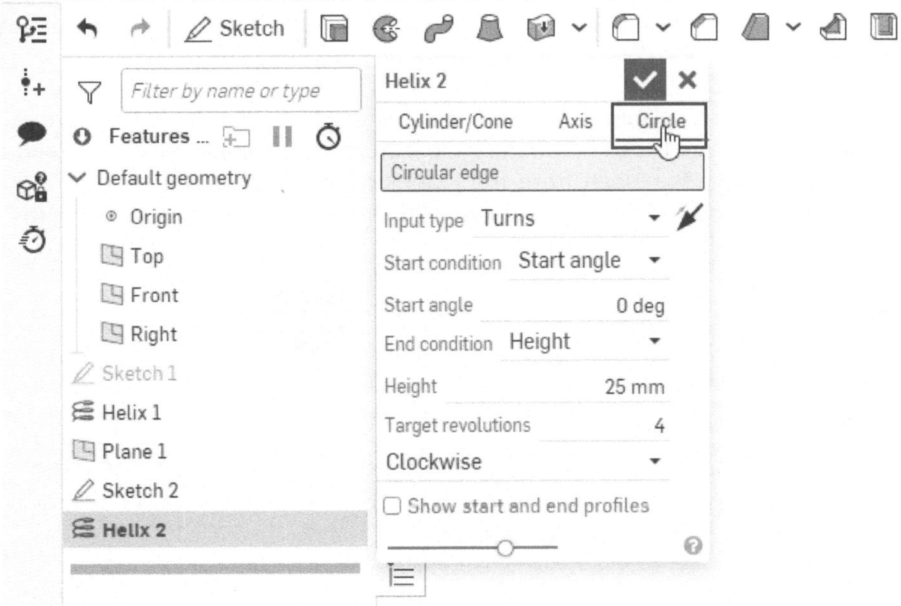

11. Select the previously created circle in the graphics area. A preview of the helix appears with default parameters, see Figure 8.84.

8.84

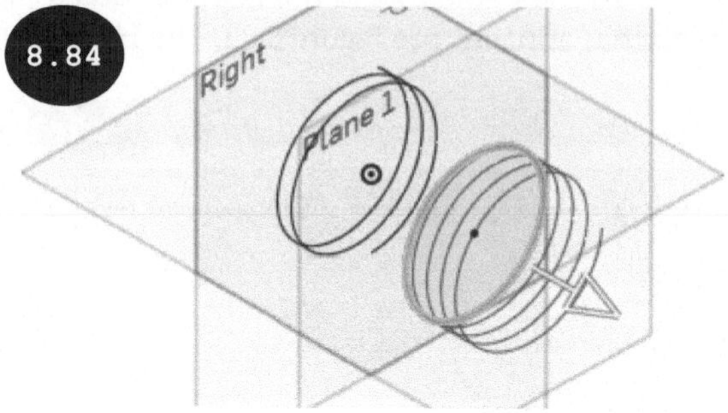

12. Select the **Turns** option in the **Input type** drop-down list to create a helix by specifying the number of revolutions or turns.

13. Enter **270** degrees in the **Start angle** field of the **Helix** dialog and press ENTER.

14. Ensure that the **Height** option is selected in the **Height** drop-down list.

15. Enter **15** mm as the total height of the helix in the **Height** field of the dialog and press ENTER. The helix preview is updated accordingly in the graphics area.

16. Enter **2.4** as the total number of revolutions for the helix in the **Target revolutions** field and press ENTER to update the preview accordingly.

17. Ensure that the **Clockwise** option is selected in the **Handedness** drop-down list of the dialog.

18. After defining all the required parameters, click the green checkmark ✓ to confirm the creation of the helix and exit the dialog.

19. Hide the display of all planes and the origin in the graphics area. To do this, hover the cursor over a plane in the Feature list and click the **Hide** icon that appears next to it, refer to Figure 8.85. The selected plane is hidden from the graphics area. Repeat this process to hide the other construction planes and the origin. Figure 8.86 shows two helices after hiding the display of the construction planes and the origin.

8.85

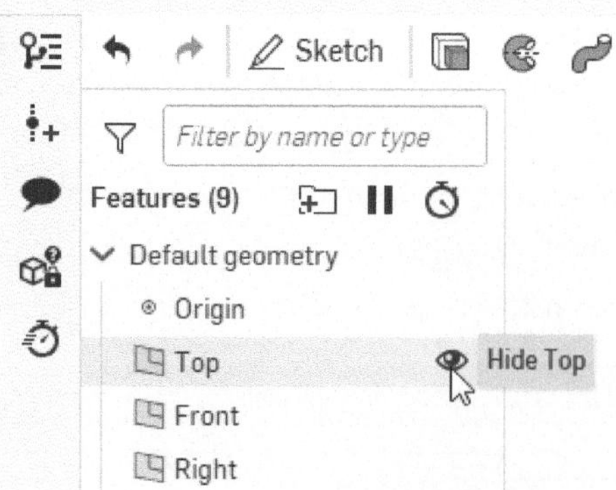

8.86

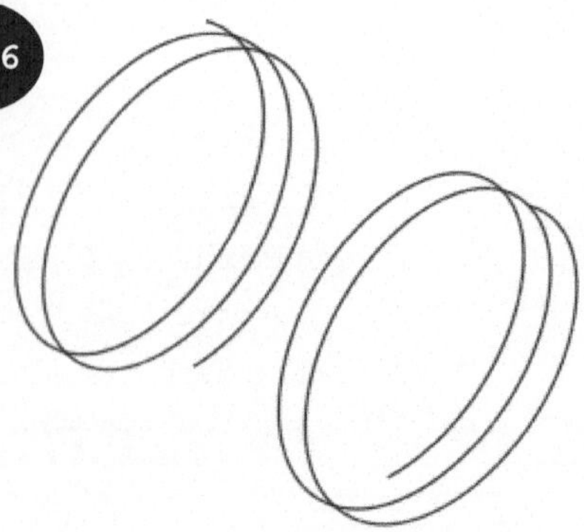

Section 5: Creating the Third Curve - Sketch

After creating the two helices, you need to create a sketch on a reference plane that is parallel to the Top plane and passes through the starting point of the first helix.

1. Click on the **Plane** tool in the **Feature** toolbar (see Figure 8.87) to open the **Plane** dialog.

8.87

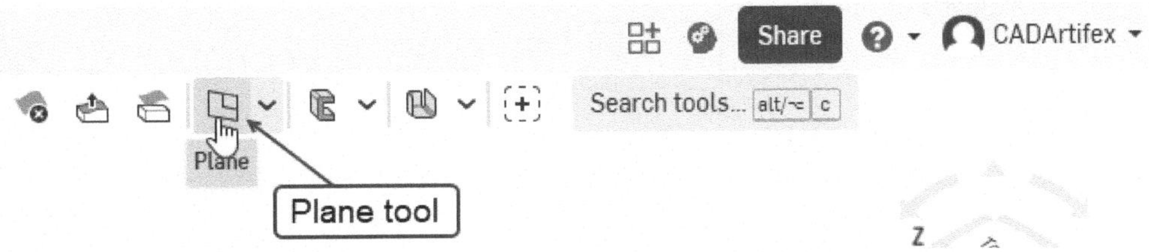

2. Select the **Plane point** option in the **Plane type** drop-down list of the dialog, see Figure 8.88.

8.88

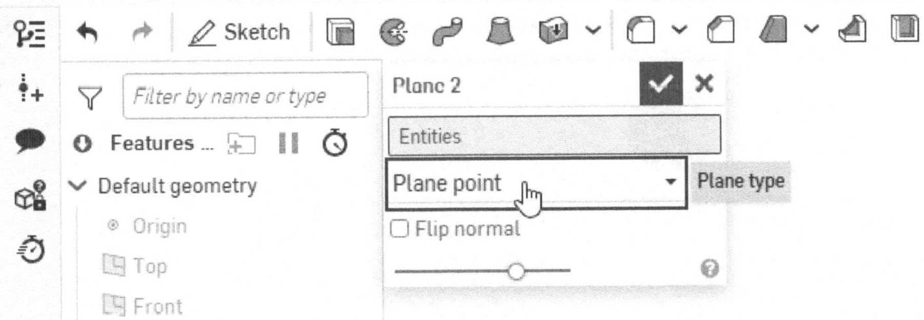

3. Select the **Top** plane in the Feature list as the first reference entity. The Top plane is highlighted in the graphics area, refer to Figure 8.89.

4. Select the start point of the first helix in the graphics area as the second reference entity, see Figure 8.89. A preview of the construction plane appears, parallel to the Top plane and passing through the start point of the first helix, see Figure 8.90.

8.89

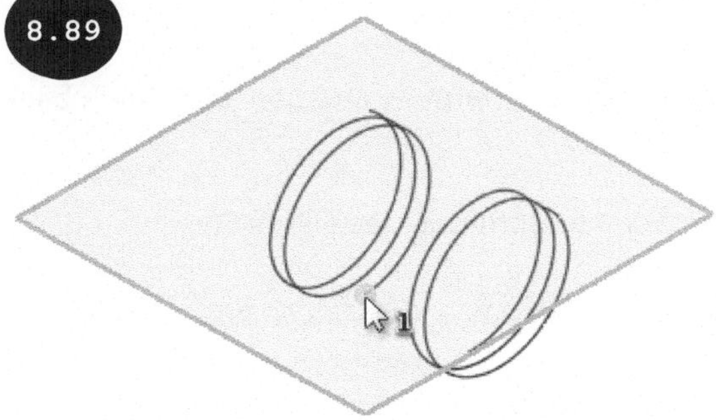

8.90

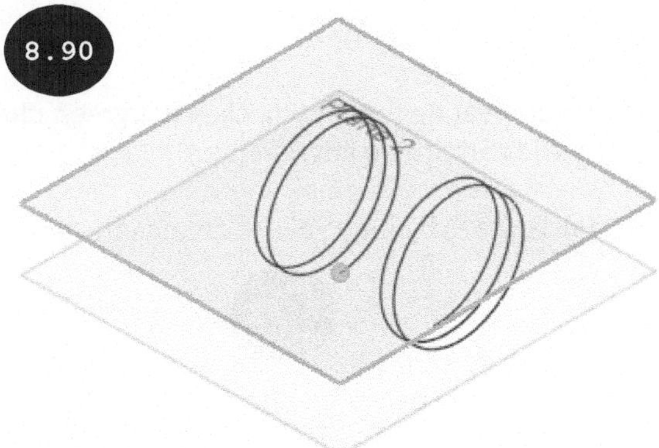

5. Click the green checkmark in the **Plane** dialog to confirm the creation of the construction plane and exit the dialog.

Now, you can create the sketch on the newly created construction plane.

6. Click on the **Sketch** tool in the **Feature** toolbar (see Figure 8.91), then select the newly created construction plane in the graphics area.

8.91

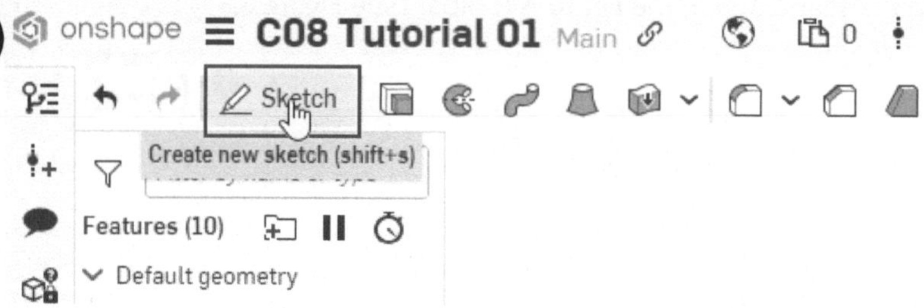

7. Press the N key to make the sketching plane normal to the viewing direction.

8. Create the sketch using the sketching tools and apply the required dimensions, see Figure 8.92. Note that both endpoints of the sketch are coincident with the start point of the respective helix.

8.92

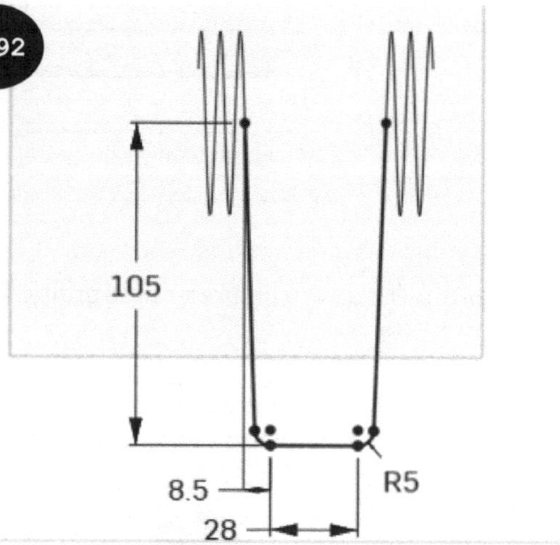

9. After creating the sketch, click the green checkmark ✓ to confirm its creation and switch back to the Part Studio environment.

10. Press the SHIFT + 7 keys to change the view orientation to isometric, see Figure 8.93.

8.93

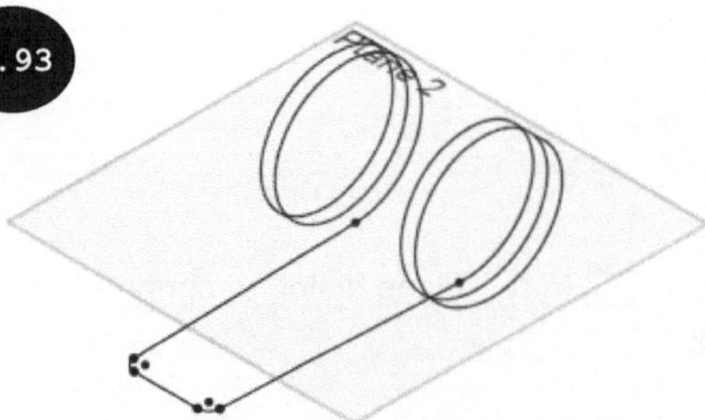

Section 6: Creating the Fourth Curve - Sketch

Now, you need to create the fourth curve on a construction plane that is parallel to the Right plane and passes through the endpoint of the first helix.

1. Invoke the **Plane** dialog by clicking the **Plane** tool in the **Feature** toolbar.
2. Select the **Plane point** option in the **Plane type** drop-down list of the dialog, see Figure 8.94.

8.94

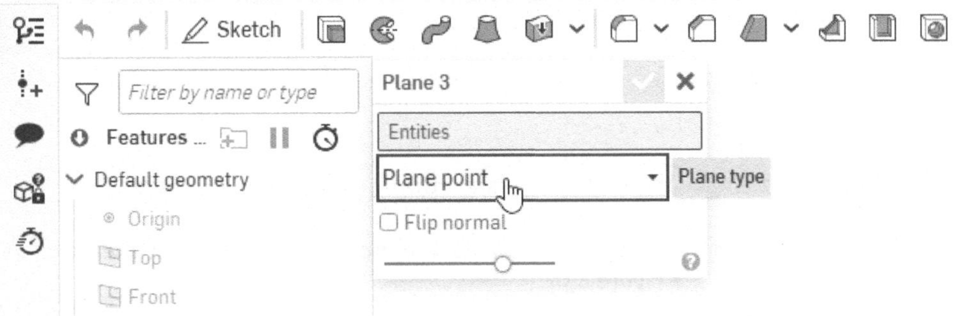

3. Select the **Right** plane in the Feature list as the first reference entity. The Right plane is highlighted in the graphics area, refer to Figure 8.95.
4. Select the endpoint of the first helix in the graphics area as the second reference entity, see Figure 8.95. A preview of the construction plane appears, parallel to the Right plane and passing through the endpoint of the first helix.

8.95

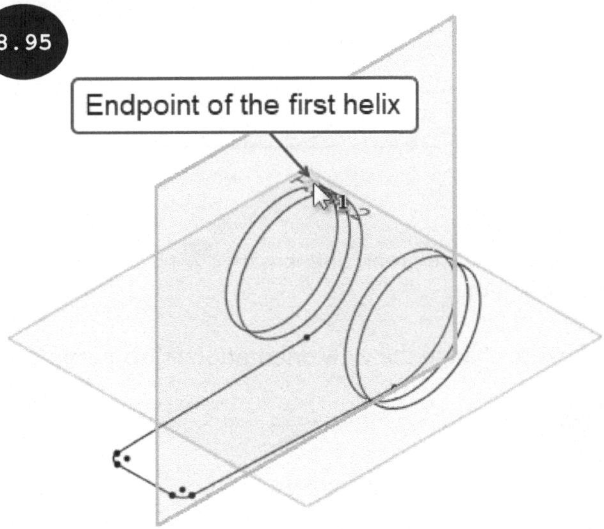

5. Click the green checkmark ✓ in the **Plane** dialog to confirm the creation of the construction plane and exit the dialog.

Now, you can create the sketch on the newly created construction plane.

6. Click on the **Sketch** tool in the **Feature** toolbar (see Figure 8.96), then select the newly created construction plane (**Plane 3**) in the graphics area.

8.96

7. Press the **N** key to make the sketching plane normal to the viewing direction.

8. Create an inclined line of length 60 mm starting from the endpoint of the helix and apply the required dimensions, see Figure 8.97.

8.97

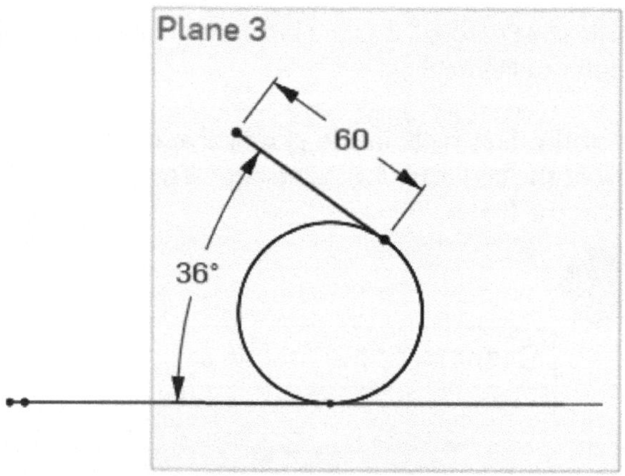

9. After creating the sketch, click the green checkmark ✓ to confirm its creation and switch back to the Part Studio environment.

10. Press the SHIFT + 7 keys to change the view orientation to isometric, see Figure 8.98.

8.98

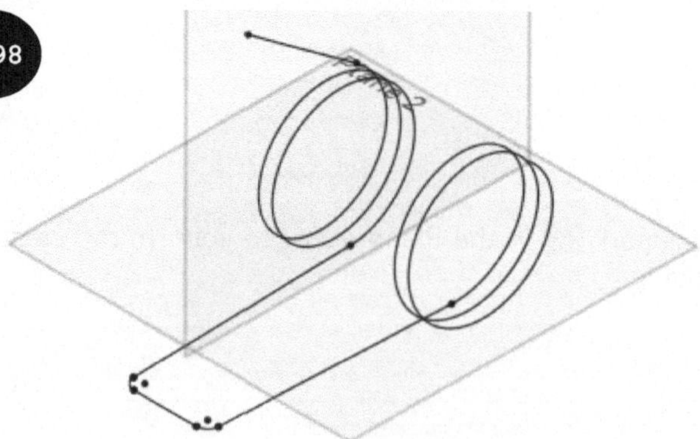

Section 7: Creating the Fifth Curve - Sketch

Now, you need to create the fifth curve on a construction plane that is parallel to the Right plane and passes through the endpoint of the second helix, in the same manner as the previously created sketch (fourth curve).

1. Create a construction plane parallel to the Right plane that passes through the endpoint of the second helix using the **Plane** tool, see Figure 8.99. In this figure, **Plane 4** is created parallel to the Right plane and passes through the endpoint of the second helix.

8.99

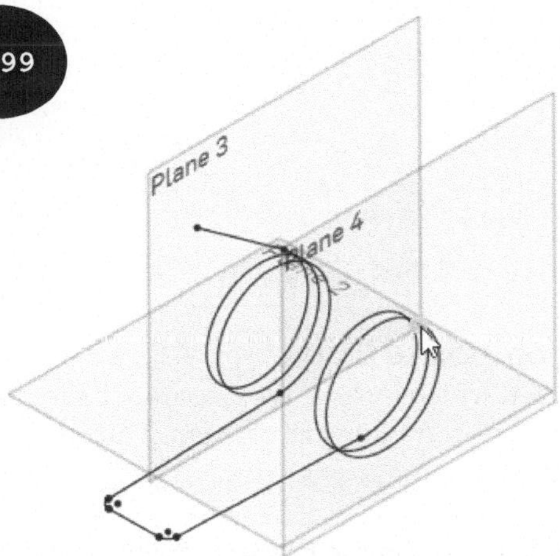

2. After creating the plane, click on the **Sketch** tool in the **Feature** toolbar (see Figure 8.100), then select the newly created construction plane (**Plane 4**) in the graphics area.

8.100

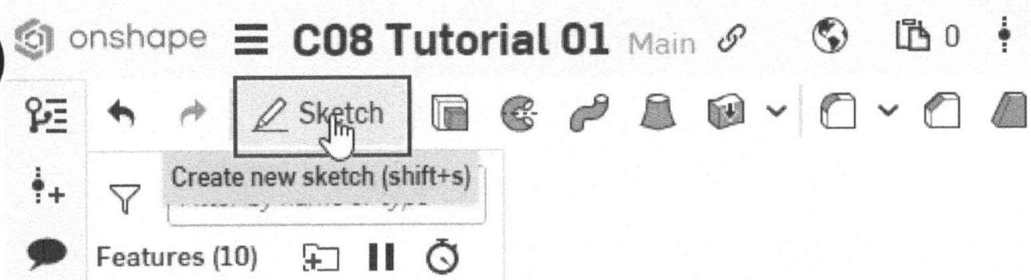

3. Press the N key to make the sketching plane normal to the viewing direction.

4. Create an inclined line of length 60 mm starting from the endpoint of the helix and apply the required dimensions, see Figure 8.101.

8.101

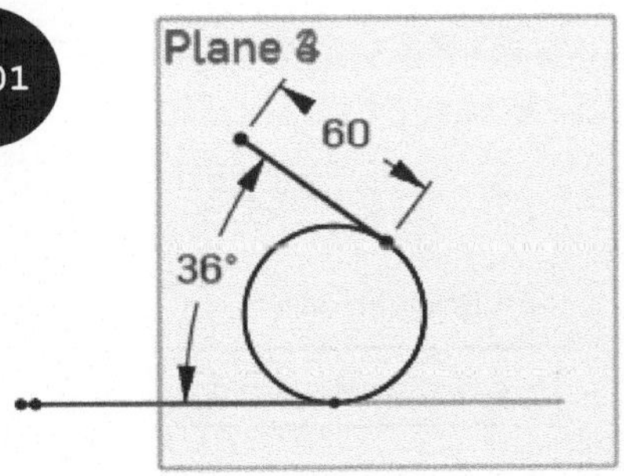

5. After creating the sketch, click the green checkmark ✓ to confirm the creation of the sketch. Next, press the SHIFT + 7 keys to change the view orientation to isometric.

6. Hide the display of all construction planes in the graphics area, see Figure 8.102.

8.102

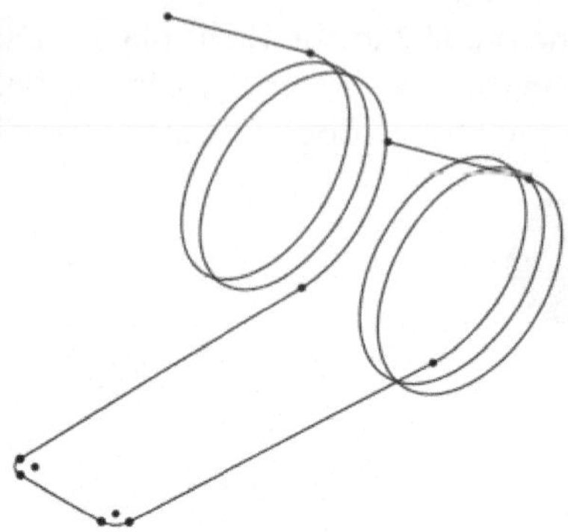

Section 8: Creating the Composite Curve

After creating a total of five curves, which include two separate helices and three individual sketches, you can create a composite curve by combining all of them. The composite curve is then used as the path for creating the sweep feature.

1. Click the arrow next to the **Plane** tool in the **Feature** toolbar and select the **Composite curve** tool from the drop-down menu that appears, see Figure 8.103. The **Composite curve** dialog appears.

8.103

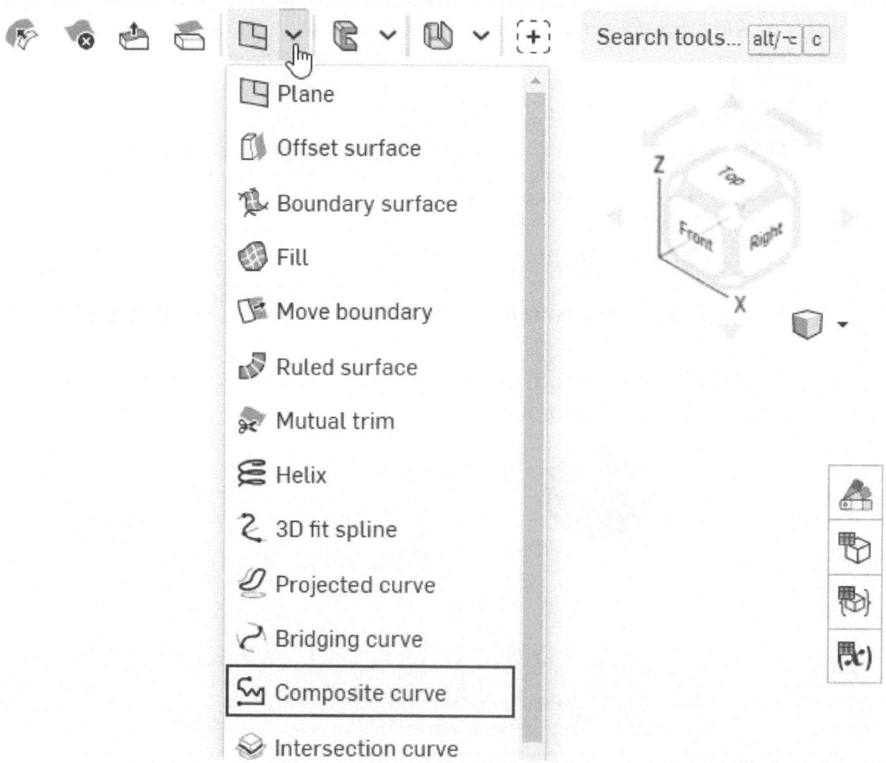

2. Select the two helices and three sketches one by one in the Feature list or in the graphics area, refer to Figure 8.104. Note that if selecting in the graphics area, you need to individually select all entities of the sketches.

8.104

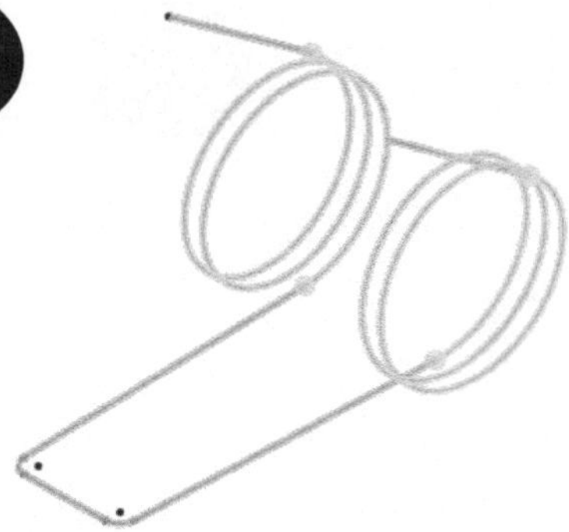

3. After selecting all the curves including sketches, click the green checkmark ✓ to confirm the creation of the composite curve and exit the dialog. Figure 8.105 shows the resultant composite curve.

8.105

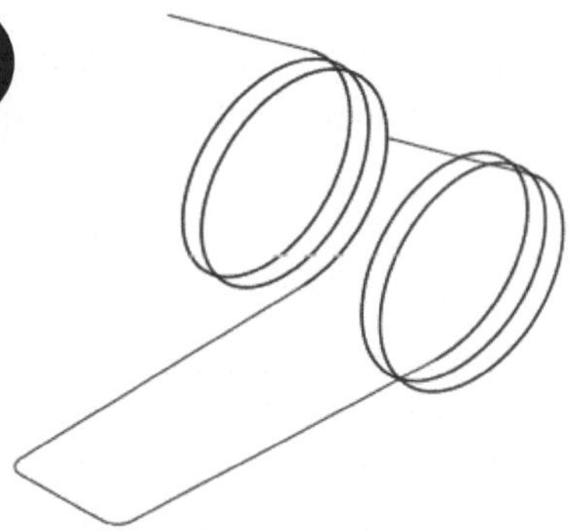

Section 9: Creating the Sweep Feature

After creating the composite curve as the path for the sweep feature, you need to create the profile on a construction plane that is normal to the curve at one of its ends. Once the profile is created, you can create the sweep feature, which involves sweeping the profile along the path.

1. Invoke the **Plane** dialog and then select the **Point normal** option in the **Plane type** drop-down list, see Figure 8.106.

8.106

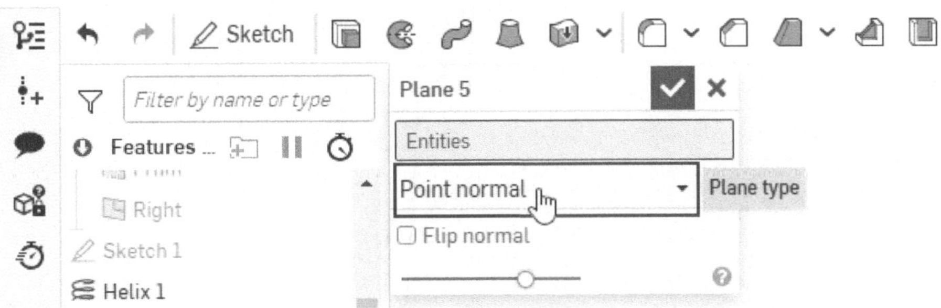

2. Select an inclined segment of the curve and its endpoint as the first and second references, see Figure 8.107. A preview of a construction plane appears, normal to the curve at the selected endpoint, see Figure 8.108.

8.107

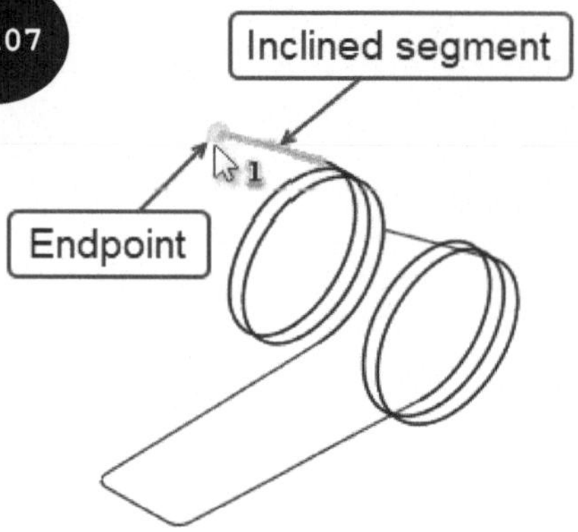

8.108

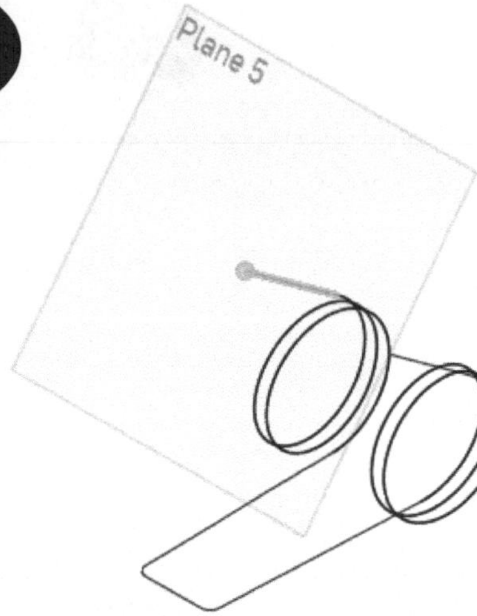

3. Click the green checkmark ✓ in the **Plane** dialog to confirm the creation of the construction plane and exit the dialog.

   Now, you can create the profile.

4. Click on the **Sketch** tool in the **Feature** toolbar, then select the newly created construction plane (**Plane 5**) as the sketching plane in the graphics area. Next, press the **N** key to make the sketching plane normal to the viewing direction.

5. Create a circle with a diameter of 6 mm as the profile of the sweep feature at the endpoint of the curve, see Figure 8.109. Note that the center of the circle is coincident with the endpoint of the curve.

8.109

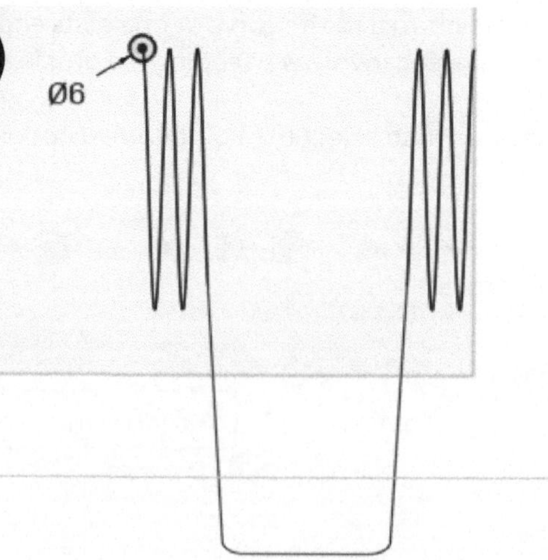

6. Click the green checkmark in the **Sketch** dialog to confirm the creation of the sketch and exit the dialog. Next, press the SHIFT + 7 keys to change the view orientation to isometric, see Figure 8.110.

8.110

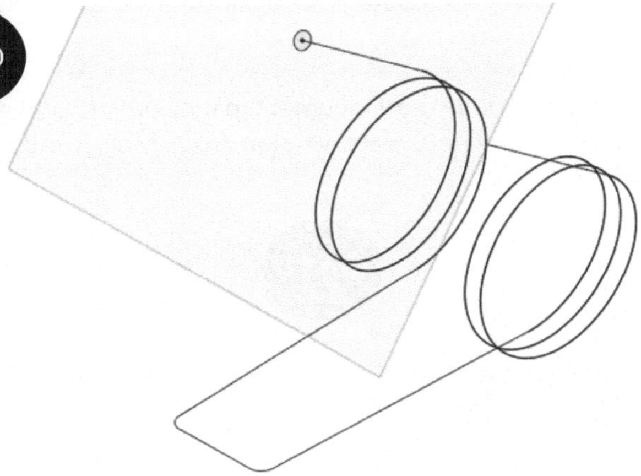

Now, you can create the sweep feature by sweeping the profile along the path.

7. Click on the **Sweep** tool in the **Feature** toolbar, see Figure 8.111. The **Sweep** dialog appears.

8.111

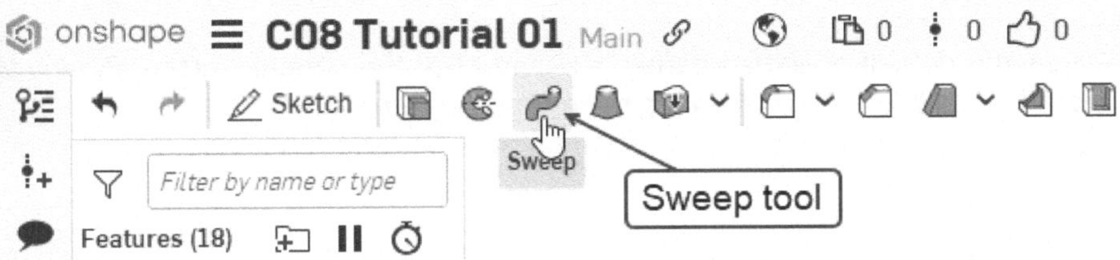

8. Select the circle as the profile of sweep feature in the graphics area.

9. Click on the **Sweep path** field in the dialog to activate it, and then select the composite curve in the graphics area. A preview of the sweep feature appears as the profile is swept along the path, see Figure 8.112.

8.112

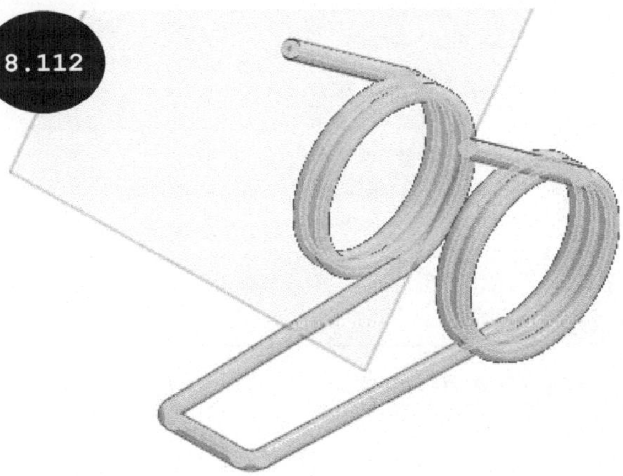

10. Click the green checkmark ✓ in the **Sweep** dialog. The sweep feature is created. Figure 8.113 shows the final model after hiding the construction planes.

    Now, you can create a version in the document to capture the current state of the design, and then close the document.

11. Click on the **Create version** tool in the **Document panel**, which is aligned vertically with the Onshape logo, see Figure 8.114. The **Create version from Main** window appears with default version name V1 in its **Name** field.

8.113

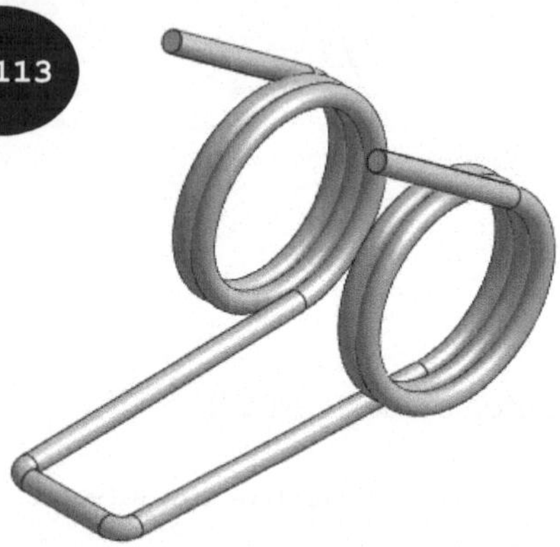

8.114

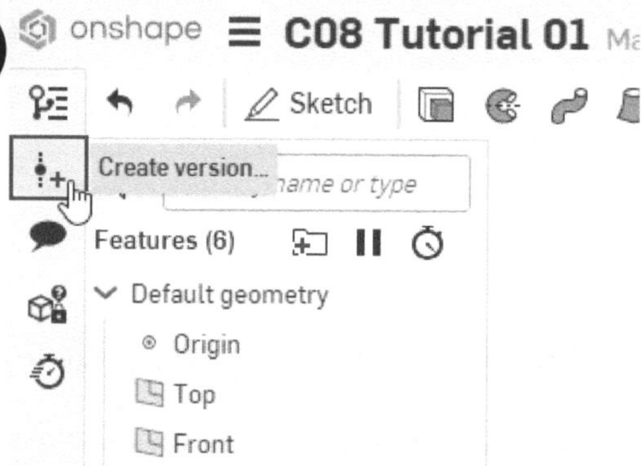

12. Accept the default specified name "V1" and click the **Create** button. A new version, "V1," is created in the document, capturing the model's current state.

    Now, you can close the document.

13. Invoke the **Document** menu by clicking on the ≡ icon next to the Onshape logo and click on the **Close document** option, see Figure 8.115. This action closes the current document.

8.115

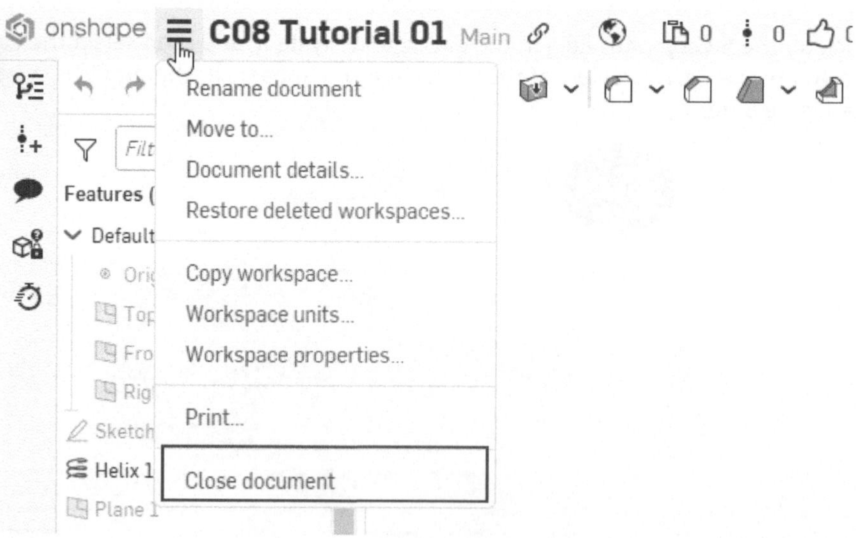

Hands-on Test Drive 1

Create a model, as shown in Figure 8.116. The different views and dimensions are given in same figure. All dimensions are in inches.

8.116

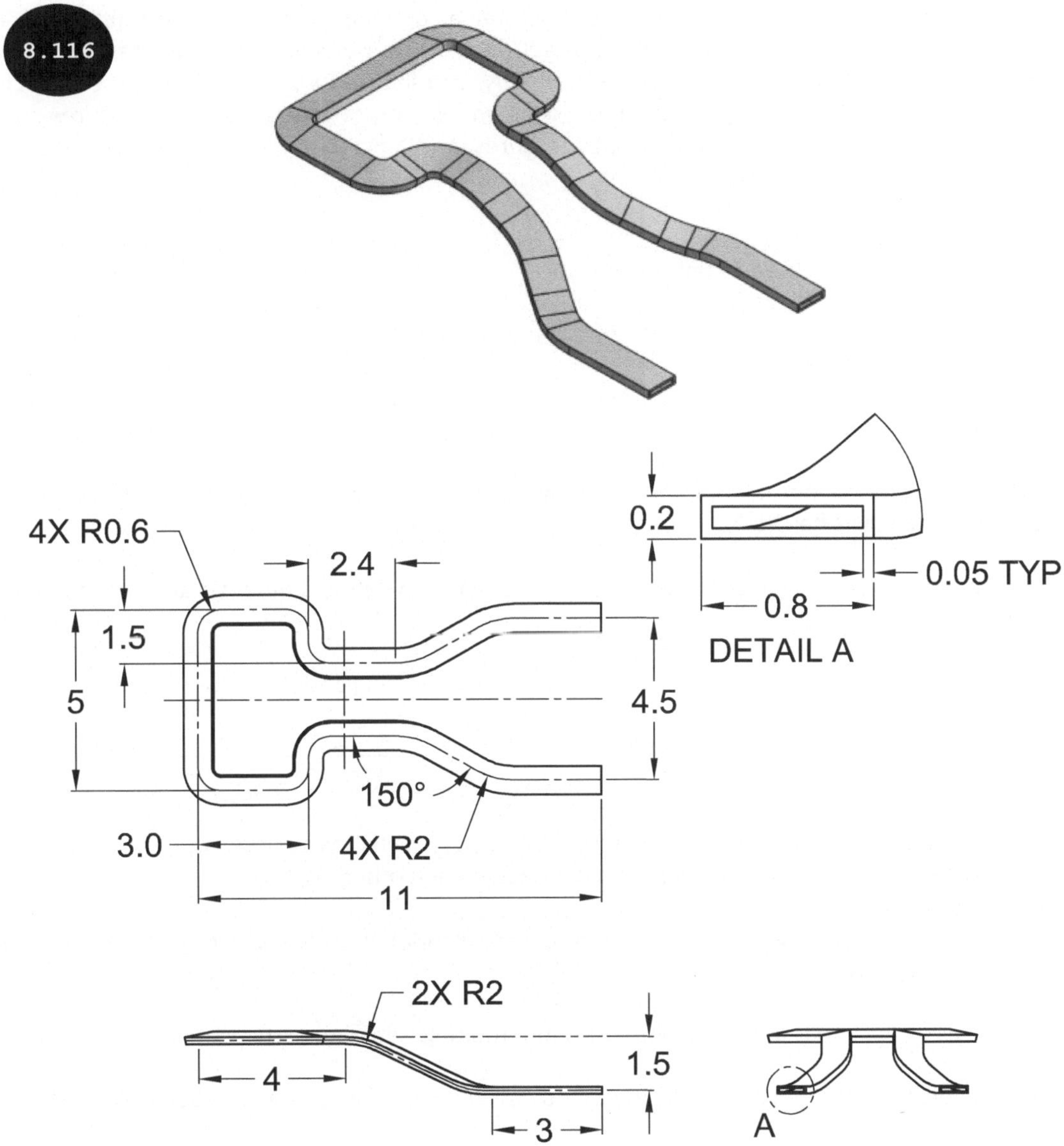

Summary

In this chapter, you learned how to create various types of curves and split models in Onshape. You explored how to create a helix using different methods, including selecting conical or cylindrical faces, axes, or circular edges. The chapter also covered creating projected curves by projecting two sketches or a sketch onto a face, as well as creating 3D fit splines through vertices and edges. You examined bridging and intersection curves, along with composite curves for combining multiple curves or sketch entities. Finally, you learned how to split parts and faces for more detailed model modifications. These skills enable you to create complex features such as internal or external threads, coils, 3D path features, and advanced geometry in your designs.

Questions

Complete and verify the following sentences:

- The _________ tool is used to create different types of helix.
- In Onshape, you can create a helix either by selecting a _________ face, an _________, or a circular edge or circle.
- The _________ option allows you to create a helix by specifying the required number of revolutions along its height.
- While creating a helix by selecting an _________, you can define different start and end radius values.
- The _________ tool allows you to create a curve by projecting one sketch onto another.
- You can create a 3D fit spline through a series of _________ or _________ using the **3D fit spline** tool.
- While creating a 3D fit spline, selecting the _________ check box creates a closed 3D fit spline, where the start and end vertices or points connect to each other.
- A _________ curve is formed by connecting two or more individual curves or sketch entities into a unified curve.
- The _________ tool is used to divide a part into multiple separate parts.
- In Onshape, the **Split** tool does not allow you to split multiple faces simultaneously. (True/False)
- You can create an intersection curve at the intersection of two or more geometries. (True/False)

CHAPTER

9

Working with Assemblies

In this chapter, the following topics will be discussed:

- Inserting the First Component of an Assembly
- Fixing the First Component
- Inserting Additional Components
- Applying Mates
- Grouping Components Together
- Activating Snap Mode
- Activating Show Mate Mode
- Patterning Assembly Components
- Establishing a Relation Between Two Mates

In the previous chapters, you explored various tools and techniques for designing realistic mechanical 3D parts. This chapter focuses on creating mechanical assemblies, which consist of two or more connected parts. Figure 9.1 illustrates an assembly with multiple interconnected parts.

9.1

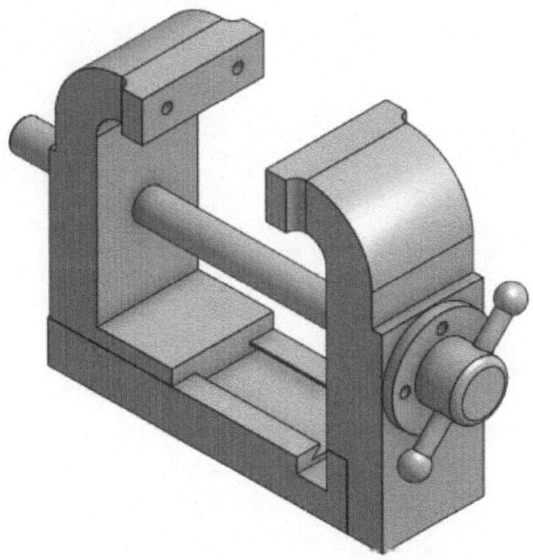

In Onshape, assemblies are created within the Assembly environment, which can be accessed directly in a design document. When a new design document is opened, the **Part Studio 1** and **Assembly 1** tabs appear at the bottom, see Figure 9.2. By default, the **Part Studio 1** tab is active, allowing you to design a 3D solid part and surface model using the tools in the **Feature** toolbar, covered in earlier chapters.

9.2

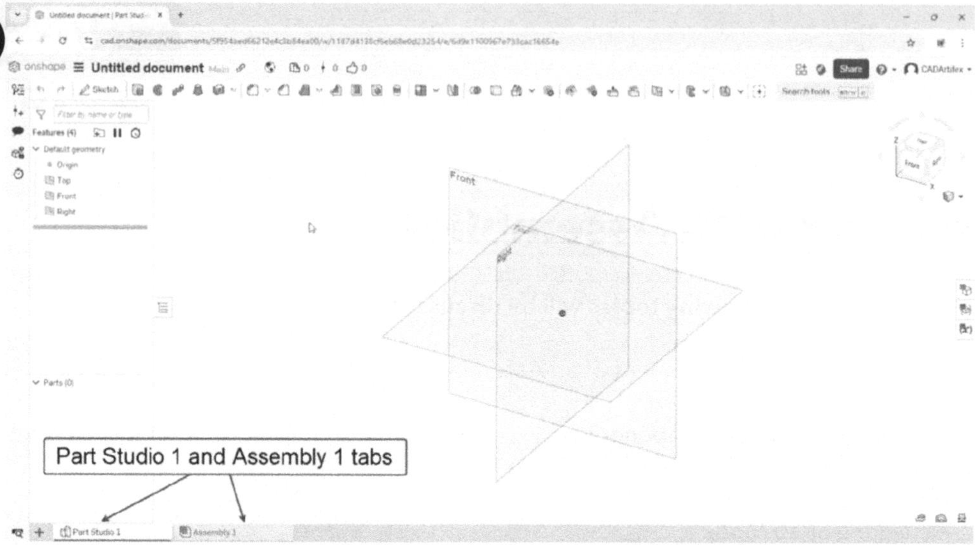

To create an assembly, click the **Assembly 1** tab at the bottom of the design document to open the Assembly environment and display the **Assembly** toolbar, see Figure 9.3.

9.3

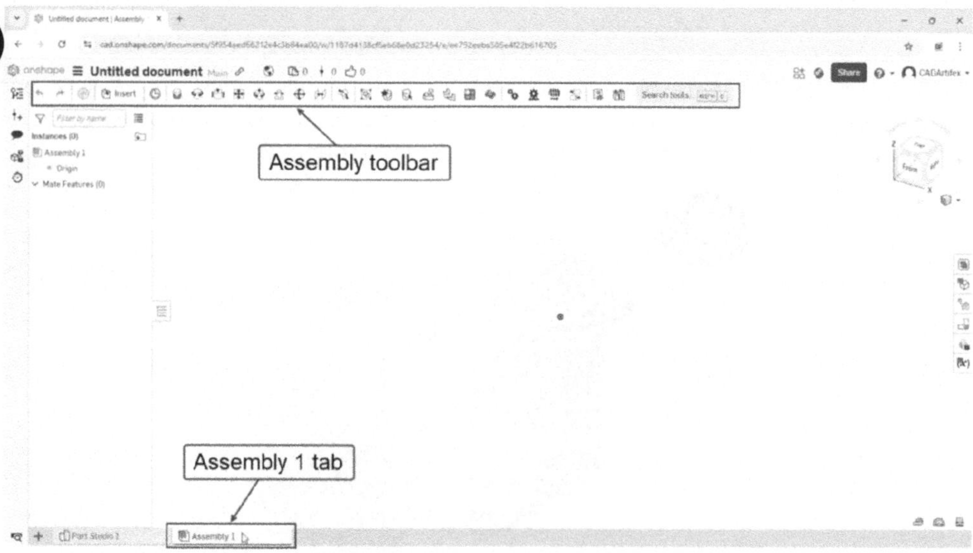

Note: In addition to the default **Part Studio 1** and **Assembly 1** tabs, you can add multiple new design tabs, such as **Part Studio**, **Assembly**, and **Drawing**, to organize all CAD data, including parts, assemblies, and drawings of a project, within a single design document.

To add a new design tab, click the **Insert new tab** + (*plus sign*) at the lower-left corner of the screen, in front of the **Part Studio 1** tab, see Figure 9.4. A menu will appear, displaying a list of available tab options. Select the desired tab, such as **Create Part Studio**, **Create Assembly**, or **Create Drawing**, to add it to the current design document. After adding a tab that represents a file (such as a part, assembly, or drawing), you can rename it as desired.

9.4

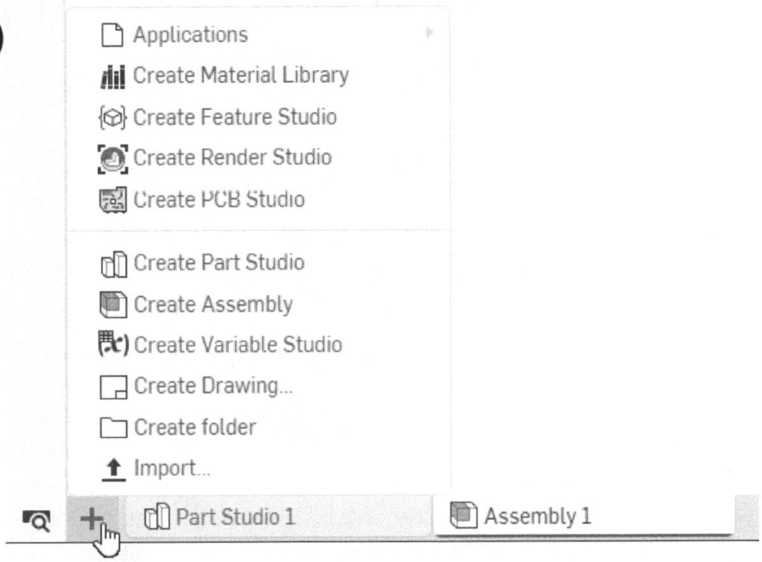

In the Assembly environment of a design document, you insert individual components of an assembly created either within the same design document or in separate design documents. Once the components are inserted, you can assemble them by applying the necessary mates. The methods for inserting components into the Assembly environment and applying various types of mates are discussed next.

Inserting the First Component of an Assembly

The method for inserting the component into the Assembly environment is discussed below:

1. After starting a design document, click the **Assembly 1** tab at the bottom to open the Assembly environment and access the **Assembly** toolbar, see Figure 9.5.

9.5

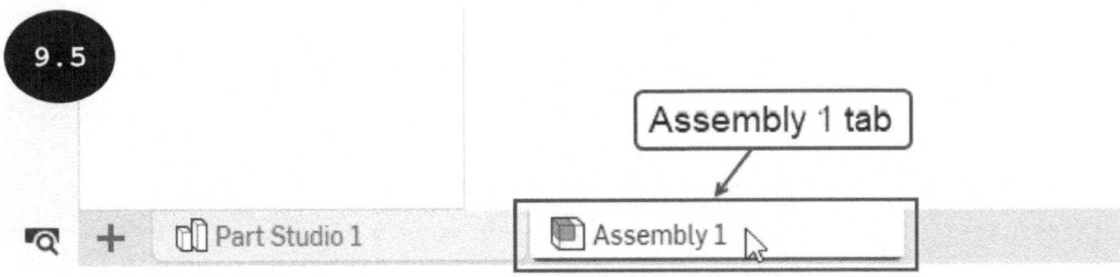

2. Click on the **Insert** tool in the **Assembly** toolbar (see Figure 9.6) or press the **I** key. The **Insert parts and assemblies** dialog appears with three tabs: **Current document**, **Other documents**, and **Standard content**, see Figure 9.7.

9.6

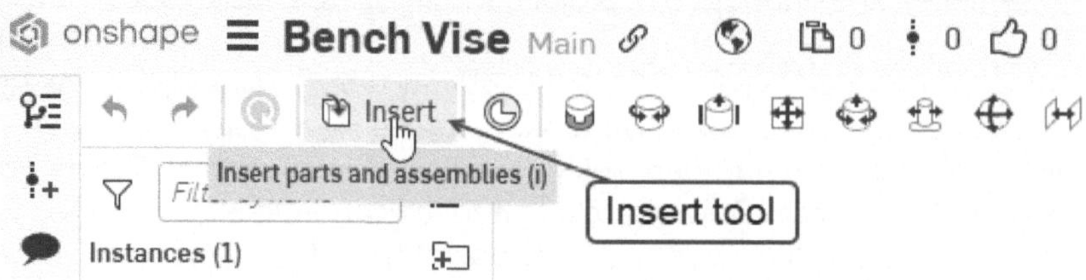

9.7

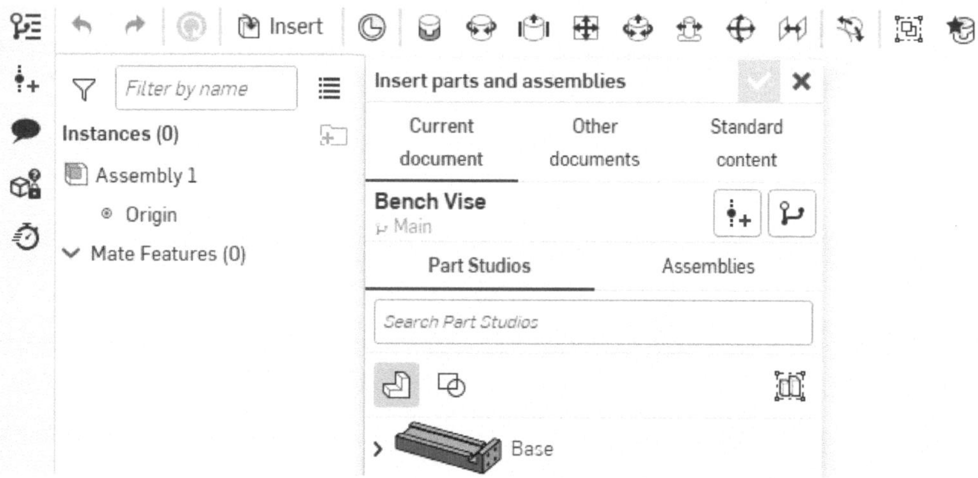

Current document: The **Current document** tab allows you to access all the parts and assemblies created within the current design document. By default, the **Part Studios** option is activated in this tab, so if the current document contains parts, they will be displayed in the dialog. To view the assemblies of the current document, click on the **Assemblies** option in this tab.

Other documents: The **Other documents** tab allows you to access parts and assemblies created in other design documents. To use this feature, click on the **Other documents** tab (see Figure 9.8) and then select the desired filter option such as **Owned by me**, **Recently opened**, **Created by me**, **Shared with me**, or **Public** to display a list of relevant design documents, see Figure 9.9.

9.8

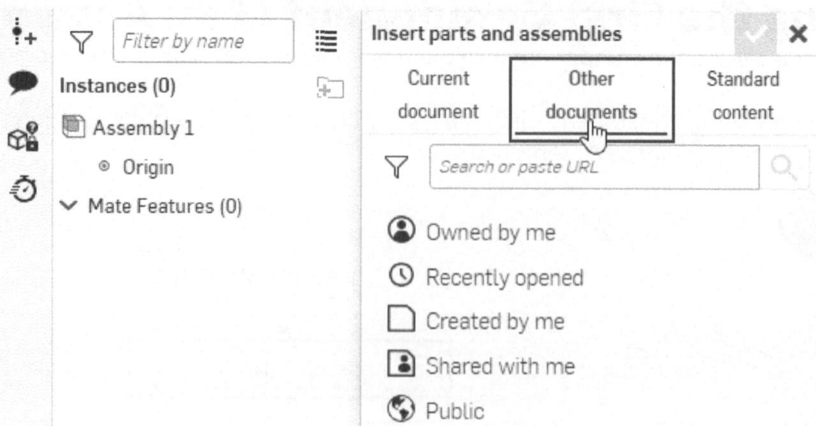

Figure 9.9 shows a list of documents displayed after activating **Created by me** in the **Other documents** tab of the dialog. This option displays all the documents you have created in Onshape.

9.9

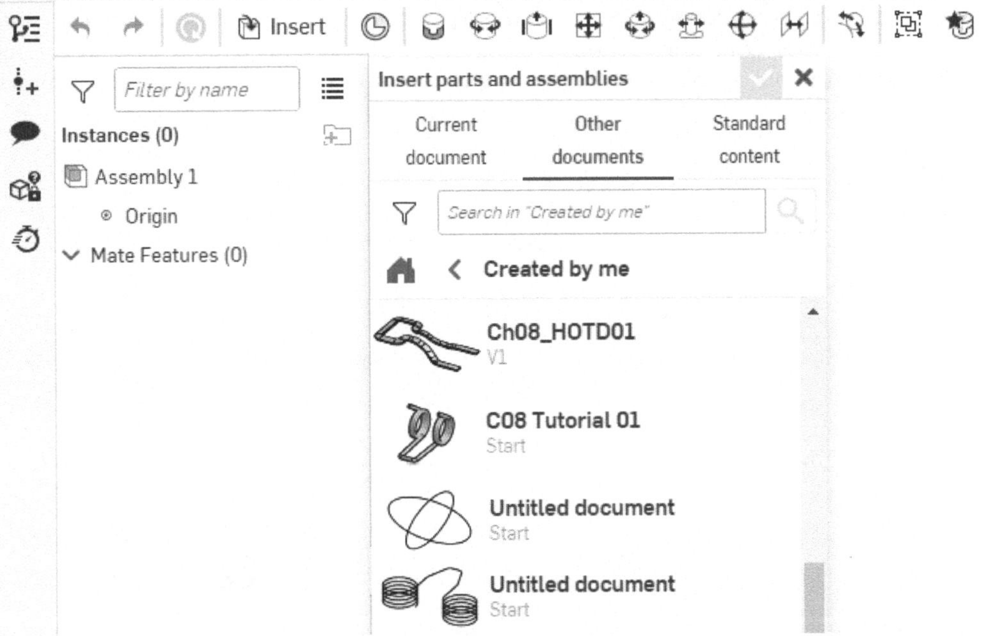

In the list of different documents, select the desired document to access all the parts and assemblies created within it, under the **Part Studios** and **Assemblies** options, respectively. You can also search for a component or document in the list using the **Search** field.

Note that if the part or assembly in the selected document is not versioned, a message will appear informing you that you need to create a version of the part or assembly before it can be inserted, refer to Figure 9.10. Click on **Create a version in** (*name of the document*) to open the **Create version** window. In this window, specify a name for the version and click the **Create** button.

9.10

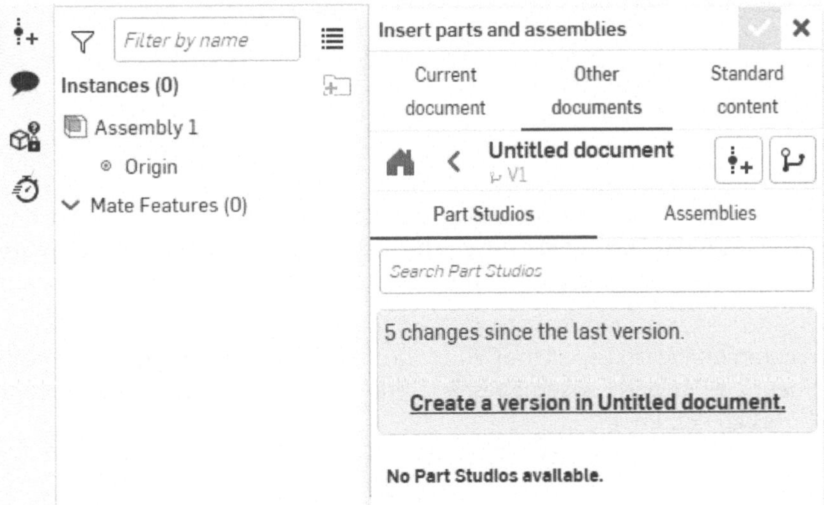

Standard content: The Standard content tab in the **Insert parts and assemblies** dialog allows you to access various Onshape-supplied standard parts, see Figure 9.11. After activating this tab, select the desired standard (such as ANSI Inch, DIN, or ISO), the category (such as Bolts & Screws, Keys, or Washers), and other related parameters of the standard part from the respective drop-down lists. Once the desired parameters are defined, you can click the **Insert** button at the bottom of the dialog to insert the standard part into the Assembly environment based on those parameters.

9.11

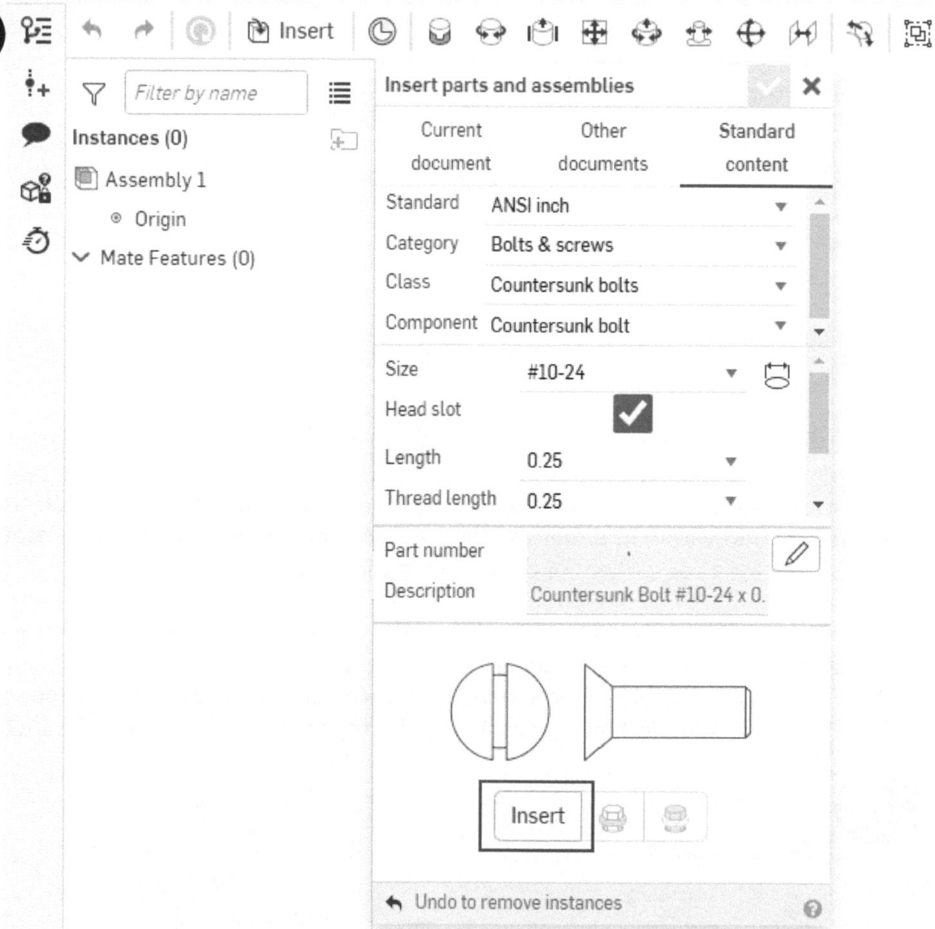

3. In the **Insert parts and assemblies** dialog, activate the desired tab (**Current document**, **Other documents**, or **Standard content**) to insert the first component either from the current document, other created document, or from the Onshape standard content library as discussed above.

Tip: It is recommended to keep all the CAD data of a project or assembly within the same document by creating all its parts, assemblies, and drawings in their respective environments within a single design document.

4. Ensure that the **Part Studios** option is activated to display a list of all parts created within the selected document as individual Part Studio files, see Figure 9.12. This figure illustrates four different components created within the current document as individual Part Studio files.

9.12

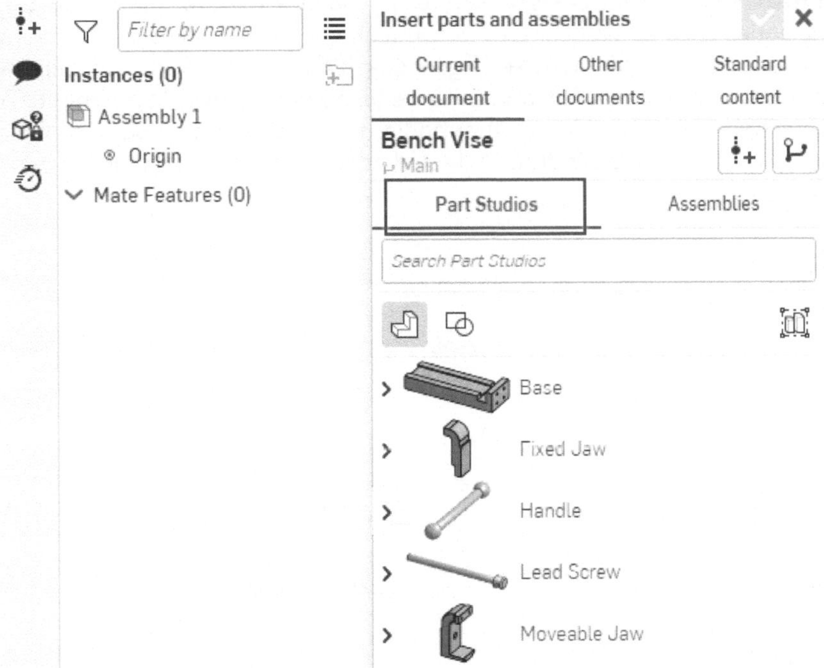

As discussed earlier, when inserting a part from another document by activating the **Other documents** tab, you need to activate the desired filter option, such as **Owned by me**, **Recently opened**, **Created by me**, **Shared with me**, or **Public**, to display a list of relevant design documents. Then, you can select the desired document from the list to display all its parts, see Figure 9.13. This figure shows two parts created within the selected design document in their respective Part Studio files (**Part Studio 1** and **Part Studio 2**).

9.13

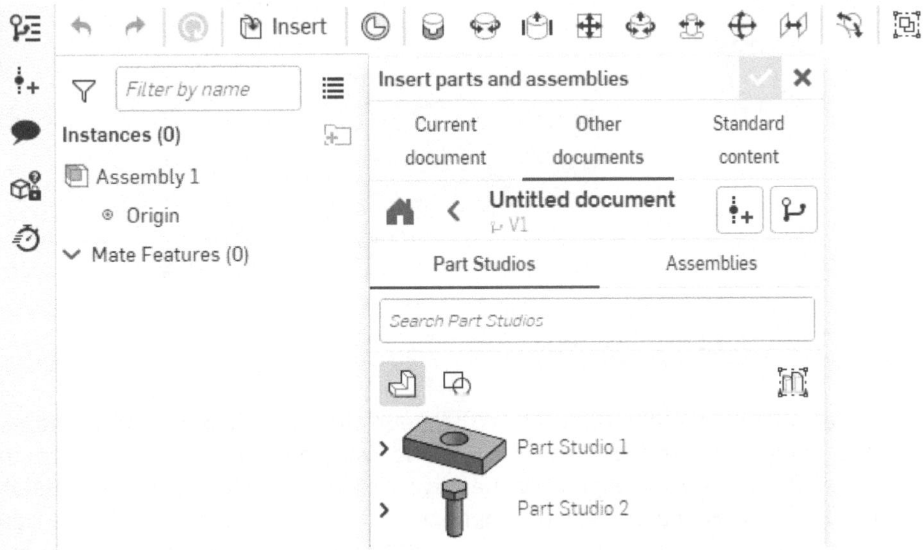

Note that if the part or assembly in the selected document is not versioned, you must first create a version by clicking the **Create a Version in** (*name of the document*) option, as discussed earlier.

Insert entire Part Studio as rigid: Activating the **Insert entire Part Studio as rigid** button will insert the entire selected Part Studio file containing multiple bodies as a single rigid component within the Assembly environment, see Figure 9.14. If the selected Part Studio file includes multiple individual bodies or parts, all of them will be inserted as a rigid component. This means that moving one body will cause all the other bodies to move together due to their rigid connection. Figure 9.14 shows Part Studio 1 of the selected document, which contains two individual bodies: Part 1 and Part 2.

9.14

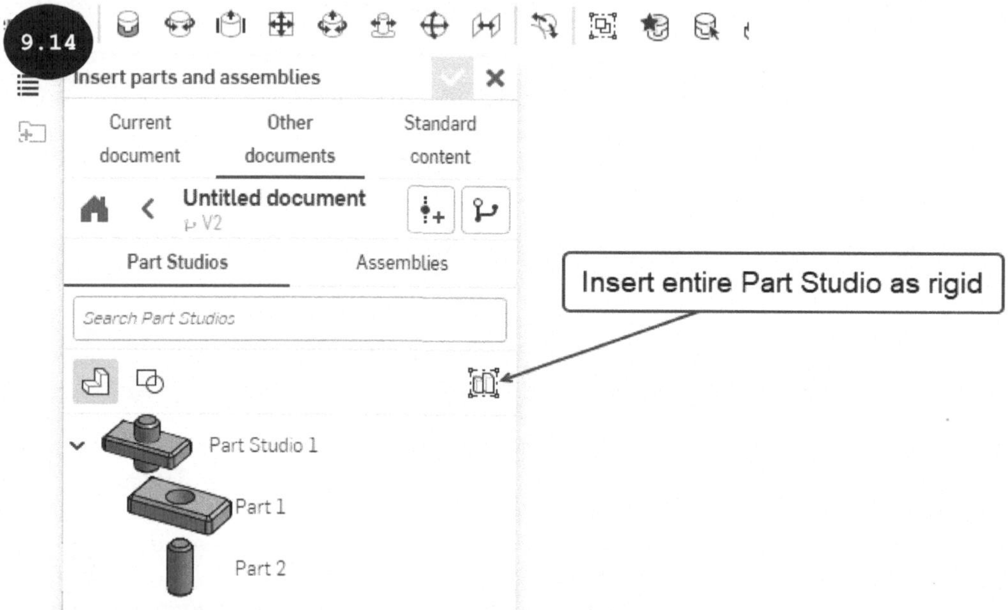

5. Select the part to be inserted in the Assembly environment. The selected part appears attached to the cursor, see Figure 9.15.

9.15

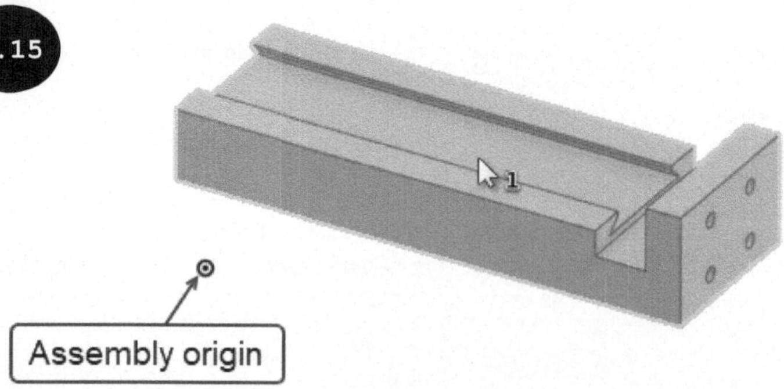

6. After selecting the part to insert, click on the green checkmark ✓ to confirm the insertion of the selected component and exit the dialog. The selected part is inserted into the Assembly environment with its origin aligned to the origin of the Assembly. Also, the name of the inserted part is listed in the Assembly list which appears at the top left of the screen, see Figure 9.16.

9.16
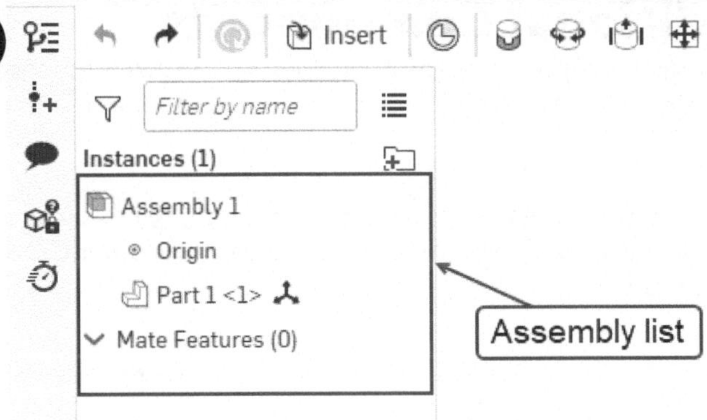

After inserting the first component of the assembly, you can continue inserting the second and subsequent components in the same manner as the first, using the **Insert** tool. However, before inserting the second component, it is recommended to first fix all the degrees of freedom of the first component in its current position, making it a fixed component. A fixed component cannot move or rotate within the graphics area.

Fixing the First Component

In Onshape, when you insert a component into the design document, it has all its degrees of freedom, meaning the component is free to move or rotate in any direction within the graphics area. As mentioned earlier, before you insert the second component into the assembly, you need to fix the first component to restrict its translational or rotational movement, so that all other components can mate with respect to it.

To fix a component, right-click on the component either in the graphics area or in the Assembly list to display a shortcut menu, see Figure 9.17. In this menu, select the **Fix** option. The selected component becomes fixed, and a fix symbol appears next to its name in the Assembly list, see Figure 9.18. This symbol indicates that all degrees of freedom are locked, preventing the component from moving or rotating in any direction.

9.17
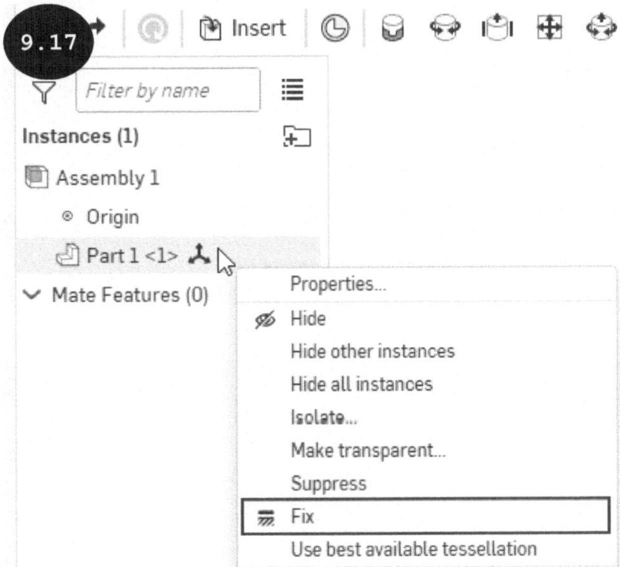

9.18
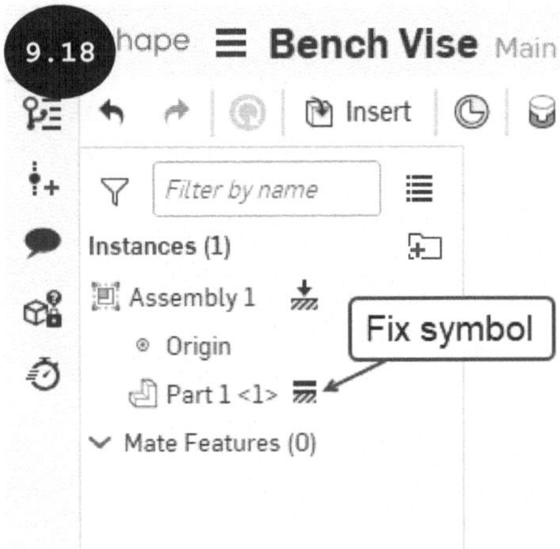

Inserting Additional Components

After inserting and fixing the first component of the assembly, you can insert the second and subsequent components one by one, using the same method as for the first component. This method is discussed below:

1. Click on the **Insert** tool in the **Assembly** toolbar (see Figure 9.19) or press the **I** key. The **Insert parts and assemblies** dialog appears with three tabs: **Current document**, **Other documents**, and **Standard content**, see Figure 9.20.

9.19

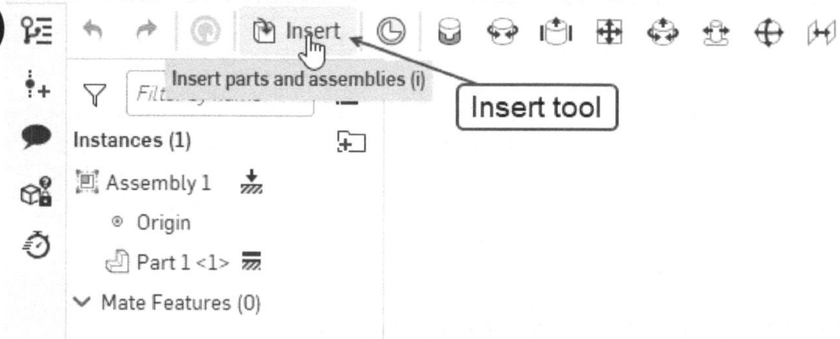

9.20

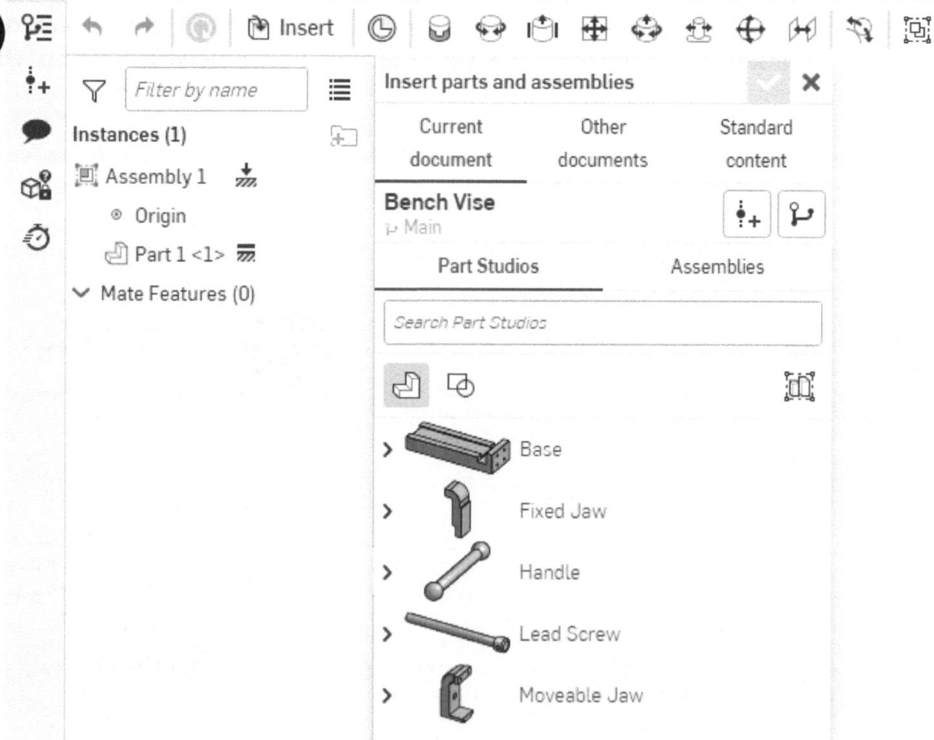

2. Activate the desired tab (**Current document**, **Other documents**, or **Standard content**) in the **Insert parts and assemblies** dialog to insert the component either from the current document, other created document, or from the Onshape standard content library as discussed earlier.

3. Select the part to be inserted in the Assembly environment. The selected part appears attached to the cursor, see Figure 9.21.

9.21

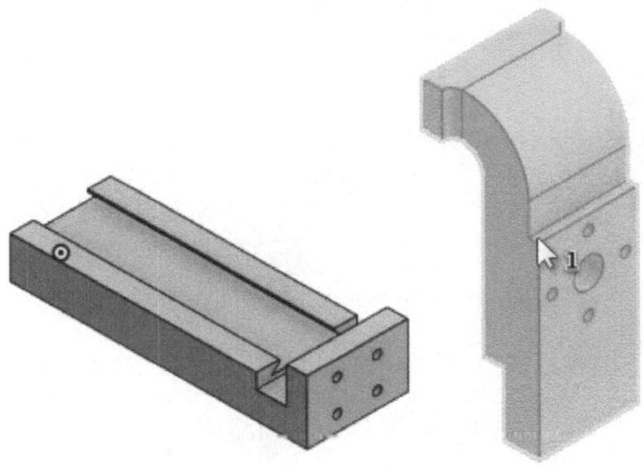

Now, you need to define the placement for the attached component in the graphics area.

4. Click anywhere in the graphics area to place the component at the desired position.

Tip: It Is recommended to define the position of the component such that it does not intersect with the existing components of the assembly.

5. After defining the position of the selected component in the graphics area, click on the green checkmark ✓ to confirm its placement and exit the dialog. The selected part is inserted into the Assembly environment at the specified position, see Figure 9.22. Additionally, the name of the inserted part appears in the Assembly list with a triad symbol, see Figure 9.23. This symbol indicates that some or all degrees of freedom of the part are not locked, allowing the part to move or rotate within its free degrees of freedom. By default, all degrees of freedom of the inserted component are free, allowing the component to move or rotate in any direction.

9.22

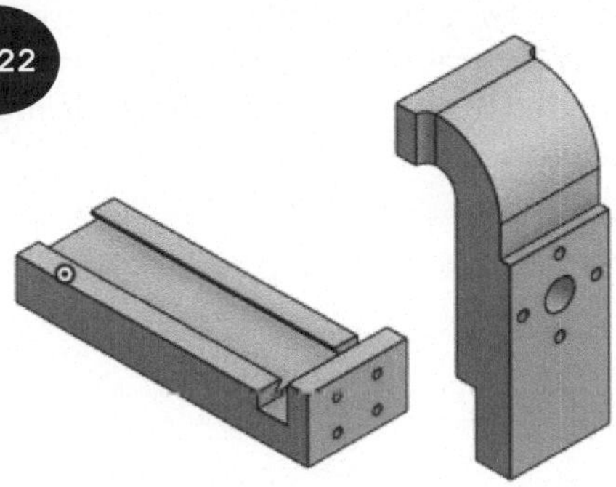

9.23

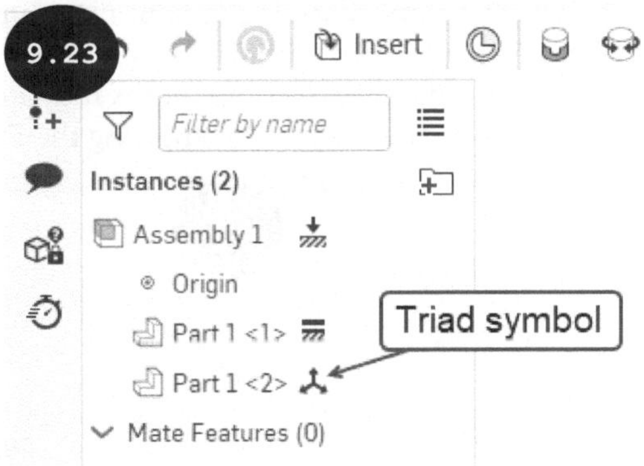

Note: To check the degrees of freedom of a component, you can move or rotate it along or about its free degrees of freedom using the Triad Manipulator. To do this, select the component in the graphics area or the Assembly list. The Triad Manipulator appears on the selected part, see Figure 9.24. You can use its translational and rotational handles to move or rotate the component along or about its free degrees of freedom. Note that the component cannot move or rotate about its fixed degrees of freedom.

9.24

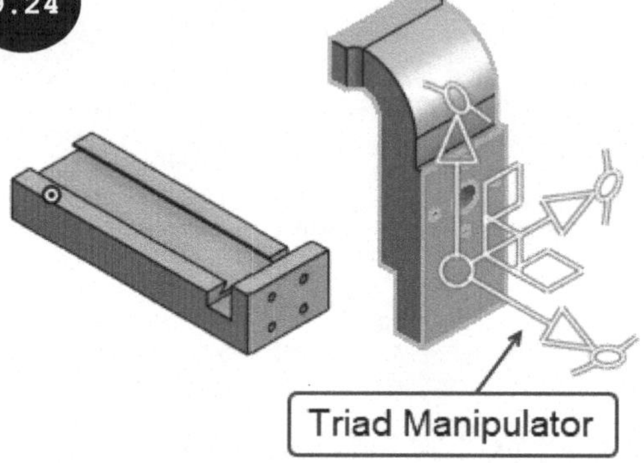

Similarly, you can insert other components of the assembly one by one. However, it is recommended to first assemble the second component with the first by applying the necessary mates before inserting the third or any subsequent components into the Assembly environment. The different types of mates and the methods for applying them are discussed next.

Applying Mates

In Onshape, you can apply various types of mates, such as Fastened, Revolute, Slider, Planar, Cylindrical, Pin Slot, Ball, Parallel, and Tangent, to define relationships between assembly components using the respective tools available in the **Assembly** toolbar. The methods for applying these mates are discussed next.

Applying the Fastened Mate

The Fastened mate is used to lock or fix components together by removing all degrees of freedom, preventing any relative motion between the components, as illustrated in Figure 9.25. This mate is typically applied between components that are welded or bolted together, with no allowable motion between them. The method for applying the Fastened mate is discussed below:

9.25

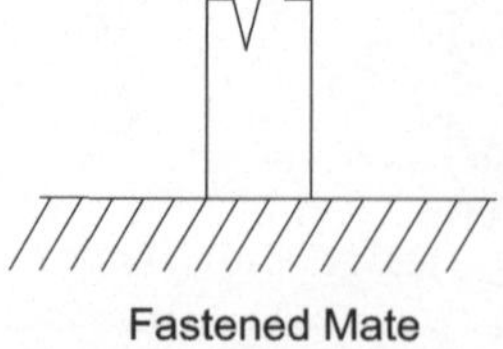

Fastened Mate
(No translational and no rotational movements)

1. Click on the **Fastened mate** tool in the **Assembly** toolbar (see Figure 9.26) or press the M key. The **Fastened** dialog appears, see Figure 9.27. By default, the **Fastened** option is selected in the **Mate type** drop-down list of the dialog, allowing you to apply the Fastened mate between two components.

9.26

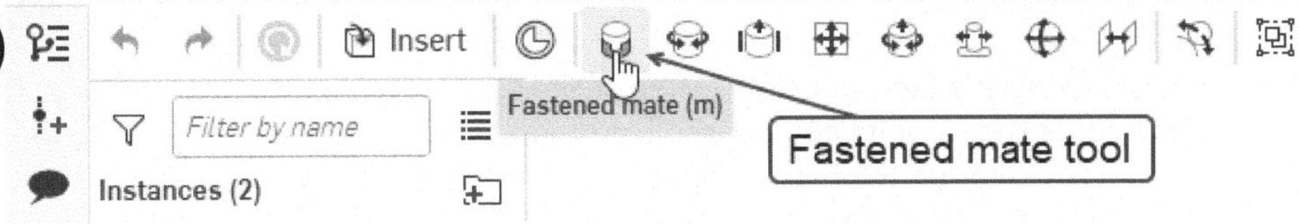

9.27

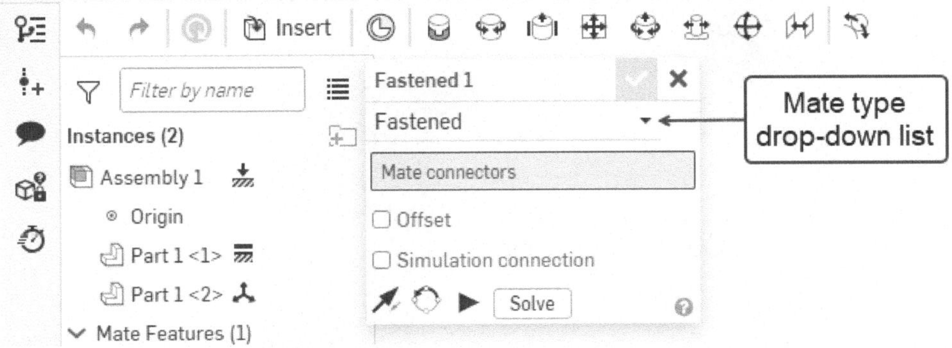

Now, you need to define the mate connector on two different components to apply the selected mate type between them.

2. Move the cursor over a face, edge, or vertex of the first component to define the mate connector on it. The respective geometry highlights and its snap points appear, see Figure 9.28. Additionally, the mate connector appears attached to the cursor on the highlighted geometry, see Figure 9.28. In this figure, the cursor is positioned over the face of a component.

9.28

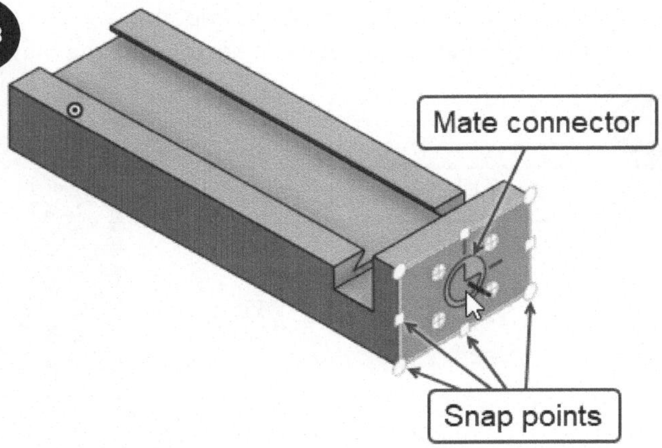

Tip: A square snap point indicates the midpoint of an edge, a circular snap point represents a corner of an edge, a four-quadrant snap point marks the center of a circular edge, and a dowel pin snap point identifies the center of the highlighted geometry.

3. Click on the desired snap point on the highlighted geometry of the component to specify the position of the mate connector.

   After defining the mate connector on the first component, proceed to define the mate connector on the second component.

4. Move the cursor over a face, edge, or vertex of the second component. The respective geometry highlights and its snap points appear, see Figure 9.29. Additionally, the mate connector appears attached to the cursor on the highlighted geometry. In this figure, the cursor is positioned over a face of the second component.

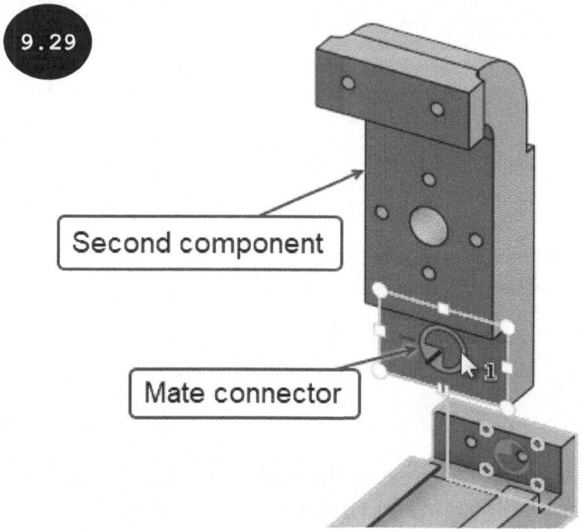

5. Click the desired snap point on the highlighted geometry of the second component to specify the position of the mate connector. The first component moves toward the second component, or vice versa, depending on the available degrees of freedom, and the mate connectors of both components coincide in the graphics area, see Figure 9.30. Also, the **Mate** Pop-up dialog appears.

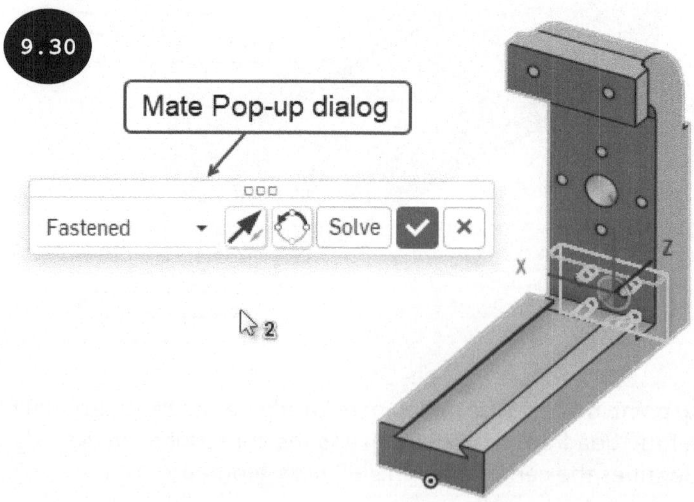

Offset: Selecting the **Offset** check box in the **Fastened** dialog enables the X, Y, and Z fields, allowing you to specify the offset distance between the components along the X, Y, and Z axes, respectively. You can also rotate the components about an axis relative to the defined mate connectors. To do this, select the required axis from the **Rotation axis** drop-down list and enter the desired rotation angle in the **Rotation angle** field, which becomes enabled in the dialog. Figure 9.31 shows the **Fastened** dialog when the **Offset** check box is selected.

9.31

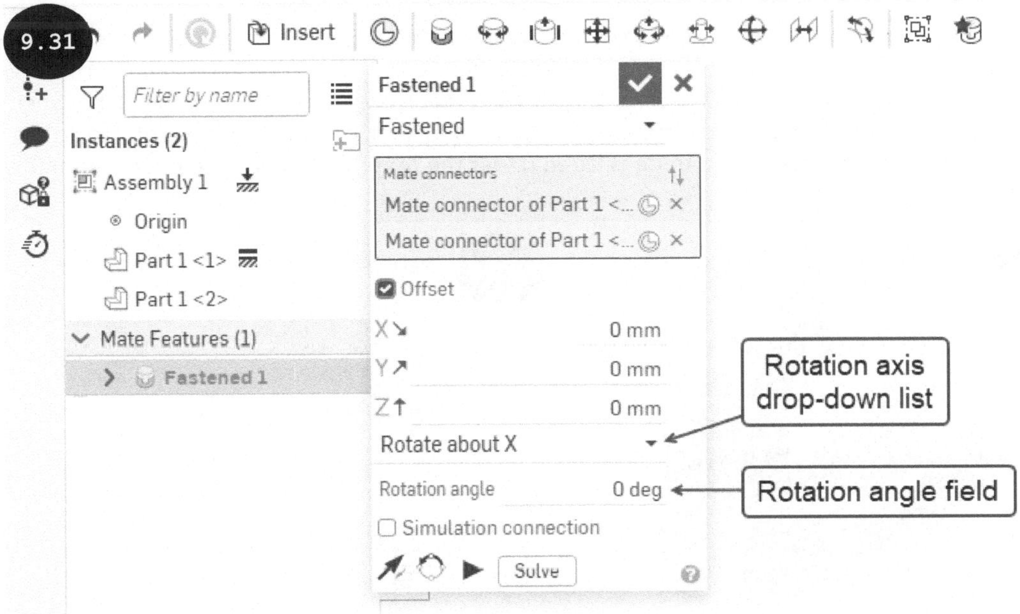

Flip primary axis: The **Flip primary axis** button is used to change the alignment between components by reversing the orientation of their primary axis (Z-axis), see Figure 9.32.

9.32

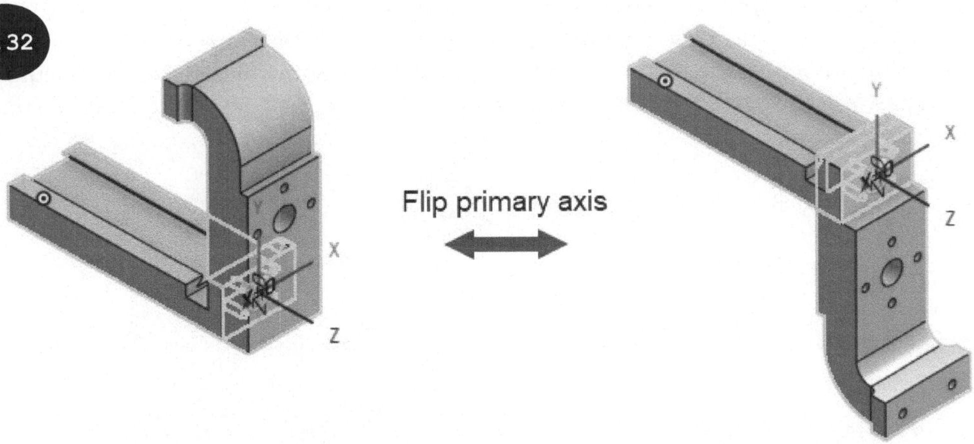

Reorient secondary axis: The **Reorient secondary axis** button rotates the movable component on the XY plane by an incremental angle of 90 degrees with each click.

Animate mate degree of freedom ►: The **Animate mate degree of freedom** button ► animates the allowable motion of the applied mate between components. It helps identify the free degrees of freedom of the movable component based on the applied mate.

Solve: The **Solve** button automatically solves all the assembly mates, including the one currently being applied.

6. After defining the mate connectors on the two components, ensure that the correct mate type, in this case, **Fastened**, is selected in the **Mate type** drop-down list. Then, click on the green checkmark ☑ to confirm and exit the dialog. The Fastened mate is applied between the components, removing all degrees of freedom and locking the components together, see Figure 9.33. Also, the applied mate is listed under the **Mate Features** node in the Assembly list, see Figure 9.34.

9.33

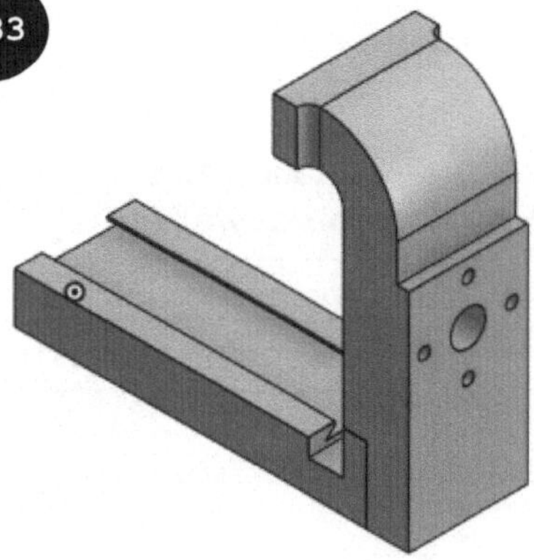

9.34

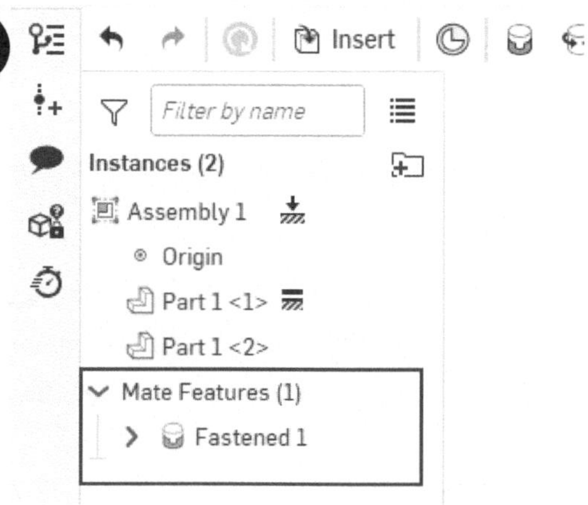

Note: By default, the symbols of applied mates are not visible in the graphics area. To toggle the visibility of an applied mate symbol, hover your cursor over the mate's name under the **Mate Features** node in the Assembly list. Then, click the **Show/Hide** icon, see Figure 9.35. Figure 9.36 illustrates the components after enabling the visibility of the Fastened mate.

9.35

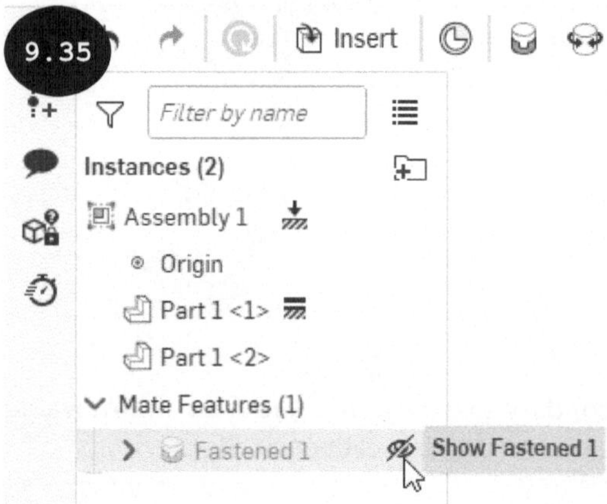

9.36

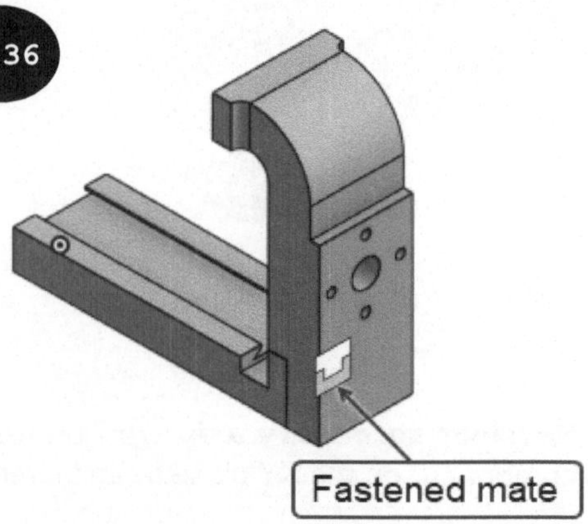

Applying the Revolute Mate

The Revolute mate allows a component to rotate about an axis by removing all degrees of freedom except one rotational degree of freedom, as illustrated in Figure 9.37. This mate type is used for rotating the component around an axis (typically the Z-axis) which is defined by the mate connectors of the components. The method for applying the Revolute mate is discussed below:

9.37

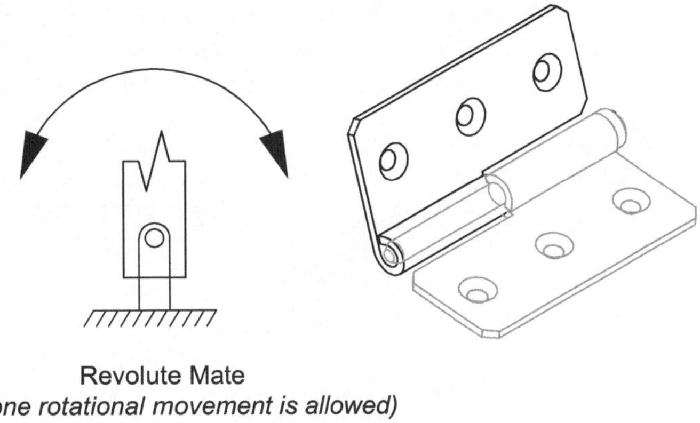

1. Click on the **Revolute mate** tool in the **Assembly** toolbar, see Figure 9.38. The **Revolute** dialog appears, see Figure 9.39. By default, the **Revolute** option is selected in the **Mate type** drop-down list of the dialog, allowing you to apply the Revolute mate between two components.

9.38

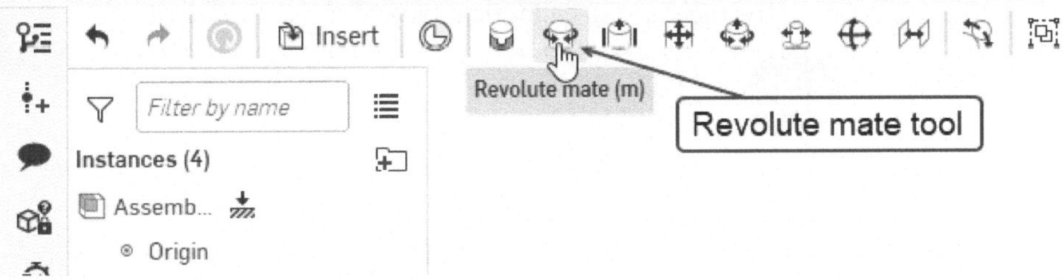

9.39

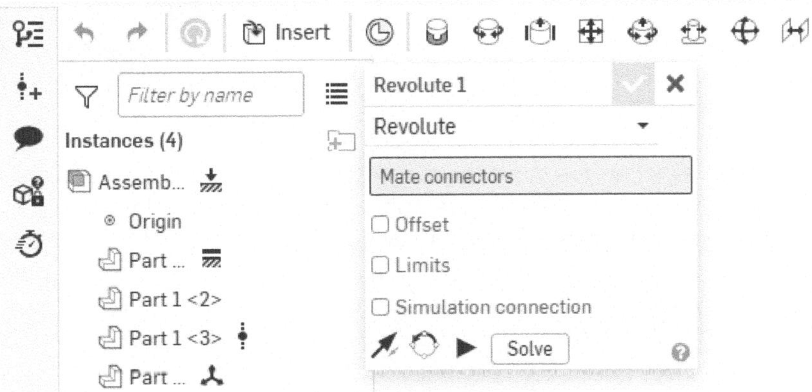

Now, you need to define the mate connector on two different components to apply the selected mate type between them. The mate connector on the first component serves as the rotational component, while the mate connector on the second component acts as the stationary component.

2. Move the cursor over a face, edge, or vertex of the first component (rotational component) to define the mate connector on it. The respective geometry highlights, and its snap points appear, see Figure 9.40. In this example, the cursor is positioned over the cylindrical face of the component, and the mate connector snaps to one of the snap points of the highlighted face.

9.40

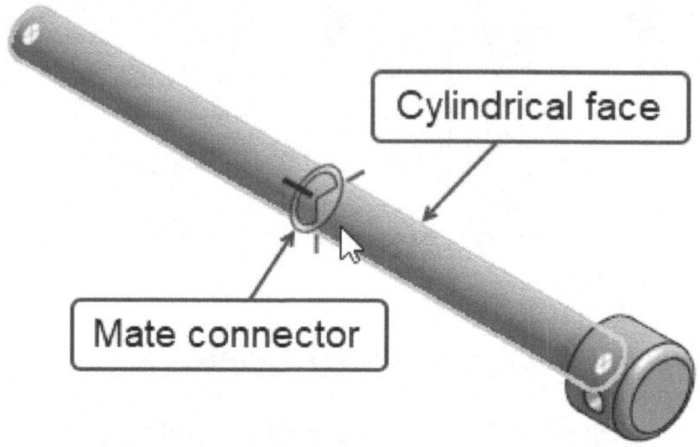

3. Click on the desired snap point on the highlighted geometry of the component to specify the position of the mate connector, see Figure 9.41. In this example, the mate connector is defined at the right snap point of the highlighted cylindrical face of the component.

9.41

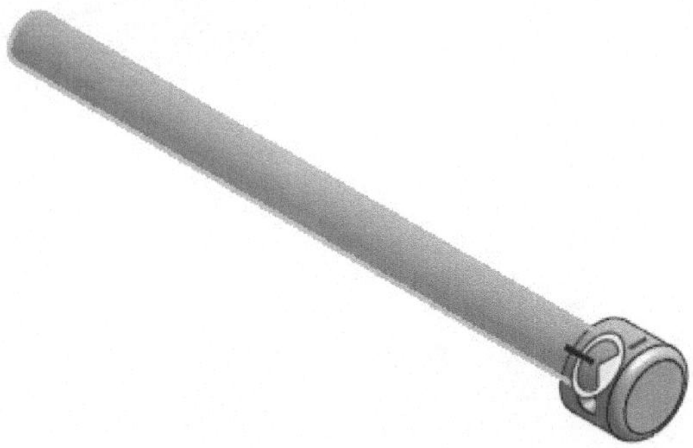

Note: Sometimes, when you move the cursor toward a snap point of the highlighted geometry to define the position of the mate connector, the snap points of other geometry on the component may get highlighted. To avoid this, you can lock the geometry whose snap point you want to select. To do this, press the SHIFT key when the snap points of the required geometry appear, then click the left mouse button on the desired snap point. Afterward, release the SHIFT key.

After defining the mate connector on the first component (rotational one), proceed to define the mate connector on the second component (stationary one).

4. Move the cursor over a face, edge, or vertex of the second component. The respective geometry highlights and its snap points appear, see Figure 9.42. In this example, the cursor is positioned over a circular edge of the component. As a result, only one snap point appears at the center of the edge, and the mate connector is snapped to it by default.

9.42

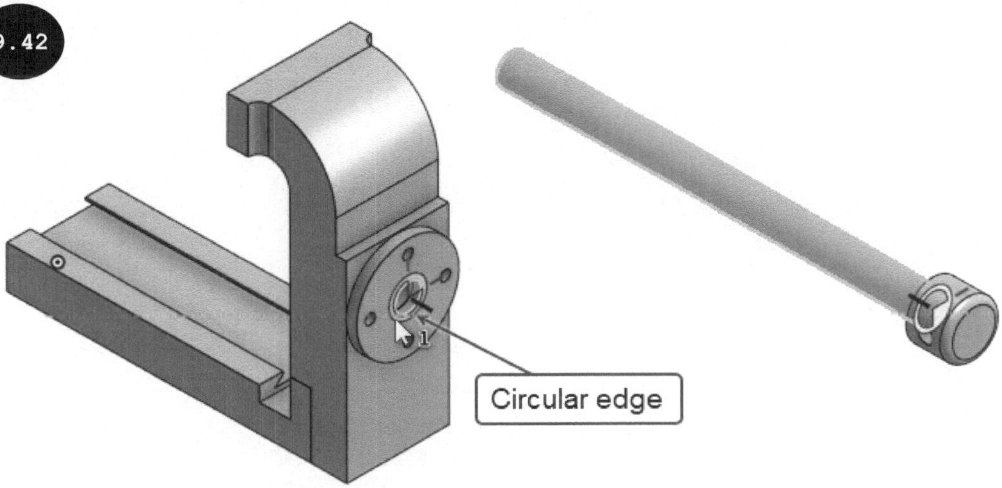

5. Click the desired snap point on the highlighted geometry of the second component to specify the position of the mate connector. The first component moves toward the second component and the mate connectors of both components coincide in the graphics area, see Figure 9.42. Also, the **Mate** Pop-up dialog appears.

9.43

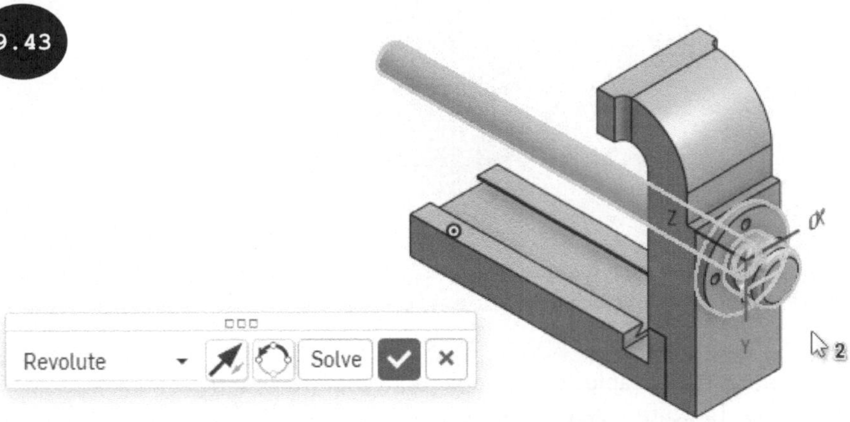

Offset: Selecting the **Offset** check box in the **Revolute** dialog enables the **Z** field (see Figure 9.44), allowing you to specify the offset distance between the components along the Z-axis (the rotational axis of the movable component), see Figure 9.45. To reverse the direction of the offset, you can enter a negative distance value in this field.

9.44

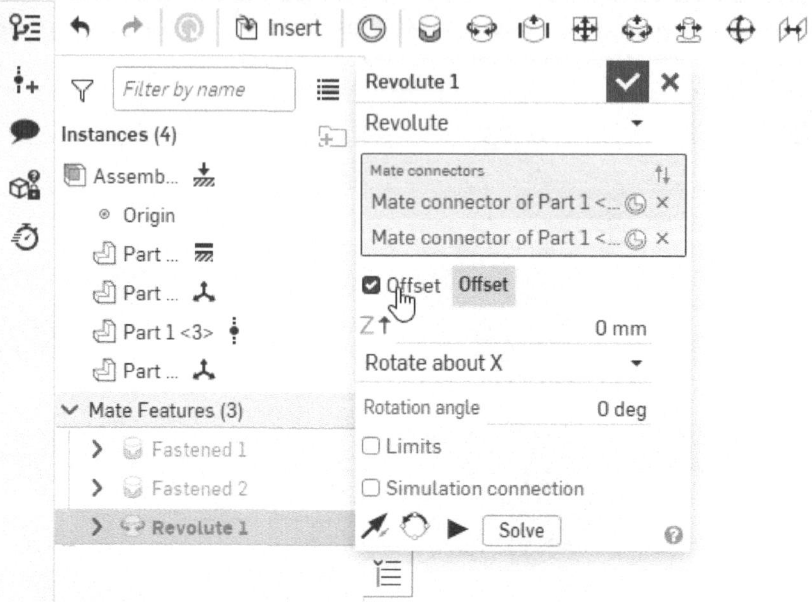

9.45

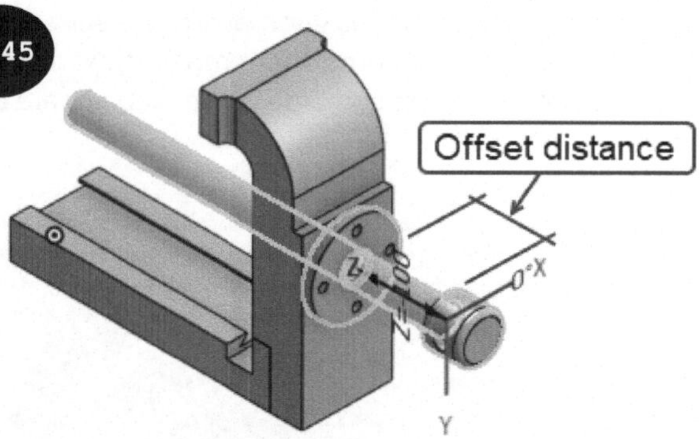

Tip: By default, the value of 0 is set as the offset distance in the Z field of the dialog. As a result, the mate connectors of both components coincide with each other in the graphics area.

You can also rotate the movable component about the X-axis or the Y-axis relative to the defined mate connectors. To do this, select the desired axis from the **Rotation axis** drop-down list and enter the desired rotation angle in the **Rotation angle** field, which becomes enabled in the dialog.

Limits: By default, in the Revolute mate, the rotational component is free to rotate a full 360 degrees about the Z-axis without any limitations. However, if needed, you can set minimum and maximum rotational limits to restrict the component's rotation within a defined range.

To set rotational limits for the rotational component, select the **Limits** check box in the **Revolute** dialog. This enables the **Limit axial Z minimum angle** and **Limit axial Z maximum angle** fields. In these fields, you can define the minimum and maximum rotational angles, respectively, refer to Figure 9.46. For example, setting **0** degrees as the minimum and **90** degrees as the maximum rotational angle will allow the component to rotate only within the **0** to **90** degrees range, see Figure 9.47.

9.46

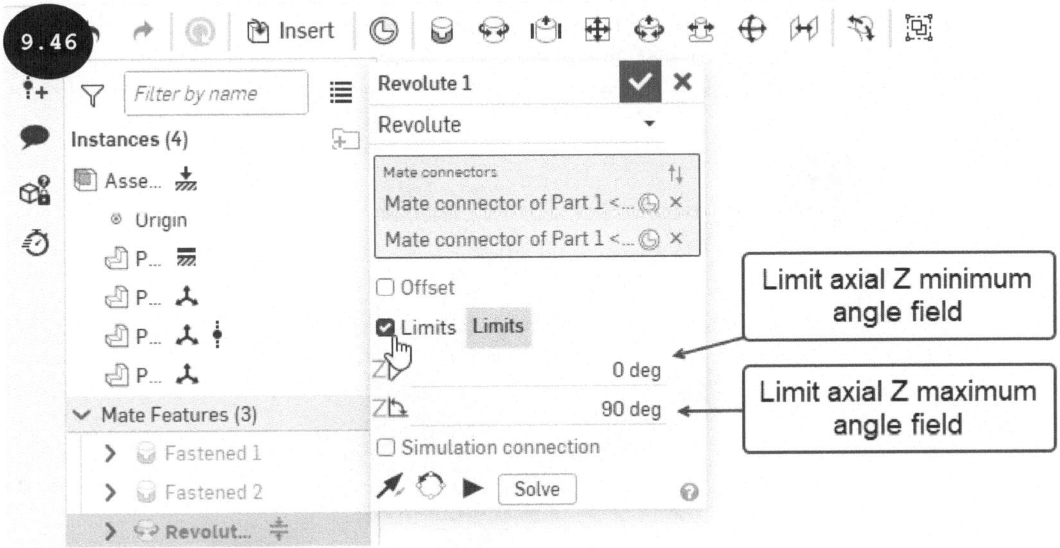

9.47

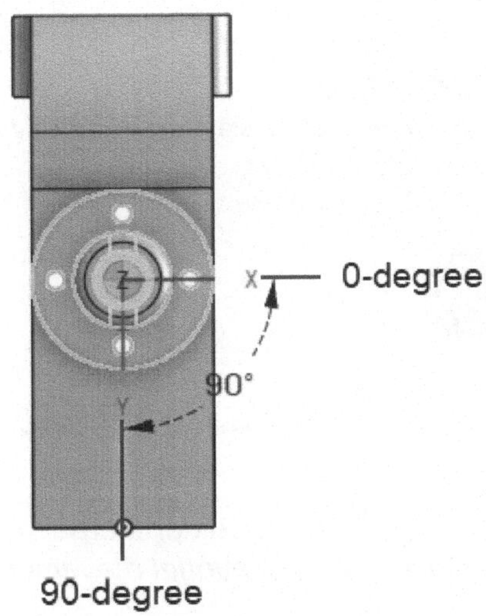

After defining these limits, you can play the animation to review the rotational limits applied to the component by clicking on the **Animate mate degree of freedom** button ▶ in the dialog.

The other options, including the **Flip primary axis** button, **Reorient secondary axis** button, **Animate mate degree of freedom** button ▶, and **Solve** button in the dialog, are the same as discussed earlier.

6. If needed, define the minimum and maximum limits for the rotational degree of freedom of the component by selecting the **Limits** check box, as discussed above.

Note: By default, the component is free to rotate about its degree of freedom (Z-axis) without any limitations, as the minimum and maximum rotational limits are set to 0 or are not defined.

7. After defining the mate connectors on the two components and other settings, click on the green checkmark to confirm and exit the dialog. The Revolute mate is applied between the components, removing all degrees of freedom except for one rotational degree of freedom, see Figure 9.48.

9.48

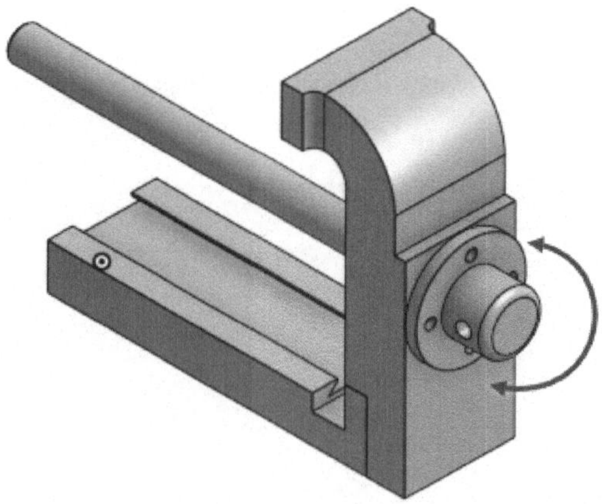

Applying the Slider Mate

The Slider mate allows a component to translate or slide along an axis (Z-axis) by restricting all degrees of freedom except for one translational degree of freedom, as illustrated in Figure 9.49. The method for applying the Slider mate is discussed below:

9.49

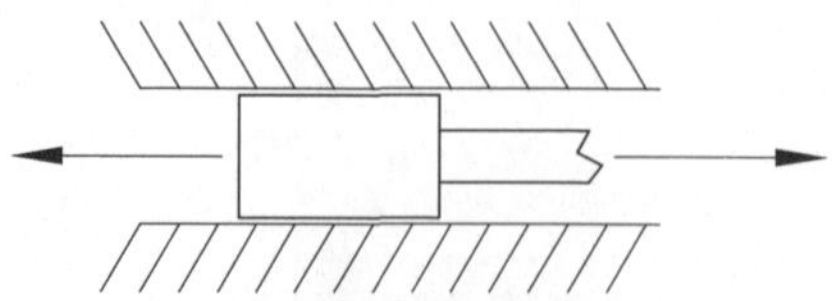

Slider Mate
(Only one translational movement is allowed)

1. Click on the **Slider mate** tool in the **Assembly** toolbar, see Figure 9.50. The **Slider** dialog appears, see Figure 9.51. By default, the **Slider** option is selected in the **Mate type** drop-down list of the dialog, allowing you to apply the Slider mate between two components.

9.50

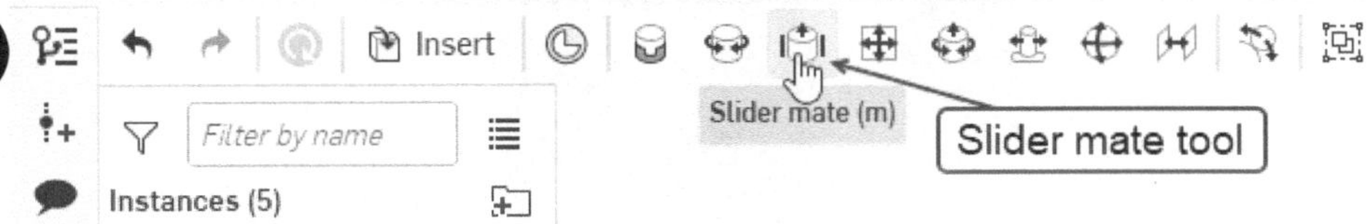

9.51

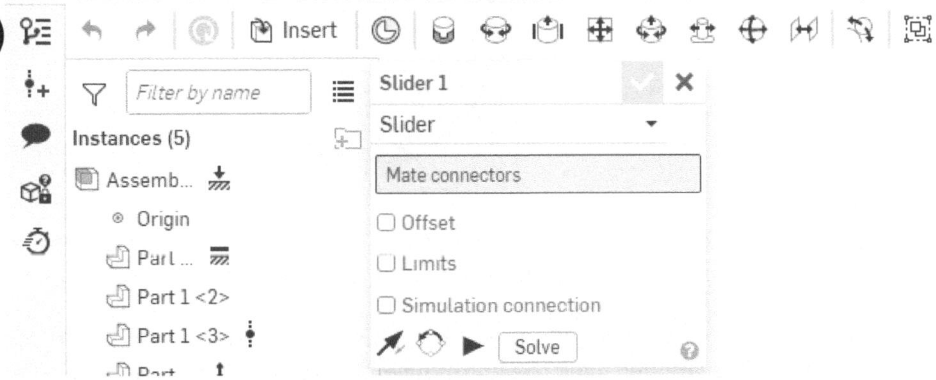

Now, you need to define the mate connector on two different components to apply the selected mate type. The mate connector on the first component serves as the slider component, while the mate connector on the second component acts as the stationary component.

2. Move the cursor over a face, edge, or vertex of the first component (slider component) to define the mate connector on it. The respective geometry highlights, and its snap points appear, see Figure 9.52. In this example, the cursor is positioned over the planar face of a component, and the mate connector snaps to one of its snap points.

9.52

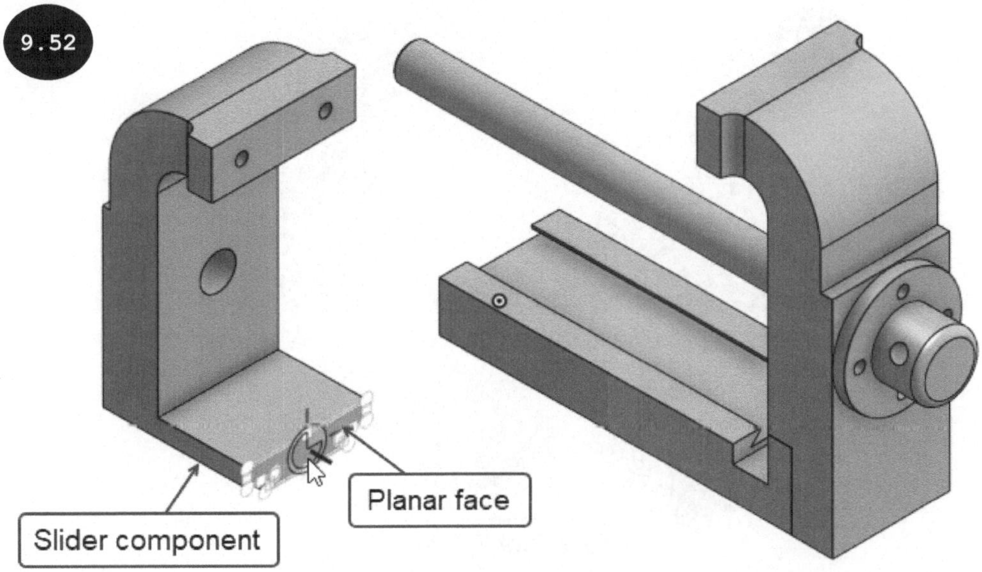

3. Click on the desired snap point on the highlighted geometry of the component to specify the position of the mate connector, see Figure 9.53. In this example, the mate connector is defined at the middle snap point of the bottom edge of the highlighted face.

9.53

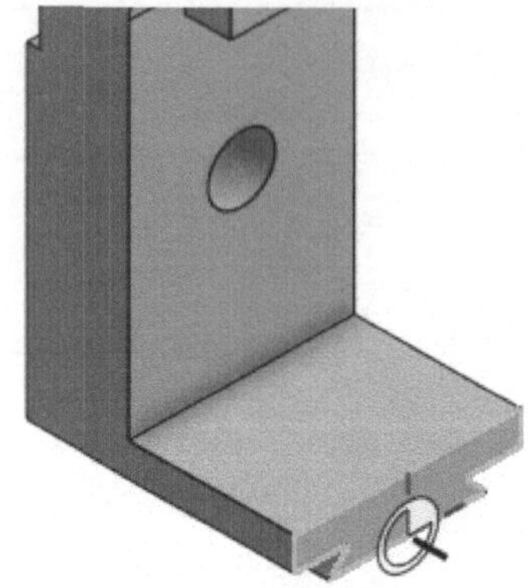

Note: Sometimes, when you move the cursor toward a snap point of the highlighted geometry to define the position of the mate connector, the snap points of other geometry on the component may get highlighted. To avoid this, you can lock the geometry whose snap point you want to select. To do this, press the SHIFT key when the snap points of the required geometry appear, then click the left mouse button on the desired snap point. Afterward, release the SHIFT key.

After defining the mate connector on the first component (slider one), proceed to define the mate connector on the second component (stationary one).

4. Move the cursor over a face, edge, or vertex of the second component. The respective geometry highlights and its snap points appear, see Figure 9.54. If needed, you can rotate the assembly by pressing and holding the right mouse button while dragging the cursor.

9.54

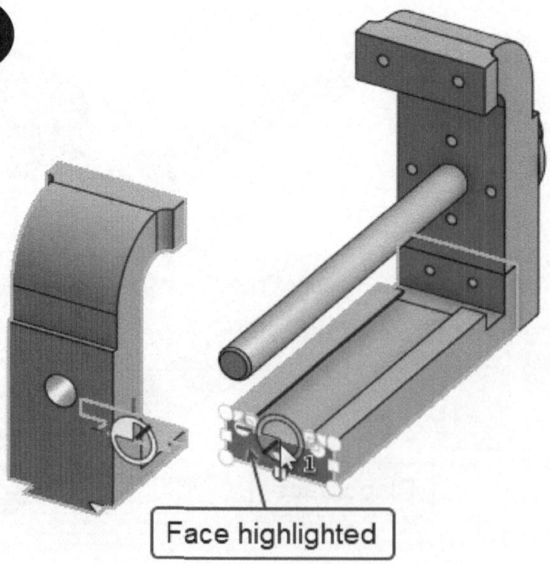

5. Press the SHIFT key to lock the highlighted geometry and then click on the desired snap point to specify the position of the mate connector, refer to Figure 9.54. The first component moves toward the second component and the mate connectors of both components coincide in the graphics area, see Figure 9.55. Also, the Mate Pop-up dialog appears.

9.55

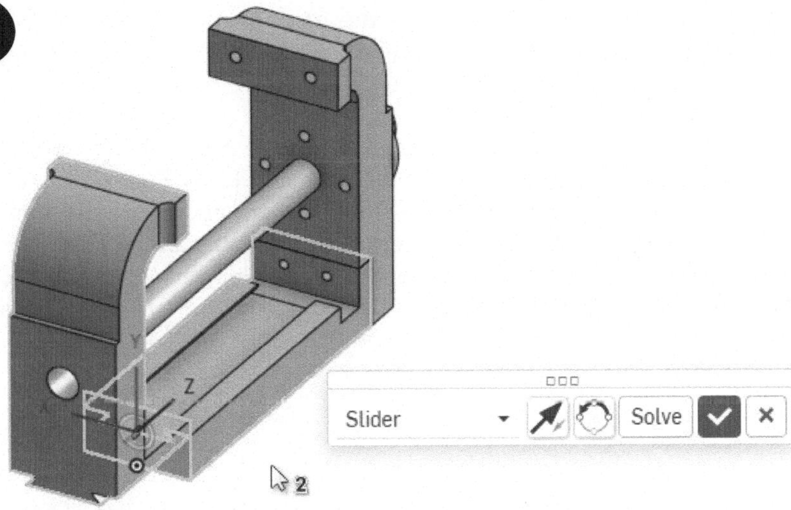

6. If you rotated the assembly while defining the mate connectors, press SHIFT + 7 to return the assembly to the isometric view.

Offset: Selecting the **Offset** check box in the **Slider** dialog enables the X and Y fields (see Figure 9.56), allowing you to specify the offset distance between the components along the X and Y axes of the slider component, respectively. To reverse the direction of the offset, enter a negative value in these fields.

9.56

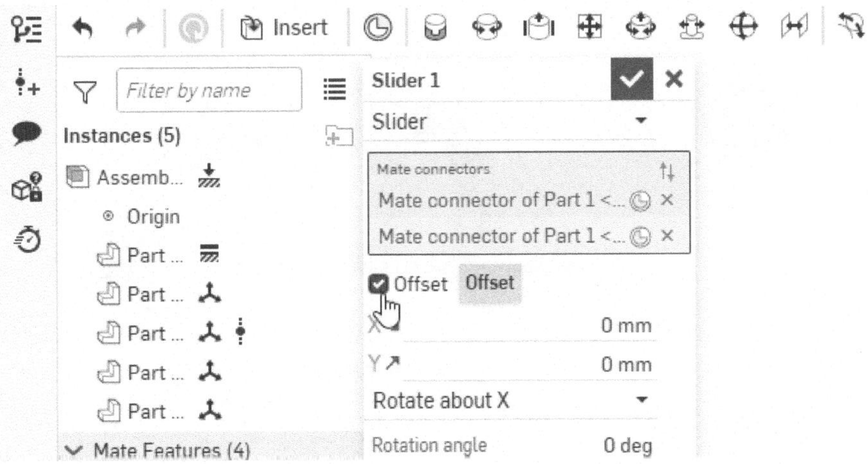

Tip: By default, the value of 0 is set as the offset distance in the X and Y fields of the dialog. As a result, the mate connectors of both components coincide with each other.

You can also set the position of the Slider component at an angle about the X, Y, or Z axis relative to the defined mate connectors. To do this, select the desired axis from the **Rotation axis** drop-down list and enter the desired rotation angle in the **Rotation angle** field, which becomes enabled in the dialog.

Limits: By default, the Slider mate allows the component to translate or slide freely along the Z-axis without any limitations. However, if needed, you can set minimum and maximum translation limits to restrict the component's movement within a defined range.

To set translation limits for the Slider component, select the **Limits** check box in the **Slider** dialog. This enables the **Limit Z minimum distance** and **Limit Z maximum distance** fields, see Figure 9.57. In these fields, you can define the minimum and maximum translation distances, respectively. For example, setting **120** distance as the minimum and **245** distance as the maximum translation distance will allow the component to slide only within the **120** to **245** distance range, refer to Figure 9.58. Note that the distances are measured from the original position of the mate connectors.

9.57

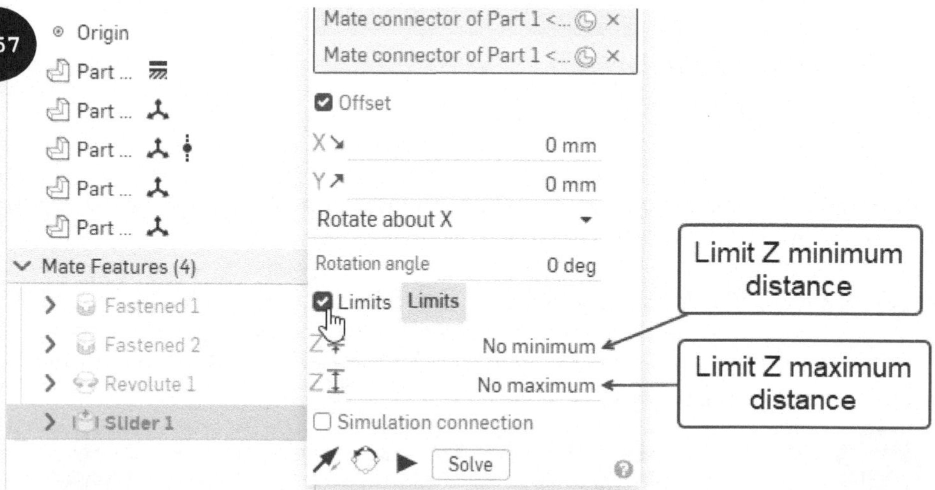

9.58

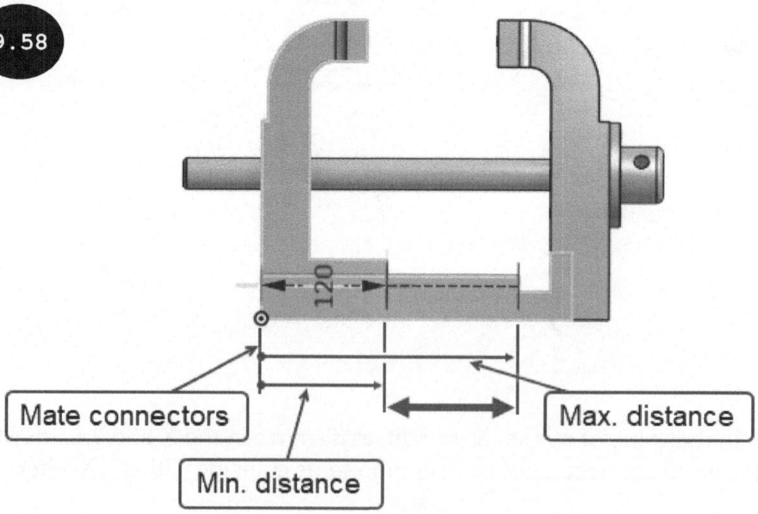

After defining these limits, you can play the animation to review the translational limits applied to the component by clicking on the **Animate mate degree of freedom** button ▶ in the dialog.

The other options, including the **Flip primary axis** button, **Reorient secondary axis** button, and **Solve** button in the dialog, are the same as discussed earlier.

7. After defining the mate connectors on the two components and other settings, click on the green checkmark ✓ to confirm and exit the dialog. The Slider mate is applied between the components, removing all degrees of freedom except for one translational degree of freedom, see Figure 9.59.

9.59

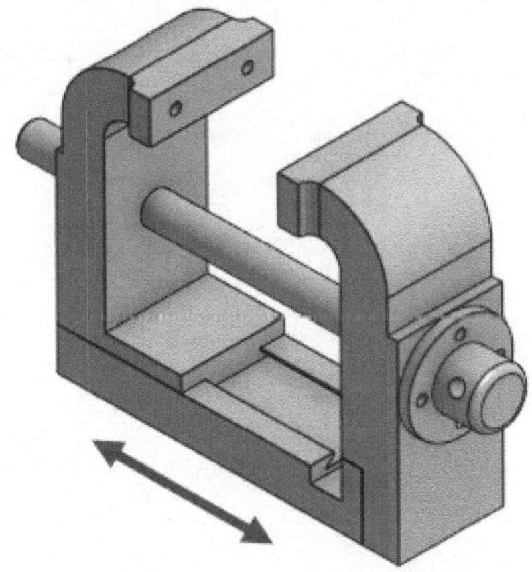

Applying the Planar Mate

The Planar mate allows a component to translate along two axes (X-axis and Y-axis) and rotate about the Z-axis, refer to Figure 9.60. In this mate, the component is restrained to a planar face of another component, restricting its movement in the direction normal to the planar face while allowing movement within the plane of the face. Additionally, the component can rotate about the Z-axis, which is normal to the planar face. The method for applying the Planar mate is discussed below:

9.60

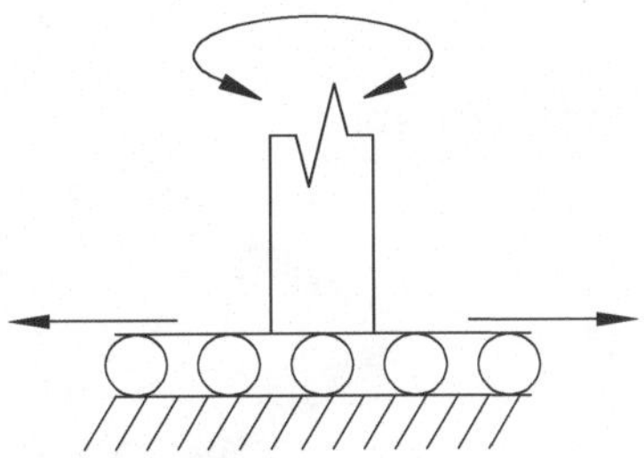

Planar Mate

(Moves freely within the plane of the face along the X and Y axes, and rotates about the Z-axis)

1. Click on the **Planar mate** tool in the **Assembly** toolbar, see Figure 9.61. The **Planar** dialog appears, see Figure 9.62. By default, the **Planar** option is selected in the **Mate type** drop-down list of the dialog, allowing you to apply the Planar mate between two components.

9.61

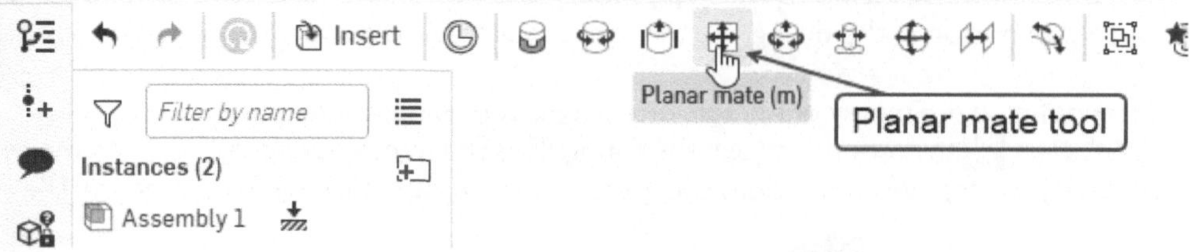

9.62

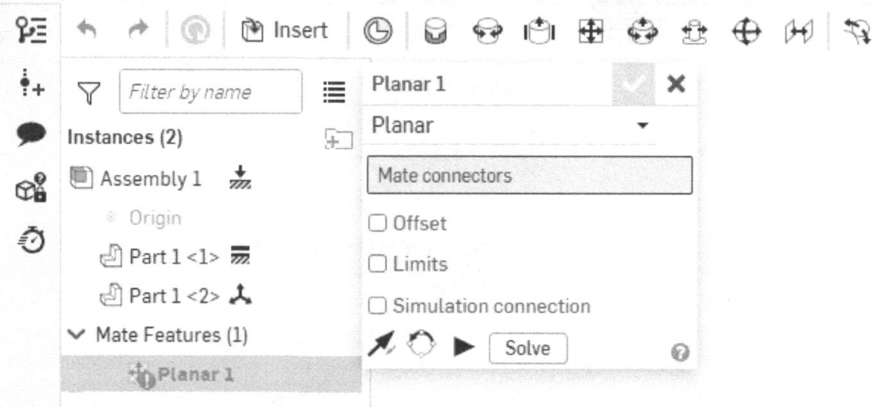

Now, you need to define the mate connector on two different components to apply the selected mate type. The mate connector on the first component serves as the moveable component, while the mate connector on the second component acts as the stationary component.

2. Move the cursor over a face, edge, or vertex of the first component (moveable component) to define the mate connector on it. The respective geometry highlights, and its snap points appear, see Figure 9.63. In this example, the cursor is positioned over a circular edge of the component. As a result, only one snap point appears at the center of the edge, and the mate connector is snapped to it by default.

9.63

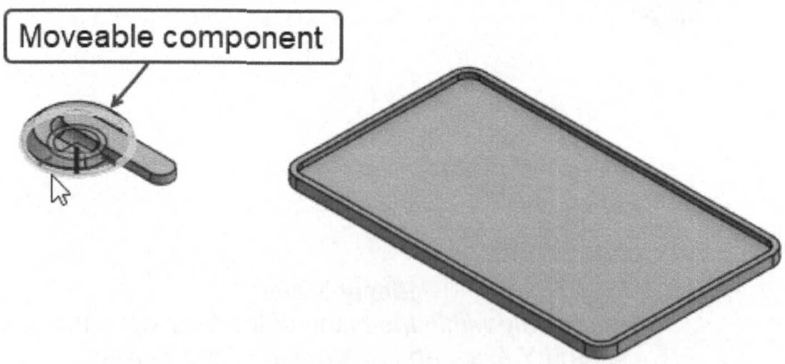

3. Press the SHIFT key to lock the highlighted geometry, then click on the desired snap point to define the position of the mate connector.

After defining the mate connector on the first component (moveable one), proceed to define the mate connector on the second component (stationary one).

4. Move the cursor over a face, edge, or vertex of the second component. The respective geometry highlights and its snap points appear, see Figure 9.64.

9.64

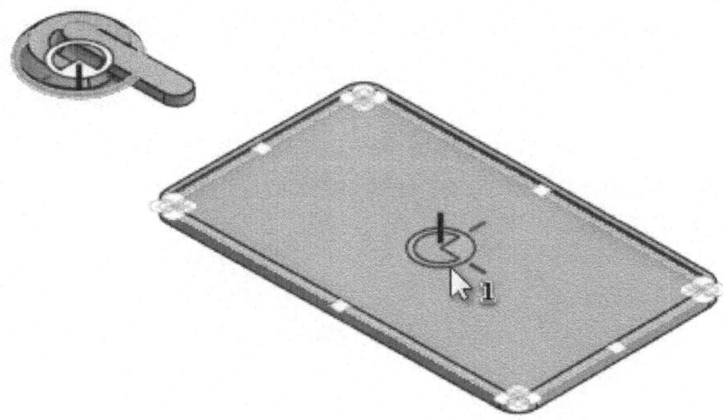

5. Press the SHIFT key to lock the highlighted geometry, then click on the desired snap point to specify the position of the mate connector. The first component moves toward the second component and the mate connectors of both components coincide, see Figure 9.65.

9.65

Offset: Selecting the **Offset** check box in the **Planar** dialog enables the **Z** field (see Figure 9.66), allowing you to specify the offset distance between the components along the Z-axis of the moveable component. To reverse the direction of the offset, you can enter a negative value in this field.

9.66

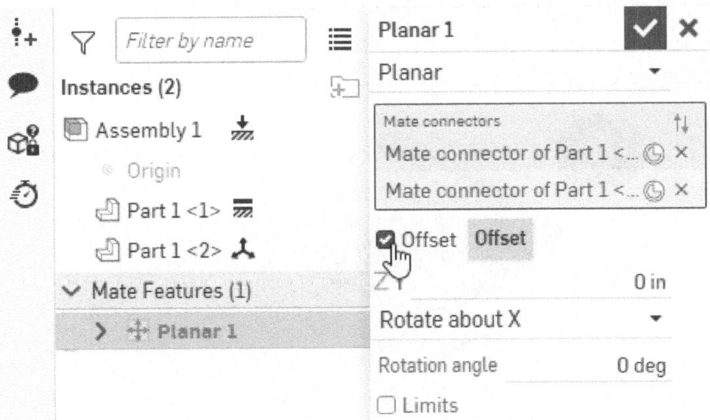

You can also set the position of the moveable component at an angle about the X or Y axis relative to the defined mate connectors. To do this, select the desired axis from the **Rotation axis** drop-down list and enter the desired rotation angle in the **Rotation angle** field of the dialog.

Limits: By default, the Planar mate allows the moveable component to translate freely along the X and Y axes and rotate about the Z-axis without any limitations. However, if needed, you can set minimum and maximum translation limits along the X and Y axes, as well as rotational limits about the Z-axis, to restrict the component's movement within a defined range.

To set translation and rotational limits for the Planar mate, select the **Limits** check box. Then, specify the minimum and maximum translation and rotational limits in their respective fields within the dialog that appears, see Figure 9.67.

9.67

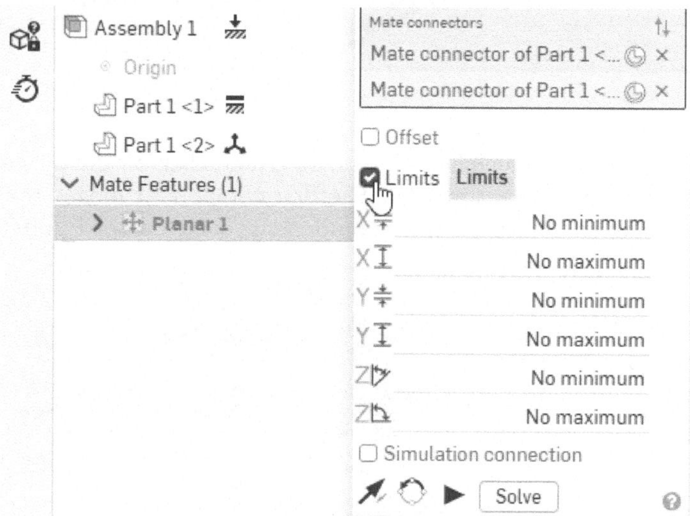

The other options, including the **Flip primary axis** button, **Reorient secondary axis** button, **Animate mate degree of freedom** button ▶, and **Solve** button in the dialog, are the same as discussed earlier.

6. After defining the mate connectors and other settings, click on the green checkmark to confirm and exit the dialog. The Planar Mate is applied between the components, removing all degrees of freedom except for two translational degrees of freedom along the X and Y axes and one rotational degree of freedom about the Z-axis, see Figure 9.68.

9.68

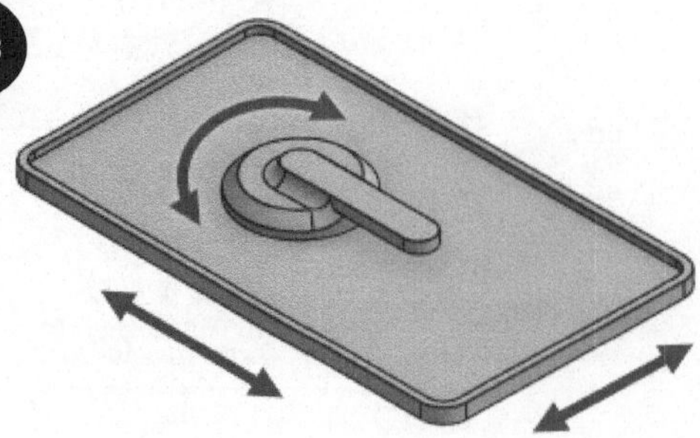

Applying the Cylindrical Mate

The Cylindrical mate allows a component to translate along the Z-axis and rotate about the same Z-axis by removing all degrees of freedom except one translational and one rotational degree of freedom, as illustrated in Figure 9.69. It is primarily used for forming a screw mechanism between components. The method for applying the Cylindrical mate is discussed below:

9.69

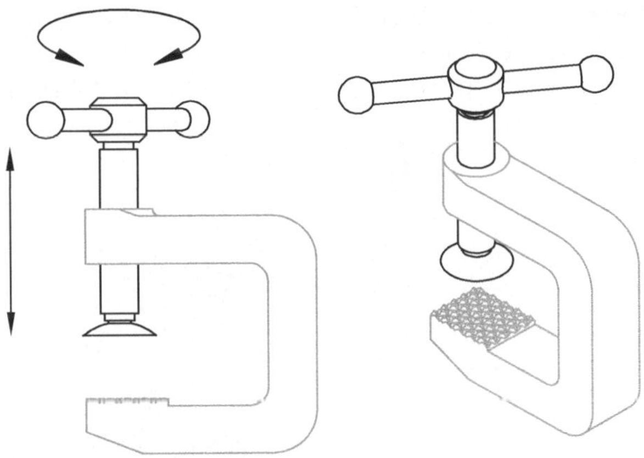

Cylindrical Mate
(One translational and one rotational movement are allowed along the same Z-axis)

1. Click on the **Cylindrical mate** tool in the **Assembly** toolbar, see Figure 9.70. The **Cylindrical** dialog appears, see Figure 9.71. By default, the **Cylindrical** option is selected in the **Mate type** drop-down list of the dialog, allowing you to apply the Cylindrical mate between two components.

9.70

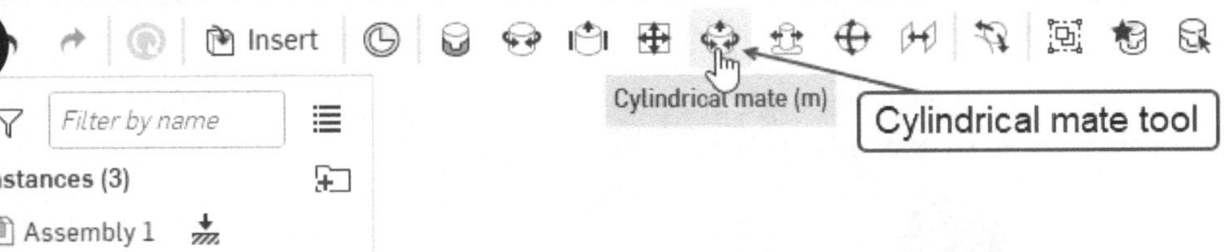

9.71

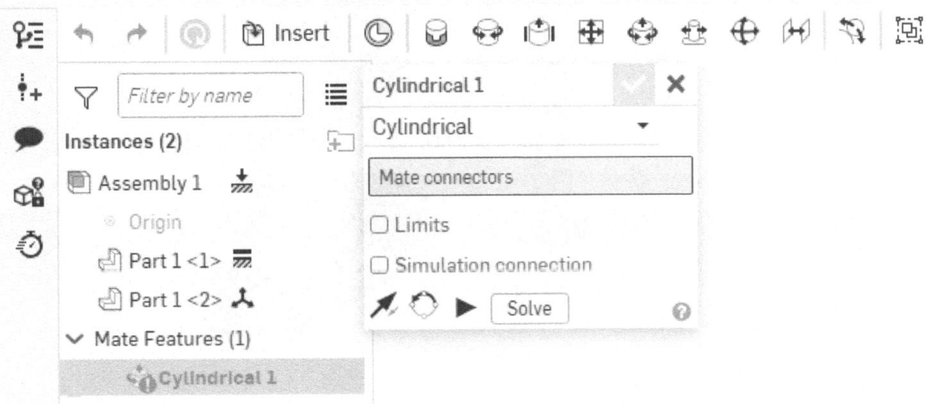

Now, you need to define the mate connector on two different components to apply the selected mate type. The mate connector on the first component serves as the moveable component, enabling both translational and rotational movements, while the mate connector on the second component acts as the stationary component.

2. Move the cursor over a face, edge, or vertex of the first component (moveable component) to define the mate connector on it. The respective geometry highlights, and its snap points appear, see Figure 9.72. In this example, the cursor is positioned over a cylindrical face of the component, and the mate connector snaps to one of the snap points of the highlighted face.

9.72

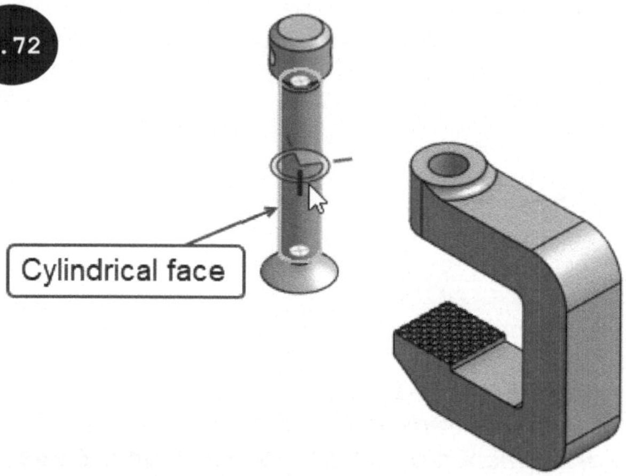

3. Press the SHIFT key to lock the highlighted geometry, then click on the desired snap point to define the position of the mate connector.

   After defining the mate connector on the first component (moveable one), proceed to define the mate connector on the second component (stationary one).

4. Move the cursor over a face, edge, or vertex of the second component. The respective geometry highlights and its snap points appear, see Figure 9.73.

9.73

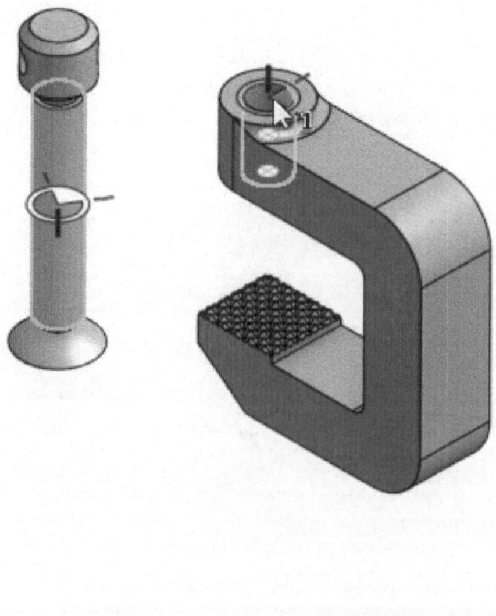

5. Press the SHIFT key to lock the highlighted geometry, then click on the desired snap point to specify the position of the mate connector. The first component moves toward the second component and the mate connectors of both components coincide, see Figure 9.74.

9.74

Limits: By default, the Cylindrical mate allows the movable component to translate and rotate freely about the Z-axis. However, you can define minimum and maximum translational and rotational limits to restrict the component's movement within a specified range, if required.

To set translation and rotational limits for the Cylindrical mate, select the **Limits** check box. Then, specify the minimum and maximum translation and rotational limits in their respective fields that appears within the dialog, see Figure 9.75.

9.75

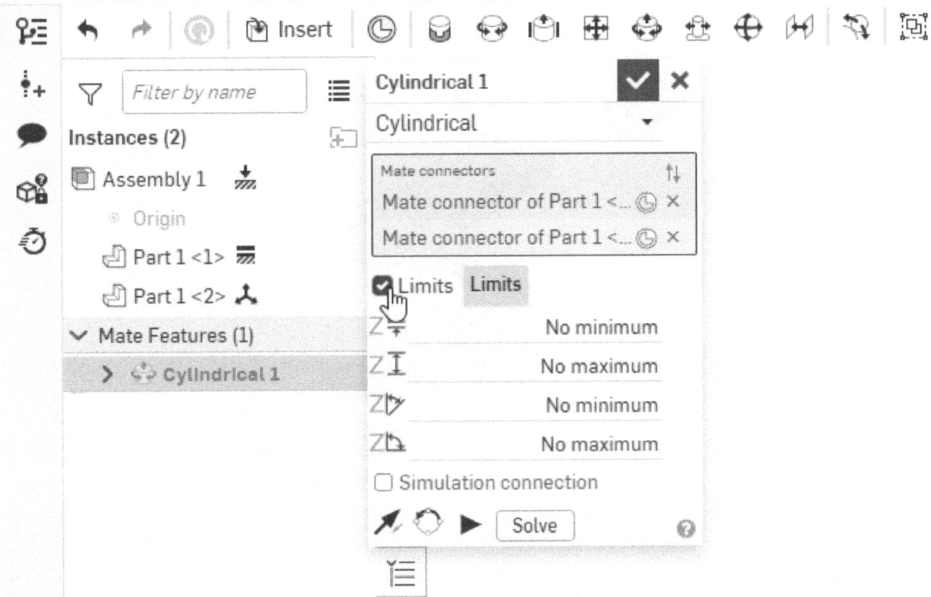

The other options, including the **Flip primary axis** button, **Reorient secondary axis** button, **Animate mate degree of freedom** button ▶, and **Solve** button in the dialog, are the same as discussed earlier.

6. After defining the mate connectors and other settings, click on the green checkmark ✓ to confirm and exit the dialog. The Cylindrical Mate is applied between the components, removing all degrees of freedom except for one translational and one rotational degree of freedom along the Z-axis, see Figure 9.76.

9.76

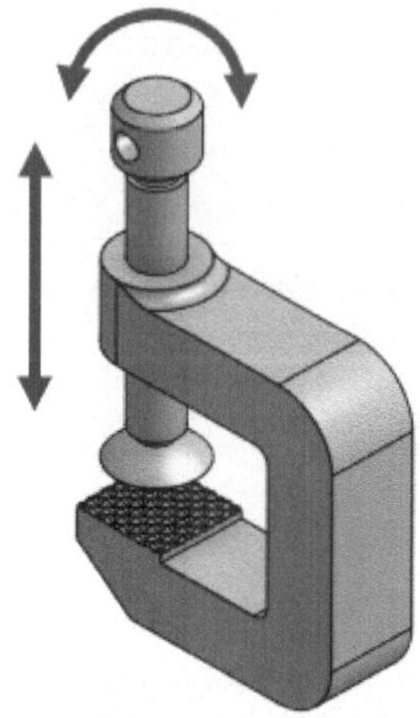

Applying the Pin Slot Mate

The Pin Slot mate allows a component to translate along one axis (X-axis) and rotate about another axis (Z-axis), restricting all other degrees of freedom except for one translational and one rotational degree of freedom, see Figure 9.77. This mate is typically used to create a pin-slot mechanism, where the pin moves along the slot and rotates about its axis. The method for applying the Pin Slot mate is discussed below:

9.77

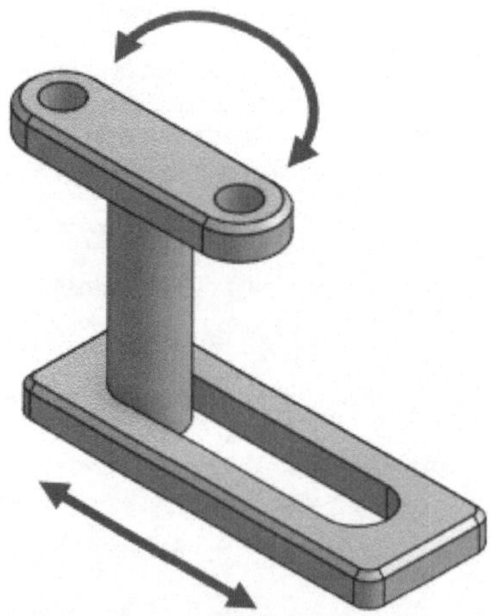

1. Click on the **Pin Slot mate** tool in the **Assembly** toolbar, see Figure 9.78. The **Pin Slot** dialog appears, see Figure 9.79.

9.78

9.79

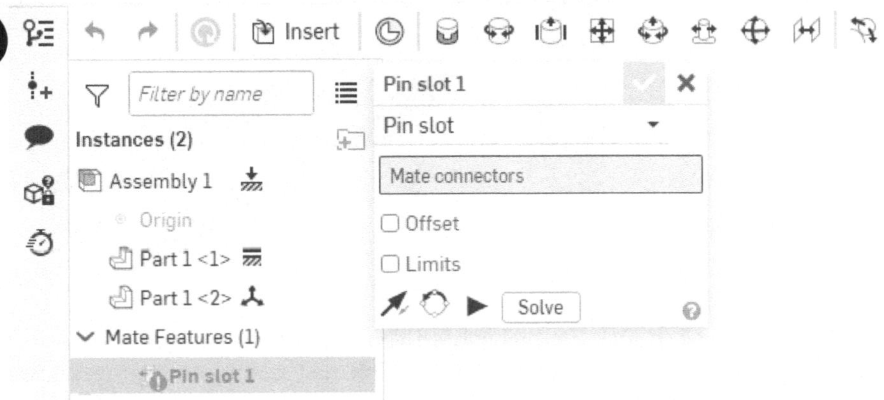

Now, you need to define the mate connector on two different components to apply the selected mate type. The mate connector on the first component serves as the moveable component, enabling both translational and rotational movements, while the mate connector on the second component acts as the stationary component.

2. Move the cursor over a face, edge, or vertex of the first component (moveable component) to define the mate connector on it. The respective geometry highlights, and its snap points appear, see Figure 9.80. In this example, the cursor is positioned over a circular edge of the component. As a result, only one snap point appears at the center of the edge, and the mate connector is snapped to it by default.

9.80

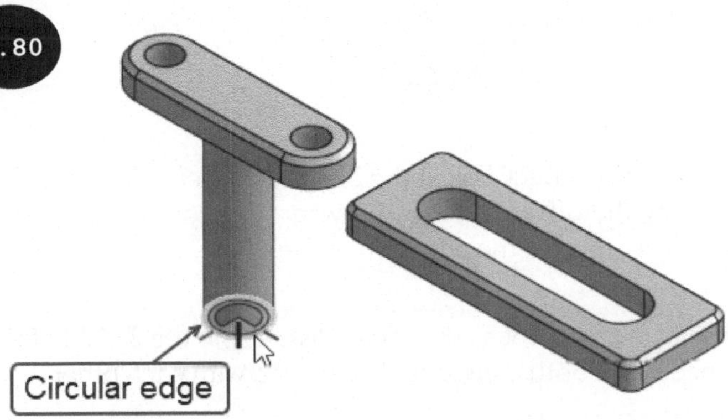

3. Press the SHIFT key to lock the highlighted geometry, then click on the desired snap point to define the position of the mate connector.

After defining the mate connector on the first component (moveable one), proceed to define the mate connector on the second component (stationary one).

4. Move the cursor over a face, edge, or vertex of the second component. The respective geometry highlights and its snap points appear, see Figure 9.81.

9.81

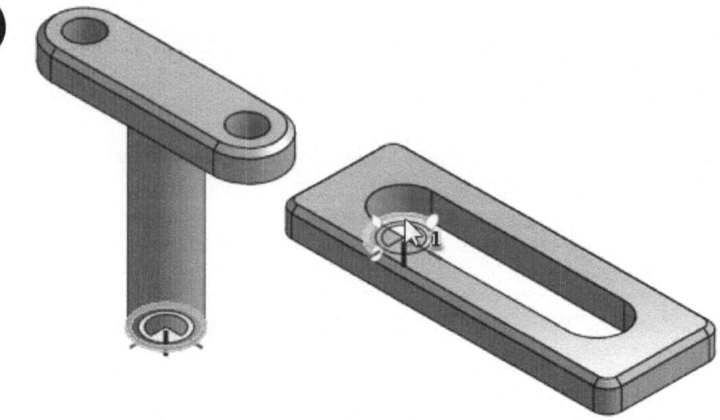

5. Press the SHIFT key to lock the highlighted geometry, then click on the desired snap point to specify the position of the mate connector. The first component moves toward the second component and the mate connectors of both components coincide, see Figure 9.82.

9.82

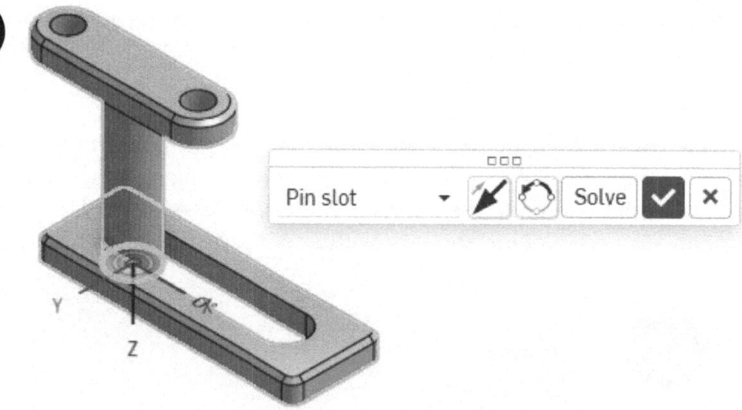

Offset: Selecting the **Offset** check box in the **Slider** dialog enables the Z field (see Figure 9.83), allowing you to specify the offset distance between the components along the Z-axis of the moveable component. To reverse the direction of the offset, enter a negative value in this field.

Tip: By default, the value of 0 is set as the offset distance in the Z field of the dialog. As a result, the mate connectors of both components coincide with each other.

9.83

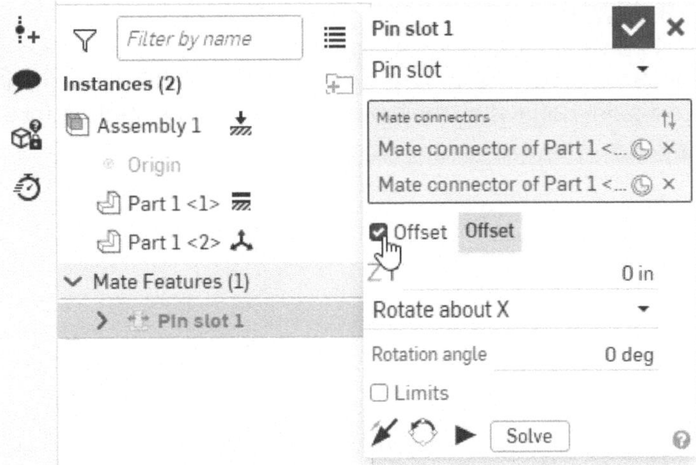

You can also set the position of the moveable component at an angle about the X or Y axis relative to the defined mate connectors. To do this, select the desired axis from the **Rotation axis** drop-down list and enter the desired rotation angle in the **Rotation angle** field, which becomes enabled in the dialog.

Limits: By default, the Pin Slot mate allows the movable component to translate freely along the X-axis and rotate freely about the Z-axis. However, you can define minimum and maximum translational and rotational limits to restrict the component's movement within a specified range, if required.

To set translation and rotational limits for the Pin Slot mate, select the **Limits** check box. Then, specify the minimum and maximum translation and rotational limits in their respective fields that appears within the dialog.

The other options, including the **Flip primary axis** button, **Reorient secondary axis** button, **Animate mate degree of freedom** button, and **Solve** button in the dialog, are the same as discussed earlier.

9.84

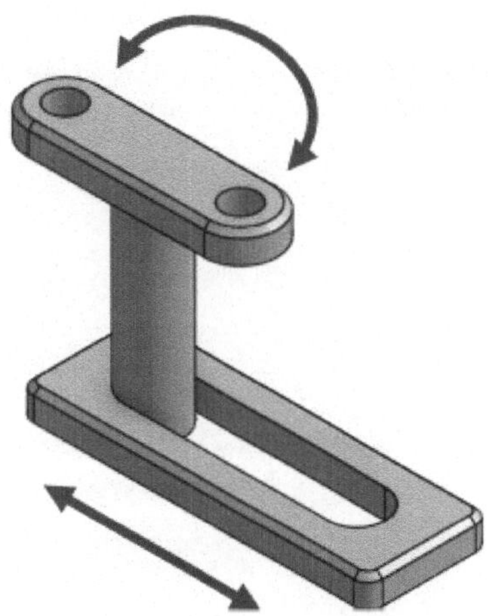

6. After defining the mate connectors and other settings, click on the green checkmark to confirm and exit the dialog. The Pin Slot Mate is applied between the components, removing all degrees of freedom except for one translational degree of freedom along the X-axis and one rotational degree of freedom about the Z-axis, see Figure 9.84.

Applying the Ball Mate

The Ball mate allows a component to rotate about all three X, Y, and Z rotational axes, see Figure 9.85. In this mate, all translational degrees of freedom are restricted, allowing the component to rotate about the three axes relative to a point defined by the mate connectors. The method for applying the Ball mate is discussed below:

9.85

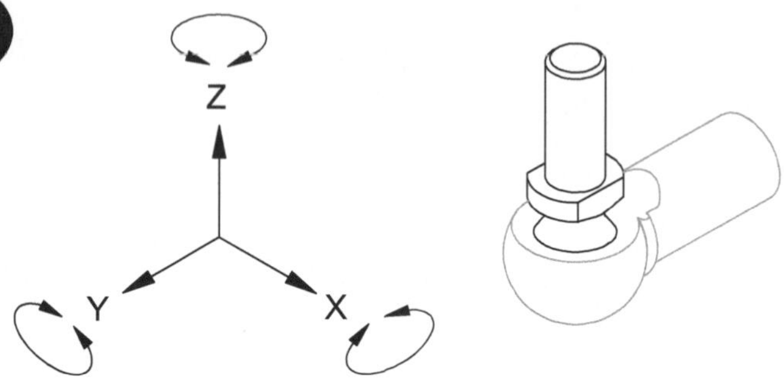

Ball Mate
(Three rotational movements are allowed)

1. Click on the **Ball mate** tool in the **Assembly** toolbar, see Figure 9.86. The **Ball** dialog appears, see Figure 9.87.

9.86

9.87

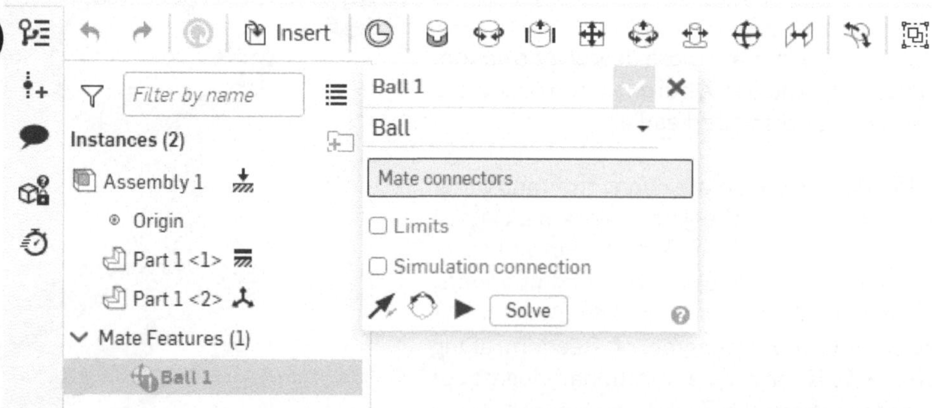

Now, you need to define the mate connector on two different components to apply the selected mate type. The mate connector on the first component serves as the rotational component, while the mate connector on the second component acts as the stationary component.

2. Move the cursor over a face, edge, or vertex of the first component (rotational component) to define the mate connector on it. The respective geometry highlights, and its snap points appear, see Figure 9.88. In this example, the cursor is positioned over a spherical face of the component, and the mate connector snaps to one of its snap points.

9.88

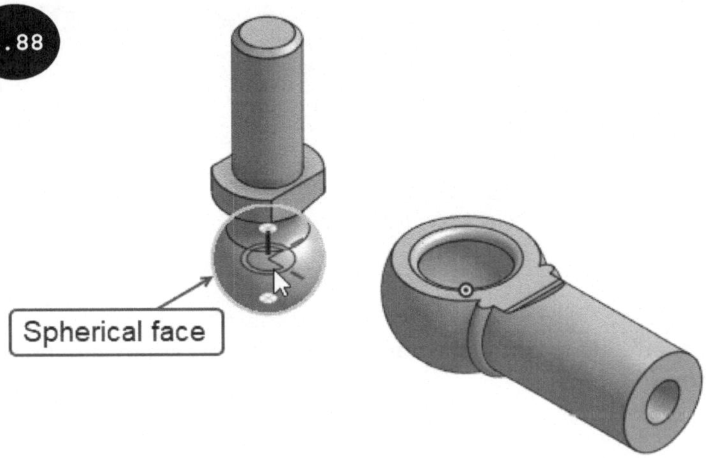

3. Press the SHIFT key to lock the highlighted geometry, then click on the desired snap point to define the position of the mate connector.

   After defining the mate connector on the first component (rotational one), proceed to define the mate connector on the second component (stationary one).

4. Move the cursor over a face, edge, or vertex of the second component, see Figure 9.89. In this example, the cursor is positioned over an inner spherical face of the component, and the mate connector snaps to one of its snap points.

9.89

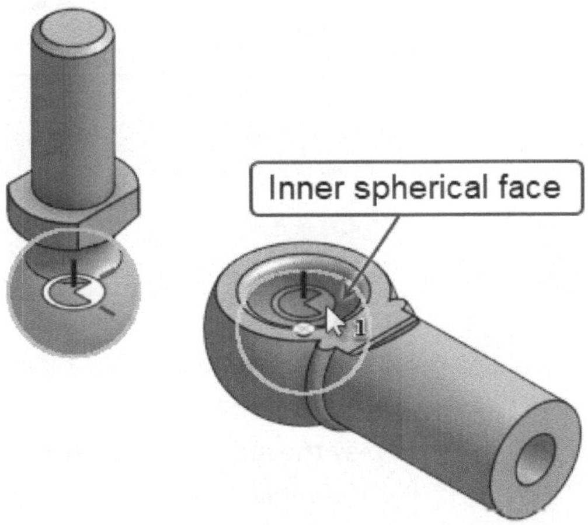

5. Press the SHIFT key to lock the highlighted geometry, then click on the desired snap point to specify the position of the mate connector. The first component moves toward the second component and the mate connectors of both components coincide, see Figure 9.90.

9.90

Tip: In Figure 9.90, the mate connectors are defined at the center snap points of the spherical faces of both components.

Limits: By default, the Ball mate allows the rotational component to rotate freely about the X, Y, and Z axes. However, you can define a maximum rotational limit to restrict the component's rotation within a specified angle, if required.

To set a maximum rotational limit for the Ball mate, select the **Limits** check box. Then, specify the maximum rotational angle in the **Limit cone maximum angle** field that appears, see Figure 9.91. Once set, the rotational component can only rotate within the defined maximum angle along all three axes.

9.91

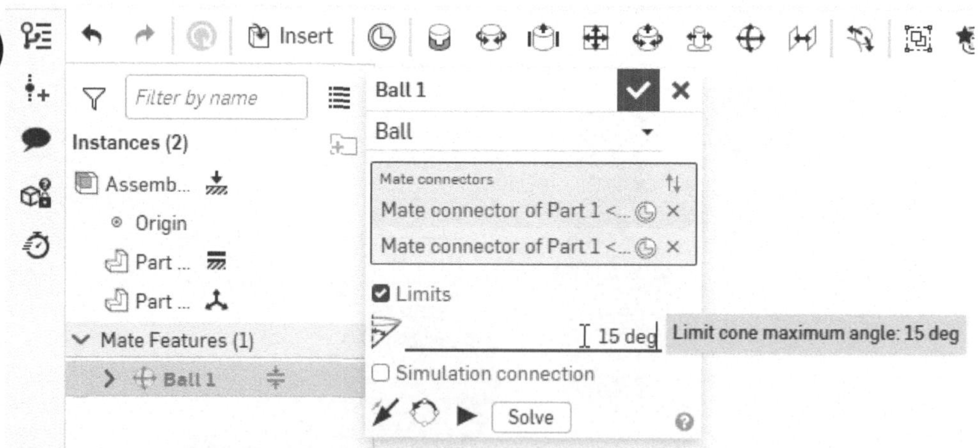

After defining rotational limit, you can play the animation to review it by clicking on the **Animate mate degree of freedom** button ▶ in the dialog.

6. After defining the mate connectors and other settings, click on the green checkmark ✅ to confirm and exit the dialog. The Ball mate is applied between the components, removing all degrees of freedom except for three rotational degrees of freedom.

Applying the Parallel Mate

The Parallel mate ensures that two components remain parallel to each other, allowing rotation about an axis normal to their planes and free translation along the X, Y, and Z axes, see Figure 9.92. The method for applying the Parallel Mate is discussed below:

9.92

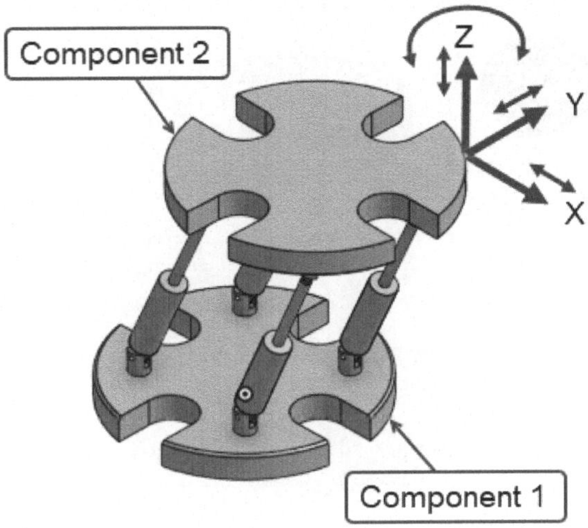

1. Click on the **Parallel mate** tool in the **Assembly** toolbar, see Figure 9.93. The **Parallel** dialog appears, see Figure 9.94.

9.93

9.94

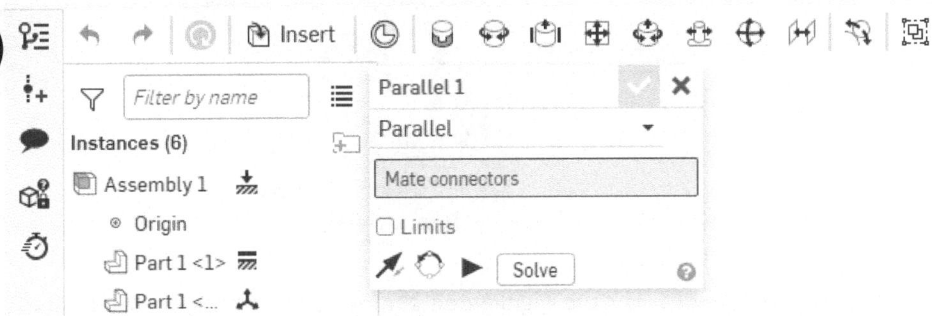

Now, you need to define the mate connector on two different components.

2. Move the cursor over a face, edge, or vertex of the first component (moveable component) to define the mate connector on it. The respective geometry highlights, and its snap points appear, see Figure 9.95. In this example, the cursor is positioned over a planar face of the component, and the mate connector snaps to one of its snap points.

9.95

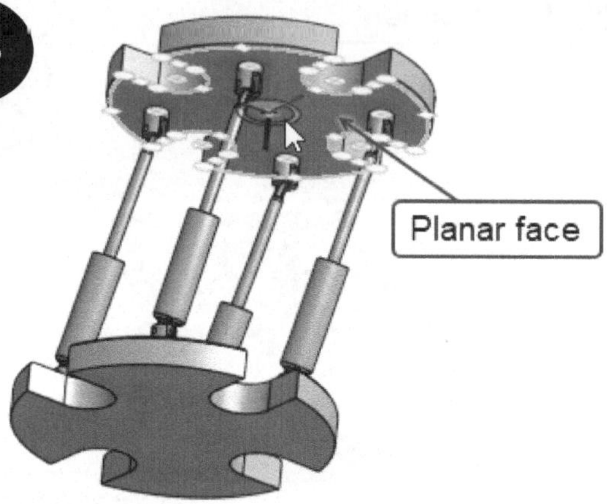

3. Press the SHIFT key to lock the highlighted geometry, then click on the desired snap point to define the position of the mate connector.

   After defining the mate connector on the first component, proceed to define the mate connector on the second component.

4. Move the cursor over a face, edge, or vertex of the second component, see Figure 9.96.

9.96

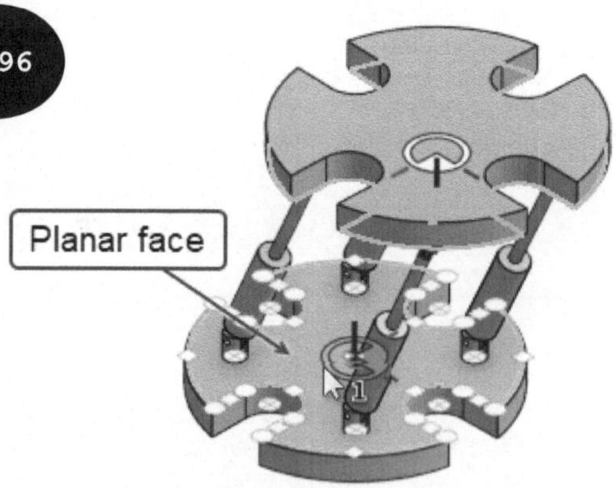

5. Press the SHIFT key to lock the highlighted geometry, then click on the desired snap point to specify the position of the mate connector. The first component moves toward the second component and the mate connectors of both components coincide, see Figure 9.97.

9.97

Limits: By default, the Parallel mate allows the moveable component to translate freely along the X, Y, and Z axes and rotate about the Z-axis without any limitations. However, if needed, you can set minimum and maximum translation limits along the X, Y, and Z axes, as well as rotational limits about the Z-axis, to restrict the component's movement within a defined range.

To set translation and rotational limits, select the **Limits** check box. Then, specify the minimum and maximum translation and rotational limits in their respective fields that appears within the dialog, see Figure 9.98.

9.98

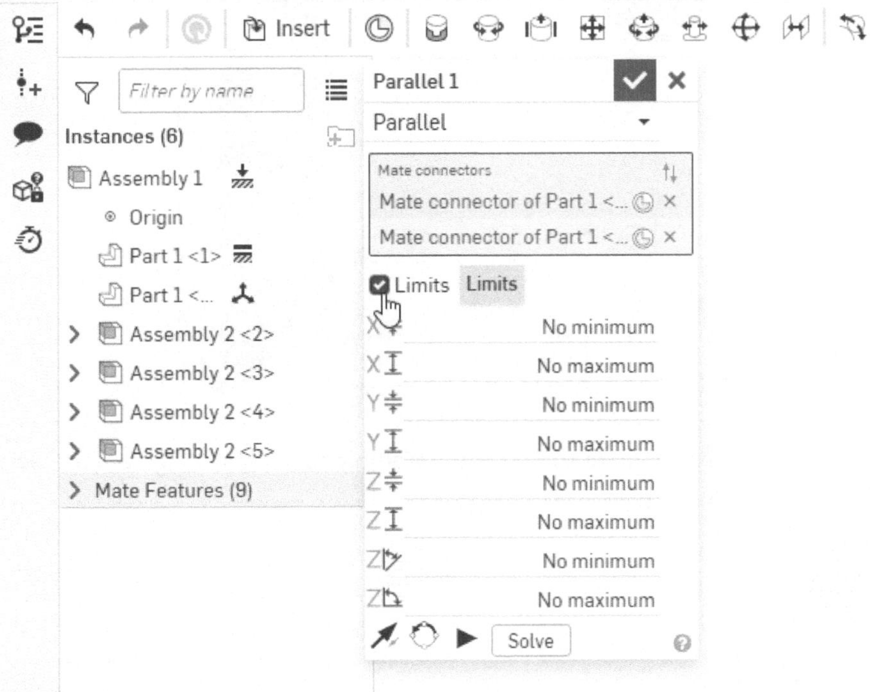

6. After defining the mate connectors and other settings, click on the green checkmark ✓ to confirm and exit the dialog. The Parallel mate is applied between the components, allowing three translational degrees of freedom and one rotational degree of freedom while maintaining the parallel relationship between them, see Figure 9.99.

9.99

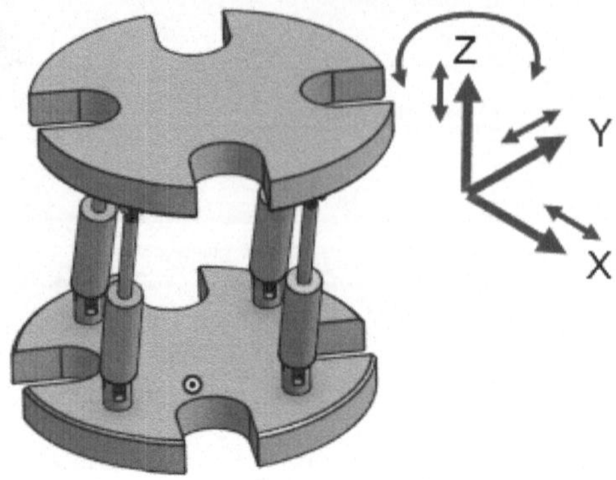

Applying the Tangent Mate

The Tangent mate ensures that entities of two different components remain tangent to each other. Figure 9.100 illustrates an example of a cam and follower mechanism. As the cam rotates, the follower moves up and down along the cam profile while maintaining a tangential relationship between the two components. The method for applying the Tangent mate is discussed below:

9.100

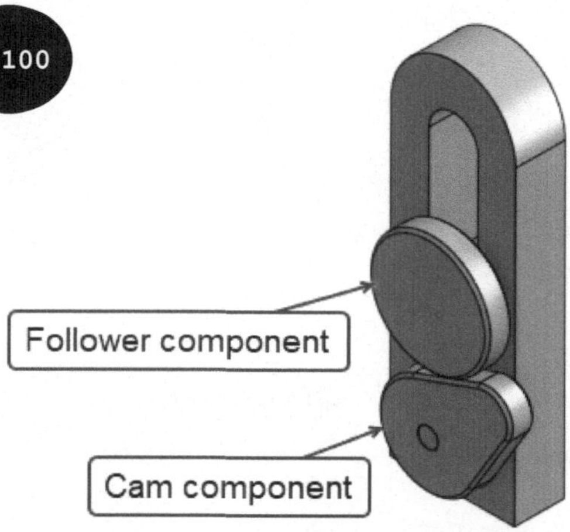

1. Click on the **Tangent mate** tool in the **Assembly** toolbar, see Figure 9.101. The **Tangent** dialog appears, see Figure 9.102.

9.101

9.102

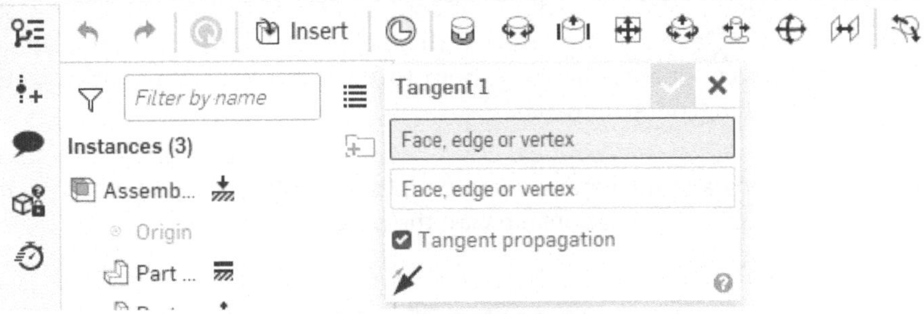

Now, you need to select entities of two different components.

2. Ensure that the **Tangent propagation** check box is selected in the dialog to automatically select all entities that are tangent to the selected one. If you wish to select an individual entity or exclude its tangent entities, you can clear this check box.

9.103

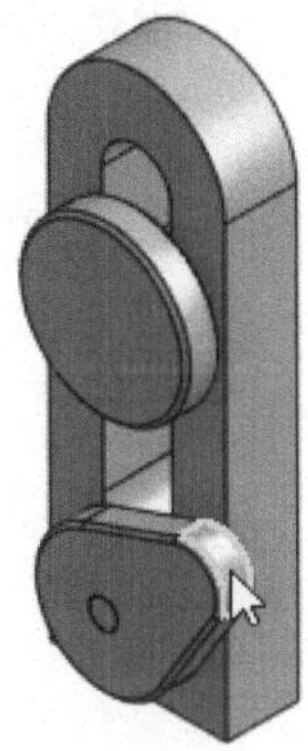

3. Move the cursor over a face, edge, or vertex of the first component, then click to select it, refer to Figure 9.103. With the **Tangent propagation** check box selected, all entities that are tangent to the selected one are also selected, forming a loop.

   Now, you can define an entity of the second component.

4. Move the cursor over a face, edge, or vertex of the second component, then click to select it, refer to Figure 9.104. Both entities of the components become tangent to each other, see Figure 9.105.

9.104

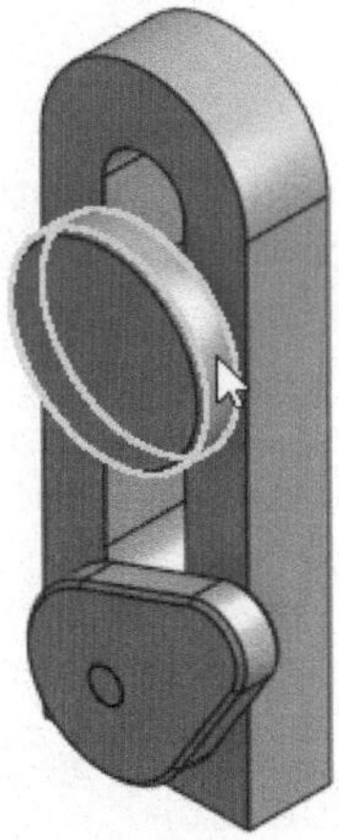

9.105

Flip primary axis : The **Flip primary axis** button is used to reverse the alignment between the selected entities of the components along their primary axis.

5. After selecting entities from two different components to be tangent to each other, click on the green checkmark ✓ to confirm and exit the dialog. The Tangent mate is applied between the entities of the components, allowing them to translate or rotate relative to each other while maintaining the tangent relationship.

Tip: After applying a mate, you can also drag the movable component along its free degree of freedom to review its relationship with the other component.

Grouping Components Together

In Onshape, you can group components such that the relative position of the components gets locked and acts as a single object. The method to group two components is discussed below:

1. Click on the **Group** tool in the **Assembly** toolbar, see Figure 9.106. The **Group** dialog appears, allowing you to select two or more components to group together.

2. Select two or more instances of similar or dissimilar components in the graphics area. The selected components are highlighted in the graphics area, and their names appear in the **Instances** field of the dialog.

3. Click on the green checkmark ✓ to confirm and exit the dialog. The selected components are grouped, locking their relative positions, and they act as a single object.

Activating Snap Mode

In Onshape, you can activate the Snap mode to automatically mate two components by dragging the mate connector of one component over another. The method to activate the Snap mode and then automatically apply a mate between the two components is discussed below:

1. Click on the **Snap mode** tool in the **Assembly** toolbar (see Figure 9.107) or press SHIFT + S. The Snap mode activates, allowing you to automatically mate two components by dragging the mate connector of one component over another. Note that it is a toggle button.

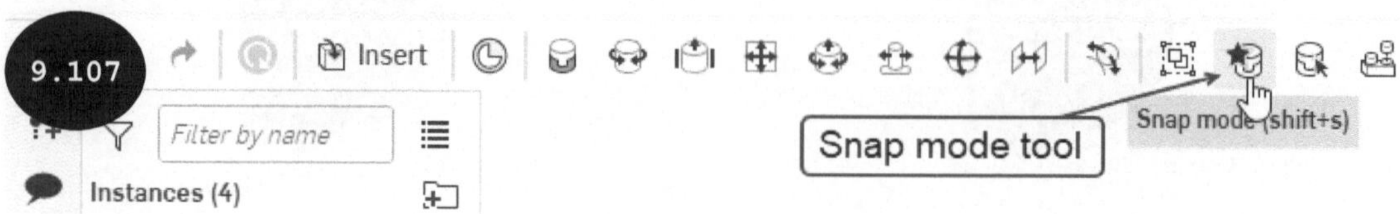

2. After activating the Snap mode, move the cursor over a face, edge, or vertex of the first component (moveable component). The respective geometry highlights, and its snap points appear, see Figure 9.108. Additionally, the mate connector snaps to one of the snap points on the geometry.

9.108

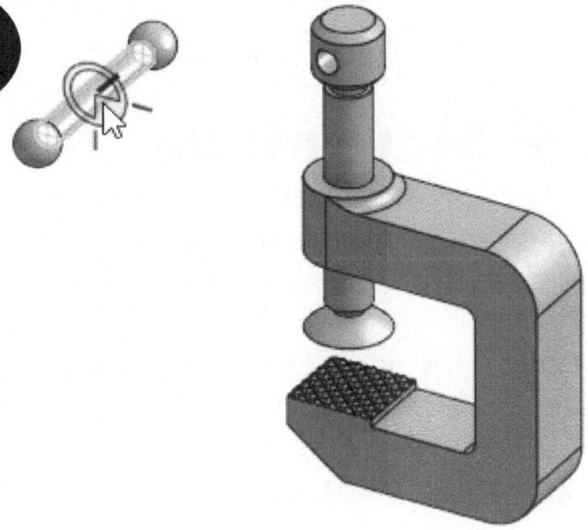

3. Drag the component toward the second component by pressing and holding the left mouse button when the mate connector snaps to the required snap point.

4. When the mate connector of the first component snaps to the desired snap point of the second component (see Figure 9.109), release the left mouse button. The mate connectors of both components coincide in the graphics area, and the **Fastened** dialog appears.

9.109

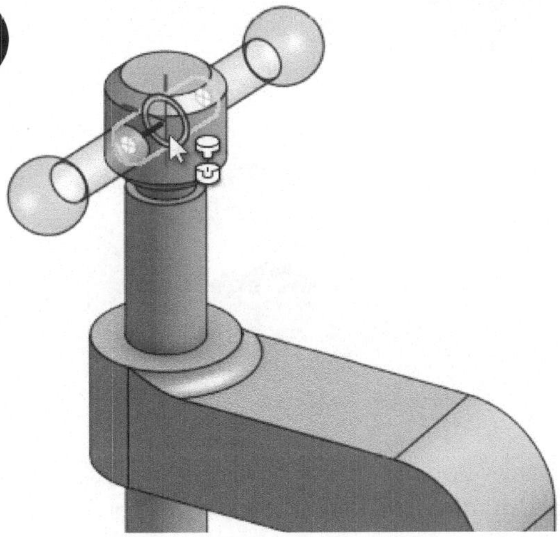

Tip: If needed, you can press the SHIFT key to lock the desired geometry of the component while defining the mate connector at one of its snap points.

5. Select the desired mate in the **Mate type** drop-down list of the dialog, then click on the green checkmark ✓ to confirm and exit the dialog. The selected mate is applied between the components relative to the defined mate connectors.

6. Similarly, you can continue dragging the mate connector of one component to another to apply the required mate type between other sets of components.

7. After applying the mates using this method, click the **Snap mode** tool in the **Assembly** toolbar or press SHIFT + S to deactivate the Snap mode.

Activating Show Mate Mode

In Onshape, you can activate the Show Mate mode to view the existing mates associated with specific components in an assembly. The method to activate the Show Mate mode and view the mates applied to a component is discussed below:

1. Click on the **Show mate mode** tool in the **Assembly** toolbar (see Figure 9.110) or press H. The Show Mate mode activates. Note that it is a toggle button.

2. After activating the Show Mate mode, hove the cursor over a component in the assembly. The mate symbols associated with the component are displayed in the graphics area, see Figure 9.111.

3. After reviewing the mates applied to the components, you can exit the Show Mate mode by clicking the **Show mate mode** tool again or pressing the H key.

Patterning Assembly Components

In Onshape, you can pattern components in the Assembly environment, similar to patterning one or more features of a component in the Part Studio environment.

In the Assembly environment, you create multiple instances of one or more components either linearly along three directions or circularly around an axis using the **Assembly linear pattern** and **Assembly circular pattern** tools, respectively. Both tools are discussed next.

Creating a Linear Component Pattern

The method for creating multiple instances of one or more components linearly along three directions is discussed below:

1. Click on the **Assembly linear pattern** tool in the **Assembly** toolbar, see Figure 9.112. The **Linear pattern** dialog appears, see Figure 9.113.

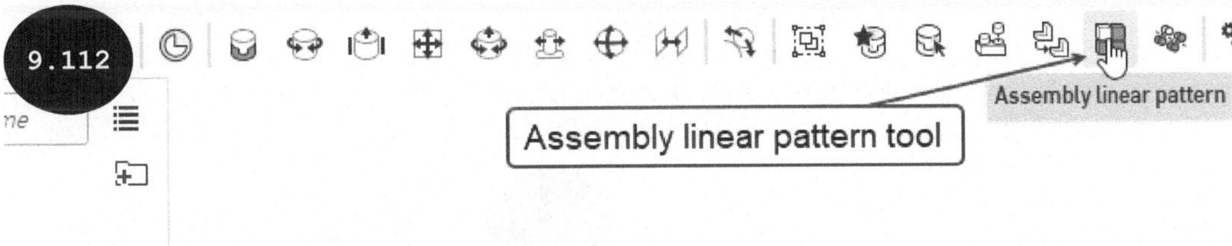

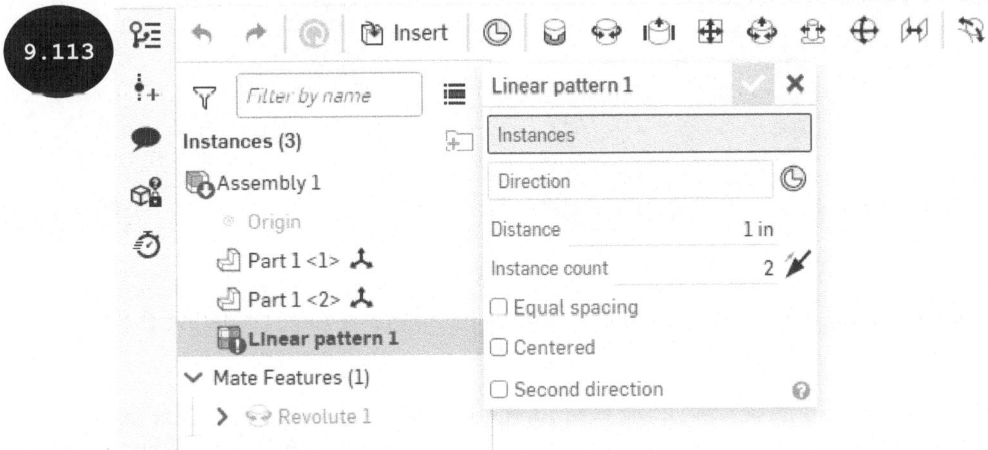

2. Select one or more components to pattern in the graphics area, see Figure 9.114. The selected components are highlighted, and their names appear in the **Instances** field of the dialog.

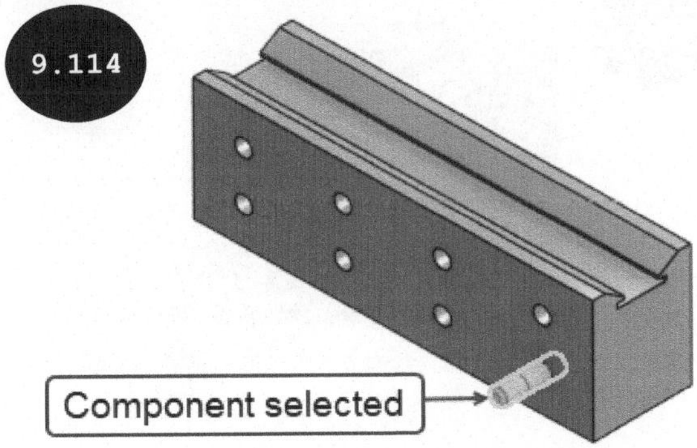

Now, you need to define the first pattern direction.

3. Click the **Direction** field to activate it, then select a linear edge or a planar face to define the first pattern direction, see Figure 9.115. In this figure, a linear edge is selected to define the pattern direction. After defining the pattern direction, a preview of the pattern appears along the selected direction with default specified parameters.

4. Specify the required parameters, such as the spacing between consecutive instances and the total number of pattern instances, in the respective fields. A preview of the pattern appears along the specified direction, see Figure 9.116. The options in this dialog are similar to those covered earlier when creating a pattern for a feature in the Part Studio environment.

9.115

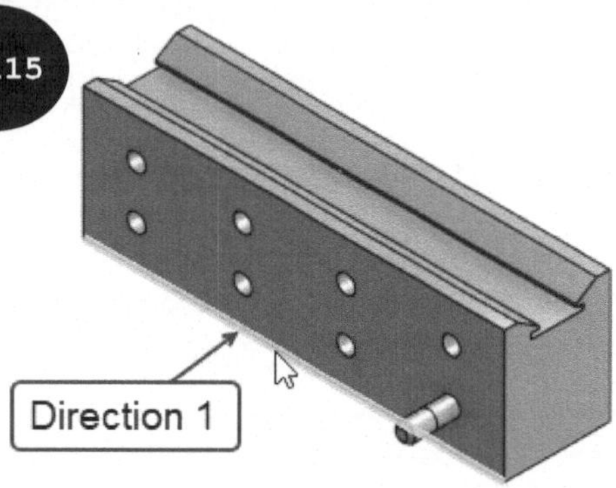

9.116

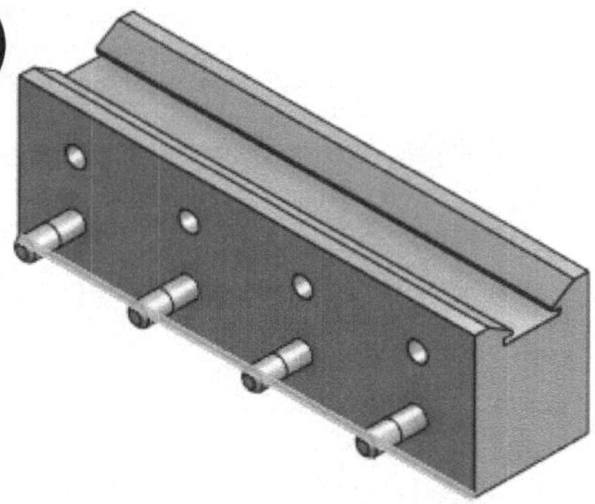

After setting the first pattern direction and its parameters, you can define the second pattern direction.

5. Select the **Second direction** check box, then choose a linear edge or planar face to define the second pattern direction. Enter the required parameters, such as the spacing between consecutive instances and the total number of pattern instances to be created along this direction. The pattern preview updates accordingly in the graphics area, see Figure 9.117.

9.117

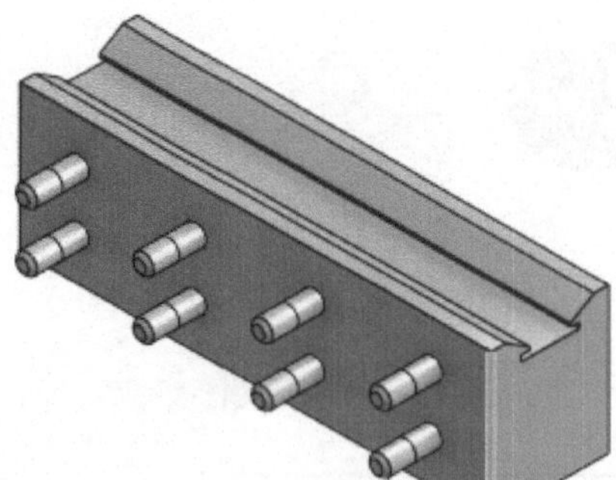

6. Similarly, you can pattern the selected component along a third direction by selecting the **Third direction** check box, if required.

7. After defining the parameters, click on the green checkmark to confirm and exit the dialog. The multiple instances of the selected component are created along the defined linear directions.

Creating a Circular Component Pattern

The method for creating multiple instances of one or more components circularly around an axis is discussed below:

1. Click on the **Assembly circular pattern** tool in the **Assembly** toolbar, see Figure 9.118. The **Circular pattern** dialog appears.

9.118

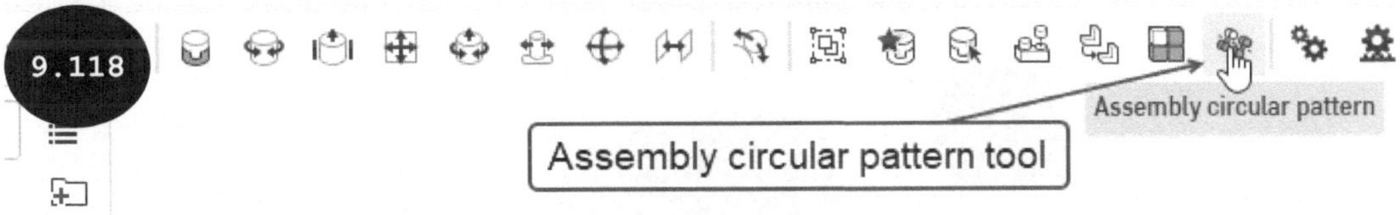

2. Select one or more components to pattern in the graphics area, see Figure 9.119. The selected components are highlighted, and their names appear in the **Instances** field of the dialog.

9.119

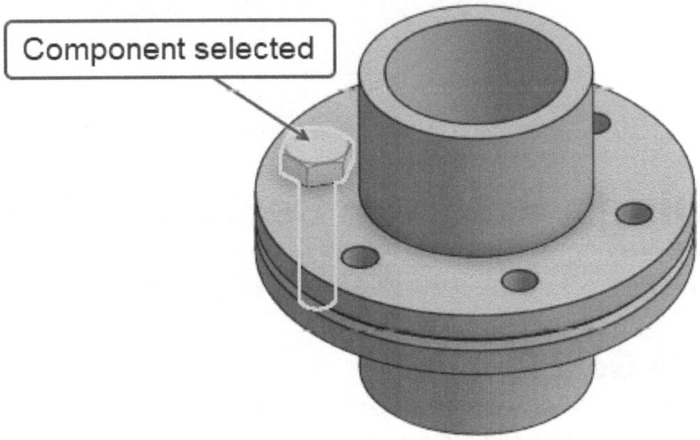

   Now, you can define a pattern axis.

3. Click the **Axis of pattern** field in the dialog to activate it, then select a circular face, a circular edge, a linear edge, or a linear sketch entity to define the pattern axis, see Figure 9.120. This figure illustrates that the outer circular face of the model being selected to define the pattern axis. After defining the pattern axis, a preview of the circular pattern appears with default parameters around the defined pattern axis, see Figure 7.121.

9.120

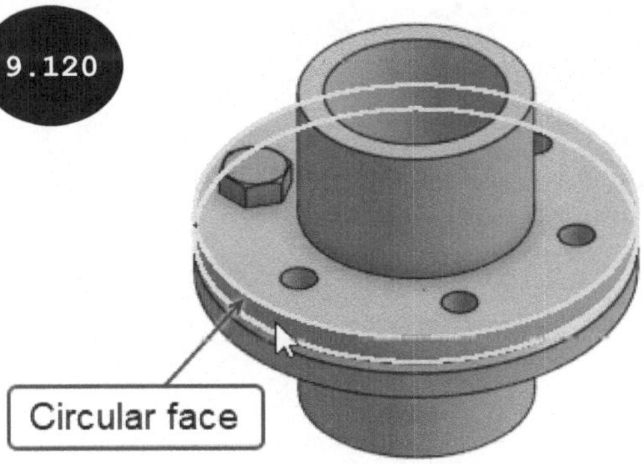

9.121

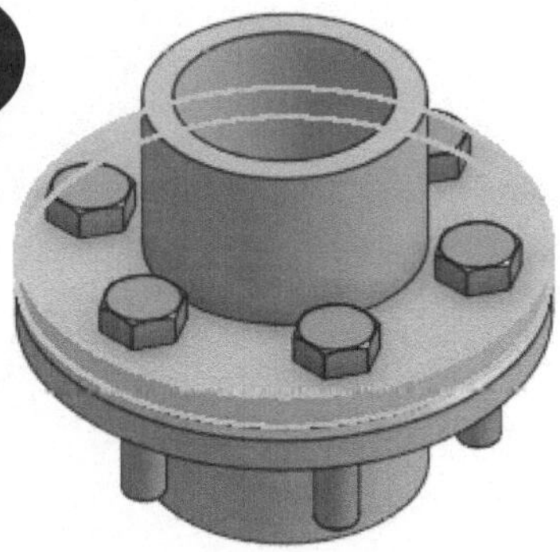

4. Specify the required parameters, such as the total angle value and number of pattern instances, in the respective fields. The pattern preview updates accordingly in the graphics area. The options in this dialog are similar to those covered earlier when creating a pattern for a feature in the Part Studio environment.

5. After defining the required parameters, click on the green checkmark ✓ to confirm and exit the dialog. The multiple instances of the selected component are created around the defined pattern axis, see Figure 9.122.

9.122

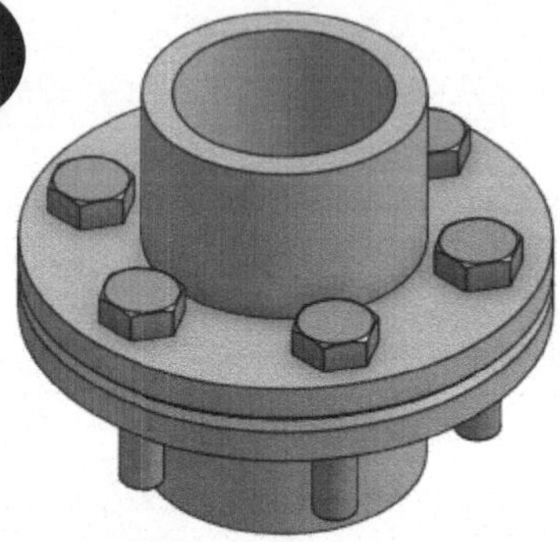

Establishing a Relation Between Two Mates

In Onshape, you can establish relations such as gear, rack and pinion, screw, and linear relations between two mates. The methods for defining these different types of relations are discussed next.

Establishing a Gear Relation

Establishing a gear relation between two mates creates a gear mechanism, allowing the components to rotate relative to each other, see Figure 9.123. You can establish a gear relation between mates that have one degree of rotational freedom, such as Revolute, Cylindrical, Planar, and Parallel mates. Among these, Revolute mates are the most suitable for applying a gear relation. The method for establishing a gear relation is discussed below:

9.123

1. Click on the **Gear relation** tool in the **Assembly** toolbar, see Figure 9.124. The **Gear** dialog appears, see Figure 9.125.

9.124

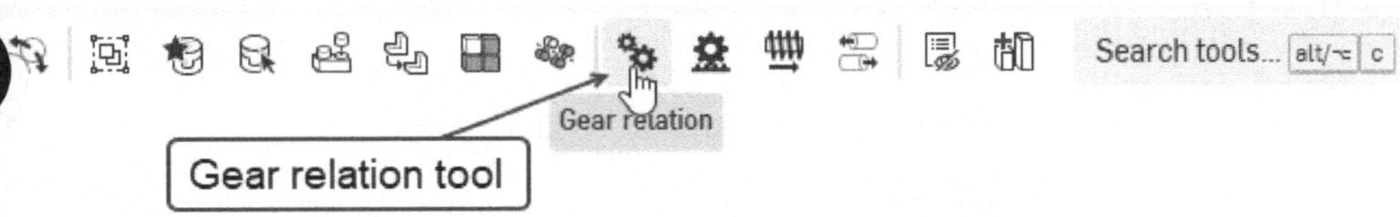

9.125

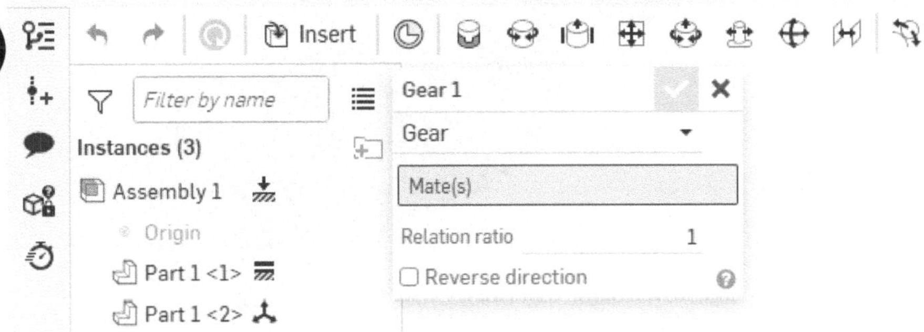

2. Select two revolute mates listed under the **Mate Features** node in the Assembly list, see Figure 9.126. The names of the selected mates appear in the **Mate(s)** field of the dialog.

9.126

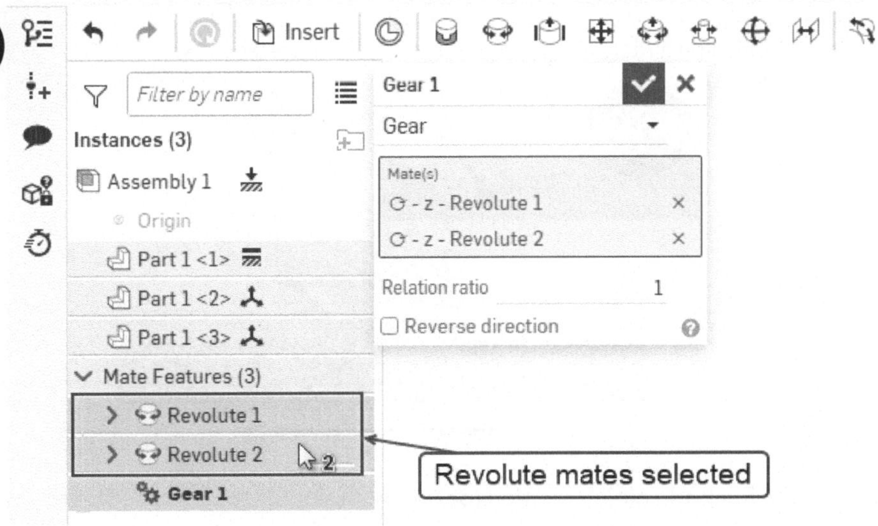

Tip: As mentioned, you can establish a gear relation using Revolute, Cylindrical, Planar, or Parallel mates, as these mates provide one degree of rotational freedom. However, Revolute mates are the most suitable choice for applying a gear relation.

3. Enter the required gear ratio in the **Relation ratio** field of the dialog.

4. If needed, you can reverse the direction of rotation for the gears by selecting the **Reverse direction** check box in the dialog.

5. After defining the required parameters, click on the green checkmark to confirm and exit the dialog. The gear relation is established between the selected mates, allowing the associated components to rotate relative to each other, see Figure 9.127.

9.127

Establishing a Rack and Pinion Relation

Establishing a rack and pinion relation between two mates creates a mechanism that converts the linear motion of one component into the rotational motion of another, and vice versa, see Figure 9.128. The method for establishing a rack and pinion relation is discussed below:

9.128

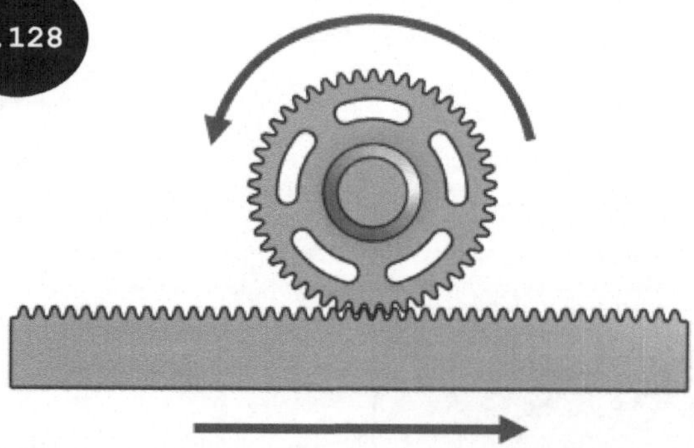

1. Click on the **Rack and pinion relation** tool in the **Assembly** toolbar, see Figure 9.129. The **Rack and pinion** dialog appears, see Figure 9.130.

9.129

9.130

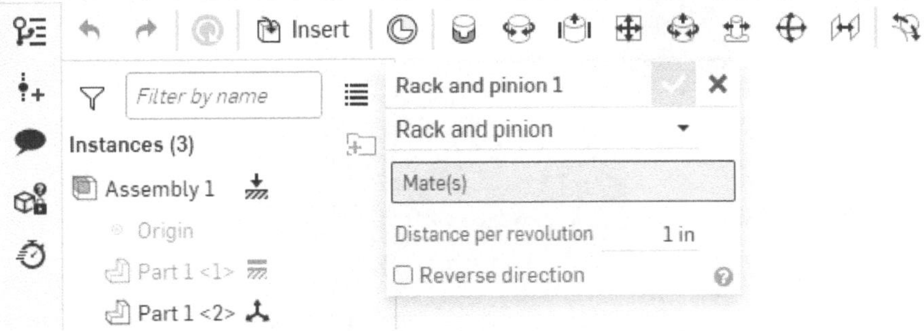

2. Select a Slider mate and a Revolute mate from the **Mate Features** node in the Assembly list, as see Figure 9.131. The selected mates appear in the **Mate(s)** field of the dialog.

9.131

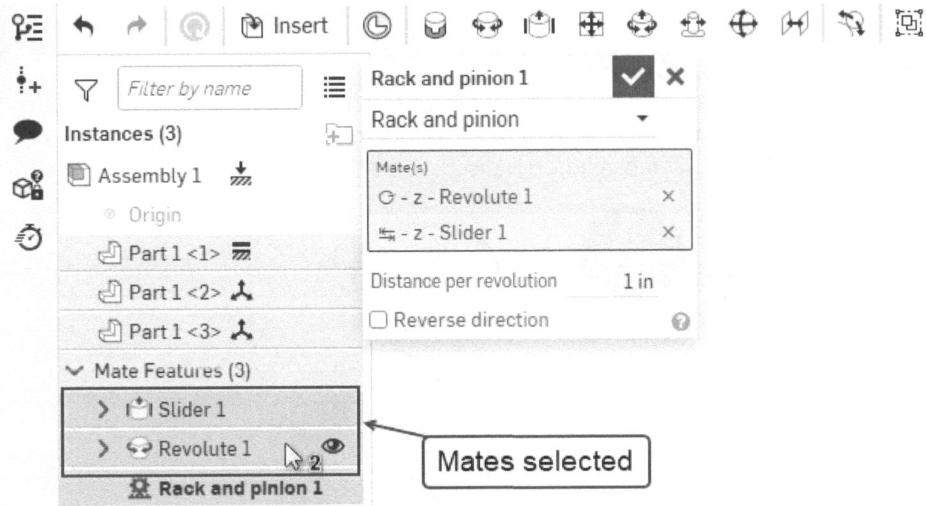

Tip: You can establish a rack and pinion relation between two mates: one with a rotational degree of freedom and the other with a linear degree of freedom. Among such mates, the combination of Revolute and Slider mates is the most suitable for applying a rack and pinion relation.

3. Enter the required distance traveled by the slider component (rack) per revolution of the revolute component (pinion) in the **Distance per revolution** field of the dialog.

4. If needed, you can reverse the direction by selecting the **Reverse direction** check box in the dialog.

5. After defining the required parameters, click on the green checkmark ✓ to confirm and exit the dialog. The rack and pinion relation is established between the selected mates, allowing the slider component (rack) to slide corresponding to each revolution of the revolute component (pinion), see Figure 9.132.

9.132

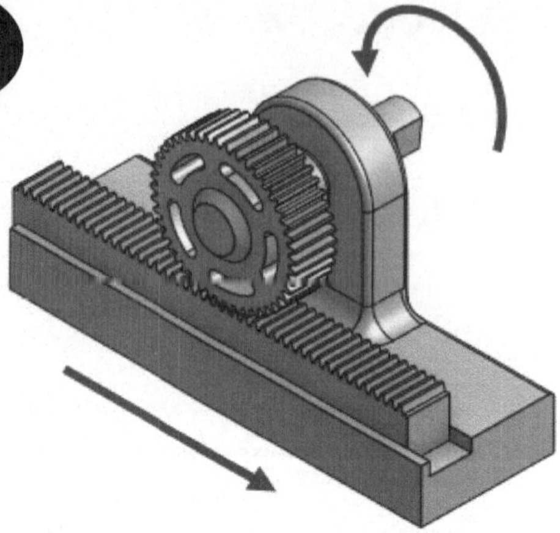

Establishing a Screw Relation

In onshape, you can establish a screw relation on a Cylindrical mate to constrain its rotational degree of freedom to the translational degree of freedom, forming a screw mechanism, see Figure 9.133. The method for establishing a screw relation is discussed below:

9.133

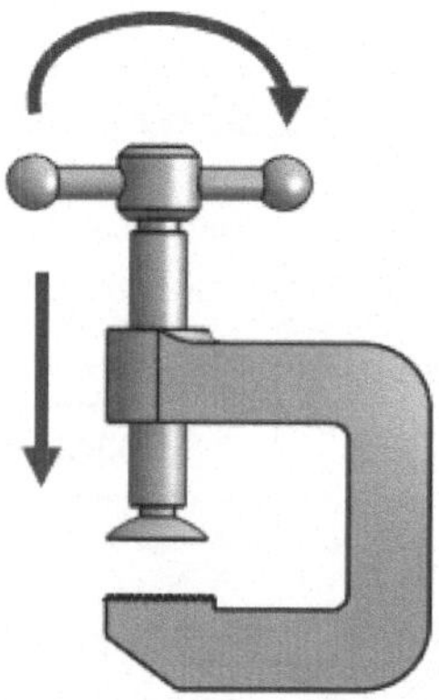

1. Click on the **Screw relation** tool in the **Assembly** toolbar, see Figure 9.134. The **Screw** dialog appears.

9.134

2. Select a Cylindrical mate from the **Mate Features** node in the Assembly list for establishing a screw relation, as see Figure 9.135. The selected mate appear in the **Mate(s)** field of the dialog.

9.135

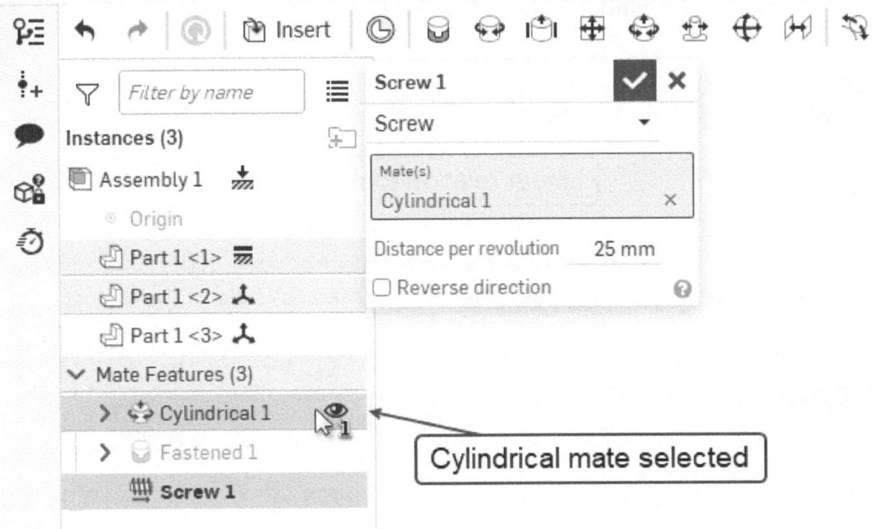

3. Enter the required distance traveled by the component per revolution in the **Distance per revolution** field of the dialog box.

4. If needed, you can reverse the direction by selecting the **Reverse direction** check box in the dialog.

5. After defining the required parameters, click on the green checkmark to confirm and exit the dialog. The screw relation is established to the selected Cylindrical mate, allowing the associated component to translate relative to its revolution.

Establishing a Linear Relation

Establishing a linear relation between two mates creates a mechanism that converts the linear motion of one component into the linear motion of another, either in the same or opposite direction, see Figure 9.136. The method for establishing a linear relation is discussed below:

9.136

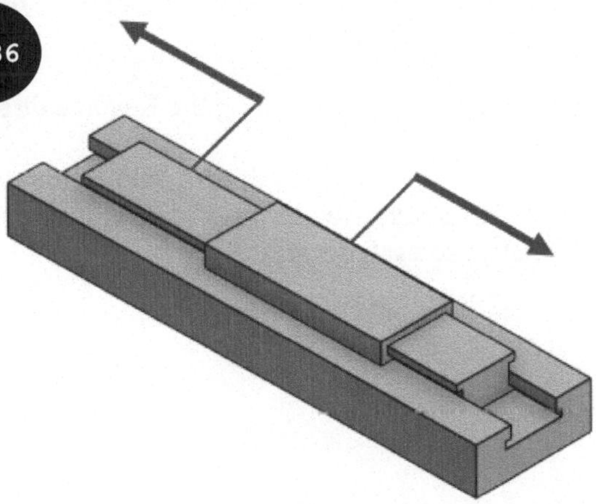

1. Click on the **Linear relation** tool in the **Assembly** toolbar, see Figure 9.137. The **Linear** dialog appears.

2. Select two Slider mates listed under the **Mate Features** node in the Assembly list, see Figure 9.138. The names of the selected mates appear in the **Mate(s)** field of the dialog.

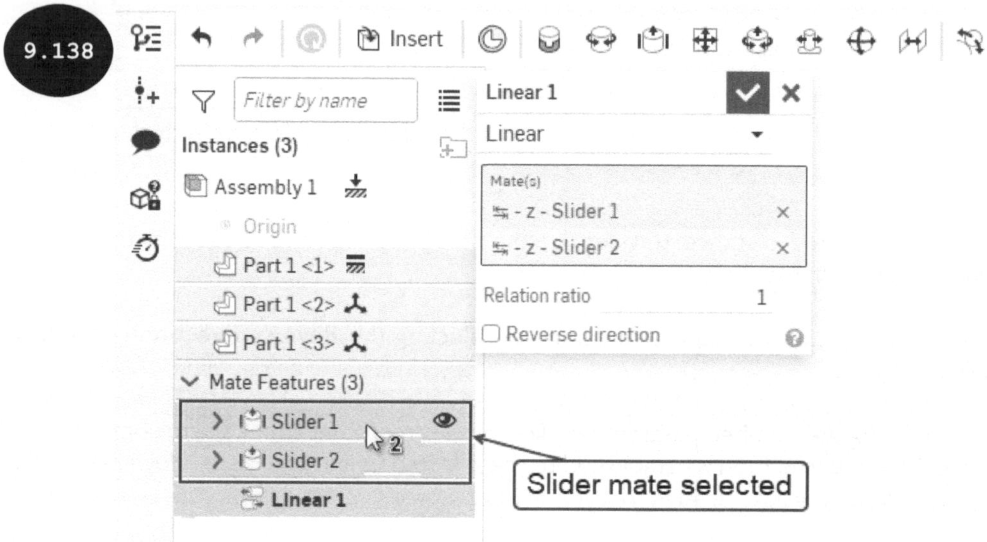

Tip: You can establish a linear relation between mates that have one degree of translational freedom, such as Slider mates, which are the most suitable mate type for applying a linear relation.

3. Enter the required ratio in the Relation ratio field of the dialog box, which defines the translational movement between the associated components.

4. If needed, you can reverse the direction by selecting the **Reverse direction** check box.

5. After defining the required parameters, click on the green checkmark ✓ to confirm and exit the dialog. The linear relation is established between the selected Slider mates, allowing the associated components to translate relative to each other.

Tutorial 1

Create an assembly, as shown in Figure 9.139 by applying the mates. Different views and dimensions of individual components of the assembly are shown in Figures 9.140 through 9.144. All dimensions are in mm.

9.139

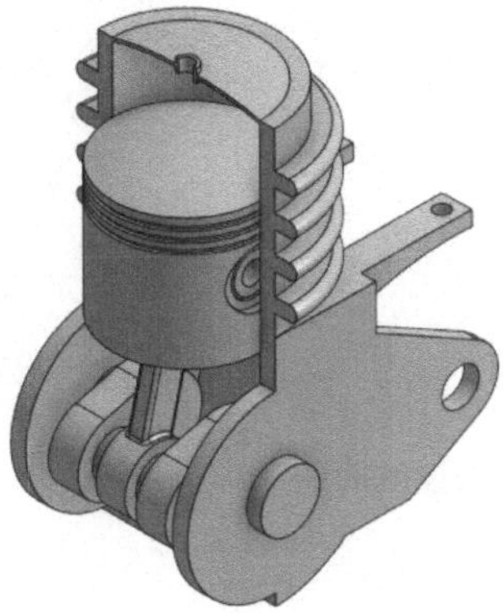

9.140

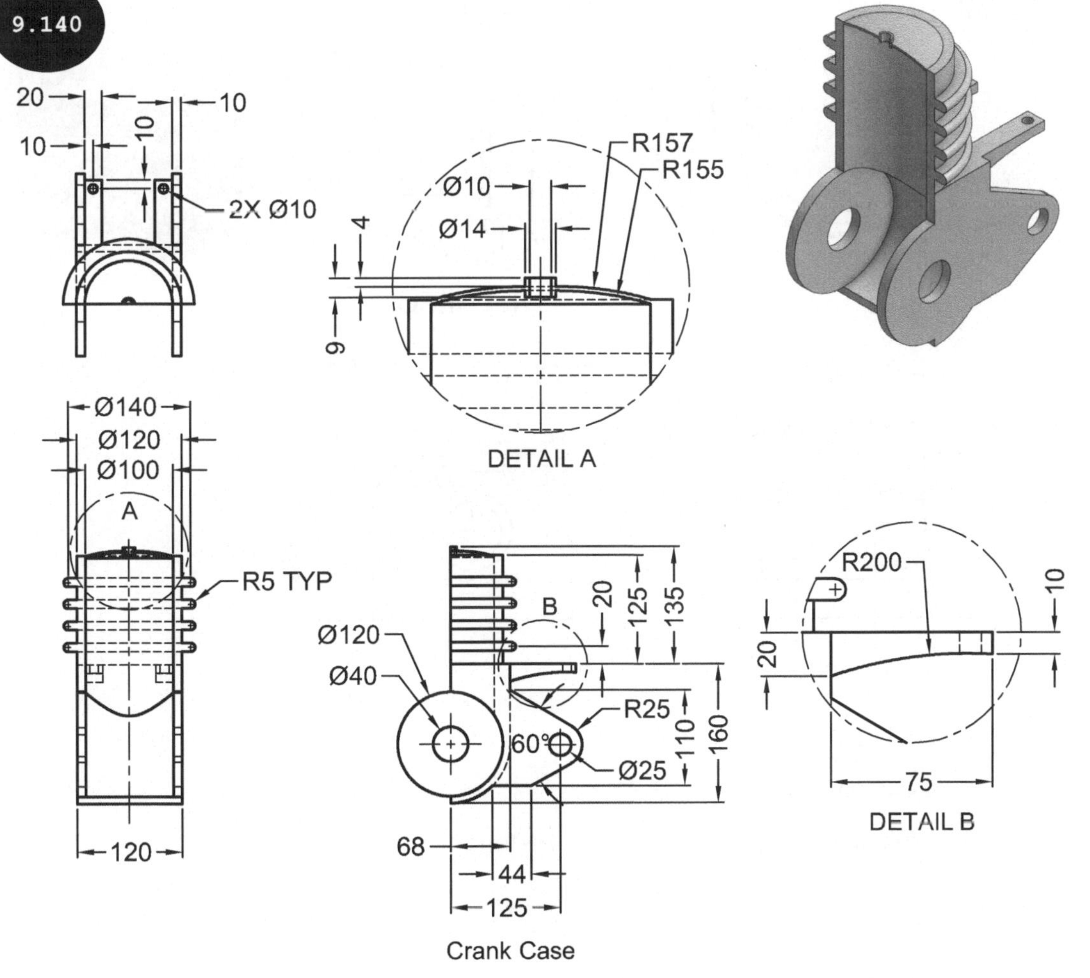

Crank Case

9.141

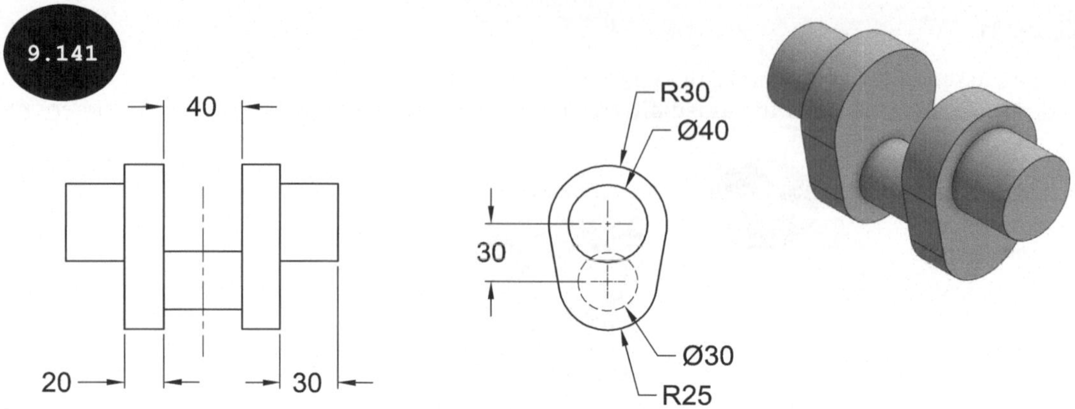

Crank Shaft

9.142

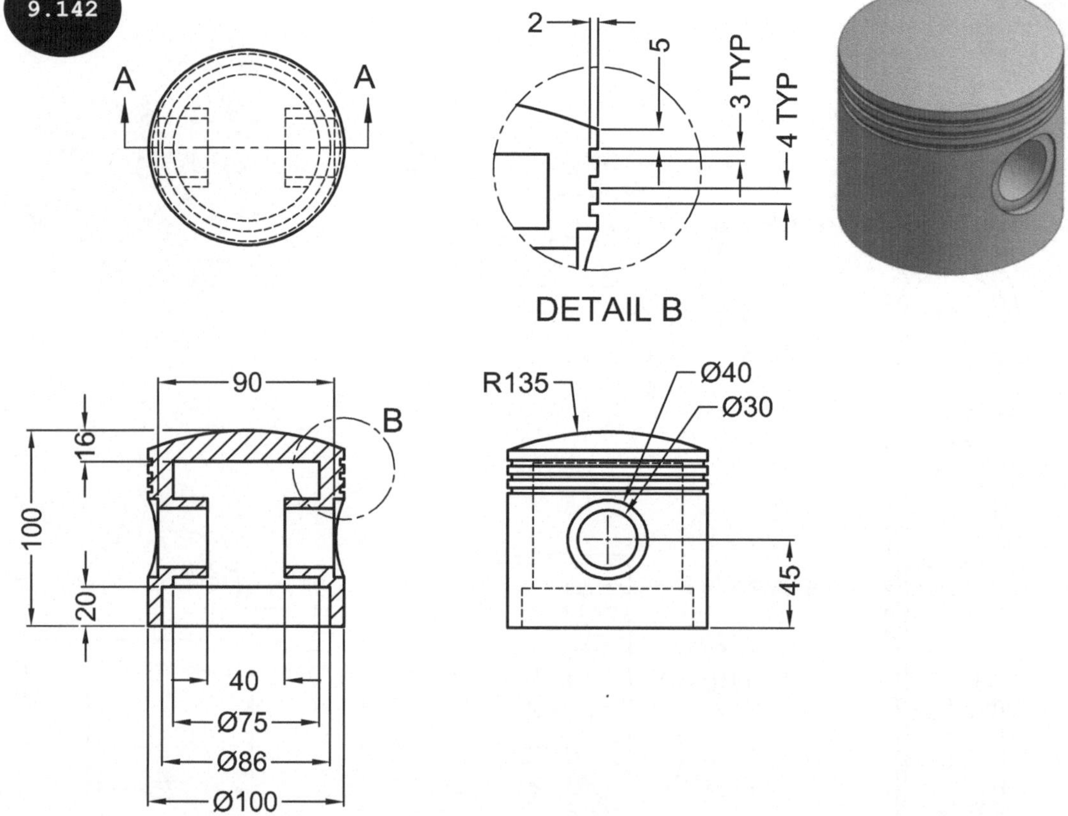

SECTION A-A

Piston

9.143

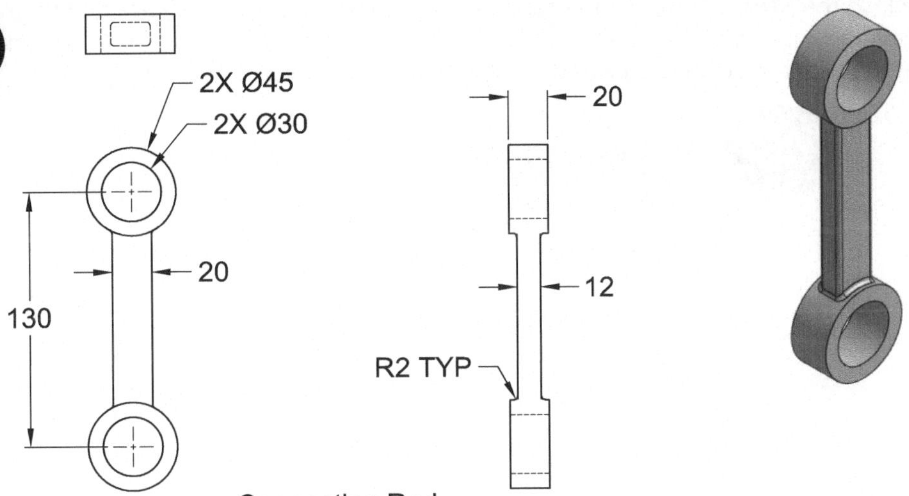

Connecting Rod

9.144

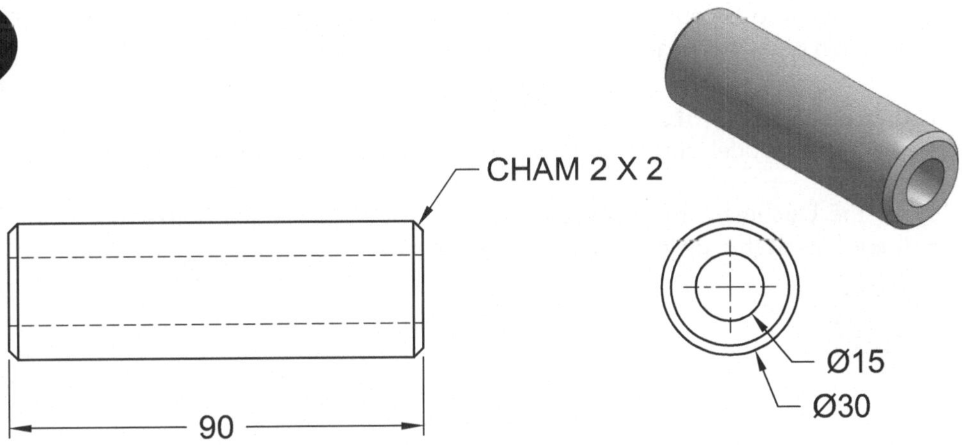

Piston Pin

Section 1: Starting a New Design Document

1. Launch Onshape (***onshape.com***) and log in to your account if you're not already logged in. The **Documents Page** appears.

Note: If you are within a document, click on the **Onshape** logo located in the top left corner of the browser to display the **Documents Page**, see Figure 9.145.

9.145

2. Click on the **Create** button at the top left corner of the **Documents Page** and then click on the **Document** option in the menu that appears, see Figure 9.146. The **New document** window appears with the default name of the document as "**Untitled document**".

9.146

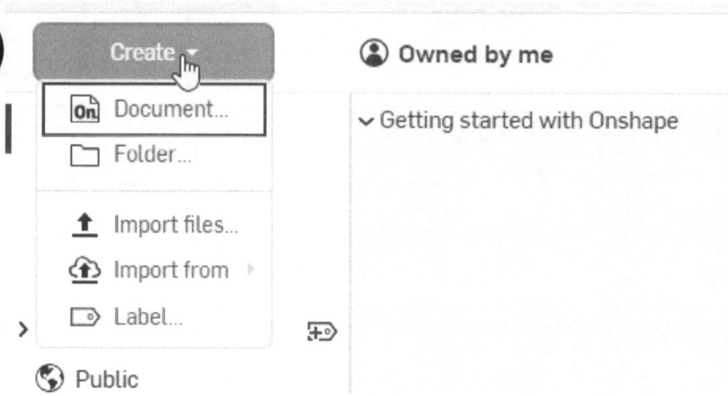

3. Enter **C09 Tutorial 01** as the name of the design document in the **New document** window, and then click on the **Create** button or the **Create Public Document** button, depending on your subscription type. A new document with the specified name is opened.

Section 2: Settings Units

Before creating the model, ensure that the document's units are properly defined.

1. Invoke the **Document** menu by clicking on the ≡ icon (three horizontal lines) next to the **Onshape** logo at the top left corner, see Figure 9.147.

9.147

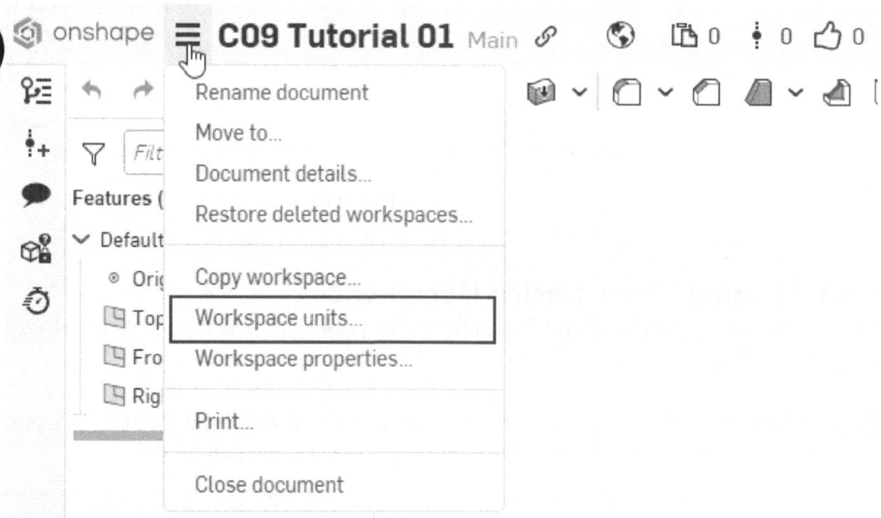

2. Click on the **Workspace units** option in the **Document** menu, refer to Figure 9.147. The **Workspace units** dialog appears.

3. Select the **Millimeter** unit in the **Length default unit** drop-down list and set its precision to **0.1** in the respective **Display decimals** drop-down list of the **Workspace units** dialog.

4. After selecting the required unit of length measurement and the decimal precision for the current design document, click on the green checkmark ✓ to confirm the selection and exit the dialog. The millimeter is defined as the unit for the length measurement.

Section 3: Creating All Components of the Assembly

In this section, you will create all components of the assembly one by one in separate Part Studio environments within the current design file.

1. Ensure that the **Part Studio 1** tab is activated to create the first component of the assembly.

2. Create the Crank Case component of the assembly as the first component, refer to Figure 9.148. You can refer to Figure 9.140 for dimensions.

9.148

Note: You can also email us at ***info@cadartifex.com*** to request access to the complete assembly of this tutorial, including all individual components. Upon receiving your email, we will share the assembly with you.

After creating the component, rename the **Part Studio 1** tab to **Crank Case**.

3. Right-click on the **Part Studio 1** tab and then select the **Rename** option in the shortcut menu that appears, see Figure 9.149. The current name appears in an edit field.

9.149

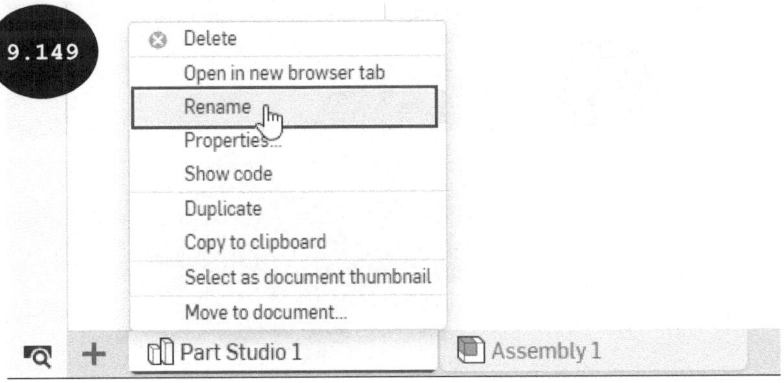

4. Enter **Crank Case** as the name of the component in the edit field, then click anywhere in the graphics area to confirm.

   Now, you can create the second component of the assembly in a new **Part Studio** tab.

5. Click on the **Insert new tab** button (+ sign) at the lower left corner of the screen to display a menu, see Figure 9.150.

9.150

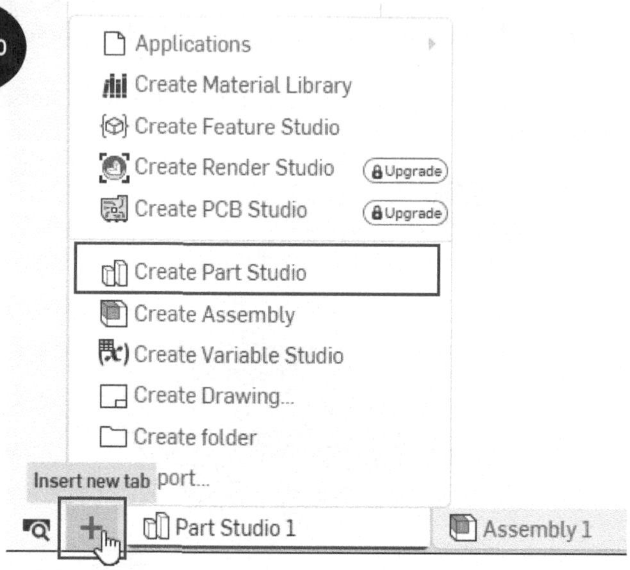

6. Select the **Create Part Studio** option in the menu, refer to Figure 9.151. A new Part Studio tab is added with a default name "**Part Studio 1**" and is activated, by default.

9.151

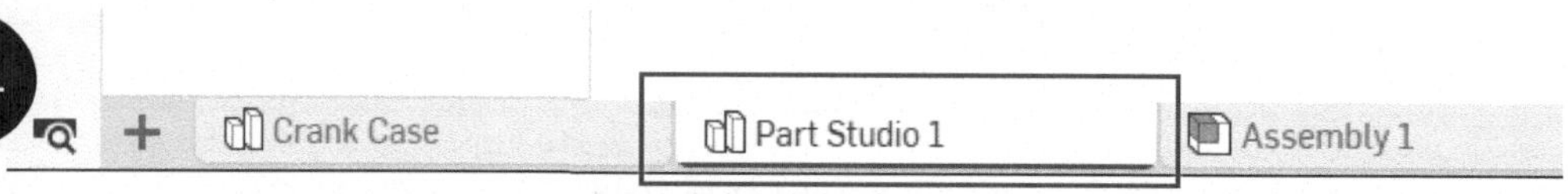

   Now, you can created the second component (Crank Shaft) in the newly added **Part Studio 1** tab.

7. Create the Crank Shaft component of the assembly as the second component, refer to Figure 9.152. You can refer to Figure 9.141 for dimensions.

9.152

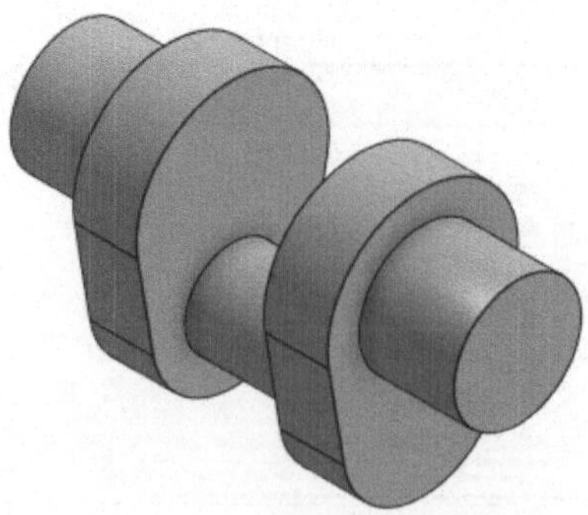

8. After creating the component, rename the **Part Studio 1** tab to **Crank Shaft** as the name of the component.

9. Similarly, create all other components of the assembly one by one in separate **Part Studio** tabs.

Note: As mentioned earlier, you can email us at info@cadartifex.com to request access to the complete assembly of this tutorial, including all individual components.

Section 4: Creating the Assembly - Single Cylinder Engine

Now, you can create the assembly (**Single Cylinder Engine**).

1. Click on the **Assembly 1** tab at the bottom of the screen to open the Assembly environment.

2. Click on the **Insert** tool in the **Assembly** toolbar, see Figure 9.153. The **Insert parts and assemblies** dialog appears, see Figure 9.154.

9.153

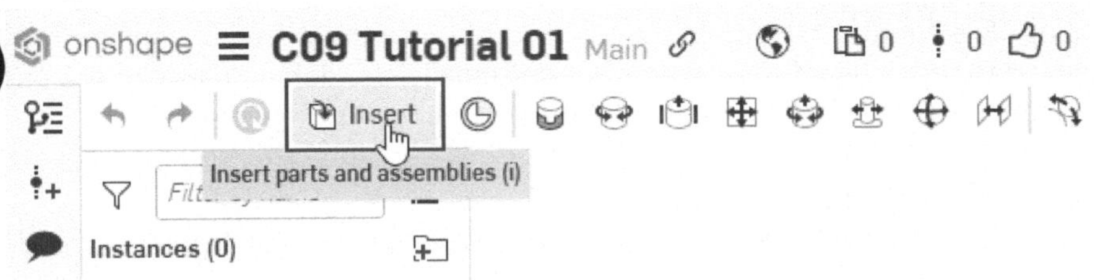

9.154

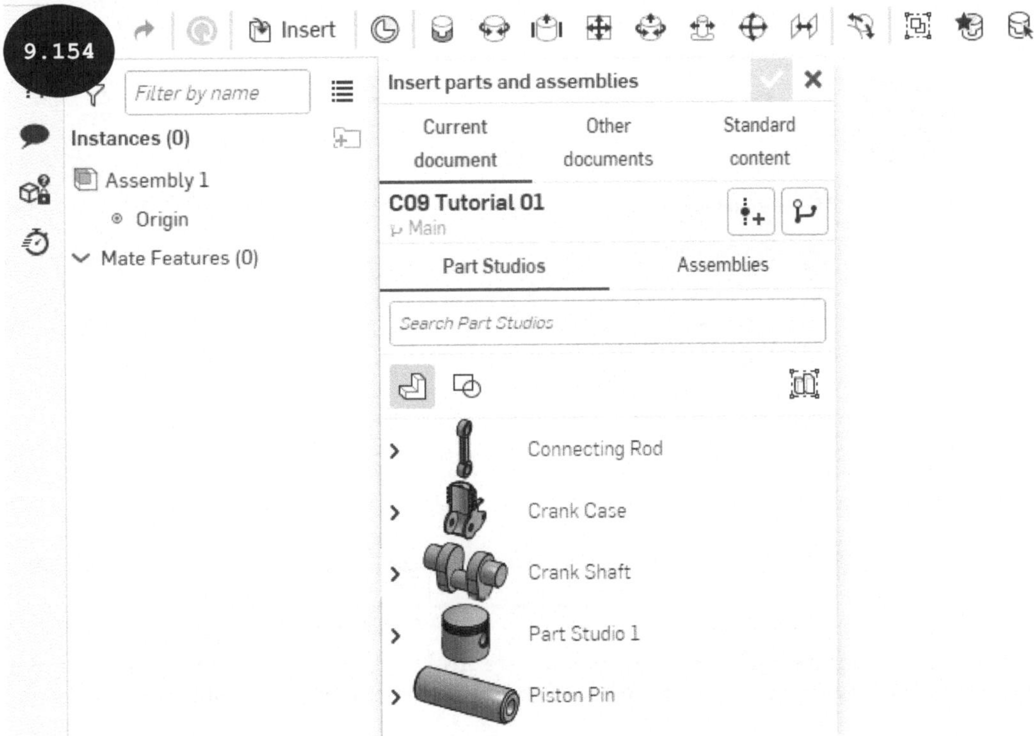

3. Ensure that the **Current document** tab is activated in the **Insert parts and assemblies** dialog to insert the components from the current document only, refer to Figure 9.154.

4. Select the **Crank Case** component from the list of components in the **Current Document** tab. The component appears attached to your cursor, see Figure 9.155.

9.155

5. Click on the green checkmark to confirm the insertion of the selected component and exit the dialog. The Crank Case component is inserted into the Assembly environment with its origin aligned to the origin of the Assembly. Additionally, the default name of the part appears in the Assembly list located at the top left of the screen, refer to Figure 9.156.

Section 5: Fixing the First Component

Now, you need to fix the Crank Case component to constrain all its degrees of freedom.

1. Right-click on the component either in the graphics area or in the Assembly list to display a shortcut menu, see Figure 9.156.

9.156

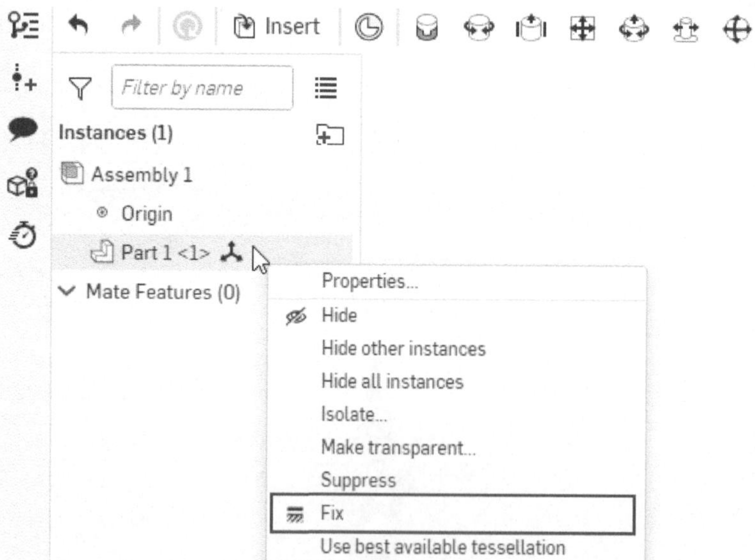

2. Select the **Fix** option in the shortcut menu, refer to Figure 9.156. The Crank Case component becomes fixed, and a fix symbol appears next to its name in the Assembly list.

Section 6: Inserting the Second Component

Now, you need to insert the second component (**Crank Shaft**) of the assembly.

1. Click on the **Insert** tool in the **Assembly** toolbar, see Figure 9.157. The **Insert parts and assemblies** dialog appears.

9.157

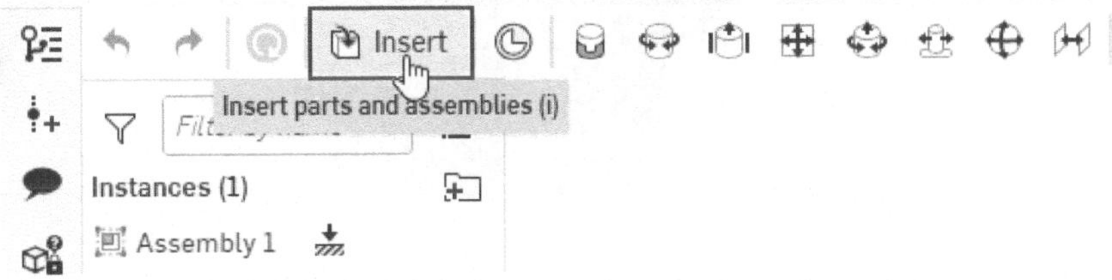

2. Select the **Crank Shaft** component from the list of components in the **Current Document** tab of the dialog. The Crank Shaft appears attached to your cursor, see Figure 9.158.

9.158

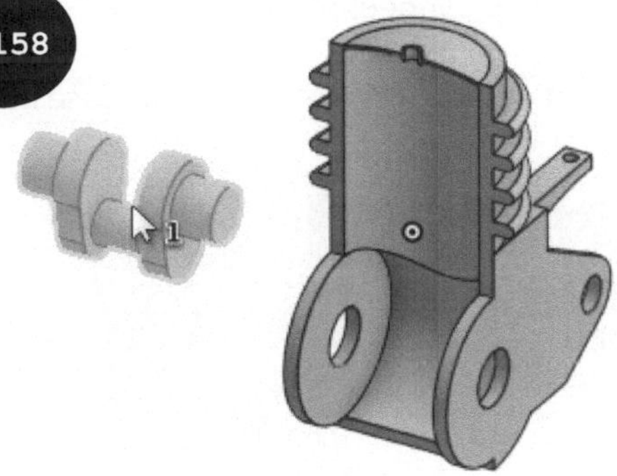

3. Click anywhere in the graphics area to place the component at the desired position.

Tip: It is recommended to define the position of the component such that it does not intersect with the existing components of the assembly.

4. After defining the position of the component, click on the green checkmark to confirm the placement and exit the dialog. The Crank Shaft is inserted at the specified position.

Section 7: Applying the Revolute Mate

Now, you need to apply a Revolute mate between the Crank Shaft and Crank Case components of the assembly to enable the Crank Shaft component to rotate about an axis.

1. Click on the **Revolute mate** tool in the **Assembly** toolbar, see Figure 9.159. The **Revolute** dialog appears.

9.159

2. Move the cursor over the rightmost circular edge of the Crank Shaft component, see Figure 9.160. The edge highlights, and the mate connector snaps to the center snap point of the edge.

9.160

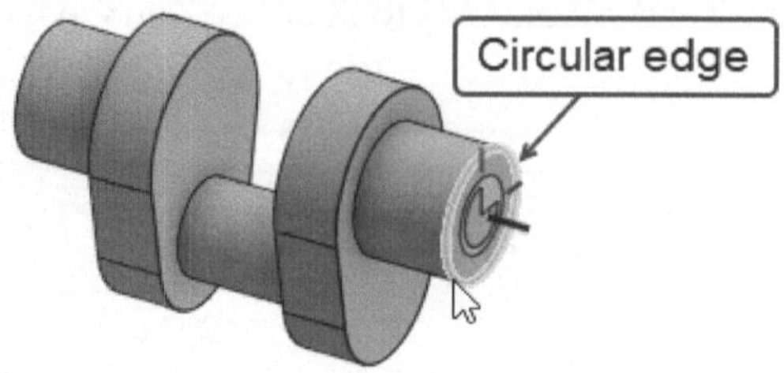

3. Click the left mouse button when the mate connector snaps to the center snap point of the circular edge, refer to Figure 9.160. The position of the mate connector is defined at the center of the circular edge.

   Now, you need to define the mate connector on the Crank Case component.

4. Move the cursor over the right circular edge of the Crank Case component, see Figure 9.161.

9.161

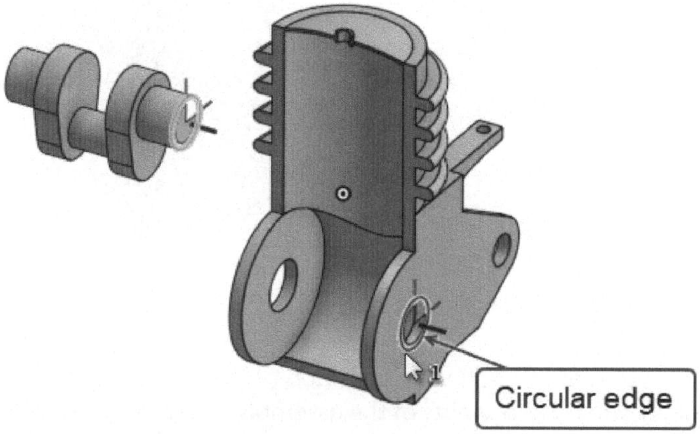

5. Click when the circular edge highlights, and the mate connector snaps to its center snap point, see Figure 9.161. The Crank Shaft component moves towards the Crank Case component, and the mate connectors of both components coincide in the graphics area, see Figure 9.162. Additionally, the **Mate** Pop-up dialog appears.

9.162

6. Select the **Offset** check box in the **Revolute** dialog to define an offset distance between the selected mate connectors, see Figure 9.163.

9.163

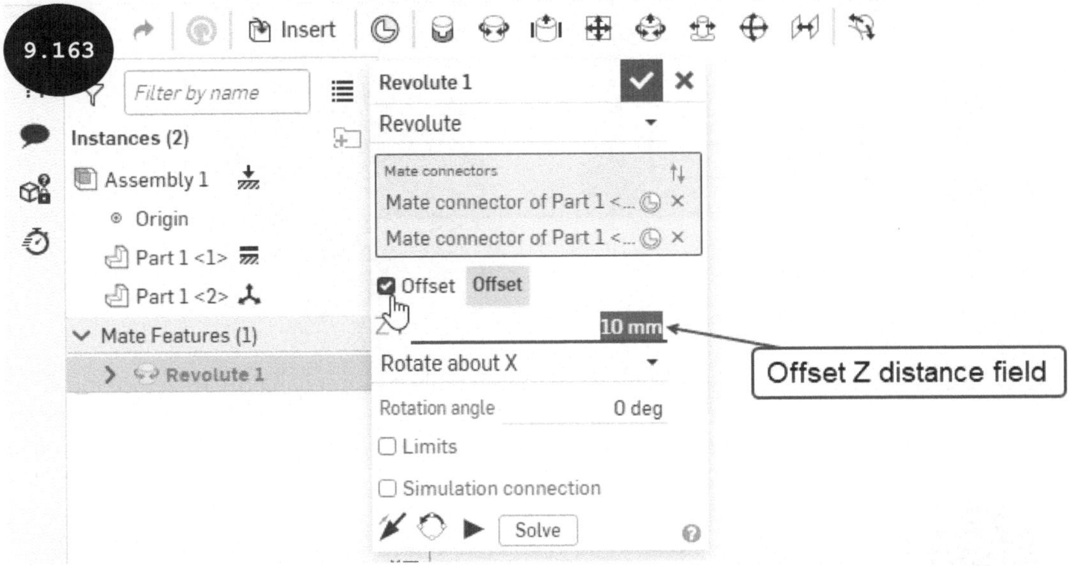

7. Enter 10 mm in the **Offset Z distance** field of the dialog (refer to Figure 9.163), then press ENTER.

8. Click on the green checkmark to confirm to settings and exit the dialog. The Revolute mate is applied between the components, removing all degrees of freedom except for one rotational degree of freedom of the Crank Shaft component, see Figure 9.164.

9.164

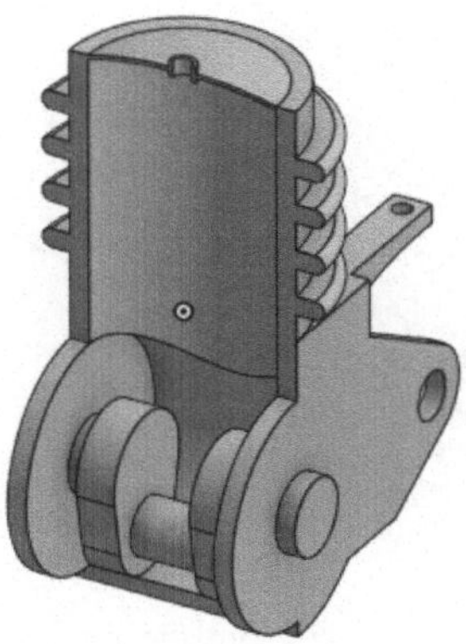

Section 8: Inserting and Assembling the Third Component

Now, you need to insert and assemble the Connecting Rod component of the assembly.

1. Insert the Connecting Rod component as the third component of the assembly using the **Insert** tool, see Figure 9.165. Position it in the graphics area to avoid intersecting with the existing components of the assembly.

9.165

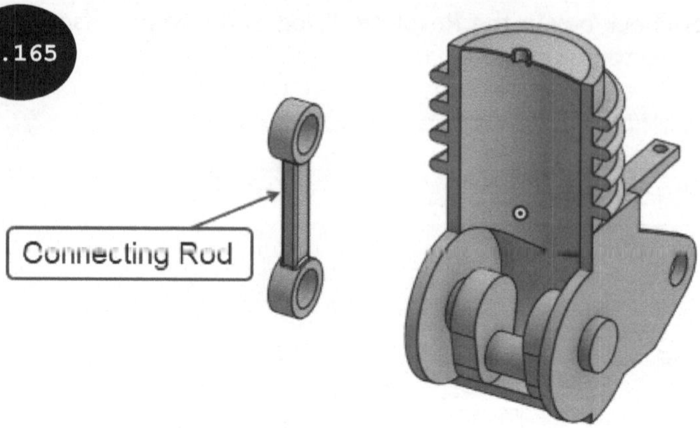

After inserting the Connecting Rod, you need to assembly it by applying the Revolute mate.

2. Click on the **Revolute mate** tool in the **Assembly** toolbar, see Figure 9.166. The **Revolute** dialog appears.

9.166

3. Hover the cursor over the lower inner circular face of the Connecting Rod, see Figure 9.167. The face highlights, and its three snap points: front, middle, and back, become visible.

9.167

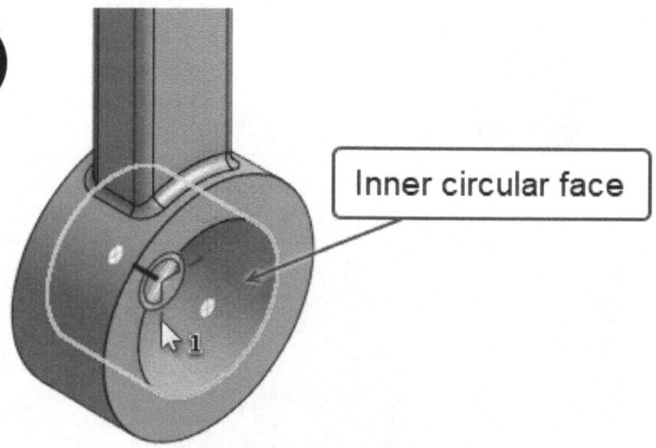

4. Press and hold the SHIFT key to lock the highlighted face, then click when the mate connector snaps to the middle snap point to define its position, refer to Figure 9.167.

   Now, you need to define the mate connector on the Crank Shaft component.

5. Move the cursor over the middle circular face of the Crank Shaft component, refer to Figure 9.168. The face gets highlighted, and its snap points appear.

9.168

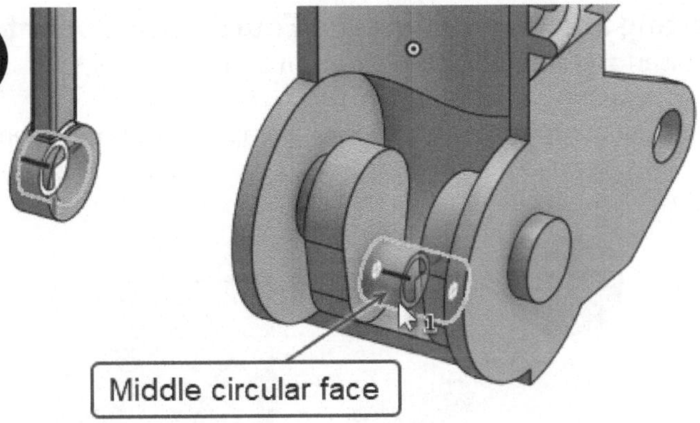

6. Press the SHIFT key, then click the left mouse button when the mate connector snaps to the middle snap point of the highlighted face (see Figure 9.168). The position of the mate connector is defined, and the Connecting Rod component moves toward the Crank Shaft component so that the defined connectors of both components coincide in the graphics area, see Figure 9.169.

9.169

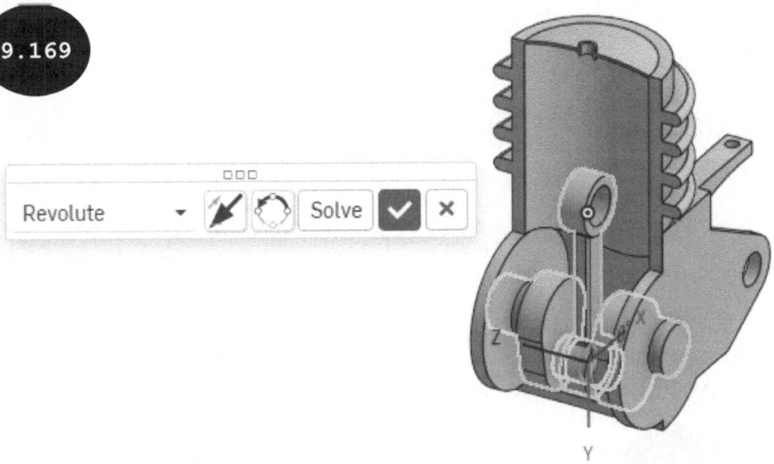

7. Click on the green checkmark ✓ to confirm and exit the dialog. The Revolute mate is applied between the components, removing all degrees of freedom except for one rotational degree of freedom of the Connecting Rod component, see Figure 9.170.

9.170

Section 9: Inserting and Assembling the Fourth Component

Now, you need to insert and assemble the Piston Pin of the assembly.

1. Insert the Piston Pin component as the fourth component of the assembly using the **Insert** tool, see Figure 9.171. Position it in the graphics area to avoid intersecting with the existing components of the assembly.

9.171

After inserting the Piston Pin, you need to assembly it by applying the Revolute mate.

2. Click on the **Revolute mate** tool in the **Assembly** toolbar, see Figure 9.172. The **Revolute** dialog appears.

9.172

3. Hover the cursor over the outer circular face of the Piston Pin, see Figure 9.173. The face highlights, and its three snap points: front, middle, and back, become visible.

9.173

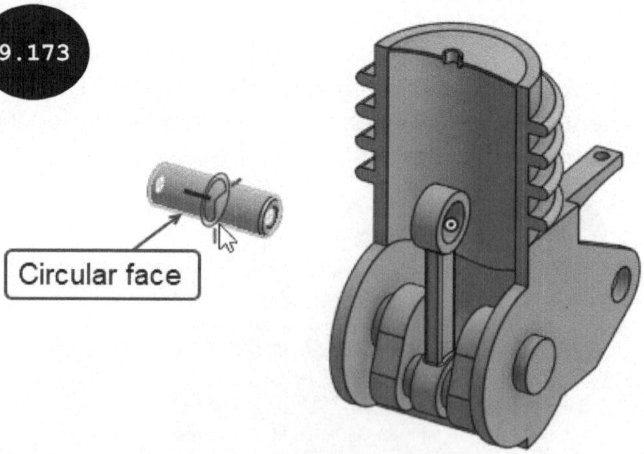

4. Press and hold the SHIFT key to lock the highlighted face, then click when the mate connector snaps to the middle snap point to define its position, refer to Figure 9.173.

Now, you need to define the mate connector on the Connecting Rod component.

5. Move the cursor over the upper inner circular face of the Connecting Rod component, see Figure 9.174. The face gets highlighted, and its three snap points appear.

9.174

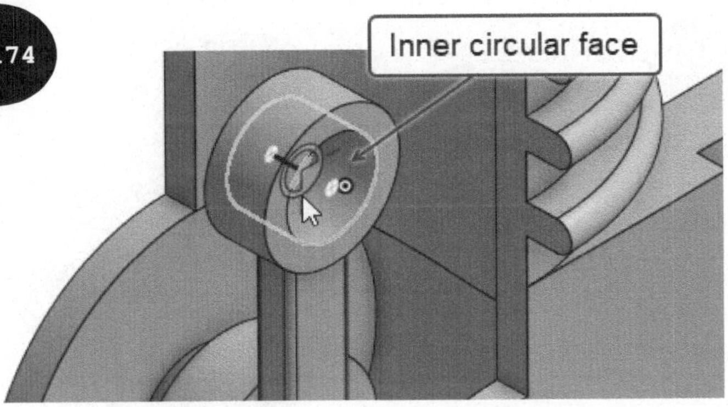

6. Press the SHIFT key, then click the left mouse button when the mate connector snaps to the middle snap point of the highlighted face (refer to Figure 9.174). The position of the mate connector is defined, and the Piston Pin component moves toward the Connecting Rod component so that the defined connectors of both components coincide, see Figure 9.175.

9.175

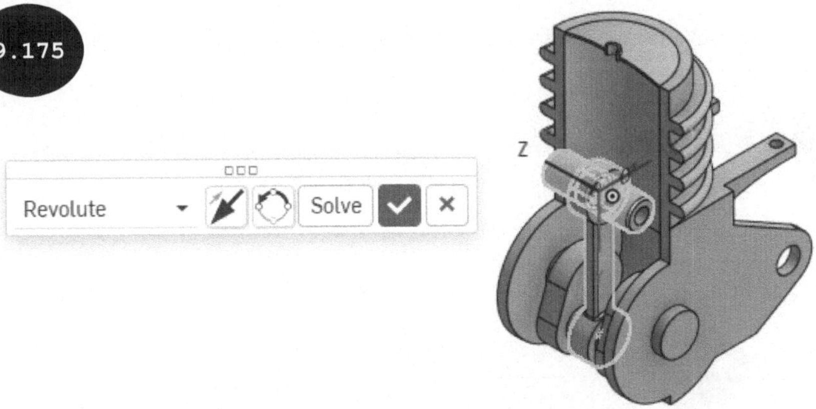

7. Click on the green checkmark ✓ to confirm and exit the dialog. The Revolute mate is applied between the components, removing all degrees of freedom except for one rotational degree of freedom of the Piston Pin component, see Figure 9.176.

9.176

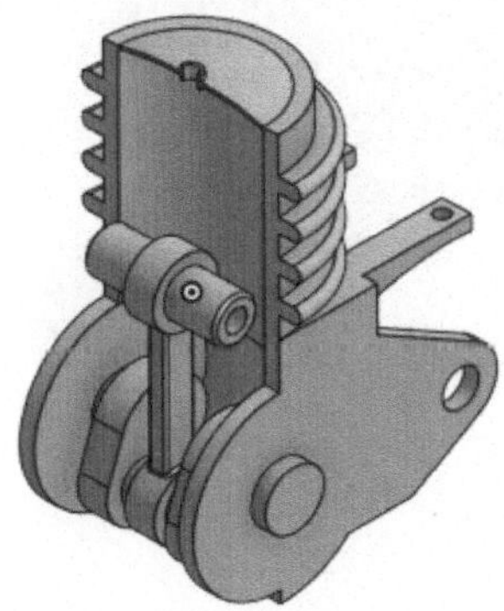

Section 10: Inserting and Assembling the Fifth Component

Now, you need to insert and assemble the Piston of the assembly.

1. Insert Piston as the fifth component of the assembly using the **Insert** tool, see Figure 9.177.

9.177

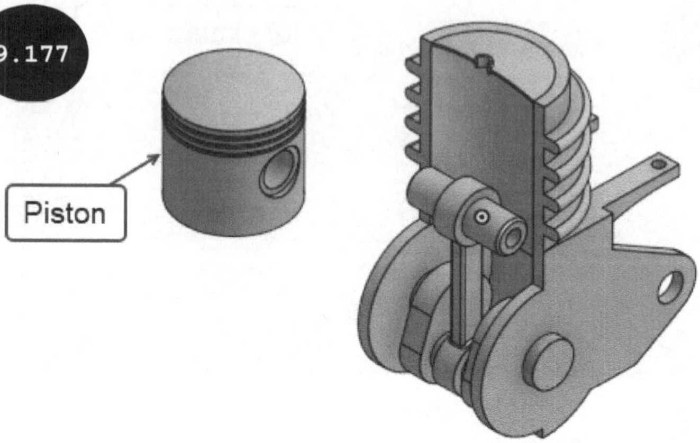

After inserting the Piston, you need to assembly it by applying the Revolute mate.

2. Click on the **Revolute mate** tool in the **Assembly** toolbar, see Figure 9.178. The **Revolute** dialog appears.

9.178

3. Hover the cursor over the right inner circular edge of the Piston, see Figure 9.179. The edge highlights, and the mate connector snaps to its center snap point.

9.179

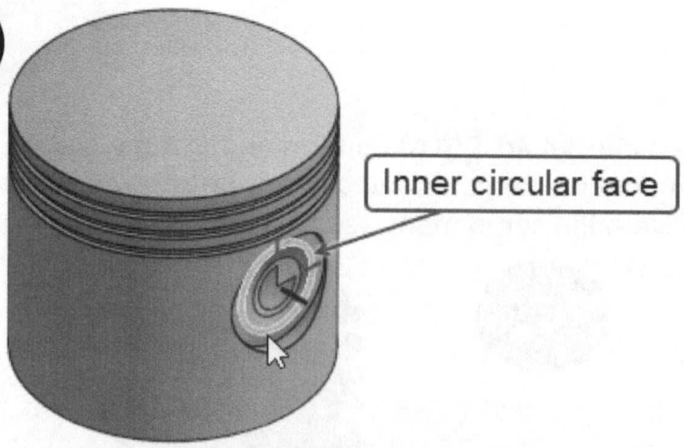

4. Click the left mouse button when the mate connector snaps to the center snap point of the edge to define its position, refer to Figure 9.179.

Now, you need to define the mate connector on the Piston Pin component.

5. Hover the cursor over the outermost right circular edge of the Piston Pin, see Figure 9.180.

9.180

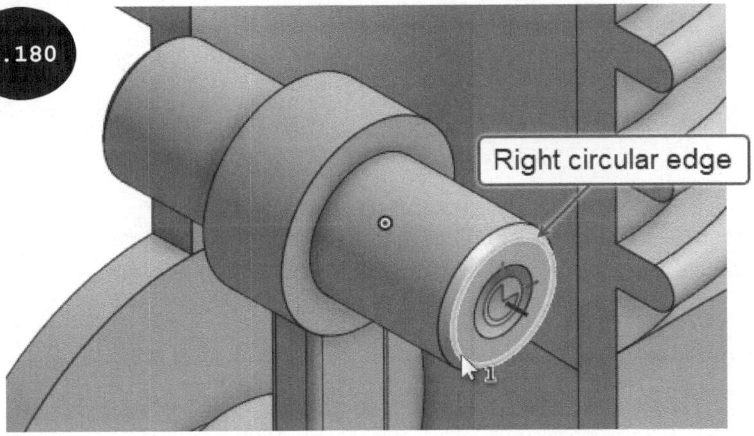

6. Click the left mouse button when the mate connector snaps to the center of the circular edge, refer to Figure 9.180. The Piston component moves toward the Piston Pin and the defined mate connectors of both components coincide, see Figure 9.181.

9.181

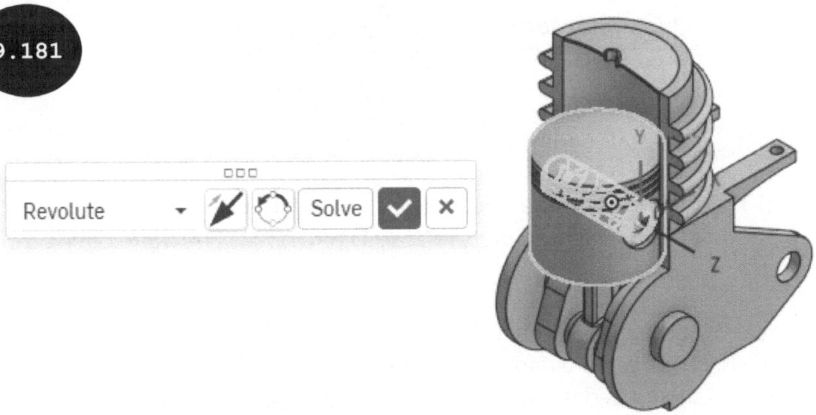

7. Click on the green checkmark ✔ to confirm and exit the dialog. The Revolute mate is applied between the components, see Figure 9.182.

9.182

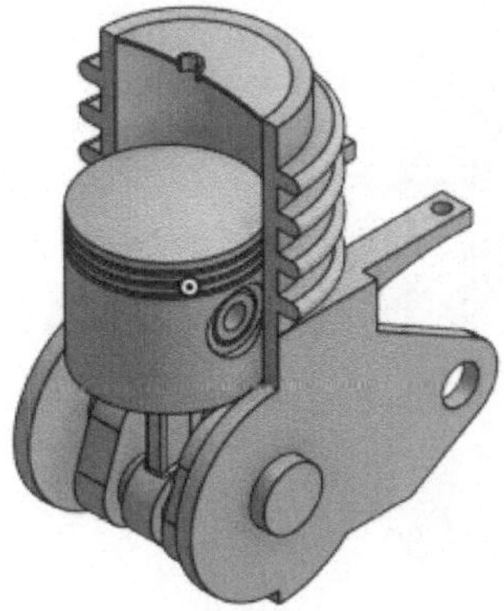

Section 11: Applying Slider Mates

Now, you need to apply the Slider mate between the Piston and Crank Case components to allow the Piston to slide along the axis of the Crank Case component.

1. Click on the **Slider mate** tool in the **Assembly** toolbar, see Figure 9.183. The **Slider** dialog appears.

9.183

2. Move the cursor over the outer circular face of the Piston (see Figure 9.184). The circular face highlights, and its three snap points (bottom, middle, and top) appear.

9.184

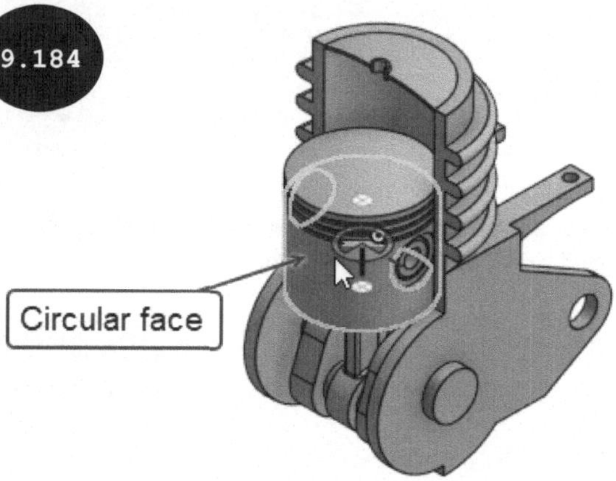

3. Press the SHIFT key, then click the left mouse button when the mate connector snaps to the middle snap point of the highlighted face, refer to Figure 9.184. The mate connector is defined on the Piston.

4. Hover the cursor over the inner circular face of the Crank Case component and then click the left mouse button when the cursor snaps to its upper snap point, see Figure 9.185. Both the defined mate connectors coincide in the graphics area, see Figure 9.186.

9.185

9.186

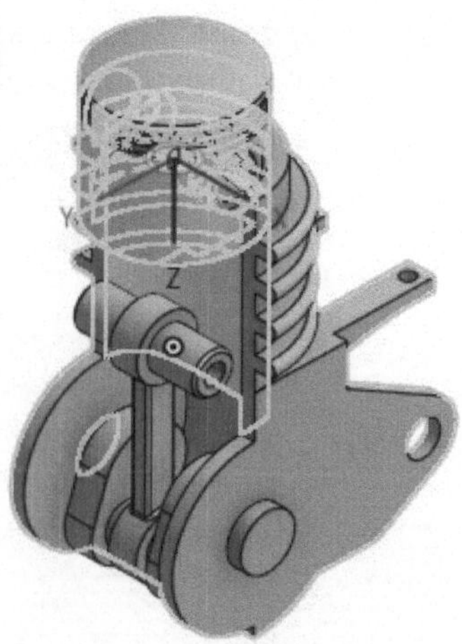

5. Click on the **Animate mate degree of freedom** button ▶ in the dialog to review to sliding motion of the Piston.

6. Click on the green checkmark ✅ to confirm and exit the dialog. The Slider mate is applied between the components, allowing the Piston to slide up and down while the Crank Shaft rotates, see Figure 9.187.

9.187

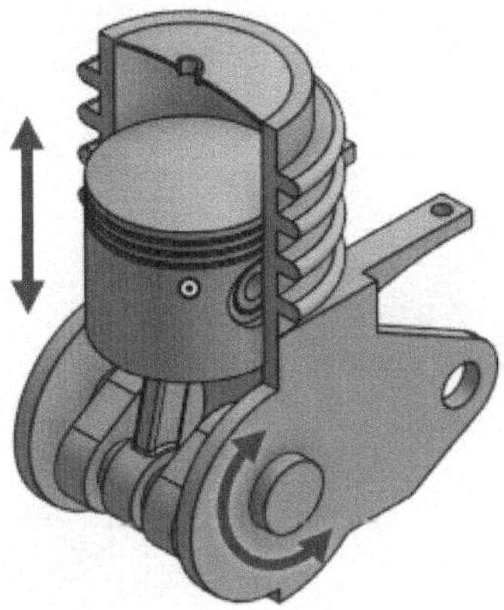

Tip: You can review the motion between the components by dragging the Crank Shaft component to rotate it. As the Crank Shaft rotates, the Piston moves up and down accordingly.

Now, you can close the document.

7. Invoke the **Document** menu by clicking on the ≡ icon next to the Onshape logo and click on the **Close document** option, see Figure 9.188. This action closes the current document.

9.188

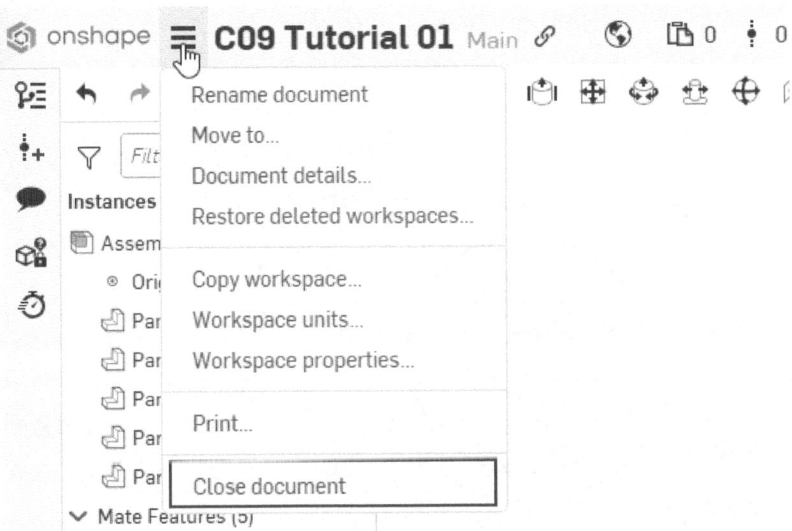

Hands-on Test Drive 1

Create an assembly, as shown in Figure 9.189 by applying all the required mates. Different views and dimensions of individual components of the assembly are shown in Figures 9.190 through 9.193. After creating the assembly, you can apply rack and pinion relation between the slider motion of the Rack component and the rotational motion of the Slotted Arm component. All dimensions are in mm.

9.189

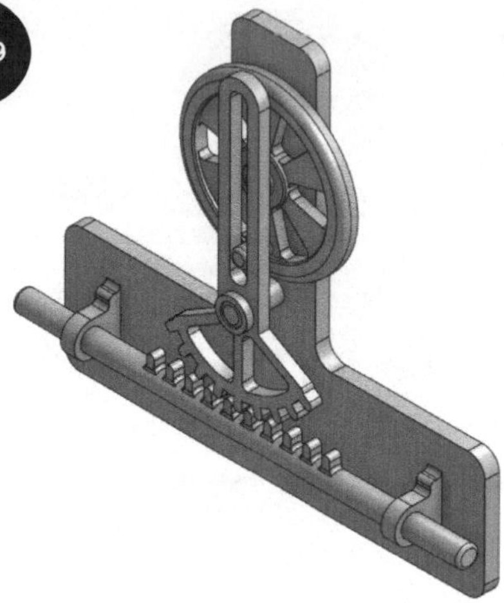

9.190

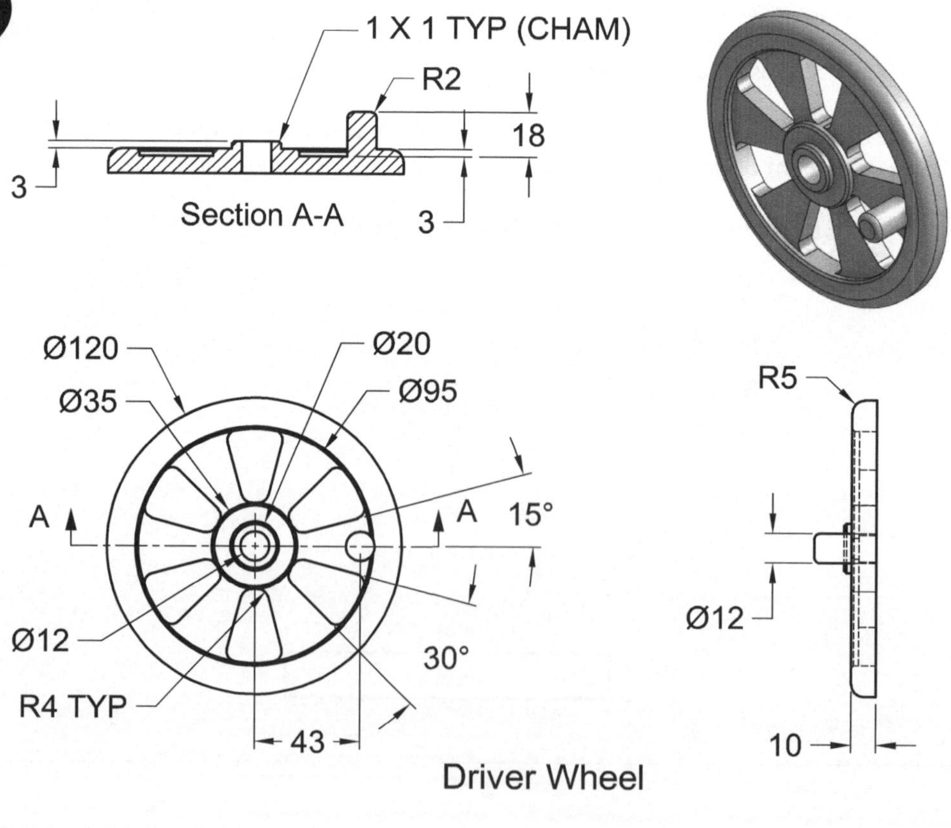

Driver Wheel

9.191

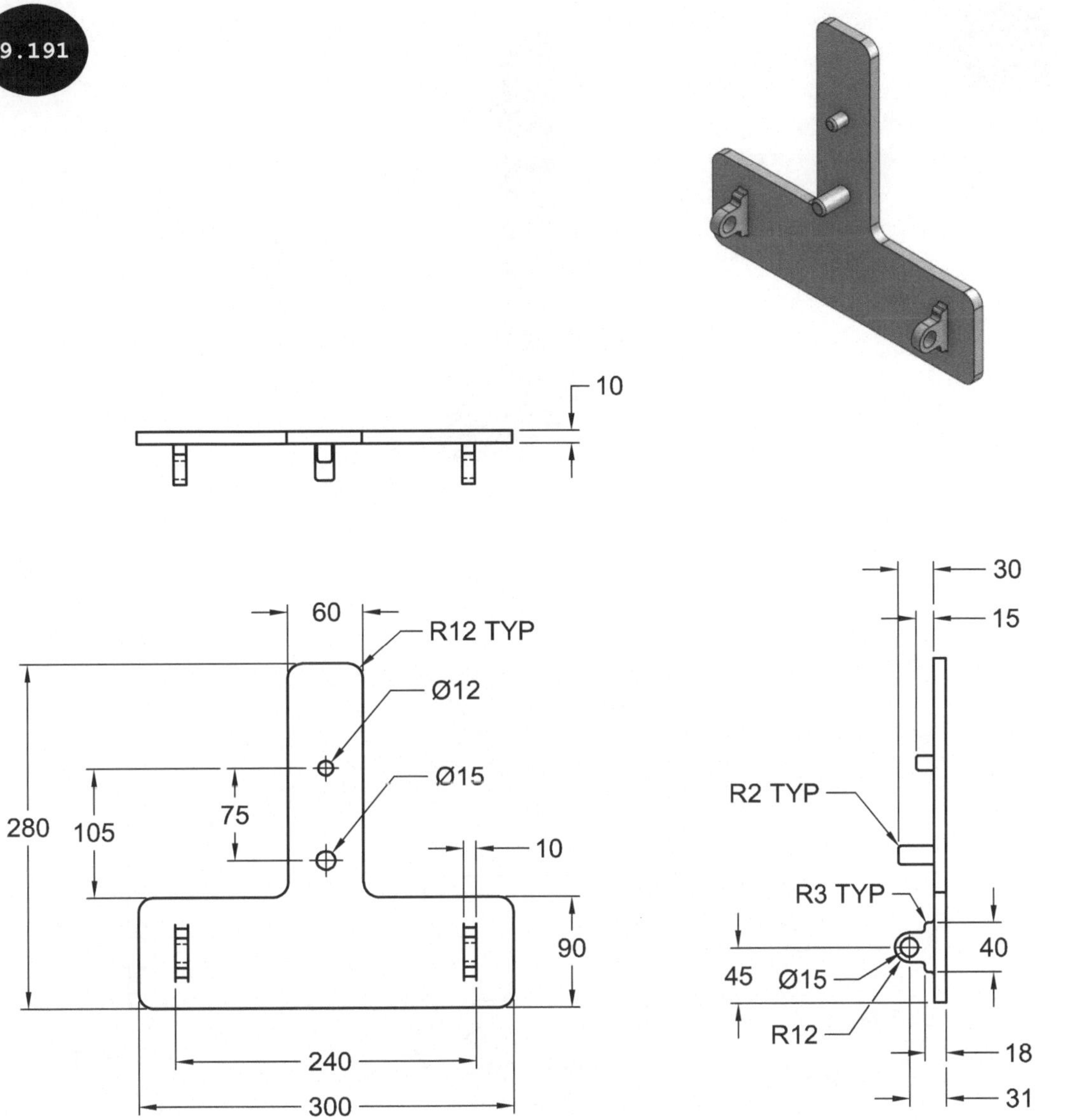

Mounting Board

9.192

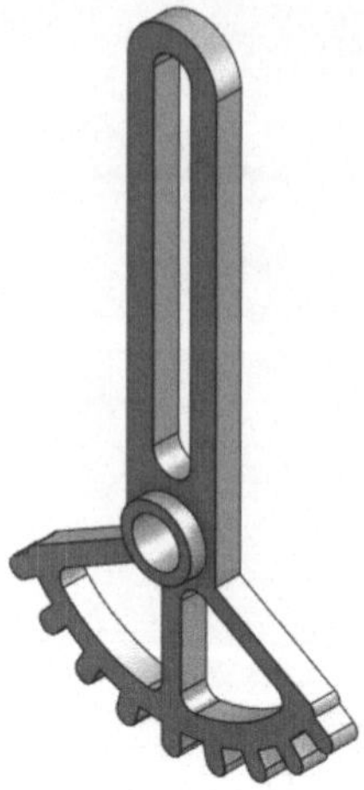

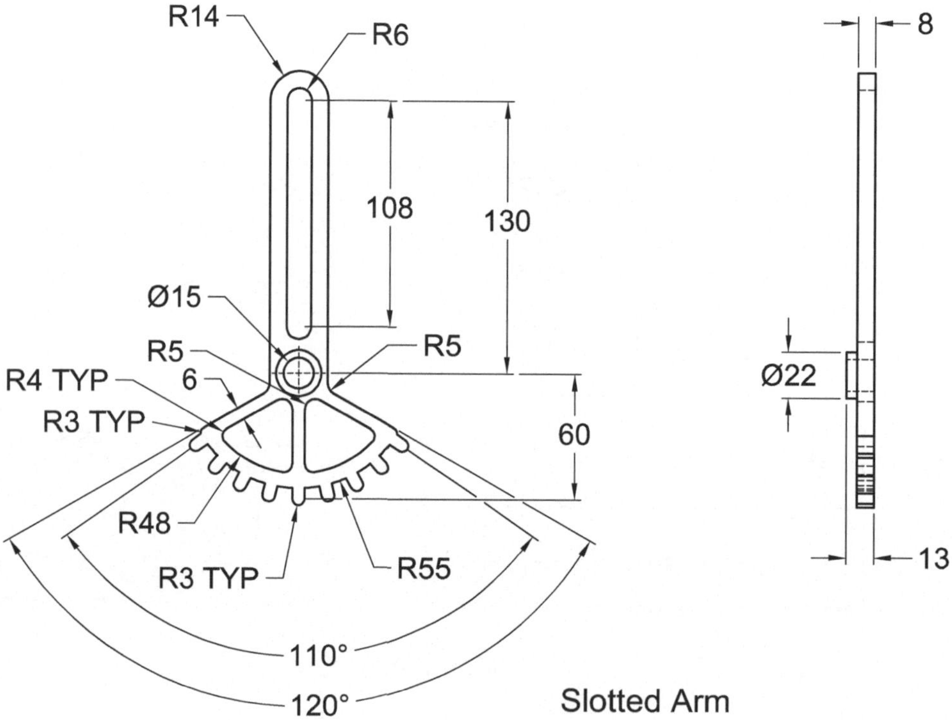

Slotted Arm

9.193

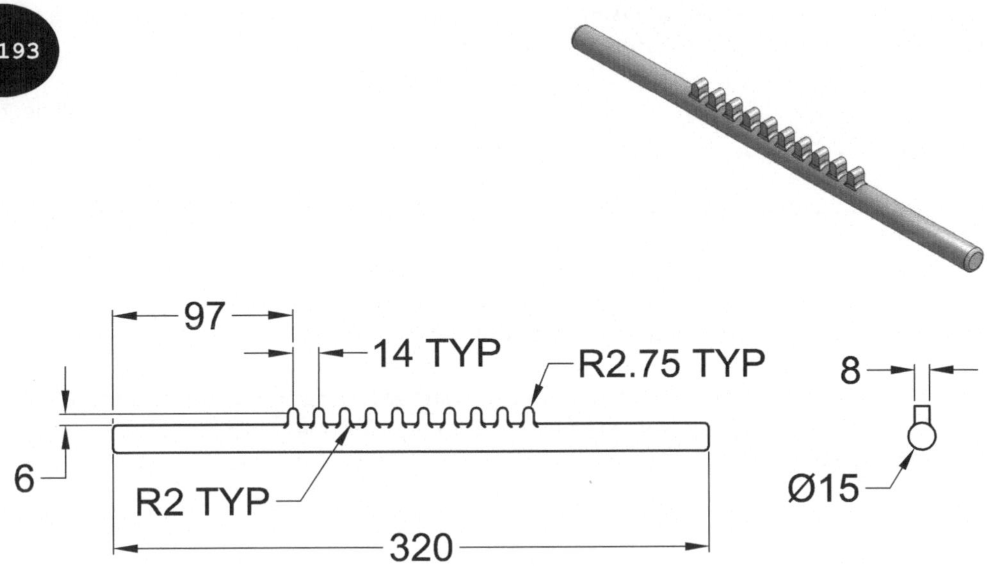

Rack

Summary

In this chapter, you learned how to assemble components by inserting and fixing the first component to establish a stable foundation and adding additional components to build the assembly. Various mates, including Fastened, Revolute, Slider, Planar, Cylindrical, Pin Slot, Ball, Parallel, and Tangent Mates, were introduced to define relationships and control movements between components.

You also explored organizing assemblies by grouping components, enabling Snap Mode for easier alignment, and using Show Mate Mode to review and refine mates. Additionally, you learned how to create Linear and Circular Component Patterns and establish advanced relations, such as Gear, Rack and Pinion, Screw, and Linear Relations, to simulate realistic mechanical behavior. These tools and techniques empower you to design, refine, and manage complex assemblies with precision.

Questions

Complete and verify the following sentences:

- The _________ tool is used to open the **Insert parts and assemblies** dialog, allowing you to add components in the Assembly environment.
- The _________ tab in the **Insert parts and assemblies** dialog provides access to all the parts and assemblies created within the current design document.
- In Onshape, you can insert various standard parts provided by Onshape into the current assembly document through the _________ tab in the **Insert parts and assemblies** dialog.

- The _________ tool is used to insert an entire Part Studio file, containing multiple bodies, as a single rigid component in the Assembly environment.
- The _________ mate is used to lock or fix two components together by removing all degrees of freedom, thereby preventing any relative motion between them.
- The _________ mate allows a component to rotate about an axis by removing all degrees of freedom except for one rotational degree of freedom.
- The _________ mate allows a component to translate along an axis by restricting all degrees of freedom except for one translational degree of freedom.
- The _________ mate allows a component to translate along the Z-axis and rotate about the same Z-axis by removing all degrees of freedom except for one translational and one rotational degree of freedom.
- In Onshape, you can apply a cam and follower mechanism between two components by using the _________ mate.
- The _________ allows you to mate two components by dragging the mate connector of one component over another.
- In Onshape, you can establish gear relations between two mates that have one _________ degree of freedom.
- In the Assembly environment of a design document, only individual components from the same design document can be inserted. (True/False)
- It is recommended to keep all the CAD data for a project or assembly within a single design document by creating the parts, assemblies, and drawings in their respective environments. (True/False)
- In Onshape, a component inserted into the design document retains all its degrees of freedom, allowing it to move or rotate freely in any direction within the graphics area. (True/False)
- In Onshape, you cannot define relative motion between two mates. (True/False)

CHAPTER

10

Working with Drawings

In this chapter, the following topics will be discussed:

- Accessing Drawing Environment
- Accessing Drawing Environment from Part/ASM
- Creating a Base View
- Creating a Projected View
- Understanding Angle of Projection
- Controlling the Display and Properties of a View
- Editing and Modifying Drawing Properties
- Creating an Auxiliary View
- Creating a Section View
- Creating an Aligned Section View
- Creating a Broken-out Section View
- Creating a Detail View
- Creating a Break View
- Creating a Crop View
- Editing and Modifying Sheet Properties
- Adding a New Sheet
- Deleting a Drawing View
- Moving a Drawing View
- Deleting a Drawing View
- Moving a View to Another Sheet
- Editing Hatch Properties of a Section View
- Adding Geometries in Drawing Views
- Applying Dimensions
- Adding a Surface Finish Symbol
- Adding a Weld Symbol
- Adding a Note
- Editing the Sheet Format
- Creating the Bill of Materials (BOM)
- Editing and Customizing the Bill of Materials
- Adding Balloons

In previous chapters, you explored creating parts and assemblies. In this chapter, you will focus on generating 2D drawings. A 2D drawing is more than just an illustration; it serves as a language for engineers to communicate ideas and details about engineered products. By creating 2D drawings, designers can convey precise and comprehensive information about components, enabling engineers on the shop floor to manufacture them accurately. The accuracy of 2D drawings is crucial, as any missing or incorrect information can result in production errors. Therefore, the designer's role in creating precise drawings is vital.

Onshape provides a dedicated Drawing environment, which ensures that you can generate accurate, error-free 2D drawings. In this environment, you can create drawings of components or assemblies, whether they are part of the same design document or from separate documents. The following sections will walk you through how to access the Drawing environment and create 2D drawings effectively.

Accessing Drawing Environment

After creating a component or an assembly in their respective environments, you can switch to the Drawing environment for creating drawings. The method for accessing the Drawing environment is discussed next.

1. Click the **Insert new tab** + (*plus sign*) at the lower-left corner of the screen, in front of the **Part Studio 1** tab, see Figure 10.1. A menu appears, displaying a list of available options.

10.1

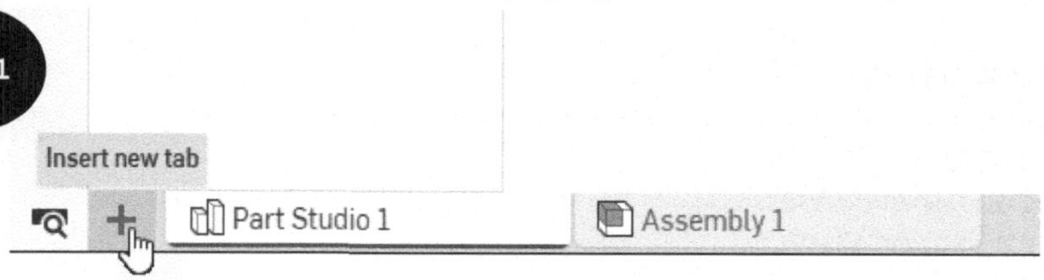

2. Select the **Create Drawing** option in the menu, see Figure 10.2. The **Create Drawing** dialog appears with two tabs: **Existing templates** and **Custom template**, see Figure 10.3.

10.2

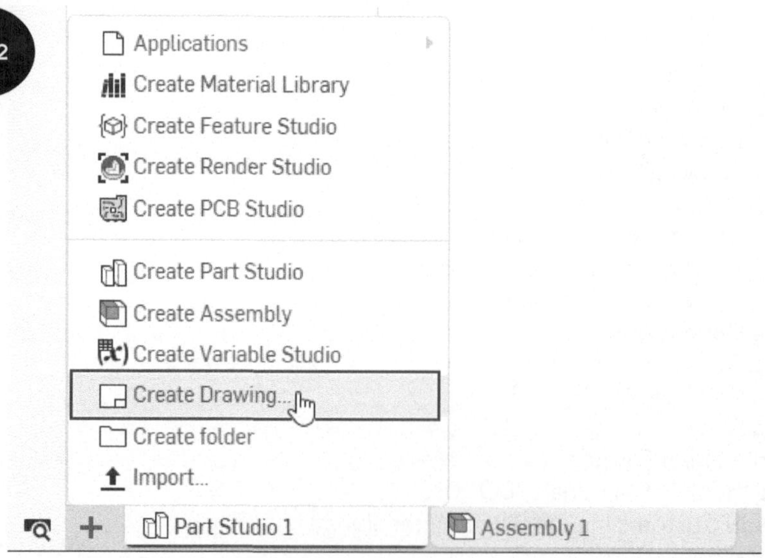

10.3

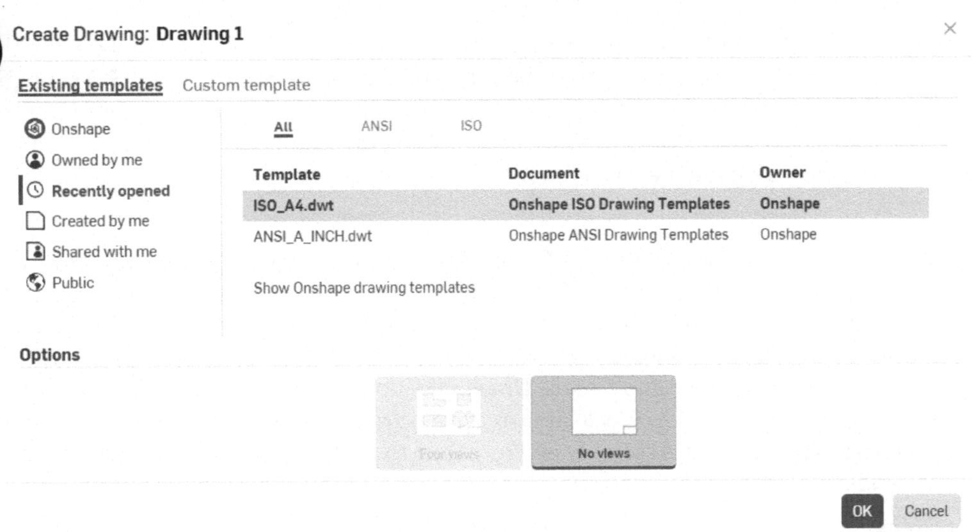

The **Create Drawing** dialog provides you with options to choose either an existing template with predefined settings to creating the drawing or a custom template tailored to your specific needs, which are discussed next.

Existing templates: By default, the **Existing templates** tab is active in the dialog, enabling you to select a standard template with predefined settings. You can select the desired filter option such as **Onshape**, **Owned by me**, **Recently opened**, **Created by me**, or **Shared with me** to display a list of relevant templates in the right panel, refer to Figure 10.3. Note that selecting the **Onshape** option specifically displays a list of all available Onshape standard templates (ANSI and ISO).

Tip: In the right panel of the **Create Drawing** window, the **All** option is selected by default, displaying a list of all available templates. Selecting **ANSI** filters the list to show only ANSI standard templates, while choosing **ISO** displays only ISO standard templates.

Custom template: The **Custom template** tab enables you to create a personalized template for your drawing. To set this up, activate the **Custom template** tab and configure the desired settings, see Figure 10.4. These include selecting the standard (ANSI or ISO), language, sheet size, units, decimal separator, angle of projection, and other preferences directly within the dialog.

10.4

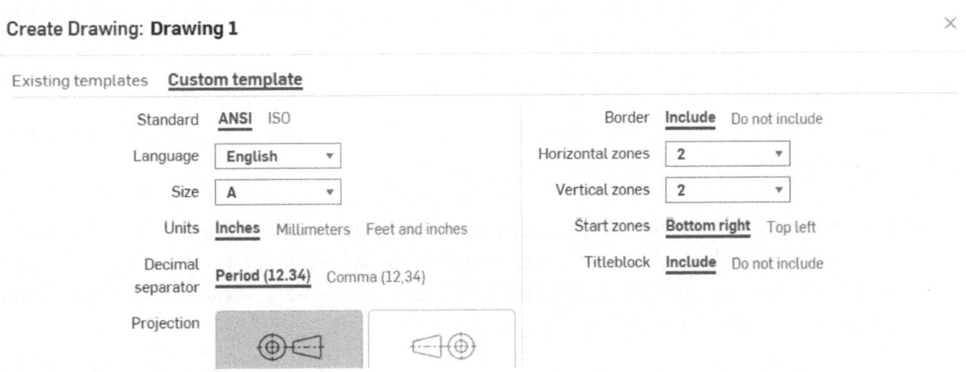

Tip: By default, when a drawing is created using the ASME standard template, the third angle of projection is applied for generating drawing views. In contrast, the ISO standard template uses the first angle of projection. However, when setting up a custom template, you can specify the desired angle of projection in the **Projection** section of the **Custom template** tab for generating the drawing views.

Options: The **Options** area in the **Create Drawing** dialog includes the **Four views** and **No views** buttons, see Figure 10.5. By default, the **No views** button is activated, enabling you to start with an empty drawing from scratch. Alternatively, the **Four views** button allows you to generate a drawing with four predefined standard views: Front, Top, Side, and Isometric. This button becomes available when the **Create Drawing** dialog is accessed from either a Part Studio or an Assembly environment. You will later explore how to directly access the Drawing environment from the Part Studio or Assembly environment to create drawings of the corresponding part or assembly.

10.5

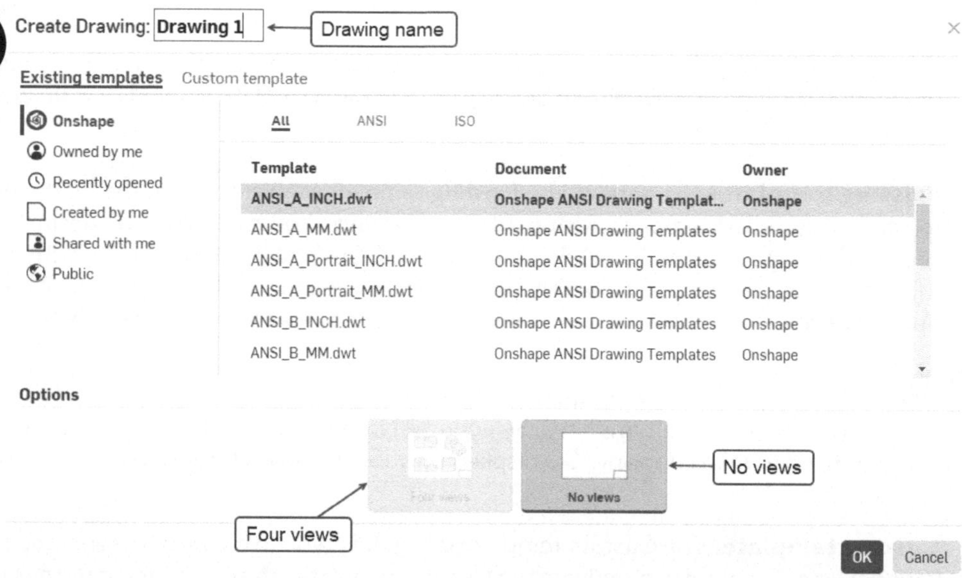

Tip: You can change the default drawing name, "**Drawing 1**," by clicking on its current name at the top of the window, refer to Figure 10.5. This will enable an edit field where you can enter a new name for the drawing as needed.

3. Select the desired pre-defined template or set up a custom one for creating the drawing as discussed above.

4. After selecting a desired template, click on the **OK** button in the dialog. The Drawing environment opens with a sheet based on the chosen template, which defines the standard, sheet size, units, angle of projection, and other parameters, see Figure 10.6. Additionally, the **Select a part or assembly** and **Insert view** dialogs appear on the screen.

10.6

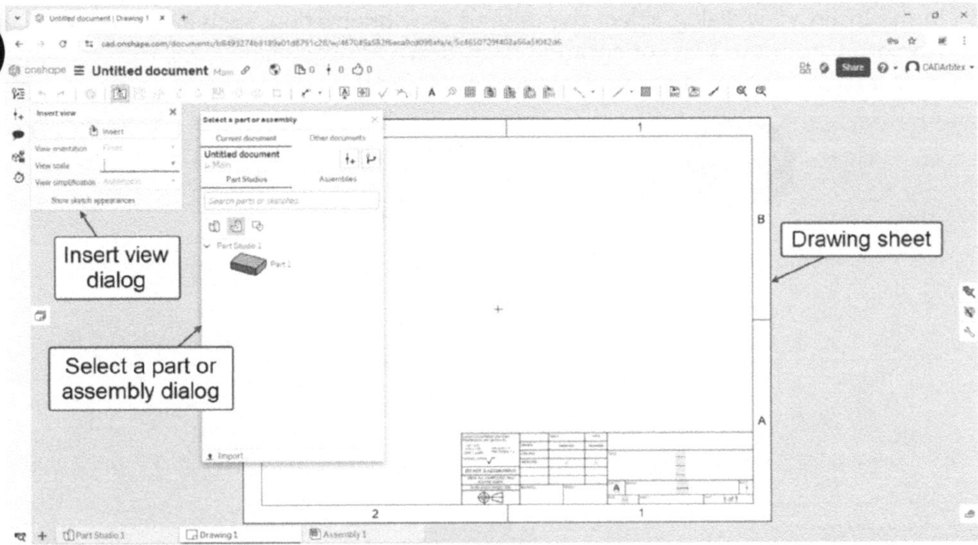

Select a part or assembly: The **Select a part or assembly** dialog allows you to select a part or an assembly to create its drawing views. By default, the **Current document** tab is active, enabling you to select a part or assembly from the current design file.

To choose a part or assembly from another document, click the **Other documents** tab. Then, select a filter option such as **Owned by me**, **Recently opened**, **Created by me**, **Shared with me**, or **Public** to display a list of relevant design documents. From this list, select the desired document to access all parts and assemblies within it under the **Part Studios** and **Assemblies** options. You can also search for a component or document in the list using the **Search** field.

5. Select the required part or assembly from the current design document or another document using the **Current document** or **Other documents** tab, respectively, as discussed above. The base view of the selected part or assembly appears attached to the cursor, see Figure 10.7. Also, the **Insert view** dialog remain displayed on the top left corner of the screen.

10.7

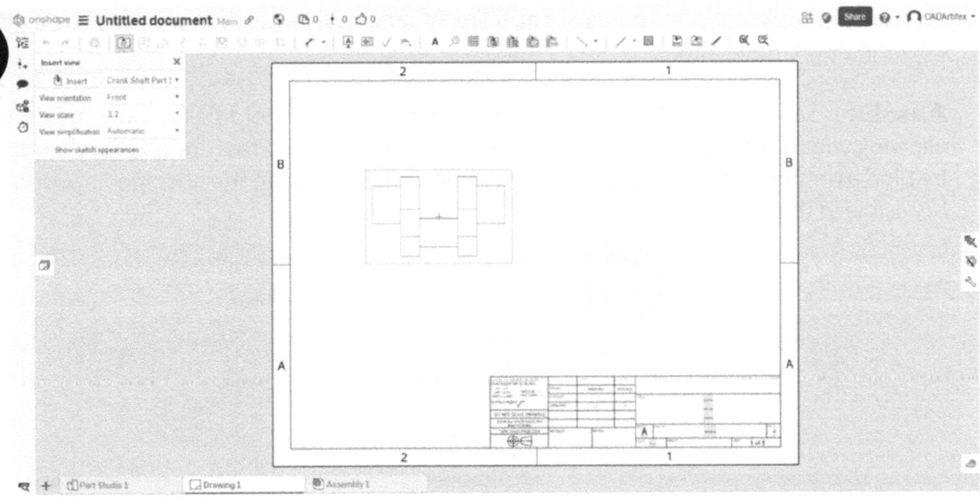

6. In the **Insert view** dialog, select the desired view orientation, such as **Front**, **Top**, **Left**, **Right**, or **Isometric**, from the **View orientation** drop-down list, see Figure 10.8. The preview of the base view, attached to the cursor, updates accordingly in the graphics area.

10.8

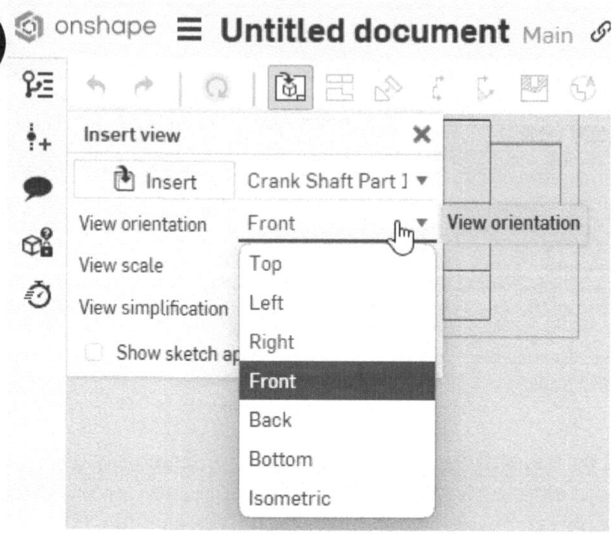

7. Select the required predefined scale for the drawing view from the **View scale** drop-down list in the **Insert view** dialog.

8. If needed, you can simplify the geometry of the selected part or assembly for display in the drawing views by choosing the appropriate option from the **View simplification** drop-down list. The available options are discussed below.

 Automatic: By default, the **Automatic** option is selected. This enables Onshape to automatically determine the optimal view simplification threshold based on the geometry of the selected part or assembly. Features or parts below the specified threshold will be hidden in the drawing views.

 None: No simplification settings are applied, meaning all features or parts will be included in the drawing views.

 Absolute: Selecting the **Absolute** option enables the **Threshold** field below the drop-down list, allowing you to specify a threshold length, see Figure 10.9. Any feature smaller than this value will be hidden in the view. Note that if the entire part is smaller than the specified threshold, it will not be visible in the view.

10.9

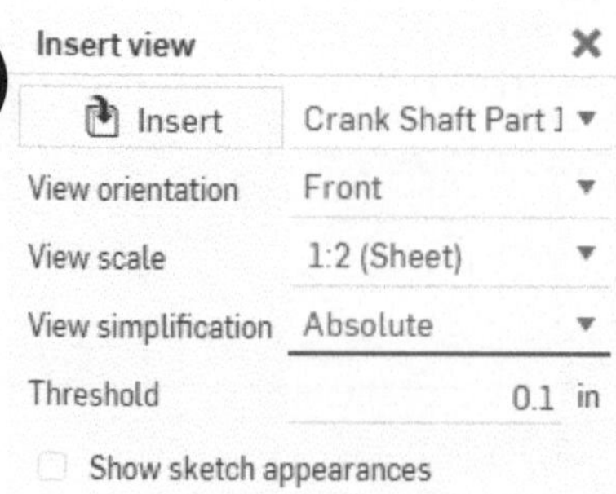

Ratio to studio: Selecting the **Ratio to studio** option enables the **Threshold** field below the drop-down list, allowing you to define a threshold length as a percentage of the total size of the Part Studio or Assembly. Any features or parts smaller than the specified threshold will be hidden in the drawing views.

Ratio to part: Selecting the **Ratio to part** option enables the **Threshold** field below the drop-down list, allowing you to define a threshold length as a percentage of the total size of the part. The features smaller than the specified threshold percentage will be hidden in the drawing views.

9. After defining the required settings, click on the drawing sheet to place the drawing view. The view is created at the specified location. Also, the **Projected view** tool automatically activates, and a projected view appears attached to the cursor as you move it. The display of the projected view changes based on the direction of the cursor movement. Figure 10.10 illustrates the different projected views that can be generated from the base view.

10.10

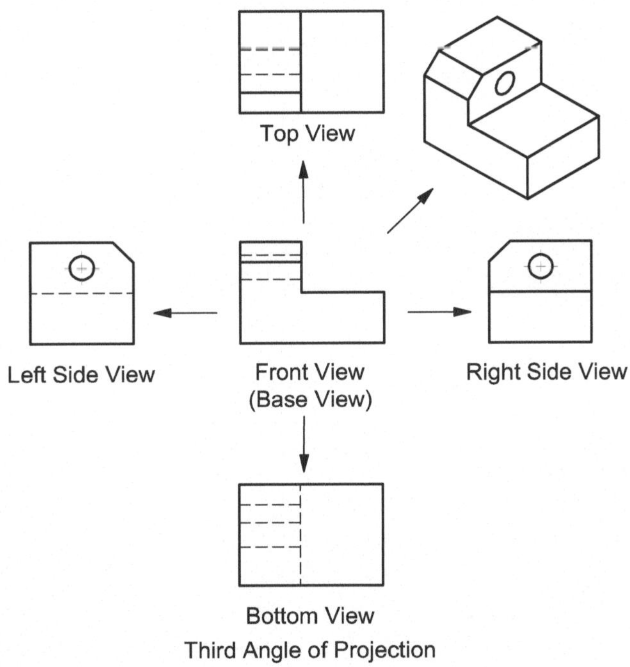

10. Click on the drawing sheet to place the projected view at the desired location. The view is created accordingly. The **Projected view** tool remains active, allowing you to generate additional projected views by first selecting a base view.

11. After creating the base view and the required projected views, press the ESC key to exit the tool.

Accessing Drawing Environment from Part/ASM

In Onshape, you can also access the Drawing environment directly from the Part Studio or Assembly environment to create drawing views of the corresponding part or assembly. The method for accessing the Drawing environment from the Part Studio is discussed below:

1. Ensure that the required **Part Studio** tab of the document is active to create drawing views of the corresponding part.

2. Right-click on the name of the part (*Part1*) in the Part list on the left side of the graphics area, then choose the **Create Drawing of Part 1** option from the shortcut menu that appears, see Figure 10.11. The **Create Drawing** dialog appears, see Figure 10.12. The options in this dialog are same as discussed earlier.

10.11

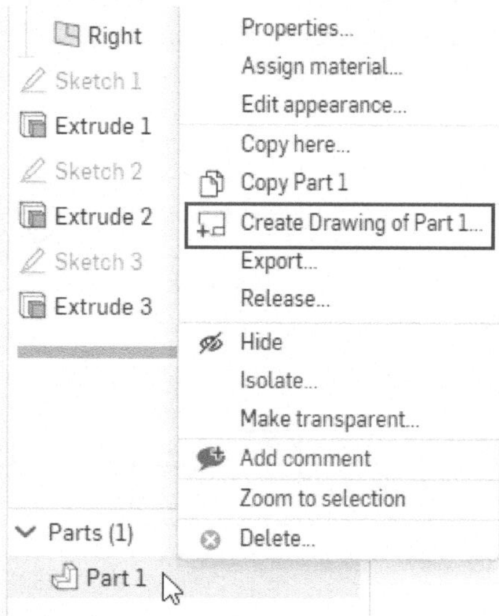

10.12

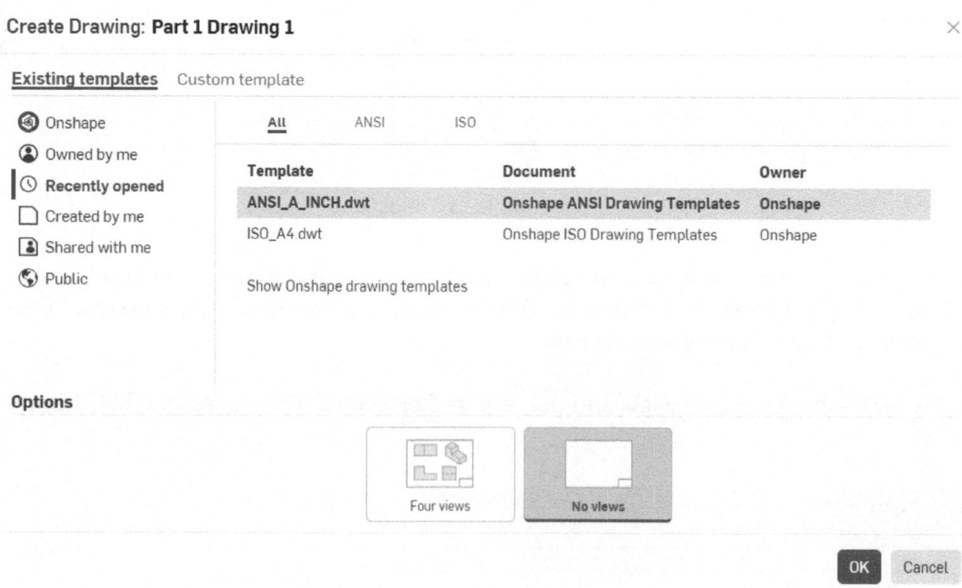

3. Choose the preferred pre-defined template or create a custom one for generating the drawing views, as discussed earlier.

4. By default, the **No views** button is selected in the **Options** area of the dialog, allowing you to start with a blank drawing sheet. If needed, you can select the **Four views** button to automatically generate the four standard views: Front, Top, Side, and Isometric on the drawing sheet.

5. After selecting a desired template, click on the **OK** button in the dialog. The Drawing environment opens with a sheet based on the chosen template and its related settings. Also, the **Insert view** dialog appears on the screen to create the base view of the part. The options in the **Insert view** dialog box are same as discussed earlier.

Note: If the **No views** button was selected in the **Options** area of the **Create Drawing** dialog when invoking the Drawing environment, the **Insert view** dialog will be displayed on the screen to create the base view of the part. On the other hand, if the **Four views** button was selected, the four standard views of the selected part would have been automatically created on the sheet, and the **Insert view** dialog wouldn't be displayed.

6. After creating the required base view and the projected views of the part (refer to Figure 10.13), press the ESC key to exit the tool.

10.13

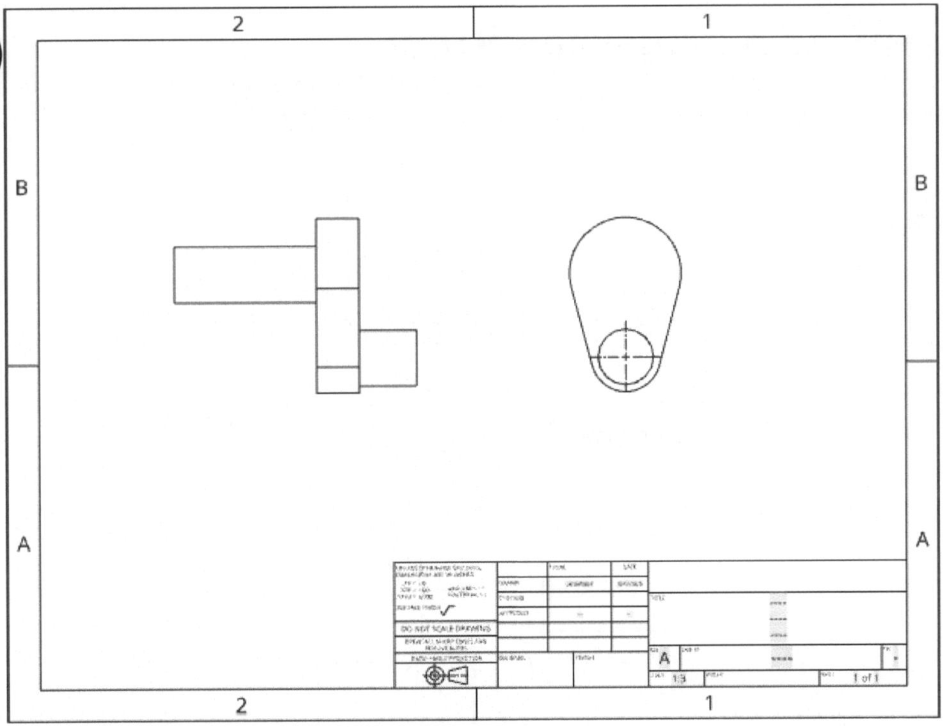

7. Similarly, you can invoke the Drawing environment from the Assembly environment to create drawing views of the corresponding assembly.

Creating a Base View

In Onshape, you can create an independent base view of a part or assembly of a desired orientation such as Front, Top, Left, Right, or Isometric using the **Insert view** dialog. This dialog opens automatically upon entering the Drawing environment, as previously discussed.

Alternatively, you can manually access the **Insert view** dialog by clicking the **Insert view** tool to create the base view of a model, see Figure 10.14.

10.14

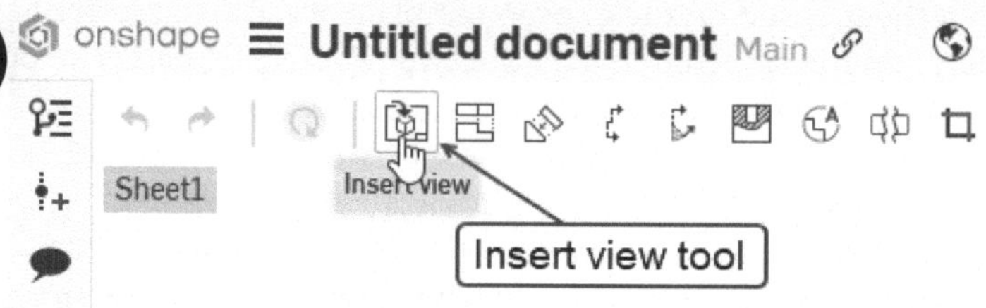

Once the **Insert view** dialog appears, you can select the desired orientation for the base view and adjust other related settings, as discussed earlier. After making the selections, click to place the view in the drawing sheet. The view is created at the specified location. Additionally, the **Projected view** tool activates automatically, and a projected view follows the cursor as you move it. You can either press the ESC key to exit the tool or continue creating the projected view, as discussed earlier.

Creating a Projected View

Projected views are orthogonal views of an object, created by viewing the object from different projection sides such as top, front, and side. Figures 10.15 and 14.16 display different projected views of an object.

10.15

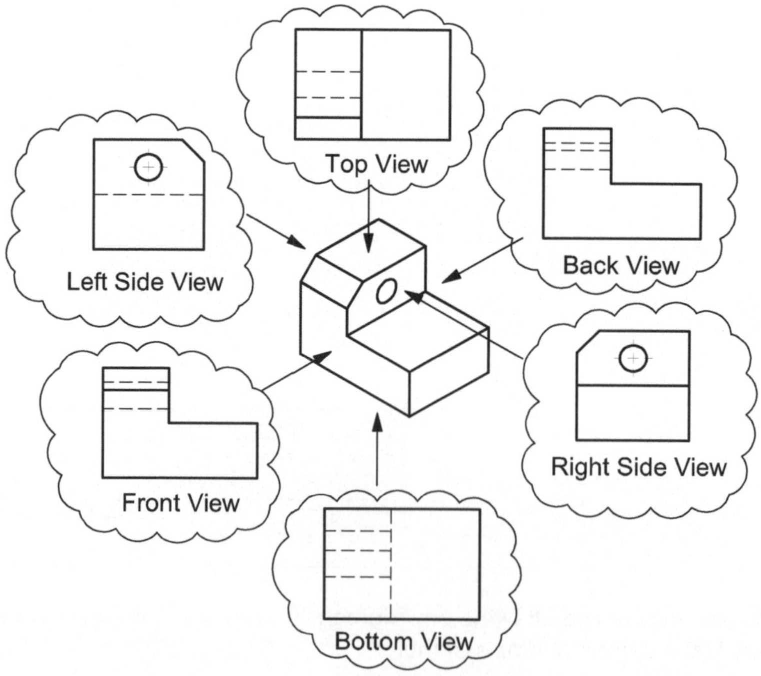

Projected Views

10.16

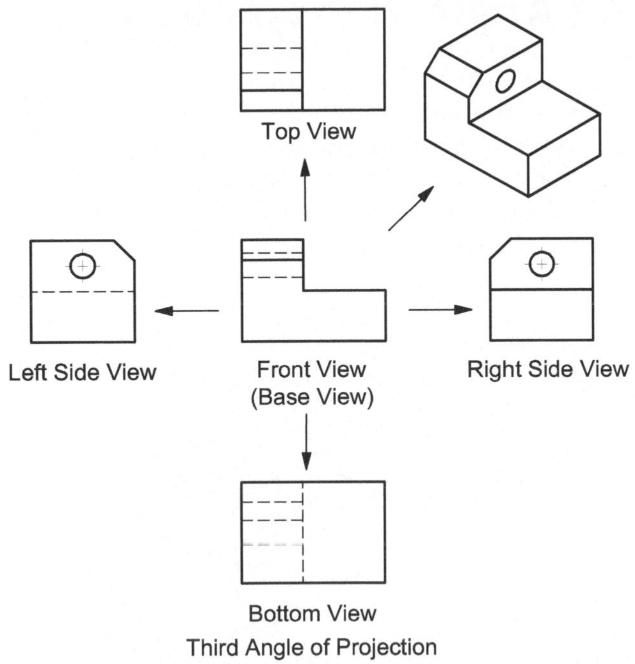

You can create the projected view of an existing view using the **Projected view** tool. As mentioned earlier, this tool activates automatically once you create the base view of a model with the **Insert view** tool. Alternatively, you can manually activate the tool by clicking on the **Projected view** tool in the **Drawing** toolbar, see Figure 10.17.

10.17

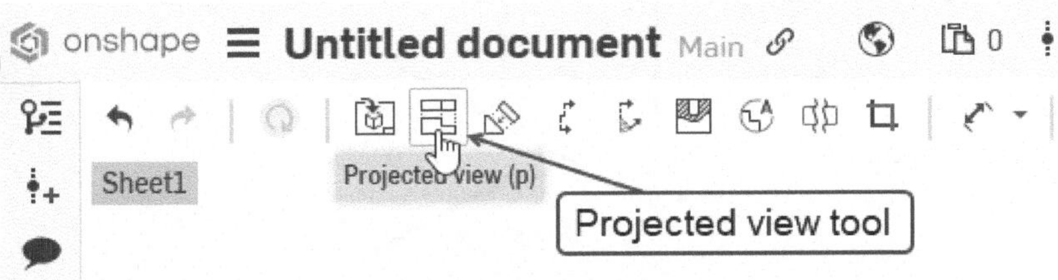

After activating the **Projected view** tool, select an existing drawing view as the parent view to create its projected view. A preview of the projected view appears attached to the cursor. Click on the drawing sheet to place the projected view at the desired location. The projected view is created, and the **Projected view** tool remains active, allowing you to create additional projected views by selecting existing views. After creating the projected views, press the ESC key to exit the tool.

Note: The creation of the projected view depends on the angle of projection defined for the drawing sheet. You can choose either the first angle of projection or the third angle of projection for creating the projected views. By default, when you create a drawing using the ISO standard template, the first angle of projection is used for generating the projected views. In contrast, when using the ASME standard template, the third angle of projection is applied. The concept of angle of projection is discussed next.

Understanding Angle of Projection

Engineering drawings follow two types of angles of projection: the first angle of projection and the third angle of projection. In the first angle of projection, the object is assumed to be placed in the first quadrant, with the viewer observing it from the direction shown in Figure 10.18. As the object is in the first quadrant, its projection views are on the respective planes, as depicted in the same Figure 10.18 When the planes of projection are unfolded, the front view appears on the upper side, and the top view appears on the bottom side. Additionally, the right-side view is on the left, and the left-side view is on the right of the front view, as shown in Figure 10.19.

10.18

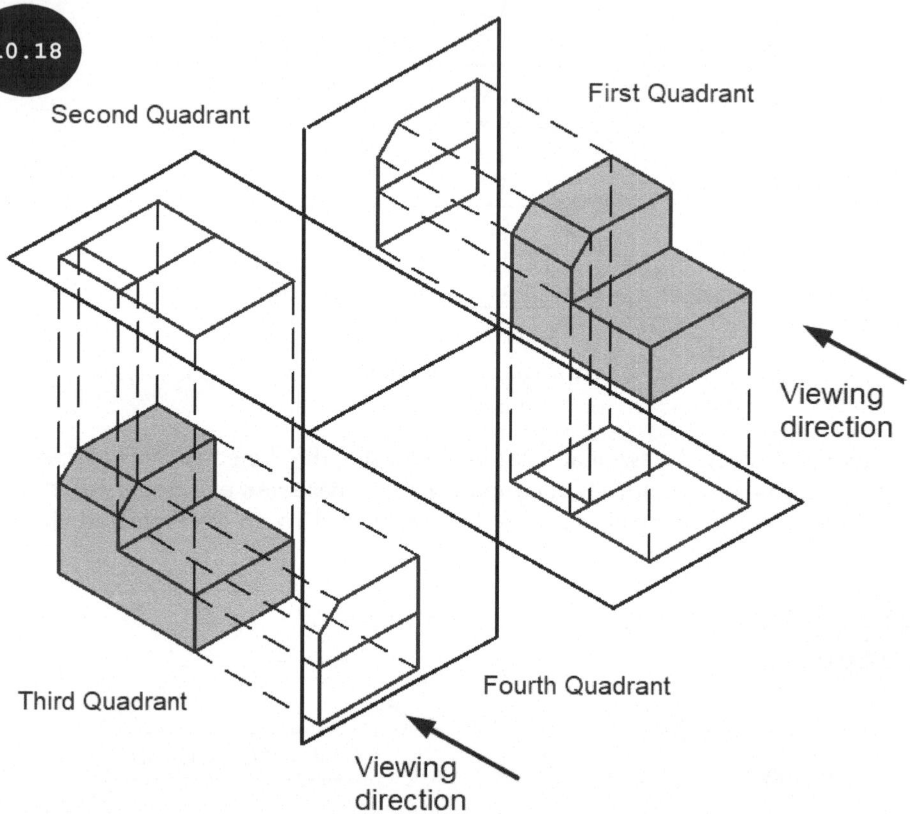

10.19

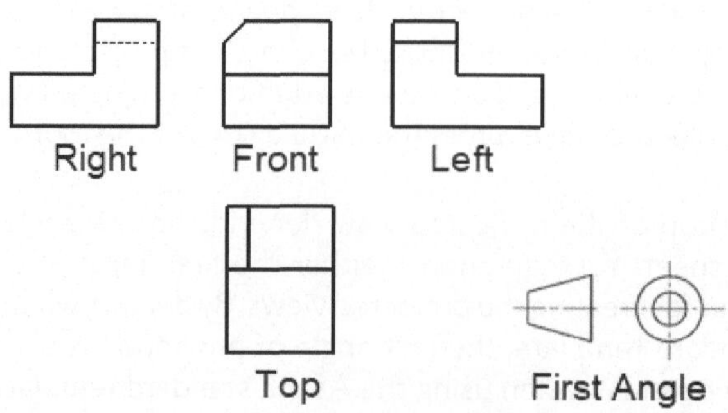

In contrast, in the third angle of projection, the object is assumed to be placed in the third quadrant, refer to Figure 10.18. Here, when the planes of projection are unfolded, the projection of the front view appears on the bottom, while the projection of the top view appears on the top side of the drawing. The right-side view appears on the right, and the left-side view appears on the left of the front view, as illustrated in Figure 10.20.

10.20

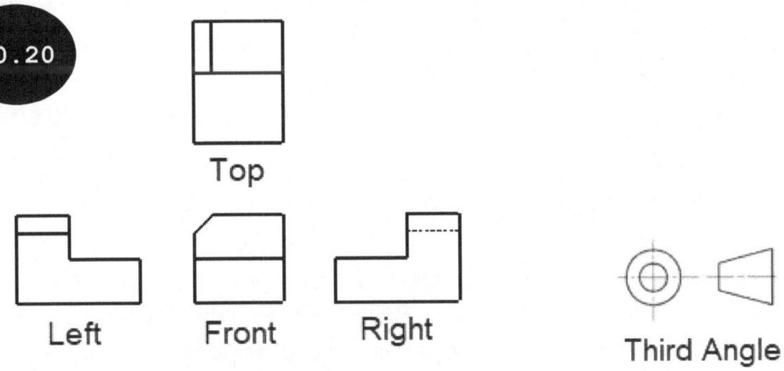

Controlling the Display and Properties of a View

In Onshape, you can modify the display style of a view to show or hide hidden edges, shaded view, threads, faulty parts, sketches, specific edges, or auto centermarks. The method for controlling the display style of a drawing view is discussed below:

1. Right-click on a drawing view whose display style you want to edit, then hover the cursor over the **Show/Hide** option in the shortcut menu that appears, see Figure 10.21. A cascading menu appears.

10.21

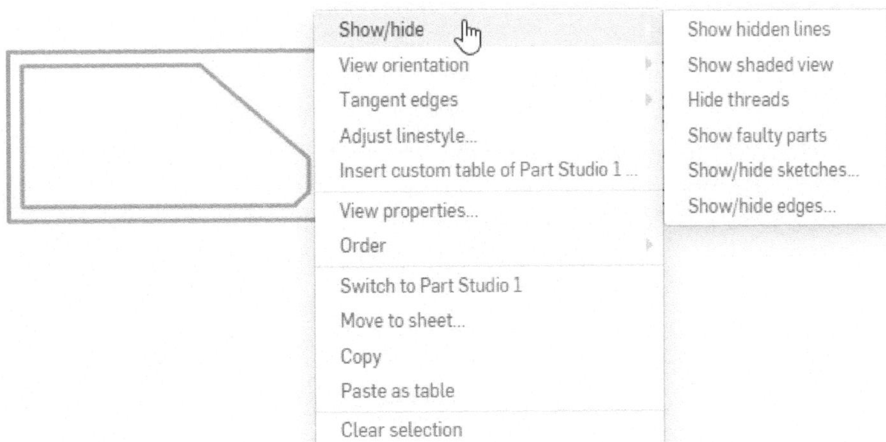

2. In this cascading menu, select the required option to control the display style of the selected view. For instance, if you want to display the hidden edges of the model in the selected view, select the **Show hidden lines** option. Figure 10.22 shows a view with and without hidden edges. Note that the availability of options, such as **Show hidden lines** or **Hide hidden lines**, depends on the current state of the view.

10.22

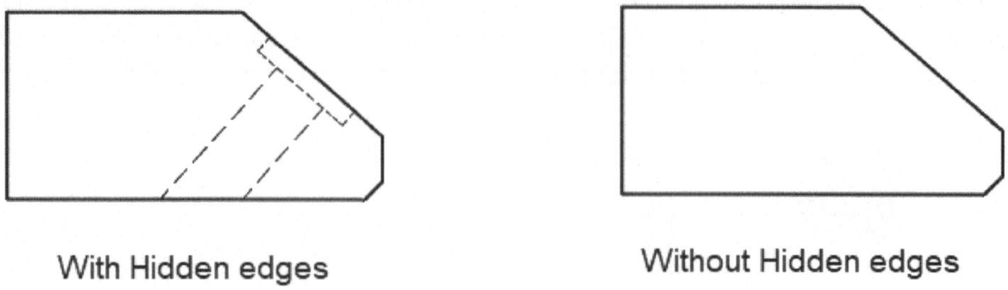

3. Likewise, you can control the display style of other views, as needed.

   Alternatively, you can control other properties of a view, such as orientation, scale, and display of tangent edges, using the **View properties** dialog. To do this, double-click on the view whose properties you want to edit. The **View properties** dialog appears, see Figure 10.23. Alternatively, right-click on a view and then click on the **View properties** option in the shortcut menu to display this dialog.

10.23

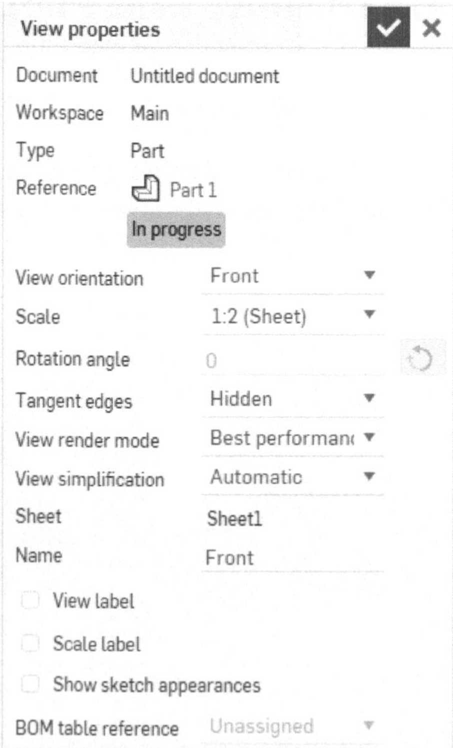

In this dialog, you can edit the default properties of the selected view as needed. For instance, to control the display of the tangent edges of the model by making them hidden or displaying them as solid or phantom lines, select the required option, **Hidden**, **Solid**, or **Phantom**, in the **Tangent edges** drop-down list. Figures 10.24 through 10.26 show a view with tangent edges displayed as solid, hidden, and displayed as phantom lines, respectively.

10.24

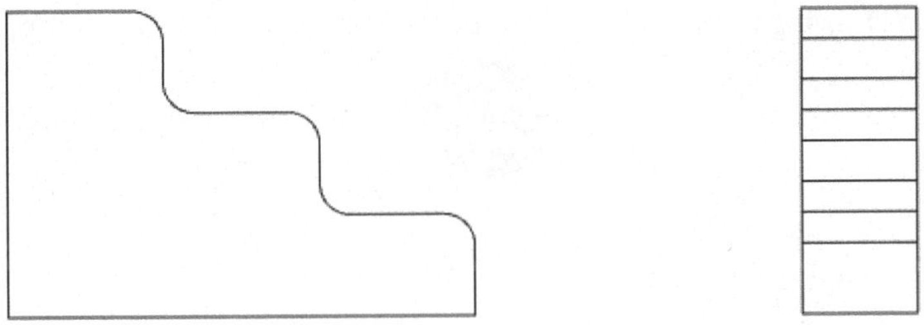

Tangent edges as solid line

10.25

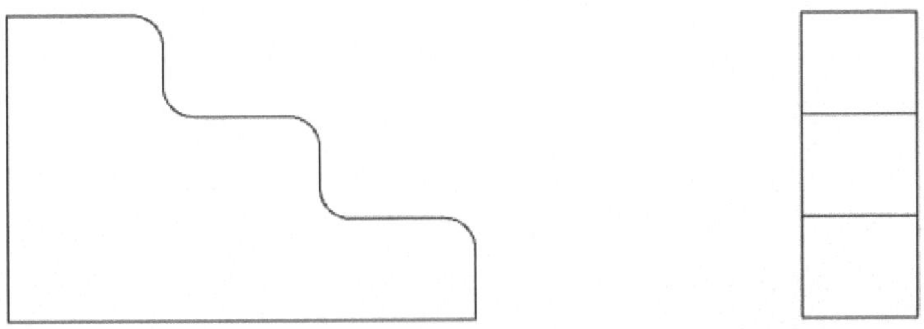

Tangent edges are hidden

10.26

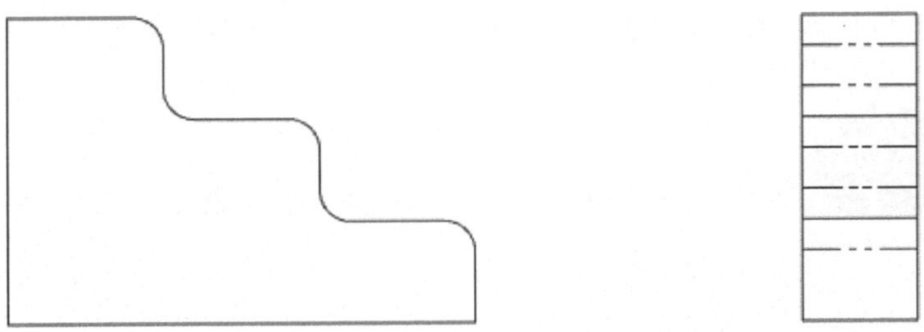

Tangent edges as phantom line

After making the necessary changes, click on the green checkmark to confirm and exit the dialog. The properties of the selected view are modified accordingly.

Editing and Modifying Drawing Properties

In Onshape, the **Drawing properties** panel allows you to modify the default properties of a drawing. These properties include settings for units and precision, dimensions, annotations, views, construction geometry, formats, tables, and inspection. The method for editing the default properties of a drawing is discussed below:

1. Click on the **Drawing properties** tool located on the middle right side of the drawing area, see Figure 10.27. The **Drawing Properties** panel appears with various tabs at its top, see Figure 10.28.

10.27

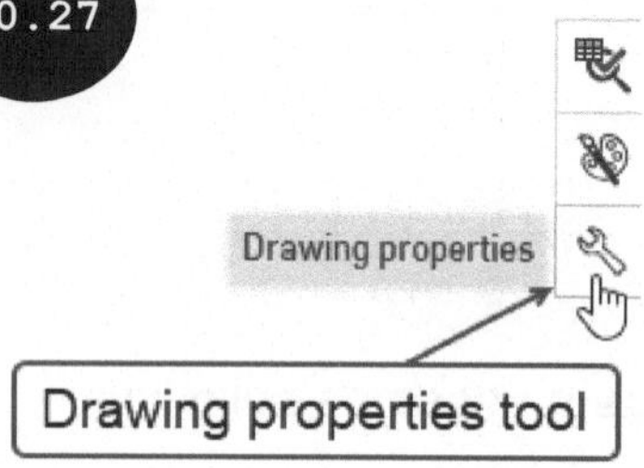

10.28

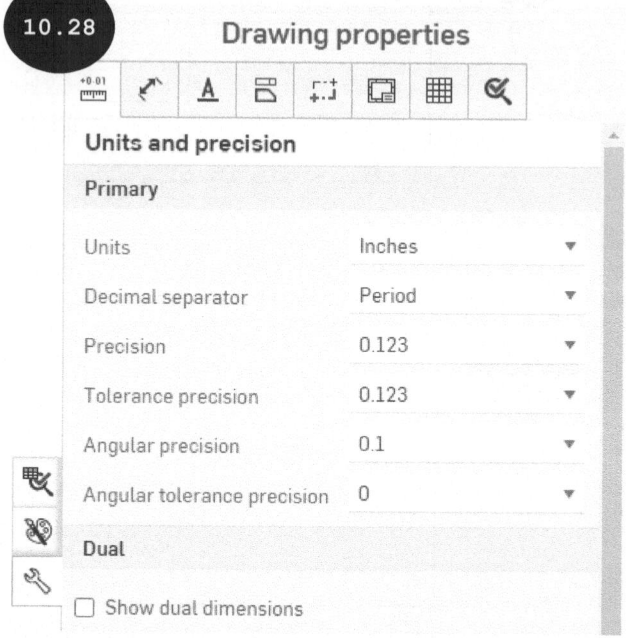

2. Activate the required tab: **Units and precision**, **Dimensions**, **Annotations**, **Views**, **Construction geometry**, **Formats**, **Tables**, and **Inspection** available at the top of the **Drawing properties** panel. The corresponding options to control the drawing properties appear in the panel, refer to Figures 10.28 and 10.29. Figure 10.28 displays the **Drawing properties** panel with options for controlling unit and precision settings, while Figure 10.29 illustrates the panel with options for adjusting dimension settings.

10.29

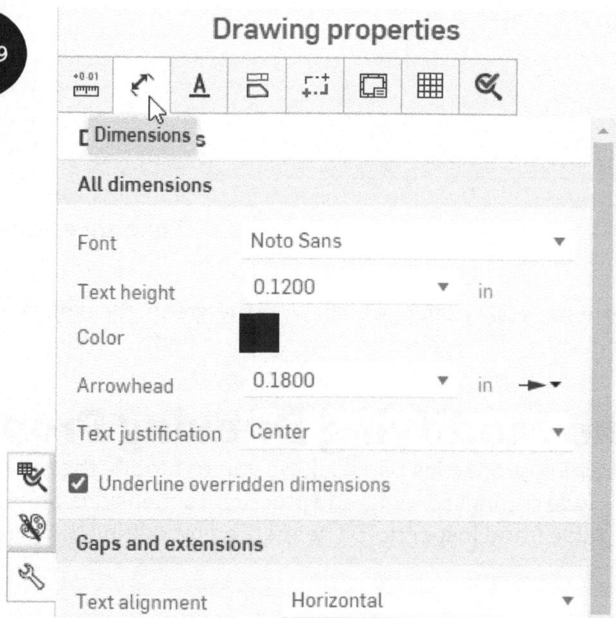

Tip: As mentioned earlier, when you create a drawing using the ISO template, the first angle of projection is used for generating the projected views, whereas the ASME template uses the third angle of projection, by default. However, you can modify the default projection angle for a drawing, if needed. To do this, click on the **Views** tab in the **Drawing properties** panel and select the required angle of projection from the **Projection angle** drop-down list.

3. After setting the required default properties for the drawing, click on the **Drawing properties** tool to close the panel.

Creating an Auxiliary View

An auxiliary view is created by projecting the edges of the model normal to a specified linear edge of an existing view, see Figure 10.30. In this example, the auxiliary view (A-A) is created perpendicular to an inclined edge of the front view, providing an accurate representation of the feature on the slanted face. The method for creating an auxiliary view is discussed below:

10.30

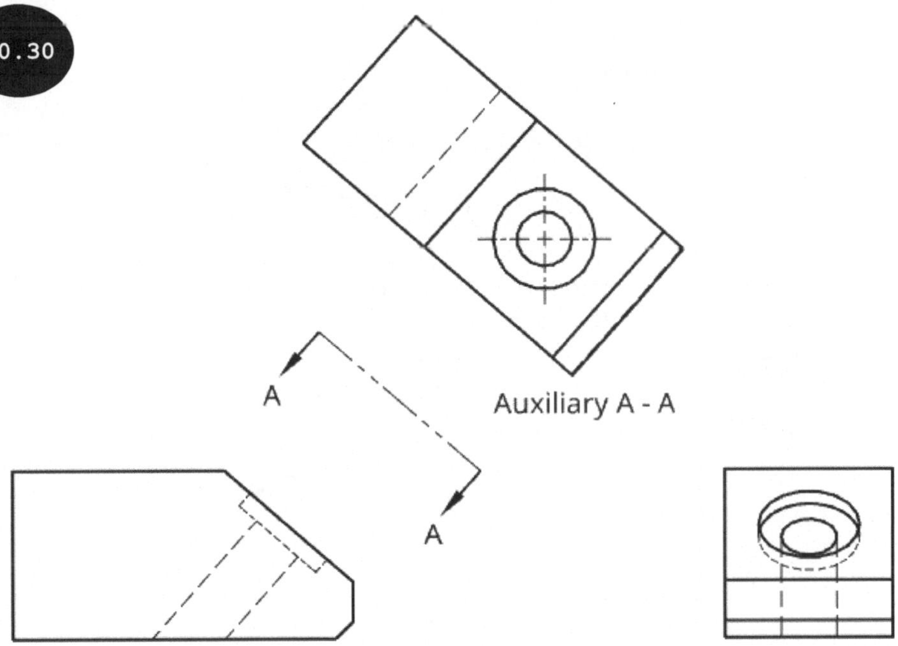

1. Click on the **Auxiliary view** tool in the **Drawing** toolbar, see Figure 10.31. The **Auxiliary view** dialog appears with two tabs: **Normal** and **In line**, see Figure 10.32.

10.31

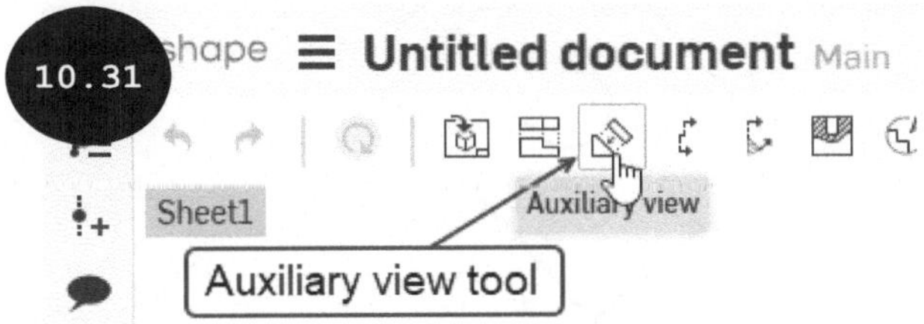

10.32

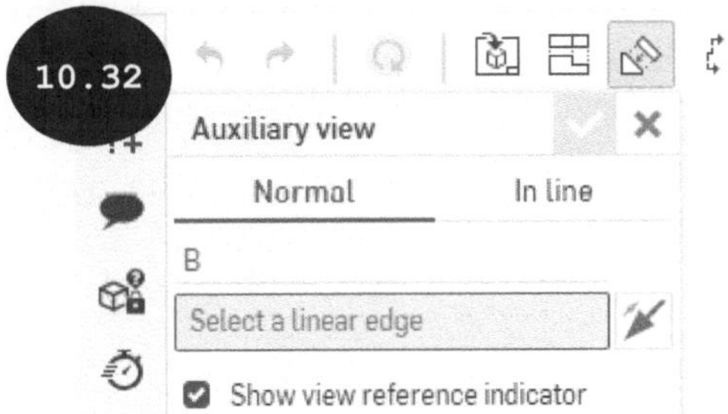

Normal: By default, the **Normal** tab is activated in the **Auxiliary view** dialog, allowing you to select a linear edge of an existing view to create an auxiliary view perpendicular to the selected edge, see Figure 10.33.

10.33

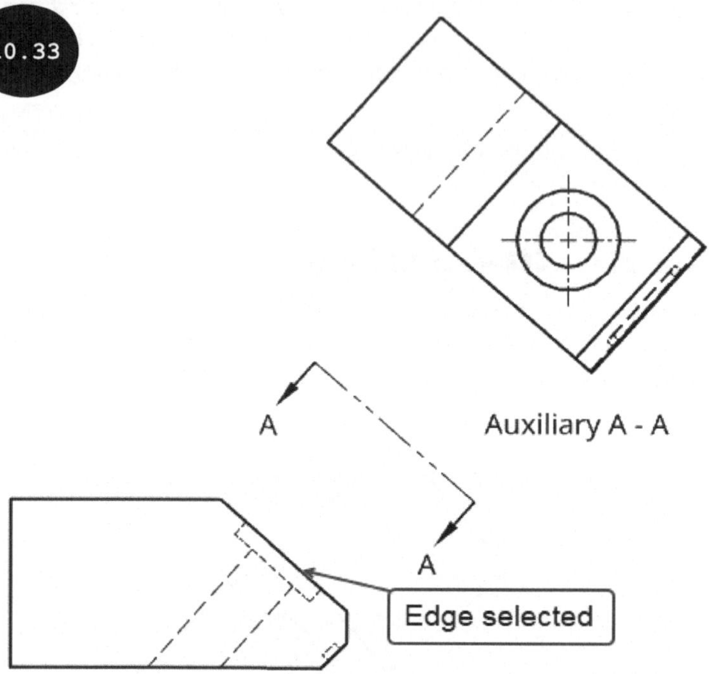

In line: The **In line** tab allows you to select a linear edge of an existing view to create an auxiliary view aligned with the selected edge, see Figure 10.34.

10.34

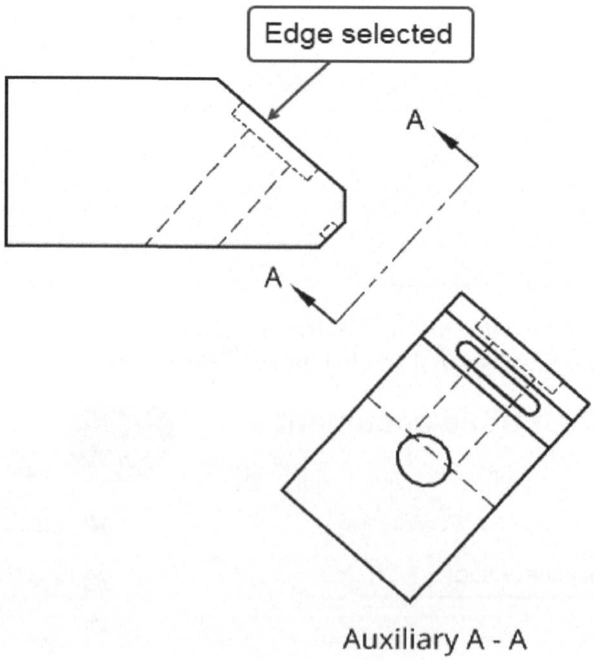

2. Activate the required tab, **Normal** or **In Line**, in the dialog to create an auxiliary view perpendicular to a linear edge of an existing view or aligned with the selected edge, respectively, as discussed.

3. Select a linear edge of an existing view to create an auxiliary view. The auxiliary view appears attached to the cursor, depending on whether the **Normal** or **In Line** tab is activated in the dialog.

4. If needed, you can reverse the viewing direction for the auxiliary view by clicking on the **Opposite direction** button in the dialog.

5. You can accept the default name of the auxiliary view, such as **A**, **B**, **C**, and so on, in the **Name** field of the dialog. If needed, you can also enter a custom name for the view in this field.

6. Move the cursor to the required location on the sheet and click to place the auxiliary view. The auxiliary view is created at the specified location.

Creating a Section View

A section view is created by cutting an object with an imaginary cutting line or section line and then viewing it from a direction perpendicular to the cut. Figure 10.35 illustrates a section view created using a section line. This view effectively highlights the internal features of the object, reduces the number of hidden-detail lines, simplifies the dimensioning of internal features, and represents the cross-section.

10.35

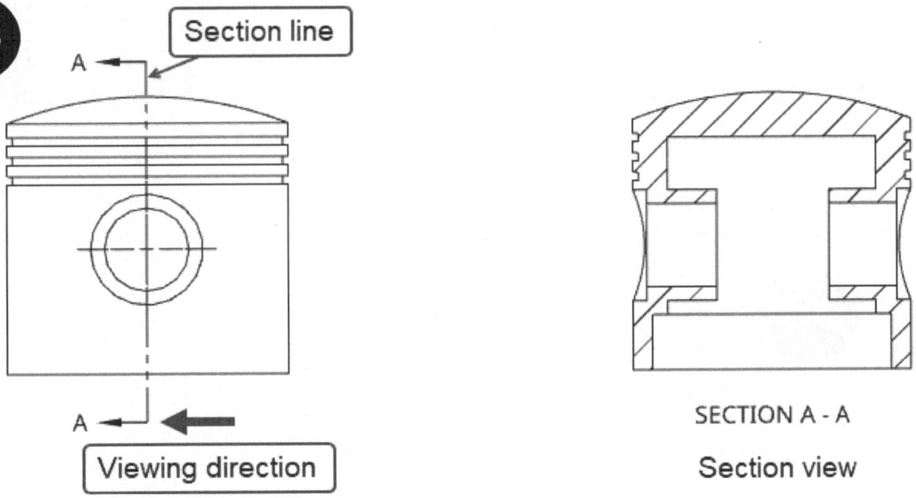

In Onshape, you can create a vertical, horizontal, and angular section view using the **Section view** tool. The method for creating each type of section view is discussed below:

1. Click on the **Section view** tool in the **Drawing** toolbar, see Figure 10.36. The **Section view** dialog appears with three tabs: **Vertical**, **Horizontal**, and **Angular**, see Figure 10.37.

10.36

10.37

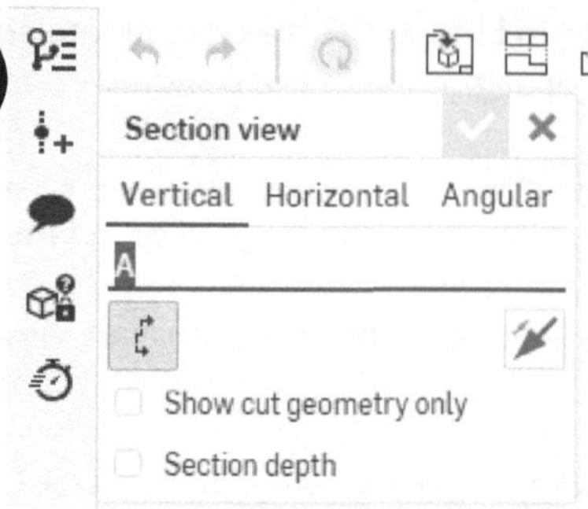

Vertical: By default, the **Vertical** tab is activated in the **Section view** dialog, allowing you to create a section view by cutting the object with a vertical section line, see Figure 10.38. Note that a section line can consist of one or more line segments.

10.38

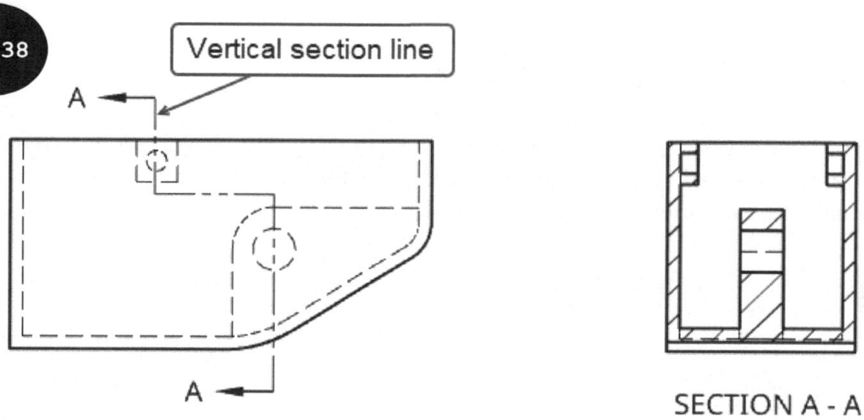

Horizontal: The **Horizontal** tab allows you to create a section view by cutting the object with a horizontal section line, see Figure 10.39. A section line can consist of one or more line segments.

10.39

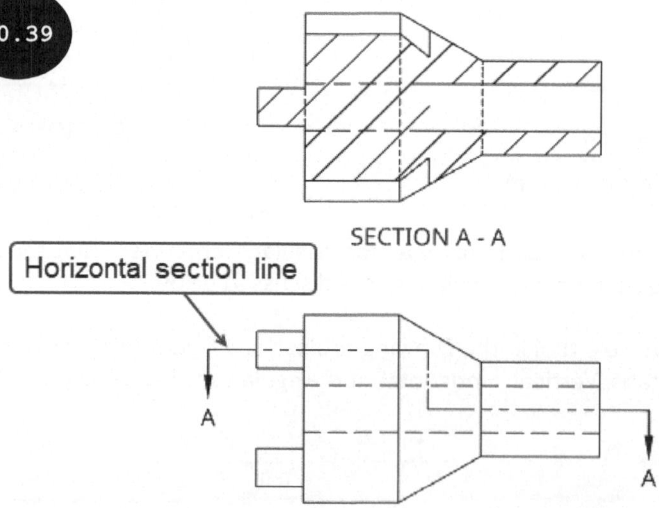

Angular: The **Angular** tab lets you create a section view by cutting the object with a section line positioned at an angle, see Figure 10.40. A section line can consist of one or more line segments. In this example, the section line consists of a single line segment.

10.40

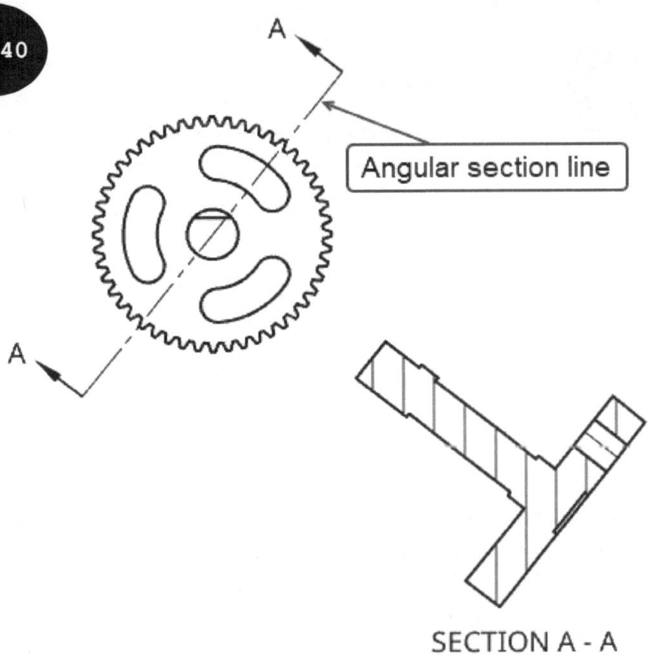

2. Activate the required tab, **Vertical**, **Horizontal**, or **Angular**, in the dialog to create a section view by cutting the object with the respective vertical, horizontal, or angular section line, as explained earlier. The respective section line (vertical, horizontal, or angular) appears attached to the cursor.

3. Move the cursor over an existing drawing view and click to set the first placement point for the section line when it snaps to an entity in the view, see Figure 10.41. The section line is placed, passing through the specified point. Additionally, as you move the cursor over the view, a jogged section line appears (see Figure 10.42), indicating that you can define an additional point to create the section line. In this example, a vertical section line is used to demonstrate the concept.

10.41

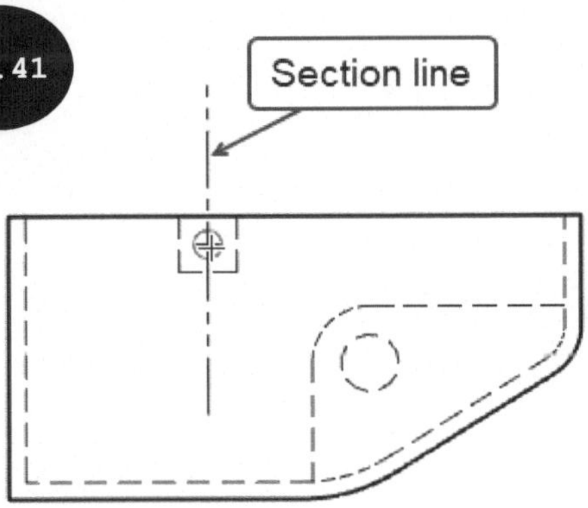

10.42

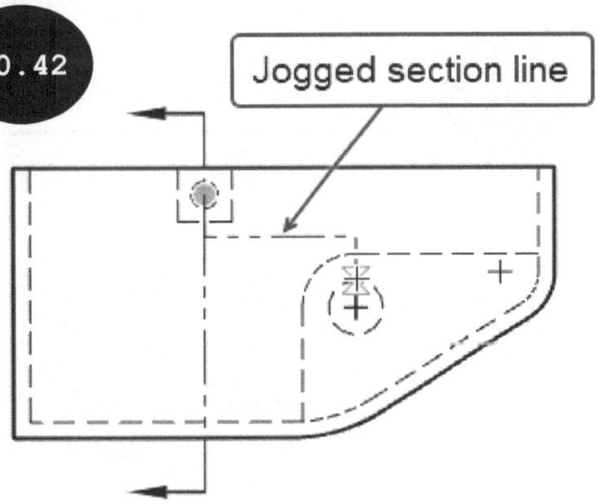

4. Click to define the second placement point for the section line, if needed. The preview of the section line updates accordingly, see Figure 10.43. Additionally, as you move the cursor over the view, another jogged section line appears, indicating that you can continue defining additional points to create the section line.

10.43

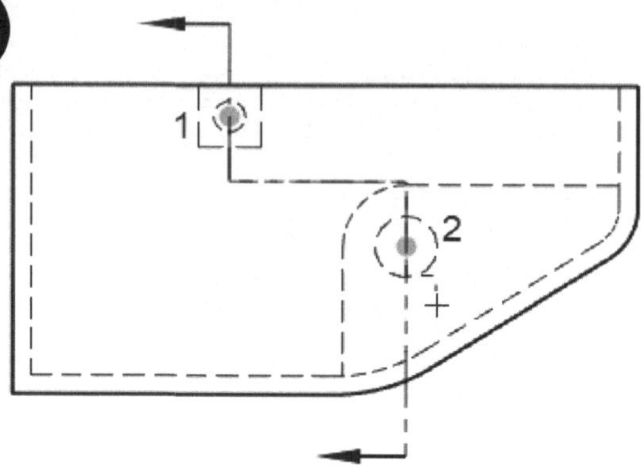

5. After defining one or more placement points for the section line (see Figures 10.44 and 10.45), move the cursor outside the view on either side of the section line. The preview of the corresponding section view appears attached to the cursor. Figure 10.44 illustrates a vertical section line with a single placement point, while Figure 10.45 depicts the vertical section line with two placement points.

10.44

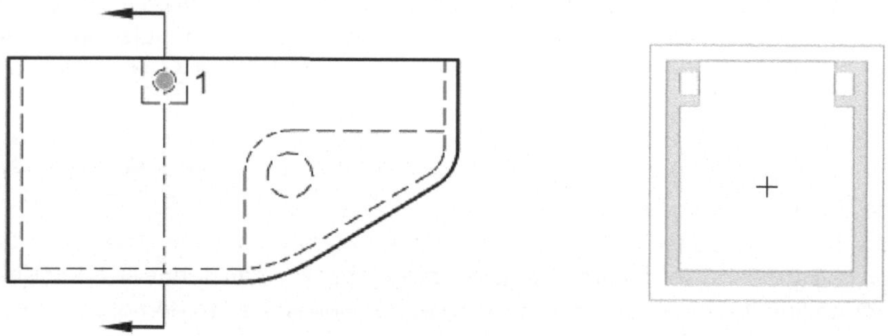

10.45

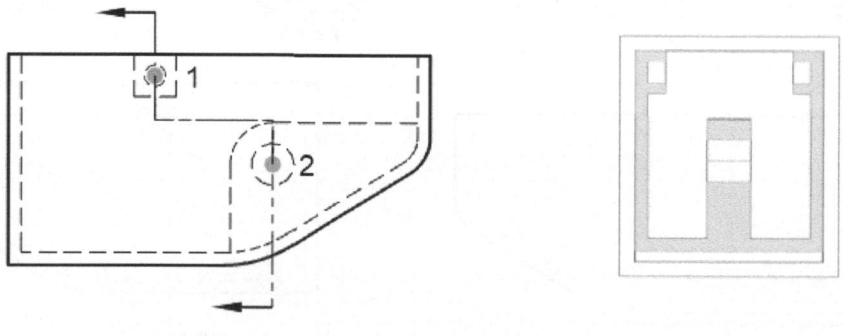

Note that the arrows on the section line indicate the viewing direction. You can reverse this direction by clicking the **Opposite direction** button in the **Section view** dialog. By default, the viewing direction is determined by the movement of the cursor on either side of the section line.

Moreover, if needed, you can enter a custom name for the section view in the **Name** field of the dialog. By default, section views are named sequentially as A, B, C, and so on.

6. Move the cursor to the desired location and click to define the placement point for the section view. The section view is then created at the specified position on the sheet, see Figure 10.46.

10.46

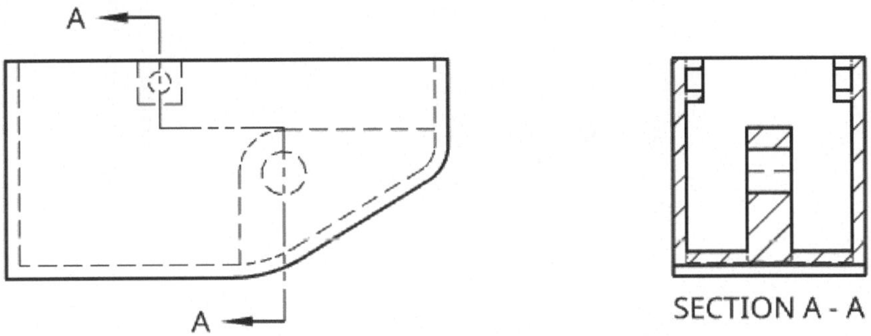

Note: In the above examples, vertical section views are shown. You can also create horizontal and angular section views in a similar manner by selecting the respective **Horizontal** or **Angular** tab in the **Section view** dialog. Figure 10.47 shows a horizontal section view, while Figure 10.48 shows an angular section view.

10.47

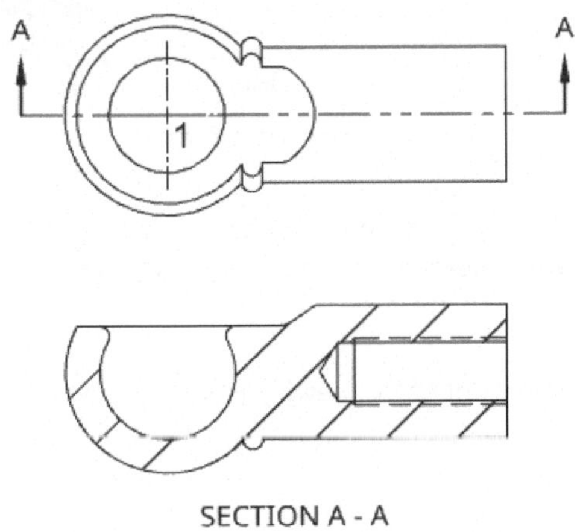

10.48

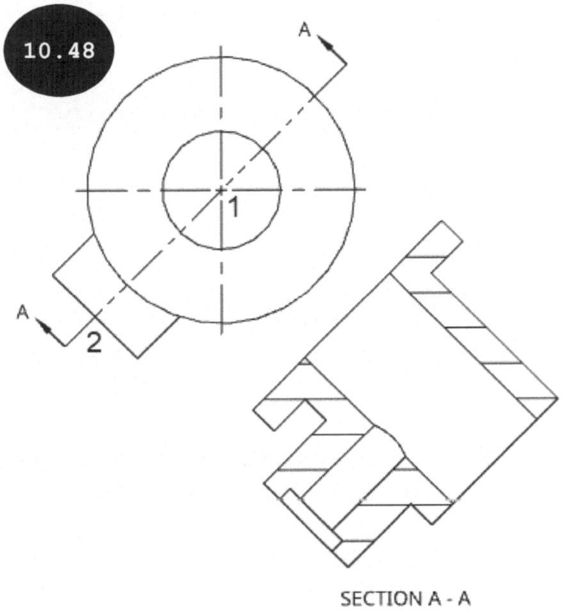

Creating an Aligned Section View

An aligned section view is created by cutting an object with a section line consisting of two non-parallel lines and then straightening the cross-section by revolving it around the center point of the section line, see Figure 10.49. The method for creating an aligned section view is discussed below.

10.49

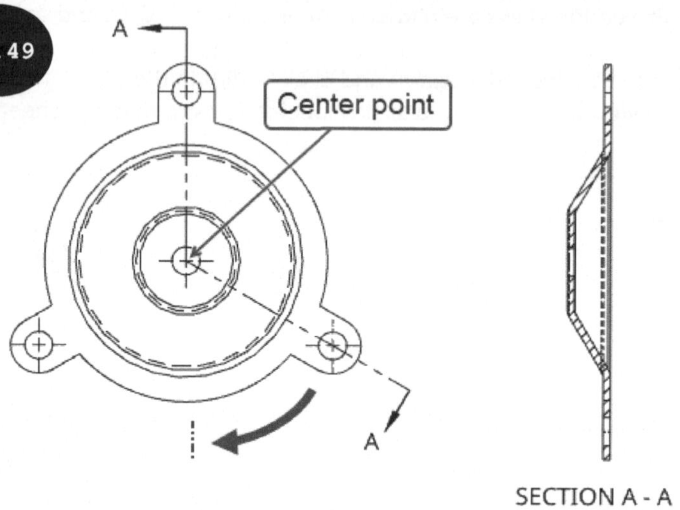

1. Click on the **Aligned section view** tool in the **Drawing** toolbar, see Figure 10.50. The **Aligned section view** dialog appears, see Figure 10.51. Additionally, a section line consisting of two non-parallel lines appears attached to the cursor, and you are prompted to specify the center point of the section line. It is because the **Center** field is activated by default in the dialog.

10.50

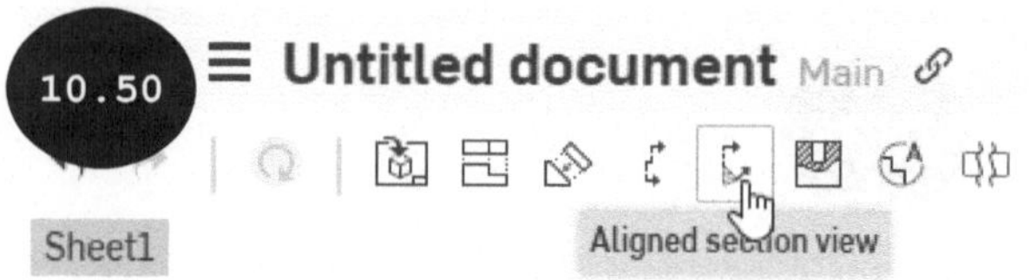

10.51

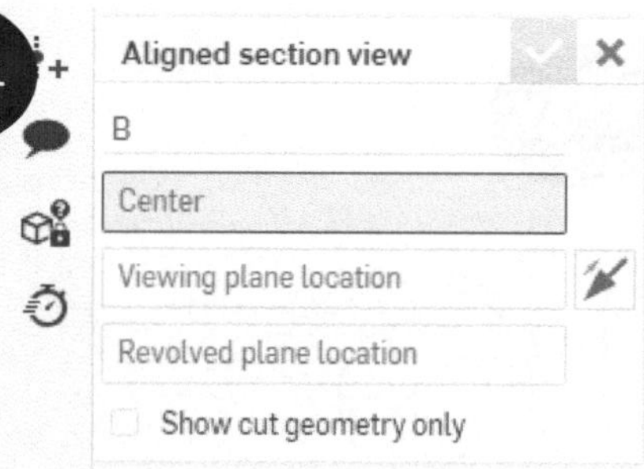

2. Click to define the center point for the section line on an existing view, refer to Figure 10.52. Once the center point is defined, the **Viewing plane location** field is automatically activated in the dialog. As a result, you are prompted to define a location for the viewing plane.

Tip: The resultant aligned section view will be created in front of the viewing plane by viewing the object from this direction.

3. Move the cursor to the desired location and click to define the placement point for the viewing plane, refer to Figure 10.52. Once the viewing plane is defined, the **Revolved plane location** field is automatically activated in the dialog to define a location for the revolved plane.

4. Move the cursor to the desired location and click to define the revolved plane, see Figure 10.52. A preview of the partial aligned section view appears as you move the cursor normal to the viewing plane, see Figure 10.52.

10.52

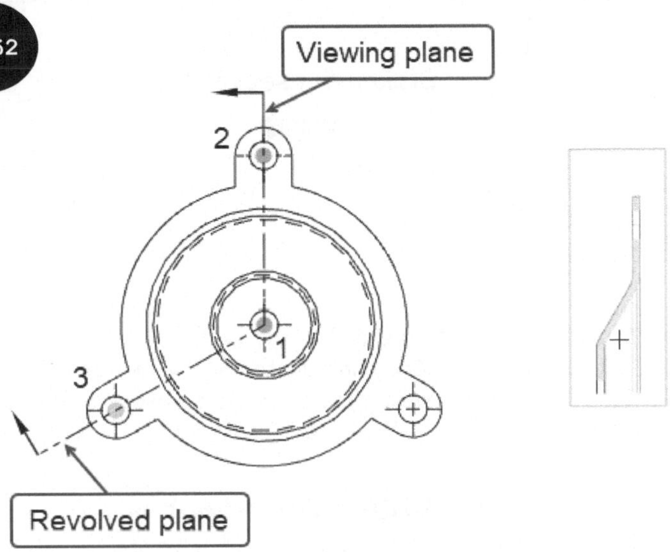

5. Click to define the placement point for the aligned section view. The aligned section view is created by straightening the cross-section of the revolved plane around the center point, see Figure 10.53.

10.53

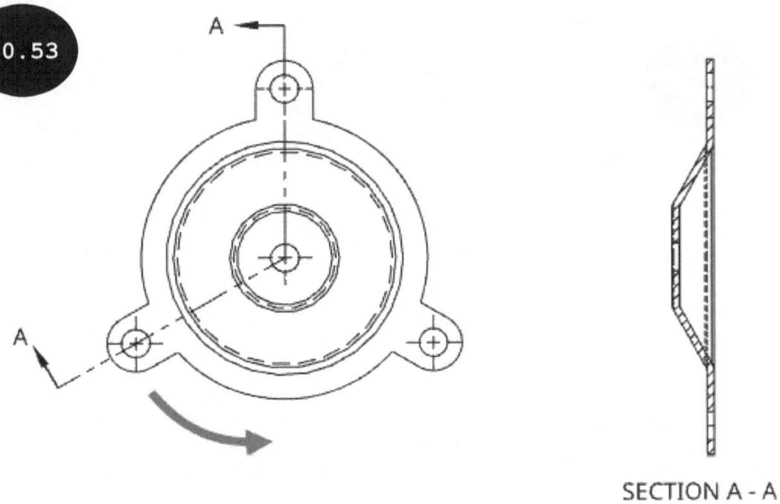

Creating a Broken-out Section View

A broken-out section view is created by removing a portion of an existing view up to a specified depth or an entity to reveal the inner details of the object, see Figure 10.54. The method for creating a broken-out section view is discussed below:

10.54

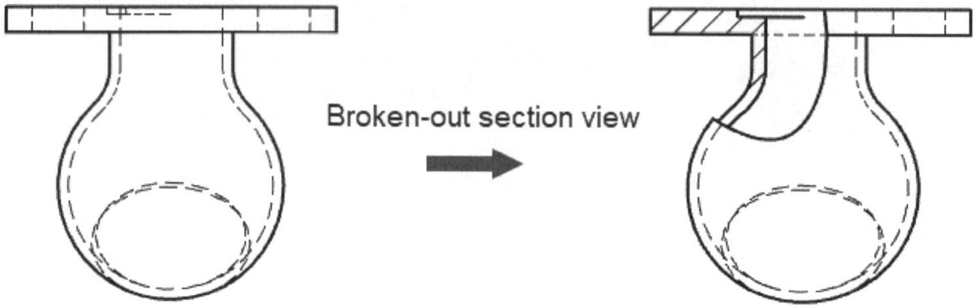

1. Click on the **Broken-out section** tool in the **Drawing** toolbar, see Figure 10.55. The **Broken-out section** dialog appears, see Figure 10.56. By default, the **Spline** tool and the **Create closed profile** field are activated in the dialog box, allowing you to create a closed profile to define the portion of a view to be removed.

10.55

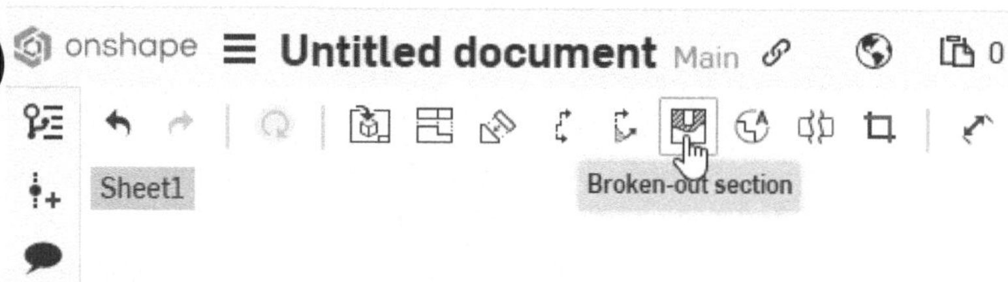

10.56

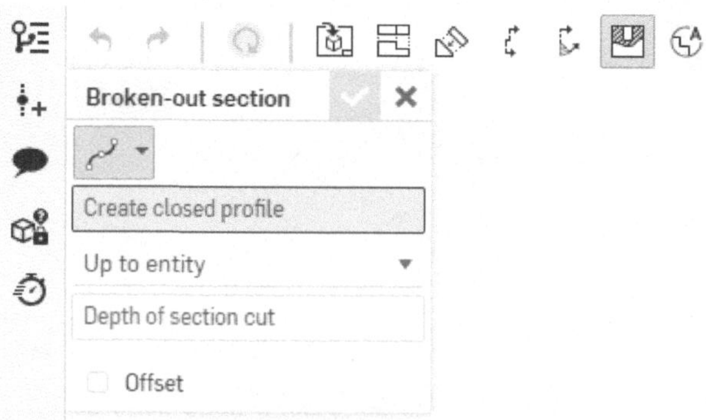

Tip: You cannot create a broken-out section view on existing section views, detail views, or aligned section views.

2. Draw a closed profile around the portion of an existing drawing view to be removed, see Figure 10.57. In this example, the closed profile is created on the Side view.

10.57

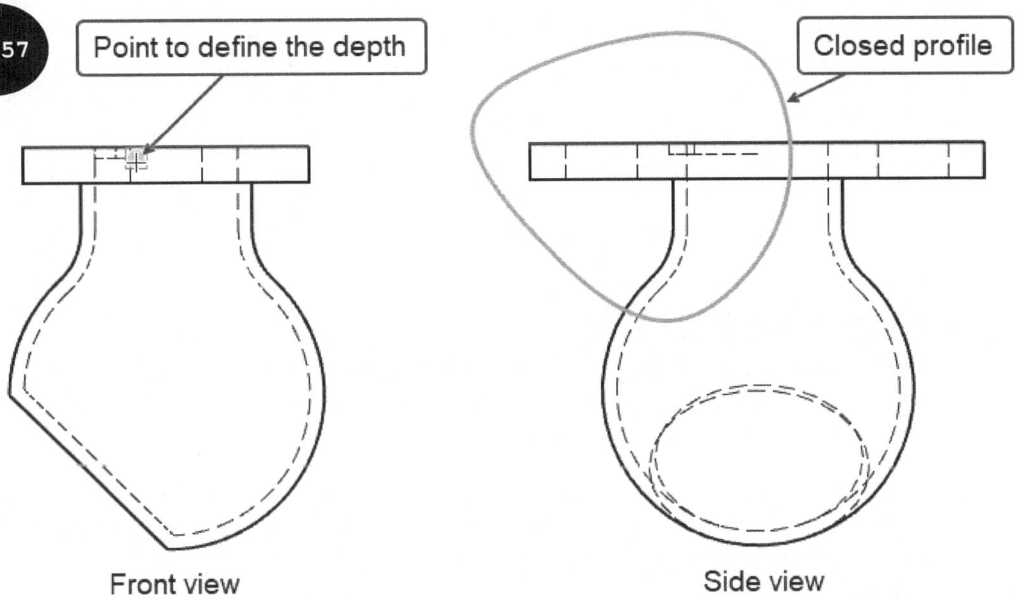

After creating a closed profile, the next step is to define the depth of the cut in the view.

3. Select the required option: **Up to entity** or **Blind** in the **End type** drop-down list of the dialog to define the depth of the cut.

   Up to entity: By default, the **Up to entity** option is selected, enabling you to select a point on another view to define the depth of the cut or the extent to which you want to remove material, refer to Figure 10.57. In this example, the point to define the depth is selected on the Front view.

   Note that when the **Up to entity** option is selected, the **Offset** check box is available in the dialog box. Selecting this check box allows you to enter an offset distance in the **Offset** field, extending the cut depth beyond the selected entity in either direction. You can reverse the offset direction by clicking the **Opposite direction** button.

   Blind: When the **Blind** option is selected, the **Depth** field becomes available in the dialog. In this field, you can enter the depth value to specify how far the material should be removed for the cut.

4. After defining the depth of the cut, click on the green checkmark to confirm and exit the dialog. The broken-out section view is created on the selected view up to a specified depth, see Figure 10.58.

10.58

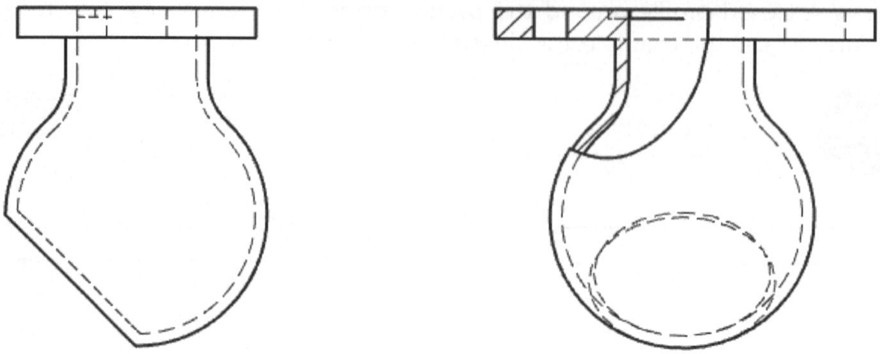

Creating a Detail View

A detail view magnifies a specific portion of an existing drawing view to clearly illustrate or dimension small features. You can define the area to be enlarged by creating a closed sketch using tools such as **Circle**, **Spline**, or **Polygon**. The method for creating a detail view is discussed below:

1. Click on the **Detail view** tool in the **Drawing** toolbar, see Figure 10.59. The **Detail view** dialog appears, see Figure 10.60. By default, the **Circle** tool is activated in the dialog, allowing you to draw a circle to define the area of a view to be enlarged.

10.59

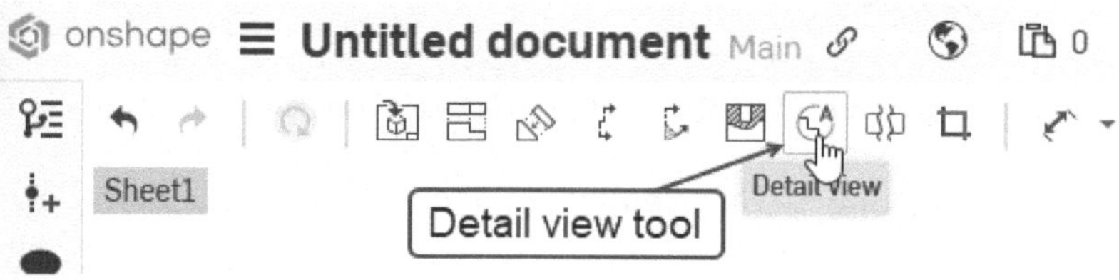

10.60

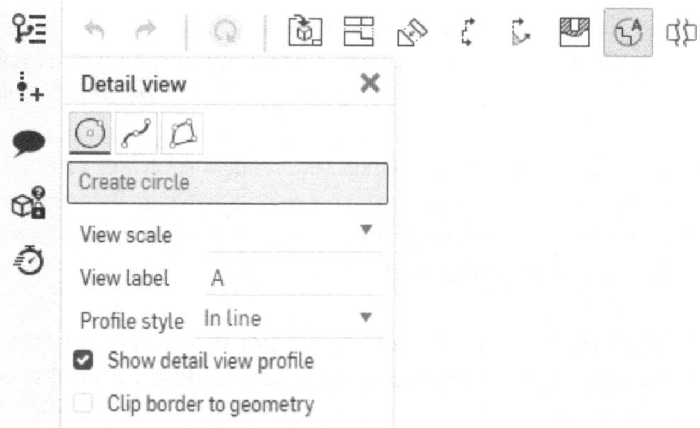

2. Click to activate the required tool: **Circle**, **Spline**, or **Polygon** in the **Detail view** dialog to create a closed sketch in the desired shape.

3. Create a closed sketch around the portion of the existing view to be enlarged, depending on the tool activated in the previous step. This could be a circle, spline, or polygon, based on your selection. An enlarged view of the defined area attaches to the cursor, see Figure 10.61. In this example, a circle is created around the portion of a view to be enlarged.

10.61

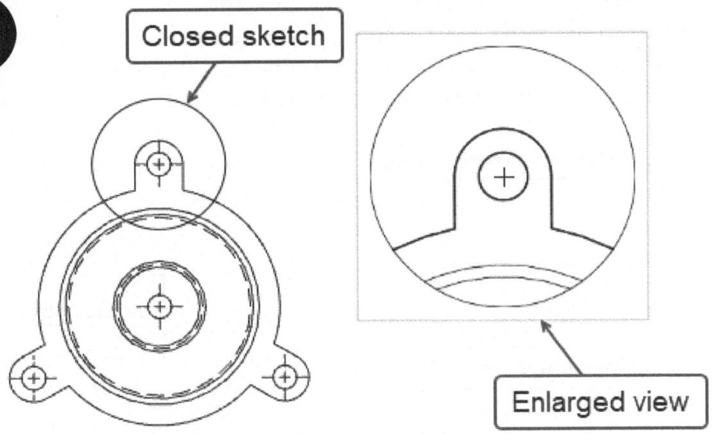

4. Select the required option (**In line**, **Connected**, or **Leader**) from the **Profile style** drop-down list to control the position of the label on the source view relative to the detail view.

   In line: The **In line** option places the label on the source view, aligned or positioned between the closed sketch created, see Figure 10.62 (a).

   Connected: The **Connected** option links the detail view to the source view with a dashed line, see Figure 10.62 (b).

   Leader: The **Leader** option attaches the label to the source view with a leader line, see Figure 10.62 (c).

10.62

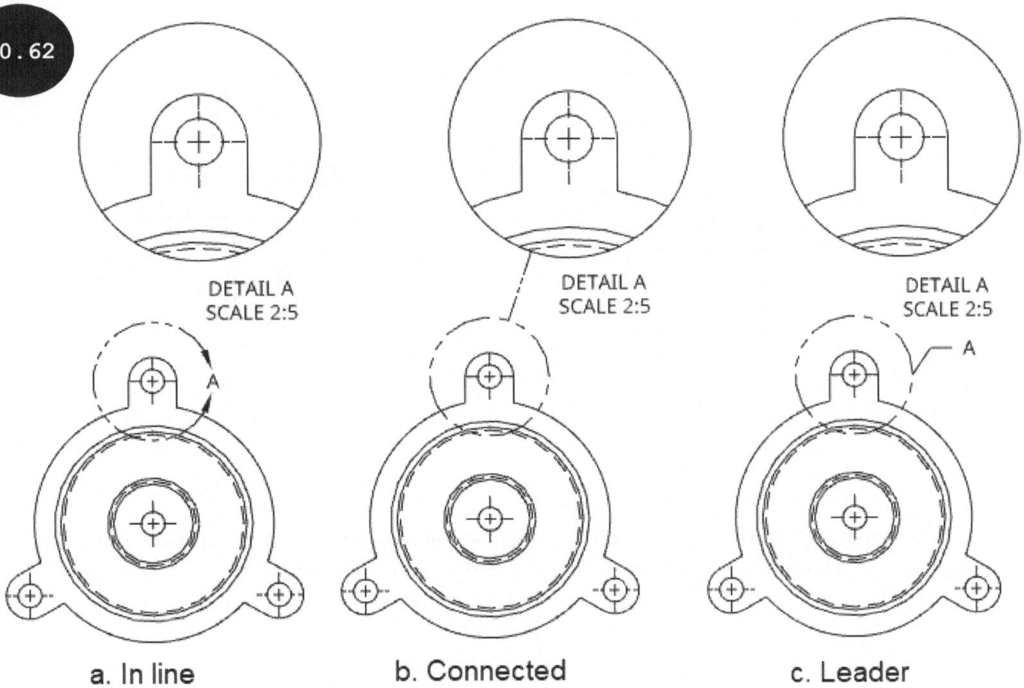

5. Ensure that the **Show detail view profile** check box is selected in the dialog to outline the detail view border, similar to the outline drawn on the source view using the circle, spline, or polygon. Figure 10.63 shows a detail view with an outline similar to the outline drawn on the source view using the spline. If you want to display the detail view without an outline, clear this check box.

10.63

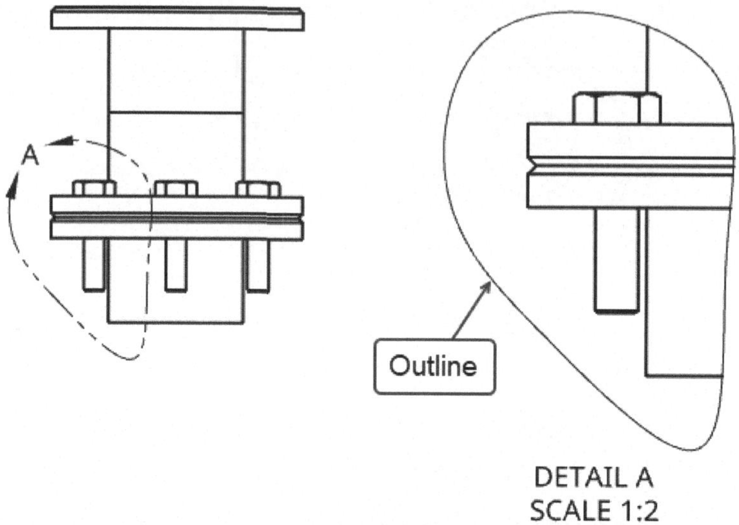

6. If you want to display the outline only on the geometry of the detail view, select the **Clip border to geometry** check box, see Figure 10.64. This check box is enabled only when the **Show detail view profile** check box is selected.

10.64

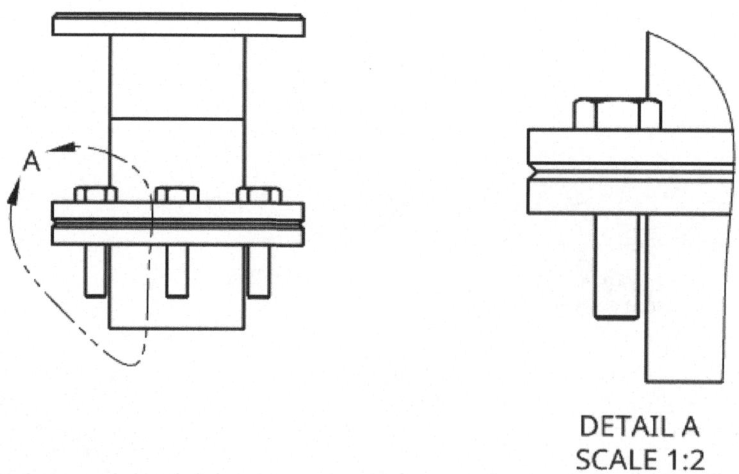

7. After selecting the required options, click to define the placement for the detail view on the sheet. A detail view of the defined portion is created at the specified location.

Creating a Break View

A break view is created by breaking an existing view using a pair of vertical or horizontal break lines, with the portion between the break lines removed, as shown in Figure 10.65. A break view is used to display a view with a large length-to-width ratio on a small-scale sheet by removing a section of the view that has the same cross-section, as illustrated in the figure. The method for creating a break view is discussed below:

10.65

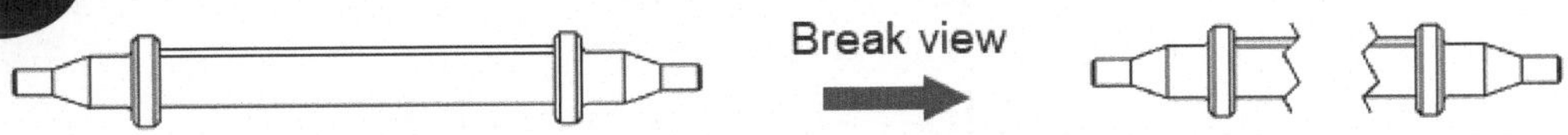

1. Click on the **Break view** tool in the **Drawing** toolbar, see Figure 10.66. The **Break view** dialog appears with two tabs: **Vertical** and **Horizontal**, see Figure 10.67.

10.66

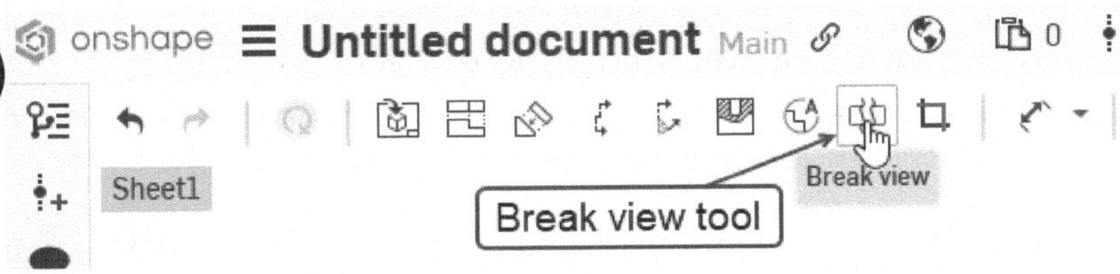

10.67

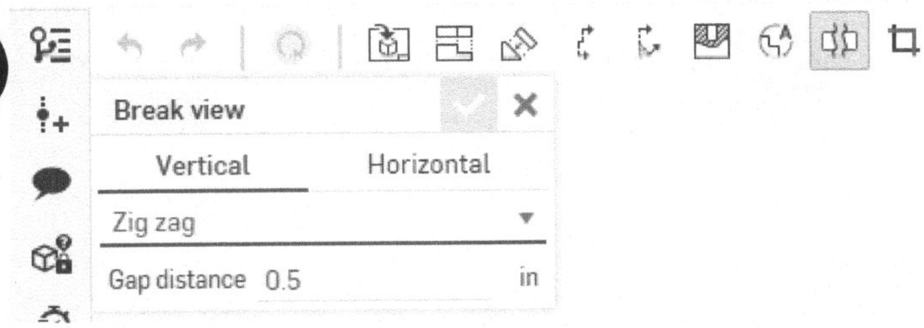

Vertical: By default, the **Vertical** tab is activated in the **Break view** dialog, allowing you to create a break view using a pair of two vertical break lines, refer to Figure 10.65.

Horizontal: The **Horizontal** tab allow you to create a break view using a pair of two horizontal break lines, see Figure 10.68.

10.68

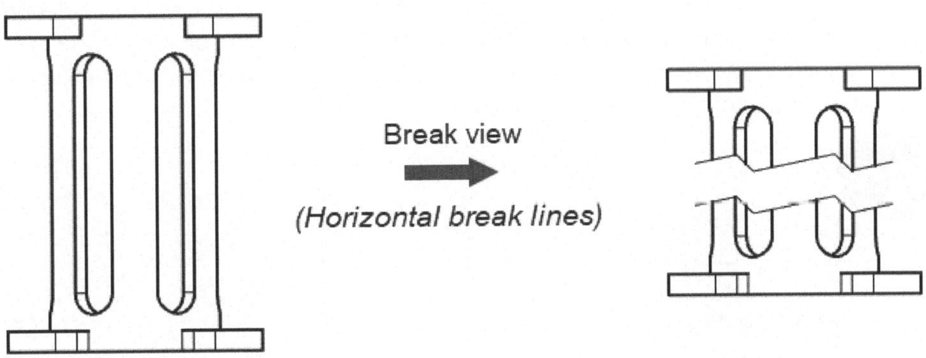

2. Activate the required tab (**Vertical** or **Horizontal**) in the dialog to break an existing view using a pair of vertical or horizontal lines, respectively, as discussed above.

3. Move the cursor over the existing view to be broken. A preview of the first vertical or horizontal break line appears attached to the cursor, depending on whether the **Vertical** or **Horizontal** tab is activated in the dialog, see Figure 69. This figure shows the preview of a vertical break line.

10.69

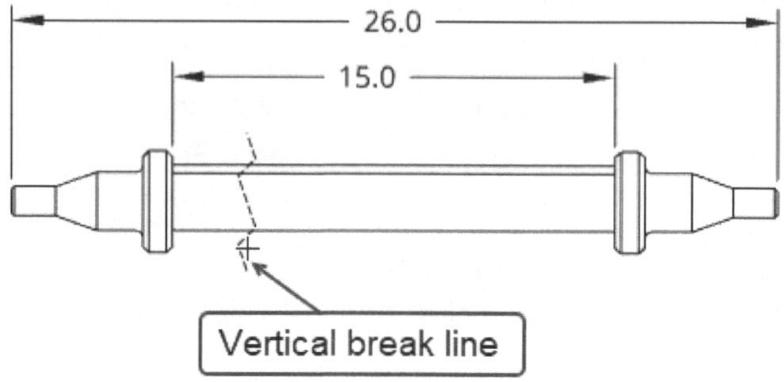

4. Specify the placement point for the first break line by clicking the left mouse button at the desired location on the view. The second break line appears attached to the cursor.

5. Specify the placement point for the second break line at the desired location on the view. The view is then broken, and the portion inside the defined break lines is removed, see Figure 10.70.

10.70

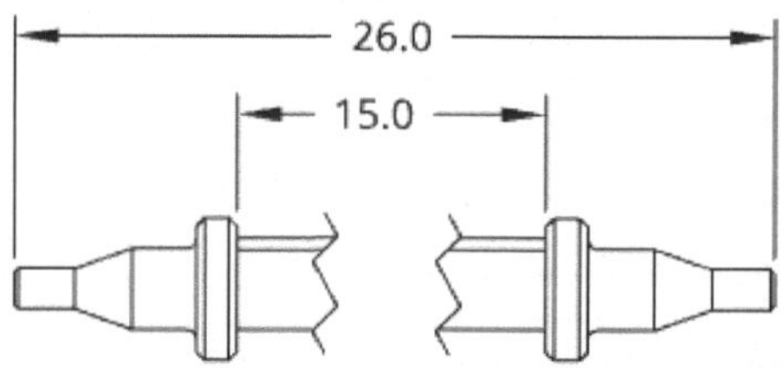

Note: It is evident from the figure above that even after breaking the view, the overall length or dimension values associated with it remain unchanged. You will learn about applying dimensions later in this chapter.

6. Define the type of break line as zig zag, small zig zag, curve, or straight by selecting the required option in the **Break line type** drop-down list of the dialog. The display of the break line updates accordingly in the view. Figure 10.70 shows the zig zag break lines, while Figure 10.71 shows the small zig zag, curve, and straight break lines.

10.71

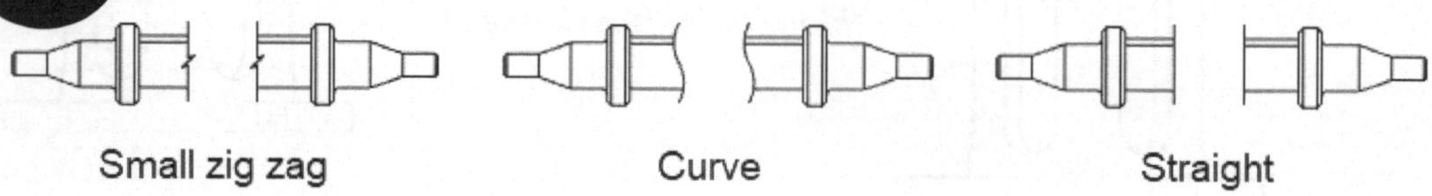

7. If needed, you can also control the gap between the break lines using the **Gap distance** field of the **Break view** dialog.

8. After selecting the required options, click on the green checkmark to confirm and exit the dialog. The break view of specified settings is created on the selected view.

Creating a Crop View

A crop view is created by cropping an existing view using a closed sketch, such that only the portion inside the closed sketch is retained in the view, see Figure 10.72. You can create the closed sketch using the **Circle**, **Spline**, or **Polygon** tool while creating the crop view. The method for creating a crop view is discussed below:

10.72

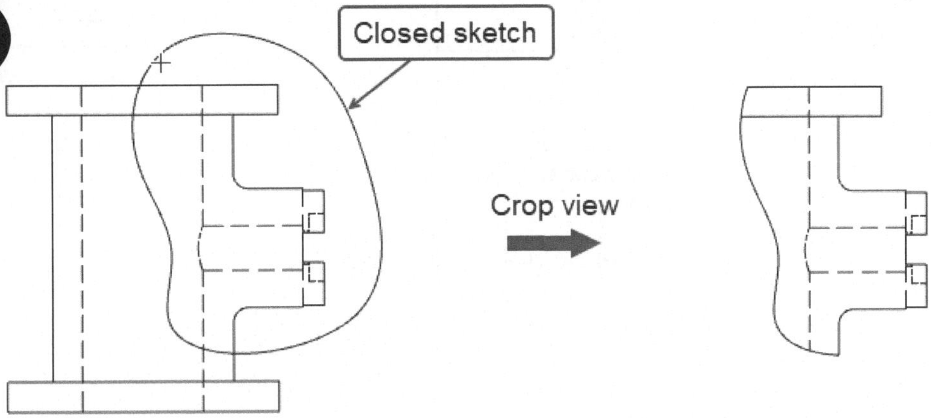

1. Click on the **Crop view** tool in the **Drawing** toolbar, see Figure 10.73. The **Crop view** dialog appears, see Figure 10.74. By default, the **Spline** tool is activated in the dialog, allowing you to draw a closed spline to define the area of a view to be cropped.

10.73

10.74

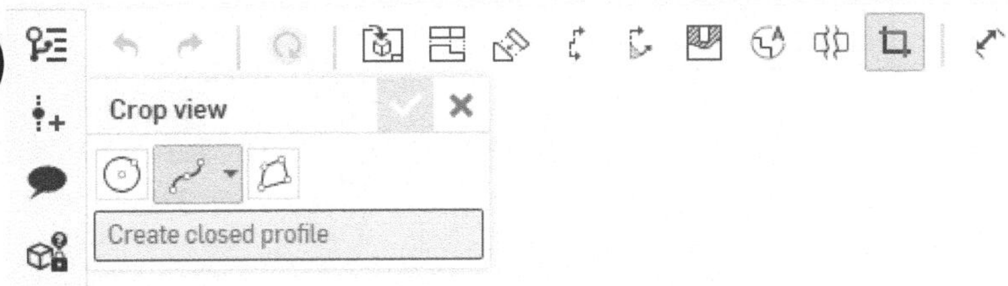

2. Click to activate the required tool: **Circle**, **Spline**, or **Polygon** in the **Crop view** dialog to create a closed sketch.

3. Create a closed sketch around the portion of the existing view to be cropped, depending on the tool activated in the previous step. This could be a circle, spline, or polygon, based on your selection. Figure 10.75 shows a closed sketch created using the **Spline** tool.

4. After creating a closed sketch around a portion of a view to be cropped, click on the green checkmark ✓ to confirm and exit the dialog. The crop view is created such that only the portion that lies inside the closed sketch is retained in the view, see Figure 10.76. Note that the scale of the view remains the same.

10.75

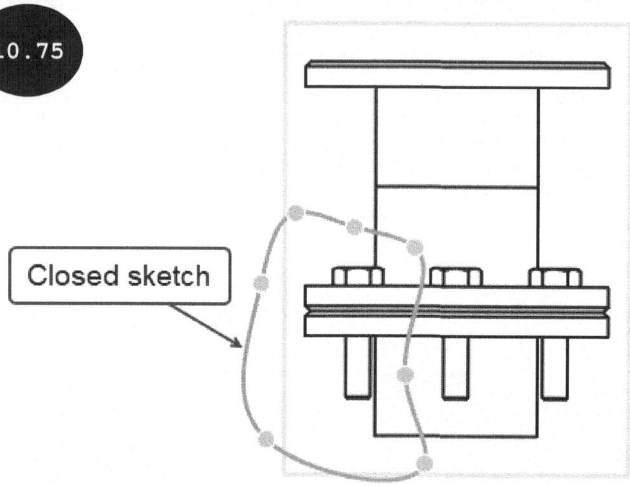

10.76

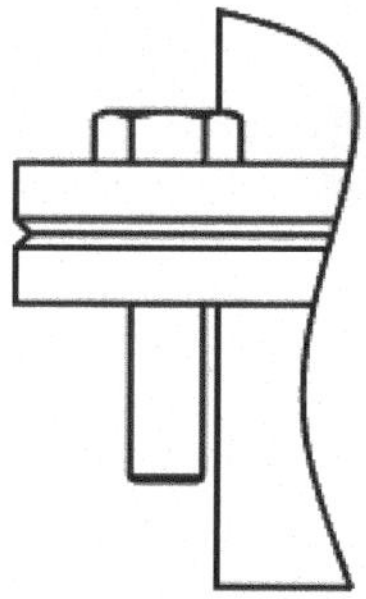

Editing and Modifying Sheet Properties

In Onshape, you can modify the default sheet properties such as sheet size and scale using the **Sheet** panel. The method for editing the default properties of a drawing is discussed below:

1. Click on the **Sheets** tool located on the middle left side of the drawing area, see Figure 10.77. The **Sheet** panel appears with a list of available drawing sheets and views, see Figure 10.78.

10.77

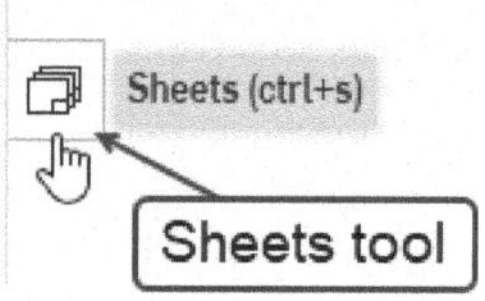

10.78

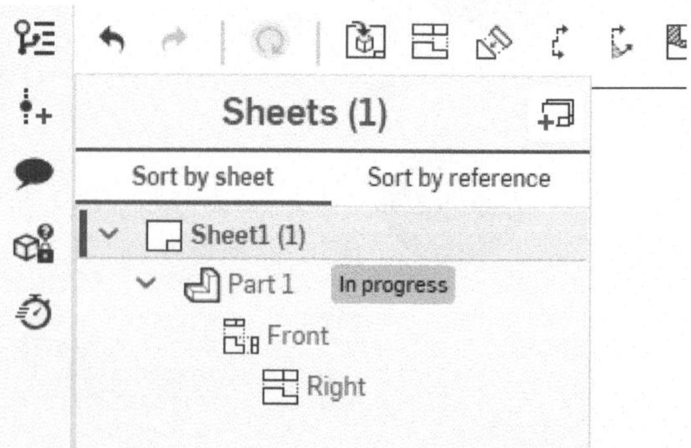

Tip: The sheet, whose title bar is highlighted with a light blue background and a vertical blue bar to its left in the **Sheet** panel, indicates that it is currently activated and displayed in the drawing area. You will learn about adding additional sheets for a drawing later in this chapter.

2. Right-click on the sheet whose properties you want to modify, then click on the **Properties** option in the shortcut menu, see Figure 10.79. The **Sheet properties** dialog appears, see Figure 10.80.

10.79

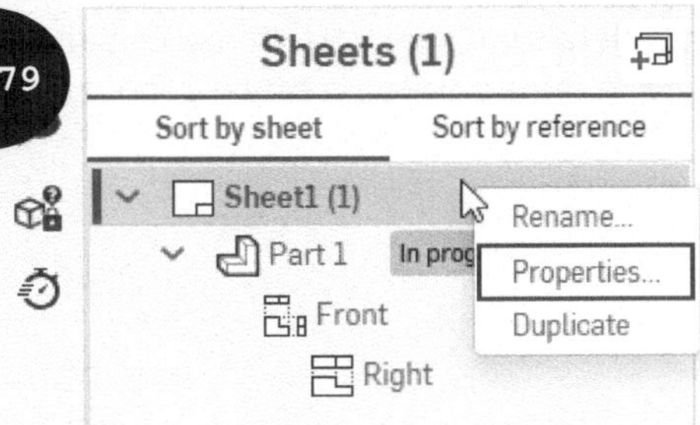

10.80

In the **Sheet properties** dialog, you can edit the sheet properties such as sheet size, scale and format.

3. After modifying the necessary sheet properties, click on the green checkmark ✓ to confirm and exit the dialog. The sheet properties update accordingly, while the **Sheet** panel remains visible.

Adding a New Sheet

In addition to the default sheet for creating drawing views of a part or assembly, you can add additional sheets as required. The method for adding a new sheet is discussed below:

1. Ensure that the **Sheet** panel is displayed on the left of the drawing area. You can display the **Sheet** panel by clicking on the **Sheets** tool located on the middle left side of the drawing area as discussed earlier.

2. Click on the **Insert sheet** tool located at the top right corner of the **Sheet** panel, see Figure 10.81. A new sheet with default properties is inserted and becomes the active sheet of the drawing.

10.81

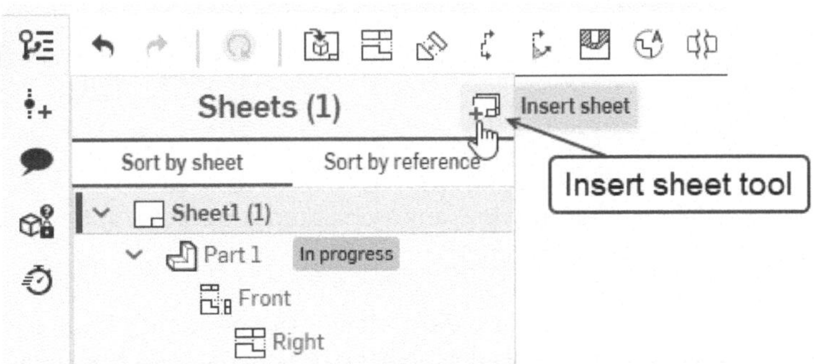

3. You can create drawing views on the currently active sheet, as discussed earlier.

4. Similarly, you can add multiple sheets for creating the drawing.

Note: You can switch between sheets by double-clicking on their names in the **Sheet** panel.

To delete a sheet, right-click on it and select **Delete** from the shortcut menu. Similarly, you can use other options in the shortcut menu to rename a sheet, create a duplicate copy, or move it up or down in the list.

5. To exit the **Sheet** panel, click on the **Sheets** tool again.

Deleting a Drawing View

To delete an existing drawing view, select the view and press the DELETE key. The selected view is removed from the drawing sheet and is no longer part of the drawing.

Alternatively, you can delete a view through the **Sheet** panel. Click on the **Sheets** tool to display the panel, select the view to be deleted, and right-click to open the shortcut menu. Then, click **Delete**, see Figure 10.82. The selected view will be removed from the sheet.

10.82

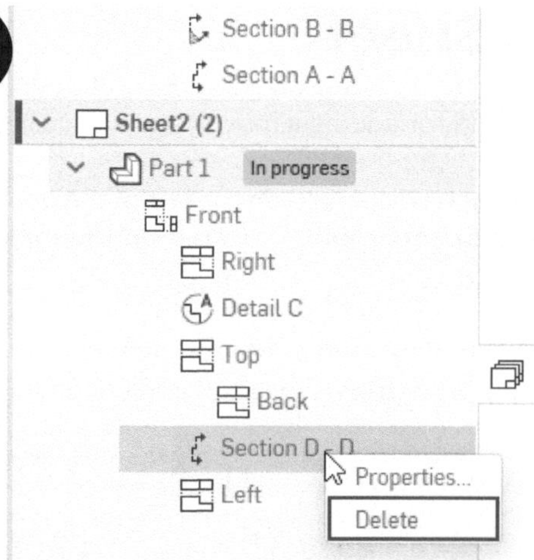

Note: When you delete a drawing view, any associated geometries such as dimensions, centerlines, or section lines are also deleted.

Additionally, if you delete a parent view, its dependent views, such as detail views and section views, are also deleted. However, projected views remain available on the drawing sheet even after deleting the parent view.

Moving a Drawing View

In Onshape, after placing a drawing view on the sheet, you may need to reposition it. To do this, press and hold the left mouse button on the view, then drag it to the desired location.

Note: When you move a view, all its dependent views such as projected and section views automatically move as well to maintain alignment with the parent view.

To break a view's alignment with its parent view, right-click on the view, then select **Suppress alignment with parent** in the shortcut menu, see Figure 10.83. Now, the view can be moved independently.

10.83

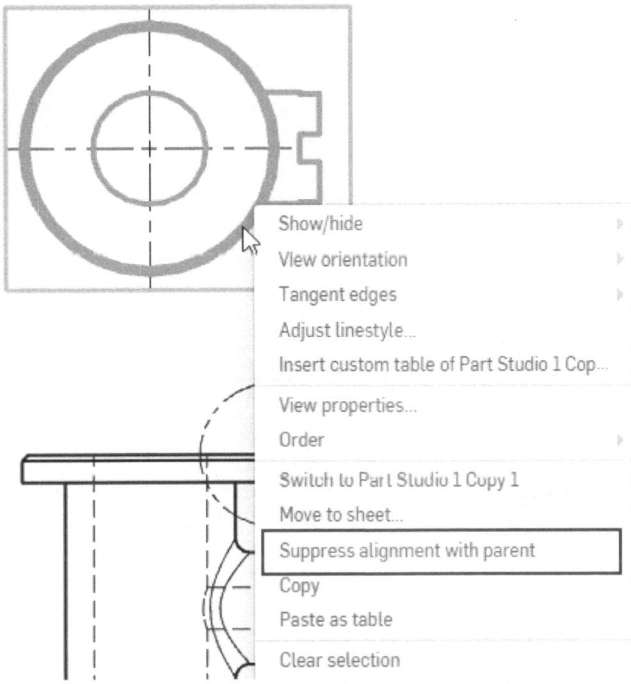

Moving a View to Another Sheet

You can also move a drawing view of one sheet to an another sheet of the drawing. To do this, right-click on the view and then select the **Move to sheet** option in the shortcut menu that appears. The **Move to sheet** dialog appears, refer to Figure 10.84. The Sheet drop-down list in this dialog displays all available sheets in the current drawing.

Open the **Sheet** drop-down list (see Figure 10.84) and select the desired sheet to move the selected view. This activates the selected sheet and displays the moved view on it. Also, the **Move to sheet** dialog remains open. Click on the green checkmark ✓ to confirm and exit the dialog.

10.84

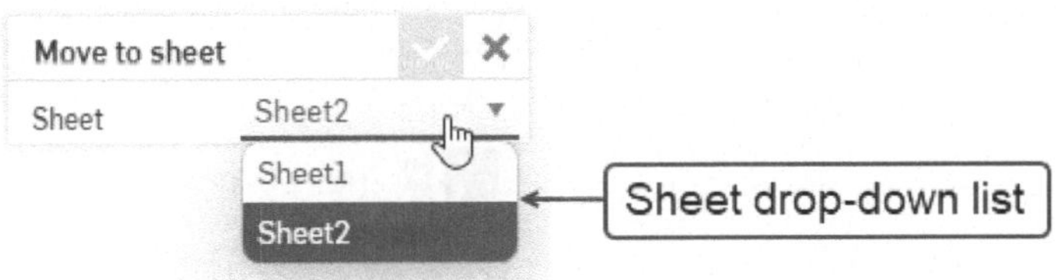

Editing Hatch Properties of a Section View

In Onshape, after creating a section view, you can edit its default hatching properties, including the hatch pattern, scale factor, and hatch angle. The method for modifying the hatch properties of a view is explained below:

1. Right-click on the section view, then select **Edit hatch section** in the shortcut menu that appears, see Figure 10.85. The **Edit hatch** dialog appears, see Figure 10.86.

10.85

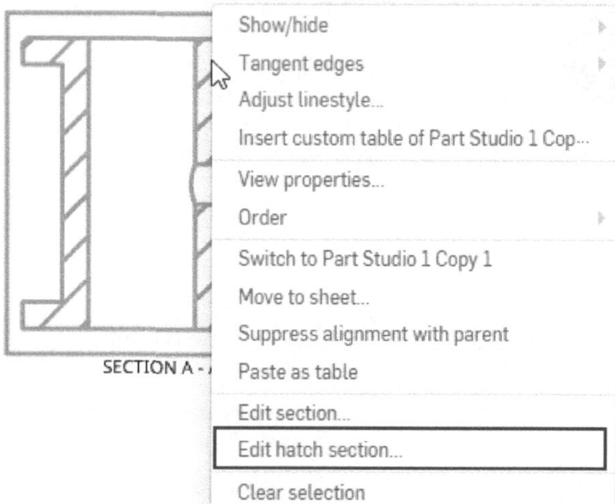

10.86

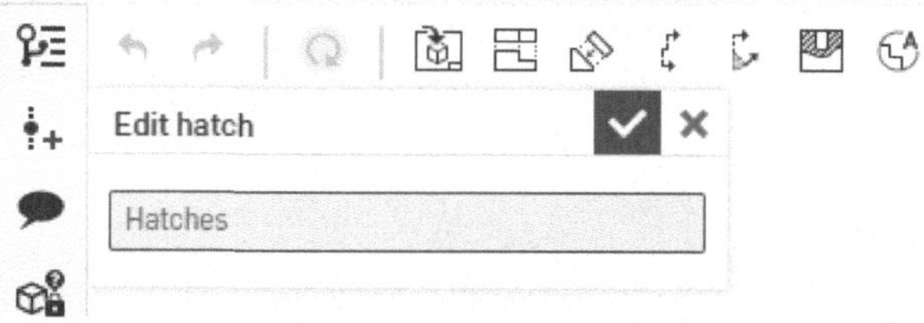

2. Select the hatch of a view. The default properties of the selected hatch appear in the dialog, with the **ANSI** tab activated by default, see Figure 10.87. You can switch to the required tab (**ANSI**, **ISO**, or **General**) to define the properties according to ANSI, ISO, or non-standard settings.

10.87

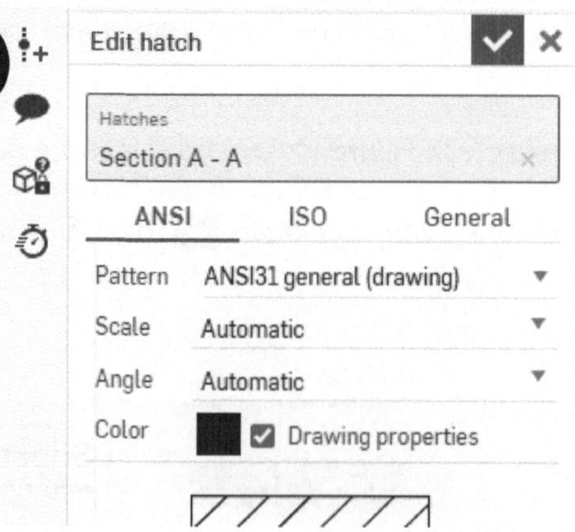

Tip: You can select the hatch of any view and modify its properties using the **Edit hatch** dialog. Additionally, you can select multiple hatches to modify their properties simultaneously.

3. Select the desired pattern type, scale, and angle from the respective drop-down lists in the Edit hatch dialog.

4. To edit the default color of the selected hatch, clear the **Drawing properties** check box, then click the Color swatch to open the **Hatches color** sub-dialog, see Figure 10.88.

10.88

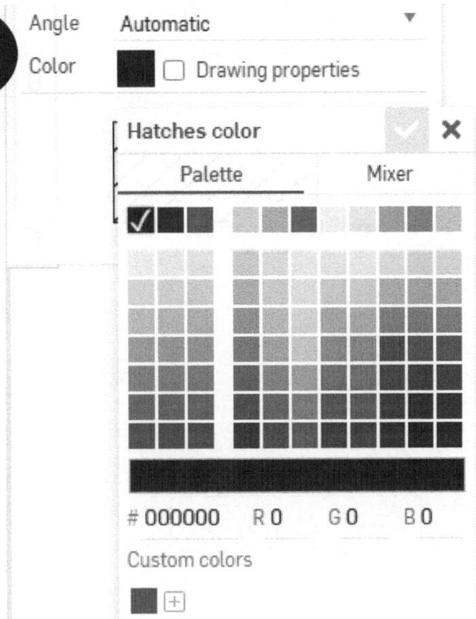

5. After selecting the required color for the selected hatch, click on the green checkmark in the **Hatches color** sub-dialog to confirm the selection. The **Edit hatch** dialog remains displayed.

6. Once the hatch properties are deafened, click on the green checkmark in the **Edit hatch** dialog to confirm the selection and exit the dialog.

Adding Geometries in Drawing Views

After creating the drawing views of a part or an assembly, you can add geometries such as centerlines, center marks, and virtual sharp corners to define geometric relationships. For example, center marks in drawing views help identify the center of rounded or circular edges, while centerlines indicate the center between two lines or edges representing hole features. The different types of geometries are discussed next.

Adding Centerlines

Centerlines are used as references for identifying the center of circular cut or hole features in drawing views, see Figure 10.89.

10.89

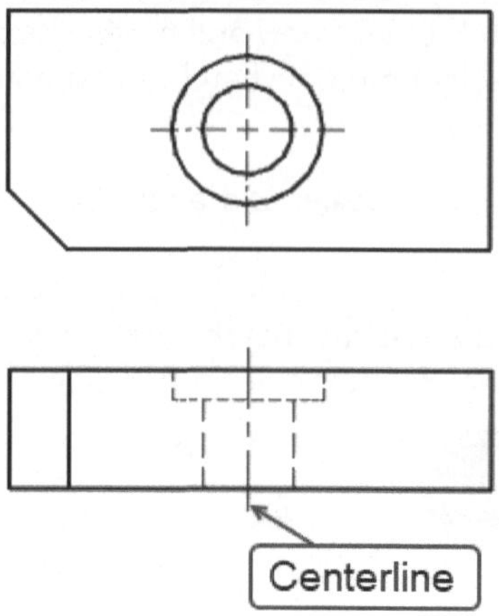

In Onshape, you can add centerlines using various tools available in the **Geometry** flyout, see Figure 10.90. These tools include: **2 point centerline**, **Edge to edge centerline**, **3 point circle centerline**, and **2 point circle centerline**.

10.90

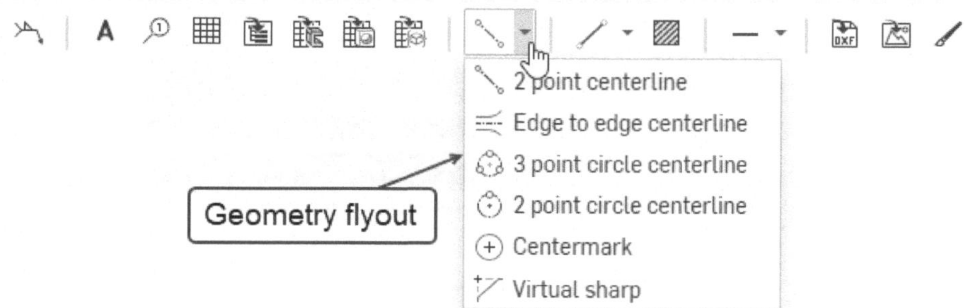

2 point centerline: The **2 point centerline** tool is used to add a centerline by selecting two points on the entities of an existing drawing view.

Edge to edge centerline: The **Edge to edge centerline** tool is used to add a centerline at the midpoint between two selected linear edges of an existing drawing view, refer to Figure 10.89.

3 point circle centerline: The **3 point circle centerline** tool is used to add a circular centerline by specifying three points on the entities of an existing drawing view, see Figure 10.91.

10.91

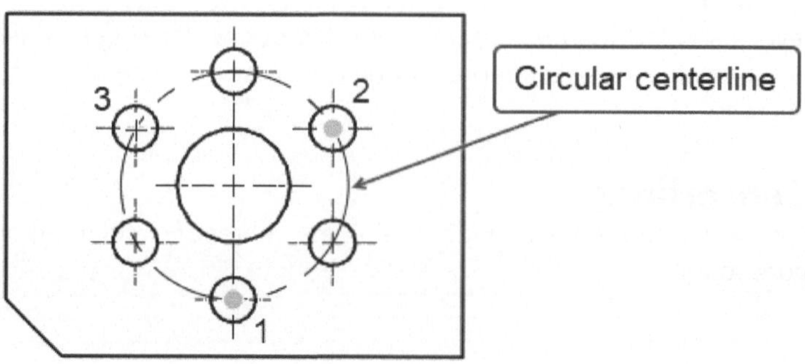

2 point circle centerline: The **2 point circle centerline** tool is used to add a circular centerline by specifying a center point and a point on an entity of an existing drawing view, see Figure 10.92.

10.92

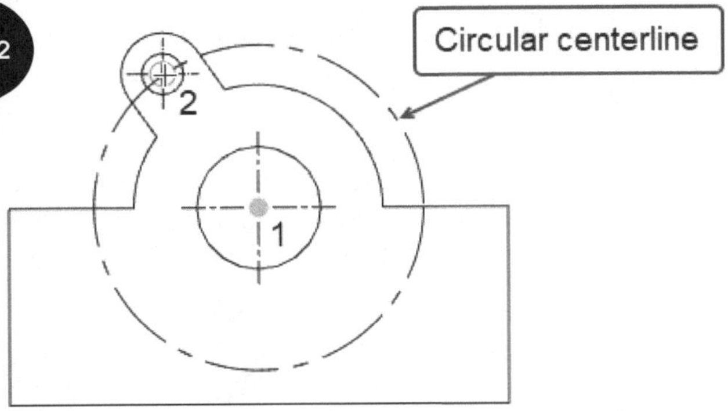

Adding Centermarks

Centermarks are used to identify the center points or Pitch Circle Diameter (PCD) of circular or patterned features in drawing views. In Figure 10.93, a circular centermark is added to represent the PCD of circular edges.

10.93

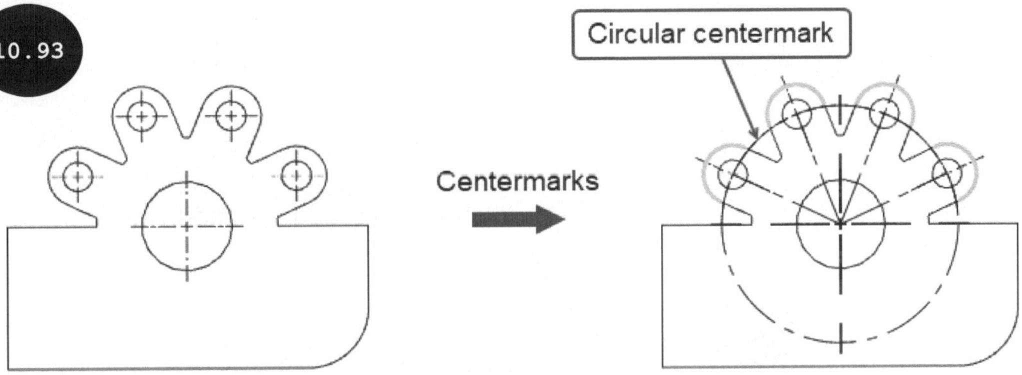

In Onshape, you can add three types of centermarks using the **Centermark** tool: Single, Circular, and Linear. The methods for creating these centermarks are discussed below:

1. Invoke the **Geometry** flyout and select the **Centermark** tool, see Figure 10.94. The **Centermark** dialog appears with three tabs: **Single**, **Circular**, and **Linear**, see Figure 10.95.

10.94

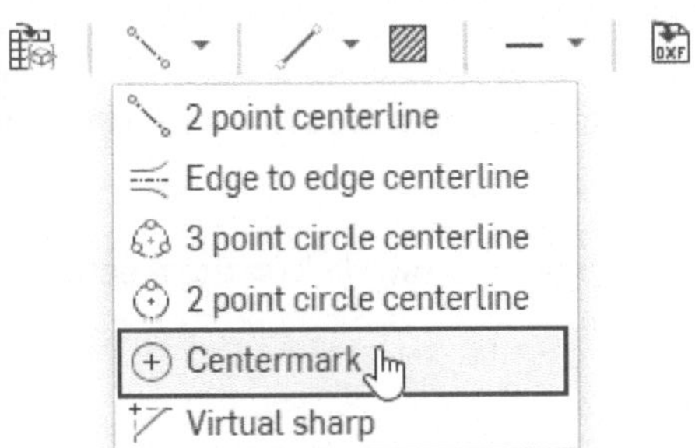

10.95

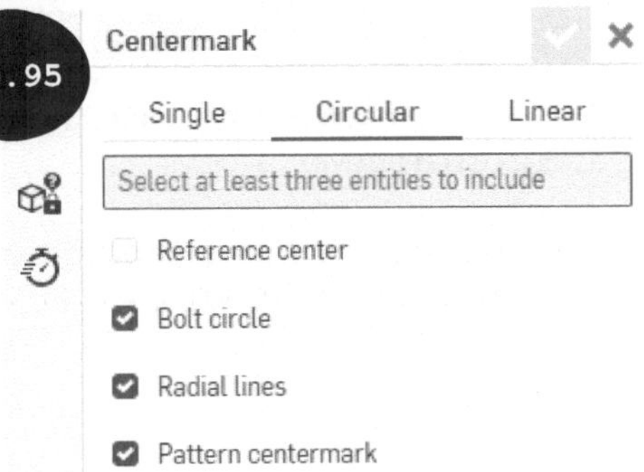

Single: The **Single** tab allows you to add a centermark at the center of one or more individual circular edges of a view.

Circular: The **Circular** tab allows you to add a circular centermark representing the PCD of at least three circular edges, see Figure 10.96. To create a circular centermark using this tab, select a minimum of three circular edges in a view.

After selecting three circular edges in a view, a preview of the circular centermark appears. You can customize this centermark by including or excluding the bolt circle, radial lines, and pattern centermark using the respective check boxes in the dialog, see Figure 10.97.

10.96

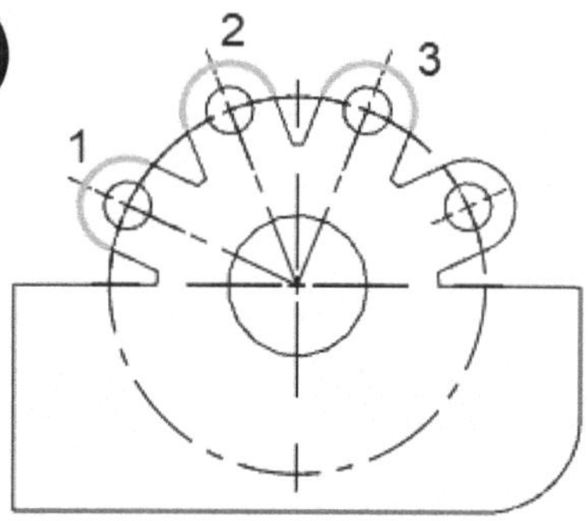

10.97

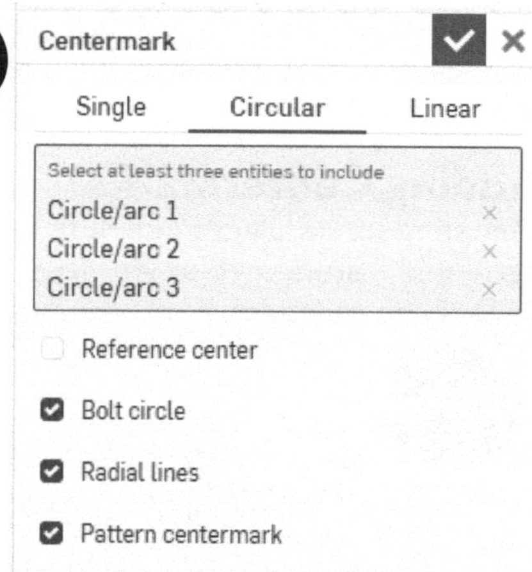

Linear: The **Linear** tab allows you to add a centermark by selecting at least two circular edges, see Figure 10.98.

10.98

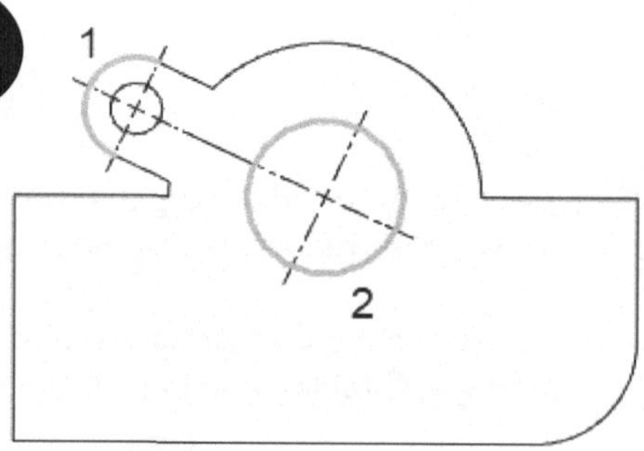

2. Activate the required tab (**Single**, **Circular**, and **Linear**) and then create a centermark accordingly, as discussed above.

3. Once the centermark is added on the selected entities of the view, click on the green checkmark to confirm and exit the dialog.

Adding a Virtual Sharp

In Onshape, you can create a virtual sharp point between two intersecting, non-parallel edges using the **Virtual sharp** tool, see Figure 10.99. This point represents the extension and intersection of the edges and serves as a reference for applying dimensions.

10.99

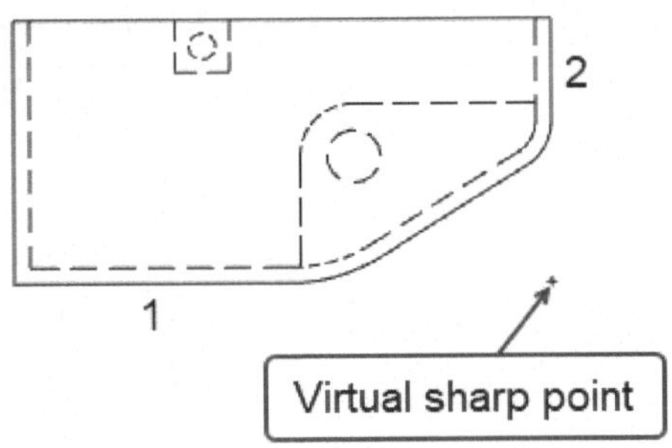

To add a virtual sharp point, invoke the **Geometry** flyout and select the **Virtual sharp** tool, see Figure 10.100. Then, select two non-parallel edges one by one, refer to Figure 10.99. A virtual sharp point forms at their intersection in the view.

10.100

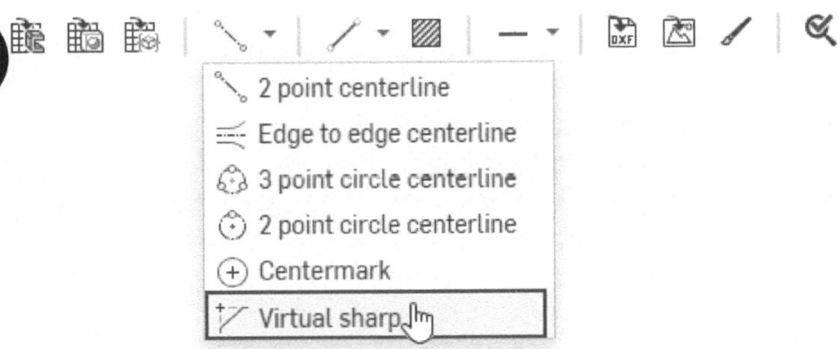

Creating a Sketch

In Onshape, you create a sketch on the current drawing sheet just as you would in the Sketching environment. This allows you to represent supplementary geometry or custom symbols, such as weld and surface symbols. The tools for creating a sketch are available in the **Sketch** drop-down menu, see Figure 10.101.

10.101

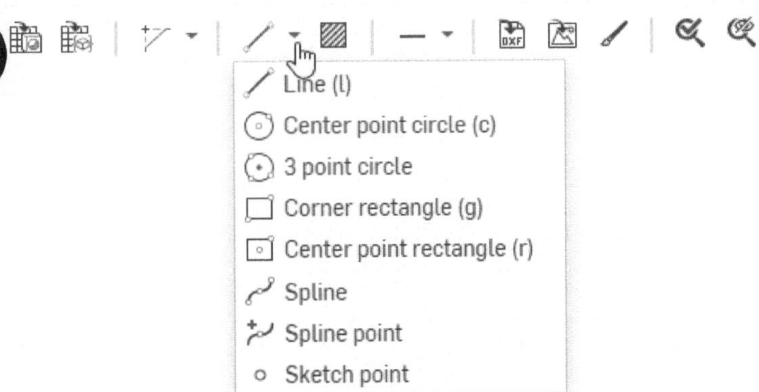

Applying Dimensions

After creating various drawing views of a component or an assembly, you need to apply dimensions to them. In Onshape, you can apply various types of dimensions using the tools available in the **Dimension** drop-down menu, see Figure 10.102.

10.102

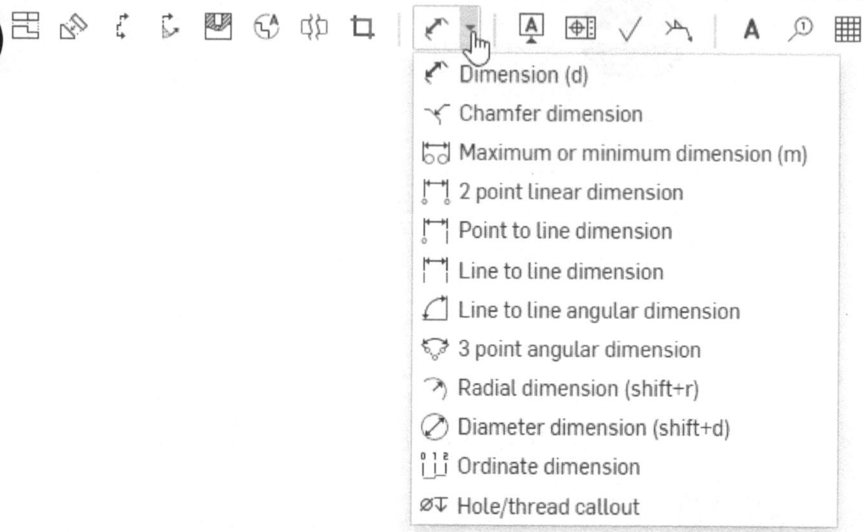

The **Dimension** tool in this flyout applies various types of dimensions, including horizontal, vertical, aligned, angular, diameter, radius, and arc length, based on the selected entity or entities. For example, selecting a circle applies a diameter dimension, while selecting two parallel lines results in a linear dimension. The methods for applying these dimensions are the same as those used for sketch entities in the Sketching environment. Figure 10.103 illustrates drawing views with dimensions applied using the **Dimension** tool.

10.103

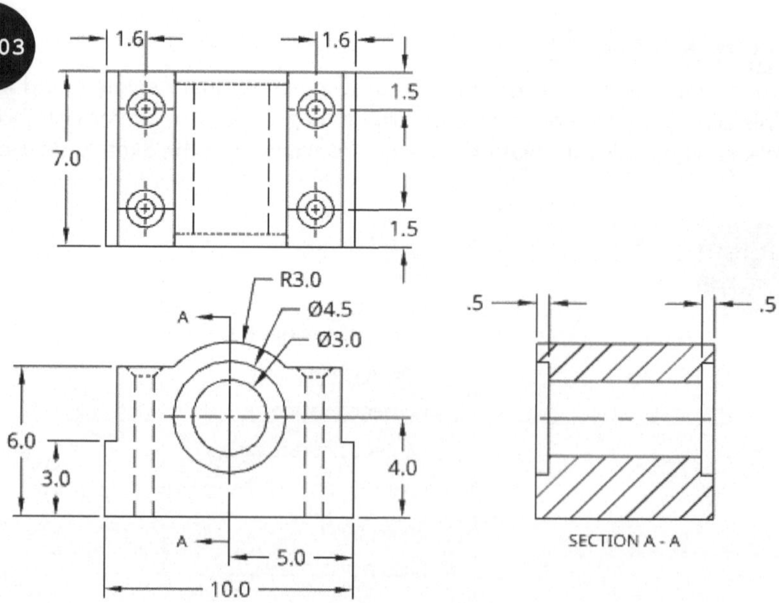

In addition to using the **Dimension** tool for various dimension types, you can also apply specific dimensions using individual tools available in the **Dimension** drop-down menu. For example, to apply linear dimensions between two points, activate the **2 point linear dimension** tool, and to apply radius dimensions, use the **Radius dimension** tool. The method for applying these dimensions remains the same as discussed earlier.

The next section covers applying chamfer dimensions, ordinate dimensions, and hole/thread callouts using their respective tools.

Applying a Chamfer dimension

The method for applying a chamfer dimension is discussed below:

1. Invoke the **Dimension** drop-down menu and click on **Chamfer dimension**, see Figure 10.104.

10.104

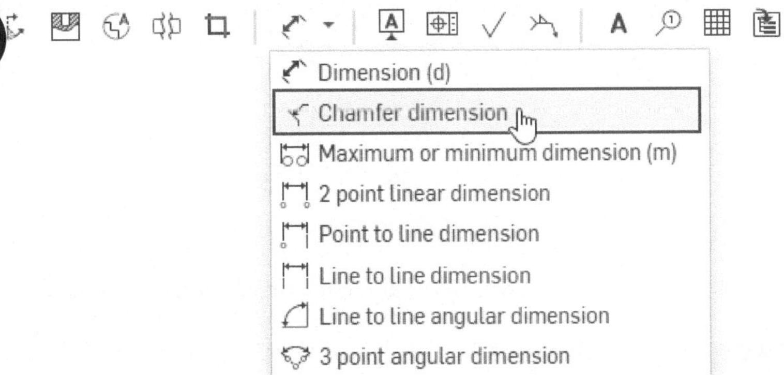

2. Select the chamfered (beveled) edge and an adjacent edge in the drawing view. A preview of the chamfer dimension appears, attached to the cursor, see Figure 10.105.

10.105

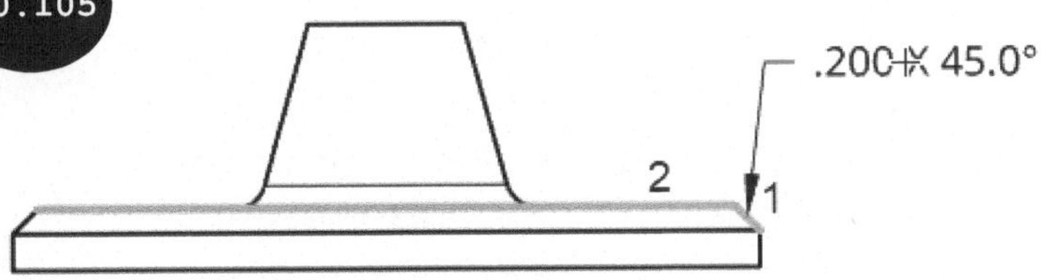

3. Click to define the placement point for the chamfer dimension on the sheet. The chamfer dimension applies, and the tool remains active.

4. Similarly, you can continue applying the chamfer dimension to other chamfered edges.

5. After applying the chamfer dimension, press the ESC key to exit the tool.

Applying Ordinate Dimensions

Ordinate dimensions are used for dimensioning machine parts for maintaining accuracy and measuring distance in the X and Y directions from a specified base point, see Figure 10.106. The method for applying ordinate dimensions is discussed below:

10.106

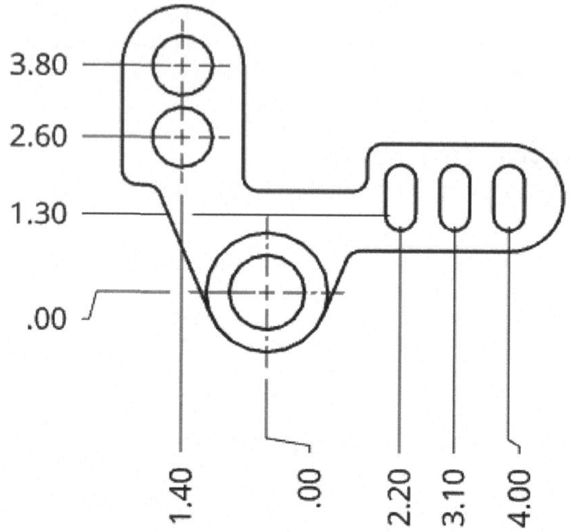

1. Invoke the **Dimension** drop-down menu and click on **Ordinate dimension**, see Figure 10.107.

10.107

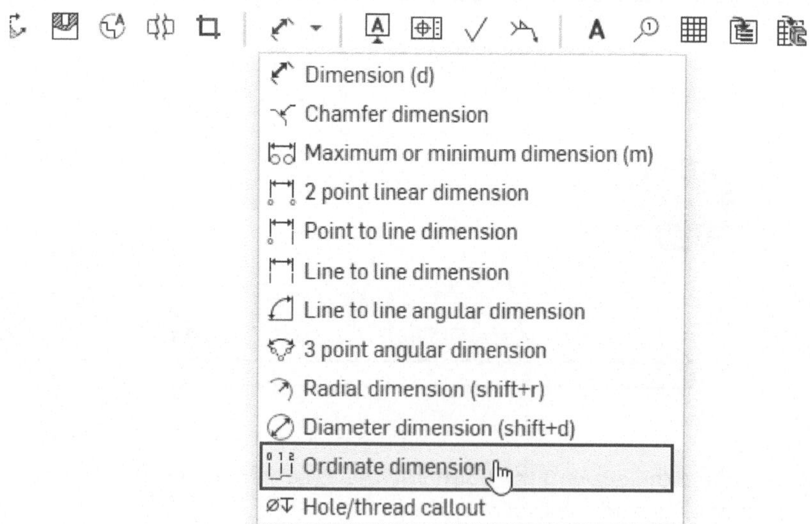

Now, define a base point (origin) to measure all other entities.

2. Click on an entity in the drawing view to set it as the origin. The zero-dimension attaches to the cursor with a leader, see Figure 10.108.

10.108

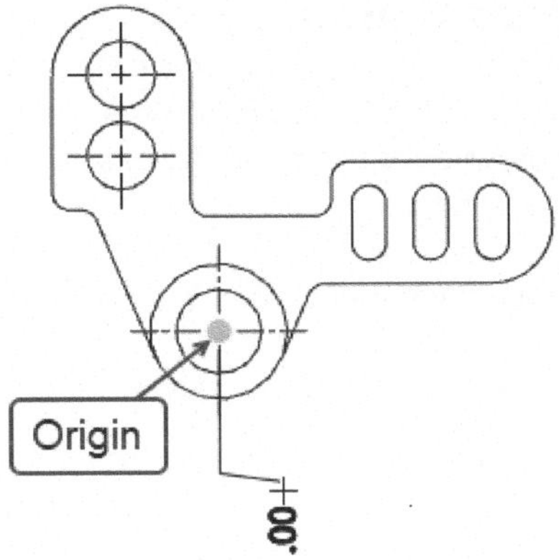

3. Move the cursor vertically or horizontally, depending on whether you want to apply horizontal ordinate dimensions or vertical ordinate dimensions, respectively.

4. Click on the drawing sheet to place the zero-dimension. The zero-dimension is applied, and a dimension leader attaches to the cursor.

   Now, you can select the entity in the view to measure from the origin (zero-dimension).

5. Click on an entity in the view to be dimensioned from the origin. The ordinate dimension is applied, measuring from the origin. Another dimension leader also appears attached to the cursor, refer to Figure 10.109.

6. Click on another entity in the view. The ordinate dimension is applied to the selected entity, measuring from the origin, refer to Figure 10.109.

7. Similarly, apply the remaining ordinate dimensions measuring from the origin in one direction (either vertically or horizontally), see Figure 10.109. In this example, horizontal ordinate dimensions are applied.

10.109

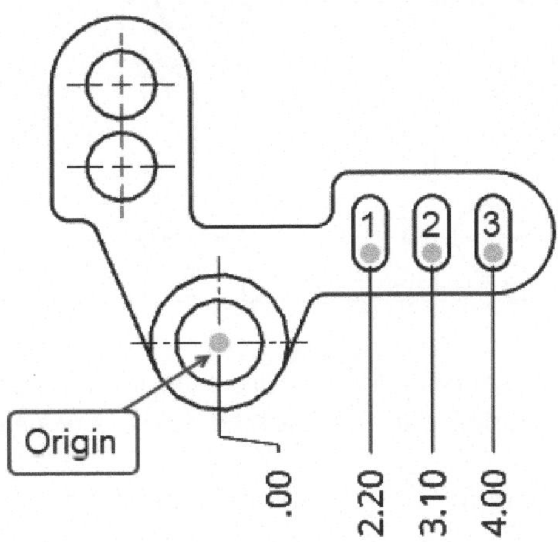

8. After applying the dimensions, press the ESC key to exit the tool.

Applying Hole/Thread Callouts

In Onshape, you can apply a callout or dimension to a hole or thread in a drawing view. A hole callout specifies details such as diameter, depth, and hole type for a standard hole, while a thread callout provides thread specifications, including thread type, size, and class. The method for applying a hole/thread callout is discussed below:

1. Invoke the **Dimension** drop-down menu and click on **Hole/thread callout**, see Figure 10.110.

10.110

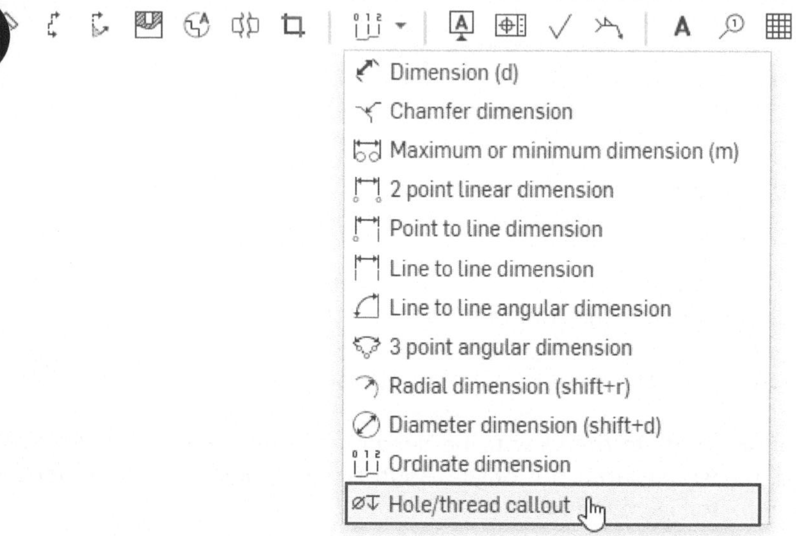

2. Select a circular edge of the hole. A preview of the hole callout appears attached to the cursor, see Figure 10.111.

10.111

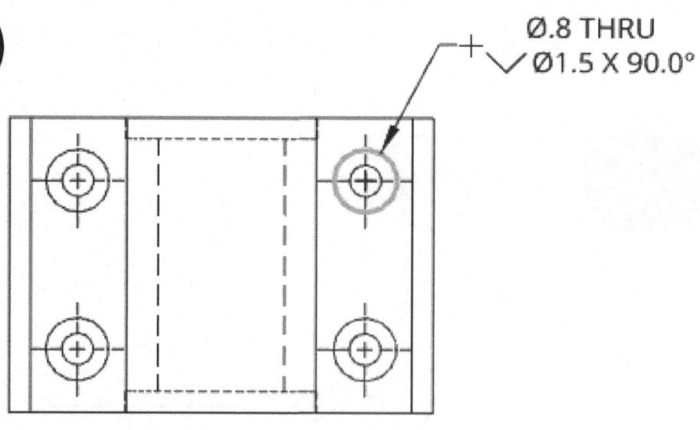

3. Click to define the placement point for the hole callout on the drawing sheet. A hole callout with the defined parameters is applied to the selected hole in the view.

4. Similarly, you can apply hole and thread callouts to other hole or thread edges in the view.

5. Press the ESC key to exit the tool.

Adding a Surface Finish Symbol

In Onshape, you can add a surface finish symbol to specify the surface finish of a model's face. A surface finish symbol consists of three components: surface roughness, waviness, and lay, see Figure 10.112. The specifications in a surface finish symbol are used for machining the respective surface of the object. You can add it to the edge of a surface in a drawing view using the **Surface finish symbol** tool. The method for adding a surface finish symbol is discussed below:

10.112

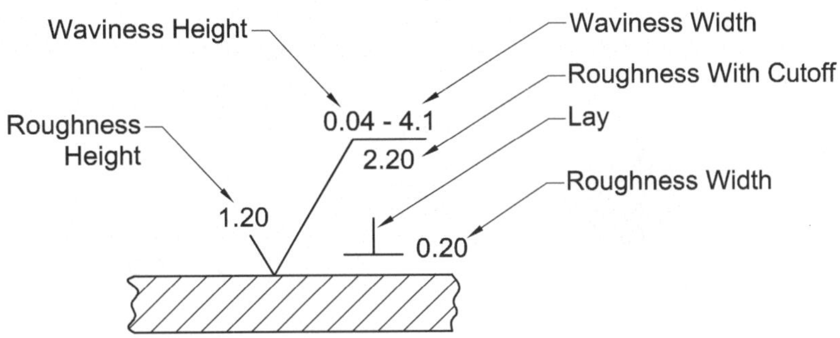

1. Click on the **Surface finish symbol** tool in the **Drawing** toolbar, see Figure 10.113. The **Surface finish** dialog appears. Also, an empty surface finish symbol appears attached to the cursor.

10.113

2. Select the required type of surface finish symbol in the **Type** drop-down list of the dialog, see Figure 10.114.

3. Specify the required specification for the surface finish such as roughness, waviness, or process, and lay in the respective fields of the dialog box.

4. Select an edge of a view to attach the surface finish symbol of the specified parameters. The symbol appears on the selected edge (see Figure 10.115), and the **Surface finish** dialog remains visible.

10.114

10.115

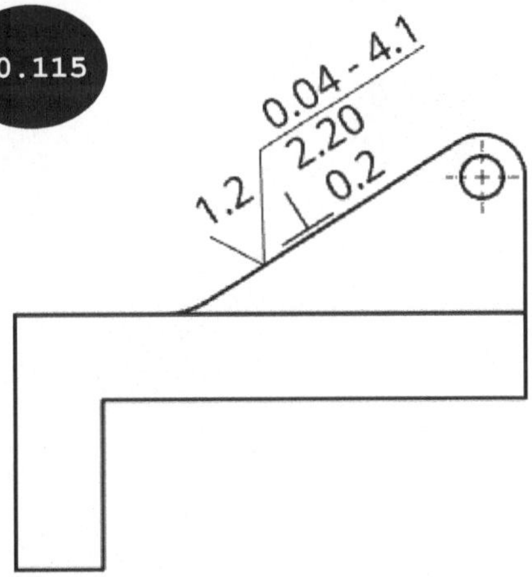

5. Similarly, you can add a surface finish symbol with the specified parameters to other required edges of the view. Press the ESC key to exit the tool.

Note: You can also add a leader to a surface finish symbol. To do this, select the symbol and drag the dot that appears in the middle of its slant leg. This action adds a leader that connects the symbol to the edge of the view, see Figure 10.116. Click to define the new position for the surface finish symbol.

To move the surface finish symbol along the edge, drag the dot that connects it to the edge of the view.

10.116

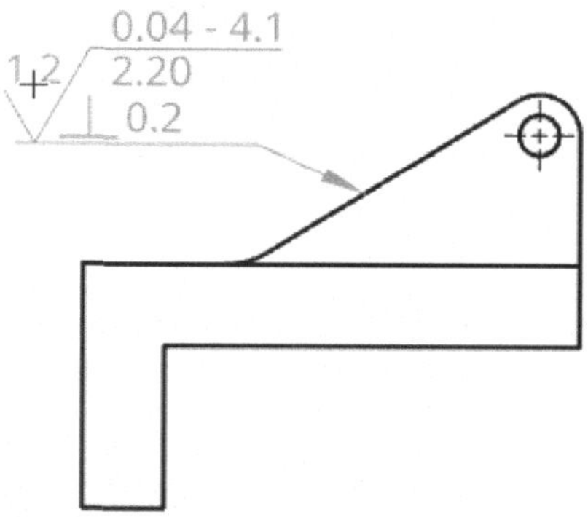

Adding a Weld Symbol

In Onshape, you can add a weld standard symbol in a drawing view to define welding parameters, including weld type, size, process, and specifications, at the joint or edge where welding is required. The method for adding a weld symbol is discussed below:

1. Click on the **Weld symbol** tool in the **Drawing** toolbar, see Figure 10.117. The **Weld symbol** dialog appears, see Figure 10.118.

10.117

10.118

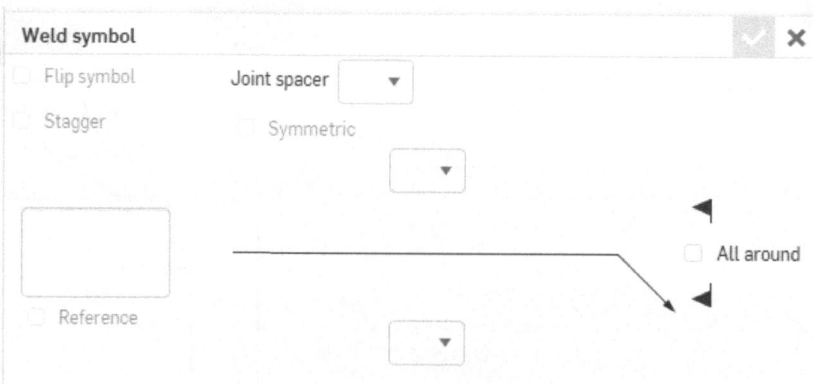

Note: The options available for defining weld parameters in the **Weld symbol** dialog box depend on the selected drawing standard (ASME or ISO) for the current drawing.

To change the weld standard, open the **Drawing properties** panel by clicking the **Drawing properties** tool located in the middle left of the screen. In the **Drawing properties** panel, go to the **Annotations** tab and scroll down to the **Weld symbols** section to edit the weld standard for the current drawing.

2. If using the ANSI drawing standard, select the required joint spacer from the **Joint spacer** drop-down list, choosing from options such as **Double V groove, Double bevel groove, Double U groove, Double J groove, Double flare V**, or **Double flare bevel**, see Figure 10.119.

10.119

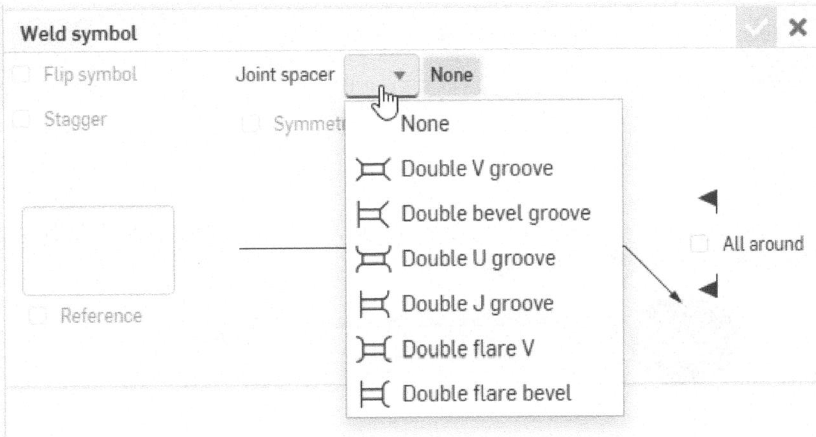

On the other hand, if using the ISO standard, you need to select the joint type from the **Joint type** drop-down list, including options like **Square groove, V groove, U groove, J groove, Bevel groove,** or **Single bevel butt broad root**.

3. Specify the required weld parameters in the dialog, then select an edge of the view to place the weld symbol. The symbol follows the cursor and attaches to the selected edge with a leader, see Figure 10.120.

10.120

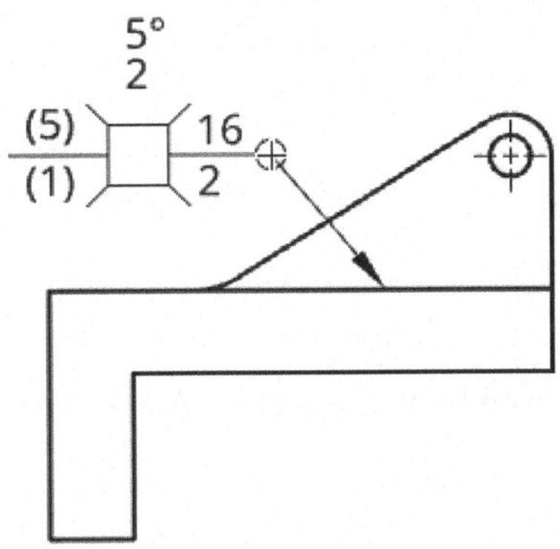

4. Click to set the position of the weld symbol on the sheet. The symbol attaches to the selected edge, and the Weld finish dialog remains visible.

5. Similarly, you can add weld symbols with the specified parameters to other required edges of the view. Press the ESC key to exit the tool.

Adding a Note

In Onshape, you can add a note anywhere on a drawing sheet or attach it to a specific edge of a view using the Text tool. Notes and text in drawings are typically used to convey additional information that is not included in the drawing views. The method for adding note is discussed below:

1. Click on the **Note** tool in the **Drawing** toolbar, see Figure 10.121.

10.121

2. Click to specify a location for adding text anywhere on the sheet. An edit box appears, along with the **Note** window, as shown in Figure 10.122.

10.122

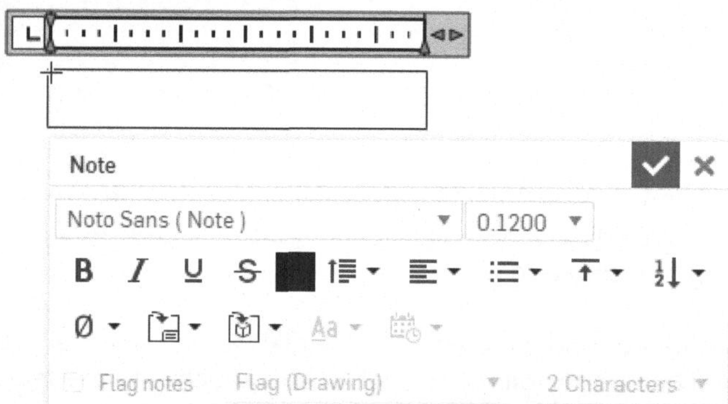

3. Enter the required note or text in the edit box. Then, use the **Note** window to adjust the font, height, color, justification, and other formatting options.

4. After writing the desired note, click on the green checkmark in the **Note** window to confirm the addition of the note. The Note tool remains active.

5. Similarly, you can add multiple notes on the sheet as needed. Press the ESC key to exit the tool.

Tip: You can also attach a note to an edge of a view with a leader using the **Note** tool.

Editing the Sheet Format

When entering the Drawing environment, you can select a desired drawing template that defines the sheet size and other related settings, along with the title block. The title block contains essential drawing details such as the project name, drawn by, checked by, approved by, date, sheet number, and more. You can create or customize the title block to match your company's standard format.

To edit the title block, ensure it is in the unlocked state. You can lock or unlock the title block using the **Drawing properties** panel.

To unlock the title block, open the **Drawing properties** panel by clicking the **Drawing properties** tool located in the middle left of the screen. In the panel, navigate to the **Formats** tab and select the **Unlocked** option from the **Lock** drop-down list, see Figure 10.123. Note that the **Unlocked** option enables editing of the title block, while the **Locked** option prevents editing by locking the title block.

10.123

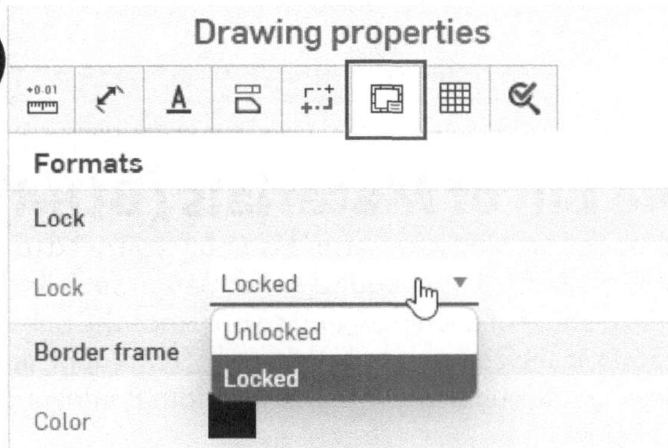

Tip: In the **Formats** tab of the **Drawing properties** panel, you can also modify other parameters, such as the color and thickness of the border frame, border zone, and title block, using the respective options.

After unlocking the title block, double-click on any editable text or field with a grey background in the title block. An edit field appears along with the Note window, as shown in Figure 10.124. In this field, you can enter the required text and format it using the Note window. Click anywhere outside the field to confirm and exit the edit mode. Similarly, you can modify other necessary information in the title block.

10.124

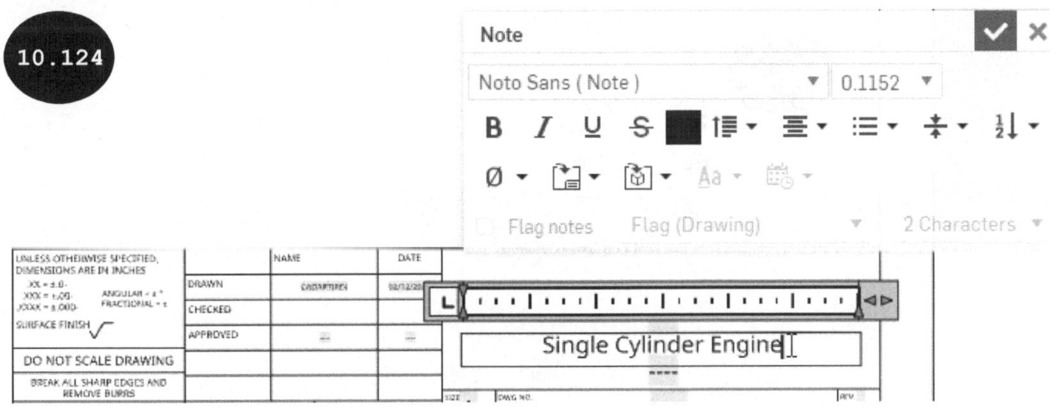

In Onshape, you can edit the title block by deleting, moving, and stretching its existing line entities. To delete a line, select it and press the DELETE key. To adjust the length of a line, select it and drag one of its endpoints. Similarly, to move a line, drag its midpoint.

In addition to modifying existing lines, you can create new line entities for the title block using the **Line** tool available in the **Drawing** toolbar. After creating new lines, you need to link them to the title block. To do this, select the newly created lines, right-click to open the shortcut menu, and choose **Move to > Title Block** to assign them accordingly, see Figure 10.125.

10.125

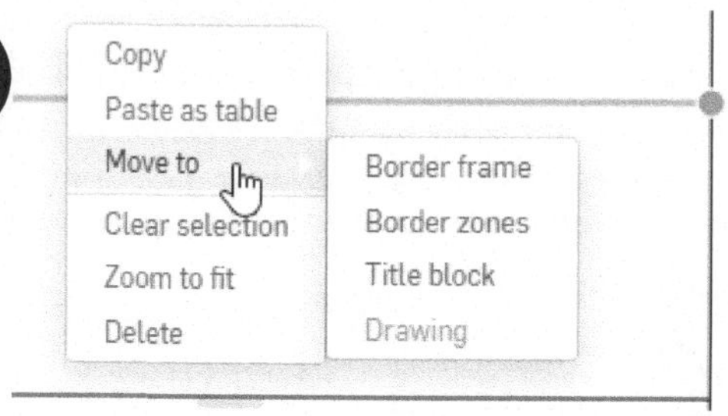

Creating the Bill of Materials (BOM)

After creating all the required drawing views of an assembly, you need to create the Bill of Materials. The Bill of Materials (BOM) contains all the required information such as the number of parts used in an assembly, part number, quantity of each part, and so on. Since the Bill of Materials (BOM) contains all the necessary information, it serves as a primary source of communication between the manufacturer and the vendors as well as the suppliers. The method for creating a Bill of Materials (BOM) for an assembly is discussed below:

1. Click on the **BOM table** tool in the **Drawing** toolbar, see Figure 10.126. The preview of a table appears attached to the cursor along with the display of the **BOM table** dialog, see Figure 10.127.

10.126

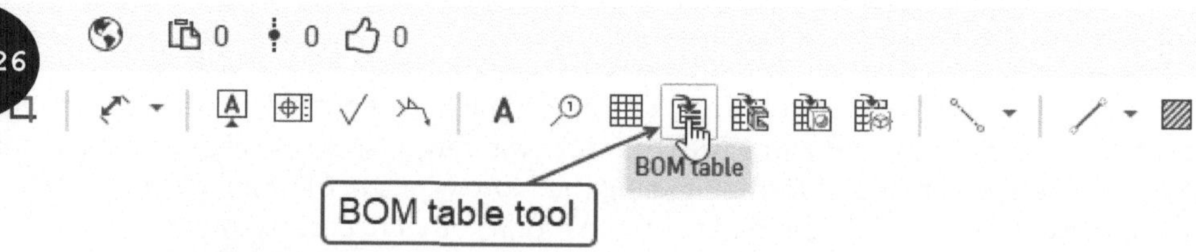

10.127

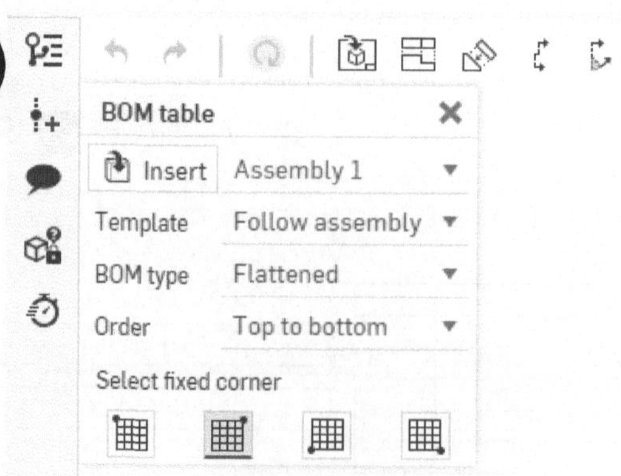

Insert: If a drawing sheet contains multiple assemblies, you can select the appropriate one for BOM creation from the **Insert** drop-down list in the dialog. Additionally, you can add a new assembly to the sheet by clicking the **Insert** button. This opens the **Select a BOM** dialog, allowing you to choose an assembly to insert into the current sheet for BOM creation.

Template: The **Template** drop-down list provides a selection of available BOM templates. You can select the desired template from this list to create the BOM.

BOM type: By default, the **Flattened** option is selected in the **BOM type** drop-down list, enabling you to create a BOM without displaying the assembly hierarchy. Selecting the **Structured - Top Level** option allows you to create a BOM that displays the assembly hierarchy for only one level. Selecting the **Structured - Multi-level** option enables you to create a BOM that includes all levels of the assembly hierarchy, including sub-assemblies.

Order: You can arrange the BOM items in either top-to-bottom or bottom-to-top order by selecting the appropriate option from the **Order** drop-down list.

Select fixed corner: Select the desired option in the **Select fixed corner** area to set one of the table's corners as a fixed or anchor point, which will be used to position the BOM on the sheet.

2. After selecting the desired BOM options, move the cursor to the preferred location on the sheet and click to place the Bill of Materials (BOM). The Bill of Materials (BOM) is placed at the specified position in the drawing sheet, see Figure 10.128.

10.128

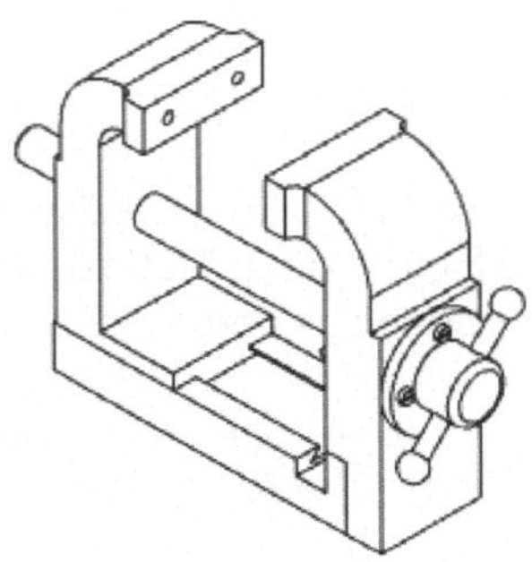

Item	Quantity	Part number	Description
1	1		
2	1		
3	1		
4	1		
5	1		
6	1		
7	4		
8	4		

Editing and Customizing the Bill of Materials

After inserting the Bill of Materials (BOM), you can add additional details such as Material, Name, Revision, Vendor, Product Line, and Mass in separate columns if needed. To do this, right-click the BOM and select "**Switch to BOM :** *assembly name*" from the shortcut menu, Figure 10.129. This opens the Assembly environment with the **Bill of materials** panel on the left, Figure 10.130.

10.129

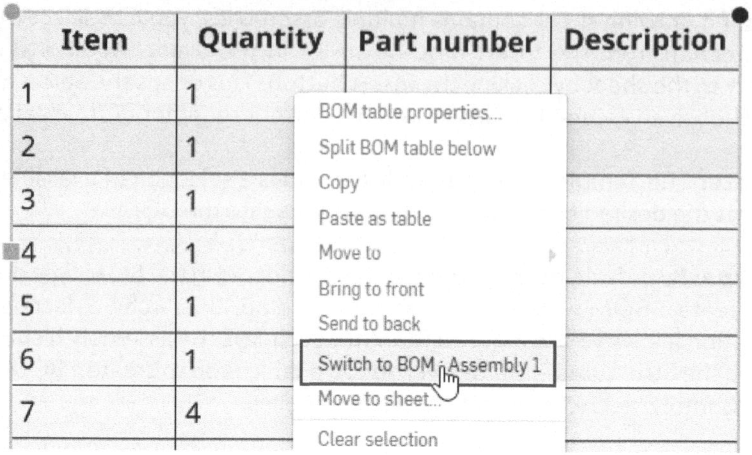

10.130

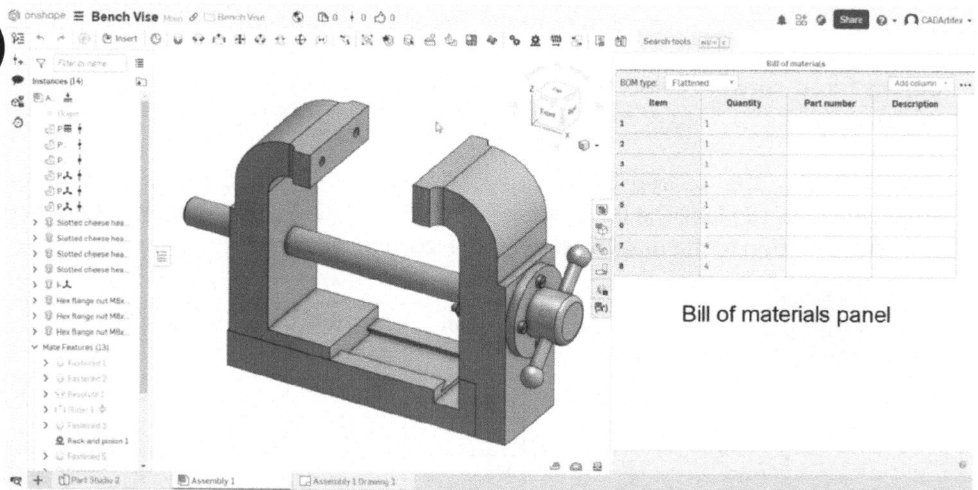

In the **Add Column** drop-down list of the **Bill of materials** panel, you can select the desired option to add the corresponding detail to the BOM in a new column, see Figure 10.131. Multiple details can be included by selecting the required options from the drop-down list one by one.

10.131

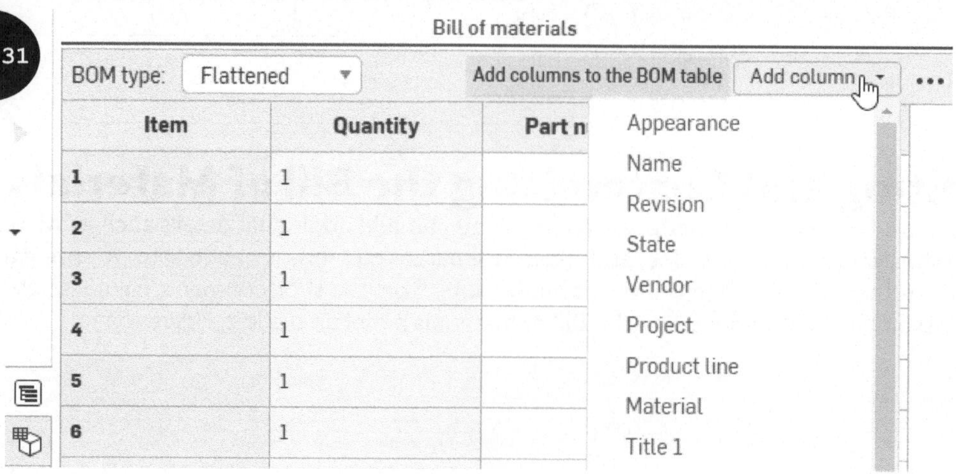

In addition to adding details, you can also delete an existing column if it is no longer needed in the BOM. To do this, right-click the title bar of the column you want to remove and select **Remove column** from the shortcut menu, see Figure 10.132. The selected column is then removed from the BOM.

You can also reposition a column by moving it left or right. To do this, right-click the column's title bar and select the desired option from the shortcut menu, see Figure 10.132.

10.132

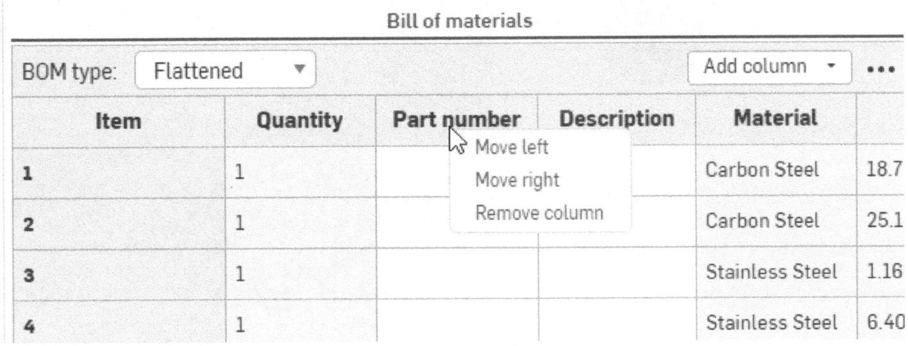

After adding the required details to the BOM, switch back to the Drawing environment by selecting the **Drawing** tab at the bottom of the screen. To reflect the changes made to the BOM in the Assembly environment within the Drawing environment, you need to update the workspace.

To do this, press CTRL + Q or click on the **Update from this Workspace** tool in the **Drawing** toolbar, see Figure 10.133. The BOM then updates in the Drawing environment to reflect the changes made in the Assembly environment, see Figure 10.134. In this example, the Material, Mass, and Revision columns are added to the BOM.

10.133

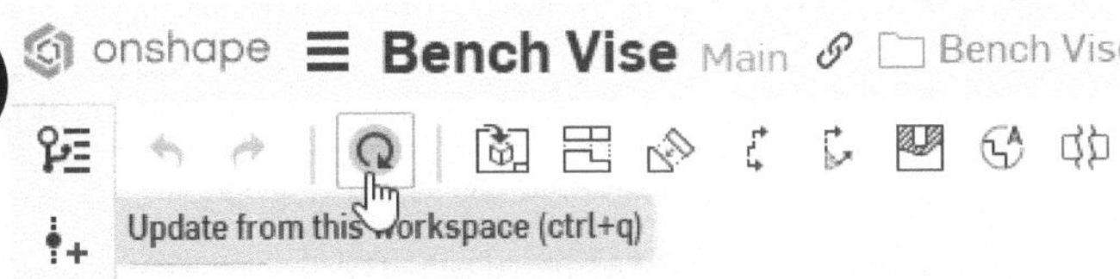

10.134

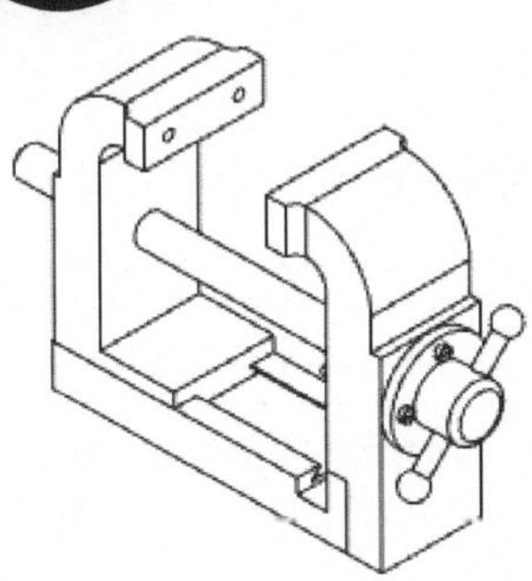

Item	Quantity	Description	Material	Mass	Revision
1	1		Carbon Steel	18.775 lb	
2	1		Carbon Steel	25.181 lb	
3	1		Stainless Steel	1.166 lb	
4	1		Stainless Steel	6.402 lb	
5	1		Carbon Steel	23.797 lb	
6	1		Stainless Steel	0.547 lb	
7	4		Stainless Steel	0.078 lb	
8	4		Stainless Steel	0.018 lb	

Adding Balloons

A balloon is connected to a component with a leader line, displaying the corresponding part number or other details such as the quantity listed in the Bill of Materials (BOM). In technical drawings, balloons are typically attached to individual components of an assembly to clearly identify them with their assigned part numbers in the BOM, refer to Figure 10.135.

10.135

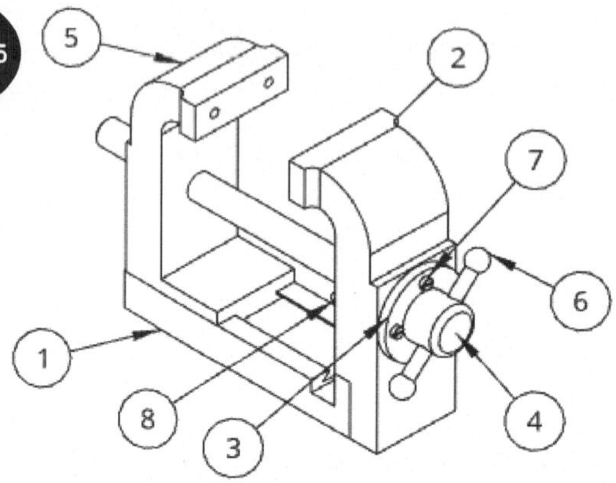

In Onshape, you can add balloons to the components of the assembly using the **Callout** tool. The method for adding balloons is discussed below:

1. Click on the **Callout** tool in the **Drawing** toolbar, see Figure 10.136. The **Callout** dialog appears, see Figure 10.137. Also, a balloon appears attached to the cursor.

10.136

10.137

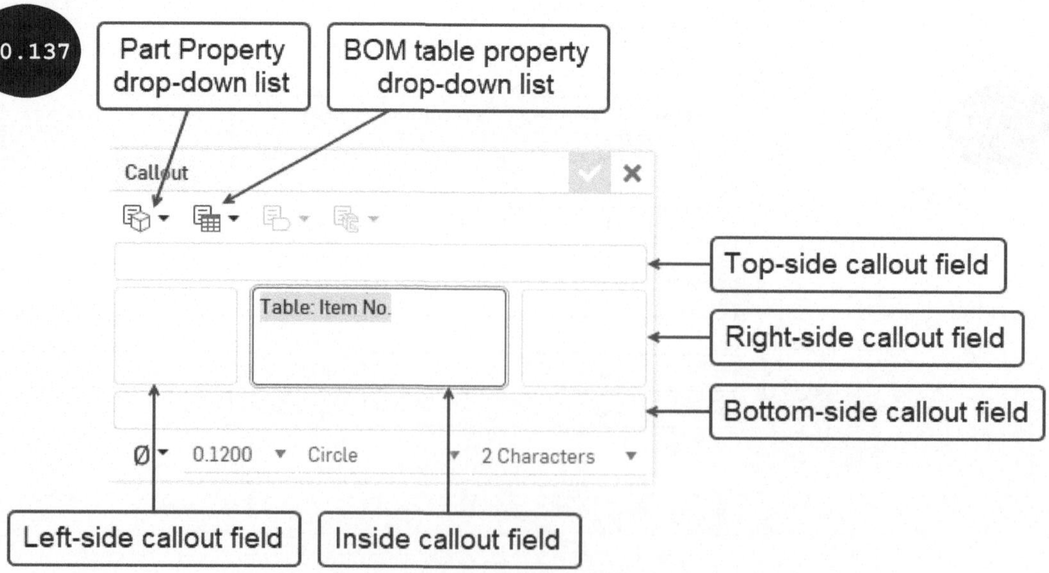

By default, the **Item No** property tag is added to the **Inside callout** field of the dialog, see Figure 10.137. As a result, the item number of the respective component is displayed inside the balloon.

You can also add a new tag to be displayed inside the callout. To do this, ensure that the **Inside callout** field is activated, then select the required tag from the **Part property** drop-down list or the **BOM tab property** drop-down list. The selected tag is then added to the **Inside callout** field.

Now, when you add a balloon to a component, its corresponding properties are automatically displayed inside the callout, see Figure 10.138. In this example, the item number and quantity of the component are shown inside the callout. Additionally, you can include custom text or keyboard characters such as forward slash (/), colon (:), and semicolon (;) in the field.

10.138

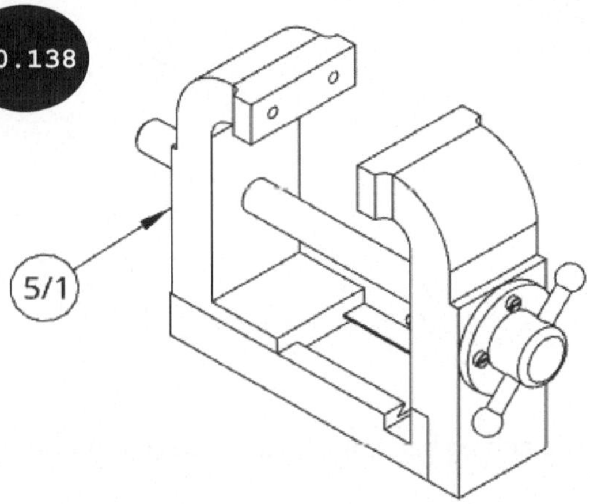

Similarly, you can add custom text and item property tags to other fields in the **Callout** dialog. The specified text or property will then appear on the corresponding side of the balloon. For example, any text or item property entered in the **Right-side** callout field of the dialog will be displayed on the right side of the balloon on the sheet.

To delete an existing property tag, select it in the field and press the DELETE key.

2. Select the desired balloon shape from the **Border shape** drop-down list in the **Callout** dialog, see Figure 10.139.

10.139

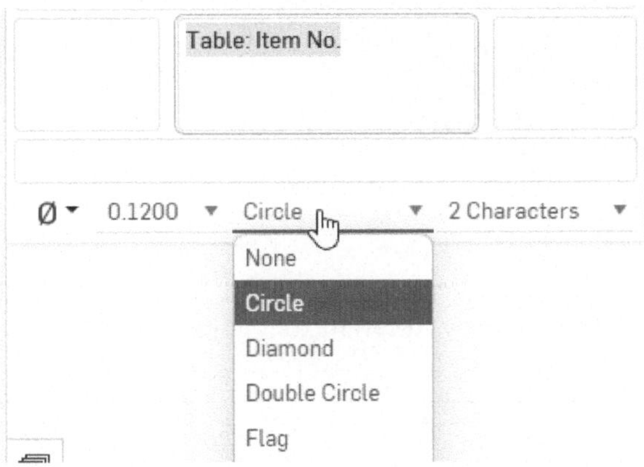

3. Specify additional settings, such as text height and border size, in the **Callout** dialog as needed.

4. Hover over the edge of the component and click to select it. A preview of the balloon appears, attached to the cursor with a leader connecting it to the selected component.

5. Move the cursor to the desired location and click to place the balloon on the sheet. The balloon appears at the specified location, displaying the assigned property tags, see Figure 10.140. In this example, the balloon has a split-circle shape, with the top portion displaying the item number and the bottom portion showing the available quantity of the component. Additionally, another balloon appears attached to the cursor.

10.140

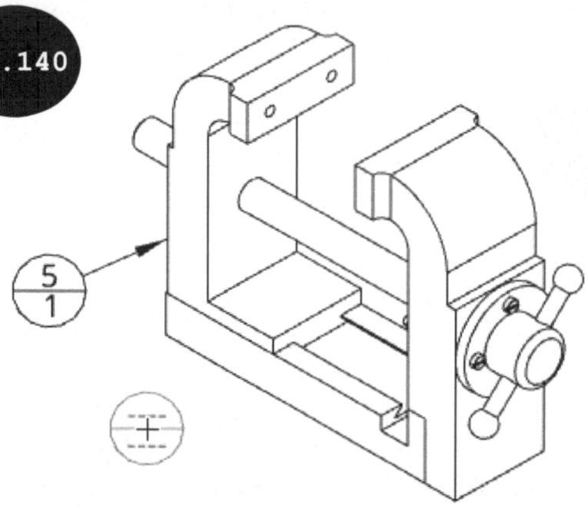

6. Similarly, you can continue adding balloons to each component of the assembly one by one, see Figure 10.141.

10.141

Item	Quantity	Material	Mass	Description
1	1	Carbon Steel	18.775 lb	
2	1	Carbon Steel	25.181 lb	
3	1	Stainless Steel	1.166 lb	
4	1	Stainless Steel	6.402 lb	
5	1	Carbon Steel	23.797 lb	
6	1	Stainless Steel	0.547 lb	
7	4	Stainless Steel	0.078 lb	
8	4	Stainless Steel	0.018 lb	

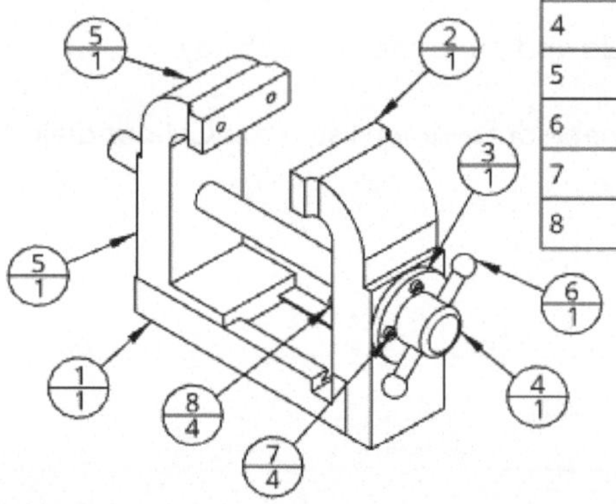

Tip: After placing the balloon, you can further adjust its position by dragging it.

Tutorial 1

Open the model created in Tutorial 2 of Chapter 6 and then create different drawing views: front, top, section, detail, and isometric, on the ANSI B INCH sheet, as shown in Figure 10.142. After creating the drawing views, apply dimensions using the dimension tools.

10.142

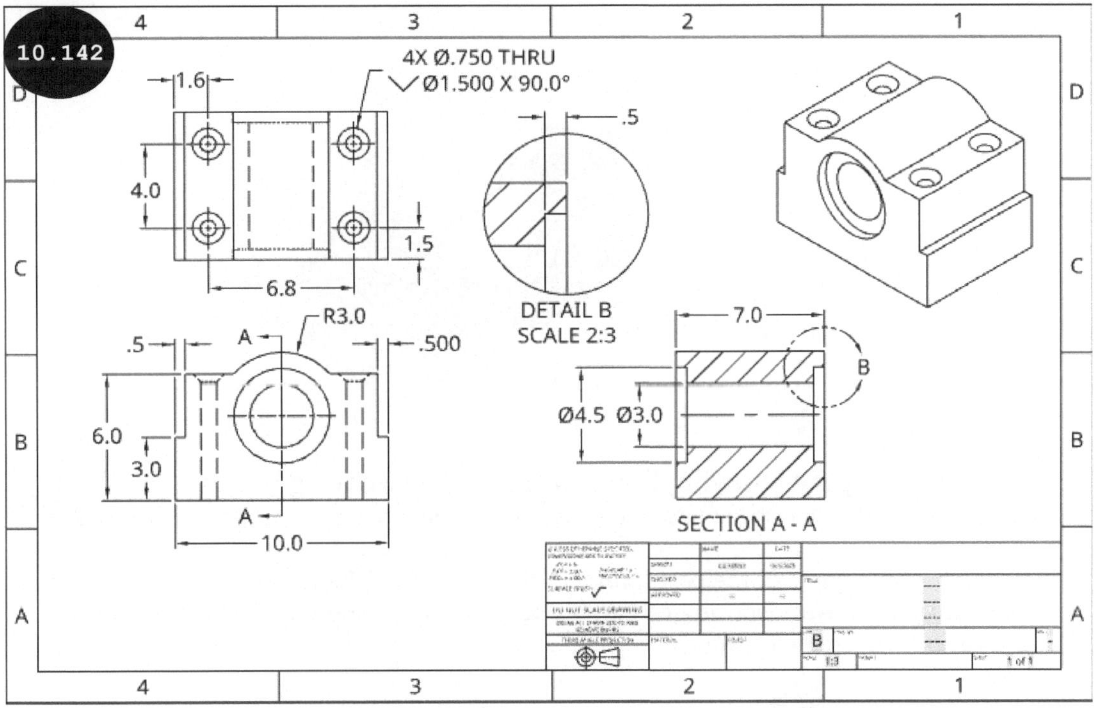

Section 1: Opening the Tutorial 2 of Chapter 6

1. Launch Onshape (***onshape.com***) and log in to your account if you're not already logged in. The **Documents Page** appears.

2. In the **Documents Page**, click on the **Created by me** option (see Figure 10.143) to filter and display all models you have created in Onshape.

10.143

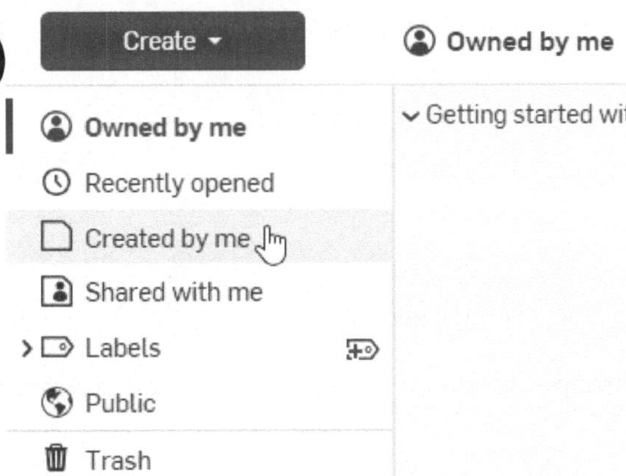

3. Scroll through the list of models in the right panel and double-click on the **C06 Tutorial 02** file. This opens the model created in Tutorial 2 of Chapter 6, see Figure 10.144.

10.144

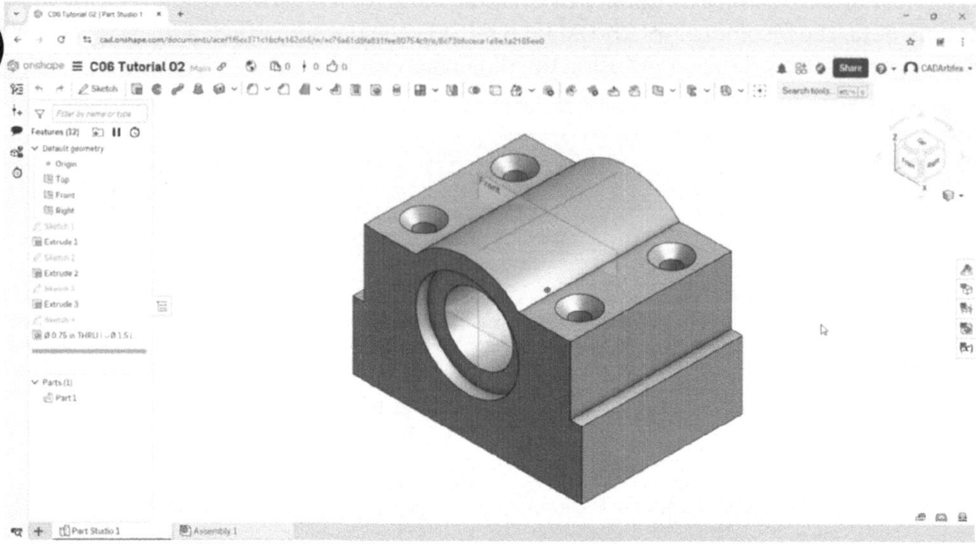

Section 2: Invoking the Drawing Environment and Creating Views

Now, you can invoke the Drawing environment and create the Front and Top views of the model.

1. Right-click on the name of the part (*Part1*) in the Part list on the left side of the graphics area, then choose the **Create Drawing of Part 1** option from the shortcut menu that appears, see Figure 10.145. The **Create Drawing** dialog appears.

10.145

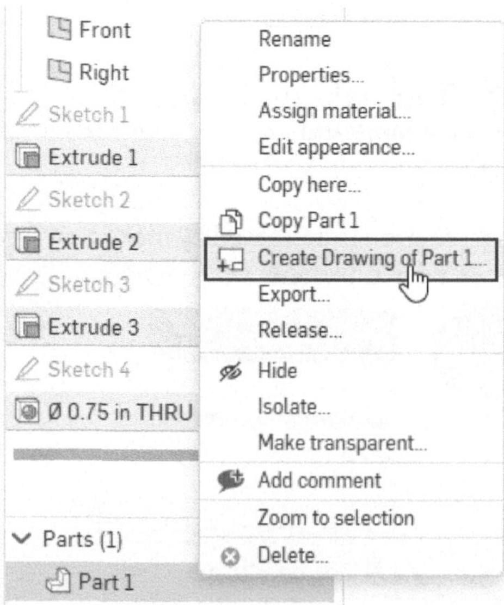

2. Click on the **Onshape** option to display a list of all the available standard templates, see Figure 10.146.

10.146

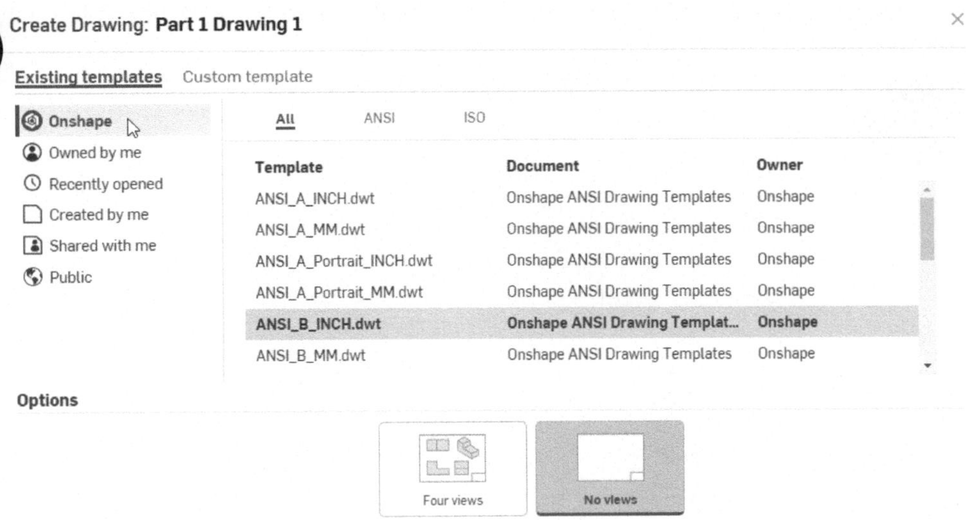

3. Select the **ANSI_B_INCH.dwt** template, ensure that the **No views** option is selected in the **Options** section of the dialog, and click **OK**. The Drawing environment opens in a new tab (**Part 1 Drawing 1**). A preview of the base view appears attached to the cursor, while the **Insert view** dialog is displayed in the top left corner of the screen.

4. Ensure that the **Front** option is selected in the **View orientation** drop-down list, then click to place the front view on the lower left of the sheet, see Figure 10.147. The front view is created and positioned at the specified location. As you move the cursor, a preview of a projected view appears attached to it, see Figure 10.147.

10.147

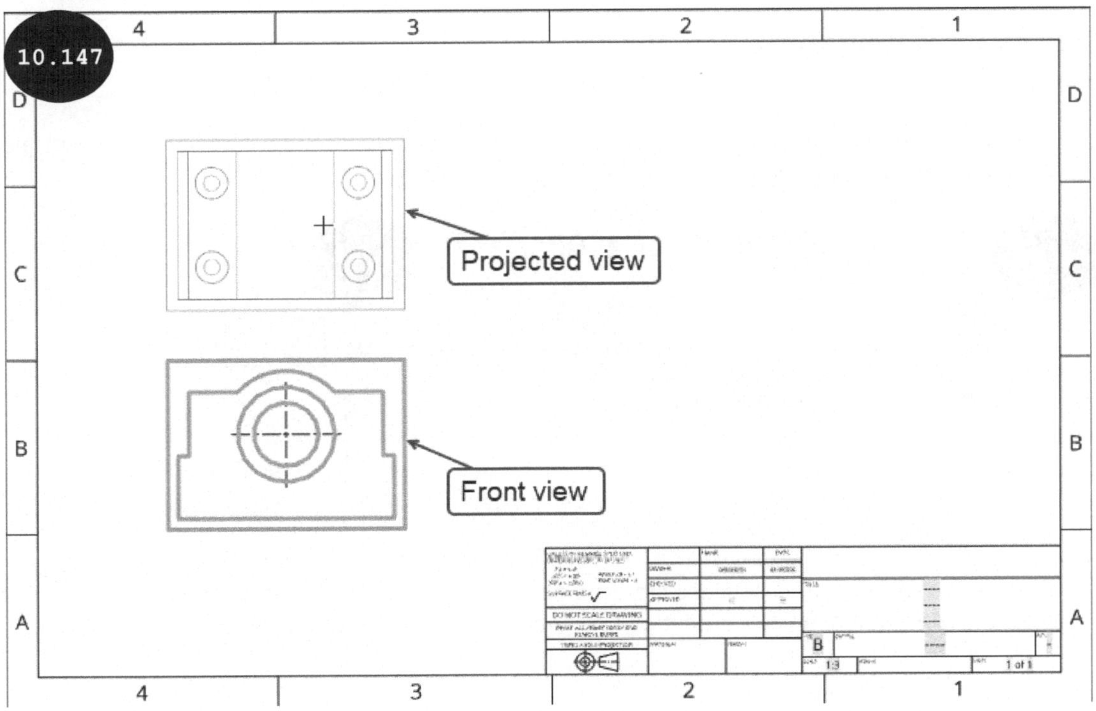

5. Move the cursor vertically upward and click to create the Top view of the model on the sheet, see Figure 10.148.

10.148

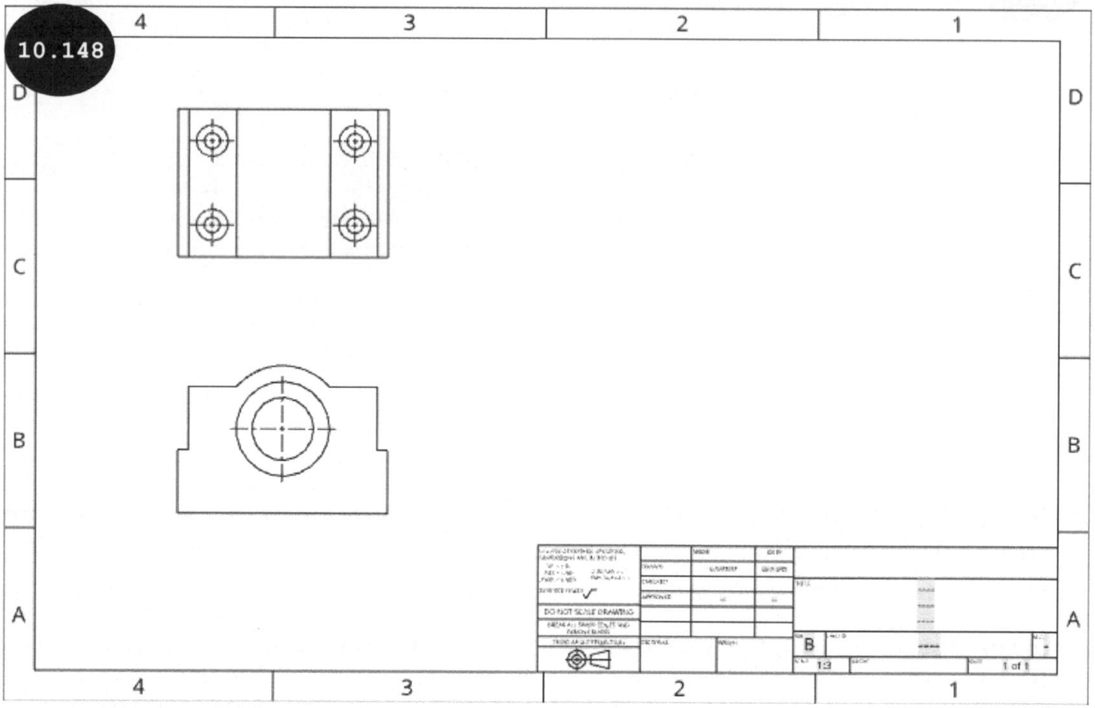

6. Press the ESC key to exit the tool.

Section 3: Creating the Section View

Now, you can create the section view using the Front view as the parent view.

1. Click on the **Section view** tool in the **Drawing** toolbar, see Figure 10.149. The **Section view** dialog appears, see Figure 10.150.

10.149

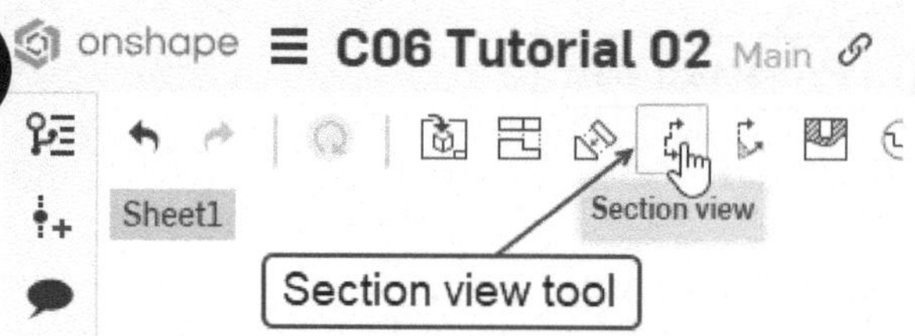

10.150

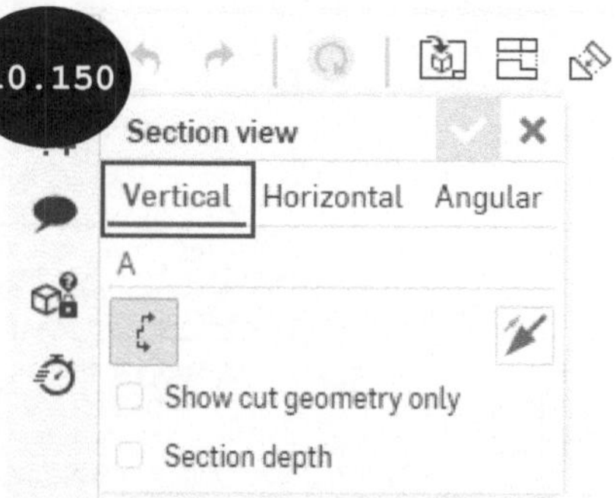

2. Ensure the **Vertical** tab is activated in the **Section view** dialog to create a vertical section view, refer to Figure 10.150. A vertical section line appears attached to the cursor.

3. Move the cursor to the center of the two concentric circular edges in the Front view and click when it snaps to the center, see Figure 10.151. The vertical section line is then placed through the center of the Front view.

10.151

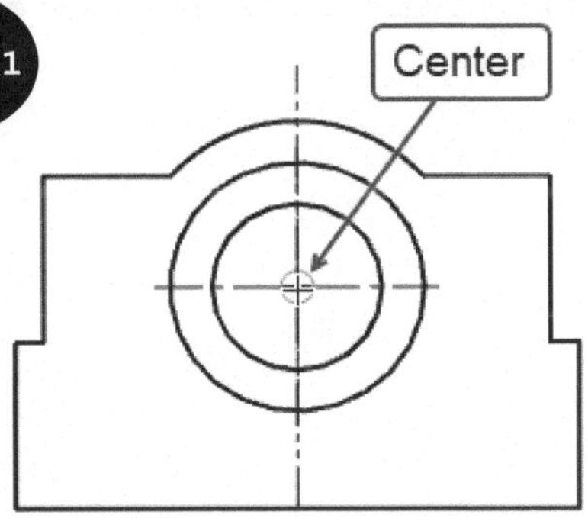

4. Move the cursor horizontally to the right. A preview of the section view appears attached to the cursor.

5. Click to position the section view on the sheet. The section view is then created and placed at the specified position, see Figure 10.152.

10.152

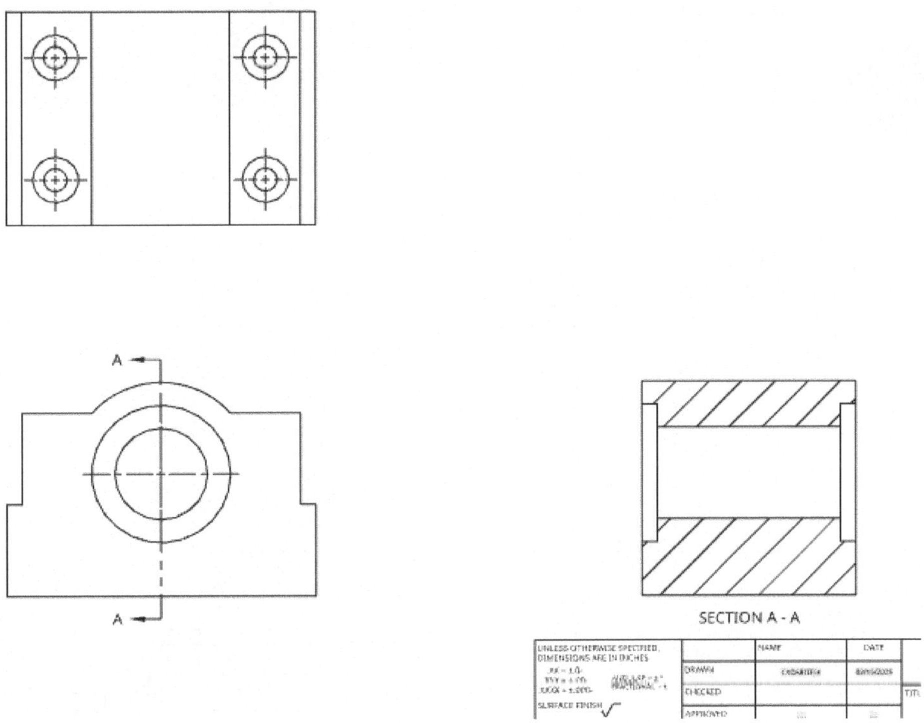

Section 4: Displaying Hidden Lines

Now, you can turn on the display of hidden lines in the Front and Top views of the model.

1. Right-click on the Front view, then hover over the **Show/hide** option in the shortcut menu, see Figure 10.153. A cascading menu appears.

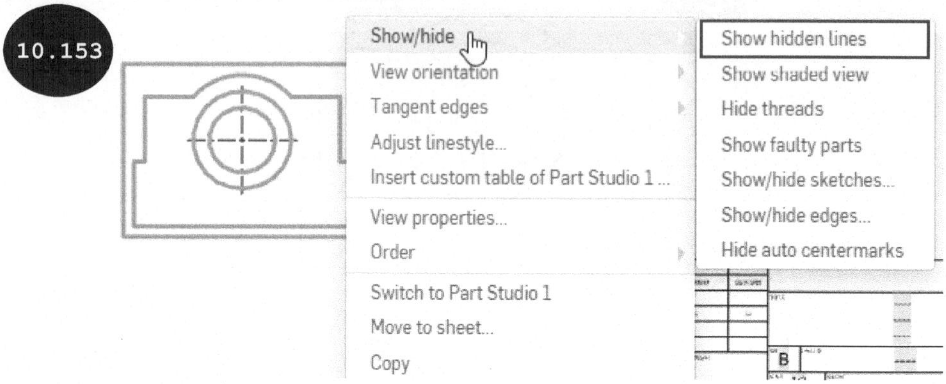

2. Select the **Show hidden lines** option in the cascading menu, refer to Figure 10.153. The hidden edges of the model become visible in the Front view as hidden lines, see Figure 10.154.

3. Similarly, turn on the display of hidden lines in the Top view of the model. Figure 10.154 shows the Front and Top views with hidden lines displayed.

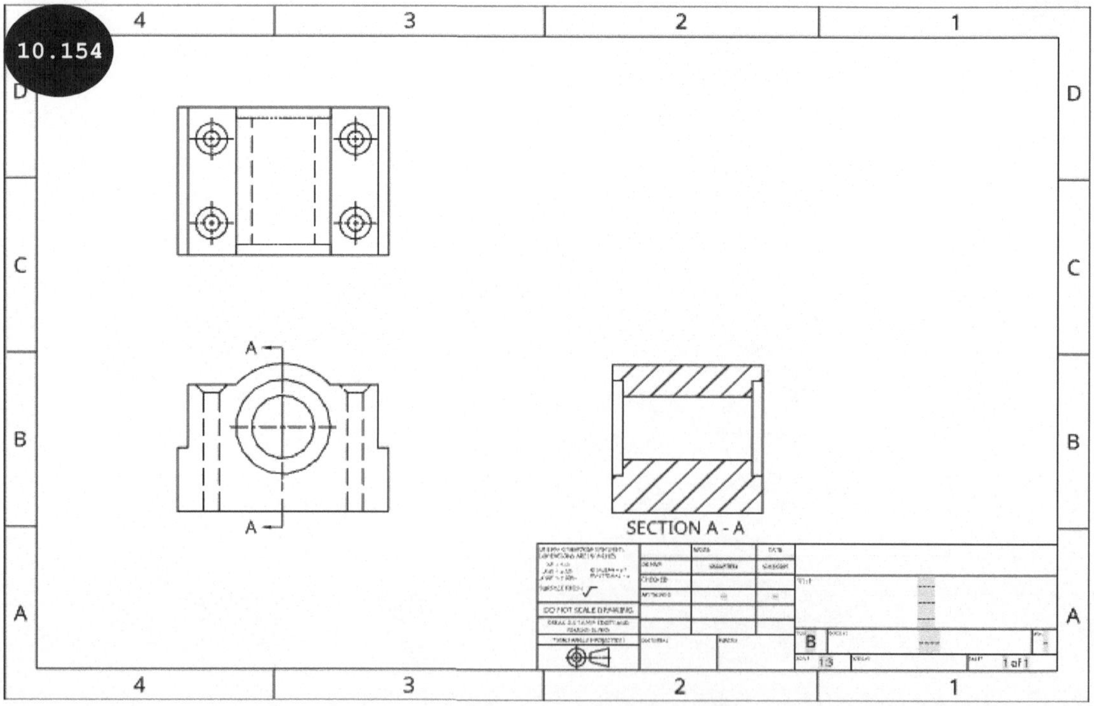

Section 5: Creating the Detail View

Now, you can create the detail view to display a small portion of the section view at a magnified scale.

1. Click on the **Detail view** tool in the **Drawing** toolbar, see Figure 10.155. The **Detail view** dialog appears, see Figure 10.156.

10.155

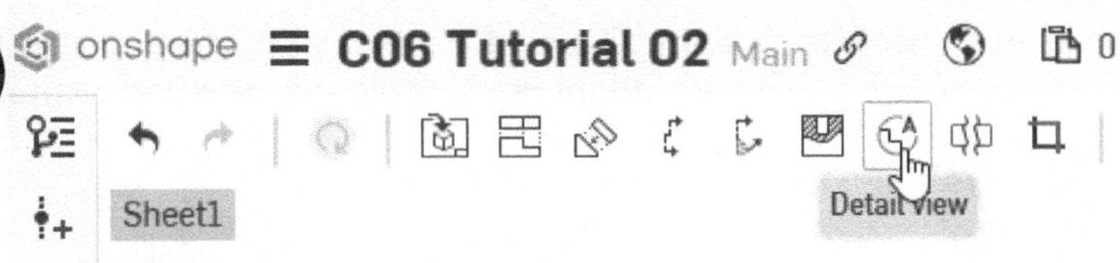

10.156

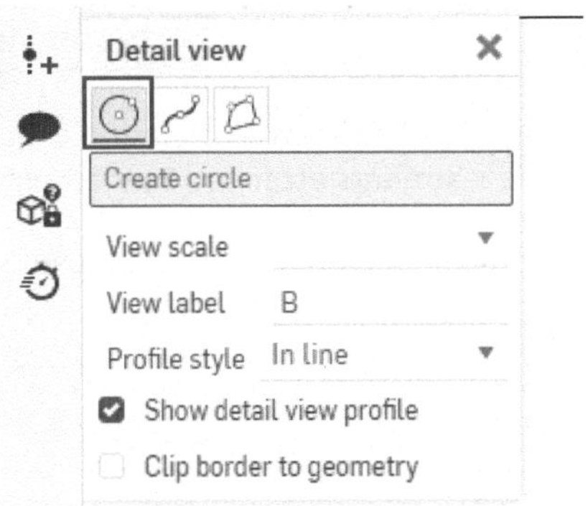

2. Ensure the **Circle** tool is active in the **Detail view** dialog to draw a circle around the portion of the view to be enlarged, see Figure 10.156.

3. Move the cursor over the top right corner or vertex of the section view and click to specify the center point of the detail view boundary when the cursor snaps to it, see Figure 10.157.

4. Move the cursor outward to set the boundary size, ensuring it covers the portion to be enlarged (see Figure 10.158), then click. A preview of the detail view for the selected portion appears attached to the cursor.

10.157

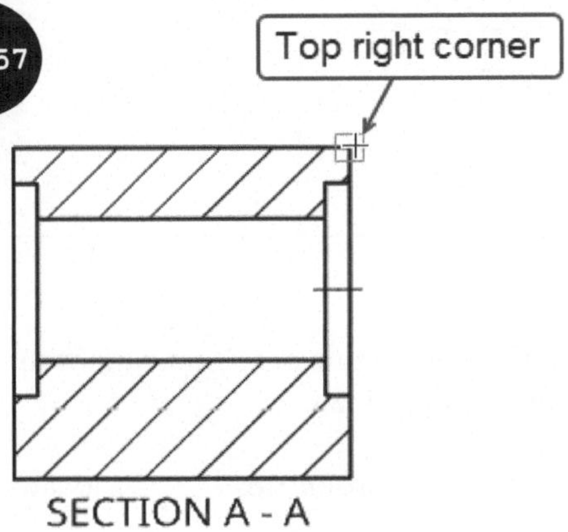

10.158

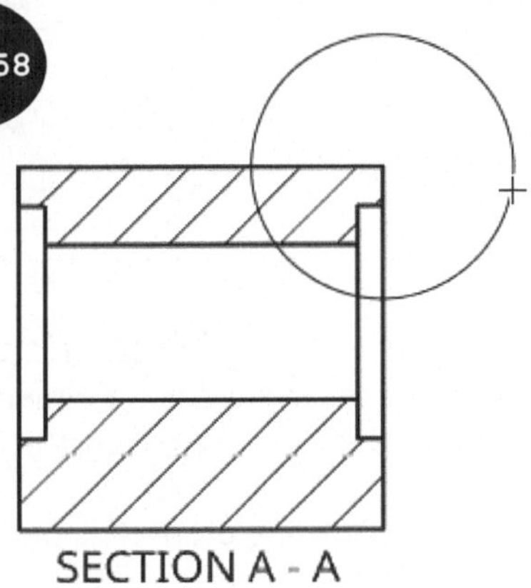

5. Accept the default scale, label, and other options in the dialog, then position the detail view on the right side of the Top view on the sheet.

Section 6: Creating the Isometric View

Now, you can create an independent isometric view of the model.

1. Click on the **Insert view** tool in the **Drawing** toolbar, see Figure 10.159. The **Insert view** dialog appears, and a preview of an independent drawing view is attached to the cursor.

10.159

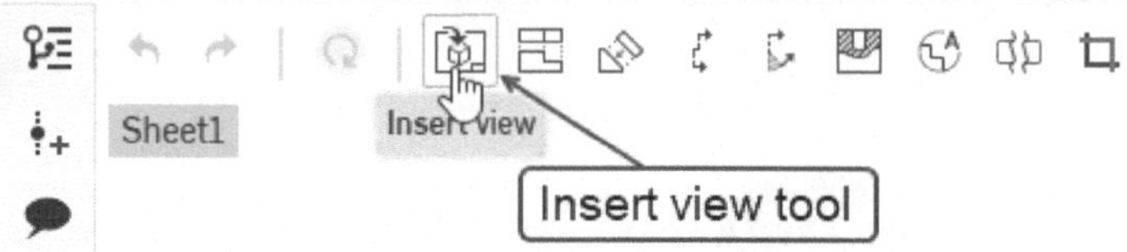

2. Select the **Isometric** option from the **View orientation** drop-down list in the **Insert view** dialog. A preview of the isometric view appears attached to the cursor.

3. Click to place the isometric view in the top right corner of the sheet, refer to Figure 10.160.

10.160

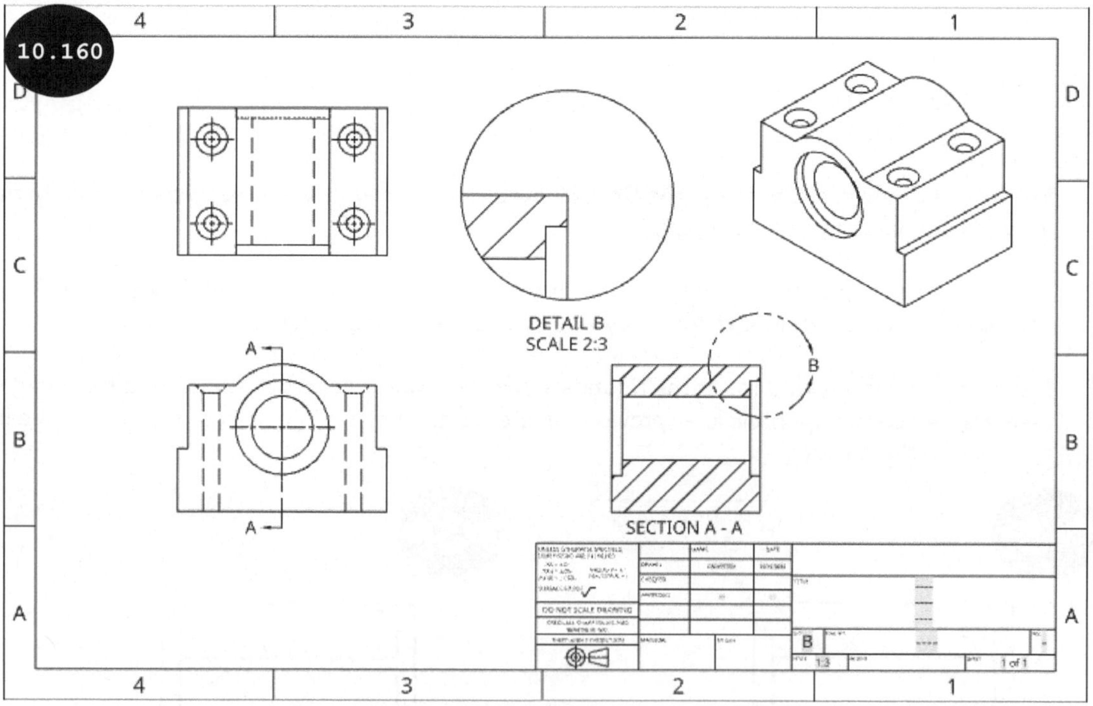

Section 7: Modifying Dimension Properties

Now, you can modify the default dimension properties, including units, precision, and other related settings, as needed before applying the dimensions to the drawing views.

1. Invoke the **Drawing properties** panel by clicking the **Drawing properties** tool located in the middle left of the screen.

2. Ensure that the **Units and precision** tab is activated, then select **0.1** in the **Precision** drop-down list to set the decimal places for the dimension value, see Figure 10.161.

10.161

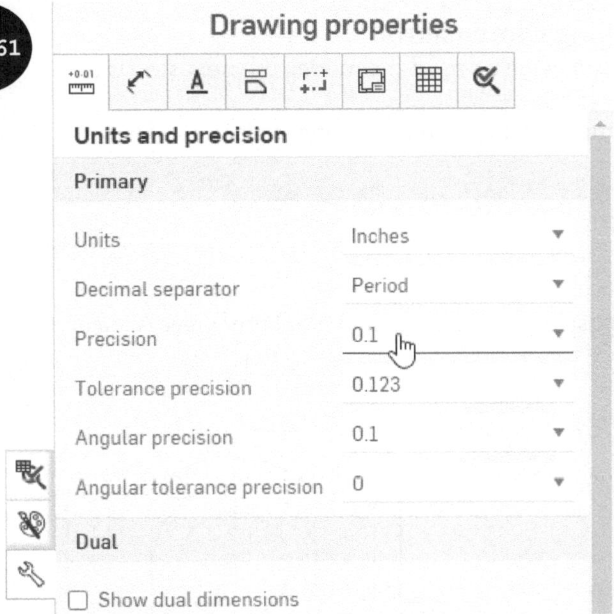

3. Click on the **Dimensions** tab in the **Drawing properties** panel, then set the text height to **0.2** inch and the arrowhead size to **0.18** inch.

4. Click on the **Annotations** tab in the **Drawing properties** panel, then scroll down to the **Hole/thread callouts** section at its bottom. Next, set the text height for hole and thread callouts to **0.2** inch.

5. Click on the **Views** tab in the **Drawing properties** panel and then set the view labels to **0.2** inches in the **All views** section.

6. Navigate to the **Section views** section in the **Views** tab, and set the arrowhead size to **0.18** inch and the cutting line label size to **0.2** inches, see Figure 10.162.

10.162

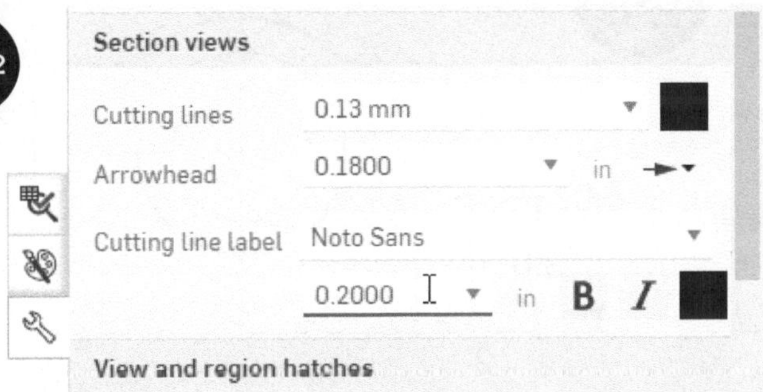

7. Navigate further to the **Detail views** section of the **Views** tab, then set the arrowhead size to **0.18** inches and the detail profile label size to **0.2** inches.

8. After making the necessary modifications in the Drawing Properties panel, click on the **Drawing Properties** tool to close it.

Section 8: Applying Dimensions

After creating all the drawing views of the model, the next step is to apply the required dimensions.

1. Click on the **Dimension** tool in the **Drawing** toolbar, see Figure 10.163.

10.163

2. Select the leftmost lower vertical edge of the Front view. A linear dimension for the selected edge appears attached to the cursor, see Figure 10.164.

10.164

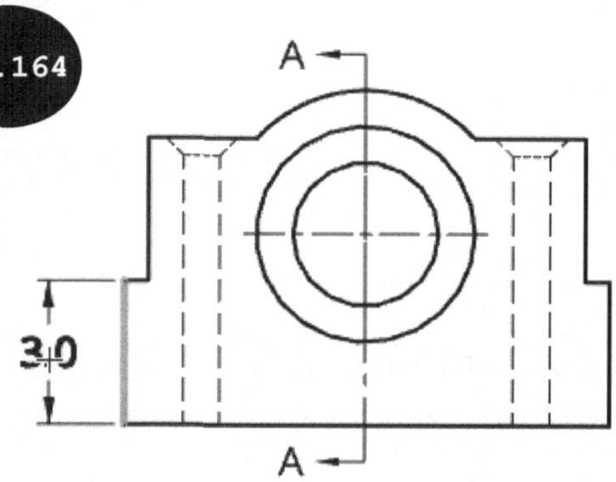

3. Click to define the placement of the dimension on the sheet. The **Dimension** tool remains activated.

4. Click on the top left vertex and the bottom left vertex of the Front view. A linear dimension between the selected vertices appears attached to the cursor, see Figure 10.165.

10.165

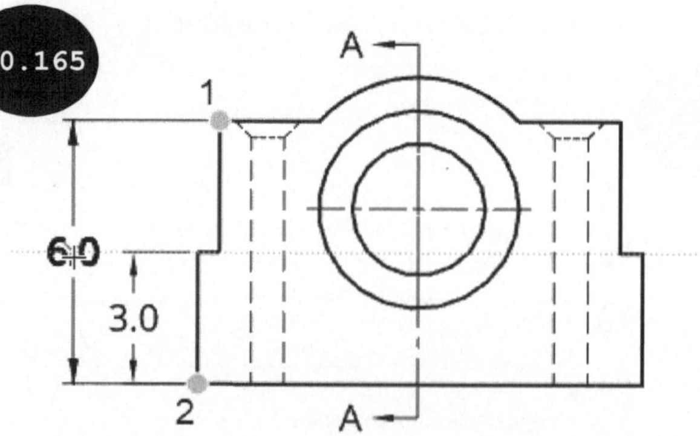

5. Similarly, apply the remaining dimensions to the drawing views. Figure 10.166 shows the drawing views after all the required dimensions have been applied using the **Dimension** tool. Next, press the ESC key to exit the tool.

10.166

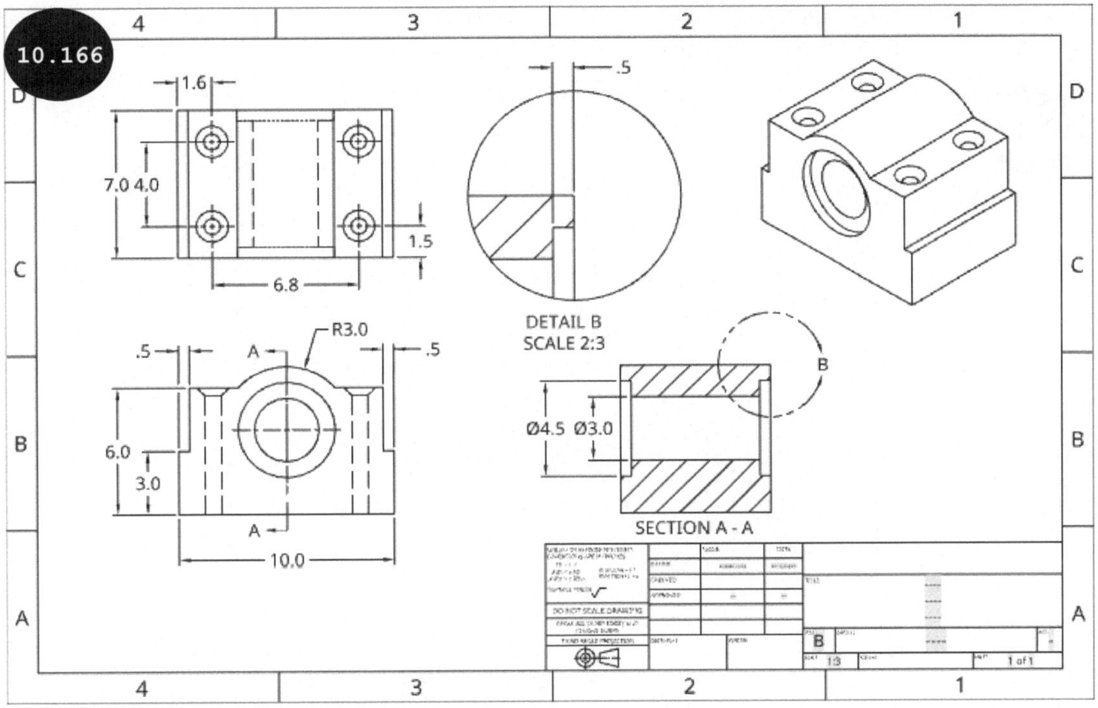

Now, you need to apply the hole callout to the hole on the Top view.

6. Invoke the **Dimension** drop-down menu and then click on the **Hole/thread callout** tool, see Figure 10.167.

10.167

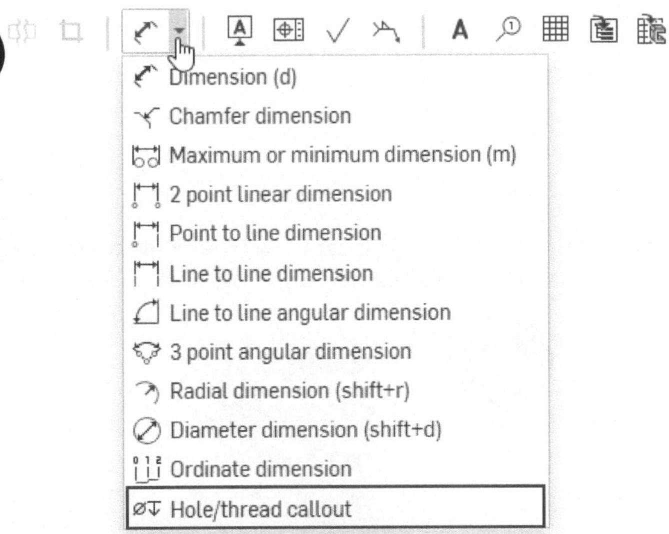

7. Click on the outer circular edge of one of the holes with similar parameters in the Top view. A hole callout appears attached to the cursor.

8. Click to define the position of the hole callout on the sheet. Press the ESC key to exit the tool. Figure 10.168 shows the drawing after applying all the dimensions, including the hole callout.

10.168

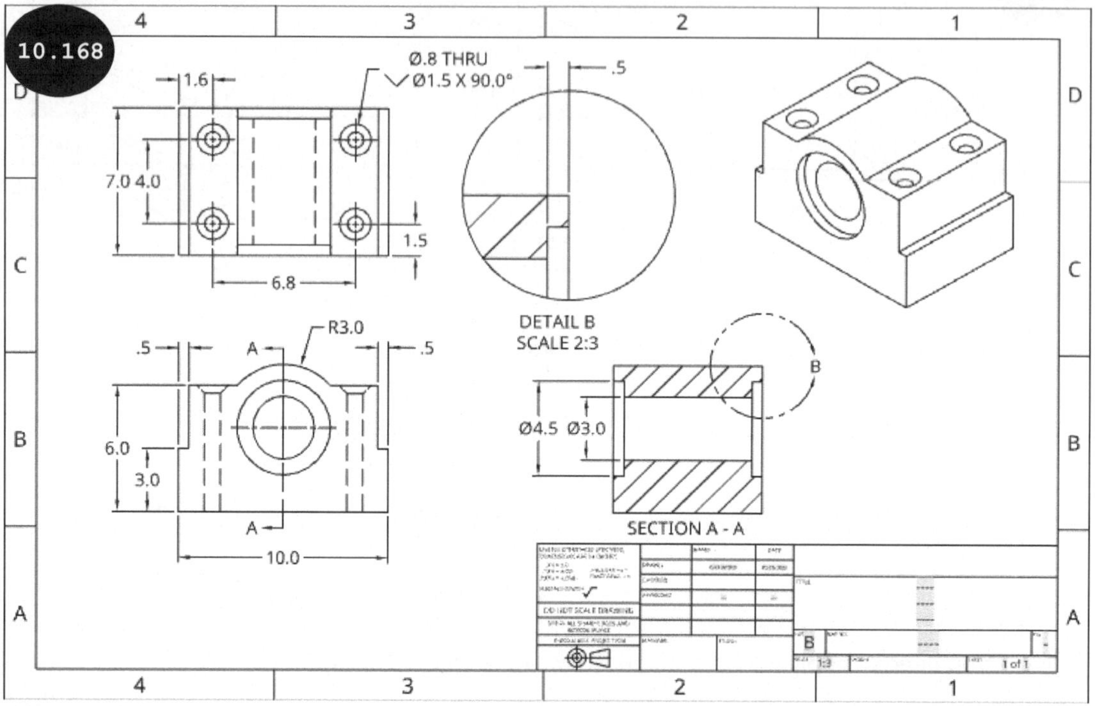

Tip: After placing the dimensions, you can further adjust their positions by dragging them to the desired location on the sheet. This allows for better clarity and organization, ensuring the dimensions do not overlap with other elements in the drawing.

Hands-on Test Drive 1

Open the assembly created in Tutorial 1 of Chapter 9, (see Figure 10.169) and then create the different drawing views: Front, Top, and Right of the assembly using the ISO_A4 sheet template, see Figure 10.170.

10.169

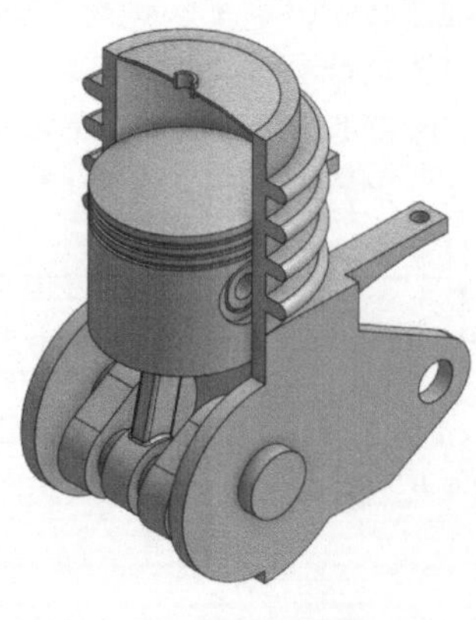

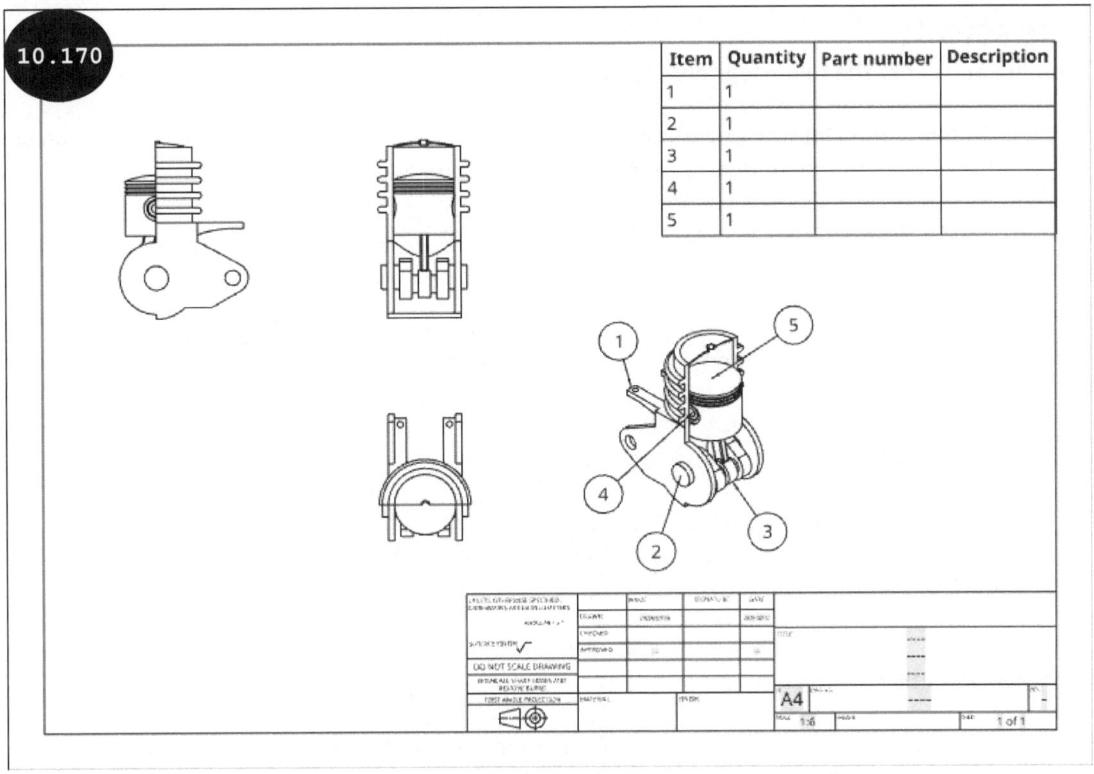

10.170

Summary

This chapter provided a comprehensive understanding of Onshape's Drawing Environment and its various tools for creating and managing technical drawings. It covered how to access the drawing environment from both Part and Assembly workspaces and the process of creating different types of views, including base, projected, auxiliary, section, aligned section, broken-out section, detail, break, and crop views.

Additionally, the chapter explained view display and property controls, modifying drawing and sheet properties, and organizing multiple sheets within a drawing. It also discussed editing hatch patterns in section views, moving views within a sheet or to another sheet, and deleting views when necessary.

The chapter further explored annotation tools such as adding centerlines, centermarks, virtual sharps, and various dimensions including chamfer, ordinate, and hole/thread callouts. It also covered surface finish symbols, weld symbols, notes, and sheet format customization.

Finally, the chapter introduced Bill of Materials (BOM) creation and customization, including adding balloons to improve clarity in assembly drawings. By mastering these tools, users can efficiently create detailed, professional drawings in Onshape for manufacturing and documentation purposes.

Questions

Complete and verify the following sentences:

- Upon entering the Drawing environment, the _________ dialog automatically opens, allowing you to select a component or an assembly for creating its drawing views.
- Engineering drawings follow two types of angles of projection: the _________ and the _________.
- In Onshape, the _________ panel enables you to modify the default properties of a drawing, including units, precision, dimensions, annotations, formats, inspection settings, and more.
- A _________ view is created by cutting an object with an imaginary cutting line and then viewing it from a direction perpendicular to the cut.
- An _________ view is created by cutting an object with a section line consisting of two non-parallel lines and then flattening the cross-section by revolving it around the center of the section line.
- A _________ view magnifies a specific portion of an existing drawing view to clearly illustrate or dimension small features.
- A _________ view is used to represent a component with a large length-to-width ratio on a smaller sheet by removing a portion of the view that maintains the same cross-section.
- The _________ tool in the **Sheet** panel is used to add additional sheets beyond the default one for creating drawing views.
- The _________ dimensions are used to ensure accuracy when dimensioning machine parts by measuring distances in the X and Y directions from a specified base point.
- In a drawing, the _________ includes essential information such as the part numbers, quantities, and details of all components used in an assembly.
- The _________ tool is used to add a balloon with a leader line to a component in a drawing view, indicating its part number or other relevant details.
- The projected view is created based on the angle of projection specified for the drawing sheet. (True/False)
- A broken-out section view cannot be created on an existing section view, detail view, or aligned section view. (True/False)
- In Onshape, once the Bill of Materials (BOM) is inserted, additional details like Material, Name, Revision, Vendor, Product Line, and Mass can be added. (True/False).

INDEX

INDEX

Symbols

A

B

E

F

G

H

I

K

L

M

N

O

P

R

S

T

U

V

W

Z

Other Publications by CADArtifex

Some of the other Publications by CADArtifex are given below:

AutoCAD Textbooks

AutoCAD 2025: A Power Guide for Beginners and Intermediate Users
AutoCAD 2024: A Power Guide for Beginners and Intermediate Users
AutoCAD 2023: A Power Guide for Beginners and Intermediate Users
and more

AutoCAD For Architectural Design Textbooks

AutoCAD 2023 for Architectural Design: A Power Guide for Beginners and Intermediate Users
AutoCAD 2022 for Architectural Design: A Power Guide for Beginners and Intermediate Users
AutoCAD 2021 for Architectural Design: A Power Guide for Beginners and Intermediate Users
and more

Autodesk Fusion 360 Textbooks

Autodesk Fusion 360: A Power Guide for Beginners and Intermediate Users (7th Edition)
Autodesk Fusion 360: A Power Guide for Beginners and Intermediate Users (6th Edition)
Autodesk Fusion 360: A Power Guide for Beginners and Intermediate Users (5th Edition)
and more

Autodesk Fusion 360 Surface and T-Spline Textbooks

Autodesk Fusion 360 Surface Design and Sculpting with T-Spline Surfaces (7th Edition)
Autodesk Fusion 360 Surface Design and Sculpting with T-Spline Surfaces (6th Edition)
and more

Autodesk Inventor Textbooks

Autodesk Inventor 2025: A Power Guide for Beginners and Intermediate Users
Autodesk Inventor 2024: A Power Guide for Beginners and Intermediate Users
Autodesk Inventor 2023: A Power Guide for Beginners and Intermediate Users
and more

Onshape Textbooks

Onshape 2025: A Power Guide for Beginners and Intermediate Users

PTC Creo Parametric Textbooks

Creo Parametric 11.0: A Power Guide for Beginners and Intermediate Users
Creo Parametric 10.0: A Power Guide for Beginners and Intermediate Users
Creo Parametric 9.0: A Power Guide for Beginners and Intermediate Users
and more

SOLIDWORKS Textbooks

SOLIDWORKS 2025: A Power Guide for Beginners and Intermediate User
SOLIDWORKS 2024: A Power Guide for Beginners and Intermediate User
SOLIDWORKS 2023: A Power Guide for Beginners and Intermediate User
SOLIDWORKS 2021: A Power Guide for Beginners and Intermediate User
and more

SOLIDWORKS Sheet Metal and Surface Design Textbooks

SOLIDWORKS Sheet Metal and Surface Design 2025 for Beginners and Intermediate Users
SOLIDWORKS Sheet Metal and Surface Design 2024 for Beginners and Intermediate Users
and more

SOLIDWORKS Simulation Textbooks

SOLIDWORKS Simulation 2025: A Power Guide for Beginners and Intermediate User
SOLIDWORKS Simulation 2024: A Power Guide for Beginners and Intermediate User
SOLIDWORKS Simulation 2023: A Power Guide for Beginners and Intermediate User
SOLIDWORKS Simulation 2022: A Power Guide for Beginners and Intermediate User
and more

Exercises Books

Some of the exercises books are given below:

100 AutoCAD Exercises - Learn by Practicing (2 Edition)
Autodesk Inventor Exercises - Learn by Practicing
Autodesk Fusion 360 Exercises Learn by Practicing (2023-24)
SOLIDWORKS Exercises - Learn by Practicing (3 Edition)

Project-Based eBook/Video Courses*

- Autodesk Fusion 360 Project-Based eBook/ Video Courses Bundle
- SOLIDWORKS Project-Based eBook/Video Courses Bundle

For more information about eBook courses, visit:* ***projects.cadartifex.com/courses*
